Developmental Psychology
Childhood and Adolescence

Second Edition

Developmental Psychology

Childhood and Adolescence

Second Edition

David R. Shaffer
University of Georgia

Brooks/Cole Publishing Company
Pacific Grove, California

Brooks/Cole Publishing Company

A Division of Wadsworth, Inc.

© 1989, 1985 by Wadsworth, Inc., Belmont, California 94002. All rights reserved. No part of this book may be reproduced, stored in a retrieval system, or transcribed, in any form or by any means— electronic, mechanical, photocopying, recording, or otherwise— without the prior written permission of the publisher, Brooks/Cole Publishing Company, Pacific Grove, California 93950, a division of Wadsworth, Inc.

Printed in the United States of America
10   9   8   7   6   5   4   3   2

Library of Congress Cataloging-in-Publication Data

Shaffer, David R. (David Reed), 1946–
  Developmental psychology.
  First ed. has subtitle: theory, research, and
applications.
  Bibliography: p.
  Includes index.
  1. Child psychology.   2. Adolescent psychology.
3. Developmental psychology.   I. Title.
BF721.S4688   1988   155.4   88-10547
ISBN 0-534-09444-9

Sponsoring Editor: *Philip L. Curson*
Editorial Assistant: *Amy Mayfield*
Production Coordinator: *Fiorella Ljunggren*
Manuscript Editor: *Rephah Berg*
Permissions Editor: *Carline Haga*
Interior and Cover Design: *Katherine Minerva*
Cover Illustration: *Katherine Minerva*
Art Coordinator: *Lisa Torri*
Interior Illustration: *Cyndie Clark-Huegel and Wayne Clark*
Cartoons: *Wayne Clark*
Photo Researcher: *Stephen Forsling*
Typesetting: *Graphic Typesetting Service*
Cover Printing: *The Lehigh Press Company*
Printing and Binding: *R. R. Donnelley & Sons Company*

(Credits continue on p. 677.)

Preface

$\mathbf{M}$y purpose in writing this book has been to produce a current and comprehensive overview of developmental psychology that reflects the best theories, research, and practical advice that developmentalists have to offer. Throughout my 16 years of teaching, I have longed for a substantive introductory text that is also interesting, accurate, up to date, and written in clear, concise language that an introductory student can easily understand. At this level, a good text should talk "to" rather than "at" its readers, anticipating their interests, questions, and concerns and treating them as active participants in the learning process. In the field of developmental psychology, a good text should also stress the processes that underlie developmental change, so that students come away from the course with a firm understanding of the causes and complexities of human development. Last but not least, a good text is a relevant text—one that shows how the theory and research that students are asked to digest can be applied to a number of real-life settings. The present volume represents my attempt to accomplish all of these objectives.

Although this book is a rigorous and research-oriented portrayal of developmental psychology, I take applications seriously, and I have striven to show how information gleaned from theory and basic research has helped us to understand and, in many cases, to solve a variety of real-world problems. For example, the laws of genetics are discussed in terms of their broad implications for human development and their contributions to the treatment and prevention of hereditary disorders. I have shown how basic research on physical/neurological growth, learning, and perceptual processes has furthered our understanding of personality development, while also suggesting a number of very useful strategies for accomplishing the objectives of preschool curricula, treating phobic reactions, promoting the development of social skills, and reducing racial and ethnic prejudice. Many helpful hints for teachers are presented and analyzed as we examine the course and content of children's intellectual development. Theory and research on parent/infant attachment are discussed in terms of their relevance to emotional development as well as their implications for the structuring of orphanages, nursery schools, and day-care centers. Many other contemporary issues and practices such as home birthing, maternal employment, mainstreaming, compensatory education, grade retention, single parenting, stepparenting, child abuse, and the importance of close friendships are examined from both a theoretical and a practical perspective. In summary, I have tried to write a book that is both rigorous and applied, one that challenges students to think about the fascinating process of human development, to share in the excitement of our young and dynamic discipline, and to acquire a knowledge of developmental principles that will serve them well in their roles as parents, teachers, nurses, day-care workers, pediatricians, or psychologists or in any other capacity by which they may one day influence the lives of developing persons.

Philosophy

Certain philosophical views are inherent in any systematic treatment of a field as broad as developmental psychology. My philosophy can be summarized as follows:

• **I believe in theoretical eclecticism.** This book will not attempt to convince its readers that any one theoretical viewpoint is "best." The psychoanalytic, behavioristic, cognitive-developmental, information-processing, ethological, and behavior genetic viewpoints (as well as several less-encompassing theories that address selected aspects of development) are all treated with respect.

• **The best information about human development comes from systematic research.** To teach this course effectively, I believe that one must convince students of the value of theory and systematic research. Although there are many ways to achieve these objectives, I have chosen to contrast modern developmental psychology with its "prescientific" origins and then to discuss and illustrate the many methodological approaches that researchers use to test their theories and answer important questions about developing children and adolescents. I've taken care to explain why there is no one "best method" for studying human development, and I've repeatedly stressed that our most

reliable findings are those that can be replicated using a variety of methods.

• **I favor a strong process orientation.** A major complaint with many developmental texts (including some best sellers) is that they describe human development without explaining why it occurs. My own process orientation is based on the belief that students are more likely to remember what develops and when if they know and understand the reasons that these developments take place.

• **Human development is a holistic process.** Although individual researchers may concentrate on particular topics such as physical development, cognitive development, or the development of moral reasoning, development is not piecemeal but holistic: human beings are at once physical, cognitive, and social creatures, and each of these components of "self" depends, in part, on the changes that are taking place in other areas of development. This holistic perspective is a central theme of modern developmental psychology—and one that is emphasized throughout the text.

• **A developmental psychology text should be a resource book for students—one that reflects current knowledge.** I have chosen to cite a fair number of very recent studies and reviews to ensure that my coverage (and any outside reading that students may undertake) will represent our current understanding of a topic or topics. However, I have tried to avoid the tendency, common in textbooks, to ignore older research simply because it is older. In fact, many of the "classics" of developmental psychology are prominently displayed throughout the text to illustrate important breakthroughs and to show how our knowledge about developing persons gradually builds on these earlier findings and insights.

Organization and Content

There are two traditional ways of presenting human development. In the *chronological,* or "ages and stages," approach, the coverage begins at conception and proceeds through the life span, using ages or chronological periods as the organizing principle. By contrast, the *topical* approach is organized around areas of development and follows each from its origins to its most mature forms. Each of these presentations has its advantages and disadvantages. On the one hand, a chronological focus highlights the holistic character of development but may obscure the links between early and later events within each developmental domain. On the other hand, a topical approach highlights developmental sequences and processes but at the risk of failing to convey that development is a holistic enterprise.

I've chosen to organize this book topically to focus intently on developmental processes and to provide the student with an uninterrupted view of the sequences of change that children experience within each developmental domain. At the same time, I consider it essential to paint a holistic portrait of the developing person. To accomplish this objective, I've stressed the fundamental interplay among biological, cognitive, social, and ecological influences in my coverage of *each and every facet of development*. So even though this text is topically organized, students will not lose sight of the whole person and the holistic character of human development.

Content.　Because the first edition of this book enjoyed success among both students and professors, I made every effort to retain in this new edition the major qualities that people have said they like. One such characteristic is the book's division into five major parts, each of which is introduced by a brief opener. Part I presents an orientation to the discipline and the tools of the trade, including a thorough discussion and illustration of research methodologies (Chapter 1) and a succinct review of psychoanalytic, behavioristic, cognitive-developmental, and ethological theories of development (Chapter 2). An important feature of this coverage is my analysis of the contributions and the limitations of each research method and each of the major developmental theories.

Parts II through V focus on the major themes, processes, and products of development: biological foundations of development (Part II), language, learning, and cognitive development (Part III), social and personality development (Part IV), and the ecology of human development (Part V).

Continuing Features

Several highlights of the first edition that distinguished my coverage from that found in other texts have been updated and retained in the second edition. Among these features are:

- A contemporary treatment of theory and research in behavior genetics in Chapter 3.
- A thorough consideration of social and environmental influences on physical development in Chapter 5.
- An entire chapter (Chapter 6) on perceptual development that traces the growth of perceptual abilities

throughout childhood and early adolescence and discusses the many social and ecological influences on this important cognitive process.

- Piaget's theory of language acquisition in Chapter 8.
- An even-handed critique of both the Piagetian and the information-processing approaches to cognitive development in Chapter 9.
- An updated analysis and evaluation of compensatory education in Chapter 10.
- The latest research on parent/infant bonding in Chapter 11.
- Extensive coverage of the development of self-knowledge and its relation to social cognition and personality development in Chapter 12.
- A contemporary view of psychological androgyny in Chapter 13.
- A thorough coverage of moral development in Chapter 14 that includes Gilligan's theory of sex differences in moral reasoning.
- Treatment of the family as a *social system* in Chapter 15, including father and sibling influences as well as the impact of ecological variables (for example, subculture and neighborhood) and important events such as divorce and remarriage.
- A current assessment of the developmental implications of schooling, covering practices such as ability grouping, peer tutoring, and grade retention, in Chapter 16.
- Consistent attention to *cross-cultural* research. Not only do students enjoy learning about the development of people in other cultures, but the cross-cultural literature also helps them to see how human beings can be so much alike, and, at the same time, so different from one another.
- Discussions throughout the text, at the most relevant junctures, of the various abnormalities and behavior problems in order to illustrate the relations between normal and atypical patterns of development. In my experience, such an integrated presentation leads to less "stigmatizing" of those individuals who are in some way atypical, without compromising the amount of material that one can present on the causes, consequences, and treatment of developmental problems and disorders.

New to This Edition

One of the most exciting things about being a developmentalist is that our discipline is constantly changing. Each successive issue of our leading journals contains new findings and fresh insights that we, as a community of scholars, must incorporate to maintain our positions as "experts" in the field. Although there was no overwhelming sentiment for a radical restructuring of the book by either the professors or the students who used the first edition, I have made several important changes in the content of this second edition—adding new topics that reflect recent trends in our discipline while condensing and reorganizing other material to make room for these additions. Among the most noteworthy of these alterations are the following:

- In Chapter 3 I've placed much more emphasis on genotype/environment interplays and their implications for human development. My purpose in exposing students to recent theories of behavior genetics is to illustrate how genotypes and environments interact to produce developmental change and how genetic and environmental *differences* combine to produce *variations* in developmental outcomes.
- Interest in the *long-term* developmental implications of prenatal and perinatal complications has grown dramatically since the first edition was published. The most recent findings on this topic are discussed in Chapter 4 of this revised edition.
- Coverage of physical growth and development (Chapter 5) now includes a major section on the development of the brain and central nervous system. Here, I've focused extensively on the plasticity issue and on the role of experiential factors in neural growth and development.
- Research on infant perceptual capabilities has exploded over the past five years. This section of Chapter 6 has been completely rewritten to reflect these exciting developments. There is also a new section on research methodology that illustrates how creative investigators have persuaded nonverbal infants to tell us what they are sensing or perceiving.
- Information-processing theory receives much more attention in the second edition than in the first. Not only has this coverage been greatly expanded in Chapter 9, where we take up the topic of cognitive development, but the book now reflects the contribution of information-processing theorists to research in perceptual development (Chapter 6), learning (Chapter 7), language development (Chapter 8), intelligence testing (Chapter 10), achievement strivings (Chapter 12), sex-role development (Chapter 13), and moral development (Chapter 14).
- The Ainsworth/Kagan debate about the role of infant temperament in emotional attachments is highlighted

in Chapter 11, as is an expanded and thoroughly updated section addressing the impact of maternal employment and alternative caregiving on children's social and emotional well-being.
- Chapter 12 has been reorganized to reflect more directly on the development of the self and on two aspects of personal/social development that are central to the developing self-concept: sociability and achievement. Moreover, the portion of the chapter on achievement behavior has been expanded to include Weiner's attributional theory of achievement and Dweck's exciting work on learned helplessness.
- Chapter 13 now features Martin and Halverson's schematic-processing model of sex typing—a viewpoint that (in my opinion) provides the "missing link" in our quest for a truly integrative theory of sex-role development. Also appearing in this revised chapter is a new section on the development of sexuality and a contemporary assessment of the sexual attitudes and behavior of today's adolescents.
- Chapter 14 has been rewritten to focus on three *interrelated* aspects of social development: aggression, altruism, and social development. Dodge's social information-processing theory of aggression is an important addition to this chapter, as is the new evidence reflecting on Gilligan's theory of female moral development.
- The impact of the computer on developing children is now highlighted in Chapter 16. Moreover, discussion of the peer group as a socializing agent has been strengthened considerably by the inclusion of a major section focusing on the developmental implications of having (or not having) friends.

Writing Style

My goal has been to write a book that talks directly to its readers and treats them as active participants in an ongoing discussion. I have tried to be relatively informal and down to earth in my writing style and to rely heavily on questions, thought problems, and a number of other exercises to stimulate student interest and involvement. Most of the chapters were "pretested" on my own students, who red-penciled whatever wasn't clear to them and suggested several of the concrete examples, analogies, and occasional anecdotes that I've used when introducing and explaining complex ideas. So, with the valuable assistance of my student-critics, I have attempted to prepare a manuscript that is substantive and challenging but that reads more like a story than like an encyclopedia.

Special Features

Among the features I've included to make the book more interesting and the material easier to learn are the following:

- **Boxes.** Each chapter contains a number of boxes that call attention to important issues, ideas, or applications. The aim of these boxes is to permit a closer and more personal examination of selected topics while stimulating the reader to think about the questions, controversies, practices, and policies under scrutiny. Some of the boxes address methodological issues (for example, characteristics of a *useful* psychological test), whereas others focus on theoretical and empirical controversies (e.g., can apes acquire language?), practical concerns (e.g., fathers as custodial parents), applications (e.g., improving children's social skills), and policy decisions (e.g., grade retention). All the boxes were carefully selected to reinforce central themes in the text.
- **Outlines and chapter summaries.** An outline at the beginning of each chapter provides the student with a preview of what will be covered. Each chapter concludes with a succinct summary that allows the student to quickly review the chapter's major points.
- **Subheadings.** Subheadings are employed *very* frequently to keep the material well organized and to divide the coverage into manageable bites.
- **Vocabulary.** Key terms appear in boldface type to alert the student that these are important concepts to learn.
- **Running glossary.** At the bottom of right-hand pages, a running glossary provides on-the-spot definitions for boldface vocabulary items as they appear in the text for the first time (and occasionally a second time if a term reappears in a later chapter and is critical at that point). These glossary items are done in a second color to command attention.
- **Glossary indexing.** Page references for running-glossary items appear in the subject index at the end of the book. So if students forget a definition, they don't have to search frantically for the page where it appeared.
- **Use of italics.** Italics are used liberally throughout the text to emphasize important points.
- **Illustrations.** Photographs, tables, and figures are used extensively. Although these features are designed, in part, to provide visual relief and to maintain student interest, they are not merely decorations. All visual aids, including the occasional cartoons, were selected to illustrate important principles and outcomes and thereby enhance the educational goals of the text.

Supplementary Aids

Instructor's Resource Manual

For the instructor, there is an Instructor's Resource Manual that summarizes key terms and chapter objectives, contains suggestions about films and reading materials, and features overhead transparency masters that can also be used as classroom handouts.

Test-item bank and testing file

An entirely new testing file is available to all instructors who adopt *Developmental Psychology.* The test file for each chapter consists of two sets of multiple-choice items, five to ten short-answer questions, three to five essay questions, and answers for *all* test items. For those instructors with access to microcomputers, the test file is also available in a version compatible with most popular formats. The Brooks/Cole sales representative has complete details.

Student Study Guide

A very thorough study guide is also available to help students master the information in the text. The study materials for each chapter include a detailed summary that highlights all important principles and concepts, a programmed Personalized System of Instruction (PSI) review, a preliminary multiple-choice self-test emphasizing concepts, a research digest and drill, and a comprehensive multiple-choice self-test covering concepts, theory, research, and applications. In addition to these more traditional review materials, there are also a number of probing "applications" exercises and conceptual vignettes that challenge students to think about and to apply what they have learned. This study guide should be a particularly helpful learning aid for the students, and I urge the instructor to take a good look at it.

Acknowledgments

So many individuals have assisted me with the planning and production of this book that I could never adequately thank them all. I am especially grateful to Ignatius J. Toner of the University of North Carolina at Charlotte, who persuaded me several years ago that I might be successful at producing a developmental text. And to urge me onward, he and his wife, Fiona Ritchie, contributed a very fine first draft of a chapter (Chapter 14) for the first edition.

I am also heavily indebted to Carol Sigelman of the University of Arizona, who, about once every six weeks, provided me with new references and with many, many useful suggestions for clarifying my presentation. It is certainly no exaggeration to say that Dr. Sigelman has had a meaningful and salutary influence on every section of this book. Thank you, Carol, for your invaluable support and assistance.

The quality of any developmental text depends to a large extent on the quality of the prepublication reviews from developmentalists around the country. Many of my colleagues have influenced this book by contributing detailed and constructive criticisms, as well as useful suggestions, references, and a lot of encouragement. Each of these experts has helped to make the final product a better one, and I thank them all. The reviewers of the first edition were Martin Banks, University of California at Berkeley; Don Baucum, Birmingham-Southern College; Jay Belsky, Pennsylvania State University; Keith Berg, University of Florida; Marvin Berkowitz, Marquette University; Dana Birnbaum, University of Maine at Orono; Kathryn Black, Purdue University; Robert Bohlander, Wilkes College; Cathryn Booth, University of Washington; Yvonne Brackbill, University of Florida; Cheryl Bradley, Central Virginia Community College; John Condry, Cornell University; David Crowell, University of Hawaii; Connie Hamm Duncanson, Northern Michigan University; Mary Ellen Durrett, University of Texas at Austin; Beverly Eubank, Lansing Community College; Beverly Fagot, University of Oregon; Larry Fenson, San Diego State University; Harold Goldsmith, University of Oregon; Charles Halverson, University of Georgia; Lillian Hix, Houston Community College; Patricia Leonhard, University of Illinois at Champaign–Urbana; Frank Laycock, Oberlin College; Mark Lepper, Stanford University; John Ludeman, Stephens College; Phil Mohan, University of Idaho; Robert Plomin, Pennsylvania State University; Judith Powell, University of Wyoming; Daniel Richards, Houston Community College; Peter Scharf, University of Seattle; and Rob Woodson, University of Texas.

The reviewers of the second edition were Kathryn Black, Purdue University; Thomas J. Brendt, Purdue University; Mary Courage, Memorial University of Newfoundland; Donald N. Cousins, Rhode Island College; Mark L. Howe, Memorial University of Newfoundland; Gerald L. Larson, Kent State University; Sharon Nelson-Le Gall, University of Pittsburgh; David Liberman, University of Houston; Richard Newman, University of California at Riverside; Scott Paris, University of Michigan; Thomas S. Parish, Kansas State University; Frederick M. Schwantes, Northern Illinois University; Renuka R. Sethi, California State College at Bakersfield; Faye B. Steuer, College of Charleston; Donald Tyrell, Franklin and Marshall College; and Joachim K. Wohlwill, Pennsylvania State University.

I am also indebted to my friend and colleague William G. Graziano, who critiqued Chapters 1 through 4 of the first edition, and to the many students who so generously volunteered to read and comment on various portions of the present manuscript. Their collective contribution to the book's readability has been substantial.

Several people have prepared helpful materials for use both within and outside of the text. I wish to thank Don Baucum of Birmingham-Southern College, who produced the test file as well as the student study guide, and Larry and Judith Fenson, who prepared the instructor's manual. Thanks are also in order to Wayne Clark and Cyndie Clark-Huegel, who illustrated the book, and to Stephen Forsling, who diligently searched for and found photographs that capture the essence of development.

Special thanks go to Geraldine Moon, who coordinated the efforts of the project's clerical staff, and to Pat Smith and Marian Farrow, who are becoming amazingly proficient at deciphering my ambiguous hieroglyphics and transforming that mess into a polished manuscript. Never once did these women complain about the volume of work I generated, although I could hardly blame them were they to hope and pray that I would soon become enamored of my own word processor. All kidding aside, it is difficult to express in words just how much the efforts of Geri, Pat, and Marian have meant to me.

Once again, the staff at Brooks/Cole showed me why they have a reputation for producing excellent textbooks. As the project neared completion (from my end, at least), Senior Production Coordinator Fiorella Ljunggren took charge, imposing impossible deadlines along with the support and encouragement to meet them. Fiorella has taught me that a manuscript does not a book make, and I've learned from our many collaborations to sincerely appreciate her dedication and professionalism. Rephah Berg was also exceptional in her role as copy editor. Having now worked with Rephah on three projects, I am convinced that no one catches errors (in logic as well as syntax) any better than she. Carline Haga has been very helpful in securing permissions, and the art department has devoted many, many hours to the task of making this volume pleasing from a visual standpoint. I am grateful to all of them, especially Katherine Minerva, who designed the book and created its handsome cover, and Lisa Torri, who coordinated the art program.

Last but certainly not least, I owe an especially important debt of gratitude to my project editors, C. Deborah Laughton and Phil Curson. C. Deborah persuaded me to sign a contract with Brooks/Cole and was there throughout the first and for most of the second edition, answering questions, solving problems, and gently prodding this recalcitrant author to keep working during important historical events (such as the World Series). C. Deborah's advice and counsel were simply invaluable, and I'll miss her very much now that she has left Brooks/Cole. (It is doubtful, however, that I will ever consent to miss the Series again.)

Phil Curson took over in midstream and promptly dispelled the myth that a change of editors is an author's worst nightmare. Phil has been very helpful to me and especially enthusiastic about this project—even though he was not its sponsoring editor. Yet, I am hardly surprised by his dedication and enthusiasm, for his efforts in behalf of the first edition were one major reason that that volume enjoyed the success it did.

David R. Shaffer

Brief Contents

Contents

Part IV
Social and Personality Development 390

Developmental Psychology

Childhood and Adolescence

Second Edition

I

This is a book about children and adolescents—a description and explanation of their behaviors, thoughts, perceptions, emotions, and abilities. At the same time, this is a book about developmental psychology—the study of how individuals develop and change over the course of their lives.

Part I consists of two chapters designed to orient you to the field of developmental psychology. Chapter 1 sets the stage. We will first discuss the meaning of development and see just how recent this concept really is. After considering how the scientific community gradually became interested in developing children, we will focus on the methods and strategies that researchers have used to detect and explain developmental change.

Perhaps the most useful tools that developmental researchers have at their disposal are the many theories that have been proposed to account for human development. In Chapter 2 we will take a closer look at the role of theory in developmental psychology as we examine several of the more influential theories of child and adolescent development.

Taken together, these opening chapters provide an orientation and some important background for the material presented throughout the text. They will help you understand what developmental psychology is and how researchers go about answering questions they may have about developing children and adolescents.

An Overview of Developmental Psychology

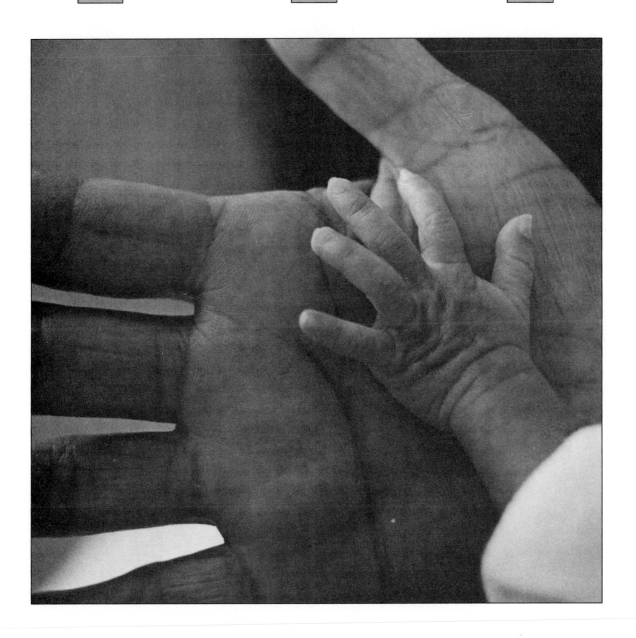

Introduction

I would like to begin this book by asking a question: Why did *you* choose to enroll in a course on human development? For many students majoring in psychology, home economics, elementary education, or nursing, the class is required and there is no way around it. Expectant parents sometimes take the course in order to learn more about babies as part of their preparation for parenthood. Occasionally students will elect the course seeking to answer specific questions about their own behavior or that of a friend or a family member. For example, a college roommate of mine, who happened to be a fisheries major, dabbled in child development hoping to discover why he and his identical twin often seemed to be thinking the same things in similar situations. Another classmate, who was Chinese, was forever asking questions about American family life. He had taken the course thinking he might acquire a better understanding of Western culture by learning how American children are raised. As our friendship blossomed, he ended up learning a lot about one grand old Western institution—poker—and we both learned a fair number of things about developing children as well.

Whatever your reasons for taking this course, at one time or another you have probably been curious about one or more aspects of human development. For example:

- Have you ever wondered what the world looks like to newborn infants? Do you suppose they can make any sense of their new surroundings?
- When do you think infants will first recognize their mothers? their fathers? themselves (in a mirror)?
- Why do many 1-year-olds seem so attached to their mothers and so fearful of strangers?
- Foreign languages are difficult for us to follow if we merely listen to conversations among people who speak these tongues. Yet infants and toddlers pay close attention to conversations and will acquire their native language in the absence of formal instruction. How is

this possible? Is language learning easier for children than for adults?
- Why do many young children think that things that move, like the sun and the wind, are alive?
- Do you suppose we could teach algebra to a fourth-grader who had learned to multiply and divide?
- Why are some people friendly and outgoing while others are shy and reserved? Does the quality of family life determine one's personality? If so, then why are children from the same family often so different from one another?

These are just a few of the issues that students say they wish to learn more about in electing a course in human development. As one perceptive sophomore recently remarked, "I want to know why all of us turn out so much alike and, at the same time, so different from one another." As we will see, her interest is shared by all developmental researchers.

The Concept of Development

Simply stated, **development** refers to systematic changes in the individual that occur between the moment of conception (when the father's sperm penetrates the mother's ovum, creating a new organism) and the day one dies. The word *systematic* implies that developmental changes are somehow orderly or patterned, so that temporary mood swings and other transitory changes in our appearance, thoughts, and behaviors are therefore excluded.

To fully appreciate the concept of development, we must seek to understand the processes that underlie and induce developmental change. One such process is **maturation,** a biological unfolding of the individual according to a plan contained in the *genes*—the hereditary material passed from parents to their offspring at conception. Evidence for the maturational guidance of human development can be seen at many points throughout the life span. For example, a primitive heart forms and begins to beat in all healthy human embryos within a month after they are conceived. The human maturational program also contributes very heavily to important developmental milestones such as the infant's ability to walk and to utter meaningful words at about 12 months of age, the 5-year-old's proficiency at staying upright on a bicycle, and the dramatic transformations of our bodies at age 9 to 16 as we reach sexual maturity. Since the brain undergoes many maturational changes, maturation is partly responsible not only for readily observable physical changes but also for psychological changes such as our increasing ability to concentrate, to solve problems, and to understand what another person may be feeling. Indeed, it seems that we may even be biologically programmed to age and eventually to die. So one reason human beings are so similar in so many noteworthy respects is that our common "species heredity" or maturational blueprints ensure that all of us will undergo many of the same developmental changes at about the same points in our lives.

A second critical developmental process is **learning,** or the means by which our experiences produce relatively permanent changes in our feelings, thoughts, and patterns of behavior. Let's consider a very simple example. Although a certain degree of physical maturation is necessary before a grade school child can become reasonably proficient at dribbling a basketball, careful instruction and many, many hours of practice are essential if this youngster is ever to approximate the feats of such wizards of the hardwoods as the Harlem Globetrotters. It turns out that most of our abilities and habits do not simply unfold as part of nature's grand plan; we often learn to feel, think, and behave in new ways from our observations of and interactions with parents, teachers, and other important people in our lives, and we are affected by the events that we experience. Stated another way, we change in response to the environments in which we live—particularly in response to the actions and reactions of the people around us. Of course, many developmental changes are the products of *both* maturation and learning. And as we will see throughout this book, some of the more lively debates about human development are arguments about which of these processes contributes more to specific developmental changes.

If development represents the systematic changes an individual experiences from conception un-

til death, the science of development is the study of these changes. Actually, we might well speak of the *sciences* of development, for this area of study is truly a multidisciplinary enterprise. **Developmental psychology,** the largest of these disciplines, is concerned with identifying and explaining the changes that individuals undergo across the life span. And yet, many biologists, sociologists, anthropologists, educators, physicians, home economists, and even historians share this interest and have contributed in important ways to our knowledge of both human and animal development. Because the science of development is multidisciplinary, we use the term *developmentalist* to refer to any scholar—regardless of discipline—who seeks to understand the developmental process.

Many human developmentalists have chosen to concentrate on one particular segment of the life span. For example, those who label themselves child developmentalists study the changes that individuals experience between conception and *puberty*—an event (or series of events) that typically occurs at 11 to 15 years of age and marks the passage from childhood into adolescence. Those who are interested in adolescent development concentrate on the changes that occur between puberty and young adulthood, when the individual leaves home to work or to study and is now reasonably independent of parental sanctions. In this text, we will consider the major developments of both these phases of life. Our two major concerns in studying child and adolescent development will be to specify *how* children and adolescents change over time and *why* these developments take place.

When social scientists began to chart the course of human development over the first several years of life, they soon discovered that no two children are exactly alike. Even newborn infants vary considerably in

---

development: the process by which organisms grow and change over the course of their lives.

maturation: developmental changes in the body or behavior that result from the aging process rather than from learning, injury, illness, or some other life experience.

learning: a relatively permanent change in behavior (or behavioral potential) that results from one's experiences or practice.

developmental psychology: the scientific study of how individuals change over time and the factors that produce these changes.

their alertness, their activity levels, and their responsiveness to other people. During the first year, some infants develop an intense fear of strangers and others do not. As they continue to mature, children clearly differ in the ages at which they reach important milestones such as walking, talking, counting, or riding a bicycle. Youngsters raised within a particular culture, a neighborhood, or even the same household often display very different interests, values, mental abilities, and patterns of social behavior. So even though some features of human development may be universal, each of us is in many ways a unique individual. Therefore, a third major concern of the child developmentalist is to identify the important ways in which children differ from one another and to explain why these developmental variations might occur.

Human Development as a Continual and Cumulative Process

In his famous poem *Paradise Lost*, John Milton wrote: "Childhood shows the man as morning shows the day." This interesting analogy can be interpreted in at least two ways. It could be translated to mean that the events of childhood have little or no real impact on one's adult life, just as a sunny summer morning often fails to forecast an impending afternoon thundershower. Yet most people do not interpret Milton's statement that way. Most take it to mean that the events of childhood play a very meaningful role in forecasting the future. Child developmentalists clearly favor this latter interpretation.

Although no one can specify precisely what adulthood holds in store from even the most meticulous examination of a person's childhood, developmentalists have learned that the first 12 to 15 years are an extremely important segment of the life span—one that sets the stage for adolescence and adulthood. And yet, how we perform on that stage will also depend on the experiences we have as adolescents and adults. Obviously, you are not the same person you were at age 10 or even at age 15. You have probably grown somewhat (either up or out), acquired new academic skills, and developed very different interests and aspirations from those you had as a fifth-grader or a high school sophomore. And the path of such developmental change stretches ever onward, through middle age and beyond, culminating in the final change that occurs when we die. In sum, human development is best described as a *continual* and cumulative process. The only thing that is constant

Table 1-1. A chronological overview of human development

Period of life	Chronological time frame
1. Prenatal period	Conception to birth
2. Infancy	First two years of life
3. Toddler period[a]	1 to 3 years of age
4. Preschool period	3 to 6 years of age
5. Middle childhood	6 to 12 or so years of age (onset of puberty marks the end of this period)
6. Adolescence	12 or so to 20 years of age (many developmentalists define the end of adolescence as the point at which the individual begins to work and is reasonably independent of parental sanctions)
7. Young adulthood	20 to 40 years of age
8. Middle age	40 to 65 years of age
9. Old age	65 years of age and older (postretirement)

[a]Because infants are often referred to as toddlers once they begin to walk, there is some overlap between infancy and toddlerhood.

Note: The age ranges listed here are approximate and may not apply to any particular individual. For example, a few 10-year-olds have experienced puberty and are properly classified as adolescents. Some teenagers are fully self-supporting with children of their own and are best classified as young adults.

is change, and the changes that occur at each major phase of life have important implications for the future.

Table 1-1 presents a chronological overview of the life span as the developmental psychologist sees it. Our focus in this text is on development during the first six periods of life—the epochs known as childhood and adolescence. By examining how children develop from the moment they are conceived until they reach young adulthood, we will each undoubtedly learn a little more about ourselves and the determinants of our behavior. Our review of the many factors that influence human development should also provide some insight into why no two children are ever exactly alike, even when they are raised together in the same home. Before we begin our journey through the world of childhood, let's note that we do not yet have answers for all the important questions you may have about developing children. Quite the contrary—developmental psychology is a young discipline with many unresolved issues. But as we proceed through the text, it should become quite clear that the developmentalists of the past half century have provided an enormous amount of very practical information about the younger set—information that can help us to become better educators, better child practitioners, and better-informed parents.

Human Development as a Holistic Process

In years gone by, it was fashionable to divide the developmentalists into three camps: (1) those who studied physical growth and development, including bodily changes and the sequencing of motor skills, (2) those who studied the cognitive aspects of development, including perception, language, learning, and thinking, and (3) those who concentrated on the psychosocial aspects of development, including emotions, personality, and the growth of interpersonal relationships. Today we know that this classification is somewhat artificial and misleading. Researchers who work in any of these three areas can't help noticing that changes in one aspect of development have important implications for other aspects. Let's consider an example.

What determines a person's popularity with peers? If you were to say that the person's social skills are important, you would be right. Social skills such as warmth, friendliness, and willingness to cooperate are characteristics that popular children typically display. However, there is much more to popularity (or peer acceptance) than meets the eye. We now have some indication that the age at which a child reaches puberty, an important milestone in physical development, has a very real effect on social life. For example, boys who reach puberty early enjoy better subsequent relations with their peers than boys who reach puberty later. Let's also note that bright children who do well in school tend to be more popular with their peers than children of average intelligence or below who perform somewhat less admirably in the classroom.

We see, then, that one's "popularity" depends not only on social skills but also on cognitive prowess and physical characteristics. As this example illustrates, development is not piecemeal but **holistic**—human beings are physical, cognitive, and social creatures, and each of these components of "self" depends, in part, on changes that are taking place in other areas of development. This holistic perspective is perhaps the dominant theme of human development today—and the theme around which our book is organized.

A Brief Overview of the Text

To this point, we have suggested that development is a cumulative process and that the many changes that each person experiences are meaningfully related to one another. How did developmentalists make these important discoveries? What methods do they use to chart the course of development? How do they decide what to study and why it may be important to look at these phenomena?

The aim of this book is to answer each of these questions by introducing you to the goals, methods, theories, findings, and practical accomplishments of modern developmental psychology. Part I sets the stage. In the remainder of this first chapter, we will see how the scientific community gradually became interested in developing children and then devised a number of strategies for detecting and explaining developmental change. In Chapter 2 we take a closer look at the role of theory in developmental psychology as we examine four major theories of human development and see that the assumptions made by developmental theorists largely determine the phenomena that they choose to study.

The rest of the text is organized around broad areas of study and research. Human beings are biological creatures, and our emphasis in Part II is on physical changes and the biological bases of development. Among the more remarkable developments of childhood and adolescence are the changes that occur in perceiving, thinking, reasoning, and remembering. These cognitive, or intellectual, developments are examined in detail in Part III. Of course, humans are also social animals, and our focus in Part IV shifts to social and personality development. And in Part V we will go beyond the individual child to consider the influence of the family and society on the development of children and adolescents.

The organization of this text around particular topics and processes reflects the specialization of modern developmental psychology: each major developmental theory emphasizes different aspects of development, and investigators typically concentrate on specific topics and processes when conducting research. Yet a division of the field into areas and topics is merely a convenient way of organizing a vast amount of information about developing persons, and it is important to remember that human development is a *holistic* process. For example, one cannot hope to understand a topic such as sex-role development without knowing how biology, learning, cognition, and important social forces

---

holistic perspective: a unified view of the developmental process that emphasizes the important interrelationships among the physical, mental, social, and emotional aspects of human development.

combine to influence a person's perception of self as a male or a female who is expected to behave like other males or females in his or her culture. So even though this text is topically organized, we will not lose sight of the whole person or the holistic nature of human development.

The reason we concentrate on research and its application in this text is that most of what we know about developmental processes comes from the results of empirical research. Today there are many excellent methods for studying human development—a variety of techniques that we are about ready to discuss in some detail. But before we do, it is necessary to take a brief look at the history of developmental psychology in order to understand and appreciate why this field has become an empirical science.

Human Development in Historical Perspective

To some extent, contemporary Western societies can be characterized as "child-centered": people often think of births as "blessed events," spend billions of dollars (pounds, francs, and so on) to care for, protect, and educate their young, and do not require children to shoulder the full responsibilities of citizenship until attaining the legal age of 14–21 (depending on the society), when they have presumably gained the wisdom and skills to "pull their own weight." Yet, childhood and adolescence were not always regarded as the very special and sensitive periods that we know them to be today. To understand how developmentalists think about and approach the study of children, it is necessary to see how the concept of childhood "developed" over time. And you may be surprised just how recent our modern viewpoint really is. Of course, only after people came to view childhood as a very special period did they begin to study children and the developmental process.

Childhood in Premodern Times

For a glimpse of childhood in the ancient past, imagine that you have just become a parent in the ninth century B.C. in the warlike city-state of Sparta. Chances are you feel relieved that the birth is over and has gone well but, at the same time, very anxious, for a moment of truth is rapidly approaching. In a few short hours, your infant will undergo a rigorous examination by the Spartan Council of Elders. The job of the elders is to inspect all newborns to determine whether the infants are sufficiently strong and healthy that they may be allowed to live. If your infant is judged weak or defective, he or she will be taken into the wilderness and left alone to die (Despert, 1965). The "lucky" infants who are pronounced healthy will soon be exposed to a strict training regimen designed to "harden" them for the grim task of serving a military state. For example, Spartan children are not permitted to display weakness of character by crying, and even very young infants are to be "toughened" by growing accustomed to cold-water baths (Despert, 1965). At 7 years of age, when American children of a future era are entering the second grade, your sons will be taken from your home and raised in a public barracks. While living in the barracks, they will very likely be beaten often or go for days at a time without food, for these are the methods used by the barracks masters to instill the discipline and mental toughness that your sons will require to become admirable warriors and credits to the Spartan nation (deMause, 1974; Despert, 1965).

Not all early societies treated their children as harshly as the citizens of Sparta. Yet, for several centuries after the birth of Christ, children were viewed as family "possessions" or resources that parents were free to use as they saw fit. In fact, it wasn't until the 12th century A.D. in Christian Europe that secular legislation equated infanticide—the killing of children—with murder (deMause, 1974)!

Currently, there is some debate about what your childhood would have been like had you grown up during the medieval era. Historian Philippe Ariès (1962) has analyzed documents and paintings from medieval Europe and concluded that European societies had *no* concept of childhood as we know it before 1600. Medieval children were not coddled or indulged to the extent that today's children are. They were often dressed in downsize versions of adult clothing and were depicted in artwork as working alongside adults (usually close relatives) in the shop or the field or as drinking and carousing with adults at parties. And except for exempting *infants* from criminal culpability for their harmdoing, medieval law generally made no distinctions between childhood and adult offenses (Borstelmann, 1983; Kean, 1937). But were medieval children really considered to be miniature adults?

Probably not. More recent and extensive examinations of medieval history reveal that childhood was generally recognized as a distinct phase of life and that children were thought to have certain needs above

Photo 1-1. Although medieval children dressed like their elders and often worked alongside them, it is doubtful that they were considered miniature adults.

and beyond those of adults (see Borstelmann, 1983; Kroll, 1977). Clearly the experiences of children were different during medieval times than today: emotional bonds between parents and their young may not have been as strong then as now, and children did routinely perform economic functions within the family that closely resemble "career" activities by today's standards. But it is almost certainly an overstatement to conclude that medieval societies had absolutely no concept of childhood and merely treated their young as miniature adults (Kroll, 1977).

Origins of Modern-Day Views on Childhood

During the 17th and 18th centuries, attitudes toward children and child rearing began to change. Religious leaders of that era stressed that children were innocent and helpless souls who should be shielded from the wild and wanton behavior of adults and adolescents. One method of accomplishing this objective was to send children to school. Although the primary purpose of schooling was to provide a proper moral and religious education, it was now recognized that important subsidiary skills such as reading and writing must be taught in order to transform the innocents into "servants and workers" who would provide society "with

a good labor force" (Ariès, 1962, p. 10). Although children were still considered family possessions, parents were now discouraged from abusing their sons and daughters and were urged to treat them with more warmth and affection (Ariès, 1962; Despert, 1965).

Early philosophical perspectives on childhood

Why did attitudes toward children change so drastically in the 17th and 18th centuries? Although the historical record is hazy on this point, it is likely that the thinking of influential social philosophers contributed in a meaningful way to the "new look" at children and child care. Lively speculation about human nature led these philosophers to carefully consider each of the following issues:

1. Are children inherently good or inherently bad?
2. Are children driven by inborn motives and instincts; or, rather, are they products of their environments?
3. Are children actively involved in determining their characters; or, rather, are they passive creatures molded by parents, teachers, and other agents of society?

Debates about these philosophical questions produced quite different perspectives on children and child rearing, ranging from Thomas Hobbes's (1651/1904)

Rousseau

Innate purity

Hobbes

Original sin

doctrine of **original sin,** which held that children are inherently selfish egoists who must be controlled by society, to Jean Jacques Rousseau's doctrine of **innate purity**—the notion that children are born with an intuitive sense of right and wrong that is often misdirected by society. These two viewpoints clearly differ in their implications for child rearing. Proponents of original sin argued that parents must actively restrain their egoistic offspring, while the innate purists viewed children as "noble savages" who should be given more freedom to follow their inherently positive inclinations.

Another view on children and child rearing was suggested by John Locke, who believed that the mind of an infant is a **tabula rasa,** or "blank slate," and that children have no inborn tendencies. In other words, children are neither inherently good nor inherently bad, and how they turn out will depend entirely on their worldly experiences. Like Hobbes, Locke argued in favor of disciplined child rearing to ensure that children would develop good habits and acquire few if any unacceptable ones.

These philosophers also differed on the question of children's participation in their own development. Hobbes maintained that children must learn to rechannel their naturally selfish interests into socially acceptable outlets; in this sense, they are passive subjects to be molded by the more powerful elements of

society—namely, parents. Locke, too, believed that the child's role is passive, since the mind of an infant is a blank slate on which experience writes its lessons. But a strikingly different view was proposed by Rousseau who believed that children are actively involved in the shaping of their intellects and personalities. In Rousseau's words, the child is not a "passive recipient of the tutor's instruction" but a "busy, testing, motivated explorer. The active searching child, setting his own problems, stands in marked contrast to the receptive one . . . on whom society fixes its stamp" (quoted in Kessen, 1965, p. 75).

Clearly these philosophers had some interesting ideas about children and how they should be raised. But how could anyone decide whether their views were correct? Unfortunately, the philosophers collected no objective data to back their contentions, and the few observations they did make were limited and unsystematic. Can you anticipate the next step in the evolution of developmental psychology?

Children as subjects: The baby biographies

As children became a proper topic for philosophical debate, the child's world began to change. The English formed societies for the prevention of cruelty to children. Education became increasingly widespread, and teachers began to use toys and picture books to facilitate the learning of their very young pupils (Despert, 1965). Pediatrics—the branch of medicine focusing on the care of infants and children—was recognized as a worthy medical specialty (deMause, 1974). Finally, philosophers, educators, and scientists from a variety of academic backgrounds began to observe the growth and development of their own children and to publish these data in works known as **baby biographies.**

Perhaps the most influential of the baby biographers was Charles Darwin, who made daily records of the early development of his son (Darwin, 1877). Darwin's curiosity about child development stemmed from his earlier theory of evolution, which had appeared in his book *The Origin of Species*. Most of us are familiar with Darwin's ideas that human beings gradually evolved from lower species. But how did this theory lead him to study children? On this point Darwin was clear. He believed that young, untrained infants shared many characteristics with their subhuman ancestors. For example, he described both babies and beasts as amoral creatures who must be disciplined before they would acquire any desirable habits. Such similarities between children and animals were intriguing to Darwin because he was a firm believer in the "biogenetic principle," or the **law of recapitulation**—the notion that an individual who develops from a single cell at conception into a marvelously complex, thinking human being as a young adult will retrace the entire evolutionary history of the species, thereby illustrating the "descent of man." In sum, Darwin argued that the way to approach thorny philosophical questions about human nature was to study the origins of humanity—both in nature and in developing children (Kessen, 1965). Consequently, he and many of his contemporaries turned to the baby biography, less out of an interest in development than as a means of answering questions about our evolutionary past.

One might suspect that the data recorded in the numerous baby biographies of the 18th and 19th centuries might have eventually led to a comprehensive theory of child development (or, at least, to a theory of infant development). Unfortunately, this proved not to be the case. Observations for many of the baby biographies were made at irregular intervals, and different biographers emphasized very different aspects of their children's behavior. Consequently, the data provided by various biographers were often not comparable. We might also note that the persons making observations in these biographical studies were generally the child's parents. This presents a problem because observers who are also kin may selectively record pleasant or positive incidents while paying much less attention to unpleasant or negative episodes. Yet another type of observer bias may result if the investigator has a number of "pet" assumptions about the nature of development and then notices or records only those observations that appear consistent with his or her point of view. Finally, almost every baby biography was based on observations of a single child, and it is difficult to know whether conclusions based on a single case would hold for other children.

Although the baby biographies were not very useful as a source of scientific information, they were a step in the right direction. Indeed, the fact that eminent scientists such as Charles Darwin were now writing about developing children implied that human development was a topic worthy of scientific scrutiny.

Emergence of a Psychology of Childhood

Introductory textbooks in virtually all academic areas typically credit someone as the "founder" of the discipline. In developmental psychology there are at least two viable candidates for this honor. One is an American psychologist G. Stanley Hall, whose most influential work was published in 1891.

Well aware of the shortcomings of baby biographies based on single children, Hall set out to collect more objective data on larger samples. Specifically, he was interested in the character of children's thinking,

---
Thomas Holbes

original sin: the idea that children are inherently negative creatures who must be taught to rechannel their selfish interests into socially acceptable outlets. *Rousseau*

innate purity: the idea that infants are born with an intuitive sense of right and wrong that is often misdirected by the demands and restrictions of society.

tabula rasa: the idea that the mind of an infant is a "blank slate" and that all knowledge, abilities, behaviors, and motives are acquired through experience.

18 + 19 C

baby biography: a detailed record of an infant's behavior over a period of time.

law of recapitulation: the notion that the developmental phases that an individual displays (ontogeny) will retrace, or recapitulate, the evolutionary history of the species (phylogeny).

and he developed a familiar research tool—the **questionnaire**—to "discover the contents of children's minds" (Hall, 1891). What he found was that children's understanding of worldly events increases rapidly over the course of childhood. Hall also discovered that the reasoning of young children is rather curious at times, deviating radically from that dictated by formal logic. Here, then, was the first large-scale scientific investigation of developing children, and it is on this basis that G. Stanley Hall merits consideration as the founder of developmental psychology.

At about the same time that Hall was using questionnaires to study children's thinking, a young European neurologist was trying a very different method of probing the mind and revealing its contents. The neurologist's approach was extremely fruitful, providing information that led him to propose a theory that revolutionized thinking about children and childhood. This neurologist was Sigmund Freud. His ideas came to be known as *psychoanalytic theory.*

In many areas of science, psychology included, new theories are often revisions or modifications of old theories. However, in Freud's day, there were few "old" theories of human behavior to modify. Freud was truly a pioneer, formulating his psychoanalytic theory from the thousands of notes he took and observations he made while treating patients for various kinds of "nervous" (emotional) disturbances.

Ever the astute observer, Freud happened to notice that patients would often describe very similar experiences or events that had been noteworthy to them while they were growing up. He then inferred that there must be important milestones in human development that all people share. As he continued to observe his patients and listen to their accounts of their lives, Freud concluded that each milestone in the life history of a patient was related in some meaningful way to earlier events. At this point, he recognized that he had the data—the pieces of the puzzle—from which to construct a comprehensive theory of human development.

The genius of Freud soon attracted many followers. Shortly after the publication of Freud's earliest theoretical monographs, the *International Journal of Psychoanalysis* was founded, and other researchers began to report their tests of Freud's thinking. By the mid-1930s much of Freud's work had been translated into other languages, and the impact of psychoanalytic theory was felt around the world. Over the years, Freud's theory proved to be quite *heuristic*—meaning that it continued to generate new research and to prompt other researchers to extend Freud's thinking. Clearly, the field of child development was alive and well by the time Freud died, in 1939.

Freud's work illustrates the role that theories play in the scientific study of human development. Although the word *theory* is an imposing term, it so happens that theories are something that everybody has. If someone were to ask you why males and females appear so very different as adults when they seem so very similar as infants, you would undoubtedly have something to say on the issue. In answering, you would be stating or at least reflecting your own underlying theory of sex differences. So a **theory** is really nothing more than a set of concepts and propositions that allow the theorist to describe and explain some aspect of experience. In the field of psychology, theories help us to describe various patterns of behavior and to explain why those behaviors occur.

Good theories have another important feature: the ability to predict future events. These theoretical predictions, or **hypotheses,** are then tested by collecting additional data. The information we obtain when testing hypotheses not only provides some clues about the theory's ability to explain new observations but may also lead to new theoretical insights that extend our knowledge even further.

Today there are many theories that contribute to our understanding of developing children, and in

Chapter 2 we will examine several of the more influential of these viewpoints. Although it is quite natural for people reading about these theories to pick a favorite, the scientist uses a rather stringent yardstick to evaluate theories: he or she will formulate hypotheses and conduct research to see whether the theory can adequately predict and explain new observations. Thus, there is no room for subjective bias when evaluating a theory. Theories in developmental psychology are only as good as their ability to predict and explain important aspects of human growth and development.

In the next section of the chapter, we will focus on the "tools of the trade"—that is, the research methods that developmentalists use to test their theories and gain a better understanding of the child's world.

Research Methods in Developmental Psychology

When detectives are assigned cases to solve, they first gather the facts, formulate hunches, and then sift through the clues or collect additional information until one of their hunches proves correct. Unraveling the mysteries of development is in many ways a similar endeavor. Investigators must carefully observe their subjects, study the information they have collected, and then use these data to draw conclusions about the ways people develop.

The focus in this section is on the methods that researchers use to gather information about developing children and adolescents. Our first task is to understand why developmentalists consider it absolutely essential to collect all these facts. We will then discuss the advantages and disadvantages of six basic fact-finding strategies: naturalistic observation, interviews, case studies, the clinical method, experiments, and natural (or quasi) experiments. Finally, we will consider the ways developmentalists use these strategies to detect and explain age-related changes in children's feelings, thoughts, and behaviors.

The Scientific Method

Modern developmental psychology is appropriately labeled a scientific enterprise because those who study developing organisms have adopted a value system we call the **scientific method** that guides their attempts at understanding. There is nothing mysterious about the scientific method. It is really more of an *attitude* or *value* than a method; the attitude dictates that,

above all, investigators must be *objective* and must allow their observations (or data) to decide the merits of their thinking. *before scientific method*

In the 17th and 18th centuries, when social philosophers were presenting their views on children and child rearing, their ideas were often interpreted as fact. It was as if people assumed that great minds always had great insights. Very few individuals questioned the word of these well-known scholars, because the scientific method was not yet an important criterion for evaluating wisdom and knowledge.

The intent here is not to criticize the early social philosophers. In fact, contemporary developmentalists (and today's children) are indebted to these men for helping to modify the ways in which society thought about and treated its young. However, so-called great minds may produce miserable ideas on occasion, and if poorly conceived notions have implications for the way human beings are to be treated, it behooves us to discover these erroneous assumptions before they harm anyone. The scientific method, then, is a value that helps to protect the scientific community and society at large against flawed reasoning. The protection comes from the practice of evaluating the merits of various theoretical pronouncements against the objective record, rather than simply relying on the academic, political, or social credibility of the theorist. Of course, this means that the theorist whose ideas are being evaluated must be equally objective and, thus, willing to discard pet notions when there is evidence that they have outlived their usefulness.

Applying the Scientific Method to the Study of Children and Adolescents

Today researchers are rather fortunate in having many methods that they can use to test their hypotheses about human development. This diversity of

questionnaire: *Hall* a research instrument that asks the persons being studied to respond to a number of written questions.

theory: a set of concepts and propositions designed to organize, describe, and explain an existing set of observations.

hypothesis: a theoretical prediction about some aspect of experience.

scientific method: an attitude or value about the pursuit of knowledge that dictates that investigators must be objective and must allow their data to decide the merits of their theorizing.

available research techniques is a strength because discoveries produced by one technique can be verified by other methods. Such *converging evidence* is extremely important, for it demonstrates that the "discovery" one has made is truly a discovery and not merely an artifact of the method used to collect the original data.

In the pages that follow, we will consider several of the methods that investigators use when trying to unravel the mysteries of development. Before we begin, here is an exercise, or "thought problem," that you may find interesting: In reviewing each method, we will consider an example of the kind of research that this approach has generated. Look carefully at these examples and select the study that you find most interesting. Then see whether you can think of a way that one or more of the other research methods might be used to provide converging evidence for the results of that study.

Naturalistic observation

A research method that many developmentalists favor is **naturalistic observation**—observing people in their common, everyday (that is, natural) surroundings. To observe children, this would usually mean going into homes, schools, or public parks and playgrounds and carefully recording what happens. Rarely will the observer try to record every event that occurs. Generally speaking, the researcher will be testing a specific hypothesis about one particular class of behavior, such as cooperation or aggression. He or she will then focus exclusively on this type of behavior and perhaps its antecedents and consequences (if they can be determined from the observational record).

Naturalistic observation is not so simple as it first appears, for a researcher using this approach must be extremely careful to guard against **observer bias**—the tendency to confirm one's hypothesis by reading too much (or too little) into naturally occurring events. In other words, the observational record must be as objective as possible, calling for a minimum of interpretation by the observer. One way to increase objectivity is to specify in advance precisely what kinds of activity qualify as examples of the behavior that you wish to study. You must also assess the **reliability** of your observations as a check on the objectivity of the procedure. Reliability is most often measured by asking a second person to observe the same events that the first observer witnesses and then comparing the observational records of the two observers. If independent observers largely agree on what occurred, the observational records are reliable. A lack of agreement indicates that the

Photo 1-2. Children's tendency to perform for an observer is one of the problems researchers must overcome when using the method of naturalistic observation.

observational scheme is unreliable and needs to be revised.

Finally, the mere presence of an unfamiliar adult observer is itself an unusual event that may make children behave rather atypically. Consider the experiences of one graduate student who attempted to take pictures of children's playground antics. What he recorded in many of his photos was somewhat less than spontaneous play. For example, one child who was playing alone with a doll jumped up when the student approached with the camera and informed him that he should take a picture of her "new trick" on the monkey bars. Another child who was playing kickball said "Get this" as he broke away from the kickball game and laid a blindside tackle on an unsuspecting onlooker. Clearly, observers should do what they can to minimize the influence they are likely to have on the behavior of their subjects. One way to approach the problem is to videotape the behavioral record for later viewing by members of the research team. Videotaping is particularly effective at minimizing the influence of an observer if the taping is done from a concealed location or if the recording equipment is in place for a long period so that children become less intrigued by this unusual machinery. If videotaping is not feasible, observers can minimize their influence by mingling with the children in their natural habitats before the actual conduct of the study. In this way, children become accustomed to the observers' presence and therefore are less likely to "perform" for them or alter their behavior in any significant way.

An example of naturalistic observation.
Several years ago, Rosalind Charlesworth and Willard Hartup (1967) used naturalistic observation to see whether nursery school children become more pleas- ?
ant to one another as they grow older. Charlesworth and Hartup first defined examples of positive social reinforcement that nursery-schoolers might dispense to one another, including such behaviors as showing affection or approval, cooperating, sharing, and giving tangible objects such as toys or snacks. Then, over a five-week period, they carefully observed a sample of 3- and 4-year-old nursery school children, noting each instance in which a child dispensed a positive social reinforcer to a classmate. The results were interesting. Not only were 4-year-olds more likely to reinforce their peers than were 3-year-olds, but they also distributed their reinforcers to a larger number of classmates. In addition, there was a strong relationship between giving and receiving social reinforcers: children who gave the most got the most, and children who infrequently reinforced their peers received few niceties in return. In other words, these children appeared to engage in a *reciprocal exchange* of positive reinforcers. Many theorists have argued that a kind of reciprocal exchange, or "equity," underlies most social encounters between adults (see, for example, Walster, Walster, & Berscheid, 1978). Charlesworth and Hartup's observations suggest that we may learn a great deal about the origins of social equity by observing the mutual give-and-take among young children at play in their peer groups.

A limitation of naturalistic observation.
From a procedural standpoint, Charlesworth and Hartup's study is an excellent piece of naturalistic observation. The investigators had rather precise definitions of the behaviors they wished to record, and they took care to ensure that their measures were reliable. They also tried to minimize their own influence on the children's behavior by allowing their subjects to get to know them and to grow accustomed to their presence. Yet, it can be argued that the knowledge we gain from any observational study is somewhat limited, no matter how carefully the investigator has designed the project.

The major limitation of observational research is its inability to differentiate among several possible causes for the observations made. Let's reconsider a major result of Charlesworth and Hartup's study: Do 4-year-olds reinforce peers more than 3-year-olds do *because* the older children have learned that peers will return their acts of kindness? Or, rather, do 4-year-olds simply

favor *group* play activities that just happen to provide more opportunities to give and receive social reinforcers? The latter explanation is not at all farfetched if the nursery school setting has few solitary (that is, one-person) toys that are sufficiently interesting to capture the imagination of the typical 4-year-old. In sum, there are many variables in the natural setting that may affect children's behavior, and it is often difficult to specify which of these variables or what combination of them is responsible for an observation or pattern of observations. But please note that this is merely a limitation of observational research, not a devastating critique. Naturalistic observation is an excellent procedure for detecting developmental trends or changes in behavior, which, once observed, may then be subjected to intensive causal analyses in later research.

Interviews, case studies, and the clinical method

Three common methods that developmentalists use to gather information and test hypotheses are the interview technique, the case study, and the clinical method. Although these approaches are similar in many respects, they differ in the extent to which the individuals who participate in the research are treated alike by the investigator.

The interview method. A researcher who opts for the interview method will ask the child (or the parents) a series of questions pertaining to one or more aspects of development. If the session is a **structured interview,** all who participate in the study are asked exactly the same questions in the same order. The purpose of this standardized, or structured, format is to

reciprocal exchange (social equity)
problem - perform

naturalistic observation: a method in which the scientist tests hypotheses by observing people as they engage in everyday activities in their natural habitats (for example, home, school, or playground).

observer bias: a tendency of an observer to over- or underinterpret naturally occurring experiences rather than simply recording the events that take place.

observer reliability: the degree of agreement between independent observers on what they have witnessed in an observational study.

structured interview: a technique in which all interviewees are asked the same questions in precisely the same order so that the responses of different participants can be compared.

treat each person alike so that the responses of different participants can be compared.

One interesting application of the interview technique is a project in which kindergarten, second-grade, and fourth-grade children responded to 24 questions designed to assess their knowledge of social stereotypes about males and females (Williams, Bennett, & Best, 1975). Each question came in response to a different short story in which the central character was described by either stereotypically masculine adjectives (for example, *aggressive, forceful, tough*) or stereotypically feminine adjectives (for example, *emotional, excitable*). The child's task was to indicate whether the character in each story was male or female. Williams and his associates found that even kindergartners could usually tell whether the stories referred to boys or girls. In other words, these 5-year-olds were quite knowledgeable about gender stereotypes, although children's thinking became much more stereotyped between kindergarten and the second grade. One implication of these results is that stereotyping of the sexes must begin very early if kindergartners are already thinking along stereotyped lines.

The interview method has some very real shortcomings. Investigators must hope that the answers they receive are honest and accurate and that they are not merely attempts by respondents to present themselves in a favorable or socially desirable manner. Clearly, inaccurate responses will lead to erroneous conclusions. When interviewing children of different ages, the investigator must also ensure that all questions are clearly understood by even the youngest respondents; otherwise, the age trends observed in one's study may represent differences in children's ability to comprehend and communicate rather than real underlying changes in children's feelings, thoughts, or behaviors.

In spite of these potential shortcomings, the structured interview can be an excellent research tool. Interviews are particularly useful when the interviewer *challenges* children to display what they know about an issue, for the socially desirable response to such a challenge is likely to be a truthful or accurate answer. In the gender stereotyping study, for example, the investigators wished to determine whether children of different ages had an understanding of common stereotypes about men and women. The participants probably considered each question a personal challenge or a puzzle to be solved and therefore were motivated to answer accurately and to display exactly what they knew about males and females. Under the circumstances, then, the

(begins early)
stereotyping of
sexes - interview technique

structured interview was an excellent method of assessing children's perceptions of the sexes.

The case study. Yet another method of researching human development is the **case study** approach. An investigator who uses this method prepares detailed descriptions of one or more individuals and then attempts to draw conclusions by analyzing these "cases." In preparing an individualized record, or "case," the psychologist will typically include many items of information about the individual, such as his or her family background, socioeconomic status, education and work history, health record, self-descriptions of significant life events, and performance on psychological tests. Much of the information included in any case history comes from interviews with the individual, although the questions asked are typically not standardized and may vary considerably from case to case.

The baby biographies of the 18th and 19th centuries are examples of case studies, each of which was based on a single subject. But perhaps the best known of the case-study researchers is Sigmund Freud, who prepared and analyzed dozens of cases and, from these records, formulated a comprehensive theory of human development—psychoanalytic theory.

Although Freud was a strong proponent of the case study and used it to great advantage, this method has three major shortcomings that seriously limit its usefulness. First, the validity of an investigator's conclusions will obviously depend on the accuracy of the information received from the "cases." Unfortunately, the potential for inaccuracy is great in a method in which adult subjects try to recall the causes and consequences of important events that happened years ago in childhood. Second, the data on any two (or more) individuals may not be directly comparable if the investigator has asked each participant different questions rather than posing a standard set of questions to all. Finally, the case study may lack *generalizability*; that is, conclusions drawn from the experiences of the particular individuals who were studied may not apply to most people. In fact, one recurring criticism of Freud's psychoanalytic theory is that it was formulated from the experiences and recollections of emotionally disturbed patients who were hardly typical of the general population. In sum, the case study can serve as a rich source of ideas about human development. However, its limitations are many, and any conclusions drawn from case studies should be verified through the use of other research techniques.

The clinical method. The **clinical method** is a close relative of the case-study approach. The investigator is usually interested in testing a particular hypothesis by presenting the research participant with a task or stimulus of some sort and then inviting a response. When the participant has responded, the investigator will typically ask a second question or introduce a new task in the hope of clarifying the participant's original answer. The questioning continues until the investigator has the information needed to evaluate his or her hypothesis. Although participants are often asked the same questions in the initial stages of the research, their answers to each question determine what the investigator asks next. Since participants' answers often differ, it is possible that no two participants will ever receive exactly the same treatment. In other words, the clinical method considers each subject to be unique.

Jean Piaget, a famous Swiss psychologist, relied extensively on the clinical method to study children's moral reasoning and general intellectual development. The data from Piaget's research are largely protocol records of his interactions with individual children. Here is a small sample from Piaget's work (1932/1965, p. 140) on the development of moral reasoning—a sample that shows that this young child thinks about lying in a very different way than adults do:

Piaget: Do you know what a lie is?
Clai: It's when you say what isn't true.
Piaget: Is 2 + 2 = 5 a lie?
Clai: Yes, it's a lie.
Piaget: Why?
Clai: Because it isn't right.
Piaget: Did the boy who said 2 + 2 = 5 know it wasn't right or did he make a mistake?
Clai: He made a mistake.
Piaget: Then if he made a mistake, did he tell a lie or not?
Clai: Yes, he told a lie.

We need only examine the richness of Piaget's thinking (as we will in Chapters 2 and 9) to see that the clinical method can provide a wealth of information about developing children. However, the clinical approach is a controversial technique that presents some thorny interpretive problems. We have already noted the difficulties in comparing cases or protocols generated by a procedure that treats each participant differently. Furthermore, the nonstandardized treatment of participants raises the possibility that the examiner's preexisting theoretical biases may affect the questions asked and the interpretations provided. Since conclusions drawn from the clinical method depend, in part, on the investigator's subjective assessments and interpretations, it is desirable to provide converging evidence for clinical insights by verifying them with other research techniques.

The experimental method

The laboratory experiment is one of the more popular methods of studying children because it permits the researcher to conduct reasonably unambiguous tests of his or her hypothesis. To introduce the essential features of this important technique, let's consider a problem that seems well suited for the **experimental method.**

———— Sigmund Freud

case study: a research method in which the investigator gathers extensive information about the life of an individual and then tests developmental hypotheses by analyzing the events of the person's life history.

clinical method: a type of interview in which a child's response to each successive question (or problem) determines what the investigator will ask next.

experimental method: a research strategy in which the investigator introduces some change in the child's environment and then measures the effect of that change on the child's behavior.

Suppose we believe that children learn a lot from watching television and that they are likely to imitate the behavior of the television characters to whom they are exposed. One hypothesis we might derive from this line of reasoning is that children who watch "helpful" television characters are likely to become more helpful themselves when they have opportunities to provide assistance to others in the near future. If we analyze our hypothesis, what we are saying is that a change in one variable (the kind of television program that children watch) will produce changes in a second variable (helpfulness).

In conducting a laboratory experiment to test this (or any) hypothesis, we would bring our participants together in a controlled environment, expose them to different treatments, and record as data their responses to the treatments. The different treatments to which we expose our participants represent the **independent variable** of our experiment. To test the hypothesis that we have proposed, our independent variable (or treatments) would be the type of television program that we show to our participants. Half of our children might view a program in which one or more characters were helpful to others, and the other half would watch a program in which the characters were not especially helpful. Children's reactions to the television shows would become the data, or **dependent variable,** in our experiment. Since our hypothesis involves helpgiving, we would want to measure (as our dependent variable) how helpful children are after watching each type of television show. A dependent variable is called "dependent" because its value presumably "depends" on the independent variable. In the present case, we are hypothesizing that future helpgiving (our dependent variable) will be greater for those children who watch programs that demonstrate helpgiving (one level of the independent variable) than for children who watch programs that show little or no helpgiving (the second level of the independent variable). If we are careful experimenters and exercise precise control over *all* other factors that may affect children's helpgiving, then the pattern of results that we have anticipated would allow us to draw a strong conclusion: watching television programs that demonstrate helpgiving *causes* children to become more helpful in the near future. Indeed, the most important advantage of the experimental method is that it permits a precise assessment of the cause-and-effect relationship that may exist between two variables.

Several years ago, the experiment we have discussed was actually conducted (Sprafkin, Liebert, & Poulos, 1975). The 6-year-olds who participated in this study watched one of two programs: an episode from the popular *Lassie* series that contained a dramatic rescue scene or a *Lassie* episode that contained no outstanding acts of helpgiving. Thus, the independent variable was the type of program the children watched. After watching one or the other show, each child began to play a game in an attempt to win a prize. While playing, he or she could hear some puppies in an adjacent area that were apparently discomforted. The dependent variable in this experiment was the amount of time children would spend away from the game giving help or comfort to the crying puppies. Note that, to help, the children had to leave the game and thereby decrease their chances of winning a prize.

Was helpgiving at all influenced by the type of program the children had watched? Indeed it was, for the children who had watched the episode in which helpgiving was emphasized spent considerably more time comforting the distressed pups than did the children who had watched the other episode. So it appears that examples of helpgiving on television can have a positive effect on the behavior of young children.

When students discuss this experiment in class, someone invariably challenges this interpretation of the results. For example, one student recently proposed an alternative explanation that "maybe the kids who watched helpgiving on TV simply liked dogs better than kids who saw a TV program with no helpgiving." In other words, she was suggesting that children's "liking for dogs" had determined the amount of help they gave and that the independent variable (type of television program) had had no effect at all! Could she have been correct? How do we know that the children in the two experimental conditions really didn't differ in some important way (such as their liking for dogs) that may have affected their willingness to help the puppies?

This question brings us to the crucial issue of **experimental control.** In order to conclude that the independent variable is causally related to the dependent variable, the experimenter must ensure that all other factors that could affect the dependent variable are *controlled*—that is, equivalent in each experimental condition. One way to equalize these extraneous factors is to do what Sprafkin et al. (1975) did: randomly assign children to their experimental treatments. The concept of *randomization,* or **random assignment,** means that each research participant has an equal probability of being exposed to each experimental treatment or condition. Assignment of individual participants to a particular treatment is accomplished by an unbiased procedure such as the flip of a coin. If the assignment is truly random, there is only a very slim chance that participants in the two (or more) experimental conditions will differ on any characteristic that might affect their performance on the dependent variable: all these "extraneous" characteristics will have been randomly distributed within each condition and equalized across the different conditions. Since Sprafkin et al. randomly assigned children to experimental conditions, they could be reasonably certain that the group of children who watched the "helpful" TV program had no greater "liking for dogs" than children who watched the "nonhelpful" TV program. So it was reasonable for them to conclude that the former group of children were the more helpful group *because* they had watched a TV program in which helpgiving was a central theme.

Surely Sprafkin et al. might have selected methods other than a laboratory experiment to explore the relationship, or **correlation,** between children's viewing of prosocial television programs and their tendency to be helpful. But even though alternative methodologies might have produced some very interesting and important findings, we will see in Box 1-1 why no method other than the experimental approach could have led these investigators to the unambiguous conclusion that watching prosocial television *causes* children to become more helpful.

A possible limitation of laboratory experiments. Critics of laboratory experimentation have argued that the tightly controlled laboratory environment is often very contrived and artificial and that children are likely to behave very differently in these surroundings than they would in a natural setting. Urie Bronfenbrenner (1977) has charged that a heavy reliance on laboratory experiments has transformed developmental psychology into "the science of the strange behavior of children in strange situations with strange adults" (p. 19). Similarly, Robert McCall (1977) notes that experiments tell us what *can* cause a developmental change but do not necessarily pinpoint the factors that *actually do* cause such changes in natural settings. Consequently, it is quite possible that conclusions drawn from laboratory experiments will not always apply to the real world.

One way around this criticism is to design experiments that seem more natural to children—experiments that take place in familiar surroundings and require children to perform highly typical or familiar activities. Bronfenbrenner (1977) has suggested several ways to make the experimental setting seem more realistic. For example, the study might take place in comfortable settings such as the home or school. Furthermore, children may behave more naturally as participants if their teachers or parents serve as the experimenter rather than a strange adult. Finally, we might urge investigators to make their procedures seem more typical or familiar to children. Researchers who study intellectual development, for example, might present their questions as a game or as a puzzle to be solved, rather than simply asking the child to take a test.

The field experiment. Perhaps the best way of determining whether a conclusion drawn from a laboratory experiment applies in the real world is to seek converging evidence by conducting an experiment in the natural environment—that is, a **field experiment.** This approach combines the advantages of na-

---

different treatments

independent variable: the aspect of a child's environment that an experimenter modifies or manipulates in order to measure its impact on the child's behavior.

reactions (data)
future
dependent variable: the aspect of a child's behavior that is measured in an experiment and assumed to be under the control of the independent variable.

experimental control: steps taken by an experimenter to ensure that all extraneous factors that could influence the dependent variable are roughly equivalent in each experimental condition; these precautions must be taken before an experimenter can be reasonably certain that observed changes in the dependent variable were caused by the manipulation of the independent variable.

random assignment: a control technique in which
(equalized) participants are assigned to experimental conditions through an unbiased procedure so that the members of the groups are not systematically different from one another.

meaningful
correlation: a relationship between two variables; correlated variables "go together," or covary, and are systematically related, although this relationship is not necessarily causal.

field experiment: an experiment that takes place in a naturalistic setting such as the home, the school, or a playground.

natural environment + experimental

Box 1-1

**The Difference between
Correlation and Causation**

There are many strategies that one can use to study the relationship between variables such as children's exposure to prosocial television and their helpgiving. Suppose, for example, that we had *interviewed* several dozen youngsters to determine each child's favorite TV shows and then *observed* the children at play, noting that those who preferred prosocial programming were much more helpful than those who favored other kinds of televised entertainment. What these data would show is that there is a meaningful relationship, or *correlation*, between children's television preferences and their helpfulness during free play. But would this correlation imply that watching prosocial television causes children to become more helpful?

No, it would not! Although we would have detected a relationship between children's preferences for prosocial programming and their helpgiving, the direction of this relationship is not at all clear. An equally plausible interpretation for our correlational finding is that being helpful leads children to prefer prosocial programs! Another possibility is that neither of these variables causes the other and that both are actually caused by a third variable that we have not measured. For example, if parental encouragement of helpgiving causes children to become more helpful *and* to prefer prosocial TV programs, then the latter two variables may be correlated, even though their relationship is not one of cause and effect. So correlational findings point to systematic relationships between variables, but they do not establish causality.

Naturalistic observation, interviews, case studies, and the clinical method are all excellent strategies for determining whether two or more variables are correlated. But since correlations do not imply causation, these methods cannot be used to establish the underlying causes of any aspect of human development. By contrast, the experimental method allows an investigator to determine whether two variables are causally related by systematically manipulating one of these variables to observe its *effect* (if any) on the other. So when Joyce Sprafkin and her colleagues manipulated children's exposure to different kinds of television programming and found that those who had watched prosocial programs became more helpful than those who had watched other programs, they were able to conclude that exposure to prosocial programming *causes* children to become more helpful, at least in the short run.

---

turalistic observation with the more rigorous control of an experiment. In addition, children are typically not apprehensive about participating in a "strange" experiment, because all the activities they undertake are everyday activities, and they may not even be aware that they are being observed.

Let's consider an example of a field experiment that provides converging evidence for the hypothesis that children who watch television programs that display **prosocial responses**—helpfulness, cooperation, and affection—will themselves become more prosocially inclined. Lynette Friedrich and Aletha Stein (1973) went into a nursery school, became acquainted with the children there, and then observed how often each child was helpful, cooperative, or affectionate toward other children. This initial measure of the child's prosocial behavior provided a *baseline* against which future increases in helpfulness or cooperation could be measured. After the baseline data were collected, the children were randomly assigned to different experimental conditions. Some of the children watched prosocial television programming *(Mister Rogers' Neighborhood)* at school, three days a week for a month. Other children spent an equal amount of time at school watching neutral films featuring circuses and farm scenes. At the end

of this month-long treatment phase, each child was observed daily in the nursery school setting for two additional weeks to determine whether the television programming had had any effects on his or her willingness to cooperate with others or to give help and affection.

The results of this field experiment clearly indicated that children who had watched the prosocial programming did, indeed, become more cooperative and affectionate toward their peers than they had been during the initial baseline period. Not only are the results of this field experiment consistent with those reported by Sprafkin et al. (1975), but they also demonstrate that the conclusions drawn from that laboratory experiment are definitely applicable to the real world.

The natural (or quasi) experiment

There are many developmental issues to which the experimental method is not easily applied. Suppose, for example, that a developmental psychologist wanted to study the effects of school desegregation on the academic performance of Black children in Macon, Georgia. If it were possible to apply the experimental method, the psychologist might randomly assign half the Black students in Macon to integrated schools, while the other half would remain in segregated schools. After a year or so, the scholastic performance of these two groups could be compared to assess the academic effects of desegregation on Black schoolchildren. However, school desegregation generally takes place at roughly the same time for everyone within a given school district. Therefore, public policy makes the researcher's proposed experiment impossible. In cases such as this one, the psychologist would attempt to study the issue in question by conducting a **natural (or quasi) experiment.**

A natural experiment is a study in which the investigator observes the consequences of some natural event or policy decision that he or she assumes will have an impact on people's lives. The "independent variable" in a natural experiment is the event, or "happening," which presumably will have consequences for those who experience it. But unlike experimental research, in which the investigator controls the independent variable and the assignment of participants to treatments, the natural experiment "does not" allow for such tight controls. Indeed, the quasi experimenter must study the effects of natural events whenever, wherever, and however they may occur.

Thomas Cook and Donald Campbell (1979) describe an interesting natural experiment centered in Winston-Salem, North Carolina. The event that took place (that is, the "treatment") was a campaign in which a large group of young children were encouraged to watch the educational television program *Sesame Street* on a regular basis. Other children, whom the campaign would not reach, served as a no-treatment control group. The dependent variable was a test of children's general knowledge. Both groups were given the test before the campaign and again, well after the treatment group had been encouraged to become regular viewers of *Sesame Street*. At the time of the pretest, children in the treatment group knew significantly *less* general information than children in the control group. At the later testing, however, children in the treatment group knew significantly *more* than children in the control group. These findings, illustrated in Figure 1-1, imply that *Sesame Street* is rather effective at furthering the general knowledge of young children.

The major limitation of a natural experiment is that the investigator often has too little information about research participants and too little control over natural events to draw firm conclusions about cause and effect. For example, in the research described by Cook and Campbell (1979), the nature of the campaign was such that children were not randomly assigned to the treatment and no-treatment groups. And as is often the

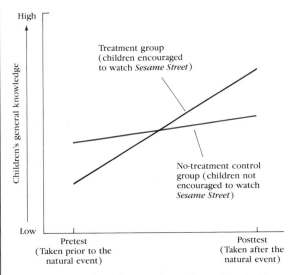

Figure 1-1. Results of the natural experiment described by Cook and Campbell (1979).

case in nonrandom assignment, the children did differ—those in the treatment group knew *less* initially than those in the control group. Unfortunately, this initial difference between the groups suggests an alternative interpretation for the results. Suppose that children in the treatment condition were both *younger* and *smarter* than children in the control group. If this were true, it might be that children in the treatment group knew less on the initial test *because they were younger* but that their knowledge increased faster over time *because they were brighter.* The implication, then, is that encouraging children in the treatment group to watch *Sesame Street* may have had little if any effect on their general knowledge. Clearly, the investigator's lack of control over important aspects of the research makes the results of natural experiments vulnerable to alternative interpretations.

Despite its inability to make *strong* statements about cause and effect, the natural experiment is never-

---

prosocial responses: behaviors such as cooperation, helping, sharing, or comforting that benefit other people.
natural (or quasi) experiment: a study in which the investigator measures the impact of some naturally occurring event that is assumed to affect people's lives.

Table 1-2. Some strengths and limitations of six general methods of collecting scientific data

Method	Strengths	Limitations
Naturalistic observation	Allows the study of phenomena as they occur in the real world; requires no intervention or treatment	Possibly subject to observer bias; cannot specify the causes of the observations that one has made
Structured interviews	Relatively quick way to gather much information; standardized format allows the investigator to make direct comparisons between data provided by different participants	Data collected may be inaccurate, may be less than completely honest, or may reflect variations in respondents' verbal skills and ability to understand the questions; cannot be used to specify cause-and-effect relationships
Case studies	Very broad method that considers many sources of data when drawing inferences and conclusions about individual participants	Data collected may be inaccurate or biased; conclusions drawn from individual "cases" may not apply to most people; cannot be used to specify cause-and-effect relationships
Clinical methods	Flexible methodology that treats subjects as unique individuals; freedom to probe can be an aid in ensuring that the participant understands the meaning of the questions one asks	Conclusions drawn may be unreliable in that participants are not all treated alike; flexible probes depend, in part, on the investigator's subjective interpretations of the participant's responses; can be used only with highly verbal participants; cannot be used to specify cause-and-effect relationships
Experiments	Allow a determination of causal relationships among variables; field experiments permit causal analyses of events in the natural environment	Precise control that is required may make experiments seem contrived or artificial and limit generalizability of results *(may not apply to most people)*
Natural experiments	Permit a study of the impact of natural events that would be difficult or impossible to simulate in an experiment; provide strong clues about cause-and-effect relationships	Lack of precise control over natural events or the participants exposed to them prevents the investigator from establishing definitive cause-and-effect relationships

theless useful in determining whether a natural event could *possibly* have had an effect on those who experience it. For example, the fact that those children who were encouraged to watch *Sesame Street* showed the greater increases in knowledge at least suggests that *Sesame Street* may have contributed to their relatively large gains. So natural experiments often provide meaningful clues about cause and effect. However, their results always remain open to alternative interpretations.

Summing up. The six fact-finding strategies we have examined are very general research techniques that scientists from many disciplines often use to collect data and evaluate their theories and hypotheses. By way of brief review, the strengths and weaknesses of each of these methods are summarized in Table 1-2. In the next section, we will consider three additional research methods that are more uniquely "developmental" in character.

Designing Research to Measure Developmental Change

Let's assume that we have chosen to study some aspect of children's development and have selected one of the six basic fact-finding strategies as a method of gathering information on that topic. As developmentalists, we are not merely interested in examining children's progress at any given phase of life; generally, we would hope to determine how children's feelings, thoughts, and behaviors *develop* or change over time. How might we design our research to chart these developmental trends? Let's briefly consider three methods: the cross-sectional comparison, the longitudinal comparison, and the sequential design.

Cross-sectional comparisons

The **cross-sectional comparison** is a method in which people who *differ in age* are studied *at the same point in time.* By comparing the responses of participants in the different age groups, investigators can often identify age-related changes in whatever aspect of development they happen to be studying.

An experiment by Brian Coates and Willard Hartup (1969) is an excellent example of a cross-sectional comparison. Coates and Hartup were interested in determining why preschool children are less proficient than first- or second-graders at learning new responses displayed by an adult model. Their hypothesis was that younger children do not spontaneously *describe* what they are observing, whereas older children will produce verbal descriptions of the modeled sequence. When asked to perform the actions they have witnessed, the preschoolers are at a distinct disadvantage because they have no verbal "learning aids" that would help them to recall and reproduce the model's behavior.

To test these hypotheses, Coates and Hartup designed an interesting cross-sectional experiment. Children from two age groups—4- and 5-year-olds and 7- and 8-year-olds—watched a short film in which an adult model displayed 20 novel responses, such as shooting at a tower of blocks with a pop gun, throwing a beanbag between his legs, and lassoing an inflatable toy with a Hula Hoop. Some of the children from each age group were instructed to describe the model's actions, and they did so as they watched the film (induced-verbalization condition). Other children were not required to describe the model's actions as they observed them (passive-observation condition). When the show ended, each child was taken to a room that contained the same toys seen in the film and was asked to demonstrate what the model had done with these toys.

Three interesting findings emerged from this experiment (the data appear in Figure 1-2). First, the 4–5-year-olds who were *not* told to describe what they had seen (that is, the passive observers) reproduced *fewer* of the model's responses than the 4–5-year-olds who described the model's behavior (the induced verbalizers) or the 7–8-year-olds in either experimental condition. This finding suggests that 4–5-year-old children may not produce the verbal descriptions that would help them to learn unless they are explicitly instructed to do so. Second, the performance of younger and older children in the induced-verbalization condition was comparable. So younger children can learn just as much

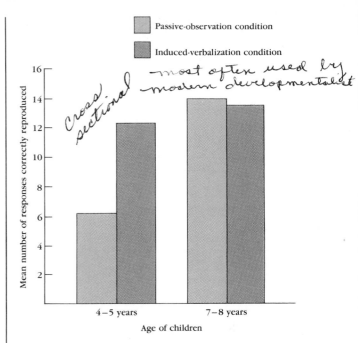

Passive-observation condition

Induced-verbalization condition

most often used by modern developmentalist

Cross sectional

Figure 1-2. Children's ability to reproduce the behavior of a social model as a function of age and verbalization instructions. *(Adapted from Coates & Hartup, 1969.)*

as older children by observing a social model *if the younger children are told to describe what they are seeing.* Finally, 7–8-year-olds in the passive-observation condition reproduced about the same number of behaviors as 7–8-year-olds in the induced-verbalization condition. This finding suggests that instructions to describe the model's actions had little effect on 7–8-year-olds, who will apparently describe what they have seen even when not told to. Taken together, the results imply that 4–5-year-olds in the natural setting may learn less from social models because they, unlike older children, do not spontaneously produce the verbal descriptions that would help them to remember what they have observed.

An important advantage of the cross-sectional method is that the investigator can collect data from children of different ages over a short time. For example, Coates and Hartup did not have to wait three years for their 4–5-year-olds to become 7–8-year-olds in or-

no "individual" study
cohort effect

cross-sectional comparison: a research design in which subjects from different age groups are studied at the same point in time.

der to test their developmental hypotheses. They merely sampled from two age groups and tested both samples simultaneously.

Cohort effects. Notice, however, that in cross-sectional research, participants at each age level are *different* people. In the language of developmental methodology, they come from different cohorts, where a **cohort** can be defined as a group of people of the same age who are exposed to similar cultural environments and historical events as they are growing up. The fact that cross-sectional comparisons always involve different cohorts presents us with a thorny interpretive problem, for any age differences that are found in the study may not always be due to age or development but, rather, may reflect other cultural or historical factors that distinguish members of different cohorts. Stated another way, cross-sectional comparisons confound age and cohort effects.

An example should clarify the issue. For years, cross-sectional research had consistently indicated that young adults score higher on intelligence tests than middle-aged adults, who, in turn, score higher than the elderly. But does intelligence decline with age, as these findings would seem to indicate? Not necessarily! More recent research (Baltes, 1968) reveals that individuals' intelligence test scores remain stable over the years and that the earlier studies were really measuring something quite different: age differences in education. The older adults in the cross-sectional studies had had less schooling and, therefore, scored lower on intelligence tests than the middle-aged and young adult samples. Their test scores had not declined but, rather, had always been lower than those of the younger adults with whom they were compared. So the earlier cross-sectional research had discovered a cohort effect, not a true developmental trend.

Despite its confounding of age and cohort effects, the cross-sectional comparison is still the design most often used by contemporary developmentalists. Not only is this approach reasonably easy and efficient in terms of the time taken to conduct one's research, but cross-sectional comparisons are likely to yield valid developmental conclusions when there is little reason to believe that the cohorts being studied have had widely different experiences while growing up. If we wished to compare 4- and 5-year-old children, for example, we could feel reasonably confident that history or the prevailing culture had not changed in any major way in the year that separates these two cohorts. It is mainly in

studies that attempt to make inferences about development over a span of several years that "cohort effects" are a serious problem.

Data on individual development. There is a second major problem with the cross-sectional study: it tells us nothing about the development of *individuals* because each person is observed *at only one point in time*. So cross-sectional comparisons cannot provide answers to questions such as "When will *my* child become more independent?" or "Will aggressive 2-year-olds become aggressive 5-year-olds?" To address issues like these, the investigator often turns to a second kind of developmental comparison, the longitudinal method.

Longitudinal comparisons

The **longitudinal comparison** is a method whereby the same children are observed repeatedly over a period of time. The time period may be very long or reasonably short. The investigators may be looking at one particular aspect of development, such as intelligence, or many. By repeatedly testing the same children, investigators can assess the "stability" of various attributes and patterns of developmental change for *each* child in the sample. In addition, they can identify general developmental trends and processes by looking for commonalities, such as the point(s) at which most children undergo various changes and the experiences, if any, that children seem to share prior to reaching these milestones. Finally, the tracking of several children over time will help investigators to understand *individual differences* in development, particularly if they are able to establish that different kinds of earlier experiences lead to very different outcomes.

One of the most famous longitudinal projects in the history of developmental psychology began in 1929 at the Fels Research Institute in Yellow Springs, Ohio. Imagine that you had been a new parent in 1929 and had responded to an ad requesting that you bring your newborn infant to the Fels Institute. The purpose of your visit: so that you and your child might participate together in an exciting new research project. When you arrive, a member of the Fels staff explains that this project is an ambitious one that will teach us a great deal about the child's world and the ways children develop. As he describes the project further, you suddenly realize that he is asking you to submit to at least one interview a year and to have your child weighed, measured, tested, and observed *for the next 18 years!* Would you volunteer? Many mothers did, for the Fels researchers began their longitudinal study with a total of 89 children, 45 males and 44 females.

Over the course of the project, the amount of information collected from each child (and from his or her mother) was simply staggering. For the first six years of the child's life, a professional interviewer made half-day, semi-annual visits to the home, interviewing the mother and watching her interact with her child. These visits continued on an annual basis when the child was between 6 and 12 years of age. In addition, each child was repeatedly observed interacting with peers in a nursery school setting between the ages of 2½ and 5 and in a day camp between the ages of 6 and 10. In each of these settings, children were rated on traits such as aggression, achievement, conformity, dependency, sex-typed play, and verbal fluency. At three-year intervals between the ages of 8 and 17, each of the Fels children took an extensive battery of personality tests. Finally, 71 of the participants were located, tested, and interviewed when they were young adults between the ages of 20 and 29.

Can you imagine the work involved in analyzing all this information? Indeed, the data were analyzed, and they allowed members of the research team to draw important conclusions about the long-term stability or instability of behaviors such as aggression, achievement, and dependency. The investigators were also able to make inferences about the effects of various methods of parenting on the child's later feelings, aspirations, and behavior. Clearly, the Fels project was an undertaking of monumental proportions. We will return to this important study on several occasions as we continue along our journey through the child's world.

Although we have portrayed the longitudinal comparison in a very favorable manner, this procedure does have several drawbacks of which you should be aware. For example, longitudinal projects can be very *costly* (imagine the bill for 18 years of research in the Fels study) and *time-consuming*. The latter point is more important than it may first appear, for the focus of theory and research in developmental psychology is constantly changing, and longitudinal questions that seem very exciting at the beginning of a long-term project may seem rather trivial by the time the project ends. As longitudinal researchers, we may also have a problem with *subject loss*; children may move away, get sick, or become bored with repeated testing, and they occasionally have parents who, for one reason or another, will not allow them to continue in the study. The result is a smaller and potentially **nonrepresentative sample** that

not only provides less information about the developmental issues in question but also may limit the conclusions of the study to those healthy children who do not move away and who remain cooperative over the long run.

There is another shortcoming of longitudinal research that students often see right away—the **cross-generational problem.** Children growing up in one era may be exposed to very different kinds of experiences than children from another era. As a consequence, the patterns of development that characterize one generation of children may not always apply to other generations.

To clarify the issue, we need only note how times have changed since the 1930s and '40s, when the Fels children were growing up. In this age of dual-career families, more youngsters are attending day-care centers and nursery schools than ever before. Modern families are smaller than those of years past, meaning that children now have fewer brothers and sisters. Families also move more frequently than they did in the 1930s and '40s, so that many children from the modern era are exposed to a wider variety of people and places than was typical in years gone by. And no matter where they may be living, today's youngsters grow up in front of television sets, an influence that was not widely available until the mid-1950s. So children of the 1930s and 1940s lived in a very different world, and we cannot be certain that these youngsters developed in precisely the same way as today's children. In other words, cross-generational changes in the environment may limit the conclusions of a longitudinal project to those children who were growing up while the study was in progress.

We have seen that the cross-sectional and longitudinal methods each have distinct advantages and disadvantages. Might it be possible to combine the best

---

cohort: a group of people of the same age who are exposed to similar cultural and historical events as they develop.

longitudinal comparison: a research design in which one group of subjects is studied repeatedly over a period of months or years.

nonrepresentative sample: a subgroup that differs in important ways from the larger group (or population) to which it belongs.

cross-generational problem: the fact that long-term changes in the environment may limit conclusions of a longitudinal project to that generation of children who were growing up while the study was in progress.

Photo 1-3. Leisure activities of the 1930s (left) and the 1980s (right). As these photos illustrate, children growing up in the 1930s had very different kinds of experiences from those of today's youth. Many believe that cross-generational changes in the environment may limit the results of a longitudinal study to the youngsters who were growing up while that research was in progress.

features of both approaches? A third kind of developmental comparison—the sequential design—tries to do just that.

The sequential comparison

Suppose that we have devised a training program designed to reduce racial prejudice among 6- to 10-year-olds. Before administering our program on a large scale, we would surely want to try it out on a smaller number of children to see whether it really works. However, there are a number of additional questions that others may have about our program, such as "When can children first understand it?" or "At what age will children respond most favorably to the technique?" Finally, educators and child-care personnel would want to know whether any immediate reductions in prejudice produced by our program will persist over time. In order to address all these issues in our research, we will need a design that measures *both* the short-term and the long-term effects of our program on children of *different ages*.

Clearly, the cross-sectional comparison cannot answer all our questions. The cross-sectional design, which employs different children at each age level, cannot tell us anything about the long-term effects of our program on an individual child. The longitudinal method can tell us about long-term effects. But since all the participants would be exposed to the program at the same age (say, age 6), a longitudinal study would not tell us whether this training would be any more (or less) effective if it were first administered when children were a little older.

The only approach that allows us to answer all our questions is a **sequential comparison** (Schaie, 1965, 1986). Sequential comparisons combine the best features of the cross-sectional and the longitudinal approaches by selecting participants of different ages and then studying each of these cohorts over time. For purposes of our proposed research, we might begin by administering our training program to a group of 6-year-olds, a group of 8-year-olds, and a group of 10-year-olds. Of course, we would want to randomly assign other 6-, 8-, and 10-year-olds to control groups that were not to be exposed to the training program. The children who were "trained" would then be observed and compared with their age mates in the control group to determine (1) whether the program was immediately effective at reducing racial prejudice and (2) if so, the age at which the program had its largest *immediate* impact. This is the information that we would obtain had we conducted a standard cross-sectional experiment.

However, our choice of the sequential design allows us to measure the enduring effects of our program by simply retesting our samples of 6- and 8-year-olds two years later. This approach has several advantages over the standard longitudinal comparison. The

Table 1-3. Summary of the cross-sectional, longitudinal, and sequential designs

	Cross-sectional method	*Longitudinal method*	*Sequential method*
Procedure	Observe people of different ages (cohorts) at one point in time	Observe people of one cohort repeatedly over time	Combine the cross-sectional and the longitudinal approaches by observing different cohorts repeatedly over time
Information gained	Differences between participants from different cohorts	Changes in individual participants over time	Changes over time in participants from different cohorts
Advantages	1. Demonstrates age differences; hints at developmental trends 2. Relatively inexpensive 3. Takes little time to conduct	1. Provides data on the development of individuals 2. Can reveal links between early experiences and later outcomes 3. Indicates how individuals are alike and how they are different in the ways they change over time	1. Helps to separate true developmental trends from cohort effects 2. Indicates whether developmental changes experienced by one cohort are similar to those experienced by other cohorts 3. Often less costly and time-consuming than the longitudinal approach
Disadvantages	1. Age trends may reflect extraneous differences between "cohorts" rather than true developmental change 2. Provides "no data" on the development of "individuals" because each participant is observed at only one point in time	1. Relatively time-consuming and expensive 2. Subject loss may yield nonrepresentative sample that limits the generalizability of one's conclusions 3. Cross-generational changes may limit one's conclusions to the cohort that was studied	1. More costly and time-consuming than cross-sectional research 2. Despite being the strongest method, may still leave questions about whether a developmental change is generalizable beyond the cohorts that were studied

first is a *time saving:* in only two years, we have learned about the long-term effects of the program on those children who are still between the target ages of 6 and 10. A standard longitudinal comparison would require four years to provide similar information. Second, the sequential design actually yields *more information* about long-term effects than the longitudinal approach does. If we had chosen the longitudinal method, we would have data on the long-term effects of a program administered *only* to 6-year-olds. However, the sequential approach allows us to determine whether the program has *comparable* long-term effects when administered to both 6- and 8-year-olds. Clearly, this combination of the cross-sectional and longitudinal methods provides a rather versatile alternative to either of those approaches (see Table 1-3 for a brief summary of the aims, implications, advantages, and disadvantages of each type of developmental comparison).

The Cross-Cultural Comparison

Developmental researchers are normally hesitant to publish a new finding or conclusion until they have studied enough children to determine that their "discovery" is reliable. However, their conclusions are frequently based on children living at one point in time within one particular culture or subculture, and it is often difficult to know whether these conclusions will apply to future generations or even to children who are currently growing up in other subcultures or in other societies around the world. Today, the generalizability of findings across samples and settings has become an important issue, for many theorists have implied that

sequential comparison: a research design in which subjects from different age groups are studied repeatedly over a period of months or years.

Photo 1-4. Cross-cultural comparisons allow us to identify similarities and differences in the development of children from different cultures and subcultures.

there are "universals" in human development—events and outcomes that all children share as they progress from infancy to adulthood.

Cross-cultural studies are those in which participants from different cultural or subcultural backgrounds are observed, tested, and compared on some aspect of their psychological functioning. Studies of this kind serve many purposes. For example, they allow the investigator to determine whether conclusions drawn about the development of children from one social context (such as middle-class, White youngsters in the Untied States) also characterize children growing up in other societies or even those from different ethnic or socioeconomic backgrounds within the same society (for example, American children of Hispanic ancestry or those from economically disadvantaged homes). So the **cross-cultural comparison** guards against the overgeneralization of research findings and, indeed, is the only way to determine whether there are truly "universals" in human development.

Although cross-cultural research has led to the discovery of several developmental outcomes that most (if not all) people share, many investigators who favor

and use this approach are looking for *differences* rather than similarities. They recognize that human beings develop in societies that have very different ideas about issues such as the age at which mothers should wean their infants, when and how children should be punished, the activities that are most appropriate for boys and for girls, the time at which childhood ends and adulthood begins, the treatment of the aged, and countless other aspects of life. They have also learned that people from various cultures differ in the ways they perceive the world, express their emotions, think, and solve problems. Ruth Benedict (1934) used the term *cultural relativism* to express her belief that a person's behavior can be understood only within the context of his or her cultural and subcultural environment. So developmental psychology in cross-cultural perspective is, in part, an attempt to discover how social groups may differ in the ways they raise their children and how these differences may then contribute to the development of culture-specific patterns of behavior, or distinct "cultural personalities."

One classic example of cultural relativism comes from Margaret Mead's (1935) study of three subcultures on the island of New Guinea. Despite their geographical proximity, these three groups were found to be very dissimilar in many respects. Mead described the Arapesh as a passive, peace-loving tribe who stood in marked contrast to their neighbors, the Mundugumor, who were especially ruthless and aggressive. The third group, the Tchambuli, were not particularly pacifistic or aggressive, although they did differ from the other two groups and from members of our own society. Among the Tchambuli, males were the passive, nurturant, and dependent sex, whereas females were dominant, independent, and assertive. This particular study is but one example of a large body of cross-cultural research indicating that the content of social development, or _what_ the children become, will depend very heavily on the specific values and child-rearing practices that are endorsed by members of their "social order."

We have now reviewed a variety of research designs and techniques, each of which has definite strengths and weaknesses. When planning a research project, developmentalists will select a method only after carefully considering what it will take to answer the questions they are asking and then comparing these needs against available resources, such as the size of their research budget, the amount of time they have to conduct the research, and the availability of research participants. The fact that investigators have so many methods from which to choose is really an advantageous arrangement in that findings obtained by one technique may then be checked (and perhaps confirmed) through the use of other methodologies. So there is no "best method" for studying children and adolescents; each of the approaches that we have considered has contributed in a meaningful way to our understanding of human development.

There is yet another important concern that investigators must heed when planning their research— the impact of their procedures on research participants. Specifically, children and adolescents serving as participants in psychological research have important rights that the investigator is ethically bound to protect.

Ethical Considerations in Developmental Research

Many years ago, Sigmund Freud proposed that children must establish a close emotional relationship with a mother figure during the first year or two of life,

or they would remain forever cold and emotionally unresponsive to other people. There is a very simple experiment that one could conduct to test this hypothesis: randomly assign one group of infants to an experimental condition in which they are locked in an attic and receive only the most basic care for the first two years of their lives. The remaining infants would be reared in their normal home environments for the same length of time. If Freud was correct, we should find that our socially isolated group would remain wary of people and unable to form close emotional attachments to others for as long as we might care to observe them. By contrast, children reared at home should show a more normal pattern of emotional responsiveness.

Now you may be thinking "Heaven forbid! Only a barbarian would propose such an experiment!" This example is admittedly extreme, but purposefully so to make a point: a researcher is never justified in exposing children to any situation or experimental procedure that is likely to harm them seriously. In the case of our hypothetical experiment, we have reason to believe that social isolation will have harmful and possibly even pathological consequences for research participants. Thus, the project represents a gross violation of **research ethics,** and it is unlikely that any developmental researcher would even contemplate such a course of action (except, of course, to make a point about ethical guidelines in research with children).

The ethical issues encountered in most research are far more subtle. Here are some of the dilemmas that developmental psychologists may have to resolve during their careers as researchers:

• Is it appropriate to expose children to situations that virtually guarantee that they will violate certain prohibitions or behave in some other socially undesirable manner?
• Can I ask children or adolescents about the ways their parents punish them, or is this line of questioning an invasion of the children's (or parents') privacy?
• Am I ever justified in deceiving children in some way, either by misinforming them about the purpose of my

looks for diff in dev. determines universals

cross-cultural comparison: a study that compares the behavior and/or development of people from different cultural or subcultural backgrounds.
research ethics: standards of conduct that investigators are ethically bound to honor in order to protect their research participants from physical or psychological harm.

Table 1-4. The rights of children and responsibilities of investigators involved in psychological research

In order to protect children who participate in psychological research and to clarify the responsibilities of researchers who work with children, the American Psychological Association (1973) has endorsed the following ethical guidelines:

1. No matter how young the child, he has rights that supersede the rights of the investigator. The investigator should measure each operation he proposes in terms of the child's rights, and before proceeding, he should obtain the approval of a committee of [the investigator's fellow scientists].

2. The final responsibility to establish and maintain ethical practices in research remains with the individual investigator. He is also responsible for the ethical practices of all [research collaborators, who, in turn,] incur parallel obligations.

4. The investigator should inform the child of all features of the research that may affect his willingness to participate.

5. The investigator should respect the child's freedom to refuse to participate in research . . . as well as to discontinue participation at any time.

6. The informed consent of parents or of those who act in the child's behalf—teachers, superintendents of institutions— should be obtained, preferably in writing. Informed consent requires that the parent or other responsible adult be told all features of the research that may affect his willingness to allow the child to participate.

9. The investigator uses no research operation that may harm the child either physically or psychologically. Psychological harm, to be sure, is difficult to define; nevertheless, its definition remains the responsibility of the investigator. When the investigator is in doubt about the possible harmful effects of the research operations, he seeks consultation from others. When harm seems possible, he is obligated to find other means of obtaining the information or to abandon the research.

10. Although we accept the ethical ideal of full disclosure of information, a particular study may necessitate concealment or deception. Whenever concealment or deception is thought to be essential to the conduct of the study, the investigator should satisfy a committee of his peers that his judgment is correct. If concealment or deception is practiced, adequate measures should be taken after the study to ensure the participant's understanding of the reasons for the concealment or deception.

11. The investigator should keep in confidence all information obtained about research participants.

Source: American Psychological Association (1973).

study or by telling them something untrue about themselves (for example, "You did poorly on this test")?

- Can I observe my participants in the natural setting without informing them that they are the subjects of a scientific investigation?

- Is it acceptable to tell children that their classmates think that an obviously incorrect answer is "correct" in order to see whether participants will conform to the judgments of their peers?

- Am I justified in using verbal punishment (disapproval) as part of my research procedure?

Before reading further, you may wish to think about these issues and formulate your own opinions. Then read Table 1-4 and reconsider each of your points of view.

Have any of your opinions changed? It would not be terribly surprising if they hadn't. As you can see, the guidelines in Table 1-4 are very general; they do not explicitly permit or prohibit specific operations or practices such as those described in the dilemmas. The responsibility for treating children fairly and protecting them from harm falls squarely on the shoulders of the " investigator."

How, then, do investigators decide whether to use a procedure that some may consider questionable on ethical grounds? They generally weigh the advantages and disadvantages of the research by carefully calculating its possible *benefits* (to humanity or to the participants) and comparing them against the potential *risks* that participants may face. If the potential benefits greatly outweigh the potential risks, and if there are no other less risky procedures that could be used to produce these same benefits, the investigator will generally proceed. However, there are safeguards against overzealous researchers who underestimate the riskiness of their procedures. In the United States, for example, universities, research foundations, and government agencies that fund research with children have set up "human-subjects review committees" to provide second (and

Photo 1-5. Ethical considerations may force an investigator to abandon procedures that cause harm or pose unforeseen risks to research participants.

sometimes third) opinions on the ethical standards and considerations of all proposed research. The function of these review committees is to reconsider the potential risks and benefits of the proposed research and, more important, to help ensure that all possible steps are taken to protect the welfare and maintain the integrity of those who may choose to participate in the project.

Although it is your right and privilege to disagree, any of the dilemmas outlined above can be resolved in ways that permit an investigator to use the procedures in question and still remain well within current ethical guidelines. For example, it is generally considered permissible to observe children in natural settings (for example, at home or at school) without

informing them that they are being studied if the investigator has previously obtained the *informed consent* (see Table 1-4, guideline 6) of the adults responsible for the children's care and safety in these settings. It is also considered permissible to ask children personal questions about themselves or their family lives as long as the investigator has taken steps to minimize the risks of invading their privacy—steps such as (1) assuring these youngsters that their answers will remain anonymous, (2) making them understand that they are not required to answer questions that they don't feel like answering, and (3) explaining to them that they may have their data discarded and immediately destroyed should they feel uncomfortable about what they have said or done.

Of course, final approval of one's procedures by a review committee does not absolve investigators of the need to reevaluate the benefits and costs of their projects, even while the research is in progress. Suppose, for example, that a researcher studying children's aggression in a playground setting came to the conclusion that his subjects had (1) discovered his own fascination with aggressive behavior and (2) begun to beat on one another in order to attract his attention. At that point, the risks to participants would have escalated far beyond the researcher's initial estimates, and he would have been ethically bound (in my opinion) to stop the research immediately.

In the final analysis, guidelines and review committees do not guarantee that research participants will be treated responsibly; only investigators can do that, by constantly reevaluating the consequences of their operations and by modifying or abandoning any procedure that may compromise the welfare or the dignity of those who have volunteered to participate.

Summary

Developmental psychology is the largest of several disciplines that seek to explain *development*— that is, the systematic changes in the individual that occur between conception and death. Developmentalists are particularly concerned with *describing* significant changes in physical growth, mental abilities, emotional expression, and social behavior and with *explaining* why these changes occur. Although we will focus mainly on the developments of childhood and adolescence in this book, it is important to recognize that human development continues throughout life and is *holistic*—meaning that changes in one aspect of development often have implications for other, seemingly unrelated aspects.

Children who lived in medieval times (and earlier) were often treated rather harshly by their elders and were afforded few of the rights, privileges, and protections of today's youth. The viewpoints of important social philosophers of the 17th and 18th centuries contributed to a more humane outlook on children and child rearing, and shortly thereafter, people began to study their sons and daughters and to report their findings in baby biographies. The scientific study of children did not emerge until nearly 1900 as G. Stanley Hall, in the United States, and Sigmund Freud, in Europe, began to collect objective data and to formulate theories about human growth and development. Soon other investigators were conducting research to evaluate and extend these theories, and the study of developmental psychology began to thrive.

Developmental psychology today is a truly objective science. Gone forever are the days when the merits of a theory depended on the social or academic prestige of the theorist. Today a developmentalist determines the adequacy of a theory by deriving hypotheses and conducting research to see whether the theory can predict and explain the new observations that he or she has made. There is no room for subjective bias in evaluating ideas; theories of human development are only as good as their ability to account for the important aspects of children's growth and development.

Developmentalists are fortunate to have available a wide variety of useful methods for studying children and detecting developmental changes. The major methods for conducting research with children include naturalistic observation, interviews, case studies, clinical approaches, experiments, and natural experiments. Developmental trends are detected by adapting one or more of these techniques to provide cross-sectional or longitudinal comparisons. The cross-sectional comparison assesses developmental change by studying children of different ages at the same point in time. The longitudinal approach detects developmental trends by repeatedly examining the same children as they grow older. The sequential design, a combination of the cross-sectional and the longitudinal approaches, offers the investigator the best features of both strategies. Each of these research techniques and designs has advantages and disadvantages, and there is no "best method" for studying children. When planning a research project, the developmentalist selects a particular technique and research design only after considering the nature of the problem under investigation, the costs involved, and the availability of research participants.

Developmentalists may face difficult ethical dilemmas when conducting research with children. No matter how important the knowledge that might be gained, a researcher is never justified in harming children or in undermining their dignity. The knowledge gained from research with children should benefit us all, but it is the responsibility of the investigator to guarantee that this knowledge does not come at the expense of the participants who so generously provide it.

References

AMERICAN PSYCHOLOGICAL ASSOCIATION. (1973). Ethical principles in the conduct of research with human participants. Washington, DC: Author.

ARIÈS, P. (1962). *Centuries of childhood*. New York: Knopf.

BALTES, P. B. (1968). Longitudinal and cross-sectional sequences in the study of age and generation effects. *Human Development, 11*, 145–171.

BENEDICT, R. (1934). *Patterns of culture*. Boston: Houghton Mifflin.

BORSTELMANN, L. J. (1983). Children before psychology: Ideas about children from antiquity to the late 1800s. In P. H. Mussen (Ed.), *Handbook of child psychology* (Vol. 1). New York: Wiley.

BRONFENBRENNER, U. (1977). Toward an experimental ecology of human development. *American Psychologist, 32*, 513–531.

CHARLESWORTH, R., & Hartup, W. W. (1967). Positive social reinforcement in the nursery school peer group. *Child Development, 38*, 993–1002.

COATES, B., & Hartup, W. W. (1969). Age and verbalization in observational learning. *Developmental Psychology, 1*, 556–562.

COOK, T. D., & Campbell, D. T. (1979). *Quasi-experimentation: Design and analysis issues for field settings*. Skokie, IL: Rand McNally.

DARWIN, C. A. (1877). A biographical sketch of an infant. *Mind, 2*, 285–294.

deMAUSE, L. (1974). The evolution of childhood. In L. deMause (Ed.), *The history of childhood*. New York: Harper & Row.

DESPERT, J. L. (1965). *The emotionally disturbed child: Then and now*. New York: Brunner/Mazel.

FRIEDRICH, L. K., & Stein, A. H. (1973). Aggressive and prosocial television programs and the natural behavior of preschool children. *Monographs of the Society for Research in Child Development, 38*(4, Serial No. 51).

HALL, G. S. (1891). The contents of children's minds on entering school. *Pedagogical Seminary, 1*, 139–173.

HOBBES, T. (1904). *Leviathan*. Cambridge: Cambridge University Press. (Original work published 1651)

KEAN, A. W. G. (1937). The history of the criminal liability of children. *Law Quarterly Review, 3*, 364–370.

KESSEN, W. (1965). *The child*. New York: Wiley.

KROLL, J. (1977). The concept of childhood in the Middle Ages. *Journal of the History of the Behavioral Sciences, 13*, 384–393.

McCALL, R. B. (1977). Challenges to a science of developmental psychology. *Child Development, 48*, 333–344.

MEAD, M. (1935). *Sex and temperament in three primitive societies*. New York: William Morrow.

PIAGET, J. (1965). *The moral judgment of the child*. New York: Free Press. (Original work published 1932)

SCHAIE, K. W. (1965). A general model for the study of developmental problems. *Psychological Bulletin, 64*, 91–107.

SCHAIE, K. W. (1986). Beyond calendar definitions of age, time, and cohort: The general developmental model revisited. *Developmental Review, 6*, 252–277.

SPRAFKIN, J. L., Liebert, R. M., & Poulos, R. W. (1975). Effects of a prosocial televised example on children's helping. *Journal of Experimental Child Psychology, 20*, 119–126.

WALSTER, E., Walster, G. W., & Berscheid, E. (1978). *Equity: Theory and research*. Newton, MA: Allyn & Bacon.

WILLIAMS, J. E., Bennett, S. M., & Best, D. L. (1975). Awareness and expression of sex stereotypes in young children. *Developmental Psychology, 11*, 635–642.

Theories of Human Development

That's only true in theory, not in practice!
ANONYMOUS
There is nothing as practical as a good theory.
KURT LEWIN

In our introductory chapter, we talked only briefly about theories, portraying them as sets of concepts and propositions that describe and explain certain aspects of our experience. We also noted that everyone is a "theorist" in one sense of the term, for each of us has a definite point of view reflecting what he or she believes to be true about many issues, observations, and events.

A *scientific* theory is a public pronouncement that indicates what a scientist believes to be true about his or her specific area of investigation (Kaplan, 1983). And the beauty of scientific theories is that they help us to organize our thinking about a broad range of observations and events. Imagine what life might be like for a researcher who plugs away at collecting data and cataloging fact after fact without somehow organizing this information around a set of concepts and propositions. Chances are that this individual would eventually be swamped by seemingly unconnected facts, thus qualifying as a trivia expert who lacks a "big picture." So theories are of critical importance in developmental psychology (or in any other scientific discipline, for that matter), for each of them provides us with a "lens" through which we might interpret any number of specific observations about developing individuals.

What are the characteristics of a good theory? Ideally, it should be concise, or **parsimonious,** and yet be able to explain a broad range of phenomena. A theory with few principles that accounts for a large number of empirical observations is much more useful than a second theory that requires many more principles and assumptions to explain the same number (or a lesser number) of observations. In addition, good theories are **falsifiable**—that is, capable of making explicit predictions about future events so that the theory can be

supported or disconfirmed. And as implied by the falsifiability criterion, good theories do not limit themselves to that which is already known. Instead, they are **heuristic**—meaning that they "build" on existing knowledge by continuing to "generate" testable hypotheses that, if confirmed by future research, will lead to a much richer understanding of the phenomena under investigation.

Clearly, a theory that simply "explains" a set of observations without making any new predictions is neither falsifiable nor heuristic and is of limited scientific value. And even if a theory is parsimonious, falsifiable, and sufficiently heuristic to formulate some hypotheses, it may still be inaccurate, or *invalid,* and may have to be discarded altogether if its predictions are consistently disconfirmed. So it may seem at times that some theoretical pronouncements *are* true only in theory, not in practice. However, there is clearly another side to this issue. Couldn't we argue that even "bad" theories that are later abandoned have served a useful purpose by stimulating the new knowledge that led to their ultimate demise? We might also note that good theories survive because they continue to generate new knowledge, much of which may have practical implications that truly benefit humanity. In this sense, there is nothing quite so practical as a *good* theory.

In this chapter we will concentrate on four broad theoretical perspectives that have each had a major impact on the science of human development: the *psychoanalytic* viewpoint, the *learning* viewpoint, the *cognitive-developmental* viewpoint, and the *ethological* viewpoint. However, there are several other theoretical viewpoints that have emerged as complements to, extensions of, or (as some would argue) replacements for the four "grand theories," and we will be considering the strengths and weaknesses of these alternative approaches throughout the text. For example, exciting new theories of **behavior genetics** are introduced in Chapter 3, where we will discuss hereditary influences on human development. And *information-processing* theory, an important new look at children's intellectual growth with roots in computer science, learning theory, and cognitive-developmental theory, is a central focus of Chapter 9, on intellectual development.

As we will see in the pages that follow, different theories emphasize different areas or aspects of human behavior. In addition, each theory makes different assumptions about human nature and the causes of development. So before reviewing the content of our four "grand theories," it may be helpful to consider some of the more basic issues or points of contention on which they differ.

Questions and Controversies about Human Development

Developmental theories have different points of view on at least five basic issues:

1. Are children inherently good or inherently bad?
2. Is nature (biological forces) or nurture (environmental forces) the primary influence on human development?
3. Are children actively involved in the developmental process; or, rather, are they passive recipients of social and biological influences?
4. Is development continuous or discontinuous?
5. Do children follow similar or different developmental paths?

1. *Assumptions about human nature.* We learned in Chapter 1 that social philosophers of the 17th and 18th centuries portrayed children as inherently bad (doctrine of *original sin*), as inherently good (doctrine of *innate purity*), or as neither bad nor good (doctrine of *tabula rasa*). As it turns out, each of these ideas remains with us today in one or more contemporary theories of human development. Although one may search a theory in vain for explicit statements about human nature, the theorist will typically emphasize either the positive or negative aspects of children's character or perhaps will note that positivity or negativity of character depends on the child's experiences. These assumptions about human nature are important, for they influence the content of each developmental theory—particularly what the theory has to say about child rearing.

2. *Nature versus nurture.* One of the oldest controversies among developmental theories is the "nature versus nurture" issue: Are human beings a product of their heredity and other biological predispositions,

or are they shaped by the environment in which they are raised? Here are two opposing viewpoints:

> Heredity and not environment is the chief maker of man. . . . Nearly all of the misery and nearly all of the happiness in the world are due not to environment. . . . The differences among men are due to differences in germ cells with which they were born [Wiggam, 1923, p. 42].

> Give me a dozen healthy infants, well formed, and my own specified world to bring them up in and I'll guarantee to take any one at random and train him to become any type of specialist I might select—doctor, lawyer, artist, merchant, chief, and yes, even beggar-man and thief, regardless of his talents, penchants, tendencies, abilities, vocations, and race of his ancestors. There is no such thing as an inheritance of capacity, talent, temperament, mental constitution, and behavioral characteristics [Watson, 1925, p. 82].

Although few contemporary developmentalists would endorse either of these radical points of view, the **nature/nurture controversy** rages on. For example, Arthur Jensen (1969) has argued that heredity accounts for 80% of the variability in human intelligence; most developmental researchers, however, consider this an overestimate. Toward the other end of the continuum, B. F. Skinner (1971) believes that many human attributes

---

parsimony: a criterion for evaluating the scientific merit of theories; a parsimonious theory is one that uses relatively few explanatory principles to explain a broad set of observations.

falsifiability: a criterion for evaluating the scientific merit of theories; a theory is falsifiable when it is capable of generating predictions that could be disconfirmed.

heuristic value: a criterion for evaluating the scientific merit of theories; a heuristic theory is one that continues to stimulate new research and new discoveries.

behavior genetics: the scientific study of how one's hereditary endowment interacts with environmental influences to determine such attributes as intelligence, temperament, and personality.

nature/nurture controversy: the debate within developmental psychology over the relative importance of biological predispositions (nature) and environmental influences (nurture) as determinants of human development.

are determined largely by <u>environment</u>, biology playing only a minor role.

Of course, there is a middle ground. The majority of child developmentalists now believe that the relative contributions of nature and nurture depend on the aspect of development in question. However, they stress that complex human attributes such as intelligence, temperament, and personality are the end products of a long and involved interplay between biological predispositions and environmental forces (see, for example, Plomin, 1986; Scarr & Weinberg, 1983). Their advice to us, then, is to <u>think less about nature versus nurture</u> and more about how these two sets of influences combine or interact to produce developmental change.

3. Activity versus passivity. Another topic of theoretical debate is the **activity/passivity issue.** Are children curious, active creatures who largely determine how agents of society treat them? Or are they passive souls on whom society fixes its stamp? Consider the implications of these opposing viewpoints. If it could be shown that children are extremely malleable—literally at the mercy of those who raise them—then perhaps individuals who turned out to be less than productive would be justified in suing their overseers for malfeasance. Indeed, one young man in the United States recently used this logic to bring a malfeasance suit against his parents. Perhaps you can anticipate the defense that the parents' lawyer would offer. Counsel would surely argue that the parents tried many strategies in an attempt to raise their child right but that he responded favorably to none of them. The implication is that this young man

played an active role in determining how his parents treated him and therefore is largely responsible for creating the climate in which he was raised.

Which of these perspectives do you consider the more reasonable? Think about it, for very soon, you will have an opportunity to state your views on this and other topics of theoretical debate.

4. Continuity versus discontinuity. Now think for a moment about the concept of developmental change. Do you think the changes we experience along the road to maturity occur very gradually? Or would you say that these changes are rather abrupt?

On one side of the **continuity/discontinuity issue** are continuity theorists, who view human development as an additive process that occurs in small steps, without sudden changes. They might represent the course of developmental change with a smooth growth curve like the one in Figure 2-1A. By contrast, discontinuity theorists believe that the developing child proceeds through a series of abrupt changes, each of which elevates the child to a new and presumably more advanced level of functioning. These levels, or "stages," are represented by the plateaus of the discontinuous growth curve in Figure 2-1B.

A second aspect of the continuity/discontinuity issue centers on whether developmental changes are quantitative or qualitative in nature. Quantitative changes are changes in degree. For example, children grow taller; they run a little faster with each passing year; and they acquire more and more knowledge about the world around them. By contrast, qualitative changes are changes

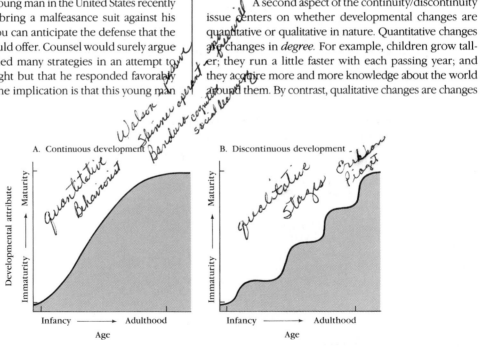

Figure 2-1. The course of development as described by continuity and discontinuity (stage) theorists. *(From Shaffer, 1977.)*

in *kind*—changes that make the individual fundamentally different in some way than he or she was before. The transformation of a tadpole into a frog is a qualitative change. Similarly, we might regard the infant who lacks language as qualitatively different from a preschooler who speaks well, or the adolescent who is sexually mature as fundamentally different from a classmate who has yet to reach puberty. Continuity theorists generally think that developmental changes are both gradual and quantitative in nature, whereas discontinuity theorists tend to view such changes as more abrupt and qualitative. Indeed, discontinuity theorists are the ones who argue that we progress through **developmental stages.** Presumably, each of these stages represents a distinct phase within a larger sequence of development—a period of the life cycle characterized by a particular set of abilities, motives, behaviors, or emotions that occur together and form a coherent pattern.

Finally, there is a third aspect of the continuity/discontinuity debate: Are there close connections between early developments and later ones, or, rather, do changes that occur early in life have little bearing on future outcomes? Continuity in this sense implies a sense of *connectedness* between earlier and later developments. Those who argue against the concept of developmental stages might see such connectedness in the stability of attributes over time, as might be indicated, for example, if aggressive toddlers become aggressive adolescents, or if particularly curious infants are recognized, as adults, for creative accomplishments. Even a theorist who proposes that we pass through qualitatively distinct stages might still see some connectedness (or continuity) in development if the abilities that characterize each successive stage are thought to evolve from and replace those of the previous stage.

Yet, there are theorists who believe that many later developments are discontinuous with, or *unconnected* to, earlier developments (see Kagan, 1980). The idea here is that a new behavior pattern may simply replace an old one without having evolved from it, as when an infant who once smiled at strangers comes to fear them, or when a teenage girl who has previously avoided boys suddenly becomes "boy crazy." In this sense, then, the discontinuity position is that many attributes and abilities that are apparent early in life will not carry over into adulthood, so that we cannot often predict what an adult will be like by knowing what he or she was like as an infant or a young child.

In sum, the debate about developmental continuities and discontinuities is a very complex one. There is the issue of whether developmental change is gradual or abrupt; the issue of whether it is qualitative or quantitative; and the issue of whether it is or is not connected to earlier developments. Theorists do not always take the continuity or the discontinuity position on all these issues, but they do often lean predominantly in one direction or the other.

5. *Similarity versus difference in development.* Finally, developmental theorists often disagree about whether the changes we experience are *universal* or *particularistic* (that is, different from person to person). Stage theorists generally assume that the stages they have proposed apply to all normal people and are therefore universal. For example, all normal humans acquire and begin to use language at 11–14 months of age, experience cognitive changes that prepare them for school at age 5 to 7 years, reach sexual maturity during the preteen or teenage period, and will show some signs of aging (for example, wrinkles, a decline in certain sensory abilities) by midlife. From this perspective, then, we all follow similar developmental paths. However, other theorists believe that developmental changes are far more varied than this. They stress that patterns of development may differ dramatically from culture to culture, from family to family, and even among members of the same family. Their message, then, is that development can (and does) proceed in many directions and is much less universal than stage theorists would have us believe.

In Chapter 1 we noted that many people find it exceedingly difficult *not* to select a "favorite" theory of human development after scanning several of these approaches for the first time. The reason that we tend to "play favorites" may be quite simple: we all make assumptions about children and the ways they develop,

---

activity/passivity issue: a debate among developmental theorists about whether children are active contributors to their own development or, rather, passive recipients of environmental influence.

continuity/discontinuity issue: a debate among theorists about whether developmental changes are best characterized as gradual, quantitative, and connected over time or, rather, are abrupt, qualitative, and often unconnected to earlier developments.

developmental stage: a distinct phase within a larger sequence of development; a period characterized by a particular set of abilities, motives, behaviors, or emotions that occur together and form a coherent pattern.

Box 2-1
**How Do You Stand on Major
Developmental Issues?**

1. Children are
   a. creatures whose basically negative or selfish impulses must be controlled.
   b. neither inherently good nor inherently bad.
   c. creatures who are born with many positive and few negative tendencies.
2. Biological influences (heredity, maturational forces) and environmental influences (culture, parenting styles, learning experiences) are thought to contribute to development. Overall,
   a. biological factors contribute more than environmental factors.
   b. biological and environmental factors are equally important.
   c. environmental factors contribute more than biological factors.
3. People are basically
   a. active beings who play a major role in determining their own abilities and traits.
   b. passive beings whose characteristics are molded either by social influences (parents and other significant people, outside events) or by biological factors beyond their control.
4. Development proceeds
   a. through stages, so that the individual changes rather abruptly into a quite different kind of person than he or she was in an earlier stage.
   b. continuously—in small increments without abrupt changes or distinct stages.
5. Traits such as aggressiveness or dependency
   a. emerge in childhood and remain largely stable over the years.
   b. first appear in childhood but often disappear or give way to quite different traits at some later time.
6. When we compare the development of different individuals, we see
   a. mainly similarities; children and adults develop along universal paths and experience similar changes at similar ages.
   b. mainly differences; different people often undergo different sequences of change and have widely different timetables of development.

Your pattern of answers:

Question					
1	2	3	4	5	6
c	b	a	a	b	a

---

and perhaps we tend to favor theories that make assumptions similar to our own. See whether you find this true of yourself by first taking the short quiz that appears in Box 2-1. At the end of the chapter (on page 67), you will find a box indicating how the major developmental theorists might answer these same questions. You can then determine whether the theory you found most appealing while reading the chapter also happened to be the one that most closely matches your own preexisting assumptions about human development. (Let's note, however, that the best way to evaluate these theories is on the demonstrated ability of each to predict and explain significant aspects of human development, not on the basis of our first impressions or preferences.)

The Psychoanalytic Viewpoint

With the possible exception of Charles Darwin's theory of evolution, no scientific theory has had a greater impact on Western thought than Sigmund Freud's psychoanalytic theory. One professor claimed that Freud's name was recognized by a larger percentage of the American people than that of any other scientific personality. And he may have been correct. Many laypersons have been exposed to at least some of Freud's ideas, and it would not be surprising if friends and relatives were to ask your opinion of Freud (and his theory) when they learn that you are taking a psychology course.

Almost no one is neutral about Sigmund Freud. His followers thought him a genius even though they didn't agree with all his ideas. Yet many of his contemporaries in the medical profession ridiculed Freud, calling him a quack, a crackpot, and other less complimentary names. What was it about this man and his theory that made him so controversial? For one thing, he emphasized the importance of sexual urges as determinants of behavior, for children as well as for adults! In this section of the chapter, we will first consider Freud's interesting perspective on human development and then compare Freud's theory with that of his best-known follower Erik Erikson.

Overview of Freud's
Psychoanalytic Theory

In Chapter 1 we saw that Freud formulated his psychoanalytic theory from the observations and notes that he made about the life histories of his mentally disturbed patients. Freud assumed that people are often reluctant to discuss very personal matters with a stranger, even if the stranger is a therapist. For this reason, he favored nontraditional methods of interviewing patients—methods such as hypnosis, free association (in which the patient discusses anything that comes to mind),

Photo 2-1. The psychoanalytic theory of Sigmund Freud (1856–1939) changed our thinking about developing children.

and *dream analysis.* While reclining on the couch, the patient would relax and talk about anything and everything that popped into his or her head. Dreams were thought to be a particularly rich source of information, for they gave some indication of a patient's **unconscious motivations.** Freud assumed that we all dream about what we really want—for example, sex and power—unhindered by social prohibitions that tend to suppress these desires when we are awake.

From his analyses of patients' dreams, slips of the tongue, unexpected free associations, and childhood memories, Freud was able to infer that all of us experience intense conflicts that influence our behavior. As biological creatures, we have goals or motives that must be satisfied. Yet society dictates that many of these basic urges are undesirable and must be suppressed or controlled. According to Freud, these "conflicts" emerge at several points during childhood and play a major role in determining the course and character of one's social and personality development.

Instincts, goals, and motives

Freud believed that all human behavior is energized by *psychodynamic* forces. Presumably each individual has a fixed amount of *psychic,* or mental, energy, which he or she uses to think, to learn, and to perform other mental functions.

According to Freud, a child needs psychic energy in order to satisfy basic urges. And what kind of urges are children born with? Bad ones! Freud viewed the newborn as a "seething cauldron"—that is, an inherently negative creature who is relentlessly "driven" by two kinds of biological **instincts** (or motives), which he called **Eros** and **Thanatos.** Eros, or the life instincts, helps the child (and the species) to survive; it directs life-sustaining activities such as respiration, eating, sex, and the fulfillment of all other bodily needs. In contrast, Thanatos—the death instincts—was viewed as a set of destructive forces present in all human beings. Freud believed that Eros is stronger than Thanatos, thus enabling us to survive rather than self-destruct. But he argued that if the psychic energy of Thanatos reached a critical point, the death instincts would be expressed in some way. For example, Freud thought that destructive acts such as arson, fist fights, murder, war, and even masochism (physical harm directed against the self) were outward expressions of the death instincts.

Three components of personality: Id, ego, and superego

According to Freud (1933), the "psychic energy" that serves the instincts is eventually divided among three components of personality—the id, ego, and superego.

The id: Legislator of the personality. At birth, the personality is all **id.** The major function of the id is to serve the instincts by seeking objects that will satisfy them.

Have you ever heard a hungry baby cry until someone comes to feed him? A Freudian would say that the baby's cries and agitated limb movements are energized by the hunger instinct. Presumably the id directs these actions as a means of attracting the mother or

---

unconscious motivations: Freud's term for feelings, experiences, and conflicts that influence a person's thinking and behavior but lie outside the person's awareness.

instinct: an inborn biological force that motivates a particular response or class of responses.

Eros: Freud's name for instincts such as respiration, hunger, and sex that help the individual (and the species) to survive.

Thanatos: Freud's name for inborn, self-destructive instincts that were said to characterize all human beings.

id: psychoanalytic term for the inborn component of the personality that is driven by the instincts.

irrational

another adult and thereby producing the object (food— or, literally, the mother's breast) that reduces hunger.

According to Freud, the id obeys the **pleasure principle** by seeking immediate gratification for instinctual needs. This impulsive thinking (also called "primary-process thinking") is rather unrealistic, however, for the id will invest psychic energy in any object that seems as if it will gratify the instincts, regardless of whether the object can actually do so. If we had never progressed beyond this earliest type of thinking, we might gleefully ingest wax fruit to satisfy hunger, reach for an empty pop bottle when thirsty, or direct our sexual energies at racy magazines and inflatable love dolls. Perhaps you can see the problem: we would have a difficult time satisfying our needs by relying on our irrational ids. Freud believed that these very difficulties lead to the development of the second major component of personality—the ego.

The ego: Executive of the personality. According to Freud (1933), the **ego** emerges when psychic energy is diverted from the id to energize important cognitive processes such as perception, learning, and logical reasoning. The goal of the rational ego is to serve the **reality principle**—that is, to find realistic ways of gratifying the instincts. At the same time, the ego must invest some of its available psychic energy to block the id's irrational thinking.

Freud stressed that the ego is both servant and master to the id. The ego's mastery is reflected by its ability to delay gratification until reality is served. But the ego continues to serve the id as an executive serves subordinates, pondering several alternative courses of action and selecting a plan that will best satisfy the id's basic needs.

The superego: Judicial branch of the personality. The **superego** is the person's moral arbiter. It develops from the ego, represents the ideal, and strives for *perfection* rather than for pleasure or reality (Freud, 1933).

Freud believed that 3–6-year-old children are gradually internalizing the moral standards of their parents, eventually adopting these guidelines as their own. These **internalized** "codes of conduct" form the child's superego. At this point, children do not need an adult to tell them when they have been bad; they are now aware of their transgressions and will feel guilty or ashamed of what they have done. Freud argued that the biggest task faced by parents when raising a child is to

ensure that the child develops a stable superego. This internal censor is presumably *the* mechanism that prevents human beings from expressing undesirable sexual and aggressive instincts in ways that could threaten society and the social order.

Dynamics of the personality. We see, then, that the superego's main function is to monitor the ego—that is, to ensure that the ego violates no moral principles. Note, however, that since the ego serves the id, the superego's major adversary is really the id. In other words, the superego attempts to persuade the ego to find socially acceptable outlets for the id's undesirable impulses—a process called **sublimation.** Sublimation might be illustrated by a person who decides to exercise vigorously or to take a cold shower in order to "drain away" unacceptable sexual urges.

Although the three components of personality may have conflicting goals or purposes, they normally do not incapacitate one another. The mature, healthy personality is best described as a dynamic set of checks and balances: the id communicates basic needs, the ego restrains the impulsive id long enough to find realistic methods of satisfying these needs, and the superego decides whether the ego's problem-solving strategies are morally acceptable. The ego is clearly "in the middle" and must serve two harsh masters by striking a balance between the opposing demands of the id and the superego.

Of course, not everyone is perfectly normal or healthy. Abnormalities or unusual quirks may arise if psychic energy is unequally distributed across the id, ego, and superego. For example, a sociopath might have a very strong id, a normal ego, and a very weak superego. By contrast, the righteous moralist may have a personality in which most of the psychic energy is controlled by a very strong superego. These are but two of the many abnormal personalities that could result from uneven distributions of psychic energy among the id, ego, and superego.

Freud's stages of psychosexual development

Freud viewed the sex instinct as the most important of the life forces because he often discovered that the mental disturbances of his patients revolved around childhood sexual conflicts that they had **repressed**—that is, forced out of conscious awareness. Sex in childhood! Certainly the notion of childhood sexuality was among the more controversial of Freud's ideas.

Photo 2-2. In the oral stage, children derive pleasure from sucking on, chewing, or biting objects.

Yet, his use of the term *sex* refers to much more than a need to copulate. Many simple bodily functions that most of us would consider rather asexual were viewed by Freud as "erotic"activities.

Although the sex instinct is presumably inborn, Freud (1940/1964) felt that its character changes over time, as dictated by biological maturation. As the sex instinct matures, its energy, or **libido,** gradually shifts from one part of the body to another, and the child enters a new stage of *psychosexual* development. Freud called these stages "psychosexual" to underscore his view that the maturation of the sex instinct leaves distinct imprints on the developing psyche (that is, the mind, or personality).

The oral stage (birth to 1 year). Freud was struck by the fact that infants spend much of the first year spitting, chewing, sucking, and biting on objects, and he concluded that the sex instinct must be centered on the mouth during this "oral" period. Indeed, he believed that oral activities are methods of gratifying the sex instinct, because children will suck, bite, or chew just about anything that comes into contact with their mouths—their thumbs, lips, toys, and parts of their mother's body—even when they are not particularly hungry or thirsty.

Freud argued that infants in the **oral stage** may adopt any of several basic methods—for example, sucking, biting, or spitting—to gratify the sex instinct. Presumably, the child will prefer one (or some combination) of these techniques over all others. This choice is thought to be important, for the child's preferred method of oral gratification may give some indication of the kind of personality that he or she will have later in life. Note the implication here: Freud is saying that *early experiences may have a long-term effect on social and personality development.* In Box 2-2 we will see why Freud believed that earlier modes of functioning are likely to surface in the adult personality.

The anal stage (1 to 3 years). In the second year of life, libido concentrates in the anal region as the sphincter muscles begin to mature. For the first time, the child has the ability to withhold or expel fecal material at will, and Freud believed that voluntary defecation becomes the primary method of gratifying the sex instinct.

During the **anal stage,** children must endure the demands of toilet training. For the first time, outside agents are interfering with instinctual impulses by insisting that the child inhibit the urge to defecate until

pleasure principle: tendency of the id to seek immediate gratification for instinctual needs, even when realistic methods for satisfying these needs are unavailable.

ego: psychoanalytic term for the rational component of the personality.

reality principle: tendency of the ego to defer immediate gratification in order to find rational and realistic methods for satisfying the instincts.

superego: psychoanalytic term for the component of the personality that consists of one's internalized moral standards.

internalization: the process of adopting the attributes or standards of other people; taking these standards as one's own.

sublimation: a mechanism by which the ego finds socially acceptable outlets for the id's undesirable impulses.

repression: a type of motivated forgetting in which anxiety-provoking thoughts and conflicts are forced out of conscious awareness.

libido: Freud's term for the biological energy of the sex instinct.

oral stage: Freud's first stage of psychosexual development (from birth to 1 year), in which children gratify the sex instinct by stimulating the mouth, lips, teeth, and gums.

anal stage: Freud's second stage of psychosexual development (from 1 to 3 years of age), in which anal activities such as defecation become the primary methods of gratifying the sex instinct.

Box 2-2
Early Experiences May Affect the Adult Personality

Freud (1940/1964) described several mechanisms that children may use to defend themselves (literally, their *egos*) against the anxieties or uncertainties of growing up. We have already discussed one such "defense" mechanism—sublimation—in which the child finds socially acceptable outlets for unacceptable motives. Freud believed that frequent use of these defense mechanisms may have long-term effects on the personality. For example, a teenage girl who habitually sublimates her sexual desires by taking cold showers may become a "cleanliness nut" as an adult.

Another important ego defense mechanism is *fixation*, or arrested development. According to Freud, the child who experiences severe conflicts at any particular stage of development may be reluctant to move or incapable of moving to the next stage, where the uncertainties are even greater. The child may then fixate at the earlier stage, and further development will be arrested or at least impaired. Freud believed that some people become fixated at the level of primary-process thinking and consequently remain "dreamers" or "unrealistic optimists" throughout their lives. Others fixate on particular behaviors. An example is the chronic thumbsucker whose oral fixation is expressed later in life in substitute activities such as smoking or oral sex. In sum, Freud was convinced that childhood fixations were important de-

terminants of many personality characteristics.

A person who experiences too much anxiety or too many conflicts at any stage of development may retreat to an earlier, less traumatic stage. Such developmental reversals are examples of an ego-defense mechanism that Freud called *regression*. Even a well-adjusted adult may regress from time to time in order to forget problems or reduce anxiety. For example, masturbation is one earlier mode of sexual functioning that a person may undertake to reduce sexual conflicts or frustrations. Dreaming is a regressive activity that enables a person to resolve conflicts and obtain pleasure through the magic of wishful thinking. Thus, regression is a third way in which earlier events, activities, and thought processes may affect the behavior of adults.

---

she has reached a designated locale. There are, of course, many strategies that parents might adopt when seeing their child through this first "social" conflict. Freud believed that the emotional climate created by parents in their attempts at toilet training is very important, for it may have a lasting effect on the child's personality.

The phallic stage (3 to 6 years). We now come to the aspect of Freudian theory that many people find so controversial. Freud's view was that 3–4-year-old children have matured to the point that their genitals have become an interesting and sensitive area of the body. Libido presumably flows to this area as children derive pleasure from stroking and fondling their genitals. What is so controversial? According to Freud, all children of this age develop a strong incestuous desire for the parent of the other sex. He called this period the **phallic stage** because he believed that the phallus (penis) assumes a critically important role in the psychosexual development of both boys and girls.

Let's examine this stage for boys. According to Freud, 3–4-year-old boys develop an intense sexual longing for their mothers. At the same time, they become jealous: if they could have their way, they would destroy their chief rivals for maternal affection, their fathers. Freud called this stage of affairs the **Oedipus complex** after the legendary Oedipus, king of Thebes, who unwittingly killed his father and married his mother.

Now, preschool boys are not as powerful as King Oedipus, and they face certain defeat in their quest to win the sexual favors of their mothers. In fact, Freud suggests that a jealous young son will have many conflicts with his paternal rival and will eventually fear that his father might castrate him for this rivaling conduct. When this *castration anxiety* becomes sufficiently intense, the boy (if development is normal) will then resolve his Oedipus complex by repressing his incestuous desire for the mother and identifying with the father. This *identification with the aggressor* lessens the chances of castration, for the boy is no longer a rival. He will try to emulate the father, incorporating all the father's attitudes, attributes, and behaviors. In so doing, the son is likely to adopt a distinct preference for the masculine sex role and become a "male" psychologically. Identification with the aggressor should also place the crowning touch on the boy's superego, for he will repress two of the most taboo of motives—incest and murder—and internalize the moral standards of his feared and respected rival. In short, the boy has become a well-behaved youngster—daddy's "little man."

And what about girls? Freud contends that, before age 3–4, girls prefer their mothers to their fathers. But once the girl discovers that she lacks a penis, she is thought to blame her closest companion, the mother, for this "castrated" condition. This traumatic discovery results in a transfer of affection from the mother to the

Photo 2-3. According to Freud, a transfer of affection from mother to father occurs in little girls between ages 3 and 5.

father. Freud believed that a girl of this age envies her father for possessing a penis and that she will choose him as a sex object in the hope that he will share with her the valued organ that she lacks (Freud assumed that a girl's *real* underlying motive was to bear her father's child, an event that would compensate for her lack of a penis, especially if the child was a male).

The female Oedipus complex (known as the **Electra complex**) bears some obvious similarities to that of the male. Children of each sex value the male phallus; girls hope to gain one, and boys hope to keep theirs. Furthermore, both boys and girls perceive the parent of the same sex as their major rival for the affection of the other parent. However, Freud was uncertain just how (or why) girls ever resolved their Electra complexes. Boys fear castration, and this intense fear forces them to renounce their Oedipus complexes by identifying with their fathers. But what do girls fear? After all, they supposedly believe that they have already been castrated, and they attribute this act of brutality to their mothers. To Freud's way of thinking, they no longer have any reason to fear the mother.

Why, then, does the Electra complex subside? Freud (1924/1961) assumed that it may simply fade away as the girl faces reality and recognizes the impossibility

of possessing her father. However, he suggested that girls will develop weaker superegos than boys because their resolution of the Electra complex is *not* based on a fear of retaliation (castration anxiety) that would force them to internalize the ethical standards of their mothers (or their fathers).

The latency period (ages 6–12). Between ages 6 and 12, the child's sex instincts are relatively quiet. The sexual traumas of the phallic stage are forgotten, and all available libido is channeled into some socially acceptable activity, such as schoolwork or vigorous play, that consumes most of the child's physical and psychic energy. This stage, which Freud called the **latency period,** continues until puberty, when the child suddenly experiences a number of biological changes that mark the beginning of Freud's final psychosexual stage.

The genital stage (age 12 onward). With the onset of puberty come maturation of the reproductive system, production of sex hormones, and, according to Freud, a reactivation of the genital zone as an area of sensual pleasure. The adolescent may openly express libido toward members of the other sex, but for the first time, the underlying aim of the sex instincts is reproduction. Throughout adolescence and young adulthood, libido is invested in activities—forming friendships, preparing for a career, courting, marrying—that prepare the individual to satisfy the fully mature sex

---

phallic stage: Freud's third stage of psychosexual development (from 3 to 6 years of age), in which children gratify the sex instinct by fondling their genitals and developing an incestuous desire for the parent of the other sex.

Oedipus complex: Freud's term for the conflict that 4- to 6-year-old boys experience when they develop an incestuous desire for their mothers and, at the same time, a jealous and hostile rivalry with their fathers.

Electra complex: female version of the Oedipus complex, in which a 4- to 6-year-old girl was said to envy her father for possessing a penis and would choose him as a sex object in the hope of sharing this valuable organ that she lacks.

latency period: Freud's fourth stage of psychosexual development (age 6 to puberty), in which sexual desires are repressed and all the child's available libido is channeled into socially acceptable outlets such as schoolwork or vigorous play.

instinct by having children. The **genital stage** is the longest of Freud's psychosexual stages. It lasts from puberty to old age, when the individual may regress to an earlier stage and begin a "second childhood."

Evaluation of Freud's theory

How plausible do you think Freud's ideas are? Do you think that we are all relentlessly driven by sexual and aggressive instincts? Could we have really experienced Oedipus or Electra complexes and simply repressed these traumatic events? And what about the role of culture in human development? In 19th- and early 20th-century Europe, there were no clinical psychologists or sex therapists, and the topic of sex was not discussed publicly in this outwardly prudish Victorian era. Could the sexual conflicts that Freud thought so important have merely been reflections of the sexually repressive culture in which his patients lived?

Few contemporary psychologists accept all of Freud's major premises and propositions. For example, there is not much evidence for the notion that the oral and anal activities of childhood predict one's later personality. Nor is there reason to believe that all children experience Oedipus and Electra complexes. To experience these conflicts, 4- to 6-year-old children would have to recognize the anatomical differences between the sexes, and there is little evidence that they do. In fact, Alan Katcher (1955) found that the majority of 4- to 5-year-olds are inept at assembling a doll so that its genitals match other parts of its body. Even 6-year-olds often made mistakes such as attaching a lower torso containing a penis to an upper body with breasts. Clearly, these "oedipal-aged" children were confused or ignorant about sex differences in genital anatomy (see also McConaghy, 1979), and it seems highly unlikely that they could be experiencing any castration anxiety or penis envy.

But we cannot reject all of Freud's ideas simply because some of them may seem a bit outlandish. Indeed, there are several reasons that Sigmund Freud will always remain an important figure in the history of the behavioral sciences. Perhaps Freud's greatest contribution was his concept of unconscious motivation. When psychology came into being in the middle of the 19th century, investigators were concerned with understanding isolated aspects of *conscious* experience, such as sensory processes and perceptual illusions. It was Freud who first noted that these scientists were studying the tip of an iceberg when he proclaimed that the vast majority of psychic experience lay below the level of conscious awareness. Freud also deserves considerable credit for focusing attention on the importance of early experience for later development. Debates continue about exactly how critical early experiences are, but few developmentalists today doubt that early experiences *can* have lasting effects. Finally, we might thank Freud for studying the emotional side of human development— the loves, fears, anxieties, and other powerful emotions that play important roles in our lives, as well as the defense mechanisms that we use to cope with emotional traumas and conflicts. Unfortunately, these aspects of life have often been overlooked by developmentalists who have tended to concentrate instead on observable behaviors or on rational thought processes.

In sum, Freud was truly a great pioneer who dared to navigate murky, uncharted waters that his predecessors had not even thought to explore. In the process, he changed our views of humankind.

Erik Erikson's Theory of Psychosocial Development

As Freud became widely read, he attracted many followers. However, Freud's pupils did not always agree with the master, and eventually they began to modify some of Freud's ideas and became important theorists in their own right. Among the best known of these *neo-Freudian* scholars is Erik Erikson.

Erikson accepts many of Freud's ideas. He agrees that people are born with a number of basic instincts and that the personality has three components: the id, ego, and superego. He also assumes that development occurs in stages and that the child must successfully resolve some crisis or conflict at each stage in order to be prepared for the crises that will emerge later in life.

However, Erikson is truly a revisionist, for his theory differs from Freud's in several important respects. First, Erikson (1963, 1972) stresses that children are *active, adaptive* explorers who seek to control their environment rather than passive creatures who are molded by their parents. He has also been labeled an ego psychologist because he believes that an individual must first understand the *realities* of the social world (an ego function) in order to adapt successfully and show a normal pattern of personal growth. This is perhaps the major difference between Freud and Erikson. Unlike Freud, who felt that the most interesting aspects of behavior stemmed from conflicts between the id and the superego, Erikson assumes that human beings are basically rational creatures whose thoughts, feelings, and actions are largely controlled by the ego.

Clearly, Erikson's thinking was shaped by his own interesting experiences. He was born in Denmark, was raised in Germany, and spent much of his adolescence wandering through Europe. After receiving his professional training, Erikson emigrated to the United States, where he studied college students, victims of combat fatigue during World War II, civil rights workers in the South, and American Indians. With this kind of cross-cultural background, it is hardly surprising that Erikson would emphasize social and cultural aspects of development in his own theory. Henry Maier (1969, p. 23) used these words to reflect Erikson's point of view:

> Culture adds the human aspect of living. Man lives by "instinctual" forces, and culture insists upon the "proper" use of these forces. [But] it is the cultural environment . . . which determines the nature of each individual's experience. The child and his parents are never alone; through the parent's conscience [many past] generations are looking upon a child's actions, helping him to integrate his relationships with their approval. . . . A culture, class, or ethnic group's basic ways of [viewing the world] are transmitted to the [child] . . . and tie the child forever to his original milieu.

In sum, Erikson believes that we are largely products of our *society* rather than our sex instincts. For this reason, his approach should be labeled a theory of *psychosocial* development.

Eight life crises

Erikson believes that all human beings face a minimum of eight major crises, or conflicts, during the course of their lives. Each crisis is primarily "social" in character and has very real implications for the future. Table 2-1 compares Freud's psychosexual and Erikson's psychosocial stages. Note that Erikson's developmental stages do not end at adolescence or young adulthood. Erikson believes that the problems of adolescents and young adults are very different from those faced by parents who are raising children or by the aged who must grapple with the specter of retirement, a sense of uselessness, and death. Most contemporary developmentalists would definitely agree.

An analysis of the first psychosocial stage—**basic trust versus mistrust**—should help to illustrate Erikson's thinking. Recall that Freud emphasized the infant's oral activities during the first year of life, and he believed that a mother's feeding practices could have a lasting impact on her child's personality development.

Erikson agrees. However, he goes on to argue that what is most important to an infant's later development is not merely the caregiver's feeding practices but, rather, her *overall responsiveness* to the infant and his needs. To develop a basic sense of trust, infants must be able to count on their primary caregivers to provide food, to relieve discomfort, to come when beckoned, to smile when smiled upon, and to display warmth and affection. And should close companions often neglect, reject, or respond inconsistently to an infant, the infant will learn a very simple lesson—other people are not to be trusted.

Erikson believes that the successful resolution of each life crisis prepares the person for the next of life's conflicts. By contrast, the individual who fails to resolve one or more of the life crises is almost certain to encounter problems in the future. For example, a child who learns to mistrust other human beings in infancy may find it exceedingly difficult to trust a prospective friend later in life. An adolescent who fails to establish a strong *personal identity* may be reluctant to commit his or her fragile sense of self to a shared identity with a prospective spouse. We see, then, that later crises become very formidable hurdles for the individual who stumbles early.

Although Erikson believes that the crises of childhood set the stage for our adult lives, we must remember that he views human beings as rational, "adaptive" creatures who struggle to the very end in their attempts to cope successfully with their social environment. Charles Dickens's Scrooge, a fictional character in *A Christmas Carol,* aptly illustrates the self-centered, "stagnated" adult—one who is failing at Erikson's seventh life crisis (and who has been unsuccessful at establishing a sense of intimacy as well). You may remember that old Scrooge was so absorbed in his own interests (making money) that he completely ignored the needs and wishes of his young storekeeper, Bob Cratchit. Scrooge's tale had a happy ending, however. By the end of the story, he had acquired a sense of intimacy and generativity that had eluded him earlier, and he was

---

genital stage: Freud's final stage of psychosexual development (from puberty onward), in which the underlying aim of the sex instinct is to establish an erotic relationship with another adult and to have children.

basic trust versus mistrust: the first of Erikson's eight psychosocial stages, in which infants must learn to trust their closest companions or else run the risk of mistrusting other people later in life.

Table 2-1. Erikson's and Freud's stages of development

Approximate age	Erikson's stage or "psychosocial" crisis	Erikson's viewpoint: Significant events and social influences	Corresponding Freudian stage
Birth to 1 year	Basic trust versus mistrust	Infants must learn to trust others to care for their basic needs. If caregivers are rejecting or inconsistent in their care, the infant may view the world as a dangerous place filled with untrustworthy or unreliable people. The mother or primary caregiver is the key social agent.	Oral
1 to 3 years	Autonomy versus shame and doubt	Children must learn to be "autonomous"—to feed and dress themselves, to look after their own hygiene, and so on. Failure to achieve this independence may force the child to doubt his or her own abilities and feel shameful. Parents are the key social agents.	Anal
3 to 6 years	Initiative versus guilt	Children attempt to act grown up and will try to accept responsibilities that are beyond their capacity to handle. They sometimes undertake goals or activities that conflict with those of parents and other family members, and these conflicts may make them feel guilty. Successful resolution of this crisis requires a balance: the child must retain a sense of initiative and yet learn not to impinge on the rights, privileges, or goals of others. The family is the key social agent.	Phallic
6 to 12 years	Industry versus inferiority	Children must master important social and academic skills. This is a period when the child compares the self with peers. If sufficiently industrious, children will acquire the social and academic skills to feel self-assured. Failure to acquire these important attributes leads to feelings of inferiority. Significant social agents are teachers and peers.	Latency

continued

now ready to face life's final crisis in a positive frame of mind. An unlikely reversal? Not necessarily! Erikson is quite the optimist; he maintains that "there is little that cannot be remedied later, there is much [in the way of harm] that can be prevented from happening at all" (1950, p. 104).

Evaluation of Erikson's theory

Many people prefer Erikson's theory to Freud's because they simply refuse to believe that human beings are dominated by sexual instincts. An analyst like Erikson, who stresses our rational, adaptive nature, is so much easier to accept. In addition, Erikson emphasizes many of the social conflicts and personal dilemmas that people may remember, are currently experiencing, or can easily anticipate. In the words of one student, "Erikson's theory is so relevant ... Freud's is a figment of his *wild* imagination."

Researchers who study such topics as the emotional development of infants, the growth of the self-concept during childhood, and the formation of a reasonably stable personal identity during adolescence have found that Erikson has captured many of the central issues of life in his eight psychosocial stages. At the same time, Erikson's theory is very imprecise about the *causes* of psychosocial development. Those who read Erikson's ideas often find themselves asking such questions as "What kinds of experiences must people have to cope with and resolve various psychosocial conflicts?" or "How exactly do the outcomes of one psychosocial stage influence personality at a later stage?" Unfortunately, Erikson is not very explicit about these important issues. So his theory is really a descriptive overview of human social and emotional development that does not adequately *explain* how or why this development takes place.

Approximate age	Erikson's stage or "psychosocial" crisis	Erikson's viewpoint: Significant events and social influences	Corresponding Freudian stage
12 to 20 years	Identity versus role confusion	This is the crossroad between childhood and maturity. The adolescent grapples with the question "Who am I?" Adolescents must establish basic social and occupational identities, or they will remain confused about the roles they should play as adults. The key social agent is the society of peers.	Early genital (adolescence)
20 to 40 years (young adulthood)	Intimacy versus isolation	The primary task at this stage is to form strong friendships and to achieve a sense of love and companionship (or a shared identity) with another person. Feelings of loneliness or isolation are likely to result from an inability to form friendships or an intimate relationship. Key social agents are lovers, spouses, and close friends (of both sexes).	Genital
40 to 65 years (middle adulthood)	Generativity versus stagnation	At this stage, adults face the tasks of becoming productive in their work and raising their families or otherwise looking after the needs of young people. These standards of "generativity" are defined by one's culture. Those who are unable or unwilling to assume these responsibilities will become stagnant and/or self-centered. Significant social agents are the spouse, children, and cultural norms.	Genital
Old age	Ego integrity versus despair	The older adult will look back at life, viewing it as either a meaningful, productive, and happy experience or as a major disappointment full of unfulfilled promises and unrealized goals. One's life experiences, particularly social experiences, will determine the outcome of this final life crisis.	Genital

Psychoanalytic Theory Today

Today psychoanalysts represent a small minority within the community of child developmentalists. Many researchers have abandoned the psychoanalytic approach (particularly Freud's theory) because it is difficult to verify or disconfirm. Suppose, for example, that we wanted to test the basic Freudian proposition that the "healthy" personality is one in which psychic energy is evenly distributed among the id, ego, and superego. How could we do it? There are objective tests that we could use to select "mentally healthy" subjects, but we have no instrument that measures psychic energy or the relative strengths of the id, ego, and superego. The point is that many psychoanalytic assertions are untestable by any method other than the interview or a clinical approach, and unfortunately, these techniques are time-consuming, expensive, and among the least objective of all methods used to study developing children.

Of course, the main reason that so many developmental researchers have abandoned the psychoanalytic perspective is that other theories seemed more compelling to them. One theory favored by many is the learning approach, to which we now turn.

The Learning Viewpoint (Behaviorism)

John B. Watson was a radical in his own time. He was the person who proclaimed that he could take a dozen healthy infants and train them to be whatever he chose—doctor, lawyer, beggar, and so on, regardless of their backgrounds or ancestry. This statement alone was sufficient to raise more than a few eyebrows. Watson (1913) also believed that the psychologists of his day were wasting their time studying subjective, "mentalis-

Photo 2-4. John B. Watson (1878–1958) was the father of behaviorism and the first social-learning theorist.

tic" concepts such as sensation, volition, and emotion. On many occasions he argued that subjective, nonobservable phenomena are best left to philosophy; surely they have no place in a *science* of psychology. Watson's point was that the larger community of scientists would never take psychology seriously unless psychologists began to study what they could see—overt behavioral responses.

A basic premise of Watson's **"behaviorism"** is that the mind of an infant is a *tabula rasa* and that *learned* associations between stimuli and responses are the building blocks of human development. According to Watson, development does not proceed through a series of stages; it is a continuous process marked by the gradual acquisition of new and more sophisticated behavioral patterns, or habits. Watson believed that only the simplest of human reflexes (for example, the sucking reflex) are inborn and that all important behavioral tendencies, including traits, talents, values, and aspirations, are learned.

The behaviorists of the 1980s are more moderate in their views. They recognize that "heredity" and "maturation" play meaningful roles in human development and that no amount of prompting or environmental enrichment could transform a severely retarded person into a lawyer or a brain surgeon. However, these contemporary learning theorists believe that biological factors merely place limits on what children are capable of learning. And to this day, theorists who favor the learning approach feel that the most significant aspects of human behavior—those habits and qualities that make us "human"—are learned.

What Is Learning?

Simply stated, **learning** is a process that produces relatively *permanent* changes in behavior or behavioral potential. These behavioral changes are the result of a person's experiences or practice, as opposed to natural causes such as maturation, fatigue, injury, or illness.

Learned responses or habits may be acquired in several ways. **Classical conditioning** is a type of learning in which a person comes to associate a neutral stimulus with a second, nonneutral stimulus that always elicits a particular response. When this association has been made, the formerly neutral stimulus will have acquired the capacity to evoke the response in question. For example, very young children are unlikely to lick their lips the first two or three times they hear the jingling of an ice-cream truck as it passes before their house. But this initially neutral jingling sound may soon begin to elicit lip licking (and perhaps a host of other behaviors as well) as soon as children associate it with ice cream, a nonneutral stimulus that does produce lip licking (see Figure 2-2). In Chapter 7 we will see that classical conditioning is a common occurrence in everyday life and may be the basis for many of our fears, attitudes, and prejudices.

Operant (or *instrumental*) **conditioning** is a second type of learning, in which a child first emits a response and then comes to associate it with a particular outcome, or consequence. Two kinds of consequences are significant in operant conditioning—reinforcers and punishments. **Reinforcers** are consequences that promote operant learning by increasing the probability that a response will occur in the future. For example, a mother who praises her son for sharing a cookie with a playmate is using praise as a reinforcer. And if the boy recognizes that sharing is what produced this pleasant outcome, he is likely to share again with his friend when the opportunity presents itself. **Punishments** are consequences that suppress a response and decrease the likelihood that it will occur in the future. For example, an infant whose hands are slapped every time she reaches for her mother's glasses may soon refrain from reaching for people's glasses, at least her mother's. An adolescent who is grounded for sassing his father will probably think twice before repeating this "mistake." In sum, operant conditioning is a very common form of learning

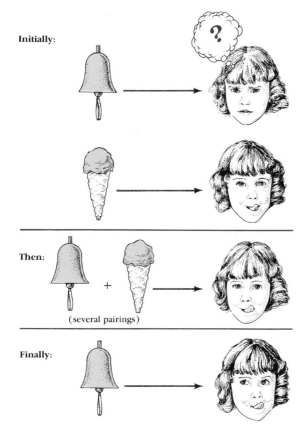

Initially:

Then:

(several pairings)

Finally:

Figure 2-2. In classical conditioning, an initially neutral stimulus (such as a bell) acquires the ability to elicit a response (such as lip licking) by virtue of its repeated association with a second, nonneutral stimulus (ice cream) that always elicits the response.

in which various acts become either more or less probable, depending on the consequences they produce.

Observational learning is a third process by which we acquire new feelings, attitudes, and behaviors. If a child watches someone do something or listens attentively to that person's reasoning, then the child may learn to do, think, or feel as the person did. Even toddlers can learn by observing other people. A 2-year-old boy may discover how to approach and pet the family dog simply by noting how his older sister does it. A young girl may acquire a negative attitude toward a minority group after hearing her parents talk about its people in a disparaging way. In the language of observational learning, the individual who is ob-

served and imitated is called a social *model*. Over the years, children are exposed to hundreds of social models and have the opportunity to learn literally thousands of responses (some good, some bad) simply by observing others perform them.

Theories of Social Learning

Although Watson argued that learned associations between stimuli and responses are the "bricks" in the "edifice of human development," he really did not have a developmental theory to work with. Since Watson's day several major theories have been proposed to explain social learning and the process of human development. The earliest of these approaches arose in the 1930s, when a group of anthropologists, psychologists, and sociologists from Yale University attempted to interpret psychoanalytic phenomena according to principles of learning outlined earlier by Clark Hull, a famous experimental psychologist who worked with animals. These "neo-Hullian" theorists rejected Freud's idea that we harbor inborn instincts. Yet, they believed that most human behaviors were performed in order to satisfy unlearned motives such as hunger or sex (that is,

---

behaviorism: a school of thinking in psychology that holds that conclusions about human development should be based on controlled observations of overt behavior rather than speculation about unconscious motives or other unobservable phenomena; the philosophical underpinning for the early theories of learning.

learning: a process that produces relatively permanent changes in behavior (or behavioral potential) that are the result of experience or practice.

classical conditioning: a form of learning in which an initially neutral stimulus is repeatedly paired with a meaningful stimulus so that the neutral stimulus eventually elicits the response originally made only to the meaningful stimulus.

operant conditioning: a form of learning in which freely emitted acts (or operants) become either more or less probable, depending on the consequences they produce.

reinforcer: any consequence of an act that increases the probability that the act will recur.

punishment: any consequence of an act that suppresses that act and/or decreases the probability that it will recur.

observational learning: learning that results from observing the behavior of others.

primary drives) or learned motives such as the need for achievement or the need for approval (that is, **secondary drives**). The neo-Hullians scoffed at the Freudian notion of oral and anal fixations that might resurface in the adult personality; yet, they viewed the personality as a collection of learned responses, or **habits,** that often persist over time because they have proved to be successful methods of reducing drives. So even though the neo-Hullians used different terminology than Freud did and made a major contribution to the science of human development by stressing that many of the motives that guide our behavior might be *learned* (rather than innate, their theory was similar in many respects to psychoanalytic theory—a viewpoint that contemporary learning theorists clearly reject. And we will begin to see the basis for this dissatisfaction in the pages that follow, as we examine the operant-learning theory of B. F. Skinner and the cognitive social-learning theory of Albert Bandura.

Skinner's operant-learning approach (radical behaviorism)

While the neo-Hullians were formulating their theory of human development, psychologist B. F. Skinner was conducting research with animals and discovering important principles that would eventually lead to a second social-learning theory—one very different from the neo-Hullian approach. For example, Skinner (1953) clearly rejects the notion that most human behavior is motivated by primary and secondary drives. In fact, he considers the term *drive* a circular motivational label that has little or no explanatory value, a sentiment shared by many contemporary researchers:

> It is not the existence of motivated behavior that is being questioned, but whether such behavior [can be] explained by ascribing it to the action of drives. The limitations of this type of analysis can be illustrated by considering a common activity such as reading . . . people spend large sums . . . purchasing reading material; . . . they [read] for hours on end; and they can become emotionally upset when deprived of reading material [such as a missed newspaper]. . . .
>
> One could ascribe [reading behavior] to the force of a "reading drive." . . . However, if one wanted to *predict* what people read, when, how long, and the order in which they choose to read different material, one would look not for drives, but for preceding inducements and expected benefits derived from reading [Bandura, 1977, p. 3; italics added].

Why, then, do people read? For any number of reasons. One person may be reading because she finds the activity pleasurable; another reader may be studying for an exam; a third may be trying to understand his income-tax form; a fourth reader may be planning a vacation. To attribute the behavior of these four individuals to a "reading drive" is surely a grossly oversimplified analysis.

According to Skinner (1953), the majority of habits that children acquire are freely emitted responses (or operants) that become either more or less probable as a function of their consequences. In other words, Skinner proposes that behavior is motivated by *external* stimuli—reinforcers or punitive events—rather than by internal forces, or drives.

In Chapter 7 we will take a closer look at the process of operant learning and its contribution to human development. For now, let's simply note that even young infants can learn to alter their behavior (that is, form new habits) in order to obtain reinforcement or to avoid punitive consequences. Consider the following demonstration. Paul Weisberg (1963) exposed 3-month-old infants to four experimental treatments to see whether he could teach some of them to babble to a caregiver. One group of infants received social stimulation in the form of smiles and gentle rubs on the chin whenever they happened to babble (*contingent* social stimulation). A second group were given the same kinds of social stimulation, but these gesures were *noncontingent;* that is, they were presented at random and did not depend on the infant's babbling behavior. Two other groups received nonsocial stimulation (the sound of chimes) that was either contingent or noncontingent on their babbling responses. Weisberg found that neither noncontingent social stimulation nor the sound of chimes was sufficient to reinforce babbling behavior. Babbling became more frequent only when it was accompanied by contingent social stimulation.

Skinner would argue that it makes little sense to attribute the babbling of these infants to a "babbling drive." Instead, the infants appear to have learned to babble because this act produced *external* stimuli (smiles and pats) that they found satisfying.

Recently a number of learning theorists have noted some serious deficiencies in Skinner's operant analysis of human behavior. For example, Albert Bandura (1977) calls Skinner's theory "radical behaviorism" because it focuses exclusively on the external stimuli (rewards and punishments) that influence our behavior and ignores all cognitive determinants of social learn-

Photo 2-5. B. F. Skinner (1904–　) proposed a social-learning theory that emphasizes the role of external stimuli in controlling human behavior.

Photo 2-6. In his theory of human development, Albert Bandura (1925–　) emphasizes the cognitive aspects of social learning.

ing. Indeed, Bandura has proposed a social-learning theory of his own—a theory that was largely based on his many reservations about Skinner's point of view.

Bandura's cognitive social-learning theory

Are we on firm ground in trying to explain human social learning on the basis of research with animals? Bandura (1977, 1986) doesn't think so. He does agree with Skinner that operant conditioning is an important type of learning, particularly for animals. However, Bandura stresses that humans are *cognitive* beings—active information processors—who, unlike animals, are likely to think about the relationships between their behavior and its consequences and are often more affected by what they *believe* will happen than by the events they actually experience. To illustrate, you need only consider your own plight as a college student. Your education is costly and time-consuming and probably imposes many demands that you find less than satisfying. Yet, you continue to tolerate the costs and unpleasantries because you can probably *anticipate* greater rewards once you obtain your degree. Your behavior is not shaped by its immediate consequences; if it were, few students would ever make it through the trials and turmoils of college. Instead, you persist as a student because you have *thought about* the long-term benefits

of obtaining a college education and have decided that they outweigh the short-term costs that you must endure.

Nowhere is Bandura's cognitive emphasis clearer than in his decision to highlight observational learning as a central "developmental process." According to Bandura, children can learn novel responses by merely observing the behavior of a model, making mental notes on what they have seen, and then using these mental representations to reproduce the model's behavior at some future time. This is clearly a form of *cognitive* learning, for as we will see in Chapter 7, children need not be reinforced or even respond in order to learn by observing others. All that is required for observational learning is that the observer pay close attention to the model's behavior and then store this information in memory so that it can be retrieved for use at a later date (Bandura, 1977, 1986).

---

primary drives: innate (nonlearned) motives such as hunger and sex that impel the organism into action.

secondary drives: all motives that are not present at birth and are acquired as a result of experience.

habits: the neo-Hullian term for the well-learned associations between various stimuli and responses that represent the stable aspects of one's personality.

Bandura suggests that observational learning permits young children to acquire any number of new responses in a variety of settings where their "models" are simply pursuing their own interests and are not trying to teach them anything in particular. In fact, many of the behaviors to which children attend (and which they may imitate) are actions that models display but would like to discourage—practices such as swearing, smoking, or eating between meals. Bandura's point is that children are continually learning both desirable and undesirable responses by "keeping their eyes (and ears) open," and he is not at all surprised that human development proceeds so very rapidly along so many paths.

Social Learning as a Reciprocal Process

Compared with psychoanalytic theory, early versions of learning theory seem rather bleak and barren. Nowhere does one find lists of habits or traits that describe the healthy or the abnormal personality. There are no "stages" in learning theory. Presumably, development proceeds in small steps without sudden changes, and this gradual learning process occurs over the entire life span. In addition, early versions of learning theory were largely tributes to Watson's doctrine of **environmental determinism**: young, unknowing children were viewed as passive recipients of environmental influence—they would become whatever parents, teachers, and other agents of society groomed them to be. In fact, B. F. Skinner, the famous "radical behaviorist" of recent times, has taken a position that many students find difficult to accept: not only are we products of our experiences, but we have little say in determining the character of those experiences. In other words, Skinner (1971) is arguing that "free will," or the concept of conscious choice, is merely an illusion.

Students are not the only ones who object to Skinner's statements or to a strict interpretation of environmental determinism. In recent years, cognitive social-learning theorists have argued that children are active, thinking creatures who contribute in meaningful ways to their own development. For example, observational learning requires *active* observation and encoding of the behaviors displayed by social models. Moreover, the child must later *decide* whether and when he or she will perform these learned responses.

Children are also active in another important respect—they are often responsible for creating the very reinforcers that strengthen new habits. Suppose that a little boy discovers he can gain control over desirable toys by assaulting his playmates. In this case, control over the desired toy is a pleasant outcome that reinforces the child's aggressive behavior. But note that the reinforcer here is produced by the child himself—through his aggressive actions. Not only has bullying behavior been reinforced (by obtaining the toy), but the character of the play environment has changed. Our bully becomes more likely to assault his playmates in the future. And the playmates may become more likely to "give in" to the bully.

In sum, cognitive learning theorists such as Albert Bandura (1977) and Richard Bell (1979) believe that human development is best described as a continuous *reciprocal interaction* between children and their environments (**reciprocal determinism**): the environment clearly affects the child, but the child's behaviors are thought to affect the environment as well. The implication is that children are *actively involved* in creating the very environments that will influence their growth and development.

Contributions and Criticisms of Learning Theory

Developmentalists have benefited from the learning viewpoint in many ways. For example, the learning theorist's emphasis on overt behavior and its immediate causes has produced important clinical insights. Many problem behaviors can now be treated rapidly by a method called *counterconditioning* in which the therapist (1) identifies the reinforcers that sustain undesirable habits and eliminates them while (2) reinforcing alternative behaviors that are more desirable. Thus, childhood phobias such as a fear of school may be eliminated in a matter of weeks, rather than the months (or years) that a psychoanalyst might take probing the child's unconscious, trying to find the underlying conflict that is producing the phobic reaction.

Perhaps the major contribution of the learning viewpoint is the wealth of information it has provided about developing children. By observing how children react to various environmental influences, learning theorists have begun to understand how and why children form emotional attachments to others, adopt sex roles, become interested in doing well at school, learn to abide by moral rules, form friendships, and so on. Much of what we know about human development stems from the research of "behavioral," or learning, theorists.

Finally, learning theorists stress *objectivity* in all phases of their work. Their units of analysis are objective behavioral responses, rather than subjective phenomena that are difficult to observe or measure. They carefully define their concepts, test hypotheses, and conduct tightly controlled experiments to provide objective evidence for the suspected causes of developmental change. The demonstrated success of their approach has encouraged researchers from all theoretical backgrounds to become more objective when studying developing children.

In spite of its strengths, however, many view the learning approach as an oversimplified account of human development. Consider its explanation of individual differences: presumably, individuals follow different developmental paths because no two persons grow up in exactly the same environment. Yet critics are quick to note that each of us comes into the world with a unique genetic inheritance. Furthermore, children mature at different rates, a factor that affects how other people respond to them and how they will react to the behavior of others. One's genetic inheritance and maturational timetable may have direct effects on development, or they may have indirect effects by determining what a person is capable of learning (or would find reinforcing) at any given point in life. Thus, learning theorists may have oversimplified the issue of individual differences in human development by downplaying the contribution of important biological factors.

Despite the popularity of recent cognitively oriented learning theories that stress the child's active role in the developmental process, some critics maintain that *no* learning theorist pays enough attention to the *cognitive* determinants of human development. Proponents of this third, or "cognitive-developmental," viewpoint believe that the child's mental abilities undergo a series of qualitative changes (or stages) that the behaviorists completely ignore. Further, they argue that a child's impressions of and reactions to the environment depend largely on his or her level of **cognitive development.** Let's now turn to this viewpoint and see what it has to offer.

The Cognitive-Developmental Viewpoint

The major contributor to the cognitive viewpoint is unquestionably Jean Piaget, a Swiss scholar who began to study children's intellectual development during the 1920s. According to Piaget, children are neither driven by undesirable instincts nor "molded" by environmental influences. Piaget and his followers view children as *constructivists*—that is, as curious, active ex-

Photo 2-7. In his cognitive-developmental theory, Swiss scholar Jean Piaget (1896–1980) focused on the growth of children's knowledge and reasoning skills.

plorers who respond to the environment according to their *understanding* of its essential features. Presumably, any two children might react very differently to some aspect of the environment if they interpret it differently. To predict how a child will respond to a mother's praise, a father's scolding, or a playmate's bossiness,

environmental determinism: the notion that children are passive creatures who are molded by their environments.

reciprocal determinism: the notion that the flow of influence between children and their environments is a two-way street; the environment may affect the child, but the child's behavior will also influence the environment.

cognitive development: age-related changes that occur in mental activities such as attending, perceiving, learning, thinking, and remembering.

one has to know how the child perceives, or construes, that behavior.

Piaget adds that a child's constructions of reality (interpretations of the environment) depend on his or her level of cognitive development. If he is correct, it follows that a child's cognitive abilities largely determine (1) how the child will respond to environmental events and thus (2) what effect these events will have on the child's development.

Origins of Piaget's Cognitive Theory

Jean Piaget was an exceptional individual. At the age of 10 he published his first scientific article, about a rare albino sparrow. Shortly thereafter he began an after-school job assisting the director of the local museum of natural history. By age 15, Piaget was publishing zoological articles about shellfish. One of these papers resulted in a job offer as curator of the Geneva Museum of Natural History. Piaget regretfully declined the position in order to finish high school.

Piaget completed a Ph.D. in zoology in 1918. His secondary interest was *epistemology* (the branch of philosophy concerned with the origins of knowledge), and he hoped desperately to be able to integrate his two interests. At that point, he felt psychology was the answer. He journeyed to Paris and spent two years at the Sorbonne studying clinical psychology, logic, and philosophy of science. During his stay in Paris, Piaget was offered a position standardizing intelligence tests at the Alfred Binet laboratories. His decision to accept this position had a profound influence on the direction of his career.

Many of us would find the task of standardizing an intelligence test rather tedious. The examiner must administer a preestablished sequence of precisely worded questions to the test taker according to a set procedure. This standardized format ensures that variations in test performance will reflect individual differences in intelligence rather than variations in the examiner's methods or the questions asked of the examinee. The person's intellectual ability is then estimated from the number and types of questions answered correctly.

However, Piaget soon discovered that he was more interested in test takers' *incorrect* answers. It seemed to him that children of about the same age were producing the same kinds of "wrong answers" for certain questions. But why? Piaget proceeded to question children about their misconceptions, using the clinical method he had learned earlier while working in a psychiatric clinic. He soon discovered that children of *different* ages produced *different* kinds of wrong answers, and he concluded that intelligence must be a multidimensional attribute. Older children are not simply "more intelligent" than younger children; their thought processes are completely different. Piaget then set up his own laboratory and attempted to determine how children progress from one mode (or stage) of thinking to another. The work of this remarkable man continued for some 60 years, until he died in 1980. We will now consider some of Piaget's most basic ideas about intelligence and its impact on human development.

Piaget's View of Intelligence

Piaget is an *organismic theorist*—one who views the child as an active creature who follows a developmental path dictated both by biological maturation and by experience. From the moment they are born, children begin to act upon and transform their environments and, in turn, are shaped (or changed) by the consequences of their actions. According to Piaget, this constant interplay between a biologically maturing child and his or her environment is responsible for the growth of intelligence.

Piaget's definition of intelligence reflects his background in biology. He viewed intelligence as a basic life function that helps the organism adapt to its environment. He added that intelligence is "a form of equilibrium toward which all [cognitive structures] tend" (1950, p. 6). So, according to Piaget, intellectual activity is undertaken with one goal in mind: to establish **equilibrium**—that is, a balanced or harmonious relationship—between one's thought processes and the environment. Piaget believed that the environment is an exciting place full of many new stimuli that are not immediately understood by the curious, active child. Any "disequilibrium" between the environment and the child's modes of thinking should prompt the child to make mental adjustments in an attempt to cope with puzzling new experiences. In sum, the Piagetian approach to intelligence is an "interactionist" viewpoint, which implies that imbalances between one's own mental abilities and the environment stimulate cognitive activity and intellectual growth.

At this point, you may be thinking that intelligence is a very complex attribute. Piaget agrees. He states that intellect consists of no fewer than three interrelated components: *content, structure,* and *function.*

Intellectual content — *thinking*

When Piaget speaks of intellectual content, he is referring to "what" the child thinks. For example, when a 4-year-old girl says that the sun is alive because it moves across the sky or that rules made by her parents apply to all children, we have some indication of the content of her thinking. According to Piaget, content (or intellectual performance) is determined by an underlying *structure* (or concept). Although Piaget's main interest during the early stages of his career was the content of children's thinking, he soon realized that studies of intellectual content cannot explain why children think the way they do or how they progress from one type of thinking to another. For these reasons, Piaget devoted most of his career to the study of intellectual structure and function.

Cognitive structures = *interpret* *schema*

A cognitive structure, or **schema,** is an organized pattern of thought or action that is used to interpret some aspect of one's experience. For example, the 4-year-old who says the sun is alive because it moves is operating on the basis of a simple cognitive schema—things that move are alive. The same child might say that a tree is dead, simply because it does not move (or because its limited movement is attributable to the wind).

According to Piaget, neonates enter the world without any innate ideas about reality, although they do come equipped with a number of inborn reflexes, such as sucking and grasping, that help them adapt to the environment. But aside from their adaptive significance, these innate reflexes serve another important function: they are soon modified by experience to become the child's first true schemata. For example, true reflexive sucking occurs only if an object comes into contact with the infant's lips. Yet, Piaget (1952), carefully observing his own son, noted:

> During the second day . . . Laurent begins to make sucking movements between meals. . . . His lips open and close as if to receive a real nippleful but without having an object [to suck]. This behavior became more frequent [with the passage of time] [pp. 25–26].

Soon Laurent began to further modify his sucking response by taking many objects into his mouth. Shortly after he was a month old, he had developed a coordinated motor habit, or *behavioral* schema:

> After a meal . . . his arms . . . instead of gesticulating aimlessly, constantly move toward his mouth. . . .

> Thirteen times in succession I have been able to observe the hand go back into the mouth. There is no longer any doubt that coordination exists . . . I remove the hand and place it near his waist. After a few minutes the lips move and the hand approaches them again. . . . [Finally] the hand enters the mouth, the thumb alone is retained, and sucking continues [1952, pp. 52–53].

This thumbsucking schema is only one of many that evolve from basic reflexes. Now you may be thinking, so what? How are these simple behavioral schemata related to what we think of as "thinking," or mental schemata? Piaget would answer that *mental schemata evolve from behavioral schemata.* We shall examine this transformation in some detail when we consider the topic of cognitive development in Chapter 9.

Intellectual functions—Piaget's mechanisms for change = *organization* + *adaptation*

Piaget believed that human beings inherit two important intellectual functions that he called "organization" and "adaptation." **Organization** refers to the child's tendency to arrange available schemata into coherent systems, or bodies of knowledge. For example, a boy may initially believe that anything that flies is a "bird." When he discovers that many things that are not birds can also fly, he may organize this new knowledge into a new, more complex mental structure such as this one:

A flying object may be

a bird ← a plane → Superman

This inclination to organize one's available schemata is inborn and automatic; children are constantly rearranging their existing knowledge to produce new and more complex mental structures.

---

equilibrium: Piaget's term for the state of affairs in which there is a balanced, harmonious relationship between one's thought processes and environmental events.

schema (plural, **schemata):** an organized pattern of thought or action that a child develops to make sense of some aspect of his or her experience; Piaget sometimes uses the term *cognitive structures* as a synonym for *schemata.*

organization: Piaget's name for the child's inborn tendency to combine and integrate available schemata into coherent systems, or bodies of knowledge.

Photo 2-8. Piaget believed that children are naturally curious explorers who try to make sense of their surroundings.

The goal of organization is to further the process of **adaptation**. The adaptive function is the child's tendency to adjust to the demands of the environment. According to Piaget, adaptation occurs in two ways: **assimilation** and **accommodation**.

Assimilation is a process in which children seek to incorporate some new experience into schemata that they already have. Imagine the reaction of an infant who is exposed for the first time to a beach ball. She may first try to grasp it with one hand and thus assimilate it into her "grasping" schema in much the same way that rattles, rubber animals, and other crib toys have been assimilated in the past. In other words, this infant is trying to adapt to a novel stimulus by construing it as something familiar—namely, something to be grasped.

By itself, assimilation would rarely allow one to adapt successfully to new experiences. Piaget (1952) believed that persons who assimilate novel aspects of the environment will also *accommodate* to that experience—that is, alter their existing schemata in response to environmental demands. For example, the infant may have to alter her grasping structure (accommodate) by

using two hands instead of one in order to assimilate a beach ball into that particular schema. Assimilation and accommodation are complementary aspects of all adaptive acts. They are inborn processes that come into play whenever the child encounters new and interesting objects, events, or situations.

We can compare the activity of cognitive schemata to the behavior of an amoeba. This one-celled animal is a perpetual "eating machine" that engulfs food particles, changes shape, and grows. Cognitive growth occurs in a somewhat similar fashion. Children extend their schemata to novel aspects of the environment, and in the process of ingesting (assimilating) this environmental "nutriment," their schemata are changed (accommodated). The product of this intellectual functioning is adaptation—a state of equilibrium between the child's cognitive schemata and the environment.

But equilibrium is short-lived, according to Piaget. Just as an amoeba repeatedly changes shape by ingesting more food, one's cognitive structures are repeatedly changing (accommodating) as new experiences are assimilated. And even during periods when they are not experiencing anything new, children are actively organizing their existing knowledge into higher-order schemata. So two kinds of activity—organization and adaptation—make possible a progressively greater understanding of the world. Piaget stressed that these intellectual functions operate in a reciprocal fashion: assimilations bring about new accommodations, which stimulate reorganizations, which, in turn, allow further assimilations, and so on. Gradually, maturing children who are developing new schemata and reorganizing this existing knowledge will have progressed to the point where they think about old issues in entirely new ways; that is, they pass from one stage of cognitive development to the next higher stage.

Stages of Cognitive Development

Piaget divided intellectual development into four major periods: the *sensorimotor* stage (birth to age 2), the *preoperational* stage (ages 2 to 7), the *concrete-operational* stage (ages 7 to 11), and the *formal-operational* stage (ages 11–12 and beyond). These stages are increasingly complex. They form what Piaget called an *invariant developmental sequence*—that is, children progress through the stages in exactly the order in which they are listed. There is no skipping of stages, because each successive stage builds on previous ones. For example, formal operations, Piaget's highest stage, includes all the aspects of its predecessor, concrete operations, with the difference that the mental abilities that characterize concrete operations are now reorganized in a way that permits the child to reason at a higher level.

Table 2-2 describes some of the key features of Piaget's four cognitive stages. Each of these periods of intellectual growth will be discussed in much greater detail when we return to the topic of cognitive development in Chapter 9.

Contributions and Criticisms of the Cognitive-Developmental Viewpoint

Like Watson and Freud, Piaget was an innovative renegade. He believed that people who studied intelligence largely ignored its most interesting features—intellectual structure and function. Of course, this view made Piaget quite unpopular among the psychometricians who were presumably measuring the least interesting aspect of intelligence, intellectual content, with their IQ tests. In addition, Piaget stressed a mentalistic concept, "cognition," that had fallen from favor among psychologists from the behaviorist tradition. So in the

beginning, Piaget and his closest associates stood alone, receiving little if any encouragement from other members of the psychological community.

Clearly the times have changed. Not only did Piaget's early theorizing interest researchers in children's thinking and hasten the development of what we know today as "cognitive psychology," but his early work linking moral development to cognitive development (see Chapter 14 for an extended discussion) has spawned a whole new area of developmental research—the study of **social cognition**. Contemporary social-cognitive theorists such as Lawrence Kohlberg and Robert Selman have found that the same mind that gradually constructs increasingly sophisticated understandings of the physical world also comes, with age, to form more complex ideas about sex differences, moral values, the significance of human emotions, the meaning and obligations of friendship, and countless other aspects of social life. The primary goals of social-cognitive researchers are to determine (1) how children come to understand the feelings, thoughts, and behaviors of themselves and other people and (2) how this knowledge then affects their own social behavior. The development of social cognition is a primary focus of Chapter 12, and the links between one's social-cognitive abilities and various aspects of social and personality development are discussed throughout the text.

Finally, Piaget was the first major developmental theorist to stress that children are active, adaptive creatures whose thought processes are very different from those of adults. Educators soon recognized the implications of this line of reasoning for their own field as they began to treat children less like little adults and more like curious explorers who should be given educational experiences that they are capable of understanding. For example, many teachers now introduce the difficult concept of number by presenting young

---

adaptation: Piaget's name for the child's inborn tendency to adjust to the demands of the environment.

assimilation: Piaget's term for the process by which children interpret new experiences by incorporating them into their existing schemata.

accommodation: Piaget's term for the process by which children modify their existing schemata in order to incorporate or adapt to new experiences.

social cognition: the study of children's thinking about the thoughts, motives, intentions, and behaviors of themselves and other people.

Table 2-2. Piaget's stages of cognitive development

Approximate age	Stage	Primary schemata or methods of representing experience	Major developments
Birth to 2 years	Sensorimotor	Infants use sensory and motor capabilities to explore and gain a basic understanding of the environment. At birth, they have only innate reflexes with which to engage the world. By the end of the sensorimotor period, they are capable of complex sensorimotor coordinations.	Infants acquire a primitive sense of "self" and "others," learn that objects continue to exist when they are out of sight (object permanence), and begin to internalize behavioral schemata to produce images, or mental schemata.
2 to 7 years	Preoperational	Children use symbolism (images and language) to represent and understand various aspects of the environment. They respond to objects and events according to the way things appear to be. Thought is egocentric, meaning that children think everyone sees the world in much the same way that they do.	Children become imaginative in their play activities. They gradually begin to recognize that other people may not always perceive the world as they do.
7 to 11 years	Concrete operations	Children acquire and use cognitive operations (mental activities that are components of logical thought).	Children are no longer fooled by appearances. By relying on cognitive operations, they understand the basic properties of and relations among objects and events in the everyday world. They are becoming much more proficient at inferring motives by observing others' behavior and the circumstances in which it occurs.
11 years and beyond	Formal operations	Children's cognitive operations are reorganized in a way that permits them to operate on operations (think about thinking). Thought is now systematic and abstract.	No longer is logical thinking limited to the concrete or the observable. Children enjoy pondering hypothetical issues and, as a result, may become rather idealistic. They are capable of systematic, deductive reasoning that permits them to consider many possible solutions to a problem and pick the correct answer.

children with different numbers of objects to stack, color, or arrange. Presumably, new concepts like number are best taught by a method in which active children can apply their existing schemata and make the critical "discoveries" for themselves.

In spite of these many contributions, Piaget and his theory have been severely criticized. Psychoanalysts, not surprisingly, argue that Piaget ignores the most important of all "mentalistic" phenomena—unconscious motivation and its impact on behavior. In addition, there is now some question about whether Piaget's stages really "hang together" as the coherent and distinct modes of thinking that he believed they were. The problem is that children do not always act as if they were at only one particular stage, implying that cognitive development may be a lot less stagelike (and perhaps less sequentially invariant) than Piaget had claimed (see Flavell, 1982, 1985). Finally, there are those individuals (particularly learning theorists) who believe that Piaget, the trained zoologist, was too preoccupied with basic biological processes and has overemphasized their role in human development. This is an interesting critique because there are others who feel that Piaget paid insufficient attention to biological factors. Who would make such a claim? The ethologists.

The Ethological Viewpoint

Ethology is the study of the biological bases of behavior, including its evolution, causation, and development (Cairns, 1979). This theoretical approach arose from the efforts of several European zoologists who argued that other theorists had overlooked or ignored important biological contributions to human and animal behavior.

According to ethologists, members of each species are born with a number of innate responses that are products of evolution. These "biologically programmed" behaviors are thought to have evolved as a result of the Darwinian process of **natural selection**. Presumably, environmental stresses or demands impinge on members of all species, ensuring that only those individuals with the most adaptive characteristics will survive to pass these attributes along to their offspring. Thus, each species-specific behavior is pre-selected—meaning that it has persisted because it serves some function that increases the chances of survival for the individual and the species (Blurton-Jones, 1972). Examples of preselected characteristics are the nest-building behavior of lovebirds, nut cracking by red squirrels, and crying to communicate discomfort by human infants.

Once an ethologist has identified an interesting behavior (or pattern of behaviors) that warrants investigation, he or she is likely to seek answers for four basic questions (Hinde, 1983): (1) What causes this behavior? (2) How did it develop? (3) What are its biological functions or consequences? and (4) How did it evolve? When conducting research, ethologists prefer the method of naturalistic observation because they believe that "biologically programmed" behaviors that affect human (or animal) development are best identified and understood if they are observed in a setting in which they have adaptive significance (Charlesworth, 1980). Stated another way, it makes little sense to look for innate responses to the natural environment in the highly artificial context of the laboratory. (Ethologists do occasionally conduct laboratory experiments, but usually only to confirm or clarify observations made in the natural environment.)

When testing a hypothesis in the field, a human ethologist makes detailed records of children's interactions, noting when the critical behavior occurred and what happened before and after the critical event. Of particular interest are any possible innate responses (for example, facial features or postural cues) that may have elicited or terminated the behavior in question. Ethologists believe that all our innate responses have the function of promoting particular kinds of experiences that will affect our development. For example, the cry of a human infant is thought to be a biologically programmed "distress signal" that brings caregivers running. Not only are infants said to be biologically programmed to convey their distress with loud, lusty cries, but ethologists also believe that caregivers are biologically predisposed to respond to such signals. So the adaptive significance of an infant's crying is to ensure (1) that the infant's basic needs (for example, hunger, thirst, safety) will be met and (2) that the infant will have sufficient contact with other human beings to form primary social and emotional relationships (Bowlby, 1973).

Although ethologists are especially critical of learning theorists for largely ignoring the biological bases of human development, they are well aware that development could not progress very far without learning. For example, the cry of an infant may be an innate signal that promotes the human contact from which emotional attachments emerge. However, these emotional attachments do not simply "happen" automatically. The infant must first *learn* to discriminate familiar faces from those of strangers before he will show any evidence of being emotionally attached to a regular companion. Presumably, the adaptive significance of this kind of discriminatory learning goes back to that period in evolutionary history when humans traveled in nomadic tribes and lived in the great outdoors. In those days, it was crucial that an infant become attached to familiar companions and fearful of strangers, for failure to cry in response to a strange face might make the infant "easy pickings" for a predatory animal.

---

ethology: the study of the bioevolutionary bases of behavior.

natural selection: the evolutionary principle that individuals who have characteristics advantageous for survival in a particular environment are the ones who are most likely to survive and reproduce; over many generations, this process of "survival of the fittest" will lead to development of new species.

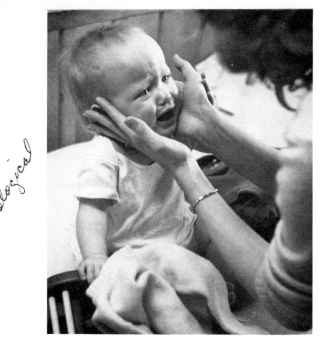

Ethological

Photo 2-9. The cry is a distress signal that attracts the attention of caregivers.

Now consider the opposite side of the coin. Some caregivers who suffer from various life stresses of their own (for example, prolonged illnesses, depression, an unhappy marriage, or even a habitually cranky baby) may be routinely inattentive or neglectful, so that the infant's cries rarely promote any contact with them. Such an infant will probably not form strong emotional attachments to her caregivers and could remain rather shy and emotionally unresponsive to other people for years to come (Ainsworth, 1979; Sroufe, Fox, & Pancake, 1983). What this infant has learned from her early experiences is that her closest companions are unreliable and are not to be trusted. Consequently, the child becomes ambivalent or wary around her caregivers and may later assume that significant others, such as teachers and peers, are equally untrustworthy individuals who should be avoided whenever possible.

How important are an individual's early experiences? Ethologists believe that they are *very* important. In fact, they have argued that there may be "critical periods" for the development of many attributes and behaviors. A **critical period** is a part of the life cycle during which the developing organism is particularly sensitive or responsive to specific environmental influences; outside this period, the same events or influences are thought to have little if any lasting effects. To illustrate, some ethologists believe that the first three years of life is a critical period for the development of social and emotional responsiveness in human beings. Presumably, we are most uniquely susceptible to forming close emotional ties during the first three years, and should we have little or no opportunity to do so during this period, we would find it difficult if not impossible to make close friends or to enter into intimate emotional relationships with other people later in life. Is there any empirical basis for this interesting and provocative claim? This is an issue that we will explore when we take up the topic of early social and emotional development in Chapter 11.

In sum, ethologists clearly acknowledge that we are largely a product of our experiences. Yet, they are quick to remind us that we are inherently biological creatures whose inborn characteristics affect the kinds of learning experiences we are likely to have.

Contributions of the Ethological Viewpoint

If this chapter had been written in 1970, it would not have included a section on ethological theory. Although ethology came into being more than 30 years ago, the early ethologists studied animal behavior; only within the past 10–15 years have proponents of ethology made a serious attempt to specify the biological bases of human conduct. Clearly, they have not yet succeeded in providing us with a comprehensive overview of all aspects of human development. However, they have made developmental researchers increasingly aware that every child has a bioevolutionary heritage that affects his or her own behavior and the reactions of others to the child.

Perhaps the most intriguing notion—one that we will discuss in detail in Chapter 11—is that infants are inherently sociable creatures who are quite capable of promoting and maintaining social interactions from the day they are born. This viewpoint contrasts sharply with that of the behaviorists, who portray the neonate as a *tabula rasa*, or with Piaget's "asocial" infant, who comes into the world equipped with only a few basic reflexes. Ethologists also believe that our evolutionary history provides us with inborn motives that affect our behavior in important ways (shades of Freud and the

Box 2-3
Is Altruism Part of Human Nature?

Darwin's notion of "survival of the fittest" seems to argue against altruism as an inborn motive. Many have interpreted Darwin's idea to mean that powerful, self-serving individuals who place their own needs ahead of others' are the ones who are most likely to survive. If this were so, evolution would favor the development of selfishness and egoism—not altruism—as basic components of human nature.

Martin Hoffman (1981) has recently challenged this point of view, listing several reasons that the concept of "survival of the fittest" actually implies altruism. His arguments hinge on the assumption that human beings are more likely to receive protection from natural enemies, satisfy all their basic needs, and successfully reproduce if they live together in cooperative social units. If this assumption is correct, cooperative, altruistic individuals would be the ones who are most likely to survive long enough to pass

along their "altruistic genes" to their offspring; individualists who "go it alone" would probably succumb to famine, predators, or some other natural disaster that they could not cope with by themselves. So over thousands of generations, natural selection would favor the development of innate social motives such as altruism. Presumably, the tremendous survival value of being "social" makes altruism, cooperation, and other social motives much more plausible as components of human nature than competition, selfishness, and the like.

It is obviously absurd to argue that infants routinely help other people. However, Hoffman believes that even newborn babies are capable of recognizing and experiencing the emotions of others. This ability, known as *empathy*, is thought to be an important contributor to altruism, for a person must recognize that others are distressed in some way before he or she is likely to help. So Hoffman is suggesting that at least one aspect of altruism—empathy—is present at birth.

Hoffman's claim is based on an experiment (Sagi & Hoffman, 1976) in

which infants less than 36 hours old listened to (1) another infant's cries, (2) an equally loud computer simulation of a crying infant, or (3) no sounds at all (silence). The infants who heard a real infant crying soon began to cry themselves, to display physical signs of agitation such as kicking, and to grimace. Infants exposed to the simulated cry or to silence cried much less and seemed not to be very discomforted. (A recent study by Martin & Clark, 1982, has confirmed these observations.)

Hoffman argues that there is something quite distinctive about the human cry. His contention is that infants listen to and experience the distress of another crying infant and become distressed themselves. Of course, this finding does not conclusively demonstrate that humans are altruistic by nature. But it does imply that the capacity for empathy may be present at birth and thus serve as a biological basis for the eventual development of altruistic behavior.

---

concept of instincts). For example, the motive of altruism presumably has evolved because it promotes survival of the species (though not necessarily the survival of the altruistic individual). Box 2-3 describes some recent observations to suggest that there may be a biological basis for certain aspects of altruism.

As we enter the 1990s, the ethological viewpoint is itself a thriving infant—one that should continue to develop and perhaps have an even stronger impact on the field of developmental psychology in the years ahead.

Criticisms of Ethology

Recall that psychoanalytic theory is often criticized as being *untestable*: How, for example, does one measure instincts or components of the personality such as the id, ego, and superego? The same criticism can be aimed at the ethologists: How does one prove that certain motives or behaviors are (1) inborn or (2) products of evolutionary history? These claims are difficult if not

impossible to confirm. In addition, ethological theory is often criticized as being a *retrospective*, or "post hoc," explanation of development. One can easily apply evolutionary concepts to explain what has already happened, but can the theory predict what is likely to happen in the future? Many developmentalists believe that it cannot.

Finally, proponents of learning theory have an interesting viewpoint on ethology. They argue that even if the bases for certain motives or behaviors are biologically programmed, these innate responses are so modified by learning that it may not be helpful to spend much time wondering about their prior evolutionary significance. Albert Bandura (1973), for example, makes

---

critical period: a brief period in the development of an organism when it is particularly sensitive to certain environmental influences; outside this period, the same influences will have little if any effect.

the following observation when comparing the aggressive behaviors of humans and animals:

> [Unlike animals], man does not rely heavily on auditory, postural, and olfactory signals for conveying aggressive intent or appeasement. He has [developed] a much more intricate system of communication—namely language—for controlling aggression. National leaders can ... better safeguard against catastrophic violence by verbal communiques than by snapping their teeth or erecting their hair, especially in view of the prevalence of baldness among the higher echelons [p. 16].

In spite of these criticisms, the ethological perspective is a valuable addition to the field of developmental psychology. It has made us aware of important biological contributors to human development and has led to several discoveries that were neither anticipated nor easily explained by other theoretical approaches.

A Final Comment on Developmental Theories

The four broad theoretical perspectives that we have reviewed differ in many respects. They make very different assumptions about human nature and about the processes and outcomes of development (see Box 2-4 for a summary of these philosophical variations); they rely on different research methods to test assumptions and hypotheses; and last but not least, *they emphasize different aspects of development.* Psychoanalytic theorists focus on social and emotional development. They have made us aware that early experiences and unconscious emotional conflicts can have a dramatic effect on the developing personality. Learning theorists are concerned mainly with the *process* of development itself. They have helped us to understand how children are influenced by their environment and how interactions between person and environment lead to the development of stable habits, traits, talents, and peculiarities. Cognitive theorists concentrate on the intellectual aspects of human development. They remind us that children are active and curious "thinkers" whose interpretations of the environment determine what kinds of learning experiences they are likely to have. Ethologists can agree, in part, with each of these arguments. But they would also emphasize that human beings are biological creatures who inherit various mannerisms, behaviors, and motives that help to steer them along particular developmental paths.

We have seen that each of these theories has definite strengths and that each is subject to criticism. Today many developmentalists can be described as *theoretical eclectics*—those who recognize that none of these theories can explain all aspects of human development but that each has contributed in important ways to what we know about developing children. The plan for the remainder of this book is to take an eclectic approach, borrowing from many theories to integrate their contributions into a unified, holistic portrait of the developing child. However, we will not shy away from theoretical controversies, for these squabbles often produce some of the most exciting breakthroughs in the field. The next chapter, for example, will show how the "nature versus nurture" controversy has helped us to understand how heredity and environment interact to affect intelligence, personality, and mental health.

Summary

A theory is a set of concepts and propositions that help to describe and explain observations one has made. Theories are particularly useful if they are *concise* and yet applicable to a wide range of phenomena. Good theories are also *precise*—that is, capable of making explicit predictions that can be evaluated in later research. Some of the basic issues addressed by theories of human development include questions about the inherent nature of human beings; the nature/nurture issue, centering on the relative contributions of biology and environment to developmental outcomes; the question whether people are actively involved in their own development; the continuity/discontinuity issue; and the question whether people tend to follow universal or particularistic developmental paths. There are four major theoretical perspectives on human development: psychoanalytic theory, learning theory (behaviorism), cognitive-developmental theory, and ethological theory.

The psychoanalytic perspective originated from the work of Sigmund Freud, who depicted children as "seething cauldrons" driven by inborn erotic and destructive instincts. At birth, the child's personality consists only of these instinctual forces (called the "id"). However, these id forces are gradually diverted into a system of rational thought, the "ego," and an irrational but ethical component of personality, the "superego."

The child is thought to pass through five psychosexual stages—oral, anal, phallic, latency, and genital—that parallel the maturation of the sex instinct. Freud assumed that the activities and conflicts that emerge at each psychosexual stage would have lasting effects on the developing personality.

Erik Erikson has revised and extended Freud's theory by concentrating less on the sex instinct and more on important sociocultural determinants of hu-man development. According to Erikson, people progress through a series of eight psychosocial stages. Each stage is characterized by a conflict, or "crisis," that the individual must successfully resolve in order to develop in a healthy direction.

The learning, or behaviorist, viewpoint originated with John B. Watson, who argued that newborn infants are *tabulae rasae* who are gradually conditioned by their experiences to feel, think, and act in certain ways. Learning theorists believe that learned associations between stimuli and responses (habits) are the building blocks of human development. Presumably, development is a continuous process marked by gradual acquisition of new and more sophisticated habits that might be acquired through classical conditioning, operant conditioning, or observational learning. B. F. Skinner believes that development reflects the operant conditioning of children who are passively molded by their experiences. By contrast, Albert Bandura views children as active information processors who learn by observation and who have a hand in creating the environments that affect their growth and development.

The cognitive-developmental viewpoint of Jean Piaget stresses that children are active explorers who have an intrinsic need to adapt to their environments. Piaget described the course of intellectual development as an invariant sequence of four stages, each of which evolves from its predecessors. According to Piaget, the child's stage of cognitive development determines how he or she will interpret various events and, thus, what the child will learn from interacting with others. The implication is that cognitive abilities play a central role in children's overall development, particularly their social and personality development.

The ethological viewpoint is that children are born with a number of adaptive responses that evolved over the course of human history and serve to channel development along particular paths. Ethologists recognize that human beings are largely products of their experiences (learning). However, they remind us that we are biological creatures whose innate characteristics affect the kind of learning experiences we are likely to have.

Although no single theoretical viewpoint offers a totally satisfactory explanation of human development, each of the four reviewed in this chapter has contributed in important ways to our understanding of developing children. Most contemporary developmentalists are eclectic, meaning that they borrow from many theories, attempting to integrate these contributions into a holistic portrait of the developing child.

References

AINSWORTH, M. D. S. (1979). Attachment as related to mother-infant interaction. In J. S. Rosenblatt, R. A. Hinde, C. Beer, & M. Busnel (Eds.), *Advances in the study of behavior* (Vol. 9). Orlando, FL: Academic Press.

BANDURA, A. (1973). *Aggression: A social learning analysis*. Englewood Cliffs, NJ: Prentice-Hall.

BANDURA, A. (1977). *Social learning theory*. Englewood Cliffs, NJ: Prentice-Hall.

BANDURA, A. (1986). *Social foundations of thought and action: A social cognitive theory*. Englewood Cliffs, NJ: Prentice-Hall.

BELL, R. Q. (1979). Parent, child, and reciprocal influences. *American Psychologist, 34*, 821–826.

BLURTON-JONES, N. (1972). Characteristics of ethological studies of human behavior. In N. Blurton-Jones (Ed.), *Ethological studies of child behavior*. London: Cambridge University Press.

BOWLBY, J. (1973). *Attachment and loss*. Vol. 2: *Separation: Anxiety and anger*. London: Hogarth Press.

CAIRNS, R. B. (1979). *Social development: The origins and plasticity of interchanges*. New York: W. H. Freeman.

CHARLESWORTH, W. R. (1980). Teaching ethology of human behavior. *Human Ethology Newsletter, 38*, 7–9.

ERIKSON, E. H. (1950). In M. J. E. Senn (Ed.), *Symposium on the healthy personality*. New York: Josiah Macy, Jr., Foundation.

ERIKSON, E. H. (1963). *Childhood and society* (2nd ed.). New York: Norton.

ERIKSON, E. H. (1972). Eight ages of man. In C. S. Lavatelli & F. Stendler (Eds.), *Readings in child behavior and child development*. San Diego, CA: Harcourt Brace Jovanovich.

FLAVELL, J. H. (1982). On cognitive development. *Child Development, 53*, 1–10.

FLAVELL, J. H. (1985). *Cognitive development* (2nd ed.). Englewood Cliffs, NJ: Prentice-Hall.

FREUD, S. (1933). *New introductory lectures in psychoanalysis*. New York: Norton.

FREUD, S. (1961). The dissolution of the Oedipus complex. In J. Strachey (Ed. and Trans.), *The standard edition of the complete psychological works of Sigmund Freud* (Vol. 19). London: Hogarth Press. (Original work published 1924)

FREUD, S. (1964). An outline of psychoanalysis. In J. Strachey (Ed. and Trans.), *The standard edition of the complete psychological works of Sigmund Freud* (Vol. 23). London: Hogarth Press. (Original work published 1940)

HINDE, R. A. (1983). Ethology and child development. In M. M. Haith & J. J. Campos (Eds.), *Handbook of child psychology*. Vol. 2: *Infancy and developmental psychobiology*. New York: Wiley.

HOFFMAN, M. L. (1981). Is altruism part of human nature? *Journal of Personality and Social Psychology, 40*, 121–127.

JENSEN, A. R. (1969). How much can we boost I.Q. and scholastic achievement? *Harvard Educational Review, 39*, 1–123.

KAGAN, J. (1980). Perspectives on continuity. In O. G. Brim, Jr., & J. Kagan (Eds.), *Constancy and change in human development*. Cambridge, MA: Harvard University Press.

KAPLAN, B. (1983). A trio of trials. In R. M. Lerner (Ed.), *Developmental psychology: Historical and philosophical perspectives*. Hillsdale, NJ: Erlbaum.

KATCHER, A. (1955). The discrimination of sex differences by young children. *Journal of Genetic Psychology, 87*, 131–143.

MAIER, H. W. (1969). *Three theories of child development*. New York: Harper & Row.

MARTIN, G. B., & Clark, R. D., III. (1982). Distress crying in neonates: Species and peer specificity. *Developmental Psychology, 18*, 3–9.

McCONAGHY, M. J. (1979). Gender permanence and the genital basis of gender: Stages in the development of constancy of gender identity. *Child Development, 50*, 1223–1226.

PIAGET, J. (1950). *The psychology of intelli-*

gence. San Diego, CA: Harcourt Brace Jovanovich.

PIAGET, J. (1952). *The origins of intelligence in children*. New York: International Universities Press.

PLOMIN, R. (1986). *Development, genetics, and psychology*. Hillsdale, NJ: Erlbaum.

SAGI, A., & Hoffman, M. L. (1976). Empathic distress in newborns. *Developmental Psychology, 12,* 175–176.

SCARR, S., & Weinberg, R. A. (1983). The Minnesota adoption studies: Genetic differences and malleability. *Child Development, 54,* 260–267.

SHAFFER, D. R. (1977). Social psychology from a social-developmental perspective. In C. Hendrick (Ed.), *Perspectives on social psychology*. Hillsdale, NJ: Erlbaum.

SKINNER, B. F. (1953). *Science and human behavior*. New York: Macmillan.

SKINNER, B. F. (1971). *Beyond freedom and dignity*. New York: Knopf.

SROUFE, L. A., Fox, N. E., & Pancake, V. R. (1983). Attachment and dependency in developmental perspective. *Child Development, 54,* 1615–1627.

WATSON, J. B. (1913). Psychology as the behaviorist views it. *Psychological Review, 20,* 158–177.

WATSON, J. B. (1925). *Behaviorism*. New York: Norton.

WEISBERG, P. (1963). Social and nonsocial conditioning of infant vocalization. *Child Development, 34,* 377–388.

WIGGAM, A. E. (1923). *The new decalogue of science*. Indianapolis: Bobbs-Merrill.

II

Human beings are biological creatures, and our emphasis in Part II is on the biological bases of development. In Chapter 3 we will discuss the concept of heredity and see that hereditary processes contribute in important ways to our physical, social, and intellectual development. We will also learn how our knowledge of genetic transmission has helped to promote healthy development by allowing us to prevent or minimize the effects of many hereditary abnormalities.

Our focus in Chapter 4 shifts to the remarkable developments that take place during the prenatal period—the nine months between conception and birth during which a single cell evolves into a recognizable human being. Although prenatal development unfolds in an orderly sequence and follows a distinct biological timetable, we will see that the 266 days before birth are truly a sensitive period in which a variety of environmental influences can interfere with nature's grand plan and produce any number of harmful consequences.

Psychological development depends to a large extent on physical development: our size, shape, strength, sensory capabilities, and muscle coordination clearly affect how we feel, think, and act. Chapter 5 describes the characteristics and capabilities of newborns and then traces their physical development from infancy through adolescence as they grow, acquire important motor skills, and become more and more like adults, both in appearance and in physical prowess.

Although in this section we concentrate on aspects of development that are heavily influenced by our biological heritage, each of the areas we will consider is subject to a variety of social and environmental influences. Thus, the three chapters in Part II also illustrate how the forces of nature and nurture combine (or interact) to determine developmental outcomes.

Biological Foundations of Development

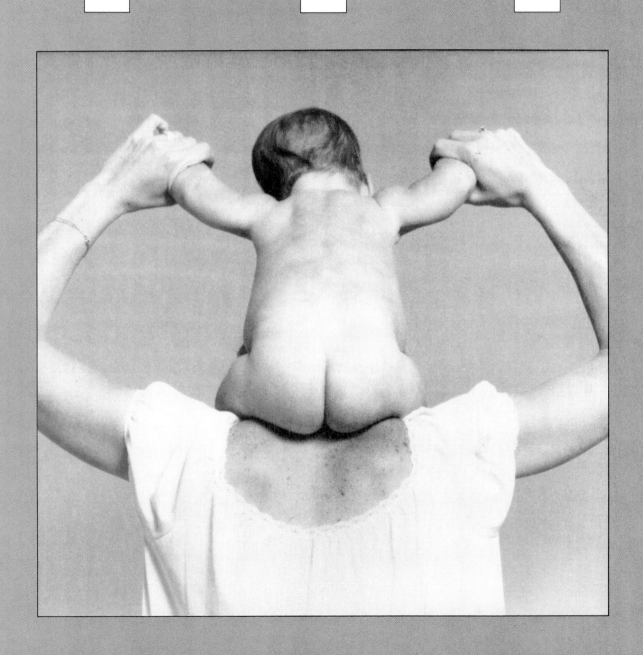

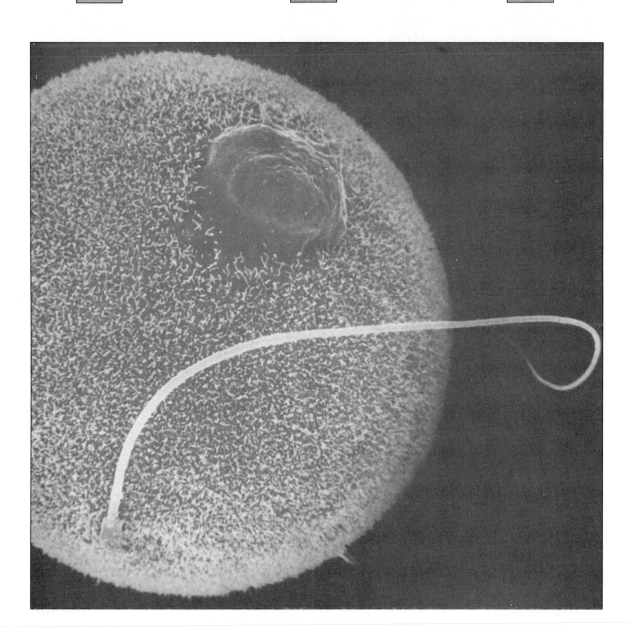

Hereditary Influences on Development

Can you remember when you were first introduced to the concept of heredity? Consider the experience of one first-grader at a parent/teacher conference. The teacher asked the boy whether he knew in which country his ancestors had lived before coming to the United States. He proudly exclaimed "The Old West" because he was "half cowboy and half Negro." Everyone present had a good laugh and then tried to convince the boy that he couldn't be of Afro-American ancestry because his parents were not—that he could only become what mom and dad already were. Evidently, the constraints of heredity did not go over too well. The child became rather distressed and asked "You mean I can't be a fireman?"

In this chapter we will consider the "constraints of heredity" in the light of what we have learned about biological bases of development over the past 300 years. In so doing, we'll see that our understanding of the fundamentals of hereditary transmission is itself a recent development and that many thorny issues remain to be resolved. After considering how hereditary information is passed from parents to children, we will explore the hereditary basis for important psychological characteristics such as intelligence, personality, and mental health. Finally, we will see that the expression "hereditary constraint" is something of a misnomer, for most complex human attributes are the result of a long and involved interplay between the forces of nature (heredity) and nurture (the environment).

Heredity in Historical Perspective

The concept of heredity dates back to at least 6000 years ago, when historical records describe farmers' attempts to produce better crops and hardier livestock by selective breeding (Burns, 1976). Before the 17th century, it was commonly assumed that children inherited their traits, talents, and peculiarities from their fathers. For example, Aristotle, writing in the fourth century B.C., argued that "nature seeks to reproduce the father exactly in the offspring but fails in different degrees. The ideal would be for male to produce male only; the first fall from this is the production of females, and thence we can proceed by gentle gradations to freaks" (1912, p. 767). According to Aristotle, fathers would fail to produce male offspring if they married too young or chose the wrong time of year for procreation. Ideally, men should be at least 37 and women 18 before they began to reproduce. Presumably, winter was the season when men would have the time and energy to reproduce themselves without generating "accidents of nature" such as daughters or small and defective sons.

The Doctrine of Preformationism

In the 17th century, the invention of the compound microscope led to the discovery of sperm and ova. The Dutch scientist Anton van Leeuwenhoek (1677) observed the movement of sperm cells under a microscope and concluded that sperm were alive. His countryman Jan Swammerdam soon proposed a *preformationist* theory, which stated that each sperm cell contained a tiny "preformed" embryo, or **homunculus,** that was nourished by the female ovum (egg) and would grow only if deposited in the womb (see Figure 3-1). Clearly, Leeuwenhoek and Swammerdam agreed with Aristotle on one important point—inheritance flowed from father to offspring, the mother serving as an incubator.

However, Swammerdam's "homunculus" theory was soon challenged by other scientists, who noted that many children resemble their mothers much more than their fathers. One group of biologists (the *ovists*) argued that preformed human embryos appeared not in the father's sperm but in the mother's ova. Presumably, sperm was little more than a "fertilizer" that triggered the growth of an embryo. The ovist viewpoint was popular in its day because it seemed to legitimize the tendency of many to blame mothers for producing deformed babies or for failing to produce male heirs.

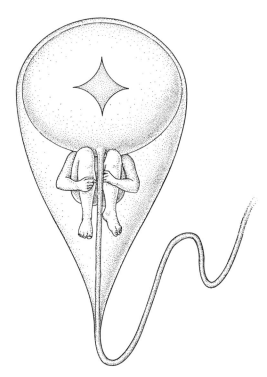

Figure 3-1. The homunculus. Leeuwenhoek believed that each sperm cell contained a preformed embryo, or "homunculus," that would grow if deposited in the womb of an adult female.

In 1759 Kaspar Wolff, a German-born anatomist, reported a set of observations that forever changed our thinking about hereditary processes (Wolff, 1759/1959). Wolff suspected that sperm and ovum unite to form a single cell that soon begins to divide. As this process of cell division was repeated thousands of times, Wolff was able to observe the gradual development of recognizable organs and body parts. This remarkable discovery implied that neither the sperm nor the ovum contained a preformed embryo. Clearly, Wolff had witnessed the evolution, or "epigenesis," of an embryo from a single fertilized ovum (that is, a zygote) to which both parents had contributed.

Modern Genetic Theories

Although Wolff's observations were hailed as a major advance in knowledge, several puzzles remained to be solved. For example, if each parent makes a roughly equivalent hereditary contribution to the off-spring, why do some children resemble one parent more than the other? The answer was more than 100 years in coming.

The work of Gregor Mendel. In 1865 Gregor Mendel reported an extensive program of research on the inheritance of color and other attributes in flowering sweet peas. During eight years of work, Mendel cross-fertilized 22 varieties of garden peas and carefully recorded the characteristics of the hybrid offspring. Fertile hybrids were then crossed to see what kinds of offspring they would produce. From his many observations, Mendel inferred the following:

1. Inherited attributes such as color of the flowers of sweet peas are produced by "characters" (later to be labeled **genes**) that are transmitted unchanged from generation to generation.
2. Each inherited attribute is determined by a pair of genes, *one of which is inherited from each parent.*
3. When an individual inherits a pair of genes that differ in their effects, one of these genes will *dominate* the other, and the characteristic of *only the dominant gene* will be expressed.
4. When a parent produces *gametes* (sperm for males and ova for females), the gene pair for each attribute divides so that each gamete contains but one member of the pair (law of segregation).

Mendel's early conclusions were brilliant insights that provided the foundation for modern genetics. Perhaps his most notable of many important contributions is the concept of genetic dominance—the principle that explains why a child may resemble one parent more than the other. According to the dominance principle, a child who inherits a different form of a particular gene from each parent will not be a "blend" of the parents' attributes. Instead, one of the parental genes will completely dominate the other, and the child will resemble the parent who contributed the dominant gene.

The work of Thomas Scott Morgan. In 1933 the zoologist Thomas Scott Morgan won the Nobel Prize in medicine for discovering that Mendel's "char-

---

homunculus: a preformed human embryo that biologists once believed to be present in each sperm cell.
genes: hereditary blueprints for development that are transmitted unchanged from generation to generation.

acters," or genes, are actual structures that are components of larger bodies, called **chromosomes,** that appear within the nuclei of all cells. Although they are not visible as separate entities, as many as 10,000–20,000 genes are said to lie like "beads on a string" along each chromosome.

Morgan's discoveries were based on his study of a relatively simple species, the vinegar fly. However, other researchers soon discovered that members of each species have a set number of chromosomes within the nucleus of each body cell. For example, normal human beings have 46 chromosomes per cell; other species have larger or smaller numbers.

The field of genetics flourished after Morgan reported that genes are located within the chromosomes of cell nuclei. Today we have a reasonably good understanding of how genes (and chromosomes) replicate themselves, allowing the human to evolve from a simple one-celled organism at conception to a complex being who enters the world with many interrelated systems, organs, and body parts. In Chapter 4 we will focus on the remarkable developments during the nine-month *prenatal* period between conception and birth. However, our immediate concern is heredity— what the child inherits from his or her parents and how this genetic inheritance affects the course of development.

Principles of Hereditary Transmission

At puberty or shortly thereafter, human females begin a process known as **ovulation:** approximately once every 28 days, an ovum ripens, leaves the ovary, and enters the fallopian tube. The average woman will ovulate some 300–500 times over the 30–40 years that she remains fertile. The vast majority of these ovulations are rather uneventful: the ripened ovum simply disintegrates when it reaches the uterus, and it leaves the body about seven to ten days later as part of the woman's menstrual flow.

Conception

Suppose, however, that a woman has sexual intercourse with a fertile male a few days before or after ovulation. When the male ejaculates, his seminal fluid may contain half again as many sperm cells (300–450 million) as there are people in the United States. These tiny, tadpolelike sperm immediately begin to swim in all directions. Perhaps as many as 5,000–20,000 of them will survive the long journey from the vagina through the uterus and into the fallopian tubes, where one may meet and penetrate the shell of a ripened ovum that is beginning its descent from the ovary (see Figure 3-2).

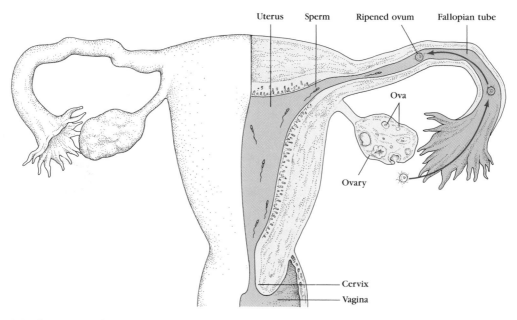

Figure 3-2. The anatomy of conception. Conception occurs in the fallopian tube as a sperm penetrates a ripened ovum that is descending from the ovary to the uterus.

Step 1
Original parent cell (for illustrative purposes this cell contains but four chromosomes).

Step 2
Each chromosome splits lengthwise, producing a duplicate.

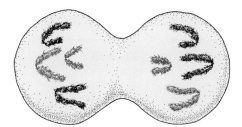

Step 3
The duplicate sets of chromosomes move to opposite ends of the parent cell, which then begins to divide.

Step 4
The cell completes its division, producing two daughter cells that have identical sets of chromosomes.

Figure 3-3. Mitosis—the way cells reproduce themselves.

This is **conception**—the beginning of a long developmental process.

      The very first development that occurs is protective: when a sperm cell penetrates the lining of the ovum, a biochemical reaction repels other sperm, thus preventing them from repeating the fertilization process. Within a few hours, the sperm cell begins to disintegrate, releasing its 23 chromosomes. At about the same time, the nucleus of the ovum releases 23 chromosomes of its own. As a new cell nucleus forms around these 23 pairs of chromosomes, the sperm and ovum become one cell—a **zygote**—that is only 1/20th the size of the head of a pin. Yet, this tiny cell may contain as many as 500,000 pairs of genes—one member of each pair coming from each parent—that provide the code, or biochemical recipe, for the zygote's development from a single cell into a recognizable human being.

Growth of the Zygote and Production of Body Cells

      As the zygote moves through the fallopian tube toward its prenatal home in the uterus, it begins to reproduce itself through the process of **mitosis.** At first

the zygote divides into two cells, but the two soon become four, four become eight, eight become sixteen, and so on. Just before each division, the cell duplicates its 46 chromosomes, and these duplicate sets move in opposite directions. The division of the cell then proceeds, resulting in two "daughter" cells, each of which has the identical 23 pairs of chromosomes (46 in all) and thus the same genetic code as the original parent cell. This remarkable process is illustrated in Figure 3-3.

---

chromosome: a threadlike structure made up of genes; in humans there are 46 chromosomes in the nucleus of each body cell.

ovulation: the process in which a female gamete (ovum) matures in one of the ovaries and is released into the fallopian tube.

conception: the moment of fertilization, when a sperm penetrates an ovum, forming a zygote.

zygote: a single cell formed at conception from the union of a sperm and an ovum.

mitosis: the process in which a cell duplicates its chromosomes and then divides into two genetically identical daughter cells.

By the time a child is born, he or she consists of billions of cells, each of which has been created through mitosis. Indeed, all the *somatic* (body) cells that make up our muscles, bones, organs, and other bodily structures are products of mitosis. Mitosis continues throughout life, creating new cells that enable us to grow and replacing old ones that are damaged. With each division, the hereditary blueprint is duplicated, so that every new cell contains an exact copy of the 46 chromosomes that we inherited at conception.

Germ Cells and Hereditary Transmission

We have learned that sperm and egg combine to form a zygote that has 46 chromosomes (23 of which come from each parent). But if cells normally contain 46 chromosomes apiece, why doesn't a person start life with 92 chromosomes, 46 coming from the father's sperm cell and 46 from the mother's ovum?

The answer is relatively simple. In addition to body cells, mature human beings have *germ* cells that serve one particular hereditary function—to produce *gametes* (sperm in males and ova in females). When male germ cells in the testes and female germ cells in the ovaries produce sperm and ova, they do so by a process called **meiosis.** In meiosis, the 23 pairs of chromosomes in the parent cell divide so that each daughter cell contains 23 single, or *unpaired,* chromosomes (see Figure 3-4). Thus, a sperm with 23 chromosomes unites with an ovum with 23 chromosomes, producing a zygote that has a full complement of 46 chromosomes (23 pairs).

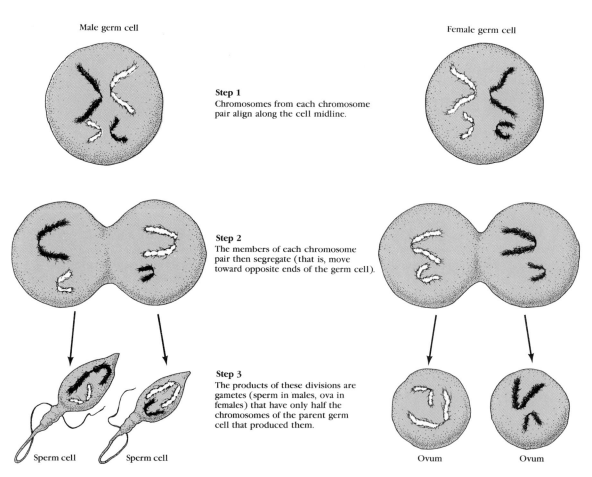

Male germ cell

Female germ cell

Step 1
Chromosomes from each chromosome pair align along the cell midline.

Step 2
The members of each chromosome pair then segregate (that is, move toward opposite ends of the germ cell).

Step 3
The products of these divisions are gametes (sperm in males, ova in females) that have only half the chromosomes of the parent germ cell that produced them.

Sperm cell   Sperm cell

Ovum   Ovum

Figure 3-4. Meiosis—the way germ cells produce sperm and ova.

Hereditary uniqueness. Full brothers and sisters have the same mother and father and have inherited 23 chromosomes from each of these parents. In view of this common heritage, why do you suppose that children from the same family do not look more alike?

Again the answer is relatively simple. When a pair of chromosomes segregates during meiosis, it is a matter of chance which of the two chromosomes will end up in a particular gamete. And because each chromosome pair segregates independently of all other pairs according to the Mendelian principle of **independent**

assortment, there are many different combinations of chromosomes that could result from the meiosis of a single germ cell. Since human germ cells contain 23 chromosome pairs, each of which is segregating independently of the others, the laws of probability tell us that there are 2^{23} possible outcomes of a meiotic division. In other words, a mature human being is capable of producing more than 8 million *different* gametes— different in that no two will carry exactly the same hereditary instructions. Because the 8 million combinations a father is capable of producing are independent of the mother's 8 million possible combinations, any couple could theoretically have 64 trillion babies without producing two children who inherited precisely the same set of genes.

In fact, the odds of exact genetic replication in two siblings born at different times are even less than 1 in 64 trillion, because of a quirk of meiosis known as the **crossing over** phenomenon. When pairs of chromosomes line up just before segregating, parts of them cross, break at the point of crossing, and exchange equivalent amounts of genetic material, much as if you were to exchange hands with a friend after a handshake. This process is illustrated in Figure 3-5. So the crossing-over phenomenon actually alters the genetic composition of a chromosome and thereby increases the number of gametes that an individual is capable of producing far beyond the figure of 8 million that would be possible if chromosomes segregated cleanly during meiosis, without exchanging genetic information.

Of course, brothers and sisters will resemble one another to some extent because their genes are drawn from a gene pool provided by the same two parents. Each brother or sister inherits half of each parent's genes, although two siblings never inherit the same half, owing to the random process by which parental chromosomes (and genes) segregate into the sperm and ovum that combine to produce each offspring. Thus,

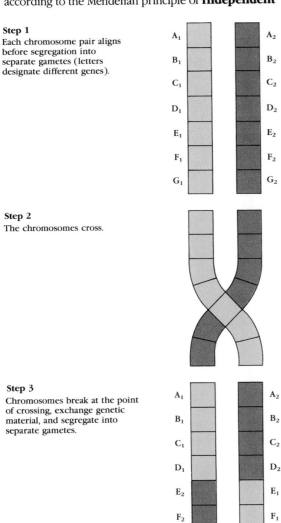

Step 1
Each chromosome pair aligns before segregation into separate gametes (letters designate different genes).

Step 2
The chromosomes cross.

Step 3
Chromosomes break at the point of crossing, exchange genetic material, and segregate into separate gametes.

Figure 3-5. The crossing-over phenomenon.

meiosis: the process in which a germ cell divides, producing gametes (sperm or ova) that each contain half of the parent cell's original complement of chromosomes; in humans, the products of meiosis contain 23 chromosomes.

independent assortment: the Mendelian principle stating that each pair of chromosomes segregates independently of all other chromosome pairs during meiosis.

crossing over: a process in which genetic material is exchanged between pairs of chromosomes.

each individual is genetically unique. The one exception to this rule is **monozygotic** (or **identical**) **twinning,** which occurs when a single zygote splits into two identical cells that develop independently. Identical twins are born in approximately 1 of every 270 pregnancies (Scheinfeld, 1967); and because they are genetically identical, monozygotic twins should show very similar

Photo 3-1. Identical, or monozygotic, twins (bottom) develop from a single zygote. Because they have inherited identical sets of genes, they will look alike, be of the same sex, and share all other inherited characteristics. Fraternal, or dizygotic, twins (top) develop from separate zygotes and have no more genes in common than siblings born at different times. Consequently, they may not look alike (as we see in this photo) and may not even be the same sex.

developmental progress if the genes that people inherit have much effect on human development.

Most twins, however, are **dizygotic** (or **fraternal**)—pairs that result when a mother releases *two* ova at approximately the same time and each is fertilized by a *different* sperm. So even though fraternal twins are born together and have shared a common prenatal environment, they have no more genes in common than any other pair of siblings. As illustrated in Photo 3-1, fraternal twins often differ considerably in appearance. Indeed, they need not even be the same sex.

Determination of gender. A hereditary basis for sex differences becomes apparent if we examine the chromosomes of typical men and women. These chromosomal portraits, or **karyotypes,** reveal that 22 of the 23 pairs of chromosomes found in human beings are similar in males and females. Gender is determined by the 23rd pair. In a normal male, the 23rd pair consists of one elongated body known as an **X chromosome** and a short, stubby companion called a **Y chromosome.** In the female, both these "sex" chromosomes are Xs (see Photo 3-2). Thus, the presence of a Y chromosome in one's hereditary blueprint means that one is a genetic male, while the absence of a Y chromosome defines a genetic female.

Pity the hundreds of thousands of women who throughout history have been belittled, tortured, divorced, or even beheaded for failing to bear their husbands a male heir! Since the father is the only parent who can provide the offspring with a Y chromosome, it is he who determines a child's gender. When the sex chromosomes segregate into gametes during meiosis, half of the sperm of a genetic (XY) male will contain an X chromosome and half will contain a Y chromosome. In contrast, the ova produced by a genetic (XX) female will normally contain a single X chromosome. Thus, the determination of gender is straightforward: if an ovum is fertilized by a sperm bearing a Y chromosome, the product is an XY zygote, which will become a male. However, if a sperm carrying an X chromosome reaches the ovum first, the result is an XX zygote, or a female.

Since half of the father's sperm contain Y chromosomes, the probability of conceiving a male child should be exactly 50/50. However, this is one case in which biology appears to defy the laws of probability. Approximately 150 males are conceived for every 100 females, perhaps because sperm bearing smaller Y chromosomes may swim faster, on average, than those bearing a larger (and presumably heavier) X chromosome.

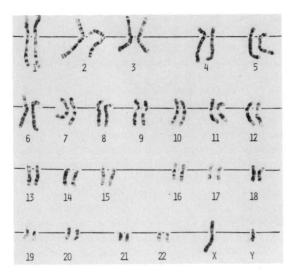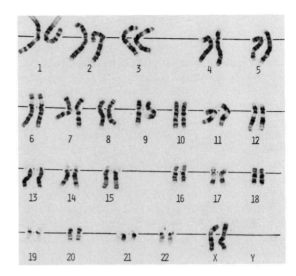

Photo 3-2. These karyotypes of a male (left) and a female (right) have been arranged so that the chromosomes could be displayed in pairs. Note that the 23rd pair of chromosomes for the male consists of one elongated X chromosome and a Y chromosome that is noticeably smaller, whereas the 23rd pair for the female consists of two X chromosomes.

And even though males are more likely to be miscarried (spontaneously aborted) during the prenatal period, they continue to outnumber females (by 106 to 100) at birth (McMillen, 1979; Stern, 1973).

Patterns of Genetic Expression

To this point, we have learned that children inherit about half a million pairs of genes and that one member of each gene pair comes from each parent. The question that can now be asked is how one's genetic inheritance, or **genotype**, affects one's **phenotype**—the way one looks, feels, thinks, and behaves. Let's begin our discussion of genetic influences by returning to an important principle discovered by Gregor Mendel more than 100 years ago—the principle of genetic dominance.

Dominant and recessive alleles

Many characteristics are determined by the interaction of a single pair of genes, or **alleles.** In human beings, eye color is a classic example. We receive one allele for eye color from each parent, and the particular combination of alleles that we have inherited determines what color our eyes will be.

Of course, the alleles that determine a characteristic like eye color may be of different kinds, as illustrated by the fact that not all people have eyes of the same color. Now suppose that you had inherited the following genotype for eye color: an allele for blue eyes

from your father and an allele for brown eyes from your mother. What color eyes would you have? If you looked in the mirror, you would immediately discover that you did *not* have one blue eye and one brown eye, and you

---

monozygotic (or identical) twins: twins that result when a single zygote divides into two separate but identical cells that each develop independently; as a result, each member of a monozygotic twin pair has inherited exactly the same set of genes.

dizygotic (or fraternal) twins: twins that result when a mother releases two ova at roughly the same time and each is fertilized by a different sperm, producing two zygotes that are genetically different.

karyotype: a chromosomal portrait created by staining chromosomes and then photographing them under a high-power microscope.

X chromosome: the longer of the two sex chromosomes; normal females have two X chromosomes, whereas normal males have but one.

Y chromosome: the shorter of the two sex chromosomes; normal males have one Y chromosome, whereas females have none.

genotype: the genetic endowment that an individual inherits.

phenotype: the ways in which a person's genotype is expressed in observable or measurable characteristics.

alleles: alternative forms of a gene that is coded for a particular trait.

could then infer that your alleles did not express themselves independently. In fact, when a person inherits alternative forms of a gene, one allele will often dominate the other, so that only the characteristic associated with the dominant form of the gene will be expressed. It happens that the allele for brown eyes is **dominant** and the weaker blue-eyed allele is said to be **recessive.** So a person who inherited a brown-eyed allele and a blue-eyed allele would have a "phenotype" of brown eyes.

Since a brown-eyed allele dominates a blue-eyed allele, we represent the brown-eyed gene with a capital *B* and the blue-eyed gene with a lower-case *b*. Considering only these two alleles, there are three possible genotypes for eye color: (1) two brown-eyed alleles (BB), (2) two blue-eyed alleles (bb), or (3) one of each (Bb). People whose genotype for an attribute consists of two genes of the same kind are said to be **homozygous** for that attribute. A person who is BB for eye color is homozygous brown and will pass only brown-eyed genes to his or her offspring. The person who is bb is homozygous blue (the only way one can have blue eyes is to inherit two recessive blue-eyed alleles) and will pass blue-eyed genes to his or her offspring. Finally, a person who is Bb is said to be **heterozygous** for eye color because he or she has two different alleles for this attribute. As we have seen, this individual will have brown eyes, because the B allele is dominant. And what kind of alleles will the heterozygous person pass along to offspring? Either a blue-eyed or a brown-eyed gene. Even though a heterozygous person has brown eyes, he or she can transmit a blue-eyed gene to children. Half the gametes produced by this individual will carry a gene

for blue eyes, and half will carry a gene for brown eyes. Therefore, *phenotype does not alter genotype.* This is what Mendel (1865/1959) had in mind when he proclaimed that genes are transmitted unchanged from one generation to another.

Can two brown-eyed individuals ever produce a blue-eyed child? The answer is yes—as long as each parent is heterozygous for eye color (that is, Bb). In Figure 3-6, the genotype of a heterozygous brown-eyed father appears at the head of the columns, and that of a heterozygous brown-eyed mother appears at the left of the rows. When the germ cells of each parent undergo meiosis, the resulting gametes will each contain only one allele for eye color—in this case, either a blue-eyed allele or a brown-eyed allele. What color eyes will the children have? The various possibilities appear in the four quadrants of the chart. If a sperm bearing a brown-eyed (B) gene unites with an ovum carrying a brown-eyed (B) gene, the result is a BB, or homozygous brown-eyed child. If a sperm containing a B gene fertilizes an ovum carrying a b gene, or if a b sperm fertilizes a B ovum, the result is a heterozygous brown-eyed (Bb) child. Finally, if both sperm and ovum carry a blue-eyed gene, the child will have blue eyes. Since each of these four combinations is equally likely to occur on any given mating, the odds are 1 in 4 that a child of two heterozygous brown-eyed parents will have blue eyes.

Eye color is but one of the many human attributes that are determined by a single gene pair in which one particular allele will dominate another.[1] Box 3-1 lists a number of other common dominant and recessive characteristics that people may inherit.

Incomplete dominance

Alternative forms of a gene do not always follow the simple dominant/recessive pattern described by Gregor Mendel. For example, some "dominant" alleles fail to mask all the effects of a "recessive" gene—that is, theirs is an **incomplete dominance.** A child who inherits heterozygous alleles of this type will have a phenotype that represents a "blending" of the two genes,

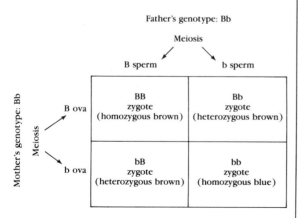

Figure 3-6. Possible genotypes and phenotypes resulting from a mating of two heterozygotes for eye color.

[1]We have talked as if each pair of alleles were responsible for determining one characteristic. Yet geneticists have discovered that some genes are *pleiotropic*—that is, they influence many characteristics. For example, a single pair of alleles is responsible for the appearance of Marfan's syndrome, a rare disorder that Abraham Lincoln may have inherited. Marfan's syndrome includes characteristics such as long, bony limbs, eye problems, a loss of hearing, and heart defects—all determined by a single pair of pleiotropic alleles.

Box 3-1
Examples of Dominant
and Recessive Traits
in Human Heredity

Our discussion of dominant and recessive genes has centered on two particular alleles, a gene for brown eyes and a gene for blue eyes. Yet eye coloring in human beings is more complex than our examples would indicate, for there are also genes for green, hazel, and gray eyes (all of which dominate a blue-eyed allele and are dominated by a gene for brown eyes). Listed below are other examples of dominant and recessive characteristics in human heredity.

Dominant traits	Recessive traits
Brown eyes	Gray, green, hazel, or blue eyes
Dark hair	Blond hair
Non-red hair (blond, brunette)	Red hair
Full head of hair	Pattern baldness*
Curly hair	Straight hair
Normal vision	Nearsightedness
Farsightedness	Normal vision
Normal vision	Color blindness
Roman nose	Straight nose
Broad lips	Thin lips
Short digits	Normal digits
Extra digits	Five digits
Double-jointedness	Normal joints
Immunity to poison ivy	Susceptibility to poison ivy
Pigmented skin	Albinism
Type A blood	Type O blood
Type B blood	Type O blood
Normal blood clotting	Hemophilia*
Normal hearing	Congenital deafness
Normal blood cells	Sickle-cell anemia*
Huntington's chorea	Normal brain and body maturation
Normal physiology	Phenylketonuria*
Normal physiology	Tay-Sachs disease*

A quick glance through the list reveals that most of the undesirable or maladaptive attributes are recessive. For that we can be thankful; otherwise genetically linked diseases and defects might soon destroy the species.

One important genetic disease produced by a *dominant* gene is Huntington's chorea, a condition that causes a gradual deterioration of the nervous system, leading to a progressive decline in one's physical and mental abilities and ultimately to death. Although some victims of Huntington's chorea die in young adulthood, normally the disease appears much later, usually after age 40. Fortunately, the dominant allele that is responsible for this lethal condition is very rare.

*This condition will be discussed elsewhere in the chapter.

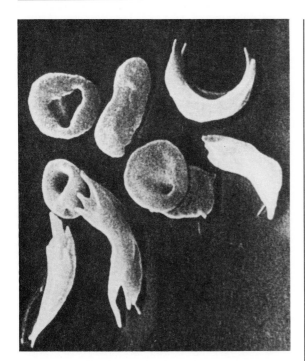

Photo 3-3. Normal (round) and "sickled" (elongated) red blood cells from a person with sickle-cell anemia.

although the stronger (or incompletely dominant) gene plays the major role in determining the child's phenotype.

The *sickle cell* trait is a noteworthy example of incomplete dominance in human heredity. About 9% of all Blacks in the United States (and relatively few Whites) are heterozygous for this attribute, carrying a recessive "sickle cell" allele (Thompson, 1975). The presence of this one recessive gene causes a substantial percentage of the person's red blood cells to assume an unusual crescent, or sickle, shape (see Photo 3-3). Sickled cells can be a problem because they tend to cluster

---

dominant allele: a relatively powerful gene that is expressed phenotypically and masks the effect of a less powerful gene.

recessive allele: a less powerful gene that is not expressed phenotypically when paired with a dominant allele.

homozygous: having inherited two alleles for an attribute that are identical in their effects.

heterozygous: having inherited two alleles for an attribute that have different effects.

incomplete dominance: condition in which a stronger allele fails to mask all the effects of a weaker allele; a phenotype results that is similar but not identical to the effect of the stronger gene.

together, distributing less oxygen throughout the circulatory system. Yet overt symptoms of circulatory distress, such as painful swelling of the joints and fatigue, are rarely experienced by these sickle-cell "carriers," unless they encounter severe emotional problems, are exposed to high altitudes, or should deprive themselves of oxygen through heavy physical exertion (Wilson, 1982).

The consequences are much more severe for those individuals who inherit *two* recessive sickle-cell genes. They will develop a severe blood disorder, called **sickle-cell anemia,** that causes massive sickling of red blood cells and inefficient distribution of oxygen at all times. Indeed, many who suffer from this painful disease will die from heart and/or kidney failure during childhood. By contrast, heterozygous individuals, who carry but one sickle-cell gene, are more phenotypically similar to the person who inherits two "normal" genes—their blood cells sickle to some extent, but they remain unaffected by this condition for the most part.

We see, then, that the "dominant" allele that produces normal red blood cells does not completely suppress the effects of a sickle-cell gene. If the dominance were complete, those who inherited a single recessive gene would not produce any sickled red blood cells.

Codominance

Some heterozygous alleles are equally strong or expressive, meaning that neither form of the gene is able to dominate the other. This type of genetic interaction is called **codominance** because the phenotype of the heterozygous individual represents an exact compromise, or combination, of the two genes that he or she has inherited.

The genes for the human blood types A and B are equally expressive. Each of these alleles dominates the gene for blood type O, but neither of the two alleles dominates the other. A heterozygous person who inherits an allele for blood type A from one parent and an allele for blood type B from the other has both A antigens and B antigens in his or her blood—a phenotype that represents an exact compromise between blood types A and B. If you have inherited the blood type known as AB, you illustrate this principle of genetic codominance.

Sex-linked characteristics

Some traits are called **sex-linked characteristics** because they are determined by genes located on the sex chromosomes. In fact, the vast majority of these sex-linked attributes are produced by recessive genes that are found only on X chromosomes. Who do you suppose is more likely to inherit these recessive X-linked traits, males or females?

The answer is males, a point we can easily illustrate with a common sex-linked characteristic, *red/green color blindness.* Many people cannot distinguish red from green, an inability caused by a recessive gene that appears only on X chromosomes. Now recall that a normal (XY) male has but one X chromosome—the one he inherited from his mother. If this X chromosome carries a recessive gene for color blindness, the male will be color-blind. Why? Because there is no corresponding gene on his Y chromosome that might counteract the effect of this "color blind" allele. By contrast, a genetic female who inherits but one gene for color blindness will not be color-blind, for the color-normal gene on her second X chromosome will dominate the color-blind gene, enabling her to distinguish red from green. Thus, a female cannot be color-blind unless *both* of her X chromosomes contain a recessive gene for color blindness.

So immediately we have reason to suspect that more males than females will be color-blind. Among White males in the United States, approximately 8 in 100 cannot distinguish red from green. This finding suggests that the ratio of "color blind" to "color normal" genes in the gene pool is approximately 1:12 (Burns, 1976). Since the odds are only 1 in 12 that any single X chromosome will contain a gene for color blindness, the likelihood that a female will inherit two of these genes (and be color-blind) is $1/12 \times 1/12$, or only 1 in 144.

There are many sex-linked characteristics other than color blindness, and most of them are disabling in some way. These include hemophilia (a disease in which the blood does not clot), diabetes, at least one kind of muscular dystrophy, degeneration of the optic nerve, and certain forms of deafness and night blindness. Because these disorders are determined by recessive genes on X chromosomes, males are much more likely than females to suffer their harmful effects.

Modifier genes and polygenic inheritance

To this point, we have considered the simplest form of genetic transmission, in which a characteristic is determined by a single pair of genes. But an allele may also act as a **modifier gene** by influencing the action or expression of other genes. For example, sex differences in pattern baldness are attributable to a modifier gene present in males. The gene(s) responsible for production of the male hormone androgen modify the gene for pattern baldness, making it dominant over the gene for normal hair. As a result, males who inherit but one gene for pattern baldness will show some degree of balding as they mature (the degree may well depend on the presence of yet other modifier genes). By contrast, females inherit a different set of genes that inhibit the production of androgen and do not alter the normally recessive nature of the gene for pattern baldness. So women must ordinarily inherit two genes for pattern baldness before they will experience a genetically based thinning of the hair (Burns, 1976).

Most complex human attributes are **polygenic**—that is, influenced by many genes rather than a single pair. One notable example is intelligence. People are not merely bright or dull; their intellectual performances are distributed at all levels between these two extremes. The current thinking is that many continuous attributes such as intelligence, height, weight, skin color, and temperament are influenced by a large number of genes, each of which contributes in a small way to one's phenotype.

A final note on genetic transmission

Our discussion so far has implied that characteristics are *determined* by the genes that people inherit. Yet, as we will see later in the chapter and throughout the text, behavioral attributes such as intelligence and temperament are strongly influenced by environmental factors. Even physical characteristics such as height and weight depend to some extent on one's medical history and the adequacy of one's diet. In sum, the genes a child inherits may be an important contributor to his or her phenotype—but hardly the sole contributor. Most human attributes are the product of a long and involved interplay between the forces of nature and nurture.

Now let's consider the exceptions to this general rule. There are a number of hereditary quirks, or aberrations, that exert a powerful (and in some cases prepotent) influence on the development of children who inherit them. In the following section, we will consider the causes and consequences of some of the more common of these hereditary abnormalities.

Chromosomal and Genetic Abnormalities

Although the vast majority of newborn infants are pronounced healthy at birth, approximately 7 of every 100 have a congenital problem of some kind (Mott, Fazekas, & James, 1985). By definition, **congenital defects** are those that are present at birth, although many of these afflictions are not detectable when the child is born. For example, Huntington's chorea is a congenital problem because the gene that produces this disease is present from the moment of conception. But as we learned in Box 3-1, the gradual deterioration of the nervous system associated with this condition is not apparent at birth and will not ordinarily appear until much later—usually after age 40.

In Chapter 4 we will consider a variety of congenital defects that are likely to result from abnormalities in the birth process or from harmful conditions to which children are exposed while developing within the womb. Here we will look only at those problems that are caused by abnormal genes and chromosomes.

Chromosomal Abnormalities

When a germ cell divides during meiosis, the distribution of its 46 chromosomes into pairs of sperm or ova is sometimes uneven. In other words, one of the resulting gametes may have too many chromosomes, while the other has too few. The vast majority of these

---

sickle-cell anemia: a genetic blood disease that causes red blood cells to assume an unusual sickled shape and to become inefficient at distributing oxygen throughout the body.

codominance: condition in which two heterozygous but equally powerful alleles produce a phenotype in which both genes are fully and equally expressed.

sex-linked characteristic: an attribute determined by a gene that appears on only one of the two types of sex chromosomes, usually the X chromosome.

modifier gene: a gene that influences the expression of other alleles.

polygenic trait: a characteristic that is influenced by the action of many genes rather than a single pair.

congenital defect: a problem that is present (though not necessarily apparent) at birth; such defects may stem from genetic and prenatal influences or from complications of the birth process.

chromosomal abnormalities are *lethal,* meaning that a zygote formed from the union of an abnormal and a normal gamete will fail to develop or will be spontaneously aborted. However, some chromosomal aberrations are not lethal, as illustrated by the finding that approximately 1 child in 200 is born with either one chromosome too many or one too few (Plomin, 1986).

Abnormalities of the sex chromosomes

Many chromosomal abnormalities involve the 23rd pair—the sex chromosomes. Occasionally males are born with an extra X or Y chromosome, producing the genotype XXY or XYY, and females will often survive if they inherit a single X chromosome (XO) or even three (XXX), four (XXXX), or five (XXXXX) X chromosomes. Each of these conditions has somewhat different implications for the child's development, as we will see in examining four of the more common sex chromosome abnormalities in Table 3-1.

In addition to the abnormalities described in the table, about 1 individual in 1000 has an X chromosome that is compressed in places and may even have separated into two or more pieces—a condition known as the **fragile-X syndrome.** Affected males usually display some degree of mental retardation (ranging from mild to severe), although a few are normal intellectually. By contrast, the majority of fragile-X females are intellectually normal, only a few showing mild retardation. Apparently, this chromosomal abnormality is a relatively simple sex-linked trait caused by a recessive gene on the X chromosome (Opitz & Sutherland, 1984). And as is true in all X-linked recessive disorders, both the incidence and the consequences of this fragile-X condition are greater in males than in females.

Autosomal abnormalities

Several hereditary abnormalities are attributable to the *autosomes*—that is, the 22 pairs of chromosomes that are similar in males and females. The most common type of autosomal abnormality occurs when an abnormal sperm or ovum carrying an extra autosome combines with a normal gamete to form a zygote that has 47 chromosomes (2 sex chromosomes and 45 autosomes). In these cases the extra chromosome appears along with one of the 22 pairs of autosomes to yield three chromosomes of that type, or a *trisomy.*

By far the most frequent of all autosomal abnormalities (occurring once in every 600 births) is **Down's syndrome,** or *trisomy-21,* a condition in which the child has inherited an extra 21st chromosome (hence the name "trisomy-21"). Children with Down's syndrome are mentally retarded, with IQs that average 50 (the average IQ among normal children is 100). They may also have congenital eye, ear, and heart defects and are usually characterized by a number of distinctive physical features, including a sloping forehead, a protruding tongue, short stubby limbs, a slightly flattened nose, and a distinctive fold to the eyelids that gives their eyes an Oriental appearance (see Photo 3-4). In years gone by, researchers often called these children "mongoloid idiots" and believed that they were largely incapable of learning. This was an unfortunate assumption, for recent research indicates that these so-called idiots reach many of the same developmental milestones as normal children, but at a slower pace (see, for example, Thompson, Cicchetti, Lamb, & Malkin, 1985). Furthermore, most of these youngsters do learn to care for their basic needs, and some have even learned to read (Hayden & Haring, 1976; Reed, 1975). They also tend to be very cheerful and affectionate companions who may have a happy childhood if they receive adequate attention and emotional support from their families or caregivers. However, they will often spend many of their adult years in an institution because their developmental handicaps usually prevent them from becoming economically self-sufficient (Cicchetti & Sroufe, 1978).

Causes of chromosomal abnormalities

Perhaps the most basic cause of chromosomal abnormalities is *uneven segregation of chromosomes* into daughter cells during mitosis and meiosis. Sometimes, for example, the meiosis of a female germ cell produces one ovum containing two X chromosomes and a second ovum with no X chromosome. Such an imbalance in the distribution of X chromosomes allows several interesting possibilities. If the first (XX) ovum is fertilized by a sperm bearing an X chromosome, the result is a poly-X (XXX) female. However, if a sperm

---

fragile-X syndrome: a sex chromosome abnormality in which individuals have a compressed or broken X chromosome; affected individuals (particularly males) may show mild to severe mental retardation.

Down's syndrome: a chromosomal abnormality (also known as trisomy-21) caused by the presence of an extra 21st chromosome; people with this syndrome have a distinct physical appearance and are moderately to severely retarded.

Table 3-1. Four common sex chromosome abnormalities

Name/genotype(s)	Incidence	Developmental implications
Female abnormalities		
Turner's syndrome; XO	1 in 3000 female births	*Appearance:* Phenotypically female but small in stature with stubby fingers and toes, a webbed neck, a broad chest, and small, underdeveloped breasts. Normal sexual development lacking at puberty, although Turner females can assume a more "womanly" appearance by taking the female hormone estrogen. *Fertility:* Sterile. *Intellectual characteristics:* Normal in verbal intelligence but frequently score below average on tests of spatial abilities such as puzzle assembly or the mental rotation of figures (see McCauley, Kay, Ito, & Treder, 1987).
Poly-X or "superfemale" syndrome; XXX, XXXX, or XXXXX	1 in 1000 female births	*Appearance:* Phenotypically female and normal in appearance. *Fertility:* Fertile; produce children with the usual number of sex chromosomes. *Intellectual characteristics:* Score below average in intelligence, with their greatest deficits on tests of verbal reasoning. Intellectual deficits are detectable as early as age 2 and are reflected by delays in reaching developmental milestones such as walking and talking (Rovet & Netley, 1983).
Male abnormalities		
Klinefelter's syndrome; XXY or XXXY	1 in 200 male births	*Appearance:* Phenotypically male with the emergence of some female secondary sex characteristics (enlargement of the hips and breasts) at puberty. Significantly taller than normal (XY) males. In the past, Klinefelter males from Eastern bloc countries may have competed as females in athletic competitions, leading to the current practice of administering sex tests to all female Olympic athletes. *Fertility:* Have underdeveloped testes and are sterile. *Intellectual characteristics:* About 20–30% of Klinefelter males are deficient in verbal intelligence, and their retardation becomes more pronounced with an increase in the number of extra X chromosomes they have inherited (Burns, 1976; Pennington & Smith, 1983).
Supermale syndrome; XYY	1 in 300 male births	*Appearance:* Phenotypic males who are significantly taller than normal (XY) males and who often develop severe acne during adolescence. *Fertility:* Typically fertile, although some of these men are not. *Intellectual characteristics:* Many XYYs score below average on intelligence tests, although their mental deficiencies are typically not profound. Even though XYYs are overrepresented among populations of convicted criminals, there is no evidence that the extra Y chromosome they have inherited makes them violent and criminally inclined (as was once believed). Crimes committed by XYYs are typically nonviolent, and XYYs are no more criminally inclined than equally dull XY males—suggesting that subnormal intelligence, not an extra Y chromosome, is the factor that may contribute most to criminality among supermales (Witkin et al., 1976).

bearing a Y chromosome reaches that ovum first, the zygote will become a Klinefelter male (XXY). And if the ovum containing no X chromosome is fertilized by an X-bearing sperm, the child will be an XO female who has Turner's syndrome. Of course, some of these abnormalities can also result from the uneven meiosis of a male germ cell.

The probability that a child will inherit Down's syndrome, Klinefelter's syndrome, or the poly-X syndrome increases dramatically if the mother is over 35. Table 3-2 illustrates the relationship of Down's syndrome to the age of the mother. Note in examining the table that mothers who have already given birth to a child with Down's syndrome are much more likely to

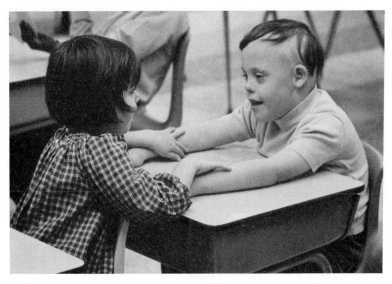

Photo 3-4. Children with Down's syndrome can live happy lives if they receive affection and encouragement from their companions.

have another child with Down's syndrome, should they give birth again, than are other women of the same age.

Why are children of older mothers more likely to have chromosomal abnormalities? One possible explanation is the **"aging ova" hypothesis.** Ova are formed only once, during prenatal development, so that a 45-year-old woman has ova that are more than 45 years old. The aging-ova hypothesis implies that a woman's ova may simply degenerate and become abnormal as she matures and nears the end of her reproductive years. Of course, an alternative explanation is that older women have had more opportunities to be exposed to *environmental hazards* (such as radiation, drugs, chemicals, and viruses) that could produce abnormalities in their ova.

A final point: It is clearly inappropriate to blame mothers for all chromosomal abnormalities. The geneticist George Burns (1976) reports that the majority of children with Turner's syndrome originate from a normal (X) ovum that is fertilized by an abnormal *sperm*— that is, one that contains neither an X nor a Y chromosome. In addition, R. E. Magenis and his associates (1977) found that 25% of children with Down's syndrome received their "extra" chromosome from their fathers rather than their mothers. The only chromosomal abnormality that is always attributable to one particular parent is the XYY, or "supermale," syndrome. In this case, the child had to receive the extra Y chromosome from his father, for the mother has no Y chromosomes to transmit to her offspring.

Genetic Abnormalities

Parents who are themselves healthy are often amazed to learn that a child of theirs could have a hereditary defect. Their surprise is certainly understandable, for most genetic problems are recessive traits that few if any close relatives have had. In addition, these problems simply will not appear unless both parents carry the harmful allele *and* the child inherits this par-

Table 3-2. Risk of Down's syndrome as a function of mother's age

	Probability that the child will have Down's syndrome	
Age of mother	At any pregnancy	After the birth of a child with Down's syndrome
–29	1 in 1000	1 in 100
30–34	1 in 600	1 in 100
35–39	1 in 200	1 in 100
40–44	1 in 65	1 in 25
45–49	1 in 25	1 in 15

Source: Adapted from Pueschel & Goldstein (1983).

Table 3-3. Brief descriptions of some major recessive hereditary defects

Defect	Description
Cystic fibrosis	A fatal disease that occurs in about 1 in 1000 births. The child lacks an enzyme that prevents mucus from obstructing the lungs and digestive tract. Many who inherit this condition die in childhood or adolescence, although advances in treatment have enabled some victims to live until their mid-30s. Over 10 million Americans are carriers who can transmit the gene for cystic fibrosis to their offspring.
Muscular dystrophy (MD)	There are more than ten forms of this genetic disease, which attacks the muscles. As the disease progresses, the individual often begins to show slurred speech, becomes unable to walk, and may gradually lose most or all motor capabilities. Occasionally MD causes death. One form, Duchenne's muscular dystrophy, is sex-linked. About 1 in 4000 males will develop Duchenne's disease; more than 100,000 Americans have inherited some form of MD.
Phenylketonuria (PKU)	The child lacks an enzyme necessary to digest foods (including milk) that contain the amino acid phenylalanine. If this condition is not detected and the child placed on a diet of milk substitutes, phenylpyruvic acid will accumulate in the body and attack the developing nervous system. Long-term effects of untreated PKU are hyperactivity and severe mental retardation. Occurs in 1 of every 10,000 Caucasian births and is much less frequent among Blacks and Orientals.
Tay-Sachs disease (infantile amaurotic idiocy)	A degenerative disease of the nervous system that will kill its victims, usually by their third birthday. Primarily affects Jewish children of Eastern European ancestry. Approximately 1 in 30 American Jews is a carrier.
Hemophilia	A sex-linked condition sometimes called "bleeder's disease." The child lacks a substance that causes the blood to clot and could bleed to death if scraped, bruised, or cut. Hemophilia was well known among the royal families of Europe and can be traced to Queen Victoria of England. Since no hemophilia is known in Victoria's ancestry, it appears that the recessive gene for hemophilia may have been a mutation that Queen Victoria then passed on to her offspring.[a] Though quite rare in females, hemophilia may occur as often as once in every 1000 male births.
Diabetes	An inherited condition in which the individual is unable to metabolize sugar properly because the body does not produce enough insulin. Two of the many forms of this disease are sex-linked. If untreated, diabetes is usually fatal. However, the disease can be controlled by taking insulin and restricting one's diet. Diabetes usually appears later in adulthood, although as many as 1 child in 2500 is diabetic.

[a]Of course, this does not mean that everyone who has hemophilia is related to Queen Victoria. A mutation, such as that producing the recessive allele for hemophilia, may occur spontaneously at any time. In at least 30% of cases of hemophilia, there is no family history of the disease. These new cases probably arise from spontaneous mutations (Apgar & Beck, 1974).

ticular gene from each parent. The exceptions to this rule are recessive defects that are sex-linked. In these cases, a male child will inherit the problem if a recessive allele should appear on the X chromosome that he inherits from his mother (recall that because a boy has only one X chromosome, he has no corresponding gene that might counteract the effect of an X-linked recessive allele).

Earlier in the chapter, we discussed two recessive hereditary defects, one that is sex-linked (color blindness) and one that is not (sickle-cell anemia). Table 3-3 describes a number of additional crippling or fatal diseases that are attributable to a single pair of recessive alleles.

Genetic abnormalities may also result from mutations. A **mutation** is a change in the chemical structure or arrangement of one or more genes that has the effect of producing a new phenotype. Many muta-

aging-ova hypothesis: the hypothesis that an older mother is more likely to have children with chromosomal abnormalities because her ova are degenerating as she nears the end of her reproductive years.

mutation: a change in the chemical structure or arrangement of one or more genes that has the effect of producing a new phenotype.

tions, such as the recessive gene for hemophilia (see Table 3-3), are harmful or even fatal, and geneticists are uncertain exactly how or why these mutations might occur. However, recent research indicates that environmental hazards such as high temperatures, toxic chemicals, and radiation can increase the rate of mutations in animals (Burns, 1976).

Evolutionary theorists believe that some mutations are beneficial. Presumably, any mutation that is stimulated by harmful conditions present in the environment can provide an "adaptive" advantage to those who inherit the mutant genes, thus enabling these individuals to survive. For example, the sickle-cell gene is a mutation that originated in Africa, Central America, and other tropical areas where malaria is widespread. Heterozygous children who inherit a single sickle-cell allele are well adapted to these environments because the mutant gene makes them more resistant to malarial infection and thus more likely to survive. Of course, the mutant sickle-cell gene is not advantageous (and can be harmful) in environments where malaria is not a problem.

Prevention and Treatment of Hereditary Abnormalities

Now try to imagine that someone in your family has a recessive genetic defect such as sickle-cell anemia and you suspect you might be a carrier. You then meet and marry a person who also believes he or she might be a carrier of this same defect. Assuming that both of you want to have children, should you now decide against it? Can you tell whether your child will be defective before birth? Is all hope lost if you produce a child who has a hereditary disease? These are issues that you and your spouse would probably wish to explore with a genetic counselor.

In recent years, a service called **genetic counseling** has been developed to help prospective parents assess the likelihood that their children will be free of hereditary defects. Although any couple who hope to have children might wish to talk with a genetic counselor about the hereditary risks their children may encounter, genetic counseling is particularly helpful for couples who have relatives with hereditary disorders or for parents who have already borne a defective child.

A genetic counselor may be a medical researcher, a geneticist, or a practitioner such as a pediatrician, obstetrician, or family doctor. He or she will usually begin by asking prospective parents why they have sought genetic counseling, thus seeking to determine whether the defect(s) that concern the couple are really hereditary in origin. If they are hereditary, the counselor will take a complete family history from each prospective parent—one that includes information about the diseases and causes of death of siblings, parents, and other blood relatives; the ethnicity and countries of origin of blood relatives who were immigrants; intermarriages that may have occurred in the past between close relatives (such as cousins); and previous problems in the childbearing process, such as miscarriages or stillbirths. The couple will also take a complete physical examination. If specific tests are available, prospective parents will be screened to determine whether they carry the genes that are responsible for producing the hereditary defect(s) that prompted them to seek counseling. From the overall profile, the genetic counselor will determine the mathematical odds that a child of the couple could inherit the defect in question and then tell the prospective parents whether there is anything they can do to reduce these odds.

Methods of detecting carriers. Fortunately, several recessive genes that produce hereditary defects can be detected by simple laboratory tests. For example, blood tests can determine whether a prospective parent carries the recessive allele for Tay-Sachs disease, sickle-cell anemia, hemophilia, phenylketonuria, or the fragile-X syndrome (Apgar & Beck, 1974; Schaeffer, 1987). In addition, chromosomal abnormalities can be detected by taking a small sample of each parent's skin (a few cells will do) and preparing karyotypes. Recent advances in the preparation of karyotypes make it possible, in some cases, to determine whether a seemingly normal individual might transmit hereditary defects to his or her children. Finally, couples who have already borne a child with a recessive hereditary disorder have already shown themselves to be carriers for that attribute.

Unfortunately, an adult may carry harmful recessive genes that are undetectable by medical tests. Certain kinds of **muscular dystrophy** are clear examples. If prospective parents are concerned about the possibility of transmitting such disorders to their children, the genetic counselor will carefully analyze their family histories and note whether any close blood relatives had the disease in question. Should a client's family history reveal several cases of the disorder, there is a good possibility that he or she carries the recessive gene for this hereditary defect. However, the likelihood that the client's child would inherit the disease is very small unless the same disorder has also occurred among the spouse's blood relatives.

An example will help to illustrate how genetic counseling works. One married couple recently requested genetic counseling and learned that they were both carriers for **Tay-Sachs disease,** a condition that normally kills an affected child within the first three years of life (see Table 3-3). The genetic counselor explained to this couple that there was 1 chance in 4 that *any* child they conceived would inherit a recessive allele from each of them and have Tay-Sachs disease. However, there was also 1 chance in 4 that the child would inherit the dominant gene from each parent, and there were 2 chances in 4 that the child would be just like its parents—phenotypically normal but a carrier of the recessive Tay-Sachs allele. After receiving this information, the young woman expressed strong reservations about having children. To her way of thinking, the 1 chance in 4 that each of her children would inherit a disease that medical science cannot treat was simply too high for her to want to take *any* chances.

At this point the genetic counselor informed the young woman that before she made a firm decision against having children, she ought to be aware of procedures that can detect many genetic abnormalities, including Tay-Sachs disease, long before her child would be born. He then told the couple that these screening procedures cannot reverse any abnormalities that are found. However, they allow expectant parents to decide whether to terminate a pregnancy rather than give birth to a defective child.

Prenatal detection of hereditary abnormalities. A common method of detecting abnormalities during the prenatal period is **amniocentesis.** A large, hollow needle is inserted into the abdomen of a pregnant woman in order to withdraw a sample of the amniotic fluid that surrounds the fetus. This fluid contains fetal body cells that can be karyotyped to determine the sex of the fetus and the presence of chromosomal abnormalities such as Down's syndrome. In addition, more than 75 genetic disorders—including Tay-Sachs disease, cystic fibrosis, Duchenne's muscular dystrophy, sickle-cell anemia, hemophilia, and Marfan's syndrome—can now be diagnosed by analyzing fetal

cells taken from the amniotic fluid or from the placenta that bonds the mother and the fetus (Golbus, 1978; Schaeffer, 1987). Although amniocentesis is not very painful and is considered a very safe procedure (Fairweather, 1978), it can trigger a miscarriage in a very small percentage of cases. In fact, the risk of miscarriage (though very small) is thought to be greater than the risk of a birth defect if the mother is under age 35 (Schaeffer, 1987).

One serious disadvantage of amniocentesis is that the procedure cannot be performed before the 14th–16th week of pregnancy, when amniotic fluid becomes sufficiently plentiful to withdraw for analysis. The results of the tests will not come back for another two weeks, leaving parents little time to consider a second-trimester abortion if the fetus is abnormal. But there is a newer technique that looks promising as an alternative to amniocentesis. This procedure, called **chorionic villus sampling** (CVS), collects tissue for the same tests as amniocentesis does and can be performed during the 8th or 10th week of pregnancy (Begley, Carey, & Katz, 1984; Schaeffer, 1987). As illustrated in Figure 3-7, a catheter is inserted through the mother's cervix into the chorion to extract fetal cells, which are then tested for hereditary abnormalities. This technique thus allows parents to know whether their fetus is abnormal by the 11th or 12th week of pregnancy, leaving them more time to carefully consider the pros and cons of a therapeutic abortion in the event the fetus has inherited a serious defect.

---

genetic counseling: a service designed to inform prospective parents about genetic diseases and to help them determine the likelihood that they would transmit such disorders to their children.

muscular dystrophy: a genetic disease that attacks the muscles and results in a gradual loss of motor capabilities (see Table 3-3).

Tay-Sachs disease: a genetic disease that attacks the nervous system, causing it to degenerate (see Table 3-3).

amniocentesis: a method of extracting amniotic fluid from a pregnant woman so that fetal body cells within the fluid can be tested for chromosomal abnormalities and other genetic defects.

chorionic villus sampling: an alternative to amniocentesis in which a catheter is inserted through the cervix to withdraw fetal cells for prenatal tests.

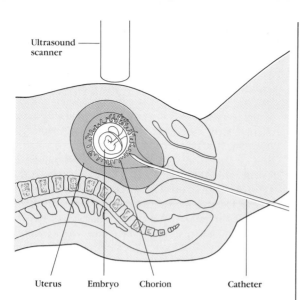

Ultrasound
scanner

Uterus   Embryo   Chorion   Catheter

Figure 3-7. In a chorionic villus sampling, a catheter is inserted through the mother's cervix to collect fetal cells for prenatal tests. *(Based on Begley, Carey, & Katz, 1984.)*

Another prenatal diagnostic technique is **ultrasound** (sonar), a method of scanning the womb with sound waves. Ultrasound provides the attending physician with an outline of the fetus in much the same way that sonar reveals outlines of the fish beneath a fishing boat. Like amniocentesis and chorionic villus sampling, ultrasound presents only a minimal risk to the developing fetus. It is particularly useful for detecting genetic defects that produce gross physical abnormalities.

Treatment of hereditary disorders. Prenatal detection of a hereditary disorder leaves many couples in a quandary, particularly if their religious background or personal beliefs argue against the option of a therapeutic abortion. If the disease in question is invariably fatal, like Tay-Sachs, the couple must decide either to violate their moral principles and terminate the pregnancy or to have a baby who will appear normal and healthy but who will show a progressive decline in all of his or her functions and die young.

This quandary may someday become a thing of the past, for geneticists are hopeful that many lethal hereditary diseases will become "curable" in the near future. And there is reason for optimism. Only 40 years ago, medical science could do little for children with another degenerative disease of the nervous system—

phenylketonuria, or **PKU.** Like Tay-Sachs disease, PKU is a metabolic disorder. Affected children lack a critical enzyme that would allow them to metabolize phenylalanine, a component of many foods, including milk. As phenylalanine gradually accumulates in the body, it is converted to a harmful substance, phenylpyruvic acid, that attacks the nervous system. In years gone by, the majority of children who inherited this disorder soon became hyperactive and severely retarded.

A major breakthrough came in the mid-1950s when scientists developed a diet low in phenylalanine that minimized the degenerative effects of PKU: children who adhered to this special diet showed much less damage to their nervous systems than they would otherwise have suffered. However, doctors could detect PKU only from its harmful effects, and unfortunately the special diet could not reverse damage already done.

In 1961 researchers discovered that the degenerative effect of PKU could be detected in its earliest stages by analyzing a blood sample taken only a few days after birth. Infants are now routinely screened for PKU, and those affected are immediately placed on the low-phenylalanine diet. The outcome of this therapeutic intervention is a happy one: children who remain on the special diet for the next several years suffer few if any of the harmful complications of what only a short time ago was considered an incurable disease.

Today the potentially devastating effects of many hereditary abnormalities can be minimized or controlled. For example, children who inherit either Turner's syndrome or Klinefelter's syndrome can be given hormones to make them more normal in appearance. Those who have blood disorders such as hemophilia or sickle-cell anemia now receive periodic transfusions that provide these patients with the clotting agents or the normal red blood cells that they lack. The discomfort experienced by children with cystic fibrosis can be lessened by antibiotics. Diabetes can be controlled by a low-sugar diet and by periodic doses of insulin, which help the patient to metabolize sugar. In sum, many abnormal children can lead approximately normal lives if their hereditary disorders are detected and treated before serious harm has been done.

How to obtain more information about genetic counseling services. Your local library may carry the *International Directory of Genetic Services,* published by the National Foundation/March of Dimes. This volume lists some 400 centers in the United States that offer genetic counseling services. For information about the services offered by centers nearest you, write to the National Foundation/March of Dimes, 1275 Mamaroneck Ave., White Plains, New York 10605.

Hereditary Influences on Behavior

We have seen that genes play a major role in determining our physical appearance and many of our metabolic characteristics. But to what extent does heredity affect such characteristics as intelligence? Can a strong case be made for genetic contributions to personality, temperament, and mental health?

In recent years, investigators from the fields of genetics, zoology, population biology, and psychology have asked the question "Are there certain abilities, traits, and patterns of behavior that depend very heavily on the particular combination of genes that an individual inherits, and if so, are these attributes likely to be modified by one's experiences?" Those who focus on these issues in their research are known as *behavior geneticists*.

Before we take a closer look at the field of **behavior genetics,** it is necessary to dispel a common myth. Although behavior geneticists view development as the process through which one's *genotype* (the set of genes one inherits) is expressed in one's *phenotype* (observable characteristics and behaviors), they are not strict hereditarians. They recognize, for example, that even physical characteristics such as height depend to some extent on environmental variables, such as the adequacy of one's diet (Fuller & Thompson, 1978). They clearly acknowledge that the long-term effects of inherited metabolic disorders such as PKU and diabetes also depend on one's environment—namely, the availability of personnel to detect and to treat these conditions. In other words, the behavior geneticist is well aware that even attributes that have a strong hereditary component are often modified in important ways by environmental influences. This is a point to keep in mind as we discuss the implications of behavior genetics research in the pages that follow.

How, then, do behavior geneticists differ from ethologists, who are also interested in the biological bases of development? The answer is relatively simple. Ethologists concentrate on inherited attributes that characterize *all* members of a species and thus conspire to make them *alike* (that is, attributes that contribute to *common* developmental outcomes). By contrast, behavior geneticists focus on the biological bases for *varia-* tion among members of a species. They are primarily concerned with determining how the unique combination of genes that each of us inherit might be implicated in making us *different* from one another. Let's now consider the methods that they use to approach this task.

Methods of Estimating Hereditary Influences

There are two major strategies that behavior geneticists use to assess hereditary contributions to behavior: *selective breeding* and *family studies*. Each of these approaches attempts to specify the **heritability** of various attributes—that is, the amount of variation in a trait or a class of behavior that is due to hereditary factors.

Selective breeding

Members of any species, particularly human beings, differ considerably in their basic abilities, peculiarities, and patterns of behavior. Could these individual differences be hereditary? Do they simply reflect the fact that no two individuals (except identical twins) inherit the same pattern of genes?

Many investigators have tried to answer this question by seeing whether they could selectively breed particular attributes in animals. A famous example of a selective breeding experiment is R. C. Tryon's (1940) attempt to show that maze-learning ability is a heritable attribute in rats. Tryon started by testing a large number of rats for ability to run a complex maze. Rats that made few errors were labeled "maze-bright"; those that made many errors were termed "maze-dull." Then, across several successive generations, Tryon mated the brightest

---

ultrasound: method of detecting gross physical abnormalities by scanning the womb with sound waves, thereby producing a visual outline of the fetus.

phenylketonuria (PKU): a genetic disease in which the child is unable to metabolize phenylalanine; if left untreated, it soon causes hyperactivity and mental retardation.

behavior genetics: the scientific study of how genotype interacts with environment to determine behavioral attributes such as intelligence, temperament, and personality.

heritability: the amount of variability in a trait that is attributable to hereditary factors.

of the maze-bright rats together, while also inbreeding the dullest of the maze-dull group. This was a well-controlled experiment in that Tryon occasionally took offspring from each group and had them raised by mothers from the other group. This *cross-fostering* procedure helps to ensure that any difference in maze-learning ability between the offspring of the two strains is due to selective breeding (heredity), rather than the type of early stimulation that the young animals received from their mother figure (environment).

Figure 3-8 shows the results of Tryon's selective breeding experiment. Note that across generations the differences in maze-running performance between the maze-bright and the maze-dull groups became increasingly apparent. By the 18th generation, the worst performer among the maze-bright group was better at running mazes than the best performer from the maze-dull group. Clearly, Tryon had shown that maze-learning ability in rats is influenced by hereditary factors. Other investigators have used the selective breeding technique to demonstrate clear genetic contributions to such attributes as activity level, emotionality, aggressiveness, and sex drive in rats, mice, and chickens (Plomin, DeFries, & McClearn, 1980).

Family studies

Since it is obviously unethical to conduct selective breeding studies with humans, the field of human behavior genetics relies on an alternative methodology known as the family study. In a typical family study, persons who live in the same household are compared to see how similar they are on one or more attributes. If the attribute in question is heritable, then the similarity between any two pairs of individuals who live in the same environment should increase as a function of their **kinship**—that is, the extent to which they have the same genes. For example, identical twins, who have the same genotype (kinship = 1.00), should be more similar on a heritable attribute than either fraternal twins or ordinary siblings, who have only half their genes in common (kinship = .50). And fraternal twins and siblings should be more similar than either half-siblings (kinship = .25) or pairs of genetically unrelated children who live in the same household (kinship = .00).

The family study can also help us to estimate the extent to which various abilities and behaviors are influenced by the environment. To illustrate, consider a case in which two genetically unrelated adopted children are raised in the same home. Their degree of kinship with each other and with their adoptive parents is .00. Consequently, there is no reason to suspect that these children will resemble each other or their adoptive parents unless their common environment plays some part in determining their standing on the ability or behavior in question. Another way the effects of environment can be inferred is to compare identical twins raised in the same environment with identical twins raised in different environments. The kinship of all pairs of identical twins, reared together or apart, is 1.00. So if identical twins reared together are more alike on an attribute than identical twins reared apart, we can infer that the environment plays a role in determining that attribute.

We are now almost ready to examine the results of several family studies in order to gauge the impact of heredity and environment on complex attributes such as intelligence, temperament, personality, and mental illness. To evaluate this research, however, one needs to know what a correlation coefficient is and how correlation coefficients can help us to determine whether an attribute is affected by hereditary factors.

Correlation coefficients and estimates of heritability

In Chapter 1 we learned that correlated variables are those that are systematically related. If one asks whether two variables are correlated, one wants to know whether those attributes "go together," or covary, in some meaningful way. An agricultural scientist might

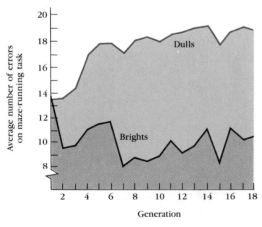

Figure 3-8. Maze-running performance by inbred maze-bright and maze-dull rats over 18 generations. *(Adapted from Plomin, DeFries, & McClearn, 1980.)*

wish to know whether crop yield is related to rainfall. A medical researcher may seek to determine whether physical exercise is related to the incidence of heart disease. A behavior geneticist conducting a family study may wish to determine whether the IQ scores of twins are related to the IQ scores of their cotwins.

Any two variables may be *positively correlated, negatively correlated,* or *uncorrelated.* A positive correlation means that high scores on variable X are associated with high scores on variable Y and that low scores on X are associated with low scores on Y. For example, height and weight are positively correlated: children who are *taller* also tend to be *heavier.* A negative correlation means that high scores on variable X are associated with low scores on variable Y and vice versa. For example, exercise is negatively correlated with the incidence of heart disease: adults who exercise *more* are *less* likely to have heart attacks. Finally, if scores on variable X are not at all associated with scores on variable Y, the two factors are said to be uncorrelated, or unrelated.

The strength, or magnitude, of a correlation can be determined statistically and is represented as a **correlation coefficient** (symbolized r) with a value between -1.00 and $+1.00$. The absolute size of a correlation coefficient (disregarding its sign) provides information about the strength of the relationship between the variables. Thus, the correlation coefficients $-.70$ and $+.70$ are equal in magnitude but opposite in direction. Both are stronger relationships than a correlation of .50. A correlation coefficient of .00 shows that the variables under consideration are unrelated. Finally, it is important to emphasize that correlation does *not* imply causation. For example, the positive correlation between the number of crimes reported in various American cities and the number of churches in those cities does not mean that churches cause crimes. In this case, a third variable, population, determines both the number of crimes in a city and the number of churches built there. Although the latter two variables are correlated, the relationship between them is not one of cause and effect.

How might the heritability of an attribute be estimated from correlations? Suppose we had conducted a study of 50 families, 25 that have a pair of identical twins and 25 that have a pair of fraternal twins. While conducting the study, we measured some aspect of personality in each twin and found that the correlation between identical twins on this trait was $+.50$ while the correlation between fraternal twins was $+.30$.

Since members of each twin pair live in the same household, we might assume that they have had highly similar environments. Therefore, the fact that identical twins are more alike on this personality dimension than fraternal twins suggests that the trait in question is affected by heredity. But just how strong is the hereditary contribution?

In recent years, behavior geneticists have proposed a statistical technique to estimate the amount of variation in a characteristic that is attributable to hereditary factors. This index, called a **heritability coefficient,** is calculated as follows:

$$H = (r \text{ identical twins} - r \text{ fraternal twins}) \times 2$$

In words, the equation reads: Heritability of an attribute equals the correlation between identical twins minus the correlation between fraternal twins, all multiplied by a factor of 2 (Plomin et al., 1980).

Now we can estimate the contribution that heredity makes to the aspect of personality that we measured in our hypothetical study. Recall that the correlation between identical twins on the attribute was $+.50$ and the correlation between fraternal twins was $+.30$. Plugging these values into the formula yields the following heritability coefficient (H):

$$H = (.50 - .30) \times 2 = .20 \times 2 = .40$$

The heritability coefficient is about .40, which, on a scale ranging from 0 (not at all heritable) to 1.00 (totally heritable), is moderate at best. We might conclude that, within the population from which our subjects were selected, this aspect of personality is influenced to some extent by hereditary factors. However, it appears that much of the variability among people on this trait is attributable to nonhereditary factors—that is, to environmental influences and to errors we may have made in measuring the trait (no measure is perfect).

---

kinship: the extent to which two individuals have genes in common.

correlation coefficient: a numerical index, ranging from -1.00 to $+1.00$, which indicates the magnitude and the direction of the relationship between two variables.

heritability coefficient: a numerical estimate, ranging from .00 to $+1.00$, of the amount of variation in an attribute that is due to hereditary factors.

Table 3-4. Average correlation coefficients for intelligence test scores from 52 family studies involving persons at three levels of kinship (genetic similarity)

Genetic relationship (kinship)	Reared together (in same household)	Reared apart (in different households)
Unrelated persons (kinship = .00)	+.23	−.01
Foster parent/child (kinship = .00)	+.20	—
Biological parent/child (kinship = .50)	+.50	—
Siblings (kinship = .50)	+.49	+.40
Twins		
Fraternal—same sex (kinship = .50)	+.53	—
Fraternal—different sex (kinship = .50)	+.53	—
Identical (kinship = 1.00)	+.87	+.75

Source: Erlenmeyer-Kimling & Jarvik (1963).

What do heritability estimates tell us?

People have often assumed that heritability coefficients tell us whether we might have inherited various traits or characteristics. *This idea is simply incorrect.* When we talk about the heritability of an attribute, we are referring to the extent to which *differences* among individuals on that attribute are related to differences in the genes they have inherited. To illustrate that *heritable* means something other than "inherited," consider that everyone inherits a nose. Agreed? Yet, the heritability of noses is .00, simply because everybody has one and there are no individual variations in "noseness" (except for those attributable to environmental events such as accidents).

In interpreting heritability coefficients, it is important to recognize that these estimates apply only to populations and *never to individuals.* So if you studied the heights of many pairs of 5-year-old twins and estimated the heritability of height to be .70, you could infer that a major reason that 5-year-olds *differ* in height is that they have inherited different genes. But since heritability estimates say nothing about individuals, it is clearly inappropriate to conclude from an *H* of .70 that 70% of Freddie Jones's height is inherited, while the remaining 30% reflects the contribution of his environment.

In sum, the term *heritable* is not a synonym for *inherited,* and a heritability estimate can tell us absolutely nothing about the development of an individual. Nevertheless, heritability coefficients are very useful statistics—the bread and butter of behavior genetics research—because they can help us to determine whether there might be a hereditary basis for the *variations* that people display on any attribute we might care to study.

Let's now consider what behavior geneticists have learned about the heritability of intelligence.

Hereditary Influences on Intellectual Performance

Earlier in the chapter, we learned that many forms of mental retardation may result should one inherit abnormal genes and chromosomes. Although most children are not mentally retarded, they do vary considerably in their performance on intelligence tests. Could it be that children make widely varying scores on these tests because they have each inherited a different set of genes?

Evidence for hereditary influences.

Over the past 60 years, more than 80 family studies have been conducted to estimate the effects of heredity on intellectual performance. Table 3-4 summarizes the findings of 52 of the more ambitious of these projects. From the data in the "Reared together" column, it is clear that the intellectual resemblance between pairs of individuals living in the same household increases as a function of their degree of kinship (that is, genetic similarity). In addition, we see that identical twins reared apart are more similar in IQ than fraternal twins reared together. Both these findings imply that heredity contributes in a meaningful way to IQ. In fact, the heritability coefficient for IQ that can be calculated from the data on twins living together is .68, a figure that suggests that the characteristics measured by intelligence tests are moderately to highly heritable.

Further evidence for the heritability of intelligence comes from longitudinal studies of twins (Wilson, 1978, 1983). By age 18 months, identical twins are already more similar than fraternal twins on tests of infant intelligence. And follow-up data collected on these children over the next 13 years show that identical twins are also more similar than fraternal twins in the age at which they reach various intellectual milestones and in the patterning of their performances across many different tests of intellectual functioning (Wilson, 1978, 1983). There was even some evidence that genetic influences on IQ became increasingly apparent over time. Consider that identical twins remained highly similar in their intellectual performances (average $r = .85$) from infancy through adolescence. By contrast, fraternal twins were most similar intellectually at age 3 ($r = .79$) and gradually became *less* similar over the years until, at age 15, they showed no greater intellectual resemblance ($r = .54$) than pairs of nontwin siblings (Wilson, 1983). A behavior geneticist can easily explain this latter finding: presumably, fraternal twins are diverging intellectually because their different genetic makeups are guiding them along separate developmental paths (Plomin, 1986).

We can conclude from these findings that genetic variations among individuals contribute in important ways to individual differences in intellectual performance. Intelligence is indeed a heritable attribute. Does this mean that the environment plays little or no part in determining intellectual performance? No, it does not! In fact, we need look no further than the family studies we have already reviewed to find evidence of environmental effects. Can you find such evidence in Table 3-4?

Evidence for environmental influences.
If we reexamine Table 3-4, we will see that at each level of kinship where data are available, individuals living together are more intellectually similar than individuals living apart. This finding clearly indicates that the environment affects intelligence. Perhaps the most striking data are those provided by individuals who are not biologically related. As expected, children who have no genes in common and who live in different environments do not resemble each other intellectually ($r = -.01$). By contrast, biologically unrelated children who live in the same household show a definite intellectual resemblance ($r = .23$), which can only be attributed to the similarity of their environments.

Recent studies of adopted children clearly show that intelligence is a product of both hereditary and environmental influences. Consider first the evidence for heredity. Several investigators have found that adopt-

ed children are more similar intellectually to their biological parents than to their adoptive parents (Horn, 1983; Plomin & DeFries, 1983). This finding can be interpreted as evidence for a genetic influence on intelligence, for adoptees share genes with their biological parents but not with adoptive caregivers.

However, an adoption study by Sandra Scarr and Richard Weinberg (1977, 1983) nicely illustrates that a heritable attribute like intelligence is highly susceptible to environmental influence. Many of Scarr and Weinberg's adoptees were Black children from lower socioeconomic backgrounds who had been placed in middle-class White homes where the adoptive parents had one or more biological children. Relatively speaking, those adoptees were more similar intellectually to their biological parents ($r = .43$) than to their adoptive parents ($r = .29$), thus confirming that intelligence is a heritable attribute. Yet, Scarr and Weinberg also found that the interracial (that is, Black and White) siblings in these adoptive homes showed some definite intellectual similarities. Since interracial siblings have no genes in common, their intellectual resemblances must be attributable to their common environments. Furthermore, the intellectual similarities between pairs of genetically unrelated Black adoptees who lived in the same home were substantial ($r = .49$), indicating that their shared environment was having a strong impact on their intellectual development. Finally, the Black adoptees had substantially *higher* IQs (by about 20 points) than what we would expect from a knowledge of their biological parents' socioeconomic backgrounds and the intellectual performances of comparable children raised in the Black community. So we see that one's *absolute score* (or phenotype) on a heritable attribute can definitely be influenced by one's environment. Since the adopting parents in the Scarr and Weinberg study were from middle-class backgrounds and highly educated, they may have provided very stimulating home environments for their interracial adoptees—environments that enabled these youngsters to flourish intellectually and outperform their less advantaged Black age mates on intelligence tests.

In the final section of this chapter, we will review some of the theories that have been proposed to explain how heredity and environment may combine or interact to influence our abilities, talents, temperaments, and other peculiarities. But first let's review the evidence that suggests that our temperaments and personalities do depend, in part, on the genes we have inherited.

Hereditary Contributions to Temperament and Personality

When psychologists speak of "personality," they are referring to a broad collection of attributes—including temperament, attitudes, values, and distinctive behavioral patterns (or habits)—that seem to characterize an individual. Unfortunately, the personality consists of so many characteristics that it is virtually impossible to measure them all with any single test. However, it is possible to focus on specific aspects of personality to see whether there is any hereditary basis for the ways we behave.

Heritability of temperament

Temperament is a term that developmentalists use to describe the predictable ways in which we respond to environmental events. Although different researchers do not always define temperament in exactly the same way, most would agree that such attributes as *activity level* (the typical vigor or pace of our behavior), *irritability,* or *emotionality* (how easily and intensely upset we become over negative events), and *sociability* (receptiveness to social stimulation) are important components of temperament (Buss & Plomin, 1984; Goldsmith et al., 1987).

Selective breeding studies conducted with various animal species indicate that temperamental characteristics such as activity, fearfulness, and sociability have a strong hereditary component (see McClearn, 1970; Plomin et al., 1980). Could the same be true of human beings?

Behavior geneticists have tried to answer this question by comparing the temperamental similarities of pairs of identical and pairs of fraternal twins. Several such studies reveal that identical twin infants and toddlers are much more alike on temperamental dimensions such as activity level, demands for attention, irritability, and sociability than pairs of fraternal twins (see, for example, Goldsmith & Campos, 1986; Wilson & Matheny, 1986). These findings imply that at least some components of human temperament are heritable. In addition, babies from different ethnic backgrounds show distinct temperamental characteristics as early as the first few days of life. In one study, Daniel Freedman (1979) compared the temperaments of newborn Caucasian and Chinese-American infants. The ethnic differences were clear: Caucasian babies were more irritable and harder to comfort than Chinese-American babies. Since the Caucasian and the Chinese-American mothers had re-

ceived the same prenatal care, it appears that the temperamental differences between their infants may well have been hereditary.

Jerome Kagan and his associates have recently conducted longitudinal studies to assess the stability of a temperamental attribute they call **behavioral inhibition**—the tendency to withdraw from unfamiliar people or situations (Kagan, Reznick, & Snidman, 1986; Reznick et al., 1986). What they found is that children who were either socially inhibited or uninhibited when first tested at age 21 months tended to remain relatively inhibited or uninhibited when retested at 4 and at 5½ years of age. Not only were the inhibited 5½-year-olds shy around peers and quite wary of a strange adult, they were also more cautious than uninhibited children about playing with novel toys that involved an element of risk (for example, a balance beam). Finally, Kagan and his associates find that inhibited children often display intense physiological arousal (for example, high heart rates) in response to novel situations that barely faze uninhibited children. As a result, they suspect that this tendency to be inhibited or uninhibited has a strong hereditary component. And regardless of whether we accept this latter speculation about the genetic basis for behavioral inhibition, Kagan's data clearly illustrate that early components of temperament can be reasonably stable over time (see also McDevitt, 1986).

Alexander Thomas and his colleagues (Thomas, Chess, & Birch, 1970; Thomas & Chess, 1977) have noted that certain temperamental attributes tend to cluster together, forming broader temperamental profiles. For example, highly active children are often very irritable and irregular in their feeding, sleeping, and bowel habits, whereas passive babies tend to be good-natured and regular in their habits. Thomas and Chess (1977) found that about two-thirds of the infants in their study could be placed into one of three categories according to their overall pattern of temperamental characteristics:

1. *The easy child.* Easygoing children are even-tempered, are typically in a positive mood, and are quite open and adaptable to new experiences. Their habits are regular and predictable.
2. *The difficult child.* Difficult children are active, irritable, and irregular in their habits. They often react very negatively (and vigorously) to changes in routine and are slow to adapt to new persons or situations.
3. *The slow-to-warm-up child.* These children are quite inactive and moody. They, too, are slow to adapt to

new persons and situations, but unlike the difficult child, they typically respond to novelty or to changes in routine with mild forms of passive resistance. For example, they may resist cuddling by directing their attention elsewhere rather than by crying or kicking.

Apparently these broader temperamental patterns may also persist over time and influence the child's adjustment to a variety of settings and situations later in life. For example, children with difficult temperaments are more likely than other children to have problems adjusting to school activities, and they are often irritable and aggressive in their interactions with peers (Rutter, 1978; Thomas, Chess, & Korn, 1982). Yet, Thomas and Chess (1977, 1986) find that early temperamental profiles can be modified by environmental factors—particularly the patterns of child rearing used by parents. For example, difficult infants who have trouble adapting to new routines often become much more adaptable if parents remain calm, exercise restraint, and allow these children to respond to novelty at a leisurely pace. By contrast, parents who are impatient and demanding with their difficult infants are the ones whose children are likely to remain difficult and to experience adjustment problems later in life.

In sum, the temperamental characteristics that we display are clearly influenced by the genes we have inherited. However, we should keep in mind that early temperamental patterns can be altered and that the changes in temperament commonly observed over the course of childhood suggest that this aspect of personality is highly susceptible to environmental influence.

Hereditary contributions to the adult personality

Psychologists have often assumed that the relatively stable traits and habits that make up our adult personalities are determined by the environment. Presumably, our feelings, attitudes, values, and characteristic patterns of behavior have been shaped by the familial and cultural contexts in which we live. Behavior geneticists would not necessarily disagree with this conclusion. However, they do believe that psychologists overestimate the impact of the environment on the developing personality while underestimating the importance of hereditary factors (Goldsmith, 1983).

Family studies of personality suggest that many attributes have a hereditary component. One example of a heritable trait is **introversion/extraversion.** In-troverts are people who are generally quiet, anxious, and uncomfortable around others. As a result, they often shun social contact. Extraverts are highly sociable people who enjoy being with others. Identical twins are moderately similar on this attribute, and their resemblance is greater than that of fraternal twins, ordinary siblings, or pairs of genetically unrelated children raised in the same household (Nichols, 1978; Scarr, Webber, Weinberg, & Wittig, 1981).

Another interesting attribute that may be influenced by heredity is **empathic concern.** A person high in empathy is a compassionate soul who recognizes the needs of others and is concerned about their welfare. In Box 2-3 we saw that newborn infants will react to the distress of another infant by becoming distressed themselves—a finding that implies that the capacity for empathy may be innate. If it is, identical twins should be more similar in empathic concern than fraternal twins.

Karen Matthews, Daniel Batson, Joseph Horn, and Ray Rosenman (1981) administered a test of empathic concern to 114 pairs of identical twins and 116 pairs of fraternal twins who ranged in age from 42 to 57 years. These twins were all males who had been raised in the same household, but most had not lived together for many years. Even though the vast majority of the twins had lived apart in different environments for long periods, the identical twins were still more alike in empathic concern ($r = .41$) than the fraternal twins ($r = .05$), suggesting that empathy is a reasonably heritable attribute. The implications of these results are interesting. In the words of the authors, "If empathic concern for others leads to altruistic motivation, the present study provides evidence for a genetic basis for individual differences in altruistic behavior" (p. 246).

---

temperament: a person's characteristic modes of response to the environment, including such attributes as activity level, irritability, and sociability.

behavioral inhibition: a temperamental characteristic reflecting one's tendency to withdraw from unfamiliar people or situations.

introversion/extraversion: the opposite poles of a personality dimension: introverts are shy, anxious around others, and ready to withdraw from social situations; extraverts are highly sociable and enjoy being with others.

empathic concern: a measure of the extent to which an individual recognizes the needs of others and is concerned about their welfare.

Table 3-5. Personality resemblances among family members at three levels of kinship

	Kinship			
	1.00 (identical twins)	.50 (fraternal twins)	.50 (nontwin siblings)	.00 (unrelated children raised in the same household)
Personality attributes (average correlations across several personality traits)	.52	.25	.20	.07

Just how heritable is the adult personality?

To what extent are our personalities influenced by the genes we have inherited? Perhaps we can get some idea by looking at personality resemblances among family members as shown in Table 3-5. Note that identical twins are more similar to each other on this composite measure of personality than fraternal twins. Were we to use the twin data to estimate the genetic contribution to personality, we might conclude that many personality traits are moderately heritable. Of course, one implication of a moderate heritability coefficient is that personality is strongly influenced by environmental factors.

What features of the environment contribute most heavily to the development of our personalities? Developmentalists have traditionally assumed that the home environment is especially important in this regard. Yet, Table 3-5 reveals that genetically unrelated individuals who live in the same home barely resemble each other on the composite personality measure (r = .07). Therefore, aspects of the home environment that all family members *share* must not contribute much to the development of personality. How, then, does environment affect personality?

Nonshared environmental influences. Behavior geneticists David Rowe and Robert Plomin (1981) argue that the environmental influences that contribute most heavily to personality are those that make individuals *different* from one another—that is, events, situations, and experiences that children within any family do *not* share. An example of a **nonshared environmental influence** within the home is a tendency of one or both parents to respond differently to sons and daughters, to first-born and later-born children, and so on. To the extent that two siblings are treated differently by parents, they will experience different environments, which will increase the likelihood that their personalities will differ in important ways. Interactions among siblings provide another source of "nonshared" environmental influence on the developing personality. For example, an older sibling who habitually dominates a younger one may become generally assertive and dominant as a result of these home experiences. But for the younger child, this home environment is a dominating environment that may foster the development of such personality traits as passivity, tolerance, and cooperation.

Measuring the effects of nonshared environments. How could we ever measure the impact of something as broad as nonshared environments? One strategy used by Denise Daniels and her associates (Daniels, 1986; Daniels & Plomin, 1985) is simply to ask pairs of adolescent siblings whether they have been treated differently by their parents and/or have experienced other important differences in their lives (for example, differences in their popularity with peers). She finds that siblings do report such differences and, more important, that these nonshared environmental influences reliably predict just how different siblings are in their personalities!

The next question, then, is "Do siblings have different experiences because they have inherited different genes?" Stated another way, is it possible that a child's heritable attributes might influence how other people respond to her, so that a "difficult" youngster, for example, is apt to be treated very differently by parents and peers than a sibling with an easy temperament would be? Although genotypes do contribute to some extent to the different experiences reported by siblings (Daniels, 1986), there is ample reason to believe that our highly individualized, unique environments are not solely attributable to our having inherited different genes. How do we know this?

The most important clue comes from studies of identical twins. Since identical twins are perfectly matched from a genetic standpoint, any *differences* between them must necessarily reflect the contribution of environmental influences that they do *not* share. Clearly, these nonshared environmental effects cannot be attributed to the twins' different genes, because identical twins have identical genotypes. So with these facts in mind, it is possible to estimate the effects of nonshared environmental influences (NSE) on any attribute:

$$NSE = 1 - r \text{ (correlation for identical twins on that attribute)}$$

The logic behind this formula is straightforward: because identical twins have identical genes, only environmental influences can keep pair members from resembling each other. "One minus the correlation for identical twins is therefore an estimate of all environmental causes that make identical twins *different*" (Rowe & Plomin, 1981, p. 521).

Table 3-5 shows that the average correlation for identical twins across several personality attributes is only $+.52$ (a figure that implies that these twins are alike in many respects and different in many others). So it seems that nonshared environmental influences (that is, $1 - .52 = .48$) are indeed important contributors to the adult personality.

Hereditary Contributions to Behavior Disorders and Mental Illness

Is there a hereditary basis for mental illness? Might some among us be genetically predisposed to commit deviant or antisocial acts? Although these ideas seemed absurd 20 years ago when I was a college student, it now appears that the answer to both questions is a qualified yes.

The evidence for hereditary contributions to abnormal behavior comes from family studies in which investigators calculate **concordance rates** for various disorders. In a twin study, for example, the concordance rate for a disorder is a measure of the likelihood that the second twin will exhibit that problem, given that the first twin does. If concordance rates are higher for identical twins than for fraternal twins, one can conclude that the disorder is influenced by heredity.

Schizophrenia is a serious form of mental illness characterized by disturbances in thinking, emotional expression, and behavior. Schizophrenics are often so deficient at forming simple concepts and making logical connections between everyday events that they are unable to distinguish fantasy from reality. As a consequence, they may experience delusions or vivid hallucinations that contribute to their apparently irrational and inappropriate behavior. A survey of several twin studies of schizophrenia suggests an average concordance rate of .46 for identical twins but only .14 for fraternal twins (Gottesman & Shields, 1982). This is a strong indication that schizophrenia is a heritable disorder. In addition, studies of adults who grew up in adoptive homes reveal that the incidence of schizophrenia (and other disorders) among these adoptees is more closely related to the incidence of schizophrenia among their biological relatives than among members of their adoptive families (Plomin et al., 1980).

In recent years, it has become increasingly apparent that heredity also contributes to abnormal behaviors and conditions such as alcoholism, criminality, depression, hyperactivity, **manic-depressive** psychosis, and a number of **neurotic disorders** (Fuller & Thompson, 1978; Mednick, Gabrielli, & Hutchings, 1984; Schwarz, 1979). Now, it is possible that you have or have had close relatives who were diagnosed as alcoholic, neurotic, manic-depressive, or schizophrenic. Rest assured that this does *not* mean that you or your children will develop these problems. Only 10–14% of children who have one schizophrenic parent ever develop any symptoms that might be labeled "schizophrenic" (Kessler, 1975). Even if you are an identical twin whose co-twin has a serious psychiatric disorder, the odds are only between 1 and 2 and 1 in 10 (depending on the disorder) that you will ever experience anything that even approaches the problem that affects your twin.

Since identical twins are often *discordant* (that is, not alike) with respect to illnesses such as schizo-

nonshared environmental influence: an environmental influence that people living together do not share and that makes these individuals different from one another.

concordance rate: the percentage of cases in which a particular attribute is present for both members of a twin pair if it is present for one member.

schizophrenia: a serious form of mental illness characterized by disturbances in logical thinking, emotional expression, and interpersonal behavior.

manic-depression: a psychotic disorder characterized by extreme fluctuations in mood.

neurotic disorder: an irrational pattern of thinking or behavior that a person may use to contend with stress or to avoid anxiety.

phrenia, it is obvious that environment must be a very important contributor to behavioral abnormalities and mental illnesses. In other words, people do not inherit particular disorders—they inherit genetic (predispositions) to develop certain illnesses or deviant patterns of behavior. And even when a child's family history suggests that such a genetic predisposition may exist, it usually takes one or more very stressful experiences (for example, rejecting parents, a failure or series of failures at school, or dissolution of the family due to divorce) to trigger the illness in question (Rutter, 1979). Clearly, this latter finding provides some basis for optimism, for it may be possible someday to prevent the onset of most heritable disorders should we (1) learn more about the adverse events that precipitate these disturbances while (2) striving to develop interventions or therapeutic techniques that will help "high risk" individuals to maintain their emotional stability in the face of environmental stress.

Another Look at the Nature/Nurture Controversy

Only 30 years ago, developmentalists were embroiled in the nature/nurture controversy: Was heredity or environment the primary determinant of human potential? Although this chapter has focused on biological influences, it should now be apparent that *both* heredity and environment contribute in important ways to developmental outcomes and that the often extreme positions taken by the hereditarians and environmentalists of yesteryear are grossly oversimplified. Today, most behavior geneticists no longer think in terms of nature *versus* nurture; they concentrate instead on trying to determine how these two important influences might combine or interact to promote developmental change. Let's now see what they have to say about the interplay between genes and environments.

Waddington's Canalization Principle
Although both heredity and environment contribute to most human traits, our genes influence some attributes more than others. Some years ago, Conrad Waddington (1966) used the term **canalization** to refer to cases where genes operate so as to limit or restrict development to a small number of outcomes. One example of a highly canalized human attribute is babbling in infancy. All infants, even deaf ones, babble in pretty much the same way over the first 8–10 months of life.

The environment has little if any effect on this highly canalized attribute, which simply unfolds according to the maturational program in our genes. By contrast, less canalized attributes such as intelligence, temperament, and personality can be deflected away from their genetic pathways in any of several directions by a variety of life experiences.

Some characteristics may be more strongly canalized during one period of the life span than during others. For example, Robert McCall (1981) suggests that intellectual development over the first two years is genetically determined; unless exposed to highly unusual environments, all infants reach the same intellectual milestones at about the same ages. However, this rigid canalization of intelligence is much less apparent during the preschool and grade school years, when children exposed to differing home and school environments often take very different developmental paths.

In sum, Waddington's canalization principle is a relatively simple idea—and yet, a very useful one that illustrates (1) that there are multiple pathways along which an individual might develop, (2) that nature and nurture combine to determine these pathways, and (3) that genes may limit the extent to which environments can influence development. Irving Gottesman makes these same points in a slightly different way in his own theory of genotype/environment interactions.

Gottesman's Range-of-Reaction Principle
When Waddington spoke about canalization, he was referring to genetically determined constraints on development that apply to *all* members of a species. Might *individual genotypes* ever operate in ways that restrict or constrain developmental outcomes? Irving Gottesman (1963) thought so. According to Gottesman's **range-of-reaction principle** genotype sets *limits* on the range of possible phenotypes that a person might display in response to different environments. This "reaction range" concept is illustrated in Figure 3-9. Here we see the effects of varying degrees of environmental enrichment on the intellectual performances (IQs) of three children: one who has high genetic potential for intellectual development (child A), one whose genetic endowment for intelligence is average (child B), and one whose potential for intellectual growth is far below average (child C). Notice that under similar environmental conditions, child A always outperforms the other two children. Child A also has the widest reaction range, in that her IQ might vary from well below average in a

restricted environment to far above average in an enriched environment. By contrast, child C has a very limited reaction range; his genetic potential for intellectual development is low and, as a result, he shows smaller variation in IQ across the three environments than do the other two children.

In sum, the range-of-reaction principle is a statement about the interplay between heredity and environment. Presumably, one's genotype sets a range of possible outcomes for any particular attribute, and the environment largely determines the point within that range where the individual will fall.

A New Look at Genotype/Environment Interactions

Up until now, we have talked as if heredity and environment were *independent* sources of influence that somehow combined to determine our observable characteristics, or phenotypes. This view is probably much too simplistic. In recent years, behavior geneticists have argued that our genes may actually influence the kinds of environments that we are likely to experience (Plomin, DeFries, & Loehlin, 1977; Scarr & McCartney, 1983). And how might genes have such an effect? In at least three ways.

Passive gene influences

Parents contribute to a child's development in two important respects: (1) by providing genes—the child's biological blueprint for development—and (2) by structuring a social, emotional, and intellectual environment in which the child will grow. In their recent theory of genotype/environment interactions, Sandra Scarr and Kathleen McCartney (1983) propose that the environments parents provide for their children depend, in part, on the parents' own genotypes. And because children share genes with their parents, the rearing environments to which they are exposed are necessarily correlated (and often compatible) with their *own* genotypes.

The following example illustrates some developmental implications of these **passive genotype/ environment interactions.** Parents who exercise regularly and who encourage this kind of animation tend to raise children who enjoy vigorous physical activities (Shaffer, 1985). Now, surely one could argue that the parents' own displays of physical activity and their inducements to exercise are potent *environmental* influences that contribute in a meaningful way to their children's activity preferences. But let's also note that

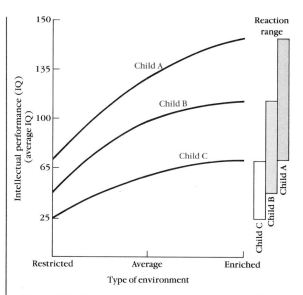

Figure 3-9. Hypothetical reaction ranges for the intellectual performances of three children in restricted, average, and intellectually enriching environments. *(Adapted from Gottesman, 1963.)*

these parents may have a genetic predisposition to enjoy physical exercise, which (1) may be passed along to their children and (2) may affect the activities that the parents will try to promote. Thus, not only are their children exposed to a rearing environment that encourages vigorous physical exercise, they may also have inherited genes that make them particularly responsive to that environment. In other words, these youngsters may come to enjoy physical exercise for both hereditary and environmental reasons—and the influences of heredity and environment are inextricably intertwined.

---

canalization: genetic restriction of phenotype to a small number of developmental outcomes; a highly canalized attribute is one for which genes channel development along predetermined pathways, so that the environment has little effect on the phenotype that emerges.

range-of-reaction principle: the idea that genotype sets limits on the range of possible phenotypes that a person might display in response to different environments.

passive genotype/environment interactions: the notion that the rearing environments that biological parents provide are influenced by the parents' own genes and hence are correlated with the child's own genotype.

⌐ elicit different reations

Evocative gene influences

Earlier, we noted that the environmental influences that contribute most heavily to personality are "nonshared" experiences that make individuals *different* from one another. Might the differences in environments that children experience be partly due to the fact that they have inherited different genes and thus may elicit different reactions from their companions?

Scarr and McCartney (1983) think so. Their notion of **evocative genotype/environment interactions** assumes that a child's heritable attributes will affect the behavior of others toward the child. For example, smily, active babies may receive more attention and social stimulation than moody and passive ones. Teachers may respond more favorably to physically attractive students than to their less attractive classmates. Clearly, these reactions of other people to the child (and the child's heritable attributes) are environmental influences that will play an important role in shaping that child's personality. So once again, we see an intermingling of hereditary and environmental influences: heredity affects the character of the social environment in which the personality develops.

Active gene influences (niche picking)

Finally, Scarr and McCartney (1983) propose that the environments children prefer and seek out will be those that are most compatible with their genetic predispositions. For example, a child with genes for sociability is likely to invite friends to the house, to be an avid party-goer, and to generally prefer activities that are socially stimulating. By contrast, the child with genes for shyness may actively avoid large social gatherings and choose instead to pursue activities such as coin collecting that can be done alone. So one implication of these **active genotype/environment interactions** is that people with different genotypes will *select* different "environmental niches" for themselves—niches that may then have a powerful effect on their social, emotional, and intellectual development.

How do genotype/environment interactions influence development?

According to Scarr and McCartney (1983), the relative importance of active, passive, and evocative gene influences will change over the course of development. During the first few years, infants and toddlers are not free to roam the neighborhood, choosing friends and building environmental niches. Most of their time is spent at home in an environment that parents structure for

them, so that passive genotype/environment interactions are particularly important early in life. But once children reach school age and venture away from home on a daily basis, they suddenly become much freer to pick their own interests, activities, friends, and hangouts. Thus, active, niche-building interactions should exert more and more influence on development as the child matures. Finally, evocative genotype/environment interactions are always important; that is, a person's heritable attributes and patterns of behavior may influence the ways other people react to him throughout life.

If Scarr and McCartney's theory has any merit, then virtually all siblings other than identical twins should become less similar over time as they emerge from the relatively similar rearing environments parents impose during the early years and begin to actively select different environmental niches for themselves. Indeed, there is some support for this assertion. Pairs of genetically unrelated adoptees who live in the same home do show some definite similarities in conduct and in intellectual performance during early and middle childhood (Scarr & Weinberg, 1978). Since these adoptees share no genes with each other or with their adoptive parents, their resemblances must be attributable to their common rearing environments. Yet, by late adolescence, genetically unrelated siblings no longer resemble each other in intelligence, personality, or any other aspect of behavior, presumably because they have selected very different environmental niches, which, in turn, have steered them along differing developmental paths (Scarr & McCartney, 1983; Scarr et al., 1981). By contrast, pairs of identical twins bear a close behavioral resemblance throughout childhood and adolescence. Why should this be? Scarr and McCartney suggest two reasons: (1) not only do identical twins elicit similar reactions from other people, but (2) their identical genotypes predispose them to prefer and to select very *similar* environments (that is, friends, interests, and activities), which will then exert comparable influences on these twin pairs and virtually guarantee that they will continue to resemble each other.

---

evocative genotype/environment interactions: the notion that our heritable attributes will affect others' behavior toward us and thus will influence the social environment in which development takes place.

active genotype/environment interactions: the notion that our genotypes affect the types of environments that we prefer and will seek out.

Box 3-2
Similarities (and Differences)
among Identical Twins Reared Apart

Raised as a strict Catholic by his mother in Czechoslovakia, Oscar Stohr became involved in the Hitler Youth Movement and remained loyal to the German Nazis during World War II. In middle age, he is now a loyal union member, employed as a factory supervisor in Germany. Jack Yufe, a store owner in California, was raised by his Jewish father and came to loathe Nazis as he grew up in a Caribbean country halfway around the world. Today, Jack holds quite liberal attitudes, whereas Oscar is very traditional and conservative.

It turns out that these two men, who seem so very different, are part of a study of *separated identical twins* being conducted by Thomas Bouchard and his associates at the University of Minnesota (see Farber, 1981). Oscar and Jack, like other twin pairs that Bouchard has examined, were separated as infants (when their parents divorced) and have lived apart from that point on. And despite their very different outlooks on life, Oscar and Jack are like other separated identical twins in that they show some remarkable similarities. For example, both men excel at sports and have difficulty with math. They have similar mannerisms and temperaments, and both tend to be absent-minded. And then there are the little things, such as their common tastes for spicy foods and sweet liqueurs, their habit of storing rubber bands on their wrists, and their preference for flushing the toilet before *and* after using it.

Bouchard and his colleagues have now studied more than 30 pairs of separated identical twins, finding that virtually all of them display some noteworthy similarities in their habits, their mannerisms, and their performances on various psychological tests. And yet, the data also show that these twins tend to differ in several respects: one twin usually displays more self-assurance or is more outgoing or aggressive or has a different outlook on life than the other.

How can separated identical twins be so different and, at the same time, so similar to each other? Perhaps the concept of *active gene influences* helps to explain the seemingly uncanny resemblances. When we learn that twins grow up in different environments, our tendency is to think of these settings as more dissimilar than they really are. In fact, identical twins raised apart are members of the same life cohort who are likely to be exposed to many of the same kinds of objects, activities, educational experiences, and historical events as they are growing up. So if identical twins are genetically predisposed to select comparable aspects of the environment for special attention, and if their "different" environments provide them with reasonably similar sets of experiences from which to build their environmental niches, then these individuals might well be expected to resemble each other in their habits, mannerisms, abilities, and interests.

Why, then, do separated identical twins often differ? According to Scarr and McCartney (1983), twins could be expected to differ on any attribute for which their rearing environments are so dissimilar as to prevent them from ever establishing comparable niches. For ex-

ample, a pair of twins might be genetically predisposed to be outgoing and sociable. But if one of them grows up with her mother in New York City and the other with a reclusive father in the Alaskan bush, the former twin will have had ample opportunity to act on her biological predispositions by mixing with other people and becoming highly extraverted, whereas her sister, lacking these opportunities, might actually become rather shy and reserved in social contexts.

The fact that separated identical twins often differ in meaningful ways helps to illustrate an important point about genotype/environment interactions and their impact on development. The point is this: although our genes may influence the kinds of life experiences we are likely to have, they do not *determine* our environments. Indeed, the events and experiences that we actually encounter will depend largely on what is available to us in the particular culture or subculture in which we are raised. And should some of the life experiences available to one person be radically discrepant from those of another, these two individuals will inevitably differ in important ways, regardless of the similarity of their genes or genetic predispositions.

Jack Yufe (left) and Oscar Stohr (right).

Even identical twins raised apart should be similar in some respects if their identical genes cause them to seek out and to prefer similar activities and experiences (see Box 3-2).

A final comment

After reading Scarr and McCartney's theory, one can easily come away with the impression that genotypes *determine* environments and therefore exert the primary influence on human development. This is not at all what the theory implies. What Scarr and McCartney are saying is that people with different genotypes are *likely* to evoke different responses from others and to select different environmental niches for themselves. But it is also true that the responses they will evoke from others and the aspects of the environment that they select when building their "niches" will depend to no small extent on the particular individuals, settings, and circumstances that are available to them. The separated identical twins that we met in Box 3-2 clearly illustrate this point. Oscar and Jack are alike in many ways because their two rearing environments permitted them access to many of the same kinds of experiences (for example, sports, math classes, spicy foods, rubber bands), thereby enabling them to develop similar habits, mannerisms, and interests. However, it was almost inevitable that Oscar and Jack would differ in their political ideologies because their sociopolitical environments were sufficiently *dissimilar* to prevent them from ever building the kinds of "niches" that would have made them social and political bedfellows.

In sum, we have seen that genotypes and environments combine to produce developmental change and that genetic and environmental differences combine to produce variations in developmental outcomes. True, genes exert some influence on those aspects of the environment that we are likely to experience. But the particular environments available to us will also limit the possible phenotypes that are likely to emerge from a particular genotype. Perhaps Donald Hebb (1980) was not too far off when he said that behavior is determined 100% by heredity and 100% by the environment, for it seems that these two sets of influences are completely and inextricably intertwined.

How exactly does the environment impinge on the individual to influence conduct and character? What environmental influences, given when, are particularly noteworthy in this regard? These are questions that we will be seeking to answer throughout the remainder of this text. We begin in our next chapter by examining how environmental events that occur even before a child is born combine with nature's grand plan to influence the course of prenatal development and the characteristics of newborn infants.

Summary

Since the dawn of recorded history, people have tried to understand how characteristics are transmitted from parents to offspring. Early theories of heredity claimed that the germ cells of either the father or the mother contained tiny preformed embryos that would begin to develop after a mating. However, biologists eventually discovered that each parent contributes equally to the creation of a child by passing hereditary "characters," or genes, to the offspring.

Development begins at conception, when a sperm cell from the father penetrates the wall of an ovum from the mother, forming a zygote. A normal zygote contains 46 chromosomes (23 from each parent), each of which consists of approximately 20,000 genes. Thus, each zygote may have as many as 500,000 pairs of genes that provide the hereditary blueprint for the development of this single cell into a recognizable human being.

Human beings consist of two kinds of cells: (1) body cells, which make up our bodies and organs, and (2) germ cells, which produce gametes—sperm in males and ova in females. Our body cells each contain duplicates of the 46 chromosomes (23 pairs) that we inherited at conception. Germ cells, which also have 23 pairs of chromosomes, divide by a process called meiosis to produce gametes that each contain 23 single (unpaired) chromosomes. Since individual gametes do not contain all the parent's chromosomes, the genetic composition of each sperm or ovum will differ. Therefore, each child inherits a unique combination of genes. The one exception is identical twins, who are formed from a single zygote that divides, creating two individuals with identical genes.

There are many ways in which one's genotype may affect phenotype—the way one looks, feels, thinks, or behaves. At least one phenotypic characteristic—gender—is determined by the 23rd pair of chromosomes (that is, the sex chromosomes). Normal females have inherited one relatively large sex chromosome (called an X chromosome) from each parent, whereas males have inherited an X chromosome and a smaller Y chromosome. An adult female (XX) can pass only X chromosomes to her offspring. However, an adult male (XY) can transmit either an X chromosome or a Y chromosome to his offspring. Thus, the father, not the mother, determines the sex of a child.

Some characteristics are determined by a single pair of genes, one of which is inherited from each parent. In dominant/recessive pairs, the individual will exhibit the phenotype of the dominant gene. If a gene pair is codominant or incompletely dominant, the individual will develop a phenotype in between those ordinarily produced by the dominant and the dominated (or recessive) genes. Sex-linked characteristics are caused by recessive genes that appear on only one of the two kinds of sex chromosomes (usually the X chromosome). Females must inherit two of these recessive genes (one on each X chromosome) in order to exhibit a sex-linked characteristic. However, males need only inherit one recessive gene to show the characteristic, because they have only one X chromosome.

Most complex human attributes such as intelligence and personality are polygenic, meaning that they are influenced by several pairs of genes rather than a single pair. In addition, the action or expression of one set of genes may be altered by the presence of modifier genes.

Occasionally children inherit abnormal genes and chromosomes. In most cases of chromosome abnormalities, the child has inherited too few or too many sex chromosomes. In about 1 in 600 births, a child inherits an extra 21st chromosome. The resulting phenotype is known as Down's syndrome, in which the child has a number of distinctive physical features and will be mentally retarded.

There are also a number of genetic diseases that children may inherit from parents who themselves are not affected but who carry the abnormal genes. In recent years, genetic counselors have had some success at using medical tests and family histories to establish the likelihood that prospective parents will have a child with a genetic problem. Many hereditary disorders cannot be detected before the child is born. However, the harmful effects of some of these diseases can be minimized by medical treatment if the condition is discovered soon after birth.

Behavior genetics is the study of how genes and environment contribute to individual variations in development. Although animals can be studied in selective breeding experiments, human behavior geneticists must conduct family studies, estimating hereditary contributions to various attributes from the similarities and differences among family members who differ in kinship. These family studies reveal that the genes people inherit exert an important influence on their intellectual performances, temperaments, personality, and tendencies to display abnormal patterns of behavior. However, family studies also show that the environment contributes in important ways to individual variations in development and that all behavioral attributes of lasting developmental significance are products of a long and involved interplay between the forces of nature and nurture.

Several theories have been proposed to explain how heredity and environment might interact to produce developmental change. For example, the range-of-reaction principle implies that heredity sets a range of developmental potentials for each attribute and the environment determines the extent of development. A more recent theory is that our genotypes influence the environments we are likely to experience—environments that then shape our conduct and character. Finally, it appears that the environments available to us may limit the phenotypes that can emerge from a particular genotype. So the current view is that heredity and environment combine to produce developmental change and that these two important influences are completely (and perhaps inseparably) intertwined.

References

APGAR, V., & Beck, J. (1974). *Is my baby all right?* New York: Pocket Books.

ARISTOTLE. (1912). *De generatione animalium* (A. Platt, Trans.). In J. A. Smith & W. D. Ross (Eds.), *The works of Aristotle* (Vol. 5). Oxford: Clarendon Press.

BEGLEY, S., Carey, J., & Katz, S. (1984, March 5). The genetic counselors. *Newsweek*, p. 69.

BURNS, G. W. (1976). *The science of genetics.* New York: Macmillan.

BUSS, A. H., & Plomin, R. (1984). *Temperament: Early developing personality traits.* Hillsdale, NJ: Erlbaum.

CICCHETTI, D., & Sroufe, L. A. (1978). An organizational view of affect: Illustration from the study of Down's syndrome infants. In M. Lewis & L. Rosenblum (Eds.), *The development of affect*. New York: Plenum.

DANIELS, D. (1986). Differential experiences of siblings in the same family as predictors of adolescent sibling personality differences. *Journal of Personality and Social Psychology, 51*, 339–346.

DANIELS, D., & Plomin, R. (1985). Differential experience of siblings in the same family. *Developmental Psychology, 21*, 747–760.

ERLENMEYER-KIMLING, L., & Jarvik, F. (1963). Genetics and intelligence. *Science, 142*, 1477–1479.

FAIRWEATHER, D. V. I. (1978). Techniques and safety of amniocentesis. In D. V. I. Fairweather & T. K. A. B. Eskes (Eds.), *Amniotic fluid: Research and clinical application*. Amsterdam: Elsevier.

FARBER, S. L. (1981). *Identical twins reared apart: A reanalysis*. New York: Basic Books.

FREEDMAN, D. G. (1979). Ethnic differences in babies. *Human Nature, 2,* 36–43.

FULLER, J. L., & Thompson, W. R. (1978). *Genetic basis of behavior.* St. Louis: Mosby.

GOLBUS, M. S. (1978). Prenatal diagnosis of genetic defects—where it is and where it is going. In J. W. Littlefield & J. DeGrouchy (Eds.), *Birth defects*. Amsterdam: Excerpta Medica.

GOLDSMITH, H. H. (1983). Genetic influences on personality from infancy to adulthood. *Child Development, 54,* 331–335.

GOLDSMITH, H. H., Buss, A. H., Plomin, R., Rothbart, M. K., Thomas, A., Chess, S., Hinde, R. A., & McCall, R. B. (1987). Roundtable: What is temperament? Four approaches. *Child Development, 58,* 505–529.

GOLDSMITH, H. H., & Campos, J. J. (1986). Fundamental issues in the study of early temperament: The Denver twin temperament study. In M. E. Lamb, A. L. Brown, & B. Rogoff (Eds.), *Advances in developmental psychology* (Vol. 4). Hillsdale, NJ: Erlbaum.

GOTTESMAN, I. I. (1963). Heritability of personality: A demonstration. *Psychological Monographs, 77*(Whole No. 572).

GOTTESMAN, I. I., & Shields, J. (1982). *Schizophrenia: The epigenetic puzzle*. Cambridge, England: Cambridge University Press.

HAYDEN, A. H., & Haring, N. G. (1976). Early intervention for high risk infants and young children: Programs for Down's syndrome children. In T. D. Tjossem (Ed.), *Intervention strategies for high risk infants and young children*. Baltimore: University Park Press.

HEBB, D. O. (1980). *Essay on mind*. Hillsdale, NJ: Erlbaum.

HORN, J. M. (1983). The Texas adoption project: Adopted children and their intellectual resemblance to biological and adoptive parents. *Child Development, 54,* 268–275.

KAGAN, J., Reznick, J. S., & Snidman, N. (1986). Temperamental inhibition in early childhood. In R. Plomin & J. Dunn (Eds.), *The study of temperament: Changes, continuities, and challenges*. Hillsdale, NJ: Erlbaum.

KESSLER, S. (1975). Psychiatric genetics. In D. A. Hamburg & K. Brodie (Eds.), *American handbook of psychiatry*. Vol. 6: *New psychiatric frontiers*. New York: Basic Books.

LEEUWENHOEK, A. van. (1677). Observations concerning little animals, etc. *Philosophical Transactions* (London), *2,* 82.

MAGENIS, R. E., Overton, K. M., Chamberlin, J., Brady, T., & Lorrien, E. (1977). Parental origin of the extra chromosome in Down's syndrome. *Human Genetics, 37,* 7–16.

MATTHEWS, K. A., Batson, C. D., Horn, J., & Rosenman, R. H. (1981). "Principles in his nature which interest him in the fortune of others . . .": The heritability of empathic concern for others. *Journal of Personality, 49,* 237–247.

McCALL, R. B. (1981). Nature-nurture and the two realms of development: A proposed integration with respect to mental development. *Child Development, 52,* 1–12.

McCAULEY, E., Kay, T., Ito, J., & Treder, R. (1987). The Turner syndrome: Cognitive deficits, affective discrimination, and behavior problems. *Child Development, 58,* 464–473.

McCLEARN, G. E. (1970). Genetic influences on behavior and development. In P. H. Mussen (Ed.), *Carmichael's manual of child psychology* (Vol. 1). New York: Wiley.

McCLEARN, G. E., & DeFries, J. C. (1973). *Introduction to behavioral genetics*. New York: W. H. Freeman.

McDEVITT, S. C. (1986). Continuity and discontinuity of temperament in infancy and early childhood: A psychometric perspective. In R. Plomin & J. Dunn (Eds.), *The study of temperament: Changes, continuities, and challenges*. Hillsdale, NJ: Erlbaum.

McMILLEN, M. M. (1979). Differential mortality by sex in fetal and neonatal deaths. *Science, 204,* 89–91.

MEDNICK, S. A., Gabrielli, W. F., Jr., & Hutchings, B. (1984). Genetic influences in criminal convictions: Evidence from an adoption cohort. *Science, 224,* 891–894.

MENDEL, G. (1959). Experiments in plant-hybridization, 1865. Reprinted in J. A. Peters (Ed.), *Classic papers in genetics*. Englewood Cliffs, NJ: Prentice-Hall.

MOTT, S. R., Fazekas, N. F., & James, S. R. (1985). *Nursing care of children and families: A holistic approach*. Reading, MA: Addison-Wesley.

NICHOLS, R. C. (1978). Heredity and environment: Major findings from twin studies of ability, personality, and interests. *Homo, 29,* 158–173.

OPITZ, J. M., & Sutherland, G. R. (1984). Conference report: International workshop on the fragile-X and X-linked mental retardation. *American Journal of Medical Genetics, 17,* 5–94.

PENNINGTON, B. F., & Smith, S. D. (1983). Genetic influences on learning disabilities and speech and language disorders. *Child Development, 54,* 369–387.

PLOMIN, R. (1986). *Development, genetics, and psychology*. Hillsdale, NJ: Erlbaum.

PLOMIN, R., & DeFries, J. C. (1983). The Colorado adoption project. *Child Development, 54,* 276–289.

PLOMIN, R., DeFries, J. C., & Loehlin, J. C. (1977). Genotype-environment interaction and correlation in the analysis of human behavior. *Psychological Bulletin, 84,* 309–322.

PLOMIN, R., DeFries, J. C., & McClearn, G. E. (1980). *Behavioral genetics: A primer.* New York: W. H. Freeman.

PUESCHEL, S. M., & Goldstein, A. (1983). Genetic counseling. In J. L. Matson & J. A. Mulick (Eds.), *Handbook of mental retardation*. Oxford: Pergamon Press.

REED, E. W. (1975). Genetic anomalies in development. In F. D. Horowitz (Ed.), *Review of child development research* (Vol. 4). Chicago: University of Chicago Press.

REZNICK, J. S., Kagan, J., Snidman, N., Gersten, M., Baak, K., & Rosenberg, A. (1986). Inhibited and uninhibited children: A follow-up study. *Child Development, 57,* 660–680.

ROVET, J., & Netley, C. (1983). The triple X chromosome syndrome in childhood: Recent empirical findings. *Child Development, 54,* 831–845.

ROWE, D. C., & Plomin, R. (1981). The importance of nonshared (E_1) environmental influences in behavioral development. *Developmental Psychology, 17,* 517–531.

RUTTER, M. (1978). Family, area, and school influences in the genesis of conduct disorders. In L. Hersov, M. Berber, & D. Shaffer (Eds.), *Aggression and antisocial behavior in childhood and adolescence*. Oxford: Pergamon Press.

RUTTER, M. (1979). Protective factors in children's responses to stress and disadvantage. In M. W. Kent & J. E. Rolf (Eds.), *Primary prevention of psychopathology*. Vol. 3: *Social competence in children*. Hanover, NH: University Press of New England.

SCARR, S., & McCartney, K. (1983). How people make their own environments: A theory of genotype–environment effects. *Child Development, 54,* 424–435.

SCARR, S., Webber, P. L., Weinberg, R. A., & Wittig, M. A. (1981). Personality resemblance among adolescents and their parents in biologically related and adoptive families. *Journal of Personality and Social Psychology, 40,* 885–898.

SCARR, S., & Weinberg, R. A. (1977). Intellectual similarities within families of both adopted and biological children. *Intelligence, 32,* 170–191.

SCARR, S., & Weinberg, R. A. (1978). The influence of family background on intellectual attainment. *American Sociological Review, 43,* 674–692.

SCARR, S., & Weinberg, R. A. (1983). The Minnesota adoption studies: Genetic differences and malleability. *Child Development, 54,* 260–267.

SCHAEFFER, C. (1987, March). Will the baby be okay? *Changing Times, 41,* 97–103.

SCHEINFELD, A. (1967). *Twins and super-twins.* Philadelphia: Lippincott.

SCHWARZ, J. C. (1979). Childhood origins of psychopathology. *American Psychologist, 34,* 879–885.

SHAFFER, D. R. (1985). Unpublished data, Department of Psychology, University of Georgia.

STERN, C. (1973). *Principles of human genetics.* New York: W. H. Freeman.

THOMAS, A., & Chess, S. (1977). *Temperament and development.* New York: Brunner/Mazel.

THOMAS, A., & Chess, S. (1986). The New York longitudinal study: From infancy to early adult life. In R. Plomin & J. Dunn (Eds.), *The study of temperament: Changes, continuities, and challenges.* Hillsdale, NJ: Erlbaum.

THOMAS, A., Chess, S., & Birch, H. G. (1970). The origin of personality. *Scientific American, 223,* 102–109.

THOMAS, A., Chess, S., & Korn, S. (1982). The reality of difficult temperament. *Merrill-Palmer Quarterly, 28,* 1–20.

THOMPSON, R. A., Cicchetti, D., Lamb, M. E., & Malkin, C. (1985). Emotional responses of Down's syndrome and normal infants in the strange situation: The organization of affective behavior in infants. *Developmental Psychology, 21,* 828–841.

THOMPSON, R. F. (1975). *Introduction to physiological psychology.* New York: Harper & Row.

TRYON, R. C. (1940). Genetic differences in maze learning in rats. *Yearbook of the National Society for Studies in Education, 39,* 111–119.

WADDINGTON, C. H. (1966). *Principles of development and differentiation.* New York: Macmillan.

WILSON, M. (1982, January 14). Sickle cell carriers at risk at high altitudes. *Athens Banner Herald,* p. 2-B.

WILSON, R. S. (1978). Synchronies in mental development: An epigenetic perspective. *Science, 202,* 939–948.

WILSON, R. S. (1983). The Louisville twin study: Developmental synchronies in behavior. *Child Development, 54,* 298–316.

WILSON, R. S., & Matheny, A. P., Jr. (1986). Behavior genetics research in infant temperament: The Louisville twin study. In R. Plomin & J. Dunn (Eds.), *The study of temperament: Changes, continuities, and challenges.* Hillsdale, NJ: Erlbaum.

WITKIN, H. A., Mednick, S. A., Schulsinger, F., Bakkestrom, E., Christiansen, K. D., Goodenough, D. R., Hirshhorn, K., Lundsteen, C., Owen, D. R., Philip, J., Rubin, D. B., & Stocking, M. (1976). Criminality in XYY and XXY men. *Science, 196,* 547–555.

WOLFF, K. F. (1959). *Theoria generationis.* In J. Needham, *A history of embryology.* New York: Abelard-Schulman. (Original work published 1759)

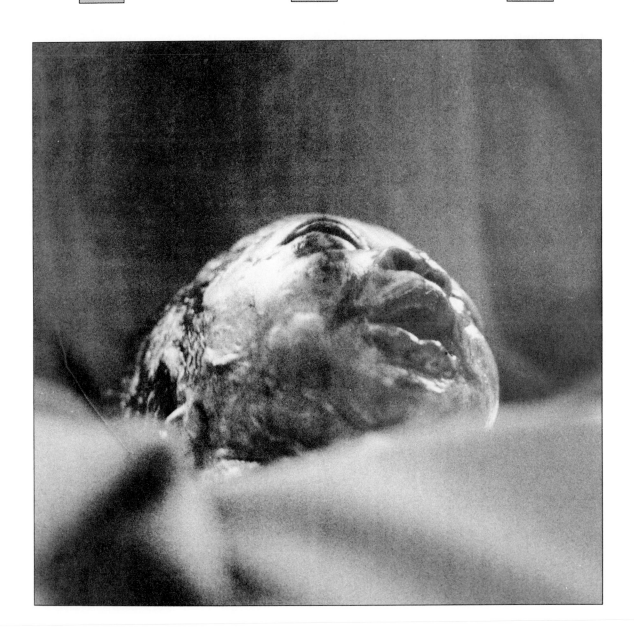

Prenatal Development and Birth

$\mathbf{T}$rue or False?

1. Human beings develop most rapidly between birth and 2 years of age.

2. The mother's womb is a protective haven that shields an unborn child from external hazards such as pollution and disease.

3. The environment has a meaningful effect on human development from the moment a child is born.

Now here is a "fill-in" item that you may find a little easier: How old are you? It turns out that this apparently straightforward question means slightly different things to different people. Many Oriental cultures date children from the moment of conception and consider them to be about 1 year old when they emerge from the womb. By contrast, we Westerners date ourselves from the moment of birth.

From a strict developmental perspective, the Oriental method of reckoning age may be the more realistic. Not only do hundreds of remarkable developments occur before a child is born, but many of these events take place within eight short weeks of conception. As we trace the miraculous evolution of a one-celled zygote into a recognizable human being, it will become apparent that human growth and development occur most rapidly during the *prenatal* period, months before birth.

When might environmental influences first occur? Once again, the answer is long before birth. **Prenatal development** does not take place in a vacuum; it occurs within the mother's uterus—an "environment" that will differ from mother to mother and may well affect the product that emerges in the delivery room. We are quite accustomed to thinking of the intrauterine environment as a safe, protective haven that enables an unborn child to take shape, grow, and become stronger in preparation for birth. This impression was created by influential scientists of the 18th century who described the womb as a kind of vacuum-packed mausoleum that "entombs" a fetus, protecting it from all external hazards (MacFarlane, 1977). Yet, we will see that the degree of safety or protection offered by the womb depends on a variety of factors, including the mother's age, health, and emotional state, the food she eats, the drugs she takes, and the chemicals or levels of radiation to which she is exposed.

In years gone by, people believed that the fetus could be affected by just about any experience that the mother might have. For example, it was once assumed, even by some physicians, that women who "failed" to bear their husbands a male heir were "at fault" because they got insufficient exercise during their pregnancies. Presumably, maternal exercise caused an unborn child to move, thereby stimulating the development of fetal muscle and increasing the probability that the fetus would become a male! Other common beliefs included the notions that a pregnant woman who often listened to music would have a musical child and that mothers who were sexually active while pregnant would produce sexually precocious children. Today we know that these ideas are unfounded, for only those maternal experiences that directly affect the intrauterine environment can influence an embryo or fetus. The reason will become clear as we look at the course of prenatal development and learn more about the interesting relationship that emerges between a mother and the unborn organism in her womb.

From Conception to Birth

In Chapter 3 we learned that development begins in the fallopian tube when a sperm penetrates the wall of a ripened ovum, forming a zygote (see Photo 4-1). From the moment of conception, it will take approximately 266 days for this tiny, one-celled zygote to become a fetus of some 200 billion cells that is ready to be born.

Prenatal development is often divided into three major phases. The first phase, called the **germinal pe-**

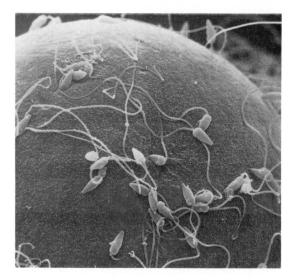

Photo 4-1. Ovum just before conception. Only one of these sperm will penetrate the egg, forming a zygote.

riod, lasts from conception until implantation—when the developing zygote becomes firmly attached to the wall of the uterus. The germinal period normally lasts about 8–14 days. The second phase of prenatal development, the **period of the embryo,** lasts from the beginning of the third week through the end of the eighth. This is the time when virtually all the major organs are formed and the heart begins to beat. The third phase, the **period of the fetus,** lasts from the ninth week of pregnancy until the child is born. During this phase, the major organ systems begin to function, and the developing organism grows rapidly.

The Germinal Period

Once conception has occurred, the fertilized ovum, or zygote, continues its journey down the fallopian tube toward the uterus. Within 24–36 hours the zygote divides by mitosis into two cells. These two cells and all their daughter cells continue to divide at periodic intervals, forming a ball-like structure, or **blastula,** that will contain 100–150 cells within seven days of conception. Cell differentiation has already begun. The inner layer of the blastula, called the **blastocyst,** will become the embryo. The outer layer of cells, or **trophoblast,** will develop into tissues that protect and nourish the embryo.

As the blastula approaches the uterus some 6–10 days after conception, small burrlike tendrils have emerged from the outer surface of the trophoblast. As nature would have it, the blastula reaches the uterus at the point in the woman's menstrual cycle when the uterine lining is engorged with small blood vessels that can provide nourishment to this primitive little creature. When the blastula comes into contact with the uterine wall, its tendrils burrow inward, tapping into the woman's blood supply. This is **implantation.** Soon cells from the uterus grow around the implanted blastula, providing a rudimentary protective covering. Within 8–14 days after conception, the site of implantation looks like a small, translucent blister on the lining of the uterus (Apgar & Beck, 1974). At this point, the germinal period comes to an end.

Implantation is a critical event in human development. Only about half of all fertilized ova are successfully implanted in the uterus, and perhaps as many as half of all implanted embryos are abnormal in some way (or burrow into a site incapable of sustaining them) and will not develop to term (Adler & Carey, 1982). So it appears that approximately 1 zygote in 4 will survive the initial phases of prenatal development.

The Period of the Embryo

From the moment of implantation, the blastula, which is still no bigger than the head of a pin, is

---

prenatal development: development that occurs between the moment of conception and the beginning of the birth process.

germinal period: first phase of prenatal development, lasting from conception until the developing organism becomes attached to the wall of the uterus.

period of the embryo: second phase of prenatal development, lasting from the third through the eighth prenatal week, during which the major organs and anatomical structures begin to develop.

period of the fetus: third phase of prenatal development, lasting from the ninth prenatal week until birth; during this period, the major organ systems begin to function and the fetus grows rapidly.

blastula: a hollow sphere of about 100–150 cells that results from the rapid division of the zygote as it moves through the fallopian tube.

blastocyst: inner layer of the blastula, which becomes the embryo.

trophoblast: outer cells of the blastula, which eventually develop into tissues that serve to protect and nourish the embryo.

implantation: the burrowing of the blastula into the lining of the uterus.

already working to ensure its continued survival. Its first accomplishment is to secrete a hormone that prevents the woman from menstruating and thereby shedding the lining of her uterus, where the blastula is implanted. This hormone circulates throughout the woman's body and is eventually detectable in her urine, where its presence is taken as a positive indication of pregnancy in a common pregnancy test.

During the second and third weeks after conception, further differentiations of the ball-like blastula take place. The outer layer, or trophoblast, forms four membranes that make it possible for the embryo to develop. One membrane, the **amnion,** is a watertight bag that surrounds the embryo, filling with fluid that seeps in from the mother's tissues. The purpose of the amnion and its amniotic fluid is to cushion the developing organism against injuries, to maintain a constant warm temperature, and to provide a weightless environment that makes it easy for the developing organism to move and to exercise its growing body (Apgar & Beck, 1974). Floating beside the tiny embryo is a balloon-shaped **yolk sac** that produces blood cells until the embryo is capable of producing its own. This yolk sac is attached to a third membrane, the **chorion,** which surrounds the amnion and the embryo. One side of the chorionic sac is covered with rootlike structures, or villi, that gather nourishment from the uterine tissues. This area eventually becomes the lining of the **placenta**—a multipurpose organ that we are about to discuss in detail. A fourth membrane, the **allantois,** forms the embryo's umbilical cord and the blood vessels in the placenta.

Function of the placenta

Once the placenta develops, it is fed by blood vessels from the mother and the embryo, although the villi of the placenta function as a barrier that prevents these two bloodstreams from mixing. This placental barrier is semipermeable, meaning that it allows some substances to pass through but not others. Gases such as oxygen and carbon dioxide, salts, and various nutrients such as sugars, proteins, and fats are small enough to cross the placental barrier. However, blood cells are too large.

As maternal blood flows into the placenta, oxygen and nutrients pass through this semipermeable membrane into the embryo's bloodstream. The embryo is connected to the placenta by means of its lifeline, the **umbilical cord,** which carries oxygen and foodstuffs to the embryo and transports carbon dioxide and met-abolic wastes from the embryo. These waste products then cross the placental barrier, enter the mother's bloodstream, and are eventually expelled from the mother's body along with her own metabolic wastes. Clearly, the placenta plays a crucial role in prenatal development, because this remarkable organ is the site of all metabolic transactions that sustain the embryo.

Development of the embryo

As the blastula becomes implanted in the wall of the uterus and as the outer protective membranes are forming, the innermost cells (or blastocyst) are rapidly differentiating into three distinct layers. The outer layer, or *ectoderm,* will eventually become the child's skin, hair, nails, oil and sweat glands, and nervous system. The middle layer, or *mesoderm,* will form muscles, bones, connective tissue, and the circulatory and excretory systems. From the inner layer, or *endoderm,* come the digestive tract, trachea, bronchi, lungs, and other vital organs such as the pancreas and liver.

During the period of the embryo, development proceeds at a breathtaking pace. About 14 days after conception, a portion of the ectoderm folds into a neural tube that soon becomes the head, brain, and spinal cord. By the end of the fourth week, the heart has formed and has already begun to beat, pushing blood through the embryo's tiny arteries and veins. The eyes, ears, nose, and mouth are also taking shape, and buds that will become arms and legs suddenly appear. Thirty days after conception, the embryo is only about 1/4 of an inch long—but 10,000 times the size of the zygote from which it developed. At no time in the future will this organism ever grow so rapidly or change so much as it has during the first prenatal month.

During the second month, the body becomes much more human in appearance as it grows about 1/30th of an inch per day. A primitive tail appears (see Photo 4-2), but it is soon enclosed by protective tissue and becomes the tip of the backbone, the coccyx. By the middle of the fifth week, the eyes have corneas and lenses. By the seventh week, the ears are well formed and the embryo has a rudimentary skeleton. Limbs are now developing from the body outward; that is, the upper arms appear first, followed by the forearms, hands, and then fingers. The legs follow a similar pattern a few days later. The brain develops rapidly during the second month, and it directs the organism's first muscular contractions by the end of the embryonic period.

During the seventh and eighth prenatal weeks, the embryo's sexual development begins with the ap-

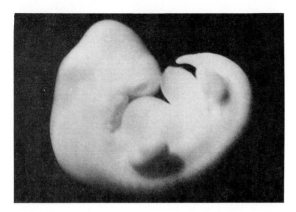

Photo 4-2. A human embryo at 38 days. The heart is now beating and the limbs are rapidly forming. Note the primitive tail (soon to become the tip of the backbone) in the upper right-hand portion of the photo.

Photo 4-3. A human embryo at 60 days. All the major organs have begun to form, and the embryo is now a fetus.

pearance of a genital ridge called the **indifferent gonad.** If the embryo is a male, a gene on its Y chromosome triggers a biochemical reaction that instructs the indifferent gonad to produce testes. If the embryo is a female, the indifferent gonad receives no such instructions and will produce ovaries. As the testes mature during the ninth and tenth prenatal weeks, they manufacture male sex hormones, which stimulate the development of a male reproductive system.[1] However, the female fetus will develop a female reproductive system even if its tiny ovaries are damaged or do not function. It appears, then, that nature's first choice is female and that "maleness" requires a "male" gene to (1) trigger the development of testes, which (2) must then function properly to produce other male sex organs.

At 60 days after conception, the embryo is slightly more than an inch long and weighs less than 1/10th of an ounce. It appears humanoid (see Photo 4-3), although its head is at least as long as the rest of its body. Apgar and Beck (1974, p. 57) offer the following description of the eight-week-old embryo:

> All of the structures which will be present when the baby is born in seven more months have already been formed, at least in beginning stages. . . . Med-

ically, the unborn baby is no longer an embryo, but a fetus; not an it, but a he or she; not an indistinct cluster of cells, but an increasingly recognizable, unique human being in the making.

The sensitive nature of embryonic development

The first two months of pregnancy are critical in several respects. This is when most miscarriages (spontaneous abortions) occur as the embryo becomes detached from the uterine wall and is expelled. Perhaps 30–50% of pregnancies end this way (Roberts & Lowe,

---

[1]One sex-linked genetic anomaly, the testicular feminization syndrome, makes a genetic male (XY) fetus insensitive to the male hormone androgen. A male fetus that inherits this condition will develop the external genitalia of a female even though testes (which will remain out of sight within the body) have evolved from the indifferent gonad (Money & Ehrhardt, 1972).

---

amnion: a watertight membrane that develops from the trophoblast and surrounds the developing embryo, serving to regulate its temperature and to cushion it against injuries.

yolk sac: a balloonlike structure that develops from the trophoblast and produces blood cells until the embryo is capable of manufacturing its own.

chorion: a membrane that develops from the trophoblast and becomes attached to the uterine tissues to gather nourishment for the embryo.

placenta: an organ, formed from the lining of the uterus and the chorion, that provides for respiration and nourishment of the unborn child and elimination of its metabolic wastes.

allantois: a membrane that develops from the trophoblast and forms the umbilical cord.

umbilical cord: a soft tube containing blood vessels that connects the embryo to the placenta.

indifferent gonad: undifferentiated tissue that produces testes in males and ovaries in females.

1975), many women miscarrying without even being aware that they are pregnant. Spontaneous abortions may be triggered by a variety of factors: the woman's uterus may be malformed or immature; the blastula may have become implanted at a site incapable of sustaining the embryo. But in the majority of cases, aborted embryos are thought to be genetically abnormal. So spontaneous abortions can be adaptive, representing "nature's way of discouraging [harmful] mutations from being incorporated into the hereditary pattern" (Browne & Dixon, 1978, p. 105).

Even genetically normal embryos that are firmly implanted in a healthy uterus are at risk during the first two months of pregnancy. Indeed, the time between two and eight weeks after conception is often labeled the "sensitive period" of pregnancy because the embryo is now particularly susceptible to the influence of **teratogens**—viruses, chemicals, drugs, and radiation—that can interfere with ongoing development and produce birth defects. Although teratogens are capable of damaging organs or body parts that have already formed, they are likely to have a much stronger impact on organs that are currently developing. Thus, the human embryo is especially susceptible to teratogens between two and eight weeks after conception because this is the time when many of its vital structures, organs, and organ systems are beginning to develop.

The Period of the Fetus

During the third prenatal month, bones begin to harden, muscles are rapidly developing, and the embryo, which has become increasingly human in appearance, is now called a *fetus*.

By the end of the third month, the fetus is already performing many interesting maneuvers in its watery environment—moving its arms, kicking its legs, making fists, twisting its body, and even turning somersaults—although these activities are not yet detected by the mother (Annis, 1978). Several organ systems are operational, allowing the fetus to swallow, to digest nu-

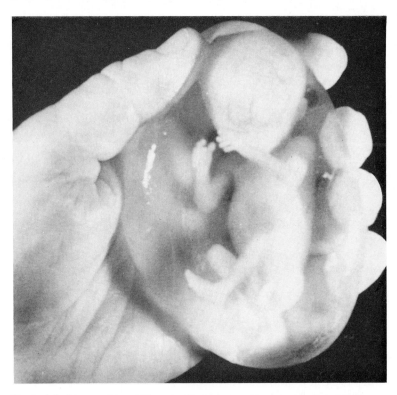

Photo 4-4. A human fetus at 12 weeks. Most organ systems are now functioning, even though the fetus is only 3 inches long and weighs less than an ounce.

Table 4-1. Infant mortality as a function of birth weight

	Birth weight		Percentage of babies who die
	In grams	*In pounds*	
Low-birth-weight babies	1000 or less	2 lb, 3 oz. or less	92
	1000–1500	2 lb, 4 oz–3 lb, 4 oz	55
	1501–2000	3 lb, 5 oz–4 lb, 6 oz	21
	2001–2500	4 lb, 7 oz–5 lb, 8 oz	6
Average-birth-weight babies	2501–3000	5 lb, 9 oz–6 lb, 9 oz	2
	3001–4500	6 lb, 10 oz–9 lb, 14 oz	1

trients, and to urinate. Gender is readily apparent, and the fetal reproductive system already contains immature ova or sperm cells. All this detail is present after 12 weeks even though the fetus is a mere 3 inches long and weighs but ½ to ¾ of an ounce (see Photo 4-4).

The second trimester. The fourth, fifth, and sixth months of pregnancy, called the "second trimester," are a period of rapid growth and development. At 16 weeks, the fetus is 8–10 inches long and weighs about 6 ounces. Its motor activity may include refined actions such as thumbsucking, as well as vigorous kicks that are strong enough to be felt by the mother. The fetal heartbeat can now be heard with a stethoscope, and the hardening skeleton can be detected by X rays or ultrasound. By the end of the fourth month, the fetus has assumed a distinctly human appearance, even though it stands absolutely no chance of surviving outside the womb.

During the fifth and sixth months, the nails begin to harden, the skin thickens, and eyebrows, eyelashes, and scalp hair suddenly appear. At 20 weeks, the sweat glands are functioning, and the fetal heartbeat is often strong enough to be heard by placing an ear on the mother's abdomen. The fetus is now about 12 inches long and weighs between 12 and 16 ounces. By the 25th week, the fetus's visual and auditory senses are apparently functional. We know this because premature infants born only 25 weeks after conception will become alert at the sound of a loud bell and blink in response to a bright light (Allen & Capute, 1986). Six months after conception, the fetus is approximately 14–15 inches long and weighs about 2 pounds.

The end of the second trimester is yet another sensitive period in human development. At some point between the 24th and 28th weeks after conception, the fetal brain and respiratory system have matured to an extent that the fetus attains the **age of viability**—the point at which survival outside the uterus *may* be possible. On March 5, 1982, Daniel Sumi made medical history by becoming the smallest baby ever to be born and subsequently live (Associated Press, 1983). This hardy young man weighed in at 13 ounces (369 grams) when he was delivered in his 27th prenatal week. (Other babies have been born earlier—as early as the 22nd week—and survived, but none of them weighed less than Daniel.) Until this birth, only one child weighing less than 1 pound had ever survived. In fact, the majority of newborns who weigh less than 3¼ pounds (1500 grams) do not survive, even with excellent medical care (Browne & Dixon, 1978; Kessner, 1973).

There is a very definite relationship between the birth weight of a child and the child's probability of surviving: the less a baby weighs at birth, the greater the likelihood that he or she will die during the birth process or soon thereafter (see Table 4-1). Each additional day that a fetus continues to develop within the uterus increases the probability of survival in the outside world.

The third trimester. The seventh, eighth, and ninth months of pregnancy—the third trimester—are a period of rapid growth. By the end of the seventh month, the fetus weighs about 4 pounds and is about 16–17 inches long. One month later, the fetus has grown to 18 inches and put on another 1 to 2½ pounds. Much of the weight gain during this period comes from a

teratogens: external agents such as viruses, drugs, chemicals, and radiation that can cross the placental barrier and harm a developing embryo or fetus.

age of viability: a point between the 24th and 28th prenatal weeks when a fetus may survive outside the uterus if excellent medical care is available.

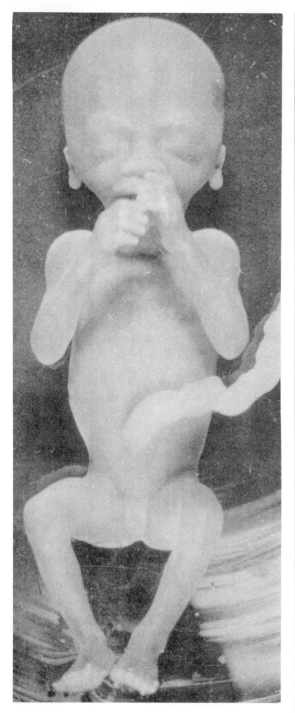

Photo 4-5. A human fetus at 210 days. By this age, survival outside the womb may be possible.

padding of fat that is deposited beneath the skin. After birth this fatty layer will help to insulate the child from changes in temperature. By the time the fetus weighs 3½ to 4 pounds, odds of survival in the event of premature birth are good. A fetus weighing at least 5 pounds at birth may not even require an incubator.

As the uterus expands during the third trimester, it assumes the shape of an inverted pear. By the middle of the ninth month, the fetus is so large that the most comfortable lie within its restricted uterine environment is likely to be a head-down posture at the base of the uterus, with the limbs curled up in the so-called fetal position. At irregular intervals over the last month of pregnancy, the mother's uterus will contract and then relax. These contractions serve to tone the uterine muscle, dilate the cervix, and help position the head of the now-inverted fetus into the gap between the pelvic bones through which it will soon be pushed. When the uterine contractions become stronger, more frequent, and regular, the prenatal period draws to a close. The mother is now in the first stage of labor, and within a matter of hours she will give birth.

Environmental Influences on Prenatal Development

The pattern of prenatal development just described is an overview of what typically occurs between conception and birth. The vast majority of unborn children follow this "normal" pattern—and for that we can be thankful. Nevertheless, there are those who encounter environmental roadblocks during the prenatal period—blocks that may be sufficiently formidable to channel their development along an abnormal path. We will now consider a number of agents and circumstances that can have an adverse effect on the unborn child.

Maternal Characteristics

Maternal age

You may recall that Aristotle cautioned women to have their babies early. He believed that women were hardiest at age 18 and that this was the time when they were most likely to bear normal, healthy children. Psychologist B. F. Skinner (1971) offered a similar recommendation, but for different reasons. Have your babies by age 20, advised Skinner, so that you can leave them in the care of professional child rearers and be completely free to pursue a career.

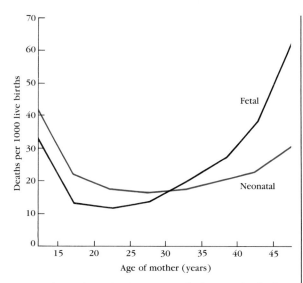

Figure 4-1. Relationship between mother's age and risk of death for the fetus or neonate. (*From Kessner, 1973.*)

Although many career-oriented mothers might applaud Skinner's suggestion, large-scale implementation of his plan could result in a sizable increase in infant mortality. As shown in Figure 4-1, there is a relationship between a mother's age and the risk of death for her fetus or **neonate** (newborn). Notice that mothers under 17 or 18 face an added risk of bearing a stillborn fetus or a baby that fails to live. Younger mothers also experience more obstetrical complications and are more likely to die during childbirth than those in their twenties (Planned Parenthood Federation of America, 1976). Why are younger mothers and their offspring at risk? Part of the problem is that some very young teens have not matured enough physically to sustain a fetus. However, the greater problem is that teenagers often do not receive adequate prenatal care. Indeed, teenage mothers and their babies are usually *not* at risk when they receive good prenatal care and competent medical supervision during the birth process (Baker & Mednick, 1984).

Mothers older than 35 also face added risks of obstetrical problems and infant mortality. At the older end of the age continuum, many of the complications of pregnancy and prenatal development are experienced by women over 35 who are having a *first* child. These older "first-timers" are more likely than women in their twenties to be ill during pregnancy, to have longer and more difficult labors, and to deliver infants

who are small, premature, or stillborn or who show any of a variety of congenital defects (Browne & Dixon, 1978; Kessner, 1973). However, we should bear in mind that the vast majority of older mothers have pregnancies that last the full nine months and produce perfectly normal babies.

The mother's emotional state

Although many women are happy to learn that they are pregnant, the fact remains that over half of all pregnancies are unplanned ("Half Our Pregnancies," 1983) and that single women and those who are unhappily married are often bitter, depressed, or angry about their pregnancies (Browne & Dixon, 1978). In fact, it is quite normal for any woman to show some symptoms of anxiety and depression while she is pregnant (Kaplan, 1986). Do these emotional states and attitudes toward pregnancy have any effect on prenatal development? Can they affect the birth process?

Although there are no direct connections between a woman's nervous system and that of her fetus, a mother's emotional state can affect her unborn child. When a mother becomes emotionally aroused, her endocrine glands secrete powerful hormones, such as adrenalin, that may cross the placental barrier and enter the fetal bloodstream. At the very least, the presence of these activating substances can significantly increase the fetus's motor activity (Sontag, 1941). And if emotional stress or anxiety lasts throughout pregnancy, expectant mothers are at risk for complications such as miscarriage, prolonged and painful labor, and premature delivery (Sameroff & Chandler, 1975). Of course, not all women who are anxious or emotionally upset will experience these problems. A mother's emotions are most likely to affect her fetus and the birth process when she is (1) extremely anxious, (2) highly dependent on others, and (3) ambivalent or negative about her pregnancy (McDonald, 1968; Stott & Latchford, 1976).

Once born, the babies of highly anxious mothers tend to be hyperactive, irritable, and quite irregular in their feeding, sleeping, and bowel habits (Sameroff & Chandler, 1975; Sontag, 1944). It has been argued that this "difficult" temperamental profile is genetically based or is caused by the activating hormones associated with the mother's heightened emotional state during pregnancy (Carey & McDevitt, 1980). However, recent re-

---

neonate: an infant from birth to approximately 1 month of age.

search hints at another possibility. Tiffany Field and her associates (Field et al., 1985) found that mothers who were highly anxious, depressed, or resentful during the last trimester of pregnancy usually remained anxious or upset after their babies were born. And compared with a group of new mothers who had had happy pregnancies, the anxious mothers were more *punitive* and *controlling* in their approach to child rearing and had infants who were *fussier* and *more variable* in mood. Brian Vaughn and his associates (Vaughn, Bradley, Joffe, Seifer, & Barglow, 1987) have recently reported a similar link between maternal anxiety late in pregnancy and infant temperament six months after birth. Yet, the most intriguing finding in this study was that the actual levels of activating hormones present in the intrauterine environment late in pregnancy did *not* predict infants' later temperamental characteristics. Although these findings are hardly definitive, they suggest that the negative temperamental qualities often observed among children of anxious mothers could be *socially* mediated. That is, mothers who have been anxious or resentful about their pregnancies may often retain some of these feelings after giving birth and then respond to their babies in ways that make these children irritable or "difficult" (Vaughn et al., 1987).

The mother's diet (nutrition)

Forty years ago, doctors often advised expectant mothers that they need not eat any more than they cared to in order to have a healthy baby. The rule of thumb in those days was that women should gain no more than 2 pounds a month while pregnant. The thinking was that excessive weight gains could be harmful for the mother and that a tiny fetus could extract the nutrients it needed even if the mother gained very little weight (15–18 pounds).

Today most obstetricians would be very concerned if a patient of theirs gained too little weight, for they are now well aware of the many harmful complications that can result from inadequate prenatal nutrition. Women are currently advised to gain 3–4 pounds during the first three months of pregnancy and approximately a pound a week thereafter—a total increase of 24–28 pounds (B. G. Brown, personal communication, Feb. 1987).

Much of what we know about nutrition and prenatal development comes from studies of expectant mothers who were severely malnourished. Severe malnutrition increases the risk of congenital defects, pro-

longed labor, stillbirth, and infant mortality during the first year. Apparently the harmful consequences of prenatal malnutrition are greatest when the nutritional deficiency occurs later in pregnancy, particularly during the last three months (see Box 4-1). Not only is this third trimester the period when an unborn child is gaining most of its eventual birth weight, but the fetus's brain cells are also rapidly multiplying and increasing in size (Tanner, 1978). So perhaps we should not be surprised to learn (1) that mothers who are severely malnourished during the third trimester are likely to deliver rather small babies or (2) that autopsies of stillborn children reveal that infants born to malnourished mothers have brain cells that are fewer and smaller than in infants whose mothers were adequately nourished (Lewin, 1975; Winick, 1976).

The long-term effects of prenatal malnutrition will depend to a large extent on the adequacy of the child's diet after birth. A malnourished infant who lives in an economically impoverished environment where nutrition *remains* inadequate is likely to show later deficits in physical growth as well as impairments in social, emotional, and intellectual development (Barrett, Radke-Yarrow, & Klein, 1982; Winick, 1976). Moreover, it appears that some of these long-term effects are linked to the infant's own behavior. Philip Zeskind and Craig Ramey (1981) have noted that fetally malnourished infants are often unresponsive, apathetic babies who become rather irritable when aroused—qualities that may make them unpleasant to deal with. As a result, these children are likely to alienate their caregivers and fail to elicit the kinds of playful stimulation and emotional support that would facilitate their social and intellectual development. Fortunately, dietary supplements given to malnourished mothers during the last half of pregnancy or to their infants soon after birth tend to make these children more active and outgoing, thereby reducing the likelihood that early malnutrition will have harmful consequences that persist over time (Barrett et al., 1982; Joos, Pollitt, Mueller, & Albright, 1983).

Teratogens

Teratology, the study of prenatal malformations and birth defects, is a young science with many unresolved issues. Not all the diseases, drugs, chemicals, and other environmental hazards that can harm a developing embryo or fetus have yet been identified. Moreover, the study of teratology is complicated by the findings that (1) few if any of the known teratogens will affect all unborn children who are exposed to them,

Box 4-1
Effects of Famine on
Infant Mortality and
Intellectual Development

Between October 1944 and March 1945, a large area of western Holland was subjected to conditions of famine. During this period of World War II, many Dutch citizens were trying to support Allied forces, and the occupying German troops retaliated by closing the roads and the rail system, thereby restricting civilian transport. This "embargo" severely limited the availability of food and other essential supplies to most large cities, and shortage of food soon became serious. Rations dropped from over 2000 calories per person per day before the famine to 500–700 calories (with a severe reduction in protein) by the time conquering Allied troops lifted the blockade.

Some 30 years later, Zela Stein and her associates (Stein & Susser, 1976; Stein, Susser, Saenger, & Marolla, 1975) examined hospital birth and death records from this period to study the effects of famine on infant mortality. And because all Dutch males must take intelligence tests when they undergo compulsory military training at age 19, it was also possible to determine whether the surviving male children born during or shortly after the famine showed any long-term intellectual deficits as a result of their early malnutrition.

The short-term effects were clear. Stein et al. (1975) found that women who were malnourished during the *last three months* of their pregnancies were much more likely to have small, underweight babies than mothers who were malnourished during their first or second trimester. The effects of malnutrition on infant mortality were almost identical, as indicated in the accompanying table.

Stein and her colleagues then compared the later intellectual performance of military inductees from the famine area with that of their peers born in parts of Holland not affected by the famine. Once again, the results were clear and somewhat surprising—malnourished males from the famine area scored no lower on the test battery than well-nourished males from nonfamine areas.

Since it is well known that malnourished fetuses often have smaller brains and fewer brain cells (see text for details), why do you suppose the malnourished males in this study showed no long-term cognitive deficits? Stein and her colleagues offer one possible explanation. They note that the mothers of these boys (and the boys themselves) were adequately nourished after the famine. Since the first two years of life is a period of rapid brain growth and development, it is certainly possible that adequate nutrition during this critical phase may compensate for any adverse effects of poor prenatal nutrition. In other words, if the fetally malnourished infant should survive, it appears that a good *postnatal* diet may help to prevent long-term deficits in neurological development and intellectual performance.

Condition	Infant mortality in first 12 months (deaths per 1000 births)
Child born before famine (mother not malnourished)	9
Mother malnourished— last 3 months of pregnancy	30
Mother malnourished— first 6 months	18
Mother malnourished—first 3 months	6
Child conceived and born after famine (mother not malnourished)	6

(2) a single teratogen may have more than one harmful effect, and (3) a particular birth defect may be caused by any of several teratogens (Abel, 1981; Spreen, Tupper, Risser, Tuokko, & Edgell, 1984).

We do know that some unborn children are more vulnerable than others to teratogenic agents. For example, a particular teratogen is more likely to produce a congenital problem of some kind if the embryo or fetus is a **later-born** or a male and if the mother is poor, undernourished, and younger than 20 or older than 40 (Apgar & Beck, 1974; Browne & Dixon, 1978).

The effects of a teratogen will also depend on the developmental stage of the embryo or the fetus. Each major organ system or body part has a critical

---

teratology: the scientific study of birth defects caused by genetic and prenatal influences or by complications of the birth process.

later-borns: children born after a mother's first child; that is, children born second (or later) to the same mother.

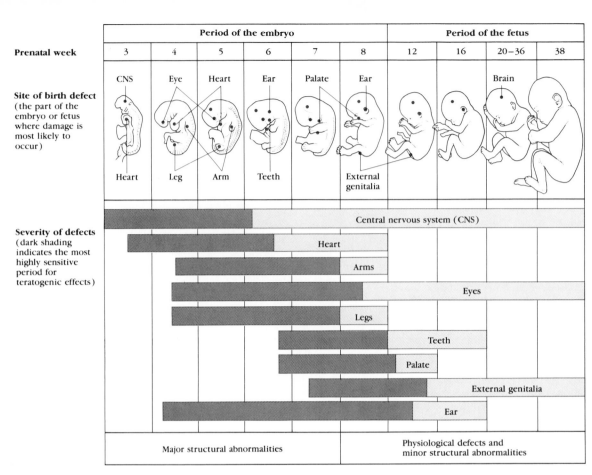

Figure 4-2. The critical periods of prenatal development. Teratogens are more likely to produce major structural abnormalities during the third through the eighth prenatal week. Note, however, that many organs and body parts remain sensitive to teratogenic agents throughout the nine-month prenatal period. (*Adapted from Moore, 1977.*)

period when it is most sensitive to teratogenic agents—namely, the time when that particular part of the body is evolving and taking shape. As we see in Figure 4-2, the most sensitive period for gross physical defects of the head and central nervous system is the third through the fifth prenatal weeks. The heart is particularly vulnerable from the middle of the third through the middle of the sixth prenatal week; the most sensitive period for many other organs and body parts is the second prenatal month. Is it any wonder, then, that the period of the embryo—when the body and organs are rapidly forming—is often called the critical (or sensitive) phase of pregnancy?

Once an organ or body part is fully formed, it becomes somewhat less susceptible to the influence of most teratogens. However, this does not mean that the structure in question is now invulnerable. Recently, Olli Heinonen and his associates (Heinonen, Slone, & Shapiro, 1977) concluded that many of the birth defects found among the 50,282 children in their sample were *anytime malformations*—problems that could have been caused by teratogens at any point during the nine-month prenatal period. Among the more common of these "anytime malformations" were defects of the central nervous system, such as microcephaly (an unusually small head often associated with mental retardation), dislocations of the hip, hernias, genital abnormalities, cataracts, and benign tumors.

We will now consider some of the more common diseases, drugs, chemicals, and other environmental teratogens that can disrupt prenatal development and produce serious birth defects.

Maternal diseases

Until the early 1940s, it was assumed that the placenta was a marvelous screening device that prevented viruses and other infectious agents from reaching the developing embryo or fetus. Today we know that this is false. Many disease agents are capable of crossing the placental barrier and doing much more damage to a developing embryo or fetus than to the mother herself. This makes sense when we remember that an unborn child has an immature immune system that cannot produce enough antibodies to effectively combat most toxins and disease agents.

Rubella. The medical community became aware of the teratogenic effect of diseases in 1941 when an Australian physician, McAllister Gregg, noticed that many mothers who had had **rubella (German measles)** early in pregnancy were delivering babies who were congenitally blind. After Gregg alerted the medical community, doctors began to notice that pregnant rubella patients were regularly bearing children with a variety of defects, including blindness, deafness, cardiac abnormalities, and mental retardation. Rubella is most dangerous during the first trimester. Studies have shown that 50–80% of babies whose mothers had rubella in the first month will have birth defects, compared with about 25% of those infected in the second month and 6% of those infected in the third month (Fuhrmann & Vogel, 1976). Rubella is less teratogenic in the fourth prenatal month, although unborn children infected at this time may later show some speech or hearing difficulties and slight mental retardation (Browne & Dixon, 1978). Today doctors stress that no woman should try to become pregnant unless she has been immunized against rubella or has already had the disease. Ideally, women should wait two to three months after a rubella vaccination before becoming pregnant, for the vaccine (which contains a weakened form of the rubella virus) is itself a teratogen that may harm an unborn child.

Other infectious diseases. Many diseases other than rubella are known teratogens (see Table 4-2 for several examples). One of the more common of these diseases, congenital **syphilis,** is most harmful in the middle and later stages of pregnancy, since syphilitic spirochetes (the microscopic organisms that transmit the disease) cannot cross the placental barrier until the 18th prenatal week. This is fortunate in one sense, for the disease can be diagnosed with a blood test and treated with antibiotics long before it could harm the fetus. However, the mother who receives no treatment runs the risk of miscarrying or of giving birth to a child who has serious eye, ear, bone, or brain damage (Miller, 1976; see also Table 4-2).

Genital herpes (herpes simplex) is another common sexually transmitted disease that is a powerful teratogen. Although the herpes virus may cross the placental barrier, most infections occur at birth as the newborn comes in contact with lesions on the mother's genitals (Hanshaw, Dudgeon, & Marshall, 1985). Unfortunately, there is no cure for this disease, which will kill about one-third of all infected neonates and cause such disabilities as blindness, permanent brain damage, or other serious neurological disorders in another 25–35%. Mothers with active herpes infections are now routinely advised to undergo a **Caesarean delivery** (a surgical procedure in which the baby is delivered through an incision in the mother's abdomen) to avoid infecting their babies.

Also of growing concern is the increasing incidence of the fatal and incurable condition known as **acquired immune deficiency syndrome (AIDS).** Though apparently caused by a virus, AIDS is difficult to transmit, seemingly requiring an exchange of bodily

---

rubella (German measles): a disease that has little effect on a mother but may cause a number of serious birth defects in unborn children who are exposed in the first 3–4 months of pregnancy.

syphilis: a common venereal disease that may cross the placental barrier in the middle and later stages of pregnancy, causing miscarriage or serious birth defects.

genital herpes: a sexually transmitted disease that can infect infants at birth, causing blindness, brain damage, or even death.

Caesarean section: surgical delivery of a baby through an incision made in the mother's abdomen and uterus.

acquired immune deficiency syndrome (AIDS): a viral disease that can be transmitted from a mother to her infant at birth and that results in a weakening of the body's immune system and, ultimately, death.

Table 4-2. Some diseases that may affect an embryo, fetus, or newborn

Sexually transmitted diseases	Description and effects
Acquired immune deficiency syndrome (AIDS)	Although AIDS is listed as a sexually transmitted disease, many mothers who transmit it to their offspring have acquired it from transfusions of contaminated blood or from their use of contaminated syringes while taking drugs. Babies born with AIDS have deficient or nonoperative immune systems and, thus, little protection against any infectious disease. The vast majority will die early in life (see text).
Gonorrhea	Major hazard is that the gonococcus organism may attack the eyes of a child passing through an infected birth canal. Infections are treated with silver nitrate eyedrops immediately after birth. If left untreated, gonorrhea can blind the child within two days.
Herpes simplex (genital herpes)	See text.
Syphilis	Untreated syphilis may cause miscarriage or several serious birth defects (see text). Occasionally babies of untreated mothers are born without showing any syphilitic symptoms. If this "latent" syphilis is not detected and treated, it will produce severe consequences 5–15 years later. The most common problems include blindness, deterioration of the central nervous system, and congestive heart failure. The vast majority of children who have long-term (tertiary) syphilis will die from its complications.

Other maternal conditions or diseases	Effects on the fetus or newborn
Chicken pox	Does not produce fetal malformations but may lead to spontaneous abortion or premature delivery. A premature infant who has chicken pox is usually very weak and likely to die.
Cholera	Interferes with the transfer of oxygen from mother to fetus. Infection during the third trimester is likely to kill the fetus, resulting in a stillbirth.
Cytomegalovirus	Produces no symptoms in adults but may produce microcephaly (small head), brain damage, and blindness in the embryo or fetus; may induce miscarriages.
Diabetes	Diabetics face a greater risk of delivering a stillborn fetus or a child who will die in the first few days after birth. Babies of diabetics may have any of a number of malformations. They are often very large because they have accumulated a large amount of fat during the third trimester. Although a diabetic mother requires special care to prevent the death of her child, more than 85% of these children currently survive.
Hepatitis	A child born to a mother with hepatitis is likely to have this disease. The infection is thought to occur during the birth process when the fetus swallows infected maternal blood that may be present as the umbilical cord separates from the placenta.

continued

Other maternal conditions or diseases	Effects on the fetus or newborn
Hypertension (chronic high blood pressure)	Increases the probability of miscarriages and infant death. The higher a woman's blood pressure, the greater the likelihood of prenatal complications.
Influenza	The more powerful strains can induce spontaneous abortion or produce a number of abnormalities during the early stages of pregnancy.
Mumps	Although this is a relatively mild disease, even in adults, perhaps as many as 27% of affected fetuses will die within the womb and be spontaneously aborted or stillborn.
Rh disease	An incompatibility between "Rh positive" fetuses, who have a protein called Rh factor in their blood, and "Rh negative" mothers, who lack this substance. During labor and delivery when they are exposed to the fetus's Rh-positive blood, Rh-negative mothers produce Rh antibodies—substances that may cross the deteriorating placental barrier and attack the fetus's red blood cells, resulting in *erythroblastosis* (Rh disease). This complication can produce serious birth defects and even death. First-borns are usually not affected because the Rh-negative mother has no Rh antibodies until giving birth to a first Rh-positive child. Rh disease can be controlled by administering *Rhogam* after the delivery—a drug that prevents the mother from forming the Rh antibodies that could harm her next Rh-positive child.
Rubella	See text.
Smallpox	This disease is particularly troublesome because the mother's immunity (by vaccination) does nothing to protect her embryo or fetus. Smallpox does not induce malformations but does increase the risk of spontaneous abortion and stillbirth.
Toxemia (eclampsia)	Toxemia of pregnancy is a disorder of unknown origin that affects about 5% of pregnant women in the United States during the third trimester. Its mildest form, called *preeclampsia,* mainly affects the mother and includes symptoms such as high blood pressure, rapid weight gain, and protein in the urine. Untreated preeclampsia may worsen and become *eclampsia,* a condition that may cause maternal convulsions and coma. About half the unborn children and 10–15% of affected mothers will die from eclampsia; surviving infants are likely to suffer brain damage.
Toxoplasmosis	About one-fourth of adults have had this mild disease, which produces symptoms similar to a common cold. The agent responsible is a parasite present in raw meat and cat feces. If a medical exam reveals that a woman has no antibodies against toxoplasmosis, she should avoid undercooked meat and locations where cat feces are likely to be present (for example, garden, pet's litter box) during her pregnancy. Toxoplasmosis can produce serious eye or brain damage and possibly even kill an unborn child.

fluids between donor and recipient. Thus, the current thinking is that prenatal transmission of AIDS from mother to infant usually occurs during the birth process, when the umbilical cord separates from the placenta, allowing an exchange of blood between mother and infant (Mott, Fazekas, & James, 1985). Studies in Africa and the United States reveal that about 50% of babies whose mothers have AIDS will themselves be born with the disease, and 95% of these infected infants will die within the first three years (Seabrook, 1987). At present, there is nothing that can be done to treat AIDS babies except to make life as comfortable as possible for them and to do what one can to limit their exposure to the many diseases that their immune systems cannot resist.

Drugs

People have long suspected that drugs taken by pregnant women could have any number of harmful effects on unborn children. Even Aristotle thought as much when he noted that many drunken mothers have feeble-minded babies (Abel, 1981). Today we know that these suspicions were often correct. Consider what Virginia Apgar has to say about drug use during pregnancy: "A woman who is pregnant, or thinks she could possibly be pregnant, should not take any drugs whatsoever unless absolutely essential—and then only when prescribed by a physician who is aware of the pregnancy" (Apgar & Beck, 1974, p. 445). Dr. Apgar is very cautious in her recommendation because even mild drugs that have few if any lasting effects on a mother may prove extremely hazardous to a developing embryo or fetus. Unfortunately, the medical community learned this lesson the hard way, as we will see in the pages that follow.

The thalidomide tragedy. In 1960 a West German drug company began to market a mild tranquilizer, sold over the counter, that was said to alleviate the periodic nausea (morning sickness) that many women experience during the first trimester of pregnancy. Presumably, the drug was perfectly safe; in tests on pregnant rats it had had no ill effects on mothers or offspring. The drug was **thalidomide.**

What came to pass quickly illustrated that drugs that appear harmless in tests with laboratory animals may turn out to be violent teratogens for human beings. Thousands of women who had used thalidomide during the first two months of pregnancy were suddenly giving birth to defective children. And the birth defects were horrible: thalidomide babies often had badly deformed

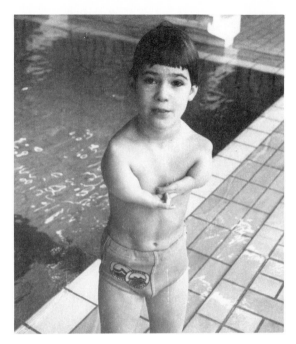

Photo 4-6. This boy has deformed arms and hands—two of the birth defects produced by thalidomide.

eyes, ears, noses, and hearts and a variety of lesser malformations, such as fusing of the fingers and toes. But perhaps the most striking of all birth defects produced by this powerful teratogen was **phocomelia**—a structural abnormality in which all or parts of the limbs are missing and the feet or hands may be attached directly to the torso like flippers.

Doctors soon discovered that the kinds of birth defects produced by thalidomide depended on when the drug was taken. Babies of mothers who had taken the drug on or around the 35th day after their last menstrual period were likely to be born without ears. Those whose mothers had used thalidomide on the 39th through the 41st day after last menstruation often had grossly deformed arms or no arms at all. If the mother had taken the drug between the 40th and the 46th day, her child might have deformed legs or no legs. However, if she had waited until the 52nd day before using thalidomide, her baby was usually not affected (Apgar & Beck, 1974).

So it took a major tragedy to establish that seemingly harmless prescription and nonprescription drugs could be powerful teratogens. Table 4-3 lists a number of commonly used medications and other substances that are either known or suspected causes of birth defects in human beings.

Sex hormones. In recent years it has become apparent that medications containing sex hormones (or their active biochemical ingredients) can affect a developing embryo or fetus. For example, oral contraceptives contain female sex hormones, and if a woman takes the pill, not knowing that she is pregnant, her unborn child faces a slightly increased risk of heart defects and other cardiovascular problems (Heinonen et al., 1977; Schardein, 1985).

One synthetic hormone that can have a tragic long-term effect on daughters is **diethylstilbestrol (DES).** From the mid-1940s through 1965, as many as 2 million women may have taken this drug to prevent miscarriages. The drug seemed safe enough—newborns whose mothers had used DES appeared to be normal in every respect. But in 1971 physicians clearly established that 17- to 21-year-old females whose mothers had used DES while pregnant were at risk for developing several abnormalities of the reproductive organs, including a rare form of cervical cancer (Hamm, 1981). Women who develop these cancerous lesions often find it difficult to conceive; and when they do, they are more likely than nonaffected mothers to miscarry or to deliver prematurely (Schardein, 1985). Clearly, the risk of cancer is not very great—fewer than 1% of DES daughters have developed the disease thus far. However, the oldest women who were exposed to DES before birth are now only 45, and we do not yet know whether they will develop cancer or other problems later in life.

Although it appears that prenatal exposure to DES does not cause cancer in males, a number of DES sons have developed abnormalities of the genital tract, and some of these men are sterile (Schardein, 1985). The U.S. Department of Health and Human Services now recommends a visit to the doctor for all individuals (male or female) who know that they were exposed to DES before birth. The affected patient should describe what is known about his or her exposure and ask the physician to record this information for future reference and consideration (Hamm, 1981).

Alcohol. In 1973 Kenneth Jones and his colleagues described a **fetal alcohol syndrome (FAS)** that affects many children of alcoholic mothers (Jones, Smith, Ulleland, & Streissguth, 1973). The most noticeable characteristics of fetal alcohol syndrome are defects

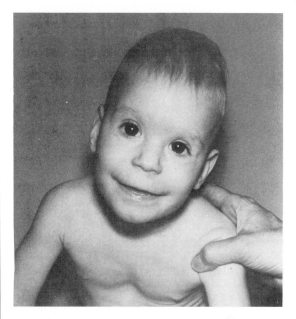

Photo 4-7. This boy's widely spaced eyes, flattened nose, and underdeveloped upper lip are three of the common physical symptoms of fetal alcohol syndrome.

such as microcephaly (small head) and malformations of the heart, limbs, joints, and face. An affected baby is likely to exhibit abnormal behaviors such as excessive irritability, hyperactivity, seizures, and tremors. At birth FAS children are smaller and lighter than normal, and their physical growth will lag behind that of normal age mates throughout childhood and adolescence. Moreover, the majority of these children score well below average in intelligence, and many are mentally retarded (Abel, 1984; Streissguth, Herman, & Smith, 1978).

---

thalidomide: a mild tranquilizer that, taken early in pregnancy, can produce a variety of malformations of the limbs, eyes, ears, and heart.

phocomelia: a prenatal malformation in which all or parts of the limbs are missing.

diethylstilbestrol (DES): a synthetic hormone, formerly prescribed to prevent miscarriage, that can produce cervical cancer in adolescent female offspring and genital-tract abnormalities (and sterility) in males.

fetal alcohol syndrome (FAS): a group of congenital problems commonly observed in the offspring of mothers who abuse alcohol during pregnancy.

Table 4-3. Partial list of drugs and treatments that affect (or are thought to affect) the fetus or the newborn

Drug	Effect
Antibiotics 　Streptomycin 　Terramycin 　Tetracycline	Heavy use of streptomycin by mothers can produce hearing loss. Terramycin and tetracycline may be associated with premature delivery, retarded skeletal growth, cataracts, and staining of the baby's teeth.
Anticoagulants	Heavy doses increase the risk of fetal hemorrhage or death.
Anticancer agents 　Amniopterin 　Amethopterin	A number of congenital anomalies have been reported.
Alcohol	Small head, facial abnormalities, heart defects, low birth weight, and mental retardation (see text).
Aspirin and other salicylates	Used in large quantities, may cause neonatal bleeding and gastrointestinal discomfort (other defects have been reported in studies with animals).
Anticonvulsants	May produce heart defects and anomalies such as cleft lip (failure of the two sides of the upper lip to grow together).
Barbiturates	All barbiturates cross the placental barrier. In clinical doses they cause the fetus or newborn to be lethargic. In large doses they may cause anoxia (oxygen starvation) or interfere with the baby's breathing.
Hallucinogens 　LSD 　Marijuana 　Mescaline	Suspected to cause chromosome damage, spontaneous abortion, and behavioral abnormalities among newborn infants (see text).
Narcotics 　Cocaine 　Codeine 　Heroin 　Methadone 　Morphine	Addiction increases the risk of premature delivery. Moreover, the fetus is often addicted to the narcotic agent, and this addiction results in a number of complications. Heavy cocaine use can seriously elevate fetal blood pressure and even induce strokes (see text).
Sex hormones 　Androgens, 　progestogens, estrogens, 　DES (diethylstilbestrol)	Sex hormones contained in birth control pills and drugs to prevent miscarriages can have a number of harmful effects, including heart malformations, cervical cancer (in female offspring), masculinization of the fetus, and other anomalies (see text).
Tranquilizers (other than thalidomide) 　Chlorpromazine 　Reserpine	May produce respiratory distress in newborns.
Tobacco	Cigarette smoking may increase the risk of spontaneous abortion, stillbirth, and infant mortality. Smokers also tend to have small babies (see text).
Vaccines	Routine immunization of the mother with live-virus vaccines should be avoided during pregnancy, except when required for rabies and cholera. The viruses in many vaccines (for example, mumps, measles, rubella, smallpox, polio) are powerful teratogens that are likely to harm the developing embryo or fetus.
Vitamins	Excessive amounts of vitamin A can cause cleft palate, malformed hearts, and other serious birth defects. The popular anti-acne drug Accutane, derived from vitamin A, is one of the most powerful of all known teratogens. Excessive doses of vitamins B_6, C, D, and K cause prenatal deformities in many animal species and could conceivably have similar effects on human beings.

How much alcohol does it take to harm an embryo or fetus? Perhaps a lot less than you might imagine. True, the symptoms of FAS are most severe when mothers are alcoholics. Yet even moderate alcohol consumption (that is, 1–3 ounces a day) by expectant mothers can retard prenatal growth and produce minor physical anomalies or abnormal behavior in newborns (Abel, 1980; Streissguth, Barr, & Martin, 1983). Today many doctors are so wary of the potentially harmful consequences of alcohol that they advise pregnant women not to drink at all (Schardein, 1985).

Tobacco. Until recently, neither doctors nor pregnant women had any reason to suspect that an after-dinner cigarette might affect an unborn child. Now we know otherwise. A recent report of the Surgeon General of the United States reviewed more than 200 studies and concluded:

> Maternal smoking directly retards the rate of fetal growth and increases the risk of spontaneous abortion, of fetal death, and of neonatal death in otherwise normal infants. More important, there is growing evidence that children of smoking mothers [particularly mothers who smoke heavily] *may* have measurable deficiencies in physical growth, intellectual development, and emotional development [U.S. Department of Health, Education and Welfare, 1979, p. ix].

Some researchers have reported that children of smokers show long-term deficits in physical growth and are more likely than children of nonsmokers to experience learning difficulties at school (see Butler & Goldstein, 1973; U.S. Department of Health, Education and Welfare, 1979). Yet, it is possible that some factor common to women who smoke other than smoking itself is responsible for these long-term effects. For example, if women who smoke have poorer diets or drink more alcohol than nonsmokers, their dietary inadequacies or alcohol consumption could be responsible for long-term consequences that researchers may have erroneously attributed to smoking.

In one recent study, Monroe Lefkowitz (1981) looked at the long-term effects of maternal smoking on 9–11-year-olds. This study was carefully controlled in that mothers who had smoked during pregnancy were comparable to those who did not smoke in age, education, income, and family size—factors known to affect physical growth and intellectual development. Data available on each child in the sample included measures of height, weight, reading ability, classroom achieve-

ments, IQ, popularity, and conduct at school. The findings were clear: 9 to 11 years after birth, the children of smokers were no smaller, no less intelligent, and no less achievement-oriented, nor were they less well behaved or popular, than the children of nonsmokers.

So the *long-term* effects of maternal smoking on the developing child are unclear at this time. Nevertheless, we do know that smoking during pregnancy can and often does retard fetal growth and will increase the risk of spontaneous abortion and neonatal death (not to mention, of course, the harmful long-term effects this habit could have on the mother herself). For these reasons, physicians today routinely advise pregnant women to stop smoking—if not forever, at least for the duration of their pregnancies.

Hallucinogens. In view of their popularity as recreational drugs, it is indeed unfortunate that we do not know more about the possible teratogenic effects of marijuana, LSD, mescaline, and other psychoactive agents. Although the evidence is not conclusive, some researchers believe that heavy use of marijuana by pregnant women can inhibit prenatal growth and produce behavioral abnormalities in newborn infants (Fried, 1980; Tinklenberg, 1975). Research on the teratogenic effects of LSD are also inconclusive: Some studies have found that women who used LSD before or during pregnancy faced an increased risk of miscarriage, stillbirth, or having babies with a variety of congenital defects, including chromosomal abnormalities (see Schardein, 1985). However, it is difficult to tell whether LSD was responsible for these complications, because the LSD users in these studies were frequently sick, undernourished, or using other known or suspected teratogens (such as alcohol and narcotic agents).

Narcotics. Although addicting agents such as codeine, heroin, methadone, and morphine do not appear to produce gross structural abnormalities, women who use these drugs are more likely than nonusers to miscarry or to deliver stillborn infants (Schardein, 1985). Moreover, the babies of narcotics addicts become addicted in the womb, and about 50% of these children are undersized (Brown, 1979). When deprived of the drug after birth, the addicted infant will experience withdrawal symptoms such as vomiting, dehydration, and convulsions that could prove fatal if not controlled. These unfortunate young addicts will normally continue to receive the addicting agent, but in progressively smaller doses. This treatment prevents severe withdrawal symptoms and allows the child to gradually overcome the addiction.

Methadone is a synthetic opiate often prescribed for addicts as an alternative to heroin. Babies born addicted to this drug are about five times as likely as nonaddicted infants to fall victim to *sudden infant death syndrome (SIDS)*, a complication in which apparently healthy infants suddenly stop breathing and die in their sleep (Chavez, Ostrea, Stryker, & Smialek, 1979).

What are the effects of today's most popular addicting drug, cocaine? Preliminary data reveal that mothers who regularly use this substance are at risk for miscarriage or premature delivery and that their babies tend to be smaller than normal, very irritable, and susceptible to serious respiratory problems (Bartol, 1986; Weiss & Mirin, 1987). Moreover, the mother's use of cocaine can induce hypertension (high blood pressure) in herself and her fetus, and cases have been reported in which unborn fetuses of cocaine-using mothers have died of strokes (Thomas, 1986). Although mothers who use cocaine are often poorly nourished and may be taking other harmful drugs, the problems seen in cocaine babies are very consistent across studies, implying that this drug is a powerful teratogen.

Finally, the behavior of babies addicted to narcotic agents is abnormal in several respects. These infants tend to be sluggish, irritable, and inattentive to the environment. In addition, they cry more often than nonaddicted infants and are less likely to cuddle when a caretaker picks them up (Strauss, Lessen-Firestone, Starr, & Ostrea, 1975). Unfortunately, these unpleasant temperamental characteristics can interfere with the emotional bonding that normally occurs between infant and parents and thus may impair the child's later social and emotional development.

Environmental hazards

Radiation. Soon after the atomic blasts of 1945 in Hiroshima and Nagasaki, scientists became painfully aware of the teratogenic effects of radiation. Not one pregnant woman who was within one-half mile of these explosions gave birth to a live child. In addition, 75% of the pregnant women who were within a mile and a quarter of the blasts had stillborn infants or seriously handicapped children who died soon after birth (Apgar & Beck, 1974). Even clinical doses of radiation such as those used in diagnostic X rays and cancer treatments can cause mutations, spontaneous abortions, or a variety of serious birth defects—particularly if the mother is exposed during the first trimester of pregnancy.

Unfortunately, no one knows just how much radiation it takes to harm an embryo or a fetus. Today expectant mothers are routinely advised to avoid exposure to X rays unless such treatment is absolutely necessary for their own survival (in these cases, it is assumed that the unborn child may be miscarried, stillborn, or seriously handicapped at birth). So serious are the potential complications of radiation exposure that Apgar and Beck (1974) advise women of childbearing age to avoid all X rays of the pelvis and abdomen except "during the first two weeks following a menstrual period, so that there is no possibility [they] could be pregnant without realizing it" (p. 110).

Chemicals and pollutants. Pregnant women routinely come in contact with potentially toxic substances in their everyday environments, including organic dyes and coloring agents, food additives, artificial sweeteners, pesticides, and cosmetic products, some of which are known to have teratogenic effects in animals (Miller, 1976; Streitfeld, 1978). Unfortunately, the risks associated with a large number of these common chemical additives and treatments remain to be determined.

Then there are the pollutants in the air we breathe and the water we drink. For example, pregnant women may be exposed to concentrations of lead, zinc, mercury, or antimony discharged into the air or water by industrial operations or present in paint and water pipes. These "heavy metals" are known to impair the physical health and mental abilities of adults and children and to have teratogenic effects (producing physical deformities and mental retardation) on developing embryos and fetuses (Miller, 1976; Rutter, 1980). Polluting chemicals called *PCBs (polychlorinated biphenyls)*, now outlawed but once widely used in plastics, carbon paper, and many other products, represent another hazard. PCBs are very stable (nonbiodegradable) compounds that concentrate in the fatty tissue of exposed organisms. Recently, Joseph Jacobson and his colleagues found that even low-level exposure to PCBs, resulting from mothers' eating of contaminated fish from Lake Michigan, was enough to make newborns smaller on average and less responsive and neurologically mature than babies whose mothers did not eat polluted fish (Jacobson, Jacobson, Fein, Schwartz, & Dowler, 1984). And seven months after birth, infants exposed to PCBs *in utero* continued to lag behind their nonexposed age mates on tests of recognition memory and information processing (Jacobson, Fein, Jacobson, Schwartz, & Dowler, 1985).

Box 4-2
How to Prevent Birth Defects:
A Checklist for Prospective Parents

In their excellent book *Is My Baby All Right?* (1974), Dr. Virginia Apgar and Joan Beck suggest several ways that prospective parents can significantly reduce the likelihood of bearing a defective child. As you read through the list, see whether you can recall why each recommendation makes good sense. In so doing, you will have reviewed much of the material on congenital defects presented in this chapter (as well as Chapter 3).

1. *If you think a close relative has a disorder that might be hereditary, you should take advantage of genetic counseling.* (Do you remember what kinds of services a genetic counselor may offer or suggest? If not, you may wish to review "Prevention and Treatment of Hereditary Abnormalities" in Chapter 3.)

2. *The ideal age for a woman to have children is between 18 and 35.* (What complications do older and younger mothers face?)

3. *Every pregnant woman needs good prenatal care supervised by a medical practitioner who keeps current on medical research in the field of tera-* tology *and who will help her deliver her baby in a reputable, modern hospital.* (We have not yet examined the birth process and its complications. When we review the pros and cons of "home births," we will see that not everyone agrees that a woman should always give birth in a hospital.)

4. *No woman should become pregnant unless she is sure that she has either had rubella or been effectively immunized against it.* (What defects can rubella cause? When during pregnancy is the disease particularly dangerous?)

5. *From the very beginning of pregnancy, a woman should do everything possible to avoid exposure to contagious diseases.* (Do you remember the teratogenic effects of congenital syphilis, gonorrhea, herpes, and other infectious agents? If not, you may wish to review Table 4-2 and the section of this chapter entitled "Maternal Diseases.")

6. *Pregnant women should avoid eating undercooked red meat or contact with any cat (or cat feces) that may carry toxoplasmosis infection.* (What are the possible consequences of toxoplasmosis for the mother? For her unborn child?)

7. *A pregnant woman should not take any drugs unless absolutely essential—and then only when prescribed* by a physician who is aware of the pregnancy. (Do you remember the effects of DES, alcohol, the hallucinogens, narcotics, and other commonly used substances? If not, you may wish to review Table 4-3 and the section of this chapter entitled "Drugs.")

8. *Unless it is absolutely essential for her own well-being, a pregnant woman should avoid radiation treatments and X-ray examinations.* (What are the possible consequences of such examinations or treatments for the unborn child? How did scientists become aware of the teratogenic effects of radiation?)

9. *Cigarettes should not be smoked during pregnancy.* (Why not? Does a mother's cigarette smoking during pregnancy have long-term effects on her children?)

10. *A prospective mother who is Rh-negative should make sure her physician takes the necessary steps to protect her unborn baby and all subsequent children from Rh disease.* (How are subsequent children protected?)

11. *A nourishing diet, rich in proteins and adequate in total calories, is essential during pregnancy.* (What are the possible effects of maternal malnutrition on the developing child? Should a pregnant woman take large amounts of extra vitamins in order to ensure that her baby will be healthy?)

Even a father's exposure to environmental toxins can affect the outcome of a pregnancy. Studies of male doctors and dentists reveal that prolonged exposure to radiation, anesthetic gases, and other toxic substances can damage a father's chromosomes and increase the likelihood of genetic defects and/or spontaneous abortions by his wife (Gunderson & Sackett, 1982).

Unfortunately, what we know about the teratogenic effects of common chemicals and pollutants may represent the tip of an iceberg, and there is a critical need for additional research on these and other potentially hazardous influences on prenatal development.

On the Prevention of Birth Defects

Reading a chapter such as this one can be frightening to anyone who wishes to have a child. It is easy to come away with the impression that "life before birth" is a veritable minefield: after all, so many hereditary accidents are possible, and even a genetically normal embryo or fetus may encounter a large number of potential hazards while developing within the womb.

But clearly there is another side to this story. Recall that the majority of genetically abnormal embryos do not develop to term. And it appears that the prenatal environment is not so hazardous when we note that more than 90% of newborn babies are perfectly normal and that many of the remaining 7–10% have minor congenital problems that are only temporary or correctable (Heinonen et al., 1977). It is true that there *is* reason for concern. However, concerned parents can significantly reduce the odds that their baby will be abnormal if they follow the simple recommendations in Box 4-2. Failure to abide by one or more of the guidelines will not necessarily mean that your child will be defective. Nor will exact compliance guarantee that the child will be healthy—accidents do happen. Following these recommendations may seem rather tedious at times and perhaps unnecessary to women who have already given birth to healthy children. However, Apgar and Beck (1974, p. 452) remind us that "each pregnancy is different. Each unborn child has a unique genetic make-up. The prenatal environment a mother provides is never quite the same for another baby. Thus, we believe no amount of effort is too great to increase the chances that a baby will be born normal, healthy, and without a handicapping birth defect."

Birth and the Perinatal Environment

The **perinatal environment** is the environment surrounding birth; it includes influences such as drugs given to the mother during delivery, practices used in the delivery, and the social environment shortly after the baby is born. As we will see, this perinatal environment is an important one that can affect a baby's well-being and the course of her future development.

The birth of a child is a dramatic and emotional event for all parties involved. During the last few weeks of pregnancy, it is natural for parents to be apprehensive about labor and childbirth, particularly if this is their first child. In fact, it is not at all uncommon for first-time mothers to fear that they will be "out of control" in the delivery room, thinking that they may be damaged or disfigured by the delivery (Grossman, Eichler, Winickoff, & Associates, 1980). Once the child is born, mothers (and fathers if present) almost always report feeling physically exhausted and relieved that the negative aspects of labor and delivery are things of the past. As they hold their newborn baby, many parents seem awestruck by the realization that *they* have actually created life.

Now let's consider the baby. In its waning hours as a fetus, a relatively carefree existence is coming to an end. Suddenly, a force stronger than the fetus is thrusting it from its comfortable lie within the uterus through a passageway that is smaller and tighter than anything it has ever experienced. After several hours of this, the child emerges into the light, draws a breath, and takes up residence in a strange new world.

Do you think babies are traumatized by the events of birth? Or are they "numb," indifferent, or awestruck? Think about this issue as we take a look at the normal birth and the typical reactions of parents to this event.

The Normal Birth

Childbirth is a three-stage process (see Figure 4-3). The **first stage of labor** begins as the mother experiences uterine contractions spaced at 10–15-minute intervals, and it ends when her cervix has fully dilated so that the fetus's head can pass through. This phase lasts an average of 8–14 hours for first-born children and 3–8 hours for later-borns. As labor proceeds, the uterus contracts more frequently and the contractions become more intense. When the head of the fetus is positioned at the cervical opening, the second phase of labor is about to begin.

The **second stage of labor,** delivery, begins as the fetus's head passes through the cervix into the vagina and ends when the baby emerges from the mother's body. This is the time when the mother may be told to bear down (push) with each contraction to assist her child through the birth canal. A quick delivery may take a half hour, whereas a long one may last more than an hour and a half.

The **third stage of labor** takes only a few minutes as the uterus once again contracts and expels the placenta from the mother's body.

The parents' experience

Although many women are exhilarated by the product of their labor, few enjoy the process; childbirth is an exhausting ordeal that can be rather painful. Obviously, physical factors such as the relative size of the mother's pelvis and the baby's head will affect the length of labor and the amount of discomfort a woman experiences. However, psychological factors such as the mother's attitude toward her pregnancy, her knowledge about the birth process, and even the presence of the father are important determinants of her reactions to childbirth.

In many Western societies, expectant mothers are advised to prepare for their day in the delivery room by attending childbirth classes. Almost all these classes inform the mother (and, ideally, her mate) what to expect during labor. They also teach breathing patterns and methods of relaxation that are thought to make the process of giving birth a little easier. The childbirth class may also give a woman the impression that she has the

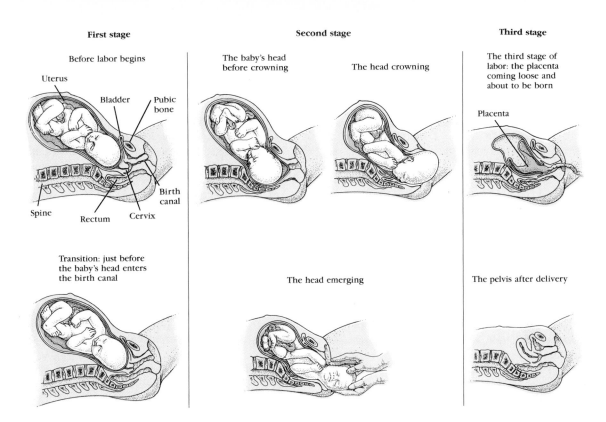

First stage

Before labor begins

Uterus
Bladder
Pubic bone
Birth canal
Spine
Rectum
Cervix

Transition: just before the baby's head enters the birth canal

Second stage

The baby's head before crowning

The head crowning

The head emerging

Third stage

The third stage of labor: the placenta coming loose and about to be born

Placenta

The pelvis after delivery

Figure 4-3. The three stages of childbirth.

support of others and will not be undertaking the rigors of childbirth on her own. Apparently this prenatal training does affect the mother's experience: women who regularly attend childbirth classes are more relaxed during labor and view the process as "easier" than those who do not receive instruction (Klusman, 1975; Wideman & Singer, 1984).

Effects of father's involvement. The father's participation is also important. When fathers (or other close companions) are present in the delivery room, women have shorter labors, experience less pain, use less medication, and feel much more positive about themselves, their families, and the childbirth process (Grossman et al., 1980; Henneborn & Cogan, 1975; Sosa, Kennell, Klaus, Robertson, & Urrutia, 1980). In addition, a father himself may benefit from his presence in the delivery room, for he, like the mother, will often display a sense of **engrossment** with the baby—an intense fascination with and a strong desire to touch, hold, and

caress this newest member of the family (Greenberg & Morris, 1974; Peterson, Mehl, & Liederman, 1979). One young father put it this way: "When I came up to see [my] wife . . . I go look at the kid and then I pick her up

perinatal environment: the environment surrounding birth, including influences such as childbirth medication, obstetrical practices, and the social stimulation a baby may receive.

first stage of labor: the period of the birth process lasting from the first regular uterine contractions until the cervix is fully dilated.

second stage of labor: the period of the birth process during which the fetus moves through the vaginal canal and emerges from the mother's body (also called the delivery).

third stage of labor: expulsion of the placenta (afterbirth).

engrossment: parents' fascination with their neonate; a desire to touch, hold, caress, and talk to the newborn baby.

and put her down . . . I keep going back to the kid. It's like a magnet. That's what I can't get over, the fact that I feel like that" (Greenberg & Morris, 1974, p. 524). Some studies find that fathers who have handled and helped care for their babies in the hospital later spend more time with them at home than other fathers who have not had these early interactions with their newborns (Greenberg & Morris, 1974). Other studies have failed to find these long-term effects on father/infant interactions but suggest that early contact with a newborn can make fathers feel closer to their wives and more a part of the "family" (Palkowitz, 1985). So a father who is present at birth may not only play an important supportive role for his wife, but is just as likely as the mother to enjoy close contact with their neonate.

Natural childbirth. Some obstetricians believe that childbirth is a perfectly natural process that should cause little if any discomfort to women who are both physically and psychologically prepared for it. The **natural childbirth** movement arose from the work of Grantly Dick-Read, in England, and Fernand Lamaze, in France. These two obstetricians were surprised to find that many women were giving birth painlessly, without medication, if they had been taught to associate childbirth with pleasant feelings and to ready themselves for the process by learning exercises, breathing methods, and relaxation techniques that we now know make childbirth easier (Dick-Read, 1933/1972; Lamaze, 1958). In recent years many women have opted for natural childbirth as scientists began to report that the painkilling drugs often given during labor could have adverse effects on a baby.

Couples who decide on a natural childbirth will typically attend classes for 8 to 12 weeks before the delivery. They will learn a set of prescribed exercises and relaxation techniques, and the father will become a coach who assists the mother to train her muscles and perfect her breathing for the event that lies ahead. The couple may also visit a delivery room and become familiar with the procedures used there so that they will be less apprehensive when the big day arrives. Although natural childbirth classes do make the childbirth process easier for couples who diligently apply themselves to the training, many women will still experience discomfort during labor—particularly those who have small pelvic openings or who are delivering large babies. Today most obstetricians tell their natural childbirth patients that they should not hesitate to authorize a physician's assistance (including anesthesia) if they are

experiencing a lot of pain. A natural childbirth patient who must resort to drugs to ease her discomfort should not feel discouraged, for her prior training may have enabled her to use smaller doses of these potentially harmful substances than she would otherwise have needed (Wideman & Singer, 1984).

Postpartum depression. There is a "down side" to the birth experience for some mothers, who may find themselves depressed, irritable, easily upset, and possibly even resentful of their babies within 3–10 days after the delivery. Most women overcome whatever **postpartum depression** they may be feeling within days or weeks, but as many as 10–15% display clinical signs of hopelessness or despair that may last for months. Surprisingly, mothers of healthy infants are just as likely to experience postpartum depression as mothers whose babies died or were abnormal (Dalton, 1980).

Any of several factors may contribute to the "baby blues." Analgesic and sedative drugs taken during childbirth are known to have a depressive effect on mood. A young mother may also feel depressed and resentful because friends and family are showering the baby with attention while ignoring her own emotional needs. Endocrinologists have suggested that postpartum depression may be a psychological reaction to hormonal changes that occur as the mother's body returns from the pregnant state to a normal menstrual cycle (Dalton, 1980). Finally, it seems that the mothers who are most likely to experience long-term depression following the birth of their babies are those who had expressed very negative feelings about their marriages or their pregnancies during the third trimester of pregnancy (Field et al., 1985). Whatever the cause, it appears that a victim of the baby blues needs the support and attention of close companions during this difficult time. Katharina Dalton (1980) finds that women who are encouraged to discuss their negative feelings freely with a sympathetic listener are often successful at overcoming them. In England, the Meet-A-Mum-Association (MAMA) has been established to provide depressed young mothers with precisely this kind of emotional support and encouragement.

The baby's experience

Is birth an unpleasant experience for a baby? Psychoanalyst Otto Rank (1929) believed that it is. After all, a perfectly contented fetus is being expelled from a soft, warm uterus where all its needs are met into a cold, bright world where, for the first time, it will experience chills, pain, hunger, and the startling rush of

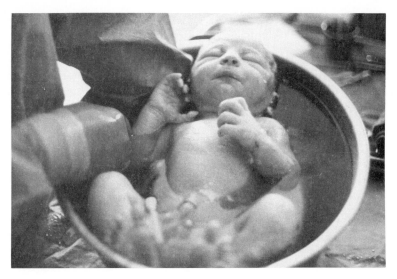

Photo 4-8. The Leboyer method of gentle birthing includes immersing the infant in a warm bath soon after birth to simulate the conditions the baby experienced in the womb.

air into the lungs. According to Rank, babies delivered after a long and complicated labor were especially traumatized by their births and were likely to remain highly anxious and neurotic throughout life.

In 1975 a French obstetrician named Frederick Leboyer attracted a lot of attention by reviving many of Rank's ideas (ideas that had even been dismissed by Rank's mentor, Sigmund Freud). In his popular book *Birth without Violence* (1975), Leboyer objects to common obstetrical practices such as a hasty severing of the umbilical cord, striking the infant to stimulate breathing, weighing the infant on cold metal scales, startling the baby by placing silver nitrate in his or her eyes, and separating the baby from the mother soon after birth—procedures that he describes as the "torture of the innocents." Leboyer believes that birth can be made much less traumatic for a child through his method of **gentle birthing.**

In a gentle birth, the delivery room is quiet and the bright lights are dimmed as the baby emerges. The infant is then placed on the mother's stomach and is caressed or massaged until the umbilical cord stops pulsating and the child is breathing freely on his or her own. After the umbilical cord is severed, the child is placed in a warm bath to simulate the conditions experienced in the womb. Every attempt is made to eliminate all possible sources of discomfort and to make the

child's first several minutes as pleasant as possible. Leboyer (1975) contends that babies who experience gentle births are happy little people who are likely to elicit highly favorable, loving reactions from their parents.

The Leboyer method of gentle birthing is highly controversial. Many obstetricians fear that potentially harmful complications may pass undetected and remain untreated if neonates are examined in dimly lit rooms (B. G. Brown, personal communication, Feb. 1987). In addition, there is no evidence that infants who experience gentle birthing are any more calm and blissful at birth or display any better developmental outcomes over the first eight months than babies who undergo standard obstetrical procedures (Hamilton, 1979; Nelson et al., 1980). Finally, there is reason to believe that birth is

natural childbirth: a delivery in which physical and psychological preparations for the birth are stressed and medical assistance is minimized.

postpartum depression: feelings of sadness, resentment, and depression that mothers may experience following a birth (also called the "baby blues").

gentle birthing: Leboyer's method of childbirth, in which the neonate is comforted, massaged, shielded from unpleasant sensory stimulation, and bathed in warm water in an attempt to reduce any traumas associated with birth.

not especially traumatic for a neonate. Aidan MacFarlane (1977) has carefully observed newborn babies and noted that most of them quiet down rapidly and begin to cope with their new surroundings soon after that first loud cry. Nevertheless, Leboyer and his followers have had an impact on obstetrical practices. Although newborn babies are rarely given warm baths in dim rooms, they are now routinely handed to their mothers for soothing and comforting soon after they are born.

The older child's experience

The birth of a child is a mixed blessing for other children in the family, who may feel deserted when the mother leaves for the hospital and neglected after she returns. Recently, Carol Kendrick and Judy Dunn (1980) found that older children are likely to seek attention by doing something naughty while the mother is feeding or caring for a new baby. These actions may well arise from jealousy, for mothers were found to pay less attention to their older children after the birth of a baby.

One implication of these findings is that parents should set time aside for their older children to let them know that they are still loved and considered important members of the family. However, this can be overdone. When Dunn and Kendrick (1981) followed up on their original sample, they found that older children (particularly girls) who were showered with attention during the weeks after the baby was born were the ones who played *least* with their baby brothers and sisters 14 months later. Surprisingly, the older children who were more positive toward their younger brothers or sisters were those whose mothers had not permitted them to brood or act naughty during the first few weeks after the birth of the baby. The challenge for parents, then, is to control the jealous reactions of the older child while making him or her feel important and wanted. Both the father and the mother can help by taking turns tending to the baby so that the other parent can spend more time with the older children. Parents might also make it easier on older children by stressing their competencies and inviting them to lend a hand in feeding, bathing, or changing the baby.

Complications of Birth

Childbirth does not always proceed as smoothly as indicated in the earlier account of the "normal" delivery. A number of factors can complicate the process, and some of these complications can have long-term effects on the child.

Anoxia. Perhaps the greatest hazard during the birth process is **anoxia,** or oxygen starvation. In many cases of anoxia, the child's supply of oxygen is interrupted because the umbilical cord has become pinched or tangled during childbirth. However, anoxia may also occur after birth if sedatives given to the mother should cross the placental barrier and interfere with the baby's breathing or if mucus ingested during childbirth becomes lodged in the baby's throat. The birth of an anoxic child is a medical emergency: if a baby's brain is deprived of oxygen for more than a few minutes, the infant may suffer serious brain damage and possibly even die. The areas of the brain most noticeably affected are those that control motor activity. Indeed, severe anoxia appears to be a major contributor to *cerebral palsy,* a motor disability in which the affected individual has difficulty controlling muscles of the arms, legs, or head (Apgar & Beck, 1974).

Children suffering from mild anoxia are often irritable at birth and may score below average on tests of motor development and concept formation during the first three years of life (Sameroff & Chandler, 1975). However, these differences between mildly anoxic and normal children eventually lessen to the point that they are no longer apparent by age 7 (Corah, Anthony, Painter, Stern, & Thurston, 1965). So at present there is no compelling evidence that *mild* anoxia has any detrimental long-term effects on children's motor abilities or intellectual development.

Abnormal positioning of the fetus. Nine times out of ten, a fetus will be born head first. Some, however, are born feet or buttocks first—a condition known as a **breech birth.** The breech presentation is hazardous because the birth process takes longer, increasing the likelihood of anoxia and its complications. Although the majority of breech babies are perfectly normal and healthy at birth, about 2% of children delivered this way will have cerebral palsy (Apgar & Beck, 1974).

Perhaps one fetus in a hundred will be lying sideways in the uterus, a position that makes normal vaginal delivery nearly impossible. The fetus must then be turned to a head-first position or else delivered by Caesarean section.

Effects of obstetric medication. In the United States, as many as 95% of mothers receive some kind of drug (and often several) while giving birth (Brackbill, 1979). These drugs may include analgesics and anesthetics to reduce pain, sedatives to relax the mother, and stimulants to induce or intensify uterine contractions. Obviously, these agents are administered in the hope of making the birth process easier for the mother. But we now know that birth medications can have undesirable consequences for the child and that some of these effects may linger as long as one year after birth (and possibly even longer).

Yvonne Brackbill and her associates (Brackbill, McManus, & Woodward, 1985) have recently summarized the results of 59 studies, finding that babies whose mothers received relatively large doses of obstetric medication were atypical in several respects: they smiled infrequently, were generally inattentive and irritable, and were difficult to feed or comfort during the first few weeks of life. Although not every study reported these effects, it is noteworthy that no study found obstetric medication to enhance infants' attention or social demeanor (Brackbill et al., 1985).

Unfortunately, parents of a heavily medicated infant may find it difficult to become very involved with or emotionally attached to such a sluggish, inattentive, and irritable companion (Murray, Dolby, Nation, & Thomas, 1981). To make matters worse, Brackbill and Broman (cited in Kolata, 1979) found that some babies of heavily medicated mothers continued to show some deficits in physical and mental development for at least one year after birth. The children most affected by obstetric medication are those whose mothers had inhaled general anesthetics, such as nitrous oxide; but even local anesthetics (for example, lidocaine) are often found to have depressive effects on the behavior of neonates (Brackbill et al., 1985).

Why might children show *any* lasting effects from a single brief exposure to birth medications? There may be several reasons. First, a dose of medication sufficient to calm or anesthetize a 140-pound woman is likely to have a much greater impact on a 7-pound baby. Second, newborn children have immature circulatory and excretory systems that may take days or even weeks to purge the body of powerful drugs. Finally, heavily medicated children get a very slow start. They are initially sluggish and unresponsive to the environment, and they may take months (or even years) to catch up with their age mates who were not so heavily medicated at birth.

In view of what we know, should we advise *all* mothers against the use of *all* obstetric medication? Probably not. Sedatives given to mothers who are "at risk" (that is, those who are small, oddly built, or delivering large babies) may make labor proceed more smoothly, thereby decreasing the likelihood of such complications as severe anoxia (Myers, 1980; Myers & Myers, 1979). We might also note that the majority of mothers receive light to moderate doses of medication that do not seriously affect their babies. To draw firm conclusions about the use of obstetric medication, we must seek to determine what drugs in what dosages are likely to have what immediate effects and what long-term consequences for the child. In the meantime, we might advise medical personnel to use medication sparingly, while encouraging expectant mothers to attend childbirth classes and to perfect the techniques taught there so that they will possibly require less medication at delivery.

Complications of Low Birth Weight

About 90% of babies in the United States are born between the 37th and 43rd weeks of pregnancy and are considered "timely" (Guttmacher, 1973). The average full-term, or "timely," infant is 19–21 inches long and weighs about 3500 grams.

Until recently, the 8–9% of infants who weighed less than 2500 grams (5½ pounds) at birth were simply labeled "premature." Yet there are actually two kinds of low-birth-weight babies. Some infants are small at birth even though they are born very close to their due dates; these babies are called **small for date** (Kopp & Parmelee, 1979). However, the majority of undersized babies are born more than three weeks before their due dates and are called "preterm," or **short gestation,** infants. Both low birth weight and short gestation are factors that affect the child's ability to survive and to develop normally outside the womb (Kopp & Parmelee, 1979).

What are the causes of low birth weight? We have already seen that mothers who smoke and drink heavily, who are malnourished, or who are in their teens are likely to deliver low-birth-weight babies. Moreover, some illnesses, such as preeclampsia (see Table 4-2), or any accident that impairs the functioning of the placenta

---

anoxia: a lack of sufficient oxygen to the brain; may result in neurological damage or death.

breech birth: a delivery in which the fetus emerges feet first or buttocks first rather than head first.

small-for-date babies: babies born close to their due dates but weighing less than 2500 grams.

short-gestation (preterm) babies: babies born more than three weeks before their due dates.

can retard fetal growth and result in a baby who is premature or small for date. Yet another frequent contributor to undersized babies is multiple births. One set of quadruplets recently born in Macon, Georgia, for example, weighed between 499 and 1089 grams each (1.1–2.4 pounds). Multiple fetuses generally gain much less weight than a singleton after the 27th week of pregnancy. And in addition to being small for date, triplets and quadruplets rarely develop to term in the uterus; in fact, they are often born 5 to 12 weeks early (Browne & Dixon, 1978).

Short-term consequences of low birth weight

The most trying task for a low-birth-weight baby is simply surviving the first few days of life. Although more and more of these infants are surviving each year, better than 50% of those who weigh less than 1000 grams (2.2 pounds) die at birth or shortly thereafter, even in the best hospitals (Paneth, Kiely, & Wallerstein, 1982). Small-for-date babies are often malformed, undernourished, or genetically abnormal—factors that will obviously hinder them as they struggle to survive. Moreover, short-gestation infants are likely to experience a number of additional problems as a consequence of their general immaturity. Their most serious difficulty is breathing. A preterm infant often has very little *surfactin,* a substance that normally coats the lungs during the last three to four weeks of pregnancy to prevent them from collapsing. A deficiency of surfactin may result in **hyaline membrane disease** (respiratory distress syndrome). Children who develop this serious respiratory ailment will breathe very irregularly, and they may stop breathing altogether.

Short-gestation infants often spend their first few weeks of life in heated *isolettes* that maintain their body temperature and protect them from infection. Isolettes are aptly named because they do isolate: the infant is fed, cleaned, and changed through a hole in the device that is much too small to allow the visiting parents to cuddle and love their baby in the usual way (see Photo 4-9). But there are also other reasons preterm infants may be difficult to love: they are likely to be tiny, wrinkled and fragile in appearance, easily upset, and difficult to comfort—in short, a far cry from the smiling, animated creatures that appear in ads for baby products. At home, mothers of preterm infants spend as much time (or more) with their babies as mothers of full-term infants but seem more emotionally detached (Brown & Bakeman, 1980; Crnic, Ragozin, Greenberg, Robinson, & Basham, 1983). One reason for this apparent detachment on the mothers' part is that preterm babies can be very difficult to interact with. Compared with full-term infants, they are reluctant to initiate social interactions and will frequently respond to a parent's bids for attention by looking away or otherwise resisting such overtures (Lester, Hoffman, & Brazelton,

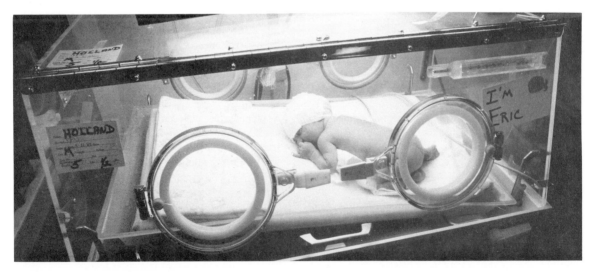

Photo 4-9. Isolettes do isolate. The holes in the apparatus allow parents and hospital staff to care for, talk to, and touch the baby, but close, tender cuddling is nearly impossible.

1985; Malatesta, Grigoryev, Lamb, Albin, & Culver, 1986). Mothers of preterm infants often remark that their babies are "hard to read," and they are apt to become rather frustrated as their persistent attempts to carry on a social dialogue are apparently rebuffed by an aloof, fussy, squirming little companion (Field, 1979; Lester et al., 1985). Although the vast majority of preterm infants are never mistreated by their caregivers, the fact remains that they are more likely than full-term infants to become targets of child abuse (Stern, 1973; Starr, 1979). So it seems that the preterm child's early isolation, forlorn and fragile appearance, and irritable and irregular behavior may impede the formation of positive emotional bonds with caregivers—sometimes to the point that the child elicits abusive rather than affectionate responses.

Only 10–15 years ago, hospitals permitted parents little if any early contact with low-birth-weight babies for fear of harming these fragile little creatures. Today, parents are encouraged to visit their child often in the hospital and to become emotionally involved during their visits by touching, caressing, and talking to their baby. The objective of these early intervention programs is to allow parents to get to know their child and to foster the development of affectionate emotional bonds between all parties involved. But there may be important additional benefits, for babies in intensive care often become less irritable and more responsive and show quicker neurological and mental development if they are periodically rocked, handled, or soothed by the sound of a mother's voice (Barnard & Bee, 1983; Rice, 1977; Rose, 1980; Schaefer, Hatcher, & Barglow, 1980).

Long-term consequences of low birth weight

Before 1975, many researchers had reported that low-birth-weight infants were likely to experience more learning difficulties later in childhood, to suffer more emotional problems, and to score lower on IQ tests than full-term infants (Caputo & Mandell, 1970; Drillien, 1969). Today we know that these conclusions are badly overstated and that the long-term prognosis for low-birth-weight children depends largely on the environment in which they are raised. Most preterm or small-for-date infants who are raised in stable, supportive homes develop healthy emotional attachments to their mothers by 12–15 months of age (Goldberg, Perrotta, Minde, & Corter, 1986; Rode, Chang, Fisch, & Sroufe, 1981) and show little evidence of serious intellectual impairment or learning difficulties later in life (Beck-

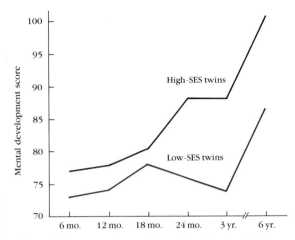

Figure 4-4. Age trends in intellectual development for low-birth-weight twins from middle-class (high SES) and lower socioeconomic (low SES) backgrounds. (*Adapted from Wilson, 1985.*)

with & Parmelee, 1986; Cohen & Parmelee, 1983). However, low-birth-weight children from unstable and economically disadvantaged backgrounds are likely to remain smaller in stature than full-term children, to experience more emotional problems, and to show long-term deficits in intellectual growth and academic achievement (Baker & Mednick, 1984; Kopp & Parmelee, 1979).

Consider what Ronald Wilson (1985) found in his study of developing twins. Although twins are generally small for date and are often preterm, Wilson focused closely on twins who were especially small (weighing under 1750 grams, or less than 3¾ pounds). In Figure 4-4, we see that these preterm, low-birth-weight babies were indeed deficient in mental development throughout the first three years of life (a score of 100 on the tests reflects average intellectual performance). Yet, the figure also shows that low-birth-weight twins from middle-class (high SES) homes eventually made up their intellectual deficits, scoring average (or slightly above) on the tests by age 6, whereas their counterparts from lower socioeconomic (low SES) backgrounds remained substantially below average in their intellectual performances. So the long-term prognosis for preterm

---

hyaline membrane disease: a serious respiratory condition in which the neonate breathes very irregularly and is at risk of dying (also called respiratory distress syndrome).

Box 4-3
Assessing the Long-Term Consequences of Prenatal and Perinatal Complications

We have now discussed many examples of what can go wrong during the prenatal and perinatal periods, as well as some steps that expectant parents can take to try to prevent such insults (see, for example, Box 4-2). Once they occur, some of these damaging effects are irreversible: a baby blinded by rubella, for example, will never regain its sight, and a child who develops cerebral palsy due to anoxia will have it for life. And yet, there are a lot of adults walking around today who turned out perfectly normal even though their mothers smoked, drank, or contracted harmful diseases while pregnant or received heavy doses of obstetric medication while in labor and childbirth. Why is this? One reason is simply that not all embryos, fetuses, and newborns who are exposed to teratogens are affected by them. But what about those who are affected? Is it possible that many of these infants will eventually overcome their early handicaps later in life?

Indeed it is, and some of the findings we have already reviewed tell us so. For example, Monroe Lefkowitz's (1981) longitudinal study found that 9 to 11 years after birth, children whose mothers had smoked during pregnancy were no longer any smaller or any less intelligent, less achievement-oriented, or less well adjusted than children of nonsmokers. Moreover, we've seen in Box 4-1 that as young adults, Dutch males whose

mothers had experienced famine during their pregnancies were no less intelligent, on average, than agemates who had received adequate prenatal nutrition. And the available literature on the long-term implications of low birth weight clearly indicates that many of these initially frail and seemingly pitiful creatures will eventually outgrow their early deficiencies.

Might we, then, characterize human infants as resilient creatures who display a *strong* capacity for recovery? Arnold Sameroff and Michael Chandler (1975) certainly think so. In fact, Sameroff and Chandler believe that most babies who display prenatal and perinatal complications will eventually recover and develop normally as long as they are not brain-damaged and have a stable and supportive environment in which to grow.

A longitudinal study by Emmy Werner and Ruth Smith (1982) provides strong support for Sameroff and Chandler's hypotheses. Werner and Smith followed up on all 670 babies born on an island in Hawaii in 1955. At birth, approximately 16% of these infants showed moderate to severe complications, another 31% showed mild complications, and 53% appeared normal and healthy. When the babies were reexamined at age 2, there was a clear relationship between severity of birth complications and developmental disorders: the more severe their neonatal complications, the more likely children were to be deficient in social and intellectual development. However, effects of the postnatal environment were already apparent. In middle-class homes, children who had shown severe birth

complications scored slightly below average on tests of intellectual development. But in lower-class homes, the intellectual performance of children who had experienced equally severe perinatal complications was *far* below average.

Werner and Smith then followed up on the children at age 10 and again at age 18. What they found was striking. By age 10, perinatal complications no longer predicted children's intellectual performance, but certain characteristics of the children's home environments did. Children from unstable, lower socioeconomic backgrounds performed rather poorly on IQ tests, whereas those from stable, supportive homes of higher socioeconomic status showed no marked deficiencies in intellectual performance. Not all the children who had experienced severe perinatal complications eventually overcame all their handicaps, even if they had been raised in stable, supportive homes. But in summarizing the results of this study, Werner and Smith noted that long-term problems related to the effects of poor environments outnumbered those attributable to perinatal stress by a factor of 10 to 1.

In sum, there is plenty of reason to be optimistic should you ever give birth to a frail, irritable, unresponsive baby that is abnormal in its appearance or behavior. Given a supportive and stimulating home environment in which to grow, a majority of these children will display a strong "self-righting" tendency and will eventually overcome their initial handicaps.

---

and small-for-date children does seem to depend very critically on the *postnatal environment* in which they are raised (see also Box 4-3).

Postmaturity

Occasionally a baby is born two or more weeks beyond the expected due date and is labeled **postmature.** Although the vast majority of postmature babies are delivered routinely and will develop normally, they

are sometimes smaller than timely babies, and they face a slightly greater risk of anoxia and its complications—perhaps because an aging placenta becomes less efficient at distributing food and oxygen to the fetus (Browne & Dixon, 1978). Should fetal monitoring indicate that a postmature baby is showing signs of malnutrition or anoxic distress, the attending physician may decide to perform a Caesarean section or to **induce labor** by surgically rupturing the amniotic sac, carefully separating the membranes from the wall of the uterus, and/or administering a drug that causes the uterus to contract.[2]

Should You Have Your Baby at Home?

Now that natural childbirth has become so popular, more and more couples are choosing to have their babies at home. Those who favor home delivery think of childbirth as a natural event that should take place in a calm, relaxed setting rather than a medical crisis (or illness) to be solved using high-technology means (Edwards & Waldorf, 1984). They believe that there are a number of distinct advantages associated with home deliveries (see Table 4-4 for a partial listing), not the least of which is freedom from the often unnecessary and potentially harmful meddling of obstetric practitioners. And it does seem that the relaxed atmosphere of the home setting may have a calming effect on many mothers, for women who deliver at home have shorter and less stressful labors and use far less obstetric medication, on average, than those who deliver in hospitals (Brackbill et al., 1985; Sagov & Brodsky, 1984). (Of course, an alternative interpretation is that mothers delivering at home may have better experiences because they have received better prenatal care and have prepared more diligently for childbirth; see Brackbill et al., 1985.)

Are home births as safe as hospital deliveries? Those who favor home birthing have examined childbirth statistics from many countries and concluded that having a baby at home is at least as safe as having one in a hospital (Sagov & Brodsky, 1984). Consider the data from Holland, where about half of all babies are born at home with the assistance of a nurse or midwife. In 1973 the mortality rates for Dutch infants were 16.3 per 1000 births for babies delivered in hospitals but only 4.5 per 1000 for babies delivered at home (MacFarlane, 1977). In addition, 60% of mothers who gave birth in hospitals experienced some postpartum depression, compared with 16% for home births. Of course, the infant mortality rate in hospitals may be artificially high in Holland (or any other country, for that matter) because all mothers who have already experienced (or are likely to experience) prenatal distress or birth complications are instructed to give birth in a hospital. Nevertheless, the low mortality rate for infants born at home suggests that the physical risks of home deliveries are

Table 4-4. Most frequently cited reasons for delivering at home by couples choosing this alternative

1. To give birth in a relaxed environment where obstetric medication is not encouraged, where friends and relatives can give the laboring woman the support she desires to give birth, and where the birth experience can become as positive a personal/family psychological event as possible.
2. To be able to choose who will be present at the delivery and to avoid unfamiliar and nonsupportive attendants, nurses, aides, students, residents, and physicians.
3. To be attended by supportive *women* attendants—midwives or physicians—who will remain with the woman throughout her labor and birth.
4. To consider alternatives to invasive intervention (for example, routine Caesarean section of breech infants or after 24 hours of ruptured membranes, or routine induction of labor at 42 weeks of gestation).
5. To avoid separation of family members after birth, including father, mother, baby, and siblings.

not great for healthy mothers who have received excellent prenatal care.

In spite of the mortality statistics, obstetricians in the United States generally advise their patients to forgo home delivery in favor of a well-equipped hospital setting (B.G. Brown, personal communication, Feb. 1987; Edwards & Waldorf, 1984). Last-minute complications can happen to anyone—even to a healthy mother who has previously given birth without incident. Therefore, most doctors believe that it is in the best interests of both mother and infant to treat all deliveries as "high risk" endeavors that may require medical intervention and the use of facilities available only at a hospital.

People in the United States who would like to have a child at home may have trouble finding an obstetrician who will take them as patients (Annas, 1984).[3]

[3]As an alternative, there are a number of certified midwives in the United States who specialize in home deliveries. A certified midwife is usually a registered nurse who has taken an additional one to two years of full-time training in nonsurgical obstetrics at an accredited college. A midwife will typically spend much more time with an expectant mother, use fewer drugs, and rely more on physical and psychological preparation for childbirth than most obstetricians do. To obtain a free list of certified midwives and the cities where they practice, write to the American College of Nurse-Midwives, 1522 K Street NW, Suite 1120, Washington, D.C. 20005.

[2]Induction of labor is a controversial practice. Mothers who are "induced" experience more discomfort and require more painkilling drugs (MacFarlane, 1977), and their babies run a greater risk of physical injury and other medical complications. For these reasons, many physicians will not induce labor unless absolutely necessary.

postmature babies: babies born two or more weeks beyond their due dates.
induced labor: the artificial initiation of uterine contractions by drugs and surgical procedures.

However, it is now possible to gain many of the advantages of a home delivery in a hospital setting if the hospital maintains a birthing room (or alternative birth center). A **birthing room** is a delivery area that is furnished like a typical bedroom. Women who give birth there are permitted (and even encouraged) to have their mates or other close companions present to provide emotional support and perhaps assist with the delivery. And infants who are healthy are often allowed to remain in the same room with their mothers ("rooming in") rather than spending their first few days in the hospital nursery. So the birthing room provides a mother and her infant with many of the comforts of home in a setting that contains all the modern facilities necessary to handle serious complications of birth (Klee, 1986).

Summary

During the 266 days between conception and birth, the unborn child passes through three successive phases. Within the first two weeks, or germinal period, the single-celled zygote becomes a multicelled blastula that travels down the fallopian tube, implants itself in the uterine lining, and begins to grow.

The second phase of prenatal development lasts from the third through the eighth week of pregnancy and is called the period of the embryo. By the end of this phase, the unborn child is only about an inch long and weighs about 1/10th of an ounce. However, it already bears some resemblance to a human being because most of its organs and body parts have formed or begun to take shape. This is a sensitive period when the organism is particularly susceptible to drugs, diseases, radiation, and other environmental hazards.

From the end of the eighth week until birth is the period of the fetus. As the fetus rapidly grows, the genitals appear, the muscles and bones develop, and all organ systems become integrated in preparation for birth. Between the 24th and 28th weeks, the brain and respiratory system mature to an extent that the fetus attains the age of viability—the point at which survival outside the uterus *may* be possible. At the beginning of the seventh month, the fetus weighs 2 pounds and is 14–15 inches long. By the end of the ninth month, the full-term fetus will have grown to 19 or 20 inches and will weigh about 7–7½ pounds.

Many environmental influences can complicate prenatal development and the birth process. Among these influences are characteristics of the mother such as age, emotional state, and quality of diet. If a mother is malnourished, particularly during the last three months of pregnancy, she runs an increased risk of having a stillborn infant or a premature baby who may fail to survive. In addition, the fetally malnourished infant may be sluggish, irritable, and neurologically immature—liabilities that could contribute to long-term deficits in social and intellectual development.

Prenatal development may also be disrupted by teratogens—drugs, diseases, chemicals, and radiation—that can attack the developing embryo or fetus and produce serious birth defects. Teratogens are dangerous throughout pregnancy; however, many of these agents are especially troublesome during the first eight weeks, when the major organs and body parts are developing. Many diseases may produce birth defects; rubella, syphilis, herpes, and toxoplasmosis are particularly harmful. A large number of drugs, including thalidomide, alcohol, tobacco, hormones, narcotics, and even some antibiotics, are known to cause congenital malformations and complications at birth. In addition, radiation and chemical pollutants such as mercury, lead, and PCBs may have adverse effects on an unborn child.

Childbirth is a three-step process that begins when the uterus contracts and prepares to push the fetus through the cervical opening and ends a few minutes after birth of the baby, when the placenta is expelled from the body. Many women feel exhilarated after giving birth, particularly if the baby's father is present or nearby to provide emotional support. Fathers who watch or participate in the birth process are apt to feel more positive about childbirth and to be more involved with their babies.

Some developmentalists believe that babies are insensitive creatures who experience little if any discomfort when they are born. Others believe that birth is extremely traumatic, and they suggest "gentle birthing" as a way of making the process less terrifying.

A new baby is a mixed blessing for an older child, who may feel neglected. Parents can make this period easier by spending time with the older child and inviting him or her to help in caring for the baby.

Complications of birth such as anoxia, breech deliveries, overuse of obstetric medication, and low birth

---

birthing room: a hospital delivery area that is furnished like a typical bedroom to provide a homelike atmosphere for childbirth.

weight may make a baby irritable and unresponsive and may contribute to problems later in childhood, particularly if the child is raised in an unstable or disadvantaged home environment. Fortunately, the problems arising from birth complications are often short-lived, provided that the child is not brain-damaged and has a stable and supportive postnatal environment in which to grow.

An increasing number of couples are choosing to forgo hospital deliveries and have their babies within the familiar surroundings of their own homes. However, many obstetricians are critical of the home birth movement, arguing that home deliveries may jeopardize the mother and her infant should complications arise. Today many hospitals maintain birthing rooms—delivery areas furnished like typical bedrooms that provide many of the comforts of home within the protective confines of a hospital.

References

ABEL, E. L. (1980). Fetal alcohol syndrome: Behavioral teratology. *Psychological Bulletin, 87,* 29–50.

ABEL, E. L. (1981). Behavioral teratology of alcohol. *Psychological Bulletin, 90,* 564–581.

ABEL, E. L. (1984). *Fetal alcohol syndrome and fetal alcohol effects.* New York: Plenum.

ADLER, J., & Carey, J. (1982, January 11). But is it a person? *Newsweek,* p. 44.

ALLEN, M. C., & Capute, A. J. (1986). Assessment of early auditory and visual abilities of extremely premature infants. *Developmental Medicine and Child Neurology, 28,* 458–466.

ANNAS, G. J. (1984). Legal aspects of home birth. In S. E. Sagov, R. I. Feinbloom, P. Spindel, & A. Brodsky (Eds.), *Home birth: A practitioner's guide to birth outside the hospital.* Rockville, MD: Aspen.

ANNIS, L. F. (1978). *The child before birth.* Ithaca, NY: Cornell University.

APGAR, V., & Beck, J. (1974). *Is my baby all right?* New York: Pocket Books.

ASSOCIATED PRESS (1983, April 30). 13 ounces at birth, boy now at 6 lbs. *Atlanta Journal.*

BAKER, R. L., & Mednick, B. R. (1984). *Influences on human development: A longitudinal perspective.* Boston: Kluwer Nijhoff.

BARNARD, K. E., & Bee, H. L. (1983). The impact of temporally patterned stimulation on the development of preterm infants. *Child Development, 54,* 1156–1167.

BARRETT, D. E., Radke-Yarrow, M., & Klein, R. E. (1982). Chronic malnutrition and child behavior: Effects of early calorie supplementation on socio-emotional functioning at school age. *Developmental Psychology, 18,* 541–556.

BARTOL, B. (1986, July 28). Cocaine babies: Hooked at birth. *Newsweek,* 56–57.

BECKWITH, L., & Parmelee, A. H. (1986). EEG patterns of preterm infants, home environment, and later IQ. *Child Development, 57,* 777–789.

BRACKBILL, Y. (1979). Obstetrical medication and infant behavior. In J. D. Osofsky (Ed.), *Handbook of infant development.* New York: Wiley.

BRACKBILL, Y., McManus, K., & Woodward, L. (1985). *Medication in maternity: Infant exposure and maternal information.* Ann Arbor: University of Michigan Press.

BROWN, J. V., & Bakeman, R. (1980). Relationships of human mothers with their infants during the first year of life: Effects of prematurity. In R. W. Bell & W. P. Smotherman (Eds.), *Maternal influence and early behavior.* Jamaica, NJ: Spectrum.

BROWN, W. A. (1979). *Psychological care during pregnancy and the postpartum period.* New York: Raven Press.

BROWNE, J. C. M., & Dixon, G. (1978). *Antenatal care.* Edinburgh: Churchill Livingstone.

BUTLER, N. R., & Goldstein, H. (1973). Smoking in pregnancy and subsequent child development. *British Medical Journal, 4,* 573–575.

CAPUTO, D. V., & Mandell, W. (1970). Consequences of low birth weight. *Developmental Psychology, 3,* 363–383.

CAREY, W. B., & McDevitt, S. C. (1980). Commentary: Measuring infant temperament. *Journal of Pediatrics, 96,* 423–424.

CHAVEZ, C. J., Ostrea, E. M., Stryker, J. C., & Smialek, Z. (1979). Sudden infant death syndrome among infants of drug-dependent mothers. *Journal of Pediatrics, 95,* 407–409.

COHEN, J. E., & Parmelee, A. H. (1983). Prediction of five-year Stanford-Binet scores in preterm infants. *Child Development, 54,* 1242–1253.

CORAH, N. L., Anthony, E. J., Painter, P., Stern, J. A., & Thurston, D. (1965). Effects of perinatal anoxia after seven years. *Psychological Monographs, 79* (3, Whole No. 596).

CRNIC, K. A., Ragozin, A. S., Greenberg, M. T., Robinson, N. M., & Basham, R. B. (1983). Social interaction and developmental competence of preterm and full-term infants in the first year of life. *Child Development, 54,* 1199–1210.

DALTON, K. (1980). *Depression after childbirth.* Oxford: Oxford University Press.

DICK-READ, G. (1972). *Childbirth without fear: The original approach to natural childbirth* (rev. ed.). New York: Harper & Row. (Original work published 1933)

DRILLIEN, C. M. (1969). School disposal and performance for children of different birthweight born 1953–1960. *Archives of Diseases in Childhood, 44,* 562–570.

DUNN, J., & Kendrick, C. (1981). Interaction between young siblings: Association with the interaction between mother and first-born child. *Developmental Psychology, 17,* 336–343.

EDWARDS, M., & Waldorf, M. (1984). *Reclaiming birth: History and heroines of American childbirth reform.* Trumansburg, NJ: Crossing Press.

FIELD, T. M. (1979). Interaction patterns of preterm and term infants. In T. M. Field, A. M. Sostek, S. Goldberg, & H. H. Shuman (Eds.), *Infants born at risk.* New York: Spectrum.

FIELD, T. M., Sandberg, D., Garcia, R., Nitza, V., Goldstein, S., & Guy, L. (1985). Pregnancy problems, postpartum depression, and early mother-infant interactions. *Developmental Psychology, 21,* 1152–1156.

FRIED, P. A. (1980). Marijuana use by pregnant women: Neurobehavioral effects on neonates. *Drug and Alcohol Dependence, 6,* 415–424.

FUHRMANN, W., & Vogel, F. (1976). *Genetic counseling.* New York: Springer-Verlag.

GOLDBERG, S., Perrotta, M., Minde, K., & Corter, C. (1986). Maternal behavior and attachment in low-birth-weight twins and singletons. *Child Development, 57,* 34–46.

GREENBERG, M., & Morris, N. (1974). Engrossment: The newborn's impact upon the father. *American Journal of Orthopsychiatry, 44,* 520–531.

GROSSMAN, F. K., Eichler, L. S., Winickoff, S. A., & Associates (1980). *Pregnancy, birth, and parenthood: Adaptations of mothers, fathers, and infants.* San Francisco: Jossey-Bass.

GUNDERSON, V., & Sackett, G. P. (1982). Paternal effects on reproductive outcome and developmental risk. In M. E. Lamb & A. L. Brown (Eds.), *Advances in developmental psychology* (Vol. 2). Hillsdale, NJ: Erlbaum.

GUTTMACHER, A. F. (1973). *Pregnancy, birth, and family planning: A guide for expectant parents in the 1970's.* New York: Viking Press.

HALF OUR PREGNANCIES ARE UNINTENTIONAL (1983, October 10). *Newsweek,* p. 37.

HAMILTON, J. S. (1979). *Crying behavior and the "nonviolent" Leboyer method of delivery.* Paper presented at biennial meeting of the Society for Research in Child Development, San Francisco.

HAMM, A. C. (1981). *Questions and answers about DES exposure during pregnancy and after birth (NIH Pub. No. 81–1118).* Washington, DC: National Institutes of Health, U.S. Department of Health and Human Services.

HANSHOW, J. B., Dudgeon, J. A., & Marshall, W. C. (1985). *Viral diseases of the fetus and newborn* (2nd ed.). Philadelphia: Saunders.

HEINONEN, O. P., Slone, D., & Shapiro, S. (1977). *Birth defects and drugs in pregnancy.* Littleton, MA: Publishing Sciences Group.

HENNEBORN, W. J., & Cogan, R. (1975). The effect of husband participation on reported pain and probability of medication during labor and birth. *Journal of Psychosomatic Research, 19,* 215–222.

JACOBSON, J. L., Jacobson, S. W., Fein, G., Schwartz, P. M., & Dowler, J. (1984). Prenatal exposure to an environmental toxin: A test of the multiple effects model. *Developmental Psychology, 20,* 523–532.

JACOBSON, S. W., Fein, G. G., Jacobson, J. L., Schwartz, P. M., & Dowler, J. (1985). The effect of intrauterine PCB exposure on visual recognition memory. *Child Development, 56,* 853–860.

JONES, K. L., Smith, D. W., Ulleland, C. N., & Streissguth, A. P. (1973). Pattern of malformation in offspring of chronic alcoholic mothers. *Lancet, 1,* 1267–1271.

JOOS, S. K., Pollitt, E., Mueller, W. H., & Albright, D. L. (1983). The bacon chow study: Maternal nutritional supplementation and infant behavioral development. *Child Development, 54,* 669–676.

KAPLAN, B. J. (1986). A psychobiological review of depression during pregnancy. *Psychology of Women Quarterly, 10,* 35–48.

KENDRICK, C., & Dunn, J. (1980). Caring for a second baby: Effects on interaction between mother and firstborn. *Developmental Psychology, 16,* 303–311.

KESSNER, D. M. (1973). *Infant death: An analysis by maternal risk and health care.* Washington, DC: National Academy of Sciences.

KLEE, L. (1986). Home away from home: The alternative birth center. *Social Science and Medicine, 23,* 9–16.

KLUSMAN, L. (1975). Reduction of pain in childbirth by the alleviation of anxiety during pregnancy. *Journal of Consulting and Clinical Psychology, 43,* 162–165.

KOLATA, G. B. (1979). Scientists attack report that obstetrical medications endanger children. *Science, 204,* 391–392.

KOPP, C. B., & Parmelee, A. H. (1979). Prenatal and perinatal influences on infant behavior. In J. D. Osofsky (Ed.), *Handbook of infant development.* New York: Wiley.

LAMAZE, F. (1958). *Painless childbirth: Psychoprophylactic method.* London: Burke.

LEBOYER, F. (1975). *Birth without violence.* New York: Knopf.

LEFKOWITZ, M. M. (1981). Smoking during pregnancy: Long-term effects on offspring. *Developmental Psychology, 17,* 192–194.

LESTER, B. M., Hoffman, J., & Brazelton, T. B. (1985). The rhythmic structure of mother-infant interactions in term and preterm infants. *Child Development, 56,* 15–27.

LEWIN, R. (1975, September). Starved brains. *Psychology Today,* pp. 29–33.

MacFARLANE, A. (1977). *The psychology of childbirth.* Cambridge, MA: Harvard University Press.

MALATESTA, C. Z., Grigoryev, P., Lamb, C., Albin, M., & Culver, C. (1986). Emotion socialization and expressive development in preterm and full-term infants. *Child Development, 57,* 316–330.

McDONALD, R. L. (1968). The role of emotional factors in obstetric complications: A review. *Psychosomatic Medicine, 30,* 222–237.

MILLER, S. S. (1976). *Symptoms: The complete home medical encyclopedia.* New York: Thomas Y. Crowell.

MONEY, J., & Ehrhardt, A. (1972). *Man and woman, boy and girl.* Baltimore: Johns Hopkins University Press.

MOORE, K. L. (1977). *The developing human.* Philadelphia: Saunders.

MOTT, S. R., Fazekas, N. F., & James, S. R. (1985). *Nursing care of children and families: A holistic approach.* Reading, MA: Addison-Wesley.

MURRAY, A. D., Dolby, R. M., Nation, R. L., & Thomas, D. B. (1981). Effects of epidural anesthesia on newborns and their mothers. *Child Development, 52,* 71–82.

MYERS, R. E. (1980). Reply to Drs. Kron and Brackbill. *American Journal of Obstetrics and Gynecology, 136,* 819–820.

MYERS, R. E., & Myers, S. E. ((1979). Use of sedative, analgesic, and anesthetic drugs during labor and delivery: Bane or boon. *American Journal of Obstetrics and Gynecology, 133,* 83–104.

NELSON, N. M., Enkin, M. W., Saigal, S., Bennet, K. J., Milner, R., & Sackett, D. L. (1980). A randomized clinical trial of the Leboyer approach to childbirth. *New England Journal of Medicine, 302,* 655–660.

PALKOWITZ, R. (1985). Fathers' birth attendance, early contact, and extended contact with their newborns: A critical review. *Child Development, 56,* 392–406.

PANETH, N., Kiely, J. L., & Wallerstein, S. (1982). Newborn intensive care and neonatal mortality in low-birth-weight infants. *New England Journal of Medicine, 307,* 149–155.

PETERSON, G. H., Mehl, L. E., & Liederman, P. H. (1979). The role of some birth-related variables in father attachment. *American Journal of Orthopsychiatry, 49,* 330–338.

PLANNED PARENTHOOD FEDERATION OF AMERICA (1976). *11 million teenagers: What can be done about the epidemic of adolescent pregnancies in the United States?* New York: Alan Guttmacher Institute.

RANK, O. (1929). *The trauma of birth.* San Diego, CA: Harcourt Brace Jovanovich.

RICE, R. D. (1977). Neurophysiological development in premature infants following stimulation. *Developmental Psychology, 13,* 69–76.

ROBERTS, C. J., & Lowe, C. R. (1975). Where have all the conceptions gone? *Lancet, 1,* 498–499.

RODE, S. S. Chang, P., Fisch, R. O., & Sroufe, L. A. (1981). Attachment patterns of infants separated at birth. *Developmental Psychology, 17,* 188–191.

ROSE, S. A. (1980). Enhancing visual recognition memory in preterm infants. *Developmental Psychology, 16,* 85–92.

RUTTER, M. (1980). Raised lead levels and impaired cognitive/behavioral functioning: A review of the evidence. *Developmental Medicine and Child Neurology, 22* (Supplement 42), 1–26.

SAGOV, S. E., & Brodsky, A. (1984). The issue of safety. In S. E. Sagov, R. I. Feinbloom, P.

Spindel, & A. Brodsky (Eds.), *Home birth: A practitioner's guide to birth outside the hospital*. Rockville, MD: Aspen.

SAMEROFF, A. J., & Chandler, M. J. (1975). Reproductive risk and the continuum of caretaking casualty. In F. D. Horowitz, M. Hetherington, S. Scarr-Salapatek, & G. Siegel (Eds.), *Review of child development research* (Vol. 4). Chicago: University of Chicago Press.

SCHAEFER, M., Hatcher, R. P., & Barglow, P. D. (1980). Prematurity and infant stimulation: A review of research. *Child Psychiatry and Human Development, 10,* 199–212.

SCHARDEIN, J. L. (1985). *Chemically induced birth defects*. New York: Dekker.

SEABROOK, C. (1987, February 19). Children—"third wave" of AIDS victims. *Atlanta Journal,* 1A, 12A.

SKINNER, B. F. (1971). *Beyond freedom and dignity*. New York: Knopf.

SONTAG, L. W. (1941). The significance of fetal environmental differences. *American Journal of Obstetrics and Gynecology, 42,* 996–1003.

SONTAG, L. W. (1944). War and the fetal maternal relationship. *Marriage and Family Living, 6,* 1–5.

SOSA, R., Kennell, J., Klaus, M., Robertson, S., & Urrutia, J. (1980). The effect of a supportive companion on perinatal problems, length of labor, and mother-infant interaction. *New England Journal of Medicine, 303,* 597–600.

SPREEN, O., Tupper, D., Risser, A., Tuokko, H., & Edgell, D. (1984). *Human developmental neuropsychology*. New York: Oxford University Press.

STARR, R. H., Jr. (1979). Child abuse. *American Psychologist, 34,* 872–878.

STEIN, Z. A., & Susser, M. W. (1976). Prenatal nutrition and mental competence. In J. D. Lloyd-Still (Ed.), *Malnutrition and intellectual development*. Littleton, MA: Publishing Sciences Group.

STEIN, Z. A., Susser, M. W., Saenger, G., & Marolla, F. (1975). *Famine and human development: The Dutch hunger winter of 1944–1945*. New York: Oxford University Press.

STERN, L. (1973). Prematurity as a factor in child abuse. *Hospital Practices, 8,* 117–123.

STOTT, D. H., & Latchford, S. A. (1976). Prenatal antecedents of child health, development, and behavior: An epidemiological report of incidence and association. *Journal of the American Academy of Child Psychiatry, 15,* 161–191.

STRAUSS, M. E., Lessen-Firestone, J. K., Starr, R. H., & Ostrea, E. M. (1975). Behavior of narcotics-addicted newborns. *Child Development, 46,* 887–893.

STREISSGUTH, A. P., Barr, H. M., & Martin, D. C. (1983). Maternal alcohol use and neonatal habituation assessed by the Brazelton scale. *Child Development, 54,* 1109–1118.

STREISSGUTH, A. P., Herman, C. S., & Smith, D. W. (1978). Stability of intelligence in the fetal alcohol syndrome: A preliminary report. *Alcoholism: Clinical and Experimental Research, 2,* 165–170.

STREITFELD, P. P. (1978). Congenital malformation: Teratogenic foods and additives. *Birth and Family Journal, 5,* 7–19.

TANNER, J. M. (1978). *Fetus into man: Physical growth from conception to maturity*. Cambridge, MA: Harvard University Press.

THOMAS, K. L. (1986, September 12). Coke, babies "simply don't mix." *Atlanta Journal,* 1B, 6B.

TINKLENBERG, J. R. (1975). *Marijuana and health hazards: Methodological issues in current research*. Orlando, FL: Academic Press.

U.S. DEPARTMENT OF HEALTH, EDUCATION AND WELFARE (1979). *Smoking and health: A report to the Surgeon General* (DHEW Pub. No. PHS 79–50066). Washington, DC: U.S. Government Printing Office.

VAUGHN, B. E., Bradley, C. F., Joffe, L. S., Seifer, R., & Barglow, P. (1987). Maternal characteristics measured prenatally are predictive of ratings of temperamental "difficulty" on the Carey Infant Temperament Questionnaire. *Developmental Psychology, 23,* 152–161.

WEISS, R. D., & Mirin, S. M. (1987). *Cocaine*. Washington, DC: American Psychiatric Press.

WERNER, E. E., & Smith, R. S. (1982). *Vulnerable but invincible: A longitudinal study of resilient children and youth*. New York: McGraw-Hill.

WIDEMAN, M. V., & Singer, J. E. (1984). The role of psychological mechanisms in preparation for childbirth. *American Psychologist, 39,* 1357–1371.

WILSON, R. S. (1985). Risk and resilience in early mental development. *Developmental Psychology, 21,* 795–805.

WINICK, M. (1976). *Malnutrition and brain development*. New York: Oxford University Press.

ZESKIND, P. S., & Ramey, C. T. (1981). Preventing intellectual and interactional sequelae of fetal malnutrition: A longitudinal, transactional, and synergistic approach to development. *Child Development, 52,* 213–218.

The Physical Self: Development of the Brain, the Body, and Motor Skills

During the 266 days since conception, the newborn child has grown from a single cell into a marvelously complex being. Now 19–21 inches long and weighing 7 to 7½ pounds, the child has entered a whole new world full of bright, colorful sights, interesting sounds, strange odors, and many, many objects to explore. Is the neonate ready for all this? Is his or her world really a "buzzing, blooming confusion," as one famous psychologist, William James, once implied? Well, perhaps it is for the first few moments. However, we will see in this chapter (and throughout the text) that the human infant is a remarkably capable organism who is well equipped at birth to attend selectively to certain aspects of this "confusing" environment and to make adaptive responses to these interesting new experiences.

On this leg of our journey through childhood,

we will first consider the mannerisms and motor capabilities of newborn infants during the *neonatal* period—the first month of life. We will then concentrate on an aspect of human development that fascinates so many parents—the transformation of the child from a largely dependent and immobile little creature into a running, jumping bundle of energy who continues to grow and who may even surpass the physical stature of his or her parents in what, to parents, may seem like a very short time.

Now for a thought question: What causes a child to grow? What factors are responsible for the development of increasingly precise motor skills that enable a child to reach for and to grasp objects, to crawl, to walk, and to run? If you think you know the answers to these questions, you may find it interesting to apply your theory of physical growth and development to each of the issues in Box 5-1. Jot down your responses, and we will see how well your theory fares as we discuss each of these topics at various points in the chapter.

The Neonate

Although many parents might argue the point, newborn infants are not very attractive. Their passage through the narrow cervix and birth canal may leave them with flattened noses, misshapen foreheads, and an assortment of bumps and bruises. As the baby is held upside down and measured, parents are apt to see a wrinkled, red-skinned little creature all covered with sticky fluid that mats its hair (if any) and may ooze from its nose and mouth as it wheezes and belts out its first cry. To make matters worse, the silver nitrate drops administered as a precaution against gonorrhea may cause the infant's eyelids to puff or swell. Although the neonate's appearance will change for the better over the first few weeks of life, it will be some time before the infant resembles the smiling, bouncing little imps who appear in baby-food commercials.

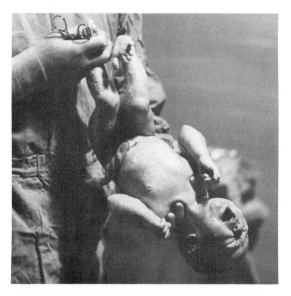

Photo 5-1. Immediately after birth, babies are not particularly attractive, but their appearance will improve over the first few weeks of life.

Box 5-1

Some Basic Questions about Physical Growth and Development

Do you know why children grow? Have you any idea why some babies are fat and others thin? What do you suppose is happening in the first 12 months of life that enables a child to crawl and eventually to stand, walk, and run? Why does a 3-year-old find it difficult to color within the lines of the figures in his coloring book? Why might a 5-year-old have trouble riding her bicycle or threading a needle?

If you can answer all these questions, you may already know quite a lot about human growth and development. But even if you think you know very little about the physical development of human beings, you may find it interesting to speculate a bit about the eight issues that appear in this box. Each issue is presented in the form of an assertion. Look each statement over and indicate whether you agree or disagree.

You can then see how well you have done on this little "pretest" as you proceed through the chapter. (If you would like immediate feedback, the answers appear after the quiz.)

Issue 1: *A baby can learn to swim before he or she can walk.*
My opinion (circle one):   T   F

Issue 2: *Babies who lose their inborn reflexes during the first year are usually brain-damaged in some way.*
My opinion: T   F

Issue 3: *Most children walk when they are ready, and no amount of encouragement will enable 6-month-old infants to walk on their own.*
My opinion: T   F

Issue 4: *Emotional traumas can seriously impair the growth and development of young children, even those who are adequately nourished, healthy, and not physically mistreated.*
My opinion: T   F

Issue 5: *The brain develops very slowly in human beings, reaching only 50% of its adult weight by age 5.*
My opinion: T   F

Issue 6: *Hormones have little effect on human growth and development until a child reaches puberty.*
My opinion: T   F

Issue 7: *A 13-year-old boy who is shorter than most of his female classmates is atypically small in stature (for males) and is likely to remain that way.*
My opinion: T   F

Issue 8: *Chubby babies are more likely than normal-weight or thin babies to be overweight as adults.*
My opinion: T   F

4. True	8. True	
3. True	7. False	
2. False	6. False	
1. True	5. False	
	Answers	

Is My Baby All Right?

The Apgar scale. In the first minute of life a baby takes his or her first test. A nurse or a doctor will check the infant's physical condition by looking at five standard characteristics that are rated from 0 to 2, recorded on a chart, and totaled (see Table 5-1). A baby's score on this **Apgar test** (named for its developer, Dr. Virginia Apgar) can range from 0 to 10, higher scores indicating a better condition. Five minutes after birth, the Apgar procedure is repeated in order to check on the first observation and/or to measure improvements in the infant's physical state.

Infants who score 7 or higher on the second testing are not in any immediate danger—they have a steady heartbeat, well-developed reflexes, and a pinkish tone to their skin and are breathing freely. However, infants scoring 4 or lower are in trouble—their heartbeats are sluggish or nonexistent, their muscles are limp, and their breathing is shallow and irregular, if they are breathing at all. These children will require immediate medical intervention in order to survive.

The Brazelton scale. The Apgar test is an excellent method of detecting severe physical or neurological irregularities that require immediate attention. A second test, the **Brazelton Neonatal Behavioral Assessment Scale,** is a more subtle measure of an infant's neurological well-being and an indication of his or her reactions to other people. The Brazelton test is typically administered on the third day of life and should be repeated several days later, after the baby has spent some time in the home setting (Brazelton, 1979). It assesses the strength of 20 infant reflexes as well as the infant's responses to 26 situations (for example, reactions to cuddling, irritability during the exam, orienting

Apgar test: a quick assessment of the newborn's heart rate, respiration, color, muscle tone, and reflexes; this simple test is performed to determine whether a neonate requires immediate medical assistance.

Brazelton Neonatal Behavioral Assessment Scale: an evaluation of a neonate's neurological status and responsiveness to other people.

Table 5-1. The Apgar test

Characteristic	Score		
	0	*1*	*2*
Heart rate	Absent	Slow (less than 100 beats per minute)	Over 100 beats per minute
Respiratory effort	Absent	Slow or irregular	Good, baby is crying
Muscle tone	Flaccid, limp	Weak, some flexion	Strong, active motion
Color	Blue or pale	Body pink, extremities blue	Completely pink
Reflex irritability	No response	Frown, grimace, or weak cry	Vigorous cry

to the examiner's face and voice, responses to a rattle). The value of this test lies in its ability to identify babies who are slow to respond to a variety of everyday experiences. If the infant is extremely unresponsive, the low Brazelton score may indicate brain damage or other neurological dysfunction. If the child is merely sluggish, particularly when responding to social stimulation, it is possible that he or she will not receive enough attention from parents to avoid later feelings of insecurity and other emotional difficulties. So a low Brazelton score is an early indication that problems may arise. Fortunately, parents of these unresponsive babies can be taught how to provide the kinds of attention and comfort that may prevent the emotional difficulties predicted by a low score on the test (see Box 5-2).

The Neonate's "Preparedness" for Life

In the past, neonates were thought to be fragile, helpless little organisms who were hardly ready for the cold, cruel world. Indeed, this may have been an adaptive attitude in an era when medical practices and procedures were rather primitive by modern standards and when a substantial percentage of newborns did die. After all, doctors could hardly blame themselves for failing to save a patient who was presumably ill equipped for survival. And parents may have felt pretty much the same way. T. Berry Brazelton (1979, p. 35) notes that "many cultures in which the neonatal death rate is high still institutionalize such practices as not speaking of the newborn as a [human] baby . . . or of not naming him until he is 3 months old and more likely to survive."

Today we know that neonates are much better prepared for life on this earth than many doctors, parents, and developmentalists had initially assumed. As we will see in Chapter 6, all the major senses are functioning reasonably well at birth. Newborns do indeed see and hear, and they also respond in predictable ways to odors, tastes, touches, and changes in temperature.

Moreover, we will see in Chapter 7 that neonates are capable of simple kinds of learning and will often remember the particularly vivid auditory and visual experiences they have had.

Yet another example of neonates' "preparedness" for life is their repertoire of inborn reflexes that help them adapt to their new surroundings from the moment of birth. A **reflex** is an unlearned and automatic response to a stimulus—a behavior (or pattern of behaviors) that is triggered by external events. Many of the neonate's inborn reflexes are reactions that are necessary for survival. Among the more obvious of these **survival reflexes** are the breathing reflex, the eyeblink (which protects the eyes against bright light or foreign particles), and the sucking and swallowing reflexes, by which the infant ingests food. Also implicated in feeding is the *rooting* reflex—an infant who is touched on the cheek will turn in that direction and search for something to suck.

In addition to the survival reflexes, the neonate also displays a number of **primitive reflexes,** which Table 5-2 describes. These reactions can be labeled "primitive" for two reasons: (1) they are controlled by "subcortical" areas of the brain—the areas that develop earliest—and (2) they gradually disappear over the first year of life as the cerebral cortex (a higher brain center) begins to direct and control behavior. Though short-lived, the subcortical reflexes are important in a diagnostic sense, for the absence or weakness of any of them is an early indication that the child's nervous system may not be functioning properly.

Some developmentalists believe that the primitive reflexes listed in Table 5-2 are remnants of our evolutionary history that have adaptive significance to this day (Bowlby, 1973; Fentress & McLeod, 1986). For example, the swimming reflex may help to keep afloat an infant who is accidentally immersed in a body of water. The grasping reflex and the Moro reflex are po-

Box 5-2
Brazelton Training: Effects on Parents and Infants

Babies who are irritable, unresponsive, and apathetic can be unpleasant companions, and they may not receive enough attention and comforting to promote the development of a warm, loving emotional bond with their parents. As a result, these "high risk" infants often develop feelings of insecurity and any number of other emotional problems. Dr. T. Berry Brazelton (1979) believes that many of these emotional difficulties can be prevented if the parents of sluggish, unresponsive babies learn how to observe, to stimulate, and to comfort their infants.

One method of teaching parents how to interact with their babies is to have them either watch or take part as the Brazelton Neonatal Behavioral Assessment Scale is administered to their child. The Brazelton test is well suited as a teaching device because it is designed to elicit many of the infant's most pleasing characteristics, such as smiling, cooing, and gazing. As the test proceeds, parents will see that their neonate can respond positively to other people, and they will also learn how to elicit these pleasant interactions. These "successful" exchanges should help parents to understand their baby while making them feel much more competent in their role as caregivers.

"Brazelton training" has proved to be an effective strategy indeed. Mothers of high-risk children who have had the Brazelton procedure demonstrated to them become more responsive in their face-to-face interactions with their babies. In addition, their infants score higher on the Brazelton test one month later than high-risk infants whose mothers were not trained (Widmayer & Field, 1980).

Other investigators (see Myers, 1982; Worobey, 1985) have found that Brazelton training also has positive effects on the parents of healthy, responsive infants. In Barbara Myers's (1982) study, either mothers or fathers in a treatment group were taught to give the Brazelton test to their neonates, while parents in a control group received no such training. When tested four weeks later, parents who had received the Brazelton training were more knowledgeable about infant behavior, more confident in their caretaking abilities, and more satisfied with their infants than control parents. In addition, fathers who had been trained reported that they were much more involved in caring for their infants at home than the fathers who had received no training.

Although many hospitals provide brief instructions on how to diaper and bathe a baby, parents are seldom told anything about the neonate's basic abilities, such as whether newborns can see, hear, or carry on meaningful social dialogues with other people. Brazelton training clearly illustrates what a new baby is capable of doing, and it appears to have a number of positive effects on both parents and their infants. This brief intervention does not always accomplish wonders (see Belsky, 1985, 1986), and even Dr. Brazelton acknowledges that more powerful and longer-term interventions are necessary for families experiencing a lot of stress (Worobey & Brazelton, 1986). Nevertheless, it appears to be a good way to help parents and babies get started on the right foot. Barbara Myers (1982), a strong proponent of the Brazelton technique, argues that "the treatment is relatively inexpensive, it only takes about an hour, and the parents reported enjoying it. This type of intervention needs to be tested [further] on other populations . . . for possible consideration as a routine portion of a hospital's postpartum care" (p. 470).

---

tentially adaptive in cultures where mothers still carry their newborn infants on their hips or in slings. In fact, ethologist John Bowlby (1973) believes that the major function of the grasping reflex is to promote close contact between the baby and the mother—contact that may help them to become emotionally attached to each other. We will explore this idea in greater detail when we consider the social world of the human infant in Chapter 11.

Living with an Infant

Thus far, we have concentrated on the experiences and capabilities of neonates who are wide awake and seem willing or even eager to discover what their new world holds in store. Yet, almost all parents will tell us that it is often difficult to coax their babies to respond to them, because neonates spend much of their time asleep or in a drowsy, inactive state. Imagine the frustration of a researcher conducting an experiment, or a mother trying to feed her baby, when the infant nods off and falls asleep just as the procedure is about to begin. This scenario is not at all unlikely, for neonates go through many changes in *state* (level of consciousness) every day, and their reactions to the world around them will obviously depend on the state they are in.

---

reflex: an unlearned and automatic response to a stimulus or class of stimuli.
survival reflexes: inborn responses such as breathing, sucking, and swallowing that enable the newborn to adapt to the extrauterine environment.
primitive reflexes: reflexes controlled by subcortical areas of the brain that gradually disappear over the first year of life.

Table 5-2. Major reflexes present in full-term neonates

Name	Response	Developmental course	Significance
I. Survival reflexes			
Breathing reflex	Repetitive inhalation and expiration	Permanent	Provides oxygen and expels carbon dioxide
Eyeblink reflex	Closing or blinking the eyes	Permanent	Protects the eyes from bright light or foreign objects
Pupillary reflex	Constriction of pupils to bright light; dilation to dark or dimly lit surroundings	Permanent	Protects against bright lights; adapts the visual system to low illumination
Rooting reflex	Turning the head in the direction of a tactile (touch) stimulus to the cheek	Gradually weakens over the first 6 months of life	Orients child to the breast or bottle
Sucking reflex	Sucking on objects placed (or taken) into the mouth	Is gradually modified by experience over the first few months of life	Allows child to take in nutrients
Swallowing reflex	Swallowing	Is permanent but modified by experience	Allows child to take in nutrients
II. Primitive (subcortical) reflexes			
Babinski reflex	Fanning and then curling the toes when the bottom of the foot is stroked	Usually disappears within the first 8 months–1 year of life	Its presence at birth and disappearance in the first year are an indication of normal neurological development
Grasping reflex	Curling of the fingers around objects (such as a finger) that touch the baby's palm	Disappears in first 3–4 months and is then replaced by a voluntary grasp	Its presence at birth and later disappearance are an indication of normal neurological development
Moro reflex	A loud noise or sudden change in the position of the baby's head will cause the baby to throw his or her arms outward, arch the back, and then bring the arms toward each other as if to hold onto something	The arm movements and arching of the back disappear over the first 6–7 months; however, the child continues to react to unexpected noises or a loss of bodily support by showing a startle reflex (which does not disappear)	Its presence at birth and later disappearance (or evolution into the startle reflex) are indications of normal neurological development
Swimming reflex	An infant immersed in water will display active movements of the arms and legs and involuntarily hold his or her breath (thus giving the body buoyancy); this swimming reflex will keep an infant afloat for some time, allowing easy rescue	Disappears in the first 4–6 months	Its presence at birth and later disappearance are an indication of normal neurological development; on a practical note, some swimming instructors have taught very young infants to adapt the swimming reflex into a primitive type of locomotion in the water (swimming), which is possible long before an infant is capable of walking
Stepping reflex	Infants held upright so that their feet touch a flat surface will step as if to walk	Disappears in the first 8 weeks unless the infant has regular opportunities to practice this response	Its presence at birth and later disappearance are taken as an indication of normal neurological development

Note: Preterm infants may show little or no evidence of subcortical reflexes at birth, and their survival reflexes are likely to be irregular or immature. However, the missing subcortical reflexes will typically appear soon after birth and will disappear a little later than they do among full-term infants.

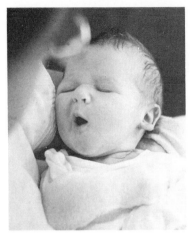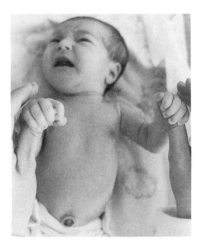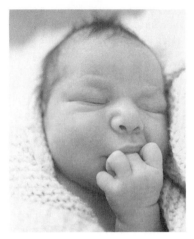

Photo 5-2. Three innate reflexes. The baby in the photograph at the left is displaying the *rooting reflex*: when an object touches the cheek, the infant will turn the head in the direction of the touch, searching for something to suck. In the center is an example of the *grasping reflex*—a curling of the fingers around objects that touch the palm. The infant in the photograph at the right illustrates the rhythmical sucking, or *sucking reflex,* that neonates display when objects are placed into their mouths.

A description of infant states

Peter Wolff (1966) carefully observed the behavior of newborn infants and described several states of consciousness that they experience during a typical day. The six major infant states are as follows:

1. *Regular sleep.* During regular sleep, babies lie still with their eyes closed and unmoving. The child's breathing is regular and the skin is pale. The infant is very passive and does not respond to mild stimuli such as soft voices or flashing lights.
2. *Irregular sleep.* In irregular sleep, the baby's breathing is irregular, and the eyes may move underneath the closed eyelids (a phenomenon known as rapid eye movements, or REMs). The child often grimaces, jerks, and twitches and may stir a bit in response to soft sounds or flashes of light.
3. *Drowsiness.* The drowsy baby who is just waking or falling asleep will intermittently open and close her eyes. Drowsy babies are fairly inactive, and their eyes have a glazed appearance when open. Breathing is regular but more rapid than in regular sleep.
4. *Alert inactivity.* The alert, inactive baby has her eyes open and scans the environment with interest. Head, trunk, and limb movements may occur, and breathing is fast and irregular. This is the state in which infants are most susceptible to conditioning.
5. *Waking activity.* Hungry or otherwise discomforted babies may awake suddenly and show sudden spurts of vigorous activity in which they twist their torsos and kick their legs. Their eyes are open, but the infants are not actively attending to their surroundings. Breathing is irregular.
6. *Crying.* Waking activity often passes into a crying state in which the infant first whimpers and then bursts forth with loud, agitated cries accompanied by vigorous kicks and arm movements.

During the first few days of life, neonates spend about 70% of their time (16–18 hours a day) sleeping and only 2–3 hours in the alert, inactive (attentive) state (Berg, Adkinson, & Strock, 1973; Hutt, Lenard, & Prechtl, 1969). Sleep cycles are typically brief, lasting from 45 minutes to 2 hours. These seven to ten daily "naps" are separated by periods of waking activity, crying, drowsiness, and alert inactivity.

Developmental changes in state

Sleep patterns. As infants develop, they spend less time sleeping and more time awake, alert, and attending to the environment. Four to six weeks after birth, babies are sleeping but 14–15 hours a day, spread over five to seven periods. Somewhere between 3 and 7 months of age, many infants reach a milestone that parents appreciate—they begin to sleep through the night and will require but two or three shorter naps during the day (Berg & Berg, 1979; Gesell et al., 1940).

At birth, infants spend approximately half their sleeping hours in **REM sleep,** a state of active, irregular sleep characterized by rapid eye movements (REMs) and brain-wave activity that is more typical of wakefulness than of regular (non-REM) sleep. However, this REM sleep becomes much less frequent by age 6 months, leveling off at about 25–30% of total sleep time thereafter.

Most adults begin their sleep cycles with a period of regular sleep, followed an hour or two later by REM sleep. When awakened from REM sleep, adults almost always report that they were dreaming. Does this mean that newborn infants are dreaming during their REM sleep? It's possible. However, the sleep cycles of neonates are roughly opposite to those of adults: babies usually drift directly into REM sleep from a drowsy, crying, or alert state, and this REM activity is followed by periods of regular sleep. Thus, REM sleep may serve a very different function for infants than for adults.

Some developmentalists believe that the purpose of REM sleep during the first few months of life is to provide the central nervous system with a source of stimulation that enables the higher brain centers to mature (Roffwarg, Muzio, & Dement, 1966). One implication of this **autostimulation theory** is that infants who are stimulated by many sights and sounds when they are awake will require less REM stimulation while they sleep. J. D. Boismier (1977) tested this hypothesis by showing one group of neonates a number of interesting visual stimuli that increased their alert inactivity. Control infants who did not attend to the stimuli were simply permitted to sleep. Boismier found that infants who received visual stimulation spent less time later in REM sleep than infants in the control group, consistent with the autostimulation theory. Perhaps the reason REM sleep declines so dramatically at 4–6 months of age is that the brain is rapidly maturing, the infant is becoming more alert, and there is simply less need for the stimulation provided by REM activity.

Crib death. Infants rarely have problems establishing regular sleeping cycles unless their central nervous system is abnormal in some way (Willemsen, 1979). Yet, every year in the United States, as many as 7,000–10,000 seemingly healthy infants suddenly stop breathing and die in their sleep.

The exact cause of this **sudden infant death syndrome (SIDS)** is unknown. We do know that low-birth-weight male infants who had scored less than 7 on the Apgar scale and who had experienced respiratory distress as neonates are most susceptible. SIDS is most likely to occur during the winter, among infants who are 2–4 months of age and who have a respiratory infection, such as a cold. Some investigators think that a virus is responsible for these "crib deaths." Others point to the fact that victims of SIDS usually have irregular respiratory patterns characterized by periods of *apnea* (spontaneous interruptions in breathing) that are very frequent and unusually long (Shannon, 1980; Steinschneider, 1975). Lewis Lipsitt (1979) believes that SIDS occurs most often at 2–4 months of age because this is the time when subcortical reflexes are diminishing in strength and voluntary cortical responses are not yet well established. Consequently, if mucus should block the nasal passages, a 2–4-month-old infant may not struggle for a breath because his innate survival reflexes are waning and his learned, protective responses to discomfort are weak or nonexistent.

Unfortunately, many parents blame themselves for crib deaths: they feel that their baby would not have died if only they had been more attentive. What, if anything, can parents do to help prevent SIDS? Proponents of the virus theory would advise them to avoid taking their young infants into crowded public places where contact with viruses is likely. Should the infant catch a virus, parents might periodically check their sleeping baby for respiratory distress. If breathing irregularities are noted, doctors may recommend installation of an *apnea monitor* in the home—a device that sounds an alarm if the baby stops breathing for more than 20–30 seconds. When they hear the alarm, parents can wake the baby, thereby coaxing him to resume normal breathing.

The course and functions of crying. The neonate's earliest cries are unlearned and involuntary responses to discomfort—distress signals by which babies make caregivers aware of their needs. Newborn infants spend about 6–7% of their time crying, although there are large individual differences in crying behavior, and the amount that any one infant cries may vary considerably from day to day (Korner, Hutchinson, Koperski, Kraemer, & Schneider, 1981).

Pediatricians and nurses are trained to listen to the vocalizations of a newborn infant, for congenital problems are sometimes detectable by the way an infant cries. For example, preterm babies and those who are malnourished or brain-damaged often emit high-pitched, nonrhythmic cries that are perceived as much more aversive than those of healthy full-term infants (Frodi et al., 1978; Zeskind, 1980). In fact, Barry Lester (1984) reports that it is even possible to discriminate preterm infants who will develop normally from those who are likely to experience later deficits in cognitive development by analyzing their crying in the first few days and weeks of life. So the cries of young infants not only reflect the babies' present biological integrity but can also help to identify those children who may require special support and attention if they are to develop normally.

Healthy babies are able to produce at least three cries: (1) a "hunger," or rhythmic, cry that starts with a whimper and becomes louder and more sustained, (2) a "mad," or angry, cry that is also rhythmic but much more intense, and (3) a "pain" cry that begins with a long shriek followed by seconds of silence (as the baby takes a deep breath) and then more vigorous crying. Peter Wolff (1969) conducted an interesting experiment to see whether young, relatively inexperienced mothers could distinguish these three kinds of cries. While he was supposedly observing the neonates in their own rooms, Wolff played a tape recording of the infant crying and waited for the mothers to respond. And respond they did: At the sound of a pain cry, mothers immediately came running to see what was wrong with their babies. However, mothers responded much more slowly (if at all) to either "hungry" or "mad" cries.

Do different cries really convey very different messages, as Wolff's study seems to imply? Maybe not. It seems that parents can *sometimes* distinguish the "pain" and the "anger" cries of their own babies but cannot discriminate those of unfamiliar infants (Wiesenfeld, Malatesta, & DeLoach, 1981). Moreover, Philip Zeskind and his associates (Zeskind, Sale, Maio, Huntington, & Weiseman, 1985) find that intense hunger cries are perceived as just as "arousing" and "urgent" as equally intense pain cries. Zeskind et al. believe that crying conveys only one very general message—"Hey, I'm distressed"—and that the effectiveness of this signal at eliciting attention depends more on the *amount* of distress it implies than on the kind of distress that the baby is experiencing.

Will parents who are especially responsive to an infant's cries produce a spoiled baby who cries a lot and enslaves them with incessant demands for attention? Apparently not, for Mary Ainsworth (Ainsworth, Bell, & Stayton, 1972) finds that mothers who are quick to respond to their infants' cries have babies who cry very little! Why should this be? Because sensitive caregivers who respond quickly to an infant's cries are also very responsive to other social signals, such as the smiles, babbles, and bright-eyed expressions that distressed infants are likely to emit once they quiet down. In other words, responsive companions are readily available to elicit and *reinforce* alternative modes of communication, which then replace crying as methods of attracting attention (Gewirtz & Boyd, 1977).

Methods of soothing a fussy baby

Although babies can be delightful companions when alert and attentive, they may also irritate the most patient of caregivers when they fuss, cry, and are difficult to pacify. Many people think that a crying baby is either hungry, wet, or in pain, and if the infant has not eaten in some time, feeding may be a very effective method of pacification. In fact, pediatricians (and thousands of parents) have discovered that the presentation of a nipplelike pacifier, without food, is often sufficient to coax the baby to suck—an inborn rhythmic activity that apparently reduces stress (Field & Goldson, 1984). Of course, the soothing effect of a pacifier will be short-lived if the baby really is hungry.

A number of researchers have found that rocking, humming, and other forms of continuous, rhythmic stimulation may quiet restless babies. Swaddling (wrapping the child snugly in a blanket) is also comforting because the wraps provide continuous tactile sensation all over the baby's body. Perhaps the infant's nervous system is programmed to respond to soft, rhythmic stimulation, for studies have shown that rocking, swaddling, and continuous rhythmic sounds have the effect of decreasing a baby's muscular activity and lowering heart and respiratory rates (Brackbill, 1975; Lipton, Steinschneider, & Richmond, 1965).

Another method of soothing crying infants is simply to pick them up. Unlike soft, rhythmic stimulation, which may put a baby to sleep, lifting an infant is likely to have the opposite effect (Korner, 1972): when babies are picked up, they become visually alert and begin to look around, particularly if their caregivers place

---

REM sleep: a state of active or irregular sleep in which the eyes move rapidly beneath the eyelids and brainwave activity is similar to the pattern displayed when awake.

autostimulation theory: a theory proposing that REM sleep in infancy is a form of self-stimulation that helps the central nervous system to develop.

sudden infant death syndrome (SIDS): the unexplained death of a sleeping infant who suddenly stops breathing (also called crib death).

them to the shoulder—an excellent vantage point for visual scanning. Anneliese Korner (1972) believes that parents who soothe their infants by picking them up may be doing them a favor, for the visual exploration that this technique allows will help babies to become familiar with their close companions and to learn more about the environment.

Just as infants differ in their temperaments, sleeping patterns, and daily rhythms (or states), they also differ in their ability to be soothed. In one study (Birns, Blank, & Bridger, 1966), 20 hungry babies 2 to 3 days old were made even more irritable when the experimenters flicked the soles of their feet. Then the investigators tried to soothe the infants by playing soft tones, rocking their bassinettes, offering them sweetened pacifiers, or immersing their feet in warm water. Some infants were easily irritated and could not be quieted by any of the soothing stimuli. Others became only mildly irritated and were quieted by any (and all) of the soothing techniques. Since these neonates had not yet received much "mothering" from human caregivers, it appears that the differences in their reactions to irritating and pacifying stimuli may be innate.

A baby who is not easily soothed can make a parent feel anxious, irritable, or downright incompetent—reactions that may cause the parent to resent the child and contribute to a poor parent/child relationship. T. Berry Brazelton (1979) believes that parents can come to enjoy even the most active and irritable of infants if they can cast aside any preconceptions they may have about the typical or "perfect" baby and learn how to adjust their parenting techniques to the characteristics of their *own* child. Indeed, the major purpose of Brazelton training (see Box 5-2) is to promote good parent/infant relations by showing parents that their child can respond positively to them and then teaching the parents how to elicit these favorable reactions.

An Overview of Maturation and Growth

Adults are often amazed at how quickly children grow. Even tiny babies don't remain tiny for long, for in the first few months of life they are gaining nearly an ounce in weight a day and an inch in length each month. Yet, the dramatic increases in height and weight that we can see are accompanied by a number of important *internal* developments in the muscles, bones, and central nervous system—changes that will largely determine the physical feats that children are capable of performing at different ages. In this section of the chapter, we will chart the course of physical development from birth through adolescence and see that there is a clear relationship between those external aspects of growth that are so noticeable and the internal changes that are much harder to detect.

Changes in Height and Weight

Babies grow very rapidly during the first two years, often doubling their birth weight by 4–6 months of age and tripling it (to about 21–22 pounds) by the end of the first year. By 2 years of age, infants are already half their eventual adult height and have quadrupled their birth weight—blossoming to 27–30 pounds. If children continued to grow at this rapid pace until age 18, they would stand about 12'3" and weigh several tons.

From age 2 until puberty, the child's growth is slow and steady, averaging 2–3 inches in height and 6–7 pounds in weight each year. During middle childhood (ages 6–11), children may seem to grow very little—over an entire year, 2 inches and 6 pounds are hard to detect on a child who stands 4 to 4½ feet tall and weighs 60 to 80 pounds (Eichorn, 1979; Lowery, 1978). However, physical growth and development are once again obvious at puberty, when adolescents enter a two- to three-year "growth spurt," during which they may post an annual gain of 10–15 pounds and 3–6 inches in height. After this initial growth spurt, there are typically small increases in height until full adult stature is attained in the mid to late teens.

Changes in Body Proportions

To a casual observer, neonates may appear to be "all head"—and for good reason. The head of a newborn is already 70% of its eventual adult size and constitutes one-quarter of the infant's total body length, the same fraction as the legs. If you asked your friends where you might find a creature whose head was as long as its legs, they might tell you to try science fiction.

As a child grows, body shape rapidly changes. Development proceeds in a **cephalocaudal** (head downward) direction, and it is the trunk that grows fastest during the first year. At 1 year of age, a child's head now accounts for only 20% of total body length. From the child's first birthday until the adolescent growth spurt, the legs are growing rapidly, accounting for more than 60% of the increase in height (Eichorn, 1979). During adolescence the trunk once again becomes the fastest-growing segment of the body, although the legs are

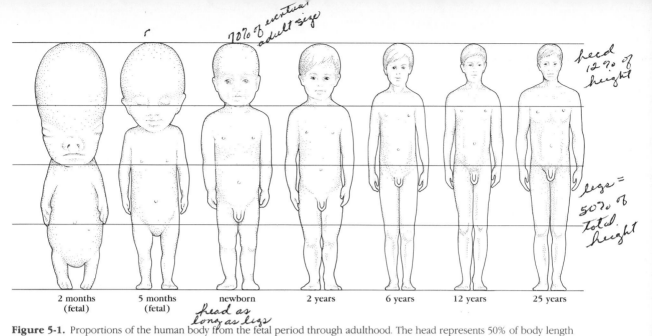

70% of eventual adult size

head 12% of height

legs = 50% of Total height

| 2 months (fetal) | 5 months (fetal) | newborn | 2 years | 6 years | 12 years | 25 years |

head as long as legs

Figure 5-1. Proportions of the human body from the fetal period through adulthood. The head represents 50% of body length at 2 months after conception but only 12–13% of one's adult stature. In contrast, the legs constitute about 12–13% of the total length of a 2-month-old fetus but 50% of the height of a 25-year-old adult.

also growing rapidly at this time. When we reach our eventual adult stature, our legs will account for 50% of total height and our heads only 12% (see Figure 5-1).

While children grow upward, they are also growing outward according to a **proximodistal** (center outward) pattern. For example, the chest and internal organs form before the arms, hands, and fingers during prenatal development. The trunk grows faster than the arms and legs during the first year. However, this center-outward sequence reverses just before puberty, when the extremities (hands and feet) begin to grow rapidly and become the first body parts to reach adult proportions, followed by the arms and legs and finally the trunk. One reason teenagers often appear so clumsy or awkward is that their hands and feet (and later their arms and legs) may suddenly seem much too large for the rest of their bodies (Tanner, 1978).

Skeletal Development

The skeletal structures that emerge during the prenatal period are initially formed from soft cartilage tissues that will gradually ossify (harden) into bony material as calcium and other minerals are deposited there. At birth, most of the infant's bones are soft, pliable, and difficult to break. One reason that neonates cannot sit up or balance themselves when pulled to a standing position is that their bones are too small and too flexible.

Fortunately for a mother and her baby, the neonate's skull consists of several soft bones that can be compressed to allow the child to pass through the cervix and the birth canal. These skull bones are separated by six soft spots, or **fontanelles,** that are gradually filled in by minerals and will ossify to form a single skull bone by about age 2.

Other parts of the body—namely, the ankles and feet and the wrists and hands—develop *more* (rather than fewer) bones as the child matures. In Figure 5-2 we see that the wrist and hand bones of a 1-year-old infant are both fewer and less well integrated (interconnected) than the corresponding skeletal equipment of an adolescent. As new bones appear, ossify, and grow, children are better able to control their extremities and

cephalocaudal development: a sequence of physical maturation and growth that proceeds from the head (cephalic region) to the tail (or caudal region).

proximodistal development: a sequence of physical maturation and growth that proceeds from the center of the body (the proximal region) to the extremities (distal regions).

fontanelles: the six soft spots in a baby's skull where the bones are not fully joined.

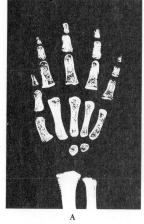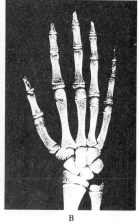

A   B

Figure 5-2. X rays showing the amount of skeletal development seen in (A) the hand of an average male infant at 12 months or an average female infant at 10 months and (B) the hand of an average 13-year-old male or an average 10½-year-old female.

will become capable of movements that will enable them to tie their shoes, write, jump, climb, ride a bicycle, and perform incredible balancing acts (of the "Look, Ma, no hands" variety) that may occasionally startle or alarm their parents.

Not all parts of the skeleton grow and harden at the same rate. The skull and the hands mature first, whereas the leg bones continue to develop until the mid to late teens. For all practical purposes, skeletal development is complete by age 18, although the width (or thickness) of the skull, leg bones, and hands will increase slightly throughout life (Tanner, 1978).

One method of estimating a child's level of physical maturation is to X-ray the wrist and hand (as in Figure 5-2). The X ray shows the number of bones and the extent of their ossification, which is then interpretable as a **skeletal age.** Using this technique, researchers have found that females mature faster than males. At birth, girls are only four to six weeks ahead of boys in their level of skeletal maturity, but by age 12 the "maturation gap" has widened to two full years (Tanner, 1978).

Muscular Development

Although one might think otherwise after listening to the claims of body builders, neonates are born with all the muscle cells they will ever have (Tanner, 1978). At birth, muscle tissue is 35% water, and it accounts for no more than 18–24% of a baby's body weight

(Marshall, 1977). However, muscle fibers soon begin to grow as the cellular fluid in muscle tissue is gradually replaced with protein and salts.

Muscular development proceeds in a cephalocaudal direction; that is, muscles in the head and neck mature earlier than those in the trunk and lower limbs. Like many other aspects of physical development, the maturation of muscle tissue occurs very gradually over childhood and then accelerates during early adolescence. One consequence of this muscular growth spurt is that members of both sexes become noticeably stronger, although increases in both muscle mass and physical strength (as measured in tests of large-muscle activity) are more dramatic for males than for females (Faust, 1977; Keough & Sugden, 1985). By the midtwenties, skeletal muscle accounts for 40% of the body weight of an average male, compared with 24% for the average female (Marshall, 1977).

The skeletal and muscular development that takes place between infancy and young adulthood helps to explain the remarkable growth of motor skills that occurs over this same period—changes that we will soon discuss in some detail. But first, we must examine another important contributor to motor skills and to virtually all other aspects of human development—the maturation of the brain and the central nervous system.

Development of the Brain and the Nervous System

At birth, a baby's brain is only 25% of its eventual adult weight. However, this remarkable organ grows rapidly over the first few years, increasing to 66% of adult weight by the end of the first year, to 76% of adult weight by age 2½, and to fully 90% of its adult weight by the child's fifth birthday (see Table 5-3). By contrast,

Table 5-3. Average weight of the brain at different ages

Age	Weight (in grams)	Percentage of adult weight
2 months after conception	3	Less than 1
5 months after conception	51	4
7 months after conception	138	10
Newborn	350	25
1 year	908	66
2½ years	1050	76
5 years	1242	90
16 years	1330–1380	100

the weight of the entire body is only 5% of adult weight at birth, 20% at age 2, and 50% at age 10.

However, an increase in brain weight is a rather gross index that tells us very little about how or when various parts of the brain will mature or how these developments will affect the child's intellectual, perceptual, and motor abilities. Let's take a closer look at the internal organization and development of the central nervous system.

Nerve Cells and Their Interconnections

The human brain and nervous system is an intricate structure consisting of billions of highly specialized cells that transmit electrical and chemical signals across trillions of **synapses,** or connective spaces between the cells. **Neurons** are the basic unit of the brain and nervous system. These are the cells that receive and transmit neural impulses. **Glia** (or neuroglia) are a second type of nerve cell that nourish the neurons and eventually encase them in insulating sheaths of myelin that facilitate the transmission of neural impulses. The brain alone may contain as many as 100 billion neurons, and glia are even more numerous (Tanner, 1978).

Production of new neurons by mitosis occurs during the prenatal period and is essentially complete by the time a full-term baby is born (Cowan, 1979; Rakic, 1985). Glia are also rapidly proliferating during the prenatal period, and they continue to form until at least age 2 and possibly longer (Tanner, 1978). If sufficient protein is available from one's diet, new brain cells will immediately begin to increase in size and weight. Indeed, the last three months of prenatal life and the first two years after birth have been termed the period of the **brain growth spurt** because more than half of one's adult brain weight is added at this time (Brierley, 1976). Between the seventh prenatal month and the child's first birthday, the brain is increasing in weight by about 1.7 grams per day—more than a milligram per minute.

One of the more interesting facts about the human nervous system is that the average infant has far more neurons and neural connections than you do. Researchers have recently discovered that as many as half the neurons produced early in life also die early in life (Janowsky & Finlay, 1986). Amid this massive cellular demise, the neurons that survive are forming connections, or synapses, with other neurons. In fact, proliferation of synapses occurs so rapidly that the number of these neural connections peaks at about age 2 and then gradually declines until age 16 (Goldman-Rakic,

Isseroff, Schwartz, & Bugbee, 1983). If we likened the developing brain to a house under construction, we might imagine a builder who merrily constructs many more rooms and hallways than he needs and then later goes back and knocks about half of them out! Although this strategy may seem a rather inefficient way to build a house, it makes some sense in the construction of an efficient nervous system. Basically, infants have many more neurons and synapses than they need, so that adjacent neural pathways come into competition with one another. Those pathways that are often used will survive, whereas those that are rarely used will disappear. Clearly it is more efficient for neural impulses to travel along one central route than to have this energy divided among several adjacent pathways that differ in their capacity to transmit such information (Cowan, Fawcett, O'Leary, & Stanfield, 1984).

Plasticity of early neural development. Another interesting characteristic of the developing nervous system is its remarkable **plasticity:** the neurons of the immature brain are not yet completely specialized and, thus, may assume any number of functions. Accordingly, young children who suffer various forms of brain damage often recover from their injuries as brain cells that might otherwise have been lost assume the functions of cells that have died (Spreen, Tupper, Risser, Tuokko, & Edgell, 1984). So it would seem to be a real advantage for neonates to have more neurons and synapses than they would ordinarily need, for these extra cells and pathways may represent a "reserve capacity" on which the infant can draw should he experience a loss of brain cells due to anoxia or other complications of birth (Huttenlocher, 1984).

Nowhere is the plasticity of the brain more apparent than among those children under the age of

---

skeletal age: a measure of physical maturation based on the child's level of skeletal development.

synapse: the connective space (juncture) between one nerve cell (neuron) and another.

neurons: nerve cells that receive and transmit neural impulses.

glia: nerve cells that nourish neurons and encase them in insulating sheaths of myelin.

brain growth spurt: the period between the seventh prenatal month and 2 years of age when more than half of the child's eventual brain weight is added.

plasticity: capacity for change; a developmental state that has the potential to be shaped by experience.

2 who have had up to half of their brains removed to control problems such as violent seizures. When this operation occurs early in life, the child suffers few if any long-term deficits in functioning—the remaining portion of her brain functions like a whole brain (see Dennis & Whitaker, 1976). But as the brain becomes more specialized over the course of childhood, it also becomes less plastic. Given proper therapy, adults who suffer brain damage often regain a substantial portion of the functions they have lost—but their recoveries are rarely as rapid or as complete as those of younger children.

Why might the brain become less plastic over time? Although the answer remains elusive, Peter Huttenlocher (1984) has offered an interesting hypothesis. Huttenlocher's view is simply that the brain's loss of plasticity stems from the loss of neurons and synapses that occurs throughout childhood. So when adolescents or adults suffer a disabling brain injury, they have fewer neural circuits standing in reserve to assume the functions previously served by those that were damaged.

Experiential effects on neural development. Some 40 years ago, Austin Riesen and his associates (Riesen, 1947; Riesen, Chow, Semmes, & Nissen, 1951) discovered that one's environment plays an important role in the organization and development of the central nervous system. Riesen's subjects were infant chimpanzees that were reared in the dark for periods ranging up to 16 months. His results were striking. Chimps raised in the dark experienced atrophy of the retina and the neurons that make up the optic nerve. This atrophy was reversible if the animal's visual deprivation did not exceed seven months but was irreversible, and often led to total blindness, if the deprivation lasted longer than one year. So neurons that are not properly stimulated will degenerate—a dramatic illustration that the "use it or lose it" principle characterizes the development of the nervous system.

If a lack of stimulation inhibits the development of the brain and nervous system, might we then foster such growth by exposing subjects to enriched environments that provide a variety of stimulation? This idea is not new by any means, for in 1815 a practitioner by the name of Spurzheim claimed that "the organs of the brain increase by [mental] exercise." For more than 20 years now, Mark Rosenzweig and his associates have been evaluating the merits of this "mental exercise" hypothesis, using animals as subjects. And as we will see in Box 5-3, the results of this research clearly illustrate

that both brain size and structure can be modified by experience.

Brain Differentiation and Growth

Not all parts of the brain develop at the same rate. At birth, the most highly developed areas are the *brain stem* and the *midbrain,* which control the child's states of consciousness, inborn reflexes, and important biological functions such as digestion, respiration, and elimination. Surrounding the midbrain are the cerebrum and cerebral cortex, the areas of the brain that are most directly implicated in bodily movements, perception, and higher intellectual activities such as learning, thinking, and production of language. The first areas of the cerebrum to mature are (1) the *primary motor areas,* which control simple motor activities such as waving the arms, and (2) the *primary sensory areas,* which control sensory processes such as vision, hearing, smelling, and tasting. Within the motor area, the nerve cells controlling the arms and upper trunk develop ahead of those controlling the legs and lower trunk. That is why infants can accomplish many things with their heads, necks, hands, and arms long before they gain enough control over the lower trunk and legs to sit up, crawl, or walk. By 6 months of age, the primary motor areas of the cerebral cortex have developed to the point that they now direct most of the infant's physical activities. At this point, inborn responses such as the palmar grasp and the Babinski reflex should disappear—a positive sign that indicates that the higher cortical centers are assuming proper control over the more primitive "subcortical" areas of the brain.

Myelinization

As brain cells proliferate and grow, some of the glia begin to produce a waxy substance called *myelin* that forms a sheath around individual neurons. This myelin sheath acts like an insulator to speed the transmission of neural impulses, thus allowing different parts of the body to communicate more efficiently with the brain.

Myelinization follows a definite chronological sequence that parallels the maturation of the nervous system. At birth or shortly thereafter, the pathways between the sense organs and the brain are reasonably well myelinated. As a result, the neonate's sensory equipment is in good working order. As neural pathways between the brain and the skeletal muscles myelinate (in a cephalocaudal and proximodistal pattern), the child becomes capable of increasingly complex mo-

Box 5-3
Raising Rats in Enriched
Environments: Effects on Brain
Growth and Development

Environmental effects on the development of the brain are dramatically illustrated in a program of research by Mark Rosenzweig and his associates (Rosenzweig, 1966, 1984; Greenough, Black, & Wallace, 1987). In Rosenzweig's initial experiment, just-weaned rat pups were taken from their mothers and placed for the next 80 days in either an *enriched* or an *impoverished* environment. The enriched environment was truly enriched. Whereas standard laboratory conditions call for three rats to a cage with a continuous supply of food and water, animals raised in the enriched environment lived in groups of 10 to 12 in a large cage that contained not only food and water but also a number of "toys"—ladders to climb, platforms and boxes to explore, exercise wheels, and so on. These toys were changed daily so that the enriched ani-

mals would not become bored with their playthings. To further enrich their early experiences, the rats were given daily exploratory sessions in novel environments and practice at maze running. By contrast, "impoverished" animals were truly deprived. Each rat lived by itself in a cage with solid walls that restricted its vision. These cages contained no playthings and were placed in a quiet, dim room. To control for genetic influences, each animal in the enriched condition had a littermate in the impoverished condition. Control groups were raised under standard laboratory conditions.

After 80 days, the rats were sacrificed and their brains were weighed, dissected, and chemically analyzed. The results were intriguing. Animals raised in the enriched environment had heavier cerebral cortexes (the "highest" brain center, which controls perception, learning, and memory) than those raised in the impoverished environment. This greater cortical development of the enriched animals was not attributable to their greater body weights, for in some

of the experiments the enriched animals actually weighed less than their impoverished brethren. Furthermore, animals raised in enriched environments had larger neurons and a more extensive network of connections among neurons than animals in the impoverished condition. Finally, there were biochemical differences between the neural tissues of the enriched and the impoverished animals—differences suggesting that the neural activity of the enriched animals was greater than that of their impoverished littermates.

Similar changes in brain size and structure have now been observed in adult rats exposed to enriched environments after spending their early days in a standard laboratory setting (Greenough et al., 1987; Rosenzweig, 1984). Although longer periods of enrichment produce smaller effects in adult rats, compared with younger ones, the fact that fully mature animals show *any* enrichment effects is a clear demonstration that the brain retains some of its plasticity later in life.

---

tor activities such as lifting the head and chest, reaching with the arms and hands, rolling over, sitting, standing, and eventually walking and running. Although myelinization proceeds very rapidly over the first few years of life, some areas of the brain are not completely myelinated until the mid to late teens or early adulthood. For example, the *reticular formation*—a part of the brain that allows us to concentrate on a subject for lengthy periods—is not fully myelinated at puberty (Tanner, 1978). This may be one reason that the attention spans of infants, toddlers, and school-age children are much shorter than those of adolescents and adults.

How important is myelinization? The answer becomes obvious when we consider the plight of those with **multiple sclerosis,** a crippling disease affecting young adults that results when the myelin sheaths surrounding individual neurons begin to disintegrate. The cause of this incurable disease is unknown, and its symptoms vary depending on the part of the nervous system that deteriorates. As the condition worsens, the patient will first lose muscular control over the affected area(s) and may eventually become paralyzed or even die. So the lesson to be learned from the tragedy of

multiple sclerosis is that, without myelinization, life as we know it would be difficult if not impossible.

Specialization of the higher brain centers

The highest brain center, the cerebrum, consists of two halves (or *hemispheres*) connected by a band of fibers called the *corpus callosum.* Each of the hemispheres is covered by a *cerebral cortex*—an outer layer of gray matter that controls sensory and motor processes, perception, and intellectual functioning. Although the left and the right cerebral hemispheres are identical in appearance, they serve different functions and control different areas of the body. The left cerebral hemisphere controls the right side of the body, and as illus-

---

myelinization: the process by which neurons are enclosed in waxy myelin sheaths that will facilitate the transmission of neural impulses.
multiple sclerosis: a crippling loss of muscular control that occurs when the myelin sheaths surrounding individual neurons begin to disintegrate.

trated in Figure 5-3, it contains centers for speech, hearing, verbal memory, decision making, and processing of language, to name a few. By contrast, the right cerebral hemisphere controls the left side of the body and contains centers for processing visual-spatial information, nonlinguistic sounds such as music, tactile (touch) sensations, and emotional expressions. Thus, the brain is a *lateralized* organ. **Cerebral lateralization** also involves a preference for using one hand or one side of the body more than the other. About 90% of adults rely on their right hands (or left hemispheres) to write, eat, and perform other motor functions, whereas these same activities are under the control of the right hemisphere among people who are left-handed. However, the fact that the brain is a lateralized organ does not mean that each hemisphere is totally independent of the other, for the corpus callosum, which connects the hemispheres, plays an important role in integrating their respective functions.

When do the two cerebral hemispheres begin to "divide the work" and become lateralized? According to Erik Lenneberg's (1967) **equipotentiality hypoth-**

esis, lateralization is a very gradual process that occurs throughout childhood and is not complete until puberty. Lenneberg's argument hinges on his observations of patients struggling to regain their linguistic capabilities after suffering traumatic injuries to the language centers of the left cerebral hemisphere. If these injuries occur *after* puberty, most affected individuals will remain mute or only partly recover their linguistic capabilities. But if the damage occurs *before* puberty, affected children are likely to regain much or all of their speech. These dramatic age differences suggested to Lenneberg that the brain is much more plastic (or less specialized) earlier in life, when areas of the right hemisphere can assume linguistic functions that would ordinarily be served by the left side of the brain.

Despite Lenneberg's interesting observations, a different picture of cerebral lateralization is beginning to emerge from recent research (see Kinsbourne & Hiscock, 1983). Consider, for example, that from the first day of life, speech sounds already elicit more electrical activity from the left side of a baby's brain, while music and other nonspeech sounds elicit greater activity from

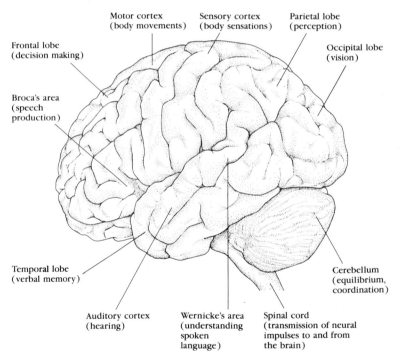

Figure 5-3. Lateral view of the left cerebral cortex and some of the functions it controls. Although the cerebellum and spinal cord are not part of the cerebral cortex, they serve important functions of their own.

the right cerebral hemisphere (Molfese, 1977). Moreover, most newborn infants display a lateral preference in their bodily movements, turning to the right rather than the left when lying on their backs (Michel, 1981). And even though very young infants are inclined to use both hands when performing motor activities, most show a clear preference for the right hand (that is, control by the left hemisphere) by 6 to 7 months of age (Ramsay, 1984, 1985). Today, many theorists believe that the two cerebral hemispheres are biologically programmed to serve different functions from the day a baby is born. According to this latter point of view, any apparent changes in lateralization that occur over time reflect children's increasing *reliance* on one hemisphere over the other to perform various tasks rather than any fundamental changes in the brain's organization or structure (Kinsbourne & Hiscock, 1983; Witelson, 1987).

Do children come to rely more and more on one particular hemisphere when performing specific tasks? Yes, indeed. Although handedness is apparent early and is reasonably well established by 2 years of age (Ramsay & Weber, 1986), lateral preferences become even stronger over time. In one experiment, preschoolers and adolescents were asked to pick up a crayon, to kick a ball, to look into a small, opaque bottle to see what was inside, and to place their ears to a box to hear a sound. Only 32% of the preschoolers, but more than half of the adolescents, showed a consistent lateral preference by relying exclusively on one side of the body to perform all four tasks (Coren, Porac, & Duncan, 1981). Recognizing shapes by touch is a spatial ability controlled by the right hemisphere and, thus, more easily accomplished with the left hand. Susan Rose (1984) finds that 3-year-olds are already better at recognizing shapes with their left than with their right hands, whereas 1-year-olds are not especially proficient at recognizing shapes with either hand. And when subjects work at complex tasks that require the use of *both* hemispheres, such as recognizing letters (a left-hemisphere function) that are inverted (a mental rotation activity controlled by the right hemisphere), 14-year-old adolescents perform much better than 10-year-olds (Merola & Liederman, 1985). So not only do children come to favor one of the two hemispheres when performing specific tasks, they also become much more proficient at integrating the respective functions served by their two cerebral hemispheres.

What are the implications for children who fail to rely on one hemisphere or the other to perform specific functions? Leslie Tan (1985) finds that 4-year-olds who have not yet established a dominant hand are more likely than their left- or right-handed age mates to be uncoordinated and delayed in their motor development. Moreover, many **dyslexic** children who are facing serious difficulties learning to read show an abnormal pattern of cerebral lateralization—one in which spatial functions (normally a right-hemisphere activity) are being served by *both* hemispheres (Witelson, 1977). This incomplete lateralization of spatial activities is thought to be a problem because the left hemisphere's processing of spatial information may be interfering with the auditory functions it normally serves, perhaps explaining why so many dyslexic youngsters struggle to match written words with their corresponding sounds and have difficulties discriminating letters that look and sound alike (for example, *b* and *d*). Although not everyone agrees that all forms of dyslexia have a neurological basis, the fact remains that many dyslexics do show irregularities in cerebral lateralization that may well be contributing to the reading difficulties they are experiencing (Kinsbourne & Hiscock, 1983; Pennington et al., 1986).

Motor Development

Perhaps the main reason that neonates seem so helpless is that they are totally incapable of moving about on their own. Oh, it is true that they may turn their heads, flail their arms, and kick their legs a bit; but the human infant is disadvantaged in comparison with the young of many species, who can follow their mothers to food (and then feed themselves) very soon after they are born.

Fortunately, the infant does not remain immobile for long. By the end of the first month, the brain and neck muscles have matured enough to permit most infants to reach the first milestone in motor development—lifting their chins while lying flat on their stomachs. Soon thereafter, children will be lifting their chests

----

cerebral lateralization: the specialization of brain functions in the left and the right cerebral hemispheres.

equipotentiality hypothesis: the notion that the cerebral hemispheres are extremely plastic early in life, so that each hemisphere can assume functions normally served by the other.

dyslexic: a general label applied to individuals who face major problems in learning to read.

as well, reaching for objects, and sitting up if someone is there to support them. Investigators who have charted the motor development of human infants over the first two years of life find that motor skills evolve in a definite sequence, which appears in Table 5-4. Although the ages at which these skills first appear vary considerably from child to child, infants who are quick to proceed through this motor sequence are not necessarily any brighter or otherwise advantaged, compared with those whose rates of motor development are average or below average. So even though the age norms in Table 5-4 are a useful standard for gauging an infant's progress as he or she begins to sit, stand, and take those first tentative steps, a child's rate of motor development really tells us very little about *future* developmental outcomes. (The one exception is the 1–2% of infants who lag 6–8 months or more behind the age norms. These youngsters sometimes have serious neurological dysfunctions that can impede their social and intellectual development.)

Basic Trends in Locomotor Development

There are two fundamental "laws" that describe motor development during the first few years of life. First, development proceeds in a *cephalocaudal* (head to foot) direction: motor activities involving the head, neck, and upper extremities appear before those

involving the legs and the lower extremities. At the same time, development advances in a *proximodistal* (center outward) direction: activities involving the trunk and shoulders appear before those involving the hands and fingers. Does this cephalocaudal/proximodistal pattern ring a bell? It should, for we have seen that both the muscles and the myelinization of neural pathways follow the same head-downward, center-outward pattern of development. Mary Shirley (1933) believed that locomotor development is a *maturational* phenomenon: as the nerves and muscles mature in a downward and outward direction, children will gradually gain control over the lower and peripheral parts of their bodies and will come to display locomotor skills in the order shown in Table 5-4.

Other Motor Milestones

The sequence of motor development described in Table 5-4 is concerned with the growth of skills that enable the child to sit, stand, and walk. Two other aspects of motor development also play important roles in the child's ability to adapt to the environment—manipulation of objects and visual/motor coordination.

Locating and grasping objects

We have learned that newborn babies are already capable of grasping objects with their palms. But as this reflexive "palmar grasp" weakens at 2–4 months of age, an infant's hand skills may seem to deteriorate. At age 3–4 months, infants enjoy slapping at objects but cannot grasp them well: the problem is that they tend to close their hands too early or too late (Bower, 1982). Moreover, very young infants lack the *eye/hand coordination* that would make them proficient at locating and grasping objects. Before 20 weeks of age, an infant who misses when reaching for an object will retract her hand from the visual field and reach all over again. Early reaching is truly a hit-or-miss proposition. By contrast, infants older than 20 weeks can extend their arms and make in-flight corrections to guide their hands to the target. So the reaching behavior of very young infants is visually *initiated,* whereas the same behavior by older infants is visually *guided* (Bower, 1982).

Do older infants actually have to watch their hands if they hope to make contact with a desired object? Apparently not. Thomas Bower (1982) describes an experiment in which the lights were extinguished just before 5-month-old infants could reach for attractive objects. Although these infants could no longer rely on visual cues to direct their hand to the target, they were

Table 5-4. Age norms (in months) for important motor milestones *maturational phenomenon*

Skill	Month when 50% of infants have mastered the skill	Month when 90% of infants have mastered the skill
Lifts head 90° while lying on stomach	2.2	3.2
Rolls over	2.8	4.7
Sits propped up	2.9	4.2
Sits without support	5.5	7.8
Stands holding on	5.8	10.0
Walks holding on	9.2	12.7
Stands alone momentarily	9.8	13.0
Stands well alone	11.5	13.9
Walks well	12.1	14.3
Walks up steps	17.0	22.0
Kicks ball forward	20.0	24.0

Source: Adapted from Frankenberg & Dodds (1967).

able to reach out and touch the object with little or no difficulty. Thus, visual cues help the infant to *locate* an object and tell him where to reach; however, vision is not necessary to control the child's reaching. (Indeed, it is fortunate that our motor responses do not require absolute visual control; otherwise we would have to watch our feet hit the ground to avoid falling flat on our faces when we walk or run.)

By the middle of the first year, infants can once again grasp small objects, but this **ulnar grasp** is a rather clumsy, clawlike grip involving the palm and outer fingers. Over the next several months, "fingering" skills gradually improve, until at 9–12 months of age the child is capable of using the thumb and forefinger to lift and fondle objects (Halverson, 1931). This **pincer grip** transforms the infant from a little fumbler into a skillful manipulator who may soon begin to corner crawling bugs and to turn knobs, dials, and rheostats, thereby discovering that he can use his newly acquired hand skills to produce any number of interesting results.

As maturation proceeds during the second year, infants become much more proficient with their hands. At 16 months of age they can scribble with a crayon, and by the end of the second year, they can copy a simple horizontal or vertical line and even build towers of five or more blocks. What is happening is that the infant is gaining control over simple movements and then integrating these skills into increasingly complex, coordinated actions (Fentress & McLeod, 1986). Building a tower, for example, requires the infant to first gain control over the thumb and the forefinger and then use the pincer grip as part of a larger action sequence that involves reaching for a block, snatching it, laying it squarely on top of another block, and then delicately releasing it. But despite their newly acquired ability to combine simple motor activities into meaningful sequences, 2- to 3-year-olds are not very good at catching and throwing a ball, eating with silverware, or drawing within the lines of their coloring books. These skills will emerge later in childhood as the muscles mature and children become more proficient at using visual information to help them coordinate their actions.

Beyond Infancy—Motor Development in Childhood

The term *toddler* aptly describes most 1–2-year-olds, who, like the notorious drunken sailor, will often fall down or trip over stationary objects when they try to get somewhere in a hurry. But as children mature, their locomotor skills increase by "leaps and bounds."

Photo 5-3. Top-heavy toddlers often lose their balance when they try to move very quickly.

By age 3, children can walk or run in a straight line and leap off the floor with both feet, although they can clear only very small (8–10-inch) objects in a single bound and cannot easily turn or stop while running. Four-year-olds can skip, hop on one foot, catch a large ball with both hands, and run much farther and faster than they could one year earlier (Corbin, 1973). By age 5, children are becoming rather graceful: like adults, they pump their arms when they run, and their balance has improved to the point that some of them can learn to ride a bicycle. One reason preschool children become more fluid in their large-muscle activities is that they are losing much of their baby fat (including their protruding bellies) as they grow in height. As a result, their centers of gravity move steadily downward, and they become

---

ulnar grasp: an early manipulatory skill in which an infant grasps objects by pressing the fingers against the palm.

pincer grip: a grasp in which the thumb is used in opposition to the fingers, enabling an infant to become more dexterous at lifting and fondling objects.

capable of coordinated actions requiring a degree of balance that is quite impossible for a top-heavy infant or toddler (Lowery, 1978).

Eye/hand and small-muscle coordination also improve rather dramatically during the preschool years. Three-year-olds find it difficult to button their clothing, tie a shoe, or copy a figure (other than a circle) on a piece of paper. Two years later, children can accomplish all these objectives and even cut a straight line with scissors, draw a person, and copy letters or numbers with a crayon.

About the time children enter the first grade (age 6–7), they can copy complex figures (such as a diamond), cut out angular patterns (paper dolls) with scissors, and print neatly and accurately (Gesell, Ames, & Ilg, 1977). Further advances in small-muscle coordination will enable the child to take up and enjoy hobbies such as assembling models, painting by the numbers, and sewing. By age 8–9, children can use most household tools (such as screwdrivers and can openers) and have become skillful performers at games such as baseball and jacks that require eye/hand coordination.

Another reason that older children outperform younger ones at "action" games such as dodgeball and Pac-Man is that they have quicker reactions than their younger playmates. In studies of *reaction time,* a stimulus such as a light suddenly appears, and the subject's task is to respond as quickly as possible by hitting a lever or pressing a button. These studies reveal that reaction time improves steadily throughout childhood (Thomas, Gallagher, & Purvis, 1981).

With each passing year, school-age children can run a little faster, jump a little higher, and throw a ball a little farther (Herkowitz, 1978; Keough & Sugden, 1985). Boys and girls are nearly equal in physical abilities until puberty, when males continue to post gains on tests of large-muscle activities, while females level off or decline (see Figure 5-4). These sex differences are, in part, attributable to biology: males have more muscle than females and might be expected to outperform them on tests of physical strength. Yet, the biological explanation does not adequately account for the *declining* performance of females, who continue to grow taller, heavier, and presumably stronger between ages 12 and 17. Jacqueline Herkowitz (1978) has suggested that the apparent physical decline of adolescent females is a product of sex-role socialization: with the widening of the hips and development of breasts, girls are strongly encouraged to become less tomboyish and more interested in traditionally feminine (and often more sedentary) activities.

There is clearly an element of truth to Herkowitz's sex-typing hypothesis. Consider, for example, that female *athletes* show no apparent decline in physical performance over time and that at least one study of females' performance in track, swimming, and cycling suggests that, as sex roles have changed over the past 30 years, women have consistently improved upon and

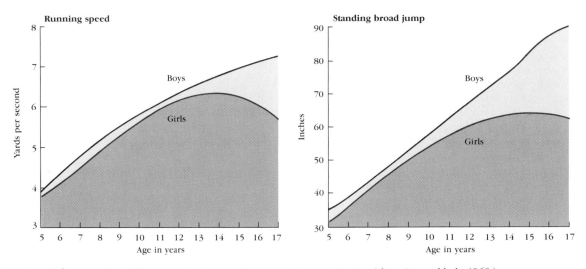

Figure 5-4. Age and sex differences on two tests of large-muscle activity. *(Adapted from Espenschlade, 1960.)*

have often shattered previous world records (Dyer, 1977). Indeed, female marathon runners are now posting times that would have beaten all the male competitors from the 1930s and 1940s! Although not all of today's young women are athletically inclined, the implications of these data are clear: adolescent females would almost certainly continue to improve on tests of large-muscle activity should they choose to remain physically active during their teenage years.

Puberty—The Physical Transition from Child to Adult

The onset of adolescence is heralded by two significant changes in physical development—the **adolescent growth spurt** and **puberty.** The term *puberty* (from the Latin *pubertas,* meaning "age of manhood" or, literally, "to grow hairy") refers to that point in life when we reach sexual maturity and become capable of producing a child. It is generally assumed that a girl becomes sexually mature at **menarche**—the time of her first menstrual period. However, James Tanner (1978) notes that young girls often menstruate without ovulating, and as a result they *may* remain functionally sterile for 12–18 months after menarche. The timing of puberty is much harder to pinpoint in males, since production of sperm is not a readily observable phenomenon. The most common index of masculine puberty is the appearance of pigmented pubic hair, an event that may occur well after the boy's penis and testicles have begun to grow (Tanner, 1978).

In this section of the chapter, we will first consider the dramatic physical changes that occur during the first two years of adolescence as the child loses that "boyish" or "girlish" look and begins to resemble an adult. And in considering the physical events of adolescence from the perspective of the teenager who experiences them, we will discover that these dramatic biological upheavals play a major role in shaping a teenager's self-concept, which, in turn, may affect the ways he or she relates to other people later in life.

The Adolescent Growth Spurt

The term *growth spurt* describes the rapid acceleration in height and weight that marks the beginning of adolescence. The timing of this event varies considerably from child to child. Girls may begin as early as age 7½ or as late as 12. The typical pattern is for a girl to start her period of rapid growth at age 10½, to

reach a peak growth rate at age 12, and to return to a slower, "prespurt" rate of growth by age 13–13½ (Tanner, 1981). Boys lag behind girls by two to three years, entering their period of rapid growth as early as age 10½ or as late as age 16. The typical pattern for males is to begin their growth spurt at age 13, to peak at age 14, and to return to a more gradual rate of growth by age 15½ or 16. Because girls mature much earlier than boys, it is not at all uncommon for females to be the tallest two or three students in a junior high school classroom.

In addition to growing taller and heavier, the body assumes an adultlike appearance during the adolescent growth spurt. Perhaps the most noticeable changes are a widening of the hips for females and a broadening of the shoulders for males. Facial features are also assuming adult proportions as the forehead protrudes, the nose and jaw become more prominent, and the lips enlarge. Gone forever is that soft-featured, innocent look that we associate with childhood.

The adolescent growth spurt is not as uniform as our overview might indicate. Body weight begins to increase first, followed four to six months later by a rapid increase in height (Tanner, 1978). The muscles are growing along with the rest of the body, although the period of greatest muscular development does not occur until a year after the maximum acceleration in height. And because this "muscle spurt" happens earlier for girls than for boys, there is a brief period when the average girl has more muscle than most of her male age mates.

Sexual Maturation

Maturation of the reproductive system occurs at roughly the same time as the adolescent growth spurt and follows a predictable sequence for members of each sex.

Sexual development in girls. For most girls, sexual maturation begins at about age 11 as fatty tissue accumulates around their their nipples, forming small "breast buds." Usually pubic hair begins to appear a little later, although as many as one-third of all girls

---

adolescent growth spurt: the rapid increase in physical growth that marks the beginning of adolescence.
puberty: the point at which a person reaches sexual maturity and is physically capable of fathering or conceiving a child.
menarche: the first occurrence of menstruation.

develop some public hair before the breasts begin to develop (Tanner, 1978).

As a girl enters her height spurt, the breasts grow rapidly and the sex organs begin to mature. Internally, the vagina becomes larger, and the walls of the uterus develop a powerful set of muscles that may one day be used to accommodate a fetus during pregnancy and to push it through the cervix and vagina during the birth process. Externally, the mons pubis (the soft tissue covering the pubic bone), the labia (the fleshy lips surrounding the vaginal opening), and the clitoris all increase in size and become more sensitive to tactile stimulation (Tanner, 1978).

The average female reaches menarche within six months of her 13th birthday—fully two years after the onset of breast development and about the time the height spurt is over (Tanner, 1978). Within a year of menarche, the young woman's breasts and pubic hair will have fully developed, and she will be grappling with the specter of axillary (armpit) hair—a feature that women in our society have been led to believe they are better off without.

Sexual development in boys. For boys, sexual maturation begins at about 11–11½ with the initial enlargement of the testes and scrotum (the saclike structure enclosing the testes). The growth of the testes is often accompanied or soon followed by the appearance of unpigmented pubic hair. About six months to a year later, the penis undergoes a period of rapid growth that coincides with the onset of the adolescent growth spurt. By the time the penis is fully developed (typically around age 14½–15), the adolescent male will reach puberty and is now capable of fathering a child.

Facial hair appears somewhat later, as outcroppings first emerge at the corners of the upper lip and then spread to the entire upper lip, to the upper cheeks, and finally to the chin and jawline. Body hair also begins to grow at this time, although that "hoped for" matting of chest hair may not appear until the late teens or early twenties—if it appears at all.

After a boy reaches sexual maturity, his voice will begin to change from the soprano of childhood to the baritone that characterizes adult males. This turn of events, which may occur gradually or abruptly, is due to growth of the larynx and lengthening of the vocal cords. Voice lowering may have its comical side: almost every man can remember at least one occasion when his voice ranged from squeaky soprano to baritone and back to soprano—sometimes within a single sentence.

Although boys are often embarrassed by this "breaking" of the voice, it is a perfectly normal sign of sexual maturity that heralds the coming of manhood.

Individual differences in sexual maturation. The sequences of sexual maturation described above are merely norms and averages that will not necessarily characterize the development of an individual child. Figure 5-5 gives us some idea of the wide variation among children in the timing of sexual maturation. Consider, for example, that an early-maturing female who develops breast buds at age 8, has pubic hair at age 11, and experiences menarche at 11½ may nearly complete her sexual maturation before the late developers in her classroom have even begun. Individual variation among males is at least as great: some boys reach sexual maturity as early as age 12½, while others *begin* later than that and do not reach puberty until their

Photo 5-4. During early adolescence, girls are maturing more rapidly than boys.

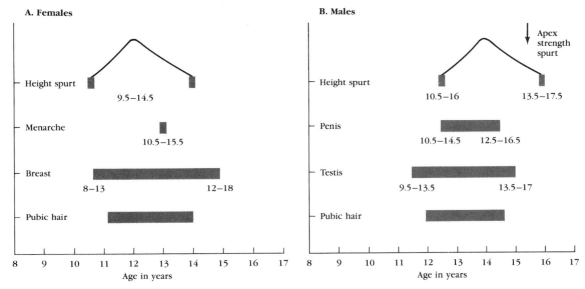

Figure 5-5. Sequence of events in the sexual maturation of females (A) and males (B). The numbers represent the variation among individuals in the ages at which each aspect of sexual maturation begins or ends. For example, we see that the growth of the penis may begin as early as age 10½ or as late as age 14½. *(From Marshall & Tanner, 1970.)*

mid to late teens. Thus, a 12-year-old girl or a 14-year-old boy might be *prepubertal* (sexually immature), *midpubertal* (rapidly maturing), or *postpubertal* (sexually mature). Biologically, this kind of variation is perfectly normal; and the age at which one attains sexual maturity has no significant effect on one's physical stature (height and weight) as an adult (Faust, 1977).

Secular trends—are we maturing earlier? Recently the females in one family were surprised when a member of the younger generation began to menstruate some two months after her 12th birthday. The inevitable comparisons soon began, as the girl learned that neither of her great-grandmothers had reached this milestone until age 15 and that her grandmother had been nearly 14 and her mother almost 13. At this point, the girl casually replied "Big deal! Lots of girls in my class have got their periods."

As it turns out, this young lady was simply "telling it like it is." In 1900, when her great-grandmother was born, the average age of first menstruation was 14–15. By 1950 most girls were reaching menarche between 13½ and 14, and today's norms have dropped even further, to age 12½ (Roche, 1979; Tanner, 1981). This secular trend toward earlier maturation started more than 100 years ago in the industrialized nations of the world, where it has recently leveled off, and it is now

happening in the more prosperous of the Third World countries as well (Tanner, 1981). In addition, people have been growing taller and heavier over the past century, as we can see in Figure 5-6.

Why have we become taller and heavier, and why do we now reach puberty earlier than ever before? James Tanner (1978) believes that these secular trends are due, in part, to improved medical care and better nutrition. Many crippling or growth-retarding illnesses have been eliminated over the past several decades, and the quality and quantity of nutrition have steadily improved. As a result, today's children are more likely than their parents or grandparents to reach their genetic potentials for maturation and growth.

Psychological Impact of Adolescent Growth and Development

What do adolescents think about the dramatic physical changes they are experiencing? For starters, they become quite concerned about their appearance and spend a great deal of time worrying about how other people will respond to them (Berscheid, Walster, & Bohrnstedt, 1973; Greif & Ulman, 1982). Generally speaking, adolescent females are most concerned about being too tall or too fat, and many well-proportioned young girls may compensate for perceived physical inadequacies by slouching, wearing flats, or trying a seem-

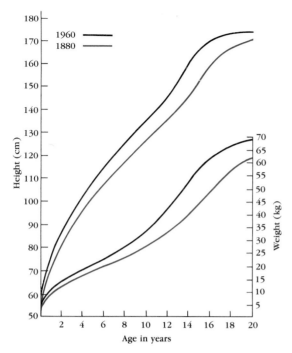

Figure 5-6. Average height and weight of North American White males, by age, in 1880 and 1960. *(From Meredith, 1963.)*

ingly endless number of fad diets (for examples of what can happen if a girl becomes overly preoccupied with her weight, see Box 5-4). Girls are also apt to worry about the condition and texture of their hair and the size of their ears, breasts, noses, and hips. Clearly, adolescent females hope to be attractive to members of the other sex, and their self-concepts depend largely on how attractive they believe themselves to be (Berscheid et al., 1973).

As for their reactions to their first menstruation, most girls are rather ambivalent (Greif & Ulman, 1982). They are often a bit excited but may be somewhat confused as well, especially if they mature very early or lack knowledge about what this event means. According to Diane Ruble and Jeanne Brooks-Gunn (1982), few girls are traumatized by menarche, but at the same time, few express delight about becoming a woman.

Although adolescent males might have you believe otherwise, they too are very concerned about their body images, particularly those characteristics that might reflect on their masculine prowess. Thus, young teenage boys hope to be tall, muscular, handsome, and hairy, and an obvious deficiency in any of these respects is

likely to make the distressed young man the butt of many jokes (Berscheid et al., 1973). Very little is known about boys' reactions to their first ejaculation, although the responses of one small sample suggests that teenage males are more positive about this sign of manhood and happier to be "grown up" than females are about their first menstruation (Gaddis & Brooks-Gunn, 1985).

Effects of body build. Body build (or physique) is a physical attribute that can affect one's self-concept and popularity with peers throughout childhood and adolescence. In one study (Staffieri, 1967), 6- to 10-year-olds were shown full-length silhouettes of **ectomorphic** (thin, linear), **endomorphic** (soft, chubby), and **mesomorphic** (athletic and muscular) physiques such as those shown in Figure 5-7. After stating which body type they preferred, the children were given a list of adjectives and asked to select those that applied to each body type. Finally, each child was asked to list the names of five classmates who could be considered good friends and three classmates whom he or she didn't like very well.

The results were clear. Not only did children prefer the mesomorphic silhouette, but they attributed positive adjectives—*brave, strong, neat,* and *helpful*—to this figure while assigning much less favorable adjectives to the ectomorphic and especially the endomorphic figure. Finally, there was a definite relationship between body build and popularity: the mesomorphs in the class turned out to be the most popular children, while the endomorphs were least popular (see also Sigelman, Miller, & Whitworth, 1986). Later research with adolescents and adults paints a similar picture—mesomorphs are generally popular individuals who often rise to positions of leadership, whereas ectomorphs and endomorphs tend to be less popular with their peers (Clausen, 1975).

Why should body build affect one's social status? Given the positive expectations that people have about mesomorphs and the less favorable stereotypes about other body types, it is likely that parents, teachers, and peers behave differently toward children with dif-

---

ectomorph: a person with a thin, linear physique and small or underdeveloped muscles.

endomorph: a person with a soft, rounded physique; one who appears chubby and nonmuscular.

mesomorph: a person with an athletic physique characterized by large bones, broad shoulders, well-developed muscles, and little fat.

Box 5-4

Two Serious Dieting Disorders of Adolescence

Twenty years ago, a young British model nicknamed "Twiggy" epitomized the height of fashion. As her name implied, Twiggy was very thin. And the attention she received from the popular media sent a none-too-subtle message to women around the Western world—skinny is beautiful, and it is a tragedy to be fat.

Unfortunately, some adolescents carry this maxim to a life-threatening extreme. *Anorexia nervosa* (or "nervous loss of appetite") is a potentially fatal eating disorder—one without any known organic cause—that may affect as many as 1 of every 200 adolescent females (and smaller numbers of males and adult females). Anorexics have a morbid fear of becoming obese and will do whatever they can to purge their bodies of fat. The typical anorexic is a quiet, obedient teenage girl who suddenly begins to starve herself soon after experiencing the bodily changes associated with menarche (or after someone happens to mention that she is getting fat). The process seems harmless at first as the young woman sets a modest goal and diets to the desired weight. But once she reaches her target, the anorexic simply continues to diet, eating less and less until she is little more than skin and bones. After she loses 20–30% of her body weight, the development of secondary sex characteristics (breasts and hips) may be scarcely noticeable, and menstruation often stops. And even though she may resemble a walking skeleton, the 60–70-pound anorexic will insist that she is well nourished and will feel that she could stand to lose a few more pounds (Minuchin, Rosman, & Baker, 1978). Imagine feeling obese at 60 pounds! Anorexia nervosa is not merely a faddish quirk that is easily overcome; in fact, only 25–30% of anorexics show any improvement without psychological help, and some 5–20% end up committing suicide or starving themselves to death

(Schleimer, 1981; Schwartz & Thompson, 1981).

Parents of anorexics are often firm, overprotective guardians who have so controlled their child's activities that she has trouble making decisions and may find it difficult to establish an identity of her own. Psychoanalytic theorists have argued that the purpose of self-starvation is to avoid growing up and having to become independent of one's parents: by remaining childlike in appearance, the anorexic attempts to be a child—someone to be cared for and nurtured. However, behaviorists view the condition as a strategy on the part of the adolescent to wrest control of her life from overprotective parents while remaining at the center of their attention.

Although psychoanalysts and behaviorists disagree on the anorexic's underlying motives, members of both groups acknowledge that anorexia nervosa is a family condition that requires family therapy. Treatment may begin by hospitalizing the anorexic and applying operant conditioning techniques to get her to eat. For example, the anorexic may be punished for weight loss by having to stay in bed and rewarded with privileges such as television or visitors on days when she has gained weight. After the patient has begun to eat, the operant therapy is followed by family therapy in which the parents and the affected child are encouraged to view themselves as autonomous individuals who each have their own unique needs, goals, and motives. The purpose of the therapy is to persuade parents to exert less control over the adolescent's activities while convincing the adolescent that she can achieve autonomy through means other than self-starvation. Although extensive treatment may be called for in some cases, many anorexics respond favorably to family therapy, eventually overcoming their condition (Andersen, 1985; Minuchin et al., 1978).

Bulimia is another serious eating disorder that is much more common than anorexia. Bulimics are binge eaters who may consume several times their normal daily caloric intake in a single sit-

ting and then purge themselves of this feast by vomiting or taking laxatives. Although anorexics are often bulimics, most who suffer from bulimia are of normal weight or are slightly overweight. Like anorexics, bulimic individuals tend to have poor body images and are overly concerned about getting fat. However, bulimics differ from anorexics in that they are usually extraverted and impulsive rather than quiet and reserved (Andersen, 1983). Bulimia is most common among college-age populations, where as many as 5% of the men and 20% of the women regularly partake in this "binge-purge" syndrome (Halmi, Falk, & Schwartz, 1981; Seabrook, 1987).

Although bulimia may seem a relatively harmless affliction, it can have any number of very serious side effects (Seabrook, 1987). For example, laxatives and diuretics used as purging agents can deplete the body of potassium and induce cardiac arrhythmia and heart attacks. Regular induction of vomiting can produce hernias, and bulimics have even drowned in their own vomit (Seabrook, 1987). Finally, binge eating is hardly a constructive approach to most problems, particularly for someone who is concerned about getting fat. Thus, it is perhaps understandable that many bulimics are depressed (about their binges and life in general) and that some turn to suicide as a solution for their problems.

Treatment for bulimia includes (1) individual psychotherapy, designed to help the patient understand the causes of binging and how these episodes might be controlled, (2) family therapy, in which family members learn how to provide the kinds of support and assistance that may lessen the chances that the patient will use food as a means of coping with stress, and (3) antidepressant medication for those bulimics who show signs of clinical depression. Although many bulimics respond favorably to treatment, it has been estimated that the majority of affected individuals never recognize that they have a potentially serious problem and, thus, may continue to binge without seeking help (Seabrook, 1987).

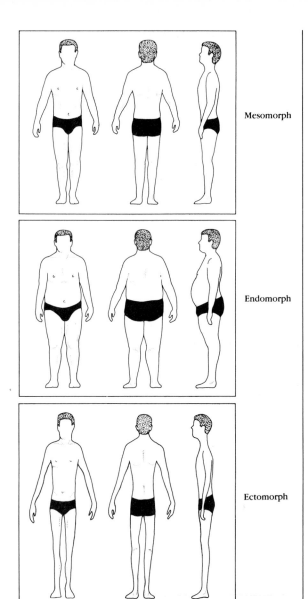

Figure 5-7. The three body types used in Staffieri's experiment.

Mesomorph

Endomorph

Ectomorph

ferent physiques, thereby contributing to a **self-ful-filling prophecy** (Langlois & Downs, 1979). For example, if teachers believe that mesomorphs are strong, friendly, and helpful and that ectomorphs are passive, shy, and inhibited, whom do you suppose they will appoint to leadership posts or encourage to run in student

elections? What are the chances that endomorphic females (who are generally presumed to be "sluggish" and "slow") would receive enthusiastic receptions were they to don those skimpy skirts and lead cheers for the football team? The point to be made is that our stereotypes about physique and its correlates will affect the way we treat our acquaintances, which, in turn, will affect their behavior. Stated another way, the social environment ends up fitting people into distinct personality (or popularity) molds that are based, in part, on physical appearances.

Does rate of maturation matter? Think back for a moment to your own adolescence—to that point when you first realized you were rapidly becoming a man or a woman. Did this happen earlier to you than to your friends, or later? Do you think the timing of these events had any meaningful effects on your personality or your social life?

Longitudinal research conducted at the University of California suggests that boys who mature early enjoy a number of social advantages over boys who mature late. Mary Cover Jones and Nancy Bayley (1950) followed the development of 16 early-maturing and 16 late-maturing male adolescents over a six-year period. They found that late maturers were more eager, anxious, and attention-seeking and were rated as less masculine and less physically attractive than early maturers. Early maturers tended to be poised and confident in social settings, and they were overrepresented among those who had won athletic honors or election to student offices. Other researchers have found that late maturers tend to feel somewhat unsure of themselves, socially inadequate, and inferior, they have lower educational aspirations than early maturers do, and they often express a need for encouragement, sympathy, and understanding (Duke et al., 1982; Livson & Peskin, 1980; Mussen & Jones, 1957; Weatherley, 1964).

Do boys who mature late eventually overcome the social disadvantages they faced as adolescents? Mary Cover Jones (1957, 1965) addressed this question by following up on the 32 boys from Jones and Bayley's project when these subjects were in their early thirties. Although many of the differences between the two groups had diminished since adolescence, the late maturers were still less sociable, less responsible, less confident, and less popular with peers than members of the early-maturing group. The late maturers showed some strengths, however, in that they were less rigid than early maturers and somewhat more innovative in their

approaches to problem solving. But on the whole, it seemed as if the social disadvantages that late-maturing males experience during adolescence may sometimes persist well into adulthood.

Why is the early-maturing male in such an advantageous position? Possibly because other people react very positively to the adultlike appearance of an early maturer, affording him privileges and responsibilities normally reserved for older individuals. Indeed, parents hold higher educational and achievement aspirations for early-maturing than for late-maturing sons (Duke et al., 1982), and they have fewer conflicts with early maturers about issues such as acceptable curfews and the boy's choice of friends (Savin-Williams & Small, 1986). Perhaps you can see how this generally positive, harmonious atmosphere might promote the poise or self-confidence that enables early maturers to become popular and to assume positions of leadership within the peer group. By contrast, if parents, teachers, and peers continue to treat a "boyish-looking" late maturer as if he were somehow less worthy of privileges or responsibility, it is easy to see how he could become unsure of himself and feel rejected.

For girls, the relationship between rate of maturation and social status is more complex. Many studies find that early-maturing females are somewhat less self-confident, outgoing, and popular than late maturers and that girls whose maturation is "on time" are the most

popular of all and have the best self-images (Aro & Taipale, 1987; Clausen, 1975; Duncan, Ritter, Dornbusch, Gross, & Carlsmith, 1985; Faust, 1960). Intuitively, these findings make a good deal of sense. Early-maturing females are very different in appearance both from their female classmates, who may tease them, and from male peers, who will not mature for several years and who may not yet be all that enthused about the early maturer's more womanly attributes. Moreover, parents report having many more conflicts about acceptable curfews and choices of friends with early-maturing than with late-maturing daughters (Savin-Williams & Small, 1986)—conflicts that may contribute to a surly, defiant attitude that colors the early maturer's relations with peers. However, the curses of early maturity appear to be short-lived for many girls. In fact, Margaret Faust (1960) finds that early maturers often rise to positions of prominence later in junior high school when the female peer group develops a strong interest in heterosexual relationships and discovers that early-maturing females tend to be popular with males.

Overall, then, the advantages of maturing early are greater for males than for females, and the psychological differences between early and late maturers become smaller and somewhat more variable over time. In interpreting the data, it is important to note that differences between early and late maturers are not large and that many *individuals* will not necessarily mirror the patterns described above. Some early-maturing males are nerds and remain nerdy over time; some early-maturing females are immensely popular throughout childhood and adolescence. As we will see in Chapters 12 and 16, many factors contribute to a person's self-image and social status, and timing of puberty is but one small term in this rather complex equation.

Causes and Correlates of Physical Growth and Development

At the beginning of the chapter, you were asked to think about *how* and *why* children grow and why they develop increasingly precise motor skills that enable them to crawl, walk, jump, and run. These thought questions normally provoke a lot of discussion in my own

---

self-fulfilling prophecy: phenomenon whereby people come to act in accordance with others' expectations of them.

classes. Typically, someone will first offer a biological explanation, arguing that our genotypes and maturational timetables determine the rate and extent of physical growth, as well as the sequencing and timing of motor development. But invariably, other students are quick to point out that environmental factors such as nutrition or opportunities to practice motor skills may also influence physical development. Although these students may not have read the pertinent literature, they are usually able to generate enough anecdotal evidence to conclude that physical growth and development represent a complex interplay between biological predispositions and a variety of environmental influences, in which biology assumes the more dominant role. Now let's consider the data that have led many developmentalists to agree with this conclusion.

Biological Mechanisms

Clearly, biological factors play a major role in the growth process. Although children do not all grow at the same rate, we have seen that the *sequencing* of both physical maturation and motor development is reasonably consistent from child to child. Apparently these regular maturational sequences that all humans share are species-specific attributes—products of our common genetic heritage.

Effects of individual genotypes. Aside from our common genetic ties to the human race, we have each inherited a unique combination of genes that will affect our physical growth and development. For example, children of tall parents tend to be taller than children of short parents, a finding that implies that stature is a heritable attribute. The proof comes from family studies: identical twins are much more similar in stature than fraternal twins, whether the measurements are taken during the first year of life, at 4 years of age, or in early adulthood (Tanner, 1978; Wilson, 1976).

Rate of maturation is also a heritable attribute. James Tanner (1978) reports that female identical twins who live together reach menarche within two months of each other, while fraternal twin sisters are often 10–12 months apart. Tanner concludes that this genetic control of growth rate "operates throughout the whole process of growth, for skeletal maturity at all ages shows the same type of family correlations as menarche. The age of eruption of the teeth is similarly controlled [by one's genotype]" (p. 126).

Of course, knowing that genotype affects "rate of maturation" and the size or shape that one assumes

is only part of the story. The next logical question is "*How* does genotype influence the growth process?" To be honest, we are not completely certain, although it appears that our genes regulate the production of hormones, which, in turn, have a major effect on physical growth and development.

Hormonal influences—the endocrinology of growth. In Chapter 4 we noted that a male fetus assumes a malelike appearance because (1) a gene on his Y chromosome triggers the development of testes, which (2) secrete a male hormone (testosterone) that is necessary for the development of a male reproductive system. By the fourth prenatal month, the thyroid gland has formed and begins to produce **thyroxine,** a hormone that is essential if the brain and nervous system are to develop properly. Babies born with a thyroid deficiency will soon become mentally handicapped if this condition goes undiagnosed and untreated (Tanner, 1978). Those who develop a thyroid deficiency later in childhood will not suffer brain damage, because their brain growth spurt is over. However, they will begin to grow very slowly, a finding that indicates that a certain level of thyroxine is necessary for normal growth and development.

Perhaps the most critical of the *endocrine* (hormone-secreting) glands is the **pituitary,** a "master gland" located at the base of the brain that sends biochemical signals to trigger the release of hormones from all other endocrine glands. For example, the thyroid gland secretes thyroxine only if instructed to do so by a hormone (thyroid-stimulating hormone, or TSH) from the pituitary. In addition to regulating the endocrine system, the pituitary produces a **growth hormone (GH)** that stimulates the rapid growth and development of body cells. Growth hormone is released in small amounts several times a day. When parents tell their children that lots of sleep helps one to grow big and strong, they are right—GH is normally secreted into the bloodstream about 60–90 minutes after a child falls asleep (Tanner, 1978). Although much remains to be learned about how GH stimulates growth, we do know that it is essential for *normal* growth and development. Children who lack this hormone do grow, and they are usually well proportioned as adults. However, they will stand only about 130 cm tall—a little over 4 feet (Tanner, 1978). Today, these youngsters can attain a more normal stature by receiving injections of GH. However, this treatment is very expensive, averaging well in excess of $1000 per inch of growth (Sternberg, 1986).

Table 5-5. Hormonal influences on growth and development

Endocrine gland	Hormones produced	Effects on growth and development
Pituitary	Activating hormones	Signal other endocrine glands to secrete their hormones ⟶ *master gland*
	Growth hormone	Helps to regulate growth from birth through adolescence
Thyroid	Thyroxine	Affects growth and development of the brain and helps to regulate growth of the body during childhood
Adrenal glands	Adrenal androgens	Stimulates the adolescent growth spurt, pubic hair, and axillary hair in females; supplements the adolescent growth spurt in males
Testes	Testosterone	Is responsible for differentiation of the male reproductive system during the prenatal period; triggers the male growth spurt and sexual maturation during adolescence
Ovaries	Estrogen Progesterone	Trigger sexual maturation in females and are responsible for regulating the menstrual cycle

As nearly as we can tell, physical growth in infancy and childhood is regulated by thyroxine and the pituitary growth hormone. However, the picture begins to change as the child approaches adolescence and the body prepares for the growth spurt that is soon to follow.

The dramatic physical changes that occur during adolescence are preceded by more subtle changes in the child's endocrine system. The process begins as the hypothalamus (a part of the brain) instructs the pituitary to activate the **adrenal glands** and the gonads (ovaries or testes). In females, androgenlike hormones secreted by the adrenal cortex trigger the adolescent growth spurt and the development of pubic and axillary hair (Tanner, 1978). At about the same time, the ovaries begin to produce *estrogen* and *progesterone,* female hormones that are responsible for the development of the breasts, uterus, and vagina, the onset of menarche and regulation of the menstrual cycle, and a widening of the hips. For males, the most important hormone is *testosterone,* a substance produced by the testes, which triggers the adolescent growth spurt as well as the growth of the penis and testes, the production of sperm, voice changes, and the development of pubic, axillary, and facial hair (Tanner, 1978). Apparently androgen from the adrenal cortex merely supplements the male growth spurt rather than triggering it. We think this to be true because in the absence of testosterone, no growth spurt takes place at all (Tanner, 1978).

Although levels of the pituitary growth hormone (GH) do *not* increase during adolescence, this substance continues to play an important role in the growth process. Apparently its function is that of a catalyst for the sex hormones, for

the usual level of GH must be present for testosterone to produce its full growth-effect on the muscles

and on the bones of the limbs and shoulders. In the absence of GH the height spurt (in males) is only about two-thirds of normal, and the shoulder width spurt even less.... In girls the height spurt is also only about two-thirds of normal in the absence of growth hormone; and the estrogen-induced growth of hip width is likewise reduced [Tanner, 1978, pp. 100–101].

Table 5-5 summarizes the hormonal influences on human growth and development.

Environmental Influences

At least four environmental factors are known to affect physical growth and development: nutrition, illnesses, emotional stress, and practice.

Nutrition

Diet is perhaps the most potent of all environmental influences on human growth and development. As you might expect, children who are inadequately nourished will grow very slowly, if at all. The dramatic impact of malnutrition on physical development can be

---

thyroxine: a hormone produced by the thyroid gland, essential for normal growth of the brain and the body.

pituitary: a "master gland" located at the base of the brain that regulates the endocrine glands and produces growth hormone.

growth hormone (GH): the pituitary hormone that stimulates the rapid growth and development of body cells.

adrenal glands: a pair of endocrine glands that secrete androgen, a hormone that triggers the adolescent growth spurt in females.

seen by comparing the heights of children before and during wartime periods when food is scarce. In Figure 5-8 we see that the average heights of schoolchildren in Stuttgart, Germany, increased during the 20 years between the two world wars. However, these secular trends were clearly reversed during the war years, when it was not always possible to satisfy the children's nutritional needs.

Short-term versus prolonged malnutrition. Prolonged malnutrition during the first five years of life may seriously retard brain growth and cause a child to remain smaller than his or her adequately nourished peers throughout life (Lewin, 1975; Tanner, 1978). These findings make sense when we recall that the first five years is a period when the brain will normally gain about 65% of its eventual adult weight and the body will grow to nearly two-thirds of its adult height (Tanner, 1978).

If malnutrition is neither prolonged nor especially severe, children will probably recover from any growth deficits by growing much faster than normal once their diet becomes adequate. James Tanner (1978) views this **catch-up growth** as a basic principle of physical development. Presumably children who experience growth deficits because of malnutrition or illness will grow very rapidly in order to regain (or catch up to) the growth trajectory that they are genetically programmed to follow. When growth catches up with its preprogrammed course, it will then slow down and follow the path dictated by heredity.

When is a child malnourished? There are actually two kinds of malnutrition. **Protein/calorie deficiency** occurs when people do not get enough protein and/or total calories to sustain normal growth. The second type of malnutrition is **vitamin/mineral deficiency:** people get enough to eat, but their diet is lacking in one or more substances that would help to maintain their health and promote normal growth.

Protein/calorie deficiencies are very common among children living in poor, underdeveloped countries in Africa, Asia, and Latin America (Winick, 1976). When children are severely malnourished, they are like-

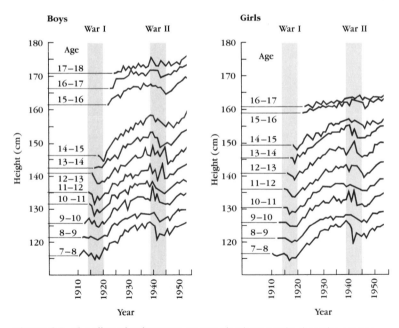

Figure 5-8. The effect of malnutrition on growth. These graphs show the average heights of Stuttgart schoolchildren aged 7–18 between 1910 and the early 1950s. Notice the trend toward increasing height between 1920 and 1940, the period between the two world wars. This secular trend was dramatically reversed during World War II, when nutrition was often inadequate. *(Based on Tanner, 1963.)*

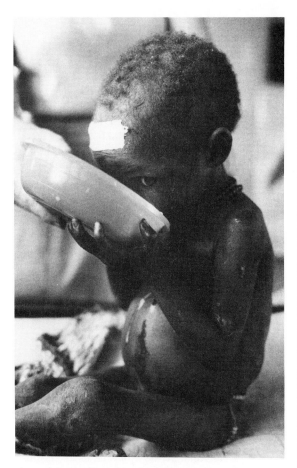

Photo 5-5. The lesions on this little boy's skin and his swollen stomach are symptoms of kwashiorkor. Without adequate protein in his diet, this child will be more susceptible to many diseases and may die from an illness that well-nourished children could easily overcome.

ly to suffer from either of two nutritional diseases—**marasmus** and **kwashiorkor**—each of which has a slightly different cause. Marasmus affects babies who get insufficient protein and too few calories, as can easily occur if a mother is malnourished and does not have the resources to provide her child with a nutritious commercial substitute for mother's milk. A victim of marasmus becomes very frail and wrinkled in appearance as growth stops and the body tissues begin to waste away. If conditions should improve, enabling these children to survive, they will remain smaller than their adequately nourished peers and will probably suffer impaired intellectual development as well (Winick, 1976).

Kwashiorkor affects children who get enough calories but little if any protein. As the disease progresses, the child's hair will thin, the face, legs, and abdomen will swell with water, and severe skin lesions may develop. In many poor countries of the world, about the only high-quality source of protein readily available to children is mother's milk. So breast-fed infants will not ordinarily suffer from marasmus unless their mothers are severely malnourished; however, they may develop kwashiorkor when they are weaned from the breast and thereby denied their primary source of protein.

In the United States, fewer than 2% of preschool children suffer from protein/calorie deficiencies, and the few who do are rarely so malnourished that they develop symptoms of marasmus or kwashiorkor. However, vitamin and mineral deficiencies may affect large numbers of children from all social classes in this relatively affluent society. One recent nutritional survey reported that the diets of many preschool children from the lower socioeconomic strata are deficient in vitamins A and C and in riboflavin (Owen, Kram, Garry, Lower, & Lubin, cited in Eichorn, 1979). Another survey conducted in ten states found that over 90% of 1–3-year-olds had diets that were deficient in iron, and 26–48% of these infants and toddlers (depending on the state) were receiving but one-third of the recommended levels (see Eichorn, 1979). The major effects of these vitamin and mineral deficiencies are to make children irritable and listless and to retard their rate of growth. A malnourished child is also less resistant to other illnesses, which could have their own adverse effects on physical growth and development.

catch-up growth: a period of accelerated growth in which children who have experienced growth deficits will grow very rapidly to "catch up to" the growth trajectory that they are genetically programmed to follow.

protein/calorie deficiency: a form of malnutrition in which children do not receive enough protein or total calories to sustain normal growth.

vitamin/mineral deficiency: a form of malnutrition in which the diet provides sufficient calories but is lacking in one or more substances that promote normal growth.

marasmus: a growth-retarding disease affecting infants who receive insufficient protein and too few calories.

kwashiorkor: a growth-retarding disease affecting children who receive enough calories but little if any protein.

Overnutrition. Dietary excess (eating too much) is yet another form of poor nutrition that may have several long-term consequences for the developing child. The most immediate effect is that the child may become **obese** and face added risk of serious medical complications such as diabetes, high blood pressure, and heart, liver, or kidney disease. Obese children may also find it difficult to make friends with age mates, who are apt to tease them about their size and shape. Indeed, we have already seen that endomorphic (chubby to fat) physiques are described in very unfavorable terms (for example, *sloppy, ugly, stupid*) by school-age children and that endomorphic youngsters are among the least popular students in grade school classrooms (Staffieri, 1967).

Although you may know (or even be) an exception to the rule, obese infants and toddlers tend to be obese during the grade school years (Shapiro et al., 1984), and obese schoolchildren are more likely than their thinner peers to be obese as adolescents and adults ("Obese Children," 1986). There is now evidence that heredity contributes to these trends, for sluggish activity levels (which hinder one from burning calories) and even a preference for sweets are moderately heritable attributes (Mayer, 1975; Milstein, 1980). Yet, a genetic predisposition toward obesity does not guarantee that one will be obese; most obese people are overweight because they consume more calories than they need ("Obese Children," 1986).

Overeating contributes to obesity in two ways: (1) by producing an excess of fat cells and (2) by depositing fatty tissue within these cells, causing them to swell (Eichorn, 1979). Fat cells are most likely to be added during two periods: from the seventh prenatal month through age 2 and during the adolescent growth spurt. And once added, a fat cell remains in the body for life, standing ready to soak up excess calories. So overeating during infancy or early adolescence clearly increases an individual's chances of becoming and remaining obese.

Crash diets for obese children are often counterproductive. Not only can severe restrictions in dietary intake interfere with the development of the brain, muscles, and bones early in life, but older children on restrictive diets may feel mistreated, rejected, and more willing to partake in binge eating should the opportunity present itself ("Obese Children," 1986). Today, many therapists favor a three-pronged approach to treating childhood obesity: (1) convincing the child that obesity is harmful and that he needs to burn more calories through strenuous exercise, (2) providing the child with strategies that he can use to alter his exercise and eating habits, and (3) asking parents to put away the snack trays, to serve fewer sweets, and to restrict eating to mealtimes without imposing strict limits on mealtime caloric intake. The idea is that an obese child won't feel mistreated and ready to binge if he can eat all he wants at mealtimes. And if he should eat no more (and, ideally, a little less) than usual, his weight should stabilize, thus allowing him to eventually outgrow his "endomorphic" physique as he becomes taller.

Illness

The very minor illnesses that all children experience have little if any effect on physical growth and development. Major diseases that keep a child in bed for several months may retard growth; but after recovering, the child will ordinarily show a growth spurt (catch-up growth) that makes up for the progress lost while he or she was sick (Tanner, 1978).

Children with frequently recurring colds, ear problems, sore throats, or skin infections tend to be smaller than their less "sickly" peers (Tanner, 1978). However, these sickly children also tend to come from economically depressed family settings where proper nutrition is lacking. So it is certainly possible that both the slow rates of growth and the recurring illnesses that characterize "sickly" children are attributable, in part, to nutritional deficiencies.

Emotional stress and lack of affection

Otherwise healthy children who experience too much stress and too little affection are likely to lag far behind their age mates in physical growth and motor development. This **failure to thrive** syndrome may characterize as many as 3% of preschool children in the United States and up to 5% of all patients admitted to pediatric hospitals (Lipsitt, 1979).

Perhaps the most intriguing research on the failure-to-thrive syndrome was reported by Lytt Gardner (1972). Gardner studied the development of healthy, nonabused children who received adequate physical care but little affection from emotionally unresponsive parents. One case involved twins—a boy and a girl—who grew normally for the first four months. Soon thereafter, the twins' father lost his job, their mother became pregnant with an unwanted baby, and the parents blamed each other for the hardships they were experiencing. The father then moved out of the house, and the mother focused her resentment on her infant son, becoming emotionally detached and unresponsive to his bids for affection (she did, however, provide him with adequate nutrition and physical care). Although his sister continued to grow normally, the boy twin at 13 months of age was about the size of an average 7-month-old infant. In other words, his growth was severely retarded, a condition that Gardner called **deprivation dwarfism.**

Gardner believes that deprivation dwarfism is directly related to the emotional deprivation that the child has experienced at home. He bases his conclusions on the behavior of many deprivation dwarfs who were hospitalized for observation and treatment. The following passage describes a typical case:

> The 15-month-old child quickly responded to the attention she received from the hospital staff. She gained weight and made up for lost growth; her emotional state improved strikingly. Moreover, *these changes were . . . unrelated to any changes in food intake.* During her stay in the hospital, she received the same standard nutrient dosage she had received at home. It appears to have been the enrichment of her social environment, not of her diet, that was responsible for the normalization of her growth [Gardner, 1972, p. 17; italics added].

Gardner's deprivation dwarfs (and most children who fail to thrive) are infants and toddlers who have suffered *severe* emotional deprivation. Yet, there is evidence that older, school-age children who experience less severe emotional traumas may also grow more slowly than normal. For example, Elsie Widdowson (1951) found that one group of orphans who were given an enriched diet actually grew *at a slower rate* than a second group who remained on the standard orphanage fare. The most likely explanation for this puzzling result is that children in the "enriched diet" group were exposed to a strict and emotionally unresponsive teacher/caretaker at precisely the time that their diet changed for the better. Thus, the lack of affection and emotional distress that these children experienced apparently interfered with normal growth even though their diet had actually improved.

Why do you suppose emotional distress inhibits physical growth and development? Apparently the answer is not related to diet, for Gardner's deprivation dwarfs who received attention in the hospital grew rapidly on the same diet on which they had "failed to thrive," and Widdowson's emotionally distressed orphans failed to thrive even though their diets had improved. Current thinking on the subject is that emotional traumas may cause a growth slowdown by inhibiting the production of pituitary growth hormone. Indeed, Gardner (1972) noted that deprivation dwarfs have abnormally low levels of growth hormone in their bloodstreams during periods of subnormal growth. And when these distressed youngsters begin to receive attention, the secretion of growth hormone resumes, enabling them to grow rapidly and make up the ground lost while they were emotionally deprived (Tanner, 1978).

Practice effects

In 1933 Mary Shirley reported that a typical American infant could sit without support at 7 months, stand while holding onto a piece of furniture at 9 months, walk when led at 11 months, and walk alone at 15 months. Modern infants develop much faster, reaching each of these important motor milestones some two to four months earlier than the children observed by Shirley in the 1930s (see Table 5-4). How might we explain these discrepant findings?

There are at least two plausible explanations for the precocious motor development of today's children. The most popular explanation is a *secular-trend hypothesis:* children today crawl and walk earlier than children of the 1930s because better nutrition and health care have accelerated the maturation process. Other theorists favor a *practice hypothesis:* modern children are quicker to develop important motor skills because they have more toys to manipulate and are less often confined to cribs and strollers than infants of the 1930s.

Much of the early literature would lead one to believe that practice plays little if any part in the development of basic motor skills. For example, Wayne and Marsena Dennis (1940) found that Hopi Indian infants who had been swaddled and bound to cradleboards for the first nine or ten months of life were no slower to take that first unaided step than Hopi infants whose parents had decided not to follow the tribal custom of tying them down. In addition, Myrtle McGraw (1935) and Arnold Gesell (Gesell & Thompson, 1929) conducted ex-

---

obesity: a medical term describing individuals who are at least 20% above the "ideal" weight for their height, age, and sex.

failure to thrive: a condition in which seemingly healthy infants fail to grow normally and are much smaller than their age mates.

deprivation dwarfism: a retardation in physical growth that is apparently triggered by emotional distress and/or a lack of love and attention.

periments in which one identical twin was allowed to practice motor skills such as climbing stairs or stacking blocks, while the cotwin was denied these experiences. The results of both studies indicated that practice had little effect on motor development: when finally allowed to perform, the unpracticed twin soon matched the skills of the cotwin who had had many opportunities to practice. The investigators concluded that physical maturation is what underlies motor development and that practice merely allows a child to perfect those skills that maturation has made possible.

Proponents of the practice hypothesis believe that this conclusion is much too strong. They note that the Hopi infants who spent their first nine or ten months on cradleboards had several months to move about and practice motor skills before they (and the unbound infants) finally began to walk. Even the "unpracticed" twins of the studies by McGraw (1935) and Gesell and Thompson (1929) were completely free to practice any number of other motor skills (such as grasping objects in their cribs, crawling, walking) that may have enabled them to climb stairs or stack blocks when they were finally given an opportunity to do so. So the critics believe that practice is essential to motor development and that children might never learn to crawl, walk, run, jump, or throw if they are denied all opportunities to rehearse these basic skills.

Evidence for the practice hypothesis. Obviously it would be grossly unethical to tie a child down for five years to see whether he could later crawl or walk without having had an opportunity to practice. However, Wayne Dennis (1960) was able to locate and study two groups of institutionalized orphans in Iran who had had very few opportunities to practice basic motor skills. The orphanages where the children lived were impoverished and understaffed. The children had no toys to play with, and they spent most of their time lying flat on their backs in their cribs. In fact, their mattresses developed hollows that made it nearly impossible for the children to roll over onto their stomachs. These orphans were never placed in a sitting position, were rarely played with, and were even fed in their cribs with their bottles propped on pillows. If a child managed to sit up, he might be taken from his crib and placed on the floor, where he was left alone (without toys) to entertain himself as best he could.

Dennis found that the motor skills of these institutionalized orphans were severely retarded. Of all infants aged 1–2, only 42% could sit alone, and *none*

could walk. In fact, only 8% of the 2–3-year-olds and 15% of the 3–4-year-olds could walk alone. Moreover, these deficits in motor development were not attributable to organic causes (for example, brain damage) or to malnutrition. (And we might also note that normal, healthy infants and toddlers from cultures that discourage motor activities will lag behind Western infants by a year or more in their acquisition of motor skills; see Kaplan & Dove, 1987.) So Dennis, who had been a very strong proponent of the maturational explanation of motor development, ended up changing his views, concluding that maturation is *necessary but not sufficient* for the development of motor skills. In other words, infants who are physically capable of sitting, crawling, or walking will not be very proficient at these activities unless they have opportunities to practice them.

Importance of an upright posture. Several years ago, Esther Thelen and Donna Fisher (1982) proposed that the age at which infants reach various motor milestones may depend very critically on the amount of time they spend in a vertical posture. This conclusion stems, in part, from Thelen's observations of infants learning to walk. Recall that neonates have a stepping reflex that normally disappears at about 2 months of age. According to Thelen (1984), this stepping motion is a precursor of walking that "goes underground" only because the growing infant's legs become too heavy for weak muscles to lift (indeed, 7-month-old infants, who normally do not "step" when held upright, will display a clear stepping motion if placed on a moving treadmill that provides a "power boost" to get their legs moving forward; see Thelen, 1986). So what Thelen is saying is that the motor patterns necessary for walking are present very early, but that infants must develop more muscle and become a little less top-heavy before they will walk. This is why vertical posturing is important. Presumably, an infant who is often placed in an upright posture will develop strength in the legs, neck, and trunk (an acceleration of muscular growth), which, in turn, will promote the development of motor skills such as standing and walking.

There is now ample support for Thelen and Fisher's hypothesis. Babies from Third World cultures who are often carried vertically in slings (or held upright on their mothers' laps) do walk earlier than Western infants, who spend much more time in a horizontal posture (Super, 1981; Thelen & Fisher, 1982). Moreover, Philip Zelazo and his associates (Zelazo, Zelazo, & Kolb, 1972) found that 2–8-week-old infants who were often held upright and encouraged to "practice" their stepping reflex subsequently walked about two months earlier than infants in a control group who did not receive this early training.

In sum, it appears that both maturation and experience are important determinants of motor development. Maturation does place limits on the age at which a child will first be capable of sitting, standing, or walking. However, it seems that experiences such as upright posturing and various forms of practice may well affect the age at which important physical capabilities are first translated into action.

Summary

Neonates are remarkably capable organisms who emerge from the womb prepared for life. They have functioning sense organs; they display some capacity for learning; and they come equipped with a repertoire of inborn reflexes (breathing, sucking, swallowing, and so on) that help them to adapt to their new surroundings. In the first five minutes of life, newborns are given the Apgar test to see how well they are breathing and otherwise adjusting to the extrauterine environment. Several days later, they often take the Brazelton Neonatal Behavioral Assessment Scale, an instrument designed to measure their reflexes, social responsiveness, and neurological well-being. This scale is particularly useful for identifying infants who are likely to experience later emotional difficulties.

The infant's state (that is, state of consciousness) changes many times during a typical day. Newborns spend nearly 70% of their time asleep; but as they mature, they spend less time sleeping and more time awake, alert, and attending to the environment. Crying is a state that tells us much about the baby. If a neonate's cries are high-pitched and nonrhythmic, he or she may be premature, malnourished, or brain-damaged. Normal, healthy infants emit at least three different cries (hunger, anger, and pain) to communicate their wants and discomforts. However, crying usually diminishes over the first year as parents learn how to soothe their crying infants, and infants learn to use other methods of communicating with their close companions.

The body is constantly changing between infancy and childhood. Height and weight increase rapidly during the first two years. Growth then becomes more gradual until early adolescence, when there is a rapid "growth spurt." The shape of the body also changes because various body parts grow at different rates and different times. For example, the head and trunk grow rapidly during the prenatal period and infancy, the limbs are growing fastest in late childhood, and the trunk is once again the fastest-growing segment of the body during adolescence.

Skeletal and muscular development parallel the changes occurring in height and weight. The bones become longer and thicker, and they gradually harden, completing their growth and development by the late teens. Muscles increase in density and size, particularly during the growth spurt of early adolescence. Development of the skeletal, muscular, and nervous systems follows a cephalocaudal (head downward) and proximodistal (center outward) pattern: structures in the upper and central regions of the body mature before those in the lower and peripheral regions.

The brain and nervous system develop very rapidly during the last three months of the prenatal period, when neurons proliferate, and the first two years of life, when neurons become organized into interconnected pathways and are encased in myelin—a waxy material that acts like an insulator to speed the transmission of neural impulses. Many neurons and synapses are formed, but only those that are often used are likely to survive. The brain has a great deal of plasticity—a characteristic that allows it to change in response to experience and to recover from many injuries. Although the brain may be organized from birth so that its two cerebral hemispheres serve different functions, children come to rely more and more on one hemisphere to perform specific tasks, and they become increasingly proficient at integrating the respective functions served by their two cerebral hemispheres.

Like the physical structures of the body, motor development proceeds in a cephalocaudal and proximodistal direction. As a result, motor skills evolve in a definite sequence, in which infants gain control over their heads, necks, and upper arms before they become proficient with their legs, feet, and hands. As the nervous system and muscles mature, children gradually acquire more control over their bodies. By age 3 they can run in a straight line, jump, and catch a large ball, although tying their shoes and copying complex figures on paper are impossible tasks. By age 5 the child is quite fluid at large-muscle activities and can draw figures or copy letters with a crayon. By age 8–9 children can easily ride bicycles and use household tools and are becoming skillful performers at games that require eye/hand coordination and speedy reaction times.

At about age 10½ for females, and age 13 for males, the adolescent growth spurt begins. Weight increases first, followed some four to six months later by a rapid increase in height. The muscles undergo a period of rapid growth about a year after the greatest growth in height.

Sexual maturation begins about the same time as the adolescent growth spurt and follows a predictable sequence for members of each sex. For females, the onset of breast and pubic-hair development is followed by a widening of the hips, enlarging of the uterus and vagina, menarche (first menstruation), and completion of breast and pubic-hair growth. For males, development of the testes and scrotum is followed by the emergence of pubic hair, the growth of the penis, the ability to ejaculate, the appearance of facial hair, and a lowering of the voice. Over the past 100 years, males and females have been growing taller and heavier and reaching sexual maturity earlier—possibly because of improved nu-

trition and health care. Yet, there are wide individual variations in the timing of sexual maturation and growth. Early-maturing males experience fewer psychological and social problems than late maturers. Among females, the psychological correlates of early or late maturing are less apparent, although early-maturing girls seem to be less popular than prepubescent classmates in grade school but tend to become more popular and self-assured later in adolescence.

Many factors affect physical growth and development. Among the important biological contributors are genotype, maturation, and hormones. Adequate nutrition, good health, and freedom from prolonged emotional traumas are also necessary to ensure normal growth and development. In addition, children must have opportunities to practice important skills such as reaching, grasping, sitting, standing, and walking if motor development is to proceed normally.

References

AINSWORTH, M. D. S., Bell, S. M., & Stayton, D. J. (1972). Individual differences in the development of some attachment behaviors. *Merrill-Palmer Quarterly, 18,* 123–143.

ANDERSEN, A. E. (1983). Anorexia nervosa and bulimia: A spectrum of eating disorders. *Journal of Adolescent Health Care, 4,* 15–21.

ANDERSEN, A. E. (1985). *Practical comprehensive treatment of anorexia nervosa and bulimia.* Baltimore: Johns Hopkins University Press.

ARO, H., & Taipale, V. (1987). The impact of timing of puberty on psychosomatic symptoms among fourteen- to sixteen-year-old Finnish girls. *Child Development, 58,* 261–268.

BELSKY, J. (1985). Experimenting with the family in the newborn period. *Child Development, 56,* 407–414.

BELSKY, J. (1986). A tale of two variances: Between and within. *Child Development, 57,* 1301–1305.

BERG, W. K., Adkinson, C. D., & Strock, B. D. (1973). Duration and frequency of periods of alertness in neonates. *Developmental Psychology, 9,* 434.

BERG, W. K., & Berg, K. M. (1979). Psychological development in infancy: State, sensory function, and attention. In J. D. Osofsky (Ed.), *Handbook of infant development.* New York: Wiley.

BERSCHEID, E., Walster, E., & Bohrnstedt, G. (1973, June). The happy American body: A survey report. *Psychology Today,* pp. 119–131.

BIRNS, B., Blank, M., & Bridger, W. H. (1966). The effectiveness of various soothing techniques on human neonates. *Psychosomatic Medicine, 28,* 316–322.

BOISMIER, J. D. (1977). Visual stimulation and the wake-sleep behavior in human neonates. *Developmental Psychobiology, 10,* 219–227.

BOWER, T. G. R. (1982). *Development in infancy.* New York: W. H. Freeman.

BOWLBY, J. (1973). *Attachment and loss.* Vol. 2: *Separation: Anxiety and anger.* London: Hogarth Press.

BRACKBILL, Y. (1975). Continuous stimulation and arousal level in infancy: Effects of stimulus intensity and stress. *Child Development, 46,* 364–369.

BRAZELTON, T. B. (1979). Behavioral competence of the newborn infant. *Seminars in Perinatology, 3,* 35–44.

BRIERLEY, J. (1976). *The growing brain.* London: NFER Publishing.

CLAUSEN, J. A. (1975). The social meaning of differential physical maturation. In D. E. Drugastin & G. H. Elder (Eds.), *Adolescence in the life cycle.* New York: Halsted Press.

CORBIN, C. (1973). *A textbook of motor development.* Dubuque, IA: William C. Brown.

COREN, S., Porac, C., & Duncan, P. (1981). Lat-

eral preference behaviors in preschool children and young adults. *Child Development, 52,* 443–450.

COWAN, W. M. (1979). The development of the brain. *Scientific American, 241,* 112–133.

COWAN, W. M, Fawcett, J. W., O'Leary, D. M., & Stanfield, B. B. (1984). Regressive events in neurogenesis. *Science, 225,* 1258–1265.

DENNIS, M., & Whitaker, H. H. (1976). Language acquisition following hemidecortication: Linguistic superiority of the left over the right hemisphere. *Brain and Language, 3,* 404–433.

DENNIS, W. (1960). Causes of retardation among institutional children: Iran. *Journal of Genetic Psychology, 96,* 47–59.

DENNIS, W., & Dennis, M. G. (1940). The effect of cradling practices upon the onset of walking in Hopi children. *Journal of Genetic Psychology, 56,* 77–86.

DUKE, P. M., Carlsmith, J. M., Jennings, D., Martin, J. A., Dornbusch, S. M., Gross, R. T., & Siegel-Gorelick, B. (1982). Educational correlates of early and late sexual maturation in adolescence. *Journal of Pediatrics, 100,* 633–637.

DUNCAN, P., Ritter, P. L., Dornbusch, S. M., Gross, R. T., & Carlsmith, J. M. (1985). The effects of pubertal timing on body image, school behavior, and deviance. *Journal of Youth and Adolescence, 14,* 227–235.

DYER, K. F. (1977). The trend of male-female performance differential in athletics, swimming, and cycling 1948–1976. *Journal of Biosocial Science, 9,* 325–338.

EICHORN, D. H. (1979). Physical development: Current foci of research. In J. D. Osofsky (Ed.), *Handbook of infant development.* New York: Wiley.

ESPENSCHLADE, A. (1960). Motor development. In W. R. Johnson (Ed.), *Science and medicine of exercise and sports.* New York: Harper & Row.

FAUST, M. S. (1960). Developmental maturity as a determinant of prestige in adolescent girls. *Child Development, 31,* 173–184.

FAUST, M. S. (1977). Somatic development of adolescent girls. *Monographs of the Society for Research in Child Development, 42*(Whole No. 169).

FENTRESS, J. C., & McLeod, P. J. (1986). Motor patterns in development. In E. M. Blass (Ed.), *Handbook of behavioral neurobiology.* Vol. 8: *Developmental psychobiology and developmental neurobiology.* New York: Plenum.

FIELD, T. M., & Goldson, E. (1984). Pacifying effects of nonnutritive sucking on term and preterm neonates during heelstick procedures. *Pediatrics, 74,* 1012–1015.

FRANKENBERG, W. K., & DODDS, J. B. (1967). The Denver development screening test. *Journal of Pediatrics, 71,* 181–191.

FRODI, A. M., Lamb, M. E., Leavitt, L. A., Donovan, W. L., Neff, C., & Sherry, D. (1978). Fathers' and mothers' responses to the faces and cries of normal and premature infants. *Developmental Psychology, 14,* 490–498.

GADDIS, A., & Brooks-Gunn, J. (1985). The male experience of pubertal change. *Journal of Youth and Adolescence, 14,* 61–69.

GARDNER, L. J. (1972). Deprivation dwarfism. *Scientific American, 227,* 76–82.

GESELL, A., Ames, L. B., & Ilg, F. L. (1977). *The child from five to ten.* New York: Harper & Row.

GESELL, A., Halverson, H. M., Thompson, H., Ilg, F. L., Costner, B. M., Ames, L. B., & Amatruda, C. S. (1940). *The first five years of life: A guide to the study of the preschool child.* New York: Harper & Row.

GESELL, A., & Thompson, H. (1929). Learning and growth in identical twins: An experimental study by the method of co-twin control. *Genetic Psychology Monographs, 6,* 1–123.

GEWIRTZ, J. L., & Boyd, E. F. (1977). Does maternal responding imply reduced infant crying? A critique of the 1972 Bell and Ainsworth report. *Child Development, 48,* 1200–1207.

GOLDMAN-RAKIC, P. S., Isseroff, A., Schwartz,

M. L., & Bugbee, N. M. (1983). The neurobiology of cognitive development. In M. M. Haith & J. J. Campos (Eds.), *Handbook of child psychology.* Vol. 2: *Infancy and developmental psychology* (4th ed.). New York: Wiley.

GREENOUGH, W. T., Black, J. E., & Wallace, C. S. (1987). Experience and brain development. *Child Development, 58,* 539–559.

GREIF, E. B., & Ulman, K. J. (1982). The psychological impact of menarche on early adolescent females: A review of the literature. *Child Development, 53,* 1413–1430.

HALMI, K. A., Falk, J. R., & Schwartz, E. (1981). Binge-eating and vomiting: A survey of a college population. *Psychological Medicine, 11,* 697–706.

HALVERSON, H. M. (1931). An experimental study of prehension in infants by means of systematic cinema records. *Genetic Psychology Monographs, 10,* 107–286.

HERKOWITZ, J. (1978). Sex-role expectations and motor behavior of the young child. In M. V. Ridenour (Ed.), *Motor development: Issues and applications.* Princeton, NJ: Princeton Book Company.

HUTT, S. J., Lenard, H. G., & Prechtl, H. E. R. (1969). Psychophysiology of the newborn. In L. P. Lipsitt & H. W. Reese (Eds.), *Advances in child development and behavior.* Orlando, FL: Academic Press.

HUTTENLOCHER, P. R. (1984). Synapse elimination and plasticity in developing human cerebral cortex. *American Journal of Mental Deficiency, 88,* 488–496.

JANOWSKY, J. S., & Finlay, B. L. (1986). The outcome of perinatal brain damage: The role of normal neuron loss and axon retraction. *Developmental Medicine and Child Neurology, 28,* 375–389.

JONES, M. C. (1957). The later careers of boys who were early- or late-maturing. *Child Development, 28,* 113–128.

JONES, M. C. (1965). Psychological correlates of somatic development. *Child Development, 36,* 899–911.

JONES, M. C., & Bayley, N. (1950). Physical maturing among boys as related to behavior. *Journal of Educational Psychology, 41,* 129–148.

KAPLAN, H., & Dove, H. (1987). Infant development among the Ache of eastern Paraguay. *Developmental Psychology, 23,* 190–198.

KEOUGH, J., & Sugden, D. (1985). *Movement skill development.* New York: Macmillan.

KINSBOURNE, M., & Hiscock, M. (1983). The normal and deviant development of functional lateralization of the brain. In M. M. Haith & J. J. Campos (Eds.), *Handbook of*

child psychology. Vol. 2: *Infancy and developmental psychobiology* (4th ed.). New York: Wiley.

KORNER, A. F. (1972). State as a variable, as obstacle and as mediator of stimulation in infant research. *Merrill-Palmer Quarterly, 18,* 77–94.

KORNER, A. F., Hutchinson, C. A., Koperski, J. A., Kraemer, H. C., & Schneider, P. A. (1981). Stability of individual differences of neonatal motor and crying patterns. *Child Development, 52,* 83–90.

LANGLOIS, J. H., & Downs, A. C. (1979). Peer relations as a function of physical attractiveness: The eye of the beholder or behavioral reality? *Child Development, 50,* 409–418.

LENNEBERG, E. H. (1967). *Biological foundations of language.* New York: Wiley.

LESTER, B. M. (1984). A biosocial model of infant crying. In L. P. Lipsitt (Ed.), *Advances in infancy research.* Norwood, NJ: Ablex.

LEWIN, R. (1975, September). Starved brains. *Psychology Today,* pp. 29–33.

LIPSITT, L. P. (1979). Critical conditions in infancy: A psychological perspective. *American Psychologist, 34,* 973–980.

LIPTON, E. L., Steinschneider, A., & Richmond, J. B. (1965). The autonomic nervous system in early life. *New England Journal of Medicine, 273,* 201–208.

LIVSON, N., & Peskin, H. (1980). Perspectives on adolescence from longitudinal research. In J. Adelson (Ed.), *Handbook of adolescent psychology.* New York: Wiley.

LOWERY, G. H. (1978). *Growth and development of children.* Chicago: Yearbook Medical Publishers.

MARSHALL, W. A. (1977). *Human growth and its disorders.* Orlando, FL: Academic Press.

MARSHALL, W. A., & Tanner, J. M. (1970). Variations in the pattern of pubertal changes in boys. *Archives of the Diseases of Childhood, 45,* 13–23.

MAYER, J. (1975). Obesity during childhood. In M. Winick (Ed.), *Childhood obesity.* New York: Wiley.

McGRAW, M. B. (1935). *Growth: A study of Johnny and Jimmy.* East Norwalk, CT: Appleton-Century-Crofts.

MEREDITH, H. V. (1963). Changes in stature and body weight of North American boys during the last 80 years. In L. P. Spiker & C. C. Spiker (Eds.), *Advances in child development and behavior* (Vol. 10). Orlando, FL: Academic Press.

MEROLA, J. L., & Liederman, J. (1985). Developmental changes in hemispheric independence. *Child Development, 56,* 1184–1194.

MICHEL, G. F. (1981). Right-handedness: A consequence of infant supine head-orientation preference. *Science, 212,* 685–687.

MILSTEIN, R. M. (1980). Responsiveness in newborn infants of overweight and normal weight parents. *Appetite, 1,* 65–74.

MINUCHIN, S., Rosman, B. L., & Baker, L. (1978). *Psychosomatic families: Anorexia nervosa in context.* Cambridge, MA: Harvard University Press.

MOLFESE, D. L. (1977). Infant cerebral asymmetry. In S. J. Segalowitz & F. A. Gruber (Eds.), *Language development and neurological theory.* Orlando, FL: Academic Press.

MUSSEN, P. H., & Jones, M. C. (1957). Self-conceptions, motivations, and interpersonal attitudes of late and early maturing boys. *Child Development, 28,* 243–258.

MYERS, B. J. (1982). Early intervention using Brazelton training with middle-class mothers and fathers of newborns. *Child Development, 53,* 462–471.

OBESE CHILDREN: A growing problem. (1986). *Science, 232,* 20–21.

PENNINGTON, B. F., McCabe, L. L., Smith, S. D., Lefly, D. L., Bookman, M. O., Kimberling, W. J., & Lubs, H. A. (1986). Spelling errors in adults with a form of family dyslexia. *Child Development, 57,* 1001–1013.

RAKIC, P. (1985). Limits of neurogenesis in primates. *Science, 227,* 1054–1055.

RAMSAY, D. S. (1984). Onset of duplicated syllable babbling and unimanual handedness in infancy: Evidence for developmental change in hemispheric specialization? *Developmental Psychology, 20,* 64–71.

RAMSAY, D. S. (1985). Fluctuations in unimanual hand preference in infants following the onset of duplicated syllable babbling. *Developmental Psychology, 21,* 318–324.

RAMSAY, D. S., & Weber, S. L. (1986). Infants' hand preference in a task involving complementary roles for the two hands. *Child Development, 57,* 300–307.

RIESEN, A. H. (1947). The development of visual perception in man and chimpanzee. *Science, 106,* 107–108.

RIESEN, A. H., Chow, K. L., Semmes, J., & Nissen, H. W. (1951). Chimpanzee vision after four conditions of light deprivation. *American Psychologist, 6,* 282.

ROCHE, A. F. (1979). Secular trends in stature, weight, and maturation. In A. F. Roche (Ed.), Secular trends in human growth, maturation, and development. *Monographs of the Society for Research in Child Development, 44,* (Whole No. 179).

ROCHE, A. F. (1981). The adipocyte-number hypothesis. *Child Development, 52,* 31–43.

ROFFWARG, H. P., Muzio, J. W., & Dement, W. C. (1966). Ontogenetic development of the human sleep-dream cycle. *Science, 152,* 604–619.

ROSE, S. A. (1984). Developmental changes in hemispheric specialization for tactual processing in very young children: Evidence from cross-modal transfer. *Developmental Psychology, 20,* 568–574.

ROSENZWEIG, M. R. (1966). Environmental complexity, cerebral change, and behavior. *American Psychologist, 21,* 321–332.

ROSENZWEIG, M. R. (1984). Experience, memory, and the brain. *American Psychologist, 39,* 365–376.

RUBLE, D. N., & Brooks-Gunn, J. (1982). The experience of menarche. *Child Development, 53,* 1557–1566.

SAVIN-WILLIAMS, R. C., & Small, S. A. (1986). The timing of puberty and its relationship to adolescent and parent perceptions of family interactions. *Developmental Psychology, 32,* 342–347.

SCHLEIMER, K. (1981). Anorexia nervosa. *Nutrition Review, 38,* 99–103.

SCHWARTZ, D. M., & Thompson, M. G. (1981). Do anorexics get well? *American Journal of Psychiatry, 138,* 319–324.

SEABROOK, C. (1987, March 23). Binge eating can be hazardous to your health. *Atlanta Journal,* p. 18.

SHANNON, D. C. (1980). Sudden infant death syndrome and near miss infants. In S. S. Gellis & B. M. Kagan (Eds.), *Current pediatric therapy.* Philadelphia: Saunders.

SHAPIRO, L. R., Crawford, P. B., Clark, M. J., Pearson, D. L., Raz, J., & Haunemann, R. L. (1984). Obesity prognosis: A longitudinal study of children from the age of 6 months to 9 years. *American Journal of Public Health, 74,* 968–972.

SHIRLEY, M. M. (1933). *The first two years: A study of 25 babies.* Vol. 1: *Postural and locomotor development.* Minneapolis: University of Minnesota Press.

SIGELMAN, C. K., Miller, T. E., & Whitworth, L. A. (1986). The early development of stigmatizing reactions to physical differences. *Journal of Applied Developmental Psychology, 7,* 17–32.

SPREEN, O., Tupper, D., Risser, A., Tuokko, H., & Edgell, D. (1984). *Human developmental neuropsychology.* New York: Oxford University Press.

STAFFIERI, J. R. (1967). A study of social stereotype of body image in children. *Journal of Personality and Social Psychology, 7,* 101–104.

STEINSCHNEIDER, A. (1975). Implications of the sudden infant death syndrome for the study of sleep in infancy. In A. D. Pick (Ed.), *Minnesota Symposia on Child Psychology* (Vol. 9). Minneapolis: University of Minnesota Press.

STERNBERG, S. (1986, December 21). Questions stunt the triumph of synthetic growth hormone. *Atlanta Journal,* pp. 1, 14.

SUPER, C. M. (1981). Cross-cultural research on infancy. In H. C. Triandis & A. Heron (Eds.), *Handbook of cross-cultural psychology.* Vol. 4: *Developmental psychology.* London: Allyn & Bacon.

TAN, L. E. (1985). Laterality and motor skills in 4-year-olds. *Child Development, 56,* 119–124.

TANNER, J. M. (1963). *Growth at adolescence.* London: Blackwell Scientific Publications.

TANNER, J. M. (1978). *Fetus into man: Physical growth from conception to maturity.* Cambridge, MA: Harvard University Press.

TANNER, J. M. (1981). Growth and maturation during adolescence. *Nutrition Review, 39,* 43–55.

THELEN, E. (1984). Learning to walk: Ecological demands and phylogenetic constraints. In L. P. Lipsitt & C. Rovee-Collier (Eds.), *Advances in infancy research* (Vol. 3). Norwood, NJ: Ablex.

THELEN, E. (1986). Treadmill-elicited stepping in seven-month-old infants. *Child Development, 57,* 1498–1506.

THELEN, E., & Fisher, D. M. (1982). Newborn stepping: An explanation for a disappearing reflex. *Developmental Psychology, 18,* 760–775.

THOMAS, J. R., Gallagher, J. D., & Purvis, G. J. (1981). Reaction time and anticipation time: Effects of development. *Research Quarterly for Exercise and Sport, 52,* 359–367.

WEATHERLEY, D. (1964). Self-perceived rate of physical maturation and personality in late adolescence. *Child Development, 35,* 1197–1210.

WIDDOWSON, E. M. (1951). Mental contentment and physical growth. *Lancet, 1,* 1316–1318.

WIDMAYER, S., & Field, T. (1980). Effects of Brazelton demonstrations on early interactions of preterm infants and their teenage mothers. *Infant Behavior and Development, 3,* 79–89.

WIESENFELD, A., Malatesta, C., & DeLoach, L. (1981). Differential parental response to familiar and unfamiliar infant distress signals. *Infant Behavior and Development, 4,* 281–285.

WILLEMSEN, E. (1979). *Understanding infancy.* New York: W. H. Freeman.

WILSON, R. S. (1976). Concordance in physical growth for monozygotic and dizygotic twins. *Annals of Human Biology, 3,* 1–10.

WINICK, M. (1976). *Malnutrition and brain*

development. New York: Oxford University Press.

WITELSON, S. F. (1977). Developmental dyslexia: Two right hemispheres and none left. *Science, 195,* 309–311.

WITELSON, S. F. (1987). Neurobiological aspects of language in children. *Child Development, 58,* 653–688.

WOLFF, P. H. (1966). The causes, controls, and organization of behavior in the neonate. *Psychological Issues, 5*(1, Whole No. 17).

WOLFF, P. H. (1969). The natural history of crying and other vocalizations in early infancy. In B. M. Foss (Ed.), *Determinants of infant behavior* (Vol. 4). London: Methuen.

WOROBEY, J. (1985). A review of Brazelton-based interventions to enhance parent-infant interaction. *Journal of Reproductive and Infant Psychology, 3,* 64–73.

WOROBEY, J., & Brazelton, T. B. (1986). Experimenting with the family in the newborn period: A commentary. *Child Development, 57,* 1298–1300.

ZELAZO, P. R., Zelazo, N. A., & Kolb, S. (1972). "Walking" in the newborn. *Science, 176,* 314–315.

ZESKIND, P. S. (1980). Adult responses to the cries of low and high risk infants. *Infant Behavior and Development, 3,* 167–177.

ZESKIND, P. S., Sale, J., Maio, M. L., Huntington, L., & Weiseman, J. R. (1985). Adult perceptions of pain and hunger cries: A synchrony of arousal. *Child Development, 56,* 549–554.

III

Language, Learning, and Cognitive Development

Some of the more remarkable developments of childhood and adolescence are the changes that occur in learning, interpreting, reasoning, remembering, and problem solving. These "cognitive," or intellectual, developments are examined in detail in Part III.

In Chapter 6 we will focus on the growth of perceptual skills and learn how children gradually become more proficient at interpreting information they receive from their sensory receptors. Chapter 7 presents an in-depth look at the learning process and describes many of the ways in which young people are influenced by their experiences.

One characteristic that distinguishes us humans from other species is our remarkable capacity for language. The development of language and communication skills is the subject of Chapter 8.

Part III concludes with an overview of intellectual development. Chapter 9 charts the growth of memory and reasoning skills from birth through adolescence. In Chapter 10, we turn to the topic of intelligence testing and consider the many factors that contribute to individual differences in intellectual performance.

As you proceed through this section, it will become obvious that all the various cognitive functions are interrelated. For example, infants and toddlers must first perceive the differences among various patterns of sound and then remember these distinctions before they can construct meaningful words and sentences. They must develop an understanding of concepts such as relative size and color before they can use the words *tall* and *green* in the same ways that adults do. So the lines that are drawn between different cognitive operations are somewhat artificial, and we will see that changes in each cognitive process have important implications for all other aspects of cognitive functioning.

Perceptual Development

Beauty is bought by judgment of the eye
not utter'd by base sale of chapmen's tongues.

SHAKESPEARE, *Love's Labours Lost*

Try to imagine that you are a neonate, only five to ten minutes old, who has just been sponged, swaddled, and handed to your mother. As you stop whimpering, you will probably open your eyes and begin to look around. Your mother or father will undoubtedly say something like "Hello, baby, how are you?" Soon someone might tickle your cheek, causing you to turn in that direction and open your mouth as if to suck (the rooting reflex). What would you make of all this sensory input? How would you interpret these experiences?

Psychologists are careful to distinguish between **sensation** and **perception.** *Sensation* refers to the process by which *information about external events is detected by the sensory receptors and transmitted to the brain.* Clearly, babies can "sense" the environment. We know, for example, that neonates will often turn their heads in the direction of sounds; they react to changes in brightness (remember the **pupillary reflex**), thus suggesting that they can see; and as countless mothers will verify, babies are apt to cry up a storm whenever they are poked by a misguided diaper pin. Although we will see that all sensory abilities improve over time, they are indeed present at birth and require only a detectable level of stimulation in order to function.

Perception, however, refers to the *interpretation of sensory input by the brain.* If you or I hear a sound, we are quick to interpret it as a voice, a piece of music, or perhaps the humming of an appliance. When an object of some kind passes into our visual field, we can easily label it as a person, a cat, or an airplane. As adults, we are accomplished perceivers. But what about the neonate? Do you think a newborn can interpret or understand the sights, sounds, tastes, touches, and smells that his or her sensory receptors detect? Can neonates *perceive* anything?

The Nativist/Empiricist Controversy

Long before anyone began to conduct experiments on sensation and perception, philosophers were debating whether neonates could perceive. *Empiricists* such as John Locke (1690/1939) believed that infants were *tabulae rasae* (blank slates) who must learn how to interpret their sensory experiences. Two hundred years later, William James (1890) added that

> *any number of sensory [inputs], falling simultaneously on a mind* which has not yet experienced them separately, will fuse into a single individual [experience] *for that mind.* The law is that all things fuse that can fuse. . . . To the infant, sounds, sights, touches, and pains, form one unanalyzed [blooming, buzzing] confusion [Vol. 1, pp. 488, 496].

In other words, James believed that the senses are "integrated" at birth and that all sensations combine to produce a global, or holistic, experience. Presumably the child's abilities to discriminate the basic senses and to interpret sensations of a particular kind will gradually develop after a long period of learning.

By contrast, the *nativists* argued that many basic perceptual abilities are already present at birth. For example, Immanuel Kant (1781/1958) believed that **spatial perception** is innate. Presumably an infant does not have to learn that receding objects will appear smaller or that approaching objects will seem to increase in size; these are spatial inferences (perceptions) that were said to be inborn and attributable to the structural characteristics of the human nervous system.

Such extreme stands on the nature/nurture issue are rare in this day and age. Although most contemporary theorists are willing to concede that babies may see some order to the universe from the moment of birth, they are also quick to remind us that the perceptual world of a human neonate is very primitive by adult standards, or even by those of a normal 2-year-old! And what is responsible for the growth of perceptual skills? Learning almost certainly has something to do with it, as the empiricists have argued; but so, too, do important biological developments such as the maturation of the sensory receptors and the central nervous system. Even though today's researchers often disagree about when various perceptual abilities first emerge, the vast majority of them are *interactionists* who believe that the growth of perceptual awareness reflects a fundamental interplay (or interaction) between the forces of nature (maturation) and nurture (experience or learning).

Since perception represents the interpretation of sensory input, a neonate's perceptual skills are obviously limited by the capabilities (or lack thereof) of her sensory equipment. How well do you think young infants can see or hear? Do you suppose that they can taste, smell, or tell the difference between colors such as red and blue? Assuming that no one knew the answers to these questions, how could we extract such information from a nonverbal creature who cannot easily express what he may see, hear, smell, taste, or feel? Stay tuned, for we will answer these questions as we explore the sensory world of human infants.

"Making Sense" of the Infant's Sensory (and Perceptual) Experiences

To estimate the sensory and perceptual capabilities of infants, one must devise tests that capitalize on the responses that infants can make. Over the years, investigators have come up with several creative methods of persuading infants to tell us what they might be sensing or perceiving. Among the more useful of these ingenious techniques are the *preference method,* the *habituation paradigm,* the *method of evoked potentials,* and the *high-amplitude sucking procedure.*

The preference method

The **preference method** is a simple procedure in which at least two stimuli are presented simultaneously to see whether infants will attend more to one of them than the other(s). This approach became popular during the early 1960s after Robert Fantz used it to determine whether very young infants could discriminate visual patterns (for example, faces, concentric circles, newsprint, and unpatterned disks). Babies were

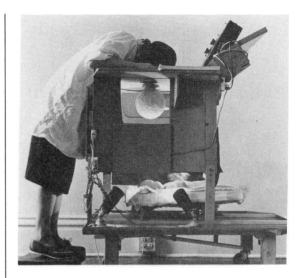

Photo 6-1. The looking chamber that Fantz used to study infants' visual preferences.

placed on their backs in a **looking chamber** (see Photo 6-1) and shown two or more stimuli. An observer located above the looking chamber then recorded the amount of time the infant gazed at each of the visual patterns. If the infant looked longer at one target than the other, it was assumed that he or she preferred that pattern.

Fantz's early results were clear. Babies less than 2 days old could easily discriminate visual forms, and they preferred to look at patterned stimuli such as faces or concentric circles rather than at unpatterned disks. Apparently the ability to detect and discriminate patterns is innate (Fantz, 1963).

---

sensation: detection of stimuli by the sensory receptors and transmission of this information to the brain.

perception: the process by which we categorize and interpret sensory input.

pupillary reflex: the reflexive action by which the pupils constrict in bright light and dilate in dark or dim surroundings.

spatial perception: interpretation of relations between objects and space.

preference method: a method used to gain information about infants' perceptual abilities by presenting two (or more) stimuli and observing which stimulus the infant prefers.

looking chamber: an enclosed criblike apparatus used to study infants' visual preferences.

Preference studies are still conducted today under the assumption that a clear preference for particular visual, auditory, tactile, or gustatory (taste) experiences implies that the infant must surely discriminate whatever stimuli are being compared. However, interpretive problems arise when infants display no distinct preferences among the target stimuli. No preference could mean that the targets are not discriminated. Yet, it may mean instead that the infant detects the differences between the stimuli but finds them equally interesting. Fortunately, there are other methods that investigators can use to resolve such interpretive ambiguities. One such method is the habituation paradigm.

The habituation method

Perhaps the most popular strategy for measuring infant sensory and perceptual capabilities is the habituation paradigm. **Habituation** is the process whereby a repetitive stimulus becomes so familiar or uninteresting that responses initially associated with it (for example, head or eye movements, changes in respiration or heart rate) are no longer apparent. Thus, habituation is a simple form of learning. As the infant stops responding to the familiar stimulus, he is telling us that he recognizes it as "old hat"—something that he has experienced before.

To test an infant's ability to discriminate two stimuli that differ in some way, the investigator first presents one of the stimuli until the infant stops attending or otherwise responding to it (habituates). Then the second stimulus is presented. If the infant discriminates this second stimulus from the first, he will indicate as much by attending closely to it, by showing a change in respiration or heart rate, or by otherwise altering his behavior in some meaningful way. And should the infant fail to react, it is assumed that the differences between the two stimuli were too subtle for him to detect. Because babies habituate to so many different kinds of stimulation—sights, sounds, odors, tastes, and tactile experiences other than those that are painful—the habituation paradigm is a most useful tool for assessing their sensory and perceptual abilities.

Evoked potentials

Yet another way of determining what infants might be capable of sensing (or perceiving) is to present them with a stimulus and record their brain waves. Electrodes are placed on the infant's scalp above those brain centers that process the kind of sensory information the investigator will be presenting. This means that responses to visual stimuli are recorded from the back of the head, at a site above the occipital lobe, whereas responses to sounds are recorded from the side of the head, above the temporal lobe. If the infant detects (senses) the particular stimulus that we present, she will show a change in the patterning of her brain waves, or **evoked potential,** shortly after its presentation. Stimuli that are not detected will produce no changes in the brain's electrical activity. This "evoked potential" procedure can even tell us whether infants can discriminate various sights or sounds, for two stimuli that are sensed as "different" will produce different patterns of electrical activity.

High-amplitude sucking

As we noted in Chapter 5, sucking is a response that all normal infants perform rather well. In fact, most infants can exert enough control over their sucking behavior to tell us what they can sense and to give us some idea of their likes and dislikes.

First used in the late 1960s (Siqueland & DeLucia, 1969), the **high-amplitude sucking method** provides infants with a special pacifier to suck—one containing electrical circuitry that will enable them to exert some control over their sensory environments. After the investigator establishes an infant's baseline sucking rate, the procedure begins. Whenever the infant sucks faster or harder than she did during the baseline observations (high-amplitude sucking), she will trip the electrical circuit in the pacifier, thereby activating machinery (for example, a slide projector or tape recorder) that introduces some kind of sensory stimulation. Should the infant detect this stimulation and find it interesting, she will continue to display bursts of high-amplitude sucking for as long as she may care to experience it. But once the infant habituates to the stimulus and her sucking returns to the baseline level, the stimulation ceases (at least until sucking resumes once again). If the investigator now introduces a second stimulus that subsequently elicits a dramatic increase in high-amplitude sucking, he could conclude that the infant has discriminated the second stimulus from the first. Finally, this basic procedure can even be modified to enable the infant to tell us which of two stimuli she prefers. Suppose, for example, that we wanted to determine whether babies prefer marches to lullabies. We could adjust the circuitry in the pacifier so that high-amplitude sucking activates one kind of music and low-amplitude (or no) sucking activates the other. By then noting what the baby does, we could draw some inferences about which of these musical compositions she prefers. Clearly, this high-amplitude sucking paradigm is a clever and versatile technique!

Let's now turn to the research literature to see what these creative new methods have taught us about babies' sensory and perceptual capabilities.

Infant Sensory Capabilities

As recently as the early 1900s, many medical texts claimed that infants were functionally blind, deaf, and impervious to pain for the first several days after birth. In exploring the sensory world of the infant, we will see why modern developmentalists can't help chuckling when they read these earlier pronouncements.

Vision

The eye of the human infant functions reasonably well at birth. Changes in illumination will elicit a *pupillary reflex,* which indicates the neonate is sensitive to brightness (Pratt, 1954). Brightness discrimination develops rapidly during the first few weeks, so that by the age of 2 months, infants can discriminate a white bar that differs only 5% in luminance from a solid white background (Peeples & Teller, 1975). Babies can also detect movement in the visual field. Even neonates are likely to track a visual stimulus with their eyes as long as the target is moving slowly (Banks & Salapatek, 1983).

Very young infants also see the world in color, not in black and white as some early theorists had assumed. Using the habituation paradigm, researchers have found that newborns discriminate many colors, although they may have some trouble telling blues from grays (Powers, Schneck, & Teller, 1981). And by 3–4 months of age, color vision is very mature: not only are infants proficient at discriminating colors, but they are now dividing the color spectrum into the same basic categories—the reds, greens, blues, and yellows—that adults do (Bornstein, Kessen, & Weiskopf, 1976; Teller & Bornstein, 1984).

By adult standards, the **visual acuity** of the neonate is poor. At birth, a baby's distance vision is about 20/300, which means that the infant sees at 20 feet what an adult with excellent vision can see at 300 feet. Many forms are difficult for a young infant to detect because she requires sharper **visual contrasts** (transitions between light and dark areas) to "see" them than adults do (Banks & Salapatek, 1983). Moreover, an infant's visual images are likely to be blurred because she has trouble

accommodating—that is, changing the shape of the lens of the eye to bring objects into focus. Until recently, investigators believed that neonates could focus reasonably well on objects 7–10 inches from their faces. However, Martin Banks (1980) has found that 1-month-old infants do not see clearly or produce sharp visual images of targets at any distance. Although visual acuity improves rapidly over the first few months of life, it may take as long as six months to a year before the infant will see as well as an adult (Banks & Salapatek, 1983).

In sum, the young infant's visual system is not operating at peak efficiency, but it is certainly working. Even newborns can sense movement, colors, changes in brightness, and a variety of visual patterns—as long as these patterned stimuli are not too finely detailed and have a sufficient amount of light/dark contrast.

Audition

Neonates hear fairly well. They are startled by loud noises and will turn away from them, but they will turn in the direction of a softer sound as if searching for its source (Field, Muir, Pilon, Sinclair, & Dodwell, 1980). However, this early ability to localize sound may be a kind of reflex, for it disappears at age 2 months and then reappears as an even more reliable response at about 4 months of age (Field et al., 1980; Muir, 1985).

Using the evoked-potential procedure, researchers have found that soft sounds that adults can hear must be made noticeably louder before a neonate will detect them (Aslin, Pisoni, & Jusczyk, 1983). In the first few hours of life, infants may hear about as well as an adult with a head cold. Their insensitivity to softer sounds could be due, in part, to fluids that have seeped into the inner ear during the birth process. Despite this minor limitation, habituation studies indicate that neo-

---

habituation: a decrease in one's response to a stimulus that has become familiar through repetition.
evoked potential: a change in patterning of the brain waves which indicates that an individual detects (senses) a stimulus.
high-amplitude sucking method: a method of assessing infants' perceptual capabilities that capitalizes on the ability of infants to make interesting events last by increasing the rate at which they suck on a special pacifier.
visual acuity: a person's ability to see small objects and fine detail.
visual contrast: the amount of light/dark transition in a visual stimulus.

nates are capable of discriminating sounds that differ in loudness, duration, direction, and frequency (Bower, 1982). They hear rather well indeed.

Young infants are particularly responsive to the sounds of a human voice. Harriet Rheingold and Judith Adams (1980) found that caregivers speak often to newborn infants and appear to enjoy these "conversations." And what do adults find so interesting about a "conversation" with a nonverbal infant? Perhaps it is simply that infants will often stop crying, open their eyes, and begin to look around or to vocalize themselves when they are spoken to (Alegria & Noirot, 1978; Rosenthal, 1982). Some investigators have even claimed that 2-day-old infants will synchronize their body movements to the stops, starts, and pauses in human speech (Condon & Sander, 1974), although other researchers dispute this claim, arguing that if there is any synchrony to these early

Photo 6-2. Young infants are particularly responsive to the sound of human voices.

interactions, it is the adult adjusting her behavior to that of the infant (Dowd & Tronick, 1986). Nevertheless, a baby's general responsiveness to the speech of his companions is a characteristic that will help him to elicit the attention and interpersonal contact that should contribute in a positive way to his social, emotional, and intellectual development.

In sum, our most appropriate response to claims that babies can't hear is to "turn a deaf ear" to them. Newborns hear very well and are capable of discriminating a staggering number of auditory stimuli. Although the baby's auditory capabilities will improve over the first 4 to 6 months of life, and some auditory skills (for example, the ability to detect very brief temporal pauses in a tone) will not mature until late in childhood (Irwin, Ball, Kay, Stillman, & Rosser, 1985), infants are remarkably well prepared for such significant achievements as (1) using voices to recognize and discriminate their companions and (2) breaking speech into smaller units—the building blocks of language. Stay tuned, for we will soon discuss these important developments.

Taste and Smell

Infants are born with some very definite taste preferences. For example, they apparently come equipped with something of a sweet tooth, for babies suck faster and longer for sweet (sugary) liquids than for bitter, sour, salty, or neutral (water) solutions (Crook, 1978). Different tastes also elicit different facial expressions from newborns. Sweets produce smiles and smacking of the lips, whereas sour substances cause infants to wrinkle their noses and purse their lips, and bitter solutions often elicit expressions of disgust—a downturning of the corners of the mouth, tongue protrusions, and even spitting (Ganchrow, Steiner, & Daher, 1983; Steiner, 1979). Moreover, these facial expressions become more pronounced as solutions become sweeter, more sour, or more bitter, suggesting that newborns can discriminate different levels or concentrations of a particular "taste."

Neonates are also capable of sensing and discriminating a variety of odors, and they will react vigorously by turning away and displaying expressions of disgust in response to unpleasant smells such as vinegar, ammonia, or rotten eggs (Rieser, Yonas, & Wilkner, 1976; Steiner, 1979). Even more remarkable are data indicating that breast-fed infants soon come to recognize their mothers by smell. Within a week, babies can discriminate the odor of their mother's feeding pad from that of an unused pad or the pad of another breast-feeding mother (MacFarlane, 1977). Indeed, breast-fed infants only 2 weeks old can easily discriminate their own mother's body odors from those of other people, whereas babies who are bottle-fed cannot, possibly because they have less contact with their mothers' bare skin (Cernoch & Porter, 1985). Like it or not, each of us has a unique "olfactory signature"—a characteristic that babies can use as an early means of "identifying" their closest companions. Ironically, Aidan MacFarlane (1977) reports that the mothers in his study often wanted to rush off and apply their deodorant when he told them he was interested in determining whether their babies could smell them.

Touch, Temperature, and Pain

Although sensitivity to touch has not been heavily researched, we learned in Chapter 5 that newborn infants will emit reflexive responses if one touches their cheeks (rooting reflex), their palms (grasping reflex), or the soles of their feet (Babinski reflex). Even while sleeping, neonates are likely to habituate to gentle strokes applied to one spot on the body but then respond once again if the tactile stimulation is shifted to a new locale—from the ear to the lips, for example (Kisilevsky & Muir, 1984). So it appears that young infants are sensitive to a variety of tactile experiences.

Later in the first year, infants are able to discriminate objects solely on the basis of touch. In one study (Streri & Pecheux, 1986a), 5-month-olds habituated to a star-shaped plywood object that they had touched repeatedly but had never seen. When later given an opportunity to fondle this object or a new one with a different shape, the infants clearly preferred to explore the novel shape rather than the one they recognized by touch.

Newborns are also quite sensitive to warmth, cold, and changes in temperature. They will refuse to suck if the milk in their bottles is too hot, and they will try to maintain their body heat by becoming more active should the temperature of a room suddenly drop (Pratt, 1954). And consider the results of an interesting study by Emily Bushnell and her associates (Bushnell, Shaw, & Strauss, 1985). Six-month-old infants first became familiar with a colored vial heated to a particular temperature. When later given a *different colored* vial heated to the *same* temperature, the infants treated it as if it were the same old stimulus that they were already familiar with. But when the color of the vial remained the same and the *temperature* changed, infants acted as if this were a novel stimulus, exploring it intently with

their eyes and hands. So not only did these 6-month-olds show that they can discriminate changes in temperature, but their intense fascination with an object's thermal characteristics implies that "temperature is an important dimension of reality for infants" (Bushnell et al., 1985, p. 598).

Do babies experience much pain? One-day-old infants who are exposed to pinpricks (like those administered in blood tests) do cry as if in pain. However, sensitivity to mild pain seems to increase rather dramatically over the first few days of life, for it takes much less aversive stimulation to bother a 5-day-old infant than a 1-day-old infant (Lipsitt & Levy, 1959).

For obvious ethical reasons, researchers have not exposed infants to severely painful stimuli. However, we know a bit about infants' reactions to intense pain from studying male babies undergoing circumcision, an operation that takes place without anesthesia. While the actual surgery is in progress, infants emit intense pain cries that are very similar to the wails of premature babies or those who are brain-damaged (Porter, Miller, & Marshall, 1986). Moreover, plasma cortisol, a physiological indicator of stress, is significantly higher just after a circumcision and for about two hours afterward than just before the surgery (Gunnar, Malone, Vance, & Fisch, 1985). But despite the trauma that these circumcised infants have experienced, they quickly recover. Not only are they capable of normal social interactions with their mothers a few minutes after the surgery is over, but they are usually sleeping quite peacefully within an hour or two of the operation (Gunnar et al., 1985).

Finally, an infant's response to painful stimuli will change rather dramatically over the first year. When given an inoculation, for example, 2-month-olds show clear expressions of pain, whereas the facial configurations of 7- to 18-month-olds suggest that these older children are angry (Izard, Hembree, & Huebner, 1987). Perhaps older infants become angry in this situation because they are more cognitively sophisticated than a 2-month-old and, thus, better able to recognize that another person is responsible for the hurt that they are experiencing.

In sum, the sensory equipment of young infants functions rather well. Even neonates are well prepared to "sense" their environments, for they are quite capable of seeing, hearing, tasting, smelling, and responding to touch, temperature, and pain from the first day of life. But how do they *interpret* this input? Can they perceive?

Our search for answers will center mainly on visual and auditory perception, simply because researchers have assumed that vision and audition are the dominant senses (for humans, at least). As a result, they have focused heavily on children's interpretations of sights and sounds, so that our current knowledge of the child's perceptual world is based largely on the visual and auditory modalities and their relations to the other senses.

Visual Perception in Infancy

We have learned that newborn infants see well enough to discriminate visual patterns. But what do they "see" when looking at these stimuli? If we show them a ☐ do they see a square; or, rather, must they learn to construct a square from an assortment of lines, angles, and edges? When do you suppose infants are capable of recognizing faces as a distinct visual form? When do they begin to distinguish the faces of close companions from those of strangers? Do you suppose neonates can perceive depth and the third dimension? Do they think receding objects shrink; or do they know that these objects remain the same size and only look smaller when moved away? These are precisely the kinds of questions that have motivated curious investigators to find ways of persuading nonverbal infants to "tell" us what they can see.

Perception of Patterns and Forms

Recall Robert Fantz's observations of infants in his looking chamber: babies only 2 days old could easily discriminate visual patterns. In fact, of all the targets that Fantz presented to them, including a drawing of a face, newsprint, a bull's-eye pattern, and unpatterned red, white, and yellow disks, the most preferred stimulus was the face! Does this finding imply that neonates already interpret faces as a meaningful pattern? Might the nativists be correct in assuming that pattern and form *perception* is innate?

Early pattern perception (0–2 months).
Other research implies that neonates' ability to "perceive" faces is more illusory than real. When Fantz (1961) later presented young infants with a face, a stimulus consisting of scrambled facial features, and a simpler stimulus that contained the same amount of light and dark shading as the facelike and scrambled-face drawings, the infants were just as interested in the scrambled face as the normal one (see Figure 6-1). What, then, made the face and the scrambled face equally interesting?

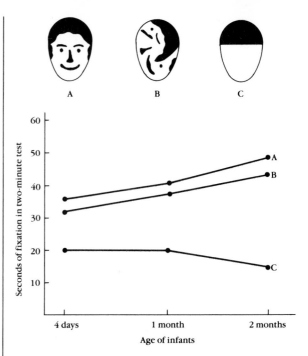

Figure 6-1. Fantz's test of young infants' pattern preferences. Infants preferred to look at complex stimuli rather than a simpler black and white oval. However, the infants did not prefer the facelike figure to the scrambled face. *(Adapted from Fantz, 1961.)*

Over the years, researchers have discovered several properties of visual stimuli that "turn babies on." For example, infants are attracted to patterns that have many boundaries between light and dark areas, or high *contrast,* particularly if these light/dark transitions are sharp (Banks & Ginsburg, 1985). Very young infants also prefer to look at moderately complex patterns rather than simpler ones and at curvilinear rather than linear features (Olson & Sherman, 1983). Thus, faces and scrambled faces may have been equally interesting to Fantz's young subjects because these targets have the same amount of contrast, curvature, and complexity (and more of all these features than the black and white oval, which failed to command much attention). Finally, young infants are especially captivated by things that move. Even newborns will track slowly moving stimuli and will spend much more time looking at a rotating object than at a comparable one that is stationary (Slater, Morison, Town, & Rose, 1985).

By analyzing the physical parameters of stimuli that babies do or do not prefer, we can estimate *what* they are seeing while scanning various targets. Figure 6-2, for example, suggests that very young infants see only a dark blob when looking at a *highly complex* checkerboard, probably because their immature eyes don't accommodate well enough to resolve the fine detail. By contrast, the infant sees a definite pattern when gazing at the *moderately complex* checkerboard (Banks & Salapatek, 1983). Martin Banks and his associates have summarized the looking preferences of very young infants quite succinctly: *babies prefer to look at whatever they see well* (Banks & Ginsburg, 1985), and the things they see best are moderately complex, high-contrast targets, particularly those that capture their attention by moving. Indeed, Banks and other prominent infant watchers such as Marshall Haith (1980) characterize the very young infant as a *stimulus seeker* who is biologically programmed to scan the environment and to explore those visual stimuli that he can detect. This inborn tendency to scan and explore is thought to play a crucial role in perceptual development, for it keeps the baby's

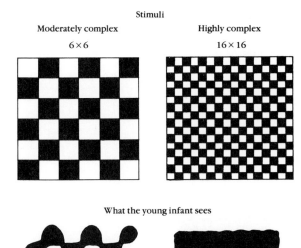

Stimuli

Moderately complex | Highly complex
6 × 6 | 16 × 16

What the young infant sees

Figure 6-2. What it might look like to the young eye. By the time these two checkerboards are processed by eyes with poor vision, only the checkerboard on the left may have any pattern left to it. Poor vision in early infancy helps to explain a preference for moderately complex rather than highly complex stimuli. *(Adapted from Banks & Salapatek, 1983.)*

visual neurons firing, thereby promoting the development of the visual areas of the brain.

To this point, we have established that even 2-day-old infants can discriminate visual patterns and will prefer some patterns to others. But do they really *perceive* forms? If shown a triangle, for example, do they see the △ that we construct; or, rather, do they detect only pieces of lines and maybe an angle (such as ∠\)?

The answers to these questions are by no means established. Although some investigators claim that 1-month-old infants can perceive whole forms if given ample time to scan them (Treiber & Wilcox, 1980), others note that very young infants are unlikely to detect forms because they limit their scanning to selected parts of whatever they are looking at (see Box 6-1). So unless the form is very small, they are unlikely to see all of it, much less put all this information together to perceive a unified whole.

Later pattern and form perception (2 months–1 year). Between the ages of 2 and 12 months, the infant's visual system is maturing rapidly, enabling her to see better and to make increasingly complex visual discriminations. This is also the period when infants are becoming rather proficient at perceiving forms.

The most basic task in perceiving a figure, or form, is to discriminate that object from its surrounding context (that is, other objects and the general "background"). How do you suppose an infant eventually recognizes that a bottle of milk in front of a centerpiece on the dining room table is not just a part of the centerpiece? What information does she use to perceive forms, and when does she begin to do so?

Philip Kellman and Elizabeth Spelke (1983; Kellman, Spelke, & Short, 1986) have been addressing these issues in some intriguing research with 4-month-olds. Infants are presented with a display consisting of a rod partly hidden by a block in front of it (see Figure 6-3, displays A and B). Will they perceive the rod as a whole object, even though part of it is not available for inspection; or, rather, will they act as though they had seen two short and separate rods?

To find out, Kellman and Spelke first presented 4-month-olds with either display A (stationary hidden rod) or display B (moving hidden rod) and allowed them to look at the display until they were no longer interested (habituation). Once they had habituated, the infants were shown displays C (a whole rod) and D (two rod segments), and their looking prefer-

Box 6-1
Visual Scanning Early in Infancy

What do young infants look at when they scan a pattern or form? To find out, Philip Salapatek (1975) developed a photographic technique to record babies' eye movements as they looked at simple geometric figures such as triangles, stars, and squares. What Salapatek soon discovered is that 1-month-old infants scanned only a small portion of each figure, usually focusing on only one angular feature or boundary—for example, one point of the star shown here. By contrast, 2-month-old infants traced a larger portion of the figure and would also scan the figure's internal areas. So 2-month-olds scanned the figures much more thoroughly than 1-month-olds did.

Daphne Maurer and Philip Salapatek (1976) next exposed 1- and 2-month-old infants to human faces and recorded their eye movements. In the sample tracings of the infants' visual behavior presented below, note that the 1-month-olds concentrated on the edges and contours of the total facial configuration and spent very little time examining internal features such as the eyes, nose, and mouth. By contrast, 2-month-old infants spent considerably more time scanning internal facial features and paid less attention to boundary areas than 1-month-olds did. Notice, too, that neither group of infants systematically scanned the whole form; hence, these infants were probably not responding to faces as unified wholes. But

1-month-old infant

2-month-old infant

Visual scanning of a geometric figure by 1- and 2-month-old infants.

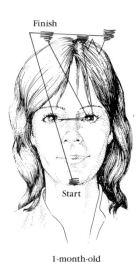
1-month-old

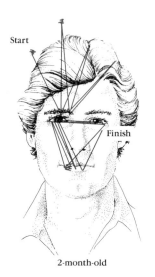
2-month-old

Visual scanning of the human face by 1- and 2-month-old infants.

as we will see in the text, perception of facial configurations is a milestone that will be reached in the not too distant future.

---

ences were recorded. Infants who had habituated to the stationary hidden rod (display A) showed no distinct preference for display C or display D in the later test. In other words, they were apparently not able to use available cues—information such as the two identical rod tips oriented along the same line—to perceive a whole rod when part of the rod was hidden. By contrast, infants *did* apparently perceive the *moving* rod (display B) as "whole," for after habituating to this stimulus, they much preferred to look at the two short rods (display D) than at a whole rod (display C, which they now treated as "old hat"). It seems that these latter infants were

inferring the rod's wholeness from its synchronized movement—the fact that its parts moved in the same direction at the same time. How soon infants are able to use motion to infer form is not known for sure, although recent research indicates that even 3-month-olds are capable of such inferences and seem to know much more about moving objects than about stationary ones (Kaufmann-Hayoz, Kaufmann, & Stucki, 1986).

By 5 to 7 months of age, infants are better able to interpret other cues to an object's wholeness so that even stationary scenes can be organized into distinct "figures" and "backgrounds." To quickly illustrate just

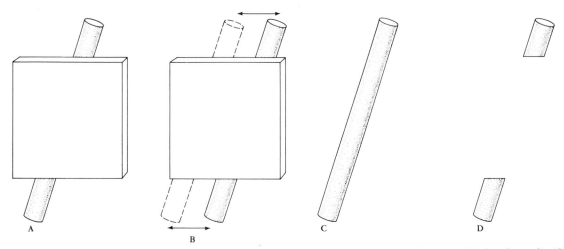

Figure 6-3. Perceiving objects as wholes. An infant is habituated to seeing a rod partially hidden by the block in front of it. The rod is either stationary (A) or moving (B). When tested afterward, does the infant treat the whole rod (C) as "old hat"? We certainly would, for we would readily interpret cues that tell us that there is one long rod behind the block and would therefore regard the whole rod as familiar. But if the infant shows more interest in the whole rod than in the two rod segments (D), he or she has apparently not been able to use available cues to perceive a whole rod. At 4 months of age, infants perceive a whole rod only if the rod moves as they are habituated to watching it. *(Adapted from Kellman & Spelke, 1983.)*

how proficient their form perception is becoming, look carefully at Figure 6-4. Do you see a square in this display? So do 5–7-month-old infants (Bertenthal, Campos, & Haith, 1980)—a remarkable achievement indeed, for the boundary of this "square" is a *subjective contour* that must be constructed mentally rather than simply detected by the visual system.

Further strides in form perception are made later in the first year, and a recent program of research by Bennett Bertenthal and associates illustrates one of these milestones. Bertenthal has wondered whether infants can perceive the human form from the barest of cues—namely, from sets of lights that can be programmed to move and thereby simulate the motions involved when a human being walks. Figure 6-5 illustrates three of these point-light displays, each of which is viewed against a black background. Display A shows 11 lights attached to points corresponding to the head and to major joints in the body—a display that adults clearly perceive as a humanlike form when the lights move as indicated in the figure. Display B is an inverted form of the same moving lights. Display C shows the same 11 lights moving in the same ways as in the other two displays, but having no explicit form. How do infants react to these stimuli?

Infants only 3 to 5 months old can clearly discriminate the three visual displays when the lights are moving, but they do not discriminate them when the lights remain stationary (Bertenthal, Proffitt, & Cutting, 1984; Bertenthal, Proffitt, Kramer, & Spetner, 1987). But there is more. At age 9 months, infants begin to pay much more attention to changes made in the patterning of the upright display (display A) than to changes of equal magnitude made in the other two displays (Bertenthal, Proffitt, Spetner, & Thomas, 1985). So it seems that young infants are detecting some coherence in each of the moving displays, whereas the 9-month-olds are attaching special significance to the "upright" display—

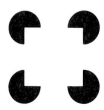

Figure 6-4. By 5–7 months of age, infants are perceiving subjective contours such as the "square" shown here. *(From Bertenthal, Campos, & Haith, 1980.)*

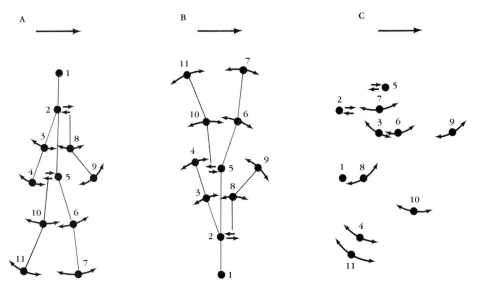

Figure 6-5. The three point-light displays used in Bertenthal's research. *(From Bertenthal, Proffitt, & Cutting, 1984.)*

as if they are now interpreting this stimulus as a representation of the human form, just as adults do.

To this point, we have focused mainly on the perception of inanimate objects and their properties. Let's now briefly consider what is known about the infant's interpretations of faces and facial expressions.

Early social perception: Faces and facial expressions. Although infants do not have an innate preference for faces, the human face is likely to be one of the more interesting objects that babies encounter on a day-to-day basis. Consider, for example, that faces have moving parts (lips, eyes) and that movement attracts immediate attention. Faces are also rich in contrast, complexity, and curvature—features that we know will capture infants' attention. Finally, faces are readily available—a baby will be exposed to the faces of caretakers several times each day, whenever he or she is fed, soothed, bathed, or diapered. So there is reason to believe that "faceness" may be one of the first "forms" that babies perceive and that infants may soon begin to discriminate the faces of familiar companions from those of strangers.

In Box 6-1 we learned that 4-week-old infants focus almost exclusively on the outer boundaries of facial stimuli, whereas 8-week-olds have at least begun to scan internal features such as the eyes, nose, and mouth. By age 9–11 weeks, infants have become much more interested in the internal features of a face than in its edges (Haith, Bergman, & Moore, 1977). Does this increasing attention to internal detail mean that 2–3-month-olds are ready to perceive faces as a meaningful configuration? It seems that way. Maria Barrera and Daphne Maurer (1981b) have found that 3-month-old infants not only recognize photographs of their mothers' faces but prefer to look at photographs of their mothers rather than at those of strangers. In a second experiment, Barrera and Maurer (1981a) found that 3-month-old infants can discriminate the faces of two strangers, even when the strangers were thought to be quite similar in appearance by a panel of adult judges. So by the tender age of 12–13 weeks, infants seem to be *perceiving* facial configurations. What's more, strangers do not "all look alike" to them.

It also appears that 3–4-month-old infants are sensitive to facial expressions. Not only can they discriminate photos of happy faces from photos of sad or angry ones (Barrera & Maurer, 1981a; LaBarbera, Izard, Vietze, & Parisi, 1976), but the happier the face, the more they like to look at it (Kuchuk, Vibbert, & Bornstein, 1986). Critics have argued that infants this young are not really perceiving whole facial expressions but are focusing instead on more limited information (Walker-Andrews, 1986). For example, infants may prefer to look at the happiest faces they see because the very broad smiles associated with happier faces provide more contrast between the model's teeth and the rest of the face than less happy faces do. Nevertheless, 3-month-old infants clearly discriminate their own mothers' happy, sad, and angry expressions when these facial configurations are accompanied by the mothers' happy, sad, or angry tone of voice. And not only do infants discriminate these three emotions, but they also become rather gleeful in response to a happy expression and distressed when exposed to angry displays (Haviland & Lelwica, 1987).

Let's note, however, that 3–4-month-old infants have a way to go yet. At this young age, they may rarely discriminate one face (or facial expression) from another unless they examine these stimuli for a long time. By contrast, 5–7-month-old infants can quickly discriminate their regular companions from strangers, are becoming more proficient at discriminating emotional expressions (for example, happy displays) that vary in intensity, and may even recognize that a line drawing of a woman's face and the woman's photograph represent the same person (Cohen, DeLoache, & Strauss, 1979; Nelson, 1987). In fact, 5–7-month-old infants are unlikely to "forget a face," even if their exposure was brief (two to three minutes) and they do not see the face again for two weeks (Fagan, 1979).

During the latter half of the first year, many infants reach another important milestone in social perception—they are able to read their mothers' emotional reactions to ambiguous situations and use this information to regulate their own behavior. This **social referencing** function is nicely illustrated in two recent studies in which 8–10-month-old infants were approached rapidly by a stranger (normally a fear-provoking event at this age). In both studies, infants responded much more favorably to the stranger's approach if their mothers had either spoken positively to the stranger or issued a warm greeting as opposed to reacting neutrally or negatively to this individual (Boccia & Campos, 1983; Feinman & Lewis, 1983). And by age 12 months, infants are already using the facial expressions of strangers to determine how they should be feeling or responding in uncertain situations. If exposed to a somewhat unpredictable, battery-operated robot, for example, infants will soon smile and approach the toy if they see a nearby stranger smiling. Yet if the stranger displays a fearful expression, the infants become wary themselves and are apt to avoid the toy (Klinnert, Emde, Butterfield, & Campos, 1986). So facial expressions clearly have meaning for 8–12-month-old infants, who are becoming rather accomplished social perceivers indeed!

Summing up. It seems that the ability to perceive faces and facial configurations follows the same general course as the perception of other visual forms and patterns. During the first two months of life, babies are *"stimulus seekers"* whose uneven scanning of the patterns they can see provides them with stimulation that will promote the further development of the visual system. Although very young infants may not actually perceive forms, they can detect very subtle differences among similar visual patterns and, thus, must see some order to the universe right from the beginning.

Between 2 and 6 months of age, the infant's visual capabilities are rapidly maturing, her scanning is becoming much more systematic, and she begins to perceive a variety of forms. Forms that move (such as faces) are probably detected first, but 6–9-month-olds can even perceive the subjective contours of stationary objects (recall the "square" of Figure 6-4). So if the very young infant is a "stimulus seeker," perhaps we are not too far off in characterizing the 3–6-month-old as a *"form constructor."*

During the latter half of the first year, infants are becoming better and better at constructing forms and at interpreting them as well. By 9–10 months of age, they apparently perceive Bertenthal's upright light display as something meaningful—a human form. They are also rather proficient at reading their mothers' facial (and vocal) expressions and at using this information to regulate their behavior in uncertain situations. So older infants are truly *"form interpreters."*

Perhaps you can see from this overview why few contemporary theorists endorse the extreme positions taken by the nativists and empiricists of yesteryear. True, neonates are biologically prepared to gaze at visual stimuli and to make visual discriminations. However, the visual *experiences* a baby has will contribute to the development of the brain and its visual centers (maturation), which, in turn, helps the infant to see more and more and to interpret her visual experiences. So the growth of pattern and form perception represents a fundamental interplay, or *interaction,* between the baby's innate endowment (a working visual sense), maturational processes, and experience (or learning).

Will this interactive model hold for spatial perception as well? Let's see whether it does.

***

social referencing: the use of others' emotional expressions to infer the meaning of otherwise ambiguous situations.

Spatial Perception

Once again, try to imagine that you are a neonate who is just about to take a first breast feeding. As you open your eyes, you see an object (the breast) before you. The question is this: Would you see a simple two-dimensional bull's-eye pattern formed by the nipple surrounded by breast tissue; or, rather, could you perceive that this object has some depth, or three-dimensionality?

Because we so easily perceive depth and the third dimension, it is tempting to conclude that neonates can too. However, empiricists have argued that poor visual acuity and an inability to bring objects into sharp focus (that is, to accommodate) prevent the neonate from making accurate spatial inferences. In addition, it appears that infants younger than 3½ months may not exhibit **stereopsis**—a convergence of the visual images of the two eyes to produce a singular, non-overlapping image that has depth (Fox, Aslin, Shea, & Dumais, 1980). All these biological limitations may make it difficult for infants to perceive depth and to locate objects in space.

However, nativists would argue that several cues to depth and distance are monocular—that is, detectable with only one eye. One important monocular depth cue is **perspective,** a principle that artists use to create the illusion of three-dimensionality on a two-dimensional surface by making linear objects converge as they recede toward the horizon (linear convergence), by drawing distant objects smaller than near objects (sizing cues), or by drawing a near figure to partly obscure one farther away (interposition). If neonates can detect these monocular perspective cues, then their world may be three-dimensional from the very beginning.

So when are infants capable of perceiving depth and making reasonably accurate inferences about size and spatial relations? Let's briefly consider four programs of research designed to answer these questions.

Experiments on depth perception

In the early 1960s, Eleanor Gibson and Richard Walk developed an apparatus they called the **visual cliff** to determine whether infants can perceive depth. The visual cliff (Photo 6-3) consists of an elevated glass platform divided into two sections by a center board. On the "shallow" side, a checkerboard pattern is placed directly under the glass. On the "deep" side, the pattern is placed several feet below the glass, creating the illusion of a sharp dropoff, or a "visual cliff." The investigator tests an infant for depth perception by placing him

Photo 6-3. An infant at the edge of the visual cliff.

on the center board and then asking the child's mother to try to coax the infant to cross both the "shallow" and the "deep" sides. If the child crawls across the shallow side but refuses to cross the deep side, then he is said to perceive depth. Presumably the infant's hesitation to cross the deep side results from a fear of the perceived dropoff.[1]

In the original "visual cliff" studies, Gibson and Walk (1960) found that most babies aged 6½ months and older would not crawl across the "deep" side to their mothers, although they showed no reluctance to cross the shallow side. Clearly, human infants are able to perceive depth by the middle of the first year.

The problem with the visual cliff is that infants must be able to crawl to show us they will avoid the cliff, and unfortunately, babies younger than 6 months can't crawl. However, Joseph Campos and his associates

---

[1]An alternative interpretation is that infants might avoid the "deep" side not because they *fear* the dropoff but simply because they see no "surface" over the cliff on which they can crawl (Rader, Bausano, & Richards, 1980). But even if this alternative interpretation is correct, the infant's refusal to cross the deep side would still imply that he or she perceives depth (that is, the surface under the glass is seen as too far away to permit any crawling).

(Campos, Langer, & Krowitz, 1970) devised a method of testing the depth perception of very young infants on the visual cliff. Campos et al. recorded changes in infants' heart rates when they were lowered face down over the "shallow" and the "deep" sides of the apparatus. Babies as young as 2 months showed a decrease in heart rate when they were over the cliff but no change in heart rate on the shallow side. A decrease in heart rate is a physiological indicator of attention that implies that the 2-month-old infants in this study considered the deep side of the apparatus more interesting than the shallow side (that is, they were probably perceiving depth although they had not yet learned to fear heights). By contrast, 1-month-old infants did not discriminate the deep and shallow sides, possibly because their visual abilities were too immature to allow them to detect the dropoff.

Although we cannot tell whether depth perception is innate from the visual-cliff research, we do know that babies are paying close attention to the deep side of the apparatus and detecting depth cues by the end of the second month.

Experiments on visual looming

As a moving object approaches, its retinal image becomes larger and larger and may expand to occupy the entire visual field (that is, may **loom**) as the object draws near the face. Do you think young infants would react to looming objects? If they do, we might infer that they can perceive movement across the third dimension.

Several years ago, Thomas Bower and his associates (Bower, Broughton, & Moore, 1970a) found that babies only 6 to 20 days old would reliably throw up their hands and retract their heads when an approaching foam rubber cube came within 8 inches of their faces. Were these "defensive" responses on the babies' part—reactions implying that the infants *perceived* the approach of the cube and were sensitive to cues for distance? Bower says yes, although Albert Yonas (1981) has another interpretation: perhaps these very young infants simply lost their balance as they leaned back to get a better look at the "nearby" cube. Indeed, Yonas's interpretation would seem to be correct, because young infants show exactly the same pattern of arm lifting and head retraction while tracking a rising stimulus that is moving *away* from them.

In his own research, Yonas finds that babies less than 1 month old rarely even blink when objects approach their faces; apparently they do not yet inter-

pret an expanding retinal image as a cue to distance or a sign that the approaching object is drawing near. Such blinking first appears at about 1 month of age and becomes much more consistent over the next three months (Yonas, 1981). Does this mean that infants must learn to infer movement across the third dimension, as the empiricists have claimed? Maybe so, but Yonas is an interactionist who believes that the maturation of the visual system plays a major role in this learning. And apparently he is right, for preterm infants, who are neurologically immature at birth, do not begin to blink at looming objects until several weeks after full-term infants do (Pettersen, Yonas, & Fisch, 1980). So it seems that a certain amount of neural maturation is necessary before infants will interpret an object's approach (or, literally, expansion of its retinal image) as a cue for depth and distance.

Experiments on size constancy

If a friend who stands 5′8″ should leave your side and walk 20 feet away from you, the image of that person on your retina will become much smaller. Yet, you realize that your friend is still 5′8″ and simply *looks* smaller because he or she is now farther away. This realization is an example of **size constancy**—the ability to detect that the dimensions of an object will remain constant over a change in distance. Obviously, a person who displays size constancy has some understanding of depth and the third dimension. Specifically, he or she recognizes that increases in distance (or depth) can compensate for decreases in the size of a retinal image to preserve an object's absolute size. So if infants show some evidence of size constancy, we can conclude that they perceive depth, distance, and the third dimension.

Because size constancy requires subjects to es-

---

stereopsis: fusion of two flat images to produce a single image that has depth.

perspective: representation of depth on a two-dimensional surface by drawing distant objects smaller than near objects and making linear features converge as they recede from the viewer.

visual cliff: an elevated platform that creates an illusion of depth, used to test the depth perception of infants.

visual looming: the expansion of the image of an object to take up the entire visual field as it draws very close to the face.

size constancy: the tendency to perceive an object as the same size from different distances despite changes in the size of its retinal image.

timate distance, it would seem that this ability could emerge only after infants become sensitive to depth and distance cues—that is, at some point after age 2 months when they first detect a visual cliff and have begun to respond more reliably to looming objects. Ross Day and Beryl McKenzie (1981) have found some evidence for size constancy among 4½-month-old infants who are looking at familiar objects. Infants were first habituated to a model of a human head placed 3 to 5 feet in front of them. If a bigger head was then substituted for the original one, the infants stared intently, thereby treating this new stimulus as novel. But if the *original* head was moved closer or farther away, the infants were not especially interested. Apparently they recognized it as the same old head, even though its retinal image was becoming larger or smaller. Let's note, however, that 4½-month-old infants will display size constancy only for *familiar* objects and only when they *watch these objects approach or recede*. Apparently, an object's motion not only helps young infants to detect form, it provides cues about the object's size as well. Not until age 6 to 8 months will infants first recognize that *stationary* objects retain their absolute size when viewed from a greater or a lesser distance (McKenzie, Tootell, & Day, 1980).

Experiments on pictorial depth cues

Recently, Albert Yonas and his associates (Granrud & Yonas, 1984; Yonas, Cleaves, & Pettersen, 1978; Yonas, Granrud, & Pettersen, 1985) have observed infants' reactions to perspective cues—the tricks that artists and photographers use to portray depth and distance on a two-dimensional surface. In the earliest of these studies, infants were exposed to a photograph of a bank of windows taken at a 45° angle. As we see in Figure 6-6, the windows on the right appear (to us at least) to be much closer than those on the left. Which side of the large photograph would infants try to touch? If they perceive pictorial cues to depth, they might be fooled into thinking that the windows on the right are closer and should reach to the right. But if they are insensitive to pictorial depth cues, they should reach out with one hand about as often as they do with the other.

What Yonas et al. (1978) found is that 7-month-olds reliably reached toward the windows that appear nearest, whereas 5-month-olds displayed no such reaching preferences. In later research, Yonas finds that 7-month-olds are also sensitive to pictorial cues such as relative size and interposition, whereas 5-month-olds are not. So it seems that somewhere between age 5 and

7 months (perhaps as early as 5½ months) infants become capable of extracting information about depth and distance from pictorial representations (see Yonas et al., 1985)—an impressive accomplishment indeed!

Conclusions

In sum, there is very little evidence that any aspect of spatial perception is innate. Although neonates will look intently at targets that approach or recede, they do not seem to be bothered by looming objects, nor do they detect depth when placed on an elevated platform (the visual cliff). Infants normally reach both these milestones by 2 to 4 months of age, aided by the maturation of the visual system, and will soon be displaying size constancy and inferring depth and distance from pic-

Figure 6-6. This bank of windows is actually a large photograph taken at a 45° angle, and the two edges of this stimulus are in fact equidistant from an infant seated directly in front of it. If infants are influenced by pictorial cues to depth, they should perceive the right edge of the photo to be nearer to them and indicate as much by reaching out to touch this edge rather than the more "distant" edge to their left. *(Adapted from Yonas, Cleaves, & Pettersen, 1978.)*

torial cues as well. But maturation alone cannot account for all the dramatic improvements in spatial perception—refinements that continue throughout the first year. Today, most researchers are interactionists who believe that a child's experiences will contribute to visual maturation *and* promote perceptual learning. Indeed, the first year is a time when infants are constantly making new and exciting discoveries about distance, depth, and spatial relations as they watch or reach for moving objects and explore sloped surfaces, stairs, and other little "visual cliffs" in the natural environment (Bertenthal & Campos, 1987; Bower, 1982).

Auditory Perception in Infancy

Although we often think of human beings as visual animals, babies are very responsive to many sounds that they hear. Not only do neonates pay attention to sounds, but it appears that they try to interpret them as well. In this section we will see that William James (1890) seems to have overstated the case when he inferred that the auditory world of the newborn is an unanalyzed buzz of confusion.

The fact that neonates will often turn their heads toward a sound has been interpreted by some as a primitive form of auditory *perception* (sounds imply sights) that is present at birth (Bower, 1982). Others disagree, noting that this auditory localization is only a reflex that soon disappears and will not reemerge as a voluntary response until about 4 months of age (Muir, 1985). So by age 4 months (and possibly even sooner), babies are apparently *interpreting* sounds as an indication that there is something out there to see, and they are turning their heads to catch a glimpse of the noise-making object.

Although there is much we do not know about infants' auditory capabilities, researchers are beginning to ask some interesting questions. When, for example, will an infant first recognize his mother's voice or prefer it to the voice of a stranger? How soon are babies capable of discriminating the various vowel and consonant sounds that make up a language? Are infants inherently musical creatures who prefer marches and melodies to nonmusical forms of auditory stimulation? These are some of the issues we will explore in the pages that follow.

Voice Recognition

Many people would undoubtedly chuckle if a mother were to claim that her week-old infant already recognizes her voice. Yet the mother might have the last laugh, for an experiment by Anthony DeCasper and William Fifer (1980) suggests that babies can recognize their mothers' voices during the first three days of life. Infants were given a special pacifier that recorded their sucking rate. At first, the experimenters simply watched to see how fast each baby sucked the pacifier. Once this "baseline" sucking rate had been established, the procedure began. For half the infants, sucking faster than the baseline rate activated a recording of the mother's voice, and sucking slower than baseline produced a recording of a female stranger. Just the opposite was true for the remaining infants: fast sucking produced the stranger's voice, and slow sucking activated a recording of the mother. DeCasper and Fifer found that their 1–3-day-old infants did whatever it took (that is, sucked faster or slower) in order to hear their own mothers. So they not only recognized the mother's voice but clearly preferred it to the voice of a female stranger. More recently, DeCasper and Spence (1986) have discovered that neonates prefer listening to stories that their mothers had read aloud many times during the last six weeks of pregnancy rather than other stories that the mothers had never recited. Thus, some auditory learning occurs before birth—a fact that may explain why newborns recognize their own mothers' voices and prefer them to the voice of another woman.

Reactions to Speech and Language

Earlier we noted that neonates become more alert when spoken to and may even synchronize their bodily movements to the rhythms in human speech. Although there is some question about how synchronized the baby's reactions to speech really are, newborn infants do show a more organized pattern of movement when responding to speech than when listening to recordings of disconnected vowel sounds and tapping noises (Condon & Sander, 1974). So babies may be programmed to recognize and react to language from the moment of birth.

Very young infants are also capable of distinguishing the various vowel and consonant sounds that make up a language. For example, Marsha Clarkson and Keith Berg (1983) found that babies can tell the difference between the vowels *a* and *i* from the second day of life. And even speech sounds that are very similar (for example, *b* and *p* or *da, ba, bi,* and *du*) are easily discriminated by 2–3-month-old infants (Eimas, 1975b; Jusczyk & Derrah, 1987).

Are adults any better than infants at discriminating the auditory components of language? The answer is yes—and no. Adults can more readily discriminate some of the sounds of the language they have acquired, a finding that indicates that auditory discriminations become more refined as the individual listens to a language and begins to reproduce its sounds (see Walk, 1981). Yet, each language uses only a subset of the sounds that human beings are capable of producing, and children will eventually lose the ability to differentiate certain sounds that are *not* components of their native tongue (Werker & Tees, 1984). For example, infants can easily discriminate the consonants *r* and *l* (Eimas, 1975a). So can you if your native language is English, French, Spanish, or German. However, Oriental languages such as Chinese and Japanese make no distinction between *r* and *l*, and as a result, native speakers of these tongues lose the ability to make this auditory discrimination.

In sum, young infants place the auditory components of language into distinct vowel and consonant categories in much the same way that adults do. However, as children mature and begin to acquire the language of their culture, they will make finer distinctions among the components of that language and may actually lose the ability to discriminate certain sounds that are not used in their native tongue. The implication is that the language we acquire will influence our auditory perception. Richard Walk (1981, p. 61) concludes that "in some respects the Biblical story of the Tower of Babel is true—we have difficulty understanding each other's speech because to learn a new language is to change our auditory perception. We are . . . a foreigner in every language but our own."

The Sound of Music

Are neonates musical creatures? Do they prefer music to other auditory stimuli? And if they do, what do they prefer: Motown or Madonna?

Unfortunately, we know very little about how newborns perceive music, although we do know that babies only 1 day old will either increase or decrease their rate of sucking on a pacifier if this strategy permits them to hear a medley of classical, modern instrumental, and "pop" music (Butterfield, cited in Walk, 1981). However, this finding may simply indicate that infants prefer any kind of sound to silence. Do babies really like music?

Apparently so. In a second study (Butterfield & Siperstein, 1972), infants either sucked or refrained

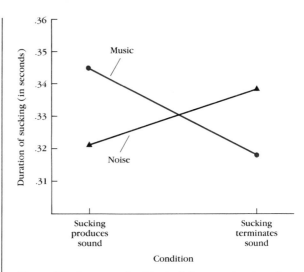

Figure 6-7. Duration of sucking by infants as a function of whether sucking produces music or noise. Clearly, newborns prefer music to noise.

from sucking when that strategy produced folk music, but they did whatever it took to *avoid* listening to nonrhythmic noise (see Figure 6-7). The investigators concluded that babies do like music and that they find noise aversive.

By the age of 4–6 months, infants begin to "bounce" to music (Moog, 1976), and they are now becoming quite skilled at discriminating melodies and at recognizing the same tune despite changes in its pitch or tempo (Chang & Trehub, 1977; Trehub, 1985). Some theorists (for example, Walk, 1981, p. 66) believe that music appreciation "is a species-specific trait and a natural part of our . . . perceptual world." But if babies are inherently musical creatures, it is likely that they prefer some kinds of music to others. Perhaps future research will allow us to determine whether infants will choose Mozart over Muzak or prefer the Motown sound to that of Madonna.

Intersensory Perception

Suppose you are playing a game in which you are blindfolded and are trying to identify objects by touch. A friend then places a small, perfectly spherical object in your hand. As you finger it, you determine that it is 1.5 to 2 inches in diameter, that it weighs at most a couple of ounces, and that it is very hard and is covered with a large number of little indentations, or "dimples."

You suddenly have an "aha" experience and conclude that the object is a _____.

A colleague who often conducts this exercise in class reports that most of his students easily identify the object as a golf ball—even if they have never touched or held a golf ball in their lives. This is an example of **cross-modal perception**—the ability to recognize by one sensory modality (in this case, touch) an object that is familiar through another (vision). As adults, we can make many cross-modal inferences of this kind. But what about human infants? Are babies capable of cross-modal perception during the first year of life? Before we examine the evidence for ourselves, let's consider what some of the major theorists would have to say.

Theories of Intersensory Perception

Recall that William James (1890) believed that the senses are integrated at birth. Presumably, sensory inputs of any kind are global experiences that are not discriminated as "visual," "auditory," "tactile," or "olfactory" experiences; the child has to learn to differentiate the senses.

Thomas Bower (1982) and Eleanor Gibson (1969) can agree, in part, with James's viewpoint. Both Bower and Gibson are **differentiation theorists:** they suggest that the senses are integrated at birth and are gradually differentiated through maturation and experience (perceptual learning). According to Bower (1982), the senses have to be integrated from the beginning—otherwise neonates would not look for sound-producing objects or reach for and try to touch objects they can see. Gibson (1969) adds that the "defining" features of various stimuli (features such as shapes, textures, forms, and patterns) are detectable by more than one modality. If she is correct, cross-modal perception may well be present at birth (or very soon thereafter).

Jean Piaget, in contrast, is an **enrichment theorist.** Piaget (1954, 1960) believes that the sensory modalities are separate at birth and will develop independently before they become more integrated at a later time (unfortunately, Piaget is not clear about when this sensory integration might occur). The enrichment perspective implies that cross-modal perception is not possible until the senses have become integrated. Presumably, a 6-week-old infant who "knows" an object by sight would be unable to recognize it by touch (as in the dark) or to discriminate it from other objects on the basis of tactile cues alone.

Which theory is correct? Let's see whether we can clarify the issue by examining the empirical record.

Are the Senses Integrated at Birth?

Suppose that you captured a baby's attention by floating a soap bubble in front of her face. Would she reach for it? If she did, how do you think she would react when the bubble disappeared at her slightest touch? Thomas Bower (1982), a differentiation theorist, would argue not only that the baby would reach for the bubble but that she would be surprised and perhaps upset when it burst. According to Bower, the baby's surprise or discomfort over the disappearing object is an indication that her senses are integrated—that is, she expects to be able to touch or feel objects she can see and reach.

Bower, Broughton, and Moore (1970b) exposed neonates to a situation similar to the soap-bubble scenario. The subjects were 8–31-day-old infants who could see an object well within reaching distance while they were wearing special goggles. Actually, this **virtual object** was an illusion created by a shadow caster. If the infant reached for it, his or her hand would feel nothing at all. Bower et al. found that the infants did reach for the virtual object and that they often became frustrated to tears when they failed to touch it. These results suggest that vision and touch are integrated: infants expect to feel objects they can see and reach, and an incongruity between vision and the tactile sense is discomforting.

Eric Aronson has studied the reactions of very young infants to incongruities between sights and sounds. Suppose, for example, that infants can see their mothers' faces and lip movements through a soundproof screen while looking straight ahead but are hearing their mothers' voices from a speaker at their own left or right. Under these circumstances, 1–2-month-old infants usually become rather agitated and many even cry (Aronson & Rosenbloom, 1971). These findings suggest that vision and audition are integrated modalities—a baby who sees his mother speak expects to hear her voice coming from the general direction of her mouth.

---

cross-modal perception: the ability to use one sensory modality to identify a stimulus or pattern of stimuli that is already familiar through another modality.

differentiation theory: a theory that the senses are integrated at birth and will gradually become more independent of one another as the child develops.

enrichment theory: a theory that the senses function independently at birth and will gradually become more integrated as the child develops.

virtual object: an intangible object (optical illusion), produced by a shadow caster, that appears to occupy a particular location in space.

Photo 6-4. According to differentiation theory, the senses are integrated at birth, and babies expect to touch and feel objects that they can see and reach. However, vision and touch are soon differentiated so that this year-old infant might even enjoy making an object disappear at her slightest touch.

In sum, the differentiation theorists appear to be right on one score—the senses are apparently integrated at birth. Yet, this sensory integration is rather loose, it seems, for young infants are not always upset by visual/tactile and visual/auditory incongruities (Bower, 1982; Walk, 1981). And even when they are upset, their emotional reactions in no way establish that they are able to use each sense to recognize objects or experiences that are already familiar through another sense. Are very young infants capable of cross-modal perception, as some differentiation theorists have claimed?

Development of Cross-Modal Perception

Although cross-modal perception has never been observed in newborns, it seems that babies only 1 month old have the ability to recognize by sight at least some of the objects that they have previously sucked. In one study, Eleanor Gibson and Arlene Walker (1984) allowed 1-month-old infants to suck either a rigid cylinder or a spongy, pliable one. Then the two objects were displayed visually so as to illustrate that the spongy cylinder would bend and that the rigid one would not. The results were clear: infants who had sucked on a spongy object preferred to look at the rigid cylinder, whereas those who had sucked on a rigid cylinder now gazed more at the pliable one. Apparently these infants could "visualize" the object they had sucked and now considered it less worthy of their inspection than the other stimulus, which was new and more interesting to them (see also Meltzoff & Borton, 1979, for another example of oral/visual matching in 1-month-olds).

Since these infants were about 30 days old, we cannot necessarily conclude that cross-modal perception is innate; either maturation or learning (or some combination of the two) could be responsible for this ability. And before we get too carried away with the remarkable proficiencies of 1-month-olds, let's note (1) that oral-to-visual perception is the only cross-modal skill that has ever been observed in infants this young and (2) that this ability is weak, at best, in very young infants and will improve dramatically over the first year (Rose, Gottfried, & Bridger, 1981). Even the seemingly related ability to match tactile sensations (from grasping) with visual ones does not appear until 5–6 months of age (Rose et al., 1981; Streri & Pecheux, 1986b). So it seems reasonable to assume that cross-modal perception is a skill (or set of skills) that babies must acquire.

Research on cross-modal transfer between the visual and auditory modalities reinforces this conclusion. By 4 months of age, infants are beginning to recognize that a pattern (or rhythm) presented in the auditory mode is the same as or different from another pattern of stimuli presented visually (Mendelson & Ferland, 1982). Moreover, 4-month-olds who can see two talking faces while hearing only one voice will reliably look at the speaker whose lip movements are synchronized with the speech (Spelke & Cortelyou, 1981). Perhaps those poorly dubbed martial arts films would bother a 4-month-old as much as they do many adults! By age 5 months, infants can even match visual and auditory cues for distance. So if they are listening to a sound track in which engine noise is becoming softer, they prefer to watch a film of a car moving away rather than one showing a vehicle approaching (Walker-Andrews & Lennon, 1985). Clearly, 4–5-month-olds know what sights jibe with many sounds, and this auditory/visual matching continues to improve over the next several months (see Allen, Walker, Symonds, & Marcell, 1977).

Another Look at the Enrichment/ Differentiation Controversy

Perhaps you can see that the data on intersensory perception are not completely consistent with either enrichment theory or differentiation theory. Apparently, the senses are *not* separate and independent at birth (as enrichment theorists believe). Rather, they are integrated early and differentiate later (the differentiation position). However, differentiation theorists were incorrect in assuming that sensory integration implies cross-modal perception, for an infant's cross-modal skills are weak at best early in life and steadily improve over time. In fact, studies of older children suggest that cross-modal judgments between vision and the **kinesthetic sense** (sensations produced by bodily movements) develop slowly and are not very accurate until 10–11 years of age (Birch & Lefford, 1963). Clearly, these latter findings seem much more consistent with Piaget's enrichment theory than with the differentiation approach.

How, then, do we interpret a pattern of data that does not clearly endorse either of our major theories? Can both theories be partly correct? Maybe so. Apparently the senses are "fused" at birth, much as William James and other differentiation theorists have argued. But over the next several weeks and months, the senses begin to differentiate. Each sense may now develop somewhat independently of the others, as enrichment theorists have argued; and as each sense continues

to develop, it will become a more effective means of categorizing the properties or distinctive features of various objects and experiences. As a result, the child should become increasingly proficient at using any of his or her senses to recognize stimuli that are already familiar through another modality, and cross-modal perception will improve.

The reason some cross-modal judgments develop so very slowly is that the senses mature at different rates. For example, the kinesthetic sense is not fully developed until late in childhood, perhaps explaining why visual-to-kinesthetic perceptual comparisons are not very accurate until age 10 or 11. In sum, the accuracy of perception across any two senses is limited by the child's perceptual capabilities in the slower-developing modality (Walk, 1981).

Infant Perception in Perspective

What remarkable perceptual competencies infants display! All the senses are functioning well at birth, and babies immediately put them to work, searching for stimuli to explore and identifying similarities and differences among these sensory inputs. Within the first few months, infants are becoming accomplished perceivers; they construct forms, react to depth and distance cues, and detect definite regularities in auditory inputs such as speech and music. And by the middle of the first year, infants have already begun to combine information from the various sensory modalities (cross-modal perception) to achieve a richer understanding of their world. Not surprisingly, then, the most notable advances later in infancy reflect the child's increasing ability to *interpret* sensory experiences—recognizing, for example, that certain patterns of movement imply animation (recall 9-month-olds' reactions to Bertenthal's point-light displays), that certain faces imply security and good times, and that certain facial expressions mean "I should be cautious" (social referencing). We have concentrated heavily on the perceptual skills of infants because infancy is a period of rapid development when most of the basic perceptual competencies emerge. Yet, we are about to see that there are other perceptual hurdles that children must overcome before they will be capable of learning to read or very proficient at such tasks as studying amid distractions or finding a well-camouflaged playmate during a game of hide-and-seek.

---

kinesthetic sense: sensations of motion produced by movements of the muscles, joints, and tendons.

Perceptual Learning and Development in Childhood

Imagine that you are walking through a snow-covered forest when you notice what appears to be movement beside a bush on your left. You stop and stare, and lo and behold, you make out the shape of a white rabbit almost perfectly camouflaged against the sterile, white backdrop of a snowbank.

Now suppose that you had a 5-year-old child with you as you walked through the forest. Assuming that the child had also seen the movement beside the bush, do you think he could have unmasked the camouflaged form as well as you did? If the child sees the form, do you think he could easily identify it as a rabbit?

Rather than trying to answer these questions immediately, we will first consider several important perceptual changes that occur between infancy and adolescence—changes in visual search, selective attention, and the perception of visual forms. You should then not only have answers for our "camouflaged rabbit" questions but also be able to cite several lines of evidence to back your conclusions.

Development of Attention

In order to perceive a white rabbit against a snowy background, the child must first focus his attention on the area where movement was seen, tune out potentially distracting stimuli such as blowing snow or the rustling of trees, and then concentrate long enough to detect the white figure against a perceptually similar background. Can 5-year-old children do these things as well as older children, adolescents, or adults? Let's see for ourselves by "focusing our attention" on the pertinent research literature.

Changes in attention span

Researchers who work with young children are careful to limit their experimental sessions to no more than a few minutes. And nursery school teachers, who must often tend to young children for hours at a time, are likely to switch topics or change classroom activities every 15 to 20 minutes. The assumption that underlies these practices is that very young children have short **attention spans**—they cannot (or will not) concentrate on any single activity for long periods.

We now know that this assumption is quite correct. In one study of children's capacity for sustained attention (Yendovitskaya, 1971), subjects were asked to put strips of colored paper in appropriately colored boxes,

and the time they devoted to this task was measured. Children aged 2½ to 3½ worked at the task for an average of 18 minutes and were easily distracted. By contrast, 5½–6-year-olds were much more persistent, often working at the task for an hour or more. Even when doing things they like, such as watching TV, 2- and 3-year-olds often get up, move about, and play with toys in between their looks at the TV set; they spend far less of their "TV time" actually watching TV than school-aged children do (Anderson, Lorch, Field, Collins, & Nathan, 1986).

The capacity for sustained attention continues to improve throughout childhood and early adolescence, and these improvements may be due, in part, to maturational changes in the central nervous system. For example, the **reticular formation,** an area of the brain responsible for the regulation of attention, is not fully **myelinated** until puberty. Perhaps this neurological development helps to explain why adolescents and young adults are suddenly able to spend hours on end cramming for upcoming exams or typing furiously to make morning deadlines on term papers.

Changes in visual search

Earlier in the chapter, we learned that neonates will scan the exterior angles and edges of visual patterns, whereas 2–3-month-olds have begun to examine a pattern's internal features. But as you might expect, the scanning patterns of a 3-month-old infant are rather unsystematic. Research with older children in the Soviet Union reveals that visual scanning becomes increasingly detailed, or "exhaustive," over the first six years of life (Zinchenko, Van Chzhi-Tsin, & Tarakanov, 1963).

Older children are also more likely to follow a set strategy when scanning visual forms and patterns. Elaine Vurpillot (1968) recorded the eye movements of 4- to 10-year-olds who were trying to determine whether two objects were "the same" or "different." Children aged 4 and 5 displayed no systematic pattern of scanning, and as a result, their judgments were often inaccurate. By contrast, children older than 6½ proceeded more slowly and systematically, looking back and forth at the corresponding features of each pair of stimuli. Not surprisingly, the older children were better able to detect the subtle (and not so subtle) differences between stimuli—information that enabled them to make accurate judgments. Similarly, older children are more likely than younger children to have a systematic plan for scanning the environment while looking for objects that are lost (Wellman, 1985).

Since visual search becomes more organized, exhaustive, and efficient over the first six to seven years of life, our hypothetical 5-year-old may have problems identifying a small white figure that appears against a snowy backdrop. Of course, this conclusion assumes that the child would notice the white figure in the first place, and that is by no means assured, as we will see in the following section.

Changes in selective attention

At any given moment our attention is **selective**—we focus on only a small portion of the total stimulation impinging on our sensory receptors. If you are now studying this chapter in preparation for an upcoming quiz, you may scarcely be aware of the humming of a nearby appliance or the sounds of traffic outside. Whenever we concentrate on something, we are trying to focus our attention on that object or event while ignoring irrelevant or distracting sensations. Does the capacity for selective attention improve much with age?

Apparently so. In one study of visual attention, George Strutt and his associates (Strutt, Anderson, & Well, 1975) asked 6-, 9-, 12-, and 20-year-olds to sort cards into piles according to the geometric design (for example, a circle or a square) printed on each card. However, some of the decks contained distracting information (for example, a star above the main form, or a vertical line through the form, or both). When no distractions were present, 6-year-olds were only slightly slower than older subjects at this card-sorting task. And although the presence of distracting stimuli hindered the performance of all subjects to some extent, the performances of the younger subjects were impeded most. The 6-year-olds, in particular, were not very good at focusing their attention on the most critical information and ignoring irrelevant inputs.

Selective attention in the auditory modality also improves with age. In one study, Eleanor Maccoby (1967) placed 5-, 7-, 9-, and 12-year-olds in situations not unlike what we might experience at noisy cocktail parties, where it is often difficult to follow one conversation as other nearby conversations compete for our attention. The children in Maccoby's experiment were required to listen to different phrases spoken simultaneously by a male and a female and then to identify what either the male or the female had said. On some occasions the children knew in advance which voice they would be asked to

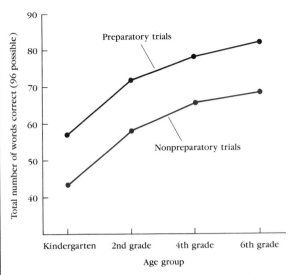

Figure 6-8. Performance on a selective attention task as a function of age. Older children were more proficient than younger children at dividing their attention between two speakers (the nonpreparatory condition) and at concentrating on one speaker while ignoring the other (preparatory condition). *(Adapted from Maccoby, 1967.)*

recall. These "preparatory" trials were similar to the situation in which we are trying to listen to one speaker while ignoring other conversations around us. On the remaining trials, the children did not know in advance which voice they would be asked to recall. These "nonpreparatory" trials were in some ways similar to a party situation in which we are trying to monitor two conversations at the same time.

The results of Maccoby's experiment appear in Figure 6-8. As you can see, older children clearly outperformed younger children on both the preparatory and the nonpreparatory trials—indicating that selective attention improves with age. In addition, performance in all age groups was much better on the

---

attention span: a person's capacity for sustaining attention to a particular stimulus or activity.

reticular formation: an area of the brain that serves to activate the organism and is thought to be important in the regulation of attention.

myelinization: the process by which neurons are encased in waxy myelin sheaths that facilitate transmission of neural impulses.

selective attention: the focusing of attention on certain aspects of experience while ignoring irrelevant or distracting sensations.

preparatory than on the nonpreparatory trials. Clearly, it is easier to understand what someone has said if we listen closely to that person and do not try to monitor another voice (or conversation) at the same time.

Since selective attention continues to improve throughout childhood, our hypothetical 5-year-old may have some difficulty visualizing a white rabbit against a snowy background, particularly if blowing snow, rustling limbs, or other irrelevant sensory inputs are present to divert his attention from the visual task at hand.

To summarize, then, learning to control attention is an important aspect of perceptual development. With age, children become better able (1) to concentrate on a task for long periods; (2) to search planfully for information that will help them to accomplish goals; and once detected, (3) to focus on this pertinent information while ignoring distractions. Let's now consider the changes that occur in children's ability to perceive visual forms—changes that depend, in part, on the control of attention.

Development of Form Perception

Earlier we learned that very young infants will gaze intently at new visual forms and, before long, will be trying to interpret them as well. During the second year, infants are acquiring language and becoming quite proficient at labeling objects and other sensory experiences they have had. In fact, "verbal" infants and toddlers will often show us that they are working hard to interpret the meaning of new visual forms by virtue of the statements they make. So if exposed to a model of a human head in which the facial features are scrambled, a 2-year-old is likely to stare intently for a few seconds and then reveal his hypotheses by gleefully exclaiming "Who hit him in the nose?" or "Who that, mommy? A monster, mommy?" (Kagan, 1971).

We see, then, that 2-year-olds seem to enjoy the opportunity to interpret or explain new visual forms. But just how precise are the perceptual abilities of a young child? Could a 2-year-old or even a 5-year-old detect and correctly identify a white rabbit in the snow? If we analyze this perceptual task, we see that it presents the child with two basic challenges. First, the perceiver must unmask a camouflaged form from a perceptually similar background. Once the form has been detected, the perceiver must then recognize that it is indeed a rabbit rather than a dog, a cat, or a squirrel. Let's now turn to the research literature to see whether 2- to 5-year-old children are likely to accomplish either of these perceptual feats.

Unmasking visual forms

Apparently, young children are not very proficient at unmasking visual forms, even when they know a hidden figure is present and they devote their attention to finding it. If you have read the children's section of your newspaper, you have undoubtedly seen "embedded figures" puzzles in which the task is to find hidden objects (for example, a spoon, a dog) in a distracting visual context. L. Ghent (1956) administered an **"embedded figures" test** to children of different ages (see Figure 6-9) and found that the ability to unmask hidden objects develops very slowly. For example, only 25% of Ghent's 8-year-olds were able to ignore the distracting background and find all the embedded figures in her relatively simple test.

Another method of testing children's ability to unmask visual forms is to present them with an incomplete figure and then gradually add information until they recognize the stimulus. Eugene Gollin (1960, 1962) showed 3- to 5-year-olds sketchy outlines of common objects such as a pig, a shoe, and a fish (see Set I of Figure 6-10). If the child did not recognize the objects, progressively more detail was added (Sets II–V) until he or she correctly identified them. Gollin found that many 3-year-olds went to Set IV before identifying the objects, while 4-year-olds identified them at Set III, and 5-year-olds were often correct at Set II. A later study (Spitz & Borland, 1971) found that people become even

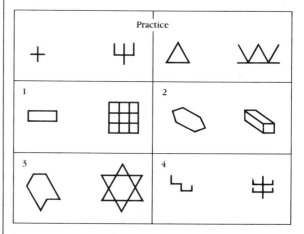

Figure 6-9. The "embedded figures" test used by Ghent to measure children's ability to unmask visual forms. On this test, the child's task is to find the figure at the left of each card within the more complex figure to the immediate right. *(From Ghent, 1956.)*

more proficient at unmasking incomplete forms between kindergarten (age 5) and late adolescence.

What do these studies imply about the 5-year-old and the white rabbit? Perhaps we could conclude that even an attentive 5-year-old might have difficulty seeing an all-white object "embedded" in a snowbank. And if the child caught a quick glimpse of the "figure" before it ran behind a bush, he might still be unable to identify it as a rabbit on the basis of such sketchy information. Let's now see whether we can determine why preschool children require so much information in order to recognize common objects such as rabbits, fish, or shoes.

Perception of wholes and parts

Many years ago, Heinz Werner (1948) argued that form perception progresses from the "global," or "diffuse," to the "discrete," or "specific." In other words, Werner believed that younger children would react to a stimulus as a whole and pay little if any attention to its parts. By contrast, older children would eventually

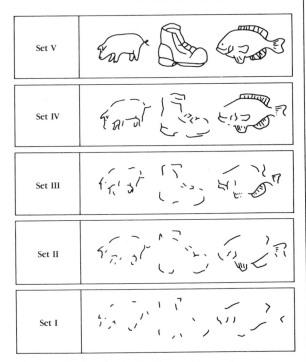

Figure 6-10. Sample stimulus figures that vary in completeness. Children are first shown figures from Set I, then Set II, and so on until they can identify the object. *(Adapted from Gollin, 1962.)*

Figure 6-11. Children's classification of ambiguous figures. When asked to define a highly ambiguous figure, preschool children are apt to label the whole object, without referring to its parts. For example, a 2–5-year-old might call this particular figure "a man," "a bird," or "some dirt." But a 6–7-year-old would respond to both the whole and its parts, perhaps by labeling this object "a bird with ears" or "a man wearing a hat."

begin to attend to the "whole" figure *and* to its parts. Presumably, increased attention to the component parts of visual stimuli should help the older child to recognize or label objects that are initially unfamiliar or ambiguous.

For example, suppose we were to show children the object in Figure 6-11 and ask them "What do you think this is?" Apparently, younger children (aged 2–4) do react to the "whole," for they are likely to call the stimulus "some dirt," "a spot," or "a bird" without labeling its parts (Ames, Metraux, Roedell, & Walker, 1974). In contrast, 6- to 7-year-olds are more apt to describe the object as "a man wearing a hat" or "a bird with ears," suggesting that they are attending to both the whole stimulus and its component parts.[2]

Why do older children respond less "holistically" to ambiguous forms and begin to pay more attention to component parts? How do they come to appreciate those aspects of visual form that they may have previously ignored? And just what "parts" of a visual

[2]The age trends described here are what we would expect for highly ambiguous forms in which both the whole object and its component parts are *novel* to children and are not very easy for them to classify. However, even 3-year-olds will respond to the whole stimulus and its parts if they view unambiguous "wholes" (say, a triangle) constructed of "parts" (three intersecting carrots) that are reasonably familiar to them (see Prather & Bacon, 1986).

---

embedded-figures test: a measure of the ability to locate hidden objects in a distracting visual context.

display are likely to capture their attention? Eleanor Gibson has proposed a theory of perceptual development that addresses these very issues. *distinctive*

Gibson's differentiation theory

According to Gibson (1969), **perceptual learning** occurs when we actively explore objects in our environment and discover their **distinctive features.** Simply defined, a distinctive feature is any cue that *differentiates* one form from another. A 3-year-old may initially confuse rabbits and cats, for both are furry animals of about the same size. However, the child will eventually discover that rabbits have long ears—a distinctive feature that differentiates them from cats, rats, squirrels, and all other small, furry animals.

Gibson believes that young children do not have to be taught to look for distinctive features; presumably perceptual learning is self-initiated and requires no external reinforcement. Thus, she views the young child as an active information seeker who is intrinsically motivated to look for the properties that differentiate objects and events.

Of course, some distinctive features are easier to detect than others. Even a 4-year-old whose attentional strategies are relatively immature soon notices large distinctive features such as the trunk of an elephant or the long ears of a rabbit. However, 4-year-olds may not easily differentiate *b* from *d* because the distinctive feature that discriminates these letters (the direction of curvature) is subtle and not very meaningful to a child of this age.

Gibson and her colleagues have conducted an experiment to study the ability of young children to distinguish different letterlike forms (Gibson, Gibson, Pick, & Osser, 1962). Children aged 4 to 8 were shown

a standard letterlike stimulus and several transformations of this "standard" form (examples appear in Figure 6-12). Their task was to pick out the stimuli that were identical to the standard. The 4- and 5-year-olds had difficulties with all the transformations in Figure 6-12: they often judged these stimuli to be identical to the standard. However, 6- to 8-year-olds were generally able to detect the "distinctive features" that differentiated the transformations from the "standard" stimulus.

Perhaps you can see the relevance of Gibson's work for elementary education—particularly reading education. Clearly, the ability to discriminate and categorize letters of the alphabet (each of which is characterized by a rather subtle but unique set of distinctive features that differentiates it from all other letters) is a major perceptual milestone—one that is necessary before children can hope to decode those funny squiggles on the printed page and become proficient readers (Gibson & Levin, 1975). Although preschool training in letter recognition (at home, at nursery school, and on educational television programs such as *Sesame Street*) does indeed help children to recognize many letters and even a few words (such as their own names), preschoolers younger than 5 to 5½ continue to confuse letters such as *b, h,* and *d* or *m* and *w* that have similar perceptual characteristics (Chall, 1983). By contrast, Gibson's subjects were beginning to detect and appreciate subtle differences in *unfamiliar* letterlike forms at precisely the time (age 6) that they are learning to read at school. So one reason that reading instruction begins in earnest in the first grade is that most 6-year-olds are now able to detect the distinctive features that differentiate letters, and they are ready to begin decoding letter combinations (words), short sentences, and very simple stories of the Dick and Jane variety (Chall, 1983; Gibson & Levin, 1975).

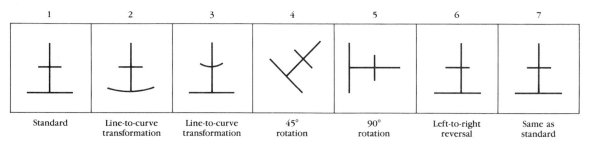

1	2	3	4	5	6	7
Standard	Line-to-curve transformation	Line-to-curve transformation	45° rotation	90° rotation	Left-to-right reversal	Same as standard

Figure 6-12. Examples of figures used to test children's ability to detect the distinctive features of letterlike forms. Stimulus 1 is the standard. The child's task is to examine each of the comparison stimuli (stimuli 2–7) and pick out those that are the same as the standard. *(Adapted from Gibson, Gibson, Pick, & Osser, 1962.)*

Photo 6-5. Perceiving the distinctive features of the letters of the alphabet is a tough task for preschool children.

In sum, Eleanor Gibson is a *differentiation* theorist. She believes that young children are constantly extracting new and more subtle information from the environment and thereby discovering the properties, patterns, and "distinctive features" that will enable them to differentiate objects and events. As this differentiation continues, a child will grow perceptually and become increasingly accurate at interpreting the broad array of stimuli that impinge on the sensory receptors.

We can now summarize the ground we have covered by returning to our 5-year-old who faces the task of detecting and identifying a stationary white object against a snowy background. A "best guess" is that the child would be much less proficient at this task than a typical adult. The reasoning is as follows:

1. Five-year-olds have much shorter attention spans than adults. Moreover, their visual search is not very exhaustive, and their focus of attention is less selective than an older person's. Taken together, these findings suggest that a 5-year-old might quickly scan the snowbank in an unsystematic fashion. And since a disorganized visual search is unlikely to detect a well-cam-

ouflaged visual form, the child may soon be attending to other distracting stimuli that are present (for example, rustling limbs or blowing snow) rather than continuing to search for the hidden object.

2. These attentional decrements may explain why young children are less proficient than adults at locating objects embedded in a distracting visual field. But even if the young child does momentarily detect a white object in the snow, he is likely to scan the form in a global, unsystematic fashion and thereby miss the "part" or "distinctive feature" (long ears) that will identify it as a rabbit (indeed, white ears may be very difficult to distinguish from a white background unless the perceiver has an opportunity to scan the figure extensively.)

Of course, the research does not imply that all 5-year-olds will always fail to perceive stationary white rabbits in snowbanks. The point is simply that this perceptual task would be more difficult for a 5-year-old than for an older child or an adult.

Environmental Influences on Perception

According to the *interactionist* view, one's experiences (or sensory environment) will contribute to perceptual development in at least two ways. By activating the sensory receptors, environmental stimuli trigger neurological responses, which, in turn, will contribute to the maturation of the brain, the sensory receptors, and the neural pathways between the brain and the sensory receptors. Moreover, the environment in which a child is raised will largely determine the kinds of input that her rapidly maturing neurological hardware will have available to analyze and interpret.

Are there experiences that an individual *must* have in order to develop a normal repertoire of perceptual skills? Are the ways that we perceive the world at all influenced by the home and cultural settings in which we live? In this final section of the chapter, we will explore each of these issues and see that one's experiences are indeed important contributors to perceptual growth and development.

perceptual learning: changes in the ability to extract information from sensory stimulation that occur as a result of experience.
distinctive feature: a dimension on which two or more objects differ and can be discriminated.

What Kinds of Experiences Are Important?

You have probably heard the expression "Use it or lose it," a cultural maxim implying that our basic abilities will deteriorate if we fail to exercise them. Students of perceptual development have tested this proposition by observing the perceptual growth of subjects (generally animals) that have been deprived of certain sensory or motor experiences. The logic underlying these "deprivation" experiments is straightforward. If subjects show a perceptual deficit of some kind after a period of sensory or motor deprivation, then the experiences that they did *not* have must be necessary for normal perceptual development.

Neurological effects of visual deprivation

In Chapter 5 we briefly discussed Austin Riesen's classic research with visually deprived chimpanzees. Recall that chimps raised in the dark experienced atrophy (degeneration) of the optic nerve, which seriously restricted their vision. This atrophy was reversible if the animal spent no more than seven months in the dark but became permanent if the deprivation lasted much longer. If dark-reared chimps were exposed to diffuse, *unpatterned* light for brief periods every day, physical degeneration of the visual system did *not* occur. Yet even these visually deprived animals later had difficulty discriminating forms such as circles and squares—a task that normal chimpanzees can easily master (Riesen, 1965).

Riesen's work is important because it indicates that the visual system requires a minimal amount of stimulation—presumably *patterned* stimulation—in order to develop normally. Although Riesen worked with chimpanzees, there is reason to believe that his findings would apply to human beings. Babies who are born with cataracts in both eyes (a cataract is an opacity of the lens of the eye that obstructs the passage of light) are often nearly blind at birth and will remain visually handicapped until the cataracts are removed. And once surgery restores their sight, these former cataract patients are like Riesen's dark-reared chimpanzees in that they have difficulty discriminating common forms such as spheres and cubes (Walk, 1981).

We even seem to require specific kinds of patterned stimulation for the neurons in the visual areas of the brain to develop properly and carry out their respective functions. It so happens that individual neurons in the **visual cortex** respond selectively to either hor-

izontal, vertical, or oblique (slanted) patterns. In other words, the visual area consists of "horizontal" cells, "vertical" cells, and "oblique" cells. Now suppose that we forced a young kitten to wear goggles all the time that allowed it to see lines in only one of the three visual orientations (for example, vertical stripes). The effect of this atypical visual environment is to change the orientation of cortical cells. Our goggle-wearing kitten would develop an abundance of "vertical" cells while losing some of those that would enable it to see lines in the horizontal and the oblique orientations (Stryker, Sherk, Leventhal, & Hirsch, 1978).

Although this research may seem rather artificial, the results probably do apply to human beings— at least to those human beings who have **visual astigmatisms** (Walk, 1981). The lenses of an astigmatic's eyes are optically distorted and will image more clearly in some visual orientations than in others. In this sense, the astigmatic's visual environment is restricted, though less severely than that of Stryker's goggle-wearing kittens. When tested, astigmatics often have trouble seeing some lines in the horizontal, the vertical, or the oblique orientation. Even when their optical errors have been corrected, astigmatics may still be unable to perceive lines equally well in all visual orientations (Mitchell, Freeman, Millodot, & Haegerstrom, 1973). This latter finding suggests that astigmatic distortions may alter the development of visual-cortical cells and produce some minor (but permanent) deficits in form perception.

Are two eyes better than one?

Because the fusion of two flat images can create an impression of depth, people have often assumed that accurate depth and distance perception requires both eyes. Yet, monocular (one-eyed) vision does not prevent depth perception, because many depth cues (for example, perspective) are detectable with only one eye. The history of collegiate and professional sports offers several examples of one-eyed participants (for example, football quarterbacks, baseball pitchers, basketball players) who have excelled at their respective sports—all of which require accurate estimation of depth and distance relations. Moreover, Richard Walk (1981) reports that a monocular infant in his sample clearly perceived depth, for she always avoided the deep side of a visual cliff. Finally, binocular infants who have one eye covered with an eyepatch are just as likely to avoid the deep side of a visual cliff as infants who can see the dropoff with both eyes. Although we have much to learn

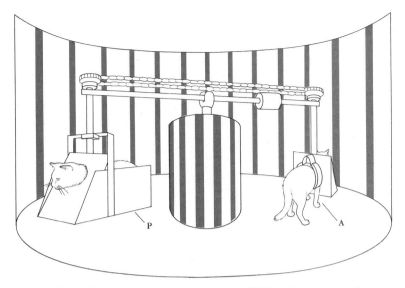

Figure 6-13. The experimental apparatus used by Held and Hein to study the effects of locomotion on visual perception. An active kitten (A) pulls its passive littermate (P). The two kittens have the same visual experiences, but only the active kitten is allowed to move about on its own. *(Adapted from Held & Hein, 1963.)*

about monocular vision, the findings to date suggest that its effects on visual perception are probably rather subtle.

Effects of movement on perception

Suppose that an infant were tied to a cradleboard so that she could see the environment but could not move. Would this inability to reach for and to explore objects have an adverse effect on her visual perception later in life?

Richard Held and Alan Hein believe that it would. Held and Hein (1963) raised kittens in the dark for 8–12 weeks and then divided them into two experimental groups. Kittens assigned to an *active* condition were permitted to move about in a lighted environment while pulling the apparatus shown in Figure 6-13. Kittens assigned to the *passive* condition merely rode in the cartlike holder and were prevented from moving about on their own. Each pair of kittens spent three hours a day in this lighted environment and the rest of their time in the dark. After several days of experience in the light, the kittens were tested to see whether they would extend their paws when lowered to a visual surface. They were also tested on the visual cliff.

The results were clear. Active kittens soon began to pass the paw-placement tests, and they *always*

avoided the deep side of the visual cliff. By contrast, passive kittens apparently did not perceive depth, for they showed absolutely no reluctance to venture out over the deep side of the apparatus. In fact, kittens in the passive group did not begin to extend their paws or to avoid the visual dropoff until they had had unrestrained access to a lighted environment for 48 hours. Held and Hein concluded that kittens (and possibly human infants) must be able to move around on their own in an environment that contains visual cues before they are likely to develop any visual/spatial skills.

However, Held and Hein may have overstated the case. Note that their "active" kittens must necessarily attend to the visual environment as they walk, whereas the "passive" kittens are freer to doze off while riding in their holders. So increased attention to the visual environment (rather than self-produced motion) may be the factor that explains the superior visual/spatial performance of Held and Hein's active kittens.

---

visual cortex: the area of the brain that receives and interprets visual impulses.

visual astigmatism: a refractive defect of the lens of the eye that prevents the formation of clear, distinct images.

There is some support for this alternative hypothesis in that children born without arms and legs can perceive depth and distance, even though their bodily movements are severely restricted (Gouin-DeCarie, 1969; James, 1890). Richard Walk (1981) suggests that "movement" may be essential for the development of visual perception, but he argues that this movement *need not be self-produced*. Presumably, even a paralyzed child might become proficient at estimating depth and distance relations if he is regularly exposed to moving stimuli that approach and recede from him.

Walk tested his **"motion hypothesis"** by rearing kittens in the dark for seven weeks and then exposing them for three hours a day to different visual environments. Kittens that were passively exposed to a static, uninteresting environment tended to doze off in their holders. When tested, these subjects showed no more depth perception than "control" kittens that had remained in the dark. Another group of dark-reared kittens were exposed to an interesting visual environment: they sat passively in holders and watched as toy cars streaked around a racetrack. When these "passive" animals were tested, they performed as well on the visual cliff as a group of "active" kittens that had been permitted to move about in a lighted environment. So all that the kittens needed to develop normal visual/spatial skills was passive exposure to *moving* objects that captured their attention.

Recently, Linda Acredolo and her associates (Acredolo, Adams, & Goodwyn, 1984) have found that human infants' knowledge of spatial relations seems to depend more on their visual tracking of objects than on their opportunities to move about on their own. Like Walk, Acredolo et al. suggest that visual tracking is more reliable and more precise under active rather than passive conditions. Yet their data suggest that it is attention to visual cues (rather than self-produced movement) that contributes most directly to visual/spatial abilities.

Taken together, these studies imply that our infant on the cradleboard will suffer no serious perceptual deficits as long as she is regularly exposed to moving objects that capture her attention. Of course, moving stimuli are very common in a typical home environment, a fact that might explain why children without arms and legs develop normal spatial abilities even though their motor activities are severely restricted.

Social and Cultural Influences

Do people who grow up in different societies and subcultures perceive the world in different ways?

An initial reaction is to say "Of course they do" and to offer the following illustration. As Shakespeare notes in the lines that open this chapter, judgments of beauty are rather subjective. Moreover, they vary from culture to culture. In the United States, for example, people are led to believe that relatively trim women represent the ideal standard of feminine loveliness. Yet men in other societies would spurn the "Hollywood starlet" types in favor of heftier women with more rounded physiques. Clearly beauty is in the eye of the beholder—and the beholder is affected by the standards of his or her culture.

Although a culture may provide evaluative standards for judging other people and their behavior, it is by no means obvious that our sociocultural backgrounds affect our perceptions of inanimate objects. For example, would an igloo-dwelling Eskimo who lives on the flat, treeless tundra of northern Canada be any more or less proficient at perceiving lines in the oblique or vertical orientation than a resident of New York City who grew up in a visual environment dominated by skyscrapers? Would a poor child who hasn't much money be any more likely than a rich child to value a dime and thereby overestimate its size? Do the child-rearing techniques that parents use have any effect on the way children process information and make judgments about the physical environment? These are some of the issues that have been explored by researchers who have looked for "social" and "cultural" influences on perception.

Perception of the physical environment

Many people from modern, industrialized societies are subject to the **oblique effect**—that is, they are better able to detect objects oriented horizontally or vertically than those in the oblique orientation. One explanation for this insensitivity to obliques is the **carpentered environment hypothesis:** People from "Westernized" societies are unlikely to see many obliques in a world full of rectangular buildings and furnishings (beds, bookcases, TV sets, and so forth) that are dominated by horizontals and verticals. However, people who live in a "noncarpentered" environment that contains many obliques should not show the "oblique effect." The implication, then, is that our architecture and the layout of objects in our everyday environment may have a dramatic effect on our visual perception.

Robert Annis and Barrie Frost (1973) tested the carpentered environment hypothesis by comparing the visual perception of Euro-Canadians with that of Cree Indians who lived in tepeelike structures in a "non-

Photo 6-6. According to the carpentered environment hypothesis, our architecture may have a dramatic effect on our visual perception.

carpentered" forested setting. As expected, the Indians, who had grown up in an environment full of obliques, were better able to detect stimuli in an oblique orientation than the Euro-Canadians, who lived in a "carpentered" environment.

Although these findings appear to confirm the carpentered environment hypothesis, a genetic interpretation is also plausible. Cree Indians have an Oriental ancestry that is very different from that of Euro-Canadians. This is an important point, because Timney and Muir (1976) found that Chinese subjects (who share a genetic ancestry with the Cree) show little or no "oblique effect," even those raised in the carpentered environment of Hong Kong. Moreover, Richard Held and his associates report that infants of European ancestry display an "oblique effect" long before their visual perception could possibly have been modified by prolonged exposure to a carpentered environment (Leehy, Moskowitz-Cook, Brill, & Held, 1975). In sum, there are clear cross-cultural differences in the ability to perceive the oblique. However, it now appears that these perceptual variations may reflect cross-cultural differences

in genotype and are probably not due to the visual characteristics of one's environment.

Of course, the cultural environment may well affect perceptual development in other ways. For example, we have already learned that the ability to discriminate certain sounds depends, in part, on one's linguistic environment. People from diverse cultural backgrounds also differ in their ability to perceive the third dimension in pictures and drawings. In Box 6-2

motion hypothesis: the notion that individuals must attend to objects that move in order to develop a normal repertoire of visual/spatial skills.

oblique effect: the finding that people are better able to detect horizontal or vertical stimuli than those in the oblique (diagonal) orientation.

carpentered environment hypothesis: the notion that people living in architectural environments dominated by horizontal and vertical elements are more susceptible to the oblique effect than people living in more natural settings.

Box 6-2
Sociocultural Influences on Picture Perception

Drawings used by William Hudson (1960) to study depth perception in pictures.

Pictures, paintings, and photographs are two-dimensional representations of a three-dimensional scene. Can children easily perceive depth and spatial relations as portrayed on a flat, two-dimensional surface? William Hudson (1960) tried to answer this question by showing a set of line drawings to groups of Black and White South Africans. Each subject scanned the drawings and then indicated his or her understanding of the depth and spatial cues by answering such questions as "Which animal is nearer the man?" and "What is the man doing (aiming at)?"

The answers to these questions may seem rather obvious to anyone who has grown up in a Western society, where two-dimensional representations of depth and spatial relations are common (indeed, recall Albert Yonas's research showing that 6–7-month-old American infants are already detecting and responding to many pictorial cues). Yet, Hudson's South African subjects often failed to give three-dimensional responses to the drawings! Hudson did find that *schoolchildren* were more likely to provide three-dimensional answers than were either preschoolers or groups of illiterate adult laborers. He concluded that education must be an important contributor to our ability to perceive depth and spatial relations in pictures.

However, later research indicates that education (or the lack thereof) cannot account for all group differences in picture perception. For example, Deregowski (1968) and Mundy-Castle (1966) have found that schoolchildren from other African societies provided fewer three-dimensional responses to Hudson's pictures than Hudson's sample of South African schoolchildren did. In fact, Hudson noted that Indian schoolchildren living in South Africa gave significantly fewer correct responses on pictorial tests of depth perception than either Black or White schoolchildren.

How can we account for these cross-cultural variations in picture perception? Perhaps they reflect societal or subcultural differences in genotype that affect visual perception (Pollack, 1976). It is also possible that children have very different *expectations* about what they are likely to see in a drawing—expectations based on the styles of artwork that are most common in their cultures. If the artwork of one's culture consists mostly of flat representations of isolated forms (people, game animals) with little or no spatial perspective, one may be unable to "see" anything other than a collection of objects in Hudson's pictures. Stated another way, a person from such a culture would not "expect" to see depth and spatial relations in a drawing.

Can our expectations, or "perceptual sets," really affect what we see in a picture or drawing? Yes, they can—and here is an example. Close your eyes and think for a second or two about a white rat. Now look at the drawing at the right, and lo and behold, you should see a white rat. However, if you had first been asked to think about an aging college professor with glasses, you would have approached the drawing with a different perceptual set and immediately perceived the "professor." Finally, note that the drawing of the "professor" is a relatively flat profile with few depth cues, whereas we (who

are proficient with depth cues) tend to perceive more three-dimensionality in the "rat" figure—its tail looks closer to us than its body.

So our perception of pictures and drawings depends, in part, on our expectations or perceptual sets. If children from different cultures have very different expectations about what they are likely to see in a drawing, it is hardly surprising that their performance may differ from ours when they are asked to interpret what we "see" as indications of depth and spatial relations.

Ambiguous figure used to demonstrate the effects of perceptual sets on the interpretation of drawings.

Source: Adapted from Reese (1963).

we take a closer look at "picture perception" and attempt to determine why a drawing may not always convey the same message to all perceivers.

Social values and perception

For years social psychologists have argued that important personal and social values may color our perceptions in any number of ways. Consider the following example. Jerome Bruner and C. C. Goodman (1947) asked 10-year-olds to adjust a spot of light until they thought it matched the size of a coin that had been presented in another part of the visual field. Children generally overestimated the sizes of all coins, and the overestimates were much greater for coins of high monetary value (dimes and quarters) than for coins of lesser value (pennies and nickels).

Bruner and Goodman also found that children from poorer homes overestimated the size of coins more than children from advantaged homes. Does this finding mean that the poorer children attached greater *value* to the coins or only that the poorer children were less *familiar* with the coins and their true sizes? Later research tends to support the value hypothesis: poorer children are more likely than advantaged children to overestimate the size of a valuable object such as a dime, but the two groups produce comparable size estimates when judging an object without value, such as a metallic "slug" (Nelson & Lechelt, cited in Burtley, 1980). So it seems that our perception of an object's physical characteristics will depend, in part, on the extent to which we value that object.

Effect of the home environment

Does a child's home environment influence perceptual development? Herman Witkin (1967) believes it does. Specifically, Witkin suggests that the techniques and strategies that parents use to raise their child will affect the child's standing on a perceptual dimension known as **field dependence/independence.**

Field dependence and field independence represent two different perceptual styles. The *field-independent person* is able to process information and perceive objects and events without being distracted by background, or "contextual," factors. By contrast, the perceptions of a *field-dependent* person are likely to be influenced by irrelevant or distracting information. One measure of field dependence/independence is Witkin's "tilted room" test. Subjects are first placed in a special chair within a small room. Then the chair and the room are tilted in different directions, and the subject's task is to align the chair with the true gravitational upright. Persons classified as field-dependent tend to concentrate on the visual context and to align the chair to the tilted environment, whereas those labeled as field-independent are better able to ignore the distracting visual "field" and align themselves with the true upright position (even though the environment will still look tilted to them). Field independents are also better than field dependents at locating objects embedded in a distracting visual context. For example, a field-independent person will soon find the hidden "termite" in Figure 6-14, whereas the field-dependent person would have to search much longer.

What aspects of home life promote field-dependent and field-independent orientations? Witkin and his associates (Witkin, 1967; Witkin, Goodenough, & Oltman, 1979) believe that domineering parents who closely supervise their child's behavior and demand that the child conform to rigidly defined rules are likely to contribute to a field-dependent orientation. By contrast, parents who are less restrictive, less rule-oriented, and generally willing to allow their children some individual initiative are probably fostering the development of a field-independent orientation.

Sex differences. Although there are vast individual differences within each sex, females tend to be more field-dependent than males (Witkin & Goodenough, 1977). Witkin suggests that this sex difference may be attributable to the ways males and females are raised. Specifically, it appears that parents are more likely to stress obedience for daughters and to restrict girls' initiative (Barry, Bacon, & Child, 1957). And according to Witkin, this is precisely the pattern of child rearing that contributes to a field-dependent orientation.

Cross-cultural studies. Cross-cultural studies also tend to support Witkin's child-rearing hypothesis. Anthropologists sometimes classify nonindustrialized societies into two basic categories: (1) *farming and pastoral* societies, in which a large number of relatively immobile families live and work together tending flocks

---

field dependence/independence: a dimension of perceptual style—namely, the extent to which the surrounding context (the field) affects a person's perceptual judgments.

Figure 6-14. Find the termite. People who are field-dependent find tasks of this sort much more difficult than people who are field-independent.

and raising crops, and (2) *hunter-gatherer* societies, in which small groups earn their livelihood by moving about in search of food (edible plants, game, and fish). Parents in farming and pastoral societies stress the kinds of values that are necessary to maintain their way of life: children are expected to be obedient and cooperative and to place the needs of the group ahead of their own personal needs and goals. As expected, Witkin and Berry (1975) found that people from this kind of society were quite field-*dependent*. Parents from hunter-gatherer societies also stress the values that would help to maintain their way of life. But for the hunter-gatherer, who most often works alone, these values include assertiveness, independence, and self-reliance rather than cooperation and obedience. Thus, Witkin and Berry (1975) were not surprised to find that children from hunter-gatherer societies were quite field-*independent*.

Perceptual style and personality. Herman Witkin and Donald Goodenough (1977) have proposed that field-dependent individuals differ from field independents on dimensions other than perceptual style. After reviewing nearly 200 studies, Witkin and Goodenough concluded that the field-dependent person is generally more interested in other people, better able to get along with others, more emotionally responsive, and somewhat less aggressive than the field-independent person. This is precisely the profile we might expect if field dependents have been encouraged by their parents to become cooperative individuals who are sen-

sitive to the needs and wishes of others. By contrast, field independents tend to be more tolerant of ambiguous situations, better able to function without explicit guidance or supervision, and more interested in achievement than field dependents. Once again, these differences "make sense" if field independents are encouraged to be independent and assertive and to pursue individual goals.

What Is Perceptual Development?

Now that we have touched on the topic of perceptual development, here is a thought question that may seem rather strange: "What is perceptual development the development of?" Although there are many ways one might choose to answer this hopelessly ambiguous question, perhaps we can agree that perceptual development is the growth of interpretive skills—a complex process that depends, in part, on the expression of individual genotypes, the maturation of the sensory receptors, the kinds of sensory experiences that the child has available to analyze and interpret, the child's emerging cognitive abilities, and the social context in which all these other variables operate. Although this chapter has focused on perceptual growth, we should remember that development is a *holistic* process and that a child's maturing perceptual abilities are likely to have a meaningful effect on many other aspects of development. Take intellectual development, for example. As we will see in Chapter 9, Jean Piaget argues that all the intellectual advances of the first two years spring from the infant's sensory and motor activities. How else, he asks, could infants ever come to understand the properties of objects without being able to see them, fondle them, and pop them into their mouths? How could infants ever become language users without first perceiving meaningful regularities in the speech they hear? And when we recall Herman Witkin's argument that children's perceptual styles will have far-reaching implications for their developing personalities, we begin to see why so many developmentalists consider perceptual growth such an important topic. Simply stated, perception is central to everything—there is nothing we do (consciously, at least) that is not influenced by our interpretation of the world around us. So it is important to understand the growth of perceptual skills because perception is truly at the heart of human development.

Summary

Sensation refers to the detection of sensory stimulation, whereas *perception* is the interpretation of what is sensed. According to the nativists, infants are born with many perceptual skills. Empiricists, however, believe that the neonate is merely a "sensory" creature and that all perceptual (interpretive) abilities must be learned. Today, most theorists have rejected these extreme positions in favor of an interactionist viewpoint. According to the interactionists, the growth of perceptual awareness reflects a fundamental interplay (interaction) between the child's sensory capabilities, maturation, and learning.

Researchers have devised several creative methods of persuading infants to tell us what they might be sensing or perceiving. Among the more useful of these approaches are the preference method, the habituation paradigm, the method of evoked potentials, and the high-amplitude sucking procedure. Applying these methods, researchers have learned that the sensory equipment of young infants is in reasonably good working order. Neonates can see patterns and colors and can detect changes in brightness. Their visual acuity is poor by adult standards but improves rapidly over the first six months. Moreover, young infants can hear very well: even newborns can discriminate sounds that differ in loudness, direction, duration, and frequency. The senses of taste and smell are also well developed at birth. Babies are born with definite taste preferences, choosing sweets over sour, bitter, or salty substances. They avoid unpleasant smells and will soon come to recognize their mothers by odor alone if they are breast-fed. Newborns are also quite sensitive to touch, temperature, and pain.

Visual perception develops rapidly during the first year. For the first two months of life, babies are "stimulus seekers" who prefer to look at moderately complex, high-contrast targets, particularly those that move. Between 3 and 6 months of age, infants are perceiving forms and beginning to recognize familiar faces. Spatial perception also improves as 3–6-month-olds begin to respond to looming objects, to display size constancy, to recognize pictorial cues to depth, and to fear heights. During the latter half of the first year, infants become increasingly proficient at interpreting visual forms and at estimating size, depth, and distance relations.

The neonate's auditory capabilities are truly remarkable. In the first three days of life, an infant can already recognize its mother's voice. Neonates are quite responsive to human speech, and they place the auditory components of language into roughly the same vowel and consonant categories that adults do. Finally, babies prefer music to unpatterned auditory stimulation, and they begin to "bounce" to music and to recognize changes in melody and tempo by 4–6 months of age.

Apparently the senses are integrated at birth and differentiated later. For the neonate, sensations from all modalities may combine to produce a "global" experience. As the senses differentiate and continue to mature, the infant becomes much more proficient at cross-modal perception—the ability to recognize by one modality an object or experience that is already familiar through another modality.

Several important perceptual changes take place between infancy and adolescence. Attentional abilities improve as children begin to examine sensory inputs more systematically. They also become more selective in what they will attend to and more proficient at concentrating on objects and tasks for long periods. As children become more attentive, they begin to identify the distinctive features that differentiate objects and events. This "perceptual learning" is a continuing process that enables the child to gradually become more proficient at interpreting the broad array of stimuli that impinge on the sensory receptors.

The environment influences perceptual development in many ways. Deprivation experiments suggest that young animals (and presumably children) must be exposed to patterned visual stimuli that capture their attention if their visual perception is to develop normally. Moreover, our social/cultural environments may influence our auditory perception, our interpretation of artwork, and our judgments about the physical characteristics of objects. Finally, it appears that the home environment contributes to the development of broad perceptual "styles" (field dependence or field independence) that may have important implications for many other aspects of development.

References

ACREDOLO, L. P., Adams, A., & Goodwyn, S. W. (1984). The role of self-produced movement and visual tracking in infant spatial orientation. *Journal of Experimental Child Psychology, 38,* 312–327.

ALEGRIA, J., & Noirot, E. (1978). Neonate orientation behavior toward human voices. *International Journal of Behavioral Development, 1,* 291–312.

ALLEN, T. W., Walker, K., Symonds, L., & Marcell, M. (1977). Intrasensory and intersensory perception of temporal sequences during infancy. *Developmental Psychology, 13,* 225–229.

AMES, L. B., Metraux, R. W., Roedell, J. L., & Walker, R. N. (1974). *Child Rorschach responses: Developmental trends from two to ten years.* New York: Brunner/Mazel.

ANDERSON, D. R., Lorch, E. P., Field, D. E., Collins, P. A., & Nathan, J. G. (1986). Television viewing at home: Age trends in visual attention and time with TV. *Child Development, 57,* 1024–1033.

ANNIS, R. C., & Frost, B. (1973). Human visual ecology and orientation anisotropies in acuity. *Science, 182,* 729–731.

ARONSON, E., & Rosenbloom, S. (1971). Space perception within a common auditory-visual space. *Science, 172,* 1161–1163.

ASLIN, R. N., Pisoni, D. B., & Jusczyk, P. W. (1983). Auditory development and speech perception in infancy. In M. M. Haith & J. J. Campos (Eds.), *Handbook of child psychology.* Vol. 2: *Infancy and developmental psychobiology.* New York: Wiley.

BANKS, M. S. (1980). The development of visual accommodation during early infancy. *Child Development, 51,* 646–666.

BANKS, M. S., & Ginsburg, A. P. (1985). Infant visual preferences: A review and new theoretical treatment. In H. W. Reese (Ed.), *Advances in child development and behavior* (Vol. 19). Orlando, FL: Academic Press.

BANKS, M. S., in collaboration with Salapatek, P. (1983). Infant visual perception. In M. M. Haith & J. J. Campos (Eds.), *Handbook of child psychology.* Vol. 2: *Infancy and developmental psychobiology.* New York: Wiley.

BARRERA, M. E., & Maurer, D. (1981a). Discrimination of strangers by the three-month-old. *Child Development, 52,* 558–563.

BARRERA, M. E., & Maurer, D. (1981b). Recognition of mother's photographed face by the three-month-old infant. *Child Development, 52,* 714–716.

BARRY, H., III, Bacon, M. K., & Child, I. L. (1957). A cross-cultural survey of some sex differences in socialization. *Journal of Abnormal and Social Psychology, 55,* 327–332.

BERTENTHAL, B. I., & Campos, J. J. (1987). New directions in the study of early experience. *Child Development, 58,* 550–567.

BERTENTHAL, B. I., Campos, J. J., & Haith, M. M. (1980). Development of visual organization: The perception of subjective contours. *Child Development, 51,* 1077–1080.

BERTENTHAL, B. I., Proffitt, D. R., & Cutting, J. E. (1984). Infant sensitivity to figural coherence in biomechanical motions. *Journal of Experimental Child Psychology, 37,* 213–230.

BERTENTHAL, B. I., Proffitt, D. R., Kramer, S. J., & Spetner, N. B. (1987). Infants' encoding of kinetic displays varying in relative coherence. *Developmental Psychology, 23,* 171–178.

BERTENTHAL, B. I., Proffitt, D. R., Spetner, N. B., & Thomas, M. A. (1985). The development of infant sensitivity to biomechanical motions. *Child Development, 56,* 531–543.

BIRCH, H. G., & Lefford, A. (1963). Intersensory development in children. *Monographs of the Society for Research in Child Development, 25*(5, Serial No. 89).

BOCCIA, M., & Campos, J. (1983, April). *Maternal emotional signalling: Its effects on infants' reactions to strangers.* Paper presented at the biennial meeting of the Society for Research in Child Development, Detroit, MI.

BORNSTEIN, M. H., Kessen, W., & Weiskopf, S. (1976). Color vision and hue categorization in young human infants. *Journal of Experimental Psychology: Human Perception and Performance, 2,* 115–129.

BOWER, T. G. R. (1982). *Development in infancy.* New York: W. H. Freeman.

BOWER, T. G. R., Broughton, J. M., & Moore, M. K. (1970a). The coordination of vision and tactile input in infancy. *Perception and Psychophysics, 8,* 51–53.

BOWER, T. G. R., Broughton, J. M., & Moore, M. K. (1970b). Infant responses to approaching objects: An indicator of response to distal variables. *Perception and Psychophysics, 9,* 193–196.

BRUNER, J. S., & Goodman, C. C. (1947). Value and need as organizing factors in perception. *Journal of Abnormal and Social Psychology, 42,* 33–44.

BURTLEY, S. H. (1980). *Introduction to perception.* New York: Harper & Row.

BUSHNELL, E. W., Shaw, L., & Strauss, D. (1985). Relationship between visual and tactual exploration by 6-month-olds. *Developmental Psychology, 21,* 591–600.

BUTTERFIELD, E. C., & Siperstein, G. N. (1972). Influence of contingent auditory stimulation upon non-nutritional suckle. In J. F. Bosma (Ed.), *Third symposium on oral sensation and perception: The mouth of the infant.* Springfield, IL: Charles C Thomas.

CAMPOS, J. J., Langer, A., & Krowitz, A. (1970). Cardiac responses on the visual cliff in prelocomotor human infants. *Science, 170,* 196–197.

CERNOCH, J. M., & Porter, R. H. (1985). Recognition of maternal axillary odors by infants. *Child Development, 56,* 1593–1598.

CHALL, J. S. (1983). *Stages of reading development.* New York: McGraw-Hill.

CHANG, H. W., & Trehub, S. E. (1977). Infants' perception of temporal grouping in auditory patterns. *Child Development, 48,* 1666–1670.

CLARKSON, M. G., & Berg, W. K. (1983). Cardiac orienting and vowel discrimination in newborns: Crucial stimulus parameters. *Child Development, 54,* 162–171.

COHEN, L. B., DeLoache, J. S., & Strauss, M. S. (1979). Infant visual perception. In J. Osofsky (Ed.), *Handbook of infant development.* New York: Wiley.

CONDON, W. S., & Sander, L. (1974). Neonate movement is synchronized with adult speech: Interactional participation and language acquisition. *Science, 183,* 99–101.

CROOK, C. K. (1978). Taste perception in the newborn infant. *Infant Behavior and Development, 1,* 52–69.

DAY, R. H., & McKenzie, B. E. (1981). Infant perception of the invariant size of approaching and receding objects. *Developmental Psychology, 17,* 670–677.

DeCASPER, A. J., & Fifer, W. P. (1980). Of human bonding: Newborns prefer their mother's voices. *Science, 208,* 1174–1176.

DeCASPER, A. J., & Spence, M. J. (1986). Prenatal maternal speech influences newborns' perception of speech sounds. *Infant Behavior and Development, 9,* 133–150.

DEREGOWSKI, J. B. (1968). Difficulties in pictorial depth perception in Africa. *British Journal of Psychology, 59,* 195–204.

DOWD, J. M., & Tronick, E. Z. (1986). Temporal coordination of arm movements in early infancy: Do infants move in synchrony with adult speech? *Child Development, 57,* 762–776.

EIMAS, P. D. (1975a). Auditory and phonetic cues for speech: Discrimination of the (r-l) distinction by young infants. *Perception and Psychophysics, 18,* 341–347.

EIMAS, P. D. (1975b). Speech perception in early infancy. In L. B. Cohen & P. Salapatek (Eds.), *Infant perception: From sensation to cognition.* Orlando, FL: Academic Press.

FAGAN, J. F., III. (1979). The origins of facial pattern recognition. In M. H. Bornstein & W. Kessen (Eds.), *Psychological development from infancy: Image to intention.* Hillsdale, NJ: Erlbaum.

FANTZ, R. L. (1961). The origin of form perception. *Scientific American, 204,* 66–72.

FANTZ, R. L. (1963). Pattern vision in newborn infants. *Science, 140,* 296–297.

FEINMAN, S., & Lewis, M. (1983). Social referencing at 10 months: A second-order effect on infants' responses to strangers. *Child Development, 54,* 878–887.

FIELD, J., Muir, D., Pilon, R., Sinclair, M., & Dodwell, P. (1980). Infants' orientation to lateral sounds from birth to three months. *Child Development, 51,* 295–298.

FOX, R., Aslin, R. N., Shea, S. L., & Dumais, S. T. (1980). Stereopsis in human infants. *Science, 207,* 323–324.

GANCHROW, J. R., Steiner, J. E., & Daher, M. (1983). Neonatal facial expressions to different qualities and intensities of gustatory stimuli. *Infant Behavior and Development, 6,* 189–200.

GHENT, L. (1956). Perception of overlapping and embedded figures by children of different ages. *American Journal of Psychology, 69,* 575–587.

GIBSON, E. J. (1969). *Principles of perceptual learning and development.* East Norwalk, CT: Appleton-Century-Crofts.

GIBSON, E. J., Gibson, J. J., Pick, A. D., & Osser, H. A. (1962). A developmental study of the discrimination of letterlike forms. *Journal of Comparative and Physiological Psychology, 55,* 897–906.

GIBSON, E. J., & Levin, H. (1975). *The psychology of reading.* Cambridge, MA: M.I.T. Press.

GIBSON, E. J., & Walk, R. D. (1960). The "visual cliff." *Scientific American, 202,* 64–71.

GIBSON, E. J., & Walker, A. S. (1984). Development of knowledge of visual-tactile affordances of substance. *Child Development, 55,* 453–460.

GOLLIN, E. S. (1960). Developmental studies of visual recognition of incomplete objects. *Perceptual and Motor Skills, 11,* 289–298.

GOLLIN, E. S. (1962). Factors affecting the visual recognition of incomplete objects: A comparative investigation of children and adults. *Perceptual and Motor Skills, 15,* 583–590.

GOUIN-DeCARIE, T. (1969). A study of the mental and emotional development of the thalidomide child. In B. M. Foss (Ed.), *Determinants of infant behavior* (Vol. 4). London: Methuen.

GRANRUD, C. E., & Yonas, A. (1984). Infants' perception of pictorially specified interposition. *Journal of Experimental Child Psychology, 37,* 500–511.

GUNNAR, M. R., Malone, S., Vance, G., & Fisch, R. O. (1985). Coping with aversive stimulation in the neonatal period: Quiet sleep and plasma cortisol levels during recovery from circumcision. *Child Development, 56,* 824–834.

HAITH, M. M. (1980). Visual competence in early infancy. In R. Held, H. Liebowitz, & H. R. Teuber (Eds.), *Handbook of sensory physiology* (Vol. 8). Berlin: Springer-Verlag.

HAITH, M. M., Bergman, T., & Moore, M. J. (1977). Eye contact and face scanning in early infancy. *Science, 198,* 853–855.

HAVILAND, J. M., & Lelwica, M. (1987). The induced affect response: 10-week-old infants' responses to three emotion expressions. *Developmental Psychology, 23,* 97–104.

HELD, R., & Hein, A. (1963). Movement-produced stimulation in the development of visually guided behavior. *Journal of Comparative and Physiological Psychology, 56,* 872–876.

HUDSON, W. (1960). Pictorial depth perception in subcultural groups in Africa. *Journal of Social Psychology, 52,* 183–208.

IRWIN, R. J., Ball, A. K. R., Kay, N., Stillman, J. A., & Rosser, J. (1985). The development of auditory temporal acuity in children. *Child Development, 56,* 614–620.

IZARD, C. E., Hembree, E. A., & Huebner, R. R. (1987). Infants' emotion expressions to acute pain: Developmental change and stability of individual differences. *Developmental Psychology, 23,* 105–113.

JAMES, W. (1890). *Principles of psychology* (2 vols.). New York: Holt.

JUSCZYK, P. W., & Derrah, C. (1987). Representation of speech sounds by young infants. *Developmental Psychology, 23,* 648–654.

KAGAN, J. (1971). *Change and continuity in infancy.* New York: Wiley.

KANT, I. (1958). *Critique of pure reason.* New York: Modern Library. (Original work published 1781)

KAUFMANN-HAYOZ, R., Kaufmann, F., & Stucki, M. (1986). Kinetic contours in infants' visual perception. *Child Development, 57,* 292–299.

KELLMAN, P. J., & Spelke, E. S. (1983). Perception of partly occluded objects in infancy. *Cognitive Psychology, 15,* 483–524.

KELLMAN, P. J., Spelke, E. S., & Short, K. R. (1986). Infant perception of object unity from translatory motion in depth and vertical translation. *Child Development, 57,* 72–86.

KISILEVSKY, B. S., & Muir, D. W. (1984). Neonatal habituation and dishabituation to tactile stimulation during sleep. *Developmental Psychology, 20,* 367–373.

KLINNERT, M. D., Emde, R. N., Butterfield, P., & Campos, J. J. (1986). Social referencing: The infant's use of emotional signals from a friendly adult with the mother present. *Developmental Psychology, 22,* 427–432.

KUCHUK, A., Vibbert, M., & Bornstein, M. H. (1986). The perception of smiling and its experiential correlates in three-month-old infants. *Child Development, 57,* 1054–1061.

LaBARBERA, J. D., Izard, C. E., Vietze, P., & Parisi, S. A. (1976). Four- and six-month-old infants' visual responses to joy, anger, and neutral expressions. *Child Development, 47,* 535–538.

LEEHY, S. C., Moskowitz-Cook, A., Brill, S., & Held, R. (1975). Orientational anisotropy in infant vision. *Science, 190,* 900–902.

LIPSITT, L. P., & Levy, N. (1959). Electrotactual

threshold in the neonate. *Child Development, 30,* 547–554.

LOCKE, J. (1939). An essay concerning human understanding. In E. A. Burtt (Ed.), *The English philosophers from Bacon to Mill.* New York: Modern Library. (Original work published 1690)

MACCOBY, E. E. (1967). Selective auditory attention in children. In L. P. Lipsitt & C. C. Spiker (Eds.), *Advances in child development and behavior.* Orlando, FL: Academic Press.

MacFARLANE, A. (1977). *The psychology of childbirth.* Cambridge, MA: Harvard University Press.

MAURER, D., & Salapatek, P. (1976). Developmental changes in the scanning of faces by young infants. *Child Development, 47,* 523–527.

McKENZIE, B. E., Tootell, H., & Day, R. H. (1980). Development of visual size constancy during the first year of human infancy. *Developmental Psychology, 16,* 163–174.

MELTZOFF, A. N., & Borton, R. W. (1979). Intermodal matching by human neonates. *Nature, 282,* 403–404.

MENDELSON, M. J., & Ferland, M. B. (1982). Auditory-visual transfer in four-month-old infants. *Child Development, 53,* 1022–1027.

MITCHELL, D. E., Freeman, R. D., Millodot, M., & Haegerstrom, G. (1973). Meridional amblyopia: Evidence for modification of the human visual system by early visual experience. *Vision Research, 13,* 535–558.

MOOG, H. (1976). *The musical experience of the pre-school child.* London: Schott.

MUIR, D. W. (1985). The development of infants' auditory spatial sensitivity. In S. E. Trehub & B. Schneider (Eds.), *Advances in the study of communication and affect.* Vol. 10: *Auditory development in infancy.* New York: Plenum.

MUNDY-CASTLE, A. C. (1966). Pictorial depth perception in Ghanaian children. *International Journal of Psychology, 1,* 289–300.

NELSON, C. A. (1987). The recognition of facial expressions in the first two years of life: Mechanisms of development. *Child Development, 58,* 889–909.

OLSON, G. M., & Sherman, T. (1983). Attention, learning, and memory in infants. In P. H. Mussen (Ed.), *Handbook of child psychology* (Vol. 2). New York: Wiley.

PEEPLES, D. R., & Teller, D. Y. (1975). Color vision and brightness discrimination in two-month-old human infants. *Science, 189,* 1102–1103.

PETTERSEN, L., Yonas, A., & Fisch, R. O. (1980). The development of blinking in response to impending collision in preterm, full-term, and postterm infants. *Infant Behavior and Development, 3,* 155–165.

PIAGET, J. (1954). *The construction of reality in the child.* New York: Basic Books.

PIAGET, J. (1960). *Psychology of intelligence.* Paterson, NJ: Littlefield, Adams.

POLLACK, R. H. (1976). Illusions and perceptual development: A tachistoscopic psychophysical approach. In K. F. Riegel & J. A. Meacham (Eds.), *The developing individual in a changing world* (Vol. 1). Hawthorne, NY: Aldine.

PORTER, F. L., Miller, R. H., & Marshall, R. E. (1986). Neonatal pain cries: Effects of circumcision on acoustic features and perceived urgency. *Child Development, 57,* 790–802.

POWERS, M. K., Schneck, M., & Teller, D. Y. (1981). Spectral sensitivity of human infants at absolute visual threshold. *Vision Research, 21,* 1005–1016.

PRATHER, P. A., & Bacon, J. (1986). Developmental differences in part/whole perception. *Child Development, 57,* 549–558.

PRATT, K. C. (1954). The neonate. In L. Carmichael (Ed.), *Manual of child psychology.* New York: Wiley.

RADER, N., Bausano, M., & Richards, J. E. (1980). On the nature of the visual-cliff-avoidance response in human infants. *Child Development, 51,* 61–68.

REESE, H. W. (1963). Perceptual set in young children. *Child Development, 34,* 151–159.

RHEINGOLD, H. L., & Adams, J. L. (1980). The significance of speech to newborns. *Developmental Psychology, 16,* 397–403.

RIESEN, A. H. (1965). Effects of visual deprivation on perceptual function and the neural substrate. In J. de Ajuriaguerra (Ed.), *Dessaferentation experimental et clinique.* Geneva: Georg.

RIESER, J., Yonas, A., & Wilkner, K. (1976). Radial localization of odors by human newborns. *Child Development, 47,* 856–859.

ROSE, S. A., Gottfried, A. W., & Bridger, W. H. (1981). Cross-modal transfer in 6-month-old infants. *Developmental Psychology, 17,* 661–669.

ROSENTHAL, M. K. (1982). Vocal dialogues in the neonatal period. *Developmental Psychology, 18,* 17–21.

SALAPATEK, P. (1975). Pattern perception in early infancy. In L. B. Cohen & P. Salapatek (Eds.), *Infant perception: From sensation to cognition* (Vol. 1). Orlando, FL: Academic Press.

SIQUELAND, E. R., & DeLucia, C. A. (1969). Visual reinforcement of nonnutritive sucking in human infants. *Science, 165,* 1144–1146.

SLATER, A., Morison, V., Town, C., & Rose, D. (1985). Movement perception and identity constancy in the new-born baby. *British Journal of Developmental Psychology, 3,* 211–220.

SPELKE, E. S., & Cortelyou, A. (1981). Perceptual aspects of social knowing: Looking and listening in infancy. In M. E. Lamb & L. R. Sherrod (Eds.), *Infant social cognition: Empirical and theoretical considerations.* Hillsdale, NJ: Erlbaum.

SPITZ, H. H., & Borland, M. D. (1971). Redundancy in line drawings of familiar objects: Effects of age and intelligence. *Cognitive Psychology, 2,* 196–205.

STEINER, J. E. (1979). Human facial expressions in response to taste and smell stimulation. In H. W. Reese & L. P. Lipsitt (Eds.), *Advances in child development and behavior* (Vol. 13). Orlando, FL: Academic Press.

STRERI, A., & Pecheux, M. (1986a). Tactual habituation and discrimination of form in infancy: A comparison with vision. *Child Development, 57,* 100–104.

STRERI, A., & Pecheux, M. (1986b). Vision-to-touch and touch-to-vision transfer of form in 5-month-old infants. *British Journal of Developmental Psychology, 4,* 161–167.

STRUTT, G. F., Anderson, D. R., & Well, A. D. (1975). A developmental study of the effects of irrelevant information on speeded classification. *Journal of Experimental Child Psychology, 20,* 127–135.

STRYKER, M. P., Sherk, H., Leventhal, A. G., & Hirsch, V. H. B. (1978). Physiological consequences for the cat's visual cortex of effectively restricting early visual experience with oriented contours. *Journal of Neurophysiology, 41,* 896–909.

TELLER, D. Y., & Bornstein, M. H. (1984). Infant color vision. In P. Salapatek & L. B. Cohen (Eds.), *Handbook of infant perception.* Orlando, FL: Academic Press.

TIMNEY, H. H., & Muir, D. W. (1976). Orientation anisotropy: Incidence and magnitude in Caucasian and Chinese subjects. *Science, 193,* 699–701.

TREHUB, S. E. (1985). Auditory pattern perception in infancy. In S. E. Trehub & B. Schneider (Eds.), *Advances in the study of communication and affect.* Vol. 10: *Auditory development in infancy.* New York: Plenum.

TREIBER, F., & Wilcox, S. (1980). Perception

of a "subjective contour" by infants. *Child Development, 51,* 915–917.

VURPILLOT, E. (1968). The development of scanning strategies and their relation to visual differentiation. *Journal of Experimental Child Psychology, 6,* 632–650.

WALK, R. D. (1981). *Perceptual development.* Pacific Grove, CA: Brooks/Cole.

WALKER-ANDREWS, A. S. (1986). Intermodal expression of expressive behaviors: Relation of eye and voice? *Developmental Psychology, 22,* 373–377.

WALKER-ANDREWS, A. S., & Lennon, E. M. (1985). Auditory-visual perception of changing distance by human infants. *Child Development, 56,* 544–548.

WELLMAN, H. M. (Ed.). (1985). *Children's searching: The development of search skill and spatial representation.* Hillsdale, NJ: Erlbaum.

WERKER, J. F., & Tees, R. C. (1984). Cross-language speech perception: Evidence for perceptual reorganization during the first year. *Infant Behavior and Development, 7,* 49–63.

WERNER, H. (1948). *Comparative psychology of mental development.* New York: International Universities Press.

WITKIN, H. A. (1967). A cognitive style approach to cross-cultural research. *International Journal of Psychology, 2,* 233–250.

WITKIN, H. A., & Berry, J. W. (1975). Psychological differentiation in cross-cultural perspective. *Journal of Cross-Cultural Psychology, 6,* 4–87.

WITKIN, H. A., & Goodenough, D. R. (1977). Field dependence and interpersonal behavior. *Psychological Bulletin, 84,* 661–689.

WITKIN, H. A., Goodenough, D. R., & Oltman, P. K. (1979). Psychological differentiation: Current status. *Journal of Personality and Social Psychology, 37,* 1127–1145.

YENDOVITSKAYA, T. V. (1971). Development of attention. In A. V. Zaporozhets & D. B. Elkonin (Eds.), *The psychology of pre-school children.* Cambridge, MA: M.I.T. Press.

YONAS, A. (1981). Infants' responses to optical information for collision. In R. N. Aslin, J. R. Alberts, and M. R. Petersen (Eds.), *Development of perception: Psychobiological perspectives.* Vol. 2: *The visual system.* Orlando, FL: Academic Press.

YONAS, A., Cleaves, W., & Pettersen, L. (1978). Development of sensitivity to pictorial depth. *Science, 200,* 77–79.

YONAS, A., Granrud, C. E., & Pettersen, L. (1985). Infants' sensitivity to relative size information for distance. *Developmental Psychology, 21,* 161–167.

ZINCHENKO, V. P., Van Chzhi-Tsin, & Tarakanov, V. V. (1963). The formation and development of perceptual activity. *Soviet Psychology and Psychiatry, 2,* 3–12.

Learning
and Development

Over the past four chapters, we have seen that human beings are biological creatures who inherit certain sensory and behavioral capacities and are "programmed" to change in a number of important ways as they mature. Yet, it should be obvious that much of what we do or what we become is attributable to factors other than genetic or maturational programming. For example, there are no hereditary codes that instruct us to feel uncomfortable in public without clothing, to use toilets, to stop at traffic signals, to brush our teeth, to prefer weekends to weekdays, or to become slightly nauseated at the thought of eating fish head soup. Clearly, these habits, feelings, and attitudes are *learned* as a result of the experiences we have had while growing up in a Western society.

In this chapter we will concentrate on the process of learning and see that it plays a very prominent role in many aspects of human development. We will also see that the ways in which developmentalists think about learning have changed rather dramatically over the years. Until the mid-1960s, learning theorists tended to endorse John Watson's behavioristic analysis of human development. You may recall from Chapter 2 that Watson described the infant as a *tabula rasa* (blank slate) who is "written upon" by experience. Indeed, Watson (1928) believed that children had little if any control over their own destiny, for he argued that they are extremely malleable organisms who are constantly being taught how to feel, think, and act by their parents, teachers, and other significant adults (all of whom are sufficiently powerful to ensure that their young charges will comply with their directives). Yet, as we proceed through the chapter, we will see that few theorists continue to subscribe to this rather passive and mechanistic portrayal of children and the developmental process. And why are they so skeptical? Simply because children are not the passive pawns of environmental influence that Watson described; instead, they are more accurately characterized as *active information processors* who have a hand in creating the very environments that will influence their growth and development.

Let's now begin our review of learning and development by trying to determine what learning is—and what it is not.

What Is Learning?

Learning is one of those deceptively simple terms that are actually quite complex and difficult to define. Most psychologists think of learning as a change in behavior (or behavior potential) that meets the following three requirements (Domjan & Burkhard, 1986):

1. The individual now thinks, perceives, or reacts to the environment in a *new way.*
2. This change is clearly the result of one's *experiences*—that is, attributable to repetition, study, practice, or the observations one has made, rather than to hereditary or maturational processes or to physiological damage resulting from injury.
3. The change is *relatively permanent.* Facts, thoughts, and behaviors that are acquired and immediately forgotten have not really been learned; and temporary changes due to fatigue, illness, or drugs do not qualify as learned responses.

There are at least three very general ways in which young children learn: (1) by *repetition,* (2) by associating a response with a particular stimulus or class of stimuli through some form of *conditioning,* and (3) by *observing* the behavior of social models. In the pages that follow, we will examine each of these relatively simple kinds of learning and their implications for human development.

not fatigued but discriminative

Habituation: Early Evidence of Information Processing

As we have seen in Chapter 6, newborn infants will eventually **habituate** (that is, stop attending or responding) to various kinds of sensory stimulation that are presented over and over. This process of becoming familiar with a sight, sound, touch, taste, or odor is a very simple form of learning. As the infant stops responding to a stimulus, he is telling us that he recognizes it as something he has experienced before. In other words, he has already encoded that stimulus (or at least one of its most noteworthy characteristics) into memory, so that its further repetition is "old hat" and nothing to get excited about.

How do we know that an infant is not merely fatigued when he stops responding to a familiar stimulus? We know because when a child has habituated to one stimulus, he will often attend to or even react vigorously to the presentation of a slightly different stimulus. In so doing, he is telling us (1) that his sensory receptors are not simply fatigued and (2) that he can tell the difference between (that is, *discriminate*) the familiar and the unfamiliar.

Developmental Trends

When does habituation first occur? Perhaps as early as the last trimester of pregnancy! Recently, Lynda Madison and her associates (Madison, Madison, & Adubato, 1986) applied vibrating stimuli to the abdomens of pregnant women and monitored fetal movements with ultrasound. After 40 repetitions, all but one of these 27–36-week-old fetuses had stopped moving in response to the vibrations as if they had now processed this stimulus as a very familiar event—something that was no longer worthy of their attention.

Although habituation may be possible even before birth, this early form of learning improves dramatically over the first year. For example, infants less than 4 months old may require many exposures to a stimulus before they habituate; and they will soon **dishabituate**—that is, begin responding once again to something they have previously recognized as familiar (Bornstein & Sigman, 1986). By contrast, 4–12-month-old infants show rapid habituation, are slow to dishabituate, and are more likely than younger infants to prefer to explore novel rather than familiar stimuli.

This trend toward rapid habituation is prob-ably related to the maturation of the sensory and motor areas of the cerebral cortex. As the brain continues to develop over the first 4–6 months and the senses mature, infants detect more and more information about a stimulus during any given exposure (Rovee-Collier, 1984). As a result, they are quicker to habituate and will show dramatic improvements in memory. In fact, 5–12-month-olds may recognize something as familiar after only one or two brief exposures, and they are likely to retain that "knowledge" for weeks or even months (Fagan, 1984; Rose, 1981).

Habituation and Later Development

Infants (and even fetuses) reliably differ in the rate at which they habituate and dishabituate (Bornstein & Sigman, 1986; Madison et al., 1986). Some infants are efficient information processors: they quickly recognize repetitive sensory inputs and are very slow to forget what they have experienced. Others are much less efficient: they require many more exposures to brand a stimulus as "familiar" and may soon forget what they have learned. Might these early individual differences in learning and information processing have any implications for later development?

Apparently so. In their recent study of fetal habituation, Madison et al. (1986) found that fetuses who habituated quickly to a vibrating stimulus made higher scores on a test of infant intelligence 4 months after birth than fetuses who had been slow to habituate. Even more interesting are a number of studies (reviewed by Bornstein & Sigman, 1986) showing that infants who habituate rapidly during the first six months of life reliably outscore their slower-habituating age mates on standardized intelligence tests and measures of language ability later in childhood. In fact, measures of early information-processing skills (habituation and dishabituation) are actually much better predictors of intellectual competencies during the preschool and grade

learning: a relatively permanent change in behavior (or behavioral potential) that results from one's experiences or practice.

habituation: a simple form of learning in which an organism eventually stops responding to a stimulus that is repeated over and over.

dishabituation: recovery of a response to a previously habituated stimulus.

school years than are the more traditional tests of infant intelligence (Bornstein & Sigman, 1986; Fagan, 1985). Why should this be? Joseph Fagan (1985) believes that the ability to detect the familiar and to retain such information may be *the fundamental intellectual process—* one that underlies complex mental activities such as the analogical reasoning and problem-solving skills that are normally measured on intelligence tests. Although more research is needed to properly evaluate Fagan's claim, the strong links between infants' early information-processing abilities and their later intellectual performance imply that habituation is indeed a most important form of learning.

Classical Conditioning

A second way that young children learn is through **classical conditioning.** In classical conditioning, a neutral stimulus that initially has no effect on the child comes to elicit a response of some sort by virtue of its association with a second, nonneutral stimulus that always elicits the response. To illustrate the process, let's consider Ivan Pavlov's famous studies of classical conditioning in animals.

Pavlov was a Russian physiologist who discovered classical conditioning while studying the digestive processes of dogs. At one point in his research, Pavlov observed that his dogs would often salivate at the appearance of a caretaker who had come to feed them. Since it was unlikely that the dogs hoped to eat the caretaker, Pavlov wondered why they were salivating. He speculated that the animals had probably associated the caretaker (an initially neutral stimulus) with food, a nonneutral stimulus that ordinarily makes dogs salivate (an unlearned, or "reflexive," response to food). In other words, salivation at the sight of the caretaker was said to be a learned response that the dogs acquired as they made a connection between the caretaker and the presentation of food.

Pavlov then designed a simple experiment to test his hypothesis. Dogs first listened to a bell, a neutral stimulus in that bells do not ordinarily make them salivate. Then this neutral stimulus was sounded just before the dogs were fed. Of course, food normally elicits salivation: in the language of classical conditioning, food is an **unconditioned stimulus (UCS)** and salivation is an unlearned or **unconditioned response (UCR)** to food. After the bell and the food had been paired several times, Pavlov then sounded the bell, withheld the food, and observed that the dogs now salivated to the sound of the bell alone. Clearly their behavior had changed as a result of their experiences. In the terminology of classical conditioning, the dogs were now emitting a **conditioned response (CR),** salivation, to an initially neutral or **conditioned stimulus (CS)**— the bell (see Figure 7-1).

As Pavlov continued to experiment with his dogs, he discovered a number of additional rules or characteristics of the conditioning process. One such rule was the principle of **stimulus generalization:** stimuli that are very similar to a CS (for example, a bell with a slightly different ring) will also elicit the conditioned response. The opposite of generalization is the principle of **discrimination:** if a stimulus is very different from the original CS (for example, a bell with a much higher- or much lower-pitched ring), the subject apparently notices the difference and will not emit the conditioned response. Finally, conditioned responses that occur repeatedly without occasionally being followed by the unconditioned stimulus will diminish in strength and eventually disappear. This gradual weakening and elimination of a conditioned response is called **extinction.**

The Classical Conditioning of Emotions and Attitudes

Although the salivary responses that Pavlov conditioned may seem rather mundane, it is quite conceivable that every one of us has learned many things through classical conditioning—things that continue to affect us today. For example, some fears, phobias, and other emotional responses may be acquired in this way. In 1920 John Watson and Rosalie Raynor presented a gentle white rat to an 11-month-old infant named Albert. Albert's initial reactions were positive ones: he crawled toward the rat and played with it as he had previously with a dog and a rabbit. Then came the conditioning phase. Every time little Albert reached for the white rat, Watson would sneak up behind him and bang a steel rod loudly with a hammer. Little Albert would then cry and shy away from the rat. In this case, a loud noise is the unconditioned stimulus (UCS) because it elicits fearful behavior (the UCR) without any learning having taken place. Did little Albert eventually associate the white rat with the loud noise and come to fear his furry playmate? Indeed he did, and he also learned to shy away from other furry things, such as cats, balls of cotton, and a fur coat. This generalization of fear to objects other than the rat illustrates that the effects of classical conditioning can be powerful indeed.

Arthur Staats (1975) has argued that many of our <u>attitudes</u> and <u>prejudices</u> are acquired by classical conditioning. Imagine, if you can, that you are an 8-year-old who overhears your father say "Those redheads are really hot-tempered. Today Red Smith smashed the Coke machine just because it gypped him out of a quarter." Your mother then concurs, noting that a redheaded acquaintance of hers is often moody and temperamental. Two days later, you accuse a redheaded playmate of cheating at marbles, and he punches you. All these experiences may serve as conditioning "trials." Over the course of three days, you have associated redheadedness with destructive behavior, moodiness, cheating, and hostility—attitudes and activities that you are likely to view in a negative light. Suddenly an initially neutral stimulus, red hair, is apt to elicit negative feelings (a conditioned response). This conditioned "attitude" may then become a full-blown **prejudice** toward redheads if future contacts and experiences with redheaded people are not more positive.

Fortunately, prejudices, fears, and other undesirable responses can often be weakened or eliminated by a treatment known as *counterconditioning*. In Box

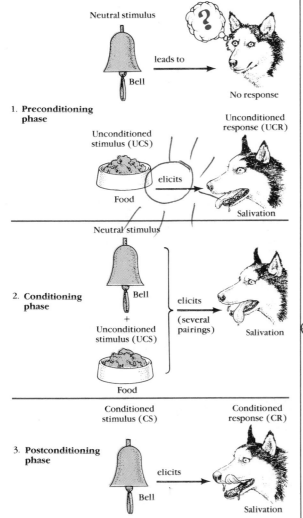

1. **Preconditioning phase**

2. **Conditioning phase**

3. **Postconditioning phase**

Figure 7-1. The three phases of classical conditioning. In the preconditioning phase, the unconditioned stimulus (UCS) always elicits an unconditioned response (UCR), while the conditioned stimulus (CS) never does. During the conditioning phase, the CS and UCS are paired repeatedly and eventually associated. At this point, the learner passes into the postconditioning phase, in which the CS alone will elicit the original response (now called a conditioned response, or CR).

// **classical conditioning:** " a type of learning in which an initially neutral stimulus is repeatedly paired with a meaningful stimulus so that the neutral stimulus comes to elicit the response originally made only to the meaningful stimulus.

unconditioned stimulus (UCS): a stimulus that elicits a particular response without any prior learning.

unconditioned response (UCR): the unlearned response elicited by an unconditioned stimulus.

conditioned response (CR): a learned response to a stimulus that was not originally capable of producing the response.

conditioned stimulus (CS): an initially neutral stimulus that comes to elicit a particular response after being paired with a UCS that always elicits the response.

stimulus generalization: the fact that one stimulus can be substituted for another and produce the same response that the former stimulus did.

discrimination: the process of differentiating and responding differently to stimuli that vary on one or more dimensions.

extinction: gradual weakening and disappearance of a learned response that occurs because the CS is no longer paired with the UCS (in classical conditioning) or the response is no longer reinforced (in operant conditioning).

prejudice: an unjustified negative attitude toward an individual based solely on the person's membership in a particular group.

Counter conditioning positive aversion

■ ■ ■

Box 7-1
Classical Conditioning as a Therapeutic Technique

Many fears, phobias, and other undesirable reactions can be weakened or eliminated by *counterconditioning*— a treatment based on classical conditioning principles. The goal of counterconditioning is to extinguish an undesirable response to a person, object, or situation and to replace it with new and more adaptive behavior.

In *positive* counterconditioning, a stimulus or situation that initially elicits an undesirable reaction (for example, fear) is gradually associated with pleasant outcomes, thereby leading to the reduction or elimination of the maladaptive behavior. For example, Mary Cover Jones (1924) used positive counterconditioning to treat a 2-year-old named Peter who, like Watson's little Albert, had acquired a strong fear of furry objects. Peter was exposed to a rabbit (a CS for fearful behavior) while he ate some of his favorite foods (a UCS for pleasant feelings). While Peter ate, the rabbit was gradually moved closer and closer until Peter was finally able to hold the rabbit by himself. In this case, the rabbit came to be associated with a pleasant UCS (desirable foods), so that Peter's fearful reaction was eventually replaced by a more desirable response (playing with the rabbit).

Aversion therapy, a second form of counterconditioning, produces changes in behavior by pairing undesirable or maladaptive responses with *unpleasant* outcomes. One area to which mild aversion therapy has been applied with some success is enuresis (bedwetting). Most children eventually learn to wake up when they have to urinate because bladder tension (an initially neutral stimulus) has often been paired with a wet bed—an unpleasant UCS that wakes them up (the UCR). However, victims of enuresis do not learn this association between bladder tension and waking, probably because wetting the bed is not sufficiently unpleasant to rouse them from their sleep.

To treat enuresis by aversive counterconditioning, the therapist must devise a method that enables the child to associate bladder tension with an alternative UCS that will wake her up. One procedure that seems to work is to have the child sleep on a special sheet containing fine electrical wires. As soon the child begins to wet, the urine (which conducts electricity) closes an electrical circuit and rings a loud buzzer or bell, a slightly unpleasant UCS that awakens the subject (Hansen, 1979). After several of these rude awakenings, the child should associate bladder tension (the CS) with waking (the CR) and stop wetting the bed.

Here, then, are two of the many ways in which classical conditioning procedures have been used to modify the undesirable behavior of children and adults. Of course, counterconditioning is hardly a cure-all, for it is often necessary to supplement these techniques with other forms of therapy—particularly when treating very strong or long-term problems such as phobic reactions, test-taking fears, smoking, and drug or alcohol addiction. Nevertheless, the relatively simple principles of learning described by Pavlov have been applied in new and creative ways to provide solutions (or partial solutions) for a number of behavior disorders.

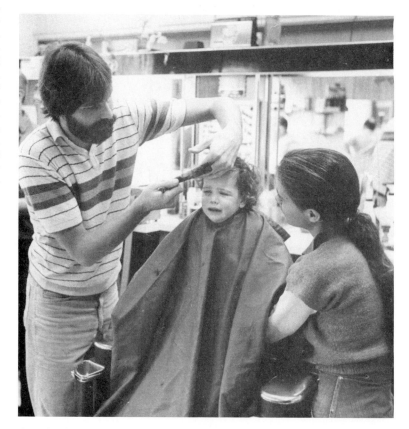

Those first haircuts are fearful events for many young children. With gentle treatment from the hairdresser—and perhaps a lollipop after the job is done—fear of the barbershop (or beauty parlor) will be weakened by counterconditioning.

7-1 we will take a closer look at this interesting therapeutic technique.

biologically programmed reflexes

Can Neonates Be Classically Conditioned?

For more than 50 years, investigators were generally unsuccessful at demonstrating classical conditioning in newborn infants; it seemed as if babies were just not susceptible to this kind of learning for the first three or four weeks of life. But after carefully reviewing the literature, Hiram Fitzgerald and Yvonne Brackbill (1976) concluded that neonates can be classically conditioned. Consider the following example. Lewis Lipsitt and Herbert Kaye (1964) paired a neutral tone (the CS) with the presentation of a nipple (a UCS that elicits sucking) to infants 2–3 days old. After several of these conditioning trials, the infants began to make sucking motions at the sound of the tone—before the nipple was presented. Clearly, their sucking qualifies as a classically conditioned response because it is now elicited by a stimulus (the tone) that does not normally elicit sucking behavior.

Fitzgerald and Brackbill point out that only a small number of responses (mostly biologically programmed reflexes such as sucking, blinking, and breathing) can be classically conditioned during the first few weeks of life and that the infant must be alert and attentive for the conditioning to have any chance of success. Moreover, very young infants display more conditioning when the time interval between the presentation of the CS and the UCS is lengthened from the 0.5 second used in studies of adults to about 1.5 seconds (Little, Lipsitt, & Rovee-Collier, 1984). This latter finding makes perfectly good sense after reviewing the habituation literature. Recall that neonates process information very slowly and, thus, may simply require more time than an older subject to associate the conditioned and unconditioned stimuli in classical conditioning experiments. But despite these early limitations in information processing, classical conditioning is almost certainly one of the ways in which very young infants learn important lessons such as that bottles or breasts give milk or that other people (notably mothers, who are soon identified by voice and/or smell) signify warmth and comfort.

Operant (Instrumental) Conditioning
stamping
shaping

In classical conditioning, learned responses are *elicited* by a conditioned stimulus. **Operant** (or instru-

behaviors = responses (operants) not elicited

mental) **conditioning** is quite different: it requires the learner to first *emit a response* of some sort (that is, *operate* on the environment) and then associate this action with the positive or negative consequences it produces.

E. L. Thorndike (1898) was the first to demonstrate instrumental conditioning in the laboratory. In one series of experiments, Thorndike placed cats in cagelike "puzzle boxes" from which they could escape and obtain food by hitting a lever on the side of the apparatus. Typically these curious and active creatures would search for a means of escape, "accidentally" trip the lever, and run out of the box to their tasty treat. As they gained more experience with these puzzle boxes, the cats soon learned to hit the lever almost immediately in order to escape from confinement and obtain the food. Thorndike concluded that the "pleasure" (that is, escape and food) associated with lever pressing had the effect of "stamping in" this particular response and "stamping out" all other impulses that did not produce the desired outcomes. In other words, lever pressing was learned because it was *instrumental* for obtaining a reward.

Although Thorndike was the pioneer in this area of study, B. F. Skinner (1953) is the person who made operant conditioning famous. Skinner has argued that most human behaviors are responses that we emit freely and voluntarily. He calls them *operants*. According to Skinner, operant behaviors are modified by their consequences. If an operant is followed by a favorable (reinforcing) outcome, it is likely to be repeated in the future. Operants that generate less favorable outcomes are not as likely to be repeated and may be suppressed (see Figure 7-2). In sum, operant conditioning is a very common form of learning in which various acts become either more or less probable depending on the consequences they produce.

suppresses + doesn't teach

Reinforcement and Punishment

In the language of operant conditioning, a **reinforcer** is any stimulus that *strengthens* a response by making it more likely to occur in the future. A rein-

acts / consequences

operant conditioning: a form of learning in which freely emitted acts (or operants) become either more or less probable depending on the consequences they produce.

reinforcer: any consequence of an act that increases the probability that the act will recur.

positive or negative

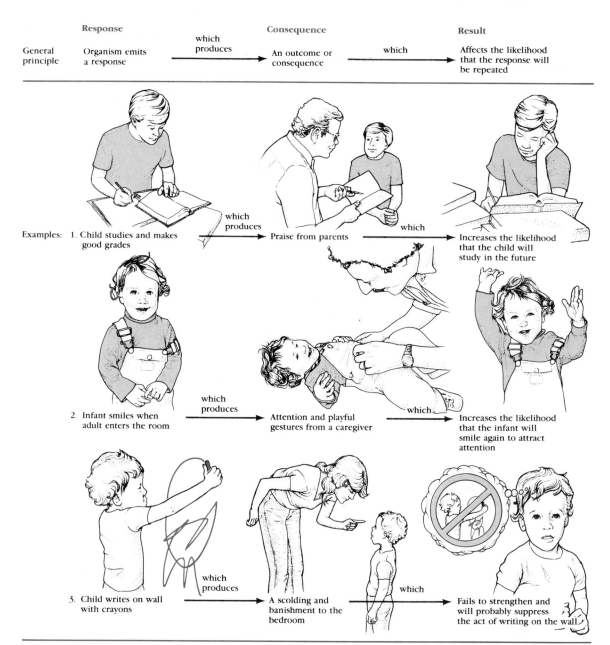

	Response	which produces	Consequence	which	Result
General principle	Organism emits a response		An outcome or consequence		Affects the likelihood that the response will be repeated

Examples:	which produces	which
1. Child studies and makes good grades	Praise from parents	Increases the likelihood that the child will study in the future
2. Infant smiles when adult enters the room	Attention and playful gestures from a caregiver	Increases the likelihood that the infant will smile again to attract attention
3. Child writes on wall with crayons	A scolding and banishment to the bedroom	Fails to strengthen and will probably suppress the act of writing on the wall

Figure 7-2. Basic principles of operant conditioning.

forcer may be something pleasant such as a piece of candy or a pat on the head. These pleasant events are called **positive reinforcers.** A reinforcer may also be something *negative,* or unpleasant, that is *removed from the situation* once the subject has made a desired response. Have you ever been in a car in which an obnoxious buzzer sounds until you buckle your seat belt? The idea here is that "buckling up" will become a stronger habit through **negative reinforcement**—we learn to fasten the belt because this act ends the irritating noise. Indeed, the desire to escape or avoid unpleasant situations is the basis for many of our habits. If a child

Box 7-2
Distinctions among
Positive Reinforcement,
Negative Reinforcement,
and Two Kinds of Punishment

Have you ever missed an item on a test and felt that the item was unnecessarily confusing or picky? While taking a "pretest" on the first day of an upper-level psychology course, I and virtually everyone else in the class missed a true/false item that read "Negative reinforcement is a form of punishment." I now know that the answer to this question is "false," but oh, did the members of the class argue about that item! As the professor tried to explain, we students were confused by the fact that a negative stimulus could be involved in reinforcement. One disgruntled classmate thought that this particular issue (and the test question) was absurd. He expressed his frustration by saying "Where I come from, positive events are rewards and negative events are punishments. Isn't that really a whole lot simpler?"

The professor answered "No, that's an oversimplification." She then proceeded to explain that reinforcements and punishments are defined by their effects: reinforcers *strengthen* responses, while punishing stimuli *weaken* or *suppress* them. Finally, she drew a table on the board that helped the class to understand how, under certain circumstances, negative stimuli could help to strengthen (reinforce) a response, while positive stimuli could be implicated in suppressing a response (punishment). Perhaps this table will help you in the same way that it helped us.

Conditions defining positive reinforcement, negative reinforcement, and punishment

Action	Type of stimulus	
	Positive (pleasant)	*Negative (unpleasant)*
Administered	Positive reinforcement (strengthens the response that produces it)	Punishment (suppresses the response that produces it)
Withdrawn	Punishment (suppresses the response that produces it)	Negative reinforcement (strengthens the response that produces it)

finds that she can prevent an aversive scolding by picking up her crayons after using them, this kind of "tidying up" should become more probable. If you find that you can avoid an incredibly boring teacher by transferring into another instructor's 8:00 A.M. section of the course, you are apt to become an early riser. In each of these examples, a behavior is strengthened through negative reinforcement—through the removal or elimination of something unpleasant. seat belt buzzer

Is *negative reinforcement* merely a fancy name for punishment? *No, it is not!* Recall that a negative reinforcer is an aversive stimulus that is *withdrawn* when the child performs a desirable act. By contrast, the most familiar form of punishment involves the *presentation* of an aversive stimulus when the child emits an undesirable response. In other words, the purpose of **punishment** is roughly opposite to that of reinforcement—to *suppress* unacceptable acts rather than to strengthen acceptable ones. Another form of punishment that parents often use is to *withhold something desirable* when the child behaves inappropriately. For example, a mother may punish roughhousing behavior by refusing to allow her children to watch their favorite TV show. By withholding this desirable activity, she is trying to suppress their roughhousing behavior and *decrease* the probability that they will repeat these acts in the future.

One reason that people tend to confuse punishment and negative reinforcement is that these two processes may often occur together. For example, a mother who scolds her son for leaving his skateboard in the kitchen is punishing that oversight; but if her aversive nagging stops when the boy takes the skateboard to his room, she has also negatively reinforced this desirable alternative response. Moreover, people generally think of positive stimuli as reinforcers and negative ones as punishments. This source of confusion can be eliminated if we recall that reinforcements and punishments are defined not by their pleasantness or unpleasantness but by their effects: reinforcers strengthen responses, and punishing stimuli inhibit or suppress them. Perhaps the table in Box 7-2 will help you to remember the differences among positive and negative reinforcement and the two kinds of punishment.

---

positive reinforcer: any stimulus whose presentation, as the consequence of an act, increases the probability that the act will recur.
negative reinforcer: any stimulus whose removal or termination, as the consequence of an act, increases the probability that the act will recur.
punishment: any consequence of an act that suppresses the response and decreases the probability that it will recur.

Students of operant conditioning believe that punishment is generally less effective than reinforcement at producing desirable changes in behavior, because punishment merely suppresses ongoing or established responses without really teaching anything new. For example, a toddler who is punished for grabbing food with her hands is likely to stop eating altogether rather than to learn to use her spoon. A much simpler way to promote this desirable alternative response is to reinforce it (Skinner, 1953).

Operant Conditioning in Infancy

Will neonates alter their behavior in order to obtain positive outcomes or to avoid unpleasant ones? Indeed they will—as long as they are capable of emitting the response that you wish to reinforce. One interesting demonstration of early operant conditioning is Butterfield and Siperstein's (1972) study of newborns' reactions to music, discussed briefly in Chapter 6. Recall that babies were first given a pacifier and their baseline sucking rates were determined. Then the procedure began. If infants sucked faster than their baseline rates, they would hear folk music, whereas sucking slower than baseline produced nonrhythmic noise. The results were clear. Babies apparently found folk tunes to be positively reinforcing, for they soon began to suck rapidly to hear the music. And if their sucking slowed to a point where it triggered nonrhythmic noise, the infants soon learned to suck a bit faster—an action that was negatively reinforced by allowing them to escape this aversive stimulation.

Although instrumental learning may begin at birth, we should remember that neonates are able (or biologically prepared) to emit only a limited number of responses (for example, sucking, kicking, grasping, and head turning) and that these are the only behaviors that will be very susceptible to operant conditioning. And because very young infants are inefficient information processors, they are apt to learn very slowly. Thus, if you hoped to teach 2-day-old infants to turn their heads to the right and offered them a nippleful of milk every time they did so, you would find that they took about 200 trials, on average, to acquire this simple head-turning response (Papousek, 1967). Older infants learn much faster: a 3-month-old will require only about 40 trials to display a simple head-turning response, and 5-month-olds can acquire this habit in fewer than 30 trials. Apparently these older subjects are simply more proficient at associating their behavior (in this case, head turning) with its consequences (a tasty treat)—an advance in information processing that seems to explain infants' increasing susceptibility to operant conditioning over the first few months of life.

Yes but may have retrieval problems

Can infants recall their previous habits?

Earlier we noted that very young infants seem to have very short memories, for they will often dishabituate to familiar stimuli within a matter of minutes. Yet, the simple act of recognizing a stimulus as "familiar" may not be terribly meaningful to a neonate or even a 2-month-old. Might young infants be better at remembering learned responses that have proved to be reinforcing in the past?

Yes, indeed, and a program of research by Carolyn Rovee-Collier (1984) makes this point quite clearly. Rovee-Collier's procedure is to place an attractive mobile over the cribs of 2–3-month-old infants and to run a ribbon from the mobile to the infants' ankles (see Photo 7-1). Within a matter of minutes, these young subjects discover that they can make the mobile move by kicking their legs, and they take great pleasure in doing so. But will they remember how to make the mobile move a week later? To succeed at this memory task, the infant not only must *recognize* the mobile but also must *recall* that it moves and that kicking is the way to get it to move. So how well do young infants remember?

The standard procedure for testing an infant's memory is to place the child back in the crib to see whether kicking occurs when he or she sees the mobile. Rovee-Collier and her associates (Earley, Griesler, & Rovee-Collier, 1985) find that 2-month-old infants remember how to make the mobile move for up to 3 days after the original learning, whereas 3-month-olds can recall this kicking response for more than a week. Clearly, a young infant's memory is much more impressive than habituation studies would have us believe.

Now we can ask "Why is it that infants eventually forget how to make the mobile move?" Is it that they simply have a limited capacity for storing such information, so that their previous learning is lost? Or is it that the learning is still there but that young infants can't retrieve this information from memory? To find out, Janet Davis and Carolyn Rovee-Collier (1983) first taught 2-month-old infants how to make the mobile move and, after 18 days, attempted to "*remind*" some of them of the kicking response *by rotating the mobile for them.* If the infants' previous learning had been lost, they should have treated the mobile as a novel stimulus, staring intently at it without kicking. But this is not what they did. Instead, they looked very *briefly* at the rotating mobile (thus indicating that they recognized it) and then kicked

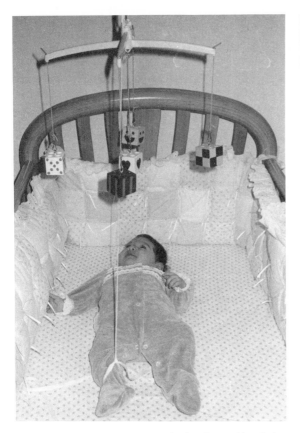

Photo 7-1. When ribbons are attached to their ankles, 2–3-month-old infants soon learn to make a mobile move by kicking their legs. But do they remember how to make the mobile move when tested days or weeks after the original learning? These are the questions that Rovee-Collier has explored in her fascinating research on infant memory.

up a storm as soon as the ribbon was attached to their ankles. By contrast, the remaining infants who received no reminder of their previous learning did not try to make the mobile move when given an opportunity to do so. The implication, then, is that even very young infants can retain meaningful information for weeks, if not longer—and a subtle reminder of this earlier learning allows them to show us how well they remember. The reason that these young subjects often seem to "forget" what they have learned is that they simply have problems retrieving stored information from memory.

Significance of early operant learning.
What impact might early learning have on infants and

foundation for strong emotional attachment.

their companions? Since even neonates are capable of associating their responses with various outcomes, they should soon learn that they can make some interesting things happen. For example, a baby may discover that crying brings forth her mother (or some other caregiver), who then unwittingly reinforces the baby's cries by giving food, attention, warmth, or comfort. Gazing, smiling, and babbling are yet other sociable gestures on which the infant may learn to rely in order to attract the attention or nurturance of caregivers. As the child is acquiring these habits, her caregivers are also learning how to react to her, so that their social interactions gradually become smoother and more satisfying for both the infant and her companions. It is fortunate, then, that babies can learn, for in so doing, they are likely to become more responsive to other people, who, in turn, are becoming more responsive to them. As we will see in Chapter 11, these early reciprocal exchanges provide a foundation for the strong emotional attachments that often develop between infants and their closest companions.

Shaping of Complex Behaviors
Many of the responses that children are expected to learn are very unfamiliar to them and may seem rather complex. For example, preschool children often have a difficult time learning to dress themselves. It looks so easy when someone does it for them, but they invariably discover that looks can be deceiving when they become tangled in their shirts and put their shoes on the wrong feet. What is likely to happen then is that the child who can't get his shirt on or his shoe tied will seek the assistance of a parent or an older sibling.

How can we condition a complex response that the child has trouble performing? A student of operant conditioning would use a procedure called **shaping.** When shaping a complex pattern of behavior, the person doing the "teaching" reinforces the child for producing *successively closer approximations* of the behavior that he or she wishes the child to learn. For example, a boy who is learning to put on his shirt might be praised for getting his arms into the sleeves, even if he quits there and doesn't button up. Gradually, the "teacher" will require him to come closer to performing the desired response, perhaps by fastening a button or

component responses

shaping: a method of teaching complex patterns of behavior by reinforcing successively closer approximations of these responses.

two, before giving any reinforcement. The next step might involve withholding praise until the boy properly aligns and fastens all the buttons on his shirt. And finally the boy might be required to align and fasten all buttons *and* tuck in his shirt before praise or some other reinforcer is administered.

Shaping is a rather effective technique that works well even with very young children. In fact, B. F. Skinner has repeatedly shown that lower animals like pigeons can be taught to play an intricate game like table tennis if one simply takes the time to reinforce successive approximations and thereby "shape" the component responses of this complex behavioral sequence.

Factors That Affect
Operant Conditioning

A number of factors can affect the initial success of operant conditioning as well as the strength or durability of habits acquired in this way. Among the more important of these influences are the timing of reinforcement, the schedule on which it is administered, and the value of the reinforcer to the child.

Timing of reinforcement. Research with animals and young children shows that reinforcement is most effective when administered immediately after

a response (Domjan & Burkhard, 1986). In fact, Stuart Millar and John Watson (1979) found that a delay of only three seconds in the presentation of a reinforcer is sufficient to prevent 6–8-month-old infants from learning to move their arms in order to see and hear an interesting audiovisual display (the reinforcer in this study). It is not that the infants are incapable of acquiring this habit, for a second group of 6–8-month-olds who were reinforced immediately after waving their arms soon learned to emit the arm-waving response.

Why do young infants fail to learn under conditions of delayed reinforcement? Probably because they simply haven't the information-processing skills to associate their actions with an outcome unless these events occur almost simultaneously. But as children mature and become more efficient information processors, they begin to notice that their actions often have delayed consequences (as when a toddler is praised later for going to the potty on his own while his parents are outside), and they will even anticipate such outcomes before they perform various acts. Indeed, older children and adults are quite susceptible to delayed reinforcement because they use verbal labels or other mediational strategies to remind themselves that certain actions are likely to pay off in the long run. This is precisely what you are doing should you say to yourself "I'll have to start studying this weekend if I hope to learn all this material and make an A on the quiz next Tuesday."

Frequency, or scheduling, of reinforcement. To this point, we have been talking mainly about cases in which a response is reinforced every time it occurs—a schedule known as **continuous reinforcement.** But in a typical home, it is unlikely that a child's desirable behaviors will be reinforced every time they occur. Parents are often not around to observe them, or they may be too preoccupied with their own activities to carefully monitor and reinforce all the child's commendable actions. As a matter of fact, adults are often inconsistent—on some occasions when they are busy or moody, they may ignore or even punish a child who has done something praiseworthy. Why, then, do children continue to perform "desirable" responses if parents and other companions are less than consistent when it comes to reinforcing them?

Extensive research with both animals and humans shows that habits may be acquired and then maintained for long periods with only occasional (that is, **partial** or *intermittent*) **reinforcement.** In fact, behaviors that have been partially reinforced will persist longer after reinforcement is totally withdrawn than behaviors that have been reinforced on a continuous schedule. In the language of operant conditioning, partial reinforcement makes a response *more resistant to extinction*. This seemingly paradoxical finding can be explained by an analogy. If you've always found water when you go to the well, a nonproductive trip or two leads you to conclude that the well has gone dry. Consequently, you are not likely to return (rapid extinction following continuous reinforcement). However, if the well has produced water, say, 60% of the time, you will not be dismayed by a "dry" trip or two and are likely to return in the future (slow extinction following partial reinforcement).

So this **"partial reinforcement" effect** helps to explain why children continue to perform commendable acts even when this praiseworthy conduct is not often reinforced by parents, teachers, and other social agents. But beware, for *undesirable* behaviors may persist for the same reason. For example, children may learn that they can nag their father until he "breaks down" and lets them do things that he was not inclined to allow. If they start several days ahead of time, persistently making their requests, occasionally a father may give in with a statement like "Oh, for Pete's sake, you can go." Although this hypothetical father may resist his children's nagging most of the time, those few occasions on which he wavers will have the effect of partially reinforcing and thus perpetuating their nagging behavior.

importance + information
Value of the reinforcer. The success of operant conditioning will also depend on the value of the stimulus that is offered as an incentive. For example, infants have little reason to value money and are less responsive to monetary incentives than older children or adults are. A girl who has just eaten all the sweets she wants is less likely to alter her behavior for another piece of candy than her brother who is hungry and hasn't had any sweets. So the learner's need for (or evaluation of) a reinforcer is an important determinant of its effectiveness at shaping operant responses.

Very general reinforcers such as praise or approval may also assume different values. If a child has always received social approval from a particular companion, then further praise from that person is not valued as much as the same level of approval from a less familiar source (Babad, 1972, 1973). This is one reason that a grandparent or a favorite aunt is often more effective than parents at persuading young children to play cooperatively, to brush their teeth, or to proceed quietly to bed. In addition, social reinforcers that provide the child with *information* about his or her performance (for example, "That's good! You can catch the ball when you hold your arms together") are much more likely to sustain an ongoing activity and promote new learning than uninformative praise or approval (for example, "Good show!"), which will soon lose its effectiveness (Martin, 1977; Perry & Garrow, 1975).

Why Do Reinforcers Reinforce?

Earlier in the chapter, we defined a reinforcer as any stimulus that strengthens a response by making it more likely to occur in the future. If you are a bit of a logician, you have probably recognized that this definition is circular: it merely describes what happens when a response becomes more probable, rather than explaining how the response was strengthened. Suppose, for example, that a man wishes to know why his 3-month-old son who is participating in Rovee-Collier's research will repeatedly kick to make an overhead mobile rotate. To say that this kicking response leads to an event (a moving mobile) that is reinforcing, which, in turn, strengthens the kicking response, does not really tell the father much about his son's behavior. Indeed, many parents would want to know why reinforcing events are reinforcing.

Literally hundreds of objects and events have been used as reinforcers in laboratory studies of operant conditioning. The list includes familiar incentives such as food, water, and sex (in animal studies), as well as less traditional activities such as playing pinball, having the brain stimulated with a mild electrical current, having the opportunity to explore visual scenes, and earning the privilege of yelling and screaming. Some of these objects and activities satisfy basic physiological needs, but others clearly do not. What do all these "incentives" have in common that makes them effective reinforcers? Why do reinforcers reinforce?

---

continuous reinforcement: a schedule of reinforcement in which every occurrence of an act is reinforced.

partial reinforcement: a schedule of reinforcement in which only some of the occurrences of an act are reinforced.

partial reinforcement effect: the finding that behaviors that have been partially reinforced are more resistant to extinction than those that have been reinforced on a continuous schedule.

learner decides on reinforcer

The Premack principle

Several years ago, David Premack (1965, 1971) proposed a theory of reinforcement that helps to explain why so many objects and events are capable of strengthening operant responses. The "**Premack principle**" of reinforcement says that *the opportunity to engage in any activity can strengthen another activity as long as the first activity is more probable than the response that one is trying to condition.* For example, food will reinforce maze running because eating is typically more probable than exploring a maze. Under ordinary circumstances maze running cannot reinforce eating. But suppose that we discovered a curious breed of malnourished animals that would rather explore new territories than eat. According to the Premack principle, we could reinforce these creatures for eating (the less probable activity) by then allowing them access to unfamiliar mazes (the more probable activity).

Teachers often use the Premack principle when they allow their students to play or to read a favorite story once they have completed their class work. Reading and playing are highly probable responses that are quite effective at reinforcing less probable activities such as schoolwork. Perhaps the most important implication of Premack's theory is that it is always the *learner*, rather than the teacher, who ultimately decides what is the most potent reinforcer for any given activity. In Box 7-3 we will see how one team of investigators kept this point in mind as they designed a highly unusual and creative program aimed at teaching fidgety nursery school children to sit still and pay more attention to their teachers.

Effect of unnecessary rewards on learning and performance

A number of activities in which children take part are valued for their own sake and do not require external prompts or rewards in order to continue. These pastimes, which might include the kicking of an overhead mobile by a 3-month-old infant, watching television, reading storybooks, and solving puzzles, are said to be *intrinsically reinforcing.*

As it turns out, many of the responses or habits that adults want children to acquire are not so intrinsically satisfying. In order to get a child to perform these responses or to develop an interest in initially unrewarding activities, parents and teachers typically offer inducements such as money, praise, or symbolic incentives (for example, gold stars for reading). These rewards, which are not inherent in the activities they are designed to encourage, are called *extrinsic* reinforcers.

There is a great deal of evidence that the offering and presentation of extrinsic reinforcement can promote new learning and motivate young children to undertake and complete activities that are *not* intrinsically satisfying to them (Danner & Lonky, 1981; Loveland & Olley, 1979; McLoyd, 1979). For example, a teacher who offers her "nonreaders" a gold star for every ten minutes that they spend reading may well increase the reading activities of these children, who would not ordinarily read on their own. But what effect would this incentive have on the class "bookworms," who read avidly because reading is intrinsically satisfying?

Mark Lepper (1983) suggests that children who perform intrinsically satisfying activities as a means of obtaining extrinsic reinforcement may come to like these activities less. In other words, intrinsic interest in an activity may be undermined if the child decides he or she is performing the activity to earn a tangible reward.

An experiment by Lepper, Greene, and Nisbett (1973) provides support for Lepper's hypothesis. Children aged 3 to 5 who showed considerable intrinsic interest in drawing with colored felt pens were promised a special certificate if they would draw a picture for a visiting adult (expected-reward condition). Other preschool children who were equally interested in drawing with felt pens engaged in the same drawing activities and either received an unexpected certificate for their work (unexpected-reward condition) or did not receive a certificate (no-reward condition). Then, 7 to 14 days later, the children were observed during free-play periods to determine whether they still wanted to draw with the felt pens. Lepper et al. found that children who had contracted to draw a picture for an extrinsic reinforcer now spent less of their free time drawing with the pens (8.6%) than children who had received no reward (16.7%) or those who had received the reward as a surprise (18.1%). Note that the reward itself did not undermine intrinsic motivation, for children in the unexpected-reward condition continued to show as much intrinsic interest in drawing as those who were not rewarded. It was only when children believed they were drawing *in order to obtain a reward* that extrinsic reinforcement undermined intrinsic interest.

Undermining one's interest in intrinsically satisfying activities is not the only undesirable effect that unnecessary rewards can have. Children who are offered such incentives for undertaking activities they already enjoy may subsequently lower their aspirations, choosing to work at easy rather than difficult assignments so as not to miss out on the rewards (Condry &

Box 7-3
A Creative Application of the Premack Principle in a Nursery School Classroom

Nursery school children can be trying pupils because they often prefer to run around yelling, screaming, and visiting one another rather than sitting quietly in their seats listening to the teacher. Many teachers will try to suppress these aversive responses by punishing them, even though punishment rarely inhibits disruptive conduct for long. How, then, can a nursery school teacher establish control over restless young children so that they will pay more attention to the lessons of the day?

One team of investigators (Homme, deBaca, Devine, Steinhorst, & Rickert, 1963) attempted to control the behavior of young preschool children by applying the Premack principle. They reasoned that disruptive behaviors that are so aversive to adults must be highly *reinforcing* for nursery school children, since they clearly prefer these activities to sitting still and listening to the teacher. If the Premack principle is correct, then highly probable behaviors such as running around, yelling, and screaming should be able to strengthen less probable responses such as sitting in one's seat and paying attention. But how? After all, these two classes of behavior seem quite incompatible.

Homme et al. solved the incompatibility problem in an ingenious way: they told the children that they could earn free time during which they could run around, yell, and scream if they sat in their seats and listened to the teacher. After three minutes of sitting quietly, a bell sounded, signaling the children to run, yell, jump, and scream. A short time later, another signal was given that informed the children that they must return to their seats and listen attentively for another three minutes. Gradually, the sitting and listening requirements were increased, and the children began to earn tokens with which they could purchase yelling and screaming time at the end of the school day. Homme et al. (1963) found that their program was extremely effective at teaching children to sit still and attend to their schoolwork—even though these desirable habits were reinforced by the very activities that the teachers were trying to inhibit. These findings provide clear support for the Premack principle and remind us that it is the learner, not the teacher, who determines which activities are the most potent reinforcers for any particular behavior.

---

extrinsic can provide reinforcement > informational → competence

Chambers, 1982). And unfortunately, this sudden tendency to forgo significant challenges is most apparent among those children who had initially displayed the strongest intrinsic interest in the rewarded activities (Pearlman, 1984).

Do these findings mean that parents and teachers should never reward a child's noteworthy accomplishments at activities that she enjoys? No, they do not! Extrinsic rewards can sustain and even increase intrinsic interest in an activity, provided that the reinforcer is given only for *"successful"* task performance rather than for merely working at the task (Pallak, Costomiris, Sroka, & Pittman, 1982). Why? Because rewards given for successes serve an important (informational) function: namely, they allow children to attribute their positive outcomes to their (competence) in that activity rather than to a desire to obtain the reward. Consequently, children are likely to perform the rewarded acts in the future because rewards given for succeeding make children feel efficacious—a feeling that is likely to increase rather than undermine their intrinsic motivation.

The implications of this line of research are clear. Extrinsic reinforcers can be used both at home and in the classroom to strengthen or sustain those activities that children will not ordinarily perform on their own. However, parents, teachers, and other social agents must guard against creating unnecessary and uninformative reward systems that are likely to decrease children's interest in activities that they already like and will perform for the fun of it.

The fact that extrinsic rewards can undermine intrinsic interest once again implies that it is the learner, rather than the teacher, who decides what events are the most potent reinforcers for any given activity. At this point, it is tempting to conclude that reinforcers "reinforce" because they are somehow pleasant or pleasurable. However, we are about to see that either pleasurable or aversive events can actually *prevent* new learning if the subject has no control over their appearance or administration. *makes many reinforcers*

controlability satisfying

Learned helplessness and the issue of control

Martin Seligman (1975, 1978) has found that a state of apathy, or **learned helplessness,** may develop

> give information > associate actions cum outcomes > control of own fate.

Premack principle: the finding that less valued (or less probable) activities can be reinforced by providing the subject access to more valued (or more probable) activities.

learned helplessness: the failure to learn how to respond appropriately in a situation because of previous exposures to uncontrollable events in the same or a similar situation.

if subjects perceive little or no connection between their actions and their outcomes. Consider the following example. Seligman and his associates administered severe electrical shocks to a group of dogs that were strapped into harnesses so that they could not escape. The next day, each dog was placed in one side of a two-compartment box and exposed to strong shocks that it could escape by merely jumping over the barrier into the other compartment. Naive dogs that have never experienced the inescapable shocks soon learn this jumping response because it is negatively reinforced (that is, jumping terminates the aversive shock). However, the dogs that had previously experienced uncontrollable shocks never did learn to escape. What these animals did learn from their prior experiences is that there was nothing they could do to control the shocks, so they did nothing. In other words, they had learned to be helpless.

Human infants can also develop these feelings of helplessness, even when the events that they cannot control are initially quite pleasant. In one study (Watson & Ramey, 1972), a group of 8-week-old infants learned to move their heads on a pressure-sensitive pillow, an act that closed an electrical switch in the pillow and caused a brightly colored mobile to rotate. The infants clearly seemed to enjoy this activity, for they smiled and cooed whenever they caused the mobiles to turn. A second group of infants were exposed to the same situation, with one important difference—they had *no* control over their mobiles, which rotated periodically on their own. Infants in this second group were at first fascinated by the rotating mobile but soon became rather apathetic; they now rarely smiled at this object and were no longer interested in watching it turn. Later the investigators exposed all their young subjects to mobiles that they could control by moving their heads. Children who had previously learned to control the mobiles were soon turning their heads and exercising control once again. However, the infants who had not been able to control the mobiles in the earlier session made *no* further attempts to exercise control—even though they now had an opportunity to do so. Apparently these children had learned that they were powerless to influence their environment, so they gave up and simply accepted their "learned helplessness."

Learning about the controllability of events is unquestionably an important aspect of human development. During the first year, most infants will discover that they can exercise some control over their caregivers by crying, cooing, or emitting other bids for attention that are likely to be reinforced with a smile, a hug, or other forms of social stimulation. Moreover, young infants tend to be wary of objects, people, or situations that they cannot control (Gunnar, 1980; Levitt, 1980), and they may stop trying to initiate social interactions with an aloof companion (Seligman, 1975). Indeed, we will see in Chapter 11 that socially responsive children gradually become rather apathetic, depressed, and uninterested in human contact if they are raised in understaffed institutions where their social gestures rarely elicit reactions from anyone. It is almost as if they felt powerless to control the behavior of their caregivers, so that they simply stopped trying and became unresponsive to other people in much the same way that Watson and Ramey's "helpless" infants ceased responding to a rotating mobile that they had previously enjoyed.

In sum, the learned-helplessness research suggests that some reinforcers may "reinforce" not because they are inherently pleasant but, rather, because they provide *information* that allows the learner to associate actions with outcomes and thereby *control* his or her own fate. In fact, this sense of control over the environment (or at least the illusion of control) may ultimately prove to be the quality that makes many reinforcers "satisfying." Surely that was true of the rotating mobile in Watson and Ramey's (1972) experiment: what the infants liked about the mobile was not that it moved but that *they could make it move.*

Punishment: The Aversive Control of Behavior

Earlier in the chapter, we defined *punishment* as an aversive event or experience that is administered in order to suppress an undesirable response. Although parents generally do not like to harm their children or see them unhappy, they will at least occasionally resort to punishment as a means of inhibiting a child's unacceptable behavior (Hoffman, 1985; Sears, Maccoby, & Levin, 1957). And there is a case to be made for its use, particularly if the prohibited act is something dangerous like playing with matches or probing electrical sockets with metallic objects. Yet, many theorists believe that punishment is a two-edged sword that may prove counterproductive and even harmful in the long run.

Operant theorists are among the strongest critics of aversive control. They believe that punishment merely suppresses an undesirable response without teaching anything new. Moreover, they argue that punishment may engender anger, hostility, or resentment and, at best, a *temporary* suppression of the behavior it is designed to eliminate. Their point is that a fear of aversive consequences can never be a totally effective deterrent, because the potential transgressor will simply inhibit unacceptable conduct until it is unlikely to be detected and punished.

In spite of these criticisms, recent research indicates that punishment, properly applied, can be an effective method of controlling undesirable behavior. In this section we will first consider how and under what circumstances punishment is likely to work. Then we will look at some of the problems that may arise from an injudicious use of punitive tactics.

How does punishment suppress a response?

There are at least two very general theories of how the administration of punishment might persuade children to suppress undesirable responses. The first, the *conditioning* viewpoint, is based on principles of classical and operant conditioning. The second, the *social information-processing* approach, is a more recent theory—one arguing that the child's *interpretation* of punitive events (and their consequences) is what determines whether he or she is likely to inhibit a punished act.

(**The conditioning viewpoint.**) Conditioning theorists have assumed that when adults punish transgressions, the aversive consequences that the child experiences will often produce some fear or anxiety. And since many transgressions are committed, detected, and punished on several occasions, it is likely that the fear or anxiety resulting from the punishment will become classically conditioned to the punished act, as shown in Figure 7-3. Once this conditioning occurs, the child should then resist the temptation to commit the punished act in order to avoid the unpleasant consequences (conditioned fear or anxiety) now associated with its performance (Aronfreed, 1976; Parke, 1972). So conditioning theorists view punitive suppression as nothing more than a conditioned avoidance response.

(**The social information-processing viewpoint.**) Social information-processing theorists agree that punishment makes children anxious or emotionally aroused. However, they believe that it is not the amount of anxiety or apprehension that the child experiences that determines whether she will inhibit a punished act— rather, the most critical determinant of future conduct is the child's *interpretation* of the uneasiness she is experiencing. If the child interprets her arousal as a fear

Step 1: Preconditioning

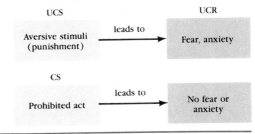

Step 2: Conditioning of fear to the prohibited act

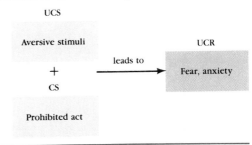

Step 3: Postconditioning and instrumental avoidance

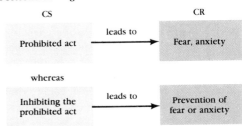

Figure 7-3. A model of the suppressive effects of punishment.

of the punitive agent or a fear of getting caught, she might well inhibit the punished act in the presence of authority figures but feel quite free to perform it when there is no one around to detect and punish these antics. By contrast, children who interpret their uneasiness as a sense of shame or guilt should now be internally motivated to avoid these dreaded emotions by inhibiting the punished act, even when there is no one else present to detect such wrongful behavior. So what the information-processing theorists are saying is that fear of detection and punishment is not enough. In order to be successful at persuading children to stop performing undesirable acts, punishment must be structured so as to inform them why these behaviors are wrong and/or why *they* should feel bad were they to perform them (Hoffman, 1985).

Which of these theories is correct? It turns out that each of them has something to offer, as we will see in the pages that follow.

When does punishment suppress a response?

Not all punishments are equally effective at suppressing or eliminating unacceptable behavior. Among the factors that influence the effectiveness of punishment are its timing, intensity, consistency, and underlying rationale, as well as the relationship between the child and the punitive agent.

Timing of punishment. Punishment is much more effective when administered "early," as the child prepares to commit the prohibited act, rather than "later," after the harm has been done (Aronfreed, 1968; Parke, 1977). In fact, the practice of delaying punishment for several hours until "Daddy comes home" is risky at best, for Justin Aronfreed (1968) found that the longer punishment is delayed, the less likely it is to prevent recurrences of the prohibited act.

Conditioning theorists can easily explain why early or immediate punishments are more effective than those administered later. If children are punished as they initiate deviant acts, the anxiety associated with punishment is conditioned to their *preparatory* or *initiating* responses. As a result, they should experience anxiety when they prepare to commit the forbidden act and should inhibit the act in order to avoid this anxiety. By contrast, punishment that occurs after the transgression is completed has the effect of conditioning anxiety to the *end* of the deviant act. So children who are punished later may experience no ill feelings as they initiate future transgressions, although they may feel bad (or anxious about being caught) after the deed is done. In addition, transgressors who are punished later may have already experienced some pleasure from performing the prohibited act, and these pleasurable effects may partly offset the aversive aspects of punishment.

Intensity of punishment. Parents often assume that their child will "have something to think about" if they punish his or her transgressions forcefully. One implication of this point of view is that mild punishment will not generate enough anxiety to convince the child that forbidden acts should be inhibited. Laboratory research with young children reveals that milder forms of punishment are generally less effective than stronger measures at inhibiting unac-

ceptable behavior (see Parke, 1977). However, we must take care not to draw inappropriate conclusions from the results of these experiments. Although the "intense" punishments (loud buzzers or noises) used in this research were certainly discomforting, they are probably a whole lot less aversive than a spanking, a week's restriction to one's room, or a parent's withdrawal of affection. There is evidence that young children tend to avoid highly punitive adults (Redd, Morris, & Martin, 1975), a finding that suggests that parents who punish their child too forcefully may produce an aloof son or daughter who is not often available to receive their instructions and guidance. And if the prohibition to be learned is difficult or subtle, the high levels of anxiety created by intense punishment may simply teach children to fear the punitive agent rather than to avoid the prohibited act.

In sum, it appears that the effectiveness of punishment increases as its intensity increases, as long as the punitive consequences are not so intense that they interfere with effective learning or are perceived by the child as "cruel and unusual."

Consistency of punishment. What will happen if an adult sometimes punishes and at other times ignores unacceptable conduct or if two parents disagree about whether a particular type of behavior warrants punishment? Laboratory research designed to answer these questions paints a clear picture: acts that are punished in an erratic or irregular fashion tend to persist for long periods and are hard to eliminate, even after the disciplinary agent begins to punish them on a regular basis (Deur & Parke, 1970; Parke, 1977).

Learning theorists can easily explain these findings. Since a prohibited act may be satisfying to the child, he or she should experience predominantly positive consequences on occasions when the act is *not* punished. In other words, inconsistent punishment may result in the "partial reinforcement" of unacceptable behavior, which will strengthen these responses and make them extremely resistant to the later use of punitive controls. So if parents or teachers decide to use punishment as a means of suppressing an undesirable response, they would be well advised to punish the misbehavior on a regular basis from the day that it first occurs.

Warmth of the punitive agent. The effectiveness of punishment also depends on the relationship between the child and the punitive agent. Punishment delivered by a person who has previously established a warm and affectionate relationship with the child is much more likely to suppress undesirable conduct than the same punishment administered by a cold or impersonal agent (Parke, 1969; Sears et al., 1957). Children who are punished by a warm, caring person may perceive the adult's act as a loss of affection and will inhibit the punished act as a means of regaining approval. However, those who are punished by a cold or rejecting adult should not be highly motivated to inhibit forbidden acts, because they have no expectation of reestablishing a warm relationship with this cool or aloof disciplinarian.

Effects of verbal rationales. It may have occurred to you that parents often give their children a rationale for the punishments they administer. Could it be that punishment becomes more effective when accompanied by an explanation that specifies why the punished act was wrong?

Both field and laboratory research suggests that this is indeed the case. Sears et al. (1957) found that mothers who combined physical punishment with the use of reasoning reported more success with punitive controls than did mothers who used punishment alone. Ross Parke (1969, 1977) reports similar findings from laboratory research and adds that factors such as the timing and intensity of punishment and the relationship between the child and the punitive agent are less important when a rationale accompanies punishment.

Why do rationales increase the effectiveness of punishments, especially mild or delayed punishments that produce little response inhibition in the absence of a rationale? Probably because rationales provide children with *information* specifying why the punished act is wrong and why they should feel guilty or shameful were they to repeat it. Consequently, a child who understands and accepts the rationale can not only avoid further guilt or shame by *refusing* to repeat the transgression but may also feel rather good about this "mature and responsible" conduct.

In sum, punitive episodes provide children with a rich array of information to process, and it is the child's *interpretation* of this input, rather than the sheer amount of anxiety he experiences, that determines the effectiveness of punitive controls. Ross Parke, an expert on punitive suppression and former proponent of the conditioning viewpoint, now stresses the *informational* value of punishment. He argues that the establishment of true *self*-restraint and long-term inhibitory controls "may re-

Photo 7-2. A child who understands why a punished act is wrong is less likely to repeat the transgression.

quire the use of cognitively-oriented training procedures. Punishment techniques that rely solely on anxiety induction, such as the noxious noises employed . . . in many experiments . . . or the more extreme forms of physical punishment sometimes used by parents may be effective mainly in securing only short-term inhibition" (1972, p. 274).

One final point: long, elaborate rationales may tax the information-processing skills of very young children and prove rather ineffective. Parke (1977) finds that brief, concrete justifications (for example, "Don't touch that toy; it's fragile and may break") will work best

information → self restraint
interpretation = effectiveness
(guilt + shame)

with 3–4-year-olds. By contrast, older children react much more positively to longer rationales, especially those that justify response inhibition in terms of the negative impact a transgression would have on other people (for example, "I will be sad if you touch the toy; you'll make me unhappy if you look at it now") (Kuczynski, 1983; Toner & Potts, 1981).

Some possible side effects of punishment

Those who have criticized the use of aversive controls are correct in arguing that punishment, when improperly applied, may produce undesirable side effects that limit its usefulness. For example, we have already seen that children may resent and will generally avoid punitive adults and that the anxiety generated by severe punishments may prevent the child from learning the lesson that the discipline was designed to teach. In addition, the children of highly punitive parents tend to be quite aggressive and difficult to control when away from the home setting in which punishment normally occurs (Eron, Walder, Huesmann, & Lefkowitz, 1974; Sears et al., 1957). Albert Bandura (1977) explains this finding by noting that punitive adults, particularly those who rely on physical punishment, are serving as aggressive models for their children. A boy who learns that he will be hit when he displeases his parents will probably direct the same kind of response toward classmates who displease him.

Administration of aversive stimuli such as a slap or a spanking may also *reinforce the punitive agent* and become habitual if this form of discipline is immediately effective at suppressing the child's undesirable behavior (Powers & Osborne, 1976). This is indeed unfortunate, for the regular use of physical punishment is often the first step along the road to child abuse (Parke & Collmer, 1975). In fact, child abuse may be a very real possibility if physical punishment is routinely administered to children who *misbehave as a means of attracting attention:* for a neglected or emotionally deprived youngster, the attention that accompanies punishment may be preferable to no attention at all.

Removing positive stimuli: The "other side" of punishment

Some of the potentially harmful effects of punishment are less likely to occur if adults choose to punish transgressions by withholding something desirable rather than administering aversive stimuli. One such punishment is the **response-cost technique,** in which

the disciplinary agent removes a tangible reinforcer that the child already has (for example, candy) or would ordinarily receive in the future (a movie next Saturday). Another alternative is the **time-out technique** (that is, time out from the opportunity to receive positive reinforcement), in which the adult "punishes" by disrupting or preventing a prohibited activity that the child seems to enjoy (for example, sending a bossy, argumentative child to her room). Although both these techniques may generate some resentment, the punitive agent is not physically abusing the child, is not serving as an aggressive model, and is not likely to unwittingly reinforce the child who misbehaves as a means of attracting attention—particularly if the time-out procedure is used.

Alternatives to punishment

Punishment is only one of many techniques that adults can use to inhibit or eliminate undesirable behavior. One successful alternative to punishment is the **incompatible-response technique,** in which the adult in charge ignores undesirable behavior—for ex-

Photo 7-3. Improperly applied, punishment can have many undesirable side effects, including an increase in the child's aggressiveness.

ample, selfish acts—and provides lavish praise or more tangible reinforcers for responses such as sharing and cooperating that are incompatible with the conduct he or she is trying to eliminate. Another proven approach is the **self-instructional technique,** in which children are told why certain acts are wrong and then taught to verbalize these rationales when they feel the urge to deviate. Both these viable alternatives to punishment have an important advantage: they produce few if any of the undesirable side effects that often accompany the use of punitive tactics. Of course, there is a time and a place for punishment: adults may occasionally have to resort to forceful or punitive strategies in order to command the attention of an unruly child. Yet, parents and teachers who try these two alternative approaches may find that they rarely have to rely on punishment in order to control children's behavior.

Observational Learning *albert Bandura*

In recent years a number of prominent developmentalists have argued that much of what we learn is acquired by observation. **Observational learning** is a relatively simple process in which the child acquires new habits by (1) observing the behavior of others (social models), (2) making mental notes of what he or she has witnessed, and (3) imitating these actions in situations where the new behaviors seem appropriate.

Albert Bandura is an important spokesman among observational-learning theorists—one who believes that the vast majority of the habits we acquire during our lifetimes are learned by observing and imitating other people. According to Bandura (1977, 1986), there are several reasons that observational learning plays such a prominent role in human development. First, learning by observation is much more efficient than the trial-and-error method. When observers can learn by watching a model perform flawlessly, they are spared the needless errors that might result from attempts to perfect the same skills and abilities on their own. Second, many complex behaviors could probably never be learned unless children were exposed to people who modeled them. Take language, for example. It seems rather implausible that parents could ever shape their child's babbles into words, not to mention grammatical speech, merely by rewarding and punishing these random vocalizations. (Indeed, we will see in Chapter 8 that parents do not often reinforce a child's speech, and when they do, they are more likely to reward its

truth value, or factual correctness, rather than its grammatical properties.) Yet, children who lack some bit of grammatical knowledge will soon alter their sentence constructions after hearing this rule of grammar reflected in the speech of a companion (Bandura & Harris, 1966; Zimmerman, 1977). Finally, observational learning permits the young child to acquire many new responses in a large number of settings where her "models" are simply pursuing their own interests and are not trying to teach her anything in particular. Of course, some of the behaviors that young children observe and may try to imitate are actions that adults display but would like to discourage—practices such as swearing, eating between meals, and smoking. Bandura's point is that children are continually learning both desirable and undesirable responses by "keeping their eyes (and ears) open," and he is not at all surprised that human development proceeds so very rapidly along so many different paths.

How Do We "Learn" by Observation?

In 1965 Bandura made what was then considered a radical statement: children can learn by merely observing the behavior of a social model, *even though they have never attempted the responses that they have witnessed or received any reinforcement for performing them.* Note the implications here: Bandura is proposing a type of "no trial" learning in which the learned response is neither elicited by a conditioned stimulus nor strengthened by a reinforcer. Impossible, said many learning theorists, for Bandura's proposition seems to ignore important principles of both classical and instrumental conditioning.

---

response-cost technique: a form of punishment in which the punitive agent removes or withholds a valuable commodity from the transgressor. *better forms of punishment*

time-out technique: a strategy in which the disciplinary agent "punishes" a child by disrupting or preventing the prohibited activity that the child seems to enjoy.

incompatible-response technique: a nonpunitive method of behavior modification in which adults ignore undesirable conduct while reinforcing acts that are incompatible with these responses. *alternatives to punishment*

self-instructional technique: a nonpunitive method of self-control in which children learn to verbalize the rationale for inhibiting an act whenever they feel the urge to perform it.

observational learning: learning that results from observing the behavior of others.

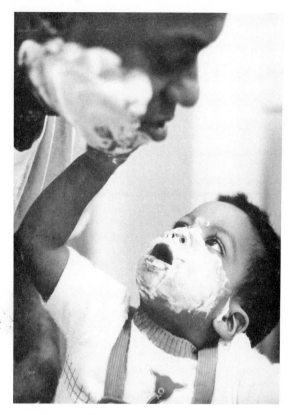

Photo 7-4. Children acquire a variety of responses through observational learning.

An example of "no trial" learning without reinforcement

But Bandura was right, although he had to conduct what is now considered a classic experiment to prove his point (Bandura, 1965). At the beginning of this experiment, nursery school children were taken one at a time to a semidarkened room to watch a short film. As they watched, they saw an adult model direct an unusual sequence of aggressive responses toward an inflatable Bobo doll, hitting the doll with a mallet while shouting "Sockeroo," throwing rubber balls at the doll while shouting "Bang, bang, bang," and so on. There were three experimental conditions. Children in the *model rewarded* condition saw the film end as a second adult appeared and gave the aggressive model some candy and a soft drink for a "championship performance." Children assigned to the *model punished* condition saw an ending in which a second adult scolded

and spanked the model for beating up on Bobo. Finally, children in the *no consequences* condition simply watched the model beat up on Bobo without receiving any reward or punishment.

When the film ended, each child was left alone in a playroom that contained a Bobo doll and many of the props that the model had used to work Bobo over. Hidden observers then watched the child, recording all instances in which he or she imitated one or more of the model's aggressive acts. These observations would reveal how willing the children were to *perform* the responses they had seen the model display. The results of this "performance" test appear on the left-hand (lighter) side of Figure 7-4. Here we see that children in the model-rewarded and the no-consequences conditions imitated more of the model's aggressive acts than children who had seen the model punished for aggressive behavior. At the very least, these results indicate that subjects in the first two conditions had learned some rather novel aggressive responses without being reinforced and without having had a previous opportunity to perform them. This looks very much like the kind of no-trial observational learning that Bandura had proposed.

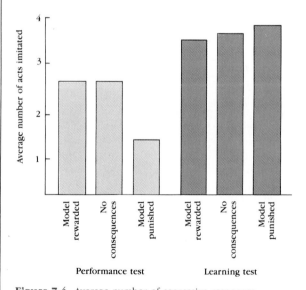

Figure 7-4. Average number of aggressive responses imitated during the performance test and the learning test for children who had seen a model rewarded, punished, or receiving no consequences for his actions. *(Adapted from Bandura, 1965.)*

The learning/performance distinction

But one question remained: Had the children in the model-rewarded and the no-consequences conditions actually *learned more* from observing the model than children who had seen the model punished? To find out, Bandura devised a second test in which he persuaded children to show just how much they had learned. Each child was offered some juice and trinkets for reproducing all of the model's behaviors that he or she could recall. The results of this "learning" test, which appear in the right-hand (darker) portion of Figure 7-4, clearly indicate that children in each of the three conditions learned about the same amount by observing the model. Apparently children in the model-punished condition had imitated fewer of the model's responses on the initial "performance" test because they felt that they too might be punished for striking Bobo. But offer them a reward, and they show that they have learned much more than their initial performances implied.

In sum, it is important to distinguish between what children *learn* by observation and their willingness to *perform* these responses. Bandura's (1965) experiment shows that reinforcement is not necessary for observational learning. What reinforcement does is to increase the likelihood that the child will perform that which he or she has already learned by observing the model's behavior.

What do children acquire in observational learning?

In many cases, young children will not imitate a model's behavior for hours, days, or even weeks after observing it. For example, a boy who wants to "shave" himself after watching his father shave will have to wait until a time when he can be alone for a while, for few parents permit their youngsters to experiment with razors. What are children acquiring that enables them to reproduce the behavior of an absent model at some point in the future—often the distant future?

According to Bandura (1977), a child who carefully observes a model will acquire **symbolic representations** of the model's behavior, which are stored in memory and retrieved at a later date to guide his or her own attempts to imitate. These symbolic representations may be *images* of the model's actions or *verbal labels* that describe these responses in an economical way. Verbal representation is particularly important, for it enables the observer to retain information that would

be difficult or impossible to remember by any other method. Imagine how hard it would be to open a combination safe if you simply formed images of the model turning the dials and did not translate these actions into a verbal label such as "L49, R37, L18"!

Apparently, symbolic coding activities do facilitate observational learning. Bandura and his associates (Bandura, Grusec, & Menlove, 1966) found that 6–8-year-olds who were told to count out loud while watching a model later reproduced *fewer* of the model's actions than age mates whose symbolic activities were not "disrupted" by counting. In addition, Brian Coates and Willard Hartup (1969) found that 4–5-year-olds who had been explicitly instructed to describe what they were observing were able to reproduce about twice as many of the model's responses as age mates who had not been instructed to describe the model's behavior.

Attentional processes: Choosing a model

Virtually all children are exposed to a large number of social models, including parents, teachers, siblings, peers, Scout leaders, and media heroes. However, Bandura (1977) notes that (1) the child must attend carefully to any model to learn by observation and (2) some models are more worthy of attention than others.

Whom are young children likely to select as social models? According to Bandura (1977), the most likely candidates are people who are warm and nurturant (socially responsive) and/or appear competent or powerful. Indeed, Joan Grusec and Rona Abramovitch (1982) found that nursery school children will often attend to and imitate their teachers (powerful, competent models) and those classmates who are typically warm, friendly, and responsive to them. Moreover, 5–8-year-olds prefer to imitate age mates or older children rather than a younger peer because they believe that a younger child is less competent than they are (see French, 1984; Graziano, Musser, & Brody, 1982).

Attainment of certain developmental milestones will also affect the child's choice of models. For example, once children are fully aware of their gender and know that it will never change (at about age 5–7), they will pay much more attention to models of their

_____ *stored in memory*

symbolic representations: the images and verbal labels that observers produce in order to retain the important aspects of a model's behavior.

Photo 7-5. Older children tend to select models of their own sex.

own sex (Ruble, Balaban, & Cooper, 1981). And as people mature, they develop certain interests, attitudes, and values and will normally prefer models who are in some way *similar* to themselves—friends or people in the same occupation, ethnic group, political party, and so on. But even though our choice of models may become somewhat more restricted over time, we will continue to learn by observing others for the rest of our lives.

Developmental Trends in Imitation and Observational Learning

Bandura's theory of observational learning assumes that an observer can construct images or other symbolic representations of a model's behavior and then use these mediators to reproduce what he or she has witnessed. When do these abilities first emerge?

Origins of imitation and imitative learning. Can newborns imitate? Apparently babies less than 7 days old are able to mimic certain facial expressions, such as surprise or sadness, as well as a few very simple motor responses, such as opening and closing their hands or sticking out their tongues (Field, Woodson, Greenberg, & Cohen, 1982; Meltzoff & Moore, 1983; Vinter, 1986). Yet, these kinds of imitative responses are much harder to elicit from a 1-month-old infant and are no longer observed among 10-week-old infants (Abravanel & Sigafoos, 1984). So the limited ca-

pacity for mimicry that newborns display may be a largely involuntary, subcortical reflex that disappears with age, only to be replaced later by voluntary imitative responses (Vinter, 1986).

Voluntary imitation of novel responses emerges and becomes much more reliable between 8 and 12 months of age (Kaye & Marcus, 1981; Piaget, 1951). Initially, the model must be present and must continue to perform a response before the child is able to imitate. But by age 12 months, about 1 infant in 10 can imitate a very simple act (such as placing a hat on a clown's head) ten minutes after seeing the model perform it (Abravanel & Gingold, 1985). This **deferred imitation**—the ability to reproduce the actions of a model at some point in the future—develops rapidly during the second year. By age 18 months, almost all infants can imitate simple acts after a ten-minute delay, and many are even showing delayed reenactments of complex responses (for example, taking a toy apart) as well (Abravanel & Gingold, 1985). And by age 20–24 months, infants have become rather proficient at reproducing modeled sequences they had observed a whole day or more earlier (Piaget, 1951).

Clearly, deferred imitation is an important developmental milestone—one indicating that children are not only constructing symbolic representations of their experiences but can also retrieve this information from memory to guide their reproduction of past events. So

18- to 24-month-old infants should now be prepared to learn a great deal by observing the behavior of their companions. But do they take advantage of this newly acquired ability?

Yes, indeed! Leon Kuczynski and his associates (Kuczynski, Zahn-Waxler, & Radke-Yarrow, 1987) recently asked mothers to record the immediate and the delayed reactions of their 16- and 29-month-old infants and toddlers to the behavior of parental and peer models in the home setting. The results were quite interesting. All the children imitated their models a fair percentage of the time, but there were age differences in the content of these imitations. Sixteen-month-olds tended to imitate affective displays, such as laughing and cheering, as well as other high-intensity antics such as jumping, shaking the head to and fro, and pounding on the table. By contrast, older infants and toddlers more often imitated *instrumental* behaviors, such as household tasks and self-care routines, and their imitations had more of a self-instructional quality to them, as if the older children were now making an active attempt (1) to acquire skills their models had displayed or (2) to understand the events they had witnessed. When imitating disciplinary encounters, for example, younger infants simply repeated verbal prohibitions and physical actions such as hand slapping, usually directing these responses to themselves. However, older infants and toddlers tended to reenact the entire scenario, including the social influence strategies the disciplinarian had used, and they usually directed these responses to another person, an animal, or a doll. So not only are older infants and toddlers making use of their imitative capabilities, but it appears that observational learning is already an important means by which they acquire basic social and instrumental competencies and gain a richer understanding of the routines and regulations that they are expected to follow.

Use of verbal mediators to represent experience. Although preschool children are rapidly acquiring language and becoming accomplished conversationalists, they are less likely than older children to rely on verbal labels as a means of representing their experiences. In the study by Coates and Hartup (1969) mentioned earlier, 4–5-year-olds and 7–8-year-olds watched a short film in which an adult model displayed a number of unusual responses, such as shooting at a tower of blocks with a pop gun and throwing a beanbag between his legs. Some of the children from each age group were told to describe the model's actions as they

observed them (induced-coding condition); others simply watched the model without having received any instructions (passive-observation condition). As we saw, the 4–5-year-olds who described what they were observing were later able to reproduce much more of the model's behavior than their counterparts in the passive-observation condition. By contrast, 7–8-year-olds reproduced the same number of the model's responses whether or not they had been told to describe what the model was doing. This latter finding suggests that 7–8-year-olds will use verbal labels to describe what they have seen, even if they are not told to. One important implication of this study is that preschool children may learn less from social models because they, unlike older children, do not spontaneously produce the verbal mediators that would help them retain what they have observed.

Television as a Modeling Influence

It has been estimated that the average American child between the ages of 2 and 11 watches 3½–4 hours of television a day (Nielsen Television Index, 1981). Given this heavy exposure to television programming, it would be surprising if media models did not influence children's thinking and behavior.

Age differences in children's reactions to television

The extent to which children will process and retain televised information depends on a number of factors, including the child's age, the content and comprehensibility of the programming, and the presence of distractors such as toys, games, and other people. Robert McCall and his associates (McCall, Parke, & Kavanaugh, 1977) found that infants and toddlers become increasingly responsive to televised models between the ages of 18 months and 3 years. Eighteen-month-olds spend a far greater percentage of their time watching live models than TV models, and they are more likely to imitate the live model during a free-play session. By contrast, 3-year-olds attend equally to live and to televised models, and they are just as likely to imitate a TV model as a live one. Nevertheless, 3- and 4-year-olds spend a smaller portion of their "TV time" actually watching the programming than older children do,

retrieval of symbolic representation

deferred imitation: the ability to reproduce a modeled sequence that has been witnessed at some point in the past.

probably because these younger children may often fail to comprehend what they are watching (Anderson & Lorch, 1983) and are easily distracted by toys, pets, or the actions of other people (Anderson, Lorch, Field, Collins, & Nathan, 1986).

What do children attend to and remember from their exposure to television? Apparently, preschoolers pay more attention to the visual than to the auditory components of television programming (Hayes, Chemelski, & Birnbaum, 1981), particularly the perceptually salient features such as fast-paced action sequences, special effects, zooms, and segments in which there are rapid changes in the scenery or the number of characters (Anderson, Lorch, Field, & Sanders, 1981). By contrast, aspects of programming that are subtle (information about a character's motives or intentions) or difficult to comprehend (adult narrations) are less likely to be noticed, understood, or retained (Calvert, Huston, Watkins, & Wright, 1982; Collins, Wellman, Keniston, & Westby, 1978).

During the elementary school years, children become less interested in the "captivating" visual effects of television programming and will attend more to features that provide information about the plot or the characters' motives and intentions. Compared with preschool children, who are apt to recall what actors have done, grade school children are much more proficient at determining the reasons these actions were undertaken and the consequences they produce (Collins et al., 1978).

What might children learn from television?

Presumably children might learn any number of new attitudes, values, and behaviors from TV if they pay close attention and construct symbolic representations of the actions they have witnessed. In recent years, child developmentalists and the public at large have become very concerned about one source of media influence in particular: the potentially negative impact of televised violence on children's interpersonal behavior.

Does televised violence affect children's behavior? Children who grow up in the United States, Canada, and other Western nations can observe violent, aggressive episodes almost any time they care to by simply turning on their TV sets. In the United States, nearly 80% of prime-time programming contains at least one violent incident, with an average rate of about 7.5 incidents per hour. In fact, the most violent TV programs are those designed for children—especially Saturday morning cartoons, which contain nearly 25 violent incidents per hour (Gerbner, Gross, Morgan, & Signorielli, 1980). And despite many popular claims to the contrary, violence rates on commercial television have remained remarkably stable since the 1960s and are *not* declining (Parke & Slaby, 1983)

Even though some people have argued that the comical violence portrayed in children's television programming is unlikely to affect the behavior of viewers, both anecdotal and research evidence suggests otherwise. Robert Liebert and his associates (Liebert, Sprafkin, & Davidson, 1982) provide several dramatic illustrations of how children have behaved in a violent or aggressive fashion after watching similar actions on television. Here is one example:

> In Los Angeles, a housemaid caught a 7-year-old boy in the act of sprinkling ground glass into the family's lamb stew. There was no malice behind the act. It was purely experimental, having been inspired by curiosity to learn whether it would really work as well as it did on television [Liebert et al., 1982, p. 7].

A number of correlational surveys paint a similar picture: children and adolescents who watch a lot of televised violence at home tend to be more aggressive than their classmates who watch little violence (Belson, 1978; Eron & Huesmann, 1980; Huesmann, 1982; Liebert et al., 1982). And one ten-year longitudinal study of children's aggression (Eron, Huesmann, Lefkowitz, & Walder, 1972) found that boys who preferred highly violent and aggressive programming at age 8 were much more aggressive at age 18 than their classmates who had not preferred to watch violent shows (see Eron, 1982, for a similar finding for girls). So it appears that heavy exposure to televised violence during early and middle childhood may promote the development of aggressive habits and dispositions that persist over time. Indeed, Eron et al. (1972) reported that children's preferences for violent programming at age 8 predicted aggression at age 18 better than any other factor they studied, including intelligence, social class, ethnicity, and parents' child-rearing practices.

We will return to the complex and controversial topic of televised violence when we take a closer look at media effects in Chapter 16. At this point, let's simply note that the televised portrayal of aggression is one potentially important influence on children's interpersonal behavior.

Positive contributions of television. Although our brief introduction to media influences has centered on a negative implication of children's exposure to television, it is important to note that this medium can have some very beneficial effects as well. For example, educational programming such as *Sesame Street* can transmit valuable information to preschool children and further their intellectual development (Ball & Bogatz, 1972). Children who often watch shows that stress positive values such as sharing, cooperating, and helping others (for example, *Fat Albert and the Cosby Kids; Mister Rogers' Neighborhood*) are likely to become more considerate, cooperative, and helpful toward their siblings and peers, particularly when adults encourage them to think about and enact the prosocial lessons they have seen on TV (Friedrich & Stein, 1975; Friedrich-Cofer, Huston-Stein, Kipnis, Susman, & Clewett, 1979). Finally, the study described in Box 7-4 illustrates how televised information can be an invaluable aid in treating childhood fears and phobias.

We have seen that children can learn many new responses from both live and televised models by merely attending to a model's behavior and retaining mental representations of what they have witnessed. Since observational learning requires neither formal instruction nor reinforcement, it probably occurs daily, even when models are simply pursuing their own interests and are not trying to teach the child anything in particular. Bandura (1977, 1986) reminds us that all developing children will learn from a variety of social models and that no two children are exposed to exactly the same pattern of modeling influences. Therefore, children should never be expected to emerge as carbon copies of their parents, siblings, or the child next door—individual differences are an inevitable consequence of observational learning.

Learning and Development Reconsidered

Many of the changes in behavior that occur as people develop are the result of learning. We learn not to dwell too long on stimuli that are already familiar (habituation). We may come to like, to dislike, or to fear almost anything if our encounters with these objects and events have occurred under pleasant or unpleasant circumstances (classical conditioning). We form habits, some good and some bad, by associating various actions with their reinforcing and punishing consequences (operant conditioning). We acquire new attitudes, values, and patterns of conduct by observing the behaviors and listening to the pronouncements of social models (observational learning). Clearly, learning is an important developmental process. And when we recall that even neonates are capable of learning and will change in response to their experiences, it is easy to see how the behaviorists of yesteryear might champion learning as the most important developmental process—the mechanism by which we become like other human beings and, at the same time, develop our own idiosyncrasies.

Another look at the behaviorist perspective

Having now reviewed basic learning processes, we are ready to take a closer and more critical look at the behaviorist view of human development. Recall that John Watson, the father of behaviorism, believed that neonates are *tabulae rasae* (blank slates) who are passively shaped, like lumps of clay, into purposeful and adaptive beings. Presumably, parents and other adults were the agents responsible for this shaping, and Watson repeatedly urged them to be firm and to take child rearing seriously, for they, as overseers, had the capacity to mold their child into anything they chose—a doctor, lawyer, scholar, and yes, even a bum or a thief—depending on the kinds of examples they set and the opportunities for learning they provided. Radical behaviorists such as B. F. Skinner largely agreed with Watson, arguing that one form of learning in particular—operant conditioning—was the central developmental process. The radical behaviorists were called "radicals" because they stressed that one need not talk about cognitive activities or even acknowledge that the child has a mind to understand operant learning and its contributions to human development. Presumably, new and more adaptive behaviors would evolve and persist because they were reinforced, whereas old and less adaptive habits would eventually wane if they were no longer reinforced or were punished. So, like Watson, Skinner and his disciples portrayed children as rather malleable and mechanical organisms who respond to environmental contingencies in much the same way that a toy robot responds to signals from a remote-control transmitter.

Almost no one today takes this passive, mechanistic theory of human development very seriously, and some of the reasons for this skepticism should be apparent from our review of the literature. Consider first that learning is often (and some would say always)

Box 7-4
Media Models as Therapists

In Box 7-1 we saw how counterconditioning procedures were used to overcome a 2-year-old's fear of furry objects. As it happens, many preschool children develop a fear of a particular class of furry objects—those big old friendly *dogs* that may frighten them by barking a hello, licking their faces, knocking them over, and occasionally nipping playfully at their heels as the children flee in terror. Children who fear dogs tend to have at least one parent who avoids dogs, so perhaps they acquire their dog-phobic reactions by observing the behavior of a fearful adult.

Albert Bandura and Frances Menlove (1968) have devised a treatment for dog phobia that they believe is both more efficient and more effective than counterconditioning. Their plan was to expose dog-phobic children to films in which one or more children react fearlessly to dogs. Presumably the observers would overcome their fears as they watched the films and learned that dogs can be pleasant companions for people like themselves.

Bandura and Menlove piloted their treatment in a nursery school. At the beginning of the project, all the children were asked to perform 14 acts to assess their fear of dogs. Each successive act required the child to initiate increasingly intimate contact with a live pooch. Forty-eight children who showed a strong fear of dogs were selected as participants for the treatment phase of the project.

The dog-phobics were then divided into three groups, each of which was exposed to a different set of films. Those assigned to the *single model* con-dition observed eight three-minute films (two a day for four days) that showed a 5-year-old boy engaging in progressively bolder interactions with a cocker spaniel. The final film showed the model fearlessly entering the dog's pen, where he petted the animal, fed it dog candies, and rested his head on the dog while taking a brief nap. Children assigned to the *multiple model* condition observed similar films, except that their materials showed several boys and girls interacting with a number of dogs ranging in size from very small to quite large. Finally, children in the *control* group did not observe a fearless model; instead, they spent an equal amount of time watching films about Disneyland and Marineland of the Pacific.

On the day after the final film, the children were once again asked to perform the 14 acts that served as a test of their fear of dogs. Bandura and Menlove found that subjects who had been exposed to fearless peer models on film were now much more willing to ap-proach and interact with a live dog than they had been during the original testing (the graph shows their results). In contrast, children in the control group showed absolutely no reduction in their fear of dogs. One month later, the children were tested a third time. This follow-up indicated that the reduced fear of dogs shown by children who had observed fearless peer models remained stable over time. The follow-up produced one other interesting outcome: children in the multiple-model condition were more willing than those who had observed a single model to initiate highly intimate contact with a dog, venturing alone into the dog's pen while feeding the dog from the hand, scratching the dog's stomach, and the like. Evidently several televised models are better than one as a means of eliminating a child's fear of a frightening object or situation.

Source: Adapted from Bandura & Menlove (1968).

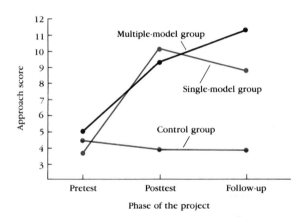

Willingness of dog-phobic children to approach a live dog at different phases of Bandura and Menlove's experiment.

an *active,* rather than a passive, process. Habituation and observational learning, for example, require subjects to actively attend to the environment and to retain what they have experienced to show any evidence of learning. Moreover, human learning is often (and some would say always) a *cognitive* process, rather than a noncog-nitive, reactive one in which responses are "stamped in" or "stamped out" by their reinforcing or punishing consequences. Nowhere is this any more apparent than in Bandura's classic research, for observational learning is clearly a cognitive activity that takes place as the observer attends to and **encodes** the model's behavior.

Reinforcement (or the promise of reinforcement) may make observers more inclined to *perform* responses that they have already acquired through observation, but reinforcement is not necessary for this learning to occur in the first place. Even within the operant-learning paradigm, children seem to treat reinforcers and punitive events as "bits of information" that help them to decide whether or not to perform various acts. Thus, the inhibitory effects of an intended punishment such as a spanking will depend more on children's *cognitive interpretations* of this event than on the amount of uneasiness or discomfort it produces. A child who is punished and who interprets her discomfort as an indication of guilt or shame may well resist the temptation to repeat the punished act—even if authority figures are not present to detect her transgression. But a second child who interprets her uneasiness as a fear of the punitive agent or as a penalty for getting caught is likely to repeat the punished act whenever the likelihood of its detection is remote.

We see, then, that children are hardly the passive pawns of environmental influence described in the earlier behavioral theories of Watson and Skinner. Instead, they are more accurately characterized as active information processors whose *interpretations* of the environment and its contingencies are what determines the impact of these events on their conduct and their eventual development. And if the links between cognition and learning were not already apparent from the examples we have cited, let's recall that infants become more proficient at all kinds of learning over the first year of life as their memories improve and they begin to process information more efficiently.

Where have all the behaviorists gone?

Although contemporary researchers generally agree that one must know how children learn in order to understand human development, very few of them continue to focus exclusively on basic learning processes in their own research. The primary interest of learning researchers today centers on the growth of mental strategies and information-processing skills that enable developing children and adolescents to learn more efficiently, to grasp increasingly complex ideas or concepts, to retain more of what they know or have experienced, and to become more adept at retrieving and using this information to answer questions, solve problems, and achieve other important objectives. In a word, many researchers from the behaviorist tradition gradually became interested in the same kinds of issues that

intrigued the cognitive-developmentalists, who were studying the growth of children's reasoning skills, memory skills, and other mental processes (Brown, Bransford, Ferrara, & Campione, 1983). In Chapter 9 we will explore these interests in some detail as we concentrate on the topic of cognitive development and see how children evolve from largely reflexive organisms at birth, into planful problem solvers who, by early to mid-adolescence, may be rather proficient at gathering and storing information and at using it to think logically about almost any issue or problem they encounter.

Must we assume, then, that infants and toddlers are hopelessly inefficient information processors who are able to learn only the simplest of rules and have little or no appreciation of abstract concepts? If we did, we would be wrong. Consider that even 1–3-year-olds are rapidly acquiring and using one of the most intricate and abstract bodies of knowledge that they will ever assimilate—namely, the rules that enable them to understand and speak a language. Think for a moment about the magnitude of this task. If we hear two foreigners conversing, their speech may seem much too rapid for us to possibly decipher; it's "Greek" to us. And we adults already use at least one language, whereas a nonverbal infant who is listening to her companions is linguistically naive. How, then, do infants and toddlers make sense of this "foreign" input to become amazingly proficient language users by the ripe old age of 4 or 5? This is the issue to which we will turn next as we explore the young child's remarkable capacity for language learning in Chapter 8.

Summary

Learning is a relatively permanent change in behavior that occurs as a result of practice or experience. It is the process by which we acquire new information, attitudes, abilities, and behaviors.

Perhaps the simplest form of learning is habituation—a process in which infants come to recognize and cease responding to stimuli that are presented over and over. Although habituation may be possible even before birth, this early form of learning improves dramatically over the first few months of life.

In classical conditioning, an initially neutral,

---

encoding: a term developmentalists use to refer to the mental representation of one's experiences.

or conditioned, stimulus (for example, a bell) is repeatedly paired with a nonneutral, or unconditioned, stimulus (for example, food) that always elicits an unconditioned response (salivation). After several such pairings, the conditioned stimulus alone will acquire the capacity to evoke what is now called a "conditioned" response (in this case, salivation). Although neonates can be classically conditioned, they process information very slowly and are less susceptible to this kind of learning than older infants are. It is important to understand classical conditioning because many of our fears, attitudes, and prejudices may be acquired in this way.

In operant, or instrumental, conditioning, the subject first emits a response and then associates this action with a particular outcome. Reinforcers are outcomes that increase the probability that a response will be repeated; punishments are outcomes that suppress an act and decrease the likelihood that it will be repeated. Even very young infants are susceptible to operant conditioning and will recall what they have learned for a period of weeks if subtly reminded of the consequences of their actions. Complex responses may be acquired through a process called "shaping" in which a subject is reinforced for emitting successively closer approximations of the desired behavior. Among the factors that determine the strength or effectiveness of operant conditioning are the timing of reinforcement, the scheduling of reinforcement, and the subject's need for (or valuation of) the stimulus offered as a reinforcer.

According to the "Premack principle" of reinforcement, the opportunity to engage in any behavior can reinforce another behavior as long as the first behavior is more probable than the second. However, stimuli offered as incentives may actually inhibit a response that a person would ordinarily perform for its intrinsic satisfaction. These findings indicate that it is the learner, rather than the teacher, who ultimately decides which stimuli are the most potent reinforcers for any given activity.

Punishment, properly applied, can be an effective means of suppressing undesirable conduct. Factors that influence the effectiveness of punishment include its timing, intensity, consistency, and underlying rationale, as well as the relationship between the subject and the punitive agent. When applied improperly, punishment may produce a number of undesirable side effects that limit its usefulness. Reinforcement of incompatible behaviors and use of self-instructional techniques are viable alternatives to punishment that produce few if any side effects.

Much of what children learn is acquired by observing the behavior of social models. This "observational learning" occurs as the child attends to the model and constructs symbolic representations of the model's behavior. These symbolic codes are then stored in memory and may be retrieved at a later date to guide the child's attempts to imitate the behavior he or she has witnessed. Reinforcement is not necessary for observational *learning*. What reinforcement does is to increase the likelihood that children will *perform* that which they have already learned by observing a model.

Voluntary imitation of simple motor acts emerges during the second half of the first year and becomes much more precise between 8 and 12 months of age. During the second year, infants have progressed to the point that they can construct symbolic representations of a modeled sequence and imitate a model who is no longer present (deferred imitation). Having achieved this milestone, they soon begin to imitate their close companions and to re-create earlier events as a means of acquiring new competencies and understanding what they have experienced. Children aged 7–8 eventually begin to use verbal labels to represent and retain what they have observed, and as a result, they may learn more from social models than younger children do.

Between the ages of 18 months and 3 years children become increasingly responsive to models on television and may acquire many new behaviors, some good and some bad, by constructing symbolic representations of the actions they have witnessed. For example, it appears that heavy exposure to TV violence during early and middle childhood may promote the development of aggressive habits or dispositions that persist over time. However, media models may also influence children in positive ways by teaching new cognitive skills, helping young viewers to overcome common fears, and promoting socially desirable behaviors such as cooperation and sharing.

Although learning is clearly an important developmental process, the behaviorists of yesteryear were incorrect in assuming that children are passive pawns of environmental influence. Our review of the literature suggested that learning is an *active* process that often occurs at a *cognitive* level. Indeed, even infants and toddlers are best described as active information processors whose *interpretations* of the environment and its contingencies are what determines the impact of these events on their behavior.

References

ABRAVANEL, E., & Gingold, H. (1985). Learning via observation during the 2nd year of life. *Developmental Psychology, 21,* 614–623.

ABRAVANEL, E., & Sigafoos, A. D. (1984). Exploring the presence of imitation during early infancy. *Child Development, 55,* 381–392.

ANDERSON, D. R., & Lorch, E. P. (1983). Looking at television: Action or reaction? In J. Bryant & D. R. Anderson (Eds.), *Children's understanding of television: Research on attention and comprehension.* Orlando, FL: Academic Press.

ANDERSON, D. R., Lorch, E. P., Field, D. E., Collins, P. A., & Nathan, J. G. (1986). Television viewing at home: Age trends in visual attention and time with TV. *Child Development, 57,* 1024–1033.

ANDERSON, D. R., Lorch, E. P., Field, D. E., & Sanders, J. (1981). The effects of TV program comprehensibility on preschool children's visual attention to television. *Child Development, 52,* 151–157.

ARONFREED, J. (1968). Aversive control of internalization. In W. J. Arnold (Ed.), *Nebraska Symposium on Motivation* (Vol. 6). Lincoln: University of Nebraska Press.

ARONFREED, J. (1976). Moral development from the standpoint of a general psychological theory. In T. Lickona (Ed.), *Moral development and behavior.* New York: Holt, Rinehart and Winston.

BABAD, E. Y. (1972). Person specificity of the "social deprivation-satiation effect." *Developmental Psychology, 6,* 210–213.

BABAD, E. Y. (1973). Effects of informational input on the "social deprivation-satiation effect." *Journal of Personality and Social Psychology, 27,* 1–5.

BALL, S., & Bogatz, J. (1972). Summative research of Sesame Street: Implications for the study of preschool children. In A. D. Pick (Ed.), *Minnesota Symposia on Child Psychology* (Vol. 6). Minneapolis: University of Minnesota Press.

BANDURA, A. (1965). Influence of models' reinforcement contingencies on the acquisition of imitative responses. *Journal of Personality and Social Psychology, 1,* 589–595.

BANDURA, A. (1977). *Social learning theory.* Englewood Cliffs, NJ: Prentice-Hall.

BANDURA, A. (1986). *Social foundations of thought and action: A social cognitive theory.* Englewood Cliffs, NJ: Prentice-Hall.

BANDURA, A., Grusec, J. E., & Menlove, F. L. (1966). Observational learning as a function of symbolization and incentive set. *Child Development, 37,* 499–506.

BANDURA, A., & Harris, M. B. (1966). Modification of syntactic style. *Journal of Experimental Child Psychology, 4,* 341–352.

BANDURA, A., & Menlove, F. L. (1968). Factors determining vicarious extinction of avoidance behavior through symbolic modeling. *Journal of Personality and Social Psychology, 8,* 99–108.

BELSON, W. A. (1978). *Television violence and the adolescent boy.* Westmead, England: Saxon House.

BORNSTEIN, M. H., & Sigman, M. D. (1986). Continuity in mental development from infancy. *Child Development, 57,* 251–274.

BROWN, A. L., Bransford, J. D., Ferrara, R. A., & Campione, J. C. (1983). Learning, remembering, and understanding. In P. H. Mussen (Ed.), *Handbook of child psychology.* Vol. 3: *Cognitive development.* New York: Wiley.

BUTTERFIELD, E. C., & Siperstein, G. N. (1972). Influence of contingent auditory stimulation upon non-nutritional suckle. In J. F. Bosma (Ed.), *Third symposium on oral sensation and perception: The mouth of the infant.* Springfield, IL: Charles C Thomas.

CALVERT, S. L., Huston, A. C., Watkins, B. A., & Wright, J. C. (1982). The relation between selective attention to television forms and children's comprehension of content. *Child Development, 53,* 601–610.

COATES, B., & Hartup, W. W. (1969). Age and verbalization in observational learning. *Developmental Psychology, 1,* 556–562.

COLLINS, W. A., Wellman, H., Keniston, A. H., & Westby, S. D. (1978). Age-related aspects of comprehension and inference from a televised dramatic narrative. *Child Development, 49,* 389–399.

CONDRY, J., & Chambers, J. (1982). Intrinsic motivation and the process of learning. In D. Greene & M. R. Lepper (Eds.), *The hidden costs of rewards.* Hillsdale, NJ: Erlbaum.

DANNER, F. W., & Lonky, E. (1981). A cognitive-developmental approach to the effects of rewards on intrinsic motivation. *Child Development, 52,* 1043–1052.

DAVIS, J. M., & Rovee-Collier, C. K. (1983). Alleviated forgetting of a learned contingency in 8-week-old infants. *Developmental Psychology, 19,* 353–365.

DEUR, J. L., & Parke, R. D. (1970). The effects of inconsistent punishment on aggression in children. *Developmental Psychology, 2,* 403–411.

DOMJAN, M., & Burkhard, B. (1986). *The principles of learning and behavior* (2nd ed.). Pacific Grove, CA: Brooks/Cole.

EARLEY, L., Griesler, P., & Rovee-Collier, C. K. (1985, April). *Ontogenetic changes in retention in early infancy.* Paper presented at the meeting of the Society for Research in Child Development, Toronto.

ERON, L. D. (1982). Parent-child interaction, televised violence, and aggression of children. *American Psychologist, 37,* 197–211.

ERON, L. D., & Huesmann, L. R. (1980). Adolescent aggression and television. *Annals of the New York Academy of Sciences, 347,* 314–331.

ERON, L. D., Huesmann, L. R., Lefkowitz, M. M., & Walder, L. O. (1972). Does television violence cause aggression? *American Psychologist, 27,* 253–263.

ERON, L. D., Walder, L. O., Huesmann, L. R., & Lefkowitz, M. M. (1974). The convergence of laboratory and field studies of the development of aggression. In J. deWit & W. W. Hartup (Eds.), *Determinants and origins of aggressive behavior.* The Hague: Mouton.

FAGAN, J. F. (1984). Infant memory: History, current trends, and relations to cognitive psychology. In M. Moscovitch (Ed.), *Infant memory: Its relation to normal and pathological memory in humans and other animals.* New York: Plenum.

FAGAN, J. F. (1985, April). *Early novelty preferences and later intelligence.* Paper presented at the meeting of the Society for Research in Child Development, Toronto.

FIELD, T. M., Woodson, R., Greenberg, R., & Cohen, D. (1982). Discrimination and imitation of facial expressions by neonates. *Science, 218,* 179–181.

FITZGERALD, H. E., & Brackbill, Y. (1976). Classical conditioning in infancy: Development and constraints. *Psychological Bulletin, 83,* 353–376.

FRENCH, D. C. (1984). Children's knowledge of the social functions of younger, older, and same-age peers. *Child Development, 55,* 1428–1433.

FRIEDRICH, L. K., & Stein, A. H. (1975). Prosocial television and young children: The effects of verbal labeling and role-playing on learning and behavior. *Child Development, 46,* 27–38.

FRIEDRICH-COFER, L. K., Huston-Stein, A., Kipnis, D. M., Susman, E. J., & Clewett, A. S. (1979). Environmental enhancement of prosocial television content: Effects on interpersonal behavior, imaginative play, and self-regulation in a natural setting. *Developmental Psychology, 15,* 637–646.

GERBNER, G., Gross, L., Morgan, M., & Signorielli, N. (1980). The "mainstreaming" of America: Violence profile no. 11. *Journal of Communication, 30,* 10–29.

GRAZIANO, W. G., Musser, L. M., & Brody, G. H. (1982). *Children's cognitions and preferences regarding younger and older peers.* Unpublished manuscript, University of Georgia.

GRUSEC, J. E., & Abramovitch, R. (1982). Imitation of peers and adults in a natural setting: A functional analysis. *Child Development, 53,* 636–642.

GUNNAR, M. R. (1980). Control, warning signals, and distress in infancy. *Developmental Psychology, 16,* 281–289.

HANSEN, G. D. (1979). Enuresis control through fading, escape, and avoidance training. *Journal of Applied Behavior Analysis, 12,* 303–307.

HAYES, D. S., Chemelski, B. E., & Birnbaum, D. W. (1981). Young children's incidental and intentional retention of televised events. *Developmental Psychology, 17,* 230–232.

HOFFMAN, M. L. (1985). Moral development. In M. H. Bornstein & M. E. Lamb (Eds.), *Developmental psychology: An advanced textbook.* Hillsdale, N J: Erlbaum.

HOMME, L. E., deBaca, P. C., Devine, J. V., Steinhorst, R., & Rickert, E. J. (1963). Use of the Premack principle in controlling the behavior of nursery school children. *Journal of the Experimental Analysis of Behavior, 6,* 544.

HUESMANN, L. R. (1982). Television violence and aggressive behavior. In D. Pearl, L. Bouthilet, & J. Lazer (Eds.), *Television and behavior: Ten years of scientific progress and implications for the eighties* (Vol. 2). Washington, DC: U.S. Government Printing Office.

JONES, M. C. (1924). A laboratory study of fear: The case of Peter. *Pedagogical Seminary, 31,* 308–315.

KAYE, K., & Marcus, J. (1981). Infant imitation: The sensorimotor agenda. *Developmental Psychology, 17,* 258–265.

KUCZYNSKI, L. (1983). Reasoning, prohibitions, and motivations for compliance. *Developmental Psychology, 19,* 126–134.

KUCZYNSKI, L., Zahn-Waxler, C., & Radke-Yarrow, M. (1987). Development and content of imitation in the second and third years of life: A socialization perspective. *Developmental Psychology, 23,* 276–282.

LEPPER, M. R. (1983). Social control processes and the internalization of social values. In E. T. Higgins, D. N. Ruble, & W. W. Hartup (Eds.), *Social cognition and social behavior: A developmental perspective.* San Francisco: Jossey-Bass.

LEPPER, M. R., Greene, D., & Nisbett, R. E. (1973). Undermining children's intrinsic interest with extrinsic reward: A test of the overjustification hypothesis. *Journal of Personality and Social Psychology, 28,* 129–137.

LEVITT, M. J. (1980). Contingent feedback, familiarization, and infant affect: How a stranger becomes a friend. *Developmental Psychology, 16,* 425–432.

LIEBERT, R. M., Sprafkin, J. N., & Davidson, E. S. (1982). *The early window: Effects of television on children and youth* (2nd ed.). New York: Pergamon Press.

LIPSITT, L. P., & Kaye, H. (1964). Conditioned sucking in the human newborn. *Psychonomic Science, 1,* 29–30.

LITTLE, A. H., Lipsitt, L. P., & Rovee-Collier, C. K. (1984). Classical conditioning and retention of the infant's eyelid response: Effects of age and interstimulus interval. *Journal of Experimental Child Psychology, 37,* 512–524.

LOVELAND, K. K., & Olley, J. G. (1979). The effect of external reward on interest and quality of task performance in children of high or low intrinsic motivation. *Child Development, 50,* 1207–1210.

MADISON, L. S., Madison, J. K., & Adubato, S. A. (1986). Infant behavior and development in relation to fetal movement and habituation. *Child Development, 57,* 1475–1482.

MARTIN, J. A. (1977). Effects of positive and negative adult-child interactions on children's task performances. *Journal of Experimental Child Psychology, 23,* 493–502.

McCALL, R. B., Parke, R., & Kavanaugh, R. (1977). Imitation of live and televised models in children 1–3 years of age. *Monographs of the Society for Research in Child Development, 42*(Serial No. 173).

McLOYD, V. C. (1979). The effects of extrinsic rewards of differential value on high and low intrinsic interest. *Child Development, 50,* 1010–1019.

MELTZOFF, A. N., & Moore, M. K. (1983). Newborn infants imitate adult facial gestures. *Child Development, 54,* 702–709.

MILLAR, W. S., & Watson, J. S. (1979). The effect of delayed feedback on infant learning reexamined. *Child Development, 50,* 747–751.

NIELSEN TELEVISION INDEX. (1981). *Child and teenage television viewing.* New York: Author.

PALLAK, S. R., Costomiris, S., Sroka, S., & Pittman, T. S. (1982). School experience, reward characteristics, and intrinsic motivation. *Child Development, 53,* 1382–1391.

PAPOUSEK, H. (1967). Experimental studies of appetitional behavior in human newborns and infants. In H. W. Stevenson, E. H. Hess, & H. L. Rheingold (Eds.), *Early behavior: Comparative and developmental approaches.* New York: Wiley.

PARKE, R. D. (1969). Effectiveness of punishment as an interaction of intensity, timing, agent nurturance and cognitive structuring. *Child Development, 40,* 213–236.

PARKE, R. D. (1972). Some effects of punishment on children's behavior. In W. W. Hartup (Ed.), *The young child* (Vol. 2). Washington, DC: National Association for the Education of Young Children.

PARKE, R. D. (1977). Some effects of punishment on children's behavior—revisited. In E. M. Hetherington & R. D. Parke (Eds.), *Contemporary readings in child psychology.* New York: McGraw-Hill.

PARKE, R. D., & Collmer, C. W. (1975). Child abuse: An interdisciplinary analysis. In E. M. Hetherington (Ed.), *Review of child development research* (Vol. 5). Chicago: University of Chicago Press.

PARKE, R. D., & Slaby, R. G. (1983). The development of aggression. In P. H. Mussen (Ed.), *Handbook of child psychology* (Vol. 4). New York: Wiley.

PEARLMAN, C. (1984). The effects of level of effectance motivation, IQ, and a penalty/reward contingency on the choice of problem difficulty. *Child Development, 55,* 2000–2016.

PERRY, D. G., & Garrow, H. (1975). The "social deprivation-satiation effect": An outcome of frequency or perceived contingency? *Developmental Psychology, 11,* 681–688.

PIAGET, J. (1951). *Play, dreams, and imitation in childhood.* New York: Norton.

POWERS, R. B., & Osborne, J. G. (1976). *Fundamentals of behavior.* St. Paul, MN: West Publishing.

PREMACK, D. (1965). Reinforcement theory. In D. Levine (Ed.), *Nebraska Symposium on Motivation* (Vol. 13). Lincoln: University of Nebraska Press.

PREMACK, D. (1971). Catching up with common sense, or two sides of a generalization: Reinforcement and punishment. In R. Glaser (Ed.), *The nature of reinforcement.* Orlando, FL: Academic Press.

REDD, W. H., Morris, E. K., & Martin, J. A. (1975). Effects of positive and negative adult-child interactions on children's social preferences. *Journal of Experimental Child Psychology, 19,* 153–164.

ROSE, S. A. (1981). Developmental changes in

infants' retention of visual stimuli. *Child Development, 52,* 227–233.

ROVEE-COLLIER, C. K. (1984). The ontogeny of learning and memory in human infancy. In R. Kail & N. E. Spear (Eds.), *Comparative perspectives on the development of memory.* Hillsdale, NJ: Erlbaum.

RUBLE, D. N., Balaban, T., & Cooper, J. (1981). Gender constancy and the effects of sex-typed televised toy commercials. *Child Development, 52,* 667–673.

SEARS, R. R., Maccoby, E. E., & Levin, H. (1957). *Patterns of child rearing.* New York: Harper & Row.

SELIGMAN, M. E. P. (1975). *Helplessness: On depression, development, and death.* New York: W. H. Freeman.

SELIGMAN, M. E. P. (1978). Comment and integration. *Journal of Abnormal Psychology, 87,* 165–179.

SKINNER, B. F. (1953). *Science and human behavior.* New York: Macmillan.

STAATS, A. W. (1975). *Social behaviorism.* Homewood, IL: Dorsey Press.

THORNDIKE, E. L. (1898). Animal intelligence: An experimental study of the association processes in animals. *Psychological Review Monographs, 2*(Whole No. 8).

TONER, I. J., & Potts, R. (1981). Effect of modeled rationales on moral behavior, moral choice, and level of moral judgment in children. *Journal of Psychology, 107,* 153–162.

VINTER, A. (1986). The role of movement in eliciting early imitations. *Child Development, 57,* 66–71.

WATSON, J. B. (1928). *Psychological care of the infant and child.* New York: Norton.

WATSON, J. B., & Raynor, R. (1920). Conditioned emotional reactions. *Journal of Experimental Psychology, 3,* 1–14.

WATSON, J. S., & Ramey, C. T. (1972). Reactions to response-contingent stimulation in early infancy. *Merrill-Palmer Quarterly, 18,* 219–228.

ZIMMERMAN, B. J. (1977). Modeling. In H. Hom & P. Robinson (Eds.), *Psychological processes in early education.* Orlando, FL: Academic Press.

Development of Language and Communication Skills

One truly remarkable achievement that sets us humans apart from the rest of the animal kingdom is our creation and use of **language.** Although animals can **communicate** with one another, their limited number of calls and gestures are merely isolated signals that convey very specific messages (for example, a greeting, a threat, a summons to congregate) in much the same way that single words or stereotyped phrases do in a human language. By contrast, human languages are amazingly *flexible* and *productive.* From a small number of individually meaningless sounds, a person who is proficient in a language can generate thousands of meaningful auditory patterns (syllables, words) that can then be combined according to a set of grammatical rules to produce an infinite number of messages. Language is also an *inventive* tool. Most of what people say or hear in any given situation is not merely a repetition of what they have said or heard before; speakers create novel utterances on the spot, and the topics they talk about may not have anything to do with their current situation or the stream of ongoing events. Indeed, language is the only form of communication by which we can easily produce a variety of messages that are blatantly untrue (as in a lie or a sarcastic utterance) or otherwise figurative in nature (as in the simile "She's like a breath of fresh air"). Yet, creative as we may be in generating new messages, other people who know the language will be able to understand any and all of our ideas as long as each of our statements adheres to the rules and conventions of the language we are speaking.

Although language is one of the most abstract bodies of knowledge we will ever acquire, children in all cultures come to understand and use this intricate form of communication very early in life. In fact, many infants are talking before they can walk. And by age 5, children not only understand most of the grammatical rules of their native tongue but are also constructing remarkably complex, adultlike sentences even though they have had no formal training in language. To a col-

lege student struggling with French, German, Spanish, or Russian, it may seem that children acquire language almost effortlessly.

The young child's remarkable capacity for language learning is a puzzling phenomenon that raises many questions. Are infants biologically programmed to acquire language? What kinds of linguistic input must they receive in order to become language users? Is there any relation between a child's cooing, gesturing, or babbling and the later production of meaningful words? How do infants and toddlers come to attach meaning to words? Do all children pass through the same steps or stages as they acquire their native language? And what must children learn to become truly effective communicators? These are but a few of the issues we will consider as we trace the development of children's linguistic skills and try to determine how youngsters become so proficient in using language at such an early age.

Two Basic Questions about Language Development

Those who study language development have tried to answer two very basic questions. The first is the "what" question—what is the normal course of language development, and just what are children acquiring that enables them to master the intricacies of their native tongue? The second is the "how" question—how is it that young children who have never had the benefit of formal schooling are nevertheless rather adept at using an abstract symbol system like language long before they ever set foot in a classroom? Before we start to grapple with these complex issues, it may be helpful to expand a bit on each of them so that we will see where we are headed and what we may be up against.

The "What" Question
What must children learn in order to become proficient users of a language? Researchers have tradi-

Photo 8-1. Animals communicate through a series of calls and gestures that convey a limited number of very specific messages.

tionally argued that four kinds of knowledge are essential: a knowledge of *phonology,* a knowledge of *semantics,* a knowledge of *syntax,* and a knowledge of *pragmatics.*

Phonology

Phonology refers to the basic units of sound, or **phonemes,** that are combined to produce words and sentences. Each language uses only a subset of the sounds that human beings are capable of generating. For example, English makes use of 45 phonemes, and no language uses more than 60. Each language has rules for combining phonemes and for pronouncing these phonemic combinations. For instance, speakers of English recognize that it is quite permissible to begin a word with *st- (stop, student)* or *sk- (skit, skull)* but not *sb-* or *sg-*. English-speaking people immediately discriminate the phonemic combinations "zip" and "sip," although Spanish speakers may not, because the Spanish language does not distinguish words on the basis of the difference between the phonemes *z* and *s.* The point for our purposes is that children must learn to hear and to pronounce a number of these speechlike sounds in order to make sense of the speech they hear and to be understood when they try to speak (de Villiers & de Villiers, 1979).

Semantics

Children must also learn how individually meaningless phonemes are combined to produce meaningful units of language called **morphemes.** Morphemes are words or grammatical markers (such as *-ed* for past tense) with "meanings" that are *arbitrarily* assigned. For example, the relation of the word *dog* to the furry, four-legged creature we know as a dog is completely arbitrary—a product of social convention.

---

language: a small number of individually meaningless signals (sounds, letters, gestures) that can be combined according to agreed-on rules to produce an infinite number of messages.

communication: the process by which one organism transmits information to and influences another.

phonology: the sound system of a language and the rules for combining these sounds to produce meaningful units of speech.

phonemes: the basic units of sound that are used in a spoken language.

morphemes: the smallest meaningful units of language; these include words and grammatical markers such as prefixes, suffixes, and verb-tense modifiers (for example, *-ed, -ing*).

We could have just as easily labeled the animal in question a "chien," which is exactly what the French have done.

Semantics refers to the expressed meaning of words and sentences. Clearly, children must recognize that words convey meaning—that words refer to particular objects, actions, and relations—before they will comprehend the speech of others and be understood when they speak. How do children learn the meanings of individual words? How do they come to understand words that express relations, such as *in, on,* and *under; front* and *back;* or *large* and *small?* When do they first realize that the furry, four-legged family pet that they know as "doggie" is also an "animal" but at the same time is a fox terrier with a proper name such as "Fang" or "Pixie"? These are some of the questions that students of language development are now trying to answer.

Syntax

Syntax refers to the form, or structure, of a language—the rules that specify how words are combined to form meaningful sentences. Each language has its own set of syntactical rules that define the function of various words in a sentence and give the sentence a meaning. Consider the following examples:

1. John hit Jim.
2. Jim hit John.

These two statements contain precisely the same words but have very different meanings. In English there is a syntactical rule that in an active sentence the noun preceding the verb names the *agent* of action, and the noun following the verb names the *object* of that action. The sentence "Jim John hit" violates the rules of word order for English and is ungrammatical, although this order is perfectly acceptable in a language like French, where the noun naming the object of an action may immediately precede the verb.

The "Jim/John" example illustrates how the meanings of individual words in a sentence interact with sentence structure to give the entire sentence a meaning. This basic principle is true of all languages even though the rules of sentence construction (syntax) vary considerably from language to language. So it would seem that children must acquire a basic understanding of the syntactical features of their native tongue before they will become very proficient at speaking or understanding that language.

Pragmatics—the fourth aspect of language learning

A knowledge of phonology, semantics, and syntax will enable children to produce grammatical sentences, but there is no guarantee that the speech they generate will be appropriate for the setting in which they find themselves. Recently, psychologists such as Elizabeth Bates (1976) and Marilyn Shatz (1983) have noted that young children must also acquire another important set of rules called the pragmatics of language—that is, the principles specifying how language is to be used in different contexts and situations. In other words, the child must learn "when" to say "what" to "whom" in order to communicate effectively and achieve his or her underlying objectives. Consider the case of a 6-year-old girl who is trying to explain a new game to her 2-year-old brother. Clearly, the older child cannot speak to this little toddler as if he were an adult or an age mate; she will have to adjust her speech to his linguistic capabilities if she hopes to be understood.

Children must learn not only *what* to say to their listeners but also *how* to say it appropriately. For example, a 3-year-old may not realize that the best way of obtaining a cookie from Grandma is to say "Grandma, may I please have a cookie?" rather than stating in a demanding tone "Gimme a cookie, Grandma!" In order to communicate most effectively, children must become "social editors" and take into account where they are, with whom they are speaking, what the listener already knows, and what the listener needs or wants to hear. These pragmatic abilities and social editing skills evolve rather gradually over the course of childhood and are now recognized as important aspects of language development.

The "How" Question

As we noted, most 5-year-olds, who have had no formal linguistic training, have already mastered the basic syntax of their language and are quite capable of understanding all but the most complex sentences that they may hear. Perhaps even more remarkable, many severely retarded children who can neither count nor remember the rules of simple games are able to construct grammatical sentences and converse rather well (Lenneberg, 1967). How is this possible? How can we account for the young child's remarkable proficiency with this totally arbitrary and abstract symbol system that we know as language?

In reviewing the various theories of language development, we will once again run headlong into the *nativist/empiricist* (nature/nurture) controversy. *Learning theorists* represent the empiricist point of view. They contend that children will gradually learn a language as they imitate the speech they hear and are reinforced by adults for successive approximations of adult language. Presumably the process begins as parents and other close companions selectively reinforce those aspects of babbling (for example, "pa-pa"; "ma-ma") that sound like words, thereby increasing the frequency of these vocalizations. Reinforcement is then gradually withheld until the child is imitating words, then word phrases, and finally grammatical utterances.

Clearly imitation must be involved in language learning, for children invariably acquire and use the same language that their caregivers do. However, *nativists* have argued that imitation cannot be the major mechanism by which children learn a language. If imitation were the central process in language learning, we wouldn't hear children producing utterances such as "poon" (for "spoon") or "I brushed my tooths" that do not appear in the speech of their older companions. Moreover, nativists contend that parents do not sit down with their children and attempt to shape their grammar; in fact, studies of vocal interactions between parents and young children suggest that parents pay little if any attention to the grammatical correctness or incorrectness of their children's statements (Slobin, 1979).

So how do the nativists account for language acquisition? Theorists such as Noam Chomsky (1968, 1980) and David McNeill (1970) propose that human beings come equipped with an inborn capacity for language learning called the **language acquisition device (LAD).** The LAD is not necessarily a particular organ or area of the brain; it is thought to consist of at least some innate knowledge (or hypotheses) about the structure of language as well as a set of cognitive and perceptual abilities that are specialized for language learning. Presumably these innate hypotheses and language-processing skills enable young children to *infer* the phonological patterns, word meanings, and rules of syntax that characterize the speech they are listening to. These inferences about the meaning and structure of linguistic information represent a "theory" of language, which children will then use to guide their own attempts to communicate (see Figure 8-1). As a child matures and has the opportunity to process more and more linguistic input, his or her underlying theory of language will become increasingly sophisticated until it approximates that used by older children and adults. For the nativists, then, language acquisition is quite natural and almost automatic, as long as children have linguistic data to process and someone with whom to communicate.

Before we can decide anything about the relative merits of the nativist and empiricist explanations of language acquisition (or any other pertinent theory, for that matter), we must review the course of language development and see what it is that children are acquiring and when. Let's begin at birth and trace the steps that infants take on their way to uttering that memorable first word.

---

semantics: the expressed meaning of words and sentences.
syntax: the structure of a language; the rules specifying how words and grammatical markers are to be combined to produce meaningful sentences.
pragmatics: principles that underlie the effective and appropriate use of language in social contexts.
language acquisition device (LAD): a set of linguistic processing skills that nativists believe to be innate; presumably the LAD enables a child to infer the rules governing others' speech and then to use these rules to produce language.

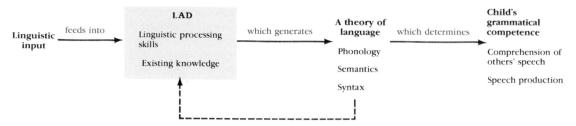

Figure 8-1. A model of language acquisition proposed by nativists.

Before Language:
The Prelinguistic Period

For the first 10 to 13 months of life, children are said to be in the **prelinguistic phase** of language development because they are not yet combining the sounds that they are capable of making into utterances that are easily interpretable as words. But even though young infants cannot produce any language, they are quite responsive to speech and other human vocalizations from the day they are born. Let's take a closer look.

The Infant's Reactions to Language

On several occasions, we have seen that young infants may be programmed to "tune in" to human speech. When spoken to, neonates will often open their eyes, gaze at the speaker, and sometimes even vocalize themselves (Rheingold & Adams, 1980; Rosenthal, 1982). By 3 days of age, an infant already recognizes his or her mother's voice and clearly prefers it to the voice of a female stranger (DeCasper & Fifer, 1980). In the first few days of life, speech elicits greater electrical activity from the left half (cerebral hemisphere) of the infant's brain, while music produces greater activity in the right half (Molfese, 1977). This early pattern, which persists into adulthood, suggests that the two hemispheres of the brain are specialized for different acoustical functions from a very early age. Finally, young infants will suck faster to hear recorded speech than to hear instrumental music or other rhythmic sounds (Butterfield & Siperstein, 1972). So babies can discriminate speech from other sound patterns, and they pay particularly close attention to speech from the very beginning.

Do different samples of speech all sound alike to the very young infant? Apparently not. Marsha Clarkson and Keith Berg (1983) found that babies only 2 days old can tell the difference between the vowels *a* and *i*, and Peter Eimas (1982) reports that 1-month-old infants are about as capable as adults of discriminating conso-

nant sounds such as *ba* and *pa* or *da* and *ta,* even though these infants have had limited exposure to speech and have never produced these sounds.

It seems, then, that the abilities to discriminate speech from nonspeech and to differentiate a variety of speechlike sounds are either (1) innate or (2) learned in the first few days and weeks of life. In either case, it would seem that young infants are remarkably well prepared for language learning.

Producing Sounds: The Infant's Prelinguistic Vocalizations

All normal and healthy infants are capable of vocalizing at birth and will typically begin to produce a variety of speechlike sounds long before they utter their first recognizable word. In recent years, **psycholinguists** have found that the vocal abilities of prelinguistic children develop in a step- or stagelike fashion over the first 10–12 months of life. Although children may differ in the ages at which they move from one stage of vocalization to another, the overall sequence of vocal development is roughly the same for virtually all prelinguistic infants.

Crying. As we noted in Chapter 5, neonates are quite capable of crying and will even emit different kinds of cries to communicate different needs. Although these earliest cries are probably reflexive responses to discomfort rather than deliberate attempts to communicate, the picture soon changes. During the third week of life, many infants begin to produce a "fake cry" that Peter Wolff (1969) describes as a "cry of low pitch and intensity; it consists of long drawn out moans which occasionally rise to more explicit cries, and then revert to poorly articulated moans" (p. 98). Wolff calls these vocalizations "fake" cries because they are often emitted when the infant does not appear to be discomforted or distressed in any way. Although **fake cries** are often used to attract attention, that is probably not their only function. Wolff (1969) believes that calm, contented infants may sometimes "fake a cry" because they have discovered that they can make interesting noises and have decided to repeat the process for the sheer pleasure of experimenting with sounds.

Cooing. At about 3–5 weeks of age, infants begin to produce a variety of new sounds that appear to be associated with pleasant states of affairs rather than with discomfort or distress. These "noncrying" vocalizations are vowellike sounds such as "oooooh," "aaaaah," or "uuuuuh" that are likely to be heard after a feeding when the baby is awake, alert, dry, and seemingly contented. Such "sounds of contentment" are called **"coos"** (and the process known as "cooing") because infants tend to repeat the same vowel sound over and over, varying their tone ever so slightly, much as pigeons and doves do when they coo.

Babbling. At 3 to 4 months of age children begin to add consonant sounds to their vocal repertoires, and by the middle of the first year, they are constructing some consonant/vowel combinations, such as *ka* or *ga*. Within weeks, infants begin to repeat these phonetic combinations and produce **babbles**—utterances such as "baba" or "papa" that sound very much like meaningful speech. But rarely are these early "words" intended as such by the 7–10-month-old infant, who is apt to follow an apparently meaningful utterance such as "papa" with a multisyllabic "papapapapapapa"—a process called **echolalia.** In the opinion of most psycholinguists, the vast majority of infants do not produce their first intelligible "word" until 10–13 months of age (de Villiers & de Villiers, 1979).

Although they have been listening to very different languages, infants the world over produce roughly the same pattern of phonemes (Sachs, 1985). Indeed, 6–10-month-olds emit a wide variety of speechlike sounds, some of which do not occur in the language that they will acquire. For example, children who hear only English may make a clicking *tsk* sound that appears in South African languages or a blowing *pf* sound that is used in Japanese, even though they have never heard these sounds in anyone's speech (de Villiers & de Villiers, 1979). However, babbling infants do not produce all the sounds that appear in their native language; some of these phonemes will be added later—after children have begun to talk.

Before uttering their first "words," infants have already begun to use sounds to refer to actions, objects, or situations. Some of these early **vocables** may be approximations of adult words; others are the child's own creations (Ferguson, 1977). For example, children might utter the vocable "mmmmmm" when they see or hear a car coming or "aacccch" when they hope to engage a companion in a bout of rough-and-tumble play. According to Charles Ferguson (1977), infants who produce these vocables are about ready to talk. They are now aware that certain speech sounds have consistent meanings, and they have begun to construct their own unique "words" (vocables) from their babbles.

Are Prelinguistic Vocalizations Related to Meaningful Speech?

Does babbling contribute to the development of meaningful speech? Many linguists are skeptical, arguing that early vocal development follows a distinct maturational timetable and that the child's first vocalizations have little if anything to do with the later development of words and sentences (Jakobson, 1968). Surely maturation must play a prominent role in phonological development, for the range of sounds that infants produce and the order in which various phonemes emerge are similar for all children, regardless of the language used by their caregivers. In fact, deaf infants, who cannot hear caregivers' speech, will babble in much the same way that hearing infants do.

But even though the order in which infants produce speechlike sounds depends, in part, on the maturation of the brain and the vocal apparatus, there are reasons to believe that babbling is meaningfully re-

---

prelinguistic stage: the period before children utter their first meaningful words.

psycholinguists: those who study the structure and development of language.

fake cries: low-pitched moans that young infants make when seeking attention or experimenting with sounds.

coos: vowellike sounds that young infants repeat over and over during periods of contentment.

babbles: vowel/consonant combinations that infants begin to produce at about 3 to 4 months of age.

echolalia: the tendency of babbling infants to repeat the same sounds over and over.

vocables: unique patterns of sound that a prelinguistic infant uses to represent objects, actions, or events.

lated to later speech. For example, 6–10-month-old infants are already adjusting their babbling to the situation in which they find themselves. They will babble at a higher pitch to their mothers than to their fathers (Lieberman, 1967) and will match the intonation of their babbling to the tonal qualities of the language they are hearing. So even though English, Arabic, French, and Chinese babies are producing the same pattern of phonemes, they are already babbling with something of an accent—and these intonational cues are clear enough to permit naive listeners to correctly guess the language of the babies' parents more often than would be expected by chance (De Boysson-Bardies, Sagart, & Durand, 1984). Let's also note that babbling overlaps with meaningful speech and that an infant's first "vocables" and discernible words are composed of the very sounds that she has been producing in the later phases of the babbling period (Ferguson, 1977; Sachs, 1985). Taken together, these findings imply that the linguistic environment has an important influence on the child's babbling, which, in turn, is related to the language (that is, words and phrases) that the child will eventually produce.

What Do Prelinguistic Infants Know about Language?

Do young infants know more about language than they can possibly tell? It now appears that they do and that one of the first things they learn about speech is a practical lesson. During the first six months, babies are most likely to coo or babble *while* their caregivers are speaking (Rosenthal, 1982). It is almost as if young infants viewed "talking" as a game of noisemaking in which the object was to "harmonize" with their speaking companions. But by 7–8 months of age, infants are typically silent while a companion speaks and will then respond with a vocalization whenever their partner stops talking. In other words, they have apparently learned their first rule in the pragmatics of language: Don't talk while someone else is speaking, for you'll soon have an opportunity to have your say.

Vocal turntaking may come about because parents who are talking to their babies will typically say something to the child, wait for the infant to smile, cough, burp, coo, or babble, and then address the infant again, thereby inviting another response (Snow & Ferguson, 1977). Of course, infants may also learn about the importance of turntaking from other contexts, or **formats,** in which they assume separate but reversible roles with their companions (Bruner, 1983). Examples of these reciprocal exchanges might include bouts of nose touching, face making, and the sharing of toys. By 9 months of age, infants clearly understand the alternation rules inherent in many games, and if such activities are interrupted by the adult's failure to take her turn, the infant is apt to vocalize, to urge the adult to resume by offering her a toy, or to wait for a second or two and take the adult's turn before looking once again at the adult (Ross & Lollis, 1987). So it seems that the ways caregivers structure their interactions with an infant may indeed help the child to recognize that many forms of social discourse, including "talking," are patterned activities that follow a definite set of rules.

Intonation as a communicative prompt. Might infants learn important lessons about language from a caregiver's tone of voice? Maybe so. Using a sound spectrograph to analyze mothers' intonational patterns during free play with their 2–6-month-olds, Daniel Stern and his associates (Stern, Spieker, & MacKain, 1982) found that adults do vary their tone of voice when trying to communicate different "messages." When the infant looked away, for example, the mother's speech assumed a rising intonation in an attempt to *recapture the baby's attention.* Sample utterances were

$$\text{"Watcha look}^{\text{ing at HUH?"}} \quad \text{or}$$

$$\text{"Look at}^{\text{ mo}^{\text{mmy!"}}}$$

When the infant gazed at the mother and smiled, rhythmic intonations with alternating rises and falls were employed to *maintain the baby's pleasant mood.* Sample utterances were

$$\text{"c}_{\text{o}}{}^{\text{mE On"}} \quad \text{or}$$

$$\text{"yo}^{\text{u}}\text{'r}_{\text{e}}\text{ the c}^{\text{UTE}}{}_{\text{s}}\text{t little thing in the w}^{\text{HOL}}\text{e world"}$$

By contrast, falling intonations were used to *elicit positive affect* (smile, bright eyes) from a somber baby—for example,

$$\text{"HEY}_{\text{ there"}}$$

It is tempting to conclude that 2–6-month-old infants not only discriminate different intonational patterns but will soon recognize that certain tones of voice have a particular "meaning" (for example, "Pay attention" or "Won't you smile for me?"). Indeed, Stern and his colleagues propose that the changing tone of the mother's voice is a signal that carries information about the mother's intentions and feelings. These signals may then be interpreted by the infant and serve as a stimulus for the development of responsive gesturing and early attempts at verbal communication.

Do preverbal infants understand the meaning of words? Although most children do not speak their first meaningful words until the end of the first year, parents are often convinced that their preverbal infants can understand at least some of what is said to them. For example, an 8-month-old boy may reliably reach for a ball when his father points to the object and says "Get the ball." Yet, a skeptic might argue that 8–9-month-old infants can respond appropriately to a familiar command without really understanding the meaning of the words in that utterance. The boy who fetches the ball in response to his father's command may be treating his dad's gestures (pointing) and verbal prompts as simple "cues for action" in much the same way that a cocker spaniel does when told to fetch a ball. How can we tell whether preverbal infants really understand the meanings of various words?

One way is to see whether young infants will focus their attention on an object when told to look at the object by a parent who is out of sight and hence cannot point or use other gestures to direct the child's attention to the target. In one such study (Thomas, Campos, Shucard, Ramsay, & Shucard, 1981), 11- to 13-month-old infants were placed in a high chair facing four objects (for example, toys and cookies). One of these objects had a name that the child's mother was sure her infant recognized and understood. Seated behind her infant, the mother then instructed her child (1) to "look at the [known word]" on some trials and (2) to look at objects designated by nonsense words that the child would *not* understand (for example, "look at the dosh") on other trials. Clearly 13-month-olds did understand the meaning of the "known" word, for they looked intently at its referent when told to do so, and they gazed very little at any of the stimuli when told to look at unknown objects such as a "dosh." By contrast, 11-month-olds did *not* understand the meaning of the "known" word, for they did not restrict their gazing to its referent when told to do so; in fact, they were just as likely to gaze at this object when told to look at the nonsense word! In a similar study, Sharon Oviatt (1980) reported a similar outcome: few infants understood the meanings of individual words before their first birthday.

In sum, 9-month-old infants may respond ap-

propriately when spoken to even though they do not yet understand the meanings of the words they are hearing. Although preverbal children are able to obey verbal commands only because they correctly interpret nonlinguistic gestures and other contextual cues, they are quite aware that a vocal command is a communicative prompt for action. By 12 to 13 months of age, infants are beginning to realize that individual words have meaning. In fact, it is probably safe to assume that children know the meaning of that eagerly awaited "first word" before they use it in their own speech. Finally, Sharon Oviatt (1980) found that infants aged 12 to 17 months understood the meaning of many nouns (for example, *rabbit*) and verbs (for example, *press it*) long before these "object" and "action" words became part of their productive vocabularies. Taken together, these findings imply that infants know much more about language than they can possibly say. Apparently, **receptive language** (comprehension) is ahead of **productive language** (expression) from the 12th or 13th month of life and possibly even sooner.

One Word at a Time: The Holophrastic Period

In the first stage of meaningful speech, the **holophrastic period,** infants utter single words that may sometimes seem to represent an entire sentence's worth of meaning (that is, **holophrases**). At first the child's productive vocabulary is limited to one or two very simple words that may be intelligible only to close companions—for example, "ba" (for "ball") or "awa" (for "I want," as the child points to food or a glass of water)—and initial language learning proceeds very

---

formats: interactions in which a young child and an older companion assume separate but reversible (reciprocal) roles.

receptive language: that which the individual comprehends when listening to others' speech.

productive language: that which the individual is capable of expressing (producing) in his or her own speech.

holophrastic period: the period when the child's speech consists of one-word utterances, some of which are thought to be holophrases.

holophrase: a single-word utterance that represents an entire sentence's worth of meaning.

slowly as infants simply expand their vocabularies "one word at a time" (Bloom, 1973). In fact, three to four months may pass before the "verbal" child develops a productive vocabulary of ten words (Nelson, 1973). But once infants reach this ten-word milestone, they begin to add new words at a faster pace. By 19 to 20 months of age, many children have working vocabularies of 50 words or more. And by age 24 months they are already producing an average of 186 words (Nelson, 1973).

The Infant's Choice of Words

What do young children talk about? Katherine Nelson (1973) studied 18 infants as they learned their first 50 words and found that their one-word utterances fell into the six general categories that appear in Table 8-1. We can see that nearly two-thirds of these first 50 words are *nominals*—words that refer to unique objects *(Mama)* or to classes of objects *(ball, doggie)*. And what kind of objects do children talk about? Nelson discovered that

> they do not learn the names of objects that are simply "there" such as tables, plates, towels, grass, or stoves. With few exceptions, all the words listed are terms applying to manipulable or movable objects. . . . [However, the objects that are named] are not only the ones the child acts upon in some way (shoes, bottle, ball), but also ones that do something themselves—trucks, clocks, buses, and animals [pp. 31–32].

In sum, children seem to talk about what interests them, and what interests them is something that moves, makes noise, or can be acted on.

Early Semantics: The Development of Word Meanings

Adults often chuckle at baby talk and consider it "cute" because young children use words differently than they do. For example, one 2-year-old boy called all furry, four-legged animals "doggie" and yet used the word *cookie* to refer only to chocolate chip cookies. If someone promised this child a cookie and gave him an Oreo, he would throw it down and look at the person as if to say "Come on, that's not a cookie!"

How do children come to infer the meaning of words? Why might they think that a cow or a horse is a "doggie" or that an Oreo is not a cookie? In recent years, psycholinguists have tried to answer these questions by looking carefully at the kinds of semantic errors (errors in word meaning) that children display in their speech.

Errors in word usage. When young children first attach a meaning to a word, it may or may not match the meaning that adults associate with the term. One kind of error that they often make is to use a word to refer to a wider variety of objects or events than an adult would. This phenomenon, called **overextension,** is illustrated by a child's use of the term *doggie* to refer to all furry, four-legged animals. **Underextension,** the opposite of overextension, is the tendency to use a general word to refer to a smaller range of objects than an adult would—for example, applying the term *cookie* only to chocolate chip cookies. Of course, children may match the adult meanings of some words from the very beginning. Indeed, many youngsters reserve the labels *daddy* and *mommy* to refer only to their parents (although others may overextend these terms to include several adult males and females). Jill and Peter de Villiers (1978) suggest that children are most likely to use a word as an adult would when that word is a proper noun (such as *Daddy*) that has a single referent.

Herbert and Eve Clark (1977) propose that children go through a series of stages in learning the

Table 8-1. Percentage of words in six categories used by children with productive vocabularies of 50 words

Word category	Description and examples	Percentage of utterances
1. General nominals	Words used to refer to classes of objects *(car, doggie, milk)*	51
2. Specific nominals	Words used to refer to unique objects *(Mommy, Rover)*	14
3. Action words	Words used to describe or accompany actions or to demand attention *(bye-bye, up, go)*	13
4. Modifiers	Words that refer to properties or quantities of things *(big, hot, mine, allgone)*	9
5. Personal/social words	Words used to express feelings or to comment about social relationships *(please, thank you, no, ouch)*	8
6. Function words	Words that have a grammatical function *(what, where, is, to, for)*	4

Source: Adapted from Nelson (1973).

Photo 8-2. A large percentage of children's "first words" are the names of objects that move, make noise, or can be acted on.

meaning of a new word. These stages are (1) underextension, (2) appropriate use (without awareness of the word's true meaning), (3) overextension, and (4) correct use. For example, a child might start off using the word *kitty* to refer only to one cat—the family pet. She may later extend *kitty* to include other cats (a seemingly appropriate use) and then overextend the term to dogs and sheep before finally understanding the meaning of *kitty* and using it only for domesticated felines.

How do children infer word meanings?
The tendency of young children to overextend or underextend the meaning of words suggests that they are forming hypotheses about what words signify and then gradually modifying these early guesses until their understanding matches an adult's. What do children attend to as they form their initial hypotheses about word meanings? According to Eve Clark's **semantic features hypothesis** (Clark, 1973), children infer the meaning

of words from the *perceptual features* of their referents. For example, a verbal infant may hear her parents describe a number of small, round objects as "cookie" and conclude from these experiences that the term *cookie* describes any object that is small and round. The next step is to overextend the word to other small, round objects such as crackers, poker chips, and coins. In sum, the semantic features hypothesis contends that a child's initial ideas about word meanings are perceptually based. Presumably, young children will assume that words serve to classify or categorize objects on the basis of their size, shape, texture, or taste or the kinds of sounds they make (Clark & Clark, 1977).

Katherine Nelson (1978) has proposed a second theory of semantic development: that children infer the meanings of words from the *functions* of their referents. Nelson would argue that a child who overextends the word *cookie* to crackers, doughnuts, and other small, round, edible objects will do so on the basis of their **functional similarity** (the fact that these objects can be eaten) rather than their perceptual similarity (the fact that they look alike).

Richard Prawat and Susan Wildfong (1980) conducted an interesting experiment to test the merits of these two theories. Young children were asked to name items that were serving functions that did not jibe with the items' perceptual characteristics. For example, children saw cereal being poured into a cuplike container and were asked whether this container was a bowl or a cup (see Figure 8-2).

The results were generally consistent with the semantic features hypothesis; that is, the 3–4-year-olds in this study were more likely to call the container a cup (the perceptual choice) than a bowl (the functional choice). Even 2–3-year-olds tend to use perceptual rath-

---

overextension: the young child's tendency to use relatively specific words to refer to a broader set of objects, actions, or events than adults do (for example, using the word *car* to refer to all motor vehicles).

underextension: the young child's tendency to use general words to refer to a smaller set of objects, actions, or events than adults do (for example, using *candy* to refer only to mints).

semantic features hypothesis: the notion that children infer the meanings of new words from the perceptual characteristics of their referents.

functional similarity hypothesis: the notion that children infer the meanings of new words from the functions served by their referents.

Figure 8-2. Is this item a cup or a bowl? If young children say it is a bowl, they apparently infer the meanings of words on the basis of the *functions* served by their referents. But if they say the container is a cup, they must be inferring word meanings on the basis of the *perceptual characteristics* of their referents. *(Adapted from Prawat & Wildfong, 1980.)*

er than functional attributes as a basis for naming objects and inferring the meanings of words (Tomikawa & Dodd, 1980). In fact, overextensions based on shared perceptual features often cut across functional lines, so that a young child might well call a small, round poker chip a "cookie"—even though poker chips and cookies serve very different functions (Bowerman, 1977).

However, children know much more about the meaning of words than their semantic errors might indicate. Two-year-olds who call all four-legged animals "doggie" can often discriminate a dog from other animals if they are given a set of animal pictures and asked to "show the doggie" (Thompson & Chapman, 1977). Perhaps the reason young children overextend words like *doggie* in their speech is that they know so very few words. A young child who sees a horse may realize that this animal is not a doggie but will nevertheless label it as such because she has no other words in her vocabulary to describe this large, four-legged creature (de Villiers & de Villiers, 1979). Children may also use this strategy to learn the names of new objects, for overextensions of a word such as *doggie* are likely to elicit reactions such as "No, Johnny, that's a *horsie*. Can you say 'horsie'? C'mon, say 'horsie'!"

Levels of semantic awareness. As adults, we can label objects in many ways. For example, we may call the family pet "Peppy" (a proper name), a collie, a dog, a mammal, or an animal. By contrast, 2–3-year-olds are likely to respond to a collie by calling it "doggie" rather than a collie (a more specific term) or an animal (a more general term).

Why are children's first words at an intermediate level of generality? Probably because adults often name objects at this level when talking with 2- to 3-year-olds, even though they may use other levels of generality when describing the same objects to an older child or an adult. For example, a mother might call a large, spotted feline a "leopard" (a specific term) when talking to her 5-year-old; however, the same animal becomes a "kitty cat" when she points it out to her infant or toddler (Mervis & Mervis, 1982). The 1- to 3-year-old has no need to distinguish leopards from house cats or golf balls from tennis balls; all "kitties" are animals that meow, and all "balls" are round objects that roll. So in naming objects at an intermediate level of generality, adults are providing verbal labels for those aspects of meaning (or "semantic features") that their young children first notice and are able to understand (Blewitt, 1983).

When a word is more than a word. Many psycholinguists believe that children use single words as holophrases—that is, one-word "sentences" that derive their meaning from the word itself and the context in which it is spoken (Dale, 1976). It does often seem that a child's one-word utterances represent much more than an attempt to label objects. For example, one 17-month-old child named Shelley used the word *ghetti* (spaghetti) three times over a five-minute period. On the first occasion, she was simply pointing at a pan on the stove and seemed to be asking "Is that spaghetti?" When her older companion showed her the pan's contents, she grinned and exclaimed "*GHETTI!*" as if to say "Heh, it *is* spaghetti!" Several minutes later, she once again approached her companion (who was now eating), tugged at his sleeve, and said "Ghetti" in a pleading way as if to request a bite of spaghetti.

Do we read too much into Shelley's speech when suggesting that she used a single word to express three different sentences' worth of meaning? Perhaps. But let's also note that on her third use of the term *ghetti,* Shelley added both a nonverbal gesture (tugging) and an intonational cue (a whine) that she had not previously used. These actions may well have been undertaken to differentiate her third utterance from the pre-

Table 8-2. Similarities in children's spontaneous two-word sentences in several languages

Function of sentence	Language				
	English	Finnish	German	Russian	Samoan
To locate or name	There book	Tuossa Rina (there Rina)	Buch da (book there)	Tosya tam (Tosya there)	Keith lea (Keith there)
To demand	More milk Give candy	Annu Rina (give Rina)	Mehr milch (more milk)	Yeshche moloko (more milk)	Mai pepe (give doll)
To negate	No wet Not hungry	Ei susi (not wolf)	Nicht blasen (not blow)	Vody nyet (water no)	Le 'ai (not eat)
To indicate possession	My shoe Mama dress	Täti auto (aunt's car)	Mein ball (my ball) Mamas hut (Mama's hat)	Mami chashka (Mama's cup)	Lole a'u (candy my)
To modify or qualify	Pretty dress Big boat	Rikki auto (broken car)	Armer wauwau (poor dog)	Papa bol'shoy (Papa big)	Fa'ali'i pepe (headstrong baby)
To question	Where ball	Missa pallo (where ball)	Wo ball (where ball)	Gde papa (where Papa)	Fea Punafu (where Punafu)

Source: Adapted from Slobin (1979).

vious two, so that her companion would not misinterpret the message, "Give Shelley some spaghetti!"

In sum, children in the holophrastic stage of language learning may be expressing rather complex ideas in their one-word utterances—ideas that we would express in sentences. Toward the end of the holophrastic period, toddlers will often string holophrases together in ways that provide a more complete picture of their desires or their assessments of a situation. For example, the phrase "Daddy [long pause] car [long pause] ride" may represent the child's description of what she and dad are doing or perhaps an attempt to coax dad to take her for a ride in the country. At this point, children are on the verge of producing their first true sentences (Clark & Clark, 1977).

From Holophrases to Simple Sentences: The Telegraphic Period

At about 18 to 24 months of age, children begin to combine words into simple "sentences" that are remarkably similar across languages (and cultures) as different as English, Finnish, German, Russian, and Samoan (see Table 8-2). These early combinations are sometimes called **telegraphic speech** because they resemble the abbreviated language of a telegram.

Although the two-word utterances in Table 8-2 are clearly ungrammatical by adult standards, they represent far more than strings of holophrases or random word combinations. Even the simplest of a child's early sentences show some systematic regularities in word order and word use. Moreover, early sentences are often quite creative. A 2-year-old who eats an Oreo and says "Allgone cookie" has created a novel statement—one that adults would not produce unless they were mimicking the child.

Why are children's earliest sentences incomplete? What kinds of messages and meanings are they trying to communicate in these telegraphic statements? And what have they learned about the pragmatics of language over the first two to two and a half years? Psycholinguists have tried to answer these questions by periodically recording and analyzing toddlers' speech. In conducting this research, investigators soon discovered that age is not a very good indicator of language development, because some children acquire language much faster than others. As a result, it is virtually impossible to specify the linguistic capabilities of the "average toddler" or the "typical 3-year-old."

According to Roger Brown (1973), the best estimate of a child's early language development is a mea-

---

telegraphic speech: early sentences that consist solely of content words and omit the less meaningful parts of speech, such as articles, prepositions, pronouns, and auxiliary verbs.

sure called the **mean length of utterance (MLU)**—the average number of morphemes that the child uses in the sentences he or she produces. Earlier we defined a morpheme as the smallest unit of speech that conveys meaning. These meaningful elements of language may be whole words, such as *cat* or *jump,* or grammatical markers such as the *-s* at the end of a noun to signify plurality or the *-ed* at the end of a verb to indicate the past tense. Thus, the phrase "See kitty" consists of only two morphemes, whereas the statements "Baby jumped" and "See doggies" each contain a total of three.

Characteristics of Telegraphic Speech

When adults send telegrams, they try to make them as short as possible because each word costs money. If you wanted to inform a friend that you were leaving Atlanta on Sunday and would be arriving home on Tuesday, you might write "Leaving Atlanta Sunday—home Tuesday." In the interest of economy, you would retain only the essential content words (typically nouns and verbs) and omit less important "function" words, such as articles, prepositions, pronouns, and auxiliary verbs. Young children follow roughly the same strategy when composing their earliest sentences.

The child's imitations of adult speech are also telegraphic. If you were to ask a 2-year-old to repeat the sentence "The doggie is chasing the kitty," she might say "Doggie chase kitty." That is, the child once again retains only the important nouns and verbs and deletes *the, is,* and the verb ending *-ing*—even though she has just heard these elements in the sentence she is trying to reproduce.

It was once thought that toddlers spoke in telegraphese because memory limitations prevented them from generating long sentences. However, the memory hypothesis was soon rejected once researchers began to note that 2–2½-year-olds were capable of producing 3-, 4-, and even 5-word "telegraphic" utterances. Thus, the current view is that toddlers omit function words and grammatical markers from their own sentences simply because they do not yet understand the meaning or purpose of these parts of speech (Reich, 1986).

A Semantic Analysis of Telegraphic Speech

The structure of the sentences that children hear will vary dramatically from culture to culture; each language has its own set of grammatical rules that permits certain word combinations and prohibits others. Yet, we have seen in Table 8-2 that toddlers who have been exposed to very different languages will produce the same kinds of two-word utterances. So children's earliest sentences are not merely shortened versions of adult language; they represent a universal "child language" that seems to have a structure of its own.

Although early attempts were made to specify the structural characteristics, or syntax, of telegraphic speech, it soon became apparent that analyses based on syntax alone grossly underestimated the young child's linguistic capabilities. Why? Because young children often use the *same* two-word utterance to convey *different* meanings (or semantic relations) in different contexts. For example, one of Lois Bloom's (1970) young subjects said "Mommy sock" on two occasions during the same day—once when she picked up her mother's sock and once while her mother was putting a sock on the child's foot. In the first instance, "Mommy sock" seems to imply a possessive relationship—"Mommy's sock." But in the second instance, the child is apparently expressing an agent/object relation such as "Mommy is putting on my sock." Syntactical analyses that focus only on sentence structure would classify these two utterances as identical, even though they almost certainly represent the child's attempt to express two very different ideas—ideas that we would communicate with different kinds of sentences. So to properly interpret telegraphic statements, one must determine the child's *meaning* or *semantic intent* by considering not only the words that she generates but also the contexts in which these utterances take place.

Roger Brown (1973) has analyzed the "telegraphese" of several young children from around the world and written a **semantic grammar** to describe the basic categories of meaning that they often express in their two-word sentences. The most common of these semantic relations appear in Table 8-3.

The child's next accomplishment is to combine these semantic relations into longer telegraphic utterances. For example, an agent/action relation such as "Mommy drink" might be added to an action/object relation such as "drink milk" to yield an agent/action/object relation of the form "Mommy drink milk." Once children reach this milestone, they are about ready to acquire and use some of the rules of syntax that will make their sentences more "grammatical" within the framework of the language they are learning.

The Pragmatics of Early Speech

There are a number of very practical lessons that children must learn before they can become effective communicators. Obviously, they must learn how to attract the attention of their companions and how to use language as a means of sustaining social interactions. They must also learn how to supplement their limited vocabularies and productive skills to make their messages clear. And last but certainly not least, children must become good listeners, for the information they receive from their conversational partners may help them to restructure any of their messages that a partner has not understood.

The development of communication skills begins long before children produce their first words. Over the first four months, babies learn to vocalize to their caregivers because cooing, laughing, excitable blurting,

Photo 8-3. Pointing is an early but very effective means of communication. By the end of the first year, children are calling attention to interesting objects and activities by pointing at them with the index finger.

and even whining are successful at attracting attention and eliciting verbal reactions from adults (Keller & Scholmerich, 1987). And by the middle of the first year, infants are already using gestures to communicate with their parents. For example, a 6-month-old child might indicate her interest in a particular toy by picking it up and showing it to an adult. At 10–11 months, infants will look in the direction in which adults are pointing, and by the end of the first year, the child begins to call the mother's attention to interesting objects and activities by pointing at them with the index finger.

How do mothers respond when their infants point? According to Eleanor Leung and Harriet Rheingold (1981), they will first determine what the child is pointing at and then name and describe whatever it is that the infant finds so fascinating. Thus, pointing is an important communicative gesture that the very young child may use to learn the *names* of interesting objects and activities—the very words that appear first in his or her vocabulary (Nelson, 1973).

When infants begin to speak, they will often combine a word and a gesture to make their "holophrases" less ambiguous for the listener. So if a 14-month-

Table 8-3. Common categories of meaning (semantic relations) expressed in children's earliest sentences

Semantic relation	Examples
Agent + action	Mommy come; Daddy sit
Action + object	Drive car; eat grape
Agent + object	Mommy sock; baby book
Action + location	Go park; sit chair
Entity + location	Cup table; toy floor
Possessor + possession	My teddy; Mommy dress
Entity + attribute	Box shiny; crayon big
Demonstrative + entity	Dat money; dis telephone

Source: Brown (1973).

mean length of utterance (MLU): average number of meaningful units (morphemes) in a child's utterances.
semantic grammar: an analysis of the semantic relations (meanings) that children express in their earliest sentences.

Box 8-1
Learning a Gestural Language

    Children who are born deaf or who lose their hearing early in childhood will have a difficult time learning to use an oral language. Contrary to popular opinion, the deaf do not learn much from lip reading. In fact, many deaf children learn no language at all until they go to school and are exposed to a gestural system known as American Sign Language (ASL).

    Even though ASL is produced by the hands rather than orally, it is a remarkably flexible medium that is similar to an oral language (Klima & Bellugi, 1975). For example, ASL has a distinct sign for each morpheme. Some signs represent entire words; others stand for grammatical morphemes (or inflections) such as the progressive ending *-ing,* the past tense *-ed,* and auxiliaries. Each sign is constructed from a limited set of gestural components in much the same way that the spoken word is constructed from a finite number of distinctive sounds (phonemes). In ASL the components that make up a sign are (1) the position of the signing hand(s), (2) the configuration of the hand(s) and fingers, and (3) the motions of the hand(s) and fingers. Syntactical rules specify how signs are to be combined to form declarative statements, to ask questions, and to negate a proposition. And like an oral language, ASL permits the user to sign plays on words (puns), metaphorical statements, and poetry. So people who are proficient in this gestural system can transmit and understand an infinite variety of highly creative messages—they are true language users.

    Deaf children learn ASL in much the same way that hearing children acquire an oral language. In fact, if their parents are deaf and communicate in sign, deaf children will acquire their first meaningful "sign" at about 9 months of age—about three months earlier than hearing children utter their first meaningful word (Bonvillian, Orlansky, & Novack, 1983). The deaf child usually begins by "babbling" in sign—that is, forming

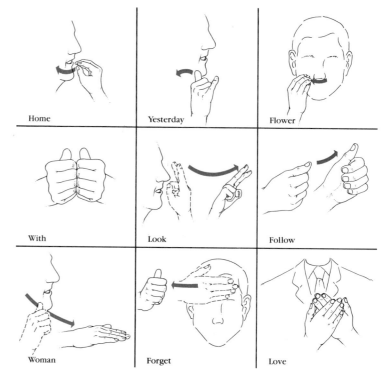

Some signs in American Sign Language.

rough approximations of signs that parents use. The child then proceeds to one-word, or "holophrastic," phrases, in which a single sign is used to convey a number of different messages, and the kinds of signs that the child first uses (nominals, action words, modifiers) are virtually identical to the categories of words that speaking children first acquire (Bonvillian et al., 1983). When deaf children begin to combine signs, their two-sign sentences are "telegraphic" statements that express the same set of semantic relations that appears in the early speech of hearing children. Finally, deaf children learning ASL and hearing children learning an oral tongue pass through roughly the same stages as they begin to acquire and use the grammatical rules of their respective languages. These striking parallels in the language learning of deaf and hearing children led Philip Dale (1976, p. 59) to conclude:

The really important aspects of language and the really important abilities the child brings to the problem of language learning are independent of the modality in which the linguistic system operates. Language is a central process, not a peripheral one. The abilities that [deaf children share with hearing children] are so general, and so powerful, that [the deaf] proceed through the same milestones of development as do hearing children.

    Today, many educators believe that deaf children should be exposed to both ASL and oral language as early as possible so that they can develop a broad range of general linguistic skills. Although this "total communication" training does not necessarily make it easier for deaf children to use the spoken language, it does make them more knowledgeable about communicating (see MacKay-Soroka, Trehub, & Thorpe, 1987) and may improve the quality of their social interactions with both their deaf and their hearing companions (Greenberg, 1984).

Table 8-4. Samples of one boy's speech at three ages

Age		
28 months (telegraphic speech)	*35 months*	*38 months*
Somebody pencil	No—I don't know	I like a racing car
Floor	What dat feeled like?	I broke my racing car
Where birdie go?	Lemme do again	It's broked
Read dat	Don't—don't hold with me	You got some beads
Hit hammer, Mommy	I'm going to drop it—inne dump truck	Who put dust on my hair?
Yep, it fit	Why—cracker can't talk?	Mommy don't let me buy some
Have screw	Those are mines	Why it's not working?

Source: Adapted from McNeill (1970).

old tugs at her father's shirtsleeve after pointing and saying "Cookie," her dad will undoubtedly realize that she is not simply naming the cookie for him. As children begin to combine words into telegraphic sentences, their use of gestures as aids to communication becomes more sophisticated. For example, 2-year-olds will often attempt to clarify the semantic relations they are trying to express by staring or pointing at the agent (or the object) of an action or by using hand and body movements to represent various actions and activities (Wilkinson & Rembold, 1981). Although we adults who are quite proficient with the spoken language may consider nonverbal gestures a rather primitive and inefficient form of communication, such an attitude is extremely shortsighted. Indeed, many deaf children come to know and use a rather sophisticated language that is based entirely on nonverbal signs and gestures (see Box 8-1).

Toddlers are also aware of many of the social and situational determinants of effective communication. For example, 2-year-olds have become rather proficient at vocal turntaking; they know that speakers "look up" at the listener when they are about to yield the floor, and they are now using this same nonverbal cue to signal the end of their own utterances (Rutter & Durkin, 1987). By age 2 to 2½, children know that they must either stand close to a listener or compensate for distance by raising their voices if they are to communicate with that person (Johnson, Pick, Siegel, Cicciarelli, & Garber, 1981; Wellman & Lempers, 1977). When talking to another toddler about some object or activity, the 2-year-old knows that he must stand close to the referent before his message is likely to be understood (Wellman & Lempers, 1977). Finally, 2-year-olds are beginning to listen carefully to the speech of their peers and will respond appropriately to many of the questions that other children ask (Garvey, 1984).

In sum, most 2–2½-year-olds have learned many practical lessons about language and communication even before they begin to use the grammatical rules of their native tongue. But although toddlers can communicate with adults and other children, their conversational skills pale in comparison with those of a 5-year-old, a 4-year-old, or even many 3-year-olds. Our next task is to determine what it is that preschool children are learning that will enable them to become rather sophisticated users of language by the ripe old age of 5, when they are about ready to enter kindergarten.

Language Learning during the Preschool Period

During the preschool period—ages 2½ to 5—children begin to produce some very lengthy sentences. Yet the most noteworthy aspect of preschool speech is not its length but its *complexity.* In Table 8-4 we see just how remarkably sophisticated a child's sentences can become over the brief span of seven to ten months.

What are children acquiring that enables them to produce complex sentences only a few short months after speaking in telegraphese? Surely they are mastering basic syntax. As we see in Table 8-4, a child of 35–38 months is now inserting articles, auxiliary verbs, and grammatical markers (for example, *-ed, -ing*) that were previously omitted, as well as negating propositions and occasionally asking a well-formed question. And although it is not as obvious from the table, we will see that preschool children are beginning to understand a number of complex semantic relations and are learning much more about the pragmatics of language and communication.

Table 8-5. Development of 14 grammatical markers in English: suffixes and function verbs

Morpheme	Meaning	Example
1. Present progressive: *-ing*	Ongoing process	He is sit*ting* down
2. Preposition: *in*	Containment	The mouse is *in* the box
3. Preposition: *on*	Support	The book is *on* the table
4. Plural: *-s*	Number	The dog*s* ran away
5. Past irregular: for example, *went*	Earlier in time relative to time of speaking	The boy *went* home
6. Possessive: *-'s*	Possession	The girl*'s* dog is big
7. Uncontractible copula *be:* for example, *are, was*	Number; earlier in time	*Are* they boys or girls? *Was* that a dog?
8. Articles: *the, a*	Definite/indefinite	He has *a* book
9. Past regular: *-ed*	Earlier in time	He jump*ed* the stream
10. Third person regular: *-s*	Number; earlier in time	She run*s* fast
11. Third person irregular: for example, *has, does*	Number; earlier in time	*Does* the dog bark?
12. Uncontractible auxiliary *be:* for example, *is, were*	Number; earlier in time; ongoing process	*Is* he running? *Were* they at home?
13. Contractible copula *be:* for example, *-'s, -'re*	Number; earlier in time	That*'s* a spaniel
14. Contractible auxiliary *be:* for example, *-'s, -'re*	Number; earlier in time; ongoing process	They*'re* running very slowly

Source: Clark & Clark (1977).

Acquiring Grammatical Morphemes

Grammatical morphemes are modifiers that give more precise meaning to the sentences we construct. These meaning modifiers usually appear sometime during the third year as children begin to pluralize nouns by adding *-s,* to signify location with the prepositional morphemes *in* and *on,* to indicate verb tense with the present progressive *-ing* or the past tense *-ed,* and to describe possessive relations with the inflection *-'s.*

Roger Brown (1973) kept records on three children as they acquired 14 grammatical morphemes that frequently appear in English sentences. He found that these three children varied considerably with respect to (1) the age at which they began to use grammatical markers and (2) the amount of time it took them to master all 14 rules. However, all three children in Brown's longitudinal study learned the 14 grammatical morphemes in precisely the order in which they appear in Table 8-5—a finding confirmed in a cross-sectional study of 21 additional children (de Villiers & de Villiers, 1973).

Why do children who have very different vocabularies learn these 14 grammatical markers in one particular order? Brown (1973) first hypothesized that

the order of acquisition might simply reflect the frequency of these 14 morphemes in parental speech. However, he soon rejected this "frequency" hypothesis when he found that the grammatical markers learned earliest appear no more often in parents' speech than the morphemes that are learned later.

Brown then considered the possibility that the morphemes acquired early may be less complex than those acquired late. A careful analysis of the semantic and syntactic complexity of each of the 14 morphemes revealed that simpler morphemes are indeed acquired earlier. For example, the present progressive *-ing,* which describes an ongoing action, appears before the past regular *-ed,* which describes both action and a sense of "earlier in time." Moreover, *-ed,* which conveys two semantic features, is acquired earlier than the uncontractible forms of the verb *to be (is, are, was, were),* which specify three semantic relations: number (singular or plural), tense (present or past), and action (ongoing process).

Young children also employ certain processing strategies that will make some morphemes easier to learn than others. For example, they seem to pay more attention to the ending of words and will find suffixes easier to learn than prefixes (Daneman & Case, 1981;

Kuczaj, 1979). They also tend to look for regularities in the language they hear and to avoid (or discount) exceptions to a general rule (Slobin, 1979). Let's examine this latter strategy, for it is responsible for many of the interesting and rather creative sentences that preschool children come up with.

Once young children have acquired a new grammatical morpheme, they will apply this rule to novel as well as to familiar contexts. For example, if the child realizes that the way to pluralize a noun is to add the grammatical inflection *-s,* he or she will have no problem solving the puzzle in Figure 8-3—these two funny-looking creatures are obviously wugs (Berko, 1958).

Since children generally avoid or discount exceptions to a rule, they will often overextend new grammatical morphemes to cases in which the adult form is irregular—a phenomenon known as **overregularization.** For example, it is quite common to hear preschool children make statements such as "I brushed my *tooths,*" "She *goed,*" or "It *runned.*" In so doing, the child is simply applying the regular morpheme for pluralization to the irregular noun *tooth* and the regular morpheme for past tense to the irregular verbs *go* and *run.*

Oddly enough, children often use the *correct* forms of many irregular nouns and verbs before they learn any grammatical morphemes. But once a new grammatical morpheme has been acquired, the child who has been correctly using irregulars such as *feet* and *went* will suddenly overregularize these words and say "foots" and "goed." Do these overgeneralizations represent giant leaps backward? Most psycholinguists say no. "Errors" of this kind merely indicate that children have discovered important new linguistic principles and are now applying them in a "creative" way to their own speech.

Mastering Transformational Rules

In addition to grammatical morphemes, each language has rules for creating variations of the basic declarative sentence. For example, people who speak English learn to transform declaratives into *wh-* questions by placing an appropriate *wh-* word *(who, what, when, where, why)* at the beginning of the sentence and then inverting the order of the subject and the auxiliary verb. Applying these rules, the declarative statement "I was eating pizza" can be modified to produce the question "What was I eating?" Other rules of **transformational grammar** that we have all mastered allow us to

This is a wug.

Now there is another one.   There are two of them.

There are two _____

Figure 8-3. A linguistic puzzle used to determine young children's understanding of the rule for forming plurals in English. *(From Berko, 1958.)*

generate *negative* sentences ("I was *not* eating pizza"), *imperatives* ("Eat the pizza!"), *relative clauses* ("I, who hate cheese, was eating pizza"), and *compound sentences* ("I was eating pizza and John was eating spaghetti").

As the child's mean length of utterance (MLU) rises above 2.5, he or she will begin to produce some variations of declarative sentences (Dale, 1976). However, young children acquire the transformational rules of their language in a step-by-step fashion, and as a result, their earliest transformations are very different from those of an adult. Let's now consider the stages that children pass through as they begin to ask questions, to negate propositions, and to generate complex sentences.

Learning to ask questions

There are two kinds of questions that are common to virtually all languages. *Yes/no questions* ask whether particular declarative statements are true or false. By contrast, *wh- questions* ask the respondent to provide information other than a yes-or-no answer. These latter queries are called *wh-* questions because, in En-

---

grammatical morphemes: prefixes, suffixes, prepositions, and auxiliary verbs that modify the meaning of words and sentences.

overregularization: the overgeneralization of grammatical rules to irregular cases where the rules do not apply (for example, saying "mouses" rather than "mice").

transformational grammar: rules of syntax that allow one to transform declarative statements into questions, negatives, imperatives, and other kinds of sentences.

Table 8-6. Transformational principles involved in generating yes/no and *wh-* questions

Declarative sentence	Transformation	Transformational rules
I. Yes/No questions		
I am swimming	Am I swimming?	1. Place the proper auxiliary verb *(am, is, are, do, does)* before the subject noun phrase
She is playing	Does she play often?	
II. Wh- questions		
They are going to church	Where are they going?	1. Insert *wh-* word at the beginning of the sentence
He sees the light	What does he see?	2. Invert the order of the subject noun and the auxiliary verb

glish, they almost always begin with a *wh-* word such as *who, what, where, when, which,* or *why.* Table 8-6 illustrates the transformational rules we use when generating yes/no and *wh-* questions.

The child's earliest questions often consist of nothing more than two- or three-word phrases uttered with a rising intonation (for example, "See doggie?"). However, a few *wh-* words are occasionally placed at the beginning of telegraphic sentences to produce simple *wh-* questions such as "Where doggie?" or "What Daddy eat?"

During the second stage of question asking, grammatical morphemes begin to appear in the child's interrogative sentences. However, word order remains a problem because the child does not yet reverse the positions of the subject and the auxiliary verb. Here are two examples of Stage 2 questions:

What Daddy is eating?
Who doggie is barking at?

Finally, children begin to place subjects and auxiliary verbs in the proper order, so that their questions sound pretty much like an adult's. However, they may occasionally produce utterances such as "Did I caught it?" or "What did you played?" because they do not yet realize that only the auxiliary verb is marked for tense in a simple interrogative sentence (Clark & Clark, 1977).

Several investigators have noted that children begin to ask "what," "where," and "who" questions long before they are requesting information about "why," "when," and "how" (Bloom, Merkin, & Wootten, 1982; Tyack & Ingram, 1977). One possible explanation for this finding is that questions of the form "what _____," "where _____," or "who _____" have concrete referents (objects, locations, and persons) that a cognitively immature toddler can easily comprehend. The implication of this line of reasoning is that children will begin to ask more "when _____," "how _____," and

"why _____" questions as they reach a point in their intellectual development at which they are better able to understand and appreciate abstract concepts such as time and causality.

Learning to produce negative sentences

The stages that children go through when learning to produce negative sentences are remarkably similar to the stages for asking questions. For example, the child's earliest negatives are formed by simply placing a negative marker at the beginning of an affirmative sentence to produce utterances such as

No sit there
Not a teddy bear

The child's next step is to move the negative marker within the sentence, placing it next to the verb stem that is to be modified. At this second stage, children are producing negatives such as

I no want milk
I not going there

Finally, children begin to combine their negative markers with auxiliary verbs such as *is, was, will, can,* and *do* to negate affirmative sentences in much the same way that adults do. Indeed, Peter and Jill de Villiers (1979) describe a delightful experiment in which young children were persuaded to argue with a talking puppet. Whenever the puppet made a declarative statement, such as "He likes bananas," the child's task was to negate the proposition (argue) in any way he or she could. Most 3–4-year-olds thoroughly enjoyed this escalating verbal warfare between themselves and the puppet. But more important, these young children were quite capable of using a wide variety of negative auxiliaries—including *wouldn't, wasn't, hasn't,* and *mustn't*—to properly negate almost any sentence the puppet produced.

Learning to produce complex sentences

When MLU reaches 3.5–4.0 (a milestone that may occur as early as age 2 or as late as 3½), children begin to produce complex sentences. The first complex constructions are often embedded sentences in which a noun phrase or a *wh-* clause serves as the object of a verb (Dale, 1976). Here are two examples:

I mean *that's a D* (noun phrase as the object)
I remember *where it is* (*wh-* clause as the object)

Within weeks, children are producing *relative clauses* that modify nouns (for example, "That's a box *that they put it in*") and joining simple sentences with the conjunctions *and, because,* and *so*—for example, "He was stuck *and* I got him out"; "I want some milk *'cause* I have a cold" (Dale, 1976; Hood & Bloom, 1979). By the end of the preschool period (age 5–6), children's oral language is very much like that of an adult. They have now acquired a working knowledge of most of the grammatical principles of their native language and are able to produce a variety of complex sentences without ever having had a formal lesson in grammar.

Semantic Development

Another reason language becomes more complex during the preschool period is that children are beginning to understand and appreciate relational contrasts such as big/little, tall/short, in/on, before/after, here/there, and I/you (de Villiers & de Villiers, 1979). The I/you distinction in conversations provides an example of how a knowledge of semantic relations comes to affect the structure of child language. To use *I* and *you* properly, the child must first understand that speakers use the term *I* to refer to the self and *you* to refer to a listener. As it turns out, the I/you contrast (including my/your and mine/yours) is among the first semantic relations that preschool children master, even though they have always been called "you" by their companions and must learn never to use this label when referring to the self (de Villiers & de Villiers, 1979).

Words that specify relations between people, objects, and events occur quite early in child language, although young children do not fully appreciate the meaning of many of these terms. For example, the word *more* is often one of the child's first words—one that is used to request a repetition of some kind ("more milk"; "more tickle"). Yet it is not until age 4–5 that children use relational terms in their full comparative sense to specify relations such as "This glass contains *more* than that one" (de Villiers & de Villiers, 1978).

Big and *little* are usually the first spatial adjectives to appear, and even 4–5-year-olds may continue to use these general terms to refer to variations in height, length, and width. Several researchers have devised linguistic games such as the argumentative-puppet technique to test children's knowledge of relational opposites like big/little, tall/short, wide/narrow, and deep/shallow. They have found that children acquire spatial opposites in the following order:

```
                tall/short          wide/narrow
big/little→                →high/low→              →deep/shallow
                long/short          thick/thin
```

There appear to be two reasons that spatial adjectives are learned in this particular order. First, children hear some adjectives more than others: *big* and *little* are by far the most frequent spatial terms in English, and even we adults seem to pay more attention to heights and lengths than to widths or thicknesses (for example, we are more apt to describe ourselves as tall or short than to mention whether we are thick or thin). Furthermore, the spatial adjectives that children acquire earliest are *less semantically complex* than those acquired later (Reich, 1986). For example, *big* and *little* refer to size (physical extent) along any and all spatial dimensions and are less precise than the adjectives *tall* and *short*, which convey two semantic relations (physical extent + verticality).

Although preschool children are becoming increasingly aware of a variety of meaningful relations and are learning how to express them orally, they continue to make some interesting semantic errors. Consider the following sentences:

1. The girl hit the boy.
2. The boy was hit by the girl.

Children younger than 5 or 6 frequently misinterpret *passive* constructions, such as sentence number 2 above. They can easily understand the *active* version of the same idea—that is, sentence 1. But if asked to point to a picture that shows "The boy was hit by the girl," preschoolers will usually select a drawing that shows a boy hitting a girl. What they have done is to assume that the first noun is the agent of the verb and that the second is the object; consequently, they interpret the passive construction as if it were an active sentence. The one exception to this rule is passives that make little sense when the child processes them as active sentences. For example, even a 3-year-old would correctly interpret "The candy was eaten by the girl" because it is nonsense to assume that the candy was the agent doing the eating (de Villiers & de Villiers, 1979).

Pragmatics and Communication Skills

During the preschool period, children are becoming increasingly aware of the pragmatics of language—that is, the rules specifying when to say what to whom in order to communicate effectively. For example, 3-year-olds already recognize that indirect commands such as "May I have some candy?" are more polite (and are probably more effective) than direct imperatives such as "Give me candy" (Bates, 1976). Some 3-year-olds can even turn declarative statements into highly successful commands, as we see in an episode described by Kenneth Reeder (1981, p. 135):

> Sheila, who is almost 3 years old, was visiting me . . . while her parents were shopping. An ice cream van, loud speaker jangling its promise of syrupy confections, stopped nearby. "Every night I get an ice cream" declared Sheila. Non-plussed, I used my stock response: "That's very nice Sheila." "Yes, even when there's a babysitter, I get an ice cream" Sheila explained patiently. I had been backed into a corner by a 3-year-old's grasp of the language as a social tool.

Three- to five-year-olds are also learning that they must tailor their messages to their audience if they hope to communicate effectively. Marilyn Shatz and Rochel Gelman (1973) recorded the speech of several 4-year-olds as they introduced a new toy to either a 2-year-old or an adult. An analysis of the tapes revealed that 4-year-old children are already proficient at adjusting their speech to their listener's level of understanding. When talking to a 2-year-old, the children used short sentences and were careful to choose phrases such as "Watch," "Look, Perry," and "Look here" that would attract and maintain the toddler's attention. By contrast, 4-year-olds explaining how the toy worked to an adult used complex sentences and were generally more polite.

Until recently, it was assumed that preschool children lacked the cognitive abilities or pragmatic skills to detect uninformative messages and to resolve most problems in communication. For example, if asked to evaluate the quality of an ambiguous message such as "Look at *that* horse" when a number of horses are in view, preschool children are more likely than their grade school counterparts to say that this is an *informative* message, thus suggesting that they are insensitive to lin-

guistic ambiguities. Moreover, 4-year-olds are less likely than 7-year-olds to restructure their own uninformative messages should these statements produce a puzzled look from a listener (Flavell, 1985). Yet, recent research suggests that the often subtle, unusual, and complex assessments of comprehension monitoring used in the laboratory may badly underestimate the communication skills of 3–5-year-olds. Consider that even 3-year-olds know that they cannot carry out a request made by a yawning adult whose speech is unintelligible, and they quickly realize that other impossible requests (such as "Bring me the refrigerator") are problematic as well (Revelle, Wellman, & Karabenick, 1985). Indeed, these young children also know how they might resolve such breakdowns in communication, for they will often say "What?" or "Huh?" to a yawning adult or will ask "How? It's too heavy!" when told to retrieve a refrigerator. There is even some evidence that young children are sensitive to some of the uninformative messages they produce, for 5-year-old kindergartners often reformulate ambiguous statements for their listeners during their turns at Show and Tell (Evans, 1985). And one reason kindergartners may detect and repair their own uninformative comments is that these messages often fail to elicit the nonverbal cues—gazes, smiles, head nods, and uh-huhs—that preschoolers have already learned to emit when they understand what they are hearing (Miller, Lechner, & Rugs, 1985).

Photo 8-4. Communication skills develop rapidly in the preschool years. Four-year-olds are already quite proficient at adjusting their messages to a listener's level of understanding.

In sum, 3–5-year-olds are better communicators than many of the older studies would have us believe. Although we will soon see that children become much more proficient at detecting and repairing uninformative messages during the grade school years, it seems that "even young preschoolers have general strategies for resolving comprehension difficulties, and . . . learn to use these strategies appropriately . . . to resolve a variety of [communication] problems" (Revelle et al., 1985, p. 662).

Refinement of Language Skills

Although 5-year-olds have learned a great deal about language in a remarkably brief period, many important strides in linguistic competence are made from ages 6 to 14—the grade school and junior high school years. Not only do schoolchildren use bigger words and produce longer and more complex utterances, they also begin to think about and manipulate language in ways that were previously impossible.

Later Syntactic Development

During middle childhood, children are correcting many of their previous syntactical errors and beginning to use a number of complex grammatical forms that did not appear in their earlier speech. For example, 5–8-year-olds are learning (or, in some cases, relearning) the correct past tenses for irregular verbs and the correct plurals for irregular nouns. They also begin to iron out the kinks in their use of personal pronouns, so that sentences such as "Him and her went" become much less frequent (Dale, 1976). Age 6–8 is the time that children begin to produce *tag questions* ("He will go, *won't he?*"; "You like candy, *don't you?*"), which are much more grammatically complex than yes/no or *wh-* questions (Dennis, Sugar, & Whitaker, 1982). And by age 7, children understand and may occasionally even produce simple passive sentences (de Villiers & de Villiers, 1979).

Clearly, middle childhood is a period of linguistic refinement: children are learning subtle exceptions to grammatical rules and coming to grips with the complex syntactical structures of their native tongue. However, this process of syntactic elaboration occurs very gradually, often continuing throughout junior high school and into the high school years (Clark & Clark, 1977).

Semantics and Metalinguistic Awareness

Children's knowledge of semantics and semantic relations continues to grow throughout the grade school years. Six-year-olds already understand some 8,000–14,000 words (Carey, 1977) and will continue to expand their productive vocabularies for many years to come. Grade school children are also becoming increasingly aware of the hierarchical relations among words and are able to label an object in many ways (for example, a big cat with spots is now recognized as a leopard, which, in turn, is a type of cat, an animal, and a living creature). Finally, school-age children gradually become more proficient at making inferences about meaning, so that they can understand more than is actually said. For example, if a 6–8-year-old hears "John did not see the rock; the rock was in the path; John fell," he is now able to infer that John must have tripped over the rock. By age 10, children can make this kind of linguistic inference (semantic integration) even when the two or more pieces of information that are necessary to draw the "appropriate" conclusion are separated by a number of intervening sentences (Johnson & Smith, 1981). And once children begin to integrate different kinds of linguistic information, they are able to detect *hidden* meanings that are not immediately obvious from the content of an utterance. For example, if a noisy 7-year-old hears her teacher remark "My, but you're quiet today," the child will probably note the contradiction between the literal meaning of the sentence and its context and thereby detect the *sarcasm* in her teacher's remark (Ackerman, 1986).

One reason that school-age children are able to "go beyond the information given" when making linguistic inferences is that they are rapidly developing **metalinguistic awareness**—an ability to think about language and to comment on its properties. This reflective ability emerges rather late—usually after age 5. Before that time, children are not even consciously aware of the relation between words and their component sounds. Questions such as "If you take the *s* sound off *scream* (or the *a* off *address*), what's left?" will leave them scratching their heads (de Villiers & de Villiers, 1979). Moreover, preschool children find it difficult to see words as arbitrarily connected to meanings. They

---

metalinguistic awareness: a knowledge of language and its properties; an understanding that language can be used for purposes other than communicating.

might think, for example, that a cow is called "cow" because it has horns—not because "cow" is what other people have arbitrarily decided to call members of this particular species.

Apparently, the emerging awareness that language is an arbitrary and rule-bound system has important educational implications, for children who score relatively high on metalinguistic tasks in kindergarten are apt to be the most proficient readers during the first and second grades (Wolf & Dickinson, 1985). Moreover, a developing knowledge of the structure and properties of language soon enables grade school children to detect and appreciate semantic ambiguities such as the "double meanings" of sentences like "The turkey is ready to eat" or "The shooting of the hunters was terrible."

At about the time children begin to think about linguistic ambiguities, they come to appreciate various jokes, riddles, and puns that are "funny" because of their play on sounds or words or the double meanings of certain syntactic structures (McGhee & Chapman, 1980). Finally, language also becomes increasingly "nonliteral" over the course of middle childhood. By age 10–11, children can appreciate and even generate some metaphors, and they are beginning to understand the proverbial meaning of figurative statements such as "When the cat's away, the mice will play" or "People who live in glass houses shouldn't throw stones" (Reynolds & Ortony, 1980; Saltz, 1979).

Growth of Communication Skills

Earlier, we examined a study (Shatz & Gelman, 1973) in which preschool children adjusted the style and content of their speech to match a listener's level of understanding. Recall that the 4-year-olds in this study were face to face with their 2-year-old or their adult companion and thus could see whether or not the listener was responding appropriately to their messages or following their instructions. Could children this young have communicated effectively with their partners if they had been asked to deliver their messages over a telephone?

Probably not. Robert Krauss and Sam Glucksberg (1977) designed an interesting set of experiments to assess the communication skills of 4–10-year-olds. Each child was asked to describe a set of unfamiliar graphic designs, printed on wooden blocks, to an age mate who had a duplicate set of designs. An opaque screen separated the speaker from the listener. The speaker's task was to stack his blocks and, at the same time, to tell the listener how to stack the duplicate blocks so that the two stacks would be identical. No restrictions were placed on communications between the speaker and the listener, and their successes were rewarded with small plastic trinkets. To learn the game, the children were given practice trials with familiar animal-shaped blocks under conditions where the speaker and listener could see each other. When they had learned the procedure, the speaker and listener were separated by the opaque screen and given eight opportunities to create identical stacks with the unfamiliar designs.

Preschool children failed miserably at this block-stacking task. As shown in Table 8-7, the younger speakers described each unfamiliar design in a holistic and idiosyncratic way, thus failing to mention *differences* among the designs that would have enabled their listeners to identify the particular stimuli that these young

Table 8-7. Typical idiosyncratic descriptions offered by preschool children when talking about unfamiliar graphic designs in the Krauss and Glucksberg communication game

Form	Child				
	1	2	3	4	5
	Man's legs	Airplane	Drapeholder	Zebra	Flying saucer
	Mother's hat	Ring	Keyhold	Lion	Snake
	Daddy's shirt	Milk jug	Shoe hold	Coffeepot	Dog

Source: Krauss & Glucksberg, 1977.

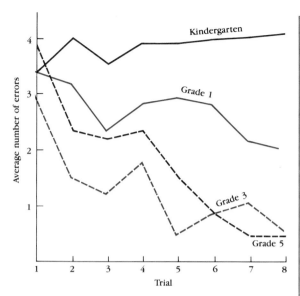

Figure 8-4. Average numbers of errors in communication for kindergarten children and for first-, third-, and fifth-graders. *(Adapted from Krauss & Glucksberg, 1969.)*

speakers were talking about. As a result, preschoolers were performing no better on the eighth block-stacking trial than they had on the first (see Figure 8-4). The third- and fifth-graders, however, were soon communicating effectively, as indicated by their nearly errorless performances over the last three or four trials. Clearly, communication skills improve rather dramatically over the course of middle childhood. But why?

Learning to generate informative messages. One reason that communication improves over time is that children gradually become more proficient at transmitting the kinds of information that will ensure that their messages are understood. Recently, Lisa Kahan and Dean Richards (1986) had 5–11-year-olds work at **referential communication** tasks similar to those used by Krauss and Glucksberg (1977). Like Krauss and Glucksberg's younger subjects, the 5–7-year-olds in this study used simple naming strategies when describing the stimuli, thereby failing to provide the critical information that a listener would need to *differentiate* one stimulus from another. By age 8, children had begun to talk about differences among the stimuli, and the 9–11-year-olds generally relied on a "differences" strategy rather than simply labeling, or naming, each object.

Older children are also better than younger

ones at anticipating what different listeners may need to know and tailoring their messages accordingly. Consider, for example, that a listener who is unfamiliar with the stimuli in a referential communication task may require more differentiating information and more message redundancy than a second person who is already familiar with these objects. Indeed, 9–10-year-olds do provide more redundant messages to "unfamiliar" than to "familiar" listeners, whereas 6–7-year-olds generally fail to adjust the content of their communications to the listener's apparent needs (Sonnenschein, 1986b).

Becoming a better listener. Of course, difficulties in communication can also arise if *listeners* fail to detect uninformative messages or, having detected them, fail to ask that they be clarified. Recently, Carol Beal (1987) found that 6–7-year-olds are reasonably proficient at repairing or revising the uninformative messages that they happen to judge as problematic; however, these younger listeners were less likely than older children to detect uninformative messages in the first place (see also Beal & Flavell, 1984). It seems that younger children often overlook problematic messages because they have at least a vague idea of what the speaker means and will assume that his intentions are clearly stated, particularly if the speaker is an adult (Beal & Flavell, 1984; Sonnenschein, 1986a). So if they hear an ambiguous statement such as "Pick up the next brown block" when two different-sized brown blocks are present, younger children are apt to conclude that "the next brown block" is an informative message and will often select the one closer to them. By contrast, 8–10-year-olds are more likely to monitor the *literal* meaning of the message they hear, to detect its ambiguity, and to request that it be clarified.

The communication skills of 5–10-year-olds can be improved by teaching young *speakers* to focus on differences among the stimuli that they are talking about (Pratt, McLaren, & Wickens, 1984; Sonnenschein & Whitehurst, 1984) and by encouraging young *listeners* to carefully monitor what they hear and to ask questions about statements they don't fully understand (see Patterson & Kister, 1981). Are speaking and listening skills closely related? Apparently so, for children who know how (or have been trained) to listen effectively are gen-

---

referential communication: communication that makes reference to objects or events that the listener is not currently experiencing.

erally able to monitor their own speech and produce informative messages (Pratt & Bates, 1982).

According to Olson and his colleagues (see Olson & Hildyard, 1983), the gradual improvements in communication skills that occur during the elementary school years are largely attributable to experiences children have had at evaluating messages that they *read* (in texts) and *write* (in themes or other homework assignments). Why should reading and writing be so important to the development of communicative abilities? Because discrepancies between the intended meaning of a message and its ambiguous literal meaning should be easier to detect (and correct) in written messages that can be scrutinized repeatedly than in oral communications, which are soon over and must be retrieved from memory. Indeed, Gary Bonitatibus and John Flavell (1985) found some support for Olson's theory: 6–7-year-olds who were just beginning to read were already much better at detecting uninformative messages when they read along as they listened than when they simply listened to the messages without having read them.

Theories of Language Development

As psycholinguists began to chart the course of language development, they were amazed that children could learn this complex symbol system at such a breathtaking pace. After all, infants are using abstract signifiers (words) to refer to objects and activities before they can even walk. By age 2, toddlers are generating hundreds of different messages in their telegraphic sentences. And by age 5, children already know and use most of the syntactical structures of their native tongue, even though they have yet to receive their first formal lesson in grammar. How do they do it? How can we possibly account for the fact that preschool children have such a rich understanding of this abstract symbol system that we call language?

At present, we have no truly definitive answers for these questions. What we do have available is a rich collection of theories, each of which has its strengths and weaknesses (Bohannon & Warren-Leubecker, 1985). In this final section of the chapter, we will review the three most influential of these approaches and see that each theory emphasizes certain mechanisms or processes that seem to play an important role in language development.

Learning Theories

Some disagreement exists among learning theorists about how children learn to talk. One group of researchers believe that language is learned through operant conditioning as adults *reinforce* children for their attempts to produce grammatical speech (Skinner, 1957; Staats & Staats, 1963). Others have argued that children acquire language by listening to and then *imitating* the speech of their older companions (Whitehurst, 1982).

The reinforcement model

In 1957 B. F. Skinner published a book entitled *Verbal Behavior* in which he argued that children learn to speak appropriately because they are reinforced for grammatical speech. Skinner believed that adults begin to shape a child's language by selectively reinforcing those aspects of babbling that are most like adult speech, thereby increasing the probability that these sounds will be repeated. Once they have "shaped" sounds into words, adults will presumably withhold further reinforcement (attention or approval) until the child begins combining words—first into primitive sentences and then into longer grammatical utterances. So caregivers were said to teach language by reinforcing successive approximations of grammatical speech until the child is talking like an adult.

Another way that parents and other companions might reinforce language is to correctly interpret what the child is trying to say. According to the **communication pressure hypothesis,** children learn to speak more clearly and grammatically because they need to communicate their needs to others (Dale, 1976). The idea here is that adults are most likely to understand grammatical speech and then unwittingly reinforce these interpretable utterances by attending to the child's requests and satisfying his needs.

Do parents really "shape" their child's language? If reinforcement theory were a plausible explanation for language learning, we should find that parents often reinforce their children's grammatical speech (perhaps by saying "Very good" or nodding approval) while discouraging ungrammatical utterances. Yet, Roger Brown and Camille Hanlon (1970) found that a mother's approval or disapproval of her child's speech depends more on its truth value than on its grammatical properties. For example, when one child referred to her mother by saying "He a girl" (truthful but grammatically incorrect), her mother replied "That's right!" When another child called attention to a lighthouse by stating

"There's the animal farmhouse" (syntactically correct but untruthful), her mother quickly corrected her. So it appears that parents pay very little attention to their child's early grammar and do not actively attempt to shape grammatical speech (see also Penner, 1987). What they are likely to reinforce when talking with their children is the *semantic* appropriateness, or "truth value," of the child's utterances.

There was a second important finding in the Brown and Hanlon (1970) study: mothers were just as likely to answer children's questions or to satisfy their needs when the children generated a primitive (ungrammatical) utterance such as "Want milk" as when they produced a well-formed version of the same idea (for example, "I want some milk"). Thus, there was no support for the communication pressure hypothesis: mothers could easily understand their children's ungrammatical statements and would often reinforce this imperfect speech by attending to the child's needs. So why does the child's language eventually become more complex? Certainly not because of any need or "pressure" to communicate effectively.

Imitation as a basis for language learning

Imitation must play some part in language learning, for children end up speaking the same language as the other members of their families and usually will even acquire an accent that characterizes the subculture or the geographical region in which they are raised. Moreover, studies of language learning suggest that young children often learn to name things by listening to the words others use and then reproducing these labels (Ammon & Ammon, 1971; Leonard, Chapman, Rowan, & Weiss, 1983).

But what about syntax? Although children may learn new words by imitating the speech they hear, there are several reasons to believe they rely on other strategies to learn the rules of syntax. If 2–3-year-olds learned to construct sentences by imitating their parents' speech, then their utterances ought to reflect at least some principles of adult grammar from the very beginning. Yet, what do children omit when they produce telegraphic statements? They drop the auxiliary verbs and other grammatical morphemes—precisely the elements they should be including if they were acquiring grammatical knowledge by imitating the speech of their close companions. Moreover, we have seen that many of the child's earliest sentences are highly creative statements such as "Allgone cookie" or "It broked" that do not appear in

adult speech and thus could not have been learned by imitation. Finally, when children do try to mimic an adult utterance, they usually condense or otherwise reformulate the statement so that it conforms to their own level of grammatical competence. Consider the following conversation in which a mother tried to teach a grammatical rule to her child by having him imitate her utterance (from McNeill, 1970, pp. 106–107).

Child: Nobody don't like me.
Mother: No, say "nobody likes me."
Child: Nobody don't like me.
[eight repetitions of this dialogue follow . . . then]
Mother: No, now listen carefully; say "*nobody likes me.*"
Child: Oh! Nobody don't likes me.

This is hardly an atypical example. Lois Bloom and her colleagues (Bloom, Hood, & Lightbown, 1974) report that children do not readily imitate a grammatical rule until they have already used that principle at least once in their spontaneous speech. So imitation may help a child to properly apply rules that he partially understands and is beginning to use, but it is probably not the mechanism by which these rules are learned in the first place (Slobin, 1979).

How do the child's companions promote language learning?

Now we begin to see why language development is such a challenging topic. If a child does not directly imitate parental speech, and if parents do not "shape" the child's language, then just what role do others play in language learning? In recent years, psycholinguists have tried to answer this question by carefully analyzing the ways older people talk to young children. Let's see what they have learned.

Opportunities to communicate. Earlier we noted that even prelinguistic infants are learning many lessons about language and communication within the context of mutual play, vocal turntaking, and other joint activities with their close companions. How important are these shared activities to the child's language development? Apparently they are very important. Michael Tomasello and Jeff Farrar (1986) recorded and analyzed linguistic interactions between 24 mothers and

---

communication pressure hypothesis: the idea that children learn to speak clearly and grammatically because clear, grammatical statements will effectively communicate their needs and desires.

their infants when the infants were 15 and 21 months of age. They found that very general measures of the mother's speech to their infants (such as total amount of speech and speech complexity) did *not* predict the infants' language proficiency or language development. Yet, one specific measure, the extent to which mothers spoke about objects to which they and their infants were *jointly attending* (such as toys that they were sharing), was a strong predictor of early language: the mothers who referred to such objects the most had children with the largest productive vocabularies. Clearly these findings make a good deal of sense, for if a child is already interested in objects the mother is talking about, he should be highly motivated to decipher the meaning of his mother's speech.

Is the child's language development affected by the willingness of close companions to initiate and maintain conversations? Apparently so, for parents who frequently encourage vocal dialogues by asking questions, making requests, or issuing commands that invite verbal responses have children who are quicker to acquire syntactical rules and produce longer utterances during the preschool period, who recognize more letters and numbers by age 5–6, and who score higher on tests of reading proficiency in second grade, compared with children from similar backgrounds whose parents are less conversant (Hoff-Ginsberg, 1986; Norman-Jackson, 1982; Price, Hess, & Dickson, 1981).

But interesting as these findings may be, several questions remain. How do children come to understand grammatical rules as they converse with others? Does it matter what close companions are saying; or, rather, could infants and toddlers learn to talk just as well if they spent thousands of hours listening to people on television? Let's see whether we can shed some light on these issues by considering what parents seem to be doing when they talk to their children.

Talking the child's language. When adults converse with one another, their sentences tend to be long and grammatically complex. By contrast, parents and older siblings address infants and toddlers with very short, simple sentences that linguists call "baby talk" or **motherese** (Gelman & Shatz, 1977). Typically these utterances are spoken slowly and in a high-pitched voice, with an emphasis on certain key words (usually words for objects or activities). Much of motherese consists of questions ("Where's the ball?") or simple imperatives ("Throw it") that may be paraphrased or repeated several times in order to attract the child's attention and

help him to understand. As it turns out, parents and other adults are quite proficient at adjusting their speech to a child's level of understanding. In one study, the language used by 20 adult strangers was recorded as each of the adults conversed with a 2-year-old boy. The results were clear: whenever the 2-year-old gave some indication that he did not understand one of the adult's statements, the adult's next sentence was shorter and less complex (Bohannon & Marquis, 1977).

Other investigators have found that mothers gradually increase both the length and complexity of their own sentences as their children's language becomes more elaborate (Newport, Gleitman, & Gleitman, 1977; Shatz, 1983). And at any given point in time, the adult's sentences are slightly longer and slightly more complex than the child's (Bohannon & Warren-Leubecker, 1985). Here, then, is a situation that might seem to be ideal for language learning. The child is constantly exposed to new semantic relations and grammatical rules that appear in simple utterances that he will probably understand—particularly if older companions frequently repeat or paraphrase the ideas they are trying to communicate. Clearly, this is a form of modeling by the parent. However, children do not acquire new grammatical principles by mimicking them directly, nor do adults make an active attempt to teach these principles by illustration. Parents speak in "motherese" for one main reason—to communicate effectively with their children.

Expansions, recasts, and topic extensions. Often adults will react to a child's telegraphic utterances by re-forming or **expanding** them so that they include the missing grammatical morphemes. For example, if the child says "Doggie go," a parent might expand this sentence by saying "Yes, the doggie is going for a walk." What the adult has done is to draw a direct comparison between the child's primitive sentence and the grammatical forms that an adult might use to express the same idea. A slightly different form of expansion occurs when adults **recast** the child's sentences into new grammatical forms. For example, a child who says "Doggie eat" might have his sentence restructured as "What is the doggie eating?" or "Yes, the doggie is hungry." These recasts are moderately novel utterances that will probably command the child's attention and thereby increase the likelihood that he will notice the new grammatical forms that appear in the adult's speech. Finally, adults often introduce new linguistic principles by merely maintaining and extending *interesting* conversations with their child (topic extension).

Photo 8-5. Older companions speak a simple, high-pitched, and repetitive language when talking to infants and toddlers—a language known as "motherese."

Do children profit from these experiences? Many psycholinguists think so. Although young children rarely mimic new grammatical forms immediately, there is some evidence that they tend to imitate expansions and recasts more readily than other kinds of adult utterances (Folger & Chapman, 1978; Scherer & Olswang, 1984). Moreover, adults who frequently expand, recast, or otherwise extend their children's speech have youngsters who are quick to acquire certain syntactical principles, particularly use of auxiliary verbs and other markers for verb tense (Barnes, Gutfreund, Satterly, & Wells, 1983; Hoff-Ginsberg, 1986; Newport et al., 1977).

Do parents expand or recast their child's utterances as part of a conscious attempt to teach language? It might seem that way, for adults regularly modify the child's ungrammatical utterances, while responding to grammatical statements with topic extensions. Yet, Sharon Penner (1987) finds that parents are not even aware that they do this and, in fact, will insist that they respond in the same way to grammatical and ungrammatical statements. Why are parents unaware of their tendency to reshape ungrammatical utterances? Simply because their expansions and recasts are ploys to com-

municate more effectively with their children rather than deliberate attempts to improve the children's grammar (Penner, 1987).

Are environmental props necessary? Adults who speak motherese and who expand and recast their child's sentences may be providing an ideal environment for language learning—one that contains a rich variety of sentences that are moderately novel but, at the same time, are related to the ideas that the child is currently expressing. Yet, we might wonder whether these modifications of adult speech are really

---

motherese: the short, simple, high-pitched (and often repetitive) sentences that adults use when talking with young children.

expansions: responding to a child's ungrammatical utterance with a grammatically improved form of that statement.

recasts: responding to a child's ungrammatical utterance with a nonrepetitive statement that is grammatically correct.

necessary for normal language acquisition. Stated another way, would children learn to talk just as well if adults spoke to them as if they were adults? Could they acquire language by merely listening to adults converse with one another or by watching and listening to people on television?

Let's consider the evidence bearing on the first question. Certain cultures (namely, the Kaluli of New Guinea and the natives of American Samoa) consider infants younger than 18 months to be largely incapable of understanding language, and no attempts are made to communicate with them (Ochs, 1982; Schieffelin & Ochs, 1983). And once these infants and toddlers begin to speak, their companions rarely if ever respond in motherese or restructure primitive sentences; instead, they converse with their children as if they were adults and insist that these youngsters try to talk as adults do. Are these children linguistically retarded? No, indeed, for they acquire a wide range of verbal skills, making great strides toward linguistic competence during the preschool period. So even though environmental props such as motherese and adult expansions may make a language a bit easier for the young child to decipher, they are not absolutely necessary for normal language development.

Could children, then, acquire language by merely listening to others converse? Apparently not. Catherine Snow and her associates (Snow et al., 1976) studied a group of Dutch children who happened to watch a great deal of German television. Despite their prolonged exposure to the German language, these Dutch-speaking subjects did not acquire any German words or grammar. De Villiers and de Villiers (1979) also cite the case of a hearing child of deaf parents who saw his parents sign to each other (but not to him) and who had little opportunity to hear any oral speech other than that on television. This child learned no formal sign language from watching his parents, and his oral speech included only a few words like *Kool-aid* that had been taken from television jingles. By age 4, this boy was combining words into highly idiosyncratic strings (for example, "That enough two wing"; "Fall that back") that clearly reflected his ignorance of most grammatical principles. After reviewing this evidence, de Villiers and de Villiers concluded that "at least some minimal exposure to [*conversations*] with speakers of the language [is absolutely] necessary for normal language acquisition" (p. 105; italics added).

In sum, parents and other companions play a crucial role in the child's language development by con-

versing with him or her and thereby introducing new linguistic principles in sentences that are tailored to the child's level of understanding. (Indeed, this tailoring of speech to the child's comprehension occurs even within those cultures where companions rarely restructure the child's utterances or talk in motherese.) But let's recall that children do not immediately mimic new linguistic forms and are not systematically reinforced for using them. How, then, do they ever acquire this information? Why do they continue to produce increasingly complex sentences? In recent years, a number of linguists have proposed a biological theory of language development—*nativism*—in an attempt to answer these questions.

The Nativist Perspective

According to the nativists, human beings are biologically programmed to acquire language. Prominent linguists such as Noam Chomsky (1968, 1980) and David McNeill (1970) have proposed that only humans have a built-in language acquisition device, or LAD—consisting of at least some inborn knowledge about the structural properties of language as well as a set of cognitive and perceptual abilities that are specialized for language learning. Presumably the LAD functions as a "language processor" that enables the child to infer the phonological, semantic, and syntactical regularities that appear in the speech of close companions. As children make inferences about semantic relations and sentence structures, they will then rely on these linguistic hypotheses to construct their own sentences.

An example will help to illustrate how a LAD might operate. Let's suppose that a 2-year-old girl reliably produces the utterance "There doggie" every time she ventures into the back yard and sees the two family pets that live there. If her companions frequently recast these (or similar) utterances to illustrate the plural form of singular nouns (for example, "What are the doggies doing?"), the LAD will eventually detect the rule for pluralization, and the child should begin to apply this principle in her own speech. In fact, nativists contend that overregularization errors such as "My *foots* are cold" or "I brushed my *tooths*" must surely mean that children have inferred the rule for pluralization on their own and are now merely demonstrating their newly acquired grammatical competence in these highly "creative" sentences. After all, these constructions would not have been taught by adults and do not appear in adult speech—unless, of course, an adult chooses to mimic a child.

If we assume that children have some unique, inborn capacity for language learning (such as a LAD), then it is easy to see how they might become rather proficient speakers without the benefit of any formal instruction. Recall that adults conversing with a child tend to adjust their speech so that it is slightly more complex than the child's. Moreover, we have seen that parents will gradually increase the complexity of their own speech as their children's utterances become more elaborate. Nativists would argue that this changing pattern of parental speech is the ideal environment for language learning, for children are constantly being exposed to new linguistic principles that will be detected by the LAD and then applied to their own speech.

The evidence for nativism

It does seem that human beings must have some unique, inborn capacity for language; after all, no subhuman species has devised anything that closely approximates a rule-bound linguistic system, whereas all normal, healthy children who are exposed to language will become language users. Now suppose that we tried to teach a chimpanzee to use a form of language and found that our subject could produce two-, three-, and even four-word strings. Would this imply that chimps have an inborn linguistic capability that is simply not used in the natural environment? In recent years psycholinguists have had to grapple with this issue, for a small number of chimpanzees have now been trained to use "linguistic" signs and symbols as a means of communicating with human beings. A portion of this intriguing research is described in Box 8-2.

Even if we were to conclude that language is unique to human beings, it remains to be shown that children are biologically programmed for language learning. Over the years, nativists have made several observations that they believe to be consistent with their biological explanation of language development. Let's examine the record for ourselves.

Brain specialization and language. As we learned in Chapter 5, the brain is a lateralized organ with major language centers located in the left cerebral hemisphere. If one of these language areas is damaged, the individual will typically experience **aphasia**—a loss of one or more language functions—and the symptoms that an aphasic displays will depend on the site and the extent of the injury. Injuries to Broca's area, near the frontal region of the left hemisphere, typically affect speech production rather than comprehension (Slobin,

1979). By contrast, patients who suffer an injury to Wernicke's area, at the back of the left hemisphere, may speak fairly well but will have difficulty understanding speech.

Apparently the left hemisphere is sensitive to some aspects of language from birth. In the first day of life, speech sounds already elicit more electrical activity from the left side of an infant's brain, while music and other nonspeech sounds produce greater activity from the right cerebral hemisphere (Molfese, 1977). Moreover, we've seen that infants are quite capable of discriminating important phonetic contrasts such as *b* and *p* or *d* and *t* during the first few weeks of life (Eimas, 1982). These findings would seem to imply that the neonate is "wired" for speech and is prepared to analyze speechlike sounds.

The critical-period hypothesis. It often seems as if preschool children acquire their first language far more easily than college students learn a foreign tongue. Is this really the case? Nativists believe it is: they have argued that human beings are most proficient at language learning during the period between age 2 and puberty.

Eric Lenneberg (1967) is perhaps the strongest proponent of the **critical-period hypothesis** for language learning. Lenneberg notes that prepubescent children can easily acquire two (or more) languages simultaneously and will speak each tongue without a trace of an accent from the other language(s). By contrast, he argues, those who acquire a second language after puberty must study intently to become fluent in that language, and they are likely to speak their new tongue with a "foreign" accent. In addition, the prognosis for recovering from traumatic aphasia depends on the age at which the injury was sustained. Children who suffer brain damage before puberty will recover most if not all of their lost language functions without special therapy, particularly if their injury occurred before age 5 (de Villiers & de Villiers, 1978). However, adolescent and adult aphasics often require extensive therapy to regain even a portion of their lost language skills. These observations suggest that the brain is particularly well suit-

---

aphasia: loss of one or more language functions due to an injury to the brain.

critical-period hypothesis: the notion that human beings are most proficient at language learning between age 2 and puberty.

Box 8-2
**Language Learning in
Chimpanzees**

Perhaps it's only natural for us humans to wonder whether chimpanzees and other primates that look so much like us could ever learn to express their ideas through some form of language. Earlier in this century, several attempts were made to raise chimpanzees like children and to teach them to speak English (Hayes, 1951; Kellogg & Kellogg, 1933). Unfortunately, these projects were destined to fail, for the vocal apparatus of a chimpanzee is structurally incapable of producing the many phonemes of human speech.

Washoe. Allen and Beatrice Gardner (1969, 1974) then tried a new approach that proved much more successful: they taught a young chimpanzee named Washoe to use the American Sign Language of the deaf (ASL).

At first Washoe learned the meanings of individual signs and increased her vocabulary one "word" at a time, just as young children do. Within a year, she was producing strings of two to three signs that expressed many of the semantic relations seen in children's telegraphic speech. Chimpanzees can also use signs to name new objects. For example, on seeing a duck for the first time, Washoe signed "water bird," and another ASL-trained chimp, Lucy, invented the sign "drink fruit" (that is, drink + fruit) to describe a watermelon. By age 4, Washoe had a productive vocabulary of 160 signs

and could understand many others that she did not produce. It is also apparent that she can carry on a simple dialogue with a human being, as we see in the following episode described by Dan Slobin (1979):

Human (pointing to Washoe's bed): What that?
Washoe: Bed.
Human: Whose?
Washoe: Mine.
Human: What color [is it]?
Washoe: Red.

Washoe also initiates conversations by describing objects and events, making requests, and asking simple questions (Gardner & Gardner, 1974; Slobin, 1979). She seems to have acquired the rudiments of a language, although she has not progressed beyond the capabilities of a 2–2½-year-old child.

The Yerkes chimps. Lana, Austin, and Sherman are chimpanzees at the Yerkes Primate Center who have learned to use hieroglyphics printed on a special keyboard to type messages to a computer (the locations of these hieroglyphic words are changed frequently to ensure that the chimps are responding to the symbolism rather than to the positions of particular keys). Lana, the first pupil, has learned to request a variety of foods, moving pictures, music, and even human contact by simply typing hieroglyphic sentences of the form "Please, machine, give _____." She asks the machine to name new objects she has never

seen before. Moreover, she recognizes when she has made a productive error in her sentences by erasing mistakes and starting the sequence over to get her message across (Rumbaugh, 1977).

The accomplishments of Austin and Sherman are more impressive. Not only can these chimps rely on abstract symbols to represent *novel* aspects of experience (for example, using hieroglyphics for the concepts "edible" and "inedible" to correctly classify foodstuffs and other objects that they have never seen before; see Savage-Rumbaugh, 1981), but they have also learned to use the hieroglyphic "language" to communicate with each other! The conversational scenario is straightforward: one chimp needs one of six tools to obtain some food that the other chimp can't see. The "requester" then asks (in machine language) for the necessary tool, and the "provider" must then decipher the message and select the appropriate implement. Left to their own natural devices (gestures and calls), the provider ends up selecting the right tool less than 10% of the time. But using the machine language, the accuracy of communication between these chimps rises to better than 90%, even when human experimenters are absent (Savage-Rumbaugh, Rumbaugh, & Boysen, 1978). Clearly, this is a form of *communication* that relies on arbitrary and abstract symbols for a meaningful exchange of information. But is it language?

Criticisms of this monkey business. Remarkable as these accom-
continued

ed for language acquisition before the onset of puberty. But why?

According to nativists, the critical period for language learning is a product of biological maturation. Lenneberg (1967) proposes that the brain is not fully specialized for language functions until it is fully mature, at puberty. Presumably a young aphasic can recover lost language skills because the right hemisphere of his or her relatively unspecialized (immature) brain is able to assume the functions that would normally be served by the damaged areas of the left hemisphere. At

puberty the prognosis changes. The brain is now completely specialized for language (and other neurological duties), so that the right hemisphere can no longer assume the linguistic functions lost when a person suffers an injury to the left side of the brain.

Linguistic universals. If language learning is unique to humans and heavily influenced by biological maturation, then all normal, healthy children should proceed through roughly the same stages when acquiring their first language. And apparently they do

Until very recently, it was assumed that only humans had a capacity for language. This viewpoint is now being challenged by the progress of several chimpanzees (and at least one gorilla) who have learned to communicate simple and sometimes inventive messages using American Sign Language.

plishments may seem, many psycholinguists are hesitant to conclude that Washoe or the Yerkes chimps have acquired a language. One of the more vocal critics, Herbert Terrace (1979; Terrace, cited in "Are Those Apes Really Talking?," 1980), actually began as an advocate of chimp language. He first taught sign language to a pupil named Nim Chimpsky (an obvious play on the name of nativist Noam Chomsky) and later discovered that Nim did not use the language to invent new sentences. Terrace then reviewed reports and videotapes of other "linguistic" chimps and concluded that all of them were simply producing either routines they had memorized or sentences that had been "cued" by the actions and gestures of a human trainer. Even Lana's, Austin's, and

Sherman's uses of hieroglyphic symbols were viewed as nonlinguistic ploys to gain a reward of some kind. The Gardners, however, insist that their pupils use language inventively and are capable of interpreting sentences that they have never seen before. Moreover, there are some exciting new developments with a rare chimpanzee species (called pygmy chimps) that is more sociable, less aggressive, and seemingly more intelligent than chimps studied previously. One pygmy chimp named Kanzi spontaneously produced prelinguistic gestures that are very similar to those of prelinguistic human infants (for example, combining pointing with vocalizations to communicate effectively; see Savage-Rumbaugh, 1984). Moreover, Kanzi has acquired some

manual signs by merely observing his mother's training, and he and his younger sister, who are now in a formal training program, are showing early signs of superior ability.

The "great debate" about the linguistic capabilities of chimpanzees will undoubtedly continue for some time unless chimps suddenly display more linguistic prowess than they have shown thus far. Clearly, the accomplishments of Washoe and the Yerkes clan are similar in many respects to the language of toddlers. However, let's keep in mind that even a severely retarded child will soon surpass the linguistic accomplishments of the brightest of chimpanzees studied to date. Obviously, human beings must have something chimps lack that enables them to acquire language as we know it. Is that something an inborn linguistic capability (or LAD) that is unique to humans? Noam Chomsky says yes and adds: "It is about as likely that an ape will prove to have a language ability as that there is an island somewhere with a species of flightless birds waiting for human beings to teach them to fly" ("Are Those Apes Really Talking?," 1980, p. 57). However, David Premack (1976) suggests that a chimp's relatively modest linguistic accomplishments may be attributable to the animal's smaller brain and more limited intellectual potential rather than to the absence of a specialized linguistic processor. It remains for future research to determine which of these two alternatives is correct.

(this is what is meant by **linguistic universals**). Even though children are typically exposed to language from the first day or two of life, they do not begin to babble for several months or to produce meaningful words for about a year. All children in all cultures show a similar pattern of phonological development. And as infants begin to "talk," they always start out with holophrastic utterances, progress to telegraphic sentences, and express precisely the same kinds of semantic and syntactic relations in their telegraphic speech (Slobin, 1979—review Table 8-2). All normal children will acquire and

use the basic syntax of their native language by the time they enter school, and they almost invariably develop the ability to think about language and its properties (that is, metalinguistic awareness) between ages 6 and 10 (de Villiers & de Villiers, 1978). Children with Down's syndrome, who mature very slowly, will proceed through these same stages of language development—though at

---

linguistic universal: an aspect of language development that all children share.

Box 8-3
On the "Invention" of Language by Children

Suppose ten children were raised in isolation by an adult caregiver who attended to their basic needs but never talked or even gestured to them in any way. Would these youngsters devise some method of communicating among themselves? No one can say for sure, for children such as these have never been studied. However, the results of two recent programs of research suggest that our hypothetical children not only would learn to communicate but might even invent their own language.

Home sign among the deaf. Susan Goldin-Meadow and Carolyn Mylander (1984) have observed the progress of ten deaf children aged 1½ to 3 years, all of whom had hearing parents who knew little if anything about sign language. Clearly, these children were exposed to very atypical linguistic environments in that they couldn't hear oral speech and their parents were unable to instruct them in the use of signs. Would these youngsters invent a system of communicating in the absence of a language model? Could they create their own unique sign languages?

Apparently so, for each of these children eventually began to use three kinds of signs: (1) *pointing gestures* to call attention to people, places, and things, (2) *characterizing signs* to represent ac-

tions, objects, or attributes (for example, digging actions to refer to a snow shovel; a fist at the mouth accompanied by chewing to represent eating; a thumb and forefinger held aloft in a circle to signify roundness), and (3) *nonverbal markers,* such as headshakes and nods, to indicate yes/no or otherwise convey semantic intent. Moreover, these youngsters soon combined their idiosyncratic signs into "sign sentences" that showed many of the structural regularities characteristic of any early child language (for example, consistent sign ordering for agents, verbs, and objects). Careful analyses of the interactions between these deaf children and their parents revealed that the "home signs" that the children used were their *own inventions* rather than imitations of parental gestures. And it is interesting to note that parents did not systematically reinforce well-formed "sign sentences"; in fact, they did exactly what parents of hearing children do—they reinforced the truth value, or "semantic appropriateness," of their child's sign sentences and paid little attention to the sentences' grammatical properties.

In sum, the highly idiosyncratic "home sign" languages that these deaf children created suggest that young human beings have a strong bias to communicate in languagelike ways—a conclusion bolstered by the research that follows.

Transforming pidgin to true language. When adult speakers of different languages are thrust together into

a single culture, they often begin to communicate in *pidgin*—a hybrid blending their contrasting tongues that enables speakers from different linguistic backgrounds to convey meaning, even though pidgin lacks the formal syntactical properties of a true language and its form may vary considerably from speaker to speaker. According to linguist Derek Bickerton (1983, 1984) the children of pidgin-speaking adults do not speak pidgin. Instead, they spontaneously invent syntactical rules that enable them to transform pidgin into true languages known as *creoles*—languages that are then used by future generations in these multilingual societies. Moreover, the syntactical rules that children develop when creolizing a pidgin are remarkably similar the world over—so similar that they cannot be attributed to chance. In fact, Bickerton believes that only a nativist model can account for these observations. In his own words: "The most cogent explanation of this similarity" of creoles the world over "is that it derives from . . . a species-specific program for language, genetically coded and expressed . . . in the structures . . . and operation of the human brain" (1984, p. 173).

So it seems that children who lack a formal linguistic model—be they deaf or subjected to marginally linguistic pidgins—will create languagelike codes to communicate with their companions. Apparently, they have some linguistic predispositions that serve them well.

---

a much slower pace. Even severely retarded children who can neither count nor grasp the rules of kindergarten games will nevertheless acquire many abstract principles of syntax and become adequate conversationalists (Lenneberg, 1967). Finally, nativists interpret the research in Box 8-3 as a rather dramatic illustration that language use is a basic aspect of human nature.

Why is language easier to learn (or perhaps even easier to invent) than counting or other sets of rules? A nativist would respond by arguing that all human beings, including retarded children, are born with certain cognitive and perceptual abilities (a LAD) that

are specialized for language learning. As these abilities mature, all children should pass through the same sequence of linguistic "milestones," and they will require nothing other than regular interactions with speaking companions in order to learn any and all languages to which they are exposed.

Problems with the nativist approach

Today almost everyone agrees that language development is influenced by biological development. However, many contemporary researchers question the notion that human beings have any innate knowledge of language, or specialized language processor (LAD), that functions most efficiently during a "critical period" between birth and puberty. Although it is true that young children can easily acquire more than one language without undue interference as long as their models for each language are consistent in the use of one tongue (as when a father speaks only English to a child and a mother only Vietnamese, for example; see Reich, 1986, for a review), evidence against the critical-period hypothesis comes from many sources. Consider that adults who receive intensive training in a foreign language require only 250–500 hours of instruction to achieve a "comfortable" level of fluency, and even the most complex languages (such as Vietnamese) require but 1300 hours of study for adults to obtain near-native levels of competence (Burke, 1974; Carroll, 1969). And in one study of American families that had moved to Holland (Snow & Hoefnagel-Hohle, 1978), adolescents and adults were quicker to acquire a working knowledge of the Dutch language than were the families' prepubescent children. Moreover, it is by no means impossible for an adult to learn to speak a foreign language without a detectable accent. In fact, controlled studies often find that adults are no worse and occasionally better than younger children at the phonological aspects of second-language learning (see Reich, 1986). Finally, if puberty were truly the end of a "critical period" for language acquisition, it would be difficult to explain the progress of many so-called "wild children" who have already reached puberty before having any opportunities to converse with anyone. Let's take a closer look.

The most intensively studied of these wild children is Genie, a young girl who was 13½ in November 1970 when found locked in an attic. Genie had been raised in isolation for the preceding 12 years by her parents, who had never spoken to her or even vocalized, except for the occasional growling sounds that her father would make to suppress her own vocalizations. Nor were there radios and TVs in the house for her to hear. Not surprisingly, Genie displayed no evidence of language at the time of her liberation. But within eight months, this postpubescent waif had learned most English phonemes, acquired a vocabulary of 200 words, and begun to generate two-word "telegraphic" sentences (Curtiss, 1977). And over the next several years, Genie's language continued to develop as she produced longer and longer sentences that were rich in their semantic content, though syntactically incomplete. Here are two examples:

M ____ say not lift my leg in dentist chair.
Mr. W____ say put face in big swimming pool.

According to Peter Reich (1986), several other postpubertal "wild children" have achieved similar levels of language proficiency (the levels normally attained by a 4-year-old) when trying to acquire an oral language. Yet, other "wild children" who never learned to speak have become quite fluent in sign language, as have many home-reared deaf adolescents who had no formal exposure to signing until after puberty (Reich, 1986). What can we say about the critical-period notion in view of these observations? Clearly a strong version of the hypothesis, which states that first-language learning is impossible after puberty, has to be incorrect. However, a weaker version of the hypothesis, which claims that language learning may be incomplete after puberty, may have some merit. Stated another way, the period between 2 years of age and puberty seems to be a *sensitive period* for first-language learning, rather than an absolutely critical period.

Several other arguments for nativism fall by the wayside on closer examination. For example, human infants are said to be "wired" for language by virtue of their ability to discriminate phonemes in the first few days and weeks of life. Is this really evidence for the existence of a LAD? If so, then rhesus monkeys and even chinchillas must have LADs, for members of these species show similar powers of auditory discrimination (Passingham, 1982). Even the amazing linguistic inventions that young children display, such as "home sign" and the creolization of pidgins (see Box 8-3), may simply mean that the large human brain is capable of detecting a wide variety of rules and creating many codes (including mathematics and computer language, both of which were invented at some point), rather than being so uniquely specialized to process and interpret language.

Finally, the most damning critique of the nativist approach may be more conceptual than empirical: we don't really *explain* language development by attributing it to a built-in language acquisition device. Recall that the concept of a LAD arose as researchers began to discover that learning theories could not explain language development. That being the case, the nativists concluded that the mechanism for language learning must be innate. Unfortunately, they have never specified *how* an inborn language processor might sift through linguistic input and infer the rules that govern language—they merely assume that these rules and relationships are eventually detected (in some unknown way) and applied to the child's own speech. Thus, the major shortcoming of the nativist approach can be illustrated by analogy: attributing advances in linguistic competence to the mysterious workings of a LAD is like saying that physical growth is biologically programmed—*and then failing to identify the underlying variables (nutrition, hormones, and so forth) that explain why growth follows the course it takes.* Clearly, the nativist approach is woefully incomplete; it is really more a description of language learning than a true explanation.

The Interactionist Perspective

It should now be apparent that neither learning theory nor the nativist approach provides a complete explanation of language development, although each of these perspectives may be partly correct. We know that children must have opportunities to converse with others before they will become proficient users of a language. Imitation obviously plays some part in the language-learning process, for children acquire the same language (and even the same accent) that their companions use. Reinforcement must also play some role, for we've seen that children talk more (and will become better readers) if their parents frequently encourage verbal interactions. Yet, if language were learned through imitation and reinforcement, it would be difficult to explain why children who hear varying kinds and amounts of linguistic input will proceed through roughly the same steps when acquiring their first language. These "linguistic universals" suggest that language learning is related in some meaningful way to biological processes. But must we attribute language development to the mysterious workings of an inborn LAD in order to explain the similarities in children's early speech?

Apparently not. In recent years, cognitive theorists such as Jean Piaget (1970) and social-communication theorists such as Elizabeth Bates (Bates & MacWhinney, 1982) and Neil Bohannon (see Bohannon & Warren-Leubecker, 1985) have argued that both biological factors and the linguistic environment combine to influence language development. According to this **interactionist** viewpoint, young children the world over may talk alike because they are all members of the same species *who share many common experiences.* What may be innate is not any specialized linguistic knowledge or processing skills but, rather, a sophisticated brain and central nervous system that matures very slowly and predisposes children to develop similar ideas at about the same age.

Piaget suggests that infants are curious explorers who form intellectual schemata to explain interesting objects and events and then end up talking about that which they know and understand. In other words, he says that language development reflects the child's cognitive development. Since cognitive development is thought to be heavily influenced by the maturation of the brain and the nervous system, all children should proceed through the same stages of intellectual growth and show some very definite similarities in the patterning of their early speech.

What role does the environment play? Piaget believes that as children develop intellectually, they will produce increasingly sophisticated utterances—statements that social-communication theorists tell us will prompt a close companion to increase the complexity of her own speech as she addresses her child. This novel linguistic input will then provide children with information they can use to form new linguistic hypotheses, produce even more complex utterances, and thereby influence the speech of their companions once again. Clearly the pattern of influence is reciprocal: the child's speech influences the speech of older companions, which, in turn, influences the child's speech, and so on. Stated another way, the interactionists are proposing that the language of young children is influenced by a linguistic environment that they have had a hand in creating.

Many observations are consistent with this interactionist theory. In our next chapter, we will see that the intellectual schemata of preverbal children are based largely on actions that these infants have witnessed or undertaken. Presumably an 8-month-old comes to know what a "ball" is by acting on it and discovering its properties. If one's cognitive competencies are reflected in language, then perhaps we should not be surprised to learn that children's first words usually focus on *objects they can manipulate or actions they have performed* (Nelson, 1973). Apparently these young infants are merely talking about aspects of their experience that they can understand.

Consider another example. Children rarely produce hypothetical statements such as "If it is cold, we will shiver" or "If it had rained, we would have been soaked" until age 4 or 5 (de Villiers & de Villiers, 1979). Indeed, these are reasonably complex statements that require (1) the capacity to think about possibilities rather than actualities and (2) an ability to shift one's frame of reference to the future or the past. In English, the syntax required to express hypotheticals is reasonably complex, much more so than the grammatically simple forms used in Russian. Nevertheless, Russian children do not begin to produce hypothetical statements until about the same age as English-speaking children do (Slobin, 1966). So the appearance of hypotheticals in children's speech depends more on an understanding of the *concept* of the hypothetical than on the intricacies of the grammar necessary to produce these utterances.

In sum, the interactionist perspective is both a synthesis and an extension of the learning and the nativist theories and is probably more accurate than either of these approaches. Like the nativists, the interactionists believe that children are biologically prepared for language learning. However, they stress that the "universals" in children's language reflect a basic interplay among biological maturation, cognitive development, and the linguistic environment rather than the workings of an inborn language processor (or LAD).

What is new about the interactionist approach is its emphasis on cognitive development and, specifically, on the impact of cognitive growth on child language and the linguistic environment. This is not to say that cognitive development explains language development; it merely places some limits on what children are likely to talk about and on what they will understand as they listen to others' speech. And even when children do grasp concepts such as time and causality, they must still discover how to express this knowledge in their own speech.

How do they make those discoveries? Here is where the interactionists propose that companions play a critically important role by promoting conversations in which they are continually introducing new linguistic concepts in sentences that are carefully tailored to the child's level of understanding. Could we educators ever devise any more effective "grammar" lessons? Probably not! And after several years (or, by one estimate, more than 9000 hours) of interacting with these responsive linguistic models, the average 6-year-old will have acquired most of the important principles of her native language and will be speaking in much the same way that her older companions do.

Summary

Students of language development have tried to answer two basic questions. The first is the "what" question: What is the normal course of language development, and just what are children acquiring that enables them to become language users? The four aspects of language that children acquire are phonology, a knowledge of the phonemes used in producing language; semantics, an understanding of the meaning of words and sentences; syntax, the rules that specify how words are combined to produce sentences; and pragmatics, the principles governing how language is to be used in different social situations. The second basic question is the "how" question: How do young children acquire a working knowledge of a highly abstract symbol system such as language? Empiricists have argued that children learn language as they imitate others' speech and are reinforced for grammatical statements. However, nativists contend that children are biologically programmed to acquire language and do not have to be reinforced for grammatical speech.

Although babies respond to speech at birth, they will not utter their first meaningful words for about a year. During this prelinguistic phase, infants vocalize by crying, cooing, and babbling. As infants continue to babble, they begin to match the intonation of their babbles to the tonal qualities of the language they hear and will eventually use sounds to represent objects and experiences, producing their own unique words, or "vocables." Although babies less than 1 year of age rarely if ever understand the meaning of individual words, they have already learned that people take turns when vocalizing to each other and that a speaker's tone of voice can be an important communicative prompt.

At about 1 year of age, infants produce their first recognizable words and enter the holophrastic phase of language development. For the next several months, children talk in one-word utterances and will expand their vocabularies one word at a time. They talk most about those things that interest them—objects that move, make noise, or can be manipulated. Young children seem to infer the meanings of words from the perceptual characteristics of their referents (size, shape, and so on) and are likely to overextend the use of words—for example, applying *doggie* to all furry, four-legged animals. Some psycholinguists believe that a child's single words are often intended as holophrases—one-word messages that represent an entire sentence's worth of meaning.

At about 18–24 months of age, children enter the telegraphic phase of language development as they begin to combine words into simple sentences. These

---

interactionist theory: the notion that biological factors and environmental influences combine to determine the course of language development.

utterances are called "telegraphic" because they typically include only nouns, verbs, and occasionally adjectives, omitting prepositions, auxiliary verbs, articles, conjunctions, and other grammatical markers. Although telegraphic sentences are not grammatical by adult standards, they represent far more than random word combinations. Not only do all children follow the same rules of word order when combining words, but they also express the same categories of meaning (semantic relations) in their earliest sentences. So telegraphic speech is not merely a shortened version of adult speech; it is a universal "child language" that has a grammar of its own.

During the preschool period (ages 2½ to 5), the child's language becomes much more similar to an adult's. As children produce longer utterances, they begin to add grammatical morphemes such as the -s for plurality, the -ed for past tense, the -ing for present progressive, articles, prepositions, and auxiliary verbs. Although individual children acquire grammatical markers at different rates, there is a striking uniformity in the order in which these morphemes appear. The preschool period is also the time when a child learns basic transformational rules that will enable him or her to change declarative statements into questions, negations, imperatives, relative clauses, and compound sentences. By the time they enter school, children have mastered most of the syntactical rules of their native language and can produce a variety of sophisticated, adultlike messages. Another reason language becomes increasingly complex during the preschool years is that youngsters are beginning to appreciate semantic and relational contrasts such as big/little, wide/narrow, more/less, and before/after. Preschool children are also communicating more effectively as they begin to detect at least some of the uninformative messages they receive and to ask for clarification. Moreover, they have learned another important pragmatic lesson: if you hope to be understood, you must tailor your message to the listener's level of understanding.

Middle childhood (ages 6–14) is a period of linguistic refinement: children learn subtle exceptions to grammatical rules and begin to understand even the most complex syntactical structures of their native language. Vocabulary continues to grow, and children gradually develop metalinguistic awareness—an ability to think about language and to comment on its properties. School-age children are also becoming much better communicators as they acquire cognitive and metalinguistic skills and begin to scrutinize the quality of messages they read and write. These cognitive advances and experiences in evaluating written communications help the grade school child to detect and clarify the uninformative oral messages that he sends and receives.

There are three major theories of language acquisition: learning theory, nativism, and the interactionist approach. Learning theorists believe that language is acquired as children imitate the speech of their companions and are reinforced for their grammatically correct imitations. However, careful analyses of conversations between parents and their young children reveal that children do not mimic the sentences they hear, nor do adults selectively reinforce their children's grammatical statements.

Nativists argue that human beings have an inborn linguistic processor, or language acquisition device, that is specialized for language learning. Presumably children require nothing other than speech to analyze and someone with whom to converse in order to learn any (and all) languages to which they are exposed. Three lines of evidence are consistent with the nativist approach. First, particular areas of the brain serve as centers of linguistic activity. Second, all children in all cultures go through the same stages of language acquisition, regardless of the structure of the language they are learning. Third, if young children lack a formal linguistic model, they may create a language of their own. But unfortunately, the nativists are not very clear about how children sift through verbal input and make the critical discoveries that will further their linguistic competencies.

Proponents of the interactionist position acknowledge that children are biologically prepared to acquire language. However, they suggest that what may be innate is not any specialized linguistic processor but, rather, a nervous system that gradually matures and predisposes children to develop similar ideas at about the same age. Thus, biological maturation is said to affect cognitive development, which, in turn, influences language development. However, interactionists stress that the environment plays a crucial role in language learning, for children will not acquire the linguistic concepts that promote language development unless they have ample opportunities to converse with responsive companions who tailor their own speech to the children's levels of understanding.

References

ACKERMAN, B. P. (1986). Children's sensitivity to comprehension failure in interpreting a nonliteral use of an utterance. *Child Development, 57,* 485–497.

AMMON, P. R., & Ammon, M. S. (1971). Effects of training black preschool children in vocabulary vs. sentence construction. *Journal of Educational Psychology, 62,* 421–426.

ARE THOSE APES REALLY TALKING? (1980, March 10). *Time,* pp. 50–57.

BARNES, S., Gutfreund, M., Satterly, D., & Wells, D. (1983). Characteristics of adult speech which predict children's language development. *Journal of Child Language, 10,* 65–84.

BATES, E. (1976). *Language and context: The acquisition of pragmatics.* Orlando, FL: Academic Press.

BATES, E., & MacWhinney, B. (1982). Functionalist approaches to grammar. In E. Wanner & L. Gleitman (Eds.), *Language acquisition: The state of the art.* Cambridge: Cambridge University Press.

BEAL, C. R. (1987). Repairing the message: Children's monitoring and revision skills. *Child Development, 58,* 401–408.

BEAL, C. R., & Flavell, J. H. (1984). Development of the ability to distinguish communicative intention and literal message meaning. *Child Development, 55,* 920–928.

BERKO, J. (1958). The child's learning of English morphology. *Word, 14,* 150–177.

BICKERTON, D. (1983). Creole languages. *Scientific American, 249,* 116–122.

BICKERTON, D. (1984). The language bioprogram hypothesis. *Behavioral and Brain Sciences, 7,* 173–221.

BLEWITT, P. (1983). Dog versus collie: Vocabulary in speech to young children. *Developmental Psychology, 19,* 602–609.

BLOOM, L. (1970). *Language development: Form and function in emerging grammars.* Cambridge, MA: M.I.T. Press.

BLOOM, L. (1973). *One word at a time: The use of single word utterances before syntax.* The Hague: Mouton.

BLOOM, L., Hood, L., & Lightbown, P. (1974). Imitation in language development: If, when and why. *Cognitive Psychology, 6,* 380–420.

BLOOM, L., Merkin, S., & Wootten, J. (1982). Wh- questions: Linguistic factors that contribute to the sequence of acquisition. *Child Development, 53,* 1084–1092.

BOHANNON, J. N., III, & Marquis, A. L. (1977). Children's control of adult speech. *Child Development, 48,* 1002–1008.

BOHANNON, J. N., III, & Warren-Leubecker, A. (1985). Theoretical approaches to language acquisition. In J. Berko Gleason (Ed.), *The development of language.* Westerville, OH: Merrill.

BONITATIBUS, G. J., & Flavell, J. H. (1985). Effect of presenting a message in written form on young children's ability to evaluate its communication accuracy. *Developmental Psychology, 21,* 455–461.

BONVILLIAN, J. D., Orlansky, M. D., & Novack, L. L. (1983). Developmental milestones: Sign language acquisition and motor development. *Child Development, 54,* 1435–1445.

BOWERMAN, M. (1977). Semantic factors in the acquisition of rules for word use and sentence construction. In D. Morehead & A. Morehead (Eds.), *Directions in normal and deficient child language.* Baltimore: University Park Press.

BROWN, R. (1973). *A first language: The early stages.* Cambridge, MA: Harvard University Press.

BROWN, R., & Hanlon, C. (1970). Derivational complexity and order of acquisition. In J. R. Hayes (Ed.), *Cognition and the development of language.* New York: Wiley.

BRUNER, J. S. (1983). *Child's talk: Learning to use language.* New York: Norton.

BURKE, S. J. (1974). Language acquisition, language learning, and language teaching. *International Review of Applied Linguistics in Language Teaching, 12,* 53–68.

BUTTERFIELD, E. C., & Siperstein, G. N. (1972). Influence of contingent auditory stimulation on non-nutritional suckle. In J. F. Bosma (Ed.), *Third symposium on oral sensation and perception: The mouth of the infant.* Springfield, IL: Charles C Thomas.

CAREY, S. (1977). The child as a word learner. In M. Halle, J. Bresnan, & G. A. Miller (Eds.), *Linguistic theory and psychological reality.* Cambridge, MA: M.I.T. Press.

CARROLL, J. B. (1969). Psychological and educational research into second language teaching to young children. In H. H. Stern (Ed.), *Languages and the young school child.* London: Oxford University Press.

CHOMSKY, N. (1968). *Language and mind.* San Diego, CA: Harcourt Brace Jovanovich.

CHOMSKY, N. (1980). *Rules and representations.* New York: Columbia University Press.

CLARK, E. V. (1973). What's in a word? On the child's acquisition of semantics in his first language. In T. E. Moore (Ed.), *Cognitive development and the acquisition of language.* Orlando, FL: Academic Press.

CLARK, H. H., & Clark, E. V. (1977). *Psychology and language: An introduction to psycholinguistics.* San Diego, CA: Harcourt Brace Jovanovich.

CLARKSON, M. G., & Berg, W. K. (1983). Cardiac orientation and vowel discrimination in newborns: Crucial stimulus parameters. *Child Development, 54,* 162–171.

CURTISS, S. (1977). *Genie: A psycholinguistic study of a modern-day "wild child."* Orlando, FL: Academic Press.

DALE, P. S. (1976). *Language development: Structure and function.* New York: Holt, Rinehart and Winston.

DANEMAN, M., & Case, R. (1981). Syntactic form, semantic complexity, and short-term memory: Influences on children's acquisition of new linguistic structures. *Developmental Psychology, 17,* 367–378.

De BOYSSON-BARDIES, B., Sagart, L., & Durand, C. (1984). Discernible differences in the babbling of infants according to target language. *Journal of Child Language, 11,* 1–16.

DeCASPER, A. J., & Fifer, W. P. (1980). Of human bonding: Newborns prefer their mothers' voices. *Science, 208,* 1174–1176.

DENNIS, M., Sugar, J., & Whitaker, H. A. (1982). The acquisition of tag questions. *Child Development, 53,* 1254–1257.

de VILLIERS, J. G., & de Villiers, P. A. (1973). A cross-sectional study of the acquisition of grammatical morphemes in child speech. *Journal of Psycholinguistic Research, 2,* 267–278.

de VILLIERS, J. G., & de Villiers, P. A. (1978). *Language acquisition.* Cambridge, MA: Harvard University Press.

de VILLIERS, P. A., & de Villiers, J. G. (1979). *Early language.* Cambridge, MA: Harvard University Press.

EIMAS, P. D. (1982). Speech perception: A view of the initial state and perceptual mechanisms. In J. Mehler, M. Garrett, & E. Walker (Eds.), *Perspectives on mental representation.* Hillsdale, NJ: Erlbaum.

EVANS, M. A. (1985). Self-initiated speech repairs: A reflection of communicative monitoring in young children. *Developmental Psychology, 21,* 365–371.

FERGUSON, C. A. (1977). Learning to produce: The earliest stages of phonological development in the child. In F. D. Minifie & L. L. Lloyd (Eds.), *Communication and cognitive abilities: Early behavioral assessment.* Baltimore: University Park Press.

FLAVELL, J. H. (1985). *Cognitive development.* Englewood Cliffs, NJ: Prentice-Hall.

FOLGER, J. P., & Chapman, R. S. (1978). A pragmatic analysis of spontaneous imitation. *Journal of Child Language, 5,* 25–38.

GARDNER, B. T., & Gardner, R. A. (1974). Comparing the early utterances of child and chimpanzee. In A. Pick (Ed.), *Minnesota Symposia on Child Psychology* (Vol. 8). Minneapolis: University of Minnesota Press.

GARDNER, R. A., & Gardner, B. T. (1969). Teaching sign language to a chimpanzee. *Science, 165,* 664–672.

GARVEY, C. (1984). *Children's talk.* Cambridge, MA: Harvard University Press.

GELMAN, R., & Shatz, M. (1977). Appropriate speech adjustments: The operation of conversational constraints on talk to two-year-olds. In M. Lewis & L. A. Rosenblum (Eds.), *Interaction, conversation, and the development of language.* New York: Wiley.

GOLDIN-MEADOW, S., & Mylander, C. (1984). Gestural communication in deaf children: The effects and noneffects of parental input on early language development. *Monographs of the Society for Research in Child Development, 49*(Serial No. 207).

GREENBERG, M. T. (1984). Pragmatics and social interaction: The unrealized nexus. In L. Feagans, C. Garvey, & R. Golinkoff (Eds.), *The origins and growth of communication.* Norwood, NJ: Ablex.

HAYES, C. (1951). *The ape in our house.* New York: Harper & Row.

HOFF-GINSBERG, E. (1986). Function and structure in maternal speech: Their relation to the child's development of syntax. *Developmental Psychology, 22,* 155–163.

HOOD, L., & Bloom, L. (1979). What, when, and how about why: A longitudinal study of early expressions of causality. *Monographs of the Society for Research in Child Development, 44*(Serial No. 181).

JAKOBSON, R. (1968). *Child language, aphasia, and phonological universals.* The Hague: Mouton.

JOHNSON, C. J., Pick, H. L., Siegel, G. M., Cicciarelli, A. W., & Garber, S. R. (1981). Effects of interpersonal distance on children's vocal intensity. *Child Development, 52,* 721–723.

JOHNSON, H., & Smith, L. B. (1981). Children's inferential abilities in the context of reading to understand. *Child Development, 52,* 1216–1223.

KAHAN, L. D., & Richards, D. D. (1986). The effects of context on referential communication strategies. *Child Development, 57,* 1130–1141.

KELLER, H., & Scholmerich, A. (1987). Infant vocalizations and parental reactions over the first 4 months of life. *Developmental Psychology, 23,* 62–67.

KELLOGG, W. N., & Kellogg, L. A. (1933). *The ape and the child.* New York: McGraw-Hill.

KLIMA, E. S., & Bellugi, I. (1975). Perception and production in a visually based language. In D. Aaronson & R. W. Rieber (Eds.), *Developmental psycholinguistics and communication disorders. Annals of the New York Academy of Science, 263,* 225–235.

KRAUSS, R. M., & Glucksberg, S. (1969). The development of communication as a function of age. *Child Development, 40,* 255–266.

KRAUSS, R. M., & Glucksberg, S. (1977). Social and nonsocial speech. *Scientific American, 236,* 100–105.

KUCZAJ, S. A., II. (1979). Evidence for a language learning strategy: On the relative ease of acquisition of prefixes and suffixes. *Child Development, 50,* 1–13.

LENNEBERG, E. H. (1967). *Biological foundations of language.* New York: Wiley.

LEONARD, L. B., Chapman, K., Rowan, L. E., & Weiss, A. L. (1983). Three hypotheses concerning young children's imitations of lexical items. *Developmental Psychology, 19,* 591–601.

LEUNG, E. H. L., & Rheingold, H. L. (1981). Development of pointing as a social gesture. *Developmental Psychology, 17,* 215–220.

LIEBERMAN, P. (1967). *Interaction, perception and language.* Cambridge, MA: M.I.T. Press.

MacKAY-SOROKA, S., Trehub, S. E., & Thorpe, L. A. (1987). Deaf children's referential messages to mother. *Child Development, 58,* 385–394.

McGHEE, P. E., & Chapman, A. J. (1980). *Children's humour.* London: Wiley.

McNEILL, D. (1970). *The acquisition of language.* New York: Harper & Row.

MERVIS, C. B., & Mervis, C. A. (1982). Leopards are kitty-cats: Object labeling by mothers for their thirteen-month-olds. *Child Development, 53,* 267–273.

MILLER, L. C., Lechner, R. E., & Rugs, D. (1985). Development of conversational responsiveness: Preschoolers' use of responsive listener cues and relevant comments. *Developmental Psychology, 21,* 473–480.

MOLFESE, D. L. (1977). Infant cerebral asymmetry. In S. J. Segalowitz & F. A. Gruber (Eds.), *Language development and neurological theory.* Orlando, FL: Academic Press.

NELSON, K. (1973). Structure and strategy in learning to talk. *Monographs of the Society for Research in Child Development, 38*(Serial No. 149).

NELSON, K. (1978). Semantic development and the development of semantic memory. In K. E. Nelson (Ed.), *Children's language.* New York: Gardner Press.

NEWPORT, E. L., Gleitman, H., & Gleitman, L. R. (1977). Mother, I'd rather do it myself: Some effects and non-effects of maternal speech style. In C. E. Snow & C. A. Ferguson (Eds.), *Talking to children: Language input and acquisition.* Cambridge: Cambridge University Press.

NORMAN-JACKSON, J. (1982). Family interactions, language development, and primary reading achievement of Black children in families of low income. *Child Development, 53,* 349–358.

OCHS, E. (1982). Talking to children in western Samoa. *Language in Society, 11,* 77–104.

OLSON, D. R., & Hildyard, A. (1983). Writing and literal meaning. In M. Martlew (Ed.), *The psychology of written language: A developmental approach.* New York: Wiley.

OVIATT, S. L. (1980). The emerging ability to comprehend language: An experimental approach. *Child Development, 51,* 97–106.

PASSINGHAM, R. E. (1982). *The human primate.* Oxford: W. H. Freeman.

PATTERSON, C. J., & Kister, M. C. (1981). The development of listener skills for referential communication. In W. P. Dickson (Ed.), *Children's oral communication skills.* Orlando, FL: Academic Press.

PENNER, S. G. (1987). Parental responses to grammatical and ungrammatical child utterances. *Child Development, 58,* 376–384.

PIAGET, J. (1970). Piaget's theory. In P. H. Mussen (Ed.), *Carmichael's manual of child psychology* (Vol. 1). New York: Wiley.

PRATT, M. W., & Bates, K. R. (1982). Young editors: Preschoolers' evaluation and production of ambiguous messages. *Developmental Psychology, 18,* 30–42.

PRATT, M. W., McLaren, J., & Wickens, G. (1984). Rules as tools: Effective generalization of verbal self-regulative communication training by first-grade speakers. *Developmental Psychology, 20,* 893–902.

PRAWAT, R. S., & Wildfong, S. (1980). The influence of functional context on children's labeling responses. *Child Development, 51,* 1057–1060.

PREMACK, D. (1976). *Intelligence in ape and man.* Hillsdale, NJ: Erlbaum.

PRICE, G. C., Hess, R. D., & Dickson, W. P. (1981). Processes by which verbal-educational abilities are affected when mothers encourage preschool children to verbalize. *Developmental Psychology, 17,* 554–564.

REEDER, K. (1981). How young children learn to do things with words. In P. S. Dale & D. Ingram (Eds.), *Child language—an international perspective.* Baltimore: University Park Press.

REICH, P. A. (1986). *Language development.* Englewood Cliffs, NJ: Prentice-Hall.

REVELLE, G. L., Wellman, H. M., & Karabenick, J. D. (1985). Comprehension monitoring in preschool children. *Child Development, 56,* 654–663.

REYNOLDS, R. E., & Ortony, A. (1980). Some issues in the measurement of children's comprehension of metaphorical language. *Child Development, 51,* 1110–1119.

RHEINGOLD, H. L., & Adams, J. L. (1980). The significance of speech to newborns. *Developmental Psychology, 16,* 397–403.

ROSENTHAL, M. K. (1982). Vocal dialogues in the neonatal period. *Developmental Psychology, 18,* 17–21.

ROSS, H. S., & Lollis, S. P. (1987). Communication within infant social games. *Developmental Psychology, 23,* 241–248.

RUMBAUGH, D. M. (1977). *Language learning by a chimpanzee: The Lana project.* Orlando, FL: Academic Press.

RUTTER, D. R., & Durkin, K. (1987). Turn-taking in mother-infant interaction: An examination of vocalizations and gaze. *Developmental Psychology, 23,* 54–61.

SACHS, J. (1985). Prelinguistic development. In J. Berko Gleason (Ed.), *The development of language.* Westerville, OH: Merrill.

SALTZ, R. (1979). Children's interpretation of proverbs. *Language Arts, 56,* 508–514.

SAVAGE-RUMBAUGH, E. S. (1981). Can apes use symbols to represent their world? *Annals of the New York Academy of Sciences, 364,* 35–59.

SAVAGE-RUMBAUGH, E. S. (1984). *Pan paniscus* and *Pan troglodytes:* Contrasts in preverbal communicative competence. In R. L. Susman (Ed.), *The pygmy chimpanzee.* New York: Plenum.

SAVAGE-RUMBAUGH, E. S., Rumbaugh, D. M., & Boysen, S. (1978). Symbolic communication between two chimpanzees *(Pan troglodytes). Science, 201,* 641–644.

SCHERER, N. J., & Olswang, L. B. (1984). Role of mother's expansions in stimulating children's language production. *Journal of Speech and Hearing Research, 27,* 387–396.

SCHIEFFELIN, B. B., & Ochs, E. (1983). A cultural perspective on the transition from prelinguistic to linguistic communication. In R. M. Golinkoff (Ed.), *The transition from prelinguistic to linguistic communication.* Hillsdale, NJ: Erlbaum.

SHATZ, M. (1983). Communication. In P. H. Mussen (Ed.), *Handbook of child psychology* (Vol. 3). New York: Wiley.

SHATZ, M., & Gelman, R. (1973). The development of communication skills: Modifications in the speech of young children as a function of listener. *Monographs of the Society for Research in Child Development, 38*(Serial No. 152).

SKINNER, B. F. (1957). *Verbal behavior.* East Norwalk, CT: Appleton-Century-Crofts.

SLOBIN, D. I. (1966). The acquisition of Russian as a native language. In F. Smith & G. A. Miller (Eds.), *The genesis of language: A psycholinguistic approach.* Cambridge, MA: M.I.T. Press.

SLOBIN, D. I. (1979). *Psycholinguistics.* Glenview, IL: Scott, Foresman.

SNOW, C. E., Arlman-Rupp, A., Hassing, Y., Jobse, J., Joosken, J., & Vorster, J. (1976). Mother's speech in three social classes. *Journal of Psycholinguistic Research, 5,* 1–20.

SNOW, C. E., & Ferguson, C. A. (Eds.), (1977). *Talking to children.* Cambridge: Cambridge University Press.

SNOW, C. E., & Hoefnagel-Hohle, M. (1978). The critical period for language acquisition: Evidence from second language learning. *Child Development, 49,* 1114–1128.

SONNENSCHEIN, S. (1986a). Development of referential communication: Deciding that a message is uninformative. *Developmental Psychology, 22,* 164–168.

SONNENSCHEIN, S. (1986b). Development of referential communication skills: How familiarity with a listener affects a speaker's production of redundant messages. *Developmental Psychology, 22,* 549–555.

SONNENSCHEIN, S., & Whitehurst, G. J. (1984). Developing referential communication: A hierarchy of skills. *Child Development, 55,* 1936–1945.

STAATS, A. W., & Staats, C. K. (1963). *Complex human behavior.* New York: Holt, Rinehart and Winston.

STERN, D., Spieker, S., & MacKain, K. (1982). Intonational contours as signals in maternal speech to prelinguistic infants. *Developmental Psychology, 18,* 727–735.

TERRACE, H. S. (1979, November). How Nim Chimpsky changed my mind. *Psychology Today,* pp. 65–76.

THOMAS, D., Campos, J. J., Shucard, D. W., Ramsay, D. S., & Shucard, J. (1981). Semantic comprehension in infancy: A signal detection approach. *Child Development, 52,* 798–803.

THOMPSON, J. R., & Chapman, R. S. (1977). Who is "Daddy" revisited? The status of two-year-olds' overextended words in use and comprehension. *Journal of Child Language, 4,* 359–375.

TOMASELLO, M., & Farrar, M. J. (1986). Joint attention and early language. *Child Development, 57,* 1454–1463.

TOMIKAWA, S. A., & Dodd, D. H. (1980). Early word meanings: Perceptually or functionally based. *Child Development, 51,* 1103–1109.

TYACK, D., & Ingram, D. (1977). Children's production and comprehension of questions. *Journal of Child Language, 4,* 211–224.

WELLMAN, H. M., & Lempers, J. D. (1977). The naturalistic communicative abilities of two-year-olds. *Child Development, 48,* 1052–1057.

WHITEHURST, G. (1982). Language development. In B. Wolman (Ed.), *Handbook of developmental psychology.* Englewood Cliffs, NJ: Prentice-Hall.

WILKINSON, L. C., & Rembold, K. L. (1981). The form and function of children's gestures accompanying verbal directives. In P. S. Dale & D. Ingram (Eds.), *Child language: An international perspective.* Baltimore: University Park Press.

WOLF, M., & Dickinson, D. (1985). From oral to written language: Transitions in the school years. In J. Berko Gleason (Ed.), *The development of language.* Westerville, OH: Merrill.

WOLFF, P. H. (1969). The natural history of crying and other vocalizations in early infancy. In B. M. Foss (Ed.), *Determinants of infant behavior* (Vol. 4). London: Methuen.

Cognitive Development

Teacher (to a class of 9-year-olds): For artwork today, I'd like each of you to draw me a picture of a person who has three eyes.
Billy: How? Nobody has three eyes!

If you were asked to account for the reaction of this 9-year-old, you might be tempted to conclude that the boy either lacks imagination or is being sarcastic. Actually, Billy's feelings about the art assignment may be rather typical (see Box 9-2), for 9-year-olds think differently than adults do, and they often find it extremely difficult to reflect on hypothetical propositions that have no basis in reality.

Our next two chapters will focus on the development of children's mental abilities. In this chapter we will chart the course of cognitive (intellectual) development from birth through adolescence and see how the changing character of children's thinking affects their relationships with other people as well as their understanding of the world around them. In Chapter 10 we will take up the topic of intelligence testing and discuss the many factors that contribute to individual differences in children's intellectual performance.

What Are Cognition and Cognitive Development?

When developmentalists talk about **cognition,** they are referring to the activity of knowing, or the mental processes by which knowledge is acquired, elaborated, stored, retrieved, and used to solve problems. The cognitive processes that help us to "know" and "understand" include a wide variety of activities, such as attending, perceiving, learning, thinking, and remembering—in short, the unobservable events and undertakings that characterize the human mind (Flavell, 1985). Almost everything we do while awake involves some kind of mental activity. We are constantly attending to objects and events, interpreting them, comparing them

with past experiences, placing them into categories, and encoding them into memory. Human beings are truly cognitive beings.

The term **cognitive development** refers to the changes that occur in children's mental skills and abilities over time. In this chapter, we will consider two very different perspectives on intelligence and intellectual development. The first of these theories is Jean Piaget's *structural-functional* approach—a model that emphasizes the biological functions and environmental influences that promote developmental changes in the organization, or "structure," of intelligence. Although many aspects of Piaget's theory have become rather controversial in recent years, the Piagetian approach remains influential and probably still qualifies as the most detailed and systematic statement on human intellectual development presently available. Consequently, a fair portion of this chapter will be devoted to Piaget's insightful and often provocative theoretical formulations.

The major alternative to Piaget's theory arose from the work of information theorists and experimental psychologists who focus not on the "structure" of intellect but, rather, on the growth of specific cognitive-processing skills such as attention, perception, and memory. Proponents of this *information-processing* theory have likened the human intellectual apparatus to a sophisticated computer system that processes, categorizes, stores, and retrieves information according to a set of programmed strategies. Their primary goals are (1) to describe how children process information to make sense of their surroundings, (2) to specify how information processing changes over time, and (3) to understand how these changes in cognitive-processing skills might contribute to developmental changes in learning, remembering, thinking, and problem solving. After exploring Piaget's monumental contributions, we will return to the information-processing approach and see why so many developmentalists are so enthusiastic about this "new look" at children's intellectual growth.

Piaget's Basic Ideas about Cognition

In Chapter 2 we learned that Piaget was a zoologist with a background in *epistemology* (the branch of philosophy concerned with the origins of knowledge) who developed a strong interest in cognitive development while standardizing intelligence tests. This job required him to administer a large number of precisely worded questions to his young test takers in order to determine the age at which the majority of them could *correctly* answer each item. However, Piaget soon became interested in the children's *wrong* answers when he discovered that children of roughly the same age were making similar kinds of mistakes—errors that were typically quite different from the incorrect responses of younger or older children. Could these age-related differences in children's error patterns reflect developmental steps, or stages, in the process of intellectual growth? Piaget thought so, and he began to suspect that *how children think* is probably a much better indicator of their cognitive abilities than *what* they may know (Flavell, 1963).

When his own three children were born, Piaget made detailed notes on their intellectual abilities, carefully observing how they reacted to various objects, events, and problems that he presented to them. Many of Piaget's ideas about intelligence and about intellectual development during infancy are based on these naturalistic observations of his own children.

Piaget's theory gradually took shape over a number of years as he broadened his horizons and began to study a larger sample of developing children. Many of Piaget's theoretical insights came from his use of the **clinical method,** a question-and-answer technique that he devised to measure the ways children attacked various problems and thought about everyday issues. By carefully questioning a large number of children in several age groups, Piaget was able to identify four methods (or patterns) of reasoning that are age-related and, in his opinion, represent different "stages" of intellectual growth.

In order to appreciate Piaget's structural-functional theory of cognitive development, it is necessary to understand what he means by *intelligence, cognitive structures* (or *schemata*), and *intellectual functions*.

What Is Intelligence?

Piaget's background in the life sciences is apparent when he defines **intelligence** as a *basic life function* that helps the organism *to adapt to its envi-*ronment. He adds that intelligence is a form of *equilibrium* toward which all cognitive structures tend (1950, p. 6). So according to Piaget, intellectual activity is undertaken with one goal in mind: to produce a balanced, or harmonious, relationship between one's thought processes and the environment (such a balanced state of affairs is called **cognitive equilibrium,** and the process of achieving it is called *equilibration*). Piaget stressed that children are active and curious explorers who are constantly challenged by many novel stimuli and events that are not immediately understood. He believed that these imbalances (or cognitive disequilibriums) between the child's modes of thinking and environmental events would prompt the child to make mental adjustments that would enable her to cope with puzzling new experiences and thereby restore cognitive equilibrium. So we see that Piaget's view of intelligence is an "interactionist" model, which implies that mismatches between one's internal mental schemes (existing knowledge) and the external environment stimulate cognitive activity and intellectual growth.

There is a very important assumption that underlies Piaget's view of intelligence: if children are to know something, they must construct that knowledge themselves. Indeed, Piaget described the child as a **constructivist**—an organism that acts on novel objects and events and thereby gains some understanding of their essential features. He adds that the child's constructions of reality (that is, interpretations of objects and events) will depend on the knowledge available to him at that

---

cognition: the activity of knowing and the processes through which knowledge is acquired.

cognitive development: changes that occur in mental activities such as attending, perceiving, learning, thinking, and remembering.

clinical method: a type of interview in which a child's response to each successive question or problem determines what the investigator will ask next (see Chapter 1 for an extended discussion of this technique).

intelligence: in Piaget's theory, a basic life function that enables an organism to adapt to its environment.

cognitive equilibrium: Piaget's term for the state of affairs in which there is a balanced, or harmonious, relationship between one's thought processes and the environment.

constructivist: one who gains knowledge by acting or otherwise operating on objects and events to discover their properties.

point in time: the more immature the child's cognitive system, the more limited his interpretation of an environmental event. Consider the following example:

> A four-year-old child and his father are watching the setting sun. "Look Daddy. It's hiding behind the mountain. Why is it going away? Is it angry?" The father grasps the opportunity to explain to his son how the world works. "Well, Mark, the sun doesn't really feel things. And it doesn't really move. It's the earth that's moving. It turns on its axis so that the mountain moves in front of the sun . . ." The father goes on to other explanations of relative motion, interplanetary bodies and such. The boy . . . firmly and definitely responds, "But *we're* not moving. *It* is. Look, it's going down" [Cowan, 1978, p. 11].

This child is making an important assumption here that dominates his attempt at understanding—namely, that the way he sees things must correspond to the way they are. Obviously, it is the sun that is moving, ducking behind the mountain as if it were a live being who was expressing some feeling or serving a definite purpose by hiding. However, the father knows the characteristics that distinguish animate from inanimate objects (and a little about astronomy as well), so that he is able to construct a very different interpretation of the "reality" that he and his son have witnessed.

Cognitive Schemata: The Structural Aspects of Intelligence

Piaget uses the term *schemata* to describe the models, or mental structures, that we create to represent, organize, and interpret our experiences. A **schema** (singular of *schemata*) is a pattern of thought or action that is similar in some respects to what the layperson calls a strategy or a concept. Piaget (1952, 1977) has described three kinds of intellectual structures: behavioral (or sensorimotor) schemata, symbolic schemata, and operational schemata.

Behavioral (or sensorimotor) schemata.

A **behavioral schema** is an organized pattern of behavior that the child uses to represent and respond to an object or experience. These are the first psychological structures to emerge, and for much of the first two years of life, an infant's knowledge of objects and events is limited to that which she can represent through overt actions. So for a 9-month-old infant, a ball is not conceptualized as a round toy that has a formal name—instead, a ball is simply an object that she and her companions can bounce and roll.

Symbolic schemata.

During the second year, children reach a point at which they can solve problems and think about objects and events without having acted on them. In other words, they are now capable of representing actions mentally and using these mental symbols, or **symbolic schemata,** to satisfy their objectives. Consider the following observation of the antics of Jacqueline, Piaget's 16-month-old daughter:

> Jacqueline had a visit from a little boy (18 months of age) . . . who, in the course of the afternoon got into a terrible temper. He screamed as he tried to get out of a playpen and pushed it backward, stamping his feet. Jacqueline stood watching him in amazement, never having witnessed such a scene before. The next day, she herself screamed in her playpen and tried to move, stamping her foot . . . several times in succession [Piaget, 1951, p. 63].

Clearly, Jacqueline was imitating the responses of her absent playmate, even though she had not performed those actions at the time they were modeled. It appears that she must have represented the model's behavior in some internal, symbolic form that preserved the original scene and guided her later imitation.

Operational schemata.

The thinking of children aged 7 and older is characterized by a third type of schema, the operational structure. A **cognitive operation** is an internal mental activity that a person performs on his or her objects of thought—an activity that is undertaken and can be mentally negated, or **reversed,** to permit a logical conclusion. To illustrate, an 8-year-old who imagines the act of flattening a ball of playdough into a disk is not fooled into thinking that he would now have more playdough as a result of spreading it out. Why? Because he can easily reverse this transformation in his head, thereby recognizing that the playdough would become the same ball if it were rolled up once again. By contrast, 5-year-olds, who cannot "operate" on their objects of thought, are constrained to make judgments on the basis of overt appearances. So were they to witness the ball-to-disk transformation, they would assume that the disk has more dough, since it now covers more area than the ball did. And even though they can imagine (with a little prompting) that the dough can be rolled up again, they do not yet recognize the logical consequences of doing so—that is, they continue to think that there is more dough in the disk.

According to Piaget, the most common cognitive operations are the mental activities implied by mathematical symbols such as $+$, $-$, $\times$, $\div$, $=$, $<$,

Figure 9-1. Reversibility is a cognitive operation that develops during middle childhood.

and >. Piaget believed that these operational abilities permit grade school children and adolescents to construct rather elaborate intellectual schemata that will enable them to think logically and systematically—first about their actual experiences and eventually about abstract or hypothetical events.

adaptation
schemata + organization = structure   *Schemata > structure*

How Is Knowledge Gained? The Functional Basis of Intelligence

How do children construct and modify their intellectual schemata? Piaget believes that all cognitive structures are created through the operation of two inborn intellectual functions that he calls *organization* and *adaptation*. **Organization** is the process by which children combine existing schemata into new and more complex intellectual structures. For example, a young infant who has "gazing," "reaching," and "grasping" reflexes will soon organize these initially unrelated schemata into a complex structure—*visually directed reach-*

ing—that enables her to reach out and discover the characteristics of many interesting objects in the environment. Although intellectual schemata may assume radically different forms at different phases of development, the process of organization is unchanging. Piaget believes that children are constantly organizing their available schemata into higher-order systems or structures.

The goal of organization is to further the adaptive function. As its name implies, **adaptation** is the process of adjusting to the demands of the environment. According to Piaget, adaptation occurs through two complementary activities, *assimilation* and *accommodation.*

Assimilation is the process by which the child tries to interpret new experiences in terms of her existing models of the world—the schemata that she already possesses. The young child who sees a horse for the first time will try to assimilate it into one of her existing schemata for four-legged animals and thus may think of this creature as a "doggie." In other words, she is trying to adapt to this novel stimulus by construing it as something familiar.

Yet, truly novel objects, events, and experiences may be difficult or impossible to interpret in terms of one's existing schemata. For example, our young child may quickly note that this big animal she is labeling a doggie has funny-looking feet and a most peculiar bark, and she may be inclined to seek a better understanding

schema: an organized pattern of thought or action that one constructs to interpret some aspect of one's experience (also called cognitive structure).

behavioral schemata: organized patterns of behavior that are used to represent and respond to objects and experiences.

symbolic schemata: internal mental symbols (such as images or verbal codes) that one uses to represent aspects of experience.

cognitive operation: an internal mental activity that one performs on objects of thought.

reversibility: the ability to reverse, or negate, an action by mentally performing the opposite action.

organization: one's inborn tendency to combine and integrate available schemata into coherent systems or bodies of knowledge.

adaptation: one's inborn tendency to adjust to the demands of the environment.

assimilation: the process of interpreting new experiences by incorporating them into existing schemata.

of the observations she has made. **Accommodation,** the complement of assimilation, is the process of modifying existing structures in order to account for new experiences. So the child who recognizes that a horse is not a dog may invent a name for this new creature or perhaps say "What dat?" and adopt the label that her companions use. In so doing, she has modified (accommodated) her schema for four-legged animals to include a new category of experience—horses.

Although Piaget distinguishes assimilation from accommodation, he believes that they occur together as complementary aspects of all intellectual acts. Every assimilation of an experience involves an accommodation to that experience. And the end product of this intellectual functioning is adaptation, a state of equilibrium between the child's cognitive structures and the environment.

In sum, Piaget describes intellectual growth as an active process in which children are repeatedly assimilating new experiences and accommodating their cognitive structures to those experiences. And even during the times when they are not experiencing anything new, children are apt to be growing intellectually as they organize their existing schemata into new and more complex structures. So two innate activities—adaptation and organization—make it possible for children to construct a progressively greater understanding of the world in which they live.

Piaget's Stages of Cognitive Development

Piaget has identified four major periods of cognitive development: the *sensorimotor* stage (birth to 2 years), the *preoperational* stage (2 to 7 years), the stage of *concrete operations* (7 to 11 years), and the stage of *formal operations* (11 years and beyond). These stages of intellectual growth represent completely different levels of cognitive functioning and form what Piaget calls an **invariant developmental sequence.** The invariant-sequence notion implies that all children progress through the stages in precisely the same order. According to Piaget, there can be no skipping of stages, because each successive stage builds on the accomplishments of previous stages.

Although Piaget believed that the *sequencing* of intellectual development is fixed, or invariant, he admitted that there are tremendous individual differences in the ages at which children enter or emerge from any

particular stage. In fact, his view was that cultural factors and other environmental influences may either accelerate or retard a child's *rate* of intellectual growth, and he considered the age norms that accompany his stages (and substages) as only rough approximations at best. So it is important to remember that any given child may spend either more or less time in a particular stage than is indicated by the "norm."

circular – intentionality – tertiary

The Sensorimotor Stage — behavioral (Birth to 2 Years)

The **sensorimotor stage** spans the first two years, or the period that psychologists refer to as infancy. The dominant cognitive structures are behavioral schemata, which evolve as infants begin to coordinate their sensory input and motor responses in order to "act on" and get to "know" the environment.

During the first two years of life, infants evolve from reflexive creatures with very limited knowledge into planful problem solvers who have already learned a great deal about themselves, their close companions, and the objects and events in their everyday world. So dramatic are the infant's cognitive advances that Piaget divides the sensorimotor period into six substages (see Table 9-1 on p. 314), which describe the child's gradual transition from a *reflexive* to a *reflective* organism. Our review will focus on three important aspects of sensorimotor development: *problem-solving skills* (or means/ends activities), *imitative abilities,* and the growth of the object concept.

Growth of problem-solving skills

Over the first eight months, infants begin to act on objects and to discover that they can make interesting things happen. However, these discoveries emerge very gradually. Piaget believes that neonates are born with only a few basic reflexes (for example, sucking, grasping) that assist them in satisfying biological needs such as hunger. During the first month, their activities are pretty much confined to exercising their innate reflexes, assimilating new objects into these reflexive schemes (for example, sucking on objects other than nipples), and accommodating their reflexes to these novel objects.

The first nonreflexive schemata emerge at 1–4 months of age as infants discover by chance that various responses that they can emit and control (for example, sucking their thumbs, making cooing sounds) are satisfying and, thus, worthy of repetition. These simple repetitive acts, called **primary circular reactions,** are

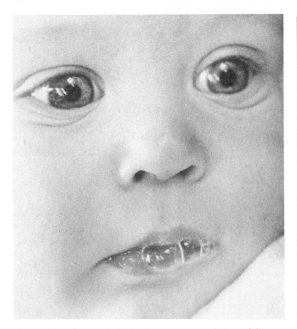

Photo 9-1. Blowing bubbles is an accommodation of the sucking reflex and one of the infant's earliest primary circular reactions.

always centered on the infant's own body. They are called "primary" because they are the first motor habits to appear and "circular" because the pleasure they bring stimulates their repetition.

Between 4 and 8 months of age, infants discover (again by chance) that they can make interesting things happen to *external objects,* such as making a rubber duck quack by squeezing it. These responses, called **secondary circular reactions,** are also repeated for the pleasure they bring. Can we argue that the child who delights in making a toy duck quack is engaging in planful or intentional thinking? Piaget says no: the secondary circular reaction is not a fully intentional response, because the result it produces was discovered by chance and was not an intended goal the first time the action was performed.

Intentionality. Truly planful responding first appears between 8 and 12 months of age as infants begin to coordinate two or more actions to achieve simple objectives. For example, if you were to place an attractive toy under a cushion, the child might lift the cushion with one hand while using the other to grab the toy. In this case, the act of lifting the cushion is not

a pleasurable response in itself; *nor is it emitted by chance.* Rather, it is part of a larger *intentional* schema in which two initially unrelated responses—lifting and grasping—are coordinated as a means to an end.

Trial-and-error experimentation. Between 12 and 18 months of age, infants begin to experiment with objects and will try to invent totally new methods of solving problems or reproducing interesting results. For example, a child who originally squeezed a rubber duck to make it quack may now decide to drop it, step on it, and crush it with a pillow to see whether these actions will have the same or different effects on the toy. These trial-and-error exploratory schemata, called **tertiary circular reactions,** signal the emergence of true curiosity.

Symbolic problem solving. A dramatic development takes place between 18 and 24 months of age: children begin to internalize their behavioral schemata to construct mental symbols, or images. Suddenly, 18–24-month-olds are capable of solving problems mentally, without resorting to trial-and-error activities. This ability, called **inner experimentation,** is illustrated in the following interaction between Piaget and his son, Laurent:

_____

accommodation: the process of modifying existing schemata in order to incorporate or adapt to new experiences.

invariant developmental sequence: a series of developments that occur in one particular order because each development in the sequence is a prerequisite for those appearing later.

sensorimotor stage: Piaget's first intellectual stage, from birth to 2 years, when infants are relying on behavioral schemata as a means of exploring and understanding the environment.

primary circular reaction: a pleasurable response, centered on the infant's own body, that is discovered by chance and performed over and over.

secondary circular reaction: a pleasurable response, centered on an external object, that is discovered by chance and performed over and over.

tertiary circular reaction: an exploratory schema in which the infant devises a new method of acting on objects to reproduce interesting results.

inner experimentation: the ability to solve simple problems on a mental, or symbolic, level without having to rely on trial-and-error experimentation.

Laurent is seated before a table and I place a bread crust in front of him, out of reach. Also, to the right of the child I place a stick, about 25 cm. long. At first, Laurent tries to grasp the bread ... and then he gives up ... Laurent again looks at the bread, and without moving, looks very briefly at the stick, then suddenly grasps it and directs it toward the bread. ... [He then] draws the bread to him [Piaget, 1952, p. 335].

Clearly, Laurent had an important insight: the stick can be used as an extension of his arm to obtain a distant object. Trial-and-error experimentation is not apparent in this case, for Laurent's "problem solving" occurred at an internal, symbolic level.

Development of imitation

Piaget recognized the adaptive significance of imitation, and he was very interested in its development. His own observations led him to believe that infants are incapable of imitating *novel* responses displayed by a model until 8 to 12 months of age (the same age at which they show some evidence of intentionality in their behavior). Moreover, the imitative schemes of infants this young are rather imprecise. Were you to bend and straighten your finger, the infant might mimic you by opening and closing her entire hand (Piaget, 1951). Indeed, precise imitations of even the simplest responses may take days (or even weeks) of practice (Kaye & Marcus, 1981), and literally hundreds of demonstrations may be required before an 8–12-month-old will "catch on" and come to enjoy sensorimotor games such as pat-a-cake.

Voluntary imitation becomes much more precise at age 12 to 18 months, as we see in the following example:

> At [1 year and 16 days of age, Jacqueline] discovered her forehead. When I touched the middle of mine, she first rubbed her eye, then felt above it and touched her hair, after which she brought her hand down a little and finally put her finger on her forehead [Piaget, 1951, p. 56].

According to Piaget, *deferred imitation*—the ability to reproduce the behavior of an *absent* model—first appears at 18 to 24 months of age. When discussing symbolic schemata, we noted an example of deferred imitation—Jacqueline's reproduction of her playmate's temper tantrum 24 hours later. Piaget believes that older infants are capable of deferred imitation because they are now constructing mental symbols, or images, of a model's behavior that are stored in memory and retrieved later to guide the child's re-creation of the modeled sequence.

Other investigators disagree with Piaget, arguing that deferred imitation begins much earlier. In Chapter 7, for example, we learned that some 12-month-olds are able to imitate simple motor acts after a 10-minute delay, and Andrew Meltzoff (1985, 1988) finds that about half of all 9- to 14-month-olds can imitate a simple act after a delay of 24 hours! But perhaps we should not be too critical of Piaget's oversights, for deferred imitation improves dramatically during the latter half of the second year, and very few infants will reenact complex behavioral sequences (such as the temper tantrum that Jacqueline witnessed) until age 18–24 months (Abravanel & Gingold, 1985).

Object permanence: Out of sight is no longer out of mind

Although 10–12-month-olds do not yet construct mental symbols, they are already forming simple *concepts* as they begin to recognize similarities and differences among objects and events and to treat perceptually similar phenomena as if they were alike (Sugarman, 1981; Younger, 1985). One of the more notable achievements of the sensorimotor period is the development of the **object concept**—the idea that people, places, and things continue to exist when they are no longer visible or detectable through the other senses.

If you were to remove your watch and cover it with a mug, you would be well aware that the watch continues to exist even though it is not visible. Objects have a permanence for us; out of sight is not necessarily out of mind. According to Piaget, babies are not initially aware of this basic fact of life. Throughout the first four months, infants will not search for attractive objects that vanish; if a watch that interests them is covered by a mug, they soon lose interest, almost as if they believed that the watch no longer existed or had lost its identity by being transformed into a mug (Bower, 1982). At age 4 to 8 months, infants will retrieve attractive objects that are partly concealed or placed beneath a transparent cover; but their continuing failure to search for objects that are completely concealed suggests that, from their perspective, disappearing objects may no longer exist.

According to Piaget, the first signs of an emerging object concept appear at 8 to 12 months of age. However, object permanence is far from complete, as we see in Piaget's demonstration with his 10-month-old daughter:

Jacqueline is seated on a mattress without anything to disturb or distract her ... I take her [toy] parrot from her hands and hide it twice in succession under the mattress, on her left [point A]. Both times Jacqueline looks for the object immediately and grabs it. Then I take it from her hands and move it very slowly *before her eyes* to the corresponding place on her right, under the mattress [point B]. Jacqueline watches this movement ... but at the moment when the parrot disappears [at point B] she turns to her left and looks where it was before [at point A] [1954, p. 51; italics added].

Jacqueline's response is typical of children at this age. When searching for a disappearing object, the 8- to 12-month-old will look in the place where it was previously found rather than the place where it was last seen. In other words, the child acts as if her behavior determined where the object is to appear, and consequently, she does not treat the object as if it existed independent of her own activity.

Between 12 and 18 months of age, the object concept improves. Infants will now track the visible movements of objects and search for them where they were last seen. However, the object concept is not complete, for the child cannot make the mental inferences necessary to understand *invisible* displacements. So if you conceal a toy in your hand, place your hand behind a barrier and deposit the toy there, remove your hand, and then ask the child to find the toy, 12- to 18-month-olds will search *where the toy was last seen*—in your hand—rather than looking behind the barrier.

By 18 to 24 months of age, the object concept is complete. Children are now capable of mentally representing invisible displacements and using these mental inferences to guide their search for an object that has disappeared.

Before we summarize the developments of the sensorimotor period, a caution is in order. In recent years, investigators have questioned several of Piaget's ideas about the object concept when they began to discover that young infants seem to understand much more about objects than Piaget had assumed. For example, even though 1–4-month-olds will not search for disappearing objects, they are typically *surprised* if an interesting toy that they have seen blocked from view by a screen is no longer present when the screen is lifted (Bower, 1982). Apparently, these very young infants have some notion that the hidden toy continues to exist, because they expected it to reappear. Why, then, did they not search for it?

Photo 9-2. Playing peek-a-boo is an exciting activity for infants who are acquiring object permanence.

Thomas Bower (1982) thinks that a simple deficit in *spatial perception* may explain why infants younger than 6–8 months fail to retrieve hidden objects. Presumably, these young infants will not look for objects that disappear behind a screen or under a cup because they suspect that two entities cannot occupy the same space and may assume that the screening object has replaced the one that disappeared. And if Bower's spatial hypothesis is correct, infants should successfully retrieve objects from behind two-dimensional barriers such as a screen before they retrieve them from three-dimensional hiding places such as a box. The rationale for this prediction is that it is harder to perceive a flat two-dimensional screen as occupying the same space and thereby "replacing" the object that has disappeared.

The research bearing on this issue is generally consistent with Bower's spatial hypothesis: by age 7 months, infants are becoming rather skillful at locating objects behind two-dimensional barriers; but not until

---

object concept: the realization that objects continue to exist when they are no longer visible or detectable through the other senses.

age 9–10 months are they equally proficient at retrieving objects from three-dimensional hiding places (Dunst, Brooks, & Doxsey, 1982; Wishart & Bower, 1985). So the inability of younger infants to locate hidden objects may reflect their lack of knowledge about spatial relations rather than ignorance of the object concept. By relying solely on studies employing search procedures. Piaget seems to have underestimated what babies may know about objects and their properties during the first 8–10 months of life.

An overview of sensorimotor development

The child's intellectual achievements during the sensorimotor period are truly remarkable. In two short years, infants have evolved from reflexive and largely immobile creatures into planful thinkers who can move about on their own, solve some problems in their heads, form simple concepts, and even communicate many of their thoughts to their companions. Clearly, deferred imitation emerges earlier than Piaget had thought, and young infants know far more about objects than he gave them credit for. Nevertheless, Piaget's description of sensorimotor development is still considered a reasonably good overview of how the human mind changes between birth and age 2 (Flavell, 1985; see Table 9-1 for a brief summary of these intellectual accomplishments).

Keep in mind that 2-year-olds are relatively unpracticed and inefficient in the use of symbolic schemata at the end of the sensorimotor period. But they will soon improve. In fact, mental symbols quickly become the most important instruments of thought as the child enters the second, or preoperational, stage of intellectual development.

Table 9-1. Summary of the substages and intellectual accomplishments of the sensorimotor period

Substage	Methods of solving problems or producing interesting outcomes	Imitation	Object concept
1. Reflex activity (0–1 month)	Exercise and accommodation of inborn reflexes	Some imitation of facial expressions[a]	Tracks moving object but ignores its disappearance
2. Primary circular reactions (1–4 months)	Repeating interesting acts that are centered on one's own body	Repetition of own behavior that is mimicked by a companion	Looks intently at the spot where an object disappeared[b]
3. Secondary circular reactions (4–8 months)	Repeating interesting acts that are directed toward external objects	Same as in Substage 2	Searches for partly concealed object
4. Coordination of secondary schemata (8–12 months)	Combining actions to solve simple problems (first evidence of intentionality)	Ability to eventually imitate novel responses after gradually accommodating a crude initial attempt at imitation	First glimmering of object permanence; searches for and finds concealed object that has *not* been visibly displaced
5. Tertiary circular reactions (12–18 months)	Experimenting to find new ways to solve problems or reproduce interesting outcomes	Systematic imitation of novel responses; deferred imitation of simple motor acts	Searches for and finds object that has been *visibly* displaced
6. Invention of new means through mental combinations (18–24 months)	First evidence of insight as the child solves problems at an internal, symbolic level	Deferred imitation of complex behavioral sequences	Object concept is complete; searches for and finds objects that have been hidden through *invisible* displacements

[a]Imitation of facial expressions such as surprise or sadness is apparently an inborn ability that may bear little relation to the voluntary imitation that appears later in the first year (Field, Woodson, Greenberg, & Cohen, 1982; Meltzoff & Moore, 1983).

[b]Some researchers believe that object permanence may be present very early and that young infants simply lack the eye/hand coordination and/or the spatial reasoning abilities that would permit them to search for and find hidden objects.

The Preoperational Stage (2 to 7 Years)

During the **preoperational stage,** children are becoming increasingly proficient at constructing and using mental symbols to think about the objects, situations, and events they encounter. But despite these advances in symbolic reasoning, Piaget's descriptions of preoperational intelligence focus mainly on the limitations or deficiencies in children's thinking. Indeed, he calls this period "preoperational" because he believes that preschool children have not yet acquired the cognitive operations (and operational schemata) that would enable them to think logically. Let's consider what Piaget has to say about the intellectual capabilities of preschool children and then contrast his somewhat negative viewpoint with a more positive outlook that is beginning to emerge from recent research.

Piaget divides the preoperational period into two substages: the *preconceptual* period (2–4 years of age) and the *intuitive* period (4–7 years).

The preconceptual period (*intuitive*)

Emergence of symbolic thought. The **preconceptual period** is marked by the appearance of the **symbolic function:** the ability to make one thing—a word or an object—stand for, or represent, something else. For example, words soon come to represent objects, persons, and events, so that the child can now easily reconstruct and make reference to the past and talk about items that are no longer present. Pretend play also blossoms at this time: toddlers often pretend to be people they are not (mommies, superheroes), and they may play these roles with props such as a shoe box or a stick that symbolize other objects such as a baby's crib or a ray gun. Although some parents are concerned when their preschool children immerse themselves in a world of make-believe and begin to invent imaginary playmates, Piaget feels that these are basically healthy activities. In Box 9-1 we will focus on children's play and see how these "pretend" activities may contribute in a positive way to the child's social, emotional, and intellectual development.

Deficits in preconceptual reasoning. Piaget calls this period "preconceptual" because he believes that the ideas, concepts, and cognitive processes of 2–4-year-olds are rather primitive by adult standards. One of the flaws that characterize the child's thinking is **animism**—a willingness to attribute life and lifelike qualities (for example, motives and intentions) to in-

animate objects. The 4-year-old who believed that the setting sun was alive, angry, and hiding behind the mountain provides a clear example of the animistic logic that children are apt to display during the preconceptual period.

Several other illogical schemata, or "preconcepts," stem from the child's **transductive reasoning.** The transductive thinker reasons from the particular to the particular: when any two events occur together (co-vary), the child is likely to assume that one has caused the other. One day when Piaget's daughter had missed her usual afternoon nap, she remarked "I haven't had a nap, so it isn't afternoon." In this case, Lucienne reasoned from one particular (the nap) to another (the afternoon) and erroneously concluded that her nap determined when it was afternoon.

According to Piaget, the most striking deficiency in children's preoperational reasoning is a characteristic that he calls **egocentrism**—a tendency to view the world from one's own perspective and to have difficulty recognizing another person's point of view. Piaget demonstrated this by first familiarizing children with an asymmetrical mountain scene (see Figure 9-2) and then asking them what an observer would see as he gazed at the scene from a vantage point other than their own. Often, 3–4-year-olds said the other person would see exactly what they saw, thus failing to consider the other's divergent perspective. Other examples of this self-focused thinking appear in the statements young children make. Here is a sample conversation in which

---

preoperational stage: Piaget's second stage of cognitive development, lasting from about age 2 to age 7, when children are thinking at a symbolic level but are not yet using cognitive operations.

preconceptual period: the early substage of preoperations, from age 2 to age 4, characterized by the appearance of primitive ideas, concepts, and methods of reasoning.

symbolic function: the ability to use symbols (for example, images and words) to represent objects and experiences.

animism: attributing life and lifelike qualities to inanimate objects.

transductive reasoning: reasoning from the particular to the particular, so that events that occur together are assumed to be causally related.

egocentrism: the tendency to view the world from one's own perspective while failing to recognize that others may have different points of view.

Box 9-1

Play Is Serious Business

Play is an intrinsically satisfying activity—something that young children do for the fun of it (Rubin, Fein, & Vandenberg, 1983). Since toddlers and preschool children spend a large percentage of their waking hours at one form of play or another, we might wonder what effects these pleasurable activities will have on their social, emotional, and intellectual development.

Piaget (1951) is one theorist who views play as an adaptive activity. Play begins early in the sensorimotor period as infants begin to repeat acts that they find satisfying or pleasurable. Piaget suggests that play activities permit children to practice their competencies in a relaxed and carefree way. Presumably the opportunity to manipulate novel objects and to play social games such as peek-a-boo will help to nurture curiosity, object permanence, inner experimentation, and other cognitive advances.

At 11–13 months of age, *pretend play* begins (Rubin et al., 1983). The earliest forms of pretend play are very simple acts in which infants pretend to engage in familiar activities such as eating, sleeping, or drinking from a cup. As children enter the preoperational stage, their play becomes much more complex. They can now substitute one object (for example, a block) for another (a car) and use language in inventive ways to construct rich fantasy worlds for themselves. Apparently, parents and other close companions make important contributions to the development of symbolic play, for the pretend activities of 2–3-year-olds are much longer in duration and more complex when the mother is available to serve as a playmate (Slade, 1987). Moreover, the themes that mothers pursue with their toddlers are also important: 2–3-year-olds will often fail to take part in unusual episodes that they do not understand (for example, saving a princess from a dragon), but they play enthusiastically when the theme revolves around familiar activities, such as setting the table or simulat-

ing naptime with a doll (Lucariello, 1987). Once again, Piaget views these simple symbolic interactions and play activities as a means for energetic young children to practice and perfect their emerging conceptual skills, thereby setting the stage for further social and intellectual growth.

Recently, investigators have begun to confirm some of Piaget's ideas about play. Jeffrey Dansky (1980) finds that preschool children who often engage in pretend play are more likely than those who rarely do to devise novel, creative uses for unusual play objects such as clothespins and matchboxes. In a similar vein, Hutt and Bhavnani (1976) found that children who were judged low in exploratory play as toddlers tended five years later to be low in curiosity and to experience problems in their personal and social adjustment. By contrast, those who had been active explorers as toddlers were more likely to score high on tests of creativity and to be judged curious and independent during the grade school years. Finally, Jennifer Connolly and Anna-Beth Doyle (1984) report that preschool children who "pretend" a lot are both more socially mature and more popular with their peers than children of the same age who "pretend" less often. After reviewing these and other studies of children's play, Rubin et al. (1983) concluded that play is clearly an adaptive activity that reflects current conceptual abilities and helps children to develop additional cognitive and social skills.

Play may also serve as a means of coping with emotional crises and reducing interpersonal conflicts. Piaget points out that young children are often obliged to follow rules and adapt to a social world that they do not fully understand. When children are upset by the imposition of a rule, they can cope with these conflicts and crises by retreating into a fantasy world that permits them to reflect on the incidents that have been so discomforting. Piaget argues that

it is primarily [emotional] conflicts that reappear in symbolic play.... If there is a [disciplinary] scene at lunch ... one can be sure that an hour or two

Role taking is a major function of symbolic play.

afterward it will be re-created with dolls and brought to a happier solution. Either the child disciplines her doll ... or in play she accepts what had not been accepted at lunch (such as finishing a bowl of soup she does not like, especially if it is the doll who finishes it symbolically).... Generally speaking, symbolic play helps in the resolution of conflicts and also in the compensation of unsatisfied needs [and *the inversion of roles*] such as obedience and authority [Piaget & Inhelder, 1969, p. 60; italics added].

The italicized portion of Piaget and Inhelder's statement hints at another major function of symbolic play—*role taking*. During the preschool period, children become cowboys, firefighters, doctors, lawyers, nurses, or space travelers by simply donning the appropriate attire and pretending to be these things. They can become powerful authority figures (such as parents) by enacting that role with dolls or with younger brothers and sisters. In other words, pretend play enables preschool children to try out roles that other people play while encouraging them to think about the feelings of the individuals who actually live these roles. In the process, they will learn from their enactments and further their understanding of the social world in which they live (Rubin et al., 1983). Play is serious business indeed!

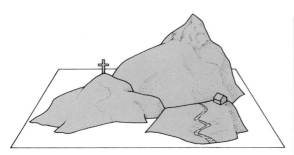

Figure 9-2. Piaget's three-mountain problem. Young, egocentric children have difficulties taking another person's perspective and will often say that a person looking at the mountains from a different vantage point will see exactly what they see from their own locations.

the egocentrism of a 4-year-old named Sandy comes through as she describes an event she has witnessed.

Sandy: Uncle David, it got on your car and scratched it.
Adult: What did?
Sandy: Come, I'll show you. *(She takes her uncle outside and shows him a scratch on the top of his new car.)*
Adult: Sandy, what made the scratch?
Sandy: Not me!
Adult (laughing): I know, Sandy, but how did the scratch get there?
Sandy: It got on the car and scratched it with its claws.
Adult: What did?
Sandy (looking around): There! *(She points to a cat that is walking across the street.)*
Adult: Oh, a cat! Why didn't you tell me that in the first place?
Sandy: I did.

In this case, Sandy assumed that her uncle shared her perspective and must already know what had caused the scratch on his car. Consequently, her speech is <u>not adapted to the needs of her listener,</u> reflecting instead her egocentric point of view.

The intuitive period – class inclusion conservation

Piaget calls the phase between age 4 and age 7 the **intuitive period.** Intuitive thought is little more than an extension of preconceptual thought, although children are now somewhat less egocentric and much more proficient at classifying objects on the basis of shared perceptual attributes such as size, shape, and color. Indeed, the child's thinking is called "intuitive" because his understanding of objects and events is based, or "centered," on their single most salient perceptual feature—the way things appear to be—rather than on logical or rational thought processes.

Classification and <u>whole/part relations.</u>
The limitations of a perceptually based, intuitive logic are apparent when 4–7-year-olds work on **class inclusion** problems that require them to think about whole/part relations. One such problem presents children with a set of wooden beads, most of which are brown, with a few white ones thrown in. If the preoperational child is asked whether these are all wooden beads, he answers yes. If asked whether there are more brown beads than white beads, he will again answer correctly. However, if he is then asked "Are there more brown beads or more wooden beads?," he will usually say "More brown beads." Notice that the child can conceive of a whole class (wooden beads) when responding to the first question and of two distinct classes (brown and white beads) when responding to the second. Yet the third question, which requires him to *simultaneously* relate a whole class to its component parts, is too difficult. The child's thinking about class inclusion is now centered on the one most salient perceptual feature—the color of the beads—so that he fails to consider that brown beads and white beads can be combined to form a larger class of wooden beads.

The conservation problem.
Other examples of children's intuitive reasoning come from Piaget's famous conservation studies (Flavell, 1963). One of these experiments begins with the child adjusting the volumes of liquid in two identical containers until each is said to have "the same amount to drink." Next the child sees the experimenter pour the liquid from one of these tall, thin containers into a short, broad container. He is then asked whether the remaining tall, thin container and the shorter, broader container have the same amount of liquid (see Figure 9-3 for an illustration of the procedure). Children younger than 6 or 7 will usually say that the tall, thin receptacle contains *more* liquid than the short, broad one. The child's thinking about liquids is apparently centered on one perceptual feature: the relative heights of the columns (tall column = more liquid). In Piaget's terminology, preoperational

intuitive period: the later substage of preoperations, from age 4 to age 7, when the child's thinking about objects and events is dominated by salient perceptual features.
class inclusion: the ability to compare a class of objects with its subclasses without confusing the two.

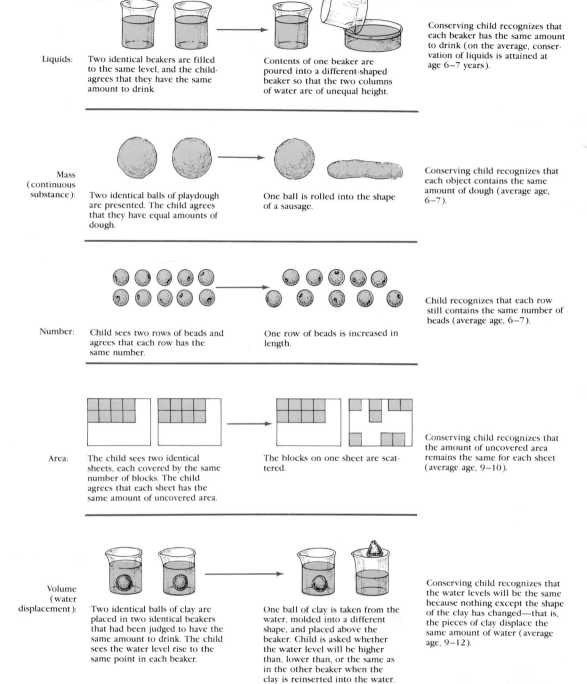

Liquids: Two identical beakers are filled to the same level, and the child agrees that they have the same amount to drink. Contents of one beaker are poured into a different-shaped beaker so that the two columns of water are of unequal height. Conserving child recognizes that each beaker has the same amount to drink (on the average, conservation of liquids is attained at age 6–7 years).

Mass (continuous substance): Two identical balls of playdough are presented. The child agrees that they have equal amounts of dough. One ball is rolled into the shape of a sausage. Conserving child recognizes that each object contains the same amount of dough (average age, 6–7).

Number: Child sees two rows of beads and agrees that each row has the same number. One row of beads is increased in length. Child recognizes that each row still contains the same number of beads (average age, 6–7).

Area: The child sees two identical sheets, each covered by the same number of blocks. The child agrees that each sheet has the same amount of uncovered area. The blocks on one sheet are scattered. Conserving child recognizes that the amount of uncovered area remains the same for each sheet (average age, 9–10).

Volume (water displacement): Two identical balls of clay are placed in two identical beakers that had been judged to have the same amount to drink. The child sees the water level rise to the same point in each beaker. One ball of clay is taken from the water, molded into a different shape, and placed above the beaker. Child is asked whether the water level will be higher than, lower than, or the same as in the other beaker when the clay is reinserted into the water. Conserving child recognizes that the water levels will be the same because nothing except the shape of the clay has changed—that is, the pieces of clay displace the same amount of water (average age, 9–12).

Figure 9-3. Some common tests of the child's ability to conserve.

children are incapable of **conservation:** they do not yet realize that certain properties of objects (such as volume, mass, or number) remain unchanged when the objects' appearances are altered in some superficial way.

Why do preoperational children fail to conserve? Simply because their thinking is not yet *operational.* According to Piaget, either of two cognitive operations is necessary for conservation. The first is *reversibility*—the ability to mentally undo, or reverse, an action. At the intuitive level, the child is incapable of mentally reversing the flow of action and therefore does not realize that the liquid in the short, broad container would attain its former height if it were poured back into a tall, thin container.

A second problem that prevents preoperational children from conserving is their **centration**—the tendency to center, or focus, on a single aspect of a problem while ignoring other information that would help them to answer correctly. Piaget suggests that children begin to overcome their "centered" thinking as they acquire a cognitive operation called **compensation**—the ability to focus on several aspects of a problem at the same time. Children at the intuitive stage are unable to attend simultaneously to both height and width when trying to solve the liquid conservation problem. Consequently, they fail to recognize that increases in the width of a column of liquid compensate for decreases in its height to preserve its absolute amount.

Does Piaget underestimate the preoperational child?

Are preschool children really as intuitive, illogical, and egocentric as Piaget assumes? Can a child who has no understanding of cognitive operations be taught to conserve? We will now consider some of the recent research designed to answer these questions.

New evidence on egocentrism.

Several experiments indicate that Piaget has badly underestimated the ability of preschool children to recognize and appreciate another person's point of view. In one study, John Flavell (Flavell, Everett, Croft, & Flavell, 1981) showed 3-year-olds a card with a dog on one side and a cat on the other. The card was then held vertically between the child (who could see the dog) and the experimenter (who could see the cat), and the child was asked which animal the experimenter could see. The 3-year-olds performed flawlessly, indicating that they could assume the experimenter's perspective and infer

that he must be seeing the cat rather than the animal they could see.

In another study (Mossler, Marvin, & Greenberg, 1976), 2–6-year-olds each watched a movie in which a boy seated at a table stated his strong desire for cookies. Then the mother entered, and she and her child watched the same movie *with the sound track turned off.* When asked what their mothers knew about the film, the 4–6-year-olds in the sample quickly recognized that their mothers had seen a "silent" film and, thus, had no way of knowing of the boy's desire for cookies. In other words, these older preoperational children were providing *nonegocentric* responses by correctly inferring what their mothers knew and then determining that their mothers' information did not match their own.

It appears, then, that preoperational children are not nearly so egocentric as Piaget had thought. However, we shouldn't assume that 4–5-year-olds are capable of seeing and appreciating another person's point of view in all circumstances and situations, particularly those in which they must infer abstract or otherwise unobservable information such as a companion's subtle motives and intentions. Rochel Gelman (1978) nicely summarizes the current viewpoint on egocentrism by noting that children become less egocentric and better able to appreciate others' points of view as they learn more and more—particularly about other people and their behavior. Perspective-taking abilities are not totally absent at one stage and suddenly present at another; they are gradually developing and becoming more refined from early in life into adulthood (Gelman, 1978).

Another look at children's causal reasoning.

Piaget is quite correct in stating that preschool children are likely to provide animistic answers to many questions and to make logical errors when thinking about cause-and-effect relationships. Yet, Merry Bullock (1985) finds that many 3-year-olds and the vast majority of 4- and 5-year-olds are reasonably proficient at discriminating animate from inanimate objects and

---

conservation: the recognition that the properties of an object or substance do not change when its appearance is altered in some superficial way.

centration: the tendency to focus on only one aspect of a problem when two or more aspects are relevant.

compensation: the ability to consider more than one aspect of a problem at a time (also called decentration).

may seem more animistic than they really are because they can't always explain how animates and inanimates differ. Moreover, recent studies of children's causal reasoning suggest that even 3-year-olds know that (1) causes precede rather than follow effects and (2) an event that always precedes an effect (100% covariation) is more likely to be its cause than are other events that occasionally precede it (Sedlak & Kurtz, 1981). And by age 5, children are even beginning to understand the concept of "randomness" by recognizing that chance outcomes are *not* predictable, whereas predetermined outcomes always are (Kuzmak & Gelman, 1986). Although these examples represent very simple kinds of causal inferences, they clearly indicate that 3–5-year-olds have some understanding of causality and will "not always" resort to animistic or transductive reasoning.

Can preoperational children conserve?

According to Piaget (1970b), children younger than 6 or 7 cannot solve conservation problems, because they have not yet acquired reversibility or compensation—the two cognitive operations that would enable them to discover the constancy of attributes such as mass and volume. Piaget has also argued that one cannot teach conservation to subjects younger than 6 or 7, for these *pre*operational children are much too intellectually immature to understand and use logical operations such as reversibility and compensation.

Are preschool children really incapable of learning to conserve? Irving Sigel and his associates (Sigel, Roeper, & Hooper, 1968) tested this hypothesis by coaxing 4–5-year-olds who had failed various conservation tests to focus on several dimensions at once (compensation training) and to think about what might happen if an action were reversed, or undone (reversibility training). The majority of children who were trained in these logical operations showed at least some modest improvement in their performance on conservation tests.

Other investigators have had much greater success with **identity training**—teaching children to recognize that the object or substance transformed in a conservation task is still the *same* object or substance, regardless of its new appearance. For example, a child being trained to recognize identities on a "conservation of liquids" task might be told "It may look like less water when we pour it from a tall, thin glass into this shorter one, but it is the *same* water, and there has to be the same amount to drink." Recently, Dorothy Field (1981) has shown that 4-year-olds who received this training not only conserved on the training task but could also

use their new knowledge about identities to solve a number of conservation problems on which they had not been trained. Field also reports that nearly 75% of the 4-year-olds who had received some kind of identity training were able to solve at least three (out of five) conservation problems that were presented to them two and one-half to five months *after* their training had ended. By contrast, only 35% of the 4-year-olds who had been trained in the logical operations of reversibility and compensation were able to conserve on this delayed posttest. We see, then, that 4-year-olds can learn to conserve and that their understanding of this "law of nature" seems to depend more on their ability to recognize identities than on their use of logical operations. In fact, 5–6-year-olds who have never been trained will often conserve by identity long before they acquire the logical operations of reversibility and compensation (Acredolo, 1982; Acredolo & Acredolo, 1979).

Summing up. Taken together, the evidence we have reviewed suggests that preschool children are not nearly as illogical or egocentric as Piaget assumed. Today, many researchers believe that Piaget underestimated the abilities of preschool children because his problems were too complex to allow them to demonstrate what they actually knew. If I were to ask you "What do quarks do?," you probably couldn't tell me unless you are a physics major. Surely, this is an unfair test of your "causal logic," just as Piaget's tests were when he questioned preschool children about phenomena (for example, "What causes the wind?") that were equally unfamiliar to them. Even when they were thinking about familiar concepts, Piaget required children to verbally justify their answers—to state rationales that these young, relatively inarticulate preschoolers were often incapable of providing (to Piaget's satisfaction, at least). Yet later research consistently indicates that Piaget's subjects may have had a reasonably good understanding of many ideas that they couldn't articulate (for example, distinctions between animates and inanimates) and would easily have displayed such knowledge on nonverbal tests of the same concepts (Bullock, 1985; Smith, 1984). Finally, information-processing theorists believe that failures on complex, multidimensional problems, such as conservation and class inclusion, stem not so much from the child's "centered" thinking or an inability to operate on one's objects of thought (as Piaget claimed) as from certain memory deficiencies that prevent young children from gathering, storing, and simultaneously comparing the many pieces of information needed to arrive at the correct answer (Case, 1985; Pascual-Leone, 1984).[1]

Clearly, Piaget was right in arguing that preschool children are more intuitive, egocentric, and illogical than older grade school children. Yet, it is now equally clear that a number of factors other than lack of cognitive operations and operational schemata may account for the poor performance of preschoolers on Piaget's own cognitive tests.

The Concrete-Operational Stage
(7 to 11 Years)

During the period of **concrete operations,** children are rapidly acquiring cognitive operations and applying these important new skills when thinking about objects, situations, and events that they have seen, heard, or otherwise experienced. Recall from our earlier discussion that a cognitive operation is an internal mental schema that enables the child to modify and reorganize her images and symbols and to reverse these transformations in her head (Flavell, 1985). For example, the operation of reversibility allows the child to mentally reverse the flow of action and thereby recognize that a column of water would once again look the same if she were to pour it back into its original container. The operations of cognitive *addition* and *subtraction* permit the child to discover the logical relation between whole classes and subclasses by mentally adding the parts to form a superordinate whole and then reversing this action (subtracting) to once again think of the whole class as a collection of subclasses. In sum, the ability to operate on one's objects of thought takes the 7- to 11-year-old far beyond the static and centered thinking of the preoperational stage.

Why does Piaget call this period *concrete* operations? Because he believes that children at this stage of development can apply their operational schemata only to objects, situations, and events that are _real or imaginable_. Indeed, we will see that 7- to 11-year-olds find it very difficult to think about any abstract idea or hypothetical proposition that has no basis in reality.

Some characteristics of
concrete-operational thinking

To this point, we have talked about two operational structures: class inclusion and conservation. Let's briefly consider two more.

---

[1]We will discuss the development of memory and its implications for problem solving in a later section of the chapter.

Mental representation of actions. According to Piaget, the concrete operator is finally able to construct accurate mental representations of a complex series of actions. Suppose, for example, that we were to ask a 5-year-old preoperational child and his 10-year-old sister to sketch a map of the route to their grandmother's house across town. Even if the younger child walks there every day, he will probably fail to produce an accurate map. His problem, according to Piaget, is that he cannot conjure up a mental representation of the entire route. By contrast, the older, operational child will find this mapmaking task rather easy, for it simply requires her to transcribe the "cognitive map" in her head (Piaget & Inhelder, 1956).

But caution is required in interpreting Piaget's mapmaking studies. In a recent experiment, Linda Anooshian and her colleagues (Anooshian, Hartman, & Scharf, 1982) found that many 3- to 6-year-olds are able to describe the steps they have taken through a familiar environment by placing photographs of the various landmarks into their proper sequence. Apparently, these preoperational children are able to represent their past actions in some internal, symbolic fashion that enables them to recall the route they traveled. Perhaps cognitive operations do help older children to think about distances, directions, and action sequences; but it appears that such operations are not absolutely necessary for either the mental representation of actions or the development of cognitive maps.

Relational logic. One of the hallmarks of concrete-operational thinking is a better understanding of relations and relational logic. For example, concrete operators are capable of **seriation,** an operation that enables them to arrange a set of stimuli along a quantifiable dimension, such as length. A related ability is

---

identity training: an attempt to promote conservation by teaching nonconservers to recognize that a transformed object or substance is the same object or substance, regardless of its new appearance.

concrete operations: Piaget's third stage of cognitive development, lasting from about age 7 to age 11, when children are acquiring cognitive operations and thinking more logically about real objects and experiences.

seriation: a cognitive operation that allows one to order a set of stimuli along a quantifiable dimension such as height or weight.

the concept of **transitivity,** which describes the relations among the elements in a serial order. If, for example, John is taller than Mark, who is taller than Sam, then John has to be taller than Sam. Although this inference seems elementary to us, children show little awareness of the transitivity principle before the stage of concrete operations.

Two additional observations are worthy of note. First, preoperational children can be trained to seriate and to make simple transitive inferences, so that the basic ability to understand the relations "less than" and "greater than" may precede the development of cognitive operations (Braine & Rumain, 1983; Gelman, 1978). Second, the transitive inferences of concrete operators are generally limited to *real objects* that are *physically present*. Indeed, 7- to 11-year-olds do not yet apply this relational logic to abstract signifiers such as the *x*s, *y*s, and *z*s that we use in algebra.

1. seriation 2. conservation (# + weight) 3. class inclusion 4. (volume)

The sequencing of concrete operations

While examining Figure 9-3, you may have noticed that some forms of conservation (for example, mass) are understood much sooner than others (area or volume). Piaget was aware of this and other developmental inconsistencies, and he coined the term **horizontal decalage** to describe them.

Why does the child display different levels of awareness or understanding on a series of conservation tasks that seem to require the same mental operations? According to Piaget, horizontal decalage occurs because problems that appear quite similar may actually differ in complexity. For example, conservation of volume (see Figure 9-3) is not attained until age 9 to 12 because it is a complex task that requires the child to simultaneously consider the operations involved in the conservation of both liquids and mass *and* then to determine whether there are any meaningful interactions between these two phenomena. Although we have talked as if concrete operations were a set of skills that appeared rather abruptly over a brief period, this is not Piaget's point of view. Piaget has always maintained that operational abilities evolve gradually and sequentially as the simpler skills that appear first are consolidated, combined, and reorganized into increasingly complex mental structures.

Carol Tomlinson-Keasey and her associates (Tomlinson-Keasey, Eisert, Kahle, Hardy-Brown, & Keasey, 1979) studied the growth of logical reasoning between ages 6 and 9. In this longitudinal study they found that various concrete-operational abilities developed very gradually and in roughly the same sequence for all the children they studied (for example, seriation appeared before conservation of number and weight, which, in turn, seemed to be necessary for the development of class-inclusion skills and the conservation of volume). However, other investigators find much less coherence, or consistency, to development during the concrete-operational period (Case, 1985; Kuhn, 1984). Apparently some children breeze through class-inclusion problems before they can seriate or conserve weight, whereas others acquire these skills in exactly the opposite order. So the sequencing of different concrete-operational skills is highly variable—a finding that challenges Piaget's assumption that the operational proficiencies acquired earliest are simpler schemata that serve as prerequisites for those developing later.

Piaget on education

After reviewing the accomplishments of the concrete-operational period, we can see why many societies begin to formally educate their young at 6 to 7 years of age. This is precisely the time when children are decentering from perceptual illusions and acquiring the cognitive operations that will enable them to comprehend arithmetic, to think about language and its properties, to classify animals, people, objects, and events, and to understand the relations between upper- and lower-case letters, letters and the printed word, words and sentences, and so on.

Although Piaget's theory is not a theory of education, it offers some helpful hints to the elementary school teacher. Perhaps the most important single proposition that educators can derive from Piaget's work is that children are naturally inquisitive souls who learn best by exploring their environments. In addition, it helps to recall that 7- to 11-year-olds think most logically and systematically about *real* objects and events and about activities that can be concretized in some way. For these reasons, Piaget advises teachers to spend less time lecturing and allow children to learn by doing. He believes that arithmetic operations may be best illustrated by having children add and subtract buttons rather than showing them how to solve problems on a blackboard. He advocates "teaching" the concepts of space and distance by allowing children to measure their heights or the widths of their desks, as opposed to lecturing them on the relations between inches, feet, and yards. In other words, Piaget contends that the teacher's job is not so much to transmit facts and concepts or to actively reinforce correct answers as to provide the setting and materials that will enable curious children to experience the *intrinsic* satisfaction of *discovering* this knowledge for themselves. Piaget sees a "discovery-based" education as critical because he believes that "the principal goal of education is to create [adults] who are capable of doing new things, not simply of repeating what other generations have done—[people] who are creative, inventive, discoverers" (Piaget, as cited in Elkind, 1977, p. 171).

The Formal-Operational Stage *flexibility* (Age 11–12 and Beyond)

By age 11 or 12, many children are entering the last of Piaget's intellectual stages—**formal operations.** Perhaps the most important characteristic of formal-operational thinking is its flexibility. No longer is thinking tied to the observable or imaginable, for formal operators can now reason quite logically about abstract ideas that may have no basis in reality.

Reactions to hypothetical propositions

One way to determine whether a preadolescent has crossed over into the stage of formal operations is to present a thought problem that violates her views about the real world. The concrete operator, whose thinking is tied to objective reality, will often balk at hypothetical propositions. In fact, she may even reply that it is impossible to think about objects that don't exist or events that could never happen. By contrast, formal operators enjoy thinking about hypotheticals and are likely to generate some very unusual and creative responses. In Box 9-2 we can see the differences between concrete-operational and formal-operational thinking as children consider a hypothetical proposition that was presented in the form of an art assignment.

Hypothetical-deductive reasoning: The systematic search for answers and solutions

The formal operator's approach to problem solving becomes increasingly systematic and abstract— much like the **hypothetical-deductive reasoning** of a scientist. We can easily compare the reasoning of formal operators with that of their younger counterparts by examining their responses to Piaget's famous "four beaker" problem:

> The child is given four similar flasks containing colorless, odorless liquids which are perceptually identical [but contain different chemicals]. We number them (1) ... (2) ... (3) ... and (4). We add a

bottle (with an eyedropper) which we call *g*. Mixing chemicals 1 + 3 + *g* will yield a yellow color. The experimenter presents to the subject two [unlabeled] glasses, one containing chemicals 1 + 3, the other containing chemical 2. In front of the subject, he pours several drops of *g* into each of the two glasses and notes the different reactions. Then the subject is asked to simply reproduce the yellow color in a test tube, using flasks 1, 2, 3, 4, and *g* as he wishes [Inhelder & Piaget, 1958, pp. 108–109].

Children at the concrete-operational stage attack this problem by *doing what they saw the experimenter do:* they mix a few drops of *g* with chemicals from each of the four flasks and thus fail to produce the yellow color. At this point, concrete operators may say something like "I tried them all and nothing works." Usually they have to be coaxed to go beyond their visual experiences to mix three chemicals, and their higher-order combinations tend to be unsystematic. In fact, concrete operators who stumble on the correct solution by this trial-and-error approach are often unable to reproduce the yellow color when asked to repeat the process.

The formal operator begins in the same way as the concrete operator, but he subsequently proceeds to test every possible combination of three chemicals when the binary combinations (that is, 1 + *g*, 2 + *g*, 3 + *g*, 4 + *g*) fail to solve the problem. Moreover, the formal operator generates the higher-order combinations according to a rational, systematic plan, often beginning with 1 + 2 + *g* and proceeding through 1 + 3 + *g*, 1 + 4 + *g*, 2 + 3 + *g*, and so on until all possible combinations have been tested and the one correct solution identified. Indeed, the systematic approach used by formal operators prepares them to find

---

transitivity: the ability to recognize relations among elements in a serial order (for example, if A > B and B > C, then A > C).

horizontal decalage: an inability to solve certain problems even though one can solve similar problems requiring the same mental operations.

formal operations: Piaget's fourth and final stage of cognitive development, from age 11 or 12 and beyond, when the individual begins to think more rationally and systematically about abstract concepts and hypothetical events.

hypothetical-deductive reasoning: a style of problem solving in which the possible solutions to a problem are generated and then systematically evaluated to determine the correct answer.

Box 9-2
Children's Responses to a
Hypothetical Proposition

Piaget (1970a) has argued that the thinking of concrete operators is reality-bound. Presumably most 9-year-olds would have a difficult time thinking about objects that don't exist or events that could never happen. By contrast, children entering the stage of formal operations were said to be quite capable of considering hypothetical propositions and carrying them to a logical conclusion. Indeed, Piaget suspected that many formal operators would even enjoy this type of cognitive challenge.

Several years ago, a group of concrete operators (9-year-old fourth-graders) and a group of children who were at or rapidly approaching formal operations (11- to 12-year-old sixth-graders) completed the following assignment:

Suppose that you were given a third eye and that you could choose to place this eye anywhere on your body. Draw me a picture to show where you would place your "extra" eye, and then tell me why you would put it there.

All the 9-year-olds placed the third eye *on the forehead between their two natural eyes.* It seems as if these children called on their concrete experiences to complete their assignment: eyes are found somewhere around the middle of the face in all people. One 9-year-old boy remarked that the third eye should go between the other two because "that's where a cyclops has his eye." The rationales for this eye placement were rather unimaginative. Consider the following examples:

Jim (age 9½): I would like an eye beside my two other eyes so that if one eye went out, I could still see with two.
Vickie (age 9): I want an extra eye so I can see you three times.
Tanya (age 9½): I want a third eye so I could see better.

In contrast, the older, formal-operational children gave a wide variety of responses that were not at all dependent on what they had seen previously. Furthermore, these children thought out the advantages of this hypothetical situation and provided rather imaginative rationales for placing the "extra" eye in unique locations. Here are some sample responses:

Ken (age 11½): (*Draws the extra eye on top of a tuft of hair.*) I could revolve the eye to look in all directions.
John (age 11½): (*Draws his extra eye in the palm of his left hand.*) I could see around corners and see what kind of cookie I'll get out of the cookie jar.

Tony (age 11): (*Draws a close-up of a third eye in his mouth.*) I want a third eye in my mouth because I want to see what I am eating.

When asked their opinions of the "three eye" assignment, many of the younger children considered it rather silly and uninteresting. One 9-year-old remarked "This is stupid. Nobody has three eyes." However, the 11–12-year-olds enjoyed the task and continued to pester their teacher for "fun" art assignments "like the eye problem" for the remainder of the school year.

So the results of this demonstration are generally consistent with Piaget's theory. Older children who are at or rapidly approaching the stage of formal operations are more likely than younger, concrete operators to generate logical and creative responses to a hypothetical proposition and to enjoy this type of reasoning.

Tanya's, Ken's, and John's responses to the "third eye" assignment.

multiple solutions to problems that have more than one answer. Although concrete operators can be trained to search for multiple solutions, they are ordinarily inclined to show "premature closure" by accepting the first solution they generate (Acredolo & Horobin, 1987).

In sum, formal-operational thinking is rational, systematic, and abstract. The formal operator can now "think about thinking" and operate on *ideas* as well as tangible objects and events. Piaget believes that these new cognitive abilities are almost certain to have a dramatic impact on the adolescent's feelings, goals, and behaviors, for teenagers are suddenly able to reflect on weighty abstractions such as morality and justice, as well as more personal concerns such as their present and

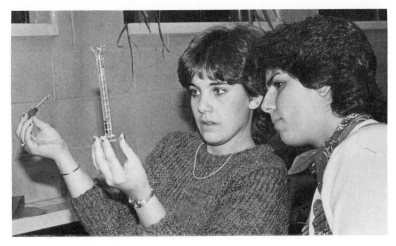

Photo 9-3. A systematic approach to problem solving is one of the characteristics of formal-operational thinking.

future roles in life, their beliefs and values, and the way things "are" as opposed to the way things "ought to be." Consequently, the adolescent approaching intellectual maturity is apt to become a bit of a philosopher, and his or her preoccupation with thinking and its products is the hallmark of the formal-operational period.

Some questions about formal operations

Piaget (1970b) has argued that the transition from concrete-operational to formal-operational reasoning takes place very gradually over a period of several years. For example, 11–13-year-olds who are entering formal operations are able to consider simple hypothetical propositions such as the three-eye problem (see Box 9-2). However, they are not yet proficient at generating and testing hypotheses, and it may be another three to four years before they are capable of the planful, systematic reasoning that is necessary to solve the "four beaker" problem or to deduce what factor determines how fast a pendulum will swing.[2] Piaget has never identified a stage of reasoning beyond formal operations, and he believes that most people will reach this highest level of intellect by age 15–18.

Does everyone reach formal operations?

Recently investigators have been finding that adolescents are much slower to acquire formal operations than Piaget had thought. In fact, Edith Neimark's (1979) review of the literature suggests that a sizable percentage of American adults do not reason at the formal level, and apparently there are some cultures—particularly those *preliterate* societies where formal schooling is rare or nonexistent—in which no one solves Piaget's formal-operational problems (Dasen, 1977; Dasen & Heron, 1981).

Why do some people fail to attain formal operations? Dasen's cross-cultural research provides one clue: they may not have had sufficient exposure to the kinds of schooling that stress logic, mathematics, and science—experiences that Piaget believes will help the child to reason at the formal level. Another possibility is that some individuals, even those who have been educated, may lack the intellectual capacity to move from concrete to formal operations. Indeed, adolescents and adults who score even slightly below average on intelligence tests will rarely if ever reason at the formal level (Inhelder, 1966; Jackson, 1965).

In the later stages of his career, Piaget (1972)

---

[2]The pendulum problem is another of Piaget's famous tests for formal-operational thinking. The subject is given a number of weights that can be tied to a string to make a pendulum. He or she is allowed to vary the length of the string, the amount of weight attached to it, and the height from which the weight is released in order to find out which of these factors, alone or in combination, will determine how

quickly the pendulum swings. The trick is to test each variable singly while holding the others constant. Formal operators, who are capable of this planful and systematic reasoning, soon discover that the critical variable is the *length* of the string: the shorter it is, the faster the pendulum swings.

suggested another possibility: perhaps nearly all adults are capable of reasoning at the formal level but will do so only on problems that hold their interest or are of vital importance to them. Indeed, Tulkin and Konner (1973) found that preliterate Bushman hunters who fail Piaget's test problems do often reason at the formal level on at least one task—tracking prey. Clearly, this is an activity of great importance to them that requires the systematic testing of inferences and hypotheses. A similar phenomenon has been observed among high school and college students: not only do 12th-graders reason more abstractly about everyday issues with which they are already familiar (Overton, Ward, Noveck, Black, & O'Brien, 1987), but physics, English, and social science majors are all more likely to perform at the formal level on problems that fall within their own academic domains or areas of expertise (De Lisi & Staudt, 1980). In sum, we must be careful not to underestimate the cognitive capabilities of adolescents and adults who fail Piaget's formal-operational tests, for their less than optimal *performances* may simply reflect either a lack of interest or a lack of experience with the test problems rather than an inability to reason at the formal level.

Are there higher stages of intellectual development? According to Piaget, formal-operational thinking is the structural equivalent of adult intelligence—the most mature form of reasoning of which human beings are capable. Not everyone agrees. Patricia Arlin (1975, 1977) has called formal operations a *problem solving* stage that describes how bright adolescents and adults think about problems that someone else presents to them. However, she believes that truly creative and insightful thinkers—people like Aristotle, Einstein, and Piaget himself—operate on a higher plane that enables them to rethink or reorganize existing knowledge and then to *ask* important questions or define totally new problems. Arlin refers to this higher intellectual ability as a **problem-finding stage.**

Several other kinds of reasoning have been proposed as examples of postformal thought. Michael Basseches (1984) cites **dialectical reasoning**—the ability to resolve logical inconsistencies or paradoxes— as one such skill. Michael Commons and his associates (Commons, Richards, & Armon, 1984) cite **systematic reasoning** as another. Should your professor ask you to compare and contrast the premises of several developmental theories (each of which is an abstract "system") for purposes of constructing a single, compre-

hensive theory (or higher-order "supersystem"), he or she is asking you to try your hand at systematic reasoning.

It turns out that college faculty members and graduate students are much more proficient at both dialectical and systematic reasoning than undergraduate students are (Basseches, 1984; Commons, Richards, & Kuhn, 1982). Do these findings indicate that there are stages of intellectual development beyond formal operations? Basseches and Commons believe they do, although other interpretations are possible. For example, a Piagetian could argue that the inability of some formal-operational undergraduates to resolve paradoxes or to construct abstract "systems" and "supersystems" simply represents a form of horizontal decalage comparable to that of a concrete operator who conserves liquids and mass but not volume. In other words, the cognitive abilities that Arlin, Basseches, and Commons have described may represent very complex formal-operational schemata rather than higher stages of intellect that are qualitatively different from formal reasoning. At this point, it is not clear whether the Piagetian perspective or the "higher stage" perspective is correct. But regardless of how this debate is eventually resolved, a task for future research will be to determine why some people are able to pose new questions, resolve paradoxes, or think at the "systematic" level while the vast majority of adults may never reach these intellectual plateaus.

An Evaluation of Piaget's Theory

Jean Piaget had a profound impact on the study of cognitive development in particular and child development in general. Perhaps the most important and far-reaching of his many insights was the realization that developing children are naturally curious beings who will *actively* explore the environment and *construct* explanations for phenomena that they don't understand. This perspective on human nature was a dramatic departure from the then-traditional view of children as passive recipients of environmental influence who must be taught the ways of the world and trained to think for themselves.

After nearly 60 years of collaborating with his young informants, Piaget died in 1980 and left us with the most detailed and integrated theory of cognitive development that currently exists. Like all good theories, this one has generated an enormous amount of research. And as often happens when theories are repeatedly scrutinized, some of this research points to problems and shortcomings in Piaget's approach. Among the more common criticisms of Piaget's theory are the issue of timing, the failure to distinguish competence and performance, the issue of whether there really are any broad stages of intellectual growth, and the question of whether Piaget really "explains" cognitive development.

The Issue of Timing

The most frequent complaint about Piaget's theory is that children do not always display various intellectual skills or enter a particular stage of development when Piaget says they should. Recall that Piaget was overly pessimistic about the cognitive abilities of preschool children and much too optimistic about the rate at which adolescents acquire formal operations and the extent to which adults use them. Do these oversights present a serious challenge to Piaget's theory?

Piagetians certainly don't think so. They note that Piaget's primary goal was to identify the normal *sequencing* of intellectual abilities and that his age norms are rough approximations at best. As it turns out, later research has generally confirmed Piaget's sequential hypotheses; that is, the general sequencing of intellectual abilities that Piaget observed in his Swiss samples also describes the course and content of intellectual growth for children from the hundreds of countries, cultures, and subcultures that have now been studied (Cowan, 1978; Flavell, 1985). Although cultural factors do influence the rate of cognitive growth, the direction of development is always from sensorimotor intellect to preoperational thinking to concrete operations to (in many cases) formal operations.

The Competence/Performance Issue

Piaget was concerned with identifying the underlying *competencies,* or cognitive structures, that presumably determined how children perform on various cognitive tasks. Indeed, he tended to assume that an individual who failed one of his problems simply lacked the underlying concepts, or thought structures, necessary for its solution.

Many researchers now believe that this latter assumption is invalid, because any number of factors other than a lack of the critical competencies might affect a child's *performance* on Piaget's tests. We've seen, for example, that 4- and 5-year-olds who seem to *know* the differences between animates and inanimates or between random phenomena and those with explicit causes were repeatedly failing Piaget's tests. Why? Because Piaget required them to explain principles that they understood but could not yet articulate. Their failures often stemmed from linguistic or communication deficiencies rather than a lack of the necessary thought structures. In a similar vein, information-processing theorists now believe that young children fail many concrete-operational tasks, not because they lack an ability to "operate" on their objects of thought (as Piaget assumed), but because they are not yet able to gather and hold all the task-relevant information in memory. Late in his career, Piaget (1972) saw the need to distinguish competence from performance when he noted that adolescents with formal-operational capabilities may apply that logic only to problems that interest them, thus arguing that motivation exerts an important influence on intellectual performance. But his earlier tendency to equate performance with competence (and to ignore other factors that might influence children's responses) is the major reason that his age norms for various cognitive milestones were often so far off target.

Does Cognitive Development Occur in Stages?

Piaget maintained that his stages of intellectual development are *holistic structures*—that is, coherent modes of thinking that are applied across a broad range of tasks. To say that a child is concrete-operational, for example, would imply that he relies on cognitive operations and thinks logically about the vast majority of intellectual problems that he encounters.

Other researchers have begun to challenge Piaget's "holistic structure" assumption and are even questioning the idea that cognitive development occurs in stages (Brainerd, 1978; Flavell, 1985). From their perspective, a "stage" of intellect implies that abrupt changes in intellectual functioning occur as the child acquires several new skills and abilities over a very brief period. Yet, our review of the literature suggests that cognitive growth doesn't happen that way: major transitions in intellect occur quite gradually, and there is often very

---

problem-finding stage: according to Arlin, a stage beyond formal operations in which the individual is now capable of using knowledge to ask questions and define new problems.

dialectical reasoning: the ability to resolve logical inconsistencies or paradoxes; thought by some to be a stage of reasoning beyond formal operations.

systematic reasoning: the ability to operate on abstract systems to construct higher-order structures (or supersystems).

little consistency in the child's performance on tasks that presumably measure the abilities that define a "stage." For example, we've seen that it may be months or even years before a 6-year-old who can seriate or conserve number will pass other concrete-operational tests such as class inclusion or conservation of volume.

Piaget's reply is to attribute inconsistencies in intellectual performance to horizontal decalage. Presumably children who can conserve liquid and mass but not volume are at a *stage* (concrete operations) where operational schemata are the dominant mental structures. Their problem is that they have not yet organized their operational structures in a way that would enable them to solve the very difficult "conservation of volume" problem.

Perhaps you can anticipate the critics' response. They would quickly note that different children acquire concrete-operational skills in different sequences—a finding that undermines Piaget's explanation of horizontal decalage as a simple "within stage" progression from basic skills (or structures) to more complex ones. Today, many cognitive theorists have taken the position that intellectual development is a complex, multifaceted process in which children are gradually acquiring skills in many different content areas— areas such as deductive reasoning, hypothesis testing, mathematical operations, verbal skills, and moral reasoning (Fischer, 1980; Flavell, 1985). Although development within each of these domains may be sequential, or even stagelike, there is no assumption of consistency across domains. Thus, a 10-year-old who enjoys solving word puzzles and playing verbal games might outperform most age mates on tests of verbal reasoning but function at a much lower level in less familiar domains, such as hypothesis testing or mathematical reasoning.

In sum, the contemporary view is that cognitive development is gradual and sequential (and some would say stagelike) *within particular intellectual domains*. However, there is very little evidence for consistency of development across domains or for broad, holistic cognitive stages of the kind that Piaget described.

Does Piaget Explain Intellectual Development?

Perhaps the major shortcoming of Piaget's theory is that it does not clearly indicate how children move from one stage of intellect to the next (Sternberg, 1984). After considering the issue, Piaget (1970b) concluded that the maturation of the brain and the nervous system helps the curious, active child to construct increasingly complex understandings of objects and events. Presumably, children are (1) constantly assimilating new experiences in ways permitted by their levels of maturation and their existing cognitive structures, (2) accommodating their thinking to these experiences, and (3) reorganizing their structures into increasingly complex mental schemata that enable them to reestablish cognitive equilibrium with novel aspects of the environment. As children continue to mature, to assimilate more complex information, and to construct and reorganize their schemata, they will eventually come to view familiar objects and events in new ways and begin the gradual transition from one stage of intellect to the next.

Clearly, this rather vague explanation of cognitive growth raises more questions than it answers. For example, we might wonder what maturational changes are necessary before children can progress from sensorimotor to preoperational functioning or from concrete operations to formal operations. What kinds of experiences must a child have before he will construct mental symbols, understand cognitive operations, or begin to operate on ideas and think about hypotheticals? Piaget is simply not very explicit about these or any other mechanisms that might enable a child to move to a higher stage of intellect. As a result, a growing number of researchers now look on his theory as an elaborate *description* of cognitive development that has little if any explanatory value (Gelman & Baillargeon, 1983).

When we critique a theory as broad as Piaget's, it is easy to lose sight of the fact that researchers have been testing and confirming many of Piaget's hypotheses for more than 60 years. Although we now recognize that this theory has some very real shortcomings and may eventually be discarded in favor of a better alternative, Piaget surely qualifies as one of the fathers of cognitive psychology and as a leading figure in the history of the behavioral sciences. Indeed, it is almost inconceivable that our knowledge of intellectual development could have progressed to its present level had Piaget pursued his early interests in zoology and never worked with developing children.

Present and Future Directions

Today researchers are branching out in several directions as they try to gain a better understanding of cognitive growth and its relation to other aspects of development. Many investigators continue to study Piagetian phenomena as they try to fill in the gaps in this influential theory. Others have looked for maturational correlates of intellectual growth and are beginning to ask some interesting questions. For example, is there any connection between the end of the brain growth spurt at age 2 and the appearance of symbolic schemata? Is it merely a coincidence that children begin to acquire and use cognitive operations at age 6 or 7—about the time that higher brain centers are rapidly myelinating and neural impulses are traveling much faster than they were during the preschool period? Do the changes in hormonal balance that occur as the body prepares for puberty have anything to do with the onset of formal-operational abilities at about the same age? Although no one can yet answer these important questions, investigators are now pursuing these early leads and continuing to search for other meaningful links between neurological maturation and intellectual growth (Epstein, 1980; Fischer, 1987).

Perhaps the best-known alternative to Piaget's theory is the *information processing* approach, a "new look" at cognitive development that arose from the work of information theorists and experimental psychologists in Canada and in the United States. Proponents of information-processing theory view cognition as an extremely complex activity involving a number of related processes. As a result, they approach the topic of intellectual development by studying the growth of specific cognitive-processing skills such as attending, perceiving, thinking, learning, and remembering.

Before we take a closer look at the information-processing approach, a caution is in order. Since much of what we know about children's ability to process and use information is itself recent information, the cognitive-processing approach lacks the elegant coherence that we saw in Piaget's work. In the following section, we will try to tie up a few of the loose ends as we discuss some of the interesting findings that are emerging from this new look at children's intellectual growth.

The Information-Processing Approach

In the mid-1950s, information theorists such as Allen Newell and Herbert Simon began to compare the human mind with that wondrous new invention called the "electric brain" (Carey, Foltz, & Allan, 1983). Simon and his colleagues noted that both the mind and the electronic computer are devices that have a finite capacity for storing, retrieving, and analyzing information.

Moreover, each of these information-processing systems consists of *hardware* and *software*. Computer hardware is the physical parameters of the machine—its keyboard (or input) system, memory, and logic units. The software consists of the plans, or programmed instructions, that tell the machine how to organize, retrieve, and operate on the information it receives. The mind's physical machinery, or "hardware," consists of the brain, nervous system, and sensory receptors. For "software" the mind relies on rules, plans, motives, and intentions—mental "programs" that affect the ways information is registered, interpreted, stored, retrieved, and analyzed.

This mind/computer analogy, then, was the framework that information theorists used while seeking to explain how children of different ages process information about objects and events to "construct" knowledge and solve problems. Over the years, computers have become increasingly sophisticated: not only do modern machines have a far greater storage (or memory) capacity than their predecessors, but they can also perform more operations more efficiently because of improvements in computer software. Information-processing theorists suggest that the same may be true of the developing mind: as the brain and nervous system mature (hardware improvements) and children adopt new strategies for attending to stimuli, interpreting them, and remembering what they have experienced (software improvements), they should become much more proficient at acting on information to solve important problems (Klahr & Wallace, 1976).

In the pages that follow, we will first consider a working model of the human information-processing system that was proposed more than 20 years ago and is still popular today. We will then trace the development of three cognitive-processing skills that are thought to have a profound influence on the course and character of children's intellectual development: (1) the ability to gather task-relevant information (attention), (2) the ability to retain and retrieve this input (memory), and (3) the strategies or rules that children use when operating on or evaluating information they have gathered and retained (hypothesis testing and problem solving).

A Model of Human Information Processing

What is happening as a person notices information and retains it for future use? Seeking to answer this question, Richard Atkinson and Richard Shiffrin (1968) assumed that humans process information in much the same way that computers do, and they formulated a model to describe the process. A slightly modified and updated version of this important and influential model appears in Figure 9-4.

As we see in the figure, incoming information is thought to flow through a number of separate but interrelated processing units. The first of these components is the **sensory store** (or sensory register). This is the system's log-in unit; it simply holds raw sensory input for a very brief period (perhaps less than a second) as a kind of "afterimage" (or echo) of what has been sensed. The contents of our sensory stores are thus extremely volatile and will soon disappear without further processing. Should we attend to this information, however, it will pass into **short-term memory (STM),** a processing unit that can store a limited amount of information (perhaps four to seven pieces) for several seconds. Hence, the capacity of short-term memory is sufficient to allow you to retain a telephone number for perhaps as long as it takes you to dial it. But unless this information is rehearsed or otherwise operated on, it too will soon be lost. Short-term memory is sometimes called *working memory* because all conscious intellectual activity is thought to take place here. So short-term, or "working," memory has two functions: (1) to store information temporarily so that (2) we can do something with it.

Finally, new information that is operated on while in short-term memory will pass into **long-term memory (LTM)**—a vast and relatively permanent storehouse of information that includes our knowledge of the world, our impressions of past experiences and events, and the strategies that we use to process information and solve problems.

An example will illustrate how the system is thought to work. Suppose that you are taking notes in your history class and you hear your instructor mention that the U.S. Constitution was ratified in 1787. Since this date is one you may need to remember, you attend to it. Consequently, the information flows from your sensory register into short-term memory, where it remains long enough for you to record it in your notebook. As you later study your notes in preparation for an upcoming exam, you will probably review this information several times and eventually register it in long-term memory, where it remains until you need it while taking your test.

Now suppose your professor asks you how many years passed between the signing of the Declaration of Independence (1776, remember?) and the ratification of the Constitution. How does the information-processing system approach this simple problem? The first step, of course, is to "log in" what the professor

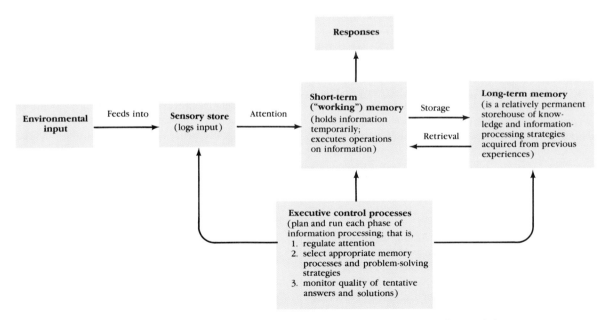

Figure 9-4. A schematic model of human information processing. *(Adapted from Atkinson & Shiffrin, 1968.)*

said through the sensory register and to attend to this input, thereby ensuring that the relevant information will flow into short-term memory. After correctly interpreting the problem, you must now search long-term memory for the two dates in question and also locate your stored knowledge of the mathematical operation of subtraction. Having found this information, you must now transfer it to short-term, or "working," memory so that you can "execute" your subtraction problem (1787 minus 1776) to derive the correct answer.

Notice that to successfully process information and use it to solve problems, you have to know what you are doing and make the right decisions. Had you not known to log the significance of the year 1787 in your notebook, this information would have soon been lost under the barrage of names and dates that followed in your history lecture. Had you lacked any knowledge of subtraction or failed to retrieve this "program" from long-term memory, you would have been unable to determine the number of years that passed between the signing of the Declaration of Independence and the ratification of the Constitution. Thus, information does not simply "flow" on its own through the various stores, or processing units, of the system; instead, we actively channel this input and make it flow. This is why the model includes **executive control processes**—the processes involved in planning and monitoring what we attend to and what we do with our knowledge.

The executive processes by which we gather, store, retrieve, and operate on information are thought to be under voluntary control and are, in fact, what most clearly distinguish human information processors from computers. When solving a problem, a computer does a whole lot less than we humans do. After all, the task-relevant information has already been logged into the machine, which solves problems that are assigned to it using strategies that are called up by a human "executive" (the programmer). All that the machine does is the necessary computations. By contrast, we humans must initiate, organize, and monitor our own cognitive processes. We decide what to attend to; we select our own strategies for retaining and retrieving this input; we call up our own "programs" for solving problems; and last but not least, we are often free to choose the very problems that we will attempt to solve.

One important implication of this information-processing model is that many factors other than a lack of the necessary logic (or cognitive structures) might account for a person's failure to solve a problem. For example, the person might not be paying attention to the most relevant information. He might not be able to hold all the relevant information in short-term memory so that he can operate on it. He might lack certain strategies that would enable him to transfer new information to long-term memory or would aid in retrieving knowledge already stored there. Of course, he may not have acquired and retained the critical rules or operations needed to solve the problem. And finally, he may lack the executive control processes that would enable him to coordinate all the necessary phases of problem solving to arrive at a logical conclusion. Clearly, this cognitive-processing analysis of the errors people make is much more elaborate than that of Piaget, who generally assumed that the reason people fail at tasks is that they lack the "cognitive structures" to solve them.

For the remainder of this chapter, we will trace the development of important cognitive-processing skills, such as attention, memory, and problem solving, and will see how the work of information-processing theorists has produced many new insights about children's intellectual development.

Attentional Processes: Getting Information into the System

Obviously a person must first detect information and attend to it before this input can be retained or used to solve problems. Since the nervous system is developing rapidly in the first few years of life, it seems reasonable to assume that the sensory register might become more efficient at gathering and holding sensory input for further analysis. However, recent research suggests that preschool children can hold just as much information in their sensory stores as older children and adults do (House, 1982) and, if anything, they retain this information slightly longer (Cowan, Suomi, & Morse,

---

sensory store: the first step in information processing, in which stimuli are noticed and are briefly available for further processing.

short-term memory (STM): the second step in information processing, in which stimuli are stored temporarily, examined, and operated on (also called working memory).

long-term memory (LTM): the third step in information processing, in which information that has been examined and interpreted is stored for future use.

executive control processes: the processes involved in regulating attention and in determining what to do with information just gathered or retrieved from long-term memory.

1982). So it is unlikely that the intellectual shortcomings that young children display are attributable to an immature or inefficient sensory register.

The growth of attention

On several occasions we have noted that toddlers and preschool children have short attention spans. When asked to work on a repetitive task, 2- to 4-year-olds will often persist for no more than a few minutes, and they are easily distracted. Even when doing things they like, such as watching television, 2- and 3-year-olds will frequently get up and wander around the room to talk to people or play with toys (Anderson, Lorch, Field, Collins, & Nathan, 1986). So very young children may fail to solve many problems because they are unable (or unwilling) to sustain their attention long enough to gather the necessary information.

Planning an appropriate attentional strategy. By about age 5, children are becoming much more persistent in their attempts to solve problems. However, their strategies for gathering information are typically unsystematic and reveal a lack of planfulness. In one study, Alice Vlietstra (1982) had 5-, 8-, and 11-year-olds examine a mock-up of a house. She then asked the children to search six similar houses until they (1) found *one* difference between the sample house and the comparison houses or (2) found *all* differences between the sample and the comparison houses. The 5-year-olds in this experiment clearly failed to follow the instructions, choosing instead to explore the stimuli in a haphazard way. The 8-year-olds searched the stimulus displays much more systematically than the 5-year-olds did, but they failed to limit their attention to "one difference" when asked to find a single difference between the sample and the comparison houses. Only the 11-year-olds were very planful; they followed the two sets of instructions equally well by confining their visual search to the information that was necessary to perform each task. In sum, the tendency of younger children to seek out and *explore* interesting new stimuli may interfere with the planful gathering of information that would help them to solve problems or perform well on tasks they are asked to undertake.

Ignoring information that is clearly irrelevant. Would young children perform as well as older children if they were told in advance which information was relevant to the task at hand? Apparently not. Patricia Miller and Michael Weiss (1981) told 7-,

10-, and 13-year-olds to remember the locations of a number of animals, each of which was hidden behind a different cloth flap. When each flap was lifted to reveal an animal, the children could also see a household object positioned either above or below the animal. Here, then, is a learning task that requires the child to attend selectively to certain information (the animals) while ignoring other potentially distracting input (the household objects). When the children were tested to see whether they had learned where each animal was located, the 13-year-olds outperformed the 10-year-olds, who, in turn, performed slightly better than the 7-year-olds. Miller and Weiss then tested to see whether children had attended to the incidental (irrelevant) information by asking them to recall which household object had been paired with each animal. They found exactly the opposite pattern on this incidental-learning test: 13-year-olds recalled *less* about the household objects than either 7- or 10-year-olds. In fact, both of the younger groups recalled as much about the irrelevant objects as about the locations of the animals. Taken together, these findings indicate that older children are much better than younger ones at concentrating on relevant information and filtering out extraneous input that may interfere with task performance.

What do children know about attention?

Do young children know more about attentional processes than their behavior would indicate? It seems that they do. Miller and Weiss (1982) asked 5-, 7-, and 10-year-olds to answer a series of questions about factors known to affect performance on an incidental-learning task (that is, a task like the "animals and objects" test in which children are told to remember only one category of objects when other, distracting stimuli are present). Although knowledge about attentional processes generally increased with age, even the 5-year-olds realized that one should at least *look first* at task-relevant stimuli and then *label* these objects as an aid to remembering them. The 7- and 10-year-olds further understood that one must *attend selectively* to task-relevant stimuli and *ignore* irrelevant information in order to do well on the problem that one was asked to undertake.

Why, then, do younger children not follow their own advice when actually working at an incidental-learning (or a similar) task? A recent study by Miller and her associates (Miller, Haynes, DeMarie-Dreblow, & Woody-Ramsey, 1986) provides some clues. It seems that

Photo 9-4. Although the ability to concentrate improves dramatically during middle childhood, grade school students are not always successful at overcoming distractions.

any strategy a 6-year-old knows about and hopes to apply is soon overwhelmed by a desire to explore those fascinating incidental stimuli that compete for his attention. By contrast, 8-year-olds are at a transitional phase: they sometimes translated what they knew into appropriate attentional strategies but were unpracticed in applying these techniques and tended to abandon them when their sporadic use did not lead to better task performance. However, the 10-year-olds in this study had apparently learned that appropriate attentional strategies do pay off, for they used them more often than 8-year-olds did and consistently outperformed their younger counterparts on tasks that required selective attention.

In sum, the development of attention is apparently a lengthy process in which a child first learns to translate what she knows into appropriate attentional strategies and then gradually comes to rely on these techniques as she encounters more and more situations that require their use to achieve important objectives.

Training children to attend

Can younger children be trained to attend more selectively to the relevant features of their environment? Apparently so. Alice Vlietstra (1982) reports that 7-year-olds become much more planful when searching for task-relevant information if they are shown how to search and then reinforced (with a marble) for following this strategy. In another recent experiment, Pamela Cole and Nora Newcomb (1983) have shown that 7-year-olds can learn to focus their attention on a central task and to shut out distracting verbal stimuli by either instructing themselves not to listen or imagining that they have shut a door between themselves and the verbal distractor.

The successful attempts to teach preschool children to conserve can also be viewed as methods of fostering selective attention. Recall that children who undergo identity training are taught to recognize that the object or substance that is transformed in a conservation task remains the same object or substance, regardless of its new appearance. In other words, they are encouraged to attend to certain task-relevant information (identities) and to ignore all potentially distracting input (altered shapes, heights, widths, and so forth) that could prevent them from conserving (Field, 1981). Since even 4-year-olds have learned to conserve simple quantities after being trained in this way, it is clear that attentional processes play a major role in determining what young children may know and understand.

Memory Processes: Retaining and Retrieving What One Has Experienced

Once children have attended to information of some kind, they must find a way to remember it if they are to learn from their experiences or use this input to solve a problem. **Memory** is a term that cognitive psychologists use to describe the processes by which people retain information and then retrieve it for use at a later time.

Investigators who study memory are careful to distinguish between recognition and recall. **Recognition memory** occurs when we encounter some in-

---

memory: the processes by which people retain information and later retrieve it for use.
recognition memory: realizing that an object or event that one experiences has been experienced before.

formation and realize that we have seen or experienced it before. **Recall memory** requires us to *retrieve* for comparative purposes a piece of information that is not currently being presented. As it turns out, recognition tasks are much easier than recall tasks. More people could correctly answer the question "Is Mick Jagger the lead singer for the Rolling Stones?" (recognition test) than the related item "Who is the lead singer for the Rolling Stones?" (recall test).

The ability to recognize the familiar is apparently inborn, for neonates who habituate to the repeated administration of a stimulus are indicating that they recognize this object or event as something they have experienced before. Moreover, the ability to *recall* interesting experiences is also apparent early in life: by 2 to 3 months of age, babies who have been taught to kick an overhead mobile will spontaneously recall this act for several days after the original training and will even remember and perform the response 18 days later if subtly "reminded" of their previous learning by seeing the mobile move (Davis & Rovee-Collier, 1983; Rovee-Collier, 1984). Both recognition memory and recall memory improve considerably over the first three years of life. For example, we learned in Chapter 7 that 5–12-month-old infants will often recognize something as familiar (that is, habituate) after only one or two brief exposures and are likely to retain this "knowledge" for weeks (Fagan, 1984). By age 2, infants will often recall interesting events that occurred several months ago (Nelson, 1984) and are quite proficient at deliberately remembering to do things that they consider important, such as reminding mother to buy them some candy as she is about to depart on a shopping trip (Somerville, Wellman, & Cultice, 1983). And by age 3, some children can even remember some experiences that they had nearly two years ago (Myers, Clifton, & Clarkson, 1987).

Despite the impressive memorial capabilities that 2–3-year-olds display, the most dramatic improvements in recall memory occur between 3 and 12 years of age. One clear sign of the memory limitations of preschool children is that their recognition memory is way ahead of their recall memory. If a 4-year-old had two minutes to study the 12 items in Figure 9-5, she would later *recognize* nearly all of them if asked to select these objects from a larger set of pictures (Brown, 1975). But if asked to *recall* the objects, she might remember only two to four of them, a far cry from the seven to nine items that an 8-year-old would recall.

Why do you suppose young children recall so little of the information that they recognize as familiar?

Figure 9-5. Imagine that you have 120 seconds in which to learn the 12 objects pictured here for an upcoming recall test. Chances are you could recall 10 or 11 of these objects when tested several minutes later, whereas an 8-year-old would recall 7–9 of them and a 4-year-old only 2–4 . What tricks or strategies might you use to make your task easier? Why do you think 4-year-olds perform so poorly on this task?

And why does recall memory improve so dramatically between infancy and early adolescence? Information-processing theorists have proposed four possible answers for these questions:

Basic capacities. One possibility is that older children and adolescents have better "computers" than young children do. They may have more "work space" for manipulating information and/or be able to do it faster.

Memory strategies. Perhaps older children and adolescents surpass young children on recall tests because they have acquired and consistently use effective strategies for getting information into long-term memory and retrieving it when they need it.

Knowledge about memory. Another hypothesis is that older children and adolescents have better recall because they know a great deal about memory. They know how long they must study to learn things thoroughly; which kinds of memory tasks take more effort; which strategies best fit each task; and so on.

Knowledge about the world. A final hypothesis attributes these developmental changes in memory to the fact that older children and adolescents know more about the world in general than young children do. Their knowledge makes many learning materials familiar, and familiar material is easier to learn and remember than unfamiliar material. They are "experts" rather than "novices."

In the pages that follow, we will evaluate the merits of each of these hypotheses.

Do basic capacities change?   *increase with age*

Do older children remember more than younger children do because they have a better "computer"—an information-processing system that has a larger capacity or is more efficient? Those who have explored this hypothesis have ruled out the idea that the capacity of long-term memory changes much over time. Basically, both young children and older ones have more long-term storage than they can possibly use, and there is no consistent evidence for an enlarging of this capacity after the first month of life (Perlmutter, 1986). A more promising idea is that the capacity of *short-term* (working) *memory* might increase with age, so that older children and adults can keep more information in mind and perform mental operations more rapidly than a younger child can.

This latter notion has been featured in the work of Juan Pascual-Leone (1984) and Robbie Case (1984, 1985), two neo-Piagetians who have tried to integrate Piaget's theory and the information-processing approach in a way that preserves the best features of both perspectives. The most traditional method of estimating the capacity of short-term memory is to assess one's **memory span.** This is done by measuring the number of items (for example, numbers) that a person can recall accurately, in order, immediately after hearing them. Studies consistently indicate that memory span increases throughout childhood: 5-year-olds can hold four or five numbers in mind, whereas 9-year-olds can recall six numbers, and adults recall an average of seven or eight (Dempster, 1981). Since short-term memory is also the site where mental operations are performed, Case prefers measures such as his **counting span** task that require subjects to operate on the information they are trying to remember. In Case's procedure, subjects are given a series of cards with different numbers of dots on them. They must count the dots on each card and remember the sum as the next card is counted, then the next, and so on. Like memory span, counting span increases with age: 5-year-olds remember an average of less than two "card sums," whereas 9-year-olds recall

about three, and 12-year-olds can keep nearly four of them in mind (Case, 1985).

What develops: Physical capacity or operating efficiency? Why do memory spans and counting spans increase with age? One possibility is that the *physical capacity* of short-term memory increases, perhaps because of maturational changes such as increased myelinization of the nervous system, which continues until adolescence. Another possibility (which may also be due, in part, to neurological development) is that children may become more proficient at recognizing the items in a memory-span task or at performing mental operations on them. If less time or effort is needed to identify and operate on the stimuli in a memory-span task, then more of one's available mental capacity can be used to store these items (Case, 1985).

At this point there is no solid evidence that the physical capacity of short-term memory increases much over childhood (Dempster, 1985). Indeed, this "capacity hypothesis" cannot explain why young children (who presumably have small storage capacities) are able to remember much more about lists of children's items than adults do (Lindberg, 1980). Robbie Case's "operating efficiency" hypothesis fares much better: children who are quick to identify and to operate on items in a memory task have longer memory spans than those who are slow to recognize or to operate on these stimuli (Case, 1985; Dempster, 1981; Howard & Polich, 1985). It seems that many information-processing skills that take a great deal of time and effort early in life become *automatized*—that is, they are accomplished with little effort—later in life. Thus, you may quickly (and almost effortlessly) arrive at an answer of 225 for the problem $9 \times 25 = \underline{\quad}$, whereas a 10-year-old might have to laboriously perform each step of the operation (that is, $9 \times 5 = 45$; leave the 5, carry the 4; $9 \times 2 = 18 + 4 = 22$; 22 and 5 = 225) and probably could not do this problem in his head. Increases in operating efficiency may be due in part to maturational changes that are occurring in the central nervous system (Case, 1985).

---

recall memory: recollecting objects, events, and experiences when examples of these bits of information are not available for comparative purposes.
memory span: a measure of the amount of information that can be held in short-term memory.
counting span: a measure of memory span that requires individuals to operate on the information they have in short-term memory.

Or it may be that older children are more familiar with numbers, numerical operations, and the like, so that they require less of their total memory capacity for performing mental activities than younger children (Flavell, 1985). Although the exact causes are unclear, there is general agreement that older children are in many ways faster and more automatic information processors than younger children (Kail, 1986; Whitney, 1986). Here, then, is one reason that memory improves over childhood.

Implications for intellectual performance. Piaget did not emphasize memory or memory development in his theory. He felt that improvements in memory stemmed from the growth of operational schemata and logical reasoning. Neo-Piagetians such as Robbie Case (1984, 1985) and Charles Brainerd (1983) argue just the opposite: improvements in logical reasoning are largely attributable to the development of memory. In fact, Case believes that increases in short-term storage that result from the automatization of information processing are what underlies the growth of logical reasoning.

Consider a 5-year-old who is struggling with a transitivity task. To answer correctly, the child must first detect and remember the critical properties of three stimuli, A, B, and C, as well as the A-to-B relation and the B-to-C relation. Clearly, this is a lot of information to keep in mind for a 5-year-old who encodes information and performs mental operations very slowly. Should the child hold all this information in short-term storage, he may not have any space left over to make the appropriate transitive inference (that is, A > or < C). Yet, if we reduce the memory demands of this problem (or, indeed, other logical puzzles such as conservation problems) by training the child what to look for and think about, he may well answer correctly (Gelman & Baillargeon, 1983). This is not to imply that increases in short-term storage guarantee logical thinking: Case is a neo-Piagetian who agrees with Piaget that children must actively construct logical schemata from their own experiences with objects and events. The point that Case is making is simply that without sufficient short-term storage to gather, hold, and then operate on all the necessary information, young children will be unable to construct logical schemes or to think rationally about many everyday events and experiences.

Development of memory strategies

In order to remember something for more than a few seconds, you must transfer this information from short-term to long-term memory. Of course, information stored in long-term memory is of little use if you are unable to retrieve it when you need it. Could some of the memory deficits that young children display stem from a failure to use planful strategies that could help them to store new information and later retrieve this input? Let's explore this idea by looking at the ways children of different ages approach the task of remembering.

Rehearsal. One very simple strategy that we adults use to retain new information is to repeat it over and over until we think we will remember it. These **rehearsal** activities really do work: stuck without paper and pencil, you are much more likely to remember someone's directions to a point across town if you repeat, or rehearse, these instructions several times.

Do young children rehearse things that they are trying to remember? Seeking to answer this question, John Flavell and his associates (see Flavell, 1985) have conducted experiments in which 5- to 10-year-olds were told to remember the order in which an experimenter pointed to a series of pictures. The results were clear: children who rehearsed (as indicated by their lip movements) performed much better than nonrehearsers on this recall task. In addition, spontaneous use of verbal rehearsal increased with age. Whereas only 10% of the 5-year-olds named the objects that they were to recall, more than half of the 7-year-olds and 85% of the 10-year-olds adopted this rehearsal strategy. In a second study, Flavell and his colleagues trained "nonrehearsers" to rehearse and found that their performance on recall tasks soon matched that of children who spontaneously rehearsed. So younger children are unlikely to produce the verbal mediators that will improve memory—that is, they show a **production deficiency** (Flavell, 1985). However, they can certainly use these mediators to their advantage if they are taught how to produce them, so there is no **mediation deficiency.**

The child's earliest attempts at spontaneous rehearsal are rather clumsy and inefficient compared with the strategies of older children. If asked to recall a list of words presented one at a time, 8-year-olds rehearse each word in just that way—one at a time. By contrast, 12-year-olds are more likely to rehearse word clusters, repeating the earlier items over and over again as they rehearse each successive word (Kunzinger, 1985; Ornstein, Naus, & Liberty, 1975). Apparently this latter form of rehearsal is a much more effective strategy, for the children who use it perform better on recall tests than those who rehearse each item singly, as it is presented.

Why do younger children not rehearse more efficiently? A study by Peter Ornstein and his associates (Ornstein, Medlin, Stone, & Naus, 1985) provides one clue. Ornstein tried to teach 7-year-olds to use the "clustering" rehearsal strategy and found that the children did so only if earlier items on the list were displayed visually so that they did not have to be retrieved from memory. By contrast, 12-year-olds relied on the clustering strategy regardless of whether earlier items were visually displayed. The implication, then, is that one's use of the most effective rehearsal techniques may depend on one's mastery of other basic competencies such as the ability to retrieve relevant materials from memory.

Categories

Semantic organization. In one sense, rehearsal is a rather unimaginative memory device because it is simply a form of mimicry or imitation. If a rehearser merely repeats the names of items to be remembered, he or she may fail to notice certain meaningful relations among the stimuli that should make them easier to recall. Consider the following example:

List 1: boat, match, hammer, coat, grass, sentence, pencil, dog, cup, picture

List 2: knife, shirt, car, fork, boat, pants, sock, truck, spoon, plate

Although these ten-item lists should be equally difficult to recall if one simply rehearses them, the second list is actually much easier for many people. The reason is that its items can be grouped into three semantically distinct categories (eating utensils, clothes, and vehicles) that can serve as cues for storage and retrieval. By contrast, **semantic organization** is harder for items in the first list (and thus they are harder to remember) because they represent ten different categories (Flavell & Wellman, 1977).

Until about age 9 or 10, children are not much better at recalling items that can be categorized (such as list 2) than those that are difficult to categorize (such as list 1). This finding suggests that young children make few attempts to organize information that they are trying to remember. And even when they begin to categorize as an aid to recall, the organizational schemes of grade school children are generally less useful than those of adults. For example, Liberty and Ornstein (1973) report that fewer than 60% of their fourth-grade sample placed words such as *flower, seed, tree* into a single category

when asked to organize 28 words that they were supposed to remember. As a result, these children recalled fewer items than young adults who had grouped the 28 words into four distinct clusters.

How do children learn to organize items in ways that could help them to remember? Perhaps this knowledge grows from experiences they have had categorizing highly related objects and events at school or watching as the teacher presents materials in a highly organized fashion. Recently, Deborah Best and Peter Ornstein (1986) found that 9-year-olds who were instructed to sort "easily categorizable" items in any way they wished were more likely to organize their materials into semantically distinct clusters than the control subjects, who were told to sort less categorizable items that could be organized, but with some difficulty. And there is more: Compared with the control subjects, those who had sorted the "easily categorizable" items were later (1) more inclined to organize subsequent lists that were difficult to categorize, (2) performing better on recall tests of these materials, and (3) more likely to preach the virtues of organizational strategies when asked to teach first-graders how to remember.

Best and Ornstein point out that classroom instructors rarely "teach" pupils to organize materials as an aid to remembering them. Instead, this important memory process seems to evolve very gradually over the grade school years as children gain more and more experience categorizing highly related items and eventually discover the benefits of organization for themselves.

Elaboration. Another effective strategy for improving recall is to add to, or elaborate on, the information that we hope to remember. **Elaboration** is particularly useful whenever our task is to associate two

---

rehearsal: a strategy for remembering that involves repeating the items one is trying to retain.

production deficiency: a failure to generate the mediators that would improve learning and memory.

mediation deficiency: an inability to use the mediators that would improve learning and memory.

semantic organization: a strategy for remembering that involves grouping or classifying stimuli into meaningful (or manageable) clusters that are easier to retain.

elaboration: a strategy for remembering that involves adding something to (or creating meaningful links between) the bits of information one is trying to retain.

or more stimuli, such as a foreign word and its English equivalent. For example, one way to remember the Spanish word for "duck," *pato* (pronounced "pot-o"), is to elaborate on the word *pato* by creating an image of a pot that is in some way linked to a duck (see Figure 9-6 for an example).

In a review of the literature, Michael Pressley (1982) found that the spontaneous use of elaborative techniques is a "latecomer to the memorizer's bag of tricks" that is rarely seen before adolescence. Moreover, a sizable percentage of adolescents do not elaborate as a strategy for improving their recall, and these "non-elaborators" typically perform at lower levels on tests of associative learning than their counterparts who use elaborative techniques.

Why is elaboration so late in developing? One popular explanation is that the very limited capacity of a younger child's short-term, or working, memory may prevent her from generating complex elaborative mediators (Pressley, 1982).[3] However, others believe that adolescents are more proficient at elaboration because they simply know more about the world than younger children do and are better able to imagine how any two (or more) stimuli might be linked. And as we will see in Box 9-3, there is now some rather dramatic evidence that a person's "knowledge base" does indeed affect his or her performance on memory tasks.

Retrieval processes. We have talked about rehearsal, organization, and elaboration as if they were only methods of *storing* information in long-term memory. Yet, these same control processes can also help us to search for and *retrieve* information from long-term storage—a fact that younger children may fail to understand. Consider the following examples.

Michael Pressley and Joel Levin (1980) prompted 6- and 11-year-olds to *elaborate* on 18 pairs of stimuli that they were trying to learn. When later taking a recall test, half the children from each age group were told to use their elaborative images to help them remember the items; the remaining children were not given any retrieval instructions. Pressley and Levin found

Figure 9-6. An example of an elaborative image that one might create to associate *pato* (pronounced "pot-o"), the Spanish word for "duck," with its English translation.

that 11-year-olds recalled nearly 65% of the items, regardless of whether they had been told to use their elaborative images to help them remember. By contrast, the 6-year-olds recalled nearly twice as many items when given retrieval instructions (42.5%) as when left to their own devices (23%). Strange as it may seem, it apparently did not occur to the latter group of 6-year-olds to use the images they had worked so hard to create as part of their retrieval strategy. In a similar study, Daniel Kee and Terace Bell (1981) found that 7-year-olds who had categorized materials they were trying to remember later failed to take full advantage of these categories as aids for recall *unless they were explicitly reminded to.* So the message that emerges from these studies is an important one: even when younger children do "organize" or "elaborate" in order to register information in long-term memory, they may still perform worse than older children on recall tests because they fail to rely on these same strategies to *retrieve* what they have worked so intently to store.

But why? One gets the feeling that younger children simply know less about memory aids and the circumstances when it is appropriate to use them. In recent years, investigators have begun to study what children know about memory and how this knowledge may influence their performance on memory tests. Let's consider what they have learned.

[3]One problem with this "capacity hypothesis" is that 5-year-olds, who have very limited "working" memories, not only can be trained to generate elaborative images but will use them to improve their performance on other problems similar to the training task (Ryan, Ledger, & Weed, 1987). So it is doubtful that young children's failures to spontaneously produce elaborative mediators stem entirely from limitations in short-term memory.

Box 9-3

Does General Knowledge Affect What We Remember?

To this point, we've seen that older children may outperform younger ones on memory-span and recall tests because (1) they can hold more information in short-term memory and (2) their strategies for encoding and retrieving information are more effective than those of younger children. Yet, there is another possibility that we should not overlook: older children have a much broader *knowledge base* than younger children and may perform better on many memory tasks because they are more familiar with the information to be retained.

Michelene Chi (1978) conducted a now-classic experiment that demonstrates just how important one's knowledge base can be to remembering. The subjects in Chi's study were six 10-year-olds, all of whom were expert chess players, and six adults, each of whom knew the game of chess but was not an expert. These subjects took part in two memory tasks. In the *digit recall* task, subjects were given a ten-second exposure to ten numbers and asked to recall as many as they could. In the *chess recall* task, they spent ten seconds looking at an arrangement of 20 chess pieces on a chessboard and were then asked to recall the location of these pieces. Notice that if one's knowledge base affects recall memory, the 10-year-old "experts" who know a lot about chess might be expected to recall more on the chess test than the "nonexpert" adults do.

The results of Chi's experiment appear in the figure. As we might expect from earlier memory-span research, adults recalled significantly more numbers than 10-year-olds did. However, just the opposite was true for the chess recall task, on which the 10-year-old "experts" performed much, much better than the adult nonexperts. In a similar study, Mark Lindberg (1980) obtained similar results: third-graders recalled more than college students about items that third-graders know more about (for example, cartoon characters and children's games), whereas college students remembered more than third-graders about items that are generally more familiar to young adults (for example, types of music and natural earth formations).

Consider the implications of these findings. On most tasks, younger children are the "novices" and older ones are the "experts." So if knowledge base affects memory performance, older children may generally outperform younger ones on recall tests, not because they have a greater memory capacity, but because they simply *know more* about the items that they must remember.

Why do we remember more about familiar information? Chi's hypothesis is that familiar input may simply be *easier to encode;* our knowledge of the material may suggest ways that the items can be grouped, stored, and then retrieved from memory. So one reason that older children may begin to generate and use more effective memory strategies is that their ever-expanding knowledge base makes it easier for them to see how the

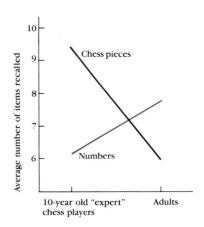

Knowledge base affects memory. Children who are chess "experts" recall more about locations of chess pieces than "novice" adults do. However, adults recall more about numbers than children do, a finding Chi (1978) attributes to adults' greater familiarity with (or knowledge of) numbers.

information they must remember can be organized or elaborated (see Lindberg, 1980).

In sum, the child's knowledge base may be a crucial variable in the development of memory (Chi, 1985). It appears that the more one knows, the more one *can* know (and remember).

[handwritten margin note: *knowing how to know*]

Development of metamemory

Metacognition is a term cognitive psychologists use to refer to what we know of the human mind and its capabilities, including our awareness of our own mental strengths and liabilities and the ways in which we monitor and control our cognitive processes. Your own store of metacognitive knowledge might include an understanding that you are better at math than at word problems; that you must selectively attend to the most relevant information if you hope to solve difficult

[handwritten margin note: *knowing about memory*]

problems; or that it is wise to double-check a proposed solution to a problem before concluding that it is correct.

One important aspect of metacognition is **metamemory**—one's knowledge of memory and memory processes. Children are displaying metamemory if

---

metacognition: one's knowledge about cognition and about the regulation of cognitive activities.

metamemory: one's knowledge about memory and memory processes.

they recognize, for example, that there are limits to what they can remember; that some things are easier to remember than others; or that certain strategies are more effective than others at helping them to remember (Flavell, 1985).

When do children first show any evidence of metamemory? Earlier, perhaps, than you might suspect. If instructed to remember where a stuffed animal (Big Bird) has been hidden so that they can later wake him up from his nap, even 2–3-year-olds will go stand near the spot where the object was placed or at least will look repeatedly at or point to that location—activities that they do not display as often if the toy is visible and they do not need to remember where it is (DeLoache, Cassidy, & Brown, 1985). So by about age 2, children have learned one simple bit of knowledge about memory: if you hope to remember something, you have to work at it!

To measure metamemory in preschool and school-age children, investigators often describe one or more memory problems and ask subjects how much information they think they will remember (anticipated performance) or which of two memory tasks will be more difficult and why (knowledge of memory processes and of the variables that affect memory). Suppose, for example, that we showed children the two sets of pictures in Figure 9-7 and asked them which girl in each set will have an easier time remembering her material. The answers should help us to determine whether children know that memory depends on the number of items to be recalled (set 1) and the ease with which these materials can be categorized (set 2).

Knowledge about memory increases rather dramatically between the ages of 4 and 11. Although a 4-year-old may know that very short lists are easier to remember than long ones and that it will take more effort to remember the longer list (Wellman, Collins, & Glieberman, 1981), children younger than age 7 usually overestimate how well they will perform on memory tasks while underestimating the amount of study that is necessary to learn the materials (Kreutzer, Leonard, & Flavell, 1975; Yussen & Levy, 1975). Not until about age 7 do children recognize that related items or those that can be organized into categories are easier to recall than unrelated items (Kreutzer et al., 1975). And although 7–9-year-olds know that rehearsing and categorizing information are more effective memory strategies than simply looking at the items or labeling them once, not until age 11 do they seem to recognize that organization is more effective than rehearsal (Justice, 1985).

Figure 9-7. Two simple metamemory questions. The child is shown the pictures in each set and asked which girl will have an easier time remembering her items. These two questions are designed to measure the child's knowledge that ease of recall depends on the amount of information one is trying to recall (set 1; girl on the left should have an easier time recalling fewer items) and how easy the information is to organize (set 2; girl on the right should have an easier time because her items can be grouped into fewer distinct categories).

Finally, it appears that younger children know very little about how they *retrieve* information from long-term memory. David Bjorklund and Barbara Zeman (1982) found that 7- and 9-year-olds had no preexisting strategies for recalling the names of children in their classroom, although they performed reasonably well at this task (75% recall). But nearly 60% of a sample of 11-year-olds professed to have a retrieval strategy, and they clearly outperformed the younger children on this exercise (88% recall). One reason that younger children may know little about retrieval is that they tend to rely on external prompts such as written notes to help them remember. But even though 7-year-olds may recognize that a written note can help them to remember something, they are less likely than 9- or 11-year-olds to know where to place such "reminders" to ensure that they will have the intended effect (Fabricius & Wellman, 1983).

What is the relation between memory and metamemory? Does a person's knowledge of the memory process determine how well he or she will perform on various memory tests? The answer is not as straightforward as we might hope. In their review of the literature, John Cavanaugh and Marion Perlmutter (1982) found several studies reporting low to moderate positive correlations between memory and metamemory. However, there are several reasons for believing that one's level of metamemory may *not* always predict one's performance on memory tests. For example, Bjorklund and Zeman's 7- to 9-year-olds were able to recall the names of more than 75% of their classmates, even though they knew very little about the strategies that might help them to retrieve this information. Apparently, *good metamemory is not required for good recall*. In addition, children who know that categorized lists are easier to remember may themselves fail to categorize items when studying for a recall test (Salatas & Flavell, 1976). So *good metamemory does not guarantee good recall*.

One reason good metamemory may not always predict good recall is that children who know more about different memory processes may not always know which strategy to choose or why one strategy is more effective than another. For example, a 7-year-old who recognizes the merits of organization may fail to categorize the material he is trying to learn if he knows that rehearsal is also an effective strategy—and one that is easier to apply. Consequently, this "knowledgeable" youngster may perform no better on a recall test than a less knowledgeable 5-year-old who knows the advantages of rehearsal but nothing about organization. Some evidence for this line of reasoning comes from attempts

to train children to use effective memory aids and other metacognitive strategies. Briefly, these studies show that merely teaching strategies is not enough; to be effective, the training must also inform the child *why* the strategy is better than others she might use and when it will be advantageous to use it. Indeed, children who receive this "informed training" when learning ways to extract and retain more information from their reading materials are soon relying on the strategies they have learned and will usually show distinct improvements in reading comprehension (a measure of retention) and other academic skills (Brown, Bransford, Ferrara, & Campione, 1983; Paris & Oka, 1986).

Summing up

After surveying the literature, we can draw four very general conclusions about the development of memory: (1) older children process information faster (or more automatically) than younger children do, thus leaving them *more space in working memory for operating on new information,* (2) older children use *more effective memory strategies* for transferring information to long-term memory and retrieving this input, (3) older children know more in general than younger children do, and their *larger knowledge base* improves their ability to learn and remember, and (4) older children know more about memory in particular, and this *greater metamemory* may enable them to select the most appropriate memory strategies or to otherwise control the flow of information between short-term and long-term memory. Of course, these four aspects of development probably interact with one another rather than evolving independently. For example, automatization of information processing may leave the child with sufficient space in working memory to use effective memory aids, such as organization or elaboration, that were just too draining earlier in childhood. Or a child's expanding knowledge base may permit faster information processing and suggest ways that information can be categorized and elaborated. The point to be made is that there is no one "best" explanation for the growth of memorial skills. All the developments that we have discussed seem to contribute in important ways to the dramatic improvements in recall memory that occur over the course of childhood.

Problem Solving: Making Use of the Information One Has Retained

Like Piaget, cognitive-processing theorists believe that children of different ages will show qualitatively different levels of performance when trying to solve various problems. However, they argue that Piaget was often vague in his description of children's levels or "stages" of problem solving, largely because his clinical method was simply too subjective and imprecise to ever provide a complete account of the growth of problem-solving skills.

Robert Siegler's (1978, 1981, 1983) **rule assessment** approach nicely illustrates how information-processing theorists study the development of logical reasoning and problem-solving skills. Siegler's most basic assumption is straightforward: when children are faced with a puzzling new experience or a problem to solve, they will first gather information and then formulate a *rule* to account for what they have witnessed. Presumably, the kind of rule that the child generates and applies to the task at hand will depend largely on the type of information that he has encoded (that is, noticed and interpreted). According to Siegler, an investigator who hopes to understand the development of problem-solving skills must first identify the rules that children use to solve problems and then determine *how* and *why* these rules change over time.

Among the tasks that Siegler uses in his rule-assessment approach is a set of balance-scale problems similar to those used by Inhelder and Piaget (1958) to assess formal-operational reasoning. The balance-scale apparatus (Figure 9-8) has four equally spaced pegs on each of its arms. Once weights are placed on various pegs, the child is asked to predict what will happen (for example, will the arms remain balanced? will the left arm go up? down?) when a brake that holds the arms motionless is released. Clearly, two aspects of this problem are important: the number of weights on each arm and the distance of those weights from the fulcrum. Siegler proposes that children might adopt any of four rules for solving balance problems and that the rule they use will depend on the type of information that they encode. The four rules are as follows:

Rule 1: The child considers only the *number of weights* and concludes that the arm with more weight will drop. If the number of weights on each arm is the same, the child concludes that the scale will remain balanced.

Rule 2: The child pays more attention to weight and consistently predicts that the arm with more weight will drop. Only when the weight on each arm is equal will the child consider the distance of the weights from the fulcrum.

Rule 3: The child always considers both weight and distance when making a prediction. But if one side has more weight while the other has its weights farther from the fulcrum, the child is conflicted and simply guesses at what will happen.

Rule 4: The child always considers both weight and distance and seems to understand that the torque on each arm is a function of weight × distance. For example, if there are three weights on the second peg to the left and two weights on the fourth peg to the right, then left torque = $3 \times 2 = 6$; right torque = $2 \times 4 = 8$; therefore, the right arm will go down.

To measure a child's strategy for solving balance problems, Siegler presents the child with the six problems in Table 9-2 and notes the patterning of responses across all six tasks. If a child consistently uses one of Siegler's four rules, then his or her answers should conform to one of the four patterns shown in the columns of the table. For example, children who make use of the "rule 1" strategy (encode only weight) will solve problems 1, 2, and 4 but will erroneously conclude that the scale will balance in problem 3 and that the right arm will drop on problems 5 and 6. By contrast, a user of rule 3 will correctly solve problems 1, 2, and 3 and respond at chance levels (guess) on problems 4, 5, and 6.

When Siegler (1981) administered his six balance-scale problems to subjects between ages 3 and 20, he found that 91% of the 4- to 20-year-olds responded as if they were using one of his four rules. Moreover, there were age differences in the use of various rules. Whereas almost no 3-year-olds used a rule, more than 80% of the 4- to 5-year-olds were encoding weight and relying on rule 1 to solve balance problems. By age 8, children were generally using rule 2 or 3, and the vast majority of 12-year-olds had settled on rule 3 as a problem-solving strategy. And although most 20-year-olds continued to use rule 3 to solve balance-scale problems,

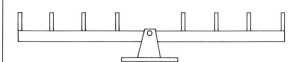

Figure 9-8. The balance-scale apparatus used by Siegler to study the development of children's problem-solving abilities.

Table 9-2. Six balance-scale problems and the patterning of answers that follows from using each of Siegler's four rules for solving such problems

Problem	Correct answer	Siegler's rule			
		1	2	3	4
1.	Balance	100% correct	100% correct	100% correct	100% correct
2.	Left down	100% correct	100% correct	100% correct	100% correct
3.	Left down	0% correct (will say balance)	100% correct	100% correct	100% correct
4.	Left down	100% correct	100% correct	33% correct (chance responding)	100% correct
5.	Left down	0% correct (will say right down)	0% correct (will say right down)	33% correct (chance responding)	100% correct
6.	Balance	0% correct (will say right down)	0% correct (will say right down)	33% correct (chance responding)	100% correct

Source: Adapted from Siegler (1981).

30% of these adults had discovered the weight × distance principle and were relying on rule 4.

At first glance, this study seems remarkably similar to Piaget's work on age differences in problem solving. However, the critical difference is that Siegler's rule-assessment approach allows the investigator to specify exactly how children are processing (or failing to process) relevant information and thus to indicate *why* they fail to solve a particular problem or set of related problems. Consider the following example.

Siegler (1976) followed up on a group of 5- and 8-year-olds, all of whom were using rule 1 (consider only number of weights) to solve balance-scale problems. If we were to infer their "stage" of reasoning from the answers they gave (as Piaget tended to do), then we would have to conclude that these children all had comparable "cognitive structures" for these problems. Yet, when Siegler provided these youngsters with experiences that showed them that the use of rule 1 was inadequate, the 8-year-olds often abandoned this rule, moving to rule 2 (or rule 3), whereas the 5-year-olds did not. But why?

Siegler hypothesized that the 8-year-olds were encoding more information than the 5-year-olds were. Presumably, the 8-year-olds were attending to both "weight" and "distance" information but relying only on weight to solve balance-scale problems. And when the "weight only" rule proved inadequate, they then began to consider the distance information that they had encoded, shifting from rule 1 to rule 2 or 3. By contrast, 5-year-olds may have encoded only the number of weights on each arm of the apparatus and completely ignored distance information. If so, they would then have no other information to consider when their weight-only rule proved inadequate, and they would be constrained to continue using this rule, or no rule.

Siegler then confirmed his hypothesis with a simple memory test: when asked to recall the number and location of the weights that they had just seen on a balance scale, the 5-year-olds remembered only the number of weights on each arm, whereas the 8-year-olds recalled both "weight" and "distance" information. Can these 5-year-olds ever be taught to use rule 2 or rule 3 when solving balance-scale problems? Yes, indeed, but only if they are first trained to encode distance information (as the 8-year-olds already do) so that they will consider this input when their experiences illus-

rule assessment: a method of assessing a child's level of cognitive functioning (or problem solving) by noting the information that he encodes and the principle, or rule, he uses to operate on this information and draw conclusions.

trate that the weight-only rule is a faulty one (Siegler, 1976). Note the implication here: the ability of 5-year-olds to learn a new rule depends not just on their current rule (or "cognitive structure" for problem solving) but on their ability to encode the relevant information as well.

Imagine how effective educators might be if they could accurately diagnose their pupils' information-processing strategies to determine exactly what each child is noticing (or failing to notice) about a problem and exactly what rule or strategy each child is using! It turns out that this rule-assessment approach has proved quite fruitful at specifying why individual children are failing to solve various arithmetic problems and at helping them to overcome their mistakes (Mayer, 1985). And in Box 9-4, we will consider several other important educational implications that stem from the work of information-processing theorists.

In sum, cognitive-processing theorists can agree with Piaget that children progress through a series of "alternative understandings" before mastering various concepts (Siegler, 1981). However, they believe that their rule-assessment approach is more precise than Piaget's theory at indicating why a child's thinking takes the form it does and at specifying the information that the child must now consider in order to move from one level of understanding to the next.

Current Status of the Information-Processing Approach

If a history of psychology were written today, Piaget's theory would surely warrant considerable space in the chapter on cognitive development. At this point, it can still be argued that Piagetian theory is the single most orderly and elaborate account of intellectual development that currently exists. Indeed, those who favor Piaget's viewpoint have questioned what they see as the "fragmented" approach of information-processing theorists, who focus intently on specific cognitive processes and view cognitive development as the simple acquisition of skills (or strategies for problem solving) in many different domains. How, they ask, can this "focus on specificity" ever provide us with a broad view of the changes that occur in children's constructions of reality—changes that take place over long periods of time?

Information-processing theorists would reply by noting that it was the many, many problems with Piaget's broad-brush account of cognitive development that stimulated their work in the first place. Although many cognitive-processing theorists are neo-Piagetians who readily acknowledge the prodigious contributions that Piaget has made, they are quite correct in their assessment that children's thinking is not nearly so homogeneous across problems, or domains, as Piaget's theory would imply. Moreover, they would challenge the assertion that their study of intellectual development is disorderly or chaotic—and with some degree of justification, for attention, memory, and problem solving all develop through predictable sequences and are becoming increasingly planful and systematic from infancy through adolescence. And even though much relevant research remains to be conducted, these important developments in information processing are helping to provide richer and more detailed explanations for the appearance and refinement of abilities such as seriation, classification, perspective taking, conservation, and hypothetical-deductive reasoning (Case, 1985; Flavell, 1985; Rosser, 1983).

In sum, the information-processing approach is itself a developing theory—one that might be described as a necessary complement to, rather than a replacement for, Piaget's earlier framework. Surely, this "new look" at cognitive growth will continue to evolve and to fill in many of the gaps that remain in Piaget's model, thereby contributing to a comprehensive theory of intellectual development that retains the best features of both approaches.

Summary

In this chapter we considered two theories of intellectual development: Jean Piaget's "structural-functional" viewpoint and the more recent "information-processing" approach. Piaget's model is a very broad and elaborate theory of intellectual growth that evolved from his naturalistic observations and conversations (clinical interviews) with developing children. According to Piaget, intellectual activity is a basic life function that helps the child to adapt to the environment. He describes children as active, inventive explorers who construct knowledge (schemata) and modify these cognitive structures through the processes of organization and adaptation. Organization is the process by which children rearrange their existing knowledge into higher-order structures, or schemata. Adaptation consists of

Box 9-4
Some Educational Implications of
Information-Processing Research

Recall that Piaget offered educators several suggestions for helping their pupils to learn. First and foremost, he argued that teachers should view children as naturally inquisitive beings who learn best by constructing their *own* knowledge from *moderately novel* aspects of experience—that is, information that challenges their current understanding and forces them to reevaluate what they already know. Indeed, if the concepts one hopes to teach are too complex, children will be unable to assimilate or accommodate to this instruction, and no new learning will occur. Moreover, Piaget stressed that a teacher's job is not so much to transmit facts, to actively structure problems, or to reinforce correct answers as to provide the climate, setting, and materials that will allow curious children the *intrinsic* satisfaction of discovering important concepts for themselves.

Information-processing theorists can certainly agree with Piaget that children are active and curious explorers who learn best by constructing knowledge from experiences that are just beyond current levels of understanding. However, their own guidelines for effective instruction are much more explicit than Piaget's and imply that teachers should take a more *active, directive* role than Piaget had envisioned. The following six implications for instruction flow directly from the information-processing research that we have reviewed.

1. *Analyze the requirements of the problems and tasks that you present to your pupils.* Know what information must be encoded and what mental operations performed to arrive at a correct answer or to otherwise grasp the lesson to be learned. Without such knowledge, it may be difficult to tell why students are making errors or to help them overcome their mistakes.

2. *Reduce short-term memory demands to a bare minimum.* Problems that require young grade school children to encode more than three or four bits of information are apt to overload their capacity for short-term storage and prevent them from thinking logically about this input. The simplest possible version of a new problem or concept is what teachers should strive to present. If a problem involves several steps, students might be encouraged to break it down into parts (or subroutines) and perhaps to record the solutions to these parts in their notes in order to reduce demands on their short-term storage. Once children grasp a concept and their information processing becomes more "automatized," they will have the short-term storage capacity to succeed at more complex versions of these same ideas or problems (Case, 1985).

3. *Treat the child's incorrect answers as opportunities to promote new learning.* Devise ways of (1) determining whether the child is encoding *all* the task-relevant information and (2) assessing the "rule" that she is using to arrive at her incorrect solution. Failures to encode pertinent information must first be overcome before the child can profit from experiences which illustrate that the rule that she favors is inadequate (Siegler, 1976).

4. *Encourage children to "have fun" using their memories.* Challenging games such as Concentration not only are enjoyable to grade school children but will help them to appreciate the advantages of being able to retain information ("clues") and to retrieve it for a meaningful purpose (solving a puzzle).

5. *Provide opportunities to learn effective memory strategies.* A teacher can do this by grouping materials into distinct categories as she talks about them or by giving children easily categorizable sets of items to sort and classify (Best & Ornstein, 1986). Question-and-answer games of the form "Tell me how dogs, cats, and fish are alike" or "How do birds and bees differ from helicopters and missiles?" are challenging to young grade

school children and will make them aware of conceptual similarities and differences on which organizational strategies depend.

6. *Structure lessons so that children are likely to acquire metacognitive knowledge and to understand why they should plan, monitor, and control their cognitive activities.* Simply teaching appropriate information-processing skills does not guarantee that your pupils will use them. If these skills are to transfer to settings other than the training task, it is important that children understand why these strategies will help them to achieve their objectives. As an instructor, you can help by making your own metacognitive knowledge more explicit ("I'll have to read this page more than once to understand it"), by offering suggestions to the child ("You might find it easier to remember the months of the year if you group them according to seasons. Summer includes . . ."), or by asking questions that remind children of strategies already taught ("Why is it important to summarize what you've read?"; "Why do you need to double-check your answer?"). All these approaches have proved quite successful at furthering children's metacognitive skills and at persuading them to apply this knowledge to the intellectual challenges that they encounter (Brown, Bransford, Ferrara, & Campione, 1983; Paris & Oka, 1986).

two complementary activities: assimilation and accommodation. Assimilation is the process by which the child attempts to fit new experiences to existing schemata. Accommodation is the process of modifying existing schemata in response to new experiences. Presumably, cognitive growth results from the interplay of these intellectual functions: assimilations stimulate accommodations, which induce the reorganization of schemata, which allow further assimilations, and so on.

Piaget believes that intellectual growth proceeds through an invariant sequence of stages that can be summarized as follows:

• *Sensorimotor period (0–2 years)*. Over the first two years, infants come to know and understand objects and events by acting on them. The sensorimotor schemata that a child creates to adapt to his or her surroundings are eventually internalized to form mental symbols that enable the child to understand the permanence of objects, to imitate the actions of absent models, and to solve simple problems at a mental level without resorting to trial and error.

• *Preoperational period (roughly 2 to 7 years)*. Symbolic reasoning becomes increasingly apparent during the preoperational period as children begin to use words and images in inventive ways in their play activities. Although 2- to 7-year-olds are becoming more and more knowledgeable about the world around them, their thinking tends to be animistic, egocentric, and unidimensional. Consequently, they may fail to solve problems that require them to consider several pieces of information simultaneously or to assume another person's point of view.

• *Concrete operations (roughly 7 to 11 years)*. During the period of concrete operations, children can think logically and systematically about concrete objects, events, and experiences. They can now add and subtract in their heads, and they recognize that the effects of many physical actions are reversible. The acquisition of these and other cognitive operations permits the child to conserve, seriate, make transitive inferences, and construct mental representations of a complex series of actions.

• *Formal operations (age 11 to 12 and beyond)*. Formal-operational reasoning is rational, abstract, and much like the hypothetical-deductive reasoning of a scientist. However, not all adolescents and adults reason at this level. Formal-operational thinking may elude those who score below average on intelligence tests or who have not been exposed to the kinds of

educational experiences that promote the development of this highest form of intellect.

Although Piaget has adequately described the general sequencing of intellectual development, his tendency to infer underlying competencies from children's intellectual performances often led him to underestimate and occasionally to overestimate the child's cognitive capabilities. Some investigators have challenged Piaget's assumption that development occurs in stages, and others have criticized his theory for failing to specify how children progress from one "stage" of intellect to the next. Although the Piagetian approach remains the most comprehensive statement on intellectual growth that currently exists, contemporary researchers recognize its shortcomings and are trying to improve on this influential theory.

Information-processing theorists approach the topic of intellectual growth by charting the development of cognitive-processing skills such as attention, memory, and problem solving. Many analogies are drawn between human information processing and the functioning of computers. The human "system" is said to consist of a sensory register to detect, or "log in," input; short-term memory, where information is stored temporarily until we can operate on it; long-term memory, where input that we operate on will remain until we retrieve it to solve problems; and executive control processes by which we plan, monitor, and control all phases of information processing.

In order to understand something or to solve a problem, one must first pay attention to the right kinds of information. Between the preschool period and adolescence, children become better able to sustain attention for longer periods, more planful and systematic in their search for information, and more knowledgeable about the strategies they can use to attend selectively to task-relevant information and ignore sources of distraction.

Memory also improves over the course of childhood. Four explanations for these improvements that have received some support are (1) that older children process information faster (or more automatically) than younger children, thus leaving more space in short-term memory for storing task-relevant information, (2) that older children use more effective strategies (rehearsal, organization, and elaboration) for transferring information to long-term memory and retrieving this input, (3) that older children have larger knowledge bases than younger ones do, which improves their ability to learn and remember, and (4) that older children know more about memory processes (metamemory), which helps them to select appropriate memory strategies.

Like Piaget, information-processing theorists have sought to explain how developing children generate hypotheses and solve problems. As children mature, they encode more and more task-relevant information and formulate increasingly sophisticated problem-solving strategies, or rules, that are based largely on the information they are encoding. Cognitive-processing theorists can agree with Piaget that children progress through a series of "alternative understandings" before mastering certain concepts, but they argue that their rule-assessment approach is better able than Piaget's theory to specify why children of different ages approach problems in different ways.

References

ABRAVANEL, E., & Gingold, H. (1985). Learning via observation during the second year of life. *Developmental Psychology, 21,* 614–623.

ACREDOLO, C. (1982). Conservation/nonconservation: Alternative explanations. In C. J. Brainerd (Ed.), *Progress in cognitive development* (Vol. 1). New York: Springer-Verlag.

ACREDOLO, C., & Acredolo, L. P. (1979). Identity, compensation, and conservation. *Child Development, 50,* 524–535.

ACREDOLO, C., & Horobin, K. (1987). Development of relational reasoning and avoidance of premature closure. *Developmental Psychology, 23,* 13–21.

ANDERSON, D. R., Lorch, E. P., Field, D. E., Collins, P. A., & Nathan, J. G. (1986). Television viewing at home: Age trends in visual attention and time with T.V. *Child Development, 57,* 1024–1033.

ANOOSHIAN, L. J., Hartman, S. R., & Scharf, J. S. (1982). Determinants of young children's search strategies in a large-scale environment. *Developmental Psychology, 18,* 608–616.

ARLIN, P. K. (1975). Cognitive development in adulthood: A fifth stage? *Developmental Psychology, 11,* 602–606.

ARLIN, P. K. (1977). Piagetian operations in problem finding. *Developmental Psychology, 13,* 297–298.

ATKINSON, R. C., & Shiffrin, R. M. (1968). Human memory: A proposed system and its control processes. In K. W. Spence & J. T. Spence (Eds.), *The psychology of learning and motivation: Advances in research and theory* (Vol. 2). Orlando, FL: Academic Press.

BASSECHES, M. (1984). *Dialectical thinking and adult development.* Norwood, NJ: Ablex.

BEST, D. L., & Ornstein, P. A. (1986). Children's generation and communication of mnemonic organizational strategies. *Developmental Psychology, 22,* 845–853.

BJORKLUND, D. F., & Zeman, B. R. (1982). Children's organization and metamemory awareness in their recall of familiar information. *Child Development, 53,* 799–810.

BOWER, T. G. R. (1982). *Development in infancy.* New York: W. H. Freeman.

BRAINE, M. D. S., & Rumain, B. (1983). Logical reasoning. In P. H. Mussen (Ed.), *Handbook of child psychology.* Vol. 3: *Cognitive development.* New York: Wiley.

BRAINERD, C. J. (1978). The stage question in cognitive-developmental theory. *Behavioral and Brain Sciences, 2,* 173–213.

BRAINERD, C. J. (1983). Working-memory systems and cognitive development. In C. J. Brainerd (Ed.), *Recent advances in cognitive-developmental theory.* New York: Springer-Verlag.

BROWN, A. L. (1975). The development of memory: Knowing, knowing about knowing, and knowing how to know. In H. W. Reece (Ed.), *Advances in child development and behavior* (Vol. 10). Orlando, FL: Academic Press.

BROWN, A. L., Bransford, T. D., Ferrara, R. A., & Campione, J. C. (1983). Learning, remembering, and understanding. In P. H. Mussen (Ed.), *Handbook of child psychology.* Vol. 3: *Cognitive development.* New York: Wiley.

BULLOCK, M. (1985). Animism in childhood thinking: A new look at an old question. *Developmental Psychology, 21,* 217–225.

CAREY, J., Foltz, K., & Allan, R. A. (1983, February 7). The mind of the machine. *Newsweek,* pp. 44–45.

CASE, R. (1984). The process of stage transition: A neo-Piagetian view. In R. J. Sternberg (Ed.), *Mechanisms of cognitive development.* New York: W. H. Freeman.

CASE, R. (1985). *Intellectual development: Birth to adulthood.* Orlando, FL: Academic Press.

CAVANAUGH, J. C., & Perlmutter, M. (1982). Metamemory: A critical examination. *Child Development, 53,* 11–28.

CHI, M. H. T. (1978). Knowledge structures and memory development. In R. S. Siegler (Ed.), *Children's thinking: What develops?* Hillsdale, NJ: Erlbaum.

CHI, M. H. T. (1985). Changing conception of sources of memory development. *Human Development, 28,* 50–56.

COLE, P. M., & Newcomb, N. (1983). Interference effects of verbal and imaginal strategies for resisting distraction on children's verbal and visual recognition memory. *Child Development, 54,* 42–50.

COMMONS, M. L., Richards, F. A., & Armon, C. (Eds.) (1984). *Beyond formal operations: Late adolescent and adult cognitive development.* New York: Praeger.

COMMONS, M. L., Richards, F. A., & Kuhn, D. (1982). Systematic and metasystematic reasoning: A case for levels of reasoning beyond Piaget's stage of formal operations. *Child Development, 53,* 1058–1069.

CONNOLLY, J. A., & Doyle, A. (1984). Relation of social fantasy play to social competence in preschoolers. *Developmental Psychology, 20,* 797–806.

COWAN, N., Suomi, K., & Morse, P. A. (1982). Echoic storage in infant perception. *Child Development, 53,* 984–990.

COWAN, P. A. (1978). *Piaget: With feeling.* New York: Holt, Rinehart and Winston.

DANSKY, J. (1980). Make-believe: A mediator of the relationship between play and associative fluency. *Child Development, 51,* 576–579.

DASEN, P. R. (1977). *Piagetian psychology: Cross-cultural contributions.* New York: Gardner Press.

DASEN, P. R., & Heron, A. (1981). Cross-cultural tests of Piaget's theory. In H. C. Triandis & A. Heron (Eds.), *Handbook of cross-cultural psychology: Developmental psychology* (Vol. 4). Newton, MA: Allyn & Bacon.

DAVIS, J. M., & Rovee-Collier, C. K. (1983). Alleviated forgetting of a learned contingency in 8-week-old infants. *Developmental Psychology, 19,* 353–365.

De LISI, R., & Staudt, J. (1980). Individual differences in college students' performance on formal operations tasks. *Journal of Ap-*

plied Developmental Psychology, 1, 163–174.

DeLOACHE, J. S., Cassidy, D. J., & Brown, A. L. (1985). Precursors of mnemonic strategies in very young children's memory. *Child Development, 56,* 125–137.

DEMPSTER, F. N. (1981). Memory span: Sources of individual and developmental differences. *Psychological Bulletin, 89,* 63–100.

DEMPSTER, F. N. (1985). Short-term memory development in childhood and adolescence. In C. J. Brainerd & M. Pressley (Eds.), *Basic processes in memory development: Progress in cognitive development research.* New York: Springer-Verlag.

DUNST, C. J., Brooks, P. H., & Doxsey, P. A. (1982). Characteristics of hiding places and the transition to stage IV performance in object permanence tasks. *Developmental Psychology, 18,* 671–681.

ELKIND, D. (1977). Giant in the nursery—Jean Piaget. In E. M. Hetherington & R. D. Parke (Eds.), *Contemporary readings in child psychology.* New York: McGraw-Hill.

EPSTEIN, H. T. (1980). EEG developmental stages. *Developmental Psychology, 13,* 629–631.

FABRICIUS, W. V., & Wellman, H. M. (1983). Children's understanding of retrieval cue utilization. *Developmental Psychology, 19,* 15–21.

FAGAN, J. F. (1984). Infant memory: History, current trends, and relations to cognitive psychology. In M. Moscovitch (Ed.), *Infant memory: Its relation to normal and pathological memory in humans and other animals.* New York: Plenum.

FIELD, D. (1981). Can preschool children really learn to conserve? *Child Development, 52,* 326–334.

FIELD, T. M., Woodson, R., Greenberg, R., & Cohen, D. (1982). Discrimination and imitation of facial expressions by neonates. *Science, 218,* 179–181.

FISCHER, K. W. (1980). A theory of cognitive development: The control and construction of hierarchies of skills. *Psychological Review, 87,* 477–531.

FISCHER, K. W. (1987). Relations between brain and cognitive development. *Child Development, 58,* 623–632.

FLAVELL, J. H. (1963). *The developmental psychology of Jean Piaget.* New York: Van Nostrand Reinhold.

FLAVELL, J. H. (1985). *Cognitive development* (2nd ed.). Englewood Cliffs, NJ: Prentice-Hall.

FLAVELL, J. H., Everett, B. H., Croft, K., & Flavell, E. R. (1981). Young children's knowledge about visual perception: Further evi

dence for the level 1–level 2 distinction. *Developmental Psychology, 17,* 99–103.

FLAVELL, J. H., & Wellman, H. M. (1977). Metamemory. In R. V. Kail & J. W. Hagen (Eds.), *Memory in cognitive development.* Hillsdale, NJ: Erlbaum.

GELMAN, R. (1978). Cognitive development. *Annual review of psychology, 29,* 297–332.

GELMAN, R., & Baillargeon, R. (1983). A review of Piagetian concepts. In P. H. Mussen (Ed.), *Handbook of child psychology.* Vol. 3: *Cognitive development.* New York: Wiley.

HOUSE, B. J. (1982). Learning processes: Developmental trends. In J. Worell (Ed.), *Psychological development in the elementary years.* Orlando, FL: Academic Press.

HOWARD, L., & Polich, J. (1985). P300 latency and memory span development. *Developmental Psychology, 21,* 283–289.

HUTT, C., & Bhavnani, R. (1976). Predictions from play. In J. S. Bruner, A. Jolly, & K. Sylva (Eds.), *Play.* New York: Penguin Books.

INHELDER, B. (1966). Cognitive development and its contribution to the diagnosis of some phenomena of mental deficiency. *Merrill-Palmer Quarterly, 12,* 299–319.

INHELDER, B., & Piaget, J. (1958). *The growth of logical thinking from childhood to adolescence.* New York: Basic Books.

JACKSON, S. (1965). The growth of logical thinking in normal and subnormal children. *British Journal of Educational Psychology, 35,* 255–258.

JUSTICE, E. M. (1985). Categorization as a preferred memory strategy: Developmental changes during elementary school. *Developmental Psychology, 21,* 1105–1110.

KAIL, R. (1986). Sources of age differences in speed of processing. *Child Development, 57,* 969–987.

KAYE, K., & Marcus, J. (1981). Infant imitation: The sensorimotor agenda. *Developmental Psychology, 17,* 258–265.

KEE, D. W., & Bell, T. S. (1981). The development of organizational strategies in the storage and retrieval of categorical items in free-recall learning. *Child Development, 52,* 1163–1171.

KLAHR, D., & Wallace, J. C. (1976). *Cognitive development: An information-processing view.* Hillsdale, NJ: Erlbaum.

KREUTZER, M. A., Leonard, C., & Flavell, J. H. (1975). An interview study of children's knowledge about memory. *Monographs of the Society for Research in Child Development, 40* (1, Serial No. 159).

KUHN, D. (1984). Cognitive development. In M. H. Bornstein & M. E. Lamb (Eds.), *Developmental psychology: An advanced textbook.* Hillsdale, NJ: Erlbaum.

KUNZINGER, E. L., III. (1985). A short-term

longitudinal study of memorial development during early grade school. *Developmental Psychology, 21,* 642–646.

KUZMAK, S. D., & Gelman, R. (1986). Young children's understanding of random phenomena. *Child Development, 57,* 559–566.

LIBERTY, C., & Ornstein, P. A. (1973). Age differences in organization and recall: The effects of training in categorization. *Journal of Experimental Child Psychology, 15,* 169–186.

LINDBERG, M. A. (1980). Is knowledge base development a necessary and sufficient condition for memory development? *Journal of Experimental Child Psychology, 30,* 401–410.

LUCARIELLO, J. (1987). Spinning fantasy: Themes, structure, and the knowledge base. *Child Development, 58,* 434–442.

MAYER, R. E. (1985). Mathematical ability. In R. J. Sternberg (Ed.), *Human abilities: An information-processing approach.* New York: W. H. Freeman.

MELTZOFF, A. N. (1985). Immediate and deferred imitation in fourteen- and twenty-four-month old infants. *Child Development, 56,* 62–72.

MELTZOFF, A. N. (1988). Infant imitation and memory: Nine-month-olds in immediate and deferred tests. *Child Development, 59,* 217–225.

MELTZOFF, A. N., & Moore, M. K. (1983). Newborn infants imitate adult facial gestures. *Child Development, 54,* 702–709.

MILLER, P. H., Haynes, V. F., DeMarie-Dreblow, D., & Woody-Ramsey, J. (1986). Children's strategies for gathering information in three tasks. *Child Development, 57,* 1429–1439.

MILLER, P. H., & Weiss, M. G. (1981). Children's attention allocation, understanding of attention, and performance on the incidental learning task. *Child Development, 52,* 1183–1190.

MILLER, P. H., & Weiss, M. G. (1982). Children's and adults' knowledge about what variables affect selective attention. *Child Development, 53,* 543–549.

MOSSLER, D. G., Marvin, R. S., & Greenberg, M. T. (1976). Conceptual perspective taking in two- to six-year-old children. *Developmental Psychology, 12,* 85–86.

MYERS, N. A., Clifton, R. K., & Clarkson, M. G. (1987). When they were very young: Almost-threes remember two years ago. *Infant Behavior and Development, 10,* 123–132.

NEIMARK, E. D. (1979). Current status of formal operations research. *Human Development, 22,* 60–67.

NELSON, K. (1984). The transition from infant to child memory. In M. Moscovitch (Ed.),

Infant memory: Its relation to normal and pathological memory in humans and other animals. New York: Plenum.

ORNSTEIN, P. A., Medlin, R. G., Stone, B. P., & Naus, M. J. (1985). Retrieving for rehearsal: An analysis of active rehearsal in children's memory. *Developmental Psychology, 21,* 633–641.

ORNSTEIN, P. A., Naus, M. J., & Liberty, C. (1975). Rehearsal and organizational processes in children's memory. *Child Development, 46,* 818–830.

OVERTON, W. F., Ward, S. L., Noveck, I. A., Black, J., & O'Brien, D. P. (1987). Form and content in the development of deductive reasoning. *Developmental Psychology, 23,* 22–30.

PARIS, S. G., & Oka, E. R. (1986). Children's reading strategies, metacognition, and motivation. *Developmental Review, 6,* 25–56.

PASCUAL-LEONE, J. (1984). Attentional, dialectic, and mental effort: Toward an organismic theory of life stages. In M. L. Commons, F. A. Richards, & C. Armon (Eds.), *Beyond formal operations: Late adolescent and adult cognitive development.* New York: Praeger.

PERLMUTTER, M. (1986). A life-span view of memory. In P. B. Baltes, D. L. Featherman, & R. M. Lerner (Eds.), *Life-span development and behavior* (Vol. 7). Hillsdale, NJ: Erlbaum.

PIAGET, J. (1950). *The psychology of intelligence.* San Diego, CA: Harcourt Brace Jovanovich.

PIAGET, J. (1951). *Play, dreams, and imitation in childhood.* New York: Norton.

PIAGET, J. (1952). *The origins of intelligence in children.* New York: International Universities Press.

PIAGET, J. (1954). *The construction of reality in the child.* New York: Basic Books.

PIAGET, J. (1970a, May). A conversation with Jean Piaget. *Psychology Today,* pp. 25–32.

PIAGET, J. (1970b). Piaget's theory. In P. H. Mussen (Ed.), *Carmichael's manual of child psychology* (Vol. 1). New York: Wiley.

PIAGET, J. (1972). Intellectual evolution from adolescence to adulthood. *Human Development, 15,* 1–12.

PIAGET, J. (1977). The role of action in the development of thinking. In W. F. Overton & J. M. Gallagher (Eds.), *Knowledge and development* (Vol. 1). New York: Plenum.

PIAGET, J., & Inhelder, B. (1956). *The child's conception of space.* New York: Norton.

PIAGET, J., & Inhelder, B. (1969). *The psychology of the child.* New York: Basic Books.

PRESSLEY, M. (1982). Elaboration and memory development. *Child Development, 53,* 296–309.

PRESSLEY, M., & Levin, J. R. (1980). The development of mental imagery retrieval. *Child Development, 51,* 558–560.

ROSSER, R. A. (1983). The emergence of spatial perspective taking: An information-processing alternative to egocentrism. *Child Development, 54,* 660–668.

ROVEE-COLLIER, C. K. (1984). The ontogeny of learning and memory in human infancy. In R. Kail & N. E. Spear (Eds.), *Comparative perspectives on the development of memory.* Hillsdale, NJ: Erlbaum.

RUBIN, K. H., Fein, G., & Vandenberg, B. (1983). *Play.* In P. H. Mussen (Ed.), *Handbook of child psychology.* Vol. 4: *Social development.* New York: Wiley.

RYAN, E. B., Ledger, G. W., & Weed, K. A. (1987). Acquisition and transfer of an integrative imagery strategy by young children. *Child Development, 58,* 448–452.

SALATAS, H., & Flavell, J. H. (1976). Behavioral and metamnemonic indicators of strategic behaviors under remember instructions in first grade. *Child Development, 47,* 81–89.

SEDLAK, A. J., & Kurtz, S. T. (1981). A review of children's use of causal inference principles. *Child Development, 52,* 759–784.

SHAFFER, D. R. (1979). *Social and personality development.* Pacific Grove, CA: Brooks/Cole.

SIEGLER, R. S. (1976). Three aspects of cognitive development. *Cognitive Psychology, 8,* 481–520.

SIEGLER, R. S. (1978). The origin of scientific reasoning. In R. S. Siegler (Ed.), *Children's thinking: What develops.* Hillsdale, NJ: Erlbaum.

SIEGLER, R. S. (1981). Developmental sequences within and between concepts. *Monographs of the Society for Research in Child Development, 46* (Serial No. 189).

SIEGLER, R. S. (1983). Information-processing approaches to development. In P. H. Mussen (Ed.), *Handbook of child psychology.* Vol. 1: *History, theory, and methods.* New York: Wiley.

SIGEL, I. E., Roeper, A., & Hooper, F. H. (1968). A training procedure for the acquisition of Piaget's conservation of quantity: A pilot study and its replication. In I. E. Sigel & F. H. Hooper (Eds.), *Logical thinking in children: Research based on Piaget's theory.* New York: Holt, Rinehart and Winston.

SLADE, A. (1987). A longitudinal study of maternal involvement and symbolic play during the toddler period. *Child Development, 58,* 367–375.

SMITH, L. B. (1984). Young children's understanding of attributes and dimensions: A comparison of conceptual and linguistic measures. *Child Development, 55,* 363–380.

SOMERVILLE, S. C., Wellman, H. M., & Cultice, J. C. (1983). Young children's deliberate reminding. *Journal of Genetic Psychology, 143,* 87–96.

STERNBERG, R. J. (1984). *Mechanisms of cognitive development.* New York: W. H. Freeman.

SUGARMAN, S. (1981). The cognitive basis of classification in very young children: An analysis of object-ordering trends. *Child Development, 52,* 1172–1178.

TOMLINSON-KEASEY, C., Eisert, D. C., Kahle, L. R., Hardy-Brown, K., & Keasey, B. (1979). The structure of concrete-operational thought. *Child Development, 50,* 1153–1163.

TULKIN, S. R., & Konner, M. J. (1973). Alternative conceptions of intellectual functioning. *Human Development, 16,* 33–52.

VLIETSTRA, A. G. (1982). Children's responses to task instructions: Age changes and training effects. *Child Development, 53,* 534–542.

WELLMAN, H. M., Collins, J., & Glieberman, J. (1981). Understanding the combination of memory variables: Developing conceptions of memory limitations. *Child Development, 52,* 1313–1317.

WHITNEY, P. (1986). Developmental trends in speed of semantic memory retrieval. *Developmental Review, 6,* 57–79.

WISHART, J. G., & Bower, T. G. R. (1985). A longitudinal study of the development of the object concept. *British Journal of Developmental Psychology, 3,* 243–258.

YOUNGER, B. (1985). The segregation of items into categories by ten-month-old infants. *Child Development, 56,* 1574–1583.

YUSSEN, S. R., & Levy, V. M. (1975). Developmental changes in predicting one's own memory span of short-term memory. *Journal of Experimental Child Psychology, 19,* 502–508.

Intelligence: Measuring Mental Performance

What does it mean to say that someone is bright or intelligent? To Piaget, it suggests that the individual has acquired a number of cognitive structures that enable him or her to solve problems and adapt successfully to the demands of the environment. Piaget thought of intelligence as a particular type of logic that children use when answering questions and thinking about everyday issues. He believed that these logical structures change with age and that all children will go through exactly the same stages of reasoning as they progress toward intellectual maturity.

By contrast, the person on the street often thinks of intelligence as an indication of how smart someone is *compared with other people*. The implication is that intelligence is a "quantity" that reflects a person's ability to learn new material or to solve various problems. Recently a group of Cornell undergraduates were asked to list the characteristics of "intelligent people." They attributed a wide range of qualities to the intellectually exceptional person, including broad general knowledge, an ability to think logically, common sense, wit, creativity, openness to new experience, and sensitivity to one's own limitations (Neisser, 1980). Presumably these students would have mentioned roughly the opposite attributes had they been asked to list the characteristics of "dull," or unintelligent, persons.

Our focus in this chapter is on *individual differences* in intelligence. We will begin by introducing yet another perspective on intellectual development—the psychometric (testing) approach—that has led to the creation and widespread use of intelligence tests. We will then consider what a person's score on an intelligence test implies about his or her ability to learn, to perform in academic settings, and to succeed at a job. Our focus will then shift to the hereditary and environmental factors that are known to affect intellectual performance, and we will evaluate the merits of preschool educational programs, such as Project Head Start, designed to promote the intellectual development of children who perform poorly on intelligence tests. Finally, we will see how people's misconceptions about the meaning of intelligence tests have sometimes led them to use these instruments in ways that are inappropriate and possibly even abusive.

What Is Intelligence?

In 1921 the *Journal of Educational Psychology* asked 17 leading investigators to define intelligence in their own words. Fourteen of these scientists were bold enough to reply, but unfortunately, their answers were contradictory and provided very little insight into what it was they were measuring with their "intelligence" tests. Although few topics in psychology have generated as much research as intelligence and intelligence testing, even today there is little consensus about what intelligence is.

It is not that the experts are in total disagreement, however, for almost everyone concedes that intelligence reflects an ability to adapt, to think abstractly, and to solve problems effectively (Sternberg & Berg, 1986). So why is there no singular definition of intelligence that everyone can endorse? Because different theorists make very different assumptions about the origins, the structure, and the stability of attributes that they consider indications of "intelligent" behavior. Let's now consider some of the more influential viewpoints on the nature of intelligence, beginning with the psychometric approach.

The Psychometric View of Intelligence

The research tradition that spawned the development of standardized intelligence tests has come to be known as the **psychometric approach.** According to psychometric theorists, intelligence can be thought of as a trait or a set of traits that characterizes some people to a greater extent than others. Indeed, the psychometrician's major goals are to identify exactly what these traits are and to measure them so that intellectual differences among individuals can be detected and described.

It turns out that there is no one psychometric view of intelligence, but many. Here are four widely cited definitions that appeared prior to 1970:

1. "The ability to carry on abstract thinking" (Terman, 1921).
2. "The . . . capacity of an individual to act purposefully and think rationally and to deal effectively with the environment" (Wechsler, 1944).
3. "Innate general cognitive ability" (Burt, 1955).
4. "All of the knowledge a person has acquired" (Robinson & Robinson, 1965).

Now let's consider the assumptions that underlie these differing points of view.

Nature/nurture and the stability of intelligence

Notice that the four definitions (particularly numbers 3 and 4) clearly differ on whether intellectual prowess is an innate capacity or an acquired attribute. Before 1960, the prevailing view was that intelligence is a potential for thinking and problem solving that is *genetically determined* and thus fixed at conception. Although a child's environment was thought to have some influence over his or her level of intellectual performance, the assumption was that individual differences in intellectual *capacity* were reasonably stable and that most of the intellectual variation among members of a population is attributable to the genes that people inherited at conception.

Most contemporary theorists can agree that our genotypes contribute in important ways to our intellectual performance. However, psychometricians gradually came to question the idea that intelligence is a "fixed" potential or a genetically determined capacity for problem solving. Why? Because their longitudinal studies revealed that a person's performance on intelligence tests may vary, and vary dramatically, over the course of childhood. Even more intriguing were observations that one's intelligence quotient, or IQ, can be modified either upward or downward depending on the experiences one has. So even if heredity does set some upper limits on intellectual development, it appears that our cognitive performances can be extremely variable over time and that environmental factors play a crucial role in determining how well people perform on intelligence tests.

Is intelligence a single attribute or many attributes?

At first glance, all four of the definitions listed above seem to imply that intelligence is a *singular* attribute or ability that is likely to affect one's performance on virtually all cognitive tests. Yet many psychometric theorists were quick to challenge this point of view, noting that intelligence tests require people to perform a *variety* of tasks, such as defining concepts, recalling lists of words or numbers, reproducing geometric designs with blocks, extracting meaning from written passages, and solving arithmetic puzzles. Couldn't these "subtests" be measuring a number of *distinct* mental abilities rather than a singular cognitive ability? Maybe so. According to the *multifactorial viewpoint,* an individual might score high on tests of some cognitive abilities (for example, verbal comprehension) and actually test below average on other, presumably independent mental skills (such as spatial or arithmetic reasoning).

One way of determining whether intelligence is a single attribute or many different attributes is to ask a group of subjects to perform a large number of mental tasks and then analyze their performances using a statistical procedure called **factor analysis.** Simply stated, factor analysis is a correlational technique for finding groups of test items that are highly correlated with one another and yet unrelated to all the remaining items on the test. Clusters of related items are called *factors,* and each factor (if any are found) will presumably represent a unique mental ability. Suppose, for example, we found that examinees performed very similarly on two tests of verbal comprehension and on three tests of arithmetic reasoning but that their "comprehension" scores were only marginally related to their "arithmetic reasoning" scores. Under these circumstances, we might conclude that verbal comprehension and arithmetic

---

psychometric approach: a theoretical perspective that portrays intelligence as a trait (or series of traits) on which individuals differ; psychometric theorists are responsible for the development of standardized intelligence tests.

factor analysis: a statistical procedure for identifying clusters of tests or test items that are highly correlated with one another and unrelated to other tests or test items.

reasoning represent distinct intellectual factors. But if subjects' verbal comprehension scores were highly correlated with their arithmetic reasoning scores (and with their scores on all other kinds of mental problems), we might conclude that intelligence is a singular attribute rather than a number of distinct mental abilities.

Early factor-analytic studies of intelligence. Charles Spearman (1927) was among the first to apply the logic of factor analysis to the study of intelligence. Spearman looked at the correlations between children's scores on a variety of cognitive tests and their grades in different subjects at school. He found that these measures were moderately correlated and therefore inferred that there must be a *general mental ability,* which he called *g,* that affects one's performance on most (if not all) cognitive tasks. However, Spearman was intrigued by the finding that individuals were often inconsistent in their intellectual performance. For example, a student who excelled at most cognitive tasks might score very low on a particular measure, such as musical aptitude or verbal memory. He then proposed that intelligence consists of two factors: *g,* or general ability, and *s,* or special abilities, each of which is specific to a particular test. Thus, one's score on a test of arithmetic reasoning would depend not only on *g* but also on the specific numerical skills (*s*) that are involved in this kind of problem solving.

Spearman's two-factor theory of intelligence was only the beginning. Several years later, Louis Thurstone (1938; Thurstone & Thurstone, 1941) factor-analyzed a battery of cognitive tests taken by eighth-graders and college students. His analyses produced seven distinct factors that he called *primary mental abilities:* spatial ability, perceptual speed (quick processing of visual information), numerical reasoning, verbal meaning (defining words), word fluency (speed at recognizing words), memory, and inductive reasoning (forming a rule that describes a set of observations). Yet, when Thurstone constructed tests to measure each of these primary mental abilities, he found that subjects' scores on the seven scales were moderately correlated. For example, a person who scored high on spatial ability might also tend to do well on tests of perceptual speed, memory, and inductive reasoning. So even though the seven primary mental abilities that Thurstone identified do seem to require different cognitive operations, the fact that they are not totally independent suggests that they may tap a common intellectual dimension of some

sort—something similar to what Spearman had called *g,* or general mental ability.

One implication of Spearman's and Thurstone's work is that there must be a reasonably small number of basic mental abilities that make up what we call "intelligence." A very different point of view has been voiced by J. P. Guilford (1967), who proposes that there may be more than 100 distinct mental abilities. He arrived at this figure by first classifying cognitive tasks along three major dimensions: (1) *content* (what must the person think about), (2) *operations* (what kind of thinking is the person asked to perform), and (3) *products* (what kind of answer is required). Guilford argued that there are four kinds of intellectual contents, five kinds of mental operations, and six kinds of intellectual products (see Table 10-1). Thus, his **"structure of intellect" model** allows for as many as 120 primary mental abilities, based on all the possible combinations of the various intellectual contents, operations, and products (that is, $4 \times 5 \times 6 = 120$).

Table 10-1. Guilford's components of mental structure: Contents, operations, and products of intellect

Contents: What the person is thinking about
1. *Figural*—properties of stimuli that we can experience through the basic senses, such as color, loudness, shape, texture
2. *Symbolic*—numbers, letters, symbols, and designs
3. *Semantic*—ideas
4. *Behavioral*—actions and expressions of other people

Operations: Mental actions or processes the person performs
1. *Cognition*—recognizing or discovering
2. *Memory*—retaining or recalling the contents of thought
3. *Divergent production*—producing a variety of ideas or solutions to a problem
4. *Convergent production*—producing a single, best solution to a problem
5. *Evaluation*—deciding whether intellectual contents are positive or negative, good or bad, and so on

Products: The outcomes (or results) of thinking
1. *Units*—a single number, letter, or word
2. *Classes*—a higher-order concept (for example, rats and gerbils are rodents)
3. *Relations*—a connection between concepts
4. *Systems*—an ordering or classification of relations
5. *Transformation*—altering or restructuring intellectual contents
6. *Implication*—making inferences from separate pieces of information

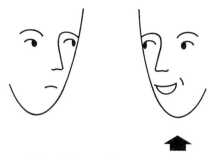

1. I'm glad you're feeling a little better.
2. You make the funniest faces!
3. Didn't I tell you she'd say "No"?

Figure 10-1. An item from one of Guilford's tests of social intelligence. The task is to read the characters' expressions and to decide what the person marked by the arrow is most probably saying to the other person. You may wish to try this item yourself (the correct answer appears below). *(Adapted from Guilford, 1967.)*

Guilford then set out to construct tests to measure each of his 120 mental abilities. For example, the test of "social intelligence" illustrated in Figure 10-1 measures the mental ability that requires the test taker to act on a *behavioral* content (the figure's facial expression), using a particular operation, *cognition,* to produce a particular product, the probable *implication* of that expression. To date, tests have been constructed to assess more than 70 of the 120 mental abilities in Guilford's model of intellect. However, the scores that people make on these presumably independent intellectual factors are often correlated, suggesting that these abilities are not nearly so independent as Guilford has assumed (Brody & Brody, 1976).

Obviously the use of factor analysis has not exactly settled the question of what intelligence is, and for some very good reasons. Since the number and type of factors that emerge from a factor analysis depend largely on the specific tests one has administered and the range of problems that these tests pose to subjects, it is hardly surprising that investigators who have administered different test batteries might draw different conclusions about the structure of intellect. Let's also recall that the "products" of a factor analysis are merely clusters of interrelated items or problems that the researcher must interpret and label. Surely a technique that allows this much subjectivity is bound to produce

Answer to task in Figure 10-1: 3.

some interpretive inconsistencies. Moreover, the names that investigators give to their factors are only "best guesses" about the meaning of these clusters, and these guesses may or may not be accurate.

What we have learned from factor-analytic studies is that intelligence is not merely a singular attribute that determines how well people perform on *all* cognitive tasks. And although we cannot say exactly how many components there are to this concept we call intelligence, most studies suggest that there are considerably fewer basic mental abilities than Guilford's figure of 120 (Brody & Brody, 1976).

A modern psychometric view of intelligence. Raymond Cattell and John Horn have influenced current thinking about intelligence by proposing that Spearman's g and Thurstone's primary mental abilities can be divided into two major dimensions of intellect: *fluid intelligence* and *crystallized intelligence* (Cattell, 1963; Horn & Cattell, 1967, 1982). **Fluid intelligence (g_f)** is described as an ability to solve abstract relational problems of the sort that are *not* taught and are relatively free of cultural influences. The kinds of problems that are used to measure (g_f) include verbal analogies, memory for lists of unrelated items (for example, paired associates such as *dog–hoe*), and tests of one's ability to recognize relationships among abstract figures. By contrast, **crystallized intelligence (g_c)** is an ability to understand relationships or solve problems that depend on knowledge acquired as a result of schooling and other life experiences. Presumably, tests of general information (for example, "At what temper-

---

g: Spearman's abbreviation for *neogenesis,* which, roughly translated, means one's ability to understand relations (or general mental ability).

s: Spearman's term for mental abilities that are specific to particular tests.

"structure of intellect" model: Guilford's factor-analytic model of intelligence, which proposes that there are 120 distinct mental abilities.

fluid intelligence (g_f): the ability to perceive relations and solve relational problems of the type that are not taught and are relatively free of cultural influences.

crystallized intelligence (g_c): the ability to understand relations or solve problems that depend on knowledge acquired from schooling and other cultural influences.

ature does water boil?"), word comprehension ("What is the meaning of *duplicate?*"), and numerical abilities are all measures of g_c, or crystallized intelligence.

The Cattell/Horn theory has a distinct developmental flavor. Crystallized intelligence is said to increase throughout the life span, since it is primarily a reflection of one's cumulative learning experiences. Fluid intelligence, in contrast, is said to increase gradually throughout childhood and adolescence as the nervous system matures. It should then level off during young adulthood and begin a steady decline with age. Many investigators have found that individuals do seem to improve with age on measures of crystallized intelligence. However, longitudinal studies of adults often fail to find the steady age-related declines in fluid intelligence that the Cattell/Horn theory predicts (Labouvie-Vief, 1977; Schaie & Hertzog, 1983, 1986).[1]

A Modern Information-Processing Viewpoint

One recurring criticism of psychometric definitions of intelligence is that they are very narrow—focusing primarily on intellectual content, or *what* the child knows, rather than on the processes by which this knowledge is acquired, retained, and used to solve problems. Moreover, psychometric assessments of intelligence (that is, intelligence tests) measure one's proficiency at mathematical, verbal, and spatial reasoning while ignoring other attributes that people commonly think of as indications of intelligence, such as common sense, persistence in problem solving, social and interpersonal skills, and the talents that underlie creative accomplishments in music, drama, and athletics (Gardner, 1983; Sternberg, Conway, Ketron, & Bernstein, 1981).

Recently, Robert Sternberg (1985) has proposed a **triarchic theory** of intelligence that emphasizes three aspects, or components, of intelligent behavior: *context, experience,* and *information-processing skills.* As we will see in reviewing this model, Sternberg's view of intelligence is much, much broader than that of the psychometric theorists.

Context. The contextual component of Sternberg's model is a relatively simple idea: whether an act qualifies as "intelligent" behavior will depend to a large extent on the social or sociocultural context in which it is displayed. According to Sternberg, intelligent people are those who can successfully adapt to their environments or who are successful at shaping their environments to suit them better. In everyday language, we might describe this kind of intelligence as practical wisdom or "street smarts." Unfortunately, this ability to tailor one's behavior to the demands of the environment is not assessed in traditional intelligence tests.

Notice that from this "contextual" perspective, what is meant by intelligent behavior may vary from one culture or subculture to another, from one historical epoch to another, and from one period of the life span to another. Sternberg describes an occasion when he attended a conference in Venezuela and showed up on time, at 8:00 A.M., only to find that he and four other North Americans were the only ones there. In North American society it is considered "smart" to be punctual for important engagements. However, strict punctuality is actually maladaptive in Latin cultures, where people are rather lax (by our standards, at least) about being on time. And consider the effects of history on assessments of intelligence. Thirty years ago, it was considered "intelligent" indeed to be able to perform arithmetic operations quickly and accurately. However, an individual who spends countless hours perfecting these same skills today might be considered somewhat less intelligent given that computers and calculators can perform these computations much faster. Finally, what is considered intelligent depends to no small extent on the age of the actor. An 8-month-old who delights at making a jack-in-the-box work might be considered rather curious, creative, and intelligent. But were you to spend ten minutes performing the very same actions, many observers would undoubtedly conclude that you are a bit slow or even retarded.

Experience and intelligence. According to Sternberg, one's experience with a task helps to determine whether one's actions qualify as intelligent behavior. Sternberg proposes that relatively novel tasks require active and conscious information processing and are the best measures of children's reasoning abilities—as long as these tasks are not so totally foreign that the child is unable to apply what he may know (as would be the case if geometry problems were presented to 5-

---

[1]Indeed, evidence from recent longitudinal studies (Dixon, Kramer, & Baltes, 1985; Schaie & Hertzog, 1983, 1986) indicates (1) that neither fluid nor crystallized intelligence shows an appreciable decline until after age 60 and (2) that some elderly individuals who remain intellectually active will retain their mental prowess and even post intellectual gains later in life.

year-olds). *Responses to novelty,* then, are an indication of the person's ability to generate good ideas or fresh insights.

In daily life, however, people may also perform more or less intelligently on familiar tasks (such as driving, balancing a checkbook, or quickly extracting the most interesting or important content from a newspaper). This second kind of intelligence reflects *automatization,* or increasing efficiency of information processing with practice. According to Sternberg, it is a sign of intelligence when we develop automatized routines or "programs of the mind" for performing our everyday tasks accurately and efficiently, so that we don't have to waste much time thinking about them.

Sternberg's theory has a most important implication for intelligence testers: in order to properly assess a person's intellectual prowess from the answers he gives, you have to know how familiar the task is to the test taker and, thus, which aspect of intelligence—response to novelty or automatization—his answer reflects. A child who struggles with and finally solves a problem after 2–3 minutes might be considered highly intelligent if the problem is novel but rather dull if this task is one that he has performed many, many times before. Similarly, if the items on an intelligence test are familiar to members of one cultural group but unfamil-

iar to members of another, the second group will perform much worse than the first, thereby reflecting a *cultural bias* in the test itself. So if one is seeking to compare the intellectual performances of people from diverse cultural backgrounds, it is imperative that one's test items be equally familiar (or unfamiliar) to all test takers.

Information-processing skills. Perhaps Sternberg's major criticism of psychometric theorists is that they estimate a person's intelligence from the quality, or correctness, of her answers while completely ignoring *how* she produces intelligent responses. Sternberg is an information-processing theorist who believes that we must now begin to focus on the components of intelligent behavior—that is, the cognitive processes by which we size up the requirements of problems, formulate strategies to solve them, and then monitor our cognitive activities until we've accomplished our goals. He argues that some people process information more efficiently than others and that our cognitive tests could be improved considerably were they to measure these differences and treat them as important aspects of intelligence.

In sum, Sternberg's triarchic theory provides us with a very rich view of the nature of intelligence. It suggests that if you want to know how intelligent Charles, Chico, and Chenghuan are, you had better consider (1) the *context* in which they are performing (that is, the culture and historical period in which they live; their ages), (2) their *experience* with the tasks and whether their behavior qualifies as responses to novelty or automatized processes, and (3) the *information-processing skills* that reflect how each of them is approaching these tasks. Unfortunately, the most widely used intelligence tests were not based on such a broad and sophisticated view of intellectual processes. But since these tests are so widely used in our society, it is important for us to understand what they do measure and why they have taken the form that they have.

---

triarchic theory: a recent information-processing theory of intelligence that emphasizes three aspects of intelligent behavior not normally tapped by IQ tests: the context of the action; the person's experience with the task (or situation); and the information-processing strategies the person applies to the task (or situation).

How Is Intelligence Measured?

When psychologists began to construct intelligence tests, at the beginning of this century, their concern was not with defining the nature of intelligence but, rather, with devising a method to determine who among groups of schoolchildren were likely to be slow learners. In this section of the chapter we will trace the development of this mental-testing movement and briefly consider the characteristics of some of the most respected and widely used intelligence tests.

Alfred Binet and the Stanford-Binet Test

French psychologist Alfred Binet and a colleague, Theophile Simon, produced the forerunner of our modern intelligence tests. In 1904, Binet and Simon were commissioned by the French government to devise a test that would identify "dull" children—slow learners who might profit from remedial instruction. Since their task was a practical one—to predict success at school—Binet and Simon began by constructing a large battery of cognitive tasks that measured skills presumed necessary for classroom learning: processes such as attention, perception, memory, reasoning, and verbal comprehension. These problems were then administered to normal schoolchildren and to those described by their instructors as dull or retarded. Items that did not discriminate between dull and normal children (for example, measures of motor skills) were systematically eliminated from the battery. After several such refinements, Binet and Simon had produced a test that sampled several cognitive abilities, could be administered in a little more than an hour, and reliably discriminated children described as dull, average, and bright by their teachers.

The concept of mental age. Binet assumed that intelligence develops with age and that older children and adolescents should be able to perform a wider variety of intellectual tasks than their younger counterparts. In 1908 the Binet-Simon test was revised and all test items were age-graded. For example, problems that were passed by most 6-year-olds but few 5-year-olds were assumed to reflect the mental performance of a typical 6-year-old; those passed by most 12-year-olds but few 11-year-olds were said to measure the intellectual skills of an average 12-year-old; and so on. This age-grading of test items for ages 3–13 allowed a more precise assessment of a child's level of intellectual functioning. A child who passed all items at the 5-year-old level but none at the 6-year-old level was said to have a **mental age (MA)** of 5 years. A child who passed all items at the 10-year-old level and half of those at the 11-year-old level would have an MA of 10½ years.

The intelligence quotient (IQ). Mental age is a useful concept that gives an absolute assessment of the child's level of intellectual development. However, a mental age, by itself, does not tell us how smart someone is. To determine whether a child is bright, average, or dull, it is necessary to compare the child's mental age with his or her chronological age. Suppose that a 7-year-old girl has a mental age of 8 years. We would consider this child reasonably bright because she can perform intellectual tasks that most 7-year-olds will fail. But the same mental age of 8 would be taken as an indication of retarded intellectual development if our test taker had a chronological age of 13.

William Stern, a German psychologist, later proposed a ratio measure of intelligence that came to be known as the **intelligence quotient,** or **IQ.** A person's IQ was calculated by dividing her mental age by her chronological age and then multiplying by 100:

$$IQ = MA/CA \times 100$$

Notice that an IQ of 100 indicates average intelligence; it means that the child has passed all the items that age mates typically pass and none of the items at the next level higher, so that *her mental age is exactly equal to her chronological age.* An IQ greater than 100 indicates

Photo 10-1. Alfred Binet (1857–1911), the father of intelligence testing.

Table 10-2. Sample problems from the Stanford-Binet

Age 3—Child should be able to:	Point to objects that serve various functions such as "goes on your feet" Name pictures of objects such as *chair, flag* Repeat a list of 2 words or digits—for example, *car, dog*
Age 4—Child should be able to:	Discriminate visual forms such as squares, circles, and triangles Define words such as *ball* and *bat* Repeat 10-word sentences Count up to 4 objects Solve problems such as "In daytime it is light; at night it is . . ."
Age 6—Child should be able to:	State the difference between familiar items such as a *bird* and a *dog* Count up to 9 objects Solve analogies such as "An inch is short; a mile is . . ."
Age 9—Child should be able to:	Solve verbal problems such as "Tell me a number that rhymes with *tree*" Solve simple arithmetic problems such as "If I buy 4 cents worth of candy and give the storekeeper 10 cents, how much money will I get back?" Repeat 4 digits in reverse order
Age 12—Child should be able to:	Define words such as *skill* and *muzzle* Repeat 5 digits in reverse order Solve verbal absurdities such as "One day we saw several icebergs that had been entirely melted by the warmth of the Gulf Stream. What is foolish about that?"

Source: Adapted from Terman & Merrill (1972).

that the child's performance is superior to that of other children her age; an IQ less than 100 means that her intellectual performance is below average.

One advantage of the IQ measure is that it allows us to compare the intellectual development of children of different ages. For example, a 6-year-old with a mental age of 3 has an IQ of 50—the same IQ as a 10-year-old with a mental age of 5. These two children are considered equally retarded even though the mental age of the second child is two years greater.

In sum, Binet had created a test that enabled him to identify slow learners and to estimate their levels of intellectual development. This information proved particularly useful to school administrators, who began to use children's mental ages as a guideline for planning curricula for both normal and retarded students.

The Stanford-Binet test.   Binet's work soon attracted the attention of psychologists in other countries. In 1916 Lewis Terman of Stanford University translated and published a revised version of the Binet scale for use with American children. This test came to be known as the *Stanford-Binet*.

Like the Binet scale, the original version of the Stanford-Binet consisted of a series of age-graded tasks designed to measure the average intellectual performance of subjects aged 3 through 13 (see Table 10-2 for some sample problems). Terman first gave his test to a sample of about 1000 middle-class American schoolchildren in order to establish performance norms against which the individual child could be compared. But unlike Binet, who classified children according to mental age, Terman favored the use of Stern's intelligence quotient, or IQ. Thus, the 1916 version of the Stanford-Binet became the first true "IQ test."

The norms for this 1916 test were based solely on the intellectual performance of White children from middle-class backgrounds. Furthermore, the earliest version of the Stanford-Binet did not adequately measure the intellectual skills of either very young children or adults. To correct these problems, investigators have revised the Stanford-Binet on several occasions. Norms for the most recent version of the test are based on a representative sample of people (2-year-olds through young adults) from many racial and socioeconomic backgrounds. The concept of mental age is no longer

mental age (MA): a measure of intellectual development that reflects the level of age-graded problems a child is able to solve.

intelligence quotient (IQ): a numerical measure of a person's performance on an intelligence test relative to the performance of other examinees of the same age.

used to determine a child's IQ on the Stanford-Binet or on any other intelligence test. Instead, individuals receive scores (called *deviation IQs*) that reflect how well or poorly they have done compared with other people of the same age. An IQ of 100 is still average. Children who pass more problems than their peers typically will have IQs above 100, whereas those who pass fewer problems than average will obtain IQs lower than 100.

The Wechsler Scales

Professor David Wechsler of the New York University–Bellevue Medical School has constructed two intelligence tests for children, both of which are now widely used. The Wechsler Intelligence Scale for Children–Revised (WISC-R) is appropriate for schoolchildren aged 6 to 16 (Wechsler, 1974). A second test, the Wechsler Preschool and Primary Scale of Intelligence (WPPSI), is designed for preschoolers between ages 4 and 6½ (Wechsler, 1967).

One reason that Wechsler constructed his own intelligence scales is that he believed the Stanford-Binet was too heavily loaded with items that require verbal skills. Wechsler suggested that many intellectual skills are predominantly *nonverbal*—abilities that are not adequately represented on Binet-type scales. He also argued that the heavy verbal bias of the Binet test discriminates against children who have certain language handicaps—for example, those for whom English is a second language or those who have reading difficulties or are hard of hearing.

Wechsler tried to overcome these problems by constructing intelligence scales that contain both verbal subtests and nonverbal, or "performance," subtests. Items on the verbal subtests are very similar to those on the Stanford-Binet. They are designed to measure the child's vocabulary, general knowledge, understanding of ideas and concepts, arithmetic reasoning, and the like. By contrast, items on the performance subtests are designed to assess predominantly nonverbal skills, such as the ability to assemble puzzles, to solve mazes, to reproduce geometric designs with colored blocks, and to rearrange sets of pictures so that they tell a meaningful story. When the examinee's performance is evaluated, he or she is assigned three scores: a verbal IQ, a performance IQ, and a full-scale IQ based on a combination of the first two measures.

Although the Wechsler scales differ in format from the Stanford-Binet, IQs derived from these instruments tend to be highly correlated. However, the Wechsler scales do tap a wider variety of intellectual skills than

the Stanford-Binet and are sensitive to inconsistencies in intellectual performance that may be early signs of brain damage or learning disorders (for example, children with reading disorders often do much worse on the verbal component of the WISC). Of course, these tests cannot specify the reasons for a child's uneven performance. They merely alert the examiner to the possibility that a problem exists—one that may call for diagnostic testing and treatment.

Distribution of IQ Scores

If a young girl scores 130 on the Stanford-Binet or the WISC, we know that her IQ is above average. But how bright is she? In order to tell, we would have to know something about the way IQs are distributed in the population at large.

One interesting feature of all modern IQ tests is that people's scores are **normally distributed** around an IQ of 100 (see Figure 10-2). This patterning of scores is hardly an accident. By definition, the average score made by examinees from each age group is set at 100, and this is the most common score that people make. Note that approximately half the population scores below 100 and half above. Moreover, roughly equal numbers of examinees will obtain IQs of 85 and 115 (15 points from the average) or 70 and 130 (30 points from average). To determine the meaning of an IQ of 130,

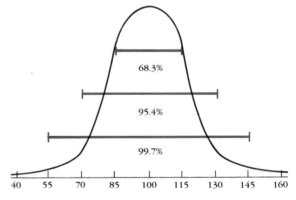

Figure 10-2. The approximate distribution of IQ scores people make on contemporary intelligence tests. These tests are constructed so that the average score made by examinees in each age group is equivalent to an IQ of 100. Note that more than two-thirds of all examinees score within 15 points of this average (that is, IQs of 85–115) and that 95% of the population score within 30 points of average (IQs of 70–130).

Table 10-3. The meaning of various IQs obtained from the Stanford-Binet

An IQ of	Equals or exceeds —% of the population	An IQ of	Equals or exceeds —% of the population
160	99.99	100	50
140	99.3	95	38
135	98	90	27
130	97	85	18
125	94	80	11
120	89	75	6
115	82	70	3
110	73	65	2
105	62	62	1

we can look at Table 10-3, which shows what percentage of the population the person outperforms by scoring at that level. Here we see that an IQ of 130 equals or exceeds the IQs of 97% of the population; it is a very high IQ indeed. Similarly, fewer than 3% of all test takers obtain IQs below 70, a cutoff that is commonly used today to define mental retardation.

Group Tests of Mental Performance

Both the Stanford-Binet and the Wechsler scales are expensive and time-consuming. These tests must be administered individually by a professional examiner, and assessing the IQ of a single examinee can take more than an hour. For measuring the intellectual performance of a large number of people—army recruits, job applicants, or thousands of students in a city's public schools—the costs of administering individual intelligence tests can become prohibitive.

During World War I, psychologists were commissioned by the U.S. Army to develop a paper-and-pencil intelligence test that could be administered to large groups of inductees to quickly weed out the very dull and to place the others into military occupations in accordance with their mental capabilities. Once developed, this first "group" test, or *Army Alpha,* was routinely used to classify and assign military personnel. As Wrightsman and Sanford (1975, p. 124) have noted, "Many of our fathers and grandfathers had their military careers—and perhaps their lives—determined by their performance on this test."

It is likely that you have taken a group test of intelligence (or scholastic aptitude) at some point in your academic career. Among the more widely used of these tests are the Lorge-Thorndike Test, which is designed for grade school and high school students, the

Scholastic Aptitude Test (SAT) and the American College Test (ACT), taken by many college applicants, and the Graduate Record Examination (GRE), often required of applicants to graduate school. These instruments are sometimes called "achievement" tests because they call for specific information that the examinee has learned at school (that is, what Cattell and Horn call crystallized intelligence) and are designed to predict future academic achievement.

Some New Approaches to Intelligence Testing

Although both the Stanford-Binet and the Wechsler scales are widely used today, new tests are constantly being developed. For example, there are now intelligence scales based on Piagetian concepts and developmental milestones (see Humphreys, Rich, & Davey, 1985). The *Kaufman Assessment Battery for Children* (K-ABC) is another recent test—one that the authors claim is fairer to minority groups and to handicapped children (that is, provides a more accurate estimate of their intellectual capabilities) than either the Stanford-Binet or the Wechsler scales (Kaufman & Kaufman, 1983).

Others have taken more radical approaches. Reuven Feuerstein (1979), for example, has argued that even though intelligence is often viewed as one's potential to learn from experience, IQ tests typically assess *what has already been learned* rather than what *can* be learned. Feuerstein's *Learning Potential Assessment Device* asks children to learn new concepts with the guid-

---

normal distribution: a symmetrical, bell-shaped curve that describes the variability of certain characteristics within a population; most people fall at or near the average score.

ance of an adult who provides hints as needed. In this test, intelligence is defined as the ability to learn quickly with minimal guidance. Sternberg (1985) finds this approach quite compatible with his triarchic theory of intelligence. For example, he argues that it really makes little sense to assess verbal *reasoning* by asking children to define words that they already know—as IQ testers often do. A better procedure would be to place unfamiliar words in a paragraph and see whether children can infer their meanings from the context, just as they must do in real life.

In sum, modern perspectives on the nature, or meaning, of intelligence are now beginning to be reflected in the content of intelligence tests. However, these new tests and testing procedures have a very short history, and it remains to be seen whether they will eventually replace more traditional assessments of mental performance, such as the WISC and the Stanford-Binet.

Assessing Infant Intelligence

None of the tests that we have reviewed can be used with children much younger than 3. Infants and toddlers have very short attention spans, and they do not talk very well. Consequently, long exams that depend heavily on the use of language are not well suited for estimating their intellectual abilities.

Over the years, attempts have been made to measure infant "intelligence" by assessing the rate at which infants reach important developmental milestones. Perhaps the best known and most widely used of the infant tests is the *Bayley Scales of Infant Development* (Bayley, 1969). This instrument, designed for infants aged 2 to 30 months, consists of three subtests: (1) the *Motor* scale, which includes problems such as grasping a cube and throwing a ball, (2) the *Mental* scale, which includes adaptive behaviors such as reaching for a desirable object, searching for a hidden toy, and following directions, and (3) the *Infant Behavioral Record,* a rating of the child's behavior on dimensions such as goal directedness, fearfulness, and social responsivity. On the basis of his or her performance, the child is given a **developmental quotient,** or **DQ,** rather than an IQ. A DQ of 100 means that the child has passed all problems (or reached all milestones) listed as appropriate for his or her age group and none for the next age group higher. A DQ of greater than 100 is a sign of accelerated development, whereas a DQ of less than 100 means that the child's developmental progress is slower than that of a typical age mate.

Do DQs predict later IQs? Today it is fashionable to criticize infant tests because these instruments generally fail to predict a child's later IQ score or scholastic achievements (Honzik, 1983; McCall, 1983). In fact, a DQ measured early in infancy may not even predict the child's developmental standing later in infancy!

Why do infant tests not do a better job of predicting children's later IQs? One possibility, discussed in Chapter 3, is that intellectual development during the first two years seems to be highly *canalized*—that is, influenced by powerful and universal maturational forces. Robert McCall (1981) is a proponent of this point of view. He argues that infants are biologically programmed to achieve various cognitive milestones in a particular sequence and that DQs indicating very rapid or very leisurely development are unstable, reflecting temporary deviations from a universal developmental path. But starting at about age 2, universal maturational forces begin to exert less of an influence over cognitive development, so that individual differences in intelligence will now become more apparent and more stable over time.

Surely there is an element of truth to McCall's theory. But perhaps the main reason infant scales are such poor predictors of later IQ is that infant tests and IQ tests tap very different kinds of abilities. The infant scales are designed to measure sensory, motor, language, and social skills, whereas standardized IQ tests such as the WISC and the Stanford-Binet emphasize more abstract abilities such as verbal reasoning, concept formation, and problem solving. So to expect an infant test to predict the later results of an IQ test is like expecting a yardstick to tell us how much someone weighs. There may be some correspondence between the two measures (a yardstick indicates height, which is correlated with weight; DQ indicates developmental progress, which is related to IQ), but the relationship is not very great.

It would be unwise, however, to throw out the "baby tests" with the bathwater, for infant scales are useful in diagnosing neurological disorders and mental retardation—even when these conditions are fairly mild and difficult to detect through standard pediatric or neurological exams (Escalona, 1968; Honzik, 1983). Moreover, Lewis and Enright (as cited by Lewis & Michalson, 1985) have found that children's earlier scores on the verbal items of the Bayley scales are related to their verbal proficiencies at age 6. So infant scales may well forecast a child's future performance on assessments of those particular skills that infant tests are designed to evaluate.

New evidence for continuity in intellectual performance. Is it foolish, then, to think that we might ever accurately forecast a child's later IQ from his or her behavior during infancy? Maybe not. Recently, Mark Bornstein and Marian Sigman (1986) have reviewed evidence suggesting that certain measures of infant attention are much better at predicting IQ during the preschool and early grade school years than are the Bayley scales or other measures of infant development. Two attributes appear especially promising: the speed at which infants *habituate* to repetitive stimuli and the extent to which infants prefer novel stimuli to familiar ones (*preference for novelty*). Indeed, measures of these two aspects of attention obtained during the first six months of life have an average correlation of .46 with IQ in childhood, particularly verbal IQ. These same measures also predict the later intellectual performance of premature infants (Rose & Wallace, 1985) and are actually much better than the Bayley scales at diagnosing mental retardation (Fagan, 1985). Perhaps we can now characterize the "smart" infant as one who prefers and seeks out novel experiences and who soaks up new information quickly—in short, an efficient information processor.

So it seems that there is some continuity between infant intelligence and childhood intelligence after all. If we think about it, there is little reason to suspect that such Bayley "mental" milestones as uncovering a toy, scribbling with a crayon, or throwing a ball would carry over into vocabulary learning or problem solving later in childhood. But the extent to which young infants prefer novelty and process information quickly is indeed related to their reasoning and problem-solving skills later in childhood.

Is IQ a Stable Attribute?

When intelligence testing became widespread, during the first half of this century, it was generally assumed that a person's IQ was a reflection of his or her mental *capacity*—an attribute that was genetically determined and therefore would remain reasonably stable over time. In other words, a child with an IQ of 120 at age 5 was expected to obtain a similar IQ when retested at age 10, 15, or 20.

How much support is there for this idea? As we have seen, infant DQs do not predict later intelligence test scores very well at all. But starting at about age 4, the IQs that children obtain are meaningfully related to their performance on IQ tests later in life.

Table 10-4. Correlations of IQs measured during the preschool years and middle childhood with IQs measured at ages 10 and 18

Age of child	Correlation with IQ at age 10	Correlation with IQ at age 18
4	.66	.42
6	.76	.61
8	.88	.70
10	—	.76
12	.87	.76

Source: Adapted from Honzik, Macfarlane, & Allen (1948).

Table 10-4 summarizes the results of a longitudinal study of more than 250 children conducted at the University of California (Honzik, Macfarlane, & Allen, 1948). In examining these correlations, we see that the shorter the interval between testings, the higher the correlation between children's IQ scores. For example, the correlation between IQs measured at ages 8 and 10 (+.88) is greater than the correlation between IQs measured at ages 6 and 10 (+.76) or at ages 8 and 18 (+.70).

At first glance, these data seem to imply that one's IQ is a very stable attribute. After all, the scores that children obtain at age 6 are clearly related to those that they obtain *12 years later at age 18!* However, it is important to note that these correlations, or "stability coefficients," are based on a large *group* of subjects, and they do not necessarily imply that the IQs of *individual children* will remain stable over time.

When individual profiles are examined, we find that many children show wide variations in IQ scores over the course of childhood. Robert McCall and his associates (McCall, Applebaum, & Hogarty, 1973) looked at the IQ scores of 140 children who had taken intelligence tests at regular intervals from age 2½ to age 17. Their findings were remarkable. More than half of these individuals displayed fluctuations in IQ over time, and the average range of variation in the IQ scores of these "fluctuators" was a whopping 28.5 points. One child in seven showed changes of at least 40 points, and changes of more than 70 points are not unknown (Hindley & Owen, 1978).

---

developmental quotient (DQ): a numerical measure of an infant's performance on a developmental schedule relative to the performance of other infants of the same age.

So it seems that IQ is reasonably stable for some children but extremely variable for many others. These findings suggest that an IQ score is not an indication of one's absolute potential for learning or intellectual capacity; if it were, the intellectual profiles of virtually all children would be highly stable, showing only minor variations due to errors of measurement.

What, then, does an IQ represent, if not one's intellectual competence or ability? Today, many experts believe that an IQ score is merely an estimate of the examinee's intellectual *performance* at one particular point in time—an estimate that may or may not be a good indication of the examinee's intellectual capabilities. The fact that IQs can wander upward or downward suggests that the environment may play a crucial role in determining intellectual performance. Indeed, the authors of the California longitudinal study were intrigued to find that the children whose IQ scores fluctuated the most were those from unstable home environments—that is, youngsters whose life experiences had also fluctuated between periods of happiness and turmoil (Honzik et al., 1948).

In reviewing several of the more widely respected intelligence tests, we have seen that these instruments vary considerably in structure and format. Some must be administered to individuals; others are appropriate for testing large groups. Many tests are heavily loaded with items requiring verbal skills; others give equal weight to nonverbal abilities. Tests are designed to serve many purposes, ranging from assessing the developmental progress of infants to predicting the ability of adults to profit from higher education or to succeed at various occupations. Although there is no simple answer to the question "How is intelligence measured?," psychologists do follow a common set of procedures when constructing and evaluating intelligence tests. In Box 10-1 we will review these important principles of test construction and see why they must be followed if a test is to be at all useful.

What Do Intelligence Tests Predict?

We have seen that IQ tests measure intellectual performance rather than competence and that a person's IQ may vary considerably over time. At this point, it seems reasonable to ask whether IQ scores can tell anything very meaningful about the people who were tested. For example, does IQ predict future academic accomplishments? Is it in any way related to a person's health, occupational status, or general life satisfaction? Research designed to answer these questions suggests some tentative answers. Let's first consider the relationship between IQ and academic achievement.

IQ as a Predictor of Scholastic Achievement

Since the original purpose of IQ testing was to estimate how well children would perform at school, it should come as no surprise that modern intelligence tests do predict academic achievement. The average correlation between children's IQ scores and their *current* grades at school is about .50 (Minton & Schneider, 1980). Moreover, assessments of IQ (or scholastic aptitude) can predict *future* academic performance. In one short-term longitudinal study, children's IQs measured in the fourth grade were highly correlated (+.73) with their scores on standardized achievement tests in the sixth grade (Crano, Kenny, & Campbell, 1972). Scholastic aptitude tests such as the ACT or SAT are also reliable predictors of the grades that high school students will make in college.

Not only do children with high IQs tend to do better in school, but they stay there longer (Brody & Brody, 1976): students who perform well on IQ tests are less likely to drop out of high school and more likely than other high school graduates to attempt and to complete college.

So intelligence test scores do predict academic achievements. Yet, it is important to note that the correlational findings we have reviewed are based on large numbers of students and that the IQ score of any particular student may not be a very good indicator of her current or future academic accomplishments. When trying to predict how well a particular student will perform in the future, a well-trained guidance counselor would undoubtedly consider the student's IQ score. However, he or she would also want to know about other variables that are related to academic success—factors such as the student's work habits, interests, and motivation to succeed. Although IQ (and aptitude) tests predict academic achievement better than *any other type of test,* judgments about an individual's future accomplishments *should never be based on a test score alone.* Indeed, studies have shown that the best single predictor of a student's future grades is not an IQ (or aptitude) score but, rather, the grades that the student has previously earned (Minton & Schneider, 1980).

Box 10-1
Principles of Test Construction

Tests designed to measure various psychological attributes vary considerably in quality. Some are virtually worthless; others are reasonably proficient at estimating how people differ along important dimensions such as anxiety, creativity, and intelligence. What makes for a good or useful test? At least four qualities: a *careful selection of items, reliability, validity,* and the establishment of *normative standards* against which to interpret an examinee's score.

Item selection. The first task when constructing any kind of psychological test is to carefully select items that reflect or represent the attribute that you hope to measure. When Binet set out to construct the first intelligence test, his purpose was to identify mentally retarded children who would not profit from traditional classroom instruction. He then selected items that seemed to tap the skills children use in completing school assignments, under the assumption that examinees who perform poorly on these tasks would also founder in the classroom. Of course, Binet would almost certainly have made different assumptions and chosen different items had his task been to assess the mechanical aptitude of students in a high school shop class. Clearly, the items that one selects for a test will depend on the purpose of that test and the assumptions that are made about the attribute(s) being measured.

Reliability. One characteristic of all useful tests is that they are highly reliable. Reliability means that *the test measures consistently,* even though different persons may administer and/or score it. If an IQ test is reliable, a person who takes it several times over a short period should obtain similar IQs on all testings. We could hardly consider a particular IQ test to be a very useful measure of intellectual functioning if a child who took it three times in a week scored 130 on Saturday, 85 on Monday, and 105 on the following Thursday.

The most common method of assessing the reliability of a test is to administer it twice to the same individuals and see how closely the two sets of scores are correlated. Fortunately, the IQ tests that we have reviewed are all fairly reliable, giving "test-retest" correlations of approximately .90. Whatever it is that these tests are measuring, they are measuring it consistently.

Validity. Good tests are not only reliable but *valid* as well. Simply stated, a test is valid if *it is measuring whatever it claims to measure.*

The validity of a test is usually estimated by comparing the scores that people make on this instrument with one or more criterion measures that are known to reflect the attribute in question. But how do we validate an IQ test when there are no absolute criteria for intellectual performance and theorists cannot even agree on what intelligence is? Admittedly, the problem is formidable—but hardly insurmountable. What is typically done is to determine whether the scores that people make on an IQ test are correlated with one or more criterion measures that are *presumed* to reflect individual differences in intelligence—measures such as grades in school, teachers' ratings of intellectual ability, and the examinees' performance on other IQ tests (or tests of academic achievement). Thus, Binet's first intelligence test was considered valid because it accomplished precisely what it was designed to do—it discriminated those students who had been labeled as dull, average, and bright by their teachers.

Normative standards. A child's performance on an IQ test has little if any meaning unless we have norms against which to compare and evaluate the child's score. These normative standards are obtained by administering the IQ test to a *standardization group*—that is, a large sample of the population for which the test was designed. Data from the standardization sample would then tell us what score represents "average" performance as well as how scores are distributed in the population as a whole.

For norms to be useful, the standardization sample must truly represent the population for which the test is intended. For example, an IQ test designed for 6–10-year-old schoolchildren in the United States should be standardized on a 6–10-year-old sample that includes the appropriate proportions of youngsters from all the racial, ethnic, socioeconomic, and geographical backgrounds that make up the population of U.S. schoolchildren. If a test is improperly standardized on a nonrepresentative segment of the population—say, schoolchildren from urban settings—the norms that result may be inappropriate for children from other groups and settings. Suppose, for example, that the item "What is an escalator?" was passed by 50% of the 7-year-olds in the urban standardization sample but by only 10% of the 7-year-olds from a rural school in Arizona. In this case, the urban norms would almost certainly underestimate the intellectual functioning of rural schoolchildren; their poor performance on the "escalator" item (and other items tapping predominantly "urban" experiences) is probably due to subcultural differences between themselves and the standardization group rather than to any true differences in their intellectual prowess. So it is not enough to merely standardize a test—the test must be standardized on a representative sample of the population to which it will be administered.

An important aspect of the standardization process is the *standardization of test procedures*. This simply means that a single testing procedure has been established and that the test apparatus, instructions, and scoring are identical for all children, regardless of who is administering the test. The purpose of this standardization is to ensure that children from all backgrounds and settings have taken the same test under exactly the same set of circumstances so that their scores may be compared.

IQ as a Predictor of Occupational Success

Do people with higher IQs land the better jobs? Are they more successful in their chosen occupations than co-workers who test lower in intelligence?

The answer to the first question seems to be yes. In one study of military personnel during World War II, recruits' IQ scores on the Army General Classification Test were clearly related to the prestige of their civilian occupations (Harrell & Harrell, 1945). Table 10-5 shows the rank order (from most to least prestigious) of some of the civilian occupations, as well as the average IQs and the range of IQs that characterized the men who worked at those jobs. Notice that the average IQ score increases as the prestige of the occupation increases—that is, the more prestigious jobs were generally held by the more intelligent men. However, a high IQ was certainly no guarantee that one would be working at a prestigious job. As we see in the "range of IQs"

Table 10-5. Average IQs and range of IQs for enlisted military personnel who had worked at various civilian occupations

Occupation	Average IQ	Range of IQs
Accountant	128.1	94–157
Lawyer	127.6	96–157
Engineer	126.6	100–151
Chemist	124.8	102–153
Reporter	124.5	100–157
Teacher	122.8	76–155
Pharmacist	120.5	76–149
Bookkeeper	120.0	70–157
Sales manager	119.0	90–137
Purchasing agent	118.7	82–153
Radio repairman	115.3	56–151
Salesman	115.1	60–153
Artist	114.9	82–139
Stock clerk	111.8	54–151
Machinist	110.1	38–153
Electrician	109.0	64–149
Riveter	104.1	50–141
Butcher	102.9	42–147
Bartender	102.2	56–137
Carpenter	102.1	42–147
Chauffeur	100.8	46–143
Cook and baker	97.2	20–147
Truck driver	96.2	16–149
Barber	95.3	42–141
Farmhand	91.4	24–141
Miner	90.6	42–139

Source: Adapted from Harrell & Harrell (1945).

column, there were some very bright men working at low-status occupations such as farmhand or miner.

We can also ask whether IQ scores predict job *performance*. Are bright lawyers, electricians, or farmhands more successful or productive than their less intelligent colleagues? Erness and Nathan Brody (1976) have reviewed the literature and concluded that the relationship between IQ and occupational success depends on the nature of the work and the range of IQs that are found in the work force. Specifically, they noted that—

1. In high-status occupations where high intelligence scores are required as a condition for training and employment, there is *no* relationship between IQ and job performance. Scientists with IQs of 150 publish no more experiments than their colleagues with IQs of 115; extremely bright lawyers win no higher percentage of their cases than lawyers whose IQs are merely "above average." However, the range of IQs among workers in high-status professions is severely restricted (everybody is reasonably bright), and it is likely that intelligence would predict job performance if individuals with low IQs were allowed to enter these professions.

2. IQ scores do seem to predict job performance in professions of intermediate status where (a) cognitive skills are helpful and (b) the range of IQs among workers is quite large. For example, bright bookkeepers outperform their relatively dull co-workers; bright life insurance agents sell more insurance than their less intelligent colleagues.

3. IQ scores are not systematically related to job performance in relatively low-status occupations that make few intellectual demands of the workers (for example, routine clerical work, factory work, and waiting on tables). However, the more intelligent workers tend to be more dissatisfied with these jobs and less likely to remain in them very long.

In sum, it appears that the relationship between IQ and the status of one's occupation is much simpler and more clear-cut than the relationship between IQ and job performance (Brody & Brody, 1976).

IQ as a Predictor of Health, Adjustment, and Life Satisfaction

Are bright people any healthier, happier, or better adjusted than those of average or below-average intelligence? A longitudinal project begun by Lewis Terman in 1922 provides some relevant information (Fincher, 1973; Terman, 1954; Terman & Oden, 1959). The subjects for Terman's study were more than 1500 California schoolchildren who had IQs of 140 or higher. The purpose of the project was to collect as much information as possible about the abilities and personal characteristics of these "gifted" children and to follow up on them every few years to see what they were accomplishing.

It soon became apparent that these children were exceptional in many respects other than intelligence. For example, they had weighed more at birth and had learned to walk and talk much sooner than most toddlers. They reached puberty somewhat early, and their general health, as determined from physicians' reports, was much better than average. The gifted children were rated by teachers as better adjusted emotionally and more morally mature than their less intelligent peers. And although they were no more popular, on the average, than their classmates, the gifted children were quicker to take charge and assume positions of leadership. Taken together, these findings demolish the stereotype of child prodigies as frail, sickly youngsters who are socially inadequate and emotionally immature (see also Janos & Robinson, 1985).

As adults, the individuals in Terman's gifted sample were still remarkable in many respects. Fewer than 5% were rated seriously maladjusted, and the incidence of problems such as ill health, psychiatric disturbance, alcoholism, and delinquent behavior was but a fraction of that normally observed in the general population (Terman, 1954). The marriage rate for these individuals was as high as it is for the population as a whole, and members of the gifted sample were more satisfied with their marriages and better adjusted sexually than were husbands and wives in general. Finally, a large percentage of these gifted individuals were high achievers, both in school and later in life. About 90% of the group had entered college, and 70% had graduated. Although many of the gifted women did not pursue a career outside the home, the occupational attainments of the gifted men were quite impressive. By age 40, 86% were working at professional or semiprofessional positions, compared with only 15–20% of California males as a whole. Many of these men were listed in *Who's Who* and *American Men of Science,* and as a group, they had taken out more than 200 patents and written some 2000 scientific reports, 100 books, 375 plays or short stories, and more than 300 essays, sketches, magazine articles, and critiques. All things considered, it would appear that the majority of Terman's gifted sample were very well-adjusted people who were living healthy, happy, and (in many cases) highly productive lives.

Interesting as Terman's results may be, they do not clearly establish that a high IQ guarantees good health, happiness, or occupational success. Psychologist David McClelland points out that

> neither Professor Terman nor anyone else has yet brought forward conclusive evidence that it is giftedness per se ... that is responsible for these happy life outcomes. [Terman's] gifted children were drawn very disproportionately from the ranks of the educated, the wealthy, and the powerful. This means that they not only had a better chance to acquire the characteristics measured in the test, but also to be happier (since they had more money), and also to have access to higher occupations and better social standing [quoted in Fincher, 1973, p. 14].

In other words, McClelland suggests that many of the positive outcomes that characterized Terman's gifted subjects may have stemmed not from their high IQs but, rather, from their superior family environments.

As it turns out, there are data to support McClelland's "family environment" hypothesis. When Terman (1954) contrasted the 150 gifted individuals who were most successful in a career (the As) with the 150 who were least successful (the Cs), he found that the childhood IQs of the members of these groups were comparable, averaging about 150. However, the academic achievements and intellectual profiles of those in the successful (A) group had remained fairly stable over time, whereas the scholastic performance and average IQ of those in the unsuccessful (C) group had declined since childhood. But why?

When Terman compared the family backgrounds of the As and Cs, he found some interesting differences. For example, the fathers of the As had more education and held better jobs than the fathers of the Cs, and twice as many of the As had siblings who had graduated from college. Moreover, the intellectual climate of the home (as indexed by number of books present and the parents' involvement in the child's learning activities) was generally richer and more stimulating for As than for Cs. Finally, twice as many Cs had experienced a disruption of family ties due to their parents' divorce, and the later divorce rate of the C subjects themselves was twice that observed among members of the A group.

So we see that a high IQ, by itself, does not guarantee good health, happiness, or success. Even among a select sample of children with superior IQs, the quality of the home environment contributes in important ways to future outcomes and accomplishments.

Box 10-2
Mental Retardation: A Closer Look

According to the American Association on Mental Deficiency, *mental retardation* is defined as "significant subaverage general intellectual functioning resulting in or associated with . . . impairments in adaptive behavior and manifested during the developmental period" (Grossman, 1983, p. 1). Translated, this means that, in order to be diagnosed as mentally retarded, an individual must, at some point before adulthood, have scored 70 or lower on an IQ test and have experienced repeated difficulties meeting age-appropriate expectations in everyday life. By these criteria about 6 to 7 million people in the United States, or 3% of the population, are retarded.

Four levels of mental retardation are recognized: mild, moderate, severe, and profound. An adult who is mildly retarded (IQ 50 or 55 to 70) is likely to have a mental age comparable to that of an 8- to 12-year-old child. Mildly retarded persons can learn both academic and practical skills in school, although they may require special instruction. And as adults, they can often work and live independently. By contrast, profoundly retarded adults (IQs below 20 or 25) have mental ages of 3 years or less. They show major delays in all aspects of development and must be cared for throughout life, often in institutional settings. So we see that there are major differences among those individuals who have been classified as "retarded."

There are many, many causes of mental deficiencies. Most severely or profoundly retarded persons (IQs below 40) have a form of *organic retardation;* that is, their retardation stems from an injury or from some biological cause such as disease or a hereditary disorder. In Chapter 3 we discussed several organic deficiencies that are hereditary, including Down's syndrome, the fragile-X syndrome, and phenylketonuria (PKU). Other forms of organic retardation are associated with prenatal and perinatal risk factors that we reviewed in Chapter 4—for example, an alcoholic mother, exposure to rubella, or severe anoxia during childbirth. Because children with organic deficiencies often have physical defects and show serious mental impairments early in life, they are usually identified and labeled as mentally retarded at some point during infancy.

The second major form of mental deficiency—*cultural-familial retardation*—is not usually detected until a child performs very poorly on an IQ test at school. These children are mildly retarded, come from poverty areas, and are apt to have a parent or sibling who is also mildly retarded (Westling, 1986). Cultural-familial retardation often appears to be due to a combination of low genetic potential and a poor (unstimulating) environment, although other factors such as perinatal stress that passed undetected may sometimes be involved. Probably 75 to 85% of mental retardation is of this type, and its exact cause is always difficult to pinpoint.

We learned from Terman's study that gifted children experience predominantly positive outcomes later in life. What happens to mentally retarded children? We get some indication from an excellent follow-up study of mildly retarded individuals (average IQ = 67) who had been placed in segregated special education classes for the mentally retarded during the 1920s and 1930s—the same era when Terman began his study of gifted children (Ross, Begab, Dondis, Giampiccolo, & Meyers, 1985). Nearly 40 years later, their life outcomes were compared with those of siblings and nonretarded age mates and with the highly favorable attainments of Terman's gifted sample.

What did the data reveal? As you might expect, the mentally retarded adults had less favorable life outcomes than the nonretarded groups. The table brings this home by comparing the jobs
continued

What about the other end of the IQ continuum? Do mentally retarded individuals have much hope of succeeding in life or achieving happiness? Although our stereotypes about mental retardation might persuade us to say no, the research presented in Box 10-2 suggests a very different conclusion.

Factors That Influence IQ Scores

Why do people differ so dramatically in the scores that they make on IQ tests? The pioneers of the mental-testing movement quickly inferred that intelligence must be a hereditary attribute—after all, family members are often very similar in their intellectual abilities and accomplishments. Yet, we have also seen that a person's IQ score may fluctuate considerably over time and that the children whose IQs fluctuate the most are often the ones who have experienced many changes in their home and family environments.

In the pages that follow, we will briefly review the classic evidence for hereditary and environmental effects on intelligence and will then take a closer look at several important sociocultural correlates of intellectual performance.

The Evidence for Heredity

In Chapter 3 we reviewed two major lines of evidence indicating that heredity affects intellectual per-

held in middle age by the mentally retarded men and their nonretarded peers. (Like the females in Terman's gifted sample, retarded women tended to marry and become homemakers.) Although about 80% of the retarded men were gainfully employed, they usually wound up in jobs that required little education or intellectual ability. Compared directly with nonretarded peers, retarded men and women fared worse on almost all counts. For example, they had lower incomes, less adequate housing, and poorer adjustment in social relationships, and they displayed greater dependency on other people.

Although at first glance these outcomes may seem rather dismal, the authors of this study found plenty of reasons for optimism. Consider, for example, that the vast majority of the mentally retarded males did work and that fewer than 20% of these workers were in the lowest job classifications, which society labels as menial. Moreover, the mentally retarded subjects were generally *self*-supporting; only about 1 in 5 reported having *any* need for public assistance in the ten years before being interviewed. Most of these mentally retarded individuals did marry, and most expressed some satisfaction with their accomplishments. So even though their life outcomes are poorer than those of nonretarded adults, these people were doing much better than stereotyped expectations of the mentally retarded would lead us to believe.

In sum, this study, like others before it, suggests that children who are labeled mildly or moderately retarded by the schools—and who do indeed have difficulty mastering academic lessons—will often simply "vanish" into the adult population after they leave school. Apparently they can adapt to the demands of adult life, displaying a fair amount of the "contextual" intelligence or "street smarts" that Sternberg talks about—and that is not measured by standardized IQ tests. As the authors put it, "It does not take as many IQ points as most people believe to be productive, to get along with others, and to be self-fulfilled" (Ross et al., 1985, p. 149).

Midlife occupations of mentally retarded, nonretarded, and gifted males

Occupational classification	Mentally retarded subjects (N = 54)	Nonretarded siblings (N = 31)	Nonretarded peers (N = 33)	Terman's gifted sample (N = 757)
Professional, managerial	1.9%	29.1%	36.4%	86.3%
Retail business, skilled trade, agricultural	29.6	32.3	39.4	12.5
Semiskilled, minor business, clerical	50.0	25.8	15.2	1.2
Slightly skilled, unskilled	18.5	13.0	9.4	0.0

Source: Adapted from Ross, Begab, Dondis, Giampiccolo, & Meyers (1985).

formance and that about half the variation in IQ scores within a particular population of test takers is due to genetic differences among these individuals:

1. *Family studies.* The intellectual resemblance between pairs of individuals living in the same home increases as a function of their kinship (that is, genetic similarity). For example, the IQ correlation for identical twins, who inherit identical genes, is substantially higher than the IQ correlations for fraternal twins and for normal siblings, who have half their genes in common.

2. *Adoption studies.* Adopted children are more similar intellectually to their biological parents than to their adoptive parents. This finding can be interpreted as evidence for a genetic influence on IQ, for adoptees share genes with their biological parents but not with their adoptive caregivers.

We also learned in Chapter 3 that a person's genotype may influence the type of environment that he or she is likely to experience. Indeed, Scarr and McCartney (1983) have proposed that people seek out environments that are compatible with their genetic predispositions, so that identical twins (who share identical genes) will select and experience more similar environments than fraternal twins or ordinary siblings do. This is a major reason that identical twins will resemble each other intellectually throughout life, whereas the intellectual resemblances between fraternal twins or ordinary siblings become progressively smaller over time (Scarr & McCartney, 1983).

Do these latter observations imply that a person's genotype *determines* his environment and thereby exerts the primary influence on his intellectual development? *No, they do not!* A child who has a genetic predisposition to seek out intellectual challenges could hardly be expected to develop a high IQ if she is raised in a barren environment that offers few such challenges for her to meet. Alternatively, a child who does not gravitate toward intellectual activities might nevertheless obtain an average or above-average IQ if raised in a stimulating environment that continually provides him with cognitive challenges that he must master. So it seems that a person's environment may either foster or inhibit the outward expression of genetic predispositions. Stated another way, heredity and environment interact to influence most human attributes—including intelligence and the course of intellectual development.

The Evidence for Environment

The evidence for environmental effects on intelligence comes from a variety of sources. For example, we learned in Chapter 3 that there is a moderate intellectual resemblance between pairs of genetically unrelated children who live in the same household. And earlier in this chapter, we saw that unstable home environments are associated with fluctuations in children's IQ scores. There are also data to indicate that a barren intellectual environment is likely to inhibit cognitive growth while a more stimulating environment can have the opposite effect.

Effects of an impoverished environment. Several investigators have studied the intellectual development of children who live in isolated, poverty-stricken communities where the literacy rate among adults is low and the educational facilities are substandard. Youngsters living in these impoverished settings scored far below average on standardized intelligence tests, and their IQs actually decreased with age (Ascher, 1935; Gordon, 1923; Sherman & Key, 1932; Wheeler, 1932). Otto Klineberg (1963) has proposed a **"cumulative deficit" hypothesis** to explain these findings. According to Klineberg's cumulative-deficit theory, impoverished environments inhibit intellectual growth, and these inhibiting effects will accumulate over time. Consequently, the longer children remain in a barren intellectual environment, the more poorly they will perform on standardized IQ tests.

Arthur Jensen (1977) tested the cumulative-deficit hypothesis by comparing the intellectual performance of economically disadvantaged Black siblings living in California and Georgia. Jensen proposed that if a "cumulative deficit" mechanism is operating, older siblings should obtain lower IQs than their younger brothers and sisters. This is precisely what he found for children in the Georgia sample, whose environmental disadvantages were markedly greater than those of the California group.[2]

Effects of environmental enrichment.

Can we promote intellectual development by enriching the environment in which children live? Apparently so, if the results of two studies of isolated mountain children are any guide (Wheeler, 1932, 1942). When children from a mountain community in eastern Tennessee were first tested in the early 1930s, they obtained an average IQ of 82. Ten years later, the children in this same community were retested. During the interval between testings, this community had changed in many ways: roads had been built, the school system had been drastically overhauled, and economic conditions had improved to the point that most people could now afford radios. In other words, this formerly isolated and impoverished community was coming into the social and economic mainstream of American life. As a result, the average IQ of children there rose by 11 points (to 93) in the ten years between testings. Other studies conducted in Hawaii and the American Midwest found similar increases in children's intellectual performance in communities where dramatic social and educational improvements had taken place (Finch, 1946; Smith, 1942).

Other investigators have charted the intellectual growth of adopted children who had been placed in their new homes before their first birthday (Scarr & Weinberg, 1977, 1983; Skodak & Skeels, 1947, 1949). Many of these adoptees came from disadvantaged family backgrounds where their biological parents were poorly educated and somewhat below average in IQ. They were placed in middle-class homes with adoptive parents who were highly educated and above average in intelligence. By the time these adoptees were 4–7 years old, they were scoring well above average on standardized IQ tests (about 110 in Scarr and Weinberg's study and 112 in Skodak and Skeels's). In fact, their intellectual performance was considerably higher than what one would expect on the basis of the IQs and educational

[2]The California children showed a small cumulative deficit on tests of verbal IQ but no age-related performance deficits on tests of nonverbal IQ.

levels of their biological parents or the IQs of other children from disadvantaged backgrounds. Since the adopting parents were known to be highly educated and above average in intelligence, it seems reasonable to assume that they were providing enriched, intellectually stimulating home environments that fostered the cognitive development of their adoptive children.

As these studies clearly indicate, the environment is a powerful force that may either promote or inhibit intellectual growth. Yet the term *environment* is a very global concept, and the evidence that we have reviewed does not really tell us which of the many life experiences that children have are most likely to affect their intellectual development. In the next section of the chapter, we will concentrate on environmental influences and see that a child's performance on IQ tests depends to some extent on parental attitudes and child-rearing practices, the structure and socioeconomic status of the family, and perhaps even the racial or ethnic group to which the family belongs.

Sociocultural Correlates of Intellectual Performance

When searching for social/cultural variables that may affect intellectual performance, it makes some sense to start with the first social system to which children are exposed—the family.

Home Environment and IQ

We have suggested that the quality of the home environment plays an important role in determining how well children perform on IQ tests. Recently, Bettye Caldwell and Robert Bradley have developed an instrument called the **HOME inventory** (Home Observation for Measurement of the Environment) that allows an interviewer/observer to visit an infant or a preschool child at home and to gain a good idea of just how intellectually stimulating (or impoverished) that home environment is (Caldwell & Bradley, 1978). The HOME inventory consists of 45 statements, each of which is scored *yes* (the statement is true of this family) or *no* (the statement is not true of this family). In order to gather the information to complete the inventory, the researcher will (1) ask the child's parent (usually the mother) to describe her daily routine and child-rearing practices, (2) carefully observe the parent as she interacts with her child, and (3) note the kinds of play materials that the parent makes available to the child. The

45 bits of information collected are then grouped into the six categories, or subscales, in Table 10-6. The home then receives a score on each subscale. The higher the scores across all six subscales, the more intellectually stimulating the home environment.

Does the HOME predict IQ?

As it turns out, there is a clear relationship between the quality of the home environment, as measured by the HOME, and children's performance on IQ tests. In fact, both Bradley and Caldwell (1976) and Helen Bee and her associates (1982) found that the quality of the home environment measured when children were either 6 or 12 months of age is a better predictor of their IQs at ages 3 and 4 than is their own first-year performance on infant intelligence tests.

Which aspects of the home environment matter most? Allen Gottfried (1984) has recently compiled the results of several longitudinal studies that have used the HOME scale to predict IQs in early childhood. He found that the best predictors of children's later IQs were the HOME subscales measuring *parental involvement* with the child, provision of *age-appropriate play materials,* and opportunities for *variety in daily stimulation.* (In fact, Bradley & Caldwell, 1984b, find that these same HOME subscales are strong predictors of children's later achievement test scores in the first grade.) Other researchers have found that the sheer amount of stimulation that parents provide is less important than whether that stimulation is *warm and responsive*—for example, a smile in return for a smile or an answer cheerfully given in response to a question (Crockenberg, 1983; Estrada, Arsenio, Hess, & Holloway, 1987). Indeed, responsive parents who take an active interest in their child's accomplishments can help premature infants to overcome early brain dysfunctions and to obtain higher IQs later in childhood than similar infants whose parents are less responsive (Beckwith & Parmelee, 1986).

In sum, an intellectually stimulating home environment is one in which parents are warm, respon-

---

cumulative-deficit hypothesis: the notion that impoverished environments inhibit intellectual growth and that these inhibiting effects accumulate over time.

HOME inventory: a measure of the amount and type of intellectual stimulation provided by a child's home environment.

Table 10-6. Subscales and sample items from the HOME inventory

Subscale 1: Emotional and Verbal Responsivity of the Mother (11 items)

Sample items: Mother responds to child's vocalizations with a verbal response

Mother's speech is clear, distinct, and audible

Mother caresses or kisses child at least once during visit

Subscale 2: Avoidance of Restriction and Punishment (8 items)

Sample items: Mother neither slaps nor spanks child during visit

Mother does not scold or derogate child during visit

Mother does not interfere with the child's actions or restrict child's movements more than three times during visit

Subscale 3: Organization of Physical and Temporal Environment (6 items)

Sample items: Child gets out of house at least four times a week

Child's play environment appears safe and free of hazards

Subscale 4: Provision of Appropriate Play Materials (9 items)

Sample items: Child has push or pull toy

Parents provide learning equipment appropriate to age—mobile, table and chairs, high chair, playpen, and so on

Mother provides toys or interesting activities for child during interview

Subscale 5: Maternal Involvement with Child (6 items)

Sample items: Mother "talks" to child while doing her work

Mother structures the child's play periods

Subscale 6: Opportunities for Variety in Daily Stimulation (5 items)

Sample items: Father provides some caretaking every day

Mother reads stories at least three times weekly

Child has three or more books of his own

Source: Adapted from Caldwell & Bradley (1978).

sive, and eager to be involved with their child (MacPhee, Ramey, & Yeates, 1984). They describe new objects, concepts, and experiences clearly and accurately, and they provide the child with a variety of play materials that are appropriate for her age or developmental level. They encourage the child to ask questions, to solve problems, and to think about what she is learning. As the child matures and enters school, they stress the importance of academic achievement and expect her to get good grades. When you stop and think about it, it is not at all surprising that children from these "enriched" home settings often have high IQs; after all, their parents are obviously concerned about their cognitive development and have spent several years encouraging them to acquire new information and to practice many of the cognitive skills that are measured on intelligence tests.

Is the home environment really all that important?

Langdon Longstreth and his associates (1981) have argued that *bright* mothers are likely to provide the most intellectually stimulating home environments. One implication of this point of view is that any correlation between the quality of the home environment and children's intellectual performance may simply reflect a hidden *genetic* effect on intelligence—that is, intelligent mothers (who just happen to provide stimulating home environments) have intelligent offspring. If this view is correct, it is possible that the quality of the home environment has few if any direct effects on children's intellectual development.

Keith Yeates and his colleagues (Yeates, MacPhee, Campbell, & Ramey, 1983) evaluated this hypothesis in a longitudinal study of 112 mothers and their 2–4-year-old children. The mothers' IQs were measured just before the birth of their children, and the children's IQs were measured at 24, 36, and 48 months of age. The HOME inventory was used to assess the quality of the families' home environments when the children were 6, 18, 30, and 42 months of age. By using a statistical procedure called multiple regression, Yeates and his associates were able to determine whether the home environment had any effect on children's IQ scores beyond that predicted on the basis of their mothers' IQs.

The results of this study were interesting and rather complex. The best predictor of a child's IQ at age 24 months was the mother's IQ, and the quality of the home environment had little if any direct effect on the intellectual performance of these toddlers. This finding is quite consistent with Longstreth's genetic reinterpretation of "home environment" effects. However, the picture had changed by the time the children were 4 years old. Now the quality of the home environment not only predicted their IQ scores but was actually a better predictor than maternal IQ. So we see that the home environment is truly an important factor in a child's intellectual development. It also seems that these environmental effects may accumulate over time, so that

Photo 10-2. Contrasting home environments. The photograph at the left shows an orderly home environment, and one in which family members are warm, responsive, and eager to be involved with one another. This is precisely the kind of setting that seems to promote children's intellectual development. In the photograph at the right we see an example of a barren, disorderly, and unattractive home environment—one that is likely to inhibit intellectual development.

the full impact of the home setting on the child's IQ may not be apparent until the child is 4 or older. Perhaps Robert McCall (1981) was right in arguing that early intellectual development is highly canalized and that environmental contributions will become more apparent only after the strong maturational forces of infancy have had their effects.

Birth Order, Family Configuration, and IQ

Two other "family" characteristics that seem to affect children's performance on IQ tests are *family size* and the child's position within the family, or *birth order.* These effects are clearly illustrated in a large-scale study conducted in Holland (Belmont & Marolla, 1973). The investigators had a very large data base indeed—military records of 386,114 males who represented nearly the entire population of young men born in Holland between 1944 and 1947. Data available for each man included an IQ score and other biographical information that was used to determine his social class, birth order, and family size. Controlling for both social class and birth order, Belmont and Marolla found that family size had a significant effect on IQ. As we see in Figure 10-3, *the brightest children tended to come from the smaller families.* When Belmont and Marolla then looked at the effects of birth order within any given family size, they found a clear birth-order effect: on the average, *first-borns outperformed second-borns, who outper-*

formed third-borns, and so on down the line. These findings are not unique to Dutch males—they have now been replicated in samples of males and females from several countries (Berbaum & Moreland, 1980; Markus & Zajonc, 1977).

One possible explanation for these birth-order and family-size effects is that first-borns and children from small families may receive more intellectual stimulation from their parents than later-borns. Indeed, this is precisely what Bradley and Caldwell (1984a) have found when they used the HOME inventory to assess the quality of home environments for first-born and later-born infants. And consider what Mary Rothbart (1971) found when she asked mothers to supervise the performance of their 5-year-olds on a series of achievement tasks. Half of the children were first-borns and half later-borns; to control for family size, all were from two-child families. Rothbart discovered that mothers spent an equal amount of time interacting with first-born and later-born children. However, the quality of the interactions differed: mothers gave more complex technical explanations to first-borns, put more pressure on first-borns to succeed, and were more anxious about their performance—perhaps explaining why first-borns outperformed later-borns on all but one of the experimental tasks. So it seems that first-borns are apt to receive more intellectual stimulation during infancy and more direct achievement training during the preschool years than later-borns do.

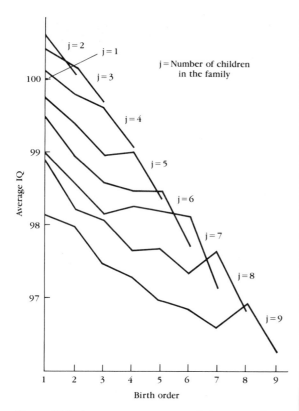

Figure 10-3. Average scores on a nonverbal measure of intelligence as a function of the examinee's birth order and the size of his family. Note that subjects from smaller families score higher on this test than subjects from large families. We also see that, within a given family size, children born early tend to obtain higher IQs than those born late. *(Adapted from Zajonc & Markus, 1975.)*

Robert Zajonc (1975; Zajonc & Markus, 1975) has proposed a slightly different explanation for these birth-order and family-size effects. According to Zajonc's **confluence hypothesis,** a child's intellectual development depends on the *average intellectual level of all family members,* including the child himself. Clearly, first-borns should have an advantage because they are initially exposed *only* to adults, whose intellectual levels are very high. By contrast, a second child experiences a less stimulating intellectual environment because she must deal with a cognitively immature older sibling as well as with her parents. The third child is further disadvantaged by the presence of *two* relatively immature older siblings. Zajonc (1975) suggests that

with each additional child, the family's intellectual environment depreciates. . . . Children who grow up

surrounded by people with higher intellectual levels [that is, first-borns and children from small families] have a better chance to achieve their maximum intellectual powers than . . . children from large families who spend more time in a world of child-sized minds . . . develop more slowly, and therefore attain lower IQs [p. 39].

Although Zajonc's confluence model is appealing for its simplicity, its predictions do not always ring true (Rodgers, 1984). For example, the model predicts that children who grow up in homes with *three* mature adults (say, two parents and a grandparent) should score higher on IQ tests than those who are exposed only to their parents; yet they don't (Brackbill & Nichols, 1982). Moreover, longer intervals between births should be to the advantage of both older and younger siblings. When children are widely spaced, the older sib has more time alone with parents, and the younger child is exposed to a much older child companion who is now reasonably mature. However, at least two recent studies have failed to confirm Zajonc's "sibling spacing" hypothesis (Brackbill & Nichols, 1982; Galbraith, 1982). So even though Zajonc's theory is an interesting explanation for birth-order and family-size effects on intelligence, it remains for future research to firmly establish its usefulness.

Finally, a caution is in order. These birth-order and family-size effects tend to be quite small and are observed only when large numbers of families are compared. Hence, the trends that emerge for the population as a whole may not apply to the members of any *particular* family. Clearly, not all first-borns are brighter than average; nor do all later-borns score lower in IQ than their older brothers and sisters.

Social-Class, Racial, and Ethnic Differences in IQ

One of the most reliable findings in the intelligence literature is that children from lower- and working-class homes average some 10–20 points below their middle-class age mates on standardized intelligence tests. Infants are apparently the only exception to this rule, as Mark Golden and his associates find no social-class differences in intellectual performance for children less than 2 years old (Golden & Birns, 1976; Golden, Birns, Bridger, & Moss, 1971).

There are also racial and ethnic differences in intellectual performance. In the United States, for example, children of Black, Native American, or Hispanic ancestry tend to score well below the White norms on standardized intelligence tests, whereas Asian-Americans score slightly higher, on average, than Whites do (Minton & Schneider, 1980; Tyler, 1965). One team of investigators (Kennedy, van de Reit, & White, 1963) administered the Stanford-Binet to 1800 Black elementary school children living in the Southeastern United States. As we see in Figure 10-4, these youngsters obtained an average IQ of 80.7, compared with the White average of 101.8. Black children living in the North or in metropolitan areas of the South do perform better on intelligence tests, obtaining an average IQ of about 85–88. Nevertheless, they continue to score some 12–15 IQ points lower than their White age mates (Loehlin, Lindzey, & Spuhler, 1975).

Before we try to interpret these social-class, racial, and ethnic differences, an important truth is worth stating here—one that is often overlooked when people discover that White and Asian-American children outperform their Black or Hispanic classmates on IQ tests. This "important truth" is that we cannot predict anything about the IQ or the future accomplishments of an *individual* on the basis of his ethnicity or color. As we see in Figure 10-4, the IQ distributions show considerable overlap between the Black and White samples. So even though the average IQ of Blacks is somewhat lower than that of Whites, the overlapping distributions mean that many Black children obtain higher IQ scores than many White children. In fact, approximately 15–25% of the Black population scores higher—in many cases, substantially higher—than *half* of the White population (Shuey, 1966).

Why Do Groups Differ in Intellectual Performance?

Over the years, psychologists have proposed three hypotheses to account for racial, ethnic, and social-class differences in IQ: (1) a *test bias* hypothesis, that standardized IQ tests do not adequately measure the intellectual capabilities of lower-class children or those from minority subcultures; (2) a *genetic* hypothesis, that group differences in IQ are hereditary; and (3) an *environmental* hypothesis, that the groups scoring lower in IQ come from culturally deprived backgrounds—that is, neighborhoods and home environments that are far less conducive to intellectual growth than those typically experienced by members of the middle class.

The test bias hypothesis

Those who favor the **"test bias" hypothesis** believe that group differences in IQ are an artifact of

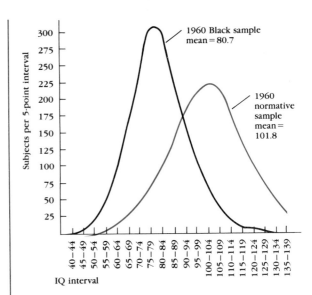

Figure 10-4. IQ distributions on the Stanford-Binet for the 1960 normative sample of White schoolchildren and for 1800 Black schoolchildren living in the Southeast. *(Adapted from Kennedy, van de Reit, & White, 1963.)*

our testing procedures. To illustrate, they point out that IQ tests currently in use were designed to measure cognitive skills (for example, assembling puzzles), general information (for example, "What is a 747?"), and cultural values (for example, "What do you do if another boy hits you?"; correct answer: Say "That's all right; it was probably accidental") that White, middle-class children are more likely to have acquired. They note that subtests measuring vocabulary and word usage may be harder for Blacks and Hispanics, who often speak a different English dialect from that of the White middle class. Not only might these children be working under a linguistic handicap while trying to understand the test instructions, but many common words do not even have the same meanings for Blacks and Hispanics as for Whites. Adrian Dove, a Black sociologist, has attempted to illustrate the kinds of biases that minority children encounter on IQ tests by constructing his own humorous ex-

---

confluence hypothesis: Zajonc's notion that a child's intellectual development depends on the average intellectual level of all family members.

"test bias" hypothesis: the notion that IQ tests have a built-in, middle-class bias that explains the substandard performance of children from lower-class and minority subcultures.

ample of a "culturally biased" test—one that relies very heavily on the language and experiences of American Blacks (see Table 10-7). If this test were to be interpreted as a valid measure of intellectual performance, the average Black would undoubtedly obtain a higher IQ score than most Whites.

Does "test bias" explain group differences in IQ? Even though standardized intelligence tests have a distinct middle-class flavor, there are reasons to believe that group differences in IQ are not solely attributable to test bias. Several attempts have now been made to construct **"culture fair" IQ tests** that do not place poor people or those from minority subcultures at an immediate disadvantage. For example, the *Raven Progressive Matrices Test* requires the examinee to scan a series of abstract designs, each of which has a missing section. The examinee's task is to complete each design by selecting the appropriate section from a number of alternatives (see Figure 10-5). These problems are assumed to be equally familiar (or unfamiliar) to people from all ethnic groups and social classes. There is no time limit on the test, and the instructions are very simple. But despite such attempts to eliminate cultural bias from the test content, middle-class Whites continue to outperform their lower-class and/or Black age mates

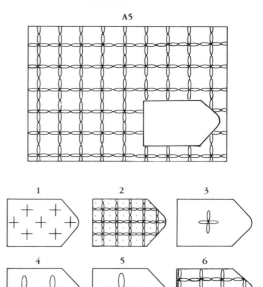

Figure 10-5. An item similar to those appearing in the Raven Progressive Matrices Test.

on these "culture fair" measures of intelligence (Jensen, 1980). Translating existing tests into the Black English dialect spoken by urban Black children also does not appear to increase the scores that these children make (Quay, 1971). And finally, IQ tests and various tests of intellectual aptitude (such as the Scholastic Aptitude Test) predict future academic successes just as well for Blacks and other minorities as for Whites (Cole, 1981; Oakland & Parmelee, 1985; Reynolds & Kaufman, 1985). Taken together, these observations imply that group differences in IQ are not entirely the result of biases in our tests and testing procedures.

Zigler's motivational hypothesis. Edward Zigler and his associates (Zigler, Abelson, Trickett, & Seitz, 1982) believe that social-class and ethnic differences in IQ are due largely to motivational factors. Presumably, lower-class and minority children score lower than they should in IQ tests because they tend to be wary of strange examiners and see little point in trying to do well on abstract and seemingly irrelevant test items—particularly if they have a history of academic failure and are anxious in testing situations.

Attempts to increase the motivation of these children by first allowing them time to play with a friendly examiner (or by mixing easy items with the harder ones

Table 10-7. Sample items from Dove's Counterbalance General "Intelligence" Test (the "Chitling Test")

1. Cheap chitlings (not the kind you purchase at a frozen food counter) will taste rubbery unless they are cooked long enough. How soon can you quit cooking them to eat and enjoy them? (A) 45 minutes, (B) 2 hours, (C) 24 hours, (D) one week (on a low flame), (E) 1 hour

2. A "handkerchief head" is: (A) a cool cat, (B) a porter, (C) an Uncle Tom, (D) a preacher

3. A "gas head" is a person who has a: (A) fast-moving car, (B) stable of "lace," (C) "process," (D) habit of stealing cars, (E) long jail record for arson

4. "Hully Gully" came from: (A) East Oakland, (B) Fillmore, (C) Watts, (D) Harlem, (E) Motor City

5. If you throw the dice and a seven is showing on the top, what is facing down? (A) seven, (B) snake eyes, (C) boxcars, (D) little Joes, (E) eleven

6. T-Bone Walker got famous for playing what? (A) trombone, (B) piano, (C) "T-flute," (D) guitar, (E) "Hambone"

Source: Adapted from Dove (1968).

Correct answers: 1, C; 2, C; 3, C; 4, C; 5, A; 6, D. How did you do on this test?

to prevent examinees from becoming discouraged by a long string of errors) have a clear effect on test performance: disadvantaged children score some 7–10 points higher than they normally would when tested in the traditional way by a strange examiner (Zigler et al., 1982; Zigler & Butterfield, 1968). However, middle-class youngsters also score higher on IQ tests when tested by a friendly examiner (Sacks, 1952). Since *all* children perform better when taking IQ tests under optimal conditions, there is some question whether Zigler's motivational hypothesis is a totally adequate explanation for group *differences* in IQ. Still, it may have some merit.

The genetic hypothesis

By far the most controversial explanation for group differences in intelligence is that they are hereditary. Those who favor the **genetic hypothesis** note that members of various social-class, ethnic, and racial groups tend to marry within their own populations rather than mating with outsiders. Although this selective mating is obviously not universal, it will nevertheless result in a restriction in the gene flow between subgroups if it continues over many generations. In other words, the argument is that people in various racial, ethnic, and social-class groupings have genotypes drawn from different gene pools. Presumably these gene pools differ in the frequency and distribution of the genes that affect mental performance.

Perhaps the strongest proponent of this genetic interpretation is Arthur Jensen of the University of California (Jensen, 1969, 1980). Jensen believes that there are two kinds of intellectual abilities, which are equally heritable within different subgroups of the population. **Level I abilities** include attentional processes, short-term memory, and associative skills—abilities that are important for simple kinds of rote learning. **Level II abilities** are those that allow one to reason abstractly and to manipulate words and symbols to form concepts and solve problems. According to Jensen, Level II abilities are highly correlated with school achievement, while Level I abilities are not. Of course, it is predominantly Level II abilities that are measured on IQ tests.

Jensen finds that Level I tasks are performed equally well by children from all races, ethnic groups, and social classes. However, middle-class and White children outperform lower-class and Black children on the more advanced Level II tasks. Since Level I and Level II tasks are equally heritable *within* each social class and ethnic group, Jensen proposes that the IQ differences *between* groups must be hereditary.

Criticisms of the genetic hypothesis.

Although Jensen's arguments may sound convincing, there are reasons to believe that genetic influences do not explain group differences in IQ. For example, Jensen's critics have noted that within-group heritability estimates imply absolutely nothing about between-group variability in an attribute (Layzer, 1972; Lewontin, 1976). As we see in Box 10-3, it is possible for individual differences *within* a group to be entirely genetic in character while differences *between* two groups are largely the result of the environments in which they are raised.

Now let's consider the idea that, owing to selective mating, members of different groups come from populations that differ in the frequency and distribution of IQ-determining genes. If this were true, we would have to assume that groups scoring low on IQ tests have fewer of these "smart genes" in their gene pool than groups that score high. Therefore, if members of a low-scoring group, such as Blacks, were to mate with members of a high-scoring group, such as Whites, the children they produce should inherit an intermediate number of IQ-determining genes and score somewhere between the Black and the White norms on IQ tests.

Data available on mixed-race children provide little support for the genetic hypothesis. Eyferth (as cited in Loehlin et al., 1975) obtained the IQ scores of illegitimate German children fathered by Black American servicemen. These mixed-race children were then compared with a group of illegitimate White children of the same age and social background. Clearly, the mixed-race group should have scored lower than their White age mates if their Black fathers had had fewer IQ-determining genes to pass along to them. However, Eyferth found that these two groups of illegitimate children did not differ in IQ.

If the genetic hypothesis were correct, we might also predict that Blacks who score extremely high on

---

"culture fair" tests: intelligence tests constructed to minimize any irrelevant cultural biases that could influence test performance.

genetic hypothesis: the notion that group differences in IQ are hereditary.

Level I abilities: Jensen's term for lower-level intellectual abilities (such as attention and short-term memory) that are important for simple association learning.

Level II abilities: Jensen's term for higher-level cognitive skills that are involved in abstract reasoning and problem solving.

Box 10-3
Why Heritability Estimates Do Not
Explain Group Differences in IQ

Let's suppose that a group of White children obtain an average IQ of 101 and their Black classmates average 87 on the same test. Further, we will assume that the heritability estimates for the Black and the White populations are comparable. Jensen might use these data to argue that the 14-point difference in IQ between the White and the Black children is attributable to the genetic differences between Blacks and Whites. On the surface, this reasoning seems to make sense because IQ is equally heritable within each group.

However, the argument is flawed. Let's recall that heritability is the amount of variation in a trait that is attributable to genetic factors. If two groups have comparable heritability estimates for a trait, this simply means that, *within* each group, the amount of variability on that trait that is attributable to genetic factors is approximately the same. It says nothing about any differences *between* the groups on that trait.

An example should clarify the point. Suppose a farmer randomly draws corn seed from a bag containing several genetic varieties. He then plants half the seed in a barren field and half in soil that is quite fertile. When the plants are fully grown, the farmer discovers that those *within* each field have grown to different heights. Since all plants within each field were grown in the same soil, their different heights reflect the genetic variability among the seeds that were planted. Therefore, the heritability estimates for plants within each plot should be very high. But notice that the plants grown in the fertile soil are taller, on the average, than those grown in the barren soil. The most logical explanation for this *between-field variation* is an environmental one: plants grown in fertile soil simply grew taller than those grown in barren soil, and this is true even though the heritability estimates for the heights of the plants *within* each field are comparable (Lewontin, 1976).

The same argument can be applied in explaining group differences in intellectual performance. Even though the heritability estimates for IQ are comparable *within* our samples of Black and White schoolchildren, the 14-point difference in average IQ *between* the groups may reflect differences in the home environments of Blacks and Whites rather than a genetic difference between the races.

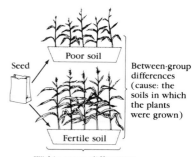

Poor soil

Seed

Fertile soil

Between-group differences (cause: the soils in which the plants were grown)

Within-group differences (cause: genetic variation in the seeds)

Why within-group differences do not necessarily imply anything about between-group differences. Here we see that the difference in the heights of the plants *within* each field reflects the genetic variation in the seeds that were planted there, whereas the difference in the *average* heights of the plants across the fields is attributable to an environmental factor—the soils in which they were grown.

IQ tests would have a higher percentage of White ancestors than would Blacks who obtain lower IQs. Yet, at least one study of extremely bright Black children found that these youngsters had no more White ancestors than is typical for the Black population as a whole (Witty & Jenkins, 1936).

Although studies of mixed-race children do not support the genetic hypothesis, neither do they disprove it. Consider, for example, that Eyferth had no data on the IQs of the Black servicemen who had fathered mixed-race children. So if these men were brighter than the average Black American, the genetic hypothesis predicts that their children would score much higher on IQ tests than mixed-race children normally do—perhaps even high enough to match the IQs of the illegitimate White children. But regardless of how we choose to interpret the results of Eyferth's study, it is worth noting that there is simply no evidence that conclusively demonstrates that *group differences* in IQ are genetically determined.

The environmental hypothesis

A third explanation for group differences in IQ is the **environmental hypothesis**—that poor people and members of various minority groups tend to grow up in environments that are much less conducive to intellectual development than those experienced by most Whites and other members of the middle class. As we saw in Chapter 5, many children from low-income families are undernourished—a circumstance that may inhibit brain growth and make them somewhat listless and inattentive. Moreover, low-income parents are often poorly educated and may have neither the time nor the money to provide an intellectually stimulating home environment for their children, particularly if they have several youngsters to feed, clothe, and care for (Gottfried, 1984). Poor people and ethnic minorities are often the targets of prejudicial and discriminatory acts that may contribute to a negative self-image and undermine their motivation to do well on tests, including IQ tests. In fact, many teachers (and some parents) expect their lower-class and minority children to perform poorly at school, and as we will see in Chapter 16, these negative expectations do seem to inhibit the intellectual performance of students from disadvantaged backgrounds.

One implication of the environmental hypothesis is that disadvantaged children who score low on IQ tests should begin to show some improvement if their environments change for the better. Indeed, E. S. Lee (1951) found a steady improvement in the IQ scores of Black schoolchildren who had migrated from the rural South, and its then substandard, segregated school systems, to Philadelphia. The longer these youngsters spent in the more stimulating, urban Northern schools, the more their IQs increased.

And what happens to children from disadvantaged backgrounds who grow up in middle-class homes? Sandra Scarr and Richard Weinberg (1976, 1977, 1983) have studied 99 Black (or interracial) children who were adopted during the first year of life by White, middle-class families. The adoptive parents in these families were above average in IQ and highly educated, and many had biological children of their own. Although Scarr and Weinberg found that the Black children averaged about 6 points lower on IQ tests than the White offspring of these same families, this small racial difference seems rather insignificant when we look at the absolute performance of the transracial adoptees. As a group, the Black adoptees obtained an average IQ of 110—10 points above the average for the population as a whole and 20 points above comparable children who are raised in the Black community. Moreover, the Black adoptees from these middle-class families were also scoring well above the national average on standardized achievement tests at school. Scarr and Weinberg (1983) concluded that

> the high IQ scores for the black and interracial children ... mean that (a) genetic differences do not account for a major portion of the IQ performance difference between racial groups, and (b) black and interracial children reared in the [middle class] culture of the tests and the schools perform as well as other adopted children in similar families [p. 261].

Recently, Elsie Moore (1986) has extended Scarr and Weinberg's research by comparing Black children adopted into middle-class White homes with similar Black children adopted into middle-class Black homes. Both these groups of Black adoptees obtained above-average IQs when they were tested at age 7 to 10. But even though the two groups were from the same social class, Black children in White homes had an average IQ of 117, whereas the average IQ of adoptees in Black homes was only 104. Why should this be?

Moore tried to find out by carefully observing the children during the session in which the IQ test was administered and by noting how their mothers interacted with them as the children tried to perform a difficult cognitive task. What she found was what she believes to be subcultural differences in parenting and in test taking, even within the same social class. For example, the children who had been placed into White homes seemed to enjoy the IQ testing session more than their counterparts from Black homes did: they were more eager to answer questions; they persisted longer at the tasks; they more often elaborated on their reasons for answering as they did; and they seemed much more confident. By contrast, children from Black homes often seemed to want to escape from the testing situation, and they sometimes shook their heads, as if to say that they didn't know an answer, even before a question was completed. These styles of test taking seemed to be linked to the parenting practices that mothers used while supervising their children's problem-solving activities. Compared with the Black mothers, White mothers provided a great deal of positive encouragement. They joked to relieve tension and even cheered and applauded when their children made some progress. However, Black mothers were more inclined to urge their children onward by showing signs of mild displeasure at a child's *lack of progress* (for example, "You could do better at this if you really tried!"), and their evaluations of their children's accomplishments were somewhat more negative than those of White mothers. Perhaps this is why their children were less comfortable during the IQ testing session than children of White mothers were.

In sum, Moore's (1986) findings suggest that even when children of different racial and ethnic groups all grow up in advantaged homes, there may still be

---

environmental hypothesis: the notion that groups differ in IQ because the environments in which they are raised are not equally conducive to intellectual growth.

subtle subcultural differences in parenting styles that contribute to group differences in IQ.

Let's note, however, that neither Scarr and Weinberg nor Elsie Moore is suggesting that White parents are better parents or that disadvantaged children would be "better off" if they were routinely placed in middle-class homes. Indeed, Scarr and Weinberg (1976) stress that

> our emphasis on IQ scores ... is not an endorsement of IQ as the ultimate human value. Although important for functioning in middle-class educational environments, IQ tests do not sample a huge spectrum of human characteristics that are requisite for social adjustment. Empathy, sociability, and altruism, to name a few, are important human attributes that are not guaranteed by a high IQ. Furthermore, successful adaptation within ethnic subgroups may be less dependent on the intellectual skills tapped by IQ measures than is adaptation in middle-class white settings [p. 739].

And even if we psychologists and educators were to assume that a high IQ is the ultimate human attribute, it would obviously be impractical (not to mention morally objectionable) to recommend that disadvantaged youths be taken from their parents and placed in more stimulating adoptive homes. However, there are other, less objectionable strategies that researchers have used to supplement the life experiences of disadvantaged children in the hope of furthering their intellectual and academic accomplishments. In our next section, we will take a closer look at these cognitive interventions and attempts at compensatory education.

Improving Intellectual Performance through Compensatory Education

During the 1960s a number of preschool educational programs were implemented in an attempt to enrich the learning experiences of disadvantaged children. Project Head Start is perhaps the best known of these **compensatory interventions.** Simply stated, the goal of **Head Start** (and similar programs) was to provide disadvantaged children with the kinds of educational experiences that middle-class youngsters were presumably getting in their homes and nursery school classrooms. It was hoped that these early interventions would compensate for the disadvantages that these chil-

dren may have already experienced and place them on a roughly equal footing with their middle-class age mates by the time they entered first grade.

The earliest reports suggested that Head Start and comparable programs were a smashing success. Children participating in compensatory education were posting an average gain of about 10 points on IQ tests, whereas the IQs of nonparticipants from similar social backgrounds remained unchanged. However, this initial optimism soon began to wane. When program participants were reexamined after completing a year or two of grade school, the gains they had made on IQ tests had largely disappeared (Bronfenbrenner, 1975; Gray & Klaus, 1970; Klaus & Gray, 1968). In other words, few if any lasting intellectual benefits seemed to be associated with these interventions—a finding that led Arthur Jensen (1969, p. 2) to conclude that "compensatory education has been tried and it apparently has failed."

However, many investigators were reluctant to accept Jensen's conclusions. They felt that it was short-sighted to place so much emphasis on IQ scores as an index of program effectiveness. After all, the ultimate goal of compensatory education is not so much to boost IQ as to improve children's academic performance. Others have argued that the impact of these early interventions might be cumulative, so that it may be several years before children who have participated in compensatory education begin to outperform their disadvantaged classmates who did not participate.

Long-Term Follow-ups

As it turns out, Jensen's critics may have been right on both counts. In 1982 Irving Lazar and Richard Darlington reported on the long-term effects of 11 early intervention programs implemented during the 1960s. The program participants were disadvantaged preschool children from several areas of the United States. At regular intervals throughout the grade school years, the investigators examined the participants' scholastic records and administered IQ and achievement tests. The participants and their mothers were also interviewed to determine the children's feelings of self-worth, attitudes about school and scholastic achievement, and vocational aspirations, as well as the mothers' aspirations for their children and their feelings about the children's progress at school. A very similar follow-up of Head Start participants is currently underway, and some preliminary results are now available (Collins, 1983). Briefly, these long-term follow-ups indicate the following:

1. Children who participate in early intervention programs show immediate gains on IQ tests and other indicators of cognitive development, whereas nonparticipants from similar social backgrounds do not. Although the cognitive gains may persist for three to four years after the program has ended, participants and nonparticipants do not differ in IQ by the time they reach junior high school.

2. Program participants tend to score somewhat higher than nonparticipants on tests of reading, language, and mathematics achievement. In addition, there is some evidence that the "achievement gap" between participants and nonparticipants widens between the first and the eighth grades.

3. Program participants are more likely to meet their school's basic requirements. In other words, they are less likely to be assigned to special education classes or to be retained in grade than their low-income classmates who did not participate in compensatory education. Program participants are also less likely than nonparticipants to drop out of high school.

4. Compensatory education seems to have long-term effects on children's attitudes about achievement. When asked to name something they have done that has made them feel proud of themselves, program participants are more likely than nonparticipants to mention their scholastic or (in the case of 15–18-year-olds) job-related successes.

5. Finally, compensatory education seems to affect maternal attitudes. Mothers of program participants are more satisfied with their children's school performance and hold higher occupational aspirations for their children than mothers of nonparticipants.

In sum, the longitudinal evaluations suggest that compensatory education has been tried and *apparently it works!* Although these programs rarely produce long-term gains in IQ, they clearly foster positive attitudes about achievement and improve children's chances of succeeding in the classroom. In fact, the lasting educational benefits of these early interventions were sufficiently impressive to persuade the Reagan administration to stand behind and continue to fund compensatory education during the early 1980s, an era of severe cutbacks in other social programs (Collins, 1983).

Importance of Parental Involvement

Some of the most successful of all the interventions are those that begin rather early and take place in the home so that parents are involved in the child's learning experiences. One notable example of these **home-based interventions** is Phyllis Levenstein's (1970) "toy demonstration" program. Levenstein worked with disadvantaged 2-year-olds and their mothers. About twice a week, members of Levenstein's research team visited participants' homes to deliver various educational toys and books. During these half-hour visits, the researcher showed the mother how to use these materials to stimulate her child. Children who took part gained an average of 17 IQ points during the seven months that the program was in effect, whereas disadvantaged "nonparticipants" showed no changes in IQ over the same period. And was this merely a temporary gain? Apparently not, for follow-up evaluations conducted during the fourth, fifth, and sixth grades revealed that Levenstein's program participants were still outperforming the disadvantaged nonparticipants on measures of IQ and academic achievement (see Lazar & Darlington, 1982).

An important advantage of a home-based intervention is that parents who become more competent at stimulating their children may continue to provide intellectually stimulating experiences long after the program formally ends. Indeed, this may be the reason that participants in Levenstein's project showed *long-term* gains in IQ. It may also explain why the younger brothers and sisters of program participants often benefit from home-based enrichment programs (Bronfenbrenner, 1975; Madden, Levenstein, & Levenstein, 1976).

Parental involvement also seems to be important to the success of interventions that begin later in the preschool period and take place in nursery school or kindergarten settings. Joan Sprigle and Lyn Schaefer (1985) have recently evaluated the long-term benefits of two such programs: *Head Start* (planned and administered by teachers and policy advisory councils) and *Learning to learn*—an intervention that educated par-

---

compensatory interventions: special educational programs designed to further the cognitive growth and scholastic achievements of disadvantaged children.

Head Start: a large-scale preschool educational program designed to provide children from low-income families with a variety of social and intellectual experiences that might better prepare them for school.

home-based interventions: compensatory interventions that take place in the home and involve one or more family members in the child's learning experiences.

Photo 10-3. Because of parental involvement, home-based interventions are among the most successful compensatory programs.

ents about the goals of the program, provided them with information about their children's progress, and repeatedly emphasized that a partnership between home and school was necessary to ensure the program's success. When the disadvantaged students who had participated in these interventions were later observed in the fourth, fifth, and sixth grades, the outcomes consistently favored the Learning to learn (LTL) program, in which parents had been heavily involved. Although LTL students did not necessarily outperform those from Head Start on IQ tests, they were making better grades in basic academic subjects (such as reading) and were less likely to have failed a grade in school or to have been placed in costly special education classes for the learning-disabled. And even though these two programs differed in ways other than degree of parental involvement, Sprigle and Schaefer believe that the greater participation of LTL parents in their children's learning activities at home contributed substantially to the success of this particular intervention.

Limitations of Compensatory Education and Implications for the Future

Now let's note what compensatory education has failed to accomplish. To date, none of these interventions has succeeded in transforming a disadvantaged population into a group of "high achievers" who score significantly above average in IQ or scholastic aptitude.

The more typical finding is that children who take part in an enrichment program will continue to score 5–15 points below the national average on IQ tests and somewhat below their grade level on measures of academic achievement (Ramey, 1982). But even though these interventions do not place program participants at the same intellectual level as their middle-class age mates, they do serve a critically important function by helping to prevent the progressive decline in IQ and academic achievement so often observed among children from disadvantaged backgrounds.

Can we ever expect to do better than this in the future? The results of Scarr and Weinberg's transracial adoption study certainly provide some hope. Yet, it is important to note that Scarr and Weinberg's adoptees may have fared so well because their enriching experiences *began very early and continued on a daily basis over a period of several years.* By contrast, a formal intervention that lasts but a few hours a week for a year or two at most is probably far too limited in scope to achieve such favorable outcomes.

Some very early and elaborate interventions have now been attempted, and the results are encouraging. In the Carolina Abecedarian Project, for example, program participants were selected from families considered to be "at risk" for producing mildly retarded children. These families were all on welfare, and most were headed by a single parent, the mother, who had scored well below average on a standardized IQ test (obtaining IQs of 70–85). The project began when the participating children were only 6 to 12 *weeks* old, and it continued for the next five years. Half of the high-risk children took part in a special day-care program designed to promote their intellectual development. The program was truly a full-time endeavor, running from 7:15 A.M. to 5:15 P.M., five days a week for 50 weeks each year. The remaining children received exactly the same dietary supplements, social services, and pediatric care given to their age mates in the experimental group, but they did not attend day care. At regular intervals over the next five years, the progress of these two groups of "high risk" children was assessed by administering the Bayley Scales of Infant Development and standardized IQ tests (Ramey, Bryant, & Suarez, 1985). Figure 10-6 summarizes the IQ data. Notice that the average IQ of children attending day care was at or slightly above the national average of 100 from age 3 onward, whereas children in the control group scored some 6–17 points below the national average over this same period. Ap-

parently, intensive interventions that continue over a period of years can have a very positive effect on the intellectual performance of disadvantaged children. And even if these gains in IQ should prove to be temporary, the results of previous studies imply that the day-care "graduates" are likely to experience much better educational outcomes in the years ahead than their age mates in the control group.

Interventions such as the Abecedarian Project are expensive to administer, and there are those who wonder whether these programs would be worth their staggering costs if we were to provide them to all disadvantaged children. However, such an attitude may be "penny-wise and pound-foolish," for Victoria Seitz and her associates found that extensive family interventions emphasizing quality day care often pay for themselves by (1) allowing more parents to get away from full-time child care to work, thereby reducing their need for public assistance, and (2) providing the foundation for cognitive growth that enables most disadvantaged children to avoid special education in school—a service that costs in excess of $1500 per pupil per year (Seitz, Rosenbaum, & Apfel, 1985). Currently, we are a long way from routinely providing the kinds of support that disadvantaged children need to improve their intellectual and academic performance (indeed, some states in the United States don't even have statewide kindergarten programs)—and the failure of earlier interventions to produce long-term gains in IQ may be one reason that such support is not more widespread (Jensen, 1981). But not only is IQ a questionable yardstick against which to gauge the success of these programs, our recent experiences with compensatory education suggest that *long-term* interventions, emphasizing both active and continuous *parental* support and quality preschool education, would almost certainly produce more favorable outcomes than the piecemeal interventions of the past.

Some Common Uses and Abuses of IQ Tests

Schools are by far the biggest users of intelligence tests. Most American children take one or more IQ tests during grade school, and their scores are generally kept on file and made readily available to teachers and counselors (Brody & Brody, 1976). Traditionally, this information has been used to identify youngsters who may have difficulties in the classroom and to sort and classify students according to their presumed intel-

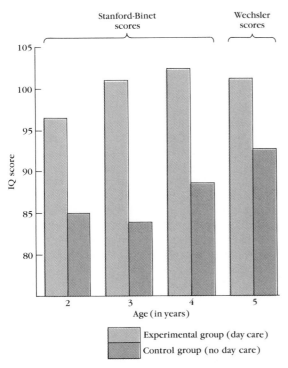

Figure 10-6. Average IQs of disadvantaged children who took part in the Abecedarian Project. *(Adapted from Ramey, Bryant, & Suarez, 1985.)*

lectual abilities. As we will see, both these uses of IQ tests have the potential for serious abuse.

The diagnostic function.   IQ tests are often used as a diagnostic tool to identify children who may have problems at school or to explain why slow learners are performing so poorly in the classroom. For example, a lackadaisical first-grader who obtains an IQ of 70 might be considered mildly retarded and a candidate for special education. However, a marginal student who obtains an IQ of 125 would seem to have some sort of motivational or emotional problem that is undermining her academic performance, and no one would recommend placing her in classes for the mentally retarded.

The sorting function.   A related use of IQ tests is to sort children into relatively homogeneous groups on the basis of their presumed mental abilities. It is often assumed that students will learn best when surrounded by classmates of comparable intellect. And since IQ scores seem to predict later academic and vocational accomplishments, it is not at all unusual for school systems to use IQ tests to channel students into the curricula for which they are presumably "best suited"—college preparatory courses for the bright children and vocational training for those who are not so bright.

Problems and pitfalls.   Perhaps you can see some of the problems involved in relying on IQ tests to diagnose, sort, and classify children. Many educators (and some school psychologists) have erroneously assumed that an IQ score reflects a relatively permanent intellectual *capacity* rather than an index of mental *performance* that may fluctuate widely over the course of childhood (Brody & Brody, 1976). If a 7-year-old boy were to obtain an IQ of 70, people would be apt to conclude that the child had a definite *lack* of ability. They might then characterize him as mildly "retarded"—a label that could follow the child throughout life and effectively bar the doors to any number of academic or vocational opportunities.

Surely many youngsters who score 70 on an IQ test are mildly retarded. But as it turns out, a low IQ merely reflects a *performance* deficit that may be caused by motivational and emotional problems or other physically based but treatable learning disabilities—factors that IQ tests are hardly designed to detect (Brody & Brody, 1976; Scarr, 1981). The implications for educa-

tional policy are clear: in the absence of other diagnostic information that points in the same direction, a low IQ score is not sufficient justification for labeling a child "retarded" or placing her in special classes.

Many of the same arguments can be made against the practice of using IQ tests to sort children into "ability groups." As we will see in Chapter 16, grade school students do not seem to learn any better or faster when surrounded by classmates who obtain similar IQs. And even if they did, many of those children whose IQs fluctuate by 20–40 points over the grade school years would undoubtedly end up in the wrong "ability" groups. Ability grouping by IQ may also have some unintended but harmful effects on children who are "correctly" classified. For example, students of average intelligence may be discouraged by their classification (or their counselors) from attempting college preparatory curricula that they are perfectly capable of mastering—particularly if they are highly motivated to do so. Moreover, children who are placed in the lower ability groups often develop negative attitudes toward themselves and school (Rutter, 1983). And when we recall that IQ scores often fail to predict the future accomplishments of *any particular individual,* we have to wonder whether intelligence tests are at all useful for sorting students into groups or channeling them into various educational curricula.

In sum, an IQ score is a potentially useful piece of information that, *when considered along with many other pieces of information,* can help to specify the causes of certain learning difficulties. But it is important to recognize that an intelligence quotient is merely an estimate of the child's intellectual performance at *one point in time*—an index that, *by itself,* tells us very little about what that child is capable of accomplishing in the years ahead. Indeed, even the educable mentally retarded usually blend into the general population after leaving school, and their later successes in life depend more on their social adjustment and motivation to succeed than on their tested mental abilities (Ross, Begab, Dondis, Giampiccolo, & Meyers, 1985; Scarr, 1981).

Summary

The psychometric, or testing, approach defines intelligence as a trait (or set of traits) that allows some people to think and solve problems more effectively than others. Relying on the factor-analytic proce-

Photo 10-4. When considered along with other pieces of information, IQ scores can be useful diagnostic tools.

dure, theorists such as Spearman, Thurstone, and Guilford have disagreed about the nature, or structure, of intellect, although almost everyone agrees that intelligence is not merely a singular attribute that determines how well people perform on *all* cognitive tasks. Robert Sternberg's recent triarchic theory criticizes psychometric theories of intelligence for their failure to consider the *contexts* in which intelligent acts are displayed, the test taker's *experience* with test items, and the *information-processing strategies* on which people rely when thinking or solving problems.

The first intelligence tests were designed to predict children's academic performance and to identify slow learners who might profit from special education. Today there are literally hundreds of intelligence tests, and instruments such as the Stanford-Binet and the Wechsler scales are widely respected and heavily used. Intelligence tests differ considerably in format and content, but most of them present the examinee with a variety of cognitive tasks and then evaluate his or her performance by comparing it with the average performance of age mates. An examinee whose performance equals that of the average age mate is assigned an in-

telligence quotient (IQ) of 100. An IQ greater than 100 indicates that the child's performance is superior to that of other children her age; an IQ less than 100 means that the child's intellectual performance is below that of a typical age mate.

IQ is a relatively stable attribute for some individuals. However, many others will show wide variations in their IQ scores over the course of childhood. The fact that IQ can wander upward or downward over time suggests that IQ tests are measuring intellectual *performance* rather than an inborn capacity for thinking and problem solving.

When we consider trends for the population as a whole, IQ scores seem to predict important outcomes such as future academic accomplishments, occupational status, and even health and happiness. However, a closer examination of individual profiles suggests that an IQ score is not always a reliable indicator of one's future health, happiness, or success. Many people with very high IQs are not very prosperous or well adjusted, while other people of average or below-average intelligence are happy, healthy, and highly successful. So a high IQ, by itself, does not guarantee success. Other factors such as one's work habits and motivation to succeed are also important contributors.

Both hereditary and environmental forces contribute heavily to intellectual performance. The evidence from family studies and studies of adopted children indicates that about half the variation among individuals in IQ is attributable to hereditary factors. But regardless of one's genetic predispositions, barren intellectual environments clearly inhibit cognitive growth, while enriched, intellectually stimulating environments can have the opposite effect.

Parents who provide a stimulating home environment by becoming involved in their child's learning activities, carefully explaining new concepts, furnishing toys that are age appropriate, and consistently encouraging the child to achieve are likely to have children who score high on IQ tests. Two other family characteristics that affect intellectual performance are family size and birth order: first-borns and children from smaller families tend to obtain slightly higher IQs than later-borns and children from large families.

On the average, children from lower-class and minority backgrounds score lower on IQ tests than White children and other members of the middle class. Apparently these group differences in IQ are not merely an artifact of our tests and testing procedures. Nor is there any conclusive evidence that they result from genetic differences among the various social-class, racial, and ethnic groups. Perhaps the best explanation for group differences in IQ is the environmental hypothesis: many poor people and minority group members score lower on IQ tests because they grow up in impoverished environments that are much less conducive to intellectual development than those of their middle-class age mates.

Several enrichment programs for disadvantaged preschoolers have now been evaluated. Although these early interventions do not produce dramatic long-term gains in IQ, they do improve children's chances of succeeding in the classroom, and they help to prevent the progressive decline in intellectual performance so often observed among students from disadvantaged backgrounds.

When considered along with other pieces of information, IQ scores can be of some assistance in diagnosing learning difficulties or in making predictions about future scholastic achievements. However, IQ is a measure of intellectual performance rather than intellectual capacity—a measure that, by itself, tells us very little about what any particular individual is likely to accomplish in the years ahead.

References

ASCHER, E. J. (1935). The inadequacy of current intelligence tests for testing Kentucky mountain children. *Journal of Genetic Psychology, 46,* 480–486.

BAYLEY, N. (1969). *Bayley Scales of Infant Development.* New York: Psychological Corporation.

BECKWITH, L., & Parmelee, A. H., Jr. (1986). EEG patterns of preterm infants, home environment, and later IQ. *Child Development, 57,* 777–789.

BEE, H. L., Barnard, K. E., Eyres, S. J., Gray, C. A., Hammond, M. A., Spietz, A. L., Snyder, C., & Clark, B. (1982). Prediction of IQ and language skill from perinatal status, child performance, family characteristics, and mother-infant interaction. *Child Development, 53,* 1134–1156.

BELMONT, L., & Marolla, F. A. (1973). Birth order, family size, and intelligence. *Science, 182,* 1096–1101.

BERBAUM, M. L., & Moreland, R. L. (1980). Intellectual development within the family: A new application of the confluence model. *Developmental Psychology, 16,* 506–518.

BORNSTEIN, M. H., & Sigman, M. D. (1986). Continuity in mental development from infancy. *Child Development, 57,* 251–274.

BRACKBILL, Y., & Nichols, P. L. (1982). A test of the confluence model of intellectual development. *Developmental Psychology, 18,* 192–198.

BRADLEY, R. H., & Caldwell, B. M. (1976). Early home environment and changes in mental test performance in children from 6 to 36 months. *Developmental Psychology, 12,* 93–97.

BRADLEY, R. H., & Caldwell, B. M. (1984a). 174 children: A study of the relationship between home environment and cognitive development during the first 5 years. In A. W. Gottfried (Ed.), *Home environment and early cognitive development: Longitudinal research.* Orlando, FL: Academic Press.

BRADLEY, R. H., & Caldwell, B. M. (1984b). The relation of infants' home environments to achievement test performance in the first grade: A follow-up study. *Child Development, 55,* 803–809.

BRODY, E. B., & Brody, N. (1976). *Intelligence: Nature, determinants, and consequences.* Orlando, FL: Academic Press.

BRONFENBRENNER, U. (1975). Is early intervention effective? Some studies of early education in familial and extrafamilial settings. In A. Montagu (Ed.), *Race and IQ.* New York: Oxford University Press.

BURT, C. (1955). The evidence for the concept of intelligence. *British Journal of Educational Psychology, 25,* 158–177.

CALDWELL, B. M., & Bradley, R. H. (1978). *Manual for the Home Observation for Measurement of the Environment.* Little Rock: University of Arkansas at Little Rock.

CATTELL, R. B. (1963). Theory of fluid and crystallized intelligence: A critical experiment. *Journal of Educational Psychology, 54,* 1–22.

COLE, N. (1981). Bias in testing. *American Psychologist, 36,* 1067–1077.

COLLINS, R. C. (1983, Summer). Head Start: An update on program effects. *Newsletter of the Society for Research in Child Development,* pp. 1–2.

CRANO, W. D., Kenny, J., & Campbell, D. T. (1972). Does intelligence cause achievement? A cross-lagged panel analysis. *Journal of Educational Psychology, 63,* 258–275.

CROCKENBERG, S. (1983). Early mother and infant antecedents of Bayley Scale performance at 21 months. *Developmental Psychology, 19,* 727–730.

DIXON, R. A., Kramer, D. A., & Baltes, P. B. (1985). Intelligence: A life-span developmental perspective. In B. B. Wolman (Ed.), *Handbook of intelligence: Theories, measurements, and applications.* New York: Wiley.

DOVE, A. (1968, July 15). The Chitling test. *Newsweek.*

ESCALONA, S. (1968). *The roots of individuality: Normal patterns of individuality.* Hawthorne, NY: Aldine.

ESTRADA, P., Arsenio, W. F., Hess, R. D., & Holloway, S. D. (1987). Affective quality of the mother-child relationship: Longitudinal consequences for children's school-relevant cognitive functioning. *Developmental Psychology, 23,* 210–215.

FAGAN, J. F. (1985). A new look at infant intelligence. In D. K. Detterman (Ed.), *Current topics in human intelligence.* Vol. 1: *Research methodology.* Norwood, NJ: Ablex.

FEUERSTEIN, R. (1979). *The dynamic assessment of retarded performers: The learning potential assessment device—theory, instruments, and techniques.* Baltimore, MD: University Park Press.

FINCH, F. H. (1946). Enrollment increases and changes in the mental level of the high school population. *Applied Psychology Monographs,* No. 10.

FINCHER, J. (1973). The Terman study is 50 years old: Happy anniversary and pass the ammunition. *Human Behavior, 2,* 8–15.

GALBRAITH, R. C. (1982). Sibling spacing and intellectual development: A closer look at the confluence models. *Developmental Psychology, 18,* 151–173.

GARDNER, H. (1983). *Frames of mind: The theory of multiple intelligences.* New York: Basic Books.

GOLDEN, M., & Birns, B. (1976). Social class and infant intelligence. In M. Lewis (Ed.), *Origins of intelligence: Infancy and early childhood.* New York: Plenum.

GOLDEN, M., Birns, B., Bridger, W., & Moss, A. (1971). Social class differentiation in cognitive development among black preschool children. *Child Development, 42,* 37–46.

GORDON, H. (1923). *Mental and scholastic tests among retarded children* (Pamphlet No. 44). London: Board of Education.

GOTTFRIED, A. W. (1984). Home environment and early cognitive development: Integration, meta-analyses, and conclusions. In A. W. Gottfried (Ed.), *Home environment and early cognitive development: Longitudinal research.* Orlando, FL: Academic Press.

GRAY, S. W., & Klaus, R. A. (1970). The early training project: A seventh-year report. *Child Development, 41,* 909–924.

GROSSMAN, H. J. (1983). *Classification in mental retardation.* Washington, D.C.: American Association on Mental Deficiency.

GUILFORD, J. P. (1967). *The nature of human intelligence.* New York: McGraw-Hill.

HARRELL, T. W., & Harrell, M. S. (1945). Army General Classification Test scores for civilian occupations. *Educational and Psychological Measurement, 5,* 229–239.

HINDLEY, C. B., & Owen, C. F. (1978). The extent of individual changes in IQ for ages between 6 months and 17 years in a British longitudinal sample. *Journal of Child Psychology and Psychiatry, 19,* 329–350.

HONZIK, M. P. (1983). Measuring mental abilities in infancy: The value and limitations. In M. Lewis (Ed.), *Origins of intelligence: Infancy and early childhood* (2nd ed.). New York: Plenum.

HONZIK, M. P., Macfarlane, J. W., & Allen, L. (1948). The stability of mental test performance between two and eighteen years. *Journal of Experimental Education, 17,* 309–324.

HORN, J. L., & Cattell, R. B. (1967). Age differences in fluid and crystallized intelligence. *Acta Psychologica, 26,* 107–129.

HORN, J. L., & Cattell, R. B. (1982). Whimsy and misunderstandings of g_f-g_c theory: A comment on Guilford. *Psychological Bulletin, 91,* 623–633.

HUMPHREYS, L. G., Rich, S. A., & Davey, T. C. (1985). A Piagetian test of general intelligence. *Developmental Psychology, 21,* 872–877.

JANOS, P. M., & Robinson, N. M. (1985). Psychosocial development in intellectually gifted children. In F. D. Horowitz & M. O'Brien (Eds.), *The gifted and talented: Developmental perspectives.* Washington, D.C.: American Psychological Association.

JENSEN, A. R. (1969). How much can we boost IQ and scholastic achievement? *Harvard Educational Review, 39,* 1–123.

JENSEN, A. R. (1977). Cumulative deficit in the IQ of blacks in the rural South. *Developmental Psychology, 13,* 184–191.

JENSEN, A. R. (1980). *Bias in mental testing.* New York: Free Press.

JENSEN, A. R. (1981). Raising the IQ: The Ra-

mey and Haskins study. *Intelligence, 5,* 29–40.

KAUFMAN, A. S., & Kaufman, N. L. (1983). *Kaufman Assessment Battery for Children: Interpretive manual.* Circle Pines, MN: American Guidance Service.

KENNEDY, W. Z., van de Reit, V., & White, J. C. (1963). A normative sample of intelligence and achievement of Negro elementary school children in the Southeastern United States. *Monographs of the Society for Research in Child Development, 28*(6, Serial No. 90).

KLAUS, R. A., & Gray, S. W. (1968). The early training project for disadvantaged children: A report after five years. *Monographs of the Society for Research in Child Development, 33*(4, Serial No. 120).

KLINEBERG, O. (1963). Negro-white differences in intelligence test performance: A new look at an old problem. *American Psychologist, 18,* 198–203.

LABOUVIE-VIEF, G. (1977). Adult cognitive development: In search of alternative interpretations. *Merrill-Palmer Quarterly, 23,* 227–263.

LAYZER, D. (1972). Science or superstition: A physical scientist looks at the IQ controversy. *Cognition, 1,* 265–300.

LAZAR, I., & Darlington, R. (1982). Lasting effects of early education: A report from the Consortium for Longitudinal Studies. *Monographs of the Society for Research in Child Development, 47*(2–3, Serial No. 195).

LEE, E. S. (1951). Negro intelligence and selective migration: A Philadelphia test of the Klineberg hypothesis. *American Sociological Review, 16,* 227–233.

LEVENSTEIN, P. (1970). Cognitive growth in preschoolers through verbal interaction with mothers. *American Journal of Orthopsychiatry, 40,* 426–432.

LEWIS, M., & Michalson, L. (1985). The gifted infant. In J. Freeman (Ed.), *The psychology of gifted children: Perspectives on development and education.* Chichester, England: Wiley.

LEWONTIN, R. C. (1976). Race and intelligence. In N. J. Block & G. Dworkin (Eds.), *The IQ controversy.* New York: Pantheon.

LOEHLIN, J. C., Lindzey, G., & Spuhler, J. N. (1975). *Race differences in intelligence.* New York: W. H. Freeman.

LONGSTRETH, L., Davis, B., Carter, L., Flint, D., Owen, J., Rickert, M., & Taylor, E. (1981). Separation of home intellectual environment and maternal IQ as determinants of child IQ. *Developmental Psychology, 17,* 532–541.

MacPHEE, D., Ramey, C. T., & Yeates, K. O. (1984). Home environment and early cognitive development: Implications for intervention. In A. W. Gottfried (Ed.), *Home environment and early cognitive development: Longitudinal research.* Orlando, FL: Academic Press.

MADDEN, J., Levenstein, P., & Levenstein, S. (1976). Longitudinal IQ outcomes of the mother-child home program. *Child Development, 47*, 1015–1025.

MARKUS, G. B., & Zajonc, R. B. (1977). Family configuration and intellectual development: A simulation. *Behavioral Science, 22*, 137–142.

McCALL, R. B. (1981). Nature-nurture and the two realms of development: A proposed integration with respect to mental development. *Child Development, 55*, 1–12.

McCALL, R. B. (1983). A conceptual approach to early mental development. In M. Lewis (Ed.), *Origins of intelligence: Infancy and early childhood* (2nd ed.). New York: Plenum.

McCALL, R. B., Applebaum, M. I., & Hogarty, P. S. (1973). Developmental changes in mental test performance. *Monographs of the Society for Research in Child Development, 38*(3, Serial No. 150).

MINTON, H. L., & Schneider, F. W. (1980). *Differential psychology.* Pacific Grove, CA: Brooks/Cole.

MOORE, E. G. J. (1986). Family socialization and the IQ test performance of traditionally and transracially adopted black children. *Developmental Psychology, 22*, 317–326.

NEISSER, U. (1980). The concept of intelligence. In R. J. Sternberg & D. K. Detterman (Eds.), *Human intelligence: Perspectives on its theory and measurement.* Norwood, NJ: Ablex.

OAKLAND, T., & Parmelee, R. (1985). Mental measurement of minority-group children. In B. B. Wolman (Ed.), *Handbook of intelligence: Theories, measurements, and applications.* New York: Wiley.

QUAY, L.C. (1971). Language dialect, reinforcement, and the intelligence-test performance of Negro children. *Child Development, 42*, 5–15.

RAMEY, C. T. (1982). In I. Lazar & R. Darlington, Lasting effects of early education: A report from the Consortium for Longitudinal Studies. *Monographs of the Society for Research in Child Development, 47*(2–3, Serial No. 195).

RAMEY, C. T., Bryant, D. M., & Suarez, T. M. (1985). Preschool compensatory education and the modifiability of intelligence: A critical review. In D. K. Detterman (Ed.), *Current topics in human intelligence.* Vol.

1: *Research methodology.* Norwood, NJ: Ablex.

REYNOLDS, C. R., & Kaufman, A. S. (1985). Clinical assessment of children's intelligence with the Wechsler scales. In B. B. Wolman (Ed.), *Handbook of intelligence: Theories, measurements, and applications.* New York: Wiley.

ROBINSON, H. B., & Robinson, N. M. (1965). *The mentally retarded child: A psychological approach.* New York: McGraw-Hill.

RODGERS, J. L. (1984). Confluence effects: Not here, not now! *Developmental Psychology, 20*, 321–331.

ROSE, S. A., & Wallace, I. F. (1985). Visual recognition memory: A predictor of later cognitive functioning in preterms. *Child Development, 56*, 843–852.

ROSS, R. T., Begab, M. J., Dondis, E. H., Giampiccolo, J. S., Jr., & Meyers, C. E. (1985). *Lives of the mentally retarded: A forty-year follow-up study.* Stanford, CA: Stanford University Press.

ROTHBART, M. K. (1971). Birth order and mother-child interaction in an achievement situation. *Journal of Personality and Social Psychology, 17*, 113–120.

RUTTER, M. (1983). School effects on pupil progress: Research findings and policy implications. *Child Development, 54*, 1–29.

SACKS, E. L. (1952). Intelligence scores as a function of experimentally established social relationships between child and examiner. *Journal of Abnormal and Social Psychology, 47*, 354–358.

SCARR, S. (1981). Testing for children: Assessment and the many determinants of intellectual competence. *American Psychologist, 36*, 1159–1166.

SCARR, S., & McCartney, K. (1983). How people make their own environments: A theory of genotype environment effects. *Child Development, 54*, 424–435.

SCARR, S., & Weinberg, R. A. (1976). IQ test performance of black children adopted by white families. *American Psychologist, 31*, 726–739.

SCARR, S., & Weinberg, R. A. (1977). Intellectual similarities within families of both adopted and biological children. *Intelligence, 32*, 170–191.

SCARR, S., & Weinberg, R. A. (1983). The Minnesota adoption studies: Genetic differences and malleability. *Child Development, 54*, 260–267.

SCHAIE, K. W., & Hertzog, C. (1983). Fourteen-year cohort-sequential analyses of adult intellectual development. *Developmental Psychology, 19*, 531–543.

SCHAIE, K. W., & Hertzog, C. (1986). Toward

a comprehensive model of adult intellectual development: Contributions of the Seattle longitudinal study. In R. J. Sternberg (Ed.), *Advances in the psychology of human intelligence* (Vol. 3). Hillsdale, NJ: Erlbaum.

SEITZ, V., Rosenbaum, L. K., & Apfel, N. H. (1985). Effects of family support intervention: A ten-year follow-up. *Child Development, 56*, 376–391.

SHERMAN, M., & Key, C. B. (1932). The intelligence of isolated mountain children. *Child Development, 3*, 279–290.

SHUEY, A. (1966). *The testing of Negro intelligence.* New York: Social Science Press.

SKODAK, M., & Skeels, H. M. (1947). A follow-up study of the development of one-hundred adopted children in Iowa. *American Psychologist, 2*, 278.

SKODAK, M., & Skeels, H. M. (1949). A final follow-up study of children in adoptive homes. *Journal of Genetic Psychology, 75*, 85–125.

SMITH, S. (1942). Language and nonverbal test performance of racial groups in Honolulu before and after a 14-year interval. *Journal of General Psychology, 26*, 51–93.

SPEARMAN, C. (1927). *The abilities of man.* New York: Macmillan.

SPRIGLE, J. E., & Schaefer, L. (1985). Longitudinal evaluation of the effects of two compensatory preschool programs on fourth- through sixth-grade students. *Developmental Psychology, 21*, 702–708.

STERNBERG, R. J. (1985). *Beyond IQ: A triarchic theory of human intelligence.* Cambridge: Cambridge University Press.

STERNBERG, R. J., & Berg, C. A. (1986). Quantitative integration: Definitions of intelligence—a comparison of the 1921 and 1986 symposia. In R. J. Sternberg & D. K. Detterman (Eds.), *What is intelligence? Contemporary viewpoints on its nature and definition.* Norwood, NJ: Ablex.

STERNBERG, R. J., Conway, B. E., Ketron, J. L., & Bernstein, M. (1981). People's conceptions of intelligence. *Journal of Personality and Social Psychology, 41*, 37–55.

TERMAN, L. M. (1921). In symposium: Intelligence and its measurement. *Journal of Educational Psychology, 12*, 127–133.

TERMAN, L. M. (1954). The discovery and encouragement of exceptional talent. *American Psychologist, 9*, 221–238.

TERMAN, L. M., & Merrill, M. A. (1972). *Stanford-Binet intelligence scale—Manual for the third revision.* Boston: Houghton Mifflin.

TERMAN, L. M., & Oden, M. H. (1959). *The gifted group at mid-life.* Stanford, CA: Stanford University Press.

THURSTONE, L. L. (1938). *Primary mental abilities*. Chicago: University of Chicago Press.

THURSTONE, L. L., & Thurstone, T. G. (1941). Factorial studies of intelligence. *Psychometric Monographs*, No. 2.

TYLER, L. E. (1965). *The psychology of human differences*. East Norwalk, CT: Appleton-Century-Crofts.

WECHSLER, D. (1944). *The measurement of adult intelligence* (3rd ed.). Baltimore: Williams & Wilkins.

WECHSLER, D. (1967). *Wechsler Preschool and Primary Scale of Intelligence*. New York: Psychological Corporation.

WECHSLER, D. (1974). *Wechsler Intelligence Scale for Children*. New York: Psychological Corporation.

WESTLING, D. L. (1986). *Introduction to mental retardation*. Englewood Cliffs, NJ: Prentice-Hall.

WHEELER, L. R. (1932). The intelligence of East Tennessee children. *Journal of Educational Psychology, 23,* 351–370.

WHEELER, L. R. (1942). A comparative study of the intelligence of East Tennessee mountain children. *Journal of Educational Psychology, 33,* 321–334.

WITTY, P. A., & Jenkins, M. D. (1936). Intra-race testing and Negro intelligence. *Journal of Psychology, 1,* 179–192.

WRIGHTSMAN, L. S., & Sanford, F. H. (1975). *Psychology: A scientific study of human behavior*. Pacific Grove, CA: Brooks/Cole.

YEATES, K. O., MacPhee, D., Campbell, F. A., & Ramey, C. T. (1983). Maternal IQ and home environment as determinants of early childhood intellectual competence: A de-velopmental analysis. *Developmental Psychology, 19,* 731–739.

ZAJONC, R. B. (1975, August). Birth order and intelligence: Dumber by the dozen. *Psychology Today*, pp. 39–43.

ZAJONC, R. B., & Markus, G. B. (1975). Birth order and intellectual development. *Psychological Review, 82,* 74–88.

ZIGLER, E., Abelson, W. D., Trickett, P. K., & Seitz, V. (1982). Is an intervention program necessary to improve economically disadvantaged children's IQ scores? *Child Development, 53,* 340–348.

ZIGLER, E., & Butterfield, E. C. (1968). Motivational aspects of changes in IQ test performance of culturally deprived nursery school children. *Child Development, 39,* 1–14.

IV

Social and Personality Development

Human beings are social animals, and our focus in Part IV shifts to social and personality development. We begin in Chapter 11 by examining the social and emotional developments of infancy and by discussing the consequences that children may face if they fail to establish affectional ties to other people during the first two or three years of life.

In Chapter 12 we will trace the development of children's knowledge about themselves and others and see that a person's understanding of the "self" and of the social environment contributes in important ways to his or her personality and social behavior.

Our attention in Chapter 13 turns to the interesting and often controversial subject of sex differences and sex-role development. We will first look beyond the myths and attempt to establish how males and females differ psychologically. Then we will consider several theories of sex-role development and try to determine whether the psychological differences between the sexes are culturally or biologically determined.

Many theorists have argued that establishing a sense of morality is the toughest task that parents face when raising a child. In Chapter 14 we will consider the topic of moral development and learn how children and adolescents come to distinguish right from wrong and to act on this distinction.

Early Emotional Growth and the Establishment of Intimate Relationships

In 1891 G. Stanley Hall stated that adolescence is the most crucial period of the life span for the development of personality. Hall characterized the teenage years as a time when interests are solidified, long-lasting friendships emerge, and important decisions are made about one's education, career, and (in those days) choice of a mate. In other words, he viewed adolescence as the period when individuals assume personal and interpersonal identities that will carry them through their adult lives.

This viewpoint was soon challenged by Sigmund Freud (1905/1930), who believed that many of the decisions that an adolescent makes about the future are predetermined by his or her reactions to earlier life experiences. In fact, Freud proclaimed that the foundations of the adult personality are laid during the first five to six years of life and that the process of personality development begins the moment that a baby is first handed to his or her parents.

Today we know that Freud was right in at least one respect: social and emotional development does begin very early in life. Although few contemporary theorists believe that our personalities are "set in stone" during the first five or six years, it is now apparent that the kinds of emotional relationships that infants develop with their close companions may well affect the ways they relate to other people later in life. Early social experiences are important experiences—and infancy is truly a sensitive period for personality development.

Our primary focus in this chapter is on a major social and emotional milestone of infancy—the development of affectional ties between children and their closest companions. We will begin by briefly reviewing what is known about infants' abilities to recognize and display emotions and will see how developmentalists define a true emotional attachment. We will then concentrate on the *process* of becoming attached and will try to determine how infants and their companions establish these close emotional ties. Next, we will consider two common fears that attached infants often display

and see why these fearful reactions often emerge during the latter part of the first year. Finally, we will review a rapidly expanding base of evidence that suggests that the kind of emotional attachments that infants are able to establish (or the lack thereof) may have important implications for their later social, emotional, and intellectual development.

Are Babies Emotional Creatures?

Do babies have feelings? Do they experience and display specific emotions such as happiness, sadness, fear, and anger the way older children and adults do? Most parents think they do. In one study, more than half the mothers of 1-month-old infants said that their babies displayed at least five distinct emotional expressions: interest, surprise, joy, anger, and fear (Johnson, Emde, Pannabecker, Stenberg, & Davis, 1982). Although one might argue that this is simply a case of proud mothers reading much too much into the behavior of their babies, there is now reliable evidence that even very young infants are indeed emotional creatures.

Facial and Vocal Expressions of Emotion

Carroll Izard and his colleagues at the University of Delaware have studied infants' emotional expressions by videotaping babies' responses to such events as grasping an ice cube, having a toy taken away, or seeing their mothers return after a separation (Izard, 1982). Izard's procedure is straightforward: he asks raters, who are unaware of the events that an infant has experienced, to tell him what emotion the child is experiencing from the facial expression that the child displays. These studies reveal that different adult raters observing the same expressions reliably see the same emotion in a baby's face. Apparently, infants are quite capable of communicating their feelings.

Izard's experiments have led him to conclude that various emotions appear at different times over the

Interest: brows raised; mouth may be rounded; lips may be pursed.

Fear: mouth retracted; brows level and drawn up and in; eyelids lifted.

Disgust: tongue protruding; upper lip raised; nose wrinkled.

Joy: bright eyes; cheeks lifted; mouth forms a smile.

Sadness: corners of mouth turned down; inner portion of brows raised.

Anger: mouth squared at corners; brows drawn together and pointing down; eyes fixed straight ahead.

Photo 11-1. Young infants display a variety of emotional expressions.

first two years. At birth, babies show interest, distress (in response to pain), disgust, and the suggestion of a smile (that is, happiness or contentment). Angry expressions appear at 3–4 months—about the same age that infants acquire sufficient control of their limbs to push unpleasant stimuli away. Sadness also emerges about this time, and fear makes its appearance at age 5–7 months, followed by shame and shyness. Finally, complex emotions such as guilt and contempt are first observed during the second year of life.

Babies can also express emotions vocally. In Chapter 5, we learned that healthy neonates produce different kinds of cries when they are hungry, "mad," or in pain and that parents are reasonably proficient at interpreting the meaning of these distress signals (Wiesenfeld, Malatesta, & DeLoach, 1981; Wolff, 1969). Very young infants also coo when contented and display "blurts" of excitation when they are happy or interested in something—signals that parents interpret as positive emotions and will attempt to prolong by talking to or playing with their babies (Keller & Scholmerich, 1987).

Critics of such demonstrations argue that the so-called emotional expressions of infancy are really nothing more than global displays of positive and negative affect. However, these critics have not adequately

explained how adults are able to show such remarkable agreement about the specific feeling an infant is experiencing (for example, distress versus disgust) when they have nothing more to go on than a tape recording of the infant's facial or vocal expressions. Moreover, babies react in predictable ways to particular kinds of experiences. During the first few weeks, soft sounds and novel visual displays are likely to elicit signs of interest and the suggestion of a smile. When given an inoculation, 2-month-old infants show the facial expression that Izard (and others) calls distress, whereas older infants react with anger (Izard, Hembree, & Huebner, 1987). And there is even some consistency to children's affective displays, for the infants who react more vigorously to a distressing event at age 2 months are likely to be the most vigorous responders when retested at ages 13–19 months (Izard et al., 1987). So it appears that early patterns of affective expression are tied to specific kinds of eliciting events and are relatively stable over time. Regardless of whether one calls them emotions (and most contemporary researchers do), it is obvious that very young infants can communicate a variety of feelings to their close companions.

By age 18–24 months, there can be *no* doubt that infants are emotional creatures. This is the age at which they begin to talk about various feelings that they or their companions have experienced and will often discuss the causes of these emotions as they enact them during pretend play (Bretherton, Fritz, Zahn-Waxler, & Ridgeway, 1986; Dunn, Bretherton, & Munn, 1987). In fact, many older infants and toddlers have already learned to fake certain affective expressions (for example, acting peeved or hurt) in order to manipulate a companion's emotions or otherwise get their own way (Bretherton et al., 1986). They are accomplished "emoters" indeed!

Recognizing Emotions: Can Babies "Read" Faces and Voices?

When do infants first notice and respond to the emotional expressions of other people? Surprising as it may seem, they are prepared to react to certain vocal signals at birth or shortly thereafter. In Box 2-3, for example, we learned that neonates who hear another infant cry will soon begin to cry themselves, thus showing some responsiveness to the distress of another baby. By age 3–4 months, infants can discriminate photos of happy faces from photos of sad or angry ones (La Barbera, Izard, Vietze, & Parisi, 1976), and the happier the face, the more they like to look at it (Kuchuk, Vibbert, & Bornstein, 1986). Although these early looking preferences do not necessarily imply that infants are interpreting various facial expressions as "happy," "angry," or "sad," they do suggest that 3-month-olds are noticing and attending to the facial parameters by which people display emotions. Finally, we learned in Chapter 6 that 3-month-olds clearly discriminate their own mothers' happy, sad, or angry expressions when these facial configurations are accompanied by the mother's happy, sad, or angry tone of voice. Not only do infants discriminate these three emotions, but they also become rather gleeful in response to a happy expression and distressed at their mothers' angry displays (Haviland & Lelwica, 1987).

The ability of infants to *interpret* emotional expressions is rather obvious by age 7–10 months—the point at which they begin to actively monitor their mothers' emotional reactions to uncertain situations and then use this information to regulate their own behavior. Indeed, this social referencing function soon extends to strangers as well: by age 12 months, infants will typically approach and play with unfamiliar toys if a nearby stranger is smiling but will often become wary and are apt to avoid these objects if the stranger displays a fearful expression (Klinnert, Emde, Butterfield, & Campos, 1986).

Emotions and Early Social Development

What role do infants' emotions play in early social development? Clearly, they serve a communicative function that is likely to affect the behavior of caregivers. For example, cries of distress summon close companions. Early suggestions of a smile or expressions of interest may convince caregivers that their baby is willing and even eager to strike up a social relationship with them. Later expressions of fear or sadness may indicate that the infant is insecure or feeling blue and needs some attention or comforting. Anger may imply that the infant wishes her companions to cease whatever they are doing that is upsetting her, whereas joy serves as a prompt for caregivers to prolong an ongoing interaction or perhaps signals the baby's willingness to accept new challenges. Thus, infant emotions are adaptive in that they promote social contact and help caregivers to adjust their behavior to the infant's needs and goals. Stated another way, the emotional expressions of infancy help infants and their close companions "get to know each other."

At the same time, the infant's emerging ability to recognize and interpret the emotions of others is a tremendously important achievement that enables the child to infer how he should be feeling or behaving in a variety of situations. The beauty of this "social referencing" is that children can *quickly* acquire knowledge in this way. For example, a sibling's joyful reaction to the family pooch should indicate that this "ball of fur" is a friend rather than an unspeakable monster. A mother's pained expression and accompanying vocal concern might immediately suggest that the knife in one's hand is an implement to be avoided. And given the frequency with which expressive caregivers direct an infant's attention to important aspects of the environment, it is likely that the information inherent in their emotional displays will contribute in a major way to the child's understanding of the world in which he lives.

What Are Emotional Attachments?

Researchers have found that the young of many species soon form close emotional ties to their mother or a "mother figure." To the layperson, this "attachment" appears to be a bond of love that is often attributed to maternal tendencies such as "mother instinct" or "mother love." Developmentalists are willing to concede that mothers and other close companions are likely to become attached to an infant long before the infant is attached to them. However, it now appears that mother love must be nurtured and that most infants are capable of promoting such a caregiver-to-infant bond from the moment of birth.

Just what is an emotional **attachment?** John Bowlby (1958, 1973) uses the term to describe the strong affectional ties that bind a person to his or her most intimate companions. According to Bowlby, people who are attached will interact often and will try to *maintain proximity to each other.* Accordingly, an 8-month-old boy who is attached to his mother may show his attachment by doing whatever it takes—crying, clinging, approaching, or following—in order to establish or to maintain contact with her. Leslie Cohen (1974) adds that attachments are *selective* in character and imply that the company of some people (**attachment objects**) is more pleasant or reassuring than that of others. For example, a 2-year-old girl who is attached to her mother should prefer the mother's company to that of a stranger whenever she is upset, discomforted, or afraid.

Although our focus in this chapter is on the attachments that develop between infants and their close companions, there are many other kinds of attachments that individuals may form. Older children, adolescents, and adults do not "cling" to their intimate companions in the same way that infants do, but we can certainly see some similarities between an infant's strong ties to his mother, a child's or adolescent's involvement with a particularly close friend, and an adult's emotional commitment to a spouse or a lover (Hazan & Shaver, 1987). Indeed, people even develop intense attachments to those cuddly kittens, puppies, or other house pets that respond to them and seem to enjoy their company. All these relationships are similar in that the attachment object is someone (or something) special with whom we are motivated to maintain contact.

How do infants and caregivers become attached to each other? Let's address this important issue by looking first at caregivers' reactions to infants.

The Caregiver's Attachment to the Infant

People sometimes find it hard to understand how a parent might become attached to a neonate. After all, newborn infants can be demanding little creatures who drool, spit up, fuss, cry, dirty their diapers on a regular basis, and often require a lot of attention at all

Photo 11-2. Infants and caregivers who are attached interact often and try to maintain proximity.

hours of the day and night. Since babies are associated with so many unpleasant consequences, why don't their parents learn to dislike them?

One reason that parents may overlook or discount the negative aspects of child care is that they have often begun to form emotional attachments to their infant *before* they experience many of the unpleasantries of parenthood. Marshall Klaus and John Kennell (1976) believe that caregivers can become *emotionally bonded* to an infant during the first few hours after birth—provided that they are given an opportunity to get to know their baby. And just what kinds of contact are necessary to promote this early emotional bonding? Let's see what Klaus and Kennell have to say.

social referencing: the use of others' emotional expressions to infer the meaning of otherwise ambiguous situations.

attachment: a close emotional relationship between two persons, characterized by mutual affection and a desire to maintain proximity.

attachment object: a close companion to whom one is attached.

Early Emotional Bonding

Several years ago, Klaus and Kennell (1976) proposed that a mother's attitude toward her infant may depend, in part, on her experiences with that child during the first few hours after giving birth. Specifically, they hypothesized that early skin-to-skin contact between mothers and their babies would make mothers more responsive to their infants and thereby promote the development of strong mother-to-infant emotional bonds.

To test this hypothesis, Klaus and Kennell (1976) studied the behavior of 28 young mothers who had just delivered full-term, healthy infants. During their three-day stay in the hospital, half of these mothers followed the traditional routine: they saw their babies briefly after delivery, visited with them 6–12 hours later, and then had half-hour feeding sessions with their infants every four hours thereafter. Mothers assigned to a second, or "extended contact," group were permitted five "extra" hours a day to cuddle their babies, including an hour of skin-to-skin contact that took place within three hours of birth.

When observed one month later, the mothers who had had extended contact with their newborns tended to stand nearer and to soothe their infants more during a routine physical examination, and they held their babies closer during feeding sessions than did mothers who had followed the traditional hospital routine. A year later, the extended-contact mothers were still more soothing, cuddling, and nurturing than mothers in the "normal routine" condition. As for the year-old infants, those who had had extended early contact with their mothers outperformed those who had not on tests of physical and mental development.

From this study and others reporting similar results (see Klaus & Kennell, 1982), Klaus and Kennell concluded that the sheer amount of early contact a mother has with her infant is less important than the timing of that contact. Indeed, their interpretation of the data is that the first 6–12 hours is a **sensitive period** for emotional bonding: presumably mothers are most likely to develop the strongest possible affection for their babies if they have had some skin-to-skin contact with them during this particular time (Kennell, Voos, & Klaus, 1979).

Why might early contact matter?

Why do mothers build these emotional bridges to their infants just after giving birth? Kennell et al. (1979) have suggested that hormones present at the time of delivery may help to focus the mother's attention on her baby and make her more susceptible to forming an early attachment. If these hormones should dissipate before a mother has any extended contact with her infant, she will presumably become less responsive to her baby, much as animals do if separated from their offspring in the first few hours after giving birth.

Although the "hormonal mediation" hypothesis may seem to account for the findings we have reviewed, there are reasons to question this interpretation of early emotional bonding. For one thing, mothers who have had close contact with their infants soon after giving birth are not always more nurturant or more involved with their babies (Svejda, Campos, & Emde, 1980), particularly if their pregnancies were unplanned (Grossmann, Thane, & Grossmann, 1981). Moreover, the hormonal hypothesis cannot explain why fathers who are present at the birth (or soon thereafter) often become so fascinated with their neonate, wishing to touch, hold, or caress the baby. Clearly, a father's initial "engrossment" with his baby seems to be a kind of emotional bonding that is very similar to that experienced by mothers and is obviously not due to the action of pregnancy hormones.

If the hormonal mediation hypothesis does not explain the early affection that parents display toward their newborn infants, then what does? One idea offered by ethologists is that caregivers are biologically predisposed to react favorably and with affection to a neonate's pleasing social overtures (Bowlby, 1973). Of course, there may be other plausible explanations for these early engrossment effects—explanations that make no reference to parents' innate predispositions. Consider a possibility suggested by social-psychological research on the interpretation of emotions. Perhaps the intense emotional arousal (fear or apprehension) that parents experience during childbirth is reinterpreted in a positive light when they are handed an infant who gazes attentively at them, grasps their fingers, and seems to snuggle in response to their caresses. If parents should then attribute these positive feelings to the baby and its behavior, it is easy to see how they might feel rather affectionate toward their neonate and become emotionally involved with him or her. However, parents who have little or no early contact with their neonates are unable to attribute their existing emotional arousal to a beautiful, responsive baby. In fact, they often end up labeling their emotions as exhaustion or as relief that the ordeal of pregnancy and childbirth is finally over (Grossman, Eichler, Winickoff, & Associates, 1980). Perhaps you can see that these latter attributions are unlikely to make parents feel especially affectionate toward the child they have just borne.

Is early contact necessary for optimal development?

Klaus and Kennell's sensitive-period hypothesis implies that new parents show a basic "readiness" to become emotionally involved with their infant during the first few hours after the baby is born. As we have seen, there is some evidence to support this proposition. However, Klaus and Kennell also implied that parents who have had little or no contact with their neonates during the sensitive period may never become as attached to these infants as they might had they had skin-to-skin contact with them during the first few hours. This second theoretical proposition is much more controversial.

In her recent review of the emotional-bonding literature, Susan Goldberg (1983) reports that mothers who have had early contact with their infants do seem to be somewhat more responsive and affectionate toward their babies for the first three days of life. But in contrast to Klaus and Kennell's research, Goldberg finds that these "early contact" effects are not large and may not last very long. In the one study in which mothers and infants were carefully observed over a nine-day period, the advantages of early contact steadily declined over time. By the ninth day after birth, early-contact mothers were no more affectionate or responsive toward their infants than mothers who had had no skin-to-skin contact with their babies for several hours after delivery. Indeed, the delayed-contact mothers showed a dramatic increase in responsiveness over the nine-day observation period—suggesting that the hours immediately after birth are not nearly so critical as Klaus and Kennell assumed (Goldberg, 1983; see also Myers, 1984).

Michael Rutter (1981) is another theorist who believes that the events of the first few hours are unlikely to have a permanent effect on mother/infant relationships. To support his claim, Rutter notes that most adoptive parents develop close emotional ties to their children even though they have rarely had *any* contact with their adoptees during the neonatal period. Indeed, the likelihood that a mother and her infant will become securely attached is just as high in adoptive families as in nonadoptive ones (Singer, Brodzinsky, Ramsay, Steir, & Waters, 1985).

In sum, research on early emotional bonding suggests that parents can become highly involved with their infants during the first few hours if they are permitted to touch, hold, cuddle, and play with their babies. As a result, many hospitals have altered their routines to allow and encourage these kinds of experiences. However, it appears that this early contact is neither crucial nor sufficient for the development of strong parent-to-infant or infant-to-parent attachments. Stable attachments between infants and caregivers are not formed in a matter of minutes, hours, or days: they build rather slowly from social interactions that take place over many weeks and months. So there is absolutely no reason for parents who have not had early skin-to-skin contact with their infant to assume that they will have problems establishing a warm and loving relationship with the child.

Infant Characteristics That Promote Caregiver-to-Infant Attachments

Since newborn infants spend so much time sleeping, crying, or in a drowsy, semiconscious state, it is tempting to think of them as inherently asocial creatures. However, ethologists John Bowlby (1969) and Konrad Lorenz (1943) have challenged this point of view, arguing that babies are indeed *sociable* companions who are born with a repertoire of reflexes, response tendencies, and other physical characteristics that are likely to elicit highly favorable reactions from their caregivers. Let's explore this idea in greater detail.

Oh, baby face: The kewpie-doll syndrome

Konrad Lorenz (1943) suggested that a baby's "kewpie doll" appearance (large forehead; chubby, protruding cheeks; soft, rounded features) makes the infant appear cute or lovable to caregivers. Thomas Alley (1981) agrees. Alley found that adults judged line drawings of babyish faces (and profiles) to be much cuter than those of 4-year-old children. When commenting on the babyish figures, Alley's subjects often described them as "adorable" or "pleasant to look at" or noted that "you receive pleasure from a cute person" (p. 653). Younger boys and girls also react positively to babyish facial features, although girls begin to show an even stronger interest in infants after reaching menarche

---

sensitive-period hypothesis: Klaus and Kennell's notion that mothers will develop the strongest possible affection for their babies if they have close contact with them within 6–12 hours after giving birth.

kewpie-doll effect: the notion that infantlike facial features are perceived as cute and lovable and will elicit favorable responses from others.

(Goldberg, Blumberg, & Kriger, 1982). Finally, infants clearly differ in physical attractiveness (Hildebrandt, 1983), and adults often respond more favorably to attractive babies than to unattractive ones (Hildebrandt & Fitzgerald, 1981; Stephan & Langlois, 1984). So it seems that infantlike facial features (or the "kewpie doll" look) may help to elicit the kinds of attention from caregivers that will promote social attachments. However, research is needed to tell us whether *parents* actually find it easier to become attached to highly attractive infants than to babies whose facial features are somewhat less than attractive.

Innate responses as sociable gestures

Not only do infants have "cute" faces, but many of their early reflexive behaviors may have an endearing quality about them (Bowlby, 1969). For example, the rooting, sucking, and grasping reflexes may lead parents to believe that their infant enjoys being close to them. Smiling, which is initially a reflexive response to almost any pleasing stimulus, seems to be a particularly potent signal to caregivers, as are cooing, excitable blurting, and spontaneous babbling (see Keller & Scholmerich, 1987). In fact, an adult's typical response to a baby's smiles and positive vocalizations is to smile at (or vocalize to) the infant (Gewirtz & Gewirtz, 1968; Keller & Scholmerich, 1987), and parents often interpret their baby's grins, laughs, and babbles as an indication that the child is contented and that they are effective care-

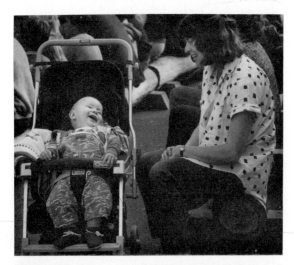

Photo 11-3. Few signals will attract as much attention as a baby's social smile.

givers. Thus, a smiling or babbling infant can reinforce caregiving activities and thereby increase the likelihood that parents or other nearby companions will want to attend to this happy little person in the future.

Even the reflexive cry, which is often described as aversive, can promote caregiver-to-infant attachments. Bowlby views the cry as a "distress signal" that elicits the approach of those who are responsible for the infant's care and safety. Presumably, responsive caregivers who are successful at quieting their babies will then become the beneficiaries of positive responses, such as smiling and babbling, that should reinforce their caregiving behavior and make them feel even closer to their contented infants.

Interactional synchrony

One thing that many parents find so fascinating about infants is that their babies often seem so responsive to them. In Chapter 6 we learned that full-term, healthy neonates are particularly responsive to the sound of the human voice (especially high-pitched "feminine" voices) and will often stop crying, open their eyes, and begin to look around or to vocalize themselves when they are spoken to. Moreover, Craig Peery (1980) reports that 1-day-old infants are already synchronizing their head movements with those of adults: frame-by-frame photographic analyses of the interactions between infants and an admiring female adult suggested that each infant reliably (1) withdrew his or her head at the approach of the adult and (2) approached the adult as she withdrew her head. Other investigators are somewhat skeptical of such claims, arguing that if there is any "synchrony" to social interactions early in infancy, it is the adult who is adjusting her behavior to that of the baby (Cohn & Tronick, 1987; Dowd & Tronick, 1986). But even so, most normal, healthy infants are highly receptive to social overtures from the first day of life—a characteristic that is likely to endear them to their close companions.

Over the next several months, caregivers and infants will ordinarily have many opportunities to interact and to develop and perfect **synchronized routines** that both parties will probably enjoy. Psychologists who have observed these exquisite interactions have likened them to "dances" in which the partners take turns responding to each other's lead. Daniel Stern (1977) has provided a written account of one such "dance" that occurred as a mother was feeding her 3-month-old infant:

A normal feeding, not a social interaction, was underway. Then a change began. While talking and looking at me, the mother turned her head and gazed at the infant's face. He was gazing at the ceiling, but out of the corner of his eye he saw her head turn toward him and he turned to gaze back at her ... now he broke rhythm and stopped sucking. He let go of the nipple ... as he eased into the faintest suggestion of a smile. The mother abruptly stopped talking and, as she watched his face begin to transform, her eyes opened a little wider and her eyebrows raised a bit. His eyes locked on to hers, and together they held motionless for an instant. . . . This silent and almost motionless instant continued to hang until the mother suddenly shattered it by saying "Hey!" and simultaneously opened her eyes wider, raising her eyebrows further, and throwing her head up toward the infant. Almost simultaneously, the baby's eyes widened. His head tilted up and, as his smile broadened, the nipple fell out of his mouth. Now she said, "Well, hello! ... Heello ... Heeelloo," so that her pitch rose and the "hellos" became longer and more emphatic on each successive repetition. With each phrase, the baby expressed more pleasure, and his body resonated almost like a balloon . . . filling a little more with each breath. The mother then paused and her face relaxed. They watched each other expectantly for a moment ... then the baby suddenly took an initiative. . . . His head lurched forward, his hands jerked up, and a fuller smile blossomed. His mother was jolted into motion. She moved forward, mouth open and eyes alight, and said "Ooooooh ... ya wanna play do ya ... yeah? . . ." And off they went [p. 3].

In this example, it was the mother who started the episode by gazing at the baby's face and capturing his attention. However, young infants are quite capable of initiating and maintaining these synchronized exchanges or even terminating them if they become overly excited or discomforted in some way. In the interaction that Stern describes, the mother soon became much more boisterous in her play and raised her voice to a level where her baby appeared apprehensive. At this point, the baby attempted to withdraw from the game by looking away. Once he had composed himself, he gazed again at his mother and "exploded into a big grin." The mother then became even more playful than before, and the baby immediately frowned and looked away. Clearly, he had had enough excitement for the moment. The mother picked up on this signal and gave the baby his nipple, and he began to feed once again. Their synchronized social exchange was suddenly over.

In sum, infants play a major role in persuading other people to love them. Babies are physically appealing; they come equipped with a number of reflexes and response capabilities that capture the attention and warm the hearts of their companions; and last but not least, they are responsive to social overtures and may soon be capable of synchronizing their behavior with that of a caregiver. Indeed, Stern (1977) believes that synchronized interactions between infants and their companions may occur several times a day and are particularly important contributors to social attachments. As an infant continues to interact with a particular caregiver, he will learn what this person is like and how he can regulate her attention. Of course, the caregiver should become more proficient at interpreting the baby's signals and will learn how to adjust her behavior to successfully capture and maintain his attention. As the caregiver and the infant practice their routines and become better "dance partners," their relationship should become more satisfying for both parties and may eventually blossom into a strong reciprocal attachment.

Problems in Establishing Caregiver-to-Infant Attachments

Although we have talked as if caregivers invariably became attached to their infants, this does not always happen. As we will see, some babies are hard to love, some caregivers are hard to reach, and some environments are not very conducive to the establishment of secure emotional relationships.

Some babies may be hard to love

Even though many neonates are remarkably proficient at attracting attention and sustaining social interactions, some babies display characteristics that could annoy and even alienate their companions. For example, premature infants are not only inalert and frequently unresponsive to others' bids for attention (Lester, Hoffman, & Brazelton, 1985), but they also tend to be physically unattractive and will often emit high-pitched, nonrhythmic cries that are perceived as much more aversive than those of healthy, full-term infants (Zeskind, 1980). Moreover, some full-term and otherwise healthy infants have difficult temperaments: they are at risk of alienating close companions because they are

synchronized routines: generally harmonious interactions between two persons in which each participant adjusts his or her behavior in response to the partner's actions.

extremely active and irritable, are irregular in their habits, and are likely to resist or ignore caregivers' social overtures (Crockenberg, 1981).

Apparently adults do often find it hard to establish stable and synchronous routines with a very irritable or unresponsive infant (Greene, Fox, & Lewis, 1983; Thoman, Acebo, & Becker, 1983). For example, Jamie Greene, Nathan Fox, and Michael Lewis (1983) report that infants who often cry during social interactions seem to disrupt the development of a positive relationship with their caregivers. Although the mothers of these fretful infants are quite willing to provide comfort and attend to basic needs, they spend less time in playful and affectionate social exchanges than mothers whose babies are less fretful and more responsive to social play.

Fortunately, most parents will eventually establish satisfying routines and become quite attached to their difficult or unresponsive infants. One way to help the process along is to identify neonates who may be difficult to love and then to teach their caregivers how to elicit favorable reactions from these sluggish or irritable companions. The Brazelton testing and training programs reviewed in Chapter 5 (see Box 5-2) were designed with these objectives in mind.

Some caregivers are hard to reach

Caregivers sometimes have personal quirks or characteristics that seriously hinder them in establishing close emotional ties to their infants. A caregiver who is chronically depressed, for example, may not be sufficiently responsive to a baby's social signals to establish a synchronous and satisfying relationship. In fact, Marian Radke-Yarrow and her associates (Radke-Yarrow, Cummings, Kuczynski, & Chapman, 1985) report that insecure attachments are the *rule* rather than the exception if the child's primary caregiver has been diagnosed as clinically depressed.

A caregiver's own family history is also an important consideration. Parents who were themselves unloved, neglected, or abused as children may expect their babies to be "perfect" and to love them right away. When the infant is irritable, fussy, and inattentive (as all infants will be at times), these emotionally insecure adults are apt to feel as if the baby has rejected them. They may then withdraw their affection—sometimes to the point of neglecting the child—or become physically abusive (Rutter, 1981; Steele & Pollack, 1974).

Problems can also arise if caregivers try to follow preconceived notions about how infants should be raised rather than adjusting their parenting to the infant's state or temperamental characteristics. For example, a father who believes that his baby requires a large amount of stimulation may end up overexciting an "excitable" infant; a mother who is afraid of spoiling her baby may be reluctant to soothe a child who has become overly excited (Korner, 1974). Unfortunately, caregivers who often misread their baby's signals and end up trying to fit a square peg into a round hole may be less likely to establish the kind of interactional synchrony with their infant that would help them to become attached to her (Sprunger, Boyce, & Gaines, 1985).

Finally, some caregivers may be disinclined to love their babies because their pregnancies were unplanned and their infants are unwanted. In one study conducted in Czechoslovakia (Matejcek, Dytrych, & Schuller, 1979), mothers who had been denied permission to abort an unwanted pregnancy were judged to be less closely attached to their children than a group of same-aged mothers of similar marital and socioeconomic status who had not requested an abortion. Although both the "wanted" and the "unwanted" children were physically healthy at birth, over the next nine years the unwanted children were more frequently hospitalized, made lower grades in school, had less stable family lives and poorer relations with peers, and were generally more irritable than the children whose parents had wanted them. Here, then, are data suggesting that failure of a caregiver to become emotionally attached to an infant could have long-term effects on the child's physical, social, emotional, and intellectual well-being.

Of course, these findings do not imply that all wanted children will be loved or that all unwanted children will remain unloved. Nevertheless, it would appear that mothers who give birth to an unplanned and unwanted child are less likely than mothers who plan their pregnancies to become closely attached to their infants.

Some environments are hazardous to the formation of healthy attachments

To this point, we have noted that the character of an adult's attachment to his or her infant is influenced by the adult's characteristics as well as those of the infant. However, we should also recognize that interactions between infants and caregivers take place within a broader social and emotional context that may affect how a particular caregiver and infant will react to each other. For example, mothers who must care for several small children with little or no assistance may find themselves unwilling or unable to devote much attention to their newest baby, particularly if the infant is at all irritable or unresponsive (Belsky, 1980; Crockenberg, 1981). Indeed, researchers have consistently reported that the more children a woman has had, the more negative her attitudes toward children become, and the more difficult she thinks her children are to raise (Garbarino & Sherman, 1980; Hurley & Hohn, 1971).

The quality of a caregiver's relationship with his or her spouse can also have a dramatic effect on parent/infant interactions. For example, parents who are depressed about an unhappy marriage sometimes look to their babies for love and attention when their spouses fail to satisfy these emotional needs (Steele & Pollack, 1974). However, they will probably fail to find the support they are seeking, for Jeffrey Cohn and Edward Tronick (1982) report that 3-month-old infants soon become wary and begin to protest should their mothers behave as if they were depressed. Cohn and Tronick suggest that the infant's negative reaction to depression may further depress the adult and make it difficult for him or her to establish a satisfying relationship with the child—a problem that may be particularly apparent if the baby has already shown a tendency to be irritable and unresponsive. Indeed, Jay Belsky (1981) finds that neonates who are at risk for later emotional difficulties (as indicated by their poor performance on the Brazelton Neonatal Behavioral Assessment Scale) are likely to have nonsynchronous interactions with their parents *only when the parents are unhappily married.* Taken together, these findings indicate that a stormy marriage is a major environmental hazard that can hinder or even prevent the establishment of close emotional ties between parents and their infants.

The Infant's Attachment to Caregivers

Although adults may become emotionally attached to an infant very soon after the baby is born, the infant will require a little more time to form a genuine attachment to caregivers. Many theories have been proposed to explain how and why infants become emotionally involved with the people around them. But before we consider these theories, we should briefly discuss the stages that babies go through in becoming attached to a close companion.

Development of Primary Social Attachments

Many years ago, Rudolph Schaffer and Peggy Emerson (1964) studied the development of social attachments by following a group of Scottish infants from early infancy to 18 months of age. Once a month, mothers were interviewed to determine (1) how the infant responded when separated from close companions in seven situations (for example, being left in a crib; being left in the presence of strangers) and (2) the persons to whom the infant's separation responses were directed. A child was judged to be attached to someone if separation from that person reliably elicited a protest.

Schaffer and Emerson found that infants pass through the following steps, or stages, as they develop close ties with their caregivers:

1. *The asocial stage (0–6 weeks).* The very young infant is somewhat "asocial" in that many kinds of social and nonsocial stimuli will produce a favorable reaction, and few produce any kind of protest. By the end of this period, infants are beginning to show a distinct preference for social stimuli, such as a smiling face.
2. *The stage of indiscriminate attachments (6 weeks to 6–7 months).* Now infants clearly enjoy human company but tend to be somewhat indiscriminate: they are apt to protest whenever *any* adult puts them down or leaves them alone. Although 3–6-month-olds are more likely to smile at their mothers than at strangers (Watson, Hayes, Vietze, & Becker, 1979), they clearly enjoy the attention they receive from just about anyone (including strangers).
3. *The stage of specific attachments (about age 7 months).* At about 7 months of age, infants begin to protest only when separated from one particular individual, usually the mother (see Figure 11-1). In addition, many infants begin to fear strangers at about this time. Schaffer and Emerson interpret these data as an indication that the infants have formed their first genuine attachments.
4. *The stage of multiple attachments.* Within weeks after forming their initial attachments, about half the infants in Schaffer and Emerson's study were becoming attached to other people (fathers, siblings, grandparents, or perhaps even a regular babysitter). By 18 months of age, very few infants were attached to only one person, and some were attached to five or more.

Schaffer and Emerson originally believed that infants who are multiply attached have a "hierarchy" of attachment objects and that the individual at the top of

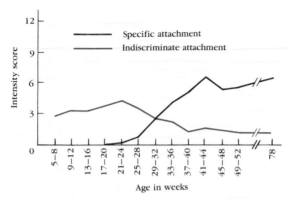

Figure 11-1. The developmental course of attachment during infancy. *(From Schaffer & Emerson, 1964.)*

the list is their most preferred companion. However, later research indicates that each of the infant's attachment objects may serve slightly different functions, so that the person whom an infant prefers most may depend on the situation. For example, most infants prefer the mother's company if they are upset or frightened (Lamb & Stevenson, 1978). However, fathers seem to be preferred as playmates, possibly because much of the time they spend with their infants is "play time," and fathers are more likely than mothers to play unusual, rough-and-tumble games that infants seem to enjoy (Clarke-Stewart, 1978; Lamb, 1981). Schaffer (1977) is now convinced that "being attached to several people does not necessarily imply a shallower feeling toward each one, for an infant's capacity for attachment is not like a cake that has to be [divided]. Love, even in babies, has no limits" (p. 100).

Theories of Attachment

If you have ever had a kitten or a puppy, you may have noticed that pets often seem especially responsive and affectionate to the person who feeds them. Might the same be true of human infants? Some theorists think so, but others disagree.

For years, theorists have argued about the reasons that babies come to "love" their caregivers. The history of this theoretical controversy is interesting because each theory makes different assumptions about the part that infants play in their social relationships and the roles that caregivers must enact in order to win the baby's affection. The four theories that have been most influential are those reviewed in Chapter 2—psychoanalytic theory, learning theory, cognitive-developmental theory, and ethological theory.

Psychoanalytic theory: Attachments develop from oral activities

According to Freud, infants are "oral" creatures who derive pleasure from activities such as sucking, biting, and mouthing objects. Presumably the infant will invest psychic energy in and become attached to any person or object that provides oral pleasure. Thus, infants were thought to become emotionally involved with their mothers because it is usually the mother who gives pleasure to the oral child by feeding her. Freud believed that infants will become securely attached to their mothers if the mother is "relaxed and generous" in her feeding practices, thereby allowing the child a "lot of oral pleasure."

Erik Erikson also believes that a mother's feeding practices would influence the strength or security of her infant's attachments. However, he suggests that a mother's *overall responsiveness* to her child's needs is more important than feeding alone. According to Erikson, a caregiver who consistently responds to an infant's needs will foster a sense of trust in other people, whereas unresponsive or inconsistent caregiving breeds mistrust. He adds that an untrusting child may well become overdependent—one who will "lean on" others, not necessarily out of love or a desire to be near but solely to ensure that his or her needs are met. Presumably children who have not learned to trust others during infancy are likely to avoid close mutual-trust relationships throughout their lives.

Before we examine the research on feeding practices and their contribution to social attachments, we need to consider another viewpoint that assumes that feeding is important—learning theory.

Learning theory: Rewardingness leads to love

Learning theorists consider the mother a logical attachment object for her baby. Not only do mothers feed their infants, they also change them when they are wet or soiled, provide warmth, tender touches, and soft, reassuring vocalizations when they are upset or afraid, and promote changes in the "scenery" in what otherwise could be a rather monotonous environment for babies who cannot get up and move about on their own. What will a baby make of all this? According to learning theorists, an infant will eventually associate the mother with pleasant feelings and pleasurable sensations, so that the mother herself becomes a source of reinforcement. Once the mother (or any other caregiver) has attained this status as a *conditioned reinforcer,* the infant is attached—he or she will now do whatever is necessary (smile, cry, coo, babble, or follow) in order to attract the caregiver's attention or to remain near this valuable and rewarding individual.

Like Freud, many learning theorists believe that feeding plays an important role in determining the quality of an infant's attachment to the primary caregiver. Robert Sears (1963) suggests two reasons that feeding may be a special kind of caregiving activity. First, the mother is often able to sit down with her infant and provide *many comforts*—including warmth and tactile, visual, and vocal stimulation, as well as satisfying the baby's hunger and thirst—*all at once*. Second, feeding is an activity that should elicit positive responses from the infant (smiling, cooing) that are likely to increase a caregiver's affection for the child. In sum, feeding is thought to be important because it provides positive reinforcers to both the caregiver and her infant—reinforcers that will strengthen their feelings of affection for each other.

Just how important *is* feeding? In 1959 Harry Harlow and Robert Zimmerman reported the results of a study designed to compare the importance of feeding and tactile stimulation for the development of social attachments in infant monkeys. The monkeys were separated from their mothers in the first day of life and reared for the next 165 days by two surrogate mothers. As you can see in Photo 11-4, each surrogate mother had a face and well-proportioned body constructed of wire. However, the body of one surrogate (the "cloth mother") was wrapped in foam rubber and covered with terrycloth. Half the infants were always fed by this warm, comfortable cloth mother, the remaining half by the rather uncomfortable "wire mother."

The research question was simple: Would these infants become attached to the "mother" who fed them, or would they instead prefer the soft, cuddly terrycloth mother? It was no contest! Infants clearly preferred the cloth mother, *regardless of which mother had fed them*. Indeed, monkeys fed by the wire mother spent more than 15 hours a day clutching the *cloth* mother, compared with only an hour or so (mostly at mealtimes) with the wire mother. Moreover, all infants ran directly to the cloth mother when they were frightened by novel stimuli (marching toy bears, wooden spiders) that were placed in their cages. Clearly, the implication of Harlow and Zimmerman's classic study is that feeding is *not* the most important determinant of an infant's attachment to caregivers.

Although Harlow's subjects were monkeys, re-

Photo 11-4. The "wire" and "cloth" surrogate mothers used in Harlow's research. This infant remains with the cloth mother even though it must stretch to the wire mother in order to feed.

search with human infants paints a similar picture. In their study of Scottish infants, Schaffer and Emerson (1964) asked each mother the age at which her child had been weaned, the amount of time it had taken to wean the child, and the feeding schedule (regular interval or demand feeding) that she had used with her baby. None of these feeding practices predicted the character of an infant's attachment to his or her mother. In fact, Schaffer and Emerson found that, in 39% of cases, the person who usually fed, bathed, and changed the child (typically the mother) was not even the child's primary attachment object! These findings are clearly damaging to any theory that states that feeding and feeding practices are the primary determinants of the child's first social attachment.

How, then, do attachments develop? Contemporary learning theorists would argue that feeding plays a role in the process but that satisfying the child's hunger is only one of the many nice things that caregivers do for their infants. Presumably the visual, tactile, and vocal stimulation that adults provide when they interact with their infants will also make these regular companions seem rather attractive or rewarding (Gewirtz, 1969). In fact, Harlow's research with infant monkeys suggests that warmth and **"contact comfort"** may be a more powerful contributor to attachments than feeding and the reduction of hunger.

In sum, learning theorists have ended up adopting a viewpoint similar to that of Erik Erikson: infants are attracted to those individuals who are quick to respond to their signals and who provide them with a variety of pleasant or rewarding experiences. Indeed, Schaffer and Emerson (1964) found that the two aspects of a mother's behavior that predicted the character of her infant's attachment to her were her *responsiveness* to the infant's behavior and the *total amount of stimulation* that she provided. Mothers who responded quickly to their infants' social signals and who often played with their babies had infants who were closely attached to them.

Cognitive-developmental theory: Attachments depend on cognitive development

Proponents of Jean Piaget's cognitive-developmental theory believe that an infant's ability to form social attachments depends, in part, on his level of intellectual development. Before an attachment can occur, the infant must be able to discriminate familiar persons (that is, potential attachment objects) from strangers. He must also recognize that close companions continue to exist even when they are absent (Schaffer, 1971). This latter ability is an example of the object concept (or *object permanence*), discussed in Chapter 9. Presumably infants who recognize that objects (or persons) have a permanent existence will develop stable schemata for people with whom they regularly interact. They should then prefer these people to all others and may even protest when they cannot locate their close companion(s). *7-9 mo   4th sensori motor substage*

yes   Is the timing of social attachments related to cognitive development? Apparently so. In their classic study of Scottish infants, Schaffer and Emerson (1964) noted that attachments normally appear during the third quarter of the first year (age 7–9 months)—precisely the time that infants begin to show some evidence of acquiring the object concept. Drawing from these observations and the work of Piaget, Schaffer (1971) then proposed that attachments will not occur until the fourth sensorimotor substage, when infants first begin to search for and find objects hidden behind a screen.

An experiment by Barry Lester and his associates (Lester, Kotelchuck, Spelke, Sellers, & Klein, 1974) was designed to evaluate Schaffer's hypothesis. In this study, 9-month-old and 12-month-old infants were given a test that measured their level of object permanence. Then each infant was exposed to a number of brief separations from the mother, the father, and a stranger. The results lend some support to the cognitive-developmental viewpoint. The 9-month-old infants who scored high (Stage 4 or above) in object permanence showed stronger protests when separated from their mothers than infants who scored lower (Stage 3 or below). Among the 12-month-old infants, those who scored high (Stage 4 or above) in object permanence showed more separation protest at the departure of *either the mother or the father* than infants whose object permanence was less well developed. Neither age group protested separations from a stranger. Using separation protest as evidence of attachments, it would appear that the cognitively advanced 9-month-olds were attached to their mothers, while the cognitively advanced yearlings were attached to *both* parents. Thus, Lester's findings not only are consistent with the developmental stages of attachment reported by Schaffer and Emerson (1964) but also indicate that the timing of the primary attachment is related to the child's level of object permanence.

Ethological theory: Attachments may be biologically programmed

Ethologists have proposed an interesting explanation for social attachments that is sometimes called "evolutionary" theory because of its distinct evolutionary overtones. The major assumption of the ethological approach is that all animals, including human beings, are born with a number of species-specific "signals," or behavioral tendencies, that promote certain social behaviors (Ainsworth, Bell, & Stayton, 1974; Bowlby, 1969, 1973). Presumably these innate signals are products of a species' evolutionary history, and each of these attributes is designed to serve some purpose that increases the chances of survival for the individual and the species.

What is the purpose of a social attachment? According to John Bowlby (1969, 1973), infant/caregiver attachments serve the same function for all species— namely, to protect the young from prolonged discomfort, from predators, and perhaps from fear itself. Of course, ethologists would argue that the long-range purpose of the primary social attachment is to ensure that the young of each successive generation live long enough to reproduce, thereby enabling the species to survive.

Origins of the ethological viewpoint.
How did ethologists ever come up with their evolutionary theory of attachment? Interestingly enough, their insights were prompted by observations of young fowl. In 1873, Spaulding first noted that chicks would follow almost any moving object—another chicken, a duck, or a human being—as soon as they were able to walk. Konrad Lorenz (1937) observed this same "following response" in young goslings, a behavior he labeled **imprinting** (or stamping in). Lorenz also noted that (1) imprinting is automatic—young fowl do not have to be taught to follow, (2) imprinting occurs only within a narrowly delimited **critical period** after the bird has hatched, and (3) imprinting is irreversible—once the bird begins to follow a particular object, it will remain attached to it.

Lorenz then concluded that imprinting was an "adaptive" response. Young birds should generally survive if they stay close to their mothers so that they are led to food and are afforded protection. Those that wander away may starve or be eaten by predators and thus fail to pass their genes to future generations. So over the course of many, many generations, then, the imprinting response eventually became an inborn, **preadapted characteristic** that attaches a young fowl to its mother, thereby increasing its chances of survival.

Attachment in humans. Although human infants do not imprint on their mothers in the same way that young fowl do, John Bowlby (1969, 1973) claims that they have inherited a number of other characteristics that help them to establish and maintain contact with their caregivers. For example, three innate responses—sucking, grasping, and following (first by keeping the caregiver in sight and later by crawling or walking)—are called **executive responses** because they are initiated by the infant and require only a minimal response from the caregiver. Two other behaviors, smiling and vocalizing (crying or babbling), serve as **signaling responses** by encouraging caregivers to approach the infant and to provide some kind of attention or comfort. Thus, the ethologists believe that infants are *active* participants in the attachment process: their role (initially, at least) is to emit a number of preprogrammed signals that are likely to attract attention or influence the behavior of caregivers.

According to Bowlby, adults are biologically programmed to respond to an infant's signals in much the same way that infants are programmed to react to the sight, sound, warmth, and touch of their caregivers.

And as a mother (or other primary caregiver) becomes more proficient at reading and reacting to her baby's signals, the infant should become ever more responsive to her. The end result of these increasingly personal interactions is the development of a *mutual* bond or attachment between the infant and his or her most intimate companion(s).

A common misunderstanding. A hasty reading of ethological theory might lead one to conclude that attachments are "automatic"—that all the child requires to form one is a caregiver with whom to interact. This view is incorrect. Although infants may be preprogrammed to beam various signals to other people, these innate responses may eventually wane if they fail to produce favorable reactions from an unresponsive caregiver (Ainsworth, Blehar, Waters, & Wall, 1978). So infants are not biologically programmed to attach themselves to the closest available human; attachments are a product of a history of interaction in which each participant has learned to respond in a meaningful way to the social signals of his or her partner. A little later in the chapter, we will see that infants may fail to establish warm, affectionate relationships with primary caregivers who are slow to react to their bids for attention.

---

contact comfort: the term used by Harlow to describe the pleasure infant monkeys derive from clinging to their mothers' bodies or to a soft, warm terrycloth mother surrogate.

imprinting: an innate or instinctual form of learning in which the young of certain species will follow and become attached to moving objects (usually their mothers).

critical period: a brief period in the development of an organism when it is particularly sensitive to certain environmental influences; outside this period, the same influences will have little if any effect.

preadapted characteristic: an innate attribute that is a product of evolution and serves some function that increases the chances of survival for the individual and the species.

executive responses: behaviors such as sucking, grasping, and following that an infant initiates in order to establish or maintain contact with a close companion.

signaling responses: behaviors such as smiling and vocalizing that an infant emits in order to attract the attention or influence the behavior of a close companion.

Comparing the four
theoretical approaches

Although the four theories we have reviewed are different in many respects, each theory has had something to offer. Even though feeding practices are not as important as psychoanalysts had originally thought, it was Sigmund Freud who stressed that we will need to know more about mother/infant interactions if we are to understand how babies form emotional attachments. Erik Erikson and the learning theorists soon pursued Freud's early leads and concluded that caregivers do play an important role in the infant's emotional development. Presumably infants are likely to view a responsive companion who provides many comforts as a trustworthy and rewarding individual who is worthy of affection. Ethologists can agree with this point of view, but they would add that the infant is an active participant in the attachment process. That is, infants are born with a number of preprogrammed responses that enable them to promote the very interactions from which attachments are likely to develop. Finally, cognitive theorists have contributed to our understanding of early emotional development by showing that the timing of social attachments is related to the child's level of intellectual development. In sum, it makes no sense to tag one of these theories as "correct" and to ignore the other three, for each theory has helped us to understand how and why infants become attached to their most intimate companions.

Primary Social attachment
+

Development of Fearful Reactions

follow a Predictable developmental course

At about the same time that infants are establishing close affectional ties to a caregiver, they often begin to display negative emotional outbursts that may puzzle or perhaps even annoy their close companions. In this section we will look at two of the common fears of infancy—*stranger anxiety* and *separation anxiety*—and try to determine why these negative reactions are likely to emerge during the second half of the first year.

Stranger Anxiety

Nine-month-old Billy is sitting on the floor in the den when his mother leads a strange person into the room. The stranger suddenly walks toward the child, bends over, and says "Hi, Billy! How are you?" If Billy is like many 9-month-olds, he may stare at the stranger for a moment and then turn away, whimper, and crawl toward his mother.

This wary reaction to a stranger, or **stranger anxiety,** stands in marked contrast to the smiling, babbling, and other positive greetings that infants often emit when approached by a familiar companion. Schaffer and Emerson (1964) noted that most of the infants in their sample reacted positively to strangers up until the time they had formed an attachment (usually at about 7 months of age) but then became fearful of strangers shortly thereafter. Studies of North American children tend to confirm this finding: wary reactions to strangers often emerge at 6–7 months of age, peak at 8–10 months, and gradually decline in intensity over the second year (Sroufe, 1977). However, stranger anxiety may never completely subside, for 2-, 3-, and even 4-year-olds are apt to show at least some signs of wariness when approached by a stranger in an unfamiliar setting (Greenberg & Marvin, 1982).

At one time, stranger anxiety was thought to be a true developmental milestone—that is, an inevi- √

Photo 11-5. Although infants become more tolerant of strangers during the second year, stranger anxiety is a reaction that may never completely subside. Unavoidable contact with an intrusive stranger is likely to upset many 2-, 3-, and even 4-year-olds.

table response to unfamiliar company that supposedly characterized all infants who had become attached to a caregiver. However, recent research indicates that infants are not always afraid of strangers and, in fact, may sometimes react rather positively to an unfamiliar companion (Bretherton, Stolberg, & Kreye, 1981; Levitt, 1980). In Box 11-1, we will consider the circumstances under which stranger anxiety is most likely to occur and see how medical personnel and child-care professionals might use this knowledge to head off outbreaks of fear and trembling in their offices.

Separation Anxiety

Not only do 7–12-month-old infants become wary of strangers, but they also begin to display obvious signs of discomfort when separated from their mothers or other familiar companions. For example, 10-month-old Tony, restrained in his playpen, is likely to cry if he sees his mother put on a coat and pick up a purse as she prepares to go shopping. If unrestrained and exposed to the same scene, 15-month-old Ben might run and cling to his mother or at least follow her to the door. As she leaves and closes the door behind her, Ben will probably cry. These reactions reflect the infants' **separation anxiety.** Separation anxiety normally appears during the latter half of the first year (at about the time infants are forming primary social attachments), peaks at 14–20 months, and gradually becomes less frequent and less intense throughout infancy and the preschool period (Kagan, 1983; Weinraub & Lewis, 1977).

Children raised in some cultural settings protest separations from their mothers at an earlier age than North American or European infants. For example, Mary Ainsworth (1967) found that Ugandan infants begin to fear separations from their mothers as early as 5–6 months of age. Why? One reason may be that Ugandan babies have much more close contact with their mothers than is typical in Western cultures—these infants sleep with their mothers, nurse for at least two years, and go wherever their mothers go, riding on the mother's hips or across her back in a cotton sling. So Ugandan infants may be quick to protest separations from their mothers because these separations are very unusual events.

Why Do Infants Fear Separations and Strangers?

We have seen that both stranger anxiety and separation anxiety emerge at about the same time as the primary social attachment and follow a predictable developmental course. Why do children who are just beginning to appreciate the pleasures of love now suddenly experience the gripping agony of fear? Let's consider three very different points of view.

The "conditioned anxiety" (or fear of separation) hypothesis. Psychoanalysts and some social-learning theorists have proposed that infants may learn to fear separations from their caregivers if prior discomforts (for example, hunger, wet diapers, and pain) have been especially frequent or intense during periods when caregivers were not present to relieve them. In other words, infants may associate prolonged or intense discomfort with the caregiver's absence and then express their "conditioned anxiety" by protesting whenever the caregiver is about to depart.

How, then, does the "conditioned anxiety" hypothesis explain the infant's fear of strangers? Quite easily. Presumably stranger anxiety actually represents the child's fear of becoming separated from or losing the person(s) to whom he or she is attached. Consistent with this point of view are the observations that wary reactions to separations and to strangers first appear just after the infant has become attached to someone (Schaffer & Emerson, 1964) and that attached infants will often cling to their mothers or other close companions when a stranger approaches (Morgan & Ricciuti, 1969).

Although this "conditioned anxiety" hypothesis is appealing for its simplicity, there are some problems with it. For example, it cannot easily explain why infants are *less* likely to protest separations from a loved one at home (where they have previously suffered many discomforts) than in a laboratory environment where they have never been before (Rinkoff & Corter, 1980). Nor does it adequately explain the *early* separation protests seen among Ugandan infants, who have rarely been separated from their mothers and therefore have had little or no opportunity to associate pain and discomfort with the mother's absence. Finally, the notion that stranger anxiety represents a "fear of separation," or a concern about losing loved ones, does not explain why infants sometimes react very positively to strangers and may

---

stranger anxiety: a wary or fretful reaction that infants and toddlers often display when approached by an unfamiliar person.

separation anxiety: a wary or fretful reaction that infants and toddlers often display when separated from the person(s) to whom they are attached.

Box 11-1
Combating Stranger Anxiety:
Some Helpful Hints for Doctors
and Child-Care Professionals

It is not at all unusual for toddlers visiting the doctor's office to break into tears and to cling tenaciously to their parents. Some youngsters who remember previous visits may be suffering from "shot anxiety" rather than stranger anxiety, but many are simply reacting fearfully to the approach of an intrusive physician who may poke, prod, and handle them in ways that are atypical and upsetting. Fortunately, there are steps that caregivers and medical personnel (or any other stranger) can take to make such visits less terrifying for an infant or toddler. What can we suggest?

1. *Keep familiar companions available.* Infants react much more negatively to strangers when they are separated from their mothers or other close companions. Indeed, most 6–12-month-olds are not particularly wary of an approaching stranger if they are sitting on their mothers' laps; however, they will frequently whimper and cry at the stranger's approach if seated only a few feet from their mothers (Morgan & Ricciuti, 1969). Clearly, doctors and nurses can expect a more constructive response from their youngest patients if they can avoid separating them from their caregivers.

Stranger anxiety is also less likely if the caregiver issues a warm greeting to the stranger or uses a positive tone of voice when talking to the infant about the stranger (Boccia & Campos, 1983; Feinman & Lewis, 1983). These actions permit the child to engage in *social referencing* and to conclude that maybe the stranger really isn't all that scary if mom and dad seem to like him. It might not hurt, then, for medical personnel to strike up a pleasant conversation with the caregiver before directing their attention to the child.

2. *Make the setting more "familiar."* Stranger anxiety occurs less frequently in familiar settings than in unfamiliar ones. For example, few 10-month-olds are especially wary of strangers at home, but most react negatively to strange companions when tested in an unfamiliar laboratory (Sroufe, Waters, & Matas, 1974). Although it may be unrealistic to advise modern physicians to make home visits, they could make at least one of their examination rooms more homelike for young children, perhaps by placing an attractive mobile in one corner and posters of cartoon characters on the wall or by having a stuffed toy or two available for the child to play with. The infant's familiarity with a strange setting also makes a difference: whereas the vast majority (90%) of 10-month-olds become upset if a stranger approaches them within a minute after being placed in an unfamiliar room, only about half will react negatively to the stranger when they have had ten minutes to grow accustomed to this setting (Sroufe et al., 1974). Perhaps trips to the doctor would become more tolerable for an infant or a toddler if medical personnel gave the child a few minutes to familiarize himself with the examination room before making their entrance.

3. *Be a less intrusive stranger.* An infant's response to a stranger often depends on the stranger's behavior. Mary Levitt (1980) finds that strange adults can easily become "friends" if they allow the infant to take the initiative and control their earliest interactions. By contrast, intrusive strangers who approach rapidly and force themselves on the child (for example, by pinning him to an examination table or trying to pick him up) are likely to elicit feelings of terror (Sroufe, 1977). Of course, busy physicians may not have the 20 minutes it can take for an apprehensive child to warm up to them on his own. But they don't need that much time anyway. Inge Bretherton and her associates (Bretherton, Stolberg, & Kreye, 1981) report that most 1–2-year-olds will respond favorably to a friendly stranger who (1) is not overly intrusive and (2) offers a toy (or suggests an activity) with which the infant is familiar. In fact, friendly strangers are apt to be more successful at establishing rapport with an infant if they cautiously take the initiative and allow the infant to regulate the pace of their activities rather than sitting back and waiting for the child to initiate an interaction with them (Bretherton et al., 1981).

4. *Try looking a little less strange to the child.* Stranger anxiety depends, in part, on the stranger's physical appearance. Jerome Kagan (1972) has argued that infants form mental representations, or *schemata,* for the faces that they encounter in daily life and are most likely to be afraid of people whose appearance is not easily assimilated into these existing schemes. So a doctor in a sterile white lab coat and a strange stethoscope around her neck (or a nurse with a pointed hat that may give her a "witchlike" look) can make infants and toddlers rather wary indeed! Pediatric professionals may not be able to alter physical features (for example, a huge nose or a facial scar) that might make children wary; but they can and often have shed their strange instruments and white uniforms in favor of more "normal" attire that will help their youngest patients to recognize them as members of the human race. Babysitters who favor the "punk" look might also do well to heed this advice if establishing rapport with their young companions is a priority.

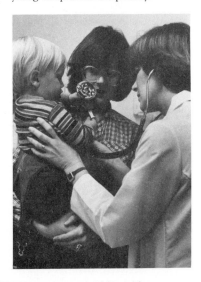

Most babies respond favorably to a friendly stranger—even a doctor—who offers a toy.

continue to do so even after they have seen their mothers leave the room (Ainsworth et al., 1978). Let's now consider a second point of view that does seem to explain these findings.

The ethological viewpoint. The ethological explanation for both stranger anxiety and separation anxiety is remarkably straightforward. John Bowlby (1973) suggests that there are a number of events that qualify as natural clues to danger. In other words, some situations have been so frequently associated with danger throughout a species' evolutionary history that a fear or avoidance response has become innate, or "biologically programmed." Among the events that infants may be programmed to fear are strange people, strange settings, and the strange circumstance of being separated from familiar companions.[1]

According to the ethological viewpoint, infants should show stronger separation protests in an unfamiliar laboratory than at home because the "strangeness" of the laboratory setting magnifies the apprehension they will ordinarily experience when separated from a caregiver. Moreover, ethologists would argue that Ugandan infants are quick to protest separations from their mothers because these separations occur so very infrequently that they qualify as highly unusual (that is, fear-provoking) events (Ainsworth, 1967).

Why, then, do stranger anxiety and separation anxiety become less intense during the second year, declining to the point where the infant will actually *initiate* separations and is able to tolerate strangers, even after her mother has left the room? Mary Ainsworth (Ainsworth et al., 1974) believes that infants become less wary of strangers and separations as they begin to use their attachment objects as **secure bases** who encourage a second preprogrammed behavior—exploring the environment. As the infant ventures away from his secure base to explore, he should eventually discover that many novel stimuli (including friendly strangers) can be interesting and enjoyable in their own right.

Are infants less likely to fear separations that they initiate themselves? Apparently so. Harriet Rheingold and Carol Eckerman (1970) found that 10-month-

olds were perfectly willing to leave their mothers and venture alone into a strange room in order to play there. However, a second group of 10-month-olds typically cried when they were placed in the same strange room and then were left alone as their mothers departed. It appears that the first group of infants were not discomforted in the strange setting because they knew where their mothers were and were using them as a secure base from which to explore the environment.

In sum, ethologists view the anxieties of infancy as preprogrammed reactions that help to protect the young of a species from harm or discomfort by ensuring that they will remain near their caregivers. Yet, the caregivers who serve this protective function are also instrumental in alleviating these programmed fears. By serving as a secure base for exploratory activities, the caregiver encourages the infant to venture into the unknown and to become increasingly familiar with the environment. As a result, the child should eventually become more tolerant of separations and much less wary of stimuli (strangers and unfamiliar settings) that have previously been a source of concern.

The cognitive-developmental viewpoint. The cognitive explanation of stranger anxiety and separation anxiety nicely complements the ethological viewpoint. Jerome Kagan (1972) believes that stranger anxiety is a natural outgrowth of the infant's perceptual and cognitive development. Kagan suggests that 6–8-month-olds have finally developed stable schemata for the faces of familiar companions and that a strange face now represents a discrepant and potentially fear-producing stimulus. He notes that children of this age will typically stare at a stranger before they begin to protest. Presumably this short visual fixation is not a fear-induced "freezing" but, rather, a period of *hypothesizing*: the infant is examining the discrepant stimulus and trying to explain what it is or what has become of the familiar faces that match his or her schema for human beings. Failing to answer these questions, the child becomes wary of the stranger and may cry in an attempt to summon familiar company. As infants mature, they are gradually exposed to many strangers, and their schemata for faces will become more generalized. Thus, a 2-year-old is unlikely to be upset at the sight of a strange face,

[1]Bowlby is not suggesting that a programmed fear of the unfamiliar is present at birth. Quite the contrary; he argues that a neonate's cognitive and perceptual capabilities are very immature and that it will take some time for the child to learn what is "familiar" and to discriminate these persons, objects, and events from those that are unfamiliar. But once such discriminations are possible, the infant's preprogrammed "fear of the unfamiliar" should be readily apparent.

secure-base phenomenon: the tendency of infants to venture away from a close companion to explore the environment.

because strangers are now easily assimilated into the infant's very broad facial schema.

Kagan's (1972, 1976) explanation of separation anxiety is equally interesting. He suggests that infants develop not only schemata for familiar faces (caregivers) but also schemata for a familiar person's probable whereabouts. In other words, the infant may schematize "familiar faces in familiar places." Kagan notes that infants are often separated from their mothers in the course of day-to-day living and generally do not protest these brief separations. For example, if a mother proceeds into the kitchen, leaving her 10-month-old son on the living room floor, the infant is likely to stop playing and watch her depart and then resume his previous activity without protesting her absence. This separation is not protested because the child is able to explain where his mother has gone; that is, he has previously developed a schema for mother-in-the-kitchen. But should the mother pick up her coat and purse and walk out the front door, the child will find it difficult to account for her whereabouts and will probably cry. In sum, cognitive theorists believe that infants are most likely to protest separations when they cannot understand where their absent companions may have gone or when they are likely to return.

The results of a home-based observational study (Littenberg, Tulkin, & Kagan, 1971) are quite consistent with Kagan's cognitive hypothesis. In this study, 15-month-old infants showed little separation protest when mother departed through a doorway she used often but considerable protest when she left through a door that she used infrequently, such as the entry to a closet or the cellar. The children were separated from their mothers in both cases, but they protested only when they could not account for the mother's whereabouts.

Kagan's theory also explains the results of an interesting study by Carl Corter and his associates (Corter, Zucker, & Galligan, 1980). Nine-month-old infants first accompanied their mothers to a strange room (room A) and shortly thereafter watched the mothers exit into a second room (room B). Few of the infants protested this separation; most of them continued to play for a while with the toys that were present before crawling into the adjoining room and finding their mothers. In cognitive terms, it is reasonable to assume that the infants had formed a schema for the mother's whereabouts once they had found her in room B. At this point, the infants and their mothers reentered room A and spent a short time together before the mother departed once again. But on this second trial, she went into an-

other room (room C) and thus violated the infant's schema for her probable whereabouts. This time the majority of the infants fussed or cried! And where did these distressed youngsters go to search for their mothers? Generally, they crawled to the doorway that matched their schemata (room B) rather than to the portal through which they had most recently seen the mother depart (room C). Here, then, is another demonstration that infants are most likely to protest separations from a caregiver when they are uncertain of her whereabouts.

Summing up. Clearly, stranger anxiety and separation anxiety are rather complex emotional responses that may stem, in part, from (1) a child's general *apprehension of the unfamiliar,* (2) her inability to *explain* who a stranger may be, what he may want, or what has become of familiar companions, and (3) perhaps even a *fear of losing those loved ones* who provide so much warmth and security. So there is no one correct explanation for these interesting fears of infancy: each of the explanations above has received some support and has helped us to understand why infants are often wary of strangers and upset when separated from their caregivers.

At this point, we might ask "Do the emotional events and experiences of infancy have any long-term effects on developing children?" Most developmental theorists believe that they do. Sigmund Freud (1905/1930) argued that the formation of a stable mother/infant emotional bond is *absolutely necessary* for normal social and personality development, a sentiment shared by ethologist John Bowlby and the best-known psychoanalytic theorist of recent times, Erik Erikson. Erikson's view is that emotional attachments provide the infant with a basic sense of trust that will permit him or her to form close affectional ties to other people later in life. Learning theorists such as Harry Harlow (who studied monkeys) and Robert Sears (who studied humans) believe that close contact with a mother figure allows the infant to acquire a repertoire of social skills that will enable him or her to interact effectively and appropriately with other members of the species. In sum, almost everyone agrees that the emotional events of infancy are very influential in shaping one's future development.

There are at least two ways to evaluate this **"early experience" hypothesis.** First, one could try to determine whether infants who do not become securely attached to their parents turn out any different from those who do. Second, one could look at what

Table 11-1. The eight episodes that make up the strange-situations test   *diff. in infant temperaments*

Number of episode	Persons present	Duration	Brief description of action
1	Mother, baby, and observer	30 seconds	Observer introduces mother and baby to experimental room, then leaves. (Room contains many appealing toys scattered about.)
2	Mother and baby	3 minutes	Mother is nonparticipant while baby explores; if necessary, play is stimulated after 2 minutes.
3	Stranger, mother, and baby	3 minutes	Stranger enters. First minute: stranger silent. Second minute: stranger converses with mother. Third minute: stranger approaches baby. After 3 minutes mother leaves unobtrusively.
4	Stranger and baby	3 minutes or less	First separation episode. Stranger's behavior is geared to that of baby.
5	Mother and baby	3 minutes or more	First reunion episode. Mother greets and/or comforts baby, then tries to settle him again in play. Mother then leaves, saying "bye-bye."
6	Baby alone	3 minutes or less	Second separation episode.
7	Stranger and baby	3 minutes or less	Continuation of second separation. Stranger enters and gears her behavior to that of baby.
8	Mother and baby	3 minutes	Second reunion episode. Mother enters, greets baby, then picks him up. Meanwhile stranger leaves unobtrusively.

Source: Ainsworth et al. (1978).

happens to infants who have had little or no contact with a mother figure during the first two years and do not become attached to anyone. In the pages that follow, we will consider the findings and implications of both these lines of inquiry.

Individual Differences in the Quality of Attachments

Mary Ainsworth and her associates (Ainsworth et al., 1978) have found that infants differ in the type (or quality) of attachments that they have with their caregivers. Ainsworth measures the quality of an infant's attachment by exposing the child to a **"strange situations" test** consisting of a series of eight episodes designed to gradually escalate the amount of stress that the baby will experience (see Table 11-1). By recording and analyzing the child's responses to these episodes— that is, exploratory activities, reactions to strangers and to separations, and, in particular, the child's behaviors when reunited with the mother—we can usually place his or her attachment into one of the following categories:

1. *Secure attachment.* About 70% of 1-year-old infants fall into this category. The **securely attached** infant actively explores while alone with the mother and is visibly upset by separation. The infant greets the mother warmly when she returns and will welcome physical contact with her. The child is outgoing with strangers while the mother is present.

2. *Insecure attachment (anxious and resistant).* About 10% of 1-year-olds fall into this category. Although they appear quite anxious and are unlikely to explore while the mother is present, they become very

early-experience hypothesis: the notion that the social and emotional events of infancy are very influential in determining the course of one's future development.

strange-situations test: a series of eight mildly stressful situations to which infants are exposed in order to determine the quality of their attachments to one or more close companions.

secure attachment: an infant/caregiver bond in which the child welcomes contact with a close companion and uses this person as a secure base from which to explore the environment.

distressed when the mother departs. When the mother returns, these infants are ambivalent: they will try to remain near her, although they resent her for having left them, but they are likely to resist contact initiated by the mother. **Anxious/resistant** infants are quite wary of strangers, even when their mothers are present.

3. *Insecure attachment (anxious and avoidant)*. These infants (approximately 20% of 1-year-olds) seem uninterested in exploring when alone with their mothers. Moreover, they show little distress when separated from the mother and will generally avoid contact with her when she returns. **Anxious/avoidant** infants are not particularly wary of strangers but may sometimes avoid or ignore them in much the same way that they avoid or ignore their mothers.

From these descriptions, it would appear that securely attached infants are reasonably happy individuals who have established an affectionate relationship with their primary caregivers. By contrast, infants in the anxious/resistant category are drawn to their mothers but seem not to trust them, while infants who are anxious and avoidant appear to derive little if any comfort from their mothers, almost as if they were somewhat "detached" from them.

How Do Infants Become Securely or Insecurely Attached?

Ainsworth's caregiving hypothesis. Ainsworth (1979) believes that the quality of an infant's attachment to his mother depends largely on the kind of "mothering" he has received. According to this **caregiving hypothesis,** mothers of *securely attached* infants are thought to be responsive caregivers from the very beginning. And evidently they are, for Ainsworth finds that these mothers are highly sensitive to their infants' signals, emotionally expressive, and likely to encourage their infants to explore; moreover, they seem to enjoy close contact with their babies (Ainsworth, 1979; Ainsworth et al., 1978). Ainsworth believes that infants learn what to expect from other people from their early experiences with primary caregivers. When a caregiver is sensitive to the infant's needs and easily accessible, the infant should derive comfort and pleasure from their interactions and become securely attached.

Mothers of *anxious and resistant* infants seem interested in their babies and willing to provide close physical contact. However, they frequently misinterpret their infants' signals and have generally failed to estab-

lish synchronized routines with them. In some cases, part of the problem may be a "difficult" infant, for Everett Waters and his associates found that infants classified as anxious/resistant at 1 year of age had often been rather irritable and unresponsive as neonates (Waters, Vaughn, & Egeland, 1980). Yet, the infant's behavior cannot be the only contributor to an anxious/resistant attachment, since many difficult babies will eventually become securely attached to their caregivers. Ainsworth (1979) has noted that mothers of anxious/resistant infants tend to be inconsistent in their caregiving. At times they react very enthusiastically to their babies, although their responses to the infant may depend more on their own moods than on the infant's emotional state. As a result, the infant becomes both saddened and resentful when he learns that he cannot necessarily count on the mother for the emotional support and comfort that he needs (see also Belsky, Rovine, & Taylor, 1984; Shiller, Izard, & Hembree, 1986).

The mothers of *anxious and avoidant* infants differ from other mothers in several respects. For example, they are very impatient with their babies, angry or resentful when the infant interferes with their own plans and activities, and quite unresponsive to the infant's signals (Ainsworth, 1979; Egeland & Farber, 1984). Moreover, they often express negative feelings about their infants, and on those occasions when they do respond positively to their children, they tend to limit their expressions of affection to brief kisses rather than hugging or cuddling (Tracy & Ainsworth, 1981). Ainsworth (1979) believes that these mothers are rigid, self-centered people who are likely to *reject* their babies. Indeed, several investigators have found that rejecting mothers (particularly those who express their rejection by abusing their infants) are the ones who are likely to have infants classified as anxious and avoidant (see Lyons-Ruth, Connell, Zoll, & Stahl, 1987; Sroufe, 1985).

Yet, caregivers need not be extremely unresponsive or actively reject their child in order to promote an anxious/avoidant relationship. Jay Belsky and his associates (Belsky, Rovine, & Taylor, 1984) find that some infants classified as anxious and avoidant have over-zealous mothers who are constantly providing them with high levels of stimulation, even during periods when the child doesn't care to be stimulated. Perhaps these infants have learned to cope with this intrusive mothering by simply turning away from or avoiding their rather insensitive caregivers so as not to become overaroused.

Caregivers or infants as architects of attachment quality? The temperament hypothesis.
To this point, we have talked as if mothers were primarily responsible for the kinds of attachments their infants form. Not everyone agrees. Jerome Kagan (1984), for example, believes that the strange-situations test may really measure individual differences in infants' temperaments rather than the quality of their attachments. Accordingly, a temperamentally "difficult" infant who resists changes in routine and is upset by novelty may become so distressed by the strange-situations procedure that he is unable to respond constructively to his mother's comforting and is thus classified as "anxious and *resistant*." By contrast, a friendly, easygoing child is apt to be classified as "securely" attached, whereas one who is shy or "slow to warm up" may appear distant or detached in the strange-situations paradigm and is apt to be classified as "anxious and *avoidant*." So Kagan's **temperament hypothesis** implies that infants, not caregivers, are the primary architects of their attachment classifications. Presumably, the attachment behaviors that a child displays reflect his or her own temperament.

However, critics of the temperament hypothesis cite several observations that are damaging to that viewpoint. For example, infants can be securely attached to one close companion and insecurely attached to another—a pattern that we should not expect if attachment classifications were merely reflections of the child's relatively stable temperamental characteristics (Sroufe, 1985). Moreover, the quality of a child's attachments to a particular caregiver can change relatively quickly if the caregiver experiences life changes (for example, divorce, a return to work) that significantly alter the way he or she interacts with the child (Thompson, Lamb, & Estes, 1982). Relatively stable aspects of temperament should not be so readily modifiable. Finally, several recent longitudinal studies have measured infant temperament, infant social behavior, and maternal caregiving over the first year to see which of these factors best predicts the quality of infant attachments at age 12 months. We will concentrate on one of these studies in particular (Goldberg, Perrotta, Minde, & Corter, 1986) because all the infants were premature and, thus, likely to display the sluggish temperamental profile that might place them at risk of developing insecure attachments. At three-month intervals over the first year, ratings were made of (1) the infants' social behaviors, (2) the mothers' caregiving styles (for example, responsiveness to social signals; ac-cessibility), and (3) the infants' temperamental characteristics. At the end of the year, the infants were tested in the strange-situations paradigm to determine the type of attachment they had to their mothers. The results were clear: the best predictor of infants' later attachment classifications was *the style of caregiving their mothers had used*, and neither infant social behaviors nor infant temperamental characteristics reliably forecasted the quality of these attachments (see also Belsky, Rovine, & Taylor, 1984, and Crockenberg & McCluskey, 1986, for similar results). And it is important to add that the majority of Goldberg's temperamentally sluggish, "at risk" infants ended up establishing *secure* attachments with their mothers rather than the anxious, insecure relationships that might have been predicted by Kagan's temperament hypothesis.

So it seems that caregivers, not infants, are the *primary* architects of the quality of infant attachments. This is not to say that infant temperament is unimportant, for we've seen that it is harder for a caregiver to be consistently sensitive and responsive to a difficult infant than to an easygoing one. Yet, the results of one recent study (Weber, Levitt, & Clark, 1986) suggest that if temperamental variables are related to the security (or insecurity) of attachments, it is the mother's temperament that makes the difference, not the child's. Of course, this latter finding is quite consistent with Ainsworth's "caregiving" hypothesis if it is reasonable to assume that a mother's temperamental characteristics will influence the type of caregiving she provides.

To this point, we have focused only on the quality of the infant's attachment to his or her mother.

---

anxious and resistant attachment: an insecure infant/caregiver bond, characterized by strong separation protest and a tendency of the child to resist contact initiated by the caregiver, particularly after a separation.

anxious and avoidant attachment: an insecure infant/caregiver bond, characterized by little separation protest and a tendency of the child to avoid or ignore the caregiver.

caregiving hypothesis: Ainsworth's notion that the type of attachment an infant develops with a particular caregiver depends primarily on the kind of caregiving he has received from that person.

temperament hypothesis: Kagan's view that the strange-situations test measures individual differences in infants' temperaments rather than the quality of their attachments.

Box 11-2
Fathers as Attachment Objects

In 1975, Michael Lamb described fathers as the "forgotten contributors to child development." And he was right. Until the mid-1970s fathers were treated as biological necessities who played only a minor role in the social and emotional development of their infants and toddlers. One reason for overlooking or discounting the father's early contributions may have been that fathers spend less time interacting with babies than mothers do (Belsky, Gilstrap, & Rovine, 1984; Parke, 1981). However, fathers appear to be just as "engrossed" with their newborn infants as mothers are (Parke, 1981), and they become increasingly responsive to their infants' social and emotional signals over the first year of the child's life (Belsky et al., 1984). How do infants react to dad's increasing involvement?

Lamb (1981) reports that many infants form attachments to their fathers during the third quarter of the first year, particularly if the fathers spend a lot of time with them. Lamb also notes that fathers and mothers respond in different ways to their babies. Mothers are more likely than fathers to hold their infants, to soothe them, to play traditional games, and to care for their needs; fathers are more likely than mothers to provide playful physical stimulation and to initiate unusual or unpredictable games that infants often enjoy (Lamb, 1981). Although many infants prefer their mothers' company when upset or afraid, fathers are generally preferred as playmates. However, the playmate role is only one of many that fathers assume. Most fathers are quite skillful at soothing and comforting their distressed infants, and they may also serve as a "secure base" from which their babies will venture to explore the environment (Hwang, 1986; Lamb, 1981). In other words, fathers are rather versatile companions who can assume any and all of the functions normally served by the other parent (of course, the same is true of mothers).

Does the kind of attachment that an infant establishes with his or her mother affect the infant's relationship with the father? Not necessarily. Mary Main and Donna Weston (1981) used the strange-situations test to measure the quality of infants' attachments to both their mothers and their fathers. They found that the quality of the child's attachment to one parent did *not* predict the type of attachment relationship that the infant had with the second parent. Of the 44 infants tested, 12 were securely attached to both parents, 11 were secure with the mother but insecure with the father, 10 were inse-

The "playmate" role is only one of many that fathers assume.

continued

Does the kind of attachment an infant has to the mother have any effect on the infant's relationship with the father? In Box 11-2 we will explore this issue as we look at some of the ways fathers contribute to their infants' social and emotional development.

Long-Term Correlates of Secure and Insecure Attachments

Does the quality of an infant's attachment relationships predict his or her later behavior? It seems to. And even though the existing data are somewhat limited in that they focus almost exclusively on infants' attachments to their mothers, the later correlates of secure and insecure attachments are very interesting indeed. For example, Susan Londerville and Mary Main (1981) found that infants who were securely attached at 12 months of age are more likely than those who were insecurely attached to obey their mothers and to cooperate with female strangers at 21 months of age. Moreover, infants who were securely attached at age 12–18 months are more curious and more creative in their symbolic play at age 2 and are more sociable with peers (Matas, Arend, & Sroufe, 1978; Pastor, 1981; Slade, 1987), and by age 3 they are even more comfortable *competing* with a strange adult at a game than are children with a history of insecure attachments (Lutkenhaus, Grossmann, & Grossmann, 1985). And it is interesting to note that, from a peer's point of view, securely attached 2–3-year-olds are much more attractive as playmates than are children who are insecurely attached. In fact, peers often respond in an overtly negative or aggressive way to playmates classified as "anxious and resistant" (Jacobson & Wille, 1986).

The relationship of early attachments to social and intellectual behavior during the *preschool* period is nicely illustrated in a study by Everett Waters and his associates. Waters, Wippman, and Sroufe (1979) first measured the quality of children's attachments at 15 months of age and then observed these children in a nursery school setting at age 3½. Children who had

cure with the mother but secure with the father, and 11 were insecurely attached to both parents.

What does the father add to a child's social and emotional development? One way to find out is to compare the social behavior of infants who are securely attached to their fathers and infants whose relationships with their fathers are insecure. Main and Weston adopted this strategy by exposing their four groups of infants to a friendly stranger in a clown outfit who spent several minutes trying to play with the child and then turned around and cried when a person at the door told the clown he would have to leave. As the clown went through his routine, the infants were each observed and rated for (1) the extent to which they were willing to establish a positive relationship with the clown (low ratings indicated that the infant was wary or distressed) and (2) signs of emotional conflict (that is, indications of psychological disturbance such as curling up in the fetal position on the floor or vocalizing in a "social" manner to a wall). The table shows the results of this stranger test. Note that infants who were securely attached to both parents were the most socially responsive group. Equally important is the finding that infants who were securely attached to *at least one parent* were more friendly toward the clown and less emotionally conflicted than infants who had insecure relationships with both parents. In sum, this study illustrates the important role that fathers play in their infants' social and emotional development. Not only are infants more socially responsive when they are securely attached to *both* the mother and the father, but it also appears that a secure attachment to the father can help to prevent harmful consequences (emotional disturbances, an exaggerated fear of other people) that could otherwise result when infants are insecurely attached to their mothers.

Average levels of social responsiveness and emotional conflict shown by infants who were either securely or insecurely attached to their mothers and fathers.

	Patterns of attachment			
Measure	Securely attached to both parents	Secure with mother, nonsecure with father	Nonsecure with mother, secure with father	Nonsecurely attached to both parents
Social responsiveness	6.04	4.87	3.30	2.45
Emotional conflict	1.17	1.00	1.80	2.50

Note: Social responsiveness ratings could vary from 1 (wary, distressed) to 9 (happy, responsive). Conflict ratings could vary from 1 (no conflict) to 5 (very conflicted).

Source: Adapted from Main & Weston (1981).

been securely attached to their mothers at age 15 months were now social leaders in the nursery school: they often initiated play activities, were generally sensitive to the needs and feelings of other children, and were very popular with their peers. Observers described these children as curious, self-directed, and eager to learn. By contrast, children who had been insecurely attached at age 15 months were socially and emotionally withdrawn, were hesitant to engage other children in play activities, and were described by observers as less curious, less interested in learning, and much less forceful in pursuing their goals. By age 4 to 5, children who had been securely attached as infants were still more curious, more responsive to peers, and much less dependent on adults than their classmates who had been insecurely attached (Arend, Gove, & Sroufe, 1979; Sroufe, Fox, & Pancake, 1983).

Fortunately, the future is not always so bleak for infants who are insecurely attached. As we saw in Box 11-2, a secure relationship with another person such as the father (or perhaps a grandparent or an older sibling) may help to prevent the undesirable consequences of an insecure attachment to the mother. In addition, it is quite possible for an initially insecure attachment to become more secure over time. One reason infants become insecurely attached in the first place is that their mothers have often withdrawn from caregiving activities because of life stresses of their own, such as health or marital problems, financial woes, and a lack of emotional support from friends and family members. Recently, researchers have been finding that initially insecure infants are likely to become securely attached if the lives of their close companions become less stressful (Vaughn, Egeland, Sroufe, & Waters, 1979). Often these positive developments take place as highly stressed and emotionally unresponsive mothers begin to receive emotional support and assistance from a close friend, a spouse, or a grandparent (Crockenberg, 1981; Feiring, Fox, Jaskir, & Lewis, 1987; Levitt, Weber, & Clark, 1986). However, it is also possible for securely attached infants to become insecurely attached if their caregivers experience life changes that make them less accessible and less responsive to their children. Ross Thompson and his colleagues (Thompson, Lamb, & Estes, 1982) have found that secure attachments sometimes change for the worse if the mother returns to work or if the child begins to receive regular caregiving from someone else (for example, a babysitter or a day-care agency). Unlike diamonds, attachments are not forever: any event that drastically alters the ways an infant and caregiver respond to each other is likely to have a significant effect on the quality of their emotional relationship.

But it would be wrong to create the impression that all mothers will undermine the security of their infants' attachments by returning to work or enrolling their children in a day-care center. As it turns out, the effects of maternal employment and alternative caregiving are bidirectional: although some securely attached infants become insecure, at least as many insecure infants will develop secure attachments to their mothers after the mother has returned to work or enrolled them in day care (Thompson et al., 1982). In the pages that follow, we will take a closer look at the effects of maternal employment and alternative caregiving and try to determine why these events and experiences do not affect all children in the same way.

Maternal Employment, Alternative Caregiving, and Children's Emotional Development

Working mothers are no longer exceptions to the rule. In the United States, over half of all mothers who live with their husbands are now employed outside the home, and the percentage of working mothers in single-parent households is even higher (Hoffman, 1984). Not only does work take a mother away from her child for several hours a day, but her infants or preschool children may also have to adjust to some form of alternative caregiving—either in-home or out-of-the-home care by a babysitter or a relative or care provided by a group day-care center (Klein, 1985). Do these daily separations and contacts with alternative caregivers have much effect on a child's social and emotional development? Let's first consider what we know about maternal employment.

Mothers who work outside the home are obviously less accessible to their children (at least during working hours) than those who remain at home full-time. One recent study found that working mothers spend much less time alone with their children than nonemployed mothers do, and the more hours these mothers worked, the less time they spent playing with their infants and toddlers (Easterbrooks & Goldberg, 1985). Nevertheless, a recent review of the literature suggests that maternal employment, in itself, is unlikely to have adverse effects on the vast majority of young children (Hoffman, 1984). Apparently working mothers can be quite successful at establishing secure relationships with their infants and toddlers if they compensate for their lack of available time for their children by being particularly sensitive and responsive when they do interact with them. Moreover, Easterbrooks and Goldberg (1985) find that families spend just as many hours together in "family" activities in households where mothers work as in those where only the father is employed. So it seems that intensive family interactions may provide all the experience an infant needs to become (or remain) securely attached to a working mother.

Yet, there is another side to this story that we should consider before drawing any firm conclusions of our own. Most studies that show no differences in the emotional development of children of employed and nonemployed mothers have focused on two-parent, middle-class families. Thus, the working mothers in these studies may be somewhat "advantaged" in that they have a spouse to assume some responsibility for child care and to encourage them as they try to establish and maintain warm, loving relationships with their infants and toddlers. Can we assume that the results of these studies would also apply to economically disadvantaged families, particularly those in which working mothers are single parents and have no spousal support?

Probably not. In one study of economically disadvantaged families (Vaughn, Gove, & Egeland, 1980), infants whose mothers had returned to work before the infants' first birthday were much more likely to develop insecure attachments than infants from similar backgrounds whose mothers cared for them at home. Moreover, the likelihood that these infants' attachments would become (or remain) insecure over time was greater when the working mother was a single parent. So an early return to work by mothers who must raise children without support from a spouse can impede the development of secure emotional attachments. In fact, even children from middle-class families often develop insecure attachments if their mothers return to work during the latter half of the first year—the period when infants are normally establishing and consolidating their primary social attachments (Benn, 1986; see also Barglow, Vaughn, & Molitor, 1987, and Belsky & Rovine, 1988).

What are the effects of a mother's return to work during the second year, after her infant has already formed an attachment to her? In their study of economically disadvantaged families, Vaughn et al. (1980) found that about half the infants whose mothers returned to work after the infants' first birthday changed attachment classifications. Yet, the direction of these changes was very interesting in that insecure infants were as likely to become securely attached after their mothers' return to work as secure infants were to become insecurely attached. Moreover, a recent short-term longitudinal study of *two-parent, middle-class* families (Owen, Easterbrooks, Chase-Lansdale, & Goldberg, 1984) found that not one infant classified as securely attached at age 12 months became insecurely attached after the mother had returned to work. Of course, it is possible that an infant from virtually any background could become insecurely attached if his mother's return to work should make her less sensitive to his social overtures and emotional needs (see Thompson et al., 1982). But the bulk of the evidence suggests that emotionally responsive mothers, particularly those who have the support of their husbands, need not worry about undermining an *already secure* relationship with an infant should they decide to return to work.

Finally, an unexpected outcome of the longitudinal study by Owen et al. (1984) is worth noting here. Infants whose mothers returned to work in the second year occasionally became more insecure in their relationships with their *fathers!* The authors explain this finding by speculating that fathers spend more time on routine household chores after their wives return to work and, as a result, may become less physically and emotionally responsive to their infants. Moreover, fathers in dual-career families tend to become less satisfied with the quality of their marital relationships after their wives return to work—a factor that could influence the ways they respond to their children (see Crouter, Perry-Jenkins, Huston, & McHale, 1987). Will these emerging insecurities eventually subside as fathers get used to the idea of their wives' working or become more proficient at striking a balance between housework and caregiving activities? At this point we cannot say, for the research that could tell us remains to be conducted. And in view of the important roles that fathers play in their children's social and emotional development, perhaps such research should become a priority.

How have children of working mothers adjusted to the alternative caregiving they receive? Is there a danger that infants in day care will form close attachments to their alternative caregivers and become less responsive to or even "detached" from their biological parents? Or could day care have the opposite effect by teaching children social skills and actually fostering their emotional development? As Box 11-3 indicates, there are no simple answers for these questions: day care affects different children in different ways.

The Unattached Infant: Effects of Restricted Social Contacts during Infancy

Some infants have very limited contacts with adults during the first year or two of life and do not appear to become attached to anyone. Occasionally these socially deprived youngsters are reared at home by very abusive or neglectful caregivers, but most of them are found in understaffed institutions where they may see a caregiver only when it is time to be fed, changed, or bathed. Will these unattached infants suffer as a result of their early experiences? If so, how are they likely to differ from children raised at home by a responsive caregiver, and what, if anything, can be done to "normalize" their developmental progress? These are the issues we will consider in the pages that follow.

We will begin by looking at the immediate and long-range effects of social deprivation on infant monkeys. Although this may seem a strange way to approach questions about socially deprived humans, there are several good reasons for reviewing the animal literature. For one thing, socially deprived humans are rather hard to come by; very few babies are raised without a primary caregiver, and it is clearly unethical to subject human infants to conditions of prolonged social deprivation when we have reason to suspect that these experiences will prove harmful to their development. But monkeys can be subjected to varying degrees of deprivation in controlled experiments that permit the investigator to infer cause-and-effect relationships. This is hardly the ideal solution, for one can never be absolutely certain that findings obtained for monkeys will hold for humans. However, monkeys do develop, and their development, like that of human infants, takes place over a period of years. Infant monkeys also form emotional attachments to their mothers—attachments that closely resemble the human infant's emotional ties to close companions. So it would seem that tightly con-

■   ■   ■

Box 11-3
Does Alternative Care Hinder
Children's Emotional Development?

The dramatic rise in maternal employment over the past 25 years means that increasing numbers of infants and toddlers have had to adjust to some form of alternative caregiving or "day care." How do children react to these arrangements? Could day care have adverse effects on a young child's social and emotional development, as some theorists (for example, Fraiberg, 1977) have feared? Or, rather, are there circumstances under which day care is likely to be a positive experience for an infant or toddler? Let's see what day-care researchers have found when addressing these issues.

Day care and the mother/ infant relationship. Although infants and toddlers are often visibly upset when they first enter day care, most children in day-care centers soon adjust to the daily routine and will often become attached to their substitute caregivers (Belsky, 1985). However, there is little evidence that these attachments undermine a child's emo-

tional relationships with parents: given a choice, most children who receive group day care continue to prefer their mothers to their substitute caregivers (Clarke-Stewart & Fein, 1983; Ragozin, 1980). Moreover, children in day-care centers are sometimes found to be more outgoing and socially competent than those who remain at home with their mothers (Clarke-Stewart & Fein, 1983), and there are even some data to indicate that *excellent* day care provided by sensitive and responsive companions can promote the intellectual development of children from disadvantaged backgrounds (Ramey, Bryant, & Suarez, 1985). In sum, these findings paint a very rosy picture, suggesting that mothers need not worry about harming their children or subverting their own emotional relationships with them should they leave their youngsters with a substitute caregiver.

However, we must be cautious in interpreting these outcomes. Most of the studies that show no differences between day-care children and children raised at home have looked at *middle-class* samples for which the alternative care was of *unusually high quality* (Anderson, Nagle, Roberts, & Smith, 1981; Clarke-

Stewart & Fein, 1983). Unfortunately, we cannot be sure that the results of these studies apply to economically disadvantaged children, who may often experience much less stimulating kinds of day care. In addition, we have already seen that some securely attached infants from middle-class homes become insecurely attached when their mothers return to work and arrange for them to receive alternative care (Barglow, Vaughn, & Molitor, 1987; Benn, 1986). So even though most youngsters are not adversely affected by alternative caregiving, the fact remains that these arrangements can undermine the emotional security of some children.

Why do children differ in their reactions to day care? Let's consider two possibilities.

Age at entry. Recently, researchers have been finding that infants from both lower-class and middle-class backgrounds (as well as those raised in communal settings, such as the Israeli kibbutz) are much more likely to develop insecure attachments to their mothers if they experience full-time (all-day) alternative care that begins prior to their first
continued

---

trolled experimental studies of socially deprived monkeys may help us to understand the behavior of those human beings who have not had an opportunity to become attached to a primary caregiver.

Harlow's Studies of Socially Deprived Monkeys

Many investigators have studied the effects of early social deprivation on rhesus monkeys, and their findings are remarkably consistent: monkeys isolated for the first six months of life or longer show extremely abnormal patterns of behavior that persist into adulthood. One of the best known of these research programs is that of Harry and Margaret Harlow (1977). The Harlows isolated rhesus monkeys at birth by placing them in individual wire cages where they could see and hear but could not touch other monkeys (partial social deprivation) or in stainless-steel cubicles in which all light was diffused, sounds were filtered, temperature

and air flow were controlled, and even feeding and cleaning of the chambers were automated (total social deprivation). These two kinds of isolation produced similar effects.

Three months of social deprivation left infants in a state of emotional shock. When removed from isolation, the infant avoided other monkeys and generally gave the appearance of being terrified by clutching at itself, crouching, or burying its head in its arms as if trying to shut out this strange new world (see Photo 11-6). The isolates also showed abnormal behaviors such as self-biting, rocking, and pulling out tufts of their hair. However, these three-month isolates eventually recovered. Daily 30-minute play periods with a normal age mate soon led to the development of effective social relationships that persisted into adolescence and adulthood.

The prognosis was not nearly as optimistic for infants isolated six months or longer. The six-month birthday (Sagi et al., 1985; Schwartz, 1983; Vaughn, Gove, & Egeland, 1980; Belsky & Rovine, 1988). Moreover, older preschool and school-age children who began day care early in infancy are sometimes found to be more aggressive toward their peers and less cooperative with adults than children who entered day care as toddlers (Belsky & Steinberg, 1978; Etaugh, 1980; Haskins, 1985). Yet, Jerome Kagan and his associates found that one group of infants who entered a very high-quality day-care program at age 3½ to 5½ months not only developed secure attachments to their mothers but were just as socially, emotionally, and intellectually mature over the first two years as a second group of children from similar social backgrounds who had been cared for at home by their mothers (Kagan, Kearsley, & Zelazo, 1978). So it seems that very early exposure to alternative caregiving need not be harmful, provided the care is excellent.

Quality of alternative care.
According to experts on alternative care, an excellent day-care facility is one that has (1) a reasonable child-to-caregiver ratio (4–12 children per adult), (2) caregivers who are warm, emotionally expressive, and responsive to children's bids for attention, (3) little staff turnover so that children can become familiar and feel comfortable with their new adult companions, (4) a curriculum made up of games and activities that are age-appropriate, and (5) an administration that is willing (or, better yet, eager) to confer with parents about the child's progress (Anderson et al., 1981; Phillips, McCartney, & Scarr, 1987). Given adequate training and resources, and some effort on the substitute caregiver's part, all these criteria can be achieved by a relative or a regular sitter providing in-home care, a nonrelative operating a day-care home, or a formal day-care center (Howes, 1988).

Regardless of the setting in which care is given, it is now apparent that the quality of alternative care that children receive does make a difference. For example, we have seen that even very young infants who experience alternative caregiving are likely to become securely attached to their parents if the care they receive is outstanding (Kagan et al., 1978). In addition, children are more likely to become attached to their substitute caregivers and to profit from the day-care curriculum when they interact with the same caregiver over a long period and when the caregiver is knowledgeable about children and responsive to their needs (Anderson et al., 1981; Howes & Stewart, 1987; Phillips et al., 1987). The size of the day-care group is also important: children who are cared for in smaller groups (15 or fewer) are more outgoing with their peers and score higher on standardized tests than those who are part of larger aggregations (Howes, 1983; Ruopp, Travers, Glantz, & Coelen, 1979).

Perhaps we can summarize by concluding that most children who receive good alternative care are unlikely to suffer any adverse effects as a result of their day-to-day separations from working parents. However, the outcome may not be so favorable for a very young infant who receives substandard day care from an unresponsive caregiver (or series of caregivers), particularly if the working mother hasn't the support of a spouse or if she lacks the time, patience, or energy to respond sensitively to her baby's needs when she does come home.

---

isolates clearly avoided normal age mates during free-play sessions, preferring instead to play by themselves with toys. What little social responsiveness they did show was directed toward other isolates, leading the Harlows to conclude that *misery prefers miserable company*. Normally reared infant monkeys usually go through a phase of aggressive play as they near their first birthday. Yet, when the isolates were attacked by other infants, they accepted the abuse without offering much defense. Bad as this behavioral pattern may sound, the effects of 12 months of social isolation were even worse. The 12-month isolates were extremely withdrawn and apathetic, and they often had to be separated from their normal age mates, who were likely to injure or even kill these passive creatures during periods of aggressive play (Harlow & Harlow, 1977).

Follow-up studies of monkeys isolated six months or longer have found that the isolates develop bizarre patterns of social and sexual behavior during adolescence and adulthood. Harlow describes the adult sexual behavior of these monkeys as follows:

> When the females were smaller than the [normally reared] males, the girls would back away and sit down facing the males [an inadequate attempt at sexual posturing], looking appealingly at their would-be consorts. Their hearts were in the right place but nothing else was.... [Isolate] males were equally unsatisfactory. They approached the females with a blind ... misdirected enthusiasm. Frequently, they would grasp the females by the side of the body and thrust laterally, leaving them working at cross purposes with reality [1962, p. 5].

Harlow and his associates initially believed that the first six months of life was a critical period for the social development of rhesus monkeys. Presumably rhesus infants who were denied social stimulation and who remained unattached to another monkey for six

Photo 11-6. Isolate monkeys often display unusual postures.

months or longer would become forever incapable of establishing normal social and emotional relationships. However, a later experiment by Steven Suomi and Harry Harlow (1972) challenged this point of view by showing that the isolation syndrome can be reversed.

Suomi and Harlow isolated four male rhesus infants for a six-month period and then exposed the isolates to 26 weeks of "therapy." The therapists in this case were younger rhesus females who were 3 months of age at the beginning of the therapy sessions. Why younger therapists? For two reasons. First, normally reared age mates are likely to attack the passive isolates and will accept these strangers only if they defend themselves. Unfortunately, the isolates do not defend themselves; instead, they withdraw and their condition worsens. By contrast, a 3-month-old infant has not yet become active and aggressive in its play; the initial response of the younger infant is to approach and cling tenaciously to the passive isolate rather than working him over. Suomi and Harlow reasoned that an emotionally disturbed isolate might be able to tolerate the presence of a relatively passive, nonaggressive infant and perhaps would even learn to respond to the younger therapist's playful antics. Once the isolate had been "drawn out of his shell," both he and his younger companion might then progress together toward the development of normal social behaviors.

For the first four weeks of the project, each isolate saw his "therapist" for two-hour periods, three days a week. Contact time was gradually increased so that, by the 12th week of therapy, each isolate and his younger therapist had contact with each other and with a second isolate/therapist pair several times a week. All the isolates were severely disturbed when they emerged from isolation, and their abnormal behaviors persisted for the first 60 days of the program. But by the end of the 26 weeks of therapy, the isolates had recovered. Their behavioral abnormalities had largely disappeared, and their play antics were virtually indistinguishable from those of their socially competent therapists. In no way did these isolates resemble the rather pitiful, socially inept creatures described in earlier reports. Melinda Novak (1979) has now used this **younger-peer therapy** to treat rhesus monkeys that were isolated for their entire first year. Novak reports that even these profoundly disturbed 12-month isolates will eventually become socially and sexually competent as adults if they are eased into a rehabilitative program with a younger therapist.

Clearly, these dramatic reversals contradict the critical-period hypothesis—a viewpoint that implied that the devastating social and emotional consequences of prolonged isolation were permanent and irreversible. Perhaps it is more accurate to say that the first six months of life is a "sensitive" period when normally reared monkeys are rapidly developing important social skills and becoming attached to their mothers. Although social deprivation interferes with these activities and produces a rather disturbed young monkey, recovery is possible if the patient is given the proper therapy.

Social Deprivation in Humans: The Institutionalized Child

Fortunately, there are both legal and ethical constraints to prevent researchers from isolating human infants for scientific purposes. Yet, in the recent past, physicians and psychologists began to discover that infants in some orphanages and foundling homes were being raised under conditions that resembled those experienced by Harlow's socially deprived monkeys. For example, it was not uncommon for an impoverished institution to have but one caregiver for every 20 infants. Moreover, the adults in these understaffed institutions rarely interacted with the infants except to bathe and change them or to prop a bottle against the infant's pillow at feeding time. Infants were often housed in separate cribs with sheets hung over the railings so that, in effect, they were isolated from the world around them. To make matters worse, babies in the more impoverished of these institutions had no crib toys to manipulate and few if any opportunities to get out of their cribs and practice motor skills. Compared with infants raised in a typical home setting, these institutionalized children received very little in the way of social or sensory stimulation.

Since the early 1940s, several investigators have reported the same reliable and quite alarming outcome: children raised for the first year of life in impoverished and understaffed institutions are likely to show signs of severe developmental retardation (Goldfarb, 1943, 1945, 1947; Provence & Lipton, 1962; Ribble, 1943; Spitz, 1945). Typically these infants appear quite normal for the first three to six months of life: they cry for attention, smile and babble at caregivers, and make all the proper postural adjustments when they are about to be picked up. But in the second half of the first year their behavior begins to change. Compared with home-reared infants, institution children seldom cry, coo, or babble; they adopt rigid body postures and often fail to accommodate to the handling of caregivers when such contact is forthcoming; their language is grossly retarded; and they often appear rather depressed, forlorn, and largely uninterested in social contact. Here is a description of one of these infants:

> Outstanding were his soberness, his forlorn appearance, and lack of animation. . . . He did not turn to adults to relieve his distress. . . . He made no demands. . . . As one made active and persistent efforts at a social exchange he became somewhat more responsive, animated and . . . active, but lapsed into his depressed . . . appearance when the adult became less active . . . if you crank his motor you can get him to go a little; but he can't start on his own [Provence & Lipton, 1962, pp. 134–135].

What are these institutionalized infants like as schoolchildren and adolescents? The answer depends, in part, on how long they remain in the bleak, barren institutional setting. William Goldfarb (1943, 1947) compared the developmental progress of two groups of children: a group who left an understaffed orphanage for foster homes during the first year of life ("foster children") and a second group who had spent their first three years at the orphanage before departing for foster homes ("institution children"). The children in these two groups were comparable in age, sex, and the socioeconomic backgrounds of their biological parents. The developmental progress of each group was periodically assessed by interviewing and observing the children and by giving them a battery of tests. The children were studied at four ages: 3½, 6½, 8½, and 12.

Goldfarb found that the institution children lagged behind the foster children in virtually all aspects of development. They scored lower than foster children on IQ tests, had more speech problems, and were remarkably dependent on adults. Moreover, they were much

Photo 11-7. Children raised in barren, understaffed institutions show many signs of developmental retardation.

more prone than the foster children to displays of temper, hyperactivity, aggression, deception, and acts of destruction. Goldfarb reported that the institution children seemed almost incapable of forming close interpersonal attachments. By adolescence they were often loners who had a difficult time relating to peers or family members.

Barbara Tizard (1977; Tizard & Hodges, 1978) has recently compared similar groups of institutionalized and early-adopted children and found that some of the developmental impairments described by Goldfarb also characterized her sample of late adoptees. The institutions in which Tizard's children lived had high ratios of staff to children, so that the children were not socially deprived. However, staff turnover was substantial, and the children rarely became attached to anyone over the first few years of life. By age 8, Tizard's institution children and late adoptees were intellectually normal and socially outgoing, and several of them had even formed emotional ties to a housemother or an adoptive parent. But despite these encouraging signs, children who had spent at least four years in the institution had few close friends and were much more unpopular, restless, and disobedient at school than children raised from late infancy in adoptive homes. So it seems that prolonged institutionalization can have adverse effects that are very difficult to overcome.

---

younger-peer therapy: a method of rehabilitating emotionally withdrawn individuals by regularly exposing them to younger but socially responsive companions.

Why Is Early Deprivation Harmful?

Studies of institutionalized children are "experiments of nature" that were not designed in a laboratory and are subject to a variety of methodological criticisms (Longstreth, 1981; Pinneau, 1955). However, the results we have reviewed are so consistent across studies that researchers have stopped arguing about whether deprivation effects are real; today the issue is "Why do they occur?"

The maternal deprivation hypothesis.

Psychologists such as John Bowlby (1973) and René Spitz (1965) believe that infants will not develop normally unless they receive the warm, loving attention of a mother figure to whom they can become attached. Presumably children raised in understaffed institutions and monkeys reared in isolation will show developmental irregularities because they have not had an opportunity to become emotionally involved with a primary caregiver.

Popular as this explanation was when it first appeared, there is no evidence that infants need to be "mothered" by a single caregiver in order to develop normally. Studies of adequately staffed institutions in the Soviet Union, the People's Republic of China, and Israel reveal that infants who are cared for by many responsive caregivers appear quite normal and are as well adjusted at 2–3 years of age as infants reared at home (Bronfenbrenner, 1970; Kessen, 1975; Levy-Shiff, 1983). Moreover, we have seen that Harlow's infant monkeys who were isolated for three months eventually recovered from their early developmental abnormalities without ever being exposed to a mother figure. All they needed was stimulation provided through daily contacts with other monkeys of the same age. In a similar vein, Freud and Dann (1951) reported that a group of six war orphans raised together from early infancy in a German concentration camp were neither mentally retarded nor socially unresponsive at 3 years of age, despite their very limited contact with their parents (who had been executed in Hitler's gas chambers) or other adult prisoners.[2] Apparently the stimulation that these orphans provided one another was sufficient to prevent

serious developmental impairments. So infants need not become attached to a single mother figure in order to develop normally.

The social stimulation hypothesis.

Could it be that impoverished understaffed institutions are breeding grounds for developmental abnormalities because they provide the infant with a monotonous *sensory* environment—one where there is little stimulation *of any kind* to encourage any sort of responsiveness? Or, rather, is it a lack of *social* stimulation that accounts for the unusual behavior and abnormal development of institutionalized children (and isolate monkeys)?

Most contemporary developmentalists favor the latter view, arguing that isolate monkeys and institutionalized humans develop abnormally because they have very little exposure to anyone who responds to their social signals. Indeed, giving isolate monkeys enriched *sensory* stimulation (in the form of slide shows) has no therapeutic effect, whereas allowing them *social* contacts with responsive peers will enable them to develop normally as they interact with these companions, become more responsive themselves, and slowly overcome their bizarre patterns of behavior (Pratt, 1967, 1969). Moreover, Sally Provence and Rose Lipton (1962) studied a sample of institutionalized infants who had toys to play with, some visual and auditory exposure to other infants, but limited contact with adult caregivers. In other words, these infants were "socially deprived" although they were certainly not "stimulus deprived." In spite of the variety of sensory stimulation that the infants received, they showed roughly the same patterns of social, emotional, and intellectual impairment that characterized the institutionalized children from earlier studies. If we contrast this finding with the normal development of Chinese, Russian, and Israeli infants who are raised by a multitude of caregivers in communal settings, we can draw an interesting conclusion: *infants apparently need sustained interactions with responsive companions in order to develop normally.* Recall that we came to the same conclusion when we looked at the origins of the primary social attachment: infants who have regular interactions with *responsive* caregivers are the ones who are likely to become securely attached to them.

Why are interactions with responsive people so important? Probably because the social stimulation an infant receives is likely to depend on the infant's own behavior: people often attend to the infant *when* he or

---

[2]These children, who were orphaned in the first few months of life, received about the same amount of attention from adults that is normally received by children in severely understaffed institutional settings. We will take a closer look at these remarkable orphans in Chapter 16 when we consider the important roles that the peer group plays in a child's social and personality development.

she cries, smiles, babbles, or gazes at them. This kind of association between one's own behavior and the behavior of caregivers may lead infants to believe that they have some *control* over their social environment. Thus, the infant may become more sociable as she learns that she can use her social signals to attract the attention and affection of her responsive companions.

Now consider the plight of institutionalized infants who may emit many signals and rarely receive a response from their overburdened or inattentive caregivers. What are these children likely to learn from their early experiences? Probably that attempts to attract the attention of others are useless, for nothing they do seems to matter to anyone. Consequently, they may develop a sense of **"learned helplessness"** and simply stop trying to exercise any control over the environment (Finkelstein & Ramey, 1977). Here, then, is a very plausible explanation for the finding that socially deprived infants are often rather passive, withdrawn, and apathetic.

Can Children Recover from Early Developmental Impairments?

Earlier we noted that severely disturbed young monkeys can overcome the effects of prolonged social isolation if they receive the proper kinds of therapy. Is the same true of human beings? Can children who start out in an understaffed institutional setting recover from their initial handicaps, and if so, what will they require in the way of corrective therapy?

There is now a wealth of evidence that socially deprived infants can recover from their handicaps if they are placed in homes where they receive ample doses of individualized attention from affectionate and responsive caregivers (Clarke & Clarke, 1976; Rutter, 1981). One notable example is a study by Wayne Dennis (1973), who compared the development of two groups of children who had lived in an understaffed Lebanese institution. Children in one group were adopted into good homes before their second birthday. Although they had developmental quotients in the mentally retarded range at the time of their adoptions, these children eventually attained IQ scores that were only slightly below average after spending several years in a stimulating home environment. By contrast, children who remained in the institution continued to score in the mentally retarded range on all intelligence tests.

The *quality* of the home environment in which children live affects their chances of recovering from early developmental impairments. Lee Willerman and

his associates found that 1-year-olds with social, motor, and mental handicaps are unlikely to recover if they live in economically disadvantaged homes where they receive little social or intellectual stimulation (Willerman, Broman, & Fiedler, 1970). However, children who are placed in "enriched" home environments may show dramatic recoveries. Audrey Clark and Jeannette Hanisee (1982) studied a group of Asian children who were adopted by highly educated and relatively affluent American parents, many of whom were teachers, ministers, or social workers. The adoptees had all been separated from their biological parents and had lived in institutions, foster homes, or hospitals before coming to the United States. Many were war orphans who had early histories of malnutrition or serious illness. But in spite of the severe environmental insults they had endured, these children made remarkable progress. After only two to three years in their highly stimulating adoptive homes, the Asian adoptees scored significantly *above* average on both a standardized intelligence test and an assessment of social maturity.

The prognosis for recovery may also depend on the *amount of time* the child has spent in a depriving early environment. It appears that prolonged social and sensory deprivation that begins early in the first year and lasts as long as three years is likely to produce serious social, emotional, and intellectual handicaps that are difficult to overcome (Dennis, 1973; Goldfarb, 1943, 1947; Rutter, 1981). For example, we have noted that Goldfarb's institution children, who had spent their first three years in an understaffed orphanage, remained somewhat socially, emotionally, and intellectually deficient as adolescents despite having lived in foster homes during the preceding eight to nine years. Do such findings imply that the first three years is a critical period for the social, emotional, and intellectual development of human beings, as Bowlby (1973) and others have argued?

At this point, no one can be certain that *all* the effects of prolonged social and emotional deprivation are *completely* reversible. However, many theorists believe that those who favor a critical-period hypothesis are being overly pessimistic. Surely it stands to reason that children who develop severe problems when de-

---

learned helplessness: the failure to learn how to respond appropriately in a situation because of previous exposures to uncontrollable events in the same or similar situations.

prived for long periods might take longer to overcome their handicaps than children whose early deprivation was relatively brief. Moreover, we have to wonder how Goldfarb's institution children would have fared had they been adopted into enriched home environments such as those of the Asian adoptees in Clark and Hanisee's (1982) study. Clearly, the fact that Goldfarb's institution children showed some deficiencies as adolescents in no way implies that they were *incapable* of recovery, as proponents of the critical-period hypothesis might have us believe.

It was only a short time ago that six months of isolation was thought to have irreversible effects on the social and emotional development of rhesus monkeys. Yet, Harry Harlow and his associates were able to perfect a therapy to treat the harmful consequences of early social deprivation and bring even their most profoundly disturbed 12-month isolates back to a state of normality. This younger-peer therapy has now been used by Wyndol Furman, Don Rahe, and Willard Hartup (1979) to modify the behavior of socially withdrawn preschool children. Children who had been identified as social isolates in a day-care setting were exposed to a series of play sessions with a partner who was either their age or 18 months younger. The findings were indeed interesting: withdrawn children who had played with a partner became much more socially outgoing in their day-care classrooms than social isolates who had not taken part in any play sessions. In addition, the improvements in sociability were greatest for those withdrawn children who had played with a *younger* partner (see Figure 11-2). So Furman et al. (1979) obtained results with humans that are similar to those reported earlier for emotionally disturbed monkeys. Although Furman's withdrawn children could hardly be classified as emotionally ill, the results of this study are sufficiently encouraging to suggest the younger-peer treatment as one possible therapy for children who are more severely disturbed.

In sum, infants who have experienced social and emotional deprivation over the first two years show a strong capacity for recovery when they are placed in a stimulating home environment and receive individualized attention from responsive caregivers. Even severely disturbed children who are adopted after spending several years in understaffed institutions will show dramatic improvements, compared with their counterparts who have remained in a barren institutional setting (Dennis, 1973; Rutter, 1981). And rather than being discouraged by handicaps that continue to plague many

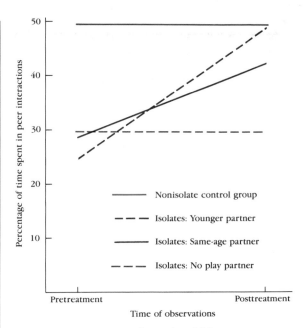

Figure 11-2. Percentages of time that children spent interacting with peers before and after engaging in play sessions with a younger or a same-age partner. *(From Furman, Rahe, & Hartup, 1979.)*

late adoptees, we could just as easily treat their partial recoveries as an encouraging sign—one that may lead to the discovery of environmental interventions and therapeutic techniques that will enable these victims of prolonged social deprivation to put their lingering deficiencies behind them.

Summary

Infants are clearly emotional creatures. At birth, babies are capable of expressing interest, distress, disgust, and pleasure (as indexed by their facial expressions). Sadness and anger first appear at 3–4 months of age, followed a few months later by clear expressions of fear, shame, and shyness. Complex emotions such as guilt and contempt emerge during the second year. Three- to four-month-olds can also discriminate others' angry displays from displays of happiness or sadness. Emotions play at least two important roles in an infant's social development. The child's own emotional expressions are adaptive in that they promote social contact with others and assist caregivers in adjusting their behavior to the infant's needs and goals. At the same time, the infant's ability to recognize and interpret the emotions of other people serves an important *social referencing* function by helping the child to infer how he or she should be feeling or behaving in a wide variety of situations.

Infants begin to form affectional ties to their close companions during the first year of life. These "bonds of love," or *attachments,* serve many purposes and are important contributors to social and emotional development. Attachments are usually reciprocal relationships, for parents and other intimate companions will often become attached to the infant.

Parents may become emotionally involved with an infant during the first few hours if they have close contact with their baby during this period. An initial bond may then be strengthened as the infant begins to emit social signals (smiles, vocalizations) that attract the attention of caregivers and make them feel that the baby enjoys their company. Eventually the infant and a close companion will establish highly synchronized interactive routines that are satisfying to both parties and are likely to blossom into a reciprocal attachment. However, some parents may have a difficult time becoming attached to their infant if the child is irritable, unresponsive, or unwanted, if they are unhappily married or have other problems that prevent them from devoting much attention to the baby, or if they follow preconceived notions about child rearing rather than adjusting their parenting to the infant's state and temperament.

Most infants have formed their primary attachment to a close companion by 6–8 months of age, and within weeks they are establishing these affectional ties with other regular companions. Many theories have been proposed to explain how and why infants form attachments. Among the most influential theories of attachment are the psychoanalytic, the learning-theory, the cognitive-developmental, and the ethological viewpoints. Although these theories make different assumptions about the roles that infants and caregivers play in the formation of attachments, each viewpoint has contributed to our understanding of early social and emotional development.

At about the time infants are becoming attached to a close companion, they often begin to display two negative emotions, or "fears." The first, stranger anxiety, is the child's wariness of unfamiliar people. It is by no means a universal reaction and is most likely to occur in response to an intrusive stranger who appears in an unfamiliar setting where loved ones are unavailable. The second, separation anxiety, is the discomfort infants may feel when separated from the person or persons to whom they are attached. As infants develop intellectually and begin to move away from attachment objects to explore the environment, they will become increasingly familiar with strangers and better able to account for the absence of familiar companions. As a result, both stranger anxiety and separation anxiety will decline in intensity toward the end of the second year.

Children differ in the security of their attachments to caregivers. A securely attached infant is one who derives comfort from close companions and can use them as safe bases for exploration. Insecurely attached infants do not venture far from their attachment objects even though they derive very little comfort or security from their contacts with them. A secure attachment is fostered by caregivers who are very responsive and affectionate toward their babies. The quality of the infant's attachments may affect his or her later behavior, and it is advantageous for the child to be attached to the father and other close companions as well as the mother. Children who are securely attached are generally more curious than insecurely attached infants and more interested in learning, more cooperative, and friendlier toward adults and peers. Moreover, these differences persist throughout the preschool period and possibly much longer. It was once feared that regular separations from attachment objects would undermine a child's emotional security. However, there is little evidence that a mother's employment outside the home or alternative caregiving by day-care workers will have such an effect, provided that the day care is of high quality and the mother is sensitive and responsive to her child when she is at home.

Some infants have had very limited contacts with caregivers during the first year or two of life, and as a result, they do not become attached to anyone. Both monkeys and children who experience little social contact during infancy are likely to be withdrawn, apathetic, and (in humans) intellectually deficient. The longer infants suffer from social and sensory deprivation, the more disturbed they become. However, both monkeys and humans have a strong capacity for recovery and may overcome many of their initial handicaps if placed in settings where they will receive ample amounts of individualized attention from responsive companions.

References

AINSWORTH, M. D. S. (1967). *Infancy in Uganda: Infant care and the growth of love*. Baltimore: Johns Hopkins University Press.

AINSWORTH, M. D. S. (1979). Attachment as related to mother-infant interaction. In J. S. Rosenblatt, R. A. Hinde, C. Beer, & M. Busnel (Eds.), *Advances in the study of behavior* (Vol. 9). Orlando, FL: Academic Press.

AINSWORTH, M. D. S., Bell, S. M., & Stayton, D. J. (1974). Infant-mother attachment and social development: Socialization as a product of reciprocal responsiveness to signals. In M. P. M. Richards (Ed.), *The integration of the child into a social world*. London: Cambridge University Press.

AINSWORTH, M. D. S., Blehar, M., Waters, E., & Wall, S. (1978). *Patterns of attachment*. Hillsdale, NJ: Erlbaum.

ALLEY, T. R. (1981). Head shape and the perception of cuteness. *Developmental Psychology, 17*, 650–654.

ANDERSON, C. W., Nagle, R. J., Roberts, W. A., & Smith, J. W. (1981). Attachment to substitute caregivers as a function of center quality and caregiver involvement. *Child Development, 52*, 53–61.

AREND, R., Gove, F. L., & Sroufe, L. A. (1979). Continuity of individual adaptation from infancy to kindergarten: A predictive study of ego-resiliency and curiosity in preschoolers. *Child Development, 50*, 950–959.

BARGLOW, P., Vaughn, B. E., & Molitor, N. (1987). Effects of maternal absence due to employment on the quality of infant-mother attachment in a low-risk sample. *Child Development, 58*, 945–954.

BELSKY, J. (1980). Child maltreatment: An ecological integration. *American Psychologist, 35*, 320–335.

BELSKY, J. (1981). Early human experience: A family perspective. *Developmental Psychology, 17*, 3–23.

BELSKY, J. (1985). Two waves of day-care research: Developmental effects and conditions of quality. In R. Ainslie (Ed.), *The child and the day care setting*. New York: Praeger.

BELSKY, J., Gilstrap, B., & Rovine, M. (1984). The Pennsylvania Infant and Family Development Project, I: Stability and change in mother-infant and father-infant interaction in a family setting. *Child Development, 55*, 692–705.

BELSKY, J., & Rovine, M. (1988). Nonmaternal care in the first year of life and the security of infant–parent attachment. *Child Development, 59*, 157–167.

BELSKY, J., Rovine, M., & Taylor, D. G. (1984). The Pennsylvania Infant and Family Development Project, III: The origins of individual differences in infant-mother attachment—maternal and infant contributions. *Child Development, 55*, 718–728.

BELSKY, J., & Steinberg, L. D. (1978). The effects of day care: A critical review. *Child Development, 49*, 929–949.

BENN, R. K. (1986). Factors promoting secure attachment relationships between employed mothers and their sons. *Child Development, 57*, 1224–1231.

BOCCIA, M., & Campos, J. J. (1983, April). *Maternal emotional signalling: Its effects on infants' reactions to strangers*. Paper presented at the biennial meeting of the Society for Research in Child Development, Detroit.

BOWLBY, J. (1958). The nature of the child's tie to his mother. *International Journal of Psychoanalysis, 39*, 350–373.

BOWLBY, J. (1969). *Attachment and loss*. Vol. 1: *Attachment*. London: Hogarth Press.

BOWLBY, J. (1973). *Attachment and loss*. Vol. 2: *Separation: Anxiety and anger*. London: Hogarth Press.

BRETHERTON, I., Fritz, J., Zahn-Waxler, C., & Ridgeway, D. (1986). Learning to talk about emotions: A functionalist perspective. *Child Development, 57*, 529–548.

BRETHERTON, I., Stolberg, U., & Kreye, M. (1981). Engaging strangers in proximal interaction: Infants' social initiative. *Developmental Psychology, 17*, 746–755.

BRONFENBRENNER, U. (1970). *Two worlds of childhood: U.S. and U.S.S.R.* New York: Russell Sage Foundation.

CLARK, E. A., & Hanisee, J. (1982). Intellectual and adaptive performance of Asian children in adoptive American settings. *Developmental Psychology, 18*, 595–599.

CLARKE, A. M., & Clarke, A. D. B. (1976). *Early experience: Myth and evidence*. New York: Free Press.

CLARKE-STEWART, K. A. (1978). And daddy makes three: The father's impact on the mother and the young child. *Child Development, 49*, 466–478.

CLARKE-STEWART, K. A., & Fein, G. G. (1983). Early childhood programs. In P. H. Mussen (Ed.), *Handbook of child psychology*. Vol. 2: *Infancy and developmental psychobiology*. New York: Wiley.

COHEN, L. J. (1974). The operational definition of human attachment. *Psychological Bulletin, 4*, 207–217.

COHN, J. F., & Tronick, E. Z. (1982). Three-month-old infants' reactions to simulated maternal depression. *Child Development, 53*, 185–193.

COHN, J. F., & Tronick, E. Z. (1987). Mother-infant face-to-face interaction: The sequence of dyadic states at 3, 6, and 9 months. *Developmental Psychology, 23*, 68–77.

CORTER, C. M., Zucker, K. J., & Galligan, R. F. (1980). Patterns in the infant's search for mother during brief separation. *Developmental Psychology, 16*, 62–69.

CROCKENBERG, S. B. (1981). Infant irritability, mother responsiveness, and social support influences on the security of infant-mother attachment. *Child Development, 52*, 857–865.

CROCKENBERG, S. B., & McCluskey, K. (1986). Change in maternal behavior during the baby's first year of life. *Child Development, 57*, 746–753.

CROUTER, A. C., Perry-Jenkins, M., Huston, T. L., & McHale, S. M. (1987). Processes underlying father involvement in dual-earner and single-earner families. *Developmental Psychology, 23*, 431–440.

DENNIS, W. (1973). *Children of the crèche*. East Norwalk, CT: Appleton-Century-Crofts.

DOWD, J., & Tronick, E. Z. (1986). Temporal coordination of arm movements in early infancy: Do infants move in synchrony with adult speech? *Child Development, 57*, 762–776.

DUNN, J., Bretherton, I., & Munn, P. (1987). Conversations about feeling states between mothers and their young children. *Developmental Psychology, 23*, 132–139.

EASTERBROOKS, M. A., & Goldberg, W. A. (1985). Effects of early maternal employment on toddlers, mothers, and fathers. *Developmental Psychology, 21*, 740–752.

EGELAND, B., & Farber, E. A. (1984). Mother-infant attachment: Factors related to its development and changes over time. *Child Development, 55*, 753–771.

ETAUGH, C. (1980). Effects of nonmaternal care on children: Research evidence and popular views. *American Psychologist, 35*, 309–319.

FEINMAN, S., & Lewis, M. (1983). Social referencing at 10 months: A second-order effect on infants' responses to strangers. *Child Development, 54*, 878–887.

FEIRING, C., Fox, N. A., Jaskir, J., & Lewis, M. (1987). The relation between social support, infant risk status, and mother-infant interactions. *Developmental Psychology, 23*, 400–405.

FINKELSTEIN, N. W., & Ramey, C. T. (1977). Learning to control the environment in infancy. *Child Development, 48*, 806–819.

FRAIBERG, S. (1977). *Every child's birthright: In defense of mothering*. New York: Basic Books.

FREUD, A., & Dann, S. (1951). An experiment

in group upbringing. In R. S. Eisler, A. Freud, H. Hartmann, & E. Kris (Eds.), *The psychoanalytic study of the child* (Vol. 6). New York: International Universities Press.

FREUD, S. (1930). *Three contributions to the theory of sex*. New York: Nervous and Mental Disease Publishing Co. (Original work published 1905)

FURMAN, W., Rahe, D. F., & Hartup, W. W. (1979). Rehabilitation of socially withdrawn preschool children through mixed-age and same-age socialization. *Child Development, 50,* 915–922.

GARBARINO, J., & Sherman, D. (1980). High-risk neighborhoods and high-risk families: The human ecology of child maltreatment. *Child Development, 51,* 188–198.

GEWIRTZ, H. B., & Gewirtz, J. L. (1968). Caretaking settings, background events, and behavior differences in four Israeli child-rearing environments: Some preliminary trends. In B. M. Foss (Ed.), *Determinants of infant behavior* (Vol. 4). London: Methuen.

GEWIRTZ, J. L. (1969). Mechanisms of social learning: Some roles of stimulation and behavior in early human development. In D. A. Goslin (Ed.), *Handbook of socialization theory and research*. Skokie, IL: Rand McNally.

GOLDBERG, S. (1983). Parent-infant bonding: Another look. *Child Development, 54,* 1355–1382.

GOLDBERG, S., Blumberg, S. L., & Kriger, A. (1982). Menarche and interest in infants: Biological and social influences. *Child Development, 53,* 1544–1550.

GOLDBERG, S., Perrotta, M., Minde, K., & Corter, C. (1986). Maternal behavior and attachment in low-birth-weight twins and singletons. *Child Development, 57,* 34–46.

GOLDFARB, W. (1943). The effects of early institutional care on adolescent personality. *Journal of Experimental Education, 12,* 107–129.

GOLDFARB, W. (1945). Effects of psychological deprivation in infancy and subsequent stimulation. *American Journal of Psychiatry, 102,* 18–33.

GOLDFARB, W. (1947). Variations in adolescent adjustment in institutionally reared children. *Journal of Orthopsychiatry, 17,* 449–457.

GREENBERG, M. T., & Marvin, R. S. (1982). Reactions of preschool children to an adult stranger: A behavioral systems approach. *Child Development, 53,* 481–490.

GREENE, J. G., Fox, N. A., & Lewis, M. (1983). The relationship between neonatal characteristics and three-month mother-infant interaction in high-risk infants. *Child Development, 54,* 1286–1296.

GROSSMAN, F. K., Eichler, L. S., Winickoff, S. A., & Associates (1980). *Pregnancy, birth, and parenthood: Adaptations of mothers, fathers, and infants*. San Francisco: Jossey-Bass.

GROSSMANN, K., Thane, K., & Grossmann, K. E. (1981). Maternal tactile contact of the newborn after various post-partum conditions of mother-infant contact. *Developmental Psychology, 17,* 158–169.

HALL, G. S. (1891). The contents of children's minds on entering school. *Pedagogical Seminary, 1,* 139–173.

HARLOW, H. F. (1962). The heterosexual affectional system in monkeys. *American Psychologist, 17,* 1–9.

HARLOW, H. F., & Harlow, M. K. (1977). The young monkeys. In *Readings in developmental psychology today* (2nd ed.). Del Mar, CA: CRM Books.

HARLOW, H. F., & Zimmerman, R. R. (1959). Affectional responses in the infant monkey. *Science, 130,* 421–432.

HASKINS, R. (1985). Public school aggression among children with varying day-care experience. *Child Development, 56,* 689–703.

HAVILAND, J. M., & Lelwica, M. (1987). The induced affect response: 10-week-old infants' responses to three emotion expressions. *Developmental Psychology, 23,* 97–104.

HAZAN, C., & Shaver, P. (1987). Romantic love conceptualized as an attachment process. *Journal of Personality and Social Psychology, 52,* 511–524.

HILDEBRANDT, K. A. (1983). Effect of facial expression variations on ratings of infants' physical attractiveness. *Developmental Psychology, 29,* 414–417.

HILDEBRANDT, K. A., & Fitzgerald, H. E. (1981). Mothers' responses to infant physical appearance. *Infant Mental Health Journal, 2,* 56–61.

HOFFMAN, L. W. (1984). Maternal employment and the young child. In M. Perlmutter (Ed.), *Minnesota Symposia on Child Psychology* (Vol. 17). Hillsdale, NJ: Erlbaum.

HOWES, C. (1983). Caregiver behavior in center and family day care. *Journal of Applied Developmental Psychology, 4,* 99–107.

HOWES, C., & Stewart, P. (1987). Child's play with adults, toys, and peers: An examination of family and child-care influences. *Developmental Psychology, 23,* 423–430.

HOWES, K. (1988). Relations between early child care and schooling. *Developmental Psychology, 24,* 53–57.

HURLEY, J. R., & Hohn, R. L. (1971). Shifts in child-rearing attitudes linked with parent-hood and occupation. *Developmental Psychology, 4,* 324–328.

HWANG, C. P. (1986). Behavior of Swedish primary and secondary caretaking fathers in relation to mother's presence. *Developmental Psychology, 22,* 749–751.

IZARD, C. E. (1982). *Measuring emotions in infants and children*. New York: Cambridge University Press.

IZARD, C. E., Hembree, E. A., & Huebner, R. R. (1987). Infants' emotion expressions to acute pain: Developmental change and stability of individual differences. *Developmental Psychology, 23,* 105–113.

JACOBSON, J. L., & Wille, D. E. (1986). The influence of attachment pattern on developmental changes in peer interaction from the toddler to the preschool period. *Child Development, 57,* 338–347.

JOHNSON, W., Emde, R. N., Pannabecker, B., Stenberg, C., & Davis, M. (1982). Maternal perception of infant emotion from birth through 18 months. *Infant Behavior and Development, 5,* 313–322.

KAGAN, J. (1972). Do infants think? *Scientific American, 226,* 74–82.

KAGAN, J. (1976). Emergent themes in human development. *American Scientist, 64,* 186–196.

KAGAN, J. (1983). Stress and coping in early development. In N. Garmezy & M. Rutter (Eds.), *Stress, coping, and development in children*. New York: McGraw-Hill.

KAGAN, J. (1984). *The nature of the child*. New York: Basic Books.

KAGAN, J., Kearsley, R. B., & Zelazo, P. R. (1978). *Infancy: Its place in human development*. Cambridge, MA: Harvard University Press.

KELLER, H., & Scholmerich, A. (1987). Infant vocalizations and parental reactions during the first four months of life. *Developmental Psychology, 23,* 62–67.

KENNELL, J. H., Voos, D. K., & Klaus, M. H. (1979). Parent-infant bonding. In J. D. Osofsky (Ed.), *Handbook of infant development*. New York: Wiley.

KESSEN, W. (1975). *Childhood in China*. New Haven, CT: Yale University Press.

KLAUS, M. H., & Kennell, J. H. (1976). *Maternal-infant bonding*. St. Louis: Mosby.

KLAUS, M. H., & Kennell, J. H. (1982). *Parent-infant bonding*. St. Louis: Mosby.

KLEIN, R. P. (1985). Caregiving arrangements by employed women with children under 1 year of age. *Developmental Psychology, 21,* 403–406.

KLINNERT, M. D., Emde, R. N., Butterfield, P., & Campos, J. J. (1986). Social referencing: The infant's use of emotional signals from a friendly adult with mother present. *Developmental Psychology, 22,* 427–432.

KORNER, A. F. (1974). The effect of the infant's state, level of arousal, sex, and ontogenetic stage on the caregiver. In M. Lewis & L. A. Rosenblum (Eds.), *The effect of the infant on its caregiver.* New York: Wiley.

KUCHUK, A., Vibbert, M., & Bornstein, M. H. (1986). The perception of smiling and its experiential correlates in three-month-old infants. *Child Development, 57,* 1054–1061.

La BARBERA, J. D., Izard, C. E., Vietze, P., & Parisi, S. A. (1976). Four- and six-month-old infants' visual responses to joy, anger, and neutral expressions. *Child Development, 47,* 535–538.

LAMB, M. E. (1975). Fathers: Forgotten contributors to child development. *Human Development, 18,* 245–266.

LAMB, M. E. (1981). The development of father-infant relationships. In M. E. Lamb (Ed.), *The role of the father in child development.* New York: Wiley.

LAMB, M. E., & Stevenson, M. (1978). Father-infant relationships: Their nature and importance. *Youth and Society, 9,* 277–298.

LESTER, B. M., Hoffman, J., & Brazelton, T. B. (1985). The rhythmic structure of mother-infant interactions in term and preterm infants. *Child Development, 56,* 15–27.

LESTER, B. M., Kotelchuck, M., Spelke, E., Sellers, M. J., & Klein, R. E. (1974). Separation protest in Guatemalan infants: Cross-cultural and cognitive findings. *Developmental Psychology, 10,* 79–85.

LEVITT, M. J. (1980). Contingent feedback, familiarization, and infant affect: How a stranger becomes a friend. *Developmental Psychology, 16,* 425–432.

LEVITT, M. J., Weber, R. A., & Clark, M. C. (1986). Social network relationships as sources of maternal support and well-being. *Developmental Psychology, 22,* 310–316.

LEVY-SHIFF, R. (1983). Adaptation and competence in early childhood: Communally-raised kibbutz children versus family raised children in the city. *Child Development, 54,* 1606–1614.

LITTENBERG, R., Tulkin, S., & Kagan, J. (1971). Cognitive components of separation anxiety. *Developmental Psychology, 4,* 387–388.

LONDERVILLE, S., & Main, M. (1981). Security of attachment, compliance, and maternal training methods in the second year of life. *Developmental Psychology, 17,* 289–299.

LONGSTRETH, L. E. (1981). Revisiting Skeels' final study: A critique. *Developmental Psychology, 17,* 620–625.

LORENZ, K. Z. (1937). The companion in the bird's world. *Auk, 54,* 245–273.

LORENZ, K. Z. (1943). The innate forms of possible experience. *Zeitschrift für Tierpsychologie, 5,* 233–409.

LUTKENHAUS, P., Grossmann, K. E., & Grossmann, K. (1985). Infant-mother attachment and style of interaction with a stranger at the age of three years. *Child Development, 56,* 1538–1542.

LYONS-RUTH, K., Connell, D. B., Zoll, D., & Stahl, J. (1987). Infants at social risk: Relations among infant maltreatment, maternal behavior, and infant attachment behavior. *Developmental Psychology, 23,* 223–232.

MAIN, M., & Weston, D. R. (1981). The quality of the toddler's relationship to mother and to father: Related to conflict and the readiness to establish new relationships. *Child Development, 52,* 932–940.

MATAS, L., Arend, R. A., & Sroufe, L. A. (1978). Continuity of adaptation in the second year: The relationship between quality of attachment and later competence. *Child Development, 49,* 547–556.

MATEJCEK, Z., Dytrych, Z., & Schuller, V. (1979). The Prague study of children born from unwanted pregnancies. *International Journal of Mental Health, 7,* 63–74.

MORGAN, G. A., & Ricciuti, H. N. (1969). Infants' responses to strangers during the first year. In B. M. Foss (Ed.), *Determinants of infant behavior* (Vol. 4). London: Methuen.

MYERS, B. J. (1984). Mother-infant bonding: The status of this critical-period hypothesis. *Developmental Review, 4,* 240–274.

NOVAK, M. A. (1979). Social recovery of monkeys isolated for the first year of life: II. Long-term assessment. *Developmental Psychology, 15,* 50–61.

OWEN, M. T., Easterbrooks, M. A., Chase-Lansdale, L., & Goldberg, W. A. (1984). The relation between maternal employment status and stability of attachments to mother and to father. *Child Development, 55,* 1894–1901.

PARKE, R. D. (1981). *Fathers.* Cambridge, MA: Harvard University Press.

PASTOR, D. L. (1981). The quality of mother-infant attachment and its relationship to toddlers' initial sociability with peers. *Developmental Psychology, 17,* 326–335.

PEERY, J. C. (1980). Neonate and adult head movement: No and yes revisited. *Developmental Psychology, 16,* 245–250.

PHILLIPS, D., McCartney, K., & Scarr, S. (1987). Child-care quality and children's social development. *Developmental Psychology, 23,* 537–543.

PINNEAU, S. R. (1955). The infantile disorders of hospitalism and anaclitic depression. *Psychological Bulletin, 52,* 429–452.

PRATT, C. L. (1967). *Social behavior of rhesus monkeys reared with varying degrees of peer experience.* Unpublished master's thesis, University of Wisconsin.

PRATT, C. L. (1969). *Effect of different degrees of early stimulation on social development.* Unpublished doctoral dissertation, University of Wisconsin.

PROVENCE, S., & Lipton, R. C. (1962). *Infants in institutions.* New York: International Universities Press.

RADKE-YARROW, M., Cummings, E. M., Kuczynski, L., & Chapman, M. (1985). Patterns of attachment in two- and three-year-olds in normal families and families with parental depression. *Child Development, 56,* 884–893.

RAGOZIN, A. S. (1980). Attachment behavior of day-care children: Naturalistic and laboratory observations. *Child Development, 51,* 409–415.

RAMEY, C. T., Bryant, D. M., & Suarez, T. M. (1985). Preschool compensatory education and the modifiability of intelligence: A critical review. In D. K. Detterman (Ed.), *Current topics in human intelligence.* Vol. 1: *Research methodology.* Norwood, NJ: Ablex.

RHEINGOLD, H. L., & Eckerman, C. D. (1970). The infant separates himself from his mother. *Science, 168,* 78–83.

RIBBLE, M. (1943). *The rights of infants.* New York: Columbia University Press.

RINKOFF, R. F., & Corter, C. M. (1980). Effects of setting and maternal accessibility on the infant's response to brief separation. *Child Development, 51,* 603–606.

RUOPP, R., Travers, J., Glantz, F., & Coelen, C. (1979). *Children at the center: Final report of the National Day Care Study.* Cambridge, MA: Abt Associates.

RUTTER, M. (1981). *Maternal deprivation revisited* (2nd ed.). New York: Penguin Books.

SAGI, A., Lamb, M. E., Lewkowicz, K. S., Shoham, R., Dvir, R., & Estes, D. (1985). Security of mother-infant, -father, and -metapelet attachments among kibbutz-reared Israeli children. In I. Bretherton & E. Waters (Eds.), Growing points of attachment theory and research. *Monographs of the Society for Research in Child Development, 50*(1–2, Serial No. 209).

SCHAFFER, H. R. (1971). *The growth of sociability.* Baltimore: Penguin Books.

SCHAFFER, H. R. (1977). *Mothering.* Cambridge, MA: Harvard University Press.

SCHAFFER, H. R., & Emerson, P. E. (1964). The development of social attachments in infancy. *Monographs of the Society for Research in Child Development, 29*(3, Serial No. 94).

SCHWARTZ, P. (1983). Length of day-care attendance and attachment behavior in eighteen-month-old infants. *Child Development, 54,* 1073–1078.

SEARS, R. R. (1963). Dependency motivation. In M. Jones (Ed.), *Nebraska Symposium on Motivation* (Vol. 11). Lincoln: University of Nebraska Press.

SHILLER, V. M., Izard, C. E., & Hembree, E. A. (1986). Patterns of emotion expression in the strange-situation procedure. *Developmental Psychology, 22,* 378–382.

SINGER, L. M., Brodzinsky, D. M., Ramsay, D., Steir, M., & Waters, E. (1985). Mother-infant attachments in adoptive families. *Child Development, 56,* 1543–1551.

SLADE, A. (1987). Quality of attachment and early symbolic play. *Developmental Psychology, 23,* 78–85.

SPAULDING, D. A. (1873). Instinct with original observation in young animals. *MacMillans Magazine, 27,* 282–283.

SPITZ, R. A. (1945). Hospitalism: An inquiry into the genesis of psychiatric conditions in early childhood. In A. Freud (Ed.), *The psychoanalytic study of the child* (Vol. 1). New York: International Universities Press.

SPITZ, R. A. (1965). *The first year of life: A psychoanalytic study of normal and deviant object relations.* New York: International Universities Press.

SPRUNGER, L. W., Boyce, W. T., & Gaines, J. A. (1985). Family-infant congruence: Routines and rhythmicity in family adaptations to a young infant. *Child Development, 56,* 564–572.

SROUFE, L. A. (1977). Wariness of strangers and the study of infant development. *Child Development, 48,* 1184–1199.

SROUFE, L. A. (1985). Attachment classification from the perspective of infant-caregiver relationships and infant temperament. *Child Development, 56,* 1–14.

SROUFE, L. A., Fox, N. E., & Pancake, V. R. (1983). Attachment and dependency in developmental perspective. *Child Development, 54,* 1615–1627.

SROUFE, L. A., Waters, E., & Matas, L. (1974). Contextual determinants of infant affectional response. In M. Lewis & L.A. Rosen-

blum (Eds.), *The origins of fear.* New York: Wiley.

STEELE, B. F., & Pollack, C. B. (1974). A psychiatric study of parents who abuse infants and small children. In R. E. Helfer & C. H. Kempe (Eds.), *The battered child.* Chicago: University of Chicago Press.

STEPHAN, C. W., & Langlois, J. H. (1984). Baby beautiful: Adult attributions of infant competence as a function of infant attractiveness. *Child Development, 55,* 576–585.

STERN, D. (1977). *The first relationship: Infant and mother.* Cambridge, MA: Harvard University Press.

SUOMI, S. J., & Harlow, H. F. (1972). Social rehabilitation of isolate reared monkeys. *Developmental Psychology, 6,* 487–496.

SVEJDA, M. J., Campos, J. J., & Emde, R. N. (1980). Mother-infant "bonding": Failure to generalize. *Child Development, 51,* 775–779.

THOMAN, E. B., Acebo, C., & Becker, P. T. (1983). Infant crying and stability in the mother-infant relationship: A systems analysis. *Child Development, 54,* 653–659.

THOMPSON, R. A., Lamb, M. E., & Estes, D. (1982). Stability of infant-mother attachment and its relationship to changing life circumstances in an unselected middle-class sample. *Child Development, 53,* 144–148.

TIZARD, B. (1977). *Adoption: A second chance.* London: Open Books.

TIZARD, B., & Hodges, J. (1978). The effect of early institutional rearing on the development of eight-year-old children. *Journal of Child Psychology and Psychiatry, 19,* 99–118.

TRACY, R. L., & Ainsworth, M. D. S. (1981). Maternal affectionate behavior and infant-mother attachment patterns. *Child Development, 52,* 1341–1343.

VAUGHN, B. E., Egeland, B. R., Sroufe, L. A., & Waters, E. (1979). Individual differences in infant-mother attachment at twelve and eighteen months: Stability and change in families under stress. *Child Development, 50,* 971–975.

VAUGHN, B. E., Gove, F. L., & Egeland, B. R.

(1980). The relationship between out-of-home care and the quality of infant-mother attachment in an economically disadvantaged population. *Child Development, 51,* 1203–1214.

WATERS, E., Vaughn, B. E., & Egeland, B. R. (1980). Individual differences in mother-infant attachment relationships at age one: Antecedents in neonatal behavior in an urban, economically disadvantaged sample. *Child Development, 51,* 208–216.

WATERS, E., Wippman, J., & Sroufe, L. A. (1979). Attachment, positive affect, and competence in the peer group: Two studies in construct validation. *Child Development, 50,* 821–829.

WATSON, J. S., Hayes, L. A., Vietze, P., & Becker, J. (1979). Discriminative infant smiling to orientations of talking faces of mother and stranger. *Journal of Experimental Child Psychology, 28,* 92–99.

WEBER, R. A., Levitt, M. J., & Clark, M. C. (1986). Individual variation in attachment security and strange situation behavior: The role of maternal and infant temperament. *Child Development, 57,* 56–65.

WEINRAUB, M., & Lewis, M. (1977). The determinants of children's responses to separation. *Monographs of the Society for Research in Child Development, 42*(4, Serial No. 172).

WIESENFELD, A., Malatesta, C., & DeLoach, L. (1981). Differential parental response to familiar and unfamiliar infant distress signals. *Infant Behavior and Development, 4,* 281–285.

WILLERMAN, L., Broman, S. H., & Fiedler, M. (1970). Infant development, pre-school IQ, and social class. *Child Development, 41,* 69–77.

WOLFF, P. H. (1969). The natural history of crying and other vocalizations in early infancy. In B. M. Foss (Ed.), *Determinants of infant behavior* (Vol. 4). London: Methuen.

ZESKIND, P. S. (1980). Adult responses to the cries of low and high risk infants. *Infant Behavior and Development, 3,* 167–177.

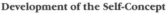

Becoming an Individual: The Self, Sociability, and Achievement

Who am I?

I'm a person who says what I think . . . not [one] who's going to say one thing and do the other. I'm really lucky. I've never [drunk or] done drugs, but I'm always high. I love life. I'm about five years ahead of my age. I've got a lot of different business interests . . . a construction company, oil wells, land . . . I'm trying everything. I travel a lot . . . it's difficult to be traveling and in school at the same time. [People] perceive me as being unusual . . . very mysterious, and I hope they see me as being a competitor, because I do all my talking on the field.

HERSCHEL WALKER, college student and running back of the Dallas Cowboys (as quoted by Blount, 1986)

How would you answer the "Who am I" question? If you are like most adults, you would probably respond by mentioning attributes such as your gender, those of your interpersonal characteristics that you consider particularly noteworthy (for example, honesty, sincerity, friendliness, or kindness), your political leanings, religious preferences (if any), and occupational aspirations or attainments, and your strongest interests and values. In so doing, you would be describing that elusive concept that psychologists call the **self.**

Although no one else knows you the way you do, it is a safe bet that much of what you know about yourself stems from your contacts and experiences with other people. When a college sophomore tells us that she is a friendly, outgoing person who is active in the Phi Mu sorority, the Young Republicans, and the Campus Crusade for Christ, she is saying that her past experiences with others and the groups to which she belongs are important determinants of her personal identity. Several decades ago, sociologists Charles Cooley (1902) and George Herbert Mead (1934) proposed that the self-concept evolves from social interactions and will undergo many changes over the course of a lifetime. They used the term **looking-glass self** to emphasize that our understanding of our identities is a reflection of how other people react to us: one's self-concept is the image seen in a social mirror.

Cooley and Mead believed that the self and social development are completely intertwined—that they emerge together and that neither can progress far without the other. Presumably, neonates experience people and events as simple "streams of impressions" and will have absolutely no concept of "self" until they realize that they exist independent of the objects and individuals that they encounter on a regular basis. Once infants make this important distinction between self and nonself, they will establish interactive routines with their close companions (that is, develop socially) and will learn that their behavior elicits predictable reactions from others. In other words, they are acquiring information about the "social self" based on the ways people respond to their overtures. As they acquire some language and begin to interact with a larger number of other people, children's self-concepts will change. Soon toddlers are describing themselves in categorical terms such as age ("I this many"), size and gender ("I big boy, not a baby"), and activities ("I'm a runner—zoom") that are reflections of how others respond to or label them. Mead (1934) concluded that

> the self has a character that is different from that of the physiological organism proper. The self is something which . . . is not initially there at birth but arises in the process of social development. That is, it develops in a given individual as a result of his relations to that process as a whole and to other individuals within the process.

Do babies really have no sense of self at birth? This issue is explored in the first section of the chapter, where we will trace the growth of the self-concept from infancy through adolescence. We will then consider what developing children know about other people and see that this aspect of social cognition parallels the development of the self-concept. Finally, we will look at some of the important "outcomes" of social development that help children to define a sense of self. In this chapter we will focus on the growth of two personal attributes—*sociability* and *instrumental competence* (or achievement)—that are very important contributors to children's self-concepts. In Chapter 13 we will examine the sex-typing process and note that the child's emerging conception of self as a male or a female may exert a powerful influence on his or her thoughts, feelings, and patterns of conduct. Our focus in Chapter 14 then shifts to moral and ethical issues—including the development of aggressive tendencies and altruistic inclinations (that is, one's willingness to cooperate, to share, and to help others)—as we follow the child's transformation from an egocentric and reputedly self-indulgent organism to a moral philosopher of sorts who has internalized certain ethical principles to evaluate his or her own conduct and the behavior of others.

Let's now return to the starting point and see how children come to know and understand this entity that we call the "self."

Development of the Self-Concept

When do infants first distinguish themselves from other people, objects, and environmental events? At what point do they sense their uniqueness and form self-images? What kinds of information do young children use to define the self? And how do their self-images and feelings of self-worth change over time? These are some of the issues we will explore as we trace the development of the **self-concept** from infancy through adolescence.

The Self as Separate from Others

Like Mead, many developmentalists believe that infants are born without a sense of self. Psychoanalyst Margaret Mahler (Mahler, Pine, & Bergman, 1975) likens the newborn to a "chick in an egg" who has no reason to differentiate the self from the surrounding environment. After all, every need that the child has is soon satisfied by his or her ever-present companions, who are simply "there" and have no identities of their own. Only as the ego begins to form, at 3–6 months of age, will infants recognize that they are separate from their caregivers. In Mahler's words, the child is now in the process of "hatching" from the mother's protective shell and spreading his wings to establish an identity of his own.

Piaget agrees that neonates are born without any knowledge of self. But as they apply their reflexive schemata to the world around them, things begin to change. During the stage of primary circular reactions (1–4 months), infants are repeating pleasurable acts that are centered on their own bodies (for example, sucking their thumbs and waving their arms). At 4–8 months (the stage of secondary circular reactions), they have begun to repeat actions centered on some aspect of the *external* environment (for example, shaking a rattle or squeezing a noise-making toy). Thus, children may learn the limits of their bodies during the first four months and recognize that they can operate on objects external to this "physical self" by the middle of the first year. If 6–8-month-old infants could talk, they might answer the "Who am I" question by saying "I am a looker, a chewer, a reacher, and a grabber who acts on objects and makes things happen."

But not everyone agrees that it takes infants 4 to 6 months to become self-aware. Indeed, we learned in Chapters 6 and 11 that newborn infants are inherently "sociable" creatures who are especially responsive to human speech and may even be capable of synchronizing certain bodily activities (head movements) with those of an adult. Moreover, very young infants also seem to have a sense of *agency*—an awareness that they can make things happen. Recall from Chapter 7 that, by age 8 weeks, babies delight at the discovery that *they* can make a brightly colored mobile rotate (by turning their heads on a pressure-sensitive pillow that activates the mobile), and they will soon become apathetic about the same mobile if they are unable to control its movement. Observations such as these have convinced some developmentalists that infants may recognize that they exist, independent of other people (or objects), during the first month or two of life, and possibly even sooner (Samuels, 1986; Stern, 1983). Yet, Mead, Mahler, and Piaget are undoubtedly correct in one sense, for any primitive self-awareness that may be present very early will become much more refined—and much more apparent to scientists who study it—over the first 4–8 months of the child's life.

self-awareness

self: the combination of attributes, motives, values, and behaviors that is unique to each individual.
looking-glass self: the idea that a child's self-concept is largely determined by the ways other people respond to the child.
self-concept: one's sense of oneself as a separate individual who possesses a unique set of characteristics.

When Do Children Recognize Themselves?

level of cognitive dev. + social experiences

Once infants know *that they are* (that they are separate from objects and close companions), they are now in a position to find out *who* or *what* they are (Harter, 1983). Although a 6-month-old infant may have a subjective sense of self (I) and nonself (they, it), we might wonder whether she perceives herself as a physical being with unique characteristics that discriminate her from other entities. In other words, does the child have a firm self-image? Can she recognize herself?

Michael Lewis and Jeanne Brooks-Gunn (1979) have studied the development of self-recognition by asking mothers to surreptitiously apply a spot of rouge to their infants' noses (while wiping the infants' ostensibly "dirty" faces) and then placing the infants before a mirror. If infants have schemata for their own faces and recognize their mirror images as themselves, they should soon notice the discrepant red dot and reach for or wipe their *own* noses. When Lewis and Brooks-Gunn subjected 9–24-month-olds to this rouge test, they found that a few of the 15–17-month-olds and the vast majority of the 18–24-month-olds touched their own noses rather than those of their mirror images. In other words, they recognized the images as reflections of themselves and inferred that they must have a strange dot on their faces—something that warranted further investigation.

By 18 months of age, many infants recognize static representations of themselves, such as a photograph taken earlier (Lewis & Brooks-Gunn, 1979). Recall that this is precisely the age when the object concept is maturing and infants are internalizing their sensorimotor schemata to form mental images. So it seems that the ability to recognize the self is closely related to the child's level of cognitive development. Even children with Down's syndrome and a variety of other mental deficiencies can recognize themselves in a mirror if they have attained a mental age of at least 18–20 months (Hill & Tomlin, 1981).

Although a certain level of cognitive development seems necessary for self-recognition, social experiences are probably of equal importance. Gordon Gallup (1979) finds that adolescent chimpanzees can easily recognize themselves in a mirror (as shown by the rouge test) unless they have been reared in complete social isolation. In contrast to normal chimps, social isolates react to their mirror images as if they were looking at another animal! So the term *looking-glass self* applies to chimpanzees as well as to humans: reflections in a "social mirror" enable normal chimps to develop a knowledge of self, whereas a chimpanzee that is denied these experiences will fail to acquire a discernible self-image.

The Preschooler's Conceptions of Self

By the time children are able to recognize themselves in a mirror or a photograph, they have already begun to notice some of the ways that people differ and to categorize themselves on these dimensions, a classification called the **categorical self.** Age is one of the first social categories that toddlers recognize and incorporate into their self-concepts—viewing themselves as "big boys" (or girls) rather than babies or adults (Edwards & Lewis, 1979). And the child's understanding of age differences becomes much more refined during the preschool period (Edwards, 1984). For example, children aged 3 to 5 who examine photographs of people aged 1 to 70 can easily classify them as "little boys and girls" (photographs of 2- to 6-year-olds), "big boys and girls" (7- to 13-year-olds), "mothers and fathers" (14- to 49-year-olds), and "grandmothers and grandfathers" (age 50 and older).

Gender is another social category that is very meaningful for young children. Two- to three-year-olds who have acquired gender labels such as *mommy* and *daddy* or *boy* and *girl* can correctly identify photographs as males and females, even though they are not always certain about their own gender identities (Brooks-Gunn & Lewis, 1982; Thompson, 1975). Further, 3- to 4-year-olds are quite aware that they are "boys" or "girls," although they often feel that they could change sex if they really wanted to (Kohlberg, 1969). And by the time they enter school, children know that they will always be males or females and have already learned many cultural stereotypes about men and women (Williams, Bennett, & Best, 1975). Clearly, one's gender identity is an extremely important aspect of "categorical self"—one that we will discuss at length in Chapter 13.

Who am I? Responses of preschool children. When asked to describe themselves, preschoolers dwell on their physical characteristics, their possessions and interpersonal relationships, and the actions they can perform (Damon & Hart, 1982). In one study (Keller, Ford, & Meachum, 1978), 3- to 5-year-olds were asked to say ten things about themselves and to complete the sentences "I am a _____" and "I am a boy/girl who _____." Approximately 50% of the children's responses to these probes and questions were action statements such as "I play baseball" or "I walk to school." By contrast, psychological descriptions such as "I'm happy" or "I like people" were rare among these 3- to 5-year-olds. So it seems that preschool children have a somewhat "physicalistic" conception of self that is based mainly on their ability to perform various acts and make things happen.

These findings would hardly surprise Erik Erikson. In his theory of psychosocial development, Erikson (1963) proposes that 2- to 3-year-olds are struggling to become independent, or autonomous, while 4- to 5-year-olds who have achieved a sense of **autonomy** are now acquiring new skills, achieving important objectives, and taking great pride in their accomplishments. According to Erikson, it is a healthy sign when preschool children define themselves in terms of their activities, for an activity-based self-concept reflects the sense of **initiative** they will need in order to cope with the difficult lessons they must learn at school.

Origins of the "private" self. When adults think about the self, they know that they have a **"public" self** (or selves) that others see and a **"private" self,** or thinking self, that is not available for public scrutiny. Do young children make this distinction be-

tween public self (or "self as known") and private self ("self as knower")?

One way to find out is to ask young children "how" or "where" they think and whether other people can observe them thinking. John Flavell (as cited in Maccoby, 1980) tried this approach and found that children older than 3½ generally know (1) that dolls can't think, even though they have heads, (2) that their own thinking goes on inside their heads, and (3) that another person cannot observe their thought processes. In addition, most 4- to 5-year-olds know that private mental activities are controlled by their brains (Johnson & Wellman, 1982), and they must also know that other people are not always able to infer what is on their minds, for even 3-year-olds will occasionally "fake" an emotion (such as anger or distress) in order to manipulate or deceive their companions (Bretherton, Fritz, Zahn-Waxler, & Ridgeway, 1986). Finally, Lev Vygotsky (1934) noted that 4- to 5-year-olds are beginning to make a clear distinction between "speech for self" and "speech for others." Speech for self, which often accompanies problem-solving activities, is now abbreviated, may be nearly inaudible, and contains many indefinite referents such as "this" or "get it" that are not likely to be understood by anyone other than the child. By contrast, communicative speech that is intended for others is boldly articulated and usually consists of complete sentences.

In sum, most 3- to 5-year-olds have at least begun to discriminate the private self-as-knower from the public self-as-known. But as we will see in the next section, their understanding of the relationship between these two aspects of self is rather primitive compared with that of an adolescent or even an 8-year-old.

Photo 12-1. Young children's sense of self is based on the activities they can perform.

categorical self: a person's classification and definition of self along such dimensions as age, size, gender, activity preferences, beliefs, and values.

autonomy: the ideal outcome of the second of Erikson's eight psychosocial crises (autonomy versus shame and doubt), in which toddlers must establish a sense of independence and self-control or else experience feelings of shame and self-doubt.

initiative: the ideal outcome of the third of Erikson's eight psychosocial crises (initiative versus guilt), in which preschool children must learn to initiate new activities and achieve important objectives or else become self-critical and experience guilt.

public self: those aspects of self that others can see or infer.

private self: those inner, or subjective, aspects of self that are known only to the individual and are not available for public scrutiny.

Conceptions of Self in Middle Childhood and Adolescence

In Chapter 9 we learned that children's thinking gradually becomes less concrete and much more abstract as they progress from middle childhood through adolescence. Is the same true of one's personal identity, or self-concept? To find out, Raymond Montemayor and Marvin Eisen (1977) asked 4th-, 6th-, 8th-, 10th-, and 12th-graders to write 20 different answers to the question "Who am I?" They found that younger children (9–10-year-olds) do describe themselves in much more concrete terms than preadolescents (11–12-year-olds), who, in turn, are more concrete and less abstract than adolescents. Generally speaking, the younger children mentioned categorical information such as names, age, gender, and address, as well as their physical attributes and favorite activities. However, adolescents defined themselves in terms of their traits, beliefs, motivations, and interpersonal affiliations. This developmental shift toward a more abstract or "psychological" view of self can be seen in the responses of three participants:

> *9-year-old:* My name is Bruce C. I have brown eyes. I have brown hair. I love! sports. I have seven people in my family. I have great! eye site. I have lots! of friends. I live at . . . I have an uncle who is almost 7 feet tall. My teacher is Mrs. V. I play hockey! I'm almost the smartest boy in the class. I love! food . . . I love! school.

> *11½-year-old:* My name is A. I'm a human being . . . a girl . . . a truthful person. I'm not pretty. I do so-so in my studies. I'm a very good cellist. I'm a little tall for my age. I like several boys . . . I'm old fashioned. I am a very good swimmer . . . I try to be helpful . . . Mostly I'm good, but I lose my temper. I'm not well liked by some girls and boys. I don't know if boys like me . . .

> *17-year-old:* I am a human being . . . a girl . . . an individual . . . I am a Pisces. I am a moody person . . . an indecisive person . . . an ambitious person. I am a big curious person . . . I am lonely. I am an American (God help me). I am a Democrat. I am a liberal person. I am a radical. I am conservative. I am a pseudoliberal. I am an Athiest. I am not a classifiable person (i.e., I don't want to be) [pp. 317–318].

On those occasions when grade school children use psychological labels to describe the self, they apply them in a concrete fashion, viewing these attributes as absolute and unchanging. For example, an 8- to 11-year-old who says that she is "kind" is likely to believe that kindness is a stable and enduring aspect of

her personality that will always characterize her interactions with others (Mohr, 1978; Rotenberg, 1982). But adolescents who describe themselves with a trait such as "kindness" may recognize that any number of extenuating circumstances can cause them to act in a way that is inconsistent with their self-descriptions. For example, a "kindly" 20-year-old might say "I help my brother with his homework, but I don't help my sister with hers because my brother really needs help, while my sister is lazy. I mean it's fair to help him and not her" (Damon & Hart, 1982, p. 858). What the adolescent has done is to integrate a stable attribute (kindness) with a belief (help only those who need help) to produce an abstract conception of self that provides a logical explanation for two actions that appear to be inconsistent.

Robert Selman (1980) has studied children's growing awareness of their *private* selves by asking them to consider the following dilemma:

> Eight-year-old Tom is trying to decide what to buy his friend Mike for a birthday present. By chance, he meets Mike on the street and learns that Mike is extremely upset because his dog Pepper has been lost for two weeks. In fact, Mike is so upset that he tells Tom "I miss Pepper so much that I never want to look at another dog . . ." Tom goes off only to pass by a store with a sale on puppies. Only two are left and these will soon be gone.

Children were first asked whether Tom should buy Mike one of the puppies. To probe their understanding of the distinction between the private self and one's public image, they were then asked questions such as "Can you ever fool yourself into thinking that you feel one way when you really feel another?" and "Is there an inside and an outside to a person?"

Selman found that children younger than 6 did not distinguish between private feelings and public behavior, responding to the questions with statements such as "If I say that I don't want to see a puppy again, then I really won't ever want to." By contrast, most 8-year-olds recognize the difference between inner states and outward appearances, and they are likely to say that Mike would really be happy to have another puppy. So somewhere between the ages of 6 and 8, children become much more aware of their subjective, "inner" selves and will think of this private self as the true self.

In early adolescence, thinking about the private self becomes much more complex. Selman (1980) proposes that young adolescents are "aware of their own self-awareness" and believe that they can *control* their inner feelings. For example, a 14-year-old might react to the loss of a pet by noting "I can fool myself into not wanting another puppy if I keep saying to myself, I don't want a puppy; I don't ever want to see another puppy." However, older adolescents eventually realize that they cannot control all their subjective experiences because their feelings and behaviors may be influenced by factors of which they are *not consciously aware*. Consider the response of one older adolescent when asked "Why did Mike say he didn't want to ever see another puppy?"

> [Mike] might not want to admit that another dog could take Pepper's place. He might feel at one level that it would be unloyal to Pepper to just go out and replace the dog. He may feel guilty about it. He doesn't want to face these feelings, so he says no dog. (Experimenter: Is he aware of this?) Probably not [Selman, 1980, p. 106].

In sum, children's understanding of their public and private selves becomes increasingly abstract from middle childhood through adolescence. The concrete 6-year-old who feels that her public image is an accurate portrayal of self will gradually become a reflective adolescent who not only distinguishes between the public and private selves but also recognizes that the private "self as knower" may not always understand why the public self behaves as it does.

Self-Esteem: The Affective Component of Self

There is another side to the self-concept that we have not considered: children's feelings about (or evaluations of) the qualities that they perceive themselves as having. This aspect of self is called **self-esteem**. Children with high self-esteem generally feel quite positive about their perceived characteristics, whereas those with low self-esteem view the self in a less favorable light.

Susan Harter (1982) has developed a 28-item self-concept scale that asks children to evaluate their competencies in four areas:

1. *Cognitive competence.* Doing well in school, feeling smart, remembering things easily, understanding what they read.
2. *Social competence.* Having a lot of friends, being popular, being important to one's classmates, feeling liked.
3. *Physical competence.* Doing well at sports, being chosen early for games, being good at new games, would rather play than watch.
4. *General self-worth.* Sure of myself, am a good person, happy the way I am, want to stay the same.

Each of the 28 items requires the child to select one of two statements that is "most like me" and then to indicate whether that statement is "sort of true for me" or "really true for me." Figure 12-1 (p. 440) shows a sample item from the cognitive competencies subscale. Each item is scored from 1 to 4. A score of 1 (far left-hand box) indicates low perceived competence on that item, and a score of 4 (far right-hand box) indicates high perceived competence. Responses to items on each of the four subscales are then summed and averaged to determine how positively the child evaluates his or her cognitive competencies, social competencies, physical competencies, and general self-worth.

Harter (1982) administered her self-concept scale to 2097 third- through ninth-graders and also asked teachers to rate each child on a similar 28-item scale. Several interesting findings emerged from this study. First, even third-graders (8-year-olds) perceive themselves in either favorable or unfavorable terms on each of the four subscales—indicating that children's feelings about the self (or self-esteem) are well established by

---

self-esteem: a person's feelings about the qualities and characteristics that make up his or her self-concept.

Figure 12-1. Sample item from Harter's self-concept scale.

Really true for me	Sort of true for me				Sort of true for me	Really true for me
☐	☐	Some kids often forget what they learn	but	Other kids can remember things easily	☐	☐

middle childhood.[1] Second, children make important distinctions about their competencies in different areas, so that their "self-esteem" depends on the situation in which they find themselves. For example, a star student who considers himself bad at sports and other physical activities may enjoy high self-esteem in the classroom while feeling inadequate on the playground. Finally, Harter found that children's evaluations of self seem to be accurate reflections of how others perceive them. For example, subjects' ratings of their cognitive competencies were positively correlated with their own achievement scores and their teachers' ratings of their cognitive competencies. Their ratings of interpersonal skills and competencies in the social area were confirmed by peers who had been asked to rate each classmate in terms of how good a friend that person was. Moreover, children who had rated themselves high in physical competencies were more frequently chosen for sporting activities and were rated higher on physical competence by gym teachers than were classmates who had rated themselves low in physical competencies. Taken together, these results suggest that both self-knowledge and self-esteem may depend to a large extent on the way others perceive and react to our behavior." This is precisely the point that Charles Cooley (1902) was making when he coined the term *looking-glass self* to explain how we construct a self-image.

Which competencies are most important? Although children evaluate their competencies in many areas, it appears that some attributes are more important than others. For example, fourth- through seventh-graders typically define their self-worth in terms of their *cognitive* and *social* competencies, so that children who enjoy the highest self-esteem are those who

do well in school and have lots of friends (Cauce, 1987; Coopersmith, 1967; Kokenes, 1974). Once again, these findings would not surprise Erik Erikson, who believed that the major psychosocial crisis that grade school children face is **industry versus inferiority.** According to Erikson, 6- to 12-year-olds are beginning to "measure" themselves against their peers to determine who they are and what they are capable of. The major goal of the grade school child is to achieve a sense of personal and interpersonal competence by acquiring important technological and social skills—reading, writing, arithmetic knowledge, an ability to cooperate, and a sense of fair play—that are necessary to win the approval of both adults and peers. Children who acquire these skills should feel good about themselves because they are developing the sense of "industriousness" that will prepare them for their next developmental hurdle—the identity crisis of adolescence. Those who fail to acquire important academic and social skills will feel inferior (that is, have low self-esteem) and may have a difficult time establishing a stable identity later in life (Erikson, 1963).

Does self-esteem change at adolescence? How stable are one's feelings of self-worth? Is a child who enjoys high self-esteem as an 8-year-old likely to feel especially good about himself as an adolescent? Or is it more reasonable to assume that the stresses and strains of adolescence cause most teenagers to doubt themselves and their competencies, thereby undermining their self-esteem?

Erik Erikson (1963) favored the latter point of view. He argued that young adolescents are likely to experience a decline in self-esteem because they are now reevaluating themselves and their goals as they search for a stable identity. Erikson proposed that the many physical, cognitive, and social changes that occur at puberty force the young adolescent to conclude "I ain't what I ought to be, I ain't what I'm gonna be, but I ain't what I was" (1950, p. 139). In other words, 12- to 15-year-olds face an **"identity crisis"** in that they are no longer sure who they are and yet must also grapple with the question "Who will I become?" A failure to

---

[1]Although 4–7-year-olds will also evaluate themselves (usually in a favorable way) on the dimensions of general competence and social acceptance, their judgments are not very accurate. Thus, the self-perceptions of younger children seem to reflect their *desire* to be liked or to be competent rather than a firm sense of self-esteem (Harter & Pike, 1984).

Photo 12-2. Children who do well in school and who have lots of friends are likely to enjoy high self-esteem.

answer these questions leaves them confused and uncertain about their self-worth. However, Erikson proposed that adolescents would eventually view themselves in more positive terms if they achieved a stable identity with which to approach the tasks of young adulthood.

Apparently some 12–14-year-olds do experience a decline in self-esteem as they leave elementary school as the oldest and most revered pupils and enter junior high, where they are the youngest and least competent (Simmons, Blyth, Van Cleave, & Bush, 1979). Moreover, one study of Canadian teenagers revealed that youngsters who are noticeably overweight are likely to suffer a precipitous decline in self-esteem early in adolescence (Mendelson & White, 1985), and another study conducted in Japan found that the 12–16-year-olds who are least satisfied with pubertal changes in their physical appearance tend to have very negative self-images (Lerner, Iwawaki, Chihara, & Sorell, 1980). But before we conclude that adolescence is hazardous to our sense of self-worth, let's note that *most* 11–14-year-olds suffer no appreciable decline in self-esteem (Dusek & Flaherty, 1981; Nottelman, 1987) and, if anything, their self-images and perceived self-worth gradually *increase* over the teenage years (see McCarthy & Hoge, 1982; O'Malley & Bachman, 1983; Savin-Williams & Demo, 1984). So Erikson's (and others') portrayal of adolescence as a period of personal stress and eroding self-esteem seems to characterize only a small minority of young people— primarily those who experience *many life changes* (for

example, a change in schools, changing body images, onset of dating, a disruption of family life) *all at once* (see Simmons, Burgeson, Carlton-Ford, & Blyth, 1987).

What, then, happened to Erikson's identity crisis? In recent years, a number of investigators have taken a close look at the adolescent's search for an identity and found that many people go through several phases, or "identity statuses," before establishing a stable self-concept. In Box 12-1 we will consider some of these findings and see that the development of a firm, future-oriented self-image is a gradual and somewhat uneven process that may begin later and take much longer than Erikson assumed.

Knowing about Others

There are some interesting parallels between the child's knowledge of self and knowledge about others. For example, infants begin to form attachments to their

---

industry versus inferiority: the psychosocial crisis of the grade school years, in which children must acquire important social and intellectual skills, or they may view themselves as incompetent.

identity crisis: Erikson's term for the uncertainty and discomfort that adolescents experience when they become confused about their present and future roles in life.

Box 12-1

Who Am I to Be? A Closer Look at the Adolescent Identity Crisis

Perhaps you can recall a time during the teenage years when you were confused about who you were, what you should be, and what you were likely to become. Do you remember how you resolved your adolescent identity crisis? Is it possible that you have not resolved it yet? And what role do you think an experience like college might play in the process of identity formation?

James Marcia (1966) has carefully analyzed what Erik Erikson had to say about the adolescent identity crisis and has concluded that, at any given point in time, adolescents and young adults can be classified into one of four "identity statuses":

1. *Identity diffusion.* The least mature of the identity statuses. Adolescents classified as diffuse either have not yet experienced an identity crisis or have failed to resolve it. No commitments have been made to important attitudes, values, or plans for the future.
2. *Identity foreclosure.* A person is classified as a foreclosure if he or she has never experienced an identity crisis but has made preliminary commitments to particular goals, values, and beliefs. This may occur when parents or other authority figures suggest an identity to the adolescent (for example, "You'll go to med school, Johnny") and he or she accepts their wishes without really evaluating them.
3. *Moratorium.* This status describes the person who is currently experiencing a strong identity crisis and is actively exploring a number of values, interests, ideologies, and prospective careers in an attempt to find a stable identity in which to grow and embrace the challenges of young adulthood.
4. *Identity achievement.* The identity achiever has resolved his or her crisis by making relatively strong commitments to an occupation, a sexual orientation, and/or a political or religious ideology. Both Marcia and Erikson believe that adolescents must experience an identity crisis and the moratorium status before achieving a stable identity. However, it is possible to progress from identity diffusion to the moratorium phase, skipping the foreclosure status.

Age trends in identity formation. Although Erikson assumed that the identity crisis occurred in early adolescence and was typically resolved by age 15–18, it appears that his age norms were overly optimistic. Philip Meilman (1979) used a structured interview to access the identity statuses of college-bound boys between 12 and 18, 21-year-old college males, and 24-year-old adult males. As shown in the graph, only 20% of the 18-year-olds, 40% of the college students, and slightly over half of the 24-year-olds had established a mature identity status. Note, however, that there was evidence of a clear developmental progression: identity diffusion and the foreclosure status became less common among older subjects, whereas nearly 25% of the 18-year-olds, 52% of the 21-year-olds, and 68% of the 24-year-olds had either reached the moratorium status or achieved stable identities.

One problem with Meilman's study is that subjects came from a very restricted sample; all were college-bound or college-educated males. Sally Archer (1982) has studied a broader cross-section of male and female 6th-, 8th-, 10th-, and 12th-graders and reported a similar set of findings. The vast majority of Archer's subjects were classified as identity-diffuse or foreclosures, the largest increase in identity achievement coming between the 10th and 12th grades. However, Archer reports that only 19% of the *continued*

continued

---

caregivers and to become wary of strangers shortly after they discover that other people are separate entities and not merely extensions of the self (Mahler et al., 1975). Yet, they recognize their companions' features and know that these people have a "permanence" about them long *before* they recognize themselves in a mirror or a photograph (Lewis & Brooks-Gunn, 1979; Pipp, Fischer, & Jennings, 1987). As we learned earlier, many 2–3-year-olds can correctly label pictures of males and females, even though they are not always certain of their own gender identities. And although 3-year-olds can easily place photographs into age categories such as "little children" and "big children," they are not always sure about the category to which they belong (Edwards & Lewis, 1979). So it seems that infants are aware of their own existence as active, independent entities fairly early in life—before they know much about others. But once this sense of "I" as an independent agent is firmly established, they begin to pay particular attention to other people, noticing how they differ and using this information to formulate a *self*-concept. Perhaps Gordon Gallup (1979) was right in arguing that a person must have some knowledge of others before he or she can understand the self.

What kinds of information do children use when forming impressions of other people? How do their impressions of others change over time? And what skills might children be acquiring that would explain these changes in **social cognition?** These are the issues we will consider in the pages that follow.

12th-graders' responses could be classified as moratoriums or identity achievement—a figure that is remarkably similar to the 24% of all 18-year-olds who had achieved these statuses in Meilman's study. Taken together, the results of these studies indicate that American youth do not experience a strong identity crisis until late adolescence. It also appears that a substantial percentage of young adults are still searching for and trying to establish a personal identity.

Effects of college attendance on identity formation. Gordon Munro and Gerald Adams (1977) compared college students with their working peers in order to assess the effects of college attendance on the process of identity formation. Although the two groups were comparable in one aspect of identity formation—the establishment of an occupational identity—the working youth were further along in terms of establishing stable religious and political identities. Munro and Adams concluded that full-time employment "might stimulate rapid movement toward identity formation, while college attendance might be seen as an extended moratorium period" (p. 523). Indeed, one recent longitudinal study found that college students often regress from identity achievement

to the moratorium status at some point in their academic careers (Adams & Fitch, 1982).

In sum, the establishment of a stable adult identity (or identities) is a very gradual process that often extends into young adulthood, particularly if the individual is exposed to a college community in which old viewpoints are likely to be challenged and new alternatives presented. However, let's not be too critical of the college environment, for the vast majority of college students emerge from their four years of higher education with "identity statuses" that are much less diffuse than those they had as entering freshmen (Waterman, 1982).

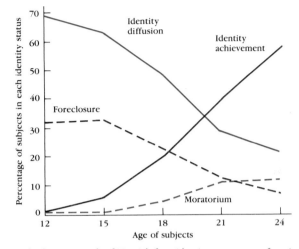

Percentages of subjects in each of Marcia's four identity statuses as a function of age. Note that resolution of the identity crisis occurs much later than Erikson assumed: only 4% of the 15-year-olds and 20% of the 18-year-olds had achieved a stable identity. *(Adapted from Meilman, 1979.)*

Age Trends in Impression Formation

Children younger than 6 or 7 are likely to characterize their friends and acquaintances in the same concrete, observable terms that they use to describe themselves. For example, preschool children often say that they like their "best friend" because (1) the friend lives nearby, so that they can play together (availability and shared activities), (2) the friend is good-looking (physical appearance), and/or (3) the friend has interesting toys (possessions). When these youngsters do use a psychological term to describe a liked or disliked other, it is typically a very general attribute such as "He is *nice*" or "She is *naughty*" that they use more as a label for the other child's recent behavior than as a description of the child's enduring qualities (Rholes & Ruble, 1984).

Apparently traitlike descriptions are much less meaningful for younger than for older children. Five- to seven-year-olds are not especially interested in playing with a child merely because he is "nice"; but describe the same child as owning an attractive toy and his popularity skyrockets. By contrast, 9-year-olds are much more inclined to want to play with a child described as "nice" than with one whose most salient quality is owning an attractive toy (Boggiano, Klinger, & Main, 1986).

Between the ages of 7 and 10, children begin

_____

social cognition: the ability to understand the thoughts, feelings, motives, and intentions of oneself and other people.

to rely less on concrete attributes (for example, possessions and physical characteristics) and more on psychological terms when describing the self and others (Livesley & Bromley, 1973; Peevers & Secord, 1973). Carl Barenboim (1981) has proposed a three-step developmental sequence to describe the changes in children's impressions during the grade school years:

1. *Behavioral comparisons phase.* If asked to talk about people they know, <u>6- to 8-year-olds</u> will compare and contrast their acquaintances in concrete <u>*behavioral* terms</u>, such as "Billy *runs* faster than Jason" or "She *draws* best in our whole class." Before this phase, children usually describe the behavior of their companions in absolute terms (for example, "Billy's fast") without making explicit comparisons.

2. *Psychological constructs phase.* As they continue to observe definite regularities in a companion's behavior, 8- to 10-year-olds should begin to base their <u>impressions on the stable *psychological* attributes,</u> or traits, that the person is now presumed to have. For example, an 8- to 10-year-old might describe well-known classmates with statements such as "He's a stubborn idiot" or "She's generous." However, children at this phase are not yet <u>comparing their acquaintances on these psychological dimensions.</u>

3. *Psychological comparisons phase.* By preadolescence (<u>age 11 or 12</u>), children should begin to <u>*compare and contrast*</u> others on important psychological dimensions. The statement "Bill is much more shy than Ted" is an example of a psychological comparison.

Barenboim evaluated his proposed developmental sequence by asking 6-, 8-, and 10-year-olds to describe three persons whom they knew well. Each of the child's descriptive statements was classified as a behavioral comparison, a psychological construct (or traitlike statement), or a psychological comparison. The children were then retested one year later, so that data were available for subjects at all ages between 6 and 11.

Several interesting findings emerged. As we see in Figure 12-2, the impressions of younger children were usually stated in behavioral terms. Use of behavioral comparisons increased between the ages of 6 and 8 and began to decline at age 9. However, 9- to 11-year-olds were relying much more heavily on psychological constructs during the same period when the use of behavioral comparisons was becoming less common. The longitudinal data were also consistent with Barenboim's proposed developmental sequence: over the year between the original test and the retest, virtually all the

subjects had either stayed at the same phase of impression formation or moved forward (for example, from behavioral comparisons to the psychological constructs phase). Note, however, that even the 11-year-olds rarely used psychological comparisons when stating their impressions of other people.

When do children begin to compare others on important psychological dimensions? To find out, Barenboim repeated his study with 10-, 12-, 14-, and 16-year-olds and found that the vast majority of 12–16-year-olds had progressed to this third level of impression formation. By contrast, fewer than 15% of the 10-year-olds *ever* used a psychological comparison when talking about their companions.

Why do children progress from behavioral comparisons to psychological constructs to psychological comparisons? Why do their own self-concepts become increasingly abstract during this same period of time? In the following section we will consider two contrasting but not altogether inconsistent points of view.

Theories of Social-Cognitive Development

The two theories that are most often used to explain developmental trends in social cognition are Piaget's cognitive-developmental approach and Robert Selman's role-taking analysis.

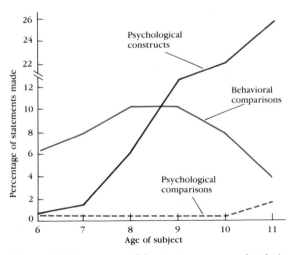

Figure 12-2. Percentages of descriptive statements classified as behavioral comparisons, psychological (traitlike) constructs, and psychological comparisons for children between the ages of 6 and 11. *(Adapted from Barenboim, 1981.)*

Cognitive-developmental theory

According to cognitive-developmental theorists, the ways children think about the self and other people largely depend on their levels of cognitive development. Recall from Chapter 9 that children younger than 6 or 7 are usually functioning at Piaget's preoperational stage—their thinking tends to be static and to center on the most salient perceptual aspects of stimuli and events. So it would hardly surprise a Piagetian to find that 4–7-year-olds describe both themselves and other people in concrete, observable terms (that is, overt appearances, possessions, and actions that the person can perform).

The thinking of 7–10-year-olds should change in many ways as these youngsters enter Piaget's concrete-operational stage. For example, egocentrism is becoming less pronounced, so that children can more readily appreciate that other people may have points of view that differ from their own. Concrete operators are also *decentering* from perceptual illusions, are becoming more proficient at *classifying* objects and events, and are beginning to recognize that certain properties of an object remain invariant despite changes in its appearance (*conservation*). Clearly, these emerging abilities to look beyond immediate appearances and to infer underlying invariances might help to explain why 8–10-year-olds are suddenly noting definite regularities in their own and others' conduct and using psychological constructs, or traits, to describe these patterns.

At age 11 to 12, children are entering formal operations and are now able to think more logically and systematically about abstractions. Although the concept of a psychological trait is itself an abstraction, it is one based on regularities in concrete, observable behaviors, perhaps explaining why *concrete* operators can think in these terms. However, a trait *dimension* is even more of a mental inference or abstraction that has few if any concrete referents. Thus, the ability to think in dimensional terms and to reliably order people along these continua (as is necessary in making psychological comparisons) implies that a person is able to operate on abstract concepts—a formal-operational ability.

Barenboim (1981) favored a cognitive-developmental interpretation when seeking to explain why children progress from behavioral comparisons to psychological constructs to psychological comparisons. And his conclusions seem quite reasonable when we recall that the shift from behavioral comparisons to psychological constructs occurs at age 8–9, soon after children have entered Piaget's concrete-operational stage and are becoming more proficient at detecting regularities, or invariances, and at classifying such events. Moreover, the shift from psychological constructs to psychological comparisons occurs at about age 12, precisely the time when children are entering formal operations and are acquiring the ability to operate on abstractions. So the points at which we see major transitions in children's impressions of the self and others are generally consistent with the Piagetian interpretations of these events.

Robert Selman (1980) has recently proposed a second "cognitive" theory to explain the development of social cognition. Specifically, Selman argues that a mature understanding of the self and other people will depend to a large extent on one particular aspect of cognitive growth—the development of **role taking** skills.

Selman's role-taking analysis of interpersonal understanding

According to Selman (1980), children will become much more proficient at understanding other people as they acquire the ability to discriminate their own perspectives from those of their companions and to see the relationships between these potentially discrepant points of view. The underlying assumption of Selman's theory is straightforward: in order to "know" a person, one must be able to assume his perspective and understand his thoughts, feelings, motives, and intentions—in short, the *internal* factors that account for his behavior. If a child has not yet acquired these important role-taking skills, she may have little choice but to describe her acquaintances in terms of their external attributes—that is, their appearance, their activities, and the things they possess.

Selman has studied the development of role-taking skills by asking children to comment on a number of interpersonal dilemmas. Here is one example (from Selman, 1976, p. 302):

> Holly is a 8-year-old girl who likes to climb trees. She is the best tree climber in the neighborhood. One day while climbing down from a tall tree, she falls . . . but does not hurt herself. Her father sees her fall. He is upset and asks her to promise not to climb trees any more. Holly promises.
> Later that day, Holly and her friends meet Shawn. Shawn's kitten is caught in a tree and can't get down.

role taking: the ability to assume another person's perspective and understand his or her thoughts and feelings.

Table 12-1. Selman's stages of social perspective taking

Stage	Typical responses to the "Holly" dilemma
0. *Egocentric or undifferentiated perspective* (roughly 3 to 6 years) Children are unaware of any perspective other than their own. They assume that whatever they feel is right for Holly to do will be agreed on by others.	Children often assume that Holly will save the kitten. When asked how Holly's father will react to her transgression, these children think he will be "happy because he likes kittens." In other words, these children like kittens themselves, and they assume that Holly and her father also like kittens. They do not recognize that another person's viewpoint may differ from their own.
1. *Social-informational role taking* (roughly 6 to 8 years) Children now recognize that people can have perspectives that differ from their own but believe that this happens *only* because these individuals have received different information. The child is still unable to think about the thinking of others and know in advance how others will react to an event.	When asked whether Holly's father will be angry because she climbed the tree, the child may say "If he didn't know why she climbed the tree, he would be angry. But if he knew why she did it, he would realize that she had a good reason." Thus, the child is saying that if both parties have exactly the same information, they will reach the same conclusion.
2. *Self-reflective role taking* (roughly 8 to 10 years) Children now know that their own and others' points of view may conflict even if they have received the same information. They are now able to consider the other person's viewpoint. They also recognize that the other person can put himself in their shoes, so that they are now able to anticipate the person's reactions to their behavior. However, the child cannot consider his own perspective and that of another person at the same time.	If asked whether Holly will climb the tree, the child might say "Yes. She knows that her father will understand why she did it." In so doing, the child is focusing on the father's consideration of Holly's perspective. But if asked whether the father would want Holly to climb the tree, the child usually says no, thereby indicating that he is now assuming the father's perspective and considering the father's concern for Holly's safety.
3. *Mutual role taking* (roughly 10 to 12 years) The child can now simultaneously consider her own and another person's points of view and recognize that the other person can do the same. At this point, each party can put the self in the other's place and view the self from that vantage point before deciding how to react. The child can also assume the perspective of a disinterested third party and anticipate how each participant (self and other) will react to the viewpoint of his or her partner.	At this stage, a child might describe the outcome of the "Holly" dilemma by taking the perspective of a disinterested third party and indicating that she knows that both Holly and her father are thinking about what each other is thinking. For example, one child remarked: "Holly wanted to get the kitten because she likes kittens, but she knew that she wasn't supposed to climb trees. Holly's father knew that Holly had been told not to climb trees, but he couldn't have known about [the kitten]. He'd probably punish her anyway just to enforce his rule."
4. *Social and conventional system role taking* (roughly 12 to 15 and older) The young adolescent now attempts to understand another person's perspective by comparing it with that of the social system in which he operates (that is, the view of the "generalized other"). In other words, the adolescent expects others to consider and typically assume perspectives on events that most people in their social group would take.	A Stage 4 adolescent might think that Holly's father would become angry and punish her for climbing the tree because fathers generally punish children who disobey. However, adolescents sometimes recognize that other people are nontraditional or may have a personal viewpoint quite discrepant from that of the "generalized other." If so, the subject might say the reaction of Holly's father will depend on the extent to which he is unlike other fathers and does not value absolute obedience.

Source: Adapted from Selman (1976).

Something has to be done right away or the kitten may fall. Holly is the only one who climbs trees well enough to reach the kitten and get it down but she remembers her promise to her father.

After listening to the dilemma, the children were asked:

1. Does Holly know how Shawn feels about the kitten?
2. How will Holly's father feel if he finds out she climbed the tree?
3. What does Holly think her father will do if he finds out she climbed the tree?
4. What would you do in this situation?

After analyzing children's responses to these questions, Selman concluded that role-taking abilities progress through a series of stages, which appear in Table 12-1.

Apparently these role-taking stages represent a true developmental sequence, for 40 of 41 boys who were repeatedly tested over a five-year period showed a steady forward progression from stage to stage with no skipping of stages (Gurucharri & Selman, 1982). Perhaps the reason these role-taking skills develop in one particular order is that they are closely related to Piaget's invariant sequence of cognitive stages (Keating & Clark, 1980). As we see in Table 12-2, preoperational children are at Selman's first or second level of role taking (stage 0 or 1), whereas most concrete operators are at the third or fourth level (stage 2 or 3) and many formal operators have reached the fifth and final level of role taking (stage 4).

Although there are meaningful links between children's role-taking stages and their performance on Piagetian cognitive measures and IQ tests (Pellegrini, 1985), it is quite possible for a person to mature intellectually and to grow less egocentric without becoming an especially skillful role taker (see Shantz, 1983). Thus, there is reason to suspect that factors other than cognitive development may also contribute to the growth of role taking. Could social experiences play such a role? Yes, indeed, for we are about to see that a child's proficiency as a role taker both influences and is influenced by the kinds of social interactions he or she has had.

Role taking and social behavior. As children acquire important role-taking skills, their relationships with other people will begin to change. For example, we've seen that preschool children (at Selman's egocentric stage) think of "friends" as people who live nearby and play together. But once they recognize that playmates may have different motives and intentions (Selman's stage 1), children begin to think of a friend as anyone who tries to do nice things for another person. Later, at stage 2, children understand that the term *friend* implies a *reciprocal* relationship in which the parties involved act with mutual respect, kindness, and affection (Furman & Bierman, 1983; Selman, 1980). Finally, young adolescents who are becoming more knowledgeable about the preferences and personalities of their acquaintances begin to view a "friend" as a person with similar interests and values who is willing to share intimate information with them (Berndt, 1982). In sum, children become much more selective about whom they call a friend as they begin to understand the viewpoints of their peers and are better able to determine who among these companions has an outlook on life that is reasonably well coordinated with their own.

Table 12-2. Percentages of children and adolescents at each of Selman's role-taking stages as a function of their level of cognitive development

Piaget's stage	Role-taking stage				
	0 Egocentric	*1* Social- informational	*2* Self- reflective	*3* Mutual	*4* Social systems
Preoperational	80	20	0	0	0
Concrete operations	0	14	32	50	4
Transitional (late concrete)	1	3	42	43	10
Early formal operations	0	6	6	65	24
Consolidated formal operations	0	12[a]	0	38	50

[a]Since only 8 consolidated formal operators were found in the sample, this figure of 12% represents only one subject.

Source: Based on Selman & Byrne (1974) and on Keating & Clark (1980).

A child's role-taking skills may also affect his or her status in the peer group. Lawrence Kurdek and Donna Krile (1982) found that the most popular children among groups of third- to eighth-graders are those who have well-developed role-taking skills. Moreover, highly sociable children and those who have established intimate friendships score higher on tests of role-taking abilities than their less sociable classmates and those without close friends (LeMare & Rubin, 1987; McGuire & Weisz, 1982).

Why are mature role takers likely to enjoy such a favorable status in the peer group? A study by Lynne Hudson and her associates (Hudson, Forman, & Brion-Meisels, 1982) provides one clue. Second-graders who had tested either high or low in role-taking ability were asked to teach two kindergarten children how to make caterpillars out of construction paper. As each tutor worked with the kindergartners, his or her behavior was videotaped for later analysis. Hudson et al. found that all the older tutors were willing to assist their younger pupils if the kindergartners *explicitly asked for help*. However, good role takers were much more likely than poor role takers to respond to a kindergartner's subtle or *indirect* requests for help. For example, exaggerated straining with scissors and frequent glances at the tutor usually elicited a helpful response from a good role taker but nothing more than a smile from a poor role taker. Apparently, good role takers are better able to infer the needs of their companions so that they can respond accordingly—an ability that may help to explain why they are so popular with their peers and quite successful at establishing close friendships.

Effects of social interactions on role taking. Although our understanding of the self and others will influence our social behavior, it appears that the reverse is also true: our social experiences can affect the way we think about the self and other people. Several years ago, Jean Piaget (1965) argued that playful interactions among grade school children promote the development of important role-taking skills. By assuming different roles while playing together, young children should become more aware of discrepancies between their own perspectives and those of their playmates. And when conflicts arise in play, children must learn to integrate their points of view with those of their companions (that is, compromise) in order for play to continue. So Piaget assumes that equal-status contacts among peers are an important contributor to social perspective taking and the growth of interpersonal understanding.

Diane Bridgeman (1981) has tested this hypothesis in an interesting study with fifth-graders. Students in a *cooperative interdependence* condition were divided into six-person study groups. Each person in each group was assigned various lessons that he or she was required to learn and then teach to the other group members. Since each student had access only to his or her own materials, the members of each group were clearly dependent on one another. Indeed, the tutors had to be good listeners and recognize what their pupils didn't understand and would need to know (a form of role taking) in order for the group members to learn all the material for which they were ultimately responsible. Students assigned to the *control* condition were required to learn exactly the same material, which was taught in the classroom by their teachers.

When tested before the experiment, students in the two conditions were found to be comparable in role-taking abilities. But by the end of the eight-week experiment, children in the cooperative learning groups had typically become better role takers, while those in the control groups had not. Apparently Piaget was right in arguing that a person's role-taking skills will depend, in part, on the kinds of social experiences that he or she has had.

Are some forms of peer contact better than others at promoting the growth of interpersonal awareness? Janice Nelson and Francis Aboud (1985) think so. Nelson and Aboud propose that disagreements among *friends* are particularly important because children tend to be more open and honest with their friends than with mere acquaintances. As a result, disagreeing friends should be more likely than disagreeing acquaintances to provide each other with the information needed to recognize and appreciate their conflicting points of view.

Nelson and Aboud tested their hypothesis in an experiment with 8–10-year-olds. Each child first took a test of "social knowledge" to measure his or her level of reasoning about interpersonal issues such as "What is the thing to do if you lose a ball that belongs to one of your friends?" After taking the test, pairs of friends and pairs of acquaintances discussed one of the interpersonal issues on which they had initially disagreed, and their discussions were tape-recorded. When the discussion was over, each member of the pair was taken aside by the experimenter and asked to offer a solution to the problem that the pair had discussed.

The results clearly showed that friends respond to conflict in a different way than acquaintances. While discussing the issue on which they disagreed,

Photo 12-3. Equal-status contacts with peers are an important contributor to role-taking skills and the growth of interpersonal understanding.

friends were more critical of their partners than acquaintances were, but they were also more likely to fully explain the rationales for their own points of view—precisely the kind of information that might be expected to promote an awareness (and perhaps an appreciation) of each other's perspectives. When tested before the discussion, pairs of friends and pairs of acquaintances made comparable scores on the social knowledge test. But after the discussion, friends' final answers to the issue they had discussed were at a higher level of social understanding than their original answers, whereas the final answers of acquaintances hadn't changed appreciably from pretest to posttest. Although these results are "early returns"—too new to have yet been replicated—they do suggest that equal-status contacts among friends may be particularly important to the development of role-taking skills and interpersonal understanding.

Postscript. Although many questions remain to be answered about the development of "self" and interpersonal awareness, this much is certain: Cooley and Mead were quite correct in suggesting that social cognition and social development are completely intertwined—that they occur together and that neither can progress very far without the other. Lawrence Kohlberg (1969) reached the same conclusion, arguing that social development produces changes in both the child's self-

concept and his or her impressions of other people. These latter developments then influence the child's future social interactions, which, in turn, will affect his or her interpretations of the self and the social environment.

Now that we have touched briefly on the topic of social cognition, it is time to consider many of the important social events, experiences, and outcomes that affect the self-concepts and social knowledge of developing children. We will begin in this chapter by looking at two aspects of social development that contribute heavily to a child's emerging sense of self-esteem: sociability and the growth of instrumental competence (or achievement).

Sociability: Development of the Social Self

Sociability is a term that researchers use to describe the child's willingness to engage others in social interaction and to seek their attention or approval. Although sociable interactions and emotional attachments are sometimes confused, they are easily distinguished. Recall that an attachment is a relatively *strong*

---

sociability: willingness to interact with others and to seek their attention or approval.

and *enduring* affectional tie between the child and a particular person (for example, the mother or father). By contrast, sociability refers to the friendly gestures that the child makes to a much wider variety of targets (peers, strange adults, teachers), and the resulting social relationships are often temporary and emotionally uninvolving (Ainsworth, 1972; Clarke-Stewart, Umeh, Snow, & Pederson, 1980). Some of the confusion surrounding these two constructs stems from the fact that both originate from the child's earliest interactions with caregivers, who usually become both attachment objects and targets for sociable gestures. But even though children may eventually become sociable with any number of other people, they will form attachments to very few.

Sociability during the First Three Years

Months before infants form their first attachments, they are already smiling, cooing, and trying to attract the attention of their companions. By 6 weeks of age, many infants prefer human company to nonsocial forms of stimulation, and they are apt to protest whenever *any* adult puts them down or walks off and leaves them alone (Schaffer & Emerson, 1964). Infants' sociable gestures are much more elaborate when they are interacting with socially skilled partners, such as their parents, than with less responsive companions, such as another infant or a toddler sibling (Vandell & Wilson, 1987). Nevertheless, even another baby may elicit a sociable response from a young infant. Touching among infants first occurs at 3 to 4 months of age (Vincze, 1971), and by the middle of the first year, infants will often smile at their tiny companions, vocalize, offer toys, and take turns gesturing to one another (Hay, Nash, & Pedersen, 1983; Vandell, Wilson, & Buchanan, 1980). Perhaps children become sociable at such an early age because other people—even little people—are likely to notice and respond to their bids for attention.

Although infants do respond to each other's gestures, investigators have wondered just how "sociable" these infant/infant interactions really are. Edward Mueller and his associates (Mueller & Lucas, 1975; Mueller & Vandell, 1979) have proposed that infants progress through three stages of sociability during the first two years. In the first, or *object-centered*, stage, infants may cluster around a single toy but will pay much more attention to the toy than to one another. But during the second, or *simple interactive*, stage, infants are now clearly reacting to the behavior of peers. In fact, one child will often try to regulate another's behavior, as we see in the following example:

Larry sits on the floor and Bernie turns and looks toward him. Bernie waves his hand and says "da," still looking at Larry. He repeats the vocalization three more times before Larry laughs. Bernie vocalizes again and Larry laughs again. This same sequence is repeated twelve more times before Bernie . . . walks off [Mueller & Lucas, 1975, p. 241].

Are these brief "action/reaction" episodes examples of true social discourse? Perhaps, but it is also possible that infants at this stage are so egocentric that they think of a peer as a particularly interesting and responsive "toy" over which they have some control (Brownell, 1986). By age 18 months however, most infants have progressed to a third, or *complementary interactive*, stage, in which their interactions are clearly social exchanges. When they now smile or vocalize, they are obviously trying to influence their playmates and will expect them to respond (Kavanaugh & McCall, 1983). Play is now characterized by role reversals and a primitive kind of reciprocity. For example, an infant who receives a toy from a playmate might immediately return the favor by offering the playmate another toy. Children are also beginning to take turns playing complementary roles, such as chaser and chasee in a game of tag. Although the first evidence of such complementary interaction may appear as early as 16 months (and even earlier with socially skilled partners, such as parents), infants become much more proficient at turntaking and other forms of cooperative exchange by the end of the second year (Brownell, 1986; Ross & Lollis, 1987).

Older infants and toddlers are also becoming more sociable with strange adults in the same ways that they are with peers (Clarke-Stewart et al., 1980). In fact, many distressed 3-year-olds can now be comforted by a strange adult (Maccoby & Feldman, 1972), and they no longer require the mother's presence in order to sustain a friendly, *competitive* interaction with a stranger (Lutkenhaus, Grossmann, & Grossmann, 1985).

Individual Differences in Sociability

Researchers who study infants and toddlers have found that some youngsters are simply more sociable than others. At least three hypotheses have been proposed to account for these individual differences in sociability: the genetic hypothesis, the "security of attachment" hypothesis, and the "ordinal position" hypothesis.

The genetic hypothesis: Sociability as a heritable attribute. There is now evidence to suggest that genotype influences one's responsiveness to other people (Goldsmith, 1983). Over the first year, identical twins are much more similar than fraternal twins in their frequency of social smiling and their fear of strangers (Freedman, 1974), and these differences in sociability are still apparent when pairs of identical and fraternal twins are retested at 18 and 24 months of age (Matheny, 1983). In fact, Sandra Scarr's (1968) study of 6–10-year-old twin pairs suggests that genetic influences on sociability are often detectable well into middle childhood. Even when identical twins have been *mistakenly reared* as fraternals, they are still (1) as similar as identical twins who have been raised as identicals on aspects of sociability such as friendliness and shyness and (2) much more similar on these same measures than are pairs of true fraternal twins (Scarr, 1968).

Although sociability appears to be a heritable attribute, environmental factors play a major role in its expression. For example, Denise Daniels and Robert Plomin (1985) recently found a significant correlation between the shyness of adopted toddlers and the sociability of their *biological* mothers: shy toddlers tended to have mothers who were low in sociability, whereas nonshy toddlers had mothers who were more outgoing. This finding argues for a genetic influence on sociability, since biological mothers and their adopted-away toddlers have genes in common. However, Daniels and Plomin also found a significant correlation between the shyness of adopted toddlers and the sociability of their *adoptive* mothers, and the magnitude of this relationship was nominally greater than that between the toddlers and their biological mothers! Since adoptive mothers and their adopted children have no genes in common, environmental factors must have been responsible for their resemblance on these sociability measures.

What early environmental events are likely to influence a child's social responsiveness? One likely candidate is the quality of the child's emotional attachments.

The "security of attachment" hypothesis.
Although attachment and sociability represent different social systems, Mary Ainsworth (1979) believes that the quality of a child's attachments will affect his or her reactions to other people. Ainsworth's position is that children who are insecurely attached to one or more unresponsive companions may be rather anxious and inhibited in the presence of others and much less sociable than children who are securely attached.

Most of the available evidence is consistent with Ainsworth's hypothesis. Infants who are securely attached to their mothers at 12 to 19 months of age are more likely than those who are insecurely attached to (1) obey their mothers, (2) cooperate with and make positive social gestures toward a strange adult, (3) act sociably around other infants, and (4) be friendly, outgoing, and popular with their peers some three years later in nursery school (LaFreniere & Sroufe, 1985; Londerville & Main, 1981; Lutkenhaus et al., 1985; Pastor, 1981). Moreover, two secure attachments are apparently better than one: toddlers who are secure with both parents are more socially responsive and less conflicted about interacting with a strange adult than are children who are insecure with one parent or both (Main & Weston, 1981). Perhaps Ainsworth is right in arguing that securely attached children are sociable children because they have learned to trust their responsive caregivers and assume that other people will also welcome their bids for attention.

The "ordinal position" hypothesis.
Several years ago, Stanley Schachter (1959) reported an interesting finding: in times of stress or uncertainty, first-borns prefer to affiliate with other people, while later-borns would rather face their problems alone. Although his subjects were adults, Schachter suspected that first-born children, who have enjoyed an exclusive relationship with their parents, are generally more sociable than later-borns.

Deborah Vandell (Vandell, Wilson, & Whalen, 1981) evaluated this **"ordinal position" hypothesis** by placing pairs of 6-month-old infants together and watching them play. Vandell found that first-borns were more likely than later-borns to approach and take turns gesturing to each other. In a similar study of 3-year-olds, Margaret Snow, Carol Jacklin, and Eleanor Maccoby (1981) found that first-borns (particularly "only" children) were both more socially outgoing and more aggressive than later-borns. The later-borns in this study often stood around watching others play, and they were somewhat more likely than first-borns to withdraw from social contacts.

There are at least two reasons that a child's ordinal position in the family may influence responsiveness to peers. For one, only children and other first-borns tend to receive more attention from parents than later-borns do (Lewis & Kreitzberg, 1979). Thus, first-

ordinal-position effect: the finding that first-borns tend to be more socially responsive to their peers than later-borns.

borns may be particularly sociable because they have had many positive social experiences at home—experiences that encourage them to be more outgoing with their peers. In addition, it is possible that later-borns have learned to be wary and somewhat inhibited around other people—particularly little people—because they are often dominated, bullied, or ridiculed by their older and more powerful siblings (Abramovitch, Corter, & Lando, 1979). Vandell et al. (1981) reported a finding that is consistent with this "social power" hypothesis: first-borns who had often interacted with an older child from outside the family were less sociable than first-borns who had had little contact with an older child. Apparently, frequent exposure to older, more powerful companions (siblings or little friends of the family) can make a child a bit hesitant to approach and interact with a new playmate.

Sociability during the Preschool Period

Between the ages of 2 and 5, children not only become more outgoing but will also direct their social gestures to a wider audience. Observational studies suggest that 2- to 3-year-olds are more likely than older children to remain near an adult and to seek physical affection, while the sociable behaviors of 4- to 5-year-olds normally consist of playful bids for attention or approval that are directed at peers rather than adults (Harper & Huie, 1985; Hartup, 1983).

Effects of nursery school on children's sociability. Does the nursery school experience have any noticeable effect on children's sociability? John Shea (1981) addressed this issue by observing 3- and 4-year-olds as they entered nursery school and began to attend classes two, three, or five days a week. As children mingled on the playground, their behavior was videotaped, and individual acts were classified on five dimensions: aggression, rough-and-tumble play, distance from the nearest child, distance from the teacher, and frequency of peer interaction. Over a ten-week observation period, children gradually ventured farther from the teacher as they became much more playful and outgoing with one another and much less forceful and aggressive. Moreover, these changes in sociability were most noticeable for the children who attended school five days a week and least apparent (but detectable nevertheless) for those who attended twice a week. Shea concluded that nursery school attendance has a very positive effect on children's reactions to other children.

However, there are exceptions to the rule. James Pennebaker and his associates (Pennebaker, Hendler, Durrett, & Richards, 1981) found that children rated *low* in sociability by their parents and teachers miss more days of nursery school because of illness than children who are rated highly sociable. This was a particularly interesting finding, for the health records of the less sociable (and presumably sickly) children indicated that they had been no less healthy than their more sociable classmates before entering nursery school. Pennebaker et al. suggest that shy and otherwise unsociable children often find the nursery school setting threatening and aversive. As a result, they may feign illnesses in order to stay home, or they may actually suffer from stress-induced disorders such as gastric problems and tension headaches. Unfortunately, these socially distressed "absentees" may be the ones who would profit most from the social curriculum of nursery school—if only they could acquire a few basic skills that would enable them to interact more effectively with their classmates. In Box 12-2 we will consider some of the strategies that researchers have used to improve the social skills of extremely unsociable children.

Who raises sociable children? Although the data are somewhat limited, it appears that parents who are warm and supportive and who *require* their children to follow certain rules of social etiquette (for example, "Be nice"; "Play quietly"; "Don't hit") are likely to raise well-adjusted sons and daughters who relate well to both adults and peers (Baumrind, 1971). By contrast, permissive parents who set few standards and exert little control over their children often raise youngsters who are aggressive and unpopular with their peers and who may resist or rebel against rules set by other adults (for example, teachers). There is also evidence that children of overprotective mothers (particularly boys) are quite sociable when interacting with adults but are often anxious and inhibited around their peers (Kagan & Moss, 1962; Martin, 1975). This finding might be explained by the fact that a highly protective mother frequently encourages her children to remain near her side. As a result, an overprotected son may be rejected as a sissy by other children, an experience that may prompt him to seek the company of friendly adults and to avoid peers.

The finding that securely attached youngsters are generally outgoing and even popular with other children suggests that sensitive, responsive caregiving contributes to the development of sociability. Kevin

MacDonald and Ross Parke (1984) believe that the character of *playful* interactions between parents and their children is especially significant in this regard, for parents' conduct while serving as "playmates" will undoubtedly influence the ways in which the child reacts to other playmates, such as siblings and peers. Clearly this idea has some merit. Nine-month-old infants whose mothers provide many opportunities for playful turn-taking are already more responsive to peer playmates than are age mates who have experienced less turntaking with their mothers (Vandell & Wilson, 1987). And in his studies of playful interactions between 3–5-year-olds and their parents, MacDonald (1987; MacDonald & Parke, 1984) finds that if parents are *directive, controlling* playmates (that is, always issuing commands and rarely allowing the child to regulate their play), their children tend to have poor social skills and nonharmonious peer interactions. Perhaps a controlling parent who is always barking orders will inhibit sociability by simply taking all the fun out of play activities. Or alternatively, these parents may be teaching their children to be bossy and dictatorial themselves—a style that is likely to elicit negative reactions from playmates and convince the child that contacts with peers are not all that pleasant.

Is Sociability a Stable Attribute?

Several longitudinal studies suggest that sociability is a reasonably stable attribute from about age 2 onward. Wanda Bronson (1985) found that, between the ages of 12 and 24 months, indicators of sociability such as a child's initial reactions to play sessions, willingness to initiate social interactions, and time spent interacting with other children become much more stable and predictable. Thus, a 12-month-old who is highly sociable today may not be tomorrow, whereas this kind of inconsistency is not often seen among 2-year-olds. Bronson also found that measures of children's sociability at 2 years of age predicted their sociability at age 3½ in nursery school, whereas sociability measured when these children were only 12–14 months of age did not. Other investigators working with older children have also found that sociability remains fairly stable over time. In other words, if a child is quite friendly and outgoing during nursery school or the early grade school years, chances are that he or she will become a highly sociable adolescent or young adult (Kagan & Moss, 1962; Schaefer & Bayley, 1963).

Merrill Roff and his associates (Roff, 1974; Roff, Sells, & Golden, 1972) have collected longitudinal data on the interpersonal behavior of thousands of developing children. One of the most reliable findings in this research is that unsociable or inappropriately sociable (that is, argumentative, aggressive) children who are *rejected by their peers* run the risk of serious emotional disturbances later in life—problems such as delinquency, neurotic and psychotic disorders, sexual deviations, and pathologically low self-esteem, to name a few. We will be returning to this intriguing relationship between poor peer relations and later emotional difficulties in Chapter 16, where we will discuss the many important roles that peers play in a child's social and personality development. But even without considering the issue further at this point, it should be apparent that the task of becoming appropriately sociable is an important developmental hurdle—one that may call for therapeutic intervention if children are extremely shy, uncomfortable, or aggressive around their peers.

Achievement: Development of the Competent Self

Two basic aims of socialization are to urge children to pursue important goals and to take pride in their accomplishments. In many Western societies, including our own, children are encouraged to be independent and competitive and to do well at whatever they may attempt—in short, to become "achievers." Although the meaning of achievement varies somewhat from society to society, a recent survey of 30 cultures reveals that people from all over the world value personal attributes such as self-reliance, responsibility, and a willingness to work hard to attain important objectives (Fyans, Salili, Maehr, & Desai, 1983).

Must these valued attributes be taught? Social-learning theorists think so, but others disagree. Psychoanalyst Robert White (1959) proposes that children are intrinsically motivated to "master" their environments. He calls this **effectance motivation**—a desire to have an effect on or to cope successfully with the environment and the people within it. We see this effectance, competence, or mastery motive in action as we watch infants struggle to turn knobs, open cabinets, and operate toys—and then notice their pleasure when they succeed. White argued that it is quite natural for

effectance motivation: an inborn motive to explore, understand, and control one's environment (sometimes called mastery motivation).

Box 12-2
Improving the Social Skills of
Unsociable Children

Unsociable children are usually deficient at a number of very basic social skills, such as successfully initiating play activities, cooperating, communicating their needs, giving help, affection, and approval to their peers, and resolving interpersonal conflicts (Asher, 1986). During the past few years, investigators have devised a number of "therapies" aimed at improving the social skills of withdrawn or otherwise unpopular children who can't seem to get along with others. Among the more common of these approaches are the following:

Reinforcing socially appropriate behaviors. In their excellent review of the literature on social-skills training, Melinda Combs and Diana Slaby (1977) point out that adults can shape socially appropriate responses such as cooperation and sharing by reinforcing these actions and ignoring examples of "inappropriate" behavior, such as aggression and solitary play. Another method of encouraging children to make social contacts is to place them in charge of valuable resources that they must dispense to the peer group. Frank Kerby and Curt Tolar (1970) tried this approach with a withdrawn 5-year-old. Each day for several days, the boy was given a large bag of candies. He was then told to ask his classmates what kind of candy they wanted and to give them the candy of their choice. After distributing all the candies, the boy was praised by his teacher and given some candy (and a nickel) for his efforts. Observations during later free-play periods revealed that this child became much more outgoing and cooperative with his peers. It seems that the candy gave him a reason to initiate social interactions. And in the process he acquired some basic social skills and enhanced his status as he dispensed valuable commodities to his classmates.

According to Combs and Slaby (1977), contingent reinforcement of socially skilled behavior is most effective if administered on a regular basis to the *entire peer group* rather than given occasionally to the unsociable children. A group-reinforcement procedure not only reinforces unsociable peers for their socially skillful acts but also allows them to see others reinforced for this kind of behavior. There are several ways for adults to structure play environments so that it becomes possible to reinforce groups of children for their appropriate social conduct. For example, they might persuade children to work at tasks or to strive for goals that require cooperation among all present. And even simple strategies such as giving children "social" toys to play with (cards, checkers, and the like) should provide ample opportunities for adults to reinforce examples of appropriate social behavior.

Modeling social skills. In Chapter 7 we learned that modeling techniques are an effective method of teaching children to approach objects (dogs) that they have previously avoided. Would a similar form of therapy help shy or solitary children overcome any fears they might have about approaching and interacting with peers?

Apparently it can. In one study (Cooke & Apolloni, 1976), live models demonstrated certain social skills—for example, smiling at others, sharing, initiating positive physical contacts, and giving verbal compliments—to withdrawn grade school children. This procedure proved effective at increasing each type of behavior that the model had enacted. The training also had two desirable side effects. First, the withdrawn children began to show increases in other positive social behaviors that had not been modeled.
continued

---

human beings to seek out challenges just for the joy of mastering them. Of course, his position is very similar to that of Piaget, who believed that children are intrinsically motivated to adapt to the environment by assimilating new experiences and then accommodating to these experiences.

Throughout this text, we have stressed that human infants are curious, active explorers who are constantly striving to understand and to exert some control over the world around them. But even though the basic propensity for competence or mastery may be innate, it is obvious that some children try harder than others to master their school assignments, their music lessons, or the positions they play on the neighborhood softball team.

How can we explain these individual differences? Is there a "motive to achieve" that children must acquire? What kinds of home and family experiences are likely to promote achievement behavior? And how do children's self-images and their expectations about succeeding or failing affect their aspirations and accomplishments? These are the issues we will consider in this final section of the chapter.

Set of 4 pictures McClellan (n Ach)

What Is Achievement Motivation?

When developmentalists talk about an "independent" person, they mean an individual who is able to accomplish many goals without assistance. The concept of achievement motivation is more complex. David McClelland and his associates (McClelland, Atkinson, Clark, & Lowell, 1953) define the **need for achievement (*n* Ach)** as a learned motive to compete and to strive for success whenever one's behavior can be evaluated against a standard of excellence. In other words,

Second, the frequency of positive social responses among *untrained* children also increased, apparently in direct response to the friendly gestures made by their classmates who had received the social-skills training. So modeling strategies can produce marked changes in a child's social skills—changes that benefit both the child and the peers with whom he or she interacts. And it seems that the modeling approach works best when the model is similar to the child, when he initially acts shy and withdrawn, and when his socially skillful actions are accompanied by some form of commentary that directs the observer's attention to the purposes and benefits of behaving appropriately toward others (Asher, Renshaw, & Hymel, 1982).

Cognitive approaches to social-skills training. Cognitive approaches to social-skills training differ from reinforcement or modeling approaches in that children are more *actively involved* in thinking about, talking about, practicing, and imagining the consequences of various social overtures (Combs & Slaby, 1977; Urbain & Kendall, 1980). One argument offered in favor of this approach is that the child's active and explicit involvement in the social-skills training procedures may increase her un-

derstanding, internalization, and generalization of the skills that are taught.

Coaching is a technique in which the therapist displays one or more social skills, explains the rationales for using them, allows children to practice such behavior, and then suggests how the children might improve on their performances. Sherri Oden and Steven Asher (1977) coached third- and fourth-grade social isolates on four important social skills—how to participate in play activities, how to take turns and share, how to communicate effectively, and how to give attention and help to peers. Not only did the children who were coached become more outgoing and positive, but follow-up measures a year later revealed that these former isolates had achieved even further gains in social status (see also Bierman, 1986; Ladd, 1981). Apparently the benefits of a coaching strategy are even greater if this approach is combined with other forms of social-skills training, such as encouraging children to work together toward the attainment of cooperative goals (Bierman & Furman, 1984).

Role-playing techniques are another type of cognitive therapy that seems to improve children's social skills. Myrna Shure and George Spivack (1974) devised a ten-week program to help preschool children generate and then evaluate

solutions to a number of interpersonal problems. Children role-played these situations with puppets and were encouraged to discuss the impact of their solutions on the feelings of all parties involved in a conflict. Shure and Spivack found that fewer aggressive solutions were offered the longer the children had participated in the program. Moreover, the children's classroom adjustment (as rated by teachers) improved as they became better able to think through the social consequences of their own actions.

Summing up. Clearly, there are several methods that might be used to improve the social skills of unsociable children and head off the potentially harmful effects of poor peer relations. Perhaps the way to treat extremely shy and withdrawn children is to begin with a technique that produces fairly immediate results—for example, contingent reinforcement or modeling. Once these isolates have been drawn out of their shells and have seen that peer contacts can be rewarding, they may then be ready for coaching or the kinds of role-playing and problem-solving experiences that are apparently quite effective at producing long-term gains in sociability and peer acceptance.

---

high "need-achievers" have learned to take pride in their ability to meet or exceed high standards, and it is this sense of self-fulfillment that motivates them to work hard, to be successful, and to outperform others when faced with new challenges.

Achievement motivation is usually measured by asking subjects to examine a set of four pictures and then write a story about each as part of a test of "creative imagination." These four pictures show people working or studying, although each is sufficiently ambiguous to suggest any number of themes (see Photo 12-4). The subject's need for achievement (*n* Ach) is determined by counting the achievement-related statements that he or she includes in the four stories (the assumption being that subjects are projecting themselves and their motives into their themes). For example, a high need-achiever might respond to Photo 12-4 by saying that

these men have been working for months on a new scientific breakthrough that will revolutionize the field of medicine, whereas a low need-achiever might say that the workers are glad the day is over so that they can go home and relax. Does this measure have any validity? Apparently so, for students who score high in achievement motivation tend to make better grades than those who score low, and they aspire to higher-status occupations as well (McClelland et al., 1953).

Recently, Susan Harter (1981) has argued that children may attempt to achieve for either of two rea-

30 item ?
intrinsic extrinsic

need for achievement (*n* Ach): a learned motive to compete and to strive for success in situations where one's performance can be evaluated against some standard of excellence.

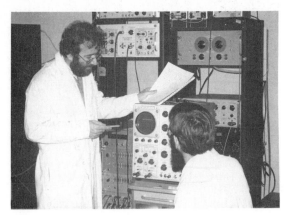

Photo 12-4. Scenes like this one were used by David McClelland and his associates to measure achievement motivation.

sons: (1) to satisfy their own needs for competence or mastery (an **intrinsic orientation** very similar to McClelland's *n* Ach) or (2) to earn *external* incentives such as grades, prizes, or approval (an **extrinsic orientation** that other theorists have called social achievement). Harter measures achievement orientation with a 30-item questionnaire that asks children whether the reasons they perform various activities are intrinsic justifications (I like challenging tasks; I like to solve problems myself) or extrinsic ones (I do things to get good grades; to win the teacher's approval). Preliminary research with this measure indicates that children who are intrinsically oriented to achieve are more likely than those who are extrinsically oriented (1) to prefer challenging problems over simpler ones and (2) to view themselves as highly competent at schoolwork and other cognitive activities.

Home and Family Influences on Mastery Motivation and Achievement

As early as 6 months of age, infants already differ in their willingness to explore the environment and their attempts to control objects, situations, and the actions of other people (Yarrow et al., 1983). Moreover, these early differences in mastery behavior are better predictors of children's intellectual performance at age 2½ than are the children's own first-year scores on infant intelligence tests (Messer et al., 1986). Although the amount of mastery behavior that young infants display is related to their level and rate of maturation (as indexed by standardized tests of infant development), social experiences will soon begin to affect the child's

curiosity and problem-solving behavior. Three especially potent influences on mastery motivation and achievement are the quality of the child's emotional relationships with caregivers, the character of the child's home environment, and the child-rearing practices that parents use while urging the child to achieve.

Quality of attachment. One of the most reliable findings in the early childhood research of the past ten years is that a secure and loving attachment to parents promotes mastery behavior. For example, infants who are securely attached to their mothers at age 12–18 months are more likely than those who are insecurely attached to venture away from the mother to successfully negotiate and explore strange environments (Cassidy, 1986; Matas, Arend, & Sroufe, 1978) and to display a strong sense of curiosity, self-reliance, and an eagerness to solve problems some four years later in kindergarten (Arend, Gove, & Sroufe, 1979). It is not that securely attached children are any more intellectually competent; instead, they seem to be more *eager* than insecurely attached children to *apply* their competencies to the new problems they encounter (Belsky, Garduque, & Hrncir, 1984). So infants apparently need the "secure base" provided by a loving, responsive parent to feel comfortable about taking risks and seeking challenges. Stated another way, a secure emotional bond with a close companion appears to be an important contributor to achievement motivation.

The home environment. The young child's tendency to explore, to acquire new skills, and to solve problems will also depend on the character of the home environment and the challenges it provides. In one study (van Doorninck, Caldwell, Wright, & Frankenberg, 1981), investigators visited the homes of 50 12-month-old infants from lower-class families and used the **HOME inventory** (described in Chapter 10) to classify the child's early environment as intellectually stimulating or unstimulating (stimulating homes were those with emotionally responsive caregivers who structured the child's play periods and provided a variety of age-appropriate toys that he or she could manipulate and control). Five to nine years later, the research team followed up on these children by looking at their standardized achievement test scores and the grades they had earned at school. As we see in Table 12-3, the quality of the home environment at 12 months of age predicted children's academic achievement several years later. Two out of three children from stimulating homes were now performing quite

Table 12-3. Relation between quality of home environment at 12 months of age and children's grade school academic achievement five to nine years later

Quality of home environment at age 12 months	Academic achievement	
	Average or high (top 70%)	Low (bottom 30%)
Stimulating	20 children	10 children
Unstimulating	6 children	14 children

Source: Adapted from van Doorninck et al. (1981).

well at school, whereas 70% of those from unstimulating homes were doing very poorly. Although the seeds of mastery motivation may well be innate, it seems that the joy of discovery and problem solving is unlikely to blossom in a barren home environment where the child has few problems to solve and limited opportunities for learning.

Which aspects of the home environment contribute most to children's propensities for achievement? Robert Bradley and Bettye Caldwell (1984) find that the HOME subscales measuring the "variety of stimulation" the child receives and the "age-appropriateness of play materials" are strong predictors of children's later first-grade achievement test scores—stronger even than the HOME subscale measuring "maternal responsivity." Why should the variety and age-appropriateness of the child's stimulation be so important? Perhaps because young children who have many different *age-appropriate* toys and experiences are likely to acquire a strong sense of competence as their attempts to control these objects and events regularly prove successful. By contrast, toys and activities that are too complex for the child may foster a sense of ineffectiveness and eventually a reluctance to try to master new challenges. Of course, Bradley and Caldwell's findings in no way minimize the importance of having warm and responsive parents; instead, they simply imply that the amount and variety of age-appropriate stimulation that the child receives at home have an effect on achievement above and beyond that predicted by factors related to parental responsiveness, such as the quality of the child's attachments. Stated another way, the security of one's attachments and the challenges provided by the home environment *both* seem to be important contributors to children's achievement strivings.

The demands that parents make of their child

and the ways they respond to his or her accomplishments can also influence the child's will to achieve. In Box 12-3 we will take a closer look at some of the child-rearing practices that seem to encourage (or discourage) the development of achievement motivation.

Beyond the Achievement Motive: Two Cognitive Determinants of Achievement Behavior

Does a high need for achievement ensure that a child will master important challenges and live up to his potential? Not necessarily. Though recognizing that the concept of achievement motivation has some value, many researchers now believe that it tells only part of the story. Two additional factors that clearly influence what a child is likely to accomplish are the *value* that the child places on achieving various goals and the child's *expectancies* of succeeding (or failing) should he pursue these objectives.

Valuation of achievement and achievement behavior. Is it naive to think that a global measure such as *n* Ach will forecast children's accomplishments on most achievement tasks? Virginia Crandall (1967) thinks so. She notes that there are many, many areas in which children might achieve, including schoolwork, sporting activities, hobbies, domestic skills, and making friends, to name a few. Presumably, a child's willingness to set high standards and to work to attain them may differ from area to area depending, in part, on the *value* of accomplishing these objectives or winning recognition for one's efforts. And it does seem obvious that we are more likely to strive for valuable or important goals than for those we consider trivial or unimportant. Indeed, Joel Raynor (1970) found that global measures of achievement motivation predict actual accomplishments only for tasks that people consider valuable or important. So the perceived value of the success we might attain—a *cognitive* variable that differs

intrinsic orientation: a desire to achieve in order to satisfy one's personal needs for competence or mastery.

extrinsic orientation: a desire to achieve in order to earn external incentives such as grades, prizes, or the approval of others.

HOME inventory: a measure of the amount and type of intellectual stimulation provided by a child's home environment.

Box 12-3
Child-Rearing Practices and
Children's Achievement Motivation

What kinds of child-rearing practices encourage achievement motivation? In their book *The Achievement Motive,* McClelland, Atkinson, Clark, and Lowell (1953) propose that parents of high need-achievers (1) stress independence training and (2) expect their children to be self-reliant at an earlier age than parents of low need-achievers.

Marian Winterbottom (1958) tested these hypotheses by measuring the achievement motivation of 29 boys aged 8 to 10 and then comparing their scores against the child-rearing strategies their mothers had used. The results supported McClelland's hypotheses: mothers of high need-achievers expected their sons to be independent at an earlier age than mothers of low need-achievers. In addition, mothers of high need-achievers were more likely than mothers of low need-achievers to reinforce self-reliance with a hug and a kiss. Winterbottom concluded that *early* independence training given with lots of warmth and affection is an important contributor to children's achievement motivation.

Bernard Rosen and Roy D'Andrade (1959) suggest that direct *achievement training* (encouraging children to do things well) is at least as important to the development of achievement motivation as independence training (encour-

aging children to do things on their own). To evaluate their hypothesis, Rosen and D'Andrade visited the homes of boys who had tested either high or low in achievement motivation and asked these 9- to 11-year-olds to work at difficult and potentially frustrating tasks—for example, building a tower of irregularly shaped blocks while blindfolded and using only one hand. To assess the kind of independence and achievement training the boys received at home, the investigators asked parents to watch their son work and to give any encouragement or suggestions that they cared to. The results were clear. Both the mothers and fathers of high need-achievers set lofty standards for their boys to accomplish while working on the experimental tasks, and they were noticeably concerned about the quality of their sons' performance. They gave many helpful hints and were quick to praise their sons for meeting one of their performance standards. In contrast, parents of low need-achievers (particularly fathers) stressed neither independence nor achievement training. They often told their sons how to perform the tasks and became rather irritated whenever the boys experienced any difficulty. Finally, the high need-achievers tended to outperform the low need-achievers and they seemed to enjoy the tasks more as well. So it appears that independence, achievement motivation, and achievement behavior are more likely to develop when parents encourage children to do things on their own *and to do them well.*

However, a caution is in order. Early independence and achievement training can backfire and cause a child to shy away from challenging tasks if parents accentuate the negative by *punishing failures and responding neutrally to successes* (Teeven & McGhee, 1972). Children who show the highest levels of achievement motivation are those who are encouraged to "do their best" by parents who *reward successes and are not overly critical of an occasional failure.*

Parents who encourage independence and achievement are likely to raise children who are motivated to achieve.

---

across individuals and achievement domains—is an important determinant of achievement behavior.

Can I achieve? The role of expectancies in achievement behavior. We are also more likely to work hard when we think we have a reasonable prospect of succeeding than when we see little chance of achieving our objectives. As we learned earlier in the chapter, grade school children are already developing positive or negative views of themselves as they evaluate their social, academic, and athletic competencies. They are also forming very specific expectations about their

likelihood of succeeding or failing at specific tasks such as arithmetic, basketball, or acting one's part in the class play. Do these expectations of doing well (or poorly) have any effect on children's behavior? Yes, indeed! In Chapter 10 we learned that IQ is an important determinant of academic achievement. Yet, it is not uncommon for children with high IQs and low academic expectancies to earn *poorer* grades than their classmates with lower IQs but higher expectancies (Battle, 1966; Crandall, 1967). In other words, expectations of success or failure are a powerful determinant of achievement behavior: children who expect to achieve usually do, whereas those who expect to fail may spend little time and effort pursuing goals that they believe to be "out of reach."

Why Do I Succeed (or Fail)? Cognitive-Attributional Theories of Achievement

Earlier we suggested that infants and toddlers are apt to view themselves as competent to master many challenges when they have had ample opportunities to *control* their environments—that is, to regulate the behavior of responsive companions and to satisfy other objectives, such as successfully operating age-appropriate toys. Just how important is this sense of personal control to children's achievement expectancies and to the value they are likely to attach to their successes and failures? Let's see what contemporary achievement theorists have to say.

Crandall best predictor of academic achievement

Locus of control and children's achievement behavior

In recent years, researchers have found that children's achievement behavior depends, in part, on their *locus of control*—that is, the extent to which they believe that their behavior influences their outcomes. Children with an internal locus of control (called **internalizers**) assume that they are personally responsible for their successes and failures. If an internalizer were to receive an A on an essay, she would probably attribute the high mark to her ability to write or to the hard work that she had expended in preparing the paper (internal causes). By contrast, children with an external locus of control (called **externalizers**) believe that their successes and failures depend more on luck, fate, or the actions of others than on their own abilities or efforts. Thus, an externalizer is likely to attribute an A grade on an essay to luck (the teacher just happened to like this one), indiscriminate grading, or some other external cause. Children's locus of control is usually measured by administering the Intellectual Achievement Responsibility Questionnaire, a 34-item scale that taps one's perceptions of responsibility for pleasant and unpleasant outcomes. Each item describes an achievement-related experience and asks the child to select an internal or an external cause for that experience (see Figure 12-3 for sample items). The more "internal" responses the child selects, the higher his internality score; children who choose few internal responses are classified as externalizers.

Virginia Crandall and her associates believe that an internal locus of control (internality) is condu-

Figure 12-3. Sample items from the Intellectual Achievement Responsibility Questionnaire.

1. *If a teacher passes you to the next grade, it would probably be*
   _____ a. because she liked you
   * _____ b. because of the work that you did

2. *When you do well on a test at school, it is more likely to be*
   * _____ a. because you studied for it
   _____ b. because the test was especially easy

3. *When you read a story and can't remember much of it, it is usually*
   _____ a. because the story wasn't well written
   * _____ b. because you weren't interested in the story

*Denotes the "internal" response for each sample item.

cive to achievement: children must necessarily assume that their efforts will lead to positive outcomes if they are to strive for success and become high achievers. Clearly there is some support for this hypothesis. In their review of more than 100 studies, Maureen Findley and Harris Cooper (1983) found that internalizers do earn higher grades and will typically outperform externalizers on standardized tests of academic achievement. In fact, one rather extensive study of minority students in the United States found that children's beliefs in internal control were a better predictor of their academic achievements than were their *n* Ach scores, their parents' child-rearing practices, or the type of classroom and the teaching styles to which these students had been exposed (Coleman et al., 1966).

Where do children's beliefs about their own control (or lack of control) over events come from? As we have already noted, these ideas may begin to form early in life as infants discover whether or not they can get companions or even toys to "respond" to them. In addition, parents who encourage self-reliance while setting clear performance standards for their children are likely to raise internalizers (Buriel, 1981; MacDonald, 1971). By contrast, protective parents who set few performance standards and allow little autonomy or freedom of expression are likely to raise youngsters who

internalizers: people who believe that they are personally responsible for their successes and failures.
externalizers: people who believe that their successes and failures depend more on external factors such as luck or fate than on their own efforts and abilities.

score higher in externality (Davis & Phares, 1969; Wichern & Nowicki, 1976). Perhaps there is a simple explanation for these findings. If children are often protected by parents who solve their problems for them and set few standards for them to live up to, it is easy to see how they might be confused about what constitutes acceptable performance and assume that parents or other adults will make those judgments for them. However, parents who stress self-reliance and set clear performance standards are creating a "predictable" world for their children—one that will enable them to determine whether their own efforts to achieve important goals have been successful or unsuccessful.

In sum, a child's propensity for achievement is heavily influenced by his or her perceptions of control over important life outcomes—perceptions that arise from early socialization experiences. High achievers do tend to feel personally responsible for their successes, just as Crandall's locus-of-control theory would predict. But it is interesting to note that high achievers may not feel personally responsible for their failures—in fact, they will often *externalize* them, blaming poor performances on tasks that are too difficult or on tests that are ambiguous. And not only does the perceived locus of control often differ for successes and failures, but children who adopt *internal* explanations for failures tend to be *low* rather than high achievers (Dweck & Elliott, 1983). Clearly, these latter findings are inconsistent with Crandall's theory, which assumes that children adopt a relatively stable locus of control and that an internal locus (or internality) is most conducive to achievement. How can we explain these puzzling outcomes? Bernard Weiner's recent attributional theory of achievement suggests some answers.

Weiner's attribution theory

Weiner (1974, 1986) has argued that human beings are active information processors who will sift through the data available to them, seeking to explain why they succeed or fail at various activities. According to Weiner, the explanations, or **causal attributions,** that we make about our achievement outcomes in one particular context will influence our *expectancies* about future successes or failures in other, similar contexts. And given the strong link between achievement expectancies and achievement behavior, it seems reasonable to assume that our beliefs about the underlying causes of our successes and failures can have a powerful effect on our motivation to persist at various achievement tasks in the future.

According to Weiner (1974, 1986), a person who is trying to explain a success or a failure might attribute that outcome to any of four causes: (1) his own *ability* (or lack of ability), (2) the amount of *effort* he expended in performing the task, (3) the *difficulty* of the task, or (4) the influence of *luck* (either good or bad). Notice that two of these four causes, ability and effort, are internal causes, or qualities of the individual, whereas the other two, task difficulty and luck, are *external,* or environmental, factors. So far, Weiner's theory sounds very similar to Crandall's theorizing about locus of control. However, Weiner proceeds to argue that these four causes also differ along a *stability* dimension. Ability and task difficulty are seen as relatively stable (unchangeable) factors; if you have high verbal ability today, you'll have roughly the same ability tomorrow; and if a particular kind of verbal problem is exceedingly difficult, similar problems are also likely to be difficult. By contrast, the amount of effort one expends on a task and the influence of luck are highly unstable (variable) from situation to situation. So Weiner categorizes the four possible causes for a success or a failure along both a locus-of-causality dimension and a stability dimension, as shown in Table 12-4.

Why is it important to distinguish the locus of an achievement-related outcome from the perceived stability of that outcome? Simply because each of these judgments has different consequences. According to Weiner, it is the stability dimension that determines achievement *expectancies.* If we should succeed at a task and attribute this outcome to a stable cause, such as our high ability or the ease of this task for us, then it is reasonable to assume that we should succeed at similar activities in the future. But if our success is attributed to an unstable cause that can vary from situation to situation (such as effort or luck), then we should not be quite so confident of attaining future successes. Conversely, if we should fail at a task and attribute this negative outcome to stable causes we can do little about (low ability or high task difficulty), we are likely to expect to fail at similar tasks in the future, whereas attrib-

Table 12-4. Weiner's classification of the four possible causes (or perceived determinants) of achievement outcomes

	Locus of causality	
Stability	*Internal cause*	*External cause*
Stable cause	Ability	Task difficulty
Unstable cause	Effort	Luck

uting a failure to an unstable cause (such as bad luck or not trying very hard) allows for the possibility of improvement and a more positive achievement expectancy. It follows, then, that a person with very high achievement expectancies is likely to attribute her successes to stable causes (such as high ability) and her failures to unstable ones (such as bad luck or insufficient effort). By contrast, a person who attributes successes to unstable causes (good luck or high effort) and failures to stable ones (low ability) is apt to have very low achievement expectancies.

Now, if the perceived stability of an achievement-related outcome determines achievement expectancies, what role does locus of causality (or control) play? According to Weiner, judgments about the internality or externality of an outcome determine its *value* to the perceiver, which, in turn, will influence his or her achievement motivation. Presumably, successes are most valuable when attributed to *internal* causes such as hard work or high ability, and few of us would feel especially proud if we succeeded because of external causes such as blind luck or a ridiculously easy task. However, *failures* attributed to internal causes (such as low ability) are damaging to our self-esteem and may make us less inclined to strive for future success. Clearly, it seems

Photo 12-5. Children are most likely to value their successes and work hard to repeat them when they attribute these outcomes to internal causes such as high ability or hard work.

fruitless to work hard to reverse a poor grade if we think we have little ability in the subject matter; in fact, the course may suddenly seem less valuable or important, and we might be inclined to drop it. But if we can attribute our poor mark to an external cause such as bad luck or an ambiguous exam, the failure should not make us feel especially critical of ourselves or undermine our feelings about the value of the course.

To summarize, then, Weiner proposes that the perceived locus of causality for achievement outcomes affects our valuation of these successes and failures, whereas our attributions about the stability of these outcomes affect our achievement expectancies. Together, these two judgments (expectancy and value) determine our willingness to undertake and persist at similar achievement-related activities in the future (see Figure 12-4 for a schematic overview of Weiner's model).

Now, if Weiner's theory is correct, high achievers should generally attribute their successes to stable, internal causes (high ability) and their failures to unstable factors (such as insufficient effort) that they can do something about. By contrast, low achievers might attribute successes to unstable causes (luck or high effort) while ascribing their failures to stable, internal causes (such as low ability) that could undermine their achievement motivation. Do high and low achievers display these different patterns of attributions?

The answer depends, in part, on the age of the child. Before age 7 or so, most children are unrealistic optimists who think that they have high ability and that they will do well on almost any task. This rosy optimism is based, in part, on wishful thinking; the more young children want to succeed, the more they believe they will succeed, even on tasks that they have repeatedly failed in the past (Stipek, Roberts, & Sanborn, 1984). Moreover, young children do not fully understand the concept of ability and how it may differ from effort. Instead, they tend to confuse the two, thinking that people who work hard have high ability, even if they accomplish very little (Nicholls & Miller, 1984; Nicholls, Patashnick, & Mettetal, 1986). Teachers may contribute to this confusion by praising young children more for their efforts than for the quality of their work, thus leading them to believe that they can accomplish anything and "be smart" by working hard (Rosenholtz & Simpson, 1984). But as children progress through the school

---

causal attributions: inferences made about the underlying causes of one's own or another person's behavior.

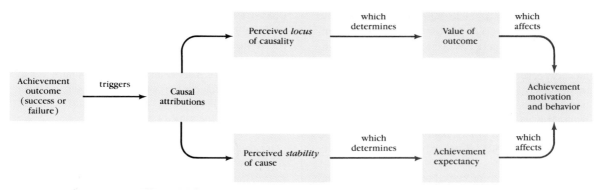

Figure 12-4. An overview of Weiner's attribution theory of achievement.

years and their grades begin to reflect the quality of their work rather than their effort expenditure, they begin to differentiate effort from ability and to make the kinds of attributions that Weiner's theory anticipates.

Do these attributions really affect children's achievement motivation and their future accomplishments? Yes, indeed, and nowhere is this any more apparent than in Carol Dweck's research on learned helplessness in grade school children.

Dweck's learned-helplessness theory

Recently, Carol Dweck and her associates have analyzed *patterns* of attributions that children display when explaining their achievement outcomes and the effects of these attributional styles on later achievement behavior. In Dweck's research, grade school children are asked to perform a series of tasks, in which their "successes" and "failures" are determined by the experimenter. Of interest are the kinds of attributions that children offer to account for these outcomes and their willingness to persist at similar achievement tasks in the future.

Dweck and her colleagues (see Dweck, 1978) find that there are reliable individual differences in the ways children react to achievement outcomes—particularly to *failure* experiences. Some children appear to be **"mastery oriented":** they tend to attribute failures to *unstable* causes such as insufficient effort and will often show increased persistence and improved performance on subsequent achievement tasks. By contrast, other children who view their failures as stemming from *stable, internal* causes (most notably a lack of ability) often show little effort expenditure and a marked deterioration of performance on future achievement tasks.

In fact, many who fall into this latter category appear to give up in the face of failure and are suddenly incapable of solving problems of the kind that they have easily mastered only a short time earlier. It appeared to Dweck that these youngsters were displaying a form of **learned helplessness:** if failures are attributed to a lack of ability that the child can do little about, then there is little reason to keep working hard at these or similar problems. Consequently, the child simply stops trying and acts helpless.

It is important to note that children who display this learned-helplessness syndrome are *not* merely the least competent members of a typical classroom. On the contrary, Dweck (1978) reports that the previous academic attainments of helpless children often equal or exceed those of their mastery-oriented classmates! Moreover, Deborah Phillips (1984) finds that about 20% of *high-ability* fifth-graders seriously underestimate their academic competencies and display symptoms of learned helplessness, such as setting modest goals for themselves, showing little persistence in academic activities, and attributing their successes to unstable causes such as high effort, rather than to stable ones such as high ability. So it appears that almost anyone, even highly competent children who have often succeeded in the past, can eventually stop trying and act helpless in the face of failure.

How does learned helplessness develop? Dweck and her colleagues (Dweck, Davidson, Nelson, & Enna, 1978) believe that the ways teachers evaluate their students can play a very important role in promoting either a "mastery" or a "helpless" orientation. If a teacher should praise students' abilities when they succeed but emphasize the nonintellectual aspects of their work (sloppiness, lack of effort) when criticizing poor performance, students are likely to conclude that they are certainly smart enough and would do better if they tried harder. In other words, this pattern of evaluation should encourage students to attribute successes to stable causes (high ability) and failures to unstable ones (insufficient effort), thereby promoting the development of a mastery orientation. Now contrast this evaluative style with one in which the teacher praises nonintellectual aspects of good performance, such as neatness or effort expenditure, while focusing on students' poor problem-solving strategies when they fail. This second pattern of evaluation seems likely to encourage youngsters to attribute successes to unstable causes (high effort) and failures to stable ones (low ability)—precisely the attributional style often observed among children displaying the helplessness syndrome. Dweck et al. have observed fifth-grade teachers as they gave their students evaluative feedback and found that teachers did indeed use different patterns with different students. Some students received the evaluative pattern thought to contribute to a mastery orientation, whereas others received the pattern thought to contribute to learned helplessness. But do these patterns really have such effects on children's achievement orientations?

Dweck et al. (1978) tried to answer this question in an interesting experiment. Fifth-graders worked on a series of 20 word puzzles (anagrams), half of which were easy and half of which were insoluble. The experimenter's evaluation of the child's performance on failure trials was then manipulated. Children assigned to the *mastery pattern* condition heard the experimenter respond to their failures by criticizing their efforts and implying that they needed to work harder. Children assigned to the *helpless pattern* condition heard the experimenter focus on the incorrectness of their solutions, as if to imply that they had little ability at this kind of task. After attempting the word puzzles and working on yet another task at which they were told that they were not doing very well, the children were asked to respond anonymously to the following attribution question: "If the man told you that you did not do very well . . . why do you think that was? (a) I did not try hard enough [effort], (b) the man was too fussy [agent], (c) I am not very good at it [ability]."

The answers children gave to this question were quite consistent with Dweck's hypothesis about the importance of evaluative feedback. As we can see in Table 12-5, 75% of the children who had received the helpless pattern of evaluation attributed their failure on the second puzzle to their own lack of ability. By contrast, 75%

Table 12-5. Percentage of children in each evaluation condition attributing failure feedback to a lack of ability, a lack of effort, or an overly fussy evaluator

| | Type of attribution | | |
Evaluative pattern	Lack of ability	Lack of effort	Fussy evaluator
Helpless pattern	75	25	0
Mastery pattern	25	65	10

of the children who had received the mastery pattern of evaluation attributed their failure to a lack of effort or externalized the blame altogether by saying that the evaluator was too fussy. These strikingly different attributional styles are all the more remarkable when we note that they took less than one hour to establish in this experiment. So it seems reasonable to conclude that similar patterns of evaluative feedback from teachers, given consistently over a period of months or years, might well contribute to the development of the contrasting "helpless" and "mastery" orientations so often observed among grade school (and older) students.

Obviously, giving up in the face of a challenge is not the kind of achievement orientation that teachers would hope to encourage. What can be done to help these "helpless" children become more persistent at achievement tasks, particularly those that are difficult to master quickly and require prolonged and concentrated effort? One solution might be to make teachers more aware of how their reactions to their students' performance are likely to affect the children's achievement orientations. Another might be to develop training programs or therapies aimed at teaching children to recognize that failures can and often should be attributed to unstable causes, such as a lack of effort, that they can easily overcome. In Box 12-4 we will see that this kind of attributional restructuring may indeed help grade school children to overcome a "helpless" orientation.

---

mastery orientation: a tendency to persist at challenging tasks because of a belief that one has high ability and/or that earlier failures can be overcome by trying harder.

learned helplessness: a tendency to give up or to stop trying after failing because these failures have been attributed to a lack of ability that one can do little about.

Box 12-4
On Helping the Helpless to Achieve

How might we encourage helpless children to persist at tasks at which they have repeatedly failed? One method favored by behavior therapists (for example, Skinner, 1968) is a programmed learning approach in which children are taught that they can succeed by receiving many success experiences on the very problems that they have previously failed. Advocates of this procedure stress the importance of structuring the therapy so that the child is *unlikely to fail,* for errors are assumed to undermine one's motivation to persist at achievement tasks.

By contrast, Carol Dweck believes that such a "success only" therapy is likely to prove ineffective. The reason for her skepticism is that helpless children tend to attribute successes to unstable causes such as high effort or luck that (1) do not necessarily imply that one will perform well in the future and (2) do not allow children to deal constructively with failure. Moreover, it is children's beliefs about the causes of their *failures* that trigger the learned-helplessness syndrome in the first place! Dweck believes that learned helplessness is likely to be overcome only if helpless children begin to attribute their failures to unstable causes—such as insufficient effort—that they

can do something about, rather than viewing them as reflecting on their lack of ability, which is not so easily modifiable. Presumably, treatments designed to accomplish this aim would persuade helpless children to try harder after experiencing failures and, thus, enable them to deal more constructively with the less-than-optimal performances that they (like all children) are likely to experience in the years ahead.

Dweck (1975) tested her hypotheses by identifying a group of 12 helpless children and exposing them to a series of math problems at which they repeatedly failed, so that they began to act helpless. At this point therapy was begun. Half the children experienced 25 sessions of *success only* therapy: they worked at math problems, invariably succeeding, and were rewarded with tokens for their accomplishments. The remaining children were exposed to 25 sessions of *attribution retraining* that were identical to the success-only sessions, with one major exception: during each training session, the child experienced three prearranged "failures." On these failure trials, the experimenter noted that the child had not worked fast enough and said "That means you should have tried harder." Thus, a rather explicit attempt was made to convince these youngsters that failures can stem from a lack of effort rather than a lack of ability. Following the 25

training sessions, subjects in both therapy groups worked the series of math problems that they had repeatedly failed at the beginning of the experiment. Their performance was recorded, as were their responses to several prearranged failures and the attributions they made to account for these failures.

The results of this experiment were quite clear. After the therapy, helpless children in the attribution-retraining condition now performed much better on the math problems that they had initially failed. They no longer gave up in the face of failure, and they were now much more inclined to attribute their failures to a lack of effort rather than to low ability. By contrast, helpless children assigned to the success-only condition showed no such improvement in performance. They continued to attribute their failures to low ability rather than to a lack of effort, and if anything, they were now even less willing to persist in the face of failure than before the therapeutic intervention. So we see that merely showing helpless children that they are capable of succeeding is not enough! To alleviate learned helplessness, one must teach children to respond more constructively to their *failures* by viewing these experiences as something that they can overcome if they try harder.

Reflections on Competence and Achievement Motivation

After reviewing a fair portion of the achievement literature, it should be clear that one's propensity for achievement involves far more than an innate mastery, or effectance, motive, even though infants obviously are interested in mastering the challenges they face. David McClelland and his associates advanced our knowledge about achievement by showing that people reliably differ in their *motivation* to achieve and by suggesting how this motive might be nurtured. However, McClelland's idea that achievement motivation is a global attribute that will forecast one's responses to virtually all achievement tasks now seems badly overstated. Virginia Crandall broke important new ground by proposing that children will try harder to master challenges in some domains than in others and by emphasizing that achievement-related cognitions such as one's *expectancies* of succeeding at a particular task and the *value* of that success are important determinants of achievement behavior. Weiner's later attribution theory grew out of Crandall's approach and focused much more intently on how specific attributions about the *causes* of achievement outcomes contribute to our achievement expectancies and to the perceived value of success and failure experiences. Finally, Dweck's learned-helplessness model begins to take us back to the starting point by demonstrating that well-ingrained attributional styles, or patterns, affect children's *motivation* to persist at challenging tasks that they have initially failed to master. So as we concluded when reviewing the various theories of attachment in Chapter 11, it makes no sense to brand any single achievement theory as "correct" and to ignore the others. Each of these theories has helped us to understand why children differ so dramatically when responding to the challenges they face.

Summary

This chapter has traced the development of children's knowledge about the self and other people (that is, social cognition) and has focused on the growth of two attributes—sociability and instrumental competence (or achievement)—that are very important contributors to children's self-concepts.

Although there is some disagreement among contemporary theorists, the prevailing point of view is that infants do not make clear distinctions between the self and nonself (objects, other people) until 4–6 months of age. But by 18–24 months of age, a self-concept is rapidly emerging as toddlers form stable self-images (as indicated by their ability to recognize themselves in a mirror) and begin to categorize themselves along socially significant dimensions such as age and sex. The self-concepts of preschoolers and young grade school children are very concrete, focusing on physical features, possessions, and the activities they can perform. Older grade school children typically describe the self in terms of psychological attributes, whereas adolescents have an even more abstract conception of self that includes not only their stable attributes but also their beliefs, attitudes, and values.

Grade school children differ in their perceived self-worth, or self-esteem. Children who feel good about their cognitive and social competencies tend to have higher self-esteem, to do better at school, and to have more friends than their classmates who feel that they are socially and intellectually inadequate. Although some adolescents (particularly those with poor body images) experience a decline in self-esteem, most do not, even though their self-concepts are apt to be changing as they approach what Erikson calls the "identity crisis" and must seek stable personal and interpersonal identities with which to meet the challenges of young adulthood.

There are some interesting parallels between children's knowledge of self and their knowledge of others. Children younger than 6 or 7 are likely to describe friends and acquaintances in the same concrete, observable terms (physical attributes and activities) that they use to describe the self. By age 8 to 10, children begin to see regularities in the behavior of both themselves and others and will often base their impressions of an acquaintance on the stable psychological constructs, or "traits," that this person is presumed to have. As they approach adolescence, their impressions become much more abstract as they begin to compare and contrast their friends and acquaintances on a number of psychological attributes. The growth of self-knowledge and interpersonal understanding is related to changes occurring in children's intellectual abilities and role-taking skills. To truly "know" a person, one must be able to assume his perspective and understand his thoughts, feelings, motives, and intentions—in short, the internal factors that account for his behavior. Both cognitive development and social experiences are important contributors to one's proficiency as a role taker.

Sociability is the child's tendency to approach and interact with other people and to seek their attention or approval. Although children become much more sociable over the first three years, some infants are more outgoing than others. Three factors that may contribute to these individual differences in sociability are the child's genotype, the security of his or her emotional attachments, and the child's ordinal position in the family.

During the preschool period, children become much more playful and outgoing with one another and much less inclined to seek the companionship of adults. Nursery school attendance often accelerates this trend, although children initially low in sociability and lacking in social skills may become even more inhibited. Warm, supportive parents who require their children to display social etiquette and who are not overly directive or controlling tend to raise appropriately sociable youngsters who establish good relations with their peers. By contrast, permissive parents and those who are highly controlling tend to have children who establish nonharmonious relations with peers. Because sociability is such a stable attribute from about age 2 onward, highly unsociable children may require therapeutic intervention to avoid the risk of poor peer relations and emotional difficulties later in life.

Children clearly differ in achievement motivation—that is, their willingness to strive for success and to master new challenges. Infants who are securely attached to responsive companions who provide them with a variety of age-appropriate stimulation are likely to become curious nursery school children who will later do well at school. Parents may also foster the development of achievement motivation by (1) encouraging their children to do things on their own and to do them well and (2) reinforcing a child's successes without becoming overly distressed about an occasional failure.

Although children differ in achievement motivation, their propensity for achievement in any given context will depend very heavily on the perceived value of success and their expectancies of succeeding. These achievement-related cognitions depend on the causal attributions that children make for their successes and failures. Mastery-oriented children tend to attribute suc-

cesses to stable, internal factors (such as high ability) and failures to unstable ones (lack of effort); consequently, they feel quite competent and will work hard to overcome failures. By contrast, helpless children often stop trying after a failure because they attribute their failures to stable, internal factors—most notably a lack of ability—that they feel they can do little about. Fortunately, these helpless children can become more mastery-oriented if they are taught that their failures can and often should be attributed to unstable causes, such as a lack of effort, that they can overcome.

References

ABRAMOVITCH, R., Corter, C., & Lando, B. (1979). Sibling interaction in the home. *Child Development, 50,* 997–1003.

ADAMS, G. R., & Fitch, S. A. (1982). Ego stage and identity status development: A cross-sequential analysis. *Journal of Personality and Social Psychology, 43,* 574–583.

AINSWORTH, M. D. S. (1972). Attachment and dependency: A comparison. In J. L. Gewirtz (Ed.), *Attachment and dependency.* Washington, DC: Winston.

AINSWORTH, M. D. S. (1979). Attachment as related to mother-infant interaction. In J. G. Rosenblatt, R. A. Hinde, C. Beer, & M. Busnel (Eds.), *Advances in the study of behavior* (Vol. 9). Orlando, FL: Academic Press.

ARCHER, S. L. (1982). The lower age boundaries of identity development. *Child Development, 53,* 1551–1556.

AREND, A., Gove, F. L., & Sroufe, L. A. (1979). Continuity of individual adaptation from infancy to kindergarten: A predictive study of ego-resiliency and curiosity in preschoolers. *Child Development, 50,* 950–959.

ASHER, S. R. (1986). An overview of intervention research with unpopular children. In S. R. Asher & J. Coie (Eds.), *Assessment of children's social status.* New York: Cambridge University Press.

ASHER, S. R., Renshaw, P. D., & Hymel, S. (1982). Peer relations and the development of social skills. In S. G. Moore (Ed.), *The young child: Reviews of research* (Vol. 3). Washington, DC: National Association for the Education of Young Children.

BARENBOIM, C. (1981). The development of person perception in childhood and adolescence: From behavioral comparisons to psychological constructs to psychological comparisons. *Child Development, 52,* 129–144.

BATTLE, E. S. (1966). Motivational determinants of academic competence. *Journal of Personality and Social Psychology, 4,* 634–642.

BAUMRIND, D. (1971). Current patterns of parental authority. *Developmental Psychology Monographs, 4*(1, Pt. 2).

BELSKY, J., Garduque, L., & Hrncir, E. (1984). Assessing performance, competence, and executive capacity in infant play: Relations to home environment and security of attachment. *Development Psychology, 20,* 406–417.

BERNDT, T. J. (1982). The features and effects of friendship in early adolescence. *Child Development, 53,* 1447–1460.

BIERMAN, K. L. (1986). Process of change during social skills training with preadolescents and its relation to treatment outcome. *Child Development, 57,* 230–240.

BIERMAN, K. L., & Furman, W. (1984). The effects of social skills training and peer involvement on the social adjustment of preadolescents. *Child Development, 55,* 157–162.

BLOUNT, R. (1986, May 4). "I'm about five years ahead of my age." *Atlanta Journal and Constitution,* pp. C17–C20.

BOGGIANO, A. K., Klinger, C. A., & Main, D. S. (1986). Enhancing interest in peer interaction: A developmental analysis. *Child Development, 57,* 852–861.

BRADLEY, R. H., & Caldwell, B. M. (1984). The relation of infants' home environments to achievement test performance in the first grade: A follow-up study. *Child Development, 55,* 803–809.

BRETHERTON, I., Fritz, J., Zahn-Waxler, C., & Ridgeway, D. (1986). Learning to talk about emotions: A functionalist perspective. *Child Development, 57,* 529–548.

BRIDGEMAN, D. L. (1981). Enhanced role-taking through cooperative interdependence: A field study. *Child Development, 51,* 1231–1238.

BRONSON, W. C. (1985). Growth in the organization of behavior over the second year of life. *Developmental Psychology, 21,* 108–117.

BROOKS-GUNN, J., & Lewis, M. (1982). The development of self-knowledge. In C. B. Kopp & J. B. Krakow (Eds.), *The child: Development in a social context.* Reading, MA: Addison-Wesley.

BROWNELL, C. A. (1986). Convergent developments: Cognitive-developmental correlates of growth in infant/toddler peer skills. *Child Development, 57,* 275–286.

BURIEL, R. (1981). The relation of Anglo- and Mexican-American children's locus of control belief to parents' and teachers' socialization practices. *Child Development, 52,* 104–113.

CASSIDY, J. (1986). The ability to negotiate the environment: An aspect of infant competence as related to quality of attachment. *Child Development, 57,* 331–337.

CAUCE, A. M. (1987). School and peer competence in early adolescence: A test of domain-specific self-perceived competence. *Developmental Psychology, 23,* 287–291.

CLARKE-STEWART, K. A., Umeh, B. J., Snow, M. E., & Pederson, J. A. (1980). Development and prediction of children's sociability from 1 to 2½ years. *Developmental Psychology, 16,* 290–302.

COLEMAN, J. S., Campbell, E. Q., Hobson, C. J., McPartland, J., Mood, A. M., Weinfeld, F. D., & York, R. L. (1966). *Equality of educational opportunity.* Report from U.S. Office of Education. Washington, DC: U.S. Government Printing Office.

COMBS, M. L., & Slaby, D. A. (1977). Social skills training with children. In B. B. Lahey & A. E. Kazdin (Eds.), *Advances in clinical child psychology.* New York: Plenum.

COOKE, T., & Apolloni, T. (1976). Developing

positive social-emotional behaviors: A study of training and generalization effects. *Journal of Applied Behavior Analysis, 9,* 65–78.

COOLEY, C. H. (1902). *Human nature and the social order.* New York: Scribner's.

COOPERSMITH, S. (1967). *The antecedents of self-esteem.* New York: W. H. Freeman.

CRANDALL, V. C. (1967). Achievement behavior in young children. In *The young child: Reviews of research.* Washington, DC: National Association for the Education of Young Children.

DAMON, W., & Hart, D. (1982). The development of self-understanding from infancy through adolescence. *Child Development, 53,* 841–864.

DANIELS, D., & Plomin, R. (1985). Origins of individual differences in infant shyness. *Developmental Psychology, 21,* 118–121.

DAVIS, W. L., & Phares, E. J. (1969). Parental antecedents of internal-external control of reinforcement. *Psychological Reports, 24,* 427–436.

DUSEK, J. B., & Flaherty, J. F. (1981). The development of the self-concept during the adolescent years. *Monographs of the Society for Research in Child Development, 46*(4, Serial No. 191).

DWECK, C. S. (1975). The role of expectations and attributions in the alleviation of learned helplessness. *Journal of Personality and Social Psychology, 31,* 674–685.

DWECK, C. S. (1978). Achievement. In M. E. Lamb (Ed.), *Social and personality development.* New York: Holt, Rinehart and Winston.

DWECK, C. S., Davidson, W., Nelson, S., & Enna, B. (1978). Sex differences in learned helplessness: II. The contingencies of evaluative feedback in the classroom, and III. An experimental analysis. *Developmental Psychology, 14,* 268–276.

DWECK, C. S., & Elliott, E. S. (1983). Achievement motivation. In P. H. Mussen (Ed.), *Handbook of child psychology.* Vol. 4: *Socialization, personality, and social development.* New York: Wiley.

EDWARDS, C. P. (1984). The age group labels and categories of preschool children. *Child Development, 55,* 440–452.

EDWARDS, C. P., & Lewis, M. (1979). Young children's concepts of social relations: Social functions and social objects. In M. Lewis & L. A. Rosenblum (Eds.), *Genesis of behavior.* Vol. 2: *The child and its family.* New York: Plenum.

ERIKSON, E. H. (1950). In M. J. E. Senn (Ed.), *Symposium on the healthy personality.* New York: Josiah Macy, Jr., Foundation.

ERIKSON, E. H. (1963). *Childhood and society* (2nd ed.). New York: Norton.

FINDLEY, M. J., & Cooper, H. M. (1983). Locus of control and academic achievement: A literature review. *Journal of Personality and Social Psychology, 44,* 419–427.

FREEDMAN, D. G. (1974). *Human infancy: An evolutionary perspective.* Hillsdale, NJ: Erlbaum.

FURMAN, W., & Bierman, K. L. (1983). Developmental changes in young children's conceptions of friendship. *Child Development, 54,* 549–556.

FYANS, L. J., Jr., Salili, F., Maehr, M. L., & Desai, K. A. (1983). A cross-cultural exploration into the meaning of achievement. *Journal of Personality and Social Psychology, 44,* 1000–1013.

GALLUP, G. G., Jr. (1979). Self-recognition in chimpanzees and man: A developmental and comparative perspective. In M. Lewis & L. A. Rosenblum (Eds.), *Genesis of behavior.* Vol. 2: *The child and its family.* New York: Plenum.

GOLDSMITH, H. H. (1983). Genetic influences on personality from infancy to adulthood. *Child Development, 54,* 331–355.

GURUCHARRI, C., & Selman, R. L. (1982). The development of interpersonal understanding during childhood, preadolescence, and adolescence: A longitudinal follow-up study. *Child Development, 53,* 924–927.

HARPER, L. V., & Huie, K. S. (1985). The effects of prior group experience, age, and familiarity on the quality and organization of preschoolers' social relationships. *Child Development, 56,* 704–717.

HARTER, S. (1981). A new self-report scale of intrinsic versus extrinsic orientation in the classroom: Motivational and informational components. *Developmental Psychology, 17,* 300–312.

HARTER, S. (1982). The perceived competence scale for children. *Child Development, 53,* 87–97.

HARTER, S. (1983). Developmental perspectives on the self-system. In P. H. Mussen (Ed.), *Handbook of child psychology.* Vol. 4: *Socialization, personality, and social development.* New York: Wiley.

HARTER, S., & Pike, R. (1984). The pictorial scale of perceived competence and social acceptance for young children. *Child Development, 55,* 1969–1982.

HARTUP, W. W. (1983). Peer relations. In P. H. Mussen (Ed.), *Handbook of child psychology.* Vol. 4: *Socialization, personality, and social development.* New York: Wiley.

HAY, D. F., Nash, A., & Pedersen, J. (1983). Interaction between six-month-old peers. *Child Development, 54,* 557–562.

HILL, S. D., & Tomlin, C. (1981). Self-recognition in retarded children. *Child Development, 53,* 1320–1329.

HUDSON, L. M., Forman, E. R., & Brion-Meisels, S. (1982). Role-taking as a predictor of prosocial behavior in cross-age tutors. *Child Development, 53,* 1320–1329.

JOHNSON, C. N., & Wellman, H. M. (1982). Children's developing conceptions of the mind and brain. *Child Development, 53,* 222–234.

KAGAN, J., & Moss, H. A. (1962). *Birth to maturity.* New York: Wiley.

KAVANAUGH, R., & McCall, R. (1983). Social influencing among 2-year-olds: The role of affiliative and antagonistic behaviors. *Infant Behavior and Development, 6,* 39–52.

KEATING, D., & Clark, L. V. (1980). Development of physical and social reasoning in adolescence. *Developmental Psychology, 16,* 23–30.

KELLER, A., Ford, L. H., Jr., & Meachum, J. A. (1978). Dimensions of self-concept in preschool children. *Developmental Psychology, 14,* 483–489.

KERBY, F. D., & Tolar, H. C. (1970). Modification of preschool isolate behavior: A case study. *Journal of Applied Behavior Analysis, 3,* 309–314.

KOHLBERG, L. (1969). Stage and sequence: The cognitive-developmental approach to socialization. In D. A. Goslin (Ed.), *Handbook of socialization theory and research.* Skokie, IL: Rand McNally.

KOKENES, B. (1974). Grade level differences in factors of self-esteem. *Developmental Psychology, 10,* 954–958.

KURDEK, L. A., & Krile, D. (1982). A developmental analysis of the relation between peer acceptance and both interpersonal understanding and perceived social self-competence. *Child Development, 53,* 1485–1491.

LADD, G. W. (1981). Effectiveness of a social learning method for enhancing children's social interaction and peer acceptance. *Child Development, 52,* 171–178.

LaFRENIERE, P. J., & Sroufe, L. A. (1985). Profiles of peer competence in the preschool: Interrelations between measures, influence of social ecology, and relation to attachment history. *Developmental Psychology, 21,* 56–69.

LeMARE, L. J., & Rubin, K. H. (1987). Perspective taking and peer interaction: Structural and developmental analyses. *Child Development, 58,* 306–315.

LERNER, R. M., Iwawaki, S., Chihara, T., & Sorell, G. T. (1980). Self-concept, self-esteem, and body attitudes among Japanese male and female adolescents. *Child Development, 51,* 847–855.

LEWIS, M., & Brooks-Gunn, J. (1979). *Social cognition and the acquisition of self.* New York: Plenum.

LEWIS, M., & Kreitzberg, V. S. (1979). Effects of birth-order and spacing on mother-infant interactions. *Developmental Psychology, 15,* 617–625.

LIVESLEY, W. J., & Bromley, D. B. (1973). *Person perception in childhood and adolescence.* London: Wiley.

LONDERVILLE, S., & Main, M. (1981). Security of attachment, compliance, and maternal training methods in the second year of life. *Developmental Psychology, 17,* 289–299.

LUTKENHAUS, P., Grossmann, K. E., & Grossmann, K. (1985). Infant-mother attachment at twelve months and style of interaction with a stranger at the age of three years. *Child Development, 56,* 1538–1542.

MACCOBY, E. E. (1980). *Social development: Psychological growth and the parent-child relationship.* San Diego, CA: Harcourt Brace Jovanovich.

MACCOBY, E. E., & Feldman, S. (1972). Mother-attachment and stranger-reactions in the third year of life. *Monographs of the Society for Research in Child Development, 37*(1, Serial No. 146).

MacDONALD, A. P. (1971). Internal-external locus of control: Parental antecedents. *Journal of Clinical and Consulting Psychology, 37,* 141–147.

MacDONALD, K. (1987). Parent-child physical play with rejected, neglected, and popular boys. *Developmental Psychology, 23,* 705–711.

MacDONALD, K., & Parke, R. D. (1984). Bridging the gap: Parent-child play interaction and peer interactive competence. *Child Development, 55,* 1265–1277.

MAHLER, M. S., Pine, F., & Bergman, A. (1975). *The psychological birth of the infant.* New York: Basic Books.

MAIN, M., & Weston, D. R. (1981). The quality of the toddler's relationships to mother and father: Related to conflict and the readiness to establish new relationships. *Child Development, 52,* 932–940.

MARCIA, J. E. (1966). Development and validation of ego identity status. *Journal of Personality and Social Psychology, 3,* 551–558.

MARTIN, B. (1975). Parent-child relations. In F. D. Horowitz (Ed.), *Review of child development research* (Vol. 4). Chicago: University of Chicago Press.

MATAS, L., Arend, R. A., & Sroufe, L. A. (1978). Continuity of adaptation in the second year: The relationship between quality of attachment and later competence. *Child Development, 49,* 547–556.

MATHENY, A. P. (1983). A longitudinal twin study of the stability of components from Bayley's Infant Behavior Record. *Child Development, 54,* 356–360.

McCARTHY, J. D., & Hoge, D. R. (1982). Analysis of age effects in longitudinal studies of adolescent self-esteem. *Developmental Psychology, 18,* 372–379.

McCLELLAND, D. C., Atkinson, J. W., Clark, R. A., & Lowell, E. L. (1953). *The achievement motive.* East Norwalk, CT: Appleton-Century-Crofts.

McGUIRE, K. D., & Weisz, J. R. (1982). Social cognition and behavioral correlates of preadolescent chumship. *Child Development, 53,* 1478–1484.

MEAD, G. H. (1934). *Mind, self, and society.* Chicago: University of Chicago Press.

MEILMAN, P. W. (1979). Cross-sectional age changes in ego identity status during adolescence. *Developmental Psychology, 15,* 230–231.

MENDELSON, B. D., & White, D. R. (1985). Development of self-body-esteem in overweight youngsters. *Developmental Psychology, 21,* 90–96.

MESSER, D. J., McCarthy, M. E., McQuiston, S., MacTurk, R. H., Yarrow, L. J., & Vietze, P. M. (1986). Relation between mastery behavior in infancy and competence in early childhood. *Developmental Psychology, 22,* 366–372.

MOHR, D. M. (1978). Development of attributes of personal identity. *Developmental Psychology, 14,* 427–428.

MONTEMAYOR, R., & Eisen, M. (1977). The development of self-conceptions from childhood to adolescence. *Developmental Psychology, 13,* 314–319.

MUELLER, E., & Lucas, T. (1975). A developmental analysis of peer interactions among toddlers. In M. Lewis & L. Rosenblum (Eds.), *Friendship and peer relations.* New York: Wiley.

MUELLER, E., & Vandell, D. L. (1979). Infant-infant interaction. In J. Osofsky (Ed.), *Handbook of infant development.* New York: Wiley.

MUNRO, G., & Adams, G. R. (1977). Ego-identity formation in college students and working youth. *Developmental Psychology, 13,* 523–524.

NELSON, J., & Aboud, F. E. (1985). The resolution of social conflict among friends. *Child Development, 56,* 1009–1017.

NICHOLLS, J. G., & Miller, A. T. (1984). Reasoning about the ability of self and others: A developmental study. *Child Development, 55,* 1990–1999.

NICHOLLS, J. G., Patashnick, M., & Mettetal, G. (1986). Conceptions of ability and intelligence. *Child Development, 57,* 636–645.

NOTTELMAN, E. D. (1987). Competence and self-esteem during transition from childhood to adolescence. *Developmental Psychology, 23,* 441–450.

ODEN, S., & Asher, S. R. (1977). Coaching children in social skills for friendship making. *Child Development, 48,* 495–506.

O'MALLEY, P. M., & Bachman, J. G. (1983). Self-esteem: Change and stability between ages 13 and 23. *Developmental Psychology, 19,* 257–268.

PASTOR, D. L. (1981). The quality of mother-infant attachment and its relationship to toddlers' initial sociability with peers. *Developmental Psychology, 17,* 326–335.

PEEVERS, B. H., & Secord, P. F. (1973). Developmental changes in attribution of descriptive concepts to persons. *Journal of Personality and Social Psychology, 27,* 120–128.

PELLEGRINI, D. S. (1985). Social cognition and competence in middle childhood. *Child Development, 56,* 253–264.

PENNEBAKER, J. W., Hendler, C. S., Durrett, M. E., & Richards, P. (1981). Social factors influencing absenteeism due to illness in nursery school children. *Child Development, 52,* 692–700.

PHILLIPS, D. (1984). The illusion of incompetence among academically competent children. *Child Development, 55,* 2000–2016.

PIAGET, J. (1965). *The moral judgment of the child.* New York: Free Press.

PIPP, S., Fischer, K. W., & Jennings, S. (1987). Acquisition of self- and mother knowledge in infancy. *Developmental Psychology, 23,* 86–96.

RAYNOR, J. O. (1970). Relationships between achievement-related motives, future orientation, and academic performance. *Journal of Personality and Social Psychology, 15,* 28–33.

RHOLES, W. S., & Ruble, D. N. (1984). Children's understanding of dispositional characteristics of others. *Child Development, 55,* 550–560.

ROFF, M. F. (1974). Childhood antecedents of adult neurosis, severe bad conduct, and psychological health. In D. F. Ricks, A. Thomas, & M. Roff (Eds.), *Life history research in psychopathology* (Vol. 3). Minneapolis: University of Minnesota Press.

ROFF, M. F., Sells, S. B., & Golden, M. M. (1972).

Social adjustment and personality development in children. Minneapolis: University of Minnesota Press.

ROSEN, B. C., & D'Andrade, R. (1959). The psychosocial origins of achievement motivation. *Sociometry, 22,* 185–218.

ROSENHOLTZ, S. J., & Simpson, C. (1984). The formation of ability conceptions: Developmental trend or social construction? *Review of Educational Research, 54,* 31–63.

ROSS, H. S., & Lollis, S. P. (1987). Communication within infant social games. *Developmental Psychology, 23,* 241–248.

ROTENBERG, K. J. (1982). Development of character constancy of self and other. *Child Development, 53,* 505–515.

SAMUELS, C. (1986). Bases for the infant's development of self-awareness. *Human Development, 24,* 36–48.

SAVIN-WILLIAMS, R. C., & Demo, D. H. (1984). Developmental change and stability in adolescent self-concept. *Developmental Psychology, 20,* 1100–1110.

SCARR, S. (1968). Environmental bias in twin studies. *Eugenics Quarterly, 15,* 34–40.

SCHACHTER, S. (1959). *The psychology of affiliation.* Stanford, CA: Stanford University Press.

SCHAEFER, E. S., & Bayley, N. (1963). Maternal behavior, child behavior, and their intercorrelations from infancy through adolescence. *Monographs of the Society for Research in Child Development, 28*(Serial No. 87).

SCHAFFER, H. R., & Emerson, P. E. (1964). The development of social attachments in infancy. *Monographs of the Society for Research in Child Development, 29*(3, Serial No. 94).

SELMAN, R. L. (1976). Social-cognitive understanding: A guide to educational and clinical practice. In T. Lickona (Ed.), *Moral development and behavior: Theory, research, and social issues.* New York: Holt, Rinehart and Winston.

SELMAN, R. L. (1980). *The growth of interpersonal understanding.* Orlando, FL: Academic Press.

SELMAN, R. L., & Byrne, D. (1974). A structural developmental analysis of role-taking in middle childhood. *Child Development, 45,* 803–806.

SHANTZ, C. U. (1983). Social cognition. In P. H. Mussen (Ed.), *Handbook of child psychology.* Vol. 3: *Cognitive development.* New York: Wiley.

SHEA, J. D. C. (1981). Changes in interpersonal distances and categories of play behavior in the early weeks of preschool. *Developmental Psychology, 17,* 417–425.

SHURE, M. D., & Spivack, G. (1978). *Problem-solving techniques in childrearing.* San Francisco: Jossey-Bass.

SIMMONS, R. G., Blyth, D. A., Van Cleave, E. F., & Bush, D. M. (1979). Entry into early adolescence: The impact of school structure, puberty, and early dating on self-esteem. *American Sociological Review, 44,* 948–967.

SIMMONS, R. G., Burgeson, R., Carlton-Ford, S., & Blyth, D. A. (1987). The impact of cumulative change in early adolescence. *Child Development, 58,* 1220–1234.

SKINNER, B. F. (1968). *The psychology of teaching.* East Norwalk, CT: Appleton-Century-Crofts.

SNOW, M. E., Jacklin, C. N., & Maccoby, E. E. (1981). Birth-order differences in peer sociability at thirty-three months. *Child Development, 52,* 589–595.

STERN, D. (1983). The early development of schemas of self, other, and "self with other." In J. D. Lictenberg & S. Kaplan (Eds.), *Reflections on self psychology.* Hillsdale, NJ: Erlbaum.

STIPEK, D. J., Roberts, T. A., & Sanborn, M. E. (1984). Preschool-age children's performance expectations for themselves and another child as a function of the incentive value of success and the salience of past performance. *Child Development, 55,* 1983–1989.

TEEVEN, R. C., & McGhee, P. E. (1972). Childhood development of fear of failure motivation. *Journal of Personality and Social Psychology, 21,* 345–348.

THOMPSON, S. K. (1975). Gender labels and early sex-role development. *Child Development, 46,* 339–347.

URBAIN, E. S., & Kendall, P. C. (1980). Review of social-cognitive problem-solving interventions with children. *Psychological Bulletin, 88,* 109–143.

VANDELL, D. L., & Wilson, K. S. (1987). Infants' interactions with mother, sibling, and peer: Contrasts and relations between interaction systems. *Child Development, 58,* 176–186.

VANDELL, D. L., Wilson, K. S., & Buchanan, N. R. (1980). Peer interaction in the first year of life: An examination of its structure, content, and sensitivity to toys. *Child Development, 51,* 481–488.

VANDELL, D. L., Wilson, K. S., & Whalen, W. T. (1981). Birth-order and social experiences differences in infant-peer interaction. *Developmental Psychology, 17,* 438–445.

van DOORNINCK, W. J., Caldwell, B. M., Wright, C., & Frankenberg, W. K. (1981). The relationship between twelve-month home stimulation and school achievement. *Child Development, 52,* 1080–1083.

VINCZE, M. (1971). The social contacts of infants and young children reared together. *Early Child Development and Care, 1,* 99–109.

VYGOTSKY, L. S. (1934). *Thought and language.* Cambridge, MA: M.I.T. Press.

WATERMAN, A. S. (1982). Identity development from adolescence to adulthood: An extension of theory and a review of research. *Developmental Psychology, 18,* 341–358.

WEINER, B. (1974). *Achievement and attribution theory.* Morristown, NJ: General Learning Press.

WEINER, B. (1986). *An attributional theory of motivation and emotion.* New York: Springer-Verlag.

WHITE, R. W. (1959). Motivation reconsidered: The concept of competence. *Psychological Review, 66,* 297–333.

WICHERN, F., & Nowicki, S. (1976). Independence training practices and locus of control orientation in children and adolescents. *Developmental Psychology, 12,* 77.

WILLIAMS, J. E., Bennett, S. M., & Best, D. L. (1975). Awareness and expression of sex stereotypes in young children. *Developmental Psychology, 11,* 635–642.

WINTERBOTTOM, M. (1958). The relation of need for achievement to learning experiences in independence and mastery. In J. Atkinson (Ed.), *Motives in fantasy, action, and society.* Princeton, NJ: Van Nostrand.

YARROW, L. J., McQuiston, S., MacTurk, R. H., McCarthy, M. E., Klein, R. P., & Vietze, P. M. (1983). Assessment of mastery motivation during the first year of life: Contemporaneous and cross-age relationships. *Developmental Psychology, 19,* 159–171.

Sex Differences and Sex-Role Development

How important is a child's gender to his or her eventual development? The answer seems to be "Very important!" Often the first bit of information that parents receive about their child is his or her sex, and the question "Is it a boy or a girl?" is the very first one that most friends and relatives ask when proud new parents telephone to announce the birth of their baby (Intons-Peterson & Reddel, 1984). Indeed, the ramifications of this gender labeling are normally swift in coming and rather direct. In the hospital nursery or delivery room, parents often call an infant son things like "big guy" or "tiger," and they are apt to comment on the vigor of his cries, kicks, or grasps. By contrast, female infants are more likely to be labeled "sugar" or "sweetie" and described as soft, cuddly, and adorable (Maccoby, 1980; MacFarlane, 1977). A newborn infant is usually blessed with a name that reflects his or her sex, and in many Western societies children are immediately adorned in either blue or pink. Mavis Hetherington and Ross Parke (1975, pp. 354–355) describe the predicament of a developmental psychologist who "did not want her observers to know whether they were watching boys or girls":

> Even in the first few days of life some infant girls were brought to the laboratory with pink bows tied to wisps of their hair or taped to their little bald heads. . . . When another attempt at concealment of sex was made by asking mothers to dress their infants in overalls, girls appeared in pink and boys in blue overalls, and "Would you believe overalls with ruffles?"

This gender indoctrination continues during the first year as parents provide their children with "sex-appropriate" clothing, toys, and hairstyles. Moreover, they often play differently with and expect different reactions from their young sons and daughters. Clearly, gender is an important attribute that frequently determines how other people will respond to an infant.

Why do people react differently to males and females—especially *infant* males and females? One explanation centers on the biological differences between the sexes. Recall that fathers determine the gender of their offspring. A zygote that receives an X chromosome from each parent is a genetic (XX) female that will develop into a baby girl, whereas a zygote that receives a Y chromosome from the father is a genetic (XY) male that will normally assume the appearance of a baby boy. Could it be that this basic genetic difference between the sexes is ultimately responsible for *sex differences in behavior*—differences that might explain why parents often do not treat their sons and daughters alike? We will explore this interesting idea in some detail in a later section of the chapter.

However, there is more to sex differences than biological heritage. Virtually all societies expect males and females to behave differently and to assume different roles. In order to conform to these expectations, the child must understand that he is a boy or that she is a girl and must incorporate this information into his or her self-concept. In this chapter we will concentrate on the interesting and controversial topic of **sex typing**—the process by which children acquire not only a gender identity but also the motives, values, and behaviors considered appropriate in their culture for members of their biological sex.

We begin the chapter by summarizing what people generally believe to be true about sex differences in personality and social behavior. As it turns out, some of these stereotypes appear to be reasonably accurate, although many others are best described as fictions or fables that have no basis in fact. We will then look at developmental trends in sex typing and see that youngsters are often well aware of sex-role stereotypes and are displaying sex-typed patterns of behavior long before they are old enough to go to kindergarten. And how do children learn so much about the sexes and sex roles at such an early age? We will address this issue by

Photo 13-1. Sex-role socialization begins very early as parents provide their infants with "gender-appropriate" clothing, toys, and hairstyles.

reviewing several influential theories of sex typing—theories that indicate how biological forces, social experiences, and cognitive development might combine or interact to influence the sex-typing process. We will then briefly consider an aspect of development that becomes quite central to our concepts of self as males or females—the growth of human sexuality. And last but not least, we will examine a new perspective on sex typing and see why many theorists now believe that traditional sex roles have outlived their usefulness in the more egalitarian social climate of our modern society.

Categorizing Males and Females: Sex-Role Standards

Most of us have learned a great deal about males and females by the time we enter college. In fact, if you and your classmates were asked to jot down ten psychological dimensions on which men and women are thought to differ, it is likely that every member of the class could easily generate such a list. Here's a head start: Which gender is most likely to display emotions? to be tidy? to be competitive? to use harsh language?

A **sex-role standard** is a value, a motive, or a class of behavior that is considered more appropriate for members of one sex than the other. Taken together, a society's sex-role standards describe how males and females are expected to behave and, thus, reflect the

stereotypes by which we categorize and respond to members of each sex.

Historically, the female's role as childbearer has been largely responsible for the sex-role standards that characterize many societies, including our own. Girls are typically encouraged to assume a nurturant, **expressive role,** for as a wife and mother, the female is often assigned the tasks of raising the children she has borne and keeping the family functioning on an even keel. To serve this end, girls are expected to become warm, friendly, cooperative, and sensitive to the needs of others (Parsons, 1955). By contrast, boys are encouraged to adopt an **instrumental role,** for as a husband and father, the male faces the tasks of providing for the family and protecting it from harm. Thus, young boys are expected to become dominant, independent, assertive, and competitive—in short, to acquire those attributes that will prepare them to make a living and to serve as intermediaries between the family and society. Roger Brown (1965) describes how this sexual "division of labor" has affected the sex-role stereotypes of American society:

> In the United States, a *real* boy climbs trees, disdains girls, dirties his knees, plays with soldiers, and takes blue for his favorite color. A *real* girl dresses dolls, jumps rope, plays hopscotch, and takes pink as her favorite color. When they go to school, real girls like English, music, and "auditorium"; real boys prefer manual training, gym, and arithmetic. In college, boys smoke pipes, drink beer, and major in engineering or physics; the girls chew gum, drink cokes, and major in fine arts. The real boy matures into a "man's man" who plays poker, goes hunting, drinks brandy, and dies in the war; the real girl becomes a "femi-

sex typing: the process by which a child becomes aware of his or her gender and acquires motives, values, and behaviors considered appropriate for members of that sex.

sex-role standard: a behavior, value, or motive that members of a society consider more typical or appropriate for members of one sex.

expressive role: a social prescription, usually directed toward females, that one should be cooperative, kind, nurturant, and sensitive to the needs of others.

instrumental role: a social prescription, usually directed toward males, that one should be dominant, independent, assertive, competitive, and goal-oriented.

nine" woman who loves children, embroiders handkerchiefs, drinks weak tea, and "succumbs" to consumption [p. 161].

Needless to say, these traditional standards of masculinity and femininity have become rather controversial in recent years. At this writing, the Equal Rights Amendment to the United States Constitution is soon to be reintroduced in the U.S. Congress, and advocates of women's rights have fought for and won major legal concessions (such as the Equal Opportunity Employment Act) that allow women more freedom to assume the instrumental role so long enjoyed by American males. But in spite of these important (and long overdue) advances, a homogenization of the sex roles is not likely in the foreseeable future. Several recent studies (see Ruble, 1983; Shaffer & Johnson, 1980; Werner & LaRussa, 1983) indicate that young adults of both sexes still endorse many traditional standards of masculinity and femininity and prefer other members of their own and the other sex who conform to these stereotypes. Table 13-1 illustrates the traits and characteristics that U.S. college students and mental health professionals assign to "typical" men and women. Note that most desirable feminine characteristics reflect warmth and emotional expressiveness, whereas the desirable masculine attributes seem to signify a competent or instrumental orientation.

Cross-cultural studies (Best et al., 1977; D'Andrade, 1966) reveal that a large number of societies endorse the sex-role standards and stereotypes shown in Table 13-1. In one rather ambitious project, Herbert Barry, Margaret Bacon, and Irvin Child (1957) analyzed the sex-typing practices of 110 nonindustrialized societies. Two judges rated each society for sex differences in the socialization of five basic attributes: nurturance, obedience, responsibility, achievement, and self-reliance. The results are summarized in Table 13-2. Note that achievement and self-reliance were more often expected of young boys, while young girls were encouraged to become nurturant, responsible, and obedient. The societies that placed the greatest emphasis on this pattern of sex typing were (1) those in which people live in large, cooperative family units where a division of labor is absolutely necessary and (2) those that depend on strength or physical prowess as a means of obtaining food and earning a living (for example, hunting; herding large animals).

Of course, these findings do not imply that self-reliance in females is frowned on or that disobe-

Table 13-1. Common stereotypes of men and women

Competency cluster (masculine descriptions are considered more desirable)

Feminine descriptions	Masculine descriptions
Not at all aggressive	Very aggressive
Not at all independent	Very independent
Does not hide emotions at all	Almost always hides emotions
Very subjective	Very objective
Very submissive	Very dominant
Very passive	Very active
Not competitive	Very competitive
Very home-oriented	Very worldly
Very sneaky	Very direct
Not adventurous	Very adventurous
Has difficulty making decisions	Can make decisions easily
Not at all self-confident	Very self-confident

Warmth-expressive cluster (feminine descriptions are considered more desirable)

Feminine descriptions	Masculine descriptions
Doesn't use harsh language	Uses very harsh language
Very tactful	Very blunt
Very gentle	Very rough
Very aware of others' feelings	Not at all aware of others' feelings
Very quiet	Very loud
Very neat	Very sloppy
Very strong need for security	Very little need for security
Enjoys art and literature	Does not enjoy art and literature
Easily expresses tender feelings	Does not easily express tender feelings

Source: Adapted from Broverman et al. (1972).

dience by young males is somehow acceptable. In fact, all five of the attributes that Barry et al. studied were encouraged of *both* boys and girls, but with different emphases on different attributes depending on the sex of the child (Zern, 1984). So it appears that the first goal of socialization is to encourage children to acquire those traits that will enable them to become well-behaved, contributing members of society. A second goal (but one that adults view as important nevertheless) is to "sex-type" the child by stressing the importance of relationship-oriented (or expressive) attributes for females and individualistic (or instrumental) ones for males.

Children in modern industrialized societies also

face strong sex-typing pressures, even though most people in these countries neither live in extended families nor depend on hunting and herding skills for their livelihood. Although parents may play a major role in this sex-typing process, they hardly stand alone. As we will see, other significant adults (for example, teachers), peers, and even the television set are important in shaping children's attitudes about the sexes and encouraging them to adopt culturally prescribed sex roles.

Some Facts and Fictions about Sex Differences

The old French maxim "Vive la différence" reflects a fact that we all know to be true: males and females are anatomically different. Adult males are typically taller, heavier, and more muscular than adult females, while females may be hardier in the sense that they live longer and are less susceptible to many diseases. But although these physical variations are fairly obvious, the evidence for sex differences in psychological functioning is not as clear as most of us might think.

Eleanor Maccoby and Carol Jacklin (1974) have conducted a major review of the literature and concluded that very few of the stereotyped views of men and women are accurate. Maccoby and Jacklin place traditional sex-role standards into the following three categories: (1) those that are probably correct, (2) open questions (stereotypes that may be overstated), and (3) those that qualify as "cultural myths" having no basis in fact. Let's begin with the stereotypes that seem to be correct.

Sex Differences That Appear to Be Real

After reviewing more than 1500 studies, Maccoby and Jacklin state that only four common sex-role stereotypes are reasonably accurate. First, females seem to have greater *verbal ability* than males. Girls develop verbal skills at an earlier age than boys, although differences between the sexes are very small until adolescence, when females' superiority in verbal ability becomes increasingly apparent. However, males outperform females on tests of *visual/spatial ability* (spatial perception; identifying the same figure from different angles) and *arithmetic reasoning*—particularly in subjects such as geometry or trigonometry that depend, in part, on visual/spatial skills. Although sex differences in some visual/spatial abilities are first detectable by age 8 to 10 (see Johnson & Meade, 1987; Linn & Petersen, 1985), males do not begin to outperform females in mathematics until early adolescence (age 12–13). Finally, Maccoby and Jacklin concluded that males are more physically and verbally *aggressive* than females.

Since the publication of Maccoby and Jacklin's influential work, researchers have identified a few additional sex-role stereotypes that seem to be accurate. For example, males are usually found to be more active than females (Eaton & Keats, 1982; Phillips, King, & Dubois, 1978), more willing to take risks (Ginsburg & Miller, 1982), more likely to initiate and to be receptive to bouts of nonaggressive rough-and-tumble play (DiPietro, 1981; Humphreys & Smith, 1987), and more vulnerable to problems such as reading disabilities, speech defects, emotional disorders, and certain forms of mental retardation (Hutt, 1972; Wittig & Petersen, 1979). From about age 5 onward, girls and women appear to be more interested in and more responsive to infants than boys and men are (Berman, 1985; Berman & Goodman, 1984; Blakemore, 1981). Girls are also less demanding than boys (Martin, 1980), are more likely to respond playfully to parents' social overtures and to comply with their requests (Gunnar & Donahue, 1980; Hetherington, Cox, & Cox, 1978), and are more likely than boys to rely on cooperation and negotiation rather than forceful, individualistic strategies when settling disputes or trying to achieve group goals (Charlesworth & Dzur, 1987; Miller, Danaher, & Forbes, 1986). After reviewing some of the more recent evidence, Maccoby (1980) suggests that perhaps there is some truth to the old wives' tale that boys are harder to raise than girls.

Table 13-2. Sex differences in the socialization of five attributes in 110 societies

| Attribute | Percentage of societies in which socialization pressures were greater for: | |
	Boys	*Girls*
Nurturance	0	82
Obedience	3	35
Responsibility	11	61
Achievement	87	3
Self-reliance	85	0

Note: The percentages for each attribute do not add to 100, because some of the societies did not place differential pressures on boys and girls with respect to that attribute. For example, 18% of the societies for which pertinent data were available did not differentiate between the sexes in the socialization of nurturance.

Source: Adapted from Barry, Bacon, & Child (1957).

Photo 13-2. Rough-and-tumble play is more common among boys than among girls.

However, let's keep in mind that these sex differences reflect *group averages* that may or may not characterize the behavior of any particular individual. For example, some males are as interested in infants as the most nurturant of females, and many girls and women are just as mathematically inclined as the best-performing boys and men. So even though the two *groups* may differ on certain attributes, there are many people within each group who do not fit the pattern. Stated another way, it is impossible to predict the aggressiveness, the mathematical skills, or the verbal abilities of any individual simply by knowing his or her gender. Only when group averages are computed do the sex differences emerge.

Attributes That May Differentiate the Sexes

The evidence for sex differences on several other social attributes is suggestive at best. As we review these findings, keep in mind that more research will be necessary before we will be able to draw any firm conclusions.

People commonly assume that females are more timid, fearful, and anxious than males, although the data

on this issue are mixed. Observational studies of children who are exposed to a variety of stressful situations usually find no sex differences in timid or fearful *behavior*. However, females are more likely than males to *report* feeling timid or fearful, and they tend to characterize their emotional reactions as deeper or more intense than males do (Diener, Sandvik, & Larsen, 1985; Maccoby & Jacklin, 1974). In childhood, girls appear to be more compliant with the demands of parents, teachers, and other authority figures. But "pushovers" they are not, for girls are no more (and are possibly less) compliant than boys with the demands and directives of age mates. And although there are data to indicate that girls are often more nurturant than boys (and perhaps more empathic as well), we will see in Chapter 14 that there is little if any evidence to support the maxim that females are more altruistic than males.

Cultural Myths

Several popular sex-role stereotypes are best described as unfounded opinions or "cultural myths" that have no basis in fact. Among the most widely accepted of these "myths" are those in Table 13-3.

Why do these inaccuracies persist? Maccoby and Jacklin (1974) propose that

> a . . . likely explanation for the perpetuation of "myths" is the fact that stereotypes are such powerful things. An ancient truth is worth restating here: if a generalization about a group of people is believed, whenever a member of the group behaves in the expected way the observer notes it and his belief is confirmed and strengthened; when a member of the group behaves in a way that is not consistent with the observer's expectations, the instance is likely to pass unnoticed, and the observer's generalized belief is protected from disconfirmation. We believe that this well-documented [selective attention] process occurs continually in relation to the expected and perceived behavior of males and females, and results in the perpetuation of myths that would otherwise die out under the impact of negative evidence [p. 355].

In other words, sex-role stereotypes are well-ingrained cognitive schemata that we use to interpret (or misinterpret) the behavior of males and females (Martin & Halverson, 1981; see also Box 13-1). People even use these schemata to classify the behavior of infants. In one study (Condry & Condry, 1976), college students watched a videotape of a 9-month-old child who was introduced as either a girl ("Dana") or a boy ("David"). As the stu-

Table 13-3. Some unfounded beliefs about sex differences

Belief	Facts
1. Girls are more "social" than boys.	The two sexes are equally interested in social stimuli, equally responsive to social reinforcement, and equally proficient at learning from social models. At certain ages, boys actually spend more time than girls with playmates.
2. Girls are more "suggestible" than boys.	Most studies of children's conformity find no sex differences. However, sometimes boys are more likely than girls to accept peer-group values that conflict with their own.
3. Girls have lower self-esteem than boys.	The sexes are highly similar in their overall self-satisfaction and self-confidence throughout childhood and adolescence. However, men and women differ in the areas in which they have their greatest self-confidence: females rate themselves higher in social competence, while males see themselves as dominant or potent.
4. Girls are better at simple repetitive tasks, whereas boys excel at tasks that require higher-level cognitive processing.	The evidence does not support these assertions. Neither sex is superior at rote learning, probability learning, or concept formation.
5. Boys are more "analytic" than girls.	Overall, boys and girls do not differ on tests of analytic cognitive style or logical reasoning, although boys do excel if the task requires visual/spatial abilities.
6. Girls lack achievement motivation.	No such differences exist! Perhaps the myth of lesser achievement motivation for females has persisted because males and females have generally directed their achievement strivings toward different goals.

Source: Adapted from Maccoby & Jacklin (1974).

dents observed the child at play, they were asked to interpret his/her reactions to toys such as a teddy bear or a jack-in-the-box. The resulting impressions of the child's behavior clearly depended on his or her presumed sex. For example, a strong reaction to the jack-in-the-box was labeled "anger" when the child was presumed to be a male and "fear" when the child had been introduced as a female.

As it turns out, the persistence of unfounded or inaccurate sex-role stereotypes has important consequences for both males and females. Some of the more negative implications of these cultural myths are discussed in the following section.

Evaluating the Accomplishments of Males and Females

In 1968 Phillip Goldberg asked female college students to judge the merits of several professional articles that were attributed to a male author ("John McKay") or to a female author ("Joan McKay"). Although these manuscripts were identical in every other respect, subjects perceived the articles written by a male to be of higher quality than those by a female.

This tendency to undervalue the accomplish-ments of females is apparent even when males and females are asked to explain their *own* successes. Females who succeed at *unfamiliar* achievement tasks are much more likely than males to attribute their favorable outcomes to luck, whereas males are more inclined to ascribe their successes to high ability (Dweck & Elliott, 1983). And in one study in which males and females were asked to explain achievements that are not easily ascribed to luck (for example, the accomplishments of a successful male or female physician), subjects of each sex tended to attribute the male's success to high ability and the female's to her untiring efforts to succeed (Feldman-Summers & Kiesler, 1974). In other words, people believe that females must try harder in order to accomplish the same feats as males. This attitude may explain the finding that employers who must choose between equally qualified male and female applicants will frequently offer a more advanced position or a higher starting salary to the male (Forisha & Goldman, 1981; Terborg & Ilgen, 1975).

When do children first begin to think that males are more competent than females? Earlier, perhaps, than you might imagine. Susan Haugh and her colleagues (Haugh, Hoffman, & Cowan, 1980) asked 3- and 5-year-

Box 13-1

Do Sex Stereotypes Color Children's Interpretations of Counterstereotypic Information?

Maccoby and Jacklin (1974) proposed that once people learn sex stereotypes, they are more likely to attend to and remember events that are consistent with these beliefs than events that would disconfirm them. Carol Martin and Charles Halverson (1981) agree. Martin and Halverson argue that gender stereotypes are well-ingrained schemata or naive theories that people use to organize and represent experience. Once established, these gender schemata should have at least two important effects on a child's (or an adult's) cognitive processes: (1) an *organizational* effect on memory, such that information consistent with the schemata will be easier to remember than counterstereotypic events, and (2) a *distortion* effect, such that counterstereotypic information will tend to be remembered as much more consistent with one's gender schemata than the information really is. For example, it should be easier for people to remember that they saw a

girl at the stove cooking (sex-consistent information) than a boy partaking in the same activity (sex-inconsistent information). And if people were to witness the latter event, they might distort what they had seen to make it more consistent with their stereotypes—perhaps by remembering the actor as a girl rather than a boy or by reconstruing the boy's activities as *fixing* the stove rather than cooking.

Martin and Halverson (1983) tested their hypotheses in an interesting study with 5- to 6-year-olds. During a first session, each child was shown 16 pictures. Half the pictures showed a child performing *gender-consistent* activities (for example, a boy playing with a truck) and half showed children displaying *gender-inconsistent* behaviors (for example, a girl chopping wood). One week later, children's memory for what they had seen was assessed.

The results of this experiment were indeed interesting. Children easily recalled the sex of the actor for scenes in which actors had performed gender-consistent activities. But when the actor's behavior was gender-*inconsistent*, these youngsters often distorted the scene by saying that the actor's sex was consistent

with the activity they recalled (for example, they were apt to say that it had been a boy rather than a girl who had chopped wood). As predicted, children's *confidence* about the sex of the actors was greater for gender-consistent scenes than for gender-inconsistent ones, suggesting that counterstereotypic information is harder to remember. But it was interesting to note that when children distorted a gender-inconsistent scene, they were just as confident about the sex of the actor (which they recalled *incorrectly*) as they were for the gender-consistent scenes in which they correctly recalled the actor's sex. So it seems that children are likely to distort counterstereotypic information to be more consistent with their stereotypes and that these memory distortions are as "real" to them as stereotypical information that has not been distorted (see Cann & Newbern, 1984, for a similar set of findings with 6- to 8-year-olds).

Why, then, do inaccurate sex stereotypes persist? Because we find disconfirming evidence harder to recall and, in fact, will often distort that information in ways that will confirm our initial (and inaccurate) beliefs.

---

olds to watch two infants on film, one of whom was presumed to be a male. When told to point to the baby who was "smart," these preschool children typically chose whichever infant had been labeled the boy. Nick Pollis and Donald Doyle (1972) found that first-grade boys were judged by their male and female classmates to be more competent at a number of unfamiliar tasks and more worthy of leadership roles than first-grade girls. Finally, kindergarten and first-grade girls already believe that they are not as good as boys at concept formation tasks and arithmetic, even though they are earning as high or even higher grades in arithmetic and have outperformed their male classmates on tests of concept learning (Entwisle & Baker, 1983; see also Entwisle, Alexander, Pallas, & Cadigan, 1987). And it is disturbing to note that the *brightest* females are often the ones who underestimate their competencies the most (Dweck & Elliott, 1983; Stipek & Hoffman, 1980).

Home influences. Parents may contribute to these sexist attitudes by virtue of the expectancies they have for their children. Jacquelynne Parsons and her associates (Parsons, Adler, & Kaczala, 1982) found that parents of 5th- through 11th-graders expect sons to achieve more than daughters in mathematics, and they believe that math classes are easier, more important, and somewhat more enjoyable for boys than for girls. Do these parental attitudes affect children's impressions of their mathematical aptitude and their prospects for future success in math? Yes, indeed! Even though the males and females in Parsons's sample *did not differ* in their previous performance in math, the children's beliefs about their own mathematical *abilities* were more in line with their parents' beliefs about their math aptitude and potential than with their own past experiences in math (see also Phillips, 1987; Stevenson & Newman, 1986). So it seems that parents' sex-stereotyped beliefs about their children's scholastic potential may be an important contributor to sex differences in children's academic self-concepts. "By attributing their daughters' performances to hard work and their sons' to high ability, parents may be teaching their sons and daughters to draw different inferences regarding their abilities from equivalent achievement experiences" (Parsons, Adler, & Kaczala, 1982, p. 320).

Scholastic influences. Teachers may also reinforce these sex-stereotyped attitudes by responding differently to the accomplishments of male and female students. In their observational study of evaluative feedback in the classroom, Carol Dweck and her associates (Dweck, Davidson, Nelson, & Enna, 1978) found that teachers' responses to boys' successes and failures were the type that promote a *mastery* orientation—that is, teachers praised a boy's ability when he succeeded while focusing more on nonintellectual factors (sloppiness, lack of effort) to account for his failures. Girls tended to receive a different evaluative pattern—teachers often stressed the nonintellectual aspects of a girl's work (neatness, high effort) when she succeeded while focusing on her intellectual shortcomings when she failed. So instructors may unwittingly provide their female students with patterns of verbal evaluation that leave girls little choice but to attribute failures to their own lack of ability. Of course, this is precisely the belief that should lead females to seriously underestimate their academic competencies and could even result in learned helplessness.

Why are the brightest female students often the ones who are most inclined to underestimate their abilities or their prospects for future academic success? A study by Jacquelynne Parsons and her associates (Parsons, Kaczala, & Meese, 1982) provides one clue. Parsons et al. looked at teachers' use of praise in five classrooms where male and female students clearly differed in their achievement expectancies. The results were indeed interesting. Teachers were more likely to praise girls whom they expected to do *poorly* than girls whom they expected to do well. But just the opposite was true for boys, who received more praise if the teacher expected them to do well rather than poorly. Notice that the pattern of praise received by female students in these classrooms does *not* reflect the teacher's true expectations about their future academic accomplishments. Perhaps you can see how a star female student who is rarely praised for her achievements might eventually conclude that she must lack ability or that academic success is not very important for girls, particularly when both the star male students and her less competent female classmates receive far more praise from the teacher than she does.

Implications for the future. Fortunately, there is some evidence that the pervasive tendency to underestimate women's competencies or to degrade their accomplishments is beginning to wane. Only 15 years ago, during the mid-1970s, young adults tended to perceive high-status professions such as medicine, architecture, and college teaching as less valuable or prestigious if they had been led to believe that the proportion of women practitioners in these fields was on the rise (Touhey, 1974). So when women were likely to make significant contributions to a high-status vocation, subjects would reassess the value or prestige of the profession rather than acknowledge the competencies of women! Yet, when my associates and I replicated this research in 1985, these sexist assessments of the value of various professions were no longer apparent (Shaffer, Gresham, Clary, & Thielman, 1986). In fact, young adults of the mid-1980s actually considered at least one high-status profession (college professor) to be higher in desirability and prestige if they had been led to believe that the proportion of women practitioners would be increasing.

Surely the underrepresentation of women in the so-called achieving roles of society (that is, politics and the professions) has helped to perpetuate the myth that females are less competent than males. However, the times are rapidly changing. According to a survey reported by the American Council on Education, when America's college class of 1985 began college, in the fall of 1980, 27% of the women said they intended to pursue careers in business, engineering, law, or medicine—a fourfold increase since 1966 (American Council on Education, 1981). So it is likely that many of the negative stereotypes about women's competencies or about their ability to succeed in heretofore "masculine" occupational pursuits will crumble over the next several decades as women achieve, in ever-increasing numbers, in virtually all walks of life. To oppose such a trend is to waste a most valuable resource—the abilities and efforts of more than half the world's population.

Developmental Trends in Sex Typing

Sex-typing research has traditionally focused on three separate but interrelated topics: (1) the development of **gender identity,** or the knowledge that one is either a boy or a girl and that gender is an unchanging attribute, (2) the development of *sex-role stereotypes*, or ideas about what males and females are supposed to be like, and (3) the development of *sex-typed* patterns of *behavior*—that is, the child's tendency to favor same-sex activities over those normally associated with the other sex. Let's look first at the child's understanding of gender and its implications.

Development of the Gender Concept

Children initially discriminate "maleness" from "femaleness" on the basis of clothing and hairstyles rather than body types and other morphological characteristics (Katcher, 1955; Thompson & Bentler, 1971). Spencer Thompson (1975) found that some 2-year-olds can readily identify the sex of people shown in pictures, even if the females are wearing short hair or pants. However, these toddlers are often uncertain about their own gender identities. By age 2½ to 3, almost all children can accurately label themselves as either boys or girls, although they have not yet developed a sense of **gender constancy**—a form of conservation in which they recognize that biological sex is unchanging. Indeed, it is not at all uncommon for 3- to 5-year-olds to think that boys can become mommies and girls daddies or that a person who alters his or her appearance (by changing hairstyle and clothing) has become a member of the other sex (Marcus & Overton, 1978; Slaby & Frey, 1975). Children normally begin to conserve gender between the ages of 5 and 7, precisely the time that they are beginning to conserve physical quantities such as liquids and mass (Marcus & Overton, 1978). Apparently 5- to 7-year-olds will apply gender constancy to themselves before they recognize that the gender of other people is invariant (Gouze & Nadelman, 1980). The sequence that youngsters seem to follow is (1) gender constancy for self, (2) gender constancy for same-sex others, and (3) gender constancy for members of the other sex (Eaton & Von Bargen, 1981).

Acquiring Sex-Role Stereotypes

Remarkable as it may seem, toddlers begin to acquire sex-role stereotypes at roughly the same time as or shortly after they first become aware of their gen-

der identities (see Huston, 1983; Weinraub et al., 1984). Deanna Kuhn and her associates (Kuhn, Nash, & Brucken, 1978) showed a male doll ("Michael") and a female doll ("Lisa") to 2½–3½-year-olds and then asked each child which of the two dolls would engage in sex-stereotyped activities such as cooking, sewing, playing with dolls, trucks, or trains, talking a lot, giving kisses, fighting, or climbing trees. Almost all the 2½-year-olds had some knowledge of sex-role stereotypes. For example, boys and girls agreed that girls talk a lot, never hit, often need help, like to play with dolls, and like to help their mothers with chores such as cooking and cleaning. By contrast, these young children felt that boys like to play with cars, like to help their fathers, like to build things, and are apt to make statements such as "I can hit you." The children who knew the most about sex-role stereotypes were the older ones (that is, the 3½-year-olds), particularly those who had some idea that gender is a stable attribute.

Over the next several years, children learn much more about the behavior of males and females and eventually begin to differentiate the sexes on *psychological* dimensions. In a well-known cross-cultural study, Deborah Best and her colleagues (1977) found that fourth- and fifth-graders in England, Ireland, and the United States generally agree that women are weak, emotional, soft-hearted, sophisticated, and affectionate, while men are ambitious, assertive, aggressive, dominating, and cruel. However, the stereotypes held by older grade school children are far more flexible than those of their younger counterparts. For example, a 7-year-old might say that carpentry is a masculine occupation that is not appropriate for a woman, whereas an 11- to 13-year-old is more likely to argue that females can and perhaps should pursue a "masculine" occupation such as carpentry if they really want to (Carter & Patterson, 1982; Meyer, 1980).

Development of Sex-Typed Behavior

The most common method of assessing the "sex-appropriateness" of children's behavior is to observe whom and what they like to play with. Sex differences in toy preferences develop very early—even before the child has established a clear gender identity or can correctly label various toys as "boy things" or "girl things" (Blakemore, LaRue, & Olejnik, 1979; Fagot, Leinbach, & Hagan, 1986; Weinraub et al., 1984). Boys aged 14 to 22 months usually prefer trucks and cars to other objects, while girls of this age would rather play with dolls and soft toys (Smith & Daglish, 1977). And by the time children enter nursery school, they generally play at sex-typed or gender-neutral activities, and they have often segregated into male and female play groups (Hartup, 1983).

Apparently children's preferences for same-sex playmates also develop very early. In nursery school, 2-year-old girls already prefer to play with other girls (La Freniere, Strayer, & Gauthier, 1984), and by age 3, boys are reliably selecting boys rather than girls as companions (Charlesworth & Hartup, 1967). Might these same-sex affiliative preferences reflect a basic incompatibility in the play behaviors of young boys and girls? To find out, Carol Jacklin and Eleanor Maccoby (1978) dressed pairs of 33-month-old toddlers in gender-neutral clothing (T-shirts and pants) and placed them together in a laboratory playroom that contained several interesting toys. Some of these dyads were same-sex pairs (two boys or two girls), and others were mixed-sex pairs (a boy and a girl). As the children played, an adult observer recorded the frequency with which they engaged in solitary activities and in socially directed play. As we see in Figure 13-1, social play varied as a function of the sex of one's playmate: boys directed more social responses to boys than to girls, while girls were more sociable with girls than with boys. Interactions between playmates in the same-sex dyads were lively and basically positive in character. By contrast, girls tended to withdraw from boys in the mixed-sex dyads. Jacklin and Maccoby suggested that there is something about boys' behavior that may scare other children and cause girls to shy away from them. Of course, an alternative interpretation for these results is that 2½- to 3-year-old boys and girls have already developed interests in different kinds of toys and games and, as a result, will respond more positively to same-sex companions, who are likely to share those interests.

Sex differences in sex-typed behavior

Many cultures, including our own, assign greater status to the male role (D'Andrade, 1966; Rosenblatt & Cunningham, 1976), and boys face stronger pressures than girls to adhere to sex-appropriate codes of conduct. Consider that fathers of baby girls are generally willing to offer a truck to their 12-month-old daughters, while fathers of baby boys are likely to withhold dolls from their sons (Snow, Jacklin, & Maccoby, 1983). Moreover, parents of 2- to 9-year-olds (particularly fathers) express more concern about their child's cross-sex play activities if the child is male (Langlois & Downs, 1980; Tauber, 1979b), and they perceive a wider

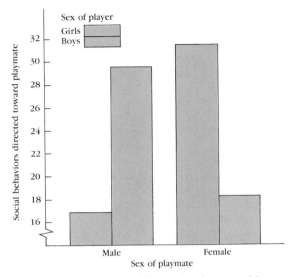

Figure 13-1. Apparently toddlers prefer playmates of their own sex, for boys are much more sociable with boys than with girls, whereas girls are more outgoing with girls than with boys. *(Adapted from Jacklin & Maccoby, 1978.)*

range of behaviors as appropriate for girls than for boys (Fagot, 1978). Perhaps it can be argued that we live in a male-oriented society where "tomboys" are at least tolerated while "sissies" are ridiculed and rejected. In other words, the male role is more clearly defined than the female role, and boys, who face stronger sex-typing pressures than girls, will soon learn what is or is not expected of them as they are criticized for deviating from approved sex-role standards. Walter Emmerich (1959) has suggested that the major accomplishment for young girls is to learn how not to be babies, whereas young boys must learn how not to be girls.

Indeed, males are quicker than females to adopt sex-typed preferences and patterns of behavior. Judith Blakemore and her associates (1979) found that 2-year-old boys already favor sex-appropriate toys while many 2-year-old girls do not. Even at age 3, girls may not always prefer feminine to masculine toys unless they are first reminded that the feminine toys are more "appropriate" for them. Finally, 3- to 4-year-old boys are more

---

gender identity: one's awareness of one's gender and its implications.

gender constancy: the realization that biological sex is invariant despite superficial changes in a person's appearance, attire, or activities.

likely than 3- to 4-year-old girls to say that they dislike opposite-sex toys (Eisenberg, Murray, & Hite, 1982).

Between the ages of 4 and 10, both males and females are becoming more aware of what is expected of them and conforming to these cultural prescriptions (Huston, 1983). Yet, girls are more likely than boys to retain an interest in cross-sex toys, games, and activities. Consider what John Richardson and Carl Simpson (1982) found when recording the toy preferences of 750 children aged 5 to 9 years as expressed in their letters to Santa Claus. Although most requests were clearly sex-typed, we see in Table 13-4 that more girls than boys were asking for "opposite sex" items. With respect to their actual sex-role preferences, young girls often wish they were boys, but it is unusual for a boy to wish he were a girl (Goldman & Goldman, 1982).

There are probably several reasons that girls are drawn to male activities and the masculine role during middle childhood. For one thing, they are becoming increasingly aware that masculine behavior is more highly valued, and perhaps it is only natural that girls would want to be what is "best" (or at least something other than a second-class citizen). And as we have noted, girls are much *freer* than boys to engage in cross-sex pursuits. Finally, it is conceivable that fast-moving masculine games and "action" toys are simply more interesting than the playthings and pastimes (dolls, dollhouses, dish sets,

Table 13-4. Percentages of boys and girls who requested popular "masculine" and "feminine" items from Santa Claus

	Percentage of boys requesting	Percentage of girls requesting
Masculine items		
Vehicles	43.5	8.2
Sports equipment	25.1	15.1
Spatial-temporal toys (construction sets, clocks, and so on)	24.5	15.6
Race cars	23.4	5.1
Real vehicles (tricycles, bikes, motorbikes)	15.3	9.7
Feminine items		
Dolls (adult female)	.6	27.4
Dolls (babies)	.6	23.4
Domestic accessories	1.7	21.7
Dollhouses	1.9	16.1
Stuffed animals	5.0	5.4

cleaning and caretaking activities) often imposed on girls to encourage their adoption of a nurturant, expressive orientation. Consider the reaction of Gina, a 5-year-old who literally squealed with delight when she received an "action garage" (complete with lube racks, gas pumps, cars, tools, and spare parts) from Santa one Christmas. At the unveiling of this treasure, Gina and her three female cousins (aged 3, 5, and 7) immediately ignored their dolls, dollhouses, and unopened gifts to cluster around and play with this unusual and intriguing toy.

In spite of their earlier interest in masculine activities, most girls come to prefer (or at least to comply with) many of the prescriptions of the feminine role as they reach puberty, become preoccupied with their changing body images, and face strong pressures to be more "ladylike" (Brown, 1957; Kagan & Moss, 1962).

How stable is sex typing?

Are highly sex-typed children likely to become highly sex-typed adults? At least one longitudinal study of middle-class children suggests that sex-typed patterns of behavior are reasonably stable over time (Kagan & Moss, 1962). For example, boys who were the most interested in masculine pursuits such as hunting or mechanics were likely to express a stronger interest in traditionally "masculine" activities as adults than men whose boyhood pastimes had been less firmly sex-typed. Girls who were the most passive and dependent in childhood were likely to be more passive and dependent as adults than women who had been reasonably active and autonomous during the grade school years. So there is some stability to sex typing and sex-typed patterns of behavior between childhood and the adult years. Highly sex-typed children do often become highly sex-typed adults.

Yet, it is important to note that an adult's sex-role behavior is hardly set in stone. Recently, investigators have been finding that the birth of a baby heralds a change in sex roles: fathers become more concerned about their breadwinner (instrumental) function, whereas mothers become more nurturant and "expressive" (Cowan & Cowan, 1987). And as adults reach middle age (and beyond), sex roles continue to evolve: males now become more compassionate and expressive and females more instrumental and autonomous (Feldman, Biringen, & Nash, 1981; Livson, 1983). So we see that sex typing is really a continuous process and that an adult's enactment of traditional sex-role behaviors may depend more on the utility of these responses at any

Photo 13-3. Girls are much freer than boys to engage in cross-sex activities.

given point in time than on any overriding personal desire to be "masculine" or "feminine."

Theories of Sex Typing and Sex-Role Development

Several theories have been proposed to account for sex differences and the development of sex roles. On the one hand, theorists who stress biological processes suggest that genetic, anatomical, and hormonal variations between the sexes are largely responsible for sex-linked behavioral differences, which, in turn, will predispose males and females to adopt gender-consistent sex roles. On the other hand, many developmentalists believe that *social* factors are crucial in determining both sex differences in behavior and the outcomes of the sex-typing process. Historically, the most influential of these "social" theories have been Freud's psychoanalytic model, social-learning theory, Kohlberg's cognitive-developmental theory, and (more recently) Martin and Halverson's gender schema (or social information-processing) theory. In this section of the chapter, we will briefly review these theories and discuss the strengths and weaknesses of each.

The Biological Approach

From a biological perspective, males and females differ in five important respects:

1. *Sex chromosomes*—XY for males, XX for females.
2. *Hormonal balance*—males higher in androgen and testosterone; females higher in estrogen.
3. *Composition of gonads*—testicular tissue for males; ovarian tissue for females.
4. *Internal reproductive system*—testes, seminal vesicles, and prostate for males; vagina, uterus, ovaries, and fallopian tubes for females.
5. *External genitalia*—penis and scrotum for males; labia and clitoris for females.

How do these physical variations affect sex typing? Some theorists have argued that genetic and hormonal differences between the sexes are responsible for several sex-linked characteristics that are apparent at birth or shortly thereafter. For example, female infants are said to be hardier, to mature faster, to talk sooner, and to be more sensitive to pain than male infants, whereas larger, more muscular males tend to sleep less, to cry more, and to be somewhat more active, more irritable, and harder to comfort than female infants (see Bell, Weller, & Waldrip, 1971; Hutt, 1972; Maccoby, 1980; Moss, 1967). If these sex differences are constitutionally based, it might seem that males and females are biologically programmed for certain activities that are congruent with the masculine or the feminine role. Could boys, for example, be predisposed toward activities such as aggression, assertiveness, and rough-and-tumble play by virtue of their higher pain thresholds, heightened activity, irritable or demanding dispositions, and muscular physiques? Could docile, undemanding, and highly verbal females be ideally suited for adoption of a nurturant, cooperative, expressive orientation?

People often assume that most sex differences are biologically determined, since biology is responsible for some (namely, the five physical characteristics listed above). A more likely possibility is that sex-linked constitutional factors *interact* with environmental events to produce sex-typed patterns of behavior (Huston, 1983). For example, parents may play more vigorously with active, muscular sons than with docile, less muscular daughters. Or perhaps they become more impatient with irritable and demanding sons who are difficult to quiet or comfort. In the first case, adults would be encouraging young boys to partake in the kinds of fast-paced, vigorous activities from which aggressive outbursts may emerge. In the second case, a parent's irritability with an agitated son could have the effect of making the child hostile or resentful toward the parent. So sex differences in aggression or any other form of sex-typed be-

Photo 13-4. Are young girls genetically predisposed toward cooperative forms of play? Biological theories of sex typing suggest that they may be.

havior may not be automatic, or "biologically programmed." Instead, it appears that a child's biological predispositions are likely to affect the *behavior* of caregivers and other close companions, which, in turn, will elicit certain reactions from the child and influence the activities and interests that the child is likely to display. The implication of this interactive model is that biological factors and social influences are completely intertwined and that both nature and nurture are important contributors to a child's sex-role development.

In the pages that follow, we will first consider some of the biological factors that contribute to sex differences and sex-typed patterns of behavior. Then we will take a look at the research suggesting that biology is not destiny.

Chromosomal differences between the sexes

Corinne Hutt (1972) believes that genetic differences between the sexes may account for the finding that boys are more vulnerable to problems such as reading disabilities, speech defects, various emotional disorders, and certain forms of mental retardation. Since genetic (XY) males have but one X chromosome, they are necessarily more susceptible to any X-linked recessive disorder for which their mother is a carrier (genetic [XX] females would have to inherit a recessive gene from each parent to show the same disorder). And since males have more genetic information (by virtue of hav-

ing some genes that appear only on a Y chromosome), they show a wider variety of attributes, including some negative ones.

Although it was once thought that gender variations in visual/spatial abilities and verbal skills might be directly attributable to genetic (or chromosomal) differences between the sexes, recent reviews of the behavior genetics literature provide little support for this point of view (see Huston, 1983; Linn & Petersen, 1985). Nevertheless, Hutt's chromosomal hypothesis should be investigated further, for psychological theories of sex typing cannot easily explain why males face greater risks of developmental disorders than females do.

Hormonal influences

In Chapter 5 we learned that hormones are powerful chemicals that play an important role in the development of bodily structures, the regulation of growth, and the functioning of organ systems. During the prenatal period, hormones trigger the development of the genitals and other organs and may have an effect on the organization and functioning of the central nervous system, most notably the brain (see Hines, 1982). Male hormones such as androgen and female hormones such as estrogen and progesterone are present in different concentrations in males and females—in other words, they are biological *correlates* of gender and gender differences. But to what extent do they influence sex typing or cause sex differences in behavior?

Some sex differences are at least partly due to the uneven distribution of sex hormones between males and females. The clearest evidence comes from animal studies which reveal that changes in a developing organism's hormonal balance are likely to have both anatomical and behavioral effects. For example, one team of investigators injected pregnant rhesus monkeys with the male hormone testosterone and noted that the female offspring showed malelike external genitalia and a pattern of social behavior that is normally more characteristic of males (Young, Goy, & Phoenix, 1964). These masculinized females often threatened other monkeys, engaged in rough-and-tumble play, and would try to "mount" a partner as males do at the beginning of a sexual encounter. Frank Beach (1965) reports that female rat pups that received testosterone injections in the first three days of life frequently displayed masculine sexual responses such as "mounting" as adults. The reverse was true for males. That is, castrated pups, which could not produce testosterone, exhibited feminine sexual characteristics such as receptive posturing as adults. Similar cross-sex mating behaviors occur among female hamsters that receive injections of the male hormone androgen as infants (Doty, Carter, & Clemens, 1971).

Although the evidence is limited, it appears that human beings may be subject to the same kinds of hormonal influences. For example, a small percentage of males are affected by a genetic anomaly known as **testicular feminization syndrome.** A male fetus who inherits this trait is insensitive to the male hormone androgen and will develop external genitalia that resemble those of a female.

John Money and his associates (Ehrhardt & Baker, 1974; Money, 1965; Money & Ehrhardt, 1972) call our attention to the reverse effect in females. Before the consequences were known, some mothers who had had problems carrying pregnancies to term were given an androgenlike drug to prevent miscarriage. This treatment had the effect of masculinizing female fetuses: if their mothers were taking the drug during the period when the genitals were developing, these genetic (XX) females were born with a female internal reproductive system and external organs that resembled those of a male (for example, a large clitoris that looked like a penis and fused labial folds that resembled a scrotum). Money and Ehrhardt (1972; Ehrhardt & Baker, 1974) have followed several of these **androgenized females** whose external organs were surgically altered and who were then raised as girls. Compared with their sisters and other female age mates, many of the androgenized girls were little tomboys who preferred to dress in slacks and shorts, showed almost no interest in jewelry and cosmetics, and clearly favored vigorous athletic activities (and male playmates) over traditionally feminine pastimes. Moreover, their attitudes toward sexuality and achievement were similar to those of males. They expressed some interest in marriage and motherhood but thought in terms of a late marriage with few children—events that should be delayed until they had established themselves in a career (they were clearly heterosexual, however, choosing males as sex partners in real life and in their fantasies). Although it could be argued that other family members had reacted to the girls' abnormal genitalia early in life, treating these girls more like boys, interviews with the girls' parents suggested that they had not (Ehrhardt & Baker, 1974). So we must seriously consider the possibility that prenatal exposure to male hormones affects the attitudes, interests, and activities of human females.[1]

Sex differences in aggression appear so early (about age 2) in so many cultures that it is difficult to attribute them solely to parental child-rearing practices (Maccoby & Jacklin, 1980). It has been suggested that males are more aggressive than females because of their higher levels of androgen and testosterone—activating male sex hormones that are thought to promote aggressive behavior. Indeed, Dan Olweus and his associates (Olweus, Mattsson, Schalling, & Low, 1980) found that 16-year-old boys who label themselves physically and verbally aggressive do have higher testosterone lev-

---

[1]Yet, it is not entirely clear that these girls' preferences for masculine activities are a result of their early exposure to androgen. Many of these androgenized females received cortisone therapy to control their androgen levels and to prevent further masculinization of their bodies, and one side effect of cortisone is to dramatically increase a person's activity level. Thus, a plausible alternative interpretation is that the high-intensity "masculine" behaviors of androgenized females are really due more to the cortisone they received than to any prenatal exposure to male sex hormones.

---

testicular feminization syndrome: a genetic anomaly in which a male fetus is insensitive to the effects of male sex hormones and will develop femalelike external genitalia.

androgenized females: females who develop malelike external genitalia because of exposure to male sex hormones during the prenatal period.

els than boys who view themselves as nonaggressive, and Elizabeth Susman and her associates (1987) found a similar link between androgen levels and aggression in a sample of 10–14-year-old males. And in their study of androgenized females, Ehrhardt and Baker (1974) report that, in the majority of families, it was the androgenized sibling who started fights with her nonandrogenized sister, rather than the other way around. However, we must be cautious in interpreting these findings, for a person's hormone level may depend on his or her experiences. For example, Irwin Bernstein and his associates (Rose, Bernstein, & Gordon, 1975) found that the testosterone levels of male rhesus monkeys rose after they had won a fight and fell after they had been defeated. So it appears that higher concentrations of the male sex hormones may be either a cause or an effect of aggressive behavior (Maccoby & Jacklin, 1980).

The "timing of puberty" effect

In recent years, investigators have found a relationship between the timing of puberty and children's performance on tests of visual/spatial abilities: both males and females who mature late perform better on spatial tests than those who mature early (Sanders & Soares, 1986; Waber, 1977). Since boys reach puberty some two years later than girls, this **"timing of puberty" effect** may help to explain why males outperform females on tests of spatial reasoning.

Why should the timing of puberty affect spatial abilities? One hypothesis is that the lateralization of spatial functions in the right cerebral hemisphere continues until puberty, so that those who mature early will be less specialized for spatial abilities than those who mature late (Waber, 1977). Although this is an interesting and highly controversial idea, the available evidence is far too limited to allow any firm conclusions.

Why biology is not destiny

Even though biological factors may predispose males and females toward different patterns of behavior, many developmentalists believe that these "forces of nature" can be modified by social experience. There are at least three lines of evidence to support this contention: John Money's work with androgenized females, Margaret Mead's cross-cultural studies of sex typing, and Nora Newcombe's recent research on the "timing of puberty" effect.

Recall that Money's androgenized females were born with the internal reproductive organs of a normal female even though their external genitalia resembled a penis and scrotum. These children are sometimes labeled boys at birth and raised as such until their abnormalities are detected. Money (1965; Money & Ehrhardt, 1972) reports that the discovery and correction of this condition (by surgery and gender reassignment) presented few if any adjustment problems for the child, provided that the sex change took place *before the age of 18 months*. But after age 3, sexual reassignment was exceedingly difficult because these genetic females had experienced prolonged masculine sex typing and had already labeled themselves as boys. These data led Money to conclude that there is a "critical period" between 18 months and 3 years of age for the establishment of gender identity. It is probably more accurate to call the first three years a *sensitive* period, for at least one group of West Indian males who had been raised as girls from birth (because of the testicular feminization syndrome) were able to accept a masculine identity at *puberty*, once their bodies assumed a more malelike appearance (Imperato-McGinley, Peterson, Gautier, & Sturla, 1979). Nevertheless, Money's findings indicate that early social labeling and sex-role socialization can play a very prominent role in determining a child's gender identity and sex-role preferences.

Margaret Mead's (1935) observations of three primitive tribes lead to the same conclusion. Mead noted that both males and females of the Arapesh tribe were taught to be cooperative, nonaggressive, and sensitive to the needs of others. This behavioral profile would be considered "expressive" or "feminine" in most Western cultures. By contrast, both men and women of the Mundugumor tribe were expected to be hostile, aggressive, and emotionally unresponsive in their interpersonal relationships—a masculine pattern of behavior by Western standards. Finally, the Tchambuli displayed a pattern of sex-role development opposite to that of Western societies: males were passive, emotionally dependent, and socially sensitive, whereas females were dominant, independent, and aggressive. In sum, members of these three tribes developed in accordance with the sex roles prescribed by their culture—even when these roles were quite inconsistent with sex-linked biological predispositions.

Nora Newcombe and Mary Bandura (1983) have recently found a "timing of puberty" effect for 11- to 12-year-old girls: those who mature late perform better on tests of spatial abilities than those who mature early. But in this study, measures of hemispheric lateralization of the brain were *unrelated* to either the timing of puberty or spatial performance. The factors that did predict the spatial abilities of these normal, nonandrogenized females were (1) timing of puberty, of course (a biological variable), and (2) measures of the girls' desire to be boys and their interest in masculine activities—interests that appear to be *socially* transmitted. Finally, timing of puberty itself was not related to the girls' preferences for the male role or masculine activities. The investigators concluded that

> the sexes differ not only in timing of puberty but also in possession of masculine personality traits and interests. . . . Since timing of puberty and [measures of masculine interests] were found to be independently related to spatial ability, either factor could potentially explain sex-differences in spatial ability. . . . Both possibilities need investigation [p. 222].

In sum, the evidence we have reviewed indicates that biology is not destiny; sex-linked biological predispositions can be modified and possibly even reversed by social and cultural influences. John Money and Anke Ehrhardt (1972) take note of this fact in their recent biosocial theory of sex typing. This theory is appropriately labeled *bio*social because it emphasizes the biological factors that determine how other people will respond to (or socialize) the child.

Money and Ehrhardt's biosocial theory

Money and Ehrhardt (1972) propose that there are a number of critical episodes or events that will affect a person's eventual preference for the masculine or the feminine sex role. The first critical event occurs at conception as the child inherits either an X or a Y chromosome from the father. Over the next six weeks, the developing embryo has only an undifferentiated gonad, and the sex chromosomes determine whether this structure becomes the male testes or the female ovaries. If a Y chromosome is present, the embryo develops testes; otherwise ovaries will form.

These newly formed gonads then determine the outcome of episode 2. The testes of a male embryo secrete two hormones—*testosterone*, which stimulates the development of a male internal reproductive system, and *mullerian inhibiting substance* (MIS), which inhibits the development of female organs. In the absence of these hormones, the embryo develops the internal reproductive system of a female.

At choice point 3 (three to four months after conception), testosterone secreted by the testes leads to the development of a penis and scrotum. If testosterone is absent (as in normal females) or if the male fetus is insensitive to the male sex hormones, the female external genitalia will form. This is the point at which a female fetus may develop the external genitalia of a male if exposed to a heavy dose of male sex hormones through drugs that the mother is taking or because of a genetic dysfunction of her own adrenal glands (of course, these androgenized females have no testes; their saclike "scrotums" are empty). Money and Ehrhardt also believe that testosterone alters the development of the brain and the nervous system, thereby suppressing the production of female sex hormones in males, with the result that males will not experience menstrual cycles at puberty.

The next major development occurs during the first three years after birth. Parents and other social agents label and begin to sex-type the child on the basis of the appearance of his or her genitals. In addition, the child will become more aware of his or her body type and learn how males and females are supposed to look. By age 3, most children have established a basic gender identity and are now well aware that they are boys or girls. Money considers this a critical development because he has found that children who undergo gender reassignment after age 3 usually experience serious adjustment problems and may never feel comfortable with their newly assigned sex.

Later, at puberty, changes in hormonal functioning are responsible for the growth of the reproductive system, the appearance of secondary sex characteristics, and the development of sexual urges. These events, in combination with one's earlier self-concept, provide the basis for an adult gender identity and sex-role preference (see Figure 13-2).

Although Money and Ehrhardt claim that social forces play a prominent and perhaps crucial role in the sex-typing process, their model focuses heavily on biological developments that people are responding to when deciding how to raise a child and does not really specify the social processes through which children acquire gender identities and sex-typed patterns of behavior. Other theorists have focused more intently on the socialization process itself, trying to identify the kinds of experiences that will convince children that they are boys who should adopt a masculine orientation or girls

---

"timing of puberty" effect: the finding that people who reach puberty late perform better on visual/spatial tasks than those who mature early.

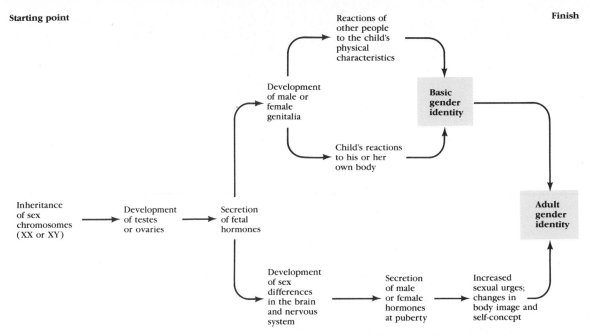

Figure 13-2. Schematic representation of Money and Ehrhardt's biosocial theory of sex typing. *(Adapted from Money & Ehrhardt, 1972.)*

who should favor feminine pursuits. The first of these "social" theories was Sigmund Freud's psychoanalytic approach—a highly controversial perspective on sex typing to which we will now turn.

Freud's Psychoanalytic Theory

Freud's explanation of psychosexual development acknowledges the contributions of both social and biological factors. Recall from our discussion of psychoanalytic theory in Chapter 2 that sexuality (the sex instinct) was said to be innate. Freud also believed that everyone is constitutionally bisexual, having inherited, in varying proportions, the biological attributes of both sexes. What, then, is responsible for the child's adoption of a gender identity consistent with his or her (predominant) biological sex?

Freud's answer was that sex typing occurs through the process of **identification.** Recall that identification is the child's tendency to emulate another person, usually the parent of the same sex. Freud argued that a 3- to 6-year-old boy will internalize masculine attitudes and behaviors when he is forced to identify with his father (the aggressor) as a means of renouncing his incestuous desires for his mother, reducing his **castration anxiety,** and thus resolving the **Oedipus**

complex. However, Freud believed that sex typing is more difficult for a girl, who already feels castrated and will experience no overriding fear that would compel her to identify with her mother and resolve her **Electra complex.** Why, then, would a girl ever develop a preference for the feminine role? For one very important reason: the object of the girl's affection, her father, is likely to reinforce his daughter for feminine behavior— an act that increases the attractiveness of the mother, who serves as the girl's model of femininity. So by trying to please her father, the girl should be motivated to incorporate her mother's feminine attributes and will eventually become "sex-typed."

Some of the evidence we have reviewed is generally consistent with Freudian theory. Recall that children are rapidly acquiring sex-role stereotypes and developing sex-typed behaviors at roughly the same age that Freud says they will (3 to 6). Moreover, boys whose fathers are absent from the home (because of divorce, military service, or death) during the oedipal period frequently have no male role model to emulate during this developmental epoch and, indeed, are often found to be less masculine in their sex-role preferences than boys from homes where the father is present (Hetherington, 1966; Roberts, Green, Williams, & Goodman,

1987). The finding that sex typing takes a little longer for girls than for boys is also in line with Freudian theory. Finally, the notion that fathers play an important role in the sex typing of their daughters has now been confirmed (Huston, 1983; Lamb, 1981).

However, the results of several other studies are very damaging to psychoanalytic theory. The idea that young children experience an Oedipus complex including castration anxiety for boys and penis envy for girls assumes that 3- to 6-year-olds are well aware of the differences between the male and female genitalia. Yet, as we saw in Chapter 2, 4- to 5-year-olds are inept at assembling dolls so that the genitals match other parts of the dolls' bodies (Katcher, 1955). These oedipal-aged children, who knew that they were boys or girls, made mistakes that showed they were ignorant about sex differences in genital anatomy (see also McConaghy, 1979). So it is hardly plausible that 3- to 6-year-olds would experience an Oedipus (or Electra) complex with castration anxiety or penis envy.

Other investigators have found that boys show a stronger identification with their fathers and heightened masculinity when fathers are warm and nurturant rather than overly punitive or threatening (Hetherington & Frankie, 1967; Mussen & Rutherford, 1963). These data are clearly inconsistent with the Freudian notion that a boy's sex-role development is furthered by a hostile relationship with a threatening father.

In sum, Freud's explanation of sex typing has not received consistent empirical support even though children begin to develop sex-role preferences at about the time that he specified. Let's now consider the social-learning interpretation of sex typing to see whether this approach looks any more promising.

Social-Learning Theory

Prominent social-learning theorists (Bandura, 1977; Mischel, 1970) have argued that children acquire their gender identities, sex-role preferences, and sex-typed behaviors in two ways: through direct tuition and observational learning. *Direct tuition* refers to the tendency of parents, teachers, and other social agents to reinforce the child's sex-appropriate responses and to punish those behaviors that they consider more appropriate for members of the other sex. Thus, boys are encouraged to be tough, assertive, and competitive and to play with action toys such as trucks or guns; girls are encouraged to be gentle and cooperative and to play with toys such as dolls or dish sets that require them to assume a nurturant, caretaking role. In addition, every child learns a variety of sex-typed attitudes and behaviors by observing the activities of same-sex models, including peers, teachers, older siblings, and media personalities, as well as the mother or the father. Walter Mischel (1970) has noted that children do not necessarily identify with (that is, hope to emulate) all the models who contribute to their sex-role development. Indeed, imitative responses that psychoanalysts call "identification" are just as easily described as examples of observational learning.

Direct tuition of sex roles

Are parents actively involved in the sex typing of their children? Yes, indeed, and the shaping of sex-typed behaviors begins rather early. Beverly Fagot (1978) studied 24 families, each of which included a mother, a father, and a single child between the ages of 20 and 24 months. Each family was observed in the home for five one-hour periods, during which the child's behaviors and the reactions of the parents were carefully recorded. Fagot noted that parental responses to certain classes of behavior *clearly depended on the sex of the toddler*. On the one hand, parents reinforced their daughters for dancing, dressing up (as women), following them around, asking for assistance, and playing with dolls. Daughters were discouraged from manipulating objects, running, jumping, and climbing. On the other hand, boys were punished for "feminine" activities (playing with dolls, seeking help) and encouraged to play with "masculine" items such as blocks, trucks, and push-and-pull toys that require large-muscle activity. Parents perceived aggression and rough-and-tumble play as more appropriate for boys than for girls, although

---

identification: Freud's term for the child's tendency to emulate another person, usually the same-sex parent.

castration anxiety: in Freud's theory, a young boy's fear that his father will castrate him as punishment for his rivalrous conduct.

Oedipus complex: Freud's term for the conflict that 4- to 6-year-old boys were said to experience when they develop an incestuous desire for their mothers and a jealous and hostile rivalry with their fathers.

Electra complex: female version of the Oedipus complex, in which a 4- to 6-year-old girl was thought to envy her father for possessing a penis and would choose him as a sex object in the hope that he would share with her this valuable organ that she lacked.

with either masculine or feminine toys. Finally, peers were especially critical of children who played with cross-sex toys, often ridiculing the offender or disrupting this "inappropriate" play. Indeed, Beverly Fagot (1985) finds that peer pressure for "sex-appropriate" play begins very early: even before establishing a basic gender identity, 21- to 25-month-old boys would belittle or disrupt each other for playing with feminine toys or with a girl, and girls of this same age were critical of other girls who chose to play with boys.

So it seems that the child's earliest preferences for sex-typed toys and activities may result from the tendency of parents (particularly fathers) to actively encourage sex-appropriate behavior and to discourage acts that they consider sex-inappropriate. As the child grows older, other people, such as teachers, Scout leaders, and especially peers, will become increasingly important as sources of reinforcement for sex-typed attitudes and behaviors.

Observational learning

According to Albert Bandura (1977), children acquire a large percentage of their sex-typed attributes by observing and imitating same-sex models. Bandura believes that there are two reasons a child might pay particular attention to models of his or her own sex. First, young children may often be reinforced for imitating same-sex siblings or parents. Indeed, you have probably heard a proud parent make statements such as "That's my little man; you're just like daddy!" or "You're as pretty as your mommy when you dress up like that!" As the child acquires a firm gender identity, a second factor comes into play. Same-sex models are now more worthy of attention because children perceive them as *similar* to themselves.

One problem with Bandura's hypothesis is that children do *not* pay more attention to same-sex models until relatively late—about 6 to 7 years of age (Ruble, Balaban, & Cooper, 1981; Slaby & Frey, 1975). In fact, John Masters and his associates (Masters, Ford, Arend, Grotevant, & Clark, 1979) found that preschool children are much more concerned about the sex-appropriateness of the *behavior* they are observing than the sex of the model who displays it. For example, 4- to 5-year-old boys will play with objects labeled "boys' toys" even after they have seen a girl playing with them. However, these youngsters are reluctant to play with "girls' toys" that boy models have played with earlier. So children's toy choices are affected more by the labels attached to the toys than by the sex of the child who served as a

they did not encourage their sons to display these behaviors. Fagot also noted that boys were more likely to be punished for feminine behaviors than girls were for masculine behaviors.

Perhaps an even more basic strategy that parents use to encourage sex-typed interests is to select gender-consistent toys for their infants and toddlers (Eisenberg, Wolchik, Hernandez, & Pasternack, 1985). A glance at the bedrooms of young boys and girls is revealing in itself: boys' rooms are likely to contain outer-space toys, sporting equipment, construction sets, and vehicles, while girls' rooms will typically include dolls, domestic toys, floral furnishings, and ruffles (Mac-Kinnon, Brody, & Stoneman, 1982). Given this early "channeling" of sex-typed interests, parents may find that additional pressures (such as differential reinforcement) are unnecessary—unless, of course, the child's play patterns and interests seem "inappropriate" to them (Eisenberg et al. 1985).

Do parents react strongly to cross-sex play? To find out, Judith Langlois and Chris Downs (1980) compared the reactions of mothers, fathers, and peers to 3–5-year-olds who were asked (by the experimenter) to play with either same-sex or cross-sex toys. Fathers showed the clearest pattern by rewarding their children for playing with the same-sex items and punishing cross-sex play. Mothers showed this same pattern with their daughters but tended to reward their sons for playing

model. But once children recognize that gender is an unchanging aspect of their personalities (at age 6 to 7), they do begin to attend selectively to same-sex models and are now likely to avoid toys and activities that members of the other sex seem to enjoy (Ruble et al., 1981).

A central tenet of social-learning theory is that a large number of same-sex models will contribute to the child's sex-role development. If this is so, we might expect that the child will become less like the same-sex parent as he or she matures and is frequently exposed to same-sex teachers, peers, media personalities, and the like. Indeed, studies of parent/child similarities reveal that school-age children and adolescents are not notably similar to either parent (Maccoby & Jacklin, 1974). One investigator (Tolar, 1968) found that college males actually resembled their mothers more than their fathers! Surely these findings are damaging to any theory (particularly the psychoanalytic approach) that claims that children acquire important personality traits by identifying with the same-sex parent.

The family as a social system. The number of children in a family and their ages and sexes affect the sex-role behaviors of *all* family members (Sutton-Smith & Rosenberg, 1970; Tauber, 1979a). For example, fathers who have two daughters tend to portray a more "masculine" image than fathers who have a son and a daughter. At first, this finding seems puzzling. But it is conceivable that fathers in girl/girl families must spend a large amount of time playing the complementary (masculine) role in order to successfully encourage the femininity of *two* girls.

The impact of siblings on sex typing is not well understood. It might seem as if both boys and girls would be more traditionally sex-typed if they had a large number of same-sex sibs to encourage and model sex-appropriate behavior. Yet, Margaret Tauber (1979a) reports that school-age girls who have older sisters and boys from all-boy families are the children who are most likely to enjoy *cross-sex* games and activities. Moreover, Harold Grotevant (1978) found that adolescent girls who have sisters develop a less "feminine" pattern of interests than girls who have brothers. These findings make some sense if children are concerned about establishing a personal niche within the family. A child with other-sex sibs could easily achieve such an individual identity by behaving in an appropriately "masculine" or "feminine" manner. However, a child who is surrounded by same-sex sibs may have to engage in cross-sex activities in order to distinguish the self from brothers (or sisters)

and avoid being categorized as one of the "boys" (or "girls").

Although we are only beginning to understand how the structure of the family affects children's sex typing, this much is clear: the child's sex-role socialization within the home depends more on the total family environment than on the influence of the same-sex parent.

Media influences. For the most part, males and females are portrayed in a highly stereotyped fashion in children's storybooks and on TV. Males are usually featured as the central characters who work at professions, make important decisions, respond to emergencies, and assume positions of leadership (Kolbe & LaVoie, 1981; Liebert, Sprafkin, & Davidson, 1982). By contrast, females are often depicted as relatively passive and emotional creatures who manage a home or work at "feminine" occupations such as waitressing or nursing.

Do these media models affect the sex-role development of young children? Indeed they do if the child is frequently exposed to these stereotyped portrayals of men and women. For example, 5- to 11-year-olds who watch more than 25 hours of television a week are more likely to choose sex-appropriate toys and to hold stereotyped views of males and females than their classmates who watch little television (Frueh & McGhee, 1975; McGhee & Frueh, 1980). Even adolescents are quite susceptible to the media typing of sex roles, particularly those aspects of masculinity and femininity portrayed in advertising (Tan, 1979). In recent years, steps have been taken to design television programming aimed at reducing the sex-role stereotypes of grade school children. We will evaluate the merits of these programs when we return to the topic of media influences in Chapter 16.

Kohlberg's Cognitive-Developmental Theory

Lawrence Kohlberg (1966) has proposed a cognitive theory of sex typing that is strikingly different from the other theories we have considered. Recall that both psychoanalytic theory and social-learning theory specify that boys learn to do "boy things" and girls learn to do "girl things" because their companions encourage these activities and discourage cross-sex behavior. Presumably children will eventually begin to identify with (or habitually imitate) same-sex models, thereby acquiring a stable gender identity and sex-appropriate attitudes and behaviors.

The cognitive theory of sex typing turns this sequence upside down. Kohlberg suggests that a child's gender identity is a cognitive judgment about the self that *precedes* his or her selective attention to (or identification with) same-sex models. Furthermore, the child's conception of gender, which is of central importance to the sex-typing process, will depend on his or her level of cognitive development. Kohlberg believes that children progress through three stages as they acquire an understanding of gender and its implications:

1. The first stage is **basic gender identity.** The child recognizes that he or she is a male or a female. Three-year-olds have usually reached this stage, although they fail to realize that gender is an unchanging attribute.
2. At the stage of **gender stability,** gender is perceived as stable over time. The child at this stage knows that boys invariably become men and that girls grow up to be women.
3. Finally, at the stage of **gender consistency,** the gender concept is complete, for the child realizes that gender is stable over time *and* across situations. Children of 6 to 7 who have reached this stage are no longer fooled by appearances. They know, for example, that one's gender cannot be altered by superficial changes such as dressing up as a member of the other sex or partaking in cross-sex activities.

According to Kohlberg, a child's basic interests and values will begin to change once he or she acquires a *mature* gender identity. For example, a boy who realizes that he will always be a male should come to value male attributes and the masculine role. At this point, he will begin to seek out male models and imitate their mannerisms in order to learn sex-appropriate patterns of behavior. The encouragement that he receives for successfully imitating males informs him that he is behaving the way boys should behave and thereby strengthens his masculine self-concept. Thus, Kohlberg's model is a cognitive-consistency theory: children are motivated to acquire values, interests, and behaviors that are consistent with their cognitive judgments about the self. It is worth repeating that for Kohlberg a child's conservation of gender (gender consistency) is the *cause*, rather than the consequence, of attending to same-sex models.

Support for Kohlberg's viewpoint. The results of several experiments are consistent with various aspects of Kohlberg's theory. For example, studies of 3- to 7-year-olds indicate that children's understanding of gender develops gradually and is clearly related to other aspects of their cognitive development such as the conservation of mass and liquids (Marcus & Overton, 1978). Ron Slaby and Karin Frey (1975) have also noted that the gender concept develops *sequentially*, progressing through the three stages Kohlberg describes (indeed, this same sequence of gender understanding has now been observed of children in many cultures; see Munroe, Shimmin, & Munroe, 1984). And there was a second interesting finding in Slaby and Frey's experiment: children who were at the highest stage of gender constancy were more likely to attend to same-sex models in a movie than were children whose gender concepts were less well developed (see also Ruble et al., 1981). Finally, the research presented in Box 13-2 suggests that a child's understanding of gender may affect his or her interpretation of sex-role stereotypes and expectations.

Limitations of Kohlberg's theory. The one major problem with Kohlberg's cognitive approach is that sex typing is already well underway before the child acquires a mature gender identity. As we have noted, 2-year-old boys prefer masculine toys before they are even aware that these playthings are more appropriate for boys than for girls (Blakemore et al. 1979). Moreover, 3-year-olds of each sex have learned many sex-role stereotypes and already prefer same-sex activities and playmates long before they begin to attend more selectively to same-sex models (Kuhn et al., 1978; Huston, 1983). And let's not forget the work of John Money (Money & Ehrhardt, 1972), who found that gender reassignment is exceedingly difficult once children have reached the age of 3 (or Kohlberg's basic identity stage) and have *tentatively* categorized themselves as boys or girls. In sum, it appears that Kohlberg overstates the case in arguing that a mature understanding of gender is necessary for sex typing and sex-role development.

Martin and Halverson's Gender Schema Theory

Carol Martin and Charles Halverson (1981) have recently proposed an information-processing model of sex typing that appears quite promising. Like Kohlberg, Martin and Halverson believe that children are intrinsically motivated to acquire interests, values, and behaviors that are consistent with their cognitive judgments about the self. However, they argue that this "self-socialization" begins as soon as the child acquires a basic gender identity at age 2 to 3 and thus is well underway by age 6 to 7, when the child achieves gender constancy. Let's take a closer look.

Martin and Halverson propose that establishment of a basic gender identity is the cornerstone of sex typing. Having reached this point, children will begin to acquire *gender schemata* (or stereotypes)—that is, organized sets of beliefs about males and females that will influence the kinds of information they will attend to, elaborate, and remember. Two kinds of gender schemata are thought to be important. Initially, children acquire a relatively superficial **"in-group/out-group" schema** as they learn which objects, behaviors, and roles are characteristic of males and females (for example, cars are for boys; girls may cry, boys shouldn't). This is the kind of information that investigators normally tap when studying children's knowledge of sex-role stereotypes. In addition, children are said to acquire an **own-sex schema,** which consists of detailed plans of action that one will need to perform various gender-consistent behaviors and to enact one's sex role. Thus, a girl who has acquired a basic gender identity will first learn to make distinctions between the sexes, such as "girls sew" and "boys build model airplanes" (in-group/out-group schema). And because she is a girl and wants to act consistently with her own self-concept, she will attend carefully to the actions involved in sewing, making them part of her own-sex schema, while paying little attention to "sex-inappropriate" behaviors, such as those involved in building model airplanes.

Once formed, gender schemata "structure" experience by providing an organization for processing social information. The idea here is that people are likely to encode and remember information consistent with their schemata and to either forget schema-inconsistent information or transform it so that it becomes consistent with their stereotypes. Support for this latter proposition was presented in Box 13-1; recall that children who heard stories in which actors performed cross-sex behaviors (for example, a girl chopping wood) tended to recall the action but to alter the scene to conform to their gender stereotypes (saying that a boy had been doing the chopping). Moreover, children do seem to be more interested in acquiring and remembering information about objects or activities that match their "own-sex" schemata. In one recent study (Bradbard, Martin, Endsley, & Halverson, 1986), 4- to 9-year-olds were given boxes of gender-neutral objects (for example, hole punches, burglar alarms, pizza cutters) and were told that these objects were all "girl" items or "boy" items.

They were then allowed several minutes to explore the objects and, one week later, were tested to determine whether they (1) remembered the gender label assigned to the objects and (2) could recall the specific information the experimenter had provided when describing the objects' functions. The findings were clear. During the initial session, boys explored more than girls if the objects had been labeled "boy" items, whereas just the reverse was true when the objects were described as things that girls enjoy. Apparently these gender labels were incorporated into children's "in-group/out-group" schemata, for they were easily recalled in the second session one week later. However, boys recalled more details about "boy" items than girls did, whereas girls recalled more than boys about these *same* objects if they had been labeled "girl" items. Finally, some of the children had been offered an incentive (a toy from a "treasure chest") for correct recall, but this inducement did *not* affect the accuracy with which they recalled the characteristics of "gender-inconsistent" items. So we see that the information-processing biases associated with gender schemata are very powerful indeed.

In sum, Martin and Halverson's gender schema theory is an interesting "new look" at the sex-typing process. Not only does this model describe how sex stereotypes might originate and persist over time, but it also indicates how these emerging "gender schemata" might contribute to the development of strong sex-role preferences and sex-typed patterns of behavior—even before the child realizes that gender is an unchanging attribute.

---

basic gender identity: the stage of gender identity in which the child first labels the self as a boy or a girl.

gender stability: the stage of gender identity in which the child recognizes that gender is stable over time.

gender consistency: the stage of gender identity in which the child recognizes that a person's gender is invariant despite changes in the person's activities or appearance (also known as gender constancy).

"in-group/out-group" schema: one's general knowledge of the mannerisms, roles, activities, and behaviors that characterize males and females.

own-sex schema: detailed knowledge or plans of action that enable a person to perform gender-consistent activities and to enact his or her sex role.

Box 13-2
Children's Conceptions of
Sex-Role Stereotypes

What do young children think about the sex-role standards and stereotypes that they have learned? Must they conform to these expectations; or, rather, do they feel free to do their own thing?

According to Lawrence Kohlberg, the answers to these questions will depend on the child's understanding of gender. Until they realize that gender is unchanging, young, egocentric children may feel that cross-sex behavior is acceptable as long as a child really wants to partake in these activities. But once the child achieves gender constancy, at age 6 to 7, he or she should become something of a chauvinist and interpret sex-role standards as absolute laws or moral imperatives that everyone should follow. Finally, Kohlberg proposes that older children who are approaching formal operations will be capable of thinking more abstractly and thus seeing the arbitrary nature of many sex-role stereotypes. In other words, preadolescents should become more flexible about sex-role standards, viewing them more as social conventions rather than moral absolutes that everyone must obey.

William Damon (1977) has tested Kohlberg's hypotheses in an interesting study of 4- to 9-year-olds. Each child was told a story about a little boy named George who insists on playing with dolls, even though his parents have told him that dolls are for girls and that boys should play with other toys. The children were then asked a series of questions about this story—questions designed to assess their own impressions of sex-role stereotypes. For example:

1. Why do people tell George not to play with dolls? Are they right?
2. Is there a rule that boys shouldn't play with dolls? Where does it come from?
3. What should George do?
4. What if George wanted to wear a dress to school? Can he do that?

Damon's findings were generally consistent with Kohlberg's cognitive explanation of stereotyping. Four-year-olds (who do not conserve gender) believe that doll play and other cross-sex behaviors are OK if that is what George really wants to do. Here are some of the answers provided by a 4-year-old named Jack:

(*Is it ok for boys to play with dolls?*) Yes. (*Why?*) Because they wanted to . . . (*So what should George do?*) Play with dolls. (*Why?*) Because it's up to him . . . (*Can boys have dresses?*) No. (*Why not?*) Because boys don't wear them. (*Does George have the right to wear a dress to school if he wants to?*) Yes, but he didn't want to. (*Is it ok if he wanted to?*) It's up to him [Damon, 1977, p. 249; italics added].

So we see that preschool children seem quite flexible about sex-role prescriptions; in fact, they view them as much less obligatory than other social-conventional rules, such as the requirement that they stay in their seats during snack periods at nursery school (Smetana, 1986).

By age 6, about the time they acquire gender constancy, children become extremely intolerant of a person who violates traditional standards of masculinity or femininity. Consider the reaction of 6-year-old Michael to George's doll play:

(*Why do you think people tell George not to play with dolls?*) Well, he should
continued

An Attempt at Integration

Perhaps some combination of the biosocial, social-learning, cognitive-developmental, and gender schema approaches provides the most accurate explanation of sex differences and the sex-typing process. Money and Ehrhardt (1972) have contributed to our understanding of sex typing by describing the important biological developments that people use to label the child as a boy or a girl and treat him or her accordingly. Yet, their biosocial model is not very explicit about the psychological determinants of sex differences and sex-role development.

Kohlberg's cognitive-developmental theory and Martin and Halverson's gender schema approach emphasize the importance of cognitive milestones and information-processing biases that occur some time after age 3, when the child acquires a basic gender identity. However, an integrative theorist would surely point out that these cognitive approaches largely ignore the important events of the first three years, when a boy, for example, develops a preference for masculine toys and activities because parents, siblings, and even his young peers frequently remind him that he is a boy, reinforce him for doing "boy things," and discourage those of his behaviors that they consider feminine. In other words, it appears that the social-learning theorists have accurately described early sex typing: very young children display gender-consistent behaviors *because other people encourage these activities.*

As a result of this early socialization (and the growth of some basic categorization skills), children acquire a basic gender identity. This is an important development, for Money's research suggests that as soon as children first label themselves as boys or girls, this self-concept is difficult to change (even though children do not yet recognize that gender itself is invariant). At

only play with things that boys play with. The things that he is playing with now is girls' stuff . . . (*Can George play with Barbie dolls if he wants to?*) No sir! . . . (*What should George do?*) He should stop playing with girls' dolls and start playing with G.I. Joe. (*Why can a boy play with G.I. Joe and not a Barbie doll?*) Because if a boy is playing with a Barbie doll, then he's just going to get people teasing him . . . and if he tries to play more, to get girls to like him, then the girls won't like him either [Damon, 1977, p. 255; italics added].

The oldest children in Damon's sample were only 9, but these youngsters were already less chauvinistic about sex-role standards and sex-typed activities. Note how 9-year-old James makes a distinction between moral rules that imply a sense of obligation and sex-role standards that are customary but non-obligatory:

(*What do you think his parents should do?*) They should . . . get him trucks and stuff, and see if he will play with those. (*What if . . . he kept on playing with dolls? Do you think they would*

punish him?) No. (*How come?*) It's not really doing anything bad. (*Why isn't it bad?*) Because . . . if he was breaking a window, and he kept on doing that, they could punish him, because you're not supposed to break windows. But if you want to you can play with dolls. (*What's the difference . . . ?*) Well, breaking windows you're not supposed to do. And if you play with dolls, you can, but boys usually don't [Damon, 1977, p. 263; italics added].

Now consider a set of observations that Kohlberg's theory does not anticipate: 12- to 13-year-olds, who should be attaining formal operations, once again become very intolerant of certain cross-sex behaviors (such as a male wearing nail polish or a female sporting a crew cut) even though they continue to be quite flexible about the hobbies or occupations that males and females might pursue (see Carter & McCloskey, 1983–84; Carter & Patterson, 1982; Stoddart & Turiel, 1985). How can we account for this second round of gender chauvinism?

One possibility is that youngsters may tend to exaggerate sex-role stereotypes in order to "get them cogni-

tively clear" during those developmental epochs when gender and gender-related issues are particularly salient to them (Maccoby, 1980). The early grade school years (age 6 to 7) are one such period, for this is when children first realize that gender is truly invariant—a *permanent* part of their personalities. And given the many gender-linked physical and physiological changes that occur at puberty, a young adolescent's sudden intolerance of personal mannerisms that imply a deviant, cross-sex identification may simply reflect a second attempt to clarify sex-role standards in his or her own mind as a prelude to establishing a mature *personal/social* (or heterosexual) identity. One implication of this point of view is that older adolescents and young adults should again become more flexible in their thinking about sex-role stereotypes once they have resolved their identity crises and now feel more comfortable with their masculine or feminine self-concepts. Support for this prediction comes from a study by Urberg (1979), who found that the sex-role stereotypes of adults were indeed much less rigid than those of high school students.

---

this point, children begin (1) to actively seek information about sex differences, (2) to organize this information into in-group/out-group gender schemata, and (3) to learn more about those behaviors that they consider appropriate for members of their *own* sex. Although social-learning processes such as differential reinforcement are still implicated in the development of sex-typed behavior, the child is now *intrinsically motivated* to perform those acts that match his or her "own-sex" gender schema and to avoid activities that are more appropriate for the other sex. Thus, 4- to 5-year-old boys, for example, will play with objects labeled "boys' toys" even if they have seen girls playing with and enjoying them (Masters et al., 1979). Their gender schemata tell them that "boy" toys are sex-appropriate, and they are inclined to approach these objects. The model's sex is of lesser importance, for these youngsters do not yet realize that her gender is invariant, and besides, they

may simply distort what they have seen to match their gender schemata (for example, recalling that it was a boy rather than a girl who had enjoyed these "boy" toys).

Once children achieve gender constancy, at age 6 to 7, their strategies for incorporating sex-typed characteristics begin to change. Rather than focusing almost exclusively on gender schemata to define what is "appropriate" or "inappropriate" for them, older children now pay closer attention to the *sex* of the models who display various attributes. Thus, a 7-year-old girl will typically select females as her models because she recognizes (1) that *she will always be a female* and (2) that she can make her own behavior more consistent with this firm, future-oriented self-image by selectively attending to other people like her (females) and then "doing what girls and women do."

In sum, biological characteristics and social-learning mechanisms such as direct tuition and observational learning play a central role in the sex-typing process. However, these factors clearly interact with one's cognitive structuring abilities and information-processing biases (gender schemata) to determine the course and the outcome of sex-role development (see Table 13-5 for a brief summary of this integrative viewpoint).

Development of Sexuality and Sexual Behavior

As children acquire knowledge about males and females and about the roles that society expects males and females to assume, they are also becoming increasingly aware of their own *sexuality*—an aspect of development that will later have a major effect on their concepts of self as men or women. In this section of the chapter, we will briefly consider the growth of human sexuality and discuss some of the changes in adolescent sexual attitudes (and behavior) over the past 60 years.

Origins of "Sexual" Activities

When do children first display signs of sexuality? Might we humans really be "sexual" beings from birth, as Freud and other psychoanalysts have assumed? Although this claim might seem a bit outrageous, consider that both male babies (Kinsey, Pomeroy, & Martin, 1948) and female babies (Bakwin, 1973) have been observed (1) to fondle their genitals, (2) to display the grunting, flushing, and sweating that accompany intense sexual arousal, and (3) to have what appear to be orgasms before becoming pale and more tranquil. In fact, parents in some cultures are well aware of the pleasure babies receive from sexual gratification and will occasionally use genital stimulation as a means of soothing a fussy or distressed infant (Ford & Beach, 1951).

Of course, infants are "sexual" beings only in the sense that their genitals are sensitive and their nervous systems allow sexual reflexes and responses. However, it will not be very long before they begin to learn what human sexuality is about and how the members of their society react to sexual behavior.

Sexual Behavior during Childhood

According to Freud, preschoolers in the *phallic stage* of psychosexual development are very interested in the functioning of their genitals and will seek bodily pleasure through masturbation. However, Freud assumed that the traumas associated with the resolution of their Oedipus or Electra complexes would force school-age children to (1) repress their sexuality and (2) rechannel their energies into schoolwork and other non-

Table 13-5. An overview of the sex-typing process from the perspective of an integrative theorist

Developmental period	Events and outcomes
Prenatal period	The fetus develops the morphological characteristics of a male or a female, which others will react to once the child is born.
Birth to 3 years	Parents and other companions label the child as a boy or a girl, frequently remind the child of his or her gender, and begin to encourage gender-consistent behavior while discouraging cross-sex activities. As a result of these social experiences and the development of very basic classification skills, the young child acquires some sex-typed behavioral preferences and the knowledge that he or she is a boy or a girl (basic gender identity).
3 to 6 years	Once children acquire a basic gender identity, they begin to seek information about sex differences, form gender schemata, and become intrinsically motivated to perform those acts that are viewed as "appropriate" for their own sex. When acquiring gender schemata, children attend to both male and female models. And once their "own sex" schemata are well established, these youngsters are apt to imitate behaviors considered appropriate for their sex, regardless of the gender of the model who displays them.
Age 6 to 7 and beyond	Children finally acquire a sense of gender consistency—a firm, future-oriented image of themselves as boys who must necessarily become men or girls who will obviously become women. At this point they begin to rely less exclusively on gender schemata and more on the behavior of same-sex models to acquire those mannerisms and attributes that are consistent with their firm categorization of self as a male or female.

erotic social activities during the long **latency period** of middle childhood. It turns out that Freud was partly right and partly wrong.

Freud was right about the sexual curiosity and sexual activities of preschool children. However, he was quite incorrect in assuming that sexuality declines during the grade school years. In fact, masturbation and other forms of sexual experimentation (including cross-sex exploits such as "playing doctor") actually *increase* with age (Rosen & Hall, 1984). Perhaps Freud was misled by the fact that preschoolers, often unaware of society's rules of etiquette, are more likely to get caught at their sex play than older children are. As Rosen and Hall (1984) put it, older children are very discreet, behaving around adults in the sexless manner that leads observers to believe that they are sexually inactive" (p. 287).

It is likely that Freud would not have been misled about the sexuality of grade school children had his patients come from *permissive* societies, where children are free to express their sexuality and are even encouraged to prepare for their roles as mature sexual beings (Ford & Beach, 1951). On the island of Ponape, for example, 4- and 5-year-olds receive a thorough "sex education" from adults and are encouraged to experiment with one another. Among the Chewa of Africa, parents believe that practice makes perfect; so, with the blessings of their parents, older boys and girls build huts and play at being husbands and wives in trial marriages. Of course, Freud might have concluded that humans are largely sexless *throughout childhood* had he worked with people from *restrictive* societies, in which all overt expressions of sexuality are actively suppressed. In New Guinea, for example, Kwoma boys are simply not allowed to touch themselves, and a boy caught having an erection is apt to have his penis beaten with a stick! Where do Western societies fall on this permissive/restrictive continuum? Most could be classified as *semirestrictive*—there are informal rules prohibiting childhood masturbation and sex play, although these rules are frequently violated and adults rarely punish children unless the violations are flagrant. Nevertheless, anthropologists such as Margaret Mead (1928) have argued that even semirestrictive societies introduce unnecessary conflicts and make the transition to adulthood much harder than it need be by perpetuating horrible myths about normal sexual activities (such as saying that masturbation causes warts or blindness) while denying children any opportunities to prepare for sexual relationships later in life.

Adolescent Sexuality

Sexuality assumes far greater importance once children experience puberty and become sexually mature: now adolescents must incorporate concepts of themselves as sexual beings into their male or female self-identities. They must also figure out how to express their sexuality in the context of interpersonal relationships. These tasks have never been easy. But they may now be more difficult than ever, given the "new morality" that has emerged over the past several decades in Western societies. What are the sexual values of today's teenagers? What is "normal" sexual behavior during adolescence? Let's see what recent research can tell us.

Teenage sexual morality. Have today's teenagers adopted a new morality that is dramatically different from the standards that their parents and grandparents held? In one sense they have, for adolescents have become increasingly liberal in their thinking about sex throughout this century—especially during the 1960s and 1970s. It seems that sexual attitudes may now be reverting ever so slightly in a conservative direction, largely as a result of the AIDS problem (Winker, 1987). But even before the specter of AIDS, it was clear that few teenagers had completely abandoned the "old" (or traditional) morality.

In his review of the literature on teenage sexuality, Philip Dreyer (1982) noted three major changes in teenagers' sexual attitudes—changes that describe what the "new morality" means to them. First, most adolescents now believe that *sex with affection* is acceptable. Thus today's youth are rejecting the maxim that premarital intercourse is always immoral, but they still believe that casual or exploitative sex is wrong (even though they may themselves have had such experiences). The second major change in teenage attitudes about sex might be termed the decline of the *double standard*—that is, the idea that sexual activity outside marriage is less objectionable for males than for females. The double standard hasn't disappeared, for college students still believe that a woman who has many sexual partners is more immoral than an equally promiscuous man (Robinson & Jedlicka, 1982). But Western

---

latency period: Freud's fourth stage of psychosexual development (age 6 to puberty) in which sexual desires are said to be repressed and the child's energy is channeled into socially acceptable outlets such as schoolwork or vigorous play.

societies have been moving for some time toward a single standard of sexual behavior for both males and females.

Finally, a third change in adolescents' sexual attitudes might be described as *increased confusion about sexual norms*. As Dreyer (1982) notes, the "sex with affection" idea is very ambiguous: must one truly be in love, or is mere liking enough to justify sexual intercourse? It is now up to the individual(s) to decide. Yet, these decisions are tough because adolescents receive mixed messages from many sources. For example, some parents stress the value of maintaining one's virginity and avoiding unpleasant consequences such as disease and pregnancy; others see sexual activity as "normal" for teenagers and will help their youngsters to obtain birth control devices. Not surprisingly, then, one's peers are likely to offer very different bits of advice when talking with an adolescent about sexual matters, al-though the average peer is probably more liberal than the typical parent. Indeed, when lamenting strong peer pressure encouraging sex, one girl offered this amusing definition of a virgin: "An awfully ugly third-grader." In years gone by, the norms of appropriate sexual conduct were much simpler: sex was fine if you were married (or perhaps engaged), but it should otherwise be avoided. This is not to say that our parents or grandparents always resisted the temptations they faced; but they probably had a lot less difficulty than today's adolescents in deciding whether what they were doing was acceptable or unacceptable.

Sexual behavior.   Not only have sexual attitudes changed, but so have patterns of adolescent sexual behavior. Today's adolescents masturbate more (or at least report masturbating more) than those of past eras (Dreyer, 1982), although many still feel guilty or

Photo 13-5. Sexual involvement has become an integral component of the adolescent's search for adult identity and emotional fulfillment.

uneasy about it (Coles & Stokes, 1985). And while only a small minority of today's 15-year-olds have experienced sexual intercourse, we see in Table 13-6 that premarital intercourse has become more common in recent years and that about half of all adolescents have had intercourse at least once before they leave high school. The table also shows that the sexual behavior of females has changed more than that of males. Oh, it is true that vestiges of the double standard persist: teenage girls are much more ambivalent about losing their virginity than teenage boys are, and girls are more insistent that emotional commitment be a prerequisite for sex (Carroll, Volk, & Hyde, 1985; Coles & Stokes, 1985). Nevertheless, college women today are about as likely as college men to have had sexual intercourse (Darling, Kallen, & VanDusen, 1984).

In sum, both the sexual attitudes and behaviors of adolescents have changed considerably since midcentury—so much so that sexual involvement is now a normal part of the adolescent's experience, an integral component of his or her search for an adult identity and emotional fulfillment (Dreyer, 1982). Many educators believe that teenage sexuality is here to stay and that our society can no longer afford to neglect sex education and counseling in the schools. And lest you wonder about the wisdom of providing sex education, the available evidence suggests that such instruction does *nothing* to promote more widespread sexual activity, although it does seem to encourage teenagers who are already sexually active to be more consistent in their use of contraception (Dawson, 1986; Marsiglio & Mott, 1986).

Psychological Androgyny: A New Look at Sex Roles

Throughout this chapter, we have used the term *sex-appropriate* to describe the mannerisms and behaviors that societies consider more suitable for members of one sex than the other. Today many psychologists believe that these rigidly defined sex-role standards are actually harmful because they constrain the behavior of both males and females. Indeed, Sandra Bem (1978) has stated that her major purpose in studying sex roles is "to help free the human personality from the restrictive prison of sex-role stereotyping and to develop a conception of mental health that is free from culturally imposed definitions of masculinity and femininity."

Table 13-6. Historical changes in the percentages of high school and college students reporting premarital sexual intercourse

	High school		College	
Period	Boys	Girls	Boys	Girls
1925–1965	25	10	55	25
1966–1973	35	35	85	65
1974–1979	56	44	74	74

Source: Dreyer (1982).

Psychologists have traditionally assumed that masculinity and femininity are at opposite ends of a single dimension: masculinity supposedly implies the absence of femininity, and vice versa. Bem challenges this assumption by arguing that a person can be androgynous—that is, both masculine and feminine, instrumental and expressive, assertive and nonassertive, competitive or noncompetitive, depending on the utility or situational appropriateness of these attributes. The underlying assumption of Bem's model is that masculinity and femininity are *two separate dimensions*. A person who has many masculine and few feminine characteristics is defined as a *masculine sex-typed individual*. One who has many feminine and few masculine characteristics is said to be *feminine sex-typed*. Finally, the **androgynous** individual is a person who has a large number of both masculine and feminine characteristics (see Figure 13-3).

Do androgynous people really exist? To find out, Bem (1974) and Spence and Helmreich (1978) have developed sex-role inventories that contain both a masculinity and a femininity scale. One testing of a large sample of college students (Spence & Helmreich, 1978) revealed that roughly 33% of the test takers were sex-typed, 27–32% were androgynous, and the remaining subjects were either "undifferentiated" (low in both masculinity and femininity) or "sex-reversed" (masculine sex-typed females or feminine sex-typed males). Judith Hall and Amy Halberstadt (1980) have constructed a similar sex-role inventory for grade school children and found that 27–32% of their 8- to 11-year-olds could be classified as androgynous. So androgynous individuals do indeed exist, and in sizable numbers.

---

androgyny: a sex-role orientation in which the individual has incorporated a large number of both masculine and feminine attributes into his or her personality.

		Femininity	
		High	Low
Masculinity	High	Androgynous	Masculine sex-typed
	Low	Feminine sex-typed	Undifferentiated

Figure 13-3. Categories of sex-role orientation (masculinity and femininity are conceptualized as separate and independent dimensions).

Is Androgyny a Desirable Attribute?

Bem (1975, 1978) has argued that androgynous people are "better off" than sex-typed people because they are not constrained by rigid sex-role concepts and are freer to respond effectively to a wider variety of situations. Seeking to test this hypothesis, Bem exposed masculine, feminine, and androgynous men and women to situations that called for independence (a masculine attribute) or nurturance (a feminine attribute). The test for masculine independence assessed the subject's willingness to resist social pressure by refusing to agree with peers who gave bogus judgments when rating cartoons for funniness (for example, several peers might say that a very funny cartoon was unfunny or that unfunny cartoons were hilarious). Nurturance, or feminine expressiveness, was measured by observing the behavior of the subject when left alone for ten minutes with a 5-month-old baby. The results confirmed Bem's hypotheses. Both the masculine sex-typed and the androgynous subjects were more independent (less conforming) on the "independence" test than feminine sex-typed individuals. Furthermore, both the feminine sex-typed and the androgynous subjects were more "nurturant" than the masculine sex-typed individuals when interacting with the baby. Thus, the androgynous subjects were quite flexible; they performed as masculine subjects did on the "masculine" task and as feminine subjects did on the "feminine" task.

If androgynous people are truly "better off," as Bem has argued, then we might expect them to be popular and to score higher on measures of self-esteem than traditional males and females do. As a matter of fact, recent research indicates that androgynous adolescents and college students do enjoy higher self-esteem and are perceived by peers to be more likable and better adjusted than classmates who are traditionally sex-typed (Major, Carnevale, & Deaux, 1981; Massad, 1981; Spence, 1982). Moreover, androgynous females are more likely than sex-typed females to attribute their achievements to ability (rather than effort or luck), to attribute their failures to factors other than lack of ability, and to show little if any decrement in performance (helplessness) after initially failing at an achievement task (Huston, 1983). Clearly, these data seem to imply that androgyny is a desirable attribute.

However, a caution is in order as we try to interpret these results. Since the androgynous person has a large number of masculine and feminine traits, we might wonder whether it is the masculine or the feminine component of androgyny that is primarily responsible for the higher levels of self-esteem and personal adjustment that seem to characterize androgynous individuals. Those who have researched the question find that it is the masculine component of androgyny that contributes most heavily to self-esteem while the feminine component has a much smaller effect (Lamke, 1982; Whitley, 1983). Perhaps this finding makes good sense when we recall that both males and females perceive masculine attributes and activities as more desirable and socially prestigeful than feminine ones.

Who Raises Androgynous Offspring?

Although the data are sketchy at this point, we are beginning to get some idea about how androgyny originates. There is some evidence that androgynous adolescents and college students come from homes in which the parents are androgynous themselves (Orlofsky, 1979; Spence & Helmreich, 1978). Moreover, parents who are *nurturant* and *highly involved* with their children and who encourage them to develop close relations with the parent of the other sex tend to foster the development of both masculine and feminine attributes (Hetherington et al., 1978; Orlofsky, 1979). Finally, daughters of working mothers perceive fewer psychological differences between males and females and are more likely to be androgynous than daughters of nonworking mothers (Hansson, Chernovetz, & Jones, 1977; Hoffman, 1984). So it appears that adults who value both masculine "instrumentality" and feminine "expressive-

Photo 13-6. Parents who are themselves androgynous are likely to raise androgynous children.

ness" and who make these feelings known are the ones who are most likely to raise androgynous offspring.

Do androgynous adults make better parents than those who are traditionally sex-typed? At first glance it may seem so if androgynous parents raise androgynous children, who, in turn, enjoy high self-esteem and are perceived as likable and well adjusted by their peers. Yet, in one study (Baumrind, 1982), 9-year-old daughters of androgynous parents were actually found to be somewhat less competent than their female classmates whose parents were traditionally sex-typed.

Does this finding imply that traditional adults make better parents than those who are androgynous? Diana Baumrind (1982) thinks so, although other interpretations are possible. For example, it may be that the benefits of having androgynous parents are minimal until adolescence, when teenagers (1) become more interested in close interpersonal relationships, in which nurturance and a concern for others are adaptive attri-

butes, and (2) are planning and preparing for a career, so that independence, assertiveness, and other "masculine" attributes might be advantageous. In fact, there is some evidence that the benefits of being androgynous are much more apparent for adolescents and young adults than for grade school children (see Perry & Bussey, 1984). So at this point, whether androgynous parents are any more or less effective than traditional parents is an open question—one that developmentalists will be trying to answer in the years ahead.

Implications and Prescriptions for the Future

The androgyny concept has generated an enormous amount of research within a brief time, and these early returns are fascinating. Perhaps the major implication of this work is that the notion of masculine superiority is a myth; androgynous individuals of each sex seem to be adaptable to a wide variety of situations, and they need not fear rejection from either same-sex or other-sex peers for having incorporated both masculine and feminine attributes into their personalities. Advocates of the women's movement have long argued that women should be freer to become more like men, and many of us may have barely noticed their support for the opposite premise—namely, that men might be "better off" if they became a little more like women. Although some people react quite negatively to the androgyny concept, thinking that it implies that a drab, unisex society is "best," it is worth repeating that androgynous females are perceived as no less feminine, nor are androgynous males perceived as any less masculine, simply because they have characteristics traditionally associated with the other sex (Major et al., 1981). In other words, the research to date provides little or no evidence of any disadvantage associated with being androgynous, and it illustrates that androgynous people are adaptive, well-adjusted individuals who are liked and respected by their peers.[2]

---

[2]Of course, it is important to remember that the behavioral patterns that are considered adaptive or nonadaptive depend to a large extent on the culture in which one is raised. In the two countries where androgyny has been studied most extensively—the United States and Canada—there are some advantages associated with being "androgynous." Yet, it is likely that an androgynous person would feel very uncomfortable indeed (and be viewed as foolhardy or maladjusted) if he or she were a citizen of a conservative Islamic society or any other culture in which the public expression of "cross-sex" attitudes and behaviors is not sanctioned and is apt to be punished.

Recently, Bem (1981) has changed her views on androgyny. She now argues that the adaptability shown by androgynous people stems not so much from having incorporated both masculine and feminine traits as from being relatively unconstrained by the implications of sex-role stereotypes. In fact, Bem believes that androgynous people are neither "masculine" nor "feminine" (or both) but, instead, are **gender aschematic.** Unlike sex-typed persons (or "gender schematics"), who have defined various beliefs, values, mannerisms, and behaviors as "appropriate" or "inappropriate" for members of their sex, gender-aschematic persons rarely think about sex-related labels or prescriptions when pursuing an interest, picking a friend, or deciding how to behave in any given situation. In short, they are free of the restrictions of gender—a state of affairs that Bem (1975) has suggested will someday come to define "a new and more human standard of psychological health."

Other theorists are not so sure that society would ever consider gender totally irrelevant or would define someone who does as a model of psychological well-being. Aletha Huston (1983) suggests that gender can never be totally irrelevant to children's social and personality development, the reason being that only females can bear children and that this biological "fact of life" has clear implications for many aspects of men's and women's lives. One problem with strong and largely untested pronouncements such as Bem's is that they could lead to a significant decline in interest in sex typing and gender-related issues—a possibility that Huston thinks undesirable in that we are only beginning to understand how genetic, hormonal, and other biological variables may affect the behavior of males and females. At the risk of sounding stodgy and conservative to some, I too think it important to continue to study sex typing and to seek a better understanding of why males and females behave as they do. Nevertheless, provocative viewpoints such as Bem's can serve a most useful function by helping "to guide the field in directions that challenge old theories and assumptions and to produce research findings with real social importance" (Huston, 1983, p. 45).

Summary

Males and females differ in several respects. Some sex differences are biological in origin, whereas others stem from socialization pressures. Interests, activities, and attributes that are considered more appropriate for members of one sex than the other are called sex-role standards (or sex-role stereotypes). Sex typing is the process by which children acquire a gender identity and assimilate the motives, values, and behaviors considered appropriate in their culture for members of their biological sex.

Some sex-role stereotypes are more accurate than others. Males tend to be more active and aggressive than females and to outperform them on tests of spatial abilities and arithmetic reasoning; females are less irritable and demanding than males, more compliant with parents' requests, and somewhat more responsive to infants, and they tend to outperform males on tests of verbal abilities. But on the whole, males and females are more similar than they are different. Among the stereotypes that have *no* basis in fact are the notions that females are more sociable, suggestible, and illogical and less analytical and achievement-oriented than males. The persistence of these "cultural myths" is particularly damaging to women. For example, members of both sexes tend to devalue women's accomplishments by attributing them to luck or hard work rather than competence. This tendency to degrade the achievements of females is well established among boys and girls by middle childhood.

Sex typing begins very early. By age 2½, most children know whether they are boys or girls, they tend to favor sex-typed toys and activities, and they are already aware of several sex-role stereotypes. By the time they enter school (or shortly thereafter), they know that gender is an unchanging aspect of their personalities, and they have learned most of the sex-role standards of their society. Boys face stronger sex-typing pressures than girls do, and consequently males are quicker to develop a preference for sex-appropriate patterns of behavior.

Several theories have been proposed to account for sex differences and the sex-typing process. Money and Ehrhardt's biosocial theory emphasizes the biological developments that occur before a child is born—developments that parents and other social agents will react to when deciding how to socialize the child. Other theorists have focused more intently on the so-

---

gender aschematic: a person who rarely thinks about sex-related labels or prescriptions when deciding how to respond to persons, events, or situations.

cialization process itself. Psychoanalytic theorists suggest that sex typing is one result of the child's identification with the same-sex parent. Social-learning theorists offer two mechanisms to explain how children acquire sex-typed attitudes and behaviors: (1) direct tuition (reinforcement for sex-appropriate behaviors and punishment for sex-inappropriate ones) and (2) observational learning. Cognitive-developmental theorists point out that the course of sex-role development will depend, in part, on the child's cognitive development. And proponents of gender schema theory have shown how children's emerging conceptions of sex-role stereotypes color their interpretations of social events and contribute to the development of sex-typed interests, attitudes, and patterns of behavior.

As Freud had thought, infants are sexual beings from the start, reacting physiologically to genital stimulation even though they have no awareness that their responses are "sexual" ones. Moreover, Freud's portrayal of preschool children as sexually curious beings was also correct, although he was very wrong in assuming that school-age children had repressed their sexual urges; in fact, sexual activity actually increases rather than declines during Freud's so-called latency period. Sexual matters become very important to adolescents, who, having reached sexual maturity, must incorporate their sexuality into their changing self-concepts. During this century, sexual attitudes have become much more permissive. The belief that premarital sex is immoral has given way to the view that sex with affection is acceptable; the double standard has weakened; and conflicting norms have increased confusion about what constitutes acceptable sexual conduct. Sexual behavior has increased as well, as more adolescents are engaging in various forms of sexual activity at earlier ages than in the past. Changes among adolescent females have been particularly marked, although females continue to be more ambivalent about their sexual involvement than males are.

The psychological attributes "masculinity" and "femininity" are generally considered to be at opposite ends of a single dimension. However, one "new look" at sex roles proposes that masculinity and femininity are two separate dimensions and that the *androgynous* person is someone who possesses a fair number of masculine *and* feminine characteristics. Recent research shows that androgynous people do exist, are relatively popular and well adjusted, and may be adaptable to a wider variety of environmental demands than people who are traditionally sex-typed.

References

AMERICAN COUNCIL ON EDUCATION. (1981, February). More college women pursue traditionally male careers. *Higher Education and National Affairs*, p. 4.

BAKWIN, H. (1973). Erotic feelings in infants and young children. *American Journal of Diseases of Children, 126*, 52–54.

BANDURA, A. (1977). *Social learning theory*. Englewood Cliffs, NJ: Prentice-Hall.

BARRY, H., III, Bacon, M. K., & Child, I. L. (1957). A cross-cultural survey of some sex differences in socialization. *Journal of Abnormal and Social Psychology, 55*, 327–332.

BAUMRIND, D. (1982). Are androgynous individuals more effective persons and parents? *Child Development, 53*, 44–75.

BEACH, F. A. (1965). *Sex and behavior*. New York: Wiley.

BELL, R. Q., Weller, G. M., & Waldrip, M. F. (1971). Newborn and preschooler: Organization of behavior and relations between periods. *Monographs of the Society for Research in Child Development, 36*(1–2, Serial No. 142).

BEM, S. L. (1974). The measurement of psychological androgyny. *Journal of Consulting and Clinical Psychology, 42*, 155–162.

BEM, S. L. (1975). Sex-role adaptability: One consequence of psychological androgyny. *Journal of Personality and Social Psychology, 31*, 634–643.

BEM, S. L. (1978). Beyond androgyny: Some presumptuous prescriptions for a liberated sexual identity. In J. A. Sherman & F. L. Denmark (Eds.), *The psychology of women: Future directions in research*. New York: Psychological Dimensions.

BEM, S. L. (1981). Gender schema theory: A cognitive account of sex-typing. *Psychological Bulletin, 88*, 354–364.

BERMAN, P. W. (1985). Young children's responses to babies: Do they foreshadow differences between maternal and paternal styles? In A. Fogel & G. F. Melson (Eds.), *Origins of nurturance*. Hillsdale, NJ: Erlbaum.

BERMAN, P. W., & Goodman, V. (1984). Age and sex differences in children's responses to babies: Effects of adults' care-taking requests and instructions. *Child Development, 55*, 1071–1077.

BEST, D. L., Williams, J. E., Cloud, J. M., Davis, S. W., Robertson, L. S., Edwards, J. R., Giles, H., & Fowlkes, J. (1977). Development of sex-trait stereotypes among young children in the United States, England, and Ireland. *Child Development, 48*, 1375–1384.

BLAKEMORE, J. E. O. (1981). Age and sex differences in interaction with a human infant. *Child Development, 52*, 386–388.

BLAKEMORE, J. E. O., LaRue, A. A., & Olejnik, A. B. (1979). Sex-appropriate toy preference and the ability to conceptualize toys as sex-role related. *Developmental Psychology, 15*, 339–340.

BRADBARD, M. R., Martin, C. L., Endsley, R. C., & Halverson, C. F., Jr. (1986). Influence of sex stereotypes on children's exploration and memory: A competence versus performance distinction. *Developmental Psychology, 22*, 481–486.

BROVERMAN, I. K., Vogel, S. R., Clarkson, F. E., & Rosenkrantz, P. S. (1972). Sex-role stereotypes: A current appraisal. *Journal of Social Issues, 28*, 59–78.

BROWN, D. G. (1957). Masculinity-femininity development in children. *Journal of Consulting Psychology, 21*, 197–202.

BROWN, R. (1965). *Social psychology*. New York: Free Press.

CANN, A., & Newbern, S. R. (1984). Sex stereotype effects in children's picture recognition. *Child Development, 55*, 1085–1090.

CARROLL, J. L., Volk, K. D., & Hyde, J. S. (1985). Differences between males and females in motives for engaging in sexual intercourse. *Archives of Sexual Behavior, 14*, 131–139.

CARTER, D. B., & McCloskey, L. A. (1983–84). Peers and the maintenance of sex-typed behavior: The development of children's conceptions of cross-gender behavior in their peers. *Social Cognition, 2*, 294–314.

CARTER, D. B., & Patterson, C. J. (1982). Sex roles as social conventions: The development of children's conceptions of sex-role stereotypes. *Developmental Psychology, 18*, 812–824.

CHARLESWORTH, R., & Hartup, W. W. (1967). Positive social reinforcement in the nursery school peer group. *Child Development, 38*, 993–1002.

CHARLESWORTH, W. R., & Dzur, C. (1987). Gender comparisons of preschoolers' behavior and resource utilization in group problem solving. *Child Development, 58*, 191–200.

COLES, R., & Stokes, G. (1985). *Sex and the American teenager*. New York: Harper & Row.

CONDRY, J., & Condry, S. (1976). Sex differences: A study in the eye of the beholder. *Child Development, 47*, 812–819.

COWAN, C. P., & Cowan, P. A. (1987). A preventive intervention for couples becoming parents. In C. F. Z. Boukydis (Ed.), *Research on support for parents and infants in the postnatal period*. New York: Ablex.

DAMON, W. (1977). *The social world of the child*. San Francisco: Jossey-Bass.

D'ANDRADE, R. G. (1966). Sex differences and cultural institutions. In E. E. Maccoby (Ed.), *The development of sex differences*. Stanford, CA: Stanford University Press.

DARLING, C. A., Kallen, D. J., & VanDusen, J. E. (1984). Sex in transition, 1900–1980. *Journal of Youth and Adolescence, 13*, 385–399.

DAWSON, D. A. (1986). The effects of sex education on adolescent behavior. *Family Planning Perspectives, 18*, 162–170.

DIENER, E., Sandvik, E., & Larsen, R. J. (1985). Age and sex effects for emotional intensity. *Developmental Psychology, 21*, 542–546.

DiPIETRO, J. A. (1981). Rough and tumble play: A function of gender. *Developmental Psychology, 17*, 50–58.

DOTY, R. L., Carter, C. S., & Clemens, L. G. (1971). Olfactory control of sexual behavior in male and early-androgenized female hamsters. *Hormones and Behavior, 2*, 325–335.

DREYER, P. H. (1982). Sexuality during adolescence. In B. B. Wolman (Ed.), *Handbook of developmental psychology*. New York: Wiley.

DWECK, C. S., Davidson, W., Nelson, S., & Enna, B. (1978). Sex differences in learned helplessness: II. The contingencies of evaluative feedback in the classroom, and III. An experimental analysis. *Developmental Psychology, 14*, 268–276.

DWECK, C. S., & Elliott, E. S. (1983). Achievement motivation. In P. H. Mussen (Ed.), *Handbook of child psychology*. Vol. 4: *Socialization, personality, and social development*. New York: Wiley.

EATON, W. O., & Keats, J. G. (1982). Peer presence, stress, and sex differences in the motor activity levels of preschoolers. *Developmental Psychology, 18*, 534–540.

EATON, W. O., & Von Bargen, D. (1981). Asynchronous development of gender understanding in preschool children. *Child Development, 52*, 1020–1027.

EHRHARDT, A. A., & Baker, S. W. (1974). Fetal androgens, human central nervous system differentiation, and behavioral sex differences. In R. C. Friedman, R. M. Rickard, & R. L. Van de Wiele (Eds.), *Sex differences in behavior*. New York: Wiley.

EISENBERG, N., Murray, E., & Hite, T. (1982). Children's reasoning regarding sex-typed toy choices. *Child Development, 53*, 81–86.

EISENBERG, N., Wolchik, S. A., Hernandez, R., & Pasternack, J. F. (1985). Parental socialization of young children's play: A short-term longitudinal study. *Child Development, 56*, 1506–1513.

EMMERICH, W. (1959). Parental identification in young children. *Genetic Psychology Monographs, 60*, 257–308.

ENTWISLE, D. R., Alexander, K. L., Pallas, A. M., & Cadigan, D. (1987). The emergent academic self-image of first graders: Its response to social structure. *Child Development, 58*, 1190—1206.

ENTWISLE, D. R., & Baker, D. P. (1983). Gender and young children's expectations for performance in arithmetic. *Developmental Psychology, 19*, 200–209.

FAGOT, B. I. (1978). The influence of sex of child on parental reactions to toddler children. *Child Development, 49*, 459–465.

FAGOT, B. I. (1985). Beyond the reinforcement principle: Another step toward understanding sex-role development. *Developmental Psychology, 21*, 1097–1104.

FAGOT, B. I., Leinbach, M. D., & Hagan, R. (1986). Gender labeling and the adoption of sex-typed behaviors. *Developmental Psychology, 22*, 440–443.

FELDMAN, S. S., Biringen, Z. C., & Nash, S. C. (1981). Fluctuations of sex-related self-attributions as a function of stage of family life cycle. *Developmental Psychology, 17*, 24–35.

FELDMAN-SUMMERS, S., & Kiesler, S. B. (1974). Those who are number two try harder: The effect of sex on attribution of causality. *Journal of Personality and Social Psychology, 30*, 846–855.

FORD, C. S., & Beach, F. A. (1951). *Patterns of sexual behavior*. New York: Harper & Row.

FORISHA, B. L., & Goldman, B. H. (1981). *Outsiders on the inside: Women and organizations*. Englewood Cliffs, NJ: Prentice-Hall.

FRUEH, T., & McGhee, P. E. (1975). Traditional sex-role development and the amount of time spent watching television. *Developmental Psychology, 11*, 109.

GINSBURG, H. J., & Miller, S. M. (1982). Sex differences in children's risk-taking behavior. *Child Development, 53*, 426–428.

GOLDBERG, P. (1968). Are women prejudiced against women? *Trans/Action, 5*, 28–30.

GOLDMAN, R., & Goldman, J. (1982). *Children's sexual thinking: A comparative study of children aged 5 to 15 years in Australia, North America, Britain and Sweden*. London: Routledge & Kegan Paul.

GOUZE, K. R., & Nadelman, L. (1980). Constancy of gender identity for self and others in children between the ages of three and seven. *Child Development, 51*, 275–278.

GROTEVANT, H. D. (1978). Sibling constellations and sex-typing of interests in adolescence. *Child Development, 49*, 540–542.

GUNNAR, M. R., & Donahue, M. (1980). Sex differences in social responsiveness between six months and twelve months. *Child Development, 51*, 262–265.

HALL, J. A., & Halberstadt, A. G. (1980). Masculinity and femininity in children: Development of the Children's Personal Attributes Questionnaire. *Developmental Psychology, 16*, 270–280.

HANSSON, R. O., Chernovetz, M. E., & Jones, W. H. (1977). Maternal employment and androgyny. *Psychology of Women Quarterly, 2*, 76–78.

HARTUP, W. W. (1983). The peer system. In P. H. Mussen (Ed.), *Handbook of child psy-*

chology. Vol. 4: *Socialization, personality, and social development*. New York: Wiley.

HAUGH, S. S., Hoffman, C. D., & Cowan, G. (1980). The eye of the very young beholder: Sex-typing of infants by young children. *Child Development, 51*, 598–600.

HETHERINGTON, E. M., (1966). Effects of parental absence on sex-typed behaviors in Negro and white preadolescent males. *Journal of Personality and Social Psychology, 4*, 87–91.

HETHERINGTON, E. M., Cox, M., & Cox, R. (1978). The aftermath of divorce. In J. H. Stevens & M. Matthews (Eds.), *Mother–child, father–child relations*. Washington, DC: National Association for the Education of Young Children.

HETHERINGTON, E. M., & Frankie, G. (1967). Effect of parental dominance, warmth, and conflict on imitation in children. *Journal of Personality and Social Psychology, 6*, 119–125.

HETHERINGTON, E. M., & Parke, R. D. (1975). *Child psychology: A contemporary viewpoint*. New York: McGraw-Hill.

HINES, M. (1982). Prenatal gonadal hormones and sex differences in human behavior. *Psychological Bulletin, 92*, 56–80.

HOFFMAN, L. W. (1984). Work, family, and the socialization of the child. In R. D. Parke (Ed.), *Review of child development research*. Vol. 7: *The family*. Chicago: University of Chicago Press.

HUMPHREYS, A. P., & Smith, P. K. (1987). Rough and tumble, friendship, and dominance in school children: Evidence for continuity and change with age. *Child Development, 58*, 201–212.

HUSTON, A. C. (1983). Sex-typing. In P. H. Mussen (Ed.), *Handbook of child psychology*. Vol. 4: *Socialization, personality, and social development*. New York: Wiley.

HUTT, C. (1972). *Males and females*. Baltimore: Penguin Books.

IMPERATO-McGINLEY, J., Peterson, R. E., Gautier, T., & Sturla, E. (1979). Androgyns and the evolution of male gender identity among male pseudohermaphrodites with 5a-reducase deficiency. *New England Journal of Medicine, 300*, 1233–1237.

INTONS-PETERSON, M. J., & Reddel, M. (1984). What do people ask about a neonate? *Developmental Psychology, 20*, 358–359.

JACKLIN, C. N., & Maccoby, E. E. (1978). Social behavior at 33 months in same-sex and mixed-sex dyads. *Child Development, 49*, 557–569.

JOHNSON, E. S., & Meade, A. C. (1987). Developmental patterns of spatial ability: An

early sex difference. *Child Development, 58*, 725–740.

KAGAN, J., & Moss, H. A. (1962). *Birth to maturity*. New York: Wiley.

KATCHER, A. (1955). The discrimination of sex differences by young children. *Journal of Genetic Psychology, 87*, 131–143.

KINSEY, A. C., Pomeroy, W. B., & Martin, C. E. (1948). *Sexual behavior in the human male*. Philadelphia: Saunders.

KOHLBERG, L. (1966). A cognitive-developmental analysis of children's sex-role concepts and attitudes. In E. E. Maccoby (Ed.), *The development of sex differences*. Stanford, CA: Stanford University Press.

KOLBE, R., & LaVoie, J. C. (1981). Sex-role stereotyping in preschool children's picture books. *Social Psychology Quarterly, 44*, 369–374.

KUHN, D., Nash, S. C., & Brucken, L. (1978). Sex-role concepts of two- and three-year-olds. *Child Development, 49*, 445–451.

La FRENIERE, P., Strayer, F. F., & Gauthier, R. (1984). The emergence of same-sex affiliative preferences among preschool peers: A developmental ethological perspective. *Child Development, 55*, 1958–1965.

LAMB, M. E. (1981). *The role of the father in child development*. New York: Wiley.

LAMKE, L. K. (1982). The impact of sex-role orientation on self-esteem in early adolescence. *Child Development, 53*, 1530–1535.

LANGLOIS, J. H., & Downs, A. C. (1980). Mothers, fathers, and peers as socialization agents of sex-typed play behaviors in young children. *Child Development, 51*, 1237–1247.

LIEBERT, R. M., Sprafkin, J. N., & Davidson, E. S. (1982). *The early window: Effects of television on children and youth*. New York: Pergamon Press.

LINN, M. C., & Petersen, A. C. (1985). Emergence and characterization of sex differences in spatial ability: A meta-analysis. *Child Development, 56*, 1479–1498.

LIVSON, F. B. (1983). Gender identity: A life-span view of sex-role development. In R. B. Weg (Ed.), *Sexuality in the later years: Roles and behavior*. Orlando, FL: Academic Press.

MACCOBY, E. E. (1980). *Social development*. San Diego, CA: Harcourt Brace Jovanovich.

MACCOBY, E. E., & Jacklin, C. N. (1974). *The psychology of sex differences*. Stanford, CA: Stanford University Press.

MACCOBY, E. E., & Jacklin, C. N. (1980). Sex differences in aggression: A rejoinder and reprise. *Child Development, 51*, 964–980.

MacFARLANE, A. (1977). *The psychology of*

childbirth. Cambridge, MA: Harvard University Press.

MacKINNON, C. E., Brody, G. H., & Stoneman, Z. (1982). The effects of divorce and maternal employment on the home environments of preschool children. *Child Development, 53*, 1392–1399.

MAJOR, B., Carnevale, P. J. D., & Deaux, K. (1981). A different perspective on androgyny: Evaluations of masculine and feminine personality characteristics. *Journal of Personality and Social Psychology, 41*, 988–1001.

MARCUS, D. E., & Overton, W. F. (1978). The development of cognitive gender constancy and sex-role preferences. *Child Development, 49*, 434–444.

MARSIGLIO, W., & Mott, F. L. (1986). The impact of sex education on sexual activity, contraceptive use, and premarital pregnancy among American teenagers. *Family Planning Perspectives, 18*, 151–162.

MARTIN, C. L., & Halverson, C. F., Jr. (1981). A schematic processing model of sex typing and stereotyping in children. *Child Development, 52*, 1119–1134.

MARTIN, C. L., & Halverson, C. F., Jr. (1983). The effects of sex-typing schemas on young children's memory. *Child Development, 54*, 563–574.

MARTIN, J. A. (1980). A longitudinal study of the consequences of early mother-infant interaction: A microanalytic approach. *Monographs of the Society for Research in Child Development, 46*(3, Serial No. 190).

MASSAD, C. M. (1981). Sex-role identity and adjustment during adolescence. *Child Development, 52*, 1290–1298.

MASTERS, J. C., Ford, M. E., Arend, R., Grotevant, H. D., & Clark, L. V. (1979). Modeling and labeling as integrated determinants of children's sex-typed imitative behavior. *Child Development, 50*, 364–371.

McCONAGHY, M. J. (1979). Gender permanence and the genital basis of gender: Stages in the development of constancy of gender identity. *Child Development, 50*, 1223–1226.

McGHEE, P. E., & Frueh, T. (1980). Television viewing and the learning of sex-role stereotypes. *Sex Roles, 6*, 179–188.

MEAD, M. (1928). *Coming of age in Samoa*. New York: William Morrow.

MEAD, M. (1935). *Sex and temperament in three primitive societies*. New York: William Morrow.

MEYER, B. (1930). The development of girls' sex-role attitudes. *Child Development, 51*, 508–514.

MILLER, P. M., Danaher, D. L., & Forbes, D.

(1986). Sex-related strategies for coping with interpersonal conflict in children aged five and seven. *Developmental Psychology, 22*, 543–548.

MISCHEL, W. (1970). Sex-typing and socialization. In P. H. Mussen (Ed.), *Carmichael's manual of child psychology* (Vol. 2). New York: Wiley.

MONEY, J. (1965). Psychosexual differentiation. In J. Money (Ed.), *Sex research: New developments*. New York: Holt, Rinehart and Winston.

MONEY, J., & Ehrhardt, A. (1972). *Man and woman, boy and girl*. Baltimore: Johns Hopkins University Press.

MOSS, H. A. (1967). Sex, age, and state as determinants of mother-infant interaction. *Merrill-Palmer Quarterly, 13*, 19–36.

MUNROE, R. H., Shimmin, H. S., & Munroe, R. L. (1984). Gender understanding and sex-role preferences in four cultures. *Developmental Psychology, 20*, 673–682.

MUSSEN, P. H., & Rutherford, E. (1963). Parent-child relations and parental personality in relation to young children's sex-role preferences. *Child Development, 34*, 589–607.

NEWCOMBE, N., & Bandura, M. M. (1983). Effect of age at puberty on spatial ability in girls: A question of mechanism. *Developmental Psychology, 19*, 215–224.

OLWEUS, D., Mattsson, A., Schalling, D., & Low, H. (1980). Testosterone, aggression, physical and personality dimensions in normal adolescent males. *Psychosomatic Medicine, 42*, 253–269.

ORLOFSKY, J. L. (1979). Parental antecedents of sex-role orientation in college men and women. *Sex Roles, 5*, 495–512.

PARSONS, J. E., Adler, T. F., & Kaczala, C. M. (1982). Socialization of achievement attitudes and beliefs: Parental influences. *Child Development, 53*, 310–321.

PARSONS, J. E., Kaczala, C. M., & Meese, J. L. (1982). Socialization of achievement attitudes and beliefs: Classroom influences. *Child Development, 53*, 322–339.

PARSONS, T. (1955). Family structure and the socialization of the child. In T. Parsons & R. F. Bales (Eds.), *Family socialization and interaction processes*. New York: Free Press.

PERRY, D. G., & Bussey, K. (1984). *Social development*. Englewood Cliffs, NJ: Prentice-Hall.

PHILLIPS, D. A. (1987). Socialization of perceived academic competence among highly competent children. *Child Development, 58*, 1308–1320.

PHILLIPS, S., King, S., & Dubois, L. (1978).

Spontaneous activities of female versus male newborns. *Child Development, 49*, 590–597.

POLLIS, N. P., & Doyle, D. C. (1972). Sex role, status, and perceived competence among first-graders. *Perceptual and Motor Skills, 34*, 235–238.

RICHARDSON, J. G., & Simpson, C. H. (1982). Children, gender, and social structure: An analysis of the contents of letters to Santa Claus. *Child Development, 53*, 429–436.

ROBERTS, C. W., Green, R., Williams, K., & Goodman, M. (1987). Boyhood gender identity development: A statistical contrast of two family groups. *Developmental Psychology, 23*, 544–557.

ROBINSON, I. E., & Jedlicka, D. (1982). Change in sexual attitudes and behavior of college students from 1965 to 1980: A research note. *Journal of Marriage and the Family, 44*, 237–240.

ROSE, R. M., Bernstein, I. S., & Gordon, T. P. (1975). Consequences of social conflict on plasma testosterone levels in rhesus monkeys. *Psychosomatic Medicine, 37*, 50–61.

ROSEN, R., & Hall, E. (1984). *Sexuality*. New York: Random House.

ROSENBLATT, P. C., & Cunningham, M. R. (1976). Sex differences in cross-cultural perspective. In B. Lloyd & J. Archer (Eds.), *Exploring sex differences*. London: Academic Press.

RUBLE, D. N., Balaban, T., & Cooper, J. (1981). Gender constancy and the effects of sex-typed televised toy commercials. *Child Development, 52*, 667–673.

RUBLE, T. L. (1983). Sex stereotypes: Issues of change in the 1970s. *Sex Roles, 9*, 397–402.

SANDERS, B., & Soares, M. P. (1986). Sexual maturation and spatial ability in college students. *Developmental Psychology, 22*, 199–203.

SHAFFER, D. R., Gresham, A., Clary, E. G., & Thielman, T. J. (1986). Sex-ratios as a basis for occupational evaluations: A contemporary view. *Social Behavior and Personality, 14*, 77–83.

SHAFFER, D. R., & Johnson, R. D. (1980). Effects of occupational choice and sex-role preferences on the attractiveness of competent men and women. *Journal of Personality, 48*, 505–519.

SLABY, R. G., & Frey, K. S. (1975). Development of gender constancy and selective attention to same-sex models. *Child Development, 46*, 849–856.

SMETANA, J. G. (1986). Preschool children's conceptions of sex-role transgressions. *Child Development, 57*, 862–871.

SMITH, P. K., & Daglish, L. (1977). Sex differences in parent and infant behavior in the home. *Child Development, 48*, 1250–1254.

SNOW, M. E., Jacklin, C. N., & Maccoby, E. E. (1983). Sex-of-child differences in father-child interaction at one year of age. *Child Development, 54*, 227–232.

SPENCE, J. T. (1982). Comment on Baumrind's "Are androgynous individuals more effective persons and parents?" *Child Development, 53*, 76–80.

SPENCE, J. T., & Helmreich, R. L. (1978). *Masculinity and femininity: Their psychological dimensions, correlates, and antecedents*. Austin: University of Texas Press.

STEVENSON, H. W., & Newman, R. S. (1986). Long-term prediction of achievement and attitudes in mathematics and reading. *Child Development, 57*, 646–659.

STIPEK, D. J., & Hoffman, J. M. (1980). Children's achievement related expectancies as a function of academic performance histories and sex. *Journal of Educational Psychology, 72*, 861–865.

STODDART, T., & Turiel, E. (1985). Children's concepts of cross-gender activities. *Child Development, 56*, 1241–1252.

SUSMAN, E. J., Inoff-Germain, G., Nottelman, E. D., Loriaux, D. L., Cutler, G. B., Jr., & Chrousos, G. P. (1987). Hormones, emotional dispositions, and aggressive attributes in young adolescents. *Child Development, 58*, 1114–1134.

SUTTON-SMITH, B., & Rosenberg, B. G. (1970). *The sibling*. New York: Holt, Rinehart and Winston.

TAN, R. S. (1979). TV beauty ads and role expectations of adolescent female viewers. *Journalism Quarterly, 56*, 283–288.

TAUBER, M. A. (1979a). Parental socialization techniques and sex differences in children's play. *Child Development, 50*, 225–234.

TAUBER, M. A. (1979b). Sex differences in parent-child interaction styles during a free-play session. *Child Development, 50*, 981–988.

TERBORG, J. R., & Ilgen, D. R. (1975). A theoretical approach to sex discrimination in traditionally masculine occupations. *Organizational Behavior and Human Performance, 13*, 352–376.

THOMPSON, S. K. (1975). Gender labels and early sex-role development. *Child Development, 46*, 339–347.

THOMPSON, S. K., & Bentler, P. M. (1971). The priority of cues in sex discrimination by children and adults. *Developmental Psychology, 5*, 181–185.

TOLAR, C. J. (1968). An investigation of parent-offspring relationships. *Dissertation Abstracts, 28*(8-B), 3465.

TOUHEY, J. C. (1974). Effects of additional women professionals on ratings of occupational prestige and desirability. *Journal of Personality and Social Psychology, 29*, 86–89.

URBERG, K. A. (1979). Sex-role conceptualization in adolescents and adults. *Developmental Psychology, 15*, 90–92.

WABER, D. P. (1977). Sex differences in mental abilities, hemispheric lateralization, and rate of physical growth at adolescence. *Developmental Psychology, 13*, 29–38.

WEINRAUB, M., Clemens, L. P., Sockloff, A.,

Ethridge, T., Gracely, E., & Myers, B. (1984). The development of sex-role stereotypes in the third year: Relationships to gender labeling, gender identity, sex-typed toy preferences, and family characteristics. *Child Development, 55*, 1493–1503.

WERNER, P. D., & LaRussa, G. W. (1983). *Persistence and change in sex-role stereotypes*. Unpublished manuscript, California School of Professional Psychology.

WHITLEY, B. E., Jr. (1983). Sex-role orientation and self-esteem: A critical meta-analytic review. *Journal of Personality and Social Psychology, 44*, 765–778.

WINKER, R. (1987, July 6). AIDS makes na-

tion's teens more cautious. *Atlanta Journal*, pp. C1–C2.

WITTIG, M. A., & Petersen, A. C. (1979). *Sex-related differences in cognitive functioning: Developmental issues*. Orlando, FL: Academic Press.

YOUNG, W. C., Goy, R. W., & Phoenix, C. H. (1964). Hormones and sexual behavior. *Science, 143*, 212–218.

ZERN, D. S. (1984). Relationships among selected child-rearing variables in a cross-cultural sample of 110 societies. *Developmental Psychology, 20*, 683–690.

14

Aggression, Altruism, and Moral Development

Suppose that a large sample of parents were asked "What is the most important aspect of a child's social development?" Surely this is a question that could elicit any number of responses. However, it's a good bet that many parents would hope above all that their children would acquire a strong sense of morality—right and wrong—to guide their everyday exchanges with other people.

What sort of moral principles and premises do parents and other adults hope to instill? We can get some clues by observing the ways they react to the behavior of young children. For example, adults often spring into action when they observe one child who appears to be harming another. Few parents would stand idly by as their 3-year-old "punches out" a playmate to gain control over a toy the other child is using. Few teachers would fail to comment on the inappropriateness of taunting, teasing, or otherwise insulting a classmate just because he shuns rough-and-tumble games in favor of more solitary activities. So children's unprovoked and intentional acts of harmdoing—or *aggression*—make up one class of behavior that many adults will strive to suppress as they attempt to instill the principle that it is inappropriate and a violation of another person's rights to purposely attempt to harm that person.

Another value that many adults try to impart and hope their children will eventually acquire is *altruism*—that is, a genuine concern for the welfare of other people. In fact, it is not at all unusual to see parents encouraging altruistic acts such as sharing, cooperating, or helping others while their children are still in diapers.

Finally, adults spend a considerable amount of time (1) describing various rules and regulations that children must obey and (2) carefully monitoring children's activities to ensure that these rules are followed (or, alternatively, that rule violations will not pass without comment). At first, parents' attempts to instill these rules of appropriate behavior may take the form of reinforcing praiseworthy conduct and punishing inappropriate acts while explaining why these transgressions are wrong and should be inhibited. Of course, the ultimate goal of this *moral socialization* is to help the child to acquire a set of personal values, or moral principles, that will enable her to monitor her own conduct, distinguishing right from wrong and acting on this distinction, even when there may be no one else present to detect and punish a transgression.

In this chapter, we will explore three interrelated aspects of social development that are often considered when making judgments about a child's ethical or moral character. We will begin with the topic of aggression, asking how it develops and changes over time and then considering some of the ways that parents and teachers might effectively control such conduct. Our focus will then shift from harmdoing to a seemingly incompatible form of social activity—the development of altruism and prosocial behavior—as we consider how young and reputedly selfish children might be persuaded to make personal sacrifices to benefit others. Finally, we will concentrate on the broader issue of moral socialization and moral development as we trace the child's evolution from a seemingly self-indulgent creature who appears to respect no rules to a moral philosopher of sorts who has internalized certain ethical principles to evaluate his own conduct and the behavior of other people.

Let's now turn to the topic of aggression.

The Development of Aggression

Although toddlers and preschool children are often appropriately sociable and cooperative playmates, they may also fight over toys, punch, kick, or tease their companions, or call them names. Why do children behave aggressively? How does aggression change over time? And what can adults do to control these hostile outbursts? These are some of the issues we will consider in the pages that follow.

What Is Aggression?

Before reading further, you may wish to jot down your own definition of *aggression* so you can compare it with the following points of view.

Could aggression be an instinct—a basic component of human nature? Freud thought so (remember the Thanatos), as did ethologist Konrad Lorenz (1966), who argued that human beings (particularly males) are biologically programmed to fight over sources of food, territories, and members of the other sex. Other theorists think of aggression as a particular class of social behavior. For example, Arnold Buss (1961) defines aggression as any response that delivers noxious stimuli to another organism. Note that this *behavioral* definition emphasizes the consequences of the action and ignores the intentions of the actor. A strict interpretation of this viewpoint suggests that klutzy dance partners who inflict pain by stepping on our toes would have to be considered aggressive. Does this seem like an aggressive act to you?

Many people would say no, because dancers usually intend no harm when they step on a partner's toes. Today, researchers generally favor an *intentional* definition of **aggression,** which states that an aggressive act is any form of behavior designed to harm or injure a living being who is motivated to avoid such treatment (Baron & Byrne, 1984). This intentional definition would classify as aggressive all acts in which harm was intended but not done (for example, a violent kick that misses its target) while excluding accidental injuries or activities such as rough-and-tumble play in which participants are enjoying themselves with no harmful intent.

Aggressive acts are often divided into two categories: **hostile aggression** and **instrumental aggression.** If an actor's major goal is to injure a victim, his or her behavior qualifies as hostile aggression. By contrast, instrumental aggression describes those situations in which one person harms another as a means to a nonaggressive end. Clearly, the same overt act could be classified as either hostile or instrumental aggression depending on the circumstances. If a young boy clobbered his sister and then teased her for crying, we might consider this hostile aggression. But these same actions could be labeled instrumentally aggressive (or a mixture of hostile and instrumental aggression) had the boy also grabbed a toy that his sister was using.

Origins of Aggression

Although infants do get angry and may occasionally strike people, it is difficult to think of these actions as having an aggressive intent. Piaget (1952) describes an incident in which he frustrated 7-month-old Laurent by placing his hand in front of an interesting object that Laurent was trying to reach. The boy then smacked Piaget's hand as if to knock it out of the way. Although this looks very much like an example of instrumental aggression, it is unlikely that Laurent intended to frighten or harm his father. Instead, he seems to have been treating his father's hand as a simple obstruction that had to be removed. Even 12- to 15-month-olds will rarely look at each other as they struggle over a toy; their attention is usually riveted on the toy itself, and their goal seems to be to gain possession of the object rather than to intimidate or harm their adversary (see Bronson, 1975; Shantz, 1987).

Near the end of the second year, things begin to change. Dale Hay and Hildy Ross (1982) observed pairs of 20–23-month-olds at play, noting all instances of conflict. Unlike their younger counterparts, these toddlers began most of their tussles by communicating with an opponent (for example, "Mine," "No! Kenny have phone") rather than treating him or her as an inanimate obstacle. As these disputes wore on, they occasionally escalated into incidents of forcible contact—actions that might be interpreted as attempts to intimidate or to force an adversary to withdraw. Although sociable reactions such as sharing were actually more common than these "shows of force," it appears as if the seeds of instrumental aggression may have already been sown by the age of 20–23 months.

Age-Related Changes in the Nature of Aggression

Much of what we know about the aggressive behavior of preschool children comes from two studies. The first is a project conducted by Florence Goodenough (1931), who asked mothers of 2- to 5-year-olds to keep diaries recording each angry outburst displayed by their children, its apparent cause, and its conse-

---

aggression: behavior performed with the intention of harming a living being who is motivated to avoid this treatment.

hostile aggression: aggressive acts for which the actor's major goal is to harm or injure a victim.

instrumental aggression: aggressive acts that are undertaken as a means to a nonaggressive end.

quences. The second is an observational study by Willard Hartup (1974), who analyzed the causes and consequences of aggressive acts that occurred over a five-week period in groups of children aged 4 to 6 and 6 to 7. These studies indicate the following:

1. Unfocused temper tantrums diminish during the preschool period and are uncommon after age 4. However, the "total" amount of aggression that children display "increases" over the preschool period, "peaking" at about age 4.

2. The tendency to retaliate in response to attack or frustration increases dramatically for children over age 3.

3. *The primary instigators of aggression vary with the age of the child.* At age 2–3 children are most often aggressive after parents have thwarted or angered them by exerting authority; older children are much more likely to aggress after conflicts with siblings or peers.

4. The form of aggression also changes over time. Children aged 2 or 3 are likely to hit or kick an adversary. Most of the squabbles among youngsters of this age concern toys and other possessions, so that their aggression is usually *instrumental* in character. Older nursery-schoolers (and young grade school children) show less and less physical aggression as they choose instead to tease, taunt, tattle, and call their victims uncomplimentary names. Although older children continue to fight over objects, an increasing percentage of their aggressive outbursts are hostile in character—designed primarily to harm another person.

Why are aggressive exchanges less common among 5-year-olds than 3- and 4-year-olds? One reason may be that parents and teachers are actively preparing older nursery-schoolers for kindergarten by refusing to tolerate aggressive acts and encouraging alternative responses such as cooperation and sharing (Emmerich, 1966). Of course, older children may have also learned from their own experiences that negotiation can be a relatively painless and efficient method of achieving the same objectives that they used to attempt through a show of force (Shantz, 1987).

Although the overall incidence of aggression declines with age, hostile aggression shows a slight increase. Hartup (1974) attributes this finding to the fact that older children (particularly grade school children) are acquiring the role-taking skills that enable them to infer the intentions of other people and to retaliate when they believe that someone means to hurt them. "To the extent that hostile aggression is dependent upon attributions about [the aggressive *intent* of another person], this type of aggression should be less evident in younger than in older children" (p. 338).

Research on children's perceptions of aggressive intent is generally consistent with Hartup's point of

Photo 14-1. As children mature, an increasing percentage of their aggressive acts qualify as examples of hostile aggression.

view. Although 3–5-year-olds may recognize that intentional harmdoing is "naughtier" than accidental or unforeseeable harmdoing (Nelson-LeGall, 1985), they are less proficient than older children at inferring an actor's hostile intentions. In one study (Dodge, Murphy, & Buchsbaum, 1984), kindergartners, second-graders, and fourth-graders were asked to judge the intentions of a child who had destroyed a peer's tower of blocks accidentally or while portraying either a hostile or a prosocial intent (that is, while trying to help clean up the room). The results were clear: kindergartners correctly discriminated the actor's true intentions less than half the time (42%). Second-graders were more accurate (57% correct), though not nearly as skilled at detecting intentional cues as the fourth-graders (72% correct).

Recently, Kenneth Dodge (1980, 1986) has argued that highly aggressive children may be highly aggressive because they often misread others' behavior and will overattribute hostile intentions to their peers. In Box 14-1 we will consider Dodge's intriguing ideas and see why aggressive youngsters are indeed likely to view their playmates as hostile adversaries who deserve to be dealt with in a forcible manner.

Is aggression a stable attribute?

We've seen that the kinds of aggression that children display will change over time. But what about aggressive dispositions? Do aggressive preschoolers remain highly aggressive throughout the grade school years, during adolescence, and as young adults?

Apparently aggression is a reasonably stable attribute from the preschool period through early adolescence. Not only are highly aggressive 3-year-olds likely to become aggressive 5-year-olds (Emmerich, 1966), but the amount of physical and verbal aggression that a child displays at ages 6 to 10 is a fairly good predictor of his or her tendency to threaten, insult, tease, and compete with peers at ages 10 to 14 (Kagan & Moss, 1962; Olweus, 1980).

On the basis of one longitudinal study of fewer than 100 individuals (Kagan & Moss, 1962), it has long been assumed that the stability of aggression from childhood to adulthood is much greater for males than for females. However, later research has questioned this assertion. Rowell Huesmann and his associates (Huesmann, Eron, Lefkowitz, & Walder, 1984) tracked one sample of 600 subjects for 22 years and found, for both males and females, that childhood measures of aggression at age 8 were solid predictors of adult aggression

at age 30 (as indexed by criminal behavior, spouse abuse, and self-reported physical aggression). Moreover, Avshalom Caspi and his colleagues (Caspi, Elder, & Bem, 1987) recently found that both boys and girls who had been moody, aggressive, and ill-tempered at age 10 tended to be ill-tempered young adults whose relations with their spouses and children were generally unpleasant and conflictual. So it seems that there is some continuity to the aggressive dispositions of female subjects after all.

Of course, these findings reflect group trends and do not necessarily imply that a highly aggressive individual cannot become relatively nonaggressive over time, or vice versa. Yet, we should not be surprised to find that aggression is a reasonably stable attribute for many children. Shortly we will see how some home settings can serve as early "training grounds" for the development of aggressive habits. And when a child who has learned to react aggressively to conflicts at home later faces similar problems at school, he may try his forceful tactics on classmates, thereby inviting counterattacks, which lead the child to assume that peers are hostile toward him. Before long, this child may find himself in the vicious cycle described in Box 14-1—a pattern that seems likely to perpetuate his aggressive inclinations.

Sex differences in aggression

Although aggression is a reasonably stable attribute for members of each sex, we noted in Chapter 13 that males seem to be more aggressive than females. Data from more than 100 studies conducted in countries all over the world reveal that boys and men are not only more physically aggressive than girls and women but more verbally aggressive as well (Maccoby & Jacklin, 1974, 1980; Tieger, 1980). Moreover, sex differences in aggression are detectable by age 2 to 2½, when children first begin to behave in ways that fit our definitions of aggression, and they are more apparent in naturalistic (that is, real-world) contexts than in contrived laboratory settings (Hyde, 1984; Maccoby & Jacklin, 1980).[1] The probability of becoming a *target* of aggression also depends on one's sex: even young children will reduce

[1]There are situations, however, in which females will approach or even equal males in aggression. For example, when they believe that no one will detect their actions, or when acting as part of a group where it is possible to diffuse personal responsibility for harmdoing among all who are present, females are just as aggressive as males (see Parke & Slaby, 1983).

Box 14-1
"You Did So Mean It!"
Attributional Biases of Highly
Aggressive Children

Kenneth Dodge (1980, 1986) has proposed a social-cognitive theory of aggression that makes a very basic assumption: a child's response to harmdoing depends not so much on the amount or kind of objective harm done as on the child's *own interpretation* of the situation and the harmdoer's intentions. Dodge suggests that every child has a data base of past experiences in which he or she has been the object of harmdoing. Presumably, these *"memory stores"* will affect the ways in which children process and interpret information about harmful acts and decide how to respond to them. Now let's suppose that a child has been harmed under ambiguous circumstances—for example, he has just been hit hard from behind by a ball as he walks across the playground. Is this harm likely to be interpreted as intentional and provoke some kind of aggressive retaliation? The answer may depend very critically on whether the victim has a reputation as an aggressive child.

According to Dodge (1986), highly aggressive children who have a history of bickering and fighting with peers are apt to carry in memory an expectancy that "other children are often hostile to me." Thus, whenever aggressive youngsters are harmed, they will be predisposed to search for social cues compatible with that expectancy. Should they then experience truly *ambiguous* harmdoing (such as being hit from behind by a ball), aggressive children should be more likely than nonaggressive ones to overattribute hostile intent to the harmdoer, which will predispose them to respond aggressively. The child's aggressive reaction may then trigger counteraggression from the harmdoing peer, which, as we see in the figure, should reinforce the aggressive child's impression that peers are hostile, thus starting the vicious cycle all over again.

Tests of the cue-distortion hypothesis. Do aggressive youngsters really distort ambiguous information about harmdoing? Are they more likely than nonaggressive children to interpret such information as implying a hostile intent? To test these hypotheses, Dodge (1980) had highly aggressive and nonaggressive boys from the second, fourth, and sixth grades each work on a jigsaw puzzle in one room while a peer worked on a similar puzzle in a second room. During a break when the boys had switched rooms to check on each other's progress, the subject heard a voice on the intercom. The voice (supposedly that of the peer who was examining the subject's puzzle) then expressed either a *hostile* intent ("Gee, he's got a lot done—I'll mess it up"), a *benign* intent ("I'll help him—Oh, no, I didn't mean to drop it"), or an *ambiguous* intent ("Gee, he's got a lot done") just before a loud crash (presumably the subject's puzzle being scattered). How did the subjects respond? Dodge found that both aggressive and nonaggressive boys reacted much more aggressively (as measured by disassembling the harmdoer's puzzle or making verbal threats) to a hostile intent than to a benign intent. So aggressive boys did not distort social cues when the harmdoer's intentions were obvious. But when the peer's intent was ambiguous, cue distortion was apparent: aggressive boys often retaliated as if the peer had acted with a hostile intent, whereas nonaggressive boys typically did nothing or said something positive, as if the peer's intentions were honorable ones. Later research indicates that highly aggressive girls distort cues about ambiguous harmdoing in roughly the same way that aggressive boys do (Dodge, Murphy, & Buchsbaum, 1984). Moreover, this kind of cue distortion is particularly strong when the aggressive child has reason to believe that the harmdoing peer just might be in a bad mood (Dodge & Somberg, 1987).

Are the expectancies of aggressive children valid ones? As it turns out, aggressive youngsters may have some very good reasons for attributing hostile intentions to their peers: not only do aggressive children provoke a large number of conflicts, but they are also more likely than nonaggressive children to be disliked (Shantz, 1986) and to become targets of aggression (Dodge & Frame, 1982). In fact, *nonaggressive* children who are harmed under ambiguous circumstances are much more likely to retaliate *if the harmdoer has a reputation as an aggressive child* (Dodge & Frame, 1982). So by virtue of their own hostile inclinations, highly aggressive children ensure that they will often be attacked by their peers.

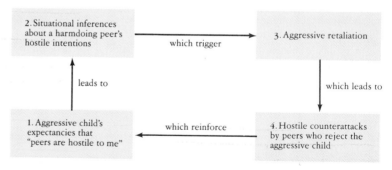

A social-cognitive model of the aggressive child's biased attributions about harmdoing and their behavioral outcomes.

the intensity of their attacks on an adversary if that person is a female (Barrett, 1979).

In Chapter 13 we explored how hormonal and other biological differences between males and females might contribute to sex differences in aggression. Yet, we also saw that biology is not destiny and that social influences seem to combine or interact with biological predispositions to shape the aggressive inclinations of both boys and girls. Let's now consider two important "social" influences on aggression: (1) the norms and values endorsed by one's society and (2) the family settings in which children are raised.

Cultural Influences

Cross-cultural studies consistently indicate that some societies (or subcultures) are more violent and aggressive than others. In the United States and Canada, religious sects such as the Amish, the Mennonites, and the Hutterites advocate cooperation and sharing while strongly discouraging aggressive behavior. Peoples such as the Arapesh of New Guinea, the Lepcha of Sikkim, and the Pygmies of the central Congo all use weapons to procure food but rarely show any kind of interpersonal aggression. When these peace-loving societies are invaded by outsiders, their members will retreat to inaccessible regions rather than stand and fight (Gorer, 1968).

In marked contrast to these groups is the Ik tribe of Uganda, whose members live in small bands and will steal from, deceive, or even kill one another in order to ensure their own survival (Turnbull, 1972). Another aggressive society is the Mundugumor of eastern New Guinea, who teach their children to be independent, combative, and emotionally unresponsive to the needs of others (Mead, 1935). These are values that serve the Mundugumor well, for during some periods of their history, the Mundugumor were cannibals who routinely killed human beings as prey and considered almost anyone other than close kinfolk to be fair game. The United States is also an aggressive society. On a percentage basis, the incidence of rape, assault, robbery, and homicide is higher in the United States than in any other stable democracy (National Commission on the Causes and Prevention of Violence, 1969).

In sum, a person's tendency toward violence and aggression will depend, in part, on the extent to which his or her society condones such behavior. Yet, not all people in pacifistic societies are kind, coopera-

tive, and helpful, nor are all members of aggressive societies prone to violence. One reason that there are dramatic individual differences in aggression within any society is that individual children are raised in very different families. In our next section, we will see how the home can sometimes serve as a breeding ground for aggression.

Familial Influences

How might one's family and the family setting contribute to violent, aggressive behavior? In the pages that follow, we will consider two interrelated avenues of influence: (1) the effects of particular child-rearing practices and (2) the more global impact of the family environment on children's aggressive inclinations.

Parental child-rearing practices and children's aggressive behavior

When investigators began to study the development of aggression, they operated under the assumption that parents' attitudes and child-rearing strategies play a major role in shaping children's aggressive behavior. Clearly, there is some truth to this assertion. One of the most reliable findings in the child-rearing literature is that *cold and rejecting* parents who *apply physical punishment in an erratic fashion and often permit their child to express aggressive impulses* are likely to raise hostile, aggressive children (Eron, 1982; Olweus, 1980; Parke & Slaby, 1983). Surely these findings make good sense. Cold and rejecting parents are frustrating their children's emotional needs and modeling a lack of concern for others by virtue of their aloofness. By ignoring many of the child's aggressive outbursts, a permissive parent is legitimizing combative activities and failing to provide many opportunities for the child to control his or her aggressive urges. And when aggression escalates to the point that a permissive parent steps in and spanks the child, the adult is serving as a model for the very behavior (aggression) that he or she is trying to suppress. So it is hardly surprising to find that parents who rely on physical punishment to discipline aggression have children who are highly aggressive outside the home setting in which the punishment normally occurs (Eron, 1982; Sears, Maccoby, & Levin, 1957). A child who learns that she will be hit when she displeases her parents will probably direct the same kind of response toward playmates who displease her.

Can the child be influencing the parent? Although parental attitudes and child-rearing practices certainly contribute to children's aggression, the stream of influence may also flow in the opposite direction, from child to parent. In Dan Olweus's (1980) child-rearing study, the best predictor of aggression among young adolescent males was their mothers' permissiveness toward, or willingness to tolerate, the boys' aggressive behavior earlier in childhood. However, the next-best predictor was not a child-rearing variable at all but, rather, a childhood measure of the boys' own temperamental impulsivity (highly active, impulsive boys tended to be the most aggressive). According to Olweus, a boy with a particularly active and impetuous temperament may simply "exhaust his mother, resulting in her becoming more permissive of aggression, which, in turn, may be conducive to a higher level of aggression in the boy" (p. 658). And should the impetuous child really anger his mother so that she can no longer ignore his conduct, she may express her negative feelings openly or resort to physical punishment as a means of altering his behavior. The implication, then, is that children have a hand in creating the very child-rearing environments that will influence their aggressive inclinations (see also Anderson, Lytton, & Romney, 1986).

Parents as managers. Another way that parents may indirectly influence their children's aggression is through their management and monitoring of the child's whereabouts, activities, and choice of friends. Gerald Patterson and Magda Stouthamer-Loeber (1984) find that *lack* of parental monitoring is consistently associated with aggressive or delinquent adolescent behaviors such as fighting with peers, sassing teachers, destruction of property, and general rulebreaking outside the house. They note that "parents of delinquents are indifferent trackers of their sons' whereabouts, the kinds of companions they keep, and the type of activities in which they engage" and that this lack of monitoring may constitute an operational definition of the "unattached parent" (p. 1305).

However, not all parents who fail to monitor their children can be described as uncaring or unconcerned. For example, Sanford Dornbusch and his associates (1985) found that heads of *mother only* households have a particularly difficult time managing the activities of their adolescent sons or daughters without the support of a spouse or some other adult in the home (see also Steinberg, 1987). And given the relation between lack of parental monitoring and deviant adolescent behavior in their own and other studies, Dornbusch et al. concluded that "raising . . . adolescents is not a task that can easily be borne by a mother alone" (p. 340).

In sum, parental awareness of and control over a child's activities may be just as important in determining a child's or an adolescent's aggressive inclinations as the particular child-rearing practices that parents have used. Moreover, Dornbusch's finding that the structure of the family affects parental monitoring suggests another interesting conclusion: to understand how aggression develops in the home setting, one must think of the family as a *social system* in which interactions among all family members (or the lack thereof) will affect the child's developmental outcomes. We will see just how true this conclusion is in the next section.

The home as a breeding ground for aggression

Gerald Patterson (1976, 1982) has observed patterns of interaction among children and their parents in families that have at least one highly aggressive child. The aggressive children in Patterson's sample fought a lot at home and at school and were generally unruly and defiant. These families were then compared with other families of the same size and socioeconomic status that had no problem children.

Patterson found that his problem children were growing up in very atypical family environments in which little if any affection is displayed and family members are constantly struggling with each other. He called these settings **coercive home environments** because a high percentage of social interactions centered on one family member's attempts to force another to stop irritating him or her. Patterson also noted that **negative reinforcement** was important in maintaining these coercive interactions: when one family member is making life unpleasant for another, the second will learn to whine, yell, scream, tease, or hit because these actions often force the antagonist to stop (and thus are reinforced). Consider the following sequence of events, which may be fairly typical in families with problem children:

1. A girl teases her older brother, who makes her stop teasing by yelling at her (yelling is negatively reinforced).
2. A few minutes later, the girl calls her brother a nasty name. The boy then chases and hits her.
3. The girl stops calling him names (which negatively reinforces hitting). She then whimpers and hits him

back, and he withdraws (negatively reinforcing her hits). The boy then approaches and hits his sister again, and the conflict escalates.

4. At this point the mother intervenes. However, her children are too emotionally disrupted to listen to reason, so she finds herself applying punitive and coercive tactics to make them stop fighting.

5. The fighting stops (thus reinforcing the mother for using punitive methods). However, the children now begin to whine, cry, or yell at the mother. These countercoercive techniques are then reinforced if the mother backs off and accepts peace at any price. Unfortunately, backing off is only a temporary solution. The next time the children antagonize each other and become involved in an unbearable conflict, the mother is likely to use even more coercion to get them to stop. The children once again apply their own methods of countercoercion to induce her to "lay off," and the family atmosphere becomes increasingly unpleasant for everyone.

Patterson finds that mothers of problem children rarely use social reinforcement or approval as a means of behavior control, choosing instead to rely almost exclusively on coercive tactics. And ironically, children who live in these highly coercive family settings eventually become resistant to punishment. They have learned to fight coercion with countercoercion and will often do so by defying the parent and repeating the very act that she is trying to suppress. Why? Because this is one of the few ways that the child can be successful at commanding the attention of an adult who rarely offers praise or shows any signs of affection. By contrast, children from noncoercive families are apt to receive much more positive attention from siblings and parents, so that they don't have to irritate other family members to be noticed. Moreover, parents from noncoercive families are more successful when they punish a child's undesirable behavior because they stand firm and will not "cave in" to countercoercion (Patterson, 1982).

So we see that the flow of influence in the family setting is *multidirectional:* coercive interactions between parents and their children and the children themselves will affect the behavior of all parties and may contribute to the development of a hostile family environment—a true breeding ground for aggression. Unfortunately, these problem families may never break out of this destructive pattern of attacking and counterattacking one another unless they receive help. In Box 14-2 we will look at one particularly effective approach

to this problem—a method that necessarily focuses on the family as a social system rather than simply concentrating on the aggressive child who has been referred for treatment.

Another possible contributor to children's aggression is the violence and destruction that they see at home while watching television. We will return to this point when we consider children's reactions to the mass media in Chapter 16.

Methods of Controlling Aggression

How might parents and teachers effectively control the aggressive antics of young children so that combative approaches to conflict do not become habitual? Over the years, a variety of solutions have been offered, including coaching strategies, the incompatible-response technique, use of the time-out procedure to punish aggressive behavior, the creation of nonaggressive play environments, and the suggestion that children be trained to empathize with the victims of aggression. But few solutions have been so highly touted as the recommendation that we offer children harmless ways to express their anger or frustrations. Let's consider this "popular" alternative first.

Catharsis: A dubious strategy

The **catharsis hypothesis** states that angry people who commit aggressive acts will "drain away" their hostile, aggressive impulses (that is, experience catharsis) and become less likely to commit another act of aggression in the near future. Freud, a proponent of this idea (for which he credited Aristotle), believed that people should be encouraged to express their aggressive urges every now and then before they build to dangerous levels and trigger a truly violent or destructive outburst. The implications of this viewpoint are clear: Presumably we could teach children to vent their anger or frustrations on inanimate objects such as Bobo dolls. In so doing, the angry child should experience catharsis

---

coercive home environment: a home in which family members often annoy one another and use aggressive tactics as a method of coping with these aversive experiences.

negative reinforcer: any stimulus whose removal or termination as the consequence of an act will increase the probability that the act will recur.

catharsis hypothesis: the notion that aggressive urges are reduced when people commit aggressive acts.

Box 14-2
**Helping Children (and Parents)
Who Are "Out of Control"**

How does one treat a problem child who is hostile, defiant, and "out of control"? Rather than focusing on the problem child, Gerald Patterson's (1976, 1982) approach is to work with the entire family. Patterson begins by carefully observing the family's interactions and determining just how family members are reinforcing one another's coercive activities. The next step is to describe the nature of the problem to parents and to teach them a new approach to managing their children's behavior. Some of the principles, skills, and procedures that Patterson stresses are the following:

1. Don't give in to the child's coercive behavior.
2. Don't escalate your own coercion when the child becomes coercive.
3. Control the child's coercion with the *time out* procedure—a method of punishment in which the child is sent to her room (or some other location) until she calms down and stops using coercive tactics.
4. Identify those of the child's behaviors that are most irritating and then establish a point system in which the child can earn credits (rewards, privileges) for acceptable conduct or lose them for unacceptable behavior. Parents with older problem children are taught how to formulate "behavioral contracts" that specify how the child is expected to behave at home and at school, as well as how deviations from this behavioral code will be punished. Whenever possible, children should have a say in negotiating these contracts.
5. Be on the lookout for occasions when you can respond to the child's prosocial conduct with warmth and affection. Although this is often difficult for parents who are accustomed to snapping at their children and accentuating the negative, Patterson believes that parental affection and approval will reinforce good conduct and eventually elicit displays of affection from the child—a clear sign that the family is on the road to recovery.

A clear majority of problem families respond quite favorably to these methods. Not only do problem children become less coercive, defiant, and aggressive, but the mother's depression fades as she gradually begins to feel better about herself, her child, and her ability to resolve family crises (Patterson, 1981). Some problem families show an immediate improvement. Others respond more gradually to the treatment and may require periodic "booster shots"—that is, follow-up treatments in which the clinician visits the family, determines why progress has slowed (or broken down), and then retrains the parents or suggests new procedures to correct the problems that are not being resolved. Clearly, this therapy works because it recognizes that "out of control" behavior stems from a *family system* in which both parents and children are influencing each other and contributing to the development of a hostile family environment. Therapies that focus exclusively on the problem child are not enough!

---

and become less likely to commit aggressive acts against other people.

Popular as this **cathartic technique** has been, it does *not* work and *may even backfire*. In one study (Walters & Brown, 1963), children who had been encouraged to slap, punch, and kick an inflatable Bobo doll were found to be much more aggressive in their later interactions with peers than were classmates who had not had an opportunity to beat on the doll. Other investigators have noted that children who are first angered by a peer and then given an opportunity to aggress against an inanimate object became no less aggressive toward the peer who had angered them in the first place (Mallick & McCandless, 1966). So cathartic techniques do not reduce children's aggressive urges. In fact, they may teach youngsters that hitting and kicking are acceptable methods of expressing their anger or frustrations.

Eliminating the payoffs for aggression

It is possible to reduce aggression by identifying and then eliminating its reinforcing consequences.

However, this approach is not as simple as it sounds, for the reinforcers that sustain aggressive acts are often very subtle. Suppose, for example, that 5-year-old Lennie wrests an attractive toy away from his 3-year-old sister, Debbie, causing her to cry. If Lennie's reward is control of the toy, his mother could teach Lennie that aggression doesn't pay by simply returning the toy to Debbie and denying him his objective. Unfortunately, this strategy wouldn't always work. If Lennie is an insecure child who feels neglected, he may well have attacked his sister *in order to attract his mother's attention*. Ironically, then, the mother would be *reinforcing* Lennie's aggression if she attended to it at all. Yet, we cannot recommend that the mother simply ignore Lennie's aggressive outbursts, for Siegal and Kohn (1959) have shown that children may interpret an adult's nonintervention as tacit approval for their aggressive deeds. So what is an adult to do?

The incompatible-response technique.

One proven method of reducing children's aggression is to ignore their hostile outbursts *while reinforcing acts that are incompatible with aggression*. In a classic study of this **incompatible-response technique,** Paul Brown and Rogers Elliot (1965) instructed nursery school teachers to turn their backs on all but the most severely aggressive exchanges among their pupils. At the same time, they were asked to reward all instances of prosocial behavior, such as sharing toys or playing together cooperatively. Within two weeks this treatment had significantly reduced the incidence of both physical and verbal aggression among the children, and the program was ended. A follow-up treatment given several weeks later brought about further reductions in aggressive behavior. In a second study, Ron Slaby (Slaby & Crowley, 1977) found that merely encouraging children to say nice things about one another produced an increase in prosocial behavior and a corresponding decrease in aggression. Clearly the reinforcement of responses that are incompatible with aggression can inhibit hostile behavior. The beauty of this nonpunitive approach is that it does not reinforce children who seek attention through their hostile acts, it does not make children angry or resentful, and it does not expose them to a punitive or aggressive model. Thus, many of the negative side effects associated with punishment can be avoided.

The "time out" procedure. Obviously parents and teachers cannot rely exclusively on the incompatible-response technique if their children are likely to do serious harm to one another. So how can they inhibit serious acts of harmdoing without "reinforcing" them with their attention? One effective strategy is the **time-out technique,** in which the adult "punishes" by disrupting or otherwise preventing the aggressive antics that the child finds reinforcing (for example, by sending the aggressor to his room until he is ready to cease the hostilities and behave appropriately). Although this approach may generate some resentment, the punitive agent is not physically abusing the child, is not serving as an aggressive model, and is not likely to unwittingly reinforce the child who misbehaves as a means of attracting attention. The time-out procedure is most effective at controlling children's hostilities when the adult in charge also reinforces cooperative or helpful acts that are incompatible with aggression (Parke & Slaby, 1983).

Modeling and coaching strategies

In Box 12-2, we learned that socially skilled behaviors that are incompatible with aggression may also be instilled by modeling or coaching strategies.

When children see a model choose a nonaggressive solution to a conflict or are explicitly coached in the use of nonaggressive methods of problem solving, they become much more inclined to enact similar solutions to their own problems. Indeed, the coaching of effective methods of conflict resolution is particularly useful when working with chronically aggressive children, for these youngsters resort to aggressive tactics because they are not very skilled at generating adequate and amicable solutions for interpersonal problems on their own (Richard & Dodge, 1982).

Creating nonaggressive environments

Another method that adults may use to reduce children's aggression is to create play areas that minimize the likelihood of interpersonal conflict. For example, providing ample space for vigorous play helps to eliminate the kinds of accidental body contacts such as tripping and shoving that often provoke aggressive incidents (Hartup, 1974). Paul Gump (1975) points out that shortages in play materials also contribute to conflicts and aggression. However, additional children can easily be assimilated into a play area without any increase in aggression if the number of slides, swings, and other toys is sufficient to prevent playmates from having to compete for scarce resources (Smith & Connolly, 1980).

Finally, toys that suggest aggressive themes (guns, knives, and so on) are likely to provoke aggressive incidents. In one study, 5- to 8-year-olds who had been encouraged to use aggressive toys in a classroom play session were more likely than those who had played with neutral toys to get into fights in other settings, such as the playground (Feshbach, 1956; see also Turner & Goldsmith, 1976). If our goal is to reduce the incidence of aggression, we may be better off in the long run to advise parents and teachers against making aggressive toys available to young children.

---

cathartic technique: a strategy for reducing aggression by encouraging children to vent their anger or frustrations on inanimate objects.

incompatible-response technique: a nonpunitive method of behavior modification in which adults ignore undesirable conduct while reinforcing acts that are incompatible with these responses.

time-out technique: a strategy in which the disciplinary agent "punishes" a child by disrupting or preventing the prohibited activity that the child seems to enjoy.

Empathy as a deterrent to aggression

Grade school children, adolescents, and adults will normally back off and stop attacking a victim who shows signs of pain or suffering (Baron, 1971; Perry & Bussey, 1977). However, many preschool children and *highly aggressive* grade school boys will continue to attack a suffering victim or one who denies that he has been hurt (Patterson, Littman, & Bricker, 1967; Perry & Perry, 1974). One possible explanation for this seemingly sadistic behavior is that preschoolers and other highly aggressive individuals do not empathize with their victims. In other words, they may not feel bad or suffer themselves when they have harmed another person.

Does **empathy** inhibit aggression? Apparently so. Grade school children who score high in empathy are rated low in aggression by their teachers, whereas classmates who test very low in empathy tend to be more aggressive (Bryant, 1982; Feshbach, 1978). Moreover, Michael Chandler (1973) found that highly aggressive 11–13-year-old delinquents who participated in a ten-week program designed to make them more aware of other people's feelings subsequently became less hostile and aggressive, compared with a second group of delinquents who had not participated in the program (see also Feshbach & Feshbach, 1982, for similar results in an empathy-training program with 9- to 11-year-olds).

In the home setting, parents can foster the development of empathy by modeling empathic concern and by using disciplinary techniques that (1) point out the harmful consequences of the child's aggressive actions while (2) encouraging the child to put himself in the victim's place and imagine how the victim feels. In the next section of the chapter, we will see that parents who rely mainly on these rational, nonpunitive disciplinary techniques tend to raise sympathetic children who seem genuinely concerned about the welfare of others.

Altruism: Development of the Prosocial Self

As we noted in opening this chapter, most adults hope their children will acquire a sense of **altruism**— that is, a genuine concern for the welfare of other people and a willingness to act on that concern. We also noted that many parents are already encouraging altruistic acts such as sharing, cooperating, or helping while their children are still in diapers! Until very recently, experts in child development would have claimed that these well-intentioned adults were wasting their time, for infants and toddlers were thought to be too egocentric to be capable of considering the needs of anyone other than themselves. But in this case the experts were wrong!

Origins of Altruism and Altruistic Concern

Long before children receive any formal moral or religious training, they may act in ways that resemble the prosocial behavior of older people. At 12 months of age, infants are often "sharing" interesting experiences by pointing, and they will occasionally offer toys to their companions (Hay, 1979; Leung & Rheingold, 1981). And by age 18 months, some children are already jumping in and trying to help with household chores such as sweeping, dusting, or setting the table (Rheingold, 1982). Demonstrations of sympathy or compassion are not at all uncommon among young children. Consider the reaction of 21-month-old John to his distressed playmate, Jerry:

> Today Jerry was kind of cranky; he just started . . . bawling and he wouldn't stop. John kept coming over and handing Jerry toys, trying to cheer him up. . . . He'd say things like "Here Jerry," and I said to John "Jerry's sad; he doesn't feel good; he had a shot today." John would look at me with his eyebrows wrinkled together like he really understood that Jerry was crying because he was unhappy. . . . He went over and rubbed Jerry's arm and said "Nice Jerry," and continued to give him toys [Zahn-Waxler, Radke-Yarrow, & King, 1979, pp. 321–322].

Clearly, John was concerned about his little playmate and did what he could to make him feel better.

Although some toddlers will often try to comfort distressed companions, others rarely do. In an attempt to explain these individual differences in compassionate behavior, Carolyn Zahn-Waxler and her associates (1979) asked mothers to keep records of (1) the reactions of their 1½- to 2½-year-olds to the distress of other children and (2) their own reactions when their child had been the cause of that distress. The results of this study were indeed interesting. Mothers of less compassionate toddlers tended to discipline acts of harmdoing with physical restraint ("I just moved him away from the baby"), physical punishment ("I swatted her a good one"), or unexplained prohibitions ("I said 'Stop that'"). By contrast, mothers of highly compassionate toddlers frequently disciplined harmdoing with *affective explanations* that helped the child to see the relation between his or her own acts and the distress they had caused (for example, "You made Doug cry; it's not nice to bite"; "You must never poke anyone's eyes!"). According to Eleanor Maccoby (1980), these affective explanations may be a form of *empathy training*—that is, the mother's scolding will distress the child and simultaneously draw attention to the discomfort of another person. Once children begin to associate their own distress with that of their victims, the foundation for compassionate behavior has been laid. All that the child now needs to learn is that he can eliminate his own conditioned discomfort by relieving the distress of others.

Developmental Trends in Altruism

Although many 2- to 3-year-olds will show some sympathy and compassion toward distressed companions, they are not particularly eager to make self-sacrificial responses, such as sharing a treasured cookie with a peer. Sharing is more likely if the recipient of the child's benevolence has previously shared with him or

Photo 14-2. Preschool children must often be coaxed to share.

her (Levitt, Weber, Clark, & McDonnell, 1985) or if a peer should actively elicit sharing through a request or a threat of some kind, such as "I won't be your friend if you won't gimme some" (Birch & Billman, 1986). But on the whole, acts of *spontaneous* self-sacrifice in the interest of others are relatively infrequent among young preschool children.

Sharing, helping, and other forms of altruism become much more common as children mature (Underwood & Moore, 1982). Observational studies in nursery schools indicate that 2½- to 3½-year-olds are more likely than their older classmates to perform acts of kindness during pretend play. However, 4–6-year-olds perform more *real* helping acts and will rarely "play-act" the role of an altruist (Bar-Tal, Raviv, & Goldberg, 1982). At age 7 to 12, children are even more altruistic and will show a greater variety of other-oriented behavior. In one study (Green & Schneider, 1974), boys from four age groups—5–6, 7–8, 9–10, and 13–14—had opportunities to (1) share candy with classmates who couldn't otherwise receive any, (2) help an experimenter who had accidentally dropped a number of pencils, and (3) volunteer to work on a project that would benefit poor children. As we see in Table 14-1, both sharing and helping increased with age. The one exception was the volunteering to work index: virtually all the boys were willing to sacrifice some of their play time in order to help needy children.

Is altruism a consistent attribute? Although many kinds of prosocial behavior become more common as children mature, we might wonder just how consistent individuals are from situation to situation. Will a child who shares cookies with the boy next door also share his bicycle with a visiting cousin? Will a youngster who refuses to cooperate or to play by the rules of a game later decline to comfort or share with one of her playmates should the opportunity present itself?

Several studies have found that there is a fair degree of consistency in children's prosocial inclinations from situation to situation. Not only are children who help or share in one situation more likely than their nonaltruistic age mates to help or share in other, similar

empathy: the ability to experience the same emotions that someone else is experiencing.

altruism: a concern for the welfare of others that is expressed through prosocial acts such as sharing, cooperating, and helping.

Table 14-1. Altruistic behavior of boys from four age groups.

Altruistic response	Age group			
	5–6	7–8	9–10	13–14
Average number of candy bars shared	1.36 (60%)	1.84 (92%)	2.88 (100%)	4.24 (100%)
Percentage of children who picked up pencils	48	76	100	96
Percentage of children who volunteered to work for needy children	96	92	100	96

Note: Figures in parentheses indicate percentage of children sharing at least one candy bar.

situations (Rushton, 1980), but there is some consistency across different kinds of prosocial activities as well. For example, sympathetic children are more cooperative than their nonsympathetic classmates (Murphy, 1937). And youngsters who have often cared for younger siblings tend to be more generous, helpful, and compassionate than those who have had few if any caregiving responsibilities (Radke-Yarrow, Zahn-Waxler, & Chapman, 1983; Whiting & Whiting, 1975).

Do girls become more altruistic than boys? People often assume that girls are (or will become) relatively generous, compassionate, and helpful, whereas boys, who are encouraged to be more autonomous and self-reliant, will tend to be (or remain) relatively selfish, unsympathetic, and aggressive (see Shigetomi, Hartmann, & Gelfand, 1981; Zarbatany, Hartmann, Gelfand, & Vinciguerra, 1985). However, several recent reviews of the literature (for example, Radke-Yarrow et al., 1983; Rushton, 1980) dispute the notion that girls and women are more altruistic than boys and men. When differences are found, females are likely to be the more helpful sex. However, the vast majority of studies find no sex differences in altruism, and boys are occasionally more helpful than girls on certain measures, such as active rescue behavior.

Does the sex of the person who needs help or comforting affect children's altruism? Apparently so, at least for young children. Rosalind Charlesworth and Willard Hartup (1967) observed the interactions of nursery school children over a five-week period and found that these youngsters generally directed their acts

of kindness to playmates of the same sex. However, the sex of a prospective recipient becomes a less important consideration during the grade school years. In one study (Ladd, Lange, & Stremmel, 1983), kindergartners and first-, third-, and fourth-graders were given an opportunity to help other children complete some schoolwork. Some of these potential recipients clearly needed more help than others. Ladd et al. found that kindergartners and first-graders often disregarded recipients' apparent needs, choosing instead to help children of their own sex. However, this same-sex bias was much less apparent among third- and fourth-graders, who typically based their helping decisions on a recipient's need for help rather than his or her gender.

Training Altruism: Cultural and Social Influences

How do children become concerned (or unconcerned) about the welfare of other people? Perhaps it can be argued that altruism begins at home, for as we've noted, a mother's reactions to harmdoing can influence the amount of compassion that her toddler displays toward distressed companions. Yet, the lessons that a mother is teaching at home may or may not be reinforced by other members of the family, the peer group, or the society in which the child is raised. All these factors must be considered when attempting to specify the reasons that some children are more altruistic than others.

Cultural influences

Cultures clearly differ in their endorsement or encouragement of altruism. In one interesting cross-cultural study, Beatrice and John Whiting (1975) observed the altruistic behavior of 3- to 10-year-olds in six cultures—Kenya, Mexico, the Philippines, Okinawa, India, and the United States. As we see in Table 14-2, the cultures in which children were most altruistic were the less industrialized societies where people tend to live in large families and everyone contributes to the family welfare. The Whitings concluded that children who are assigned important responsibilities, such as producing and processing food or caring for infant brothers and sisters, are likely to develop a cooperative, altruistic orientation at an early age.

Another possible explanation for the very low altruism scores among children from industrialized nations is that many Western societies place a tremendous emphasis on competition and stress individual rather than group goals. By contrast, Native American and Mex-

Table 14-2. Prosocial behavior in six cultures: Percentages of children in each culture who scored above the median altruism score for the cross-cultural sample as a whole

Type of society	Percentage scoring high in altruism
Nonindustrialized	
Kenya	100
Mexico	73
Philippines	63
Industrialized	
Okinawa	29
India	25
United States	8

ican children (and, indeed, children from many nonindustrialized societies) are taught to suppress individualism, to cooperate with others, and to avoid interpersonal conflicts. The impact of these cultural teachings is apparent in a number of contexts. For example, Anne Marie Tietjen (1986) finds that children from a cooperative society in New Guinea typically become less other-oriented and more self-centered in their thinking about prosocial issues once they have spent three years attending Westernized schools. And when children are asked to play games in which partners must cooperate to earn scores high enough to win a prize, Mexican children, who are taught to cooperate, clearly outperform their more competitive Mexican-American and Anglo-American age mates (Kagan & Masden, 1971, 1972). In fact, many 7- to 9-year-old American children are so competitive at these games that they will attempt to lower their partner's outcomes even though they receive no direct benefits for doing so (Kagan & Masden, 1972). Apparently this competitive orientation can be acquired very early and may interfere with prosocial activities such as sharing. In a study of nursery school children, Eldred Rutherford and Paul Mussen (1968) found that boys who were judged highly competitive by their teachers were less likely than other preschoolers to share candy with their two best friends.

Although cultures may differ in the emphasis they place on altruism, most people in most societies endorse the **norm of social responsibility**—a rule of thumb prescribing that one should help others who need help (Krebs, 1970). Let's now consider some of the ways that parents, teachers, and other social agents might persuade young children to adopt this important value and to become more concerned about the welfare of other people.

Reinforcing altruism

Perhaps the most obvious method of promoting altruism among young children is to reward them for their generous or helpful acts. In one study (Fischer, 1963), 4-year-olds were given material reinforcement (bubble gum) or social reinforcement (verbal approval) for sharing marbles with a child they did not know. Material reinforcement produced much more sharing than social reinforcement. Apparently a small amount of praise from an *unfamiliar* experimenter is simply not enough of a reinforcer to elicit self-sacrificing responses from preschool children.

Yet, verbal reinforcement can promote altruistic behavior if it is administered by a warm and charitable person whom children respect and admire (Slaby & Crowley, 1977; Yarrow, Scott, & Waxler, 1973). Perhaps verbal approval is effective under these circumstances because children hope to live up to standards set by a liked and respected person, and praise that accompanies their kindly acts suggests that they are accomplishing that objective.

Another way that adults might subtly reinforce altruism is to structure play activities so that children are likely to discover the benefits of cooperating and helping one another. Indeed, Terry Orlick (1981) finds that preschool children who have been trained to play cooperative games in which they must join forces to achieve various goals are later more cooperative in other contexts (for example, with peers on the playground) than age mates who have spent an equal amount of time playing very similar but individualistic games that do not require cooperation. Orlick also finds that youngsters in his "cooperative activities" program usually became more generous about sharing treats and possessions—even when the peers who would benefit from their acts of kindness were unknown to them. By contrast, children who participated in traditional (individualistic) activities often became stingier with their possessions as the training wore on. So it seems that a program designed to teach children to cooperate not only accomplishes that objective but may also promote completely different forms of altruism, such as sharing. If our goal is to increase our children's prosocial behavior, perhaps we should place a little less emphasis on individual pursuits while trying harder to persuade

---

norm of social responsibility: the principle that we should help others who are in some way dependent on us for assistance.

young children to "pull together" to achieve important objectives.

Practicing and preaching altruism

Social-learning theorists have assumed that adults who encourage altruism and who practice what they preach will affect children in two ways. By practicing altruism, the adult model may induce the child to perform similar acts of kindness. In addition, regular exposure to the model's **altruistic exhortations** provides the child with opportunities to internalize principles such as the norm of social responsibility that should contribute to the development of an altruistic orientation.

When young children observe charitable or helpful models, they generally become more altruistic themselves—particularly if they have established a warm and friendly relationship with these benevolent companions (Rushton, 1980; Yarrow et al., 1973). Moreover, it appears that exposure to an altruistic model can have long-term effects on children's behavior. Elizabeth Midlarsky and James Bryan (1972) found that a model who donated valuable tokens to a charity increased children's willingness to donate candy to the same charity, even though the candy donations were solicited ten days later in a different setting by a person the children had never seen. Other investigators have noted that children who observe charitable models are more generous than those who observe selfish models, even when they are tested *two to four months later* (Rice & Grusec, 1975; Rushton, 1975). Taken together, these findings suggest that encounters with altruistic models promote the development of prosocial habits and altruistic values.

Although most parents encourage their children to be kind, generous, or helpful to others, they don't always practice what they preach. How do children respond to these inconsistencies? Bryan and Walbek (1970) have addressed this issue by exposing grade school children to models who behaved either charitably or selfishly and who preached either charity ("It's good to donate to poor children") or greed ("Why should I give my money to other people?"). When the children were given an opportunity to donate their own valuable resources to charity, the size of their donations was determined by the model's behavior rather than his exhortations. In other words, children who saw a model refuse to donate while preaching charity (or greed) showed a low level of altruism themselves, while those who observed a charitable model who exhorted greed (or charity) gave sizable amounts to charity. These findings have important implications for child rearing: par-

Photo 14-3. Children learn many prosocial responses by observing the behavior of helpful models.

ents would be well advised to back up their verbal exhortations with altruistic deeds if they hope to instill a strong sense of altruistic concern in their children.

Creating an altruistic self-concept

Can we promote altruism by persuading children to think of themselves as generous or helpful individuals? Joan Grusec and Erica Redler (1980) tried to answer this question by first urging 5- and 8-year-olds to (1) donate marbles to poor children, (2) share colored pencils with classmates who hadn't any, and (3) help an experimenter with a dull and repetitive task. Once children had made an initial donation or begun to work on the repetitive task, either they were told that they were "nice" or "helpful" persons (self-concept training condition) or nothing was said (control condition). One to two weeks later, the children were asked by another adult to donate drawings and craft materials to help cheer up sick children at a local hospital.

Grusec and Redler found that self-concept training had a much greater effect on the 8-year-olds than the 5-year-olds. The 8-year-olds who were told that they must be "nice" or "helpful" individuals were more likely than those in the control condition to share their possessions and to make drawings for sick children.

Why was the self-concept training so effective with 8-year-olds but not with 5-year-olds? The research we reviewed in Chapter 12 provides a very strong clue. Recall that 8-year-olds are just beginning to describe the self in psychological terms and to see these "traits" as relatively stable aspects of their character. Thus, when told that they are "nice" or "helpful," older children may incorporate these traitlike attributions into their self-concepts and try to live up to this new self-image by sharing with or helping others.

Cognitive and Affective Contributors to Altruism

In Chapter 12 we saw that children with well-developed role-taking skills appear to be more helpful or charitable than poor role takers because they are better able to infer a companion's needs for assistance or comforting. Moreover, the link between role taking and altruism is quite clear in studies showing that young grade school children who receive training to further their role-taking skills subsequently become more charitable or helpful than age mates who receive no training (see Iannotti, 1978). However, role taking is only one of several abilities that seem to play a part in the development of altruistic behavior. Two other contributors are children's level of **prosocial moral reasoning** and their empathic reactions to the distress of other people.

Prosocial moral reasoning

Recently, researchers have begun to chart the development of children's reasoning about prosocial issues and its relationship to altruistic behavior. For example, Nancy Eisenberg and her colleagues have presented children with stories in which the central character has to decide whether to help or comfort someone when the prosocial act would be personally costly to the helpgiver. The following story illustrates the kinds of dilemmas children were asked to think about (Eisenberg-Berg & Hand, 1979):

> One day a girl named Mary was going to a friend's birthday party. On her way she saw a girl who had fallen down and hurt her leg. The girl asked Mary to go to her house and get her parents so that [they] could come and take her to a doctor. But if Mary did . . . , she would be late to the party and miss the ice-cream, cake, and all the games. What should Mary do?

As illustrated in Table 14-3, reasoning about these prosocial moral dilemmas may progress through as many as five levels between early childhood and adolescence. Notice that preschoolers' responses are frequently *hedonistic:* these youngsters often say that Mary should go to the party so as not to miss out on the goodies. But as children mature, they tend to become increasingly responsive to the needs and wishes of others—so much so that some high school students feel that they could no longer respect themselves were they to ignore the appeal of a person in need in order to pursue their own interests.

Does the level of a child's prosocial moral reasoning predict his or her altruistic inclinations? Yes, indeed! Eisenberg-Berg and Hand (1979) found that preschoolers who had begun to consider the needs of others when responding to the prosocial dilemmas later displayed more *spontaneous* sharing with peers than did their nursery school classmates whose prosocial reasoning was more hedonistic. And in a later study of older subjects, Eisenberg (1983) found that mature moral reasoners among her high school sample might even help someone they *disliked* if that person really needed their assistance, whereas immature moral reasoners were apt to ignore the needs of a person they did not like.

Why are mature moral reasoners so sensitive to the needs of others—even disliked others? Although we don't yet know the answer to this question, it's possible that morally mature individuals experience strong empathic responses to the distress of other people and that these emotional reactions trigger some form of altruistic behavior. In the following section, we will consider what researchers have learned about the relationship between empathy and altruism.

Empathy

Empathy refers to a person's ability to experience the emotions of other people. According to Martin Hoffman (1981), empathy is a universal human response that has a neurological basis and can be either fostered or suppressed by environmental influences. Hoffman believes that empathic arousal will eventually become an important mediator of altruism, a viewpoint shared by Eleanor Maccoby:

---

altruistic exhortations: verbal encouragements to help, comfort, share, or cooperate with others.
prosocial moral reasoning: the thinking that people display when deciding whether to help, share with, or comfort others when these actions could prove costly to themselves.

Table 14-3. Levels of prosocial moral reasoning

Level	Brief description	Age range
1. Hedonistic (self-centered) *pre school + young elem*	Concern is for oneself; helpgiving is most likely when it will in some way benefit the self	Preschool and young elementary school children
2. Needs-oriented *elementary*	Will base helping decisions on the needs of others; not much evidence of sympathy or guilt for not helping at this level	Elementary school children and a few preschoolers
3. Approval-oriented *elementary + some high school*	Concern is for performing altruistic acts that other people see as good or praiseworthy; being good or socially appropriate is important	Elementary school and some high school students
4. Empathic or transitional *high school*	Judgments now include evidence of sympathetic responding, evidence of guilt for failing to respond, and evidence of feeling good for having done the right thing; vague references are made to abstract principles, duties, and values	High school students and some older elementary school children
5. Strongly internalized *small minority of high schoolers*	Justifications for helping are based on strongly internalized values, norms, convictions, and responsibilities; to violate one's internalized principles will now undermine self-respect	A small minority of high school students and virtually no elementary school children

Source: Adapted from Eisenberg, Lennon, & Roth (1983).

With empathic distress the process would work in the following way: A twelve-month-old has cried on hundreds of different occasions and the sound of crying has repeatedly been associated with the child's own distress. And so by a process of [classical conditioning], the sound of crying—anyone's crying—can now evoke feelings of distress . . . and even tears. If the young listener thinks of a way to make the other person stop crying, he or she will feel better. From the standpoint of simple self-interest, then, we should expect children to learn to perform such "altruistic" actions [Maccoby, 1980, p. 347].

Although infants and toddlers do seem to recognize and will often react to the distress of their companions (Zahn-Waxler et al., 1979; see also Box 2-3), their responses are not always helpful ones. In fact, the evidence for a link between empathy and altruism is weak at best for young children, though much stronger for preadolescents, adolescents, and adults (Underwood & Moore, 1982).

One possible explanation for these age trends is that younger children who empathize with a distressed companion may lack the role-taking skills to fully understand and appreciate why they too are feeling distressed. For example, when kindergartners see slides showing a boy becoming depressed after his dog runs away, they usually attribute his sadness to an external cause (the dog's disappearance) rather than to a more "personal" or internal one, such as the boy's longing for his pet (Hughes, Tingle, & Sawin, 1981). And although kindergartners report that they feel sad after seeing the slides, they usually provide egocentric explanations for their empathic arousal (for example, "I might lose my dog"). However, 7–9-year-olds are beginning to associate their own empathic emotions with those of the story character as they put themselves in his place and infer the psychological basis for his sadness (for example, "I'm sad because he's sad . . . because if he really liked the dog, then . . ."). So empathy may become an important mediator of altruism once children become more proficient at inferring others' points of view (role taking) and understanding the causes of their own empathic emotions.

How does empathic arousal mediate altruism? One possibility is that a child's empathic distress causes him to reflect on altruistic lessons he has learned—

lessons such as the Golden Rule, the maxim that one good turn deserves another (reciprocity), or even the knowledge that other people approve of helping behavior. As a result of this reflection, the child is likely to assume some personal *responsibility* for aiding a victim of distress and would now feel guilty were he to callously ignore that obligation (Chapman, Zahn-Waxler, Cooperman, & Iannotti, 1987). Notice that this "felt responsibility" hypothesis may also help to explain why the link between empathy and altruism becomes stronger with age. Since older children are apt to have learned (and internalized) more altruistic principles than younger children, they should have much more to reflect on as they experience empathic distress. Consequently, they should be more likely than younger children to feel responsible for helping a distressed person and to follow through by rendering the necessary assistance.

Who Raises Altruistic Children?

Studies of unusually charitable adults indicate that these "altruists" have enjoyed a warm and affectionate relationship with parents who themselves were highly concerned about the welfare of others. For example, Christians who risked their lives to save Jews from the Nazis during World War II reported that they had had close ties to moralistic parents who always acted in accordance with their ethical principles (London, 1970). Moreover, interviews of White "freedom riders" from the U.S. civil rights movement of the 1960s reveal that the "fully committed" activists (that is, volunteers who gave up their homes and/or careers to work full-time for the cause) differed from "partially committed" (part-time) activists in two important ways: they had enjoyed warmer relations with their parents, and they had had parents who advocated altruism and backed up these exhortations by performing many kind and compassionate acts. By contrast, parents of partially committed civil rights workers had often preached but rarely practiced altruism (Rosenhan, 1970; see also Clary & Miller, 1986). Clearly, these findings are reminiscent of the laboratory evidence we have reviewed, which indicates that warm and compassionate models who practice what they preach are especially effective at eliciting prosocial responses from young children.

Parental reactions to a child's harmdoing also play a significant role in the development of altruism. For example, we've noted that mothers of less compassionate infants and toddlers react to harmdoing in punitive or forceful ways, whereas mothers of compassionate toddlers rely more heavily on nonpunitive,

affective explanations in which they persuade the child to accept personal responsibility for her harmdoing and urge her to direct some sort of comforting or helpful response toward the victim (Zahn-Waxler et al., 1979). Research with older children paints a similar picture: parents who continue to rely on these rational, nonpunitive disciplinary techniques tend to raise children who are sympathetic, self-sacrificing, and concerned about the welfare of other people, whereas the frequent use of more forceful and punitive forms of discipline appears to inhibit altruism and lead to the development of self-centered values (Brody & Shaffer, 1982; Dlugokinski & Firestone, 1974).[2]

If we think about it, there are several reasons that rational discipline that is heavy on reasoning might inspire children to become more altruistic. First, it encourages the child to assume another person's perspective (role taking) and to experience that person's distress (empathy training). It also teaches the child to perform helpful or comforting acts that make both the self and the other person feel better. And last but not least, these reparative responses might convince older (grade school) children that they are "nice" or "helpful" people, a positive self-image that they may try to perpetuate by performing other acts of kindness in the future.

What Is Morality (and Moral Development)?

Now that we have looked at the development of aggressive inclinations and the growth of prosocial concerns, it is time to focus on a broader aspect of socialization—one that encompasses both the encouragement of altruistic values and the inhibition of aggression. Of course, the topic to which I am referring is the child's moral education and moral development.

The **moral development** of each successive generation is of obvious significance to society. One of the reasons that people can live together in peace is that they have evolved codes of ethics that sanction certain

[2]Indeed, we will see later in the chapter that these same rational, nonpunitive disciplinary techniques (which other researchers call "induction") contribute not only to one's altruistic concern but to all aspects of moral development.

---

moral development: the process by which children acquire society's standards of right and wrong.

practices and prohibit others. Although moral standards may vary from culture to culture (Garbarino & Bronfenbrenner, 1976), every society has devised rules that its constituents must obey in order to remain members in good standing. Thus, the moral education of each succeeding generation serves two important functions: (1) to maintain the social order while (2) making it possible for the individual to function appropriately within his or her culture (or subculture).

Sigmund Freud once argued that moral education is the largest hurdle that parents face when raising a child, and many of his contemporaries agreed. In one of the first social psychology texts, William McDougall (1908) suggested:

> The fundamental problem of social psychology is the moralization of the individual into the society into which he was born as an amoral and egoistic infant. There are successive stages, each of which must be traversed by every individual before he can attain the next higher: (1) the stage in which . . . [innate] impulses are modified by the influence of rewards and punishments, (2) the stage in which conduct is controlled . . . by social praise or blame, and (3) the highest stage in which conduct is regulated by an ideal that enables a man to act in a way that seems to him right regardless of the praise or blame of his immediate social environment [p. 6].

The third stage in McDougall's theory suggests that people do not go through life submitting to society's moral dictates because they expect rewards for complying or fear punishments for transgressing. Rather, they eventually *internalize* the moral principles that they have learned and will behave in accordance with these ideals even when authority figures are not present to enforce them. As we will see, many contemporary theorists consider **internalization** to be a very important part of the development of moral controls.

A definition of morality

Virtually all adults have some idea about what morality is, although the ways they define the term will depend, in part, on their general outlooks on life. A theologian, for example, might emphasize the relationship between human beings and their Creator. A philosopher's definition of morality may depend on his or her assumptions about human nature. Psychologists are generally concerned with the feelings, thoughts, and actions of people who are facing moral dilemmas. But most adults would probably agree that **morality** implies *a set of principles or ideals that help the individual to distinguish right from wrong and to act on this distinction.*

How psychologists look at morality

Psychological research has focused on three basic components of morality: the *affective*, or emotional, component, the *cognitive* component, and the *behavioral* component. Psychoanalytic theorists emphasize the emotional aspects of moral development. According to Freud, the kind of emotional relationship a child has with his or her parents will determine the child's willingness to internalize parental standards of right and wrong. Freud also believed that a child who successfully internalizes the morality of his parents will experience negative emotions such as shame or guilt—that is, **moral affect**—if he violates these ethical guidelines. Cognitive-developmental theorists have concentrated on the cognitive aspects of morality, or **moral reasoning,** and have found that the ways children think about right and wrong may change rather dramatically as they mature. Finally, the research of social-learning and social information-processing theorists has helped us to understand how children learn to resist temptation and to practice **moral behavior,** inhibiting actions such as lying, stealing, and cheating that violate moral norms.

Photo 14-4. Resisting temptation is a difficult feat to accomplish, especially when there is no one around to help the child exercise will power.

We will begin by examining each of these theories and the research it has generated. As we see how each theory approaches the topic of moral development, we will be looking at the relationships among moral affect (that is, guilt, shame), moral reasoning, and moral behavior. This information should help us to decide whether a person really has a unified "moral character" that is stable over time and across situations. Finally, we will consider how various child-rearing practices may affect a child's moral development and, in so doing, will attempt to integrate much of the information we have reviewed.

Psychoanalytic Explanations of Moral Development

According to Freud (1935/1960), the personality consists of three basic components—the id, the ego, and the superego. Recall from Chapter 2 that the id is impulsive and hedonistic. Its purpose is to gratify the instincts. The function of the ego is to restrain the id until "realistic" means for satisfying needs can be worked out. The superego is the final component of the personality to develop. Its role is to serve as the child's moral arbiter, or *internal* censor, by monitoring the acceptability of the ego's thoughts and actions. Indeed, Freud argued that a well-developed superego is a harsh master that will punish the ego for moral transgressions by producing feelings of guilt, shame, or loss of self-esteem. So a child who is morally mature should resist temptation to violate moral norms in order to avoid these dreaded forms of negative moral affect.

Freud's Theory of Oedipal Morality

According to Freud, the superego develops during the phallic stage (age 3–6), when children were said to experience a hostile rivalry with the same-sex parent that stemmed from their incestuous desire for the other-sex parent (that is, an Oedipus complex for males and an Electra complex for females). Freud proposed that hostilities arising from the Oedipus complex would build until a boy came to fear his father and would be forced to identify with him in order to reduce this fear. By identifying with the father, the boy would internalize many of his father's attributes, including the father's moral standards. Thus, Freud assumed that the male superego would emerge during the preschool period and mature by the age of 6 to 7, when most boys would have resolved their oedipal conflicts.

Girls were assumed to experience similar conflicts during the phallic stage as they began to compete with their mothers for the affection of their fathers. But Freud argued that girls are never quite as afraid of their mothers as boys are of their fathers, because in the worst of all imaginable circumstances, their mothers could never castrate them. The implication is that a girl might find it difficult to resolve her Electra complex because she experiences no overriding fear that would absolutely force her to identify with her mother. For this reason, Freud believed that females develop weaker superegos than males do!

Studies of moral development provide very little support for any of Freud's hypotheses. Cold, threatening parents do not raise children who are morally mature. Quite the contrary; parents who rely on punitive forms of discipline, such as spankings, tend to have youngsters who often misbehave and who rarely express feelings of guilt, remorse, shame, or self-criticism (Brody & Shaffer, 1982; Hoffman, 1970). Furthermore, there is simply no evidence that males develop stronger superegos than females. In fact, investigators who have left children alone so that they are tempted to violate a prohibition usually find no sex differences in moral behavior, or they find differences favoring females (Hoffman, 1975b). Finally, there is little evidence that children are morally mature at age 6 or 7, when they have supposedly resolved their oedipal conflicts. As we will see later in the chapter, at least one aspect of morality—moral reasoning—continues to develop well into young adulthood. In view of the repeated failures to confirm these and other Freudian hypotheses, many develop-

---

internalization: the process of adopting the attributes or standards of other people—taking these standards as one's own.

morality: a set of principles or ideals that help the individual to distinguish right from wrong and to act on this distinction.

moral affect: the emotional component of morality, including feelings such as guilt, shame, and pride in ethical conduct.

moral reasoning: the cognitive component of morality; the thinking that people display when resolving moral dilemmas and deciding whether various acts are right or wrong.

moral behavior: the behavioral component of morality; actions that are consistent with one's moral standards in situations in which one is tempted to violate a prohibition.

mentalists now believe that it is time to lay Freud's theory of **oedipal morality** to rest.

Erikson's Views on Moral Development

Other psychoanalysts such as Erik Erikson (1963) have rejected Freud's theory of oedipal morality and argued that children internalize the moral principles of *both* parents in order to win their approval and to avoid losing their love. According to Erikson, both the ego and the superego play important roles in moral development. The superego dictates to the ego the kinds of behavior that are morally acceptable and unacceptable. But unless the ego is strong enough to inhibit the id's undesirable impulses, the child will be unable to resist the id, regardless of the strength of the superego. So Erikson assumes that moral behavior is a product of both the internalized rules of the superego and the restraining forces of the ego that permit the child to obey these rules.

Since the ego is the rational component of the personality—the seat of all higher intellectual functions—Erikson is arguing that moral development depends, in part, on intellectual development. The cognitive-developmentalists definitely agree.

Cognitive-Developmental Theory: The Child as a Moral Philosopher

Cognitive-developmentalists study morality by looking at the development of *moral reasoning*—that is, the thinking that children display when deciding whether various acts are right or wrong. The most basic assumption of the cognitive approach is that moral development depends very heavily on the child's cognitive development. Moral reasoning is said to progress through an **invariant sequence** of "stages," each of which is a consistent way of thinking about moral issues that is different from the stages preceding or following it. Presumably each moral stage evolves from and replaces its immediate predecessor, so that there can be no "skipping" of stages. If these assumptions sound familiar, they should, for they are the same ones that Piaget made about his stages of intellectual development.

In this section of the chapter we will consider two cognitive-developmental theories of moral reasoning—Jean Piaget's model and Lawrence Kohlberg's revision and extension of Piaget's approach.

Piaget's Theory of Moral Development

According to Piaget (1932/1965), moral maturity implies both a respect for rules and a sense of social justice—that is, a concern that all people be treated fairly and equitably under the socially defined rules of order. Piaget studied the development of a respect for rules by rolling up his sleeves and playing marbles with a large number of Swiss children. As he played with children of different ages, Piaget would ask them questions about the rules of the game—questions such as "Where do these rules come from? Must everyone obey a rule? Can these rules be changed?" Once he had identified developmental stages in the understanding and use of rules, he proceeded to study children's conceptions of social justice by presenting them with moral dilemmas in the form of stories. Here is one example:

> *Story A.* A little boy who is called John is in his room. He is called to dinner. He goes into the dining room. But behind the door there was a chair, and on the chair there was a tray with 15 cups on it. John couldn't have known that there was all this behind the door. He goes in, the door knocks against the tray, bang go the 15 cups, and they all get broken.
>
> *Story B.* Once there was a little boy whose name was Henry. One day when his mother was out he tried to reach some jam out of the cupboard. He climbed onto a chair and stretched out his arm. But the jam was too high up, and he couldn't reach it. . . . While he was trying to get it, he knocked over a cup. The cup fell down and broke [Piaget, 1932/1965, p. 122].

Having heard the stories, subjects were asked "Are these children equally guilty?" and "If not, which child is naughtier? Why?" Subjects were also asked how the naughtier child should be punished. Through the use of these research techniques, Piaget formulated a theory of moral development that includes a premoral period and two moral stages.

The premoral period

According to Piaget, preschool children show little concern for or awareness of rules. In a game of marbles, these **premoral** children do not play systematically with the intent of winning. Instead, they seem to make up their own rules, and they think the point of the game is to take turns and have fun. Toward the end of the premoral period (ages 4 to 5), the child becomes more aware of rules by watching older children and imitating their rule-bound behavior. But the premoral child does not yet understand that rules represent a cooperative agreement about how a game should be played.

The stage of moral realism, or heteronomous morality

Between the ages of 5 and 10, the child develops a strong respect for rules and a belief that they must be obeyed at all times. Children at this **heteronomous** stage assume that rules are laid down by authority figures such as God, the police, or their parents, and they think these regulations are sacred and unalterable. Try breaking the speed limit with a 6-year-old at your side and you may see what Piaget was talking about. Even if you are rushing to the hospital in a medical emergency, the young child may note that you are breaking a "rule of the road" and consider your behavior unacceptable conduct that deserves to be punished. In sum, heteronomous children think of rules as *moral absolutes*. They believe that there are a "right" side and a "wrong" side to any moral issue, and right always means following the rules.

Children at this first moral stage are apt to judge the naughtiness of an act by its objective consequences rather than the actor's intent. For example, Piaget found that many 5–9-year-olds judged John, who accidentally broke 15 cups while performing a well-intentioned act, to be naughtier than Henry, who broke one cup while stealing jam. Perhaps this focus on ob-

Photo 14-5. According to Piaget, young children display a form of "moral realism" by judging the naughtiness of an act by its objective consequences rather than the actor's intent.

jective harm done, or **moral realism,** stems from the fact that young children may be punished if and when their behavior produces harmful consequences. For example, a girl who bumps into a table without doing any harm is less likely to be reprimanded for her clumsiness than a second youngster who nudges the table and knocks over a number of her mother's plants in the process.

Heteronomous children favor **expiatory punishment**—punishment for its own sake with no concern for its relation to the nature of the forbidden act. For example, a 6-year-old might favor spanking a boy who had broken a window rather than making the boy pay for the window from his allowance. Moreover, the heteronomous child believes in **immanent justice**—the idea that violations of social rules will invariably be punished in one way or another. So if a 6-year-old boy were to fall and skin his knee while stealing cookies, he might conclude that this injury was the punishment he deserved for his transgression. Life for the morally realistic person is fair and just.

The stage of moral relativism, or autonomous morality

By age 9 or 10 most children have reached Piaget's second moral stage—the stage of moral relativ-

---

oedipal morality: Freud's theory that moral development occurs during the phallic period (ages 3 to 6) when children internalize the moral standards of the same-sex parent as they resolve their Oedipus or Electra conflicts.

invariant sequence: a series of developments that occur in one particular order because each development in the sequence is a prerequisite for those appearing later.

premoral period: in Piaget's theory, the first 4 to 5 years of life, when children have little respect for or awareness of socially defined rules.

heteronomous morality: Piaget's first stage of moral development, when children think of rules as moral absolutes that are not to be challenged (also known as the stage of moral realism).

moral realism: a characteristic of Piaget's heteronomous stage; when judging whether acts are right or wrong, children focus on the objective harm done rather than on the actor's intentions.

expiatory punishment: punitive consequences that bear no relation to the nature of the forbidden act.

immanent justice: the notion that unacceptable conduct will invariably be punished.

ism, or **autonomous morality.** Older, autonomous children now realize that social rules are arbitrary agreements that can be challenged and even changed with the consent of the people they govern. They also feel that rules can be violated in the service of human needs. Thus, a driver who speeds during a medical emergency will no longer be considered a wrongdoer, even though she is breaking the law. Judgments of right and wrong now depend more on the actor's intent to deceive or to violate social rules than on the objective consequences of the act itself. For example, 10-year-olds reliably say that Henry, who broke one cup while stealing some jam (bad intent), is naughtier than John, who broke 15 cups while coming to dinner (good or neutral intent).

When deciding how to punish a transgression, the morally autonomous individual usually favors **reciprocal punishments**—that is, treatments that shape the punitive consequences to the "crime" so that the rule breaker will understand the implications of a transgression and perhaps be less likely to repeat it. So an autonomous child may decide that the boy who deliberately breaks a window should pay for it out of his allowance (and learn that windows cost money) rather than simply submitting to a spanking. Children at this higher stage of moral reasoning no longer believe in immanent justice, because they have learned from experience that violations of social rules often go undetected and unpunished.

Moving from heteronomous to autonomous morality

According to Piaget, both cognitive maturation and social experience play a role in the transition from heteronomous to autonomous morality. The cognitive advances that are necessary for this shift are a general decline in egocentrism and the development of role-taking skills that will enable the child to view moral issues from several perspectives. The kind of social experience that Piaget considers important is *equal status* contact with peers. Beginning at about age 6, the child spends four to six hours a day at school surrounded by other children of approximately the same age. When with peers, conflicts will often arise because members of the group will not always agree on how they should play games or solve problems. Since everyone has roughly equal status, children will soon learn that they must compromise on a course of action, often without any assistance from adults, if they are to play together co-

operatively or accomplish other group goals. While settling disputes, each child will assume the roles of "governor" and "governed" and see that rules are merely social contracts that derive their power from the mutual consent of the group members rather than from an external authority figure. In sum, Piaget believes that equal-status contacts with peers lead to a more flexible morality because they (1) lessen the child's unilateral respect for adult authority, (2) increase his or her self-respect and respect for peers, and (3) illustrate that rules are arbitrary agreements that can be changed with the consent of the people they govern.

And what role do parents play? According to Piaget, parents may actually slow the progress of moral development by reinforcing the child's unilateral respect for authority figures. If, for example, a parent enforces a demand with a threat or a statement such as "Do it because *I* told you to," it is easy to see how the young moral realist might conclude that rules are "absolutes" that derive their "teeth" from the parent's power to enforce them. Although Piaget believes that the peer group plays the greater role in the development of autonomous morality, he suggests that parents could help by relinquishing some of their power to establish a more egalitarian relationship with their children.

Tests of Piaget's Theory

Many researchers have used Piaget's methods in an attempt to replicate his findings, and much of the evidence they have collected is consistent with his theory. In Western cultures, there is a clear relationship between children's ages and stages of moral reasoning: younger children are more likely than older children to think about rules as moral absolutes, to believe in immanent justice, and to consider the objective consequences of an act rather than the actor's intent when making moral judgments (Hoffman, 1970; Lickona, 1976). Apparently the child's level of moral reasoning does depend, in part, on his or her level of cognitive development. For example, IQ and moral maturity are positively correlated (Lickona, 1976), and children who score high on tests of role taking tend to make more advanced moral judgments than age mates whose role-taking skills are less well developed (Ambron & Irwin, 1975; Selman, 1971). Finally, there is even some support for Piaget's "peer participation" hypothesis: popular children who often take part in social activities and who assume positions of leadership in the peer group tend to make mature moral judgments (Keasey, 1971).

Yet, in spite of this supportive evidence, there is reason to believe that Piaget's theory has some very real shortcomings. Let's take a closer look.

Do younger children ignore an actor's intentions?

Recent research indicates that younger children can and often do consider an actor's intentions when evaluating his behavior. One problem with Piaget's moral-decision stories is that they confounded intentions and consequences by asking whether a person who caused a small amount of harm in the service of bad intentions was naughtier than one who caused a larger amount of damage while serving good intentions. Since younger children give more weight to concrete evidence that they can see than to abstract information that they must infer (Surber, 1982), it is hardly surprising that they would consider the person who did more damage to be the naughtier of the two.

Sharon Nelson (1980) unconfounded information about an actor's motives and intentions in an interesting experiment with 3-year-olds. Each child listened to stories in which a character threw a ball to a playmate. The actor's intent was described as *good* (his friend had nothing to play with) or *bad* (the actor was mad at his friend), and the consequences of his act were described as *positive* (the friend caught the ball and was happy to play with it) or *negative* (the ball hit the friend in the head and made him cry). To ensure that these young subjects would understand the actor's motives, they were shown drawings such as Figure 14-1, which happens to depict a negative intent. The children were then asked to evelute the "goodness" or "badness" of the actor's behavior.

The results were rather interesting. As we see in Figure 14-2, Nelson's 3-year-olds did consider acts that produced positive consequences to be more favorable

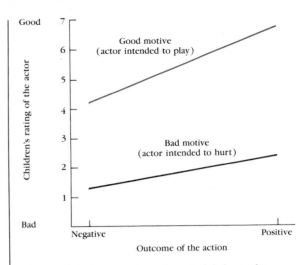

Figure 14-2. Average ratings of an actor's behavior for actors who produced positive or negative outcomes while serving either good or bad intentions. *(Adapted from Nelson, 1980.)*

than those producing negative outcomes. Yet the more interesting finding was that the good-intentioned actor who had wanted to play was evaluated much more favorably than the actor who intended to hurt his friend, *regardless of the consequences of his actions*. In a later study using a very similar methodology (Nelson-LeGall, 1985), 3–4-year-olds judged negative consequences that the actor could have foreseen to be more "intentional" and naughtier than the same consequences produced by an actor who could not have foreseen them. Moreover, 5-year-olds already know that harmdoing stemming from negligence is more blameworthy than that which is purely accidental (Shultz, Wright, & Schleifer, 1986). Taken together, these findings are clearly inconsistent with Piaget's view of younger children as "moral realists" who focus exclusively on objective harm done to assign moral responsibility. Apparently, even *preschool* children can and often do consider an actor's

Figure 14-1. Example of drawings used by Nelson to convey an actor's intentions to preschool children. *(Adapted from Nelson, 1980.)*

autonomous morality: Piaget's second stage of moral development, in which children realize that rules are arbitrary agreements that can be challenged and even changed with the consent of the people they govern (also called the stage of moral relativism).

reciprocal punishment: punitive consequences that are tailored to the forbidden act so that a rulebreaker will understand the implications of a transgression.

intentions when making moral judgments if this information is clear to them.

Do younger children respect all rules (and adult authority)?

According to Piaget, young children think of rules as sacred and obligatory prescriptions that are laid down by respected authority figures and are not to be questioned or changed. However, Elliot Turiel (1978) notes that children actually encounter two kinds of rules: (1) **moral rules,** which focus on the rights and privileges of individuals, and (2) **social-conventional rules,** which are determined by consensus and serve to govern interpersonal behavior within a particular social setting. The procedures followed while playing marbles are examples of social-conventional rules, whereas prescriptions such as "Thou shalt not steal (shove, hit, lie)" are examples of moral rules. Do children treat these two kinds of rules as equivalent? ~no

Apparently not. Judith Smetana (1981, 1985) finds that even 2½–6-year-olds make important distinctions between moral and social-conventional rules—distinctions that are also seen in Oriental cultures such as Korea, where respect for adult authority is much more heavily emphasized than in Western societies (Song, Smetana, & Kim, 1987). Basically, young children view moral transgressions such as hitting, stealing, or refusing to share as much more serious and deserving of punishment than social-conventional violations such as not staying in one's seat at nursery school or not saying grace before eating. When asked whether a violation would be OK if there were no rule against it, children said that moral transgressions are always wrong but that social-conventional violations are OK in the absence of any explicit prohibitions. So not only do preschoolers fail to see social-conventional rules as sacred and unalterable, they actually show a strong respect for moral prescriptions by age 2½ to 3—much sooner than Piaget had assumed they would.

Finally, 6–10-year-olds, who should be at Piaget's heteronomous stage of morality, are quite capable of questioning adult authority (Laupa & Turiel, 1986; Tisak, 1986). For example, most children of this age believe that their parents are justified in making and enforcing rules about moral issues such as stealing; but they feel a parent is unjustified and is behaving inappropriately when he or she imposes rules that seriously restrict their choice of friends or that arbitrarily require them to perform various household chores. So heteronomous children do have ideas about what constitutes legitimate authority, and those ideas are not based solely on an unwavering respect for the sanctity or wisdom of adults as Piaget had assumed.

Piaget was among the first to suggest that children's moral reasoning may develop in stages. His early work stimulated an enormous amount of research and several new insights, some of which were inconsistent with his original theory. One theorist who was profoundly influenced by Piaget and who has contributed many of these new insights is Lawrence Kohlberg of Harvard University.

Kohlberg's Theory of Moral Development

Kohlberg (1963, 1969, 1981) has refined and extended Piaget's theory of moral development by asking 10-, 13-, and 16-year-old boys to resolve a series of "moral dilemmas." Each dilemma challenged the respondent by requiring him to choose between (1) obeying a rule, law, or authority figure and (2) taking some action that conflicts with these rules and commands while serving a human need. The following story is the best known of Kohlberg's moral dilemmas:

> In Europe, a woman was near death from a special kind of cancer. There was one drug that doctors thought might save her. It was a form of radium that a druggist in the same town had recently discovered. The drug was expensive to make, but the druggist was charging $2000, or 10 times the cost of the drug, for a small (possibly life-saving) dose. Heinz, the sick woman's husband, borrowed all the money he could, about $1000, or half of what he needed. He told the druggist that his wife was dying and asked him to sell the drug cheaper or to let him pay later. The druggist replied "No, I discovered the drug, and I'm going to make money from it." Heinz then became desperate and broke into the store to steal the drug for his wife.
>
> Should Heinz have done that?

Kohlberg was actually less interested in the subject's decision (that is, what Heinz should have done) than in the underlying rationale, or "thought structures," that the subject used to justify his decision. To determine the "structure" of a subject's moral reasoning, Kohlberg asked probing questions. Should Heinz be punished for stealing the drug? Did the druggist have a right to charge so much? Would it be proper to charge the druggist with murder? If so, should his punishment be greater if the woman who died was an important person? And so on.

Kohlberg's first discovery was that moral development is far from complete when the child reached age 9 to 10, or Piaget's autonomous stage. Indeed, moral reasoning seemed to evolve and become progressively more complex throughout adolescence and into young adulthood. Careful analyses of his subjects' responses to several dilemmas led Kohlberg to conclude that moral growth progresses through an *invariant sequence* of three moral levels, each of which is composed of two distinct moral stages. According to Kohlberg, the order of these moral levels and stages is invariant because each depends on the development of certain cognitive abilities that evolve in an invariant sequence. Like Piaget, Kohlberg assumes that each succeeding stage evolves from and replaces its predecessor; once the individual has attained a higher stage of moral reasoning, he or she should never regress to earlier stages.

Before looking at Kohlberg's sequence of stages, it is important to emphasize that each stage represents a particular perspective, or *method of thinking* about moral dilemmas, rather than a particular type of moral decision. Decisions are not very informative in themselves, because subjects at each moral stage might well endorse either of the alternative courses of action when resolving one of these ethical dilemmas.

The basic themes and defining characteristics of Kohlberg's three moral levels and six stages are as follows:

egocentric point of view

Level 1: Preconventional morality. At this level, morality is truly external. The child conforms to rules imposed by authority figures in order to avoid punishment or to obtain personal rewards. The preconventional level consists of two stages:

Stage 1: Punishment-and-obedience orientation. At this stage, the child determines the goodness or badness of an act on the basis of its consequences. The child will defer to authority figures and obey their commands in order to avoid punishment. There is no true conception of rules, however; if the child can get away with an act, it is not considered bad. The seriousness of a violation depends on the magnitude of its consequences (that is, the amount of punishment received or the amount of objective harm done).

Stage 2: Naive hedonism, or instrumental orientation. A person at the second stage of moral development conforms to rules in order to gain rewards or to satisfy personal needs. Doing things for others is "right" if the actor will benefit in the long run. This low-level reciprocity is quite pragmatic; "You scratch my back and

I'll scratch yours" is the guiding philosophy of the individual at Stage 2. The seriousness of a violation now depends, in part, on the actor's intent.

dominant level   escalates til 23 then declines

Level 2: Conventional morality. At this level, the individual strives to obey the rules set forth by others (such as parents, peers, social groups) in order to win praise and recognition for virtuous conduct or to maintain social order.   *reasoned   "role-taking ability"*

Stage 3: "Good boy" or "good girl" orientation. Moral behavior is that which pleases, helps or is approved of by others. Actions are evaluated on the basis of the actor's intent. "He means well" is a common expression of moral approval at this stage. A primary objective of a Stage 3 respondent is to be thought of as a "nice" person.   *principled*

Stage 4: Authority and social-order-maintaining morality. At this stage, one accepts and conforms to social rules and conventions in order to avoid censure by legitimate authorities. The reason for conformity is not so much a fear of punishment as a belief that rules and laws maintain a social order that is worth preserving. Thus, behavior is judged as "good," or moral, to the extent that it conforms to rules that maintain social order.

Level 3: Postconventional morality, or *the morality of self-accepted moral principles.* The individual who has attained this third level of moral reasoning is personally committed to a set of principles that are often shared

subjects fairly consistent in reasoning stage

moral rules: standards of acceptable and unacceptable conduct that focus on the rights and privileges of individuals.

social-conventional rules: standards of conduct determined by social consensus that serve to regulate behavior within a particular social context.

preconventional morality: Kohlberg's term for the first two stages of moral reasoning, in which moral judgments are based on the consequences of an act for the actor rather than the relationship of that act to society's rules and customs.

conventional morality: Kohlberg's term for the third and fourth stages of moral reasoning, in which moral judgments are based on a desire to maintain good interpersonal relations (Stage 3) or to comply with formal laws and customs (Stage 4).

postconventional morality: Kohlberg's term for the fifth and sixth stages of moral reasoning, in which moral judgments are based on social contracts and democratic law (Stage 5) or on universal principles of ethics and justice (Stage 6).

moral stages ← → cognitive development

structure of reasoning = stages
not decisions

Box 14-3.

Examples of How Subjects at Each of Kohlberg's Six Moral Stages Might Respond to the Heinz Dilemma

Stage 1: Punishment-and-obedience orientation

Protheft: It isn't really bad to take it—he did ask to pay for it first. He wouldn't do any other damage or take anything else and the drug he'd take is only worth $200, not $2000.

Antitheft: Heinz doesn't have permission to take the drug. He can't just go and break through a window. He'd be a bad criminal doing all that damage. That drug is worth a lot of money and stealing anything so expensive would be a big crime.

Note: Both these answers disregard Heinz's intentions and judge the act in terms of its consequences. The "pro" answer minimizes the consequences while the "con" answer maximizes them. The implication is that big crimes warrant severe punishment.

Stage 2: Instrumental hedonism

Protheft: Heinz isn't really doing any harm to the druggist, and he can always pay him back. If he doesn't want to lose his wife, he should take the drug.

Antitheft: The druggist isn't wrong; he just wants to make a profit like everybody else. That's what you're in business for, to make money.

Note: Heinz's intentions are apparent in the pro answer, while the intentions of the druggist come out in the con answer. Both Heinz and the druggist are "right" for satisfying their own needs or goals.

Stage 3: "Good boy" or "good girl" morality

Protheft: Stealing is bad, but this is a bad situation. Heinz is only doing something that it is natural for a good husband to do. You can't blame him for doing something out of love for his wife. You'd blame him if he didn't save her.

Antitheft: If Heinz's wife dies, he can't be blamed. You can't say he is heartless for failing to commit a crime. The druggist is the selfish and heartless one. Heinz tried to do everything he really could.

Note: Both the pro and con answers seek to resolve the dilemma by doing what others would approve of under the circumstances. In either case, Heinz is described as a well-intentioned person who is doing what is right.

Stage 4: Authority and social-order-maintaining morality

Protheft: The druggist is leading the wrong kind of life if he just lets somebody die; so it's Heinz's duty to save her. But Heinz can't just go around breaking laws—he must pay the druggist back

continued

---

with others and yet transcend particular authority figures. In other words, moral standards are internalized and become the person's own.

Stage 5: Morality of contract, individual rights, and democratically accepted law. There is a flexibility in moral judgments at this stage. Moral actions are those that express the will of the majority or maximize social welfare. To be acceptable, rules must be arrived at by democratic procedures and must be impartial. Laws that are imposed or that compromise the rights of the majority are considered unjust and worthy of challenge. By contrast, the person at Stage 4 will not ordinarily challenge an established law and may be suspicious of those who do. This fifth stage of moral reasoning represents the official morality of the United States Constitution.

Stage 6: Morality of individual principles of conscience. At this "highest" stage of moral reasoning, the individual defines right and wrong on the basis of the self-chosen ethical principles of his or her own conscience. These principles are not concrete rules such as the Ten Commandments. They are abstract moral guidelines or principles of universal justice (and respect for individual rights) that are to be applied in all situations. Deviations from one's self-chosen moral standards produce feelings of guilt or self-condemnation; for example, the Stage 6 conscientious objector may refuse to conform to a draft law that violates his pacifist beliefs. To comply would bring self-degradation, a punishment that may be much more aversive to the conscientious objector than a short prison sentence.

Examples of how subjects at each stage might respond to the Heinz dilemma appear in Box 14-3. Although these particular responses were constructed for illustrative purposes, they represent precisely the kinds of logic that Kohlberg's subjects often use to justify stealing or not stealing the drug.

Tests of Kohlberg's Theory

The data from which Kohlberg fashioned his theory of moral development came from his doctoral research, in which boys aged 10, 13, and 16 each spent up to two hours resolving nine moral dilemmas. In analyzing the data, Kohlberg found that each child showed a fairly consistent pattern of reasoning when justifying his answers to different dilemmas. The kinds of judgments that these boys made seemed to fall into six general categories, which became Kohlberg's six moral stages.

and take his punishment for stealing.

Antitheft: It's natural for Heinz to want to save his wife, but it's still always wrong to steal. You have to follow the rules regardless of your feelings or the special circumstances.

Note: The obligation to the law transcends special interests. Even the pro answer recognizes that Heinz is morally wrong and must pay for his transgression.

Stage 5: Morality of contract, individual rights, and democratically accepted law

Protheft: Before you say stealing is wrong, you've got to consider this whole situation. Of course the laws are quite clear about breaking into a store. And even worse, Heinz would know that there were no legal grounds for his actions. Yet, it would be reasonable for anybody in this kind of situation to steal the drug.

Antitheft: I can see the good that would come from illegally taking the drug, but the ends don't justify the means. You can't say that Heinz would be completely wrong to steal the drug, but even these circumstances don't make it right.

Note: The judgments are no longer black and white. The pro answer recognizes that theft is legally wrong but that an emotional husband may be driven to steal the drug—and that is understandable (although not completely moral). The con answer recognizes exactly the same points. Heinz would be committing an immoral act in stealing the drug, but he would do so with good intentions.

Stage 6: Morality of individual principles of conscience

Protheft: When one must choose between disobeying a law and saving a human life, the higher principle of preserving life makes it morally right to steal the drug.

Antitheft: With many cases of cancer and the scarcity of the drug, there might not be enough to go around to everybody who needs it. The correct course of action can only be the one that is "right" by all people concerned. Heinz ought to act, not on emotion or the law, but according to what he thinks an ideally just person would do in this case.

Note: Both the pro and con answers transcend the law and self-interest and appeal to higher principles (individual rights, the sanctity of life) that all "reasonable" persons should consider in this situation. The pro answer is relatively straightforward. However, it is difficult to conceive of a "con" Stage 6 response unless the drug was scarce and Heinz would be depriving other equally deserving people of life by stealing the drug to save his wife.

Age trends in the use of Kohlberg's moral stages

If Kohlberg's stages represent a true developmental sequence, then we might expect that the use of Stage 1 and Stage 2 reasoning will decline with age, while judgments at stages 3 through 6 will become more frequent. Figure 14-3 presents age trends in the use of Kohlberg's moral stages for a sample of American males. Note that preconventional reasoning (stages 1 and 2) declines sharply with age: 80% of the moral judgments of 10-year-olds were preconventional (stages 1 and 2), as opposed to about 18% at age 16–18 and only 3% at age 24. The use of conventional reasoning (stages 3 and 4) increased until about age 22 and then stabilized at roughly 90% of all moral statements. Postconventional reasoning also increased with age. Whereas the 10- to 16-year-olds in this sample never used Stage 5 or Stage 6 reasoning, approximately 10% of the moral judgments of the 24-year-olds were at the postconventional level (Stage 5). Finally, a few of the 16–24-year-old subjects made statements that Kohlberg had originally interpreted as examples of Stage 6. However, a careful analysis of the rationales underlying these judgments suggested that they were more appropriately classified as Stage 3, 4, or 5 (Colby, Kohlberg, Gibbs, & Lieberman, 1983).[3]

Similar age trends have been reported in Mexico, the Bahamas, Taiwan, Turkey, Honduras, India, Kenya, and Nigeria (see Colby & Kohlberg, 1987, for a review). In all these cultures, adolescents and young adults typically reason about moral issues at a higher level than children do. So it seems that Kohlberg's levels and stages of moral reasoning are "universal"—as we would expect if they represent a true developmental sequence based, in part, on one's intellectual development.

Although Kohlberg has argued that his stages represent an invariant developmental sequence, he believes that only a small minority of any group will actually reach the postconventional level. In fact, the dominant level of moral reasoning among adults from virtually all societies is conventional morality (stages 3 and 4),

---

[3]Because Stage 6 reasoning is so rare and virtually no one functions consistently at this level, Kohlberg now treats it as a hypothetical construct—that is, the stage to which people would progress were they to develop beyond Stage 5. In fact, later versions of Kohlberg's scoring system no longer contain guidelines for assessing Stage 6 reasoning.

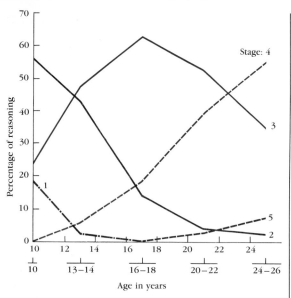

Figure 14-3. Use of Kohlberg's moral stages by male subjects aged 10 through 26 years. *(From Colby et al., 1983.)*

and it is not at all unusual to find that people from rural villages in nonindustrialized countries show absolutely no evidence of postconventional reasoning (Harkness, Edwards, & Super, 1981; Tietjen & Walker, 1985). Kohlberg suggests that fixation (or arrested development) may occur at any stage if the individual is not exposed to persons or situations that force a reevaluation of current moral concepts. And what kinds of experiences might have such an effect? Apparently, education does. People who have a university education reason at higher levels than those who do not, and the differences in moral reasoning between high school and college students become greater with each successive year of school that the college students complete (Rest & Thoma, 1985). Having a position of leadership or authority is also an experience that seems to promote the growth of moral reasoning. Even in preliterate societies, tribal leaders who must often resolve interpersonal conflicts tend to reason at somewhat higher levels than their followers (Harkness et al., 1981; Tietjen & Walker, 1985). Finally, people in many nonindustrialized societies tend to be governed at the village or tribal level and need to be concerned only with the customs and conventions of their immediate social group. So it is possible that these individuals do not reason at the postconventional level on moral issues because they have little if any experi-

ence with the kinds of social and political compromise among rival ethnic, racial, religious, and political factions that seem to contribute to Stage 5 reasoning—the social contract orientation. Nevertheless, their conventional (mostly Stage 3) moral reasoning is perfectly adaptive and hence "mature" within their own social systems (Harkness et al., 1981).

Are Kohlberg's stages an invariant sequence?

Although Kohlberg's early research and the cross-cultural studies are generally consistent with his developmental scheme, they do not establish that his moral stages develop in a fixed or invariant sequence. The major problem with the cross-sectional studies is that subjects at each age level were *different* children, and we cannot be certain that a 24-year-old at Stage 5 has progressed through the various moral levels and stages in the order specified by Kohlberg's theory. How can we evaluate the invariant-sequence hypothesis? By examining two important sources of evidence: (1) experimental attempts to modify children's moral judgments and (2) longitudinal studies of the moral development of individual children.

The experimental evidence. If Kohlberg's stages represent an invariant sequence, as he has proposed, then children might be influenced by models who reason about moral issues at one stage higher than their own. However, reasoning that is less advanced should be rejected as too simplistic, and moral judgments that are two stages higher should be too difficult for subjects to comprehend.

Most of the available evidence is consistent with these hypotheses. When exposed to moral reasoning that is one stage above (+ 1) or one stage below (− 1) their own, children generally favor and are more influenced by the more sophisticated set of arguments (Rest, 1983). Moreover, relatively few children understand or appreciate moral reasoning that is two stages higher (+ 2) than their own (see Turiel, 1966; Walker, 1982).

Other researchers (for example, Berkowitz, Gibbs, & Broughton, 1980; Maitland & Goldman, 1974) have found that adolescents who are asked to discuss moral issues and reach a consensus show greater advances in their own moral reasoning (particularly those subjects who scored lower than their peers before the discussions) than age mates who think about the same issues on their own and make individual moral judgments. And it is important to note that the advance in moral reasoning shown by the "changers" in these discussions is not merely a modeling effect. Berkowitz and Gibbs (1983) report that change is unlikely to occur unless the discussions are characterized by **transactive interactions**—that is, exchanges in which each discussant performs mental operations on the reasoning of his or her partner (for example, "Your reasoning misses an important distinction"; "Here's an elaboration of your position"; "We can combine our positions into a common view"). This latter finding is crucial, for it reinforces Kohlberg's contention that social experiences promote moral growth by introducing *cognitive* challenges to one's current reasoning—challenges to which the *less mature* individual will adapt by assimilating and accommodating to the other person's logic. Why do the more mature discussants not move in the direction of their less mature partners? Because the challenges introduced by their less mature counterparts are based on reasoning that they have already rejected. Indeed, their lack of change in the face of such logic provides additional support for Kohlberg's invariant-sequence hypothesis.

The longitudinal evidence. Clearly the most compelling evidence for Kohlberg's invariant-sequence hypothesis would be a demonstration that individual children progress through the moral stages in precisely the order that Kohlberg says they should. Ann Colby and her associates (Colby et al., 1983) have recently reported the results of a 20-year longitudinal study of 58 American males who were 10, 13, or 16 years old at the beginning of the project. These boys responded to nine of Kohlberg's moral dilemmas when the study began and again in five follow-up sessions administered at three- to four-year intervals. Colby et al. found that subjects proceeded through the stages in the order Kohlberg predicted and that no subject ever skipped a stage between testings. Furthermore, the answers a subject gave during any single testing were remarkably consistent in that about 70% fell within the subjects' dominant moral stage, the remainder falling at an immediately adjacent level (that is, either one stage higher or one stage lower than the person's dominant stage). Similar results have been reported in a nine-year longitudinal study of adolescents in Israel and a twelve-year longitudinal project conducted in Turkey (Colby & Kohlberg, 1987). So it would appear that Kohlberg's moral stages do represent a true developmental sequence.

The relationship of Kohlberg's stages to cognitive development

According to Kohlberg (1963), the young, preconventional child reasons about moral issues from an egocentric point of view. At Stage 1 the child thinks that certain acts are bad because they are punished. At Stage 2 the child shows a limited awareness of the needs, thoughts, and intentions of others but still judges self-serving acts as "right," or appropriate. However, conventional reasoning clearly requires an ability to role-take, or assume the perspective of others. For example, a person at Stage 3 must necessarily recognize others' points of view before she will evaluate intentions that would win their approval as "good," or morally acceptable. Furthermore, postconventional, or "principled," morality would seem to require much more than a decline in egocentrism and a capacity for reciprocal role taking: the person who bases moral judgments on abstract principles must be able to reason abstractly rather than simply adhering to concrete moral norms. So Kohlberg believes that the highest level of cognitive development, *formal operations*, is necessary for principled moral reasoning (stages 5 and 6).

Much of the available research is consistent with Kohlberg's hypotheses. For example, John Moir (1974) administered Kohlberg's "dilemmas test" and several measures of role taking to a group of 11-year-old girls, many of whom showed a mixture of Stage 2 (preconventional) and Stage 3 (conventional) reasoning on the moral dilemmas. Moir found a very substantial positive correlation between role-taking abilities and moral maturity; girls who were more proficient at role taking were more likely to reason at Kohlberg's conventional level (Stage 3). In another study of 10–13-year-olds, Lawrence Walker (1980) found that the only subjects who had reached Kohlberg's third stage of moral reasoning ("good boy/good girl" morality) were those who were quite proficient at reciprocal role taking. However, not all the proficient role takers had reached Stage 3 in their moral reasoning. So Walker's results imply that reciprocal-role-taking skills are *necessary but not sufficient* for the development of conventional morality.

Carol Tomlinson-Keasey and Charles Keasey

---

transactive interactions: verbal exchanges in which individuals perform mental operations on the reasoning of their discussion partners.

(1974) administered Kohlberg's moral dilemmas and three tests of cognitive development to sixth-grade girls (age 11–12) and to college women. An interesting pattern emerged. All the subjects who reasoned at the postconventional level (Stage 5) on the dilemmas showed at least some formal-operational thinking on the cognitive tests. But not all the formal operators reasoned at the postconventional level on the dilemmas test. This same pattern also emerged in a later study by Deanna Kuhn and her associates (Kuhn, Kohlberg, Langer, & Haan, 1977). So it seems that formal operations are *necessary but not sufficient* for the development of postconventional morality.

In sum, Kohlberg's moral stages are clearly related to one's level of cognitive development. Proficiency at role taking may be necessary for the onset of conventional morality, and formal operations appear to be necessary for postconventional, or "principled," morality. Yet, it is important to emphasize that intellectual growth does not guarantee moral development, for a person who has reached Piaget's highest stages of intellect may continue to reason at the preconventional level about moral issues. The implication, then, is that both *intellectual growth* and *relevant social experiences* (exposure to persons or situations that force a reevaluation of one's current moral concepts) are necessary before children can progress from preconventional morality to Kohlberg's higher stages.

Some lingering questions about Kohlberg's approach

The relationship between moral reasoning and moral behavior. One common criticism of Kohlberg's theory is that it is based on subjects' responses to hypothetical and somewhat artificial dilemmas that they do not have to face themselves (Baumrind, 1978). Would children reason in the same way about the moral dilemmas they actually encounter? Would an individual who said that Heinz should steal the drug actually do so if he were in Heinz's shoes? Can we ever predict a person's moral behavior from a knowledge of his or her stage of moral reasoning?

Many researchers have found that the moral judgments of young children do *not* predict their actual behavior in situations where they are induced to cheat or violate other moral norms (Nelson, Grinder, & Biaggio, 1969; Santrock, 1975; Toner & Potts, 1981). However, studies of older grade school children, adolescents, and young adults often find at least some

consistency between moral reasoning and moral conduct (see Blasi, 1980, 1983, for reviews of the evidence). Kohlberg (1975), for example, found that only 15% of those students who reasoned at the postconventional level actually cheated when given an opportunity, compared with 55% of the "conventional" students and 70% of those at the preconventional level. Moreover, experimental participants who are at Kohlberg's Stage 4 are more likely to refuse to shock an experimental confederate who seems to be in pain than are their age mates at Stage 3 (Kohlberg & Candee, 1984). Yet, Kohlberg is hardly surprised that moral reasoning often fails to predict moral behavior; after all, he argues that subjects at any of his moral stages may favor either course of action when resolving an ethical dilemma. It is the *structure* of their reasoning that sets them apart into different "stages" of moral development, not the decisions they reach.

In sum, Kohlberg expects a significant but imperfect relationship between moral reasoning and moral behavior, and this is precisely what the data seem to show (Blasi, 1980). A person who reasons at Stage 5 will often act differently in moral situations than one who reasons at Stage 4, Stage 3, or Stage 2. However, the relationships between moral reasoning and moral conduct that are reported in this research are based on *group* trends, and it is not always possible to specify how an *individual* will behave from a knowledge of his or her stage of moral reasoning.

Situational influences on moral reasoning. One interesting aspect of Kohlberg's research is that subjects are fairly consistent in the type (or stage) of reasoning that they use to resolve different moral issues. Does this coherence simply reflect the fact that all Kohlberg's dilemmas are abstract and hypothetical? Would subjects be so consistent when reacting to more common moral issues—ones that they have often experienced?

Lawrence Walker and his associates (Walker, de Vries, & Trevethan, 1987) sought to answer these questions by asking each of 240 6–65-year-olds to resolve three of Kohlberg's hypothetical dilemmas and a fourth, *real life* dilemma that the subject had faced and had considered very important to himself or herself. The results were interesting: 62% of the participants reasoned at the same stage when resolving real-life and hypothetical dilemmas, whereas 20% reasoned at a higher stage on the hypothetical dilemmas than on the real one, and 18% reasoned at a higher stage on the real dilemma than on the hypothetical ones. Yet, even when subjects operated at different levels on the hypothetical and the real-life dilemmas, they still ended up reasoning at adjacent stages on the two types of issues (for example, Stage 3 on the real-life dilemma and a mix of Stage 3 and Stage 4 reasoning on the hypothetical ones). So it seems that there is some underlying consistency to moral reasoning after all—a coherence that is not merely attributable to the abstract and hypothetical nature of Kohlberg's moral-decision stories.

F-3   M-4

The question of sex differences. Some investigators have reported an interesting sex difference in moral reasoning; adult females are typically at Stage 3 of Kohlberg's stage sequence, while adult males are usually at Stage 4 (Holstein, 1976; Kohlberg, 1969; Parikh, 1980). Does this mean that females are less morally mature than males (as Freud had assumed)? Carol Gilligan (1977, 1982) says no, arguing that Kohlberg's moral stages were derived from interviews with males and that they may not capture the essence of feminine moral reasoning. In Box 14-4 we will consider the basis for Gilligan's provocative claim as we examine the kinds of moral judgments that her female subjects displayed when deciding whether to have abortions.

Summing up. Kohlberg's theory is an important statement about the moral development of children, adolescents, and young adults. He has identified a sequence of moral stages that is related to cognitive development and appears to be universal across cultures.[4] Moreover, each of Kohlberg's stages does seem to be a reasonably consistent and coherent mode of thinking that is likely to determine how an individual at that stage will reason about both hypothetical and real-life moral issues. So is this influential theory the final word on moral development?

No, indeed! Despite its many strengths, there are those who argue that Kohlberg's singular focus on moral cognition makes his theory woefully incomplete. Indeed, we have already seen that one's level of moral reasoning often fails to forecast moral behavior (recall that even 15% of Kohlberg's postconventional moral reasoners were willing to cheat on a test when given an

opportunity), and critics such as Norma Haan (Haan, Aerts, & Cooper, 1985) are hardly surprised by such inconsistencies. Haan and her colleagues point out that moral dilemmas in everyday life tend to arouse powerful emotions—affective reactions that Kohlberg largely ignores, even though they may have a powerful influence on our moral conduct. According to Haan et al., what we should ultimately be interested in when we study morality is (1) how people actually behave when confronted with a moral dilemma and (2) the factors that cause them to behave as they do. In our next section of the chapter, we will examine a third theory—the social-learning approach—that attempts to specify some of the important cognitive, social, and emotional influences on a child's moral conduct and eventual moral development.

Morality as a Product of Social Learning

Unlike psychoanalytic theorists, who assume that the development of the superego implies a consistent moral orientation, social-learning theorists propose a "**doctrine of specificity.**" The implications of these opposing viewpoints can be seen in the following example. Suppose we expose a young girl to two tests of moral conduct. In the first test, the child is told not to play with some attractive toys and is then left alone with them. The second test is one in which the child is left to play a game that is "rigged" in such a way that she must cheat in order to win a valuable prize. Each situation requires the child to resist the temptation to do something she is not supposed to do before we would label her behavior morally responsible. If morality is a general attribute, as the psychoanalysts contend, our subject should either resist temptation on both of the tests or transgress on both. However, if morality is specific to the situation, the child might resist temptation on both tests, transgress on both, or resist on one and transgress on the other.

Prominent social-learning theorists such as Justin Aronfreed (1976) and Albert Bandura (1977) think

---

[4]Perhaps it is more accurate to say that the first four stages of Kohlberg's sequence are "universal," for as we have noted, postconventional reasoning does not exist in some societies, and only a small minority of adults in any society ever reach the postconventional level.

doctrine of specificity: a viewpoint shared by many social-learning theorists which holds that moral reasoning and moral behavior depend more on the situation one faces than on an internalized set of moral principles.

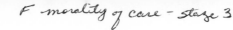

Box 14-4
A Different Voice? Gilligan's Theory of Female Moral Development

Do females have a different perspective on moral issues than males do? Carol Gilligan (1977, 1982) claims that they do, and she suggests that these sex differences in moral orientation stem from the different ways in which boys and girls are raised. Gilligan argues that boys are taught to be independent, assertive, and achievement-oriented—experiences that encourage them to consider moral dilemmas as inevitable conflicts of interest between *individuals* that laws and other social conventions are designed to resolve. She calls this orientation the *morality of justice*—a perspective that approximates Stage 4 reasoning in Kohlberg's scheme. By contrast, girls are brought up to be nurturant, empathic, and concerned about the needs of others—in short, to define their sense of "goodness" in terms of their *relationships* with

other people. So for females, morality implies a sense of caring or compassionate concern for human welfare—a *morality of care* that approximates Stage 3 reasoning in Kohlberg's scheme. According to Gilligan, the morality of care that women adopt is neither more nor less mature than the rule-bound, justice orientation of men. Instead she views these two moral orientations as "separate but equal" and suggests that females go through a different series of moral stages than males do.

Gilligan's next step was to study the moral judgments of females by asking pregnant women to discuss an important dilemma that they were currently facing—should they continue their pregnancies or have abortions? After analyzing the responses of her 29 subjects, Gilligan proposed that women's moral judgments progress through a sequence of three levels. At the first level, *self-interest* guides moral decisions, and the needs and wishes of others are largely ignored. One of Gilligan's subjects illustrated this reasoning by stating that all she

could think about was to abort her unborn fetus because having a baby would interfere with her plans to finish school. At the second level (*self-sacrifice*), women are now willing to sacrifice their own self-interests for the welfare of others, as when one young woman chose to abort a baby she wanted because the father insisted she do so. Finally, many women eventually reach a third moral level in which blatant self-sacrifice is considered "immoral" in its power to hurt the self. Presumably, the principle of *nonviolence*—an injunction against hurting anyone—becomes the premise underlying all moral judgments. This "mature" morality of care is reflected in the thinking of one 25-year-old: "I would not be doing myself or the child a favor by having this child . . . I don't need to pay off my imaginary debts to the world through this child, and I don't think that it is right to bring a child into the world and use it for that purpose" (Gilligan, 1977, p. 505). Note that the concern here does seem to

continued

---

of moral behavior as a class of "socially acceptable" responses that are self-reinforcing (for example, it feels good to help) or instrumental for avoiding guilt, anxiety, or punishment. Bandura argues that specific moral responses or habits are acquired in much the same way as any other type of social behavior—through direct tuition and observational learning. Thus, if the girl in our example had often been punished for violating verbal prohibitions (or rewarded for following instructions) and had been reinforced in the past for her honesty (or exposed to honest models), she might well resist temptation on both of the "moral conduct" tests. But inconsistent behavior could occur if one of these moral habits (for example, complying with verbal instructions) had been established while the other (honesty) had not.

How Consistent Are Moral Conduct and Moral Character?

Perhaps the most extensive study of children's moral conduct is one of the oldest—the Character Education Inquiry reported by Hugh Hartshorne and Mark May (1928–1930). The purpose of this five-year project

was to investigate the moral "character" of 10,000 children aged 8–16 by tempting them to lie, cheat, or steal in a variety of situations. The most noteworthy finding of this massive investigation was that children tended *not* to be consistent in their moral behavior; a child's willingness to cheat in one situation did not predict his willingness to lie, cheat, or steal in other situations. Of particular interest was the finding that children who cheated in a particular setting were just as likely as those who did not to state that cheating is wrong! Hartshorne and May concluded that "honesty" is largely specific to the situation rather than a stable character trait.

This "doctrine of specificity" has been questioned by other researchers. Roger Burton (1963, 1984) reanalyzed Hartshorne and May's data using newer and more sophisticated statistical techniques. His analyses provide some support for behavioral consistency. For example, a child's willingness to cheat or not cheat in one context (for example, on tests in class) is reasonably consistent, although the same child might behave very differently in highly unrelated contexts (for example, at competitive games on the playground). A similar conclusion was drawn by Nelson, Grinder, and Mutterer

be to hurt neither oneself nor, ultimately, an "unwanted" baby. Gilligan argues that this Level III morality of care is every bit as abstract and "postconventional" as Kohlberg's highest stages, even though Kohlberg's scheme might place it at Stage 3 (and hence less mature) because of its focus on personal and interpersonal obligations.

Has research supported Gilligan's claims that there are sex differences in moral reasoning, moral orientations, and moral development? Not very convincingly, it hasn't. As we have noted in the text, some investigators have reported sex differences in moral reasoning. However, the vast majority of studies comparing the moral judgments of males and females fail to find any sex differences (see Thoma, 1986, and Walker, 1984, 1986, for recent reviews). So the bulk of the evidence simply does not support the notion that Kohlberg's theory or the techniques he used to assess levels of moral reasoning are in any way biased against girls and women.

Of course, it is still possible that females may develop along a different path and will come to emphasize a "morality of care" to a greater extent than males do. Yet, there is virtually no evidence for such a claim and, indeed, there is evidence to the contrary. When asked to resolve real-life moral dilemmas that they have faced, *both* males and females tend to raise issues of compassion and interpersonal responsibility about *as often as* or *more often than* they talk about abstract issues of justice and rights (see Ford & Lowery, 1986; Walker, de Vries, & Trevethan, 1987). So it seems that persons of each sex will frequently rely on Kohlberg's "morality of justice" *and* Gilligan's "morality of care" to make moral decisions—a finding which suggests that the moral-developmental paths taken by boys and girls are probably much more similar than Gilligan has assumed.

Although Gilligan's ideas about sex differences in moral reasoning have not been supported, her work is valuable nonetheless. Perhaps the most important

lessons she has taught us are (1) that there is much more to morality than a concern with laws, rules, rights, and justice and (2) that reasoning based on compassionate concerns and interpersonal responsibility can be just as "principled," and hence mature, as the "justice" orientation that Kohlberg has emphasized in his research. What Gilligan has given us, then, is a broader view of the meaning of morality. Perhaps it is now appropriate to describe a moral person, whether male or female, as "one whose moral choices reflect reasoned and deliberate judgments that ensure justice will be accorded to each person while maintaining a passionate concern for the well-being and care of each individual" (Brabeck, 1983, p. 289).

(1969), who tempted sixth-graders to violate six different prohibitions and found that "temptation behavior is at least moderately consistent across a variety of tasks" (p. 265). And earlier in the chapter, we noted that there is some consistency to children's altruistic inclinations as well. So it seems that moral behaviors *of a particular kind* (for example, cheating on exams; helping needy others) are not nearly so situationally specific as Hartshorne and May had thought. Moreover, it appears that both the consistency of moral behaviors and the correlations among measures of moral affect, moral reasoning, and moral conduct become progressively stronger (or more apparent) between the grade school years and young adulthood (Shaffer, 1988).

In sum, the "doctrine of specificity" is clearly an overstatement, for all three aspects of morality become more consistent and more highly interrelated as children mature. However, this is not to imply that morality ever becomes a wholly stable and **unitary** attribute, for a person's willingness to lie, cheat, or violate other moral norms may always depend to some extent on situational factors, such as the importance of the objective one might achieve by transgressing or the

amount of encouragement provided by peers for deviant conduct (Burton, 1976). Stated another way, the moral character of even the most mature of adults is unlikely to be perfectly consistent across all settings and situations (Shaffer, 1988).

Learning to Resist Temptation

From society's standpoint the most important index of morality is the extent to which an individual is able to resist pressures to violate moral norms, *even when the possibility of detection and punishment is remote* (Hoffman, 1970). A person who resists temptation in the absence of external surveillance not only has learned a moral rule but also is internally motivated to abide by that rule. How do children acquire moral standards, and what motivates them to obey these learned codes of conduct? Social-learning theorists have at-

[handwritten: most imp index of morality]

---

unitary morality: the notion that moral affect, moral reasoning, and moral behavior are interrelated components of a "moral character" that is consistent across situations.

Photo 14-6. Sometimes it is difficult to tell whether children are working together, helping each other, or using each other's work. Although there is some consistency to moral behavior, a child's conduct in any particular situation is likely to be influenced by factors such as the importance of the goal that might be achieved by breaking a moral rule and the probability of being caught should he or she commit a transgression.

tempted to answer these questions by studying the effects of reinforcement, punishment, and social modeling on children's moral behavior.

The resistance-to-temptation paradigm

When studying children's resistance to temptation, an experimenter will first establish a prohibition of some sort and then leave the child alone so that he or she is tempted to violate that edict. A common procedure is to inform children that they are not to touch certain attractive toys but that they are free to play with any number of other, unattractive objects. Once a child has learned the prohibition and refrains from playing with the attractive items, the experimenter leaves the room and thereby tempts the child to violate the rule. As we will see, this **"forbidden toy" paradigm** has proved quite useful at determining whether various forms of praise, punishment, and other disciplinary techniques affect the child's willingness to comply with rules and regulations.

Reinforcement as a determinant of moral conduct

We have seen on several occasions that the frequency of many behaviors can be increased if these acts are reinforced. Moral behaviors are certainly no exception. For example, David Perry and Ross Parke (1975) found that children were more likely to obey a prohibition against touching attractive toys if they had been reinforced for playing with other, unattractive items. So the practice of rewarding alternative behaviors that are incompatible with prohibited acts can be an effective method of instilling moral controls. In addition, punishment administered by a warm, loving (socially reinforcing) parent is more successful at producing resistance to temptation than the same punishment given by a cold, rejecting parent (Sears et al., 1957). Thus, the effectiveness of punishment as a means of establishing moral prohibitions will depend, in part, on the disciplinarian's past history as a *reinforcing* agent.

The role of punishment in establishing moral prohibitions

Although reinforcing acceptable behaviors is an effective way to promote desirable conduct, adults will often fail to recognize that a child has *resisted* a temptation and is deserving of praise. By contrast, people are quick to inform a child of his or her misdeeds by *punishing* moral transgressions. Is punishment an effective way to foster the development of **inhibitory**

control? As we will see, the answer depends on the kind of punishment that is administered and on the child's *interpretation* of this aversive experience.

Early research. Ross Parke and his associates have used the "forbidden toy" paradigm to study the effects of punishment on children's resistance to temptation. During the first phase of a typical experiment, subjects are punished (usually by hearing a loud and noxious buzzer) whenever they touch an attractive toy; however, nothing happens when they play with unattractive toys. Once the child has learned the prohibition, the experimenter leaves the room. The child is then surreptitiously observed to determine whether he or she plays with the forbidden objects.

Parke (1977) found that not all punishments are equally effective at promoting the development of moral controls. You may recall that we discussed much of this research when we looked at the effects of punishment in Chapter 7. By way of review, Table 14-4 briefly summarizes the conditions under which punishment was most effective at inhibiting the child's undesirable conduct after the disciplinarian had left the room.

Yet, the most important discovery made by Parke and his associates is that all forms of punishment become more effective when accompanied by a cognitive rationale that provides the transgressor with reasons for inhibiting a forbidden act. In fact, rationales alone are more effective than mild punishments at persuading children not to touch attractive toys. However, let's not conclude that parents should abandon punishment in favor of rationales, for a combination of a punishment and a rationale is much more effective than either of these treatments by itself (Parke, 1977).

Explaining the effects of cognitive rationales. Why do rationales increase the effectiveness of punishment, especially mild or delayed punishments that produce little moral restraint by themselves? Probably because rationales provide children with information specifying why the punished act is wrong and why *they* should feel guilty or shameful were they to repeat it. So when these youngsters think about committing the forbidden act in the future, they should experience a general uneasiness (stemming from previous disciplinary encounters), should be inclined to make an *internal* attribution for this emotional arousal (for example, "I'd feel guilty were I to deviate"; "I'd violate my positive self-image"), and should now be more likely to

Table 14-4. Characteristics of punishment and the punitive context that influence a child's resistance to temptation

Timing of punishment	Punishment administered as children initiate deviant acts is more effective than punishment given after the acts have been performed. Early punishment makes children apprehensive as they prepare to commit a transgression, so that they are less likely to follow through. By contrast, late punishment makes children apprehensive *after* the act is completed, so that they may perform the act again and only then feel anxious.
Intensity of punishment	High-intensity punishment (a loud buzzer or forceful *NO!*) is more effective at inhibiting undesirable conduct than mild punishments are. However, a caution is in order, for very intense punishments such as a forceful spanking can backfire by making children hostile toward the punitive agent and willing to deviate "out of spite" when the disciplinarian is not around to oversee their activities.
Consistency of punishment	To be effective, punishment must be administered consistently. Satisfying acts that are punished erratically or inconsistently persist for long periods and are difficult to eliminate even after the punitive agent begins to punish them on a regular basis.
Relationship to the punitive agent	Punishment is more effective at establishing moral prohibitions when administered by someone who has previously established a warm and friendly (rewarding) relationship with the child.

inhibit the forbidden act and to feel rather good about their "mature and responsible" conduct. By contrast, children who receive no rationales or who have been exposed to reasoning that focuses their attention on the negative consequences they can expect for future transgressions (for example, "You'll be spanked again if

---

"forbidden toy" paradigm: a method of studying children's resistance to temptation by noting whether youngsters will play with forbidden toys when they believe that this transgression is unlikely to be detected.

inhibitory control: an ability to display acceptable conduct by resisting the temptation to commit a forbidden act.

you do it") will experience just as much uneasiness when they think about committing the forbidden act. However, these youngsters should tend to make *external* attributions for their emotional arousal (for example, "I'm worried about getting caught and punished")—attributions that might make them comply with moral norms in the presence of authority figures but should do little to inhibit deviant behavior if there is no one around to detect and punish a transgression.

We see, then, that fear of detection and punishment is not enough to persuade children to resist temptation in the absence of external surveillance. In order to establish truly internalized, *self*-controls, adults must structure disciplinary encounters to include an appropriate rationale—a rationale that informs the child why the prohibited act is wrong and why *she* should feel guilty or shameful were she to repeat it (Hoffman, 1985). Stated another way, true *self*-restraint is largely under *cognitive* control—the ability to resist temptation depends on what's in children's heads rather than on the amount of fear or uneasiness in their guts.

Although rational forms of punishment can be quite successful at inhibiting children's undesirable conduct, we should not necessarily assume that punitive tactics are the most effective or efficient way to establish moral controls. The major problem with punitive techniques is that they often have undesirable side effects that limit their usefulness (for example, making children angry or resentful, modeling coercive, antisocial modes of problem solving; or even reinforcing a child who deviates in order to attract attention). In Box 14-5 we will consider two alternative techniques that adults can use to promote children's resistance to temptation while avoiding many of the undesirable side effects associated with punishment.

Effects of social models on children's moral behavior

Social-learning theorists have generally assumed that modeling influences play an important role in the child's moral development. And they are undoubtedly correct, for as we have seen, young children often imitate the compassionate and helpful acts of altruistic models. But helpful acts are *active* responses that will capture a child's attention. Will children learn *inhibitory controls* from models who exhibit socially desirable behavior in a "passive" way by failing to commit forbidden acts?

Apparently they will, as long as they recognize that the "passive" model is actually resisting the temptation to violate a moral norm. Nace Toner and his associates (Toner, Parke, & Yussen, 1978) exposed preschool and second-grade boys to rule-following models and found that this experience did indeed promote resistance to temptation. In fact, some of the children who had been exposed to the rule-following models were still following the rule when retested a week later. In a similar study, Joan Grusec and her associates (Grusec, Kuczynski, Rushton, & Simutis, 1979) found that a model who resists temptation can be particularly effective at inspiring children to behave in kind if he clearly verbalizes that he is following a rule and states a rationale for not committing the deviant act. Finally, the type of rationale that the model provides is also important. Rule-following models whose rationales match the child's customary level of moral reasoning are more influential than models whose rationales are beyond that level (Toner & Potts, 1981).

Of course, a model who violates a moral norm may *disinhibit* observers by giving them reason to think that they too can break the rule, particularly if the model is not punished for his deviant acts (Rosenkoetter, 1973). Thus, social models play two roles in a child's moral development, sometimes leading him or her to resist temptation and at other times serving as "bad influences" who encourage inappropriate conduct.

Finally, an experiment by Nace Toner and his associates produced a very interesting outcome: 6- to 8-year-olds who were persuaded to serve as models of moral restraint for other children became more likely than age mates who had not served as exemplary models to obey rules during later tests of resistance to temptation (Toner, Moore, & Ashley, 1978). It was almost as if serving as a model had produced a change in children's self-concepts, so that they now defined themselves as "people who follow rules." The implications for child rearing are obvious: perhaps parents could succeed in establishing inhibitory controls in their older children by appealing to their maturity and persuading them to serve as models of self-restraint for their younger brothers and sisters.

Who Raises Children Who Are Morally Mature?

About 20 years ago, Martin Hoffman (1970) carefully reviewed the child-rearing literature to determine whether the techniques that parents use to discipline transgressions have any effect on the moral de-

Box 14-5
Nonpunitive Methods of
Promoting Self-Control

In recent years, social-learning and social information-processing theorists have searched for nonpunitive methods of persuading children to comply with rules and to display self-restraint. Two such strategies that appear especially promising are (1) the self-instructional approach and (2) moral self-concept training.

blue prints for action
Self-instructional strategies. If a child's willingness to resist temptation is truly under cognitive control, as social-learning and social information-processing theorists have argued, then it should be possible to teach young children how to *instruct themselves* to follow rules and to resist temptations. To test this hypothesis, Walter Mischel and Charlotte Patterson (1976) asked preschool children to work on a very dull task in the presence of a talking "clown box" that tried to persuade these youngsters to break their promise to work. Children who had been taught to say to themselves "I'm not going to look at Mr. Clown box . . . when Mr. Clown box says to look at him" were better able than those who had received no self-instructional strategy to resist this tempting distraction and keep on working.

In another study of children's self-control (Toner & Smith, 1977), preschool girls played a "waiting" game in which they received one piece of candy for every 30 seconds they waited. As long as the child continued to wait, candies would accumulate in front of her. But if she told the experimenter to stop so she could enjoy her treats, the game was over and could not be restarted. As the game began, the girls were either (1) given no further instructions, (2) told to talk about how good the candy would taste, or (3) told to instruct themselves "It is good if I wait." The results were clear. Children who instructed themselves that it was a good idea to wait did indeed show much more self-restraint than their peers in the other two conditions, who had a difficult time

resisting the temptation to eat their candies.

In sum, we see that even very simple plans or "blueprints for action" that children have available for use in the face of temptation will enhance their ability to live up to their promises, to follow rules, and to delay immediate gratification.

Instilling a "moral" self-concept. The idea that moral self-restraint is under cognitive control implies that we should be able to promote compliance with moral rules by convincing children that they are "good" or "honest" people who are inhibiting the temptation to lie, cheat, or steal because they want to (an internal attribution). Indeed, children who incorporate attributions of "goodness," "honesty," or "strength of character" into their self-concepts may strive to live up to these positive self-images and could become highly self-critical or remorseful should they violate a rule.

Apparently this kind of moral self-concept training does indeed work. William Casey and Roger Burton (1982) found that 7–10-year-olds became much more honest while playing games if being "honest" was stressed and the players had learned to remind themselves to follow the rules. Yet, when honesty was *not* stressed, the players were likely to cheat— even when they had been told to periodically remind themselves to comply with the rules. Moreover, David Perry and his associates (Perry, Perry, Bussey, English, & Arnold, 1980) found that 9–10-year-olds who had been told that they were especially good at carrying out instructions and following rules (moral self-concept training) behaved very differently after succumbing to a nearly irresistible temptation (leaving a boring task to watch an exciting TV show) than did peers who had not been told they were especially good. Specifically, children who had heard positive attributions about themselves were more inclined than control subjects to *punish their own transgressions* by giving back many of the valuable prize tokens they had been paid for working at the boring task. So it seems that labeling

children as "good" or "honest" not only may increase the likelihood that they will resist temptations but also contributes to children's feelings of guilt or remorse should they behave inappropriately and violate their positive self-images. Indeed, Perry et al. (1980) suggest that the expectation of feeling guilty or remorseful over deviant conduct may be what motivates children with positive self-concepts to resist temptations in the first place.

Summing up. Clearly, children can become effective allies in their own moral socialization if they are often encouraged to be "good" or "honest" persons and have learned how to instruct or remind themselves of the rules that they must follow in order to behave appropriately and to maintain a "good" or "honest" self-image. Unlike punishment, which is easily applied after a transgression, the nonpunitive strategies that we have reviewed will require a substantial amount of planning on the part of the adult. But despite the effort that one must expend, the potential advantages of these alternatives to punishment are many. For example, a parent who is obviously concerned about helping the child to *prevent future transgressions* is apt to be perceived as caring and loving—an impression that should increase the child's motivation to comply with parental requests. Moreover, self-concept training and the use of self-instruction should help to convince the child that "I'm resisting this temptation because I want to" and thus lead to the development of truly *internalized* controls rather than a response inhibition based on a fear of detection and punishment. And last but not least, these nonpunitive techniques produce few if any of the undesirable side effects that often accompany punishment.

velopment of their children. Much of the research that he reviewed was designed to test the hypothesis that **love-oriented discipline** (withdrawing affection or approval), which generates anxiety over a loss of love, would prove more effective at furthering the child's moral development than **power-assertive discipline** (physical punishment or withholding privileges), which generates anger or resentment.

Hoffman discovered that neither love withdrawal nor power assertion is particularly effective at promoting moral development. In fact, parents who often rely on power-assertive techniques have children who can be described as morally immature. The one disciplinary strategy that seems to foster the development of moral affect (guilt, shame), moral reasoning, and moral behavior is an approach called **inductive discipline,** which

affective   cognitive   behavioral

> includes techniques in which the parent gives explanations or reasons for requiring the child to change his behavior. Examples are pointing out physical requirements of the situation or the harmful consequences of the child's behavior for himself or others. These techniques are . . . an attempt to . . . convince the child that he should change his behavior in the prescribed manner. Also included are techniques that appeal to conformity-inducing agents that already exist with the child. Examples are appeals to the child's pride, strivings for mastery and to be "grown up," and concern for others [Hoffman, 1970, p. 286].

Hoffman noted that inductive parents who regularly stress the needs and emotions of others as part of their discipline have children who show the highest levels of moral maturity. This "other-oriented" induction is accomplished by

> directly pointing out the nature of the consequences (e.g., If you throw snow on their walk, they will have to clean it up all over again; Pulling the leash like that can hurt the dog's neck; That hurts my feelings); pointing out the relevant needs or desires of others (e.g., he is afraid . . . , so please turn the lights back on); or explaining the motives underlying the other person's behavior toward the child (e.g., Don't yell at him. He was only trying to help) [Hoffman, 1970, p. 286].

Table 14-5 summarizes the relationships among the three patterns of parental discipline (power assertion, love withdrawal, and induction) and various measures of children's moral development. Clearly these data confirm Hoffman's conclusion: parents who rely on

inductive discipline tend to have children who are morally mature, whereas frequent use of power assertion may actually inhibit the child's moral development.

Why is inductive discipline effective?

Hoffman believes there are several reasons that the use of inductive tactics is such an effective disciplinary strategy. First, the inductive disciplinarian provides *cognitive standards* (or rationales) that children can use to evaluate their conduct. And when the inductive discipline is other-oriented, parents are furnishing their child with the kinds of experiences that should foster the development of empathy and reciprocal role taking—two cognitive abilities that contribute to the growth of mature moral reasoning. Second, use of inductive discipline allows parents to talk about the *affective* components of morality, such as guilt and shame, that are not easily discussed with a child who is made emotionally insecure by love-oriented discipline or angry by power-assertive techniques. Finally, parents who use inductive discipline are likely to explain to the child (1) what he or she *should have done* when tempted to violate a prohibition and (2) what he or she *can now do* to make up for a transgression. So it appears that induction is an effective method of moral socialization because it clearly illustrates the affective, cognitive, and behavioral aspects of morality and may help the child to integrate them.

Does induction promote moral maturity; or, rather, do morally mature children elicit more inductive forms of discipline from their parents? Since the child-rearing studies are correlational in nature, either of these possibilities could explain Hoffman's findings. Yet, Hoffman (1975a) contends that parents exert far more constraints on their children's behavior than children exert on parents. In other words, he believes that parental use of inductive discipline promotes moral maturity rather than the other way around. And there is some experimental support for Hoffman's point of view in that other-oriented induction is much more effective than other forms of discipline at persuading children to keep their promises and to comply with rules imposed by unfamiliar adults (Kuczynski, 1983). And yet, children clearly have a hand in determining how they are treated by their overseers. For example, youngsters who have a history of conduct disorders are more likely than normal children to elicit coercive, punitive forms of discipline when they misbehave—both from their mothers and from other adults who have been asked to monitor their activities (see Anderson et al., 1986; Brunk & Heng-

Table 14-5. Relationships between parents' use of three disciplinary strategies and children's moral development

Direction of relationship between parent's use of a disciplinary strategy and children's moral maturity	Type of discipline		
	Power assertion	Love withdrawal	Induction
+ (positive correlation)	7	8	38
− (negative correlation)	32	11	6

Note: Table entries represent the number of occasions on which a particular disciplinary technique was found to be associated (either positively or negatively) with a measure of children's moral affect, reasoning, or behavior.

Source: Adapted from Brody & Shaffer (1982).

geler, 1984). The child's reactions to previous disciplinary encounters are also important. Ross Parke (1977) finds that children who had ignored a disciplinarian or who had pleaded for mercy were dealt with much more forcefully during the next disciplinary encounter than those who had reacted to the earlier discipline by offering to undo the harm they had done. So it is likely that moral socialization in the home is a two-way street: while inductive discipline may indeed promote the development of moral controls, children with a history of good conduct who respond more favorably to disciplinary encounters are the ones who are apt to be treated in a rational, nonpunitive manner by their parents.

Finally, it is important to note that few if any parents are totally inductive, love-oriented, or power-assertive in their approach to discipline; most make at least some use of all three disciplinary techniques. Although parents classified as "inductive" rely heavily on inductive methods, they will occasionally take punitive measures whenever punishment is necessary to command the child's attention or to discipline repeated transgressions. So the style of parenting that Hoffman calls induction may be very similar to the "rationale + mild punishment" treatment that is so effective at producing resistance to temptation in the laboratory.

A child's-eye view of discipline

What do you suppose children think about various disciplinary strategies? Do they feel (as many developmentalists do) that physical punishment and love withdrawal are ineffective methods of promoting moral restraint? Would they favor inductive techniques? Or is it conceivable that children would prefer their parents to adopt a more permissive attitude and not be so quick to discipline transgressions?

Michael Siegal and Jan Cowen (1984) addressed these issues by asking 100 children and adolescents between the ages of 4 and 18 to listen to stories describing different kinds of inappropriate conduct and to evaluate several strategies that mothers had used to discipline these antics. Five kinds of transgressions were described: (1) simple disobedience (the child refused to clean his room), (2) causing physical harm to others (the child punched a playmate), (3) causing physical harm to oneself (ignoring an order not to touch a hot stove), (4) causing psychological harm to others (making fun of a physically disabled person), and (5) causing physical damage (breaking a lamp while roughhousing). The four disciplinary techniques on which mothers were said to have relied were *induction* (reasoning with the culprit by pointing out the harmful consequences of his or her actions), *physical punishment* (hitting or spanking the child), *love withdrawal* (telling the culprit she wanted nothing more to do with him or her), and *permissive nonintervention* (ignoring the incident and assuming that the child would learn important lessons on his or her own). Each participant heard 20 stories that resulted from pairing each of the four maternal disciplinary strategies with each of the five transgressions. After listening to or reading each story, the subject indicated whether the mother's approach to the problem was "very wrong," "wrong," "half right—half wrong," "right," or "very right."

The results were indeed interesting. Although

---

love-oriented discipline: a form of discipline in which an adult withholds attention, affection, or approval in order to modify or control a child's behavior.

power-assertive discipline: a form of discipline in which an adult relies on his or her superior power (for example, by administering spankings or withholding privileges) to modify or control a child's behavior.

inductive discipline: a nonpunitive form of discipline in which an adult relies on cognitive rationales to modify or control a child's behavior.

the perceived appropriateness of each disciplinary technique varied somewhat across transgressions, the most interesting findings overall were that (1) induction was the most preferred disciplinary strategy for subjects of all ages (even preschoolers), and (2) physical punishment was the next most favorably evaluated technique. In other words, all participants seemed to favor a rational disciplinarian who relies heavily on reasoning that is occasionally backed by power assertion. By contrast, love withdrawal and permissiveness were favorably evaluated by no age group. And it is interesting to note that the younger children in the sample (that is, the 4- to 9-year-olds) favored *any* form of discipline, even love withdrawal, over a permissive attitude on the mother's part (which they viewed as "wrong" or "very wrong"). Apparently young children see the need for adults to step in and restrain their inappropriate conduct, for they were quite bothered by the stories in which youngsters were generally free to do their own thing, largely unencumbered by adult constraints.

We see, then, that the disciplinary style that children evaluate most favorably (induction backed by occasional use of power assertion) is the one most closely associated with measures of moral maturity in the child-rearing studies and with resistance to temptation in the laboratory. Perhaps another reason that inductive discipline promotes moral maturity is simply that children view this approach as the "right" way to deal with transgressions and they may be highly motivated to accept influence from a disciplinarian whose "world view" matches their own. By contrast, children who favor induction but are usually disciplined in other ways may see little justification for internalizing the values and exhortations of a disciplinarian whose very methods of inducing compliance seem unwise, unjust, and hardly worthy of their respect.

Summary

This chapter focuses on three interrelated aspects of social development that are often considered when making judgments about a child's moral character: the emergence and control of aggressive inclinations, the development of altruism and prosocial behavior, and the broader (or more inclusive) topic of moral socialization and moral development.

Aggression is defined as any act designed to harm or injure another living being who is motivated to avoid such treatment. Aggression emerges during the second year as older infants and toddlers begin to quarrel with siblings and peers over toys and other possessions. During the preschool period, children become less likely to throw temper tantrums or to hit and more likely to resort to verbally aggressive tactics such as name-calling or ridiculing. Although young grade school children continue to fight over possessions, they gradually become more proficient at inferring others' aggressive intent, so that an increasing percentage of their aggressive exchanges are person-directed hostile outbursts. Boys are more physically and verbally aggressive than girls and are more likely than girls to become targets of aggression. However, one's characteristic level of aggression (or aggressiveness) is a reasonably stable attribute for both boys and girls: an aggressive 6-year-old is likely to be relatively high in aggression as an adolescent or a young adult.

A person's aggressive inclinations will depend, in part, on the cultural, subcultural, and family settings in which he or she is raised. Cold and rejecting parents who rely on physical punishment and often permit aggression are likely to raise highly aggressive children. However, the socialization of aggression is a two-way street, for characteristics of the child (such as an active, impetuous temperament) can affect the child-rearing practices that parents use. Highly aggressive youngsters who are "out of control" often live in coercive home environments where family members are constantly struggling with one another. In order to help these highly combative children, it is often necessary to treat the entire family.

Proceeding in accordance with the catharsis hypothesis—the belief that children become less aggressive after letting off steam against an inanimate object—is an ineffective control tactic that may instigate aggressive behavior. Some proven methods of controlling children's aggression are (1) the incompatible-response technique, (2) use of the time-out procedure to punish aggression, (3) coaching and modeling nonaggressive solutions to conflict, (4) creating play environments that minimize the likelihood of conflict, and (5) encouraging children to recognize the harmful effects of their aggressive acts and to empathize with the victims of aggression.

Although infants and toddlers will occasionally offer toys to playmates, help their parents with household chores, and try to soothe distressed companions, examples of altruism become increasingly common over the course of childhood. By middle childhood, there is some consistency in children's prosocial inclinations:

those who are most helpful or compassionate in one situation are likely to be the most prosocially inclined in other, similar situations.

Like "aggression," a person's "altruistic" tendencies are influenced by the cultural and family settings in which he or she is raised. Parents can promote altruistic behavior by encouraging their child to perform acts of kindness, by reinforcing the child's prosocial deeds, and by practicing what they preach. Older children may incorporate altruism into their self-concepts if adults tell them that they are "kindly" or "helpful" people whenever they behave charitably. Empathy and role-taking skills both contribute to the development of altruistic behavior, and parents who discipline harmdoing with nonpunitive, affective explanations that point out the negative effects of misconduct for the child's victims are likely to raise children who become sympathetic, self-sacrificing, and concerned about the welfare of others.

Morality has been defined in many ways, although almost everyone agrees that it implies a set of principles or ideals that help the individual to distinguish right from wrong and to act on this distinction. Morality has three basic components: moral affect, moral reasoning, and moral behavior.

Psychoanalytic theorists emphasize the affective, or "emotional," aspects of morality. According to Freud, the character of the parent/child relationship largely determines the child's willingness to internalize the moral standards of his or her parents. This internalization is said to occur during the phallic stage and to result in the development of the superego. Once formed, the superego functions as an internal censor that will reward the child for virtuous conduct and punish moral transgressions by making the child feel anxious, guilty, or shameful. Many tests of Freudian theory have now been conducted, and most of the evidence does *not* support Freud's explanation of moral development.

Cognitive-developmental theorists have emphasized the cognitive component of morality by studying the development of moral reasoning. Jean Piaget was the pioneer. He formulated a two-stage model of moral development based on changes that occur in children's conceptions of rules and their sense of social justice. Although Piaget did identify some important processes and basic trends in the development of moral reasoning, recent research suggests that his two-stage theory is too simplistic. Lawrence Kohlberg believes that moral development progresses through an invariant sequence of three moral levels, each composed of two distinct stages.

According to Kohlberg, the order of progression through the levels and stages is invariant because each of these modes of thinking depends, in part, on the development of certain cognitive abilities that evolve in a fixed sequence. Each successive stage represents a reorganization of previous stages; and once the individual has attained a higher stage of moral reasoning, he or she will not regress to earlier stages.

Attempts to verify the cognitive theories reveal that moral reasoning is related to cognitive development. Moreover, children progress through the first four of Kohlberg's six stages in the order that Kohlberg specifies. Yet, most people never reach Kohlberg's highest moral stages, which seem to require a special kind of environmental support in order to develop.

Social-learning theorists emphasize the behavioral component of morality, and their research has helped us to understand how children are able to resist temptation and to inhibit acts that violate moral norms. Among the processes that are important in establishing inhibitory controls are reinforcing the child for acceptable behavior and punishing unacceptable conduct. However, some punishments are more effective than others. The most effective punitive tactics are those that include cognitive rationales explaining why the punished act is wrong and why the child should want to inhibit such conduct. Nonpunitive techniques such as teaching the child how to instruct herself to avoid temptations or convincing the child that she is a "good" or "honest" person are also quite effective at promoting moral self-restraint. Indeed, any technique that induces children to make internal attributions for their uneasiness in the face of temptation or for their compliance with rules is apt to contribute to their moral development. Children may also acquire inhibitory controls by observing models who show moral restraint or by serving as rule-following models for other children.

Martin Hoffman has looked at the relationship between parental disciplinary practices and children's moral development. His findings indicate that warm and loving parents who rely mainly on inductive discipline tend to raise children who are morally mature. Induction is an effective method of moral socialization because it often illustrates and may help the child to integrate the affective, cognitive, and behavioral aspects of morality. And because children generally prefer induction to other disciplinary techniques, viewing it as the wise choice for handling most transgressions, they may be highly motivated to accept influence from an inductive adult whose methods they can respect.

References

AMBRON, S. R., & Irwin, D. M. (1975). Role-taking and moral judgment in five- and seven-year-olds. *Developmental Psychology, 11,* 102.

ANDERSON, K. E., Lytton, H., & Romney, D. M. (1986). Mothers' interactions with normal and conduct-disordered boys: Who affects whom? *Developmental Psychology, 22,* 604–609.

ARONFREED, J. (1976). Moral development from the standpoint of a general psychological theory. In T. Lickona (Ed.), *Moral development and behavior.* New York: Holt, Rinehart and Winston.

BANDURA, A. (1977). *Social learning theory.* Englewood Cliffs, NJ: Prentice-Hall.

BARON, R. A. (1971). Magnitude of victim's pain cues and level of prior anger arousal as determinants of adult aggressive behavior. *Journal of Personality and Social Psychology, 17,* 236–243.

BARON, R. A., & Byrne, D. (1984). *Social psychology: Understanding human interaction.* Newton, MA: Allyn & Bacon.

BARRETT, D. E. (1979). A naturalistic study of sex differences in children's aggression. *Merrill-Palmer Quarterly, 25,* 193–203.

BAR-TAL, D., Raviv, A., & Goldberg, M. (1982). Helping behavior among preschool children: An observational study. *Child Development, 53,* 396–402.

BAUMRIND, D. (1978). A dialectical materialist's perspective on knowing social reality. In W. Damon (Ed.), Moral development. *New Directions for Child Development* (No. 2). San Francisco: Jossey-Bass.

BERKOWITZ, M. W., & Gibbs, J. C. (1983). Measuring the developmental features of moral discussion. *Merrill-Palmer Quarterly, 29,* 399–410.

BERKOWITZ, M. W., Gibbs, J. C., & Broughton, J. M. (1980). The relation of moral judgment stage disparity to developmental effects of peer dialogues. *Merrill-Palmer Quarterly, 26,* 341–357.

BIRCH, L. L., & Billman, J. (1986). Preschool children's food sharing with friends and acquaintances. *Child Development, 57,* 387–395.

BLASI, A. (1980). Bridging moral cognition and moral action: A critical review of the literature. *Psychological Bulletin, 88,* 1–45.

BLASI, A. (1983). Moral cognition and moral action: A theoretical perspective. *Developmental Review, 3,* 178–210.

BRABECK, M. (1983). Moral judgment: Theory and research on differences between males and females. *Developmental Review, 3,* 274–291.

BRODY, G. H., & Shaffer, D. R. (1982). Contributions of parents and peers to children's moral socialization. *Developmental Review, 2,* 31–75.

BRONSON, W. C. (1975). Developments in behavior with age mates during the second year of life. In M. Lewis & L. A. Rosenblum (Eds.), *The origins of behavior: Friendship and peer relations.* New York: Wiley.

BROWN, P., & Elliot, R. (1965). Control of aggression in a nursery school class. *Journal of Experimental Child Psychology, 2,* 103–107.

BRUNK, M. A., & Henggeler, S. W. (1984). Child influences on adult controls: An experimental investigation. *Developmental Psychology, 20,* 1074–1081.

BRYAN, J. H., & Walbek, N. (1970). Preaching and practicing self-sacrifice: Children's actions and reactions. *Child Development, 41,* 329–353.

BRYANT, B. K. (1982). An index of empathy for children and adolescents. *Child Development, 53,* 413–425.

BURTON, R. V. (1963). The generality of honesty reconsidered. *Psychological Review, 70,* 481–499.

BURTON, R. V. (1976). Honesty and dishonesty. In T. Lickona (Ed.), *Moral development and behavior.* New York: Holt, Rinehart and Winston.

BURTON, R. V. (1984). A paradox in theories and research in moral development. In W. M. Kurtines & J. L. Gewirtz (Eds.), *Morality, moral behavior, and moral development.* New York: Wiley.

BUSS, A. H. (1961). *The psychology of aggression.* New York: Wiley.

CASEY, W. M., & Burton, R. V. (1982). Training children to be consistently honest through verbal self-instructions. *Child Development, 53,* 911–919.

CASPI, A., Elder, G. H., Jr., & Bem, D. J. (1987). Moving against the world: Life-course patterns of explosive children. *Developmental Psychology, 23,* 308–313.

CHANDLER, M. J. (1973). Egocentrism and antisocial behavior: The assessment and training of social perspective taking skills. *Developmental Psychology, 9,* 326–332.

CHAPMAN, M., Zahn-Waxler, C., Cooperman, G., & Iannotti, R. J. (1987). Empathy and responsibility in the motivation of children's helping. *Developmental Psychology, 23,* 140–145.

CHARLESWORTH, R., & Hartup, W. W. (1967). Positive social reinforcement in the nursery school peer group. *Child Development, 38,* 993–1002.

CLARY, E. G., & Miller, J. (1986). Socialization and situational influences on sustained altruism. *Child Development, 57,* 1358–1369.

COLBY, A., & Kohlberg, L. (1987). *The measurement of moral judgment.* Vol. 1: *Theoretical foundations and research validation.* Cambridge: Cambridge University Press.

COLBY, A., Kohlberg, L., Gibbs, J., & Lieberman, M. (1983). A longitudinal study of moral judgment. *Monographs of the Society for Research in Child Development, 48*(Nos. 1–2, Serial No. 200).

DLUGOKINSKI, E. L., & Firestone, I. J. (1974). Other centeredness and susceptibility to charitable appeals: Effects of perceived discipline. *Developmental Psychology, 10,* 21–28.

DODGE, K. A. (1980). Social cognition and children's aggressive behavior. *Child Development, 51,* 162–170.

DODGE, K. A. (1986). A social information processing model of social competence in children. In M. Perlmutter (Ed.), *Minnesota Symposia on Child Psychology* (Vol. 18). Hillsdale, NJ: Erlbaum.

DODGE, K. A., & Frame, C. L. (1982). Social cognitive biases and deficits in aggressive boys. *Child Development, 53,* 620–635.

DODGE, K. A., Murphy, R. R., & Buchsbaum, K. (1984). The assessment of intention-cue detection skills in children: Implications for developmental psychopathology. *Child Development, 55,* 163–173.

DODGE, K. A., & Somberg, D. R. (1987). Hostile attributional biases among aggressive boys are exacerbated under conditions of threats to the self. *Child Development, 58,* 213–224.

DORNBUSCH, S. M., Carlsmith, J. M., Bushwall, S. J., Ritter, P. L., Liederman, H., Hastorf, A. H., & Gross, R. T. (1985). Single parents, extended households, and the control of adolescents. *Child Development, 56,* 326–341.

EISENBERG, N. (1983). Children's differentiations among potential recipients of aid. *Child Development, 54,* 594–602.

EISENBERG, N., Lennon, R., & Roth, K. (1983). Prosocial development: A longitudinal study. *Developmental Psychology, 19,* 846–855.

EISENBERG-BERG, N., & Hand, M. (1979). The relationship of preschoolers' reasoning about prosocial moral conflicts to prosocial behavior. *Child Development, 50,* 356–363.

EMMERICH, W. (1966). Continuity and stability in early social development: II. Teacher's ratings. *Child Development, 37,* 17–27.

ERIKSON, E. H. (1963). *Childhood and society* (2nd ed.). New York: Norton.

ERON, L. D. (1982). Parent-child interaction, television violence, and aggression of children. *American Psychologist, 37,* 197–211.

FESHBACH, N. (1978). Studies of the development of children's empathy. In B. Maher (Ed.), *Progress in experimental personality research.* Orlando, FL: Academic Press.

FESHBACH, N., & Feshbach, S. (1982). Empathy training and the regulation of aggression: Potentialities and limitations. *Academic Psychology Bulletin, 4,* 399–413.

FESHBACH, S. (1956). The catharsis hypothesis and some consequences of interaction with aggressive and neutral play objects. *Journal of Personality, 24,* 449–461.

FISCHER, W. F. (1963). Sharing in pre-school children as a function of the amount and type of reinforcement. *Genetic Psychology Monographs, 68,* 215–245.

FORD, M. R., & Lowery, C. R. (1986). Gender differences in moral reasoning: A comparison of the use of justice and care orientations. *Journal of Personality and Social Psychology, 50,* 777—783.

FREUD, S. (1960). *A general introduction to psychoanalysis.* New York: Washington Square Press. (Original work published 1935)

GARBARINO, J., & Bronfenbrenner, U. (1976). The socialization of moral judgment and behavior in cross-cultural perspective. In T. Lickona (Ed.), *Moral development and behavior.* New York: Holt, Rinehart and Winston.

GILLIGAN, C. (1977). In a different voice: Women's conceptions of self and morality. *Harvard Educational Review, 47,* 481–517.

GILLIGAN C. (1982). *In a different voice: Psychological theory and women's development.* Cambridge, MA: Harvard University Press.

GOODENOUGH, F. L. (1931). *Anger in young children.* Minneapolis: University of Minnesota Press.

GORER, G. (1968). Man has no "killer" instinct. In M. F. A. Montague (Ed.), *Man and aggression.* New York: Oxford University Press.

GREEN, F. P., & Schneider, F. W. (1974). Age differences in the behavior of boys on three measures of altruism. *Child Development, 45,* 248–251.

GRUSEC, J. E., Kuczynski, L., Rushton, J. P., & Simutis, Z. (1979). Learning resistance to temptation through observation. *Developmental Psychology, 15,* 233–240.

GRUSEC, J. E., & Redler, E. (1980). Attribution, reinforcement, and altruism: A developmental analysis. *Developmental Psychology, 16,* 525–534.

GUMP, P. V. (1975). Ecological psychology and children. In M. Hetherington (Ed.), *Review of child development research* (Vol. 5). Chicago: University of Chicago Press.

HAAN, N., Aerts, E., & Cooper, B. A. B. (1985). *On moral grounds: The search for practical morality.* New York: New York University Press.

HARKNESS, S., Edwards, C. P., & Super, C. M. (1981). Social roles and moral reasoning: A case study in a rural African community. *Developmental Psychology, 17,* 595–603.

HARTSHORNE, H., & May, M. S. (1928–1930). *Studies in the nature of character.* Vol. 1: *Studies in deceit.* Vol. 2: *Studies in self-control.* Vol. 3: *Studies in the organization of character.* New York: Macmillan.

HARTUP, W. W. (1974). Aggression in childhood: Developmental perspectives. *American Psychologist, 29,* 336–341.

HAY, D. F. (1979). Cooperative interactions and sharing among very young children and their parents. *Developmental Psychology, 15,* 647–653.

HAY, D. F., & Ross, H. S. (1982). The social nature of early conflict. *Child Development, 53,* 105–113.

HOFFMAN, M. L. (1970). Moral development. In P. H. Mussen (Ed.), *Carmichael's manual of child psychology* (Vol. 2). New York: Wiley.

HOFFMAN, M. L. (1975a). Moral internalization, parental power, and the nature of parent-child interaction. *Developmental Psychology, 11,* 228–239.

HOFFMAN, M. L. (1975b). Sex differences in moral internalization and values. *Journal of Personality and Social Psychology, 32,* 720–729.

HOFFMAN, M. L. (1981). Is altruism part of human nature? *Journal of Personality and Social Psychology, 40,* 121–137.

HOFFMAN, M. L. (1985). Moral development. In M. H. Bornstein & M. E. Lamb (Eds.), *Developmental psychology: An advanced textbook.* Hillsdale, NJ: Erlbaum.

HOLSTEIN, C. (1976). Irreversible, stepwise sequence in the development of moral judgment: A longitudinal study of males and females. *Child Development, 47,* 51–61.

HUESMANN, L. R., Eron, L. D., Lefkowitz, M. M., & Walder, L. O. (1984). Stability of aggression over time and generations. *Developmental Psychology, 20,* 1120–1134.

HUGHES, R., Jr., Tingle, B. A., & Sawin, D. B. (1981). Development of empathic understanding in children. *Child Development, 52,* 122–128.

HYDE, J. S. (1984). How large are gender differences in aggression? A developmental meta-analysis. *Developmental Psychology, 20,* 722–736.

IANNOTTI, R. J. (1978). Effect of role-taking experiences on role-taking, empathy, altruism, and aggression. *Developmental Psychology, 14,* 119–124.

KAGAN, J., & Moss, H. A. (1962). *Birth to maturity.* New York: Wiley.

KAGAN, S., & Masden, M. C. (1971). Cooperation and competition of Mexican, Mexican-American, and Anglo-American children of two ages and four instructional sets. *Developmental Psychology, 5,* 32–39.

KAGAN, S., & Masden, M. C. (1972). Rivalry in Anglo-American and Mexican children of two ages. *Journal of Personality and Social Psychology, 24,* 214–220.

KEASEY, C. B. (1971). Social participation as a factor in the moral development of preadolescents. *Developmental Psychology, 5,* 216–220.

KOHLBERG, L. (1963). The development of children's orientations toward a moral order: I. Sequence in the development of moral thought. *Vita Humana, 6,* 11–33.

KOHLBERG, L. (1969). Stage and sequence: The cognitive-developmental approach to socialization. In D. A. Goslin (Ed.), *Handbook of socialization theory and research.* Skokie, IL: Rand McNally.

KOHLBERG, L. (1975, June). The cognitive-developmental approach to moral education. *Phi Delta Kappan,* pp. 670–677.

KOHLBERG, L. (1981). *Essays on moral development* (Vol. 1). New York: Harper & Row.

KOHLBERG L., & Candee, D. (1984). The relationship of moral judgment to moral action. In W. M. Kurtines & J. L. Gewirtz (Eds.), *Morality, moral behavior, and moral development.* New York: Wiley.

KREBS, D. L. (1970). Altruism—an examination of the concept and a review of the literature. *Psychological Bulletin, 73,* 258–302.

KUCZYNSKI, L. (1983). Reasoning, prohibitions, and motivations for compliance. *Developmental Psychology, 19,* 126–134.

KUHN, D., Kohlberg, L., Langer, J., & Haan, N. (1977). The development of formal operations in logical and moral judgment. *Genetic Psychology Monographs, 95,* 97–188.

LADD, G. W., Lange, G., & Stremmel, A. (1983). Personal and situational influences on children's helping behavior: Factors that mediate compliant helping. *Child Development, 54,* 488–501.

LAUPA, M., & Turiel, E. (1986). Children's conceptions of adult and peer authority. *Child Development, 57,* 405–412.

LEUNG, E. H. L., & Rheingold, H. L. (1981). Development of pointing as a social gesture. *Developmental Psychology, 17,* 215–220.

LEVITT, M. J., Weber, R. A., Clark, M. C., & McDonnell, P. (1985). Reciprocity of exchange in toddler sharing behavior. *Developmental Psychology, 21,* 122–123.

LICKONA, T. (1976). Research on Piaget's theory of moral development. In T. Lickona (Ed.), *Moral development and behavior.* New York: Holt, Rinehart and Winston.

LONDON, P. (1970). The rescuers: Motivational hypotheses about Christians who saved Jews from the Nazis. In J. Macaulay & L. Berkowitz (Eds.), *Altruism and helping behavior.* Orlando, FL: Academic Press.

LORENZ, K. (1966). *On aggression.* San Diego, CA: Harcourt Brace Jovanovich.

MACCOBY, E. E. (1980). *Social development: Psychological growth and the parent-child relationship.* San Diego, CA: Harcourt Brace Jovanovich.

MACCOBY, E. E., & Jacklin, C. N. (1974). *The psychology of sex differences.* Stanford, CA: Stanford University Press.

MACCOBY, E. E., & Jacklin, C. N. (1980). Sex differences in aggression: A rejoinder and reprise. *Child Development, 51,* 964–980.

MAITLAND, K. A., & Goldman, J. R. (1974). Moral judgment as a function of peer group interaction. *Journal of Personality and Social Psychology, 30,* 699–704.

MALLICK, S. K., & McCandless, B. R. (1966). A study of the catharsis of aggression. *Journal of Personality and Social Psychology, 4,* 591–596.

McDOUGALL, W. (1908). *An introduction to social psychology.* London: Methuen.

MEAD, M. (1935). *Sex and temperament in three primitive societies.* New York: William Morrow.

MIDLARSKY, E., & Bryan, J. H. (1972). Affect expressions and children's imitative altruism. *Journal of Experimental Research in Personality, 6,* 195–203.

MISCHEL, W., & Patterson, C. J. (1976). Substantive and structural elements of effective plans for self-control. *Journal of Personality and Social Psychology, 34,* 942–950.

MOIR, J. (1974). Egocentrism and the emergence of conventional morality in preadolescent girls. *Child Development, 45,* 299–304.

MURPHY, L. B. (1937). *Social behavior and child personality: An exploratory study of some roots of sympathy.* New York: Columbia University Press.

NATIONAL COMMISSION ON THE CAUSES AND PREVENTION OF VIOLENCE. (1969). *To establish justice, to insure domestic tranquility.* New York: Award Books.

NELSON, E. A., Grinder, R. E., & Biaggio, A. M. B. (1969). Relationships between behavioral, cognitive-developmental, and self-report measures of morality and personality. *Multivariate Behavioral Research, 4,* 483–500.

NELSON, E. A., Grinder, R. E., & Mutterer, M. L. (1969). Sources of variance in behavioral measures of honesty in temptation situations: Methodological analyses. *Developmental Psychology, 1,* 265–279.

NELSON, S. A. (1980). Factors influencing young children's use of motives and outcomes as moral criteria. *Child Development, 51,* 823–829.

NELSON-LeGALL, S. A. (1985). Motive-outcome matching and outcome foreseeability: Effects on attribution of intentionality and moral judgments. *Developmental Psychology, 21,* 332–337.

OLWEUS, D. (1980). Familial and temperamental determinants of aggressive behavior in adolescent boys: A causal analysis. *Developmental Psychology, 16,* 644–660.

ORLICK, T. D. (1981). Positive socialization via cooperative games. *Developmental Psychology, 17,* 426–429.

PARIKH, B. (1980). Moral judgment development and its relation to family factors in Indian and American families. *Child Development, 51,* 1030–1039.

PARKE, R. D. (1977). Some effects of punishment on children's behavior–revisited. In E. M. Hetherington & R. D. Parke (Eds.), *Contemporary readings in child psychology.* New York: McGraw-Hill.

PARKE, R. D., & Slaby, R. G. (1983). The development of aggression. In P. H. Mussen (Ed.), *Handbook of child psychology.* Vol. 4: *Socialization, personality, and social development.* New York: Wiley.

PATTERSON, G. R. (1976). The aggressive child: Victim and architect of a coercive system. In E. J. Mash, L. A. Hamerlynck, & L. C. Handy (Eds.), *Behavior modification and families.* Vol. 1: *Theory and research.* New York: Brunner/Mazel.

PATTERSON, G. R. (1981). Mothers: The unacknowledged victims. *Monographs of the Society for Research in Child Development, 45*(5, Serial No. 186).

PATTERSON, G. R. (1982). *Coercive family processes.* Eugene, OR: Castilia Press.

PATTERSON, G. R., Littman, R. A., & Bricker, W. (1967). Assertive behavior in children: A step toward a theory of aggression. *Monographs of the Society for Research in Child Development, 32*(5, Serial No. 113).

PATTERSON, G. R., & Stouthamer-Loeber, M. (1984). The correlation of family management practices and delinquency. *Child Development, 55,* 1299–1307.

PERRY, D. G., & Bussey, K. (1977). Self-reinforcement in high- and low-aggressive boys following acts of aggression. *Child Development, 48,* 653–657.

PERRY, D. G., & Parke, R. D. (1975). Punishment and alternative response training as determinants of response inhibition in children. *Genetic Psychology Monographs, 91,* 257–279.

PERRY, D. G., & Perry, L. C. (1974). Denial of suffering in the victim as a stimulus to violence in aggressive boys. *Child Development, 45,* 55–62.

PERRY, D. G., Perry, L. C., Bussey, K., English, D., & Arnold, G. (1980). Processes of attribution and children's self-punishment following misbehavior. *Child Development, 51,* 545–551.

PIAGET, J. (1952). *The origins of intelligence in children.* New York: International Universities Press.

PIAGET, J. (1965). *The moral judgment of the child.* New York: Free Press. (Original work published 1932)

RADKE-YARROW, M., Zahn-Waxler, C., & Chapman, M. (1983). Children's prosocial dispositions and behavior. In P. H. Mussen (Ed.), *Handbook of child psychology.* Vol. 4: *Socialization, personality, and social development.* New York: Wiley.

REST, J. R. (1983). Morality. In P. H. Mussen (Ed.), *Handbook of child psychology.* Vol. 3: *Cognitive development.* New York: Wiley.

REST, J. R., & Thoma, S. J. (1985). Relation of moral judgment development to formal education. *Developmental Psychology, 21,* 709–714.

RHEINGOLD, H. L. (1982). Little children's participation in the work of adults, a nascent prosocial behavior. *Child Development, 53,* 114–125.

RICE, M. E., & Grusec, J. E. (1975). Saying and doing: Effects on observer performance. *Journal of Personality and Social Psychology, 32,* 584–593.

RICHARD, B. A., & Dodge, K. A. (1982). Social maladjustment and problem solving in school-aged children. *Journal of Consulting and Clinical Psychology 50,* 226–233.

ROSENHAN, D. L. (1970). The natural socialization of altruistic autonomy. In J. L. Macaulay & L. Berkowitz (Eds.), *Altruism and helping behavior.* Orlando, FL:

Academic Press.

ROSENKOETTER, L. I. (1973). Resistance to temptation: Inhibitory and disinhibitory effects of models. *Developmental Psychology, 8,* 80–84.

RUSHTON, J. P. (1975). Generosity in children: Immediate and long-term effects of modeling, preaching, and moral judgment. *Journal of Personality and Social Psychology, 31,* 459–466.

RUSHTON, J. P. (1980). *Altruism, socialization, and society.* Englewood Cliffs, NJ: Prentice-Hall.

RUTHERFORD, E., & Mussen, P. H. (1968). Generosity in nursery school boys. *Child Development, 39,* 755–765.

SANTROCK, J. W. (1975). Moral structure: The interrelations of moral behavior, moral judgment, and moral affect. *Journal of Genetic Psychology, 127,* 201–213.

SEARS, R. R., Maccoby, E. E., & Levin, H. (1957). *Patterns of child rearing.* New York: Harper & Row.

SELMAN, R. L. (1971). The relation of role-taking to the development of moral judgment in children. *Child Development, 42,* 79–91.

SHAFFER, D. R. (1988). *Social and personality development* (2nd ed.). Pacific Grove, CA: Brooks/Cole.

SHANTZ, C. U. (1987). Conflicts between children. *Child Development, 58,* 283–305.

SHANTZ, D. W. (1986). Conflict, aggression, and peer status: An observational study. *Child Development, 57,* 1322–1332.

SHIGETOMI, C. C., Hartmann, D. P., & Gelfand, D. M. (1981). Sex differences in children's altruistic behavior and reputations for helpfulness. *Developmental Psychology, 17,* 434–437.

SHULTZ, T. R., Wright, K., & Schleifer, M. (1986). Assignment of moral responsibility and punishment. *Child Development, 57,* 177–184.

SIEGAL, A. E., & Kohn, L. G. (1959). Permissiveness, permission, and aggression: The effect of adult presence or absence on aggression in children's play. *Child Development, 30,* 131–141.

SIEGAL, M., & Cowen, J. (1984). Appraisals of intervention: The mother's versus the culprit's behavior as determinants of children's evaluations of discipline techniques. *Child Development, 55,* 1760–1766.

SLABY, R. G., & Crowley, C. G. (1977). Modification of cooperation and aggression through teacher attention to children's speech. *Journal of Experimental Child Psychology, 23,* 442–458.

SMETANA, J. G. (1981). Preschool children's conceptions of moral and social rules. *Child Development, 52,* 1333–1336.

SMETANA, J. G. (1985). Preschool children's conceptions of transgressions: Effects of varying moral and conventional domain-related attributes. *Developmental Psychology, 21,* 18–29.

SMITH, P. K., & Connolly, K. J. (1980). *The ecology of preschool behavior.* New York: Cambridge University Press.

SONG, M., Smetana, J. G., & Kim, S. Y. (1987). Korean children's conceptions of moral and conventional transgressions. *Developmental Psychology, 23,* 577–582.

STEINBERG, L. (1987). Single parents, stepparents, and the susceptibility of adolescents to antisocial peer pressure. *Child Development, 58,* 269–275.

SURBER, C. F. (1982). Separable effects of motives, consequences, and presentation order on children's moral judgments. *Developmental Psychology, 18,* 257–266.

THOMA, S. J. (1986). Estimating gender differences in the comprehension and preference of moral issues. *Developmental Review, 6,* 165–180.

TIEGER, T. (1980). On the biological bases of sex differences in aggression. *Child Development, 51,* 943–963.

TIETJEN, A. M. (1986). Prosocial reasoning among children and adults in a Papua New Guinea society. *Developmental Psychology, 22,* 861–868.

TIETJEN, A. M., & Walker, L. J. (1985). Moral reasoning and leadership among men in a Papua New Guinea society. *Developmental Psychology, 21,* 982–992.

TISAK, M. S. (1986). Children's conceptions of parental authority. *Child Development, 57,* 166–176.

TOMLINSON-KEASEY, C., & Keasey, C. B. (1974). The mediating role of cognitive development in moral judgment. *Child Development, 45,* 291–298.

TONER, I. J., Moore, L. P., & Ashley, P. K. (1978). The effect of serving as a model of self-control on subsequent resistance to deviation in children. *Journal of Experimental Child Psychology, 26,* 85–91.

TONER, I. J., Parke, R. D., & Yussen, S. R. (1978). The effect of observation of model behavior on the establishment and stability of resistance to deviation in children. *Journal of Genetic Psychology, 132,* 283–290.

TONER, I. J., & Potts, R. (1981). Effect of modeled rationales on moral behavior, moral choice, and level of moral judgment in children. *Journal of Psychology, 107,* 153–162.

TONER, I. J., & Smith, R. A. (1977). Age and overt verbalization in delay maintenance behavior in children. *Journal of Experimental Child Psychology, 24,* 123–128.

TURIEL, E. (1966). An experimental test of the sequentiality of developmental stages in the child's moral judgments. *Journal of Personality and Social Psychology, 3,* 611–618.

TURIEL, E. (1978). The development of concepts of social structure: Social convention. In J. Glick & A. Clarke-Stewart (Eds.), *The development of social understanding.* New York: Gardner Press.

TURNBULL, C. M. (1972). *The mountain people.* New York: Simon & Schuster.

TURNER, C. W., & Goldsmith, D. (1976). Effects of toy guns and airplanes on children's antisocial free play behavior. *Journal of Experimental Child Psychology, 21,* 303–315.

UNDERWOOD, B., & Moore, B. (1982). Perspective-taking and altruism. *Psychological Bulletin, 91,* 143–173.

WALKER, L. J. (1980). Cognitive and perspective-taking prerequisites for moral development. *Child Development, 51,* 131–139.

WALKER, L. J. (1982). The sequentiality of Kohlberg's stages of moral development. *Child Development, 53,* 1330–1336.

WALKER, L. J. (1984). Sex differences in the development of moral reasoning: A critical review. *Child Development, 55,* 677–691.

WALKER, L. J. (1986). Sex differences in the development of moral reasoning: A rejoinder to Baumrind. *Child Development, 57,* 522–526.

WALKER, L. J., de Vries, B., & Trevethan, S. D. (1987). Moral stages and moral orientations in real-life and hypothetical dilemmas. *Child Development, 58,* 842–858.

WALTERS, R. H., & Brown, M. (1963). Studies of reinforcement of aggression: Transfer of responses to an interpersonal situation. *Child Development, 34,* 562–571.

WHITING, B. B., & Whiting, J. W. M. (1975). *Children of six cultures.* Cambridge, MA: Harvard University Press.

YARROW, M. R., Scott, P. M., & Waxler, C. Z. (1973). Learning concern for others. *Developmental Psychology, 8,* 240–260.

ZAHN-WAXLER, C., Radke-Yarrow, M., & King, R. A. (1979). Child rearing and children's prosocial initiations toward victims of distress. *Child Development, 50,* 319–330.

ZARBATANY, L., Hartmann, D. P., Gelfand, D. M., & Vinciguerra, P. (1985). Gender differences in altruistic reputation: Are they artifactual? *Developmental Psychology, 21,* 97–101.

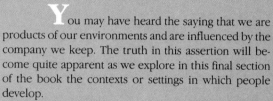

The Ecology
of Development

You may have heard the saying that we are products of our environments and are influenced by the company we keep. The truth in this assertion will become quite apparent as we explore in this final section of the book the contexts or settings in which people develop.

Virtually all children are raised in a family setting, although families differ considerably and no two individuals ever experience exactly the same family environment. Chapter 15 concentrates on the family as an agent of socialization and outlines the many ways in which families (and the cultural contexts in which families live) influence the social, emotional, and intellectual development of their young.

Of course, the family is only one source of influence for developing children, who soon reach a point in their lives when they spend many of their waking hours away from the watchful eyes of parents and other family members. In our sixteenth and final chapter we will look beyond the family to see how children and adolescents react to the messages they receive from television, their schooling, and the society of their peers.

The Family

Have humans always been social animals? Although no one can answer this question with absolute certainty, the archeological record provides some strong clues. Apparently our closest evolutionary ancestors (dating back before the Neanderthals) were already living in small bands, or tribal units, that provided increased protection against common enemies and allowed individuals to share the many labors necessary for their survival (Weaver, 1985). Of course, there are no written records of social life among these early collectives. But it is clear that, at some point during the prehistoric era, early human societies (and perhaps even the protohuman aggregations) evolved codes of conduct that defined the roles of various tribal members and sanctioned certain motives and practices while prohibiting others. Once a workable social order was established, it then became necessary to "socialize" each succeeding generation.

Socialization is the process by which children acquire the beliefs, values, and behaviors deemed significant and appropriate by the older members of their society. The socialization of each generation serves society in at least three ways. First, it is a means of regulating children's behavior and controlling their undesirable or antisocial impulses. Second, the socialization process helps to promote the personal growth of the individual. As children interact with and become like other members of their culture, they acquire the knowledge, skills, motives, and aspirations that should enable them to adapt to their environment and function effectively within their communities. Finally, socialization perpetuates the social order. Socialized children become socialized adults who will impart what they have learned to their own children.

All societies have developed various mechanisms, or institutions, for socializing their young. Examples of these socializing institutions are the family, the church, the educational system, children's groups (for example, Boy and Girl Scouts), and the mass media.

Central among the many social agencies that impinge on the child is that institution we call the family. More than 99% of children in the United States are raised in a family of one kind or another (U.S. Department of Commerce, 1979), and most children in most societies grow up in a home setting with at least one biological parent or other relative. Often children have little exposure to people outside the family for several years until they are placed in day care or nursery school or until they begin formal schooling. So it is fair to say that the family has a clear head start on other institutions when it comes to socializing a child. And since the events of the early years are very important to the child's social, emotional, and intellectual development, it is perhaps appropriate to think of the family as society's most important instrument of socialization.

Our focus in this chapter is on the family as a social system—an institution that both influences and is influenced by its young. What is a family and what functions do families serve? How does the birth of a child affect other family members? Do the existing (or changing) relationships among other members of the family have any effect on the care and training that a young child receives? Are some patterns of child rearing better than others? Do parents decide how they will raise their children—or might children be influencing their parents? Does the family's socioeconomic status affect parenting and parent/child interactions? Do siblings play an important part in the socialization process? How do children react to divorce, maternal employment, or a return to the two-parent family when a single parent remarries? And why do some parents mistreat their children? These are the issues we will consider as we look at the important roles that families play in the cognitive, social, and emotional development of their children.

Basic Features and Functions of the Family

The characteristics of a family are difficult to summarize in a sentence or two. Many family sociologists prefer to think of the family unit as a social system consisting of three basic roles: wife/mother, husband/father, and child/sibling. Of course, there are many variations on this traditional **nuclear family.** In the United States, for example, there are nearly as many childless married couples as there are families with children, and about 40–50% of American children will spend some time in a **single-parent home** (Clarke-Stewart, 1982; Glick, 1984). Although the nuclear family is the norm in contemporary Western society, people in many cultures (and subcultures) live in **extended families**—an arrangement in which grandparents, parents and their children, aunts, uncles, nieces, and nephews may live under the same roof and share responsibility for maintaining the household. In fact, the extended family is a common arrangement for Black Americans—and an adaptive one in that large numbers of economically disadvantaged Black mothers must work, are often supporting their offspring without the father, and can surely use the assistance they receive from grandparents, siblings, uncles, aunts, and cousins who may live with them (or nearby) and serve as surrogate parents for young children (Wilson, 1986). Until recently, family researchers have largely ignored extended families or looked upon them as unhealthy contexts for child rearing. That view is now changing, thanks in part to research showing how support from members of extended families (for example, grandparents) can help disadvantaged single mothers to cope with the stresses of child rearing, to become more sensitive caregivers, and to establish secure emotional relationships with their infants and toddlers (see Crockenberg, 1987; Egeland & Sroufe, 1981). Indeed, it would not be surprising to see an explosion of research on the extended family in the years ahead, for the high incidence of divorce and the ever-increasing numbers of children born out of wedlock are making the extended family arrangement more and more common among all segments of American society (Wilson, 1986).

The Functions of a Family

Families serve society in many ways. They produce and consume goods and services, thereby playing a role in the economy. Traditionally, the family has served as an outlet for the sexual urges of its adult members and as the means of replenishing the population. Indeed, few societies sanction the birth of "illegitimate" children (that is, those born out of wedlock), who are often treated as second-class citizens and called uncomplimentary names such as "bastard." Historically, families have cared for their elderly, although this function is now less common in Western societies with the advent of institutions such as Social Security, socialized medical care, and nursing homes. But perhaps the most widely recognized functions of the family—those that are served in all societies—are the caregiving, nurturing, and training that parents and other family members provide for young children.

The Goals of Parenting

After studying the child-rearing practices of many diverse cultures, Robert LeVine (1974, p. 238) concluded that families in all societies have three basic goals for their children:

1. The **survival goal**—to promote the physical survival and health of the child, ensuring that the child will live long enough to have children of his or her own.
2. The **economic goal**—to foster the skills and behavioral capacities that the child will need for economic self-maintenance as an adult.

---

socialization: the process by which children acquire the beliefs, values, and behaviors considered desirable or appropriate by the society to which they belong.

nuclear family: a family unit consisting of a wife/mother, a husband/father, and their dependent child(ren).

single-parent family: a family unit consisting of one parent (either the mother or the father) and the parent's dependent child(ren).

extended family: a group of blood relatives from more than one nuclear family (for example, grandparents, aunts, uncles, nieces, and nephews) who live together, forming a household.

survival goal: LeVine's first priority of parenting—to promote the physical health and safety (survival) of young children.

economic goal: LeVine's second priority of parenting—to promote skills that children will need for economic self-sufficiency.

3. The **self-actualization goal**—to foster behavioral capabilities for maximizing other cultural values (for example, morality, religion, achievement, wealth, prestige, and a sense of personal satisfaction).

According to LeVine, these universal goals of parenting form a hierarchy. Parents and other caregivers are initially concerned about maximizing the child's chances of survival, and higher-order goals such as teaching the child to talk, count, or abide by moral rules are placed on the back burner until it is clear that the youngster is healthy and is likely to survive. When physical health and security can be taken for granted, then parents begin to encourage those characteristics that are necessary for economic self-sufficiency. Only after survival and the attributes necessary for economic productivity have been established do parents begin to encourage the child to seek status, prestige, and self-fulfillment.

LeVine's ideas stem from his observations of child-rearing practices in societies where infants often die before their second birthday. Regardless of whether one is observing African Bushmen, South American Indians, or Indonesian tribes, parents in societies where infant mortality is high tend to maintain close contact with their infants 24 hours a day, often carrying them on their hips or their backs in some sort of sling or cradleboard. LeVine suggests that these practices increase the infants' chances of survival by reducing the likelihood of their becoming ill or dehydrated, crawling into the river or the campfire, or ambling off to be captured by a predator. Although infants are kept close at all times, their parents rarely chat with or smile at them and may seem almost uninterested in their future psychological development. Could this pattern of psychologically aloof yet competent physical caregiving be a defensive maneuver that prevents parents from becoming overly attached to an infant who might well die? Perhaps so, for many cultures in which infant mortality is high still institutionalize practices such as not speaking to neonates as if they were human beings or not naming them until late in the first year, when it is more probable that they will survive (Brazelton, 1979).

The next task that parents face is to promote those characteristics and competencies that will enable children to care for themselves and their own future families. Anthropologist John Ogbu (1981) points out that the economy of a culture (that is, the way in which people support themselves, or subsist) will determine how families socialize their young. To illustrate his point,

Photo 15-1. In many cultures, parents increase their babies' chances of survival by keeping them close at all times.

he cites a well-known cross-cultural study by Herbert Barry and his associates (Barry, Child, & Bacon, 1959), who hypothesized that societies that depend on an agricultural or pastoral economy (those that accumulate food) would stress obedience, cooperation, and responsibility when raising their children. By contrast, groups that do not accumulate food (hunting, trapping, and fishing societies) were expected to train their children to be independent, assertive, and venturesome. In other words, both types of society were expected to emphasize the values, competencies, and attributes that are necessary to maintain their way of life. Barry et al. used existing anthropological records to review the economic characteristics and child-rearing techniques of 104 **preliterate societies** all over the world. As predicted, they found that agricultural and pastoral societies did place strong pressures on their children to be cooperative and obedient, whereas hunting and fishing societies stressed assertiveness, self-reliance, and individual achievement.

Even in industrial societies such as the United States, a family's social position or socioeconomic status affects child-rearing practices. For example, parents from the lower socioeconomic strata, who typically work for a boss and must defer to his or her authority, tend to stress obedience, neatness, cleanliness, and respect for power—attributes that should enable their children to function effectively within a blue-collar economy. By contrast, middle-class parents, particularly those who work for themselves or who are professionals, are more likely to stress ambition, curiosity, creativity, and independence when raising their children (Kohn, 1979). The latter finding would hardly surprise LeVine, who would argue that middle-class parents who have the resources to promote their child's eventual economic security are freer to encourage his or her initiative, achievement, and personal self-fulfillment (the third set of parenting goals) at a very early age.

Some Cautionary Comments about the Study of Families

As we progress through the chapter looking at the ways families influence the development of their young, there are several important points to keep in mind. First, there is no "best way" to study families; each of the methods that investigators have used has very definite strengths and weaknesses (see Box 15-1), and the most convincing information that we have about family effects consists of findings that have been replicated using several methods.

In addition, much of the research that we will review assumes that the child-rearing practices that parents use largely determine how their children will behave. But as we will see, this unidirectional model of family effects is much too simplistic. Not only do children seem to influence the behavior and the child-rearing strategies of their parents, but there is also reason to believe that a family is a complex social system in which each family member influences the thinking and behavior of every other family member.

Finally, some of the research that we will examine might seem to suggest that certain patterns of parenting are better or "more competent" than others. Now let's see why many family researchers are reluctant to endorse this conclusion.

The Middle-Class Bias

Many of the findings that we will review were collected from White, middle-class samples in Western cultures and apply most directly to the development of White, middle-class children. Should we assume that the patterns of child rearing that are most effective for these youngsters are "better" than other parenting techniques? If we do, we may be making a serious mistake, for as John Ogbu (1981) aptly notes, what passes as "competent parenting" for middle-class youngsters may fall far short of the mark if applied to children in other sociocultural groups.

Consider the case of disadvantaged children who grow up in urban ghettos in the United States. According to Ogbu (1981), these youngsters are encouraged to look upon conventional jobs as indications of success. However, they may also have to acquire a very different set of competencies if they are to function effectively within the "street economy" of their subculture. Thus, while Johnny from the suburbs may strive to perfect skills such as reading and math that will prepare him for a traditional job, Johnny from the ghetto may come to view academics as somewhat less important and choose instead to pursue other "survival strategies" such as fighting, hustling, becoming a respected member of a neighborhood street gang, or even working on his jump shot. It is not that ghetto youngsters are any less interested than middle-class age mates in being successful and attaining power, money, or self-esteem; they simply differ in the means they choose to achieve these ends—often pursuing strategies suggested to them by the subculture in which they live.

Ogbu notes that ghetto parents are extremely warm and affectionate toward their infants but tend to use harsh and inconsistent punishment with their preschool and school-age children. Although the latter practices tend to be frowned on by middle-class parents (and researchers), they may be very functional within the ghetto environment. Harsh, inconsistent discipline and a generally confrontive parental style should foster the development of assertiveness, self-reliance, and a mistrust of authority figures—precisely the attributes that ghetto youngsters may need in order to make it within their street culture. Of course, Ogbu is not im-

---

self-actualization goal: LeVine's third priority of parenting—to promote the child's cognitive and behavioral capacity for maximizing such cultural values as morality, achievement, prestige, and personal satisfaction.

preliterate society: a society in which there is little or no formal schooling, so that many children never learn to read and write.

Investigators who study family relationships have traditionally used one of three research strategies: the *interview* or *questionnaire* technique, *direct observation* of family interactions, or *laboratory analog studies* (that is, experimental simulations of parent/child interactions). Although these approaches have generated a lot of very useful information about families, it is important to understand the strengths and weaknesses of each.

Interview and questionnaire studies. In an interview or questionnaire study, parents are asked to recall and describe the child-rearing practices they have used and to indicate the ways their children have acted at different times and in a variety of situations. The major advantage of this approach is that one can collect an enormous amount of information about a parent and his or her children in a short time.

Unfortunately, the interview/questionnaire method can generate inaccurate and misleading data if parents cannot recall how they or their child behaved earlier or if they confuse the child-rearing practices they used while raising different children. When asked to describe the previous behavior of any one of their children, parents are likely to become confused about which child did what and when, and thus they may end up providing a composite description of all their children. Finally, most parents have heard noted authorities express opinions about "proper" child-rearing practices, and often the practices advocated by experts differ from those that the parent has used. If even a small percentage of parents say that they relied on these "socially desirable" practices rather than the ones that they actually used, this response bias could obscure any real relationships that may exist between parenting styles and behavior of young children.

Today few investigators rely exclusively on the interview or questionnaire technique when studying family relations. Perhaps the most common research strategy is to observe family members interacting with one another at home or in the laboratory and to supplement these observations with questionnaire data or interviews.

Observational methodologies. One excellent method of studying family relations and learning how family members influence one another is to observe them interacting at home or in the laboratory. Researchers who conduct observational studies are able to look at *behavioral sequences* among various family members and determine who did what to whom with what effect. By focusing on behavioral sequences, the investigator can answer questions such as: What does the mother typically do when her son ignores her? Does she raise her voice to ensure that he listens; threaten to take away a cherished privilege; spank him? How does the child respond to his mother's influence attempts? Does he comply; argue with her; cry? Does the father become involved in these exchanges; how; when? Of course, use of an observational methodology requires the researcher to assess the *reliability* of his or her observations (see Chapter 1 for a discussion of the reliability issue). And unfortunately

continued

---

plying that ghetto children will grow up to be deviant or abnormal by anyone's standards. His point is simply that the practices that qualify as "competent parenting" will depend on the particular abilities that children will need for success within any given culture or subculture. So let's keep this point in mind and not automatically assume that deviations from middle-class patterns of child rearing are somehow "deficient" or "pathological."

The Directionality Issue

Until very recently, social scientists have assumed that influence within families was a one-way street—from parents, who did the shaping, to their children, whose personalities were molded by the caregiving practices and disciplinary techniques of their elders. Indeed, much of the work that we will discuss has attempted to determine the correspondence between various patterns of parenting and the development of young children. When relationships were found, it was generally assumed that the behavior of parents determined the behavior of their children.

Today we have reason to believe that most, if not all, social relationships display a pattern of **reciprocal influence.** Parents do indeed influence the behavior of their children. But at the same time, children play an important role in shaping the child-rearing practices used by their parents.

A study by Kathleen Anderson and her associates (Anderson, Lytton, & Romney, 1986) nicely illustrates how children can influence the behavior of their adult overseers. Anderson and her colleagues worked with 6- to 11-year-old boys and their mothers. Some of these boys were quite normal in their social behavior, whereas others had been diagnosed as "*conduct-disordered*"—that is, they were defiant and aggressive and had a history of truancy, destructive behavior, or other serious problems. The procedure was straightforward: each mother interacted for 15 minutes (1) with her own normal or conduct-disordered son, (2) with another normal boy, and (3) with another boy with conduct disorders. During each of the three sessions, the mother was simply to oversee the child's

the mere presence of an observer making notes and recording data can affect the ways family members relate to one another. For example, Leslie Zegoib and her associates (Zegoib, Arnold, & Forehand, 1975) report that mothers are warmer, more patient, and more involved with their children when they know they are being observed. Moreover, siblings and peer playmates are less likely to issue commands or to tease, quarrel, or threaten each other when observers are present (Brody, Stoneman, & Wheatley, 1984). Some investigators have tried to minimize these "observer effects" by capturing family interactions on videotape recorders placed in unobtrusive locations in the lab or the home. Another strategy is to mingle with the family for a few days before any data are collected so the family members will gradually become accustomed to the observer's presence and behave more naturally.

The analog experiment.
In a laboratory analog, an adult experimenter behaves in a way that simulates a particular pattern of child rearing and then observes the effect of this experimental manipulation on the child's behavior. For example, we've seen in Chapter 14 how Ross Parke and his associates used the analog technique to study the impact of various forms of punishment on children's resistance to temptation.

One problem with this approach is that the sequential complexities of parent/child interactions are difficult if not impossible to simulate in a situation where the child interacts on a *single occasion* with a *strange* adult. Moreover, the experimental tasks that children face in an analog and the rules they must follow are often very dissimilar to those they encounter at home, at school, or on the playground. Consider that children are often required to play with unattractive objects and to refrain from touching attractive toys in laboratory tests of resistance to temptation. Such a "prohibition" may seem arbitrary or irrational to youngsters whose experience in the home and at school suggests that it is acceptable to play with whatever toys are present in their play areas. Finally, prevailing ethical standards prevent experimenters from exposing children to the kinds of *intense* child-rearing practices (for example, spanking, ridicule, name-calling, and rejection) that may occur in the home setting. So laboratory simulations of a particular child-rearing strategy are often rather weak approximations of their naturalistic referents, and they may have very different effects on the behavior of young children (Brody & Shaffer, 1982).

In spite of these limitations, the laboratory analog serves an important "sufficiency" function by demonstrating that various child-rearing practices can (and often do) have immediate effects on children's behavior. Clearly, the observational and interview methodologies are invaluable because they provide data on the relations between the patterns of child rearing that *parents* use and the behavior of *their* children. Once these relations are known, the experimental analog can then be used to tease apart the effects of the many child-rearing practices that make up a general style or pattern of parenting and thus allow us to draw meaningful conclusions about the ways parents and children are likely to influence each other.

behavior as he played and as he worked on some simple computations. The results were clear. Regardless of whether a mother's own son was conduct-disordered or well-behaved, she was much more coercive and demanding when paired with a conduct-disordered boy than when interacting with a normal boy. Why? Because the conduct-disordered boys were much less compliant with requests—in short, their lack of cooperation and seemingly defiant attitude brought out the worst in *every* mother with whom they interacted. And yet mothers of conduct-disordered boys, who were very negative and coercive with their own sons, were as calm and positive as mothers of normal boys when interacting with a normal, well-behaved child.

We see, then, that children do have a say in determining how they are treated by parents and other adults (see Bell & Chapman, 1986, for a recent review of these "child effects" on adult behavior). In fact, children may have nearly as much effect on the behavior of their parents as parents have on the behavior of their children.

Reconceptualizing Family Effects: The Family as a Social System

Another limitation of the early research on families is that investigators concentrated on mother/child and father/child interactions and failed to treat the family as a true **social system.** Jay Belsky (1981) notes that the family consisting of a mother, a father, and a first-born child is a complex entity. Not only does the infant enter into a reciprocal relationship when alone with each parent, but the presence of *both* parents "transforms the mother-infant dyad into a *family system* [comprising] a husband-wife as well as mother-infant

reciprocal infuence: the notion that each person in a social relationship influences and is influenced by the other person(s).
family social system: the complex network of relationships, interactions, and patterns of influence that characterizes a family with three or more members.

and father-infant relationships" (p. 17). As it turns out, the mere presence of the second parent does affect the way the first parent interacts with his or her child. For example, fathers talk less and display less affection toward their infants and toddlers when the mother is present (Hwang, 1986), and mothers are less likely to initiate play activities or to hold their youngsters when the father is around (Belsky, 1981), particularly if the child is male (Liddell, Henzi, & Drew, 1987). In early adolescence, mother/son interactions are less conflict-ridden in the presence of the father, whereas the entry of the mother into father/son interactions often erodes the quality of that contact by causing the father to withdraw and become less involved in the boy's activities (Gjerde, 1986). Finally, the quality of the marriage (that is, the husband/wife relationship) can affect parent/child interactions, which, in turn, can have an effect on the quality of the marriage. So the patterns of influence in even the simplest of nuclear families are a whole lot more complex than researchers have generally assumed (see Figure 15-1). Of course, the social system becomes much more intricate with the birth of the second child and the addition of sibling/sibling and sibling/parent relationships.

We should also recognize that families exist within a larger cultural or subcultural setting and that the ecological niche a family occupies (for example, the family's religion, its social class, and the values that prevail within a subculture or even a neighborhood) can affect family interactions and the development of a family's children (Bronfenbrenner, 1986). According to Belsky (1981), future advances in the study of family relations will stem from *interdisciplinary* efforts in which developmentalists, family sociologists, and community psychologists pool their expertise to gain a better understanding of the ways in which families (within particular social contexts) influence and are influenced by their young. Focusing narrowly on parent/child interactions is not enough!

The Changing Family System in a Changing World

To date, most family research is based on traditional nuclear families consisting of a mother, a father, and one or more children. And perhaps this emphasis is understandable in that the nuclear family remains the dominant living arrangement in modern industrialized societies. In the United States, for example, nearly 80% of children live in an intact family setting with their

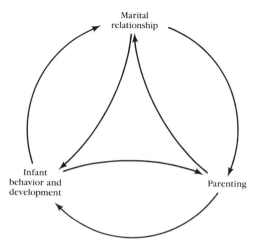

Figure 15-1. A model of the family as a social system. As implied in the diagram, a family is bigger than the sum of its parts. Parents affect infants, who affect each parent and the marital relationship. Of course, the marital relationship may affect the parenting the infant receives, the infant's behavior, and so on. Clearly, families are complex social systems. As an exercise, you may wish to rediagram the patterns of influence within a family after adding a sibling or two. *(From Belsky, 1981.)*

parents, stepparents, or legal guardians such as foster parents or grandparents (U.S. Bureau of the Census, 1982). The major changes in the American nuclear family are that (1) more mothers are working outside the home and (2) people are having fewer children.

Although most children live in nuclear families, the number of single-parent households is steadily increasing. Mavis Hetherington (1981) reports that the number of children living in single-parent homes doubled between 1960 and 1978 (rising from 5.8 million to 11.7 million), and it is worth repeating that 40–50% of all children born in the 1980s will spend some time living in a single-parent family. Two trends are responsible for this dramatic increase in the number of single-parent households: (1) the increasing number of children born out of wedlock and (2) the large number of divorces. Of these two factors, divorce is by far the major contributor. Only 16% of single-parent homes are the result of an illegitimate birth. However, the divorce rate in the United States doubled between 1965 and 1978, and it is now estimated that nearly 50% of marriages between young adults will end in divorce, a sizable majority of these divorces involving children under age 18 (Glick, 1984).

As these statistics clearly indicate, marital disruptions and restructuring of family ties are experiences that many children are now facing or will face in the years ahead. How do they cope? Does a divorce leave permanent emotional scars? Is it possible that children may be better off in a single-parent home than in a strife-ridden nuclear family where the parents are constantly bickering? These are issues that family researchers are currently exploring as they study the impact of divorce on both parents and children.

Although recent research has increased our knowledge about the effects of divorce and family dissolution, much less is known about how children are affected by a common by-product of divorce: the remarriage of the custodial parent. Over 6 million children now live in stepparent homes, and these **reconstituted families** form about 11% of all American households (Santrock, Warshak, Lindbergh, & Meadows, 1982). Later in the chapter, we will take a closer look at the reconstituted family and see whether there is any evidence for the Cinderella syndrome—the notion that many stepparents are cool, aloof caregivers who tend to favor their own biological offspring and may even abuse a stepchild.

In sum, modern families are more diverse than ever before. Our stereotyped image of the model family—the traditional "Leave It to Beaver" nuclear aggregation with a breadwinning father, a housewife mother, and at least two children—is just that: a stereotype. By one estimate, this "ideal" family represented 70% of American households in 1960 but only 12% in 1980 (Klineberg, 1984).

Fortunately, the ways researchers think about and study family relations are changing almost as fast as the families themselves. Our upcoming review of the "family" literature is a blend of (1) the old unidirectional research in which parents were assumed to mold the character of their children and (2) the "new look" at the family as a complex social system in which each family member interacts with and thereby influences every other family member. The older research is definitely worth reviewing, for it gives us some idea of how various patterns of child rearing contribute to positive or negative developmental outcomes. But as we discuss this work, let's keep in mind that children are active participants in the socialization process who play a major role in determining the character of the home environment to which they are exposed.

Interactions between Parents and Their Infants

A child begins to influence the behavior of other family members long before he or she is born. Adults who have hoped to conceive and who eagerly anticipate their baby's arrival will often plan for the blessed event by selecting names for the infant, buying or making baby clothes, decorating a nursery, moving to larger quarters, changing or leaving jobs, and preparing older children in the family for the changes that are soon to come (Grossman, Eichler, Winickoff, & Associates, 1980). Of course, the impact of an unborn child may be far less pleasant for an unwed mother or a couple who do not want their baby, who cannot afford a child, or who receive very little encouragement and support from friends, relatives, and other members of the community.

How is the birth of a child likely to influence the mother, the father, and the marital relationship? Do the changes that parents experience affect their reactions to the baby? Are some parents more capable than others of coping with a difficult infant? Is there any truth to the claim that shaky marriages can be strengthened by having a child? In attempting to answer these questions, we will see why researchers like to think of families as complex entities that they are only now beginning to understand. However, this much is certain: the arrival of an infant transforms the marital dyad into a rather intricate social system that can influence the behavior and emotional well-being of all family members.

The Transition to Parenthood

The birth of a baby is a highly significant event that alters the behavior of both mothers and fathers and may affect the quality of their marital relationship. As we noted in Chapter 13, the onset of parenthood often produces changes in sex-role behaviors. Even among egalitarian couples who have previously shared household tasks, new mothers typically become more "expressive," will partake in more traditionally feminine activities, and now feel more "feminine," whereas new fathers are apt to focus more intently on their role as a provider (Cowan & Cowan, 1987). If both parents previously worked, it is nearly always the mother who stays home to look after the baby. However, it is interesting to note that new fathers often report feeling more "fem-

---

reconstituted families: new families that form after the remarriage of a single parent.

inine" after the birth of a baby, owing perhaps to the increased nurturance and affection they display while interacting with their infants (Feldman & Aschenbrenner, 1983).

How does the birth of a child affect the marital relationship? Many family sociologists believe that the advent of parenthood is a "crisis" of sorts for a marriage. Couples must now cope with greater financial responsibilities, a possible loss of income, changes in sleeping habits, and less time to themselves—events that may be perceived as aversive and could well disrupt the bond between husbands and wives. Indeed, Jay Belsky and his associates (Belsky, Lang, & Rovine, 1985) find that marital satisfaction usually does decline after the birth of a baby. Moreover, this decline in marital bliss is generally steeper for women than for men, probably because the burden of child-care responsibilities typically falls more heavily on the mother. Nevertheless, there are tremendous individual differences in couples' adjustment to parenthood: some couples experience a significant reduction in intimacy and spousal affection after the birth of a first child, whereas others report that becoming a new parent is only mildly stressful.

What factors might account for these differences? After reviewing the available literature, Belsky (1981) concluded that the impact of a new baby on the marital relationship tends to be less severe or disruptive when parents are older, conceive after the marriage ceremony, and have been married longer before conceiving. Moreover, the parents' own family histories have an effect. If both husband and wife were treated in a warm and accepting manner by their own parents, their marriage is unlikely to suffer as they make the transition to parenthood. But if either the husband or wife was raised in an aloof or rejecting manner, the couple are apt to experience some marital discord after their child is born (Belsky & Isabella, 1985).

Of course, the behavior of the infant can also influence the couple's adjustment to parenthood. Parents of temperamentally difficult infants who cry a lot, have feeding problems, and are often "on the move" report more disruption of normal activities and greater dissatisfaction in their marital relationships than parents of "quiet" or "easy" babies (Levitt, Weber, & Clark, 1986; Sirignano & Lachman, 1985; Wilkie & Ames, 1986). Moreover, many parents of infants who require special care (for example, babies with Down's syndrome or those with illnesses that demand constant monitoring) have problems with their spouses and believe that rearing a "special" child has made their marriages worse

(Cain, Kelly, & Shannon, 1980; Gath, 1978). But for every set of parents who experience marital disharmony as a result of caring for a special child, there is at least one other couple who say that their abnormal infant has brought them closer together! So it appears that the arrival of a baby who requires special attention may disrupt the balance of a vulnerable marriage without shaking the foundation of one that is already on firm ground (Gath, 1978).

Effects of Parents on Their Infants

In recent years, a number of investigators have begun to collect longitudinal data on parent/child interactions in an attempt to determine how parents affect the social, emotional, and intellectual development of their infants and toddlers. The results of these studies are remarkably consistent: warm and sensitive mothers who often talk to their infants and try to stimulate their curiosity are contributing in a positive way to the establishment of secure emotional attachments (Ainsworth, 1979; Goldberg, Perrotta, Minde, & Corter, 1986) as well as to the child's curiosity and willingness to explore (Belsky, Garduque, & Hrncir, 1984; Cassidy, 1986), sociability (Waters, Wippman, & Sroufe, 1979), and intellectual growth (Bradley, Caldwell, & Elardo, 1979). Indeed, Jay Belsky (1981) argues that maternal warmth/sensitivity is *the* most influential dimension of mothering in infancy: It not only fosters healthy psychological functioning during this developmental epoch, but it also lays the foundation on which future experience will build" (p. 8).

Although there are many exceptions to the rule, mothers who are themselves adolescents tend to express much less favorable attitudes about child rearing than those in their twenties. Indeed, Susan Crockenberg (1987) finds that teenage mothers who were rejected by their own parents and who lack the support of a spouse or other close companions are likely to be harsh and insensitive caregivers. And even when adolescent mothers do have a close companion to provide social support, their parenting still tends to be less sensitive and responsive than that of older women. Part of the problem is that these young mothers, who are not very knowledgeable about babies and child rearing, usually seek advice and support from other unknowledgeable sources—namely, their own adolescent peers (Garcia Coll, Hoffman, & Oh, 1987). Very young mothers also provide less stimulating home environments for their infants and toddlers than older mothers do, perhaps explaining why children born to teenagers are likely to show some deficits in intellectual functioning during the preschool and grade school years (Baldwin & Cain, 1980; Garcia Coll et al., 1987).

Are older mothers who delay childbearing until they are well established in their careers any less sensitive and responsive to their infants than mothers in their twenties? Probably not. Arlene Ragozin and her associates (Ragozin, Basham, Crnic, Greenberg, & Robinson, 1982) observed the behavior of mothers aged 16 to 38 as they interacted with their 4-month-old first-born infants. As shown in Figure 15-2, older mothers were actually more responsive to these children than younger mothers were, and the older mothers reported that they derived more satisfaction from interacting with their infants as well. Clearly these data argue against the popular belief that women in their twenties are the ones who are best suited psychologically for the responsibilities of motherhood.

Father/infant interactions

Until very recently, investigators have concentrated on mother/infant interactions and all but ignored the influence of fathers. One reason for this emphasis is that mothers attend more to their infants than fathers do, even when the fathers are home from work (Parke & Tinsley, 1984). In their early study of father/infant interactions, Freda Rebelsky and Cheryl Hanks (1971) attached microphones to ten infants and recorded how often their fathers spoke to them between the ages of 2 weeks and 3 months. On an average day, the fathers in this study addressed their infants only 2.7 times for a total of approximately 40 seconds. Even today, with more

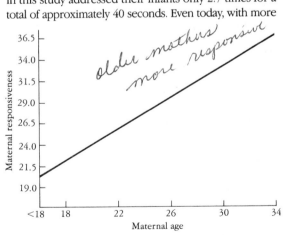

Figure 15-2. Relationship between maternal age and mothers' responsiveness to their 4-month-old first-born infants. *(Adapted from Ragozin et al., 1982.)*

mothers than ever working outside the home, it is still the mother who attends most closely to the needs of a very young infant (Coverman & Sheley, 1986).

Although fathers may have little contact with their infants during the first month or two after birth, they typically become much more involved with them over the next several months (Easterbrooks & Goldberg, 1984). Whereas mothers are likely to hold, soothe, care for, and play quietly with their infants, fathers are much more boisterous, often choosing to initiate physically stimulating, rough-and-tumble activities that infants seem to enjoy (Lamb, 1981). By assuming the role of "special playmate," the father is in a unique position to influence the activities and preferences of his children—particularly sons, for fathers tend to spend more time with sons than with daughters (Barnett & Baruch, 1987; Parke & Tinsley, 1984). Indeed, fathers of 12-month-old infants are already beginning to encourage their children (particularly sons) to play with sex-typed toys and to avoid playful activities that are considered more appropriate for children of the other sex (Snow, Jacklin, & Maccoby, 1983). However, let's note that fathers are more than mere playmates; they are often successful at soothing or comforting a distressed infant, and they may also serve as a "secure base" from which their infant will venture to explore the environment. Finally, we learned in Chapter 11 that a secure attachment to the father can help to offset the social deficiencies and emotional disturbances that could otherwise result when an infant is insecurely attached to the mother (Main & Weston, 1981). So fathers can become important contributors to their infants' development when they take an active part in child rearing and *apply* their competencies.

Indirect effects

The notion that families are social systems implies that parents may have **"indirect effects"** on their children by virtue of their ability to influence the behavior of their spouses. Consider how a father might indirectly influence the mother/infant relationship. If husband and wife are experiencing marital tension, the father's negativity toward the mother may disrupt the mother's caregiving routines and interfere with her ability to enjoy her infant (Belsky, 1981). Indeed, Frank Ped-

---

indirect parental effect: an occasion when one parent influences the behavior of his or her spouse, which, in turn, influences the behavior of their children.

Photo 15-2. Fathers play a central role in a child's life, serving as playmates, caregivers, and confidants, as well as an important source of emotional security.

ersen and his associates (Pedersen, Anderson, & Cain, 1977) found that both mothers and fathers were likely to be unresponsive or negative toward their 5-month-old infants in families characterized by marital strife. So it would seem that unhappily married couples are ill advised to have children as a means of solidifying a shaky marriage. Not only is this practice unlikely to strengthen the marital bond, but it is almost guaranteed to lead to poor parent/child relations.

Of course, the indirect effects of either parent may often be positive ones. For example, fathers tend to be much more involved with their infants when mothers believe that the father should play an important role in the child's life (Palkowitz, 1984) and when the two parents talk frequently about the baby (Belsky, Gilstrap, & Rovine, 1984; Lamb & Elster, 1985). In these studies, it appeared that mothers (who served as the infants' primary caregivers) were exerting an indirect influence on father/infant interactions by encouraging fathers to become more knowledgeable and concerned about the development of their children. Apparently the influence of parents on each other is often reciprocal, for mothers who have a close, supportive relationship with their husbands tend to be more patient with their infants and more sensitive to their needs than mothers who receive little support from their spouses and feel that they are raising their children on their own. In fact, intimate support from the husband seems to be more important to a mother's life satisfaction than any other kind of social support that she might receive—particularly if her in-

fant is temperamentally difficult (Levitt et al., 1986). The picture that emerges, then, is that happily married couples seem to function as sources of *mutual* support and encouragement, so that many child-rearing problems are easier to overcome (Crnic, Greenberg, Ragozin, Robinson, & Basham, 1983; Goldberg & Easterbrooks, 1984). Indeed, parents of babies who are at risk for later emotional problems (as noted by the child's sluggish and disorganized performance on the Brazelton Neonatal Behavioral Assessment Scale) will typically establish "synchronous" and satisfying relationships with their infants *unless they are unhappily married* (Belsky, 1981).

After examining the data on parent/infant interactions, we see that even the simplest of families is a true social system that is bigger than the sum of its parts. Not only does each family member influence the behavior of every other, but the relationship that any two family members have can indirectly affect the interactions and relationships among all other members of the family. Clearly, socialization within the family setting is not merely a two-way street—it is more accurately described as the busy intersection of many avenues of influence.

Parental Effects on Preschool and School-Age Children

During the second and third years, parents spend less time caring for and playing with their child as they begin to impose restrictions on the child's activities and try to teach him or her how to behave (or how not to behave) in a variety of situations. According to Erik Erikson (1963), this is the period when socialization begins in earnest. Parents must now limit the child's autonomy in the hope of instilling a sense of social propriety and self-control, while taking care not to undermine the child's curiosity, initiative, and feelings of personal competence.

Two Major Dimensions of Child Rearing

Erikson believed that two aspects of parenting are especially important during the preschool and school-age years: parental warmth and parental control (that is, permissiveness/restrictiveness).

A number of studies suggest that parents do differ on the two attributes that Erikson thought to be so important. Let's first consider the dimension of parental control.

Permissiveness/restrictiveness refers to the amount of autonomy that parents allow their children. Restrictive parents limit their children's freedom of expression by imposing many demands and actively surveying their children's behavior to ensure that these rules and regulations are followed. Permissive parents are much less controlling. They make relatively few demands of their children and allow them considerable freedom in exploring the environment, expressing their opinions and emotions, and making decisions about their own activities. A common finding is that parents become less restrictive as their children mature, although some parents loosen the reins more than others (Schaefer & Bayley, 1963).

Parental warmth (or **warmth/hostility**) refers to the amount of affection and approval that a parent displays toward a son or a daughter. Parents described as warm and nurturant are those who often smile at, praise, and encourage their child while limiting their criticisms, punishments, and signs of disapproval. By contrast, the hostile or rejecting parent is one who is quick to criticize, belittle, punish, or ignore a child while limiting his or her expressions of affection and approval. It is important to note that measures of parental warmth reflect the character of an adult's reactions to the child *across a large number of situations.* For example, a parent who is cool and critical when a child misbehaves but warm and accepting in most other contexts would be classified as high in parental warmth. One who is warm and nurturant whenever her child praises her but

critical, punitive, or indifferent in many other situations would be considered a more aloof or rejecting parent.

These two dimensions of child rearing are reasonably independent, so that we find parents who are warm and restrictive, warm and permissive, cool (rejecting) and restrictive, and cool and permissive. Are these aspects of parenting related in any meaningful way to the child's social, emotional, and intellectual development?

Patterns of Parental Control

Perhaps the best-known research on the effects of parental control is that of Diana Baumrind (1967, 1971, 1977). Baumrind's sample consisted of 134 preschool children and their parents. Each child was observed on several occasions in nursery school and at home. These data were used to rate the child on several behavioral dimensions (for example, sociability, self-reliance, achievement, moodiness, and self-control). Parents were also interviewed and observed while interacting with their children at home. When Baumrind analyzed the parental data, she found that individual parents generally used one of three patterns of parental control, which can be summarized as follows:

1. **Authoritarian parenting.** A very restrictive pattern of parenting in which adults impose many rules on their children, expect strict obedience, will rarely if ever explain to the child why it is necessary to comply with all these regulations, and will often rely on punitive, forceful tactics (that is, power assertion or love withdrawal) to gain compliance.

2. **Authoritative parenting.** A more flexible style of parenting in which adults allow their chil-

---

permissiveness/restrictiveness: a dimension of parenting that describes the amount of autonomy (or freedom of expression) that a parent allows a child.

warmth/hostility: a dimension of parenting that describes the amount of affection and approval that a parent displays toward a child.

authoritarian parenting: a restrictive pattern of parenting in which adults set many rules for their children, expect strict obedience, and do not explain why it is necessary to comply with these regulations.

authoritative parenting: a flexible style of parenting in which adults allow their children autonomy but are careful to explain the restrictions they impose and will ensure that their children follow these guidelines.

dren considerable freedom but are careful to provide rationales for the restrictions they impose and will ensure that the children follow these guidelines. Authoritative parents are responsive to their children's needs and points of view. However, they expect the child to comply with the spirit of the restrictions they impose and will use both power, if necessary, and reason (that is, inductive discipline) to ensure that he does.

3. **Permissive parenting.** A lax pattern of parenting in which adults make relatively few demands, permit their children to freely express their feelings and impulses, do not closely monitor their children's activities, and rarely exert firm control over their behavior.

On the basis of her observations in the nursery school setting, Baumrind identified three groups of preschool children: *energetic-friendly, conflicted-irritable,* and *impulsive-aggressive.* As shown in Table 15-1, these patterns of child behavior were closely related to

Table 15-1. Patterns of parental control and corresponding patterns of children's behavior

Parental classification	Children's behavioral profile
Authoritative parenting	*Energetic-friendly* Self-reliant Self-controlled Cheerful and friendly Copes well with stress Cooperative with adults Curious Purposive Achievement-oriented
Authoritarian parenting	*Conflicted-irritable* Fearful, apprehensive Moody, unhappy Easily annoyed Passively hostile Vulnerable to stress Aimless Sulky, unfriendly
Permissive parenting	*Impulsive-aggressive* Rebellious Low in self-reliance and self-control Impulsive Aggressive Domineering Aimless Low in achievement

parents' patterns of control. Authoritative parents generally had energetic-friendly youngsters who were cheerful, socially responsive, self-reliant, achievement-oriented, and cooperative with adults and peers. By contrast, children of authoritarian parents tended to fall into the conflicted-irritable category: they were moody and seemingly unhappy much of the time, easily annoyed, relatively aimless, and not very pleasant to be around. Finally, permissive parents often had children classified as impulsive-aggressive. These youngsters (particularly the boys) tended to be bossy and self-centered, rebellious, aggressive, rather aimless, and quite low in independence and achievement.

What do Baumrind's findings imply about parental control? For one thing, it appears that restrictive parenting is preferable to a laissez-faire approach, for children of extremely permissive parents are often aimless and defiant little terrors—in a word, spoiled brats. Moreover, the ways in which parents introduce and enforce restrictions are also important. Note that both authoritative and authoritarian parents set many standards for their children and are quite controlling. But there is a clear difference in the way control is exercised. The authoritarian parent dominates the child, allowing little if any freedom of expression, whereas the authoritative parent is careful to permit the child enough autonomy so that he or she can develop initiative, self-reliance, and a feeling of pride in personal accomplishments. Baumrind's results indicate that maintaining a firm sense of control over a child can be a very beneficial childrearing practice. It is only when the controlling parent severely restricts the child's autonomy and uses arbitrary or irrational methods of control that the child is likely to be surly or sulky in social situations and lacking in initiative and achievement.

Although Baumrind's findings clearly favor the authoritative pattern of control, one might legitimately wonder whether children of authoritarian or permissive parents might eventually "outgrow" the emotional conflicts and behavioral disturbances they displayed as preschoolers. Seeking to answer this question, Baumrind (1977) observed her subjects (and their parents) once again when the children were 8 to 9 years old. As we see in Table 15-2, children of authoritative parents were still relatively high in both *cognitive competencies* (that is, shows originality in thinking, has high achievement motivation, likes intellectual challenges) and *social skills* (for example, is sociable and outgoing, participates actively and shows leadership in group activities), whereas children of permissive parents were relatively unskilled

Table 15.2. Relationship between patterns of parental control during the preschool period and children's cognitive and social competencies during the grade school years

Pattern of parenting during preschool period	Children's competencies at age 8–9	
	Girls	*Boys*
Authoritative	Very high cognitive and social competencies	High cognitive and social competencies
Authoritarian	Average cognitive and social competencies	Average social competencies; low cognitive competencies
Permissive	Low cognitive and social competencies	Low social competencies; very low cognitive competencies

in both areas. Finally, Baumrind's latest follow-up on these youngsters suggests that the patterns of cognitive and social competencies they displayed as grade school children tend to persist into adolescence (see also Dornbusch, Ritter, Leiderman, Roberts, & Fraleigh, 1987).

One limitation of Baumrind's research is that almost all the parents in her sample were reasonably warm and accepting. As it turns out, the effects of either restrictive or permissive parenting will depend, in part, on the extent to which the parent displays warmth and affection toward the child (Becker, 1964). Children of *restrictive and rejecting* parents are often found to be extremely withdrawn and inhibited, and they may even show **masochistic** or suicidal tendencies. By contrast, children of *permissive and rejecting* parents tend to be very hostile and rebellious toward authority figures and prone to engage in delinquent acts such as alcohol and drug abuse, sexual misconduct, truancy, and a variety of criminal offenses (Patterson & Stouthamer-Loeber, 1984; Pulkkinen, 1982). What these findings seem to suggest is that the undesirable effects of either extremely restrictive (authoritarian) or extremely permissive parenting are exaggerated when parents are also cool and aloof toward their children or unconcerned about their welfare.

How important is it that a child be (or feel) accepted by his or her parents? This is the issue to which we will now turn.

Parental Warmth/Hostility

Although most parents are warm and loving, a small minority in any sample are clearly rejecting—expressing a lack of concern or feelings of dislike for their youngsters, who are often perceived as burdensome (Maccoby, 1980). Throughout this text, we have taken care to note the relationship between parental warmth and various aspects of children's social, emo-

tional, and intellectual development. Here are but a few of the attributes that characterize the children of warm and accepting parents:

1. They are securely attached at an early age. Of course, secure attachments are an important contributor to the growth of curiosity, exploratory competence, problem-solving skills, and positive social relations with both adults and peers (see Chapter 11).
2. They tend to be competent students during the grade school years—students who make steady scholastic progress and score average or above on IQ tests (Estrada, Arsenio, Hess, & Holloway, 1987; see Chapter 10).
3. They are relatively altruistic, especially when their parents preach altruistic values and practice what they preach (see Chapter 14).
4. They are generally obedient, noncoercive youngsters who get along reasonably well with parents and peers (see Chapter 12).
5. They tend to be high in self-esteem and role-taking skills, and when they are disciplined, they usually feel that their parents' actions are justified (Brody & Shaffer, 1982; Coopersmith, 1967).
6. They are satisfied with their gender identities and are likely to be firmly sex-typed or androgynous (Mussen & Rutherford, 1963; see Chapter 13).
7. They will often refer to internalized norms rather than fear of punishment as a reason for complying with moral rules (Brody & Shaffer, 1982).

---

permissive parenting: a pattern of parenting in which adults make few demands of their children and rarely attempt to control their behavior.

masochist: a person who derives pleasure from beatings or other forms of abuse administered by the self or others.

Photo 15-3. Warmth and affection are crucial components of effective parenting.

Now compare this behavioral profile with that of a group of "unwanted" Czechoslovakian children whose mothers had tried repeatedly to gain permission to abort them during the prenatal period. Compared with a group of "wanted" Czech children from similar family backgrounds, the unwanted children had less stable ties to their mothers and fathers and were described by the researchers as anxious, emotionally frustrated, and irritable (Matejcek, Dytrych, & Schuller, 1979). Although they were all physically healthy at birth, the unwanted children were more likely than those in the "wanted" group to have spotty medical histories that had required them to be hospitalized. Children in the unwanted group made significantly poorer grades at school even though they were comparable in intelligence to their "wanted" classmates. Finally, the unwanted children were less well integrated into the peer group and more likely to require psychiatric attention for serious behavior disorders. (For another look at the long-term consequences of cool, aloof parenting, see Box 15-2.)

Is parental warmth alone likely to lead to positive developmental outcomes? Probably not, for we've seen that children of warm but permissive parents tend to be low in both cognitive and social competencies (Baumrind, 1971, 1977). Nevertheless, warmth and affection are clearly important components of effective parenting. As Eleanor Maccoby (1980) has noted,

Parental warmth binds children to their parents in a positive way—it makes children responsive and more willing to accept guidance. If the parent-child relationship is close and affectionate, parents can exercise what control is needed without having to apply heavy disciplinary pressure. It is as if parents' responsiveness, affection, and obvious commitment to their children's welfare have earned them the right to make decisions and exercise control [p. 394].

A "Child's Eye" View of Effective Parenting

What attributes do children view as indications of competent parenting? One strong clue comes from John Weisz's (1980) analyses of letters submitted by 7- to 17-year-olds to a newspaper contest entitled "Why Mom Is the Greatest." The dominant theme in these essays was children's genuine appreciation of the *warmth* and *affection* that their mothers displayed. And although these youngsters also valued the autonomy their mothers allowed them, the adolescents in the sample acknowledged that it was desirable for their mothers to monitor and to exercise some *control* over their activities. Apparently the older contestants recognized that maternal restraints reflect love and concern about their welfare, whereas extreme permissiveness may indicate laxity or disinterest.

Although Weisz's findings are based on only

Box 15-2
Parental Rejection as a Contributor
to Adult Depression

Several years ago, Thomas Crook, Allen Raskin, and John Eliot (1981) proposed that adults who are clinically depressed and view themselves as inferior or worthless are often the product of a home environment in which they were clearly rejected by one or both parents. To evaluate their hypothesis, Crook et al. asked 714 adults who were hospitalized for depression to describe their childhood relationships with their mothers and fathers by indicating whether each of 192 statements characterized the behavior of either or both parents (for example, Did your mother [father] worry about you when you were away? Threaten not to love you if you misbehaved? Often make you feel guilty? Set firm standards? Consistently enforce her [his] rules? Often ridicule you?). As a comparison group, 387 nondepressed adults answered the same questions. Since an adult's self-reports of childhood experiences may be distorted and unreliable, the investigators also interviewed siblings, relatives, and long-time friends of the subjects as a check on the accuracy of their reflections. Data collected from these "independent sources" were then used to rate each subject's mother and father on the warmth/hostility and the autonomy/control (permissiveness/restrictiveness) dimensions.

The results of this study were straightforward. Subjects hospitalized for depression rated *both their mothers and their fathers* as less "accepting" and more "hostile," "detached," and "rejecting" than nondepressed adults in the comparison sample. Although the parents of depressed patients were not rated as any more "restrictive" or "controlling" than parents of nondepressed adults, they were perceived as exercising control in a more derisive way, often choosing to ridicule, belittle, or withdraw affection from their children. So even the guidance and discipline that depressed adults received during childhood were administered in a hostile, rejecting manner.

Data collected from the "independent sources" were quite consistent with the subjects' own reports. Both the mothers and fathers of the depressed patients were described as less affectionate and less involved with their children than the parents of nondepressed adults.

More recently, Monroe Lefkowitz and Edward Tesiny (1984) have conducted a *prospective* study to determine whether parental rejection measured *during childhood* would predict a person's depressive tendencies in adolescence. Mothers and fathers of 8-year-old girls completed a child-rearing questionnaire containing items designed to assess their satisfaction with their child and her behavior (extremely low scores were taken as indications of parental rejection). Ten years later, these girls (who were now 18-year-old adolescents) completed the Depression scale of the Minnesota Multiphasic Personality Inventory, a well-known diagnostic test. As expected, girls whose mothers and fathers were rejecting during childhood scored significantly higher on the Depression scale as adolescents than did their counterparts whose parents were not so rejecting.

In sum, it appears that a primary contributor to adult depression is a family setting in which one or both parents treat the child as if he or she were unworthy of their love and affection. Perhaps it is fair to say that parents who blatantly reject their children are committing an extremely powerful form of child abuse—one that could leave emotional scars that will last a lifetime.

---

244 letters written by children who had obviously established good relationships with their mothers, it is interesting to note that these youngsters stressed the very attributes—warmth and the rational exercise of control—that developmentalists consider important dimensions of effective parenting. In fact, statements indicative of aloof or authoritarian parenting almost never appeared in the letters of these young respondents. Since the data apply only to mothers, it would be interesting to see whether children mention the same attributes and child-rearing practices when they tell us "why Dad is the greatest."

Social-Class Differences in Parenting

Social class, or *socioeconomic status* (SES), refers to one's position within a society that is stratified according to status or power. In many countries, such as India, a person's social standing is determined at birth by the status of his or her parents. If you were to grow up in this kind of society, you would be compelled by virtue of your origins to pursue one of a limited number of occupations, to live in a designated neighborhood, and to marry someone who occupies a similar position in the social hierarchy.

This scenario sounds rather dismal to those of us who live in Western industrialized societies, where the most common measures of social class—family income, prestige of father's occupation, and parents' educational level—are indications of the family's achievements. In the United States, we are fond of saying that virtually anyone can rise above his or her origins if that person is willing to work extremely hard toward the pursuit of success. Indeed, this proverb is the cornerstone of the American dream.

However, sociologists tell us that the "American dream" is a belief that is more likely to be endorsed by members of the middle and upper classes—those elements of society that have the economic resources to maintain or improve on their lofty economic status (Hess, 1970). As we will see, many people from the lower and working classes face very different kinds of problems, pursue different goals, and often adopt different values. In short, they live in a different world than middle-class people do, and these ecological considerations may well affect the methods and strategies that they use to raise their children.

Social-class differences in attitudes, values, and lifestyles

Perhaps the most obvious differences between middle- and lower-class families are economic: middle-class families usually have more money and material possessions. A more subtle difference between **high-SES** (middle- and upper-class) families and **low-SES** (lower- and working-class) families centers on their feelings of power and influence. People from the lower socioeconomic strata often believe that, without material resources, they have few opportunities to get ahead and no direct access to those in power, and consequently they feel that their lives are largely controlled by the "advantaged" members of society. In order to qualify for housing, financial, or medical assistance, they must often live where the bureaucrats tell them to live or otherwise do as the bureaucrats say. Many low-SES parents cannot afford the luxury of health or disability insurance, and their resources are likely to be insufficient to cope with problems such as an accident, an extended illness, or the loss of a job. Is it any wonder, then, that many lower- and working-class adults feel insecure or helpless and are apt to develop an external locus of control (Hess, 1970; Phares, 1976)?

A low income may also mean that living quarters are crowded, that family members must occasionally make do without adequate food or medical care, and that parents are constantly tense or anxious about living under these marginal conditions. Eleanor Maccoby (1980) suggests that low-income living is probably more *stressful* for parents and that stress affects the ways in which parental functions are carried out. Indeed, Rand Conger and his associates (Conger, McCarty, Yang, Lahey, & Kropp, 1984) have recently found a rather strong association between the number of environmental stresses that a family experiences (for example, lesser education of parents, low income, many children, being a single parent, relying on welfare payments) and the treatment that children receive from their mothers. Specifically, the greater the number of environmental stressors the family was experiencing, the less supportive mothers were when interacting with their children, the more likely they were to make derogatory statements about their youngsters or to threaten, slap, push, or grab them, and the more authoritarian they became when expressing their views on child rearing.

So stress can indeed affect the ways adults react to their children. And when we consider that low-SES families are more likely to experience major and prolonged life stresses such as inadequate housing, losses of employment due to economic uncertainties, anxieties about being able to pay bills or put food on the table, and family disruptions because of divorce or desertion, we have good reason to suspect that low-SES parents may end up raising their children differently than middle- and upper-class parents do.

Patterns of child rearing in high-SES and low-SES families

Eleanor Maccoby (1980) has reviewed the child-rearing literature and concluded that high-SES parents differ from low-SES parents in at least four respects:

1. Low-SES parents tend to stress obedience and respect for authority, neatness, cleanliness, and staying out of trouble. Higher-SES parents are more likely to stress happiness, curiosity, independence, creativity, and ambition.
2. Lower-SES parents are more restrictive and authoritarian, often setting arbitrary standards and enforcing them with power-assertive forms of discipline. Higher-SES parents tend to be either permissive or authoritative, and they are more likely to use inductive forms of discipline.
3. Higher-SES parents talk more with their children, reason with them more, and may use somewhat more complex language than lower-SES parents.
4. Higher-SES parents tend to show more warmth and affection toward their children.

According to Maccoby, these relationships seem to be true in many cultures and across racial and ethnic groups within the United States. However, there is some evidence that differences between high-SES and low-SES parenting are much more pronounced for boys than for girls. For example, John Zussman (1978) found that lower-class parents were more likely than middle-class parents to use power assertion with their sons, although parents from both social classes used very low levels of power assertion with their daughters.

Of course, we should keep in mind that these class-linked differences in parenting represent *group averages* rather than absolute contrasts: some middle-class parents are highly restrictive, power-assertive, and aloof in their approach to child rearing, whereas many lower- and working-class parents function more like their counterparts in the middle class (Laosa, 1981). But on the average, it appears that lower- and working-class parents are somewhat more critical, more punitive, and more intolerant of disobedience than parents from the middle and upper socioeconomic strata.

Undoubtedly, many factors contribute to social-class differences in child rearing. Earlier we saw that the stresses associated with low-income living may cause parents to become more punitive and less responsive to a child's needs—in short, to seem somewhat aloof or uninvolved with their children. And as John Ogbu (1981) and others have noted, the way a family earns its livelihood may affect the strategies that parents use to raise their children. Low-SES parents may emphasize respect, obedience, neatness, and staying out of trouble because these are precisely the attributes that they view as critical for success in the blue-collar economy. By contrast, high-SES parents may reason or negotiate more with their children while emphasizing individual initiative and achievement because these are the skills, attributes, and abilities that high-SES parents find necessary in their own roles as businesspersons, white-collar workers, or high-salaried professionals. Finally, let's note that the children themselves may contribute to social-class differences in child rearing. Low-SES mothers, who are often younger and may receive less adequate prenatal care, are more likely than middle-class mothers to deliver prematurely or to experience other complications of childbirth (Kessner, 1973). As a result, low-SES families are more likely to have irritable, unresponsive, or otherwise difficult babies who may be harder to care for and love.

When we look at the data, it may seem that high-SES parenting is somehow "better" or more competent. After all, the responsive, authoritative parenting often observed in middle-class families produces highly sociable children who are curious, outgoing, intellectually capable, and well-behaved. Yet there is another side to this issue—one that researchers in Western societies sometimes fail to consider. Perhaps middle-class parenting is "better" for children who are expected to grow up and become productive members of a middle-class subculture. However, a middle-class pattern of parenting that stresses individual initiative, intellectual curiosity, and competitiveness may actually represent "incompetent" parenting among the Temne of Sierra Leone,

a society in which everyone must pull together and suppress individualism if the community is to successfully plant, harvest, and ration the meager crops on which its livelihood absolutely depends (Berry, 1967). And since many children from Western, industrialized societies will choose a career within the so-called blue-collar economy, it hardly seems reasonable to conclude that a pattern of child rearing that prepares them for this undertaking is in some way deficient or "incompetent."

The closest thing to a general law of parenting is that warm, sensitive, and responsive caregiving seems to be associated with positive developmental outcomes in virtually all the cultures and subcultures that social scientists have studied. But people are being somewhat **ethnocentric** when they suggest that a particular pattern or style of child rearing (for example, authoritative parenting) that produces favorable outcomes in one context (middle-class Western societies) is the optimal pattern for children in all other cultures and subcultures. Louis Laosa (1981, p. 159) makes this same point, noting that "indigenous patterns of child care throughout the world represent largely successful adaptations to conditions of life that have long differed from one people to another. Women are 'good mothers' by the only relevant standards, those of their own culture."

Effects of Siblings and the Family Configuration

Perhaps the one aspect of family socialization that we know least about is the effects that siblings have on one another. The vast majority of American children grow up with siblings, and there is certainly no shortage of speculation about the roles that brothers and sisters play in a child's life. For example, parents are often concerned about the fighting and bickering that their youngsters display, and they may wonder whether this rivalrous conduct is good for their children. At the same time, the popular wisdom is that "only" children are

---

high-SES: a term that refers to the middle and upper classes—that is, the economically advantaged members of society.

low-SES: a term that refers to the lower and working classes—that is, the economically disadvantaged members of society.

ethnocentrism: the tendency to view one's own culture as "best" and to use one's own cultural standards as a basis for evaluating other cultures.

likely to be lonely, overindulged "brats" who would profit both socially and emotionally from having siblings to teach them that they are not nearly as "special" or important as they think they are.

Although our knowledge about sibling influences is not extensive, we will see that brothers and sisters may often play an important role in a child's life. Moreover, it appears that the influence that siblings are likely to have will depend, in part, on whether they are older or younger than the child.

The Nature of Sibling Interactions

Do children respond differently to siblings than to parents? Linda Baskett and Stephan Johnson (1982) tried to answer this question by visiting with 47 families in their homes. Each family was observed for 45 minutes on five occasions. The children in these two- or three-child families ranged from 4 to 10 years of age.

Baskett and Johnson found that interactions between children and their parents were much more positive in character than those that occurred between siblings. Children often laughed with, talked to, and showed affection toward their parents, and they were more likely to comply with parental commands. By contrast, hitting, yelling, and other annoying physical antics were more often directed toward siblings. Although positive social responses outnumbered negative ones in both parent/child and sibling/sibling interactions, brothers and sisters were more coercive than parents and tended to respond less positively to a child's social overtures.

Other observational studies (for example, Abramovitch, Corter, Pepler, & Stanhope, 1986; Berndt & Bulleit, 1985) reveal that there are reliable differences in the behavior of older and younger siblings. Older siblings are generally more domineering and aggressive, whereas younger siblings are more compliant. However, older siblings also initiate more helpful, playful, and other prosocial behaviors, a finding that may reflect the pressure parents place on older children to demonstrate their maturity by looking after a younger brother or sister.

Origins and Determinants
of Sibling Rivalry

Sibling rivalry—a spirit of competition, jealousy, or resentment among siblings—often begins rather early, while the younger child is still in diapers. Several investigators (for example, Dunn & Kendrick, 1982; Stewart, Mobley, Van Tuyl, & Salvador, 1987) have found

that older toddlers and preschool children receive less attention from their mothers after the birth of a baby and are likely to respond to this "neglect" by crying, clinging to the mother, demanding attention, and sometimes even hitting the mother or the infant. So most first-borns are not entirely thrilled to have an attention-grabbing new baby in the home. They resent losing the mother's attention, may harbor animosities toward the baby for stealing it, and will do whatever they can in an attempt to make their feelings known and to recapture the mother's love.

Fortunately, most children adjust fairly quickly to a younger sibling, becoming much less anxious and less inclined to display the problem behaviors that they showed initially. Fathers seem to play an important role in this adjustment process by increasing (or at least maintaining) their rates of interaction with their first-borns as mothers are decreasing theirs (Stewart et al., 1987). Mothers can also help by appealing to the older child's maturity and encouraging him or her to assist in caring for the baby. Setting aside a little "quality time" to let the older child know that she is still loved and considered important is also a useful strategy for mothers to pursue (Dunn & Kendrick, 1982). Yet some caution is required here, for Dunn and Kendrick (1982) found that older girls whose parents showered them with attention in the weeks after a baby was born were the ones who played *least* with and were *most negative* toward their baby brother or sister 14 months later. The older children who were most positive toward their younger siblings (both 14 months later and at age 6) were those whose mothers had not permitted them to brood or respond negatively toward the baby (Dunn, 1984). We see, then, that parents may have to tread a thin line between two traps: becoming so attentive toward the new baby that they deprive the older child of attention or undermine his security and becoming so indulgent of the first-born that he resents any competition from the younger sib.

Actual confrontations among siblings become more commonplace as the younger child reaches 8–12 months of age and is now more mobile, more intrusive, and thus better able to compete with the older sib for toys or to otherwise disrupt her play activities (Dunn & Munn, 1985; Stewart et al., 1987). Indeed, these kinds of squabbles among siblings increase in both frequency and intensity once the younger child reaches 18 to 24 months of age and is suddenly quite proficient at "holding his own" by hitting or teasing the older sibling or by directing a parent's attention to the older sib's mis-

Photo 15-4. Coercive and rivalrous conduct between siblings is a normal aspect of family life.

conduct (Dunn & Munn, 1985). Several investigators have found that *same-sex* siblings tend to display more positive social behaviors (such as smiling, sharing, and showing affection) and fewer negative behaviors and are more inclined to feel close to each other than cross-sex siblings (see Abramovitch et al., 1986; Dunn & Kendrick, 1981; Furman & Buhrmester, 1985a, 1985b). Apparently this "sex of sibling" effect can appear very early and may be indirectly attributable to the behavior of mothers. In their study of 14-month-old infants and their older siblings, Dunn and Kendrick (1981) reported that mothers spent much more time playing with the younger child when he or she *differed* in gender from the older sibling. Thus, an infant sibling of the other sex may represent a greater threat to the older child's security, which, in turn, leads him or her to resent the other-sex sib and to respond less positively to this little intruder.

Conflict among siblings is seen throughout childhood, particularly among those who are nearly the same age (Furman & Buhrmester, 1985a; Minnett, Vandell, & Santrock, 1983). And there is some evidence that sibling rivalries may intensify over the course of childhood, for John Santrock and Ann Minnett (1981) found that interactions between older female sibs (for example, an 8-year-old and a 12-year-old) were more negative in tone and included fewer positive acts than interactions between pairs of younger sisters (for example, a 4-year-old and an 8-year-old).

In some ways, sibling relationships are rather paradoxical. For example, Furman and Buhrmester (1985a, 1985b) found that siblings who are similar in age report more warmth and closeness than other sibling pairs but, at the same time, more friction and conflict (conflict being especially prevalent among opposite-sex sibs who are close in age). Moreover, grade school children view their sibling relations as more conflict-ridden and less satisfying than their relations with either parent, their grandparents, or their friends. Yet, when children were asked to rate the *importance* of different social relationships and the *reliability* of their various social alliances, siblings were viewed as more important and more reliable than friends! Even young adolescents, who are often depicted as "peer-oriented," continue to perceive their siblings as important and intimate associates (Buhrmester & Furman, 1987). So siblings are significant people in a child's life—people to whom a youngster can turn for support and companionship, even though relations with them have often been rather stormy.

Perhaps these seemingly paradoxical data make perfectly good sense if we carefully reexamine the findings on the nature of sibling/sibling interactions. Yes, rivalrous conduct and conflicts among siblings are a very normal part of family life. However, the observational record consistently shows that brothers and sisters often do nice things for one another and that these acts of kindness and affection are typically much more common than hateful or rivalrous conduct (see, for example, Abramovitch et al., 1986; Baskett & Johnson, 1982).

Positive Effects of Sibling Interactions

One recent survey of child-rearing practices in 186 societies found that older children were the prin-

---

sibling rivalry: the spirit of competition, jealousy, and resentment that may arise between two or more siblings.

cipal caregivers for infants and toddlers in 57% of the groups studied (Weisner & Gallimore, 1977). Even in industrialized societies such as the United States, older siblings (particularly females) are often asked to look after and care for their younger brothers and sisters (Cicirelli, 1982). So there is reason to believe that older children may play a major role in the lives of younger siblings, often serving as their teachers, playmates, and advocates and occasionally as their disciplinarians.

Siblings as attachment objects.

Do infants become attached to their older brothers and sisters? To find out, Robert Stewart (1983) exposed 10–20-month-old infants to a variation of Ainsworth's "strange situations" test. Each infant was left with a 4-year-old sibling in a strange room that a strange adult soon entered. The infants typically showed signs of distress as their mothers departed, and they were wary in the company of the stranger. Stewart noted that these distressed infants would often approach their older brother or sister, particularly when the stranger appeared. Moreover, a majority of the 4-year-olds offered some sort of comforting or caregiving to their baby brothers and sisters. In a later study, Stewart and Marvin (1984) replicated these results and showed that the preschoolers who were most inclined to comfort an infant sibling were those who had developed the role-taking skills to understand and appreciate the basis for the infant's distress. So it appears that older preschool children can become important sources of emotional support who help younger siblings to cope with uncertain situations when their parents are not around. Moreover, infants are likely to venture much farther away to explore a strange environment if a sensitive and attentive older sibling is nearby to serve as a "secure base" for exploration (Samuels, 1980; Stewart & Marvin, 1984).

Siblings as social models.

In addition to providing a sense of security and facilitating the child's exploratory competencies, older siblings serve as models for their younger brothers and sisters. As early as 12 to 20 months of age, infants are already becoming very attentive to their older sibs, often choosing to imitate their actions or to take over toys that the older children have abandoned (Abramovitch, Corter, & Pepler, 1980; Samuels, 1977). By contrast, an older child will typically focus on parents as social models and will pay little attention the behavior of a younger sib, unless they happen to be playing together or the younger sibling is interfering with the older child's activities (Baskett, 1984; Samuels, 1977).

Siblings as teachers.

Do older siblings take it upon themselves to oversee a younger sib's activities and to promote his or her competencies? Yes, indeed. In one study (Brody, Stoneman, & MacKinnon, 1982), 8- to 10-year-olds played a popular board game with (1) a younger (4½–7-year-old) sibling, (2) an 8- to 10-year-old peer, and (3) a younger sib and a peer. As the children played, observers noted how often each child assumed the following roles: *teacher, learner, manager* (child requests or commands an action), *managee* (child is the target of management), and *equal-status playmate*. Brody et al. found that older children dominated the sibling/sibling interactions by assuming the teacher and manager roles much more often than younger sibs did. Yet, when playing with a peer, these 8- to 10-year-olds took the role of equal-status playmate and rarely tried to dominate their friends. When all three children played together, it was the older sibling rather than the peer who assumed responsibility for "managing" the younger child, although neither the older sib nor the peer did much teaching in this situation. So older siblings are likely to make an active attempt to instruct their younger brothers and sisters, particularly when playing alone with them. Although the teaching that older sibs performed in this study may seem rather trivial, other research indicates that younger siblings who experience little difficulty in learning to read are likely to have older brothers and sisters who played "school" with them and who taught them important lessons such as the ABCs (Norman-Jackson, 1982).

Do older children benefit from teaching their younger siblings? Indeed they may. Studies of peer tutoring, in which older children teach academic lessons to younger pupils, consistently find that the tutors show significant gains in academic achievement—bigger gains than those posted by age mates who have not had an opportunity to tutor a younger child (Feldman, Devin-Sheehan, & Allen, 1976). Moreover, Robert Zajonc and his associates (Zajonc, Markus, & Markus, 1979) report that first-born children with younger sibs tend to score higher on tests of intelligence and academic achievement than "only" children who have no younger siblings to tutor. Finally, Delroy Paulhus and David Shaffer (1981) found that the greater the number of younger siblings (up to three) that college women have had an opportunity to tutor, the higher these women score on the Scholastic Aptitude Test (SAT).

So it appears that the teacher/learner roles that siblings often assume at play are beneficial to all parties involved: older siblings learn by tutoring their younger brothers and sisters, while the young tutees seem to profit from the instruction they receive.

Configural Effects: Characteristics of First-Born, Later-Born, and Only Children

For more than 100 years social scientists have speculated that a child's **ordinal position** within the family will affect his or her personality (Henderson, 1981). One popular notion was that first-born children, who initially enjoy an exclusive relationship with their parents, will remain forever closer to their mothers and fathers than later-borns. Another was that later-borns will eventually become more likable and popular than first-borns because they have had to acquire important social skills in order to negotiate with their older and more powerful siblings. Do these claims have any merit? Do first-borns reliably differ from later-borns, and if so, why?

Characteristics of first-borns

There is now a great deal of evidence that first-borns are more achievement-oriented than later-borns. First-borns are overrepresented among populations of eminent people and college students (Schachter, 1963; Warren, 1966), and they tend to score higher than later-borns on tests of IQ (Zajonc, Markus, & Markus, 1979), English and mathematics achievement (Paulhus & Shaffer, 1981), and verbal reasoning (Kellaghan & Mac-Namara, 1972). In addition, first-borns score somewhat higher on tests of achievement motivation and hold higher educational aspirations than later-borns (Glass, Neulinger, & Brim, 1974; Sampson & Hancock, 1967).

In Chapter 12 we learned that first-born toddlers, nursery school children, and college students are more sociable than later-borns. However, they also tend to be less confident in social situations, and first-born males are more likely than later-borns to exhibit behavior disorders and to be rated by teachers as anxious and as aggressive toward their peers (Lahey, Hammer, Crumrine, & Forehand, 1980; Schachter, 1959). As a result, many first-borns are not terribly popular, even though they may be outgoing and will often seek others' attention or approval.

First-born children (particularly females) tend to be more obedient and somewhat more socially responsible than later-borns. Brian Sutton-Smith and B.

G. Rosenberg (1970) propose that this obedience may stem from the special and exclusive early relationship that first-borns have had with their parents. Parents seem to expect more of their first-borns and are often critical of their behavior (Baskett, 1985; Rothbart, 1971). However, they also appear to be more attentive and affectionate toward their first-born children (Jacobs & Moss, 1976), a finding that may help to explain why first-borns often feel closer to their parents than later-borns do (Sutton-Smith & Rosenberg, 1970).

Characteristics of later-borns

It is difficult to characterize later-borns because they occupy many different sibling statuses (for example, second-born female in a family of two; fourth-born and male in a family with three older sisters) and are not really a homogeneous group. In two-child families, the behavior of the later-born child is clearly influenced by the sex of his or her sibling. For example, a boy who has an older sister is likely to develop more "feminine" interests than a boy with an older brother (Sutton-Smith & Rosenberg, 1970).

As a group, later-borns seem to establish better relations with peers than first-borns do. In one study of 1750 first-born, middle-born, and last-born schoolchildren (Miller & Maruyama, 1976), the investigators found that the "babies of the family" (that is, last-borns) were most popular with their classmates, while middle-borns enjoyed intermediate popularity, and first-borns were least popular.

Let's keep in mind that these "ordinal position" effects represent group averages. Many first-borns are extremely popular with their peers, just as many later-borns are highly obedient, socially responsible, and motivated to achieve. Only when group averages are compared do the differences between first-borns and later-borns emerge.

Explaining ordinal-position effects

It appears that parents contribute to ordinal-position effects by treating first-borns differently than later-borns. Many investigators believe that first-time parents will devote more attention to first-borns because they feel unpracticed at child rearing and are especially concerned about whether they are raising their child appropriately. But after raising one child success-

---

ordinal position: the child's order of birth among siblings (also called birth order).

fully, parents gain considerable self-confidence and are not so apprehensive about the development of later-borns (Lasko, 1954; Schachter, 1959). Indeed, parents do have higher expectations for first-borns than for later-borns (Baskett, 1985), and they exert greater pressures on first-borns to be responsible and to work to the best of their ability (Lasko, 1954; Rothbart, 1971). In one study of children's achievement behavior (Hilton, 1967), mothers of first-borns were more likely than mothers of later-borns to stress achievement and to tailor their reactions to the child's performance. That is, mothers of first-borns were *extremely* warm and affectionate when their 4-year-olds succeeded on a cognitive task but were also more likely than mothers of later-borns to act peeved and to *withhold affection* if their child performed poorly on a task. Perhaps this pattern helps to explain why first-borns are so obedient and interested in pleasing their parents and are also higher in achievement motivation than later-borns.

Why are first-borns *more sociable* and yet *less popular* than later-borns? Many researchers believe that these findings are attributable to the character of sibling interactions. If you grew up with brothers and sisters, you know very well that power is unequally distributed among siblings. We have already seen that older sibs will try to dominate younger brothers and sisters in order to achieve their objectives—a tendency that may suppress the affiliative tendencies of later-borns and make them somewhat cautious and concerned about interacting with others (Abramovitch et al., 1986; Brody et al., 1982). Indeed, there is some evidence that older siblings who reliably use their greater power to impose their will on a younger brother or sister tend to employ these same tactics with peers (Berndt & Bulleit, 1985)—a move that is not likely to enhance their popularity or status in the peer group. Moreover, socially cautious later-borns may eventually become more popular than first-borns because

> if later-born children are to obtain . . . a fair share of positive outcomes, they must develop their interpersonal skills—powers of negotiation, accommodation, tolerance, and a capacity to accept less favorable outcomes—to a degree not found in first-born children . . . who may simply take or achieve what they want quite arbitrarily. . . . The acquisition of [these] interpersonal skills should facilitate social interactions with peers and thereby increase a [later-born] child's popularity [Miller & Maruyama, 1976, pp. 123–124].

Characteristics of only children

Are "only" children who grow up without siblings the spoiled, selfish, overindulged brats that people often presume them to be? Hardly! After reviewing the pertinent literature, Toni Falbo and Denise Polit (1986) found that only children (1) are about as intellectually competent and well behaved as first-borns and (2) generally establish very good relations with peers. Since only children are first-borns, they are subjected to the same relatively intense achievement training that other first-borns receive, perhaps explaining their tendency to be obedient, well-behaved, and instrumentally competent. Moreover, these singletons have no younger sibs that they can bully and, like later-borns, may soon learn that they must negotiate and be accommodating if they hope to play successfully with *peer* playmates, most of whom are probably at least as powerful as they are. So, important as siblings may be to children who have them, it is quite possible for a child to develop normally and even flourish without brothers and sisters. Indeed, the generally positive social outcomes that only children display suggest that many singletons are able to gain through their peer alliances whatever they may miss by not having siblings at home.[1]

The Impact of Divorce

Earlier in the chapter, we saw that nearly 50% of contemporary American marriages will end in divorce and that about 40–50% of American children born in the 1980s will spend some time in a single-parent household—usually one headed by the mother. Only recently have investigators begun to conduct longitudinal studies to determine how children cope with a divorce and whether this dissolution of the nuclear family is likely to have any long-term effects on their social, emotional, and intellectual development. Let's see what they have learned.

The Immediate Effects

Psychologically, a divorce is not a singular life event; instead, it is best described as a series of stressful experiences for the entire family that begins with marital conflict before the legal separation and includes many, many changes in roles, routines, and responsibilities

---

[1] The many ways that peers contribute to a child's development are a central focus of Chapter 16.

afterward (Hetherington & Camara, 1984). In her review of the literature, Mavis Hetherington (1981) finds that the dissolution of the nuclear family is a very painful experience for most children. At first, youngsters are likely to feel angry, fearful, depressed, or guilty about a divorce, and these initial reactions often strike hardest at young, egocentric preschoolers, who are likely to perceive themselves as somehow responsible for the breakup of their parents' marriages. Although adolescents may experience considerable pain and anger when their parents divorce, they are better able to infer why the divorce has occurred, to resolve any loyalty conflicts that may arise, and to understand and cope with the financial and other practical problems that the family now faces. Yet, it may be as long as a year after the divorce before children of any age recover from the initial shock and begin to feel more positively about themselves and their new living arrangements (Hetherington, 1981).

The Crisis Phase

Hetherington (1981) proposes that most children go through two phases when adjusting to a divorce: the **crisis phase,** which often lasts a year or more, and the **adjustment phase,** in which they settle down and begin to adapt to life in a single-parent home.

The emotional upheaval that accompanies the crisis phase is likely to affect the relationship that children have with their custodial parent. Hetherington and her associates (Hetherington, Cox, & Cox, 1982) find that the parenting practices of divorced mothers frequently deteriorate in the first year after the divorce, typically becoming much more coercive. Divorced mothers are apt to feel overburdened with the tasks of providing for their families and fulfilling all the responsibilities of homemaking and child rearing—almost as if they were shouldering the burden of two adults (indeed, they often are) with little or no time for themselves. Consequently, they are likely to become edgy, impatient, less sensitive to their children's needs, and more forceful and punitive in their approach to child rearing. And the children, who may already be emotionally devastated by dissolution of their family, will frequently react to their mother's coercive parenting by becoming cranky, disobedient, and downright disrespectful. The low point in mother/child relations often comes about a year after the divorce. One divorced mother described her family's ordeal as "struggle for survival," while another characterized her experiences with her children as like "getting bitten to death by

ducks" (Hetherington et al., 1982, p. 258). Not surprisingly, the stresses resulting from a divorce and this new **coercive lifestyle** will often disrupt a child's relations with peers and undermine the quality of his or her work at school (Hetherington et al., 1982; Kinard & Reinherz, 1986).

The issue of sex differences

Although the finding is by no means universal (see Kurdek, Blisk, & Siesky, 1981), it seems that the effects of marital disharmony and divorce are generally more powerful and enduring for boys than for girls. Even before the divorce occurs, boys are already showing more behavioral disruptions than girls (Block, Block, & Gjerde, 1986). And at least two longitudinal studies found that girls had largely recovered from their social and emotional disturbances two years after a divorce, whereas boys, who improved dramatically over this same period, were nevertheless continuing to show signs of emotional stress and problems in their relationships with parents, siblings, teachers, and peers (Hetherington et al., 1982; Wallerstein & Kelly, 1980b).

Why might marital turmoil and dissolution strike harder at boys? The most popular explanation is that boys tend to feel closer to fathers than girls do (recall that fathers often spend more time with sons than with daughters), so that they experience more frustration and a deeper sense of loss when the father is no longer readily available to them (Lamb, 1981). Indeed, the finding that boys seem to fare better after a divorce if they live with their fathers (see Box 15-3) is consistent with this point of view.

On staying together for the good of the children

The conventional wisdom used to be that unhappily married couples should remain together for the

---

crisis phase: the period during and immediately after a divorce (often lasting a year or more), when many children suffer emotional distress and disruptions in their schoolwork and interpersonal relations.

adjustment phase: the period following the crisis phase, when the emotional conflicts surrounding a divorce begin to subside and children are adapting to life in a single-parent home.

coercive relationship: a pattern of interaction in which the two parties often annoy each other and use assertive or aggressive tactics as a method of coping with these unpleasant experiences.

good of the children. Yet, Jack Block and his associates (1986) have found that children of divorce begin to show the behavioral disturbances that we associate with family dissolution *well before* (often years before) their unhappily married parents actually separate. Moreover, longitudinal research suggests that after the first year, children in single-parent homes are usually better adjusted than those who remain in conflict-ridden nuclear families (Hetherington et al., 1982; Wallerstein & Kelly, 1980b). Hetherington (1981) believes that an eventual escape from conflict may be the most positive outcome of divorce for many children. Judith Wallerstein and Joan Kelly (1980a) definitely agree, adding that "today's conventional wisdom holds . . . that an unhappy couple might well *divorce* for the good of the children; that an unhappy marriage for the adults is also unhappy for the children; and that a divorce that promotes the happiness of the adults will benefit the children as well" (p. 67).

Coping with a divorce: The role of the noncustodial parent

Though no longer present in the home, divorced fathers often continue to play an important role in their children's development. In fact, Hetherington (1981) believes that the quality of the child's eventual adjustment to a divorce depends to a large extent on how much support the family receives from the noncustodial parent.

Photo 15-5. Youngsters who live in conflict-ridden nuclear families often suffer physically and emotionally. In the long run, children of divorce are usually better adjusted than those whose unhappily married parents stay together "for the sake of the children."

Let's first consider the *financial* support. After a divorce, mother-headed families must often get by on a fraction of the income they had when the father was present. This often necessitates a move to more modest housing in a poorer neighborhood and, thus, may take the family away from important sources of social support such as friends and neighbors. And if the mother begins to work at the time of the divorce or soon thereafter, she may have much less time to devote to her children than ever before. Of course, this apparent withdrawal of attention and affection often comes during a period of intense emotional strife, when children are in greatest need of parental support. Moreover, the lack of monetary resources for trips, toys, treats, and other amenities to which children may be accustomed can be a significant contributor to family quarrels and bickering. So it should hardly come as a surprise that children who adjust well to a divorce often live in homes where the family finances and level of economic support are not seriously undermined by marital separation (Desimone-Luis, O'Mahoney, & Hunt, 1979; Menaghan & Lieberman, 1986).

The amount of *emotional* support that the noncustodial parent provides is perhaps the most important contributor to the child's eventual adjustment. If parents continue to squabble after a divorce and are generally hostile toward each other, the quality of the mother's parenting is apt to suffer. This is the circumstance under which children of divorce are most likely to show serious disruptions in their academic performance and interpersonal relationships, particularly if a disruptive father visits his children on a regular basis. By contrast, children from divorced families may experience few if any long-term problems in adjusting when their parents maintain reasonably warm and friendly relations. Mothers who have cordial ex-husbands tend to be more involved with their children and more sensitive to their needs, particularly when the parents agree on child-rearing strategies and disciplinary issues (Hetherington et al., 1982). Regular visits from *supportive* fathers also help children (particularly sons) to make a positive adjustment to their new life in a single-parent home (Hess & Camara, 1979; Rosen, 1979). In summarizing this research, Hetherington (1981, p. 50) suggests that "a continued, mutually supportive relationship including involvement of the father with the child is the most effective support system for divorced mothers in their parenting role."

How do children react to a divorce when the father is the custodial parent? In recent years, investi-

Box 15-3
The Father as a Custodial Parent

Although the overwhelming majority of children from broken homes live with their mothers, about 10% of custody hearings now award children to the father, and joint custody is becoming more and more common (National Center for Health Statistics, 1980). How do fathers fare as custodial parents? Are they able to cope with the emotional distress that their children may be experiencing? Do they establish good relations with their children? Are children in father-custody homes any different from those living in mother-headed families?

Fathers who have custody of their children report many of the same problems as divorced mothers do: they feel overburdened with responsibilities, are somewhat depressed, and are concerned about their competence as parents and their ability to cope with their children's emotional needs (Hethering-

ton, 1981). As a group, custodial fathers are more likely than custodial mothers to make use of alternative caregiving and support systems such as babysitters, relatives, day-care facilities, or even the noncustodial parent (Santrock & Warshak, 1979). Single-parent fathers typically demand more assistance with household tasks and more independence from their children than custodial mothers do. But most fathers in single-parent households perceive their relationships with their children to be reasonably sound (Hetherington (1981), and they are more likely than custodial mothers to report that their children are well-behaved (Ambert, 1982).

As for the children, it appears that both boys and girls react differently to the parenting they receive when the father is the custodial parent. For boys, the differences are positive ones. John Santrock and Richard Warshak (1979) report that boys are much less coercive and demanding with custodial fathers than in mother-headed families. Moreover, boys in father-custody homes are more inde-

pendent than girls, while just the reverse is true when the mother is the custodial parent. If there is a weakness in the father-custody arrangement, it is centered on the father/daughter relationship. Custodial fathers are often quite concerned about their ability to cope with the problems and emotional needs of their daughters and the fact that their daughters have no feminine role model in the home (Mendes, 1976; Santrock & Warshak, 1979). And they have reason to be concerned, for at least two studies have found that (1) girls in families where the father has custody are less well adjusted than girls who live with their divorced mothers, whereas (2) boys in father-custody homes are better adjusted than those who live with their mothers (Peterson & Zill, 1986; Santrock & Warshak, 1979). As Hetherington (1981, p. 50) points out, "These findings need to be replicated and will have important implications for custody assignments if they are confirmed."

gators have tried to answer this question by comparing the behavior of children growing up in father-headed and mother-headed single-parent homes. In Box 15-3 we will look at this research and see that fathers may be more competent as single parents than many people (and the legal system) have generally assumed.

Long-Term Reactions to Divorce

Several years ago, Lawrence Kurdek and his associates (1981) asked 8- to 17-year-olds how they felt about their parents' divorce at four years and again at six years after the marriage was dissolved. They found that many children still had negative feelings about the divorce, even though the youngsters now understood that they had not been personally responsible for the breakup. Children generally described their parents in positive or neutral terms (thus harboring few grudges), and most of them felt that the divorce had not adversely affected their peer relationships. In fact, those who had shown positive changes in their feelings about the divorce during the interval between the fourth and sixth years often reported that having friends whose parents were also divorced had helped them to cope with their

earlier feelings of bitterness and resentment. Finally, Kurdek et al. found that the older children in their sample had made the most positive adjustments to divorce, particularly those youngsters who tested high in interpersonal understanding (that is, role-taking skills) and who had an internal locus of control. Judith Wallerstein's (1984) study of adolescents ten years after their parents' divorces tended to corroborate several of Kurdek's findings. However, Wallerstein reported that many of her subjects were still burdened by painful memories and were more likely than adolescents from intact families to fear that their own marriages would be unhappy.

In sum, divorce tends to be a very unsettling life event—one that few children feel very positive about, even after ten years have elapsed. But despite their sentiments, it seems that a conflict-ridden nuclear family is often more detrimental to the child's development than the absence of a divorced parent. Indeed, the children of divorce may actually benefit in the long run if the dissolution of a bad marriage leads to an overall reduction in stress that enables either or both parents to be more sensitive and responsive to their needs (Hetherington, 1981; Wallerstein & Kelly, 1980b).

Delinquency among Children from Single-Parent Homes

Although the vast majority of children who are raised by their mothers adapt to single parenting and turn out to be reasonably well adjusted, at least one study of a representative sample of adolescents from all over the United States found that delinquent behavior is much more common among *both* male and female teenagers from single-parent homes (Dornbusch et al., 1985; see also Steinberg, 1987). Data from this national sample also suggested a possible explanation for this outcome: compared with parents in intact families, single parents exerted less influence over teenagers' choices of friends, their activities, and the hours they kept. This is an important finding, for we learned in Chapter 14 that lack of parental monitoring of an adolescent's activities is an important contributor to deviant and antisocial conduct. The survey by Dornbusch et al. produced yet another interesting outcome: the presence of another adult (for example, a grandparent) in a mother-headed household was associated with greater parental control over the adolescent's activities and low levels of delinquent behavior. Clearly, these findings suggest "that there are functional equivalents of two-parent families—non-traditional groupings that can do the job of parenting—and that the raising of *adolescents* is not a task that can easily be borne by a mother alone" (Dornbusch et al., 1985, p. 340).

Children in Reconstituted Families

Within three to five years of a divorce, about 75% of all children from broken homes will experience yet another major change in their lives: a return to the nuclear family when the custodial parent remarries and they suddenly acquire a stepparent—and perhaps new siblings as well (Glick, 1984). Apparently children from divorced families want to live in two-parent homes, even if it means having their mothers marry someone other than their fathers (Santrock et al., 1982). But are children happy with their new living arrangements once the custodial parent remarries? Do they prosper in these reconstituted families; or, rather, are they more likely to experience problems with their stepparent that could affect their cognitive, social, and emotional development?

Most studies of reconstituted families have compared the progress of children from *stepfather* homes to that of age mates in single-parent or intact families. The bulk of this research suggests that boys may make a slightly better adjustment to life with a stepfather than girls do. Compared with boys in single-parent homes, boys with stepfathers are less likely to show personality disorders or deficiencies in cognitive development (Chapman, 1977; Santrock, 1972).[2] Moreover, boys in stepfather families feel closer to their surrogate father, are less anxious and/or angered about this living arrangement, and seem to enjoy higher self-esteem than girls do (Clingempeel, Ievoli, & Brand, 1984; Santrock et al., 1982).

Much less is known about children's reactions to *stepmothers* because stepmother families are relatively uncommon (recall that biological fathers receive custody of their children in only 10% of all custody hearings). However, the data that are available suggest that the transition from a father-headed single-parent home to a two-parent stepmother family is also more difficult for girls than for boys, particularly if the biological mother maintains frequent contact with her daughter (Clingempeel & Segal, 1986; Furstenberg & Seltzer, 1983). Yet, the emotional disruption that daughters may initially experience in stepmother families is often short-lived, for "over time, the relative childrearing roles of biological mother and stepmother [are] effectively negotiated, and girls may [actually] benefit from a support system augmented by a second mother figure" (Clingempeel & Segal, 1986, p. 482).

Apparently these sex differences in children's responses to remarriage are not due solely to the behavior of stepparents, for these substitute caregivers are no less attentive and authoritative with their stepdaughters than with stepsons. Part of stepdaughters' anxiety in *stepfather* homes may result from the behavior of their biological mothers, who are somewhat less attentive and authoritative than mothers in intact homes (Santrock et al., 1982). And what kind of parenting do *stepfathers* provide? The parenting behavior of stepfathers in Santrock's sample was at least as competent (by middle-class standards) as that given by biological fathers to their daughters and somewhat more competent than that given by biological fathers to their sons (Santrock et al., 1982). Finally, the often transitory problems in *stepmother*/stepdaughter relations stem not from an indifferent treatment of daughters by stepmothers but, rather, from the stepmothers' intrusive and somewhat premature attempts to establish good motherly relations with these girls, who are often closely attached to

---

[2]Girls show little distinct improvement in cognitive functioning upon moving from a single-parent to a stepfather home. However, they function better than boys do in single-parent homes and have less room for improvement.

their biological mothers and may now be experiencing rather intense loyalty conflicts (Clingempeel & Segal, 1986).

On the basis of very limited evidence, then, it appears that boys in stepparent families may actually fare rather well, whereas girls are probably no worse and possibly better off (in the long run) than they would be in a single-parent home. Finally, there is little or no support for the notion that most stepparents are cool, aloof disciplinarians who are unconcerned about their stepchildren. On the contrary, the stepparents who have been studied to date seem to be competent parents who are involved with their stepchildren and sensitive to their needs.

A final note: Although the overwhelming majority of children in reconstituted families successfully adapt to this arrangement and become well-adjusted young men and women, there is some evidence that the incidence of deviant or delinquent behavior is higher among adolescents in stepparent homes than among age mates living with both biological parents (see Dornbusch et al., 1985; Garbarino, Sebes, & Schellenbach, 1984; Steinberg, 1987). How might we explain this finding? One possibility is that adolescents, who are becoming increasingly independent, simply view rules imposed by a stepparent as more intrusive or unwarranted than those coming from a natural parent. Indeed, the adolescent may even feel bitter and resentful toward a biological parent (and more inclined to deviate) if this lifelong advocate lends support to any unpleasant restrictions imposed by "that outsider" in their home. Clearly, the issue of deviant conduct among adolescents from reconstituted families is a topic that begs for additional research. Yet, it is important to emphasize that most adolescents who are raised by stepparents are perfectly normal teenagers who are unlikely to display any psychopathological tendencies.

Maternal Employment—Revisited

We have previously seen that a majority of mothers now work outside the home and that this arrangement need not disrupt the emotional development of their children. Infants and toddlers are likely to become securely attached to their working mothers if they have quality day care and receive responsive caregiving when their mothers return home from work. Moreover, children of working mothers (particularly daughters) tend to be more independent and to hold higher educational and occupational aspirations and less stereotyped views of men and women than children whose mothers are not employed (Hoffman, 1984). Finally, studies of toddlers (Schachter, 1981), grade school children (Gold & Andres, 1978b), and adolescents (Gold & Andres, 1978a) consistently indicate that children whose mothers work are as confident in social settings as children whose mothers remain at home and are somewhat more sociable with peers.

Does maternal employment have any effect on a child's cognitive development? The answer to this question is by no means clear at present. Although some

Photo 15-6. Maternal employment is an integral part of today's family life and, for economic reasons, a necessary one for many families.

studies report no differences in either cognitive or scholastic performance between children of homemakers and those whose mothers work, other recent research seems to suggest that maternal employment is associated with lower academic achievement for boys, but not for girls (Bronfenbrenner, 1986; Hoffman, 1984). But perhaps most sobering of all is a report published by the U.S. Department of Education (Ginsburg, cited in "Study: Children with Working Mothers," 1983) indicating that both male and female high school students from two-parent families in which the mother works score significantly lower on tests of academic achievement than their classmates whose mothers have never worked. This latter study is particularly important because it is based on a large national sample, and the findings seem to hold in every region of the country for families from all racial and socioeconomic backgrounds.

Clearly, these are provocative results that we should interpret cautiously until they are replicated in other large, national samples. But even if these findings are confirmed in future research, it may make little sense to advise working mothers that they should abandon their careers in order to stay home with their children. Economic realities have forced many mothers to work, and in one survey the vast majority of working women (76%) stated that they would continue to work even if they did not have to (Dubnoff, Veroff, & Kulka, 1978). One implication of the latter finding is that many women might resent a life of full-time mothering if they were pressured to assume that role, and it is possible that they would vent their frustrations on their children. Indeed, Francine Stuckey and her associates (Stuckey, McGhee, & Bell, 1982) found that the amount of complaining and criticism among mothers, fathers, and their preschool children was significantly greater in families with *unemployed mothers who wanted to work* than in families where the mothers either were unemployed and preferred it that way or were employed and happy about it. Moreover, later research has consistently indicated that when mothers are satisfied with their working (or nonworking) statuses, they express predominantly favorable impressions of their children and have pleasant interactions with them (Alvarez, 1985; Lerner & Galambos, 1985). But if mothers are dissatisfied with their roles (either as homemakers or as working parents), they are apt to be aloof, impatient, and intolerant with their children, which, in turn, makes the children more cranky and temperamentally difficult (Lerner & Galambos, 1985). So it seems that family interactions are most likely to be amiable and conducive to the child's development when the mother's employment status matches her attitudes about working.

In sum, maternal employment is an integral part of modern family life—a role that often satisfies a mother's personal needs as well as providing for the economic welfare of the family. Although most children are not adversely affected by a mother's working outside the home, additional research is needed to discover exactly how, why, and under what circumstances maternal employment is likely to have any detrimental effects. Once these parameters are known, it should then be possible to help working mothers to adjust their caregiving routines or obtain outside support (day care, tutoring, and the like) so that they can promote their children's cognitive and academic competencies while continuing in the careers that they must or desperately hope to pursue.

When Parenting Breaks Down: The Problem of Child Abuse

In recent years, researchers and child-care professionals have coined terms such as *the mistreated child* or **battered-child syndrome** to describe those youngsters who are burned, bruised, beaten, starved, suffocated, neglected, sexually abused, or otherwise mistreated by their caregivers. Child abuse is a very serious problem in the United States—one that has always existed but has been widely acknowledged as "serious" only since the 1960s (Hudson, 1986).Between 1968 and 1972, the number of *reported* cases of seriously battered children rose from 721 to 30,000 in the state of Michigan and from 4000 to nearly 40,000 in California (Kempe & Kempe, 1978). Since many cases of child abuse are neither detected nor reported, these statistics may represent the tip of the iceberg. Raymond Starr (1979) estimates that every year, in the United States, as many as 1.4–1.9 *million* children are subjected to forms of violence or neglect that could cause them serious physical or emotional harm.

Clearly, there are many factors that contribute to a problem as widespread as child abuse. To date, researchers have attempted to understand the battered-child syndrome by seeking answers for three basic questions: (1) Who gets abused? (2) Who are the abusers? (3) Under what circumstances is abuse most likely to occur?

Who Is Abused?

Although just about any child could become a target of neglect or abuse, some youngsters are more vulnerable than others. For example, children who react to discipline by defying or ignoring an adult are likely to elicit stronger and stronger forms of punishment from the disciplinarian—until the line between spanking and physical abuse has been crossed. According to Ross Parke and Nancy Lewis (1981), adults who rely on physically coercive methods to deal with defiance are at serious risk of becoming child abusers.

Children of all ages can contribute to their own abuse—even tiny infants! Babies who are emotionally unresponsive, hyperactive, irritable, or ill face far greater risks of being abused than quiet, healthy, and responsive infants who are easy to care for (Egeland & Sroufe, 1981; Sherrod, O'Connor, Vietze, & Altemeier, 1984). Indeed, *premature* babies, who are often active, irritable, and unresponsive, represent nearly 25% of the population of battered infants—even though only 8% of infants are born prematurely (Klein & Stern, 1971). Of course, this does not mean that 25% of all premature infants are abused but, rather, that the premature baby is more likely than a full-term infant to display certain characteristics that may trigger abusive responses from *some* caregivers. The emphasis on "some" caregivers is important, for the vast majority of difficult children are not mistreated by their parents or guardians, while other seemingly normal and happy children do become targets of abuse. Thus, the implication is that certain people may be "primed" to become abusive when their children irritate or anger them.

Who Are the Abusers?

Strange as it may seem, only about 1 child abuser in 10 has a serious mental illness that is difficult to treat (Kempe & Kempe, 1978). The fact is that people who abuse their children come from all races, ethnic groups, and social classes, and many of them appear to be rather typical, loving parents—except for their tendency to become extremely irritated with their children and to do things they will later regret.

However, overt appearances can be very deceiving. Ann Frodi and Michael Lamb (1980) presented videotapes of smiling and crying infants to groups of abusive and nonabusive mothers who were matched for age, marital status, and the number of children they had had. While the subjects watched the tapes, their physiological responses were monitored. Afterward, each subject described the emotional reactions that she had experienced while observing the infants. Frodi and Lamb reported that their nonabusive parents showed increases in physiological arousal to the infant's cries but not to his or her smiles: cries were described as unpleasant, while smiles generally made the nonabusers feel happy. By contrast, the abusive parents had much stronger physiological reactions to both cries and smiles, and they felt less happy and less willing to interact with a smiling infant than nonabusers. Frodi and Lamb suggest that child abusers may find all of an infant's social signals aversive. Thus, even a smile might trigger a hostile response from an abusive caregiver.

Some child abusers may react very negatively to their infants because they themselves were abused, neglected, or unloved as children and may never have learned how to give and receive affection (Belsky, 1980; Steele & Pollack, 1974). Byron Egeland (1979; Egeland, Sroufe, & Erickson, 1983) found that abusive mothers in his sample, many of whom had been neglected or abused by their own parents, were likely to misinterpret their babies' behavior. For example, when the infant cried to communicate needs such as hunger, nonabusive mothers treated these vocalizations as a sign of discomfort (correct interpretation), whereas abusive mothers often inferred that the baby was criticizing or rejecting them! Although such an interpretation may be understandable given the abusive mothers' own histories of being rejected or abused during childhood, perhaps you can see how their misreading of an infant's emotional signals might contribute to further distress and irritability on the part of the baby, whose "nasty temperament" may then elicit abusive responses.

Harry Harlow and his associates have observed a similar phenomenon among rhesus monkeys: female monkeys who were either abused as infants or raised without caregivers later became indifferent or abusive toward their own offspring (Harlow, Harlow, Dodsworth, & Arling, 1966; Suomi, 1978). Not only did they push their babies away, refusing to let them nurse, but some of the reluctant caregivers even killed their infants by biting off their fingers and toes. Apparently these abusive mother monkeys who had never received

---

battered children: the victims of child abuse—that is, children who are beaten, bruised, neglected, or otherwise mistreated by their caregivers.

love from a caregiver simply did not know how to attend to an infant or how to respond to its signals. They treated infants as if they were irritants.

Indeed, this tendency to misinterpret emotional signals and to respond inappropriately to others' distress can already be observed in abused infants and toddlers. In a recent study of day-care children, Mary Main and Carol George (1985) observed the reactions of abused and nonabused 1- to 3-year-olds to the fussing and crying of classmates. As shown in Figure 15-3, nonabused toddlers typically reacted to a peer's distress by attending carefully to the other child and/or by displaying concern. By contrast, not one abused toddler showed any concern in response to the distress of an age mate. Instead, the abused toddlers were likely to emit disturbing patterns of behavior, often becoming angry at this fussing and then *physically attacking* the crying child. So it seems that abused children are apt to be abusive companions who have apparently learned from their own experiences that distress signals are particularly irritating to others and will typically elicit angry responses rather than displays of sympathy and compassion.

Fortunately, many human beings who were abused or neglected during childhood learn how to respond appropriately to other people long before they have children of their own. In fact, recent research indicates that individuals who were rejected, mistreated, or otherwise emotionally deprived as children are likely to become angry, punitive, or abusive parents *only* if they are currently experiencing other kinds of social or environmental stresses (Conger, Burgess, & Barrett, 1979; Crockenberg, 1987). Let's now consider some of the social and situational factors that can contribute to child abuse.

Social-Situational Triggers: The Ecology of Child Abuse

Child abuse is most likely to occur in families under stress. Consider, for example, that battered children often come from a large family in which overburdened caregivers have many small children to attend to (Light, 1973). The probability of abuse under these stressful circumstances is further compounded if the mother is relatively young, is poorly educated, and receives little child-rearing assistance from the father, a friend or relative, or some other member of her social network (Crockenberg, 1987; Egeland et al., 1983). Other significant life changes such as the death of a family member, the loss of a job, or moving to a new home can disrupt social and emotional relationships within a family and thereby contribute to neglectful or abusive parenting (Bronfenbrenner, 1986; Conger et al., 1979; Steinberg, Catalano, & Dooley, 1981). Finally, children are much more likely to be abused or neglected if their parents are unhappily married (Belsky, 1980; Kempe & Kempe, 1978).

Of course, families are embedded in a broader social context (for example, a neighborhood, a community, and a culture) that may well affect a child's chances of being abused. Some areas can be labeled **"high risk" neighborhoods** because they have much higher rates of child abuse than other neighborhoods of the same demographic and socioeconomic backgrounds. What are these high-risk areas like? According to James Garbarino and Deborah Sherman (1980), they tend to be deteriorating neighborhoods in which families "go it alone" without interacting much with their neighbors or making use of community services such as Scouting or recreation centers. Unlike mothers in low-risk areas, those in high-risk areas take very little pride in their neighborhoods and see them as poor places to raise children. Garbarino and Sherman (1980) describe the high-risk neighborhood as a physically unattractive and socially impoverished setting in which parents not only are struggling financially but also are isolated from formal and informal support systems (for example, friends, relatives, the church, and a sense of "community"). Although the quality of a neighborhood will depend, in

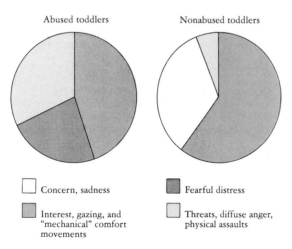

Figure 15-3. Responses to the distress of peers observed in abused and nonabused toddlers in the day-care setting. (The circles show the mean proportion of responses falling in each category for the nine abused and nine nonabused toddlers.) *(Adapted from Main & George, 1985.)*

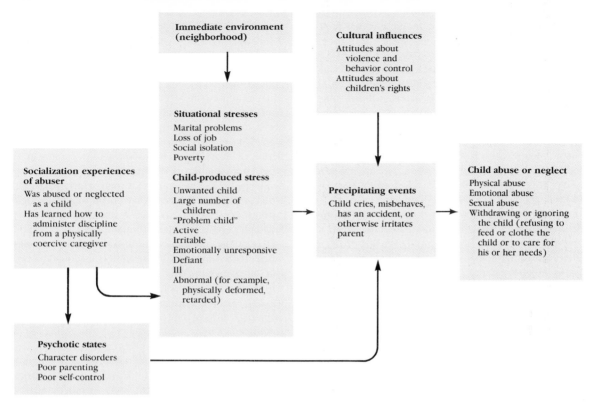

Figure 15-4. A social-ecological model of child abuse. *(Adapted from Gelles, 1973.)*

part, on the people who live there, let's also note that the actions of government and industry can have an effect. For example, a decision to rezone a low-risk area or to locate a highway there can lead to a destruction of play areas, declining property values, a loss of pride in the neighborhood, and the eventual isolation of families from friends, community services (which may no longer exist), and other bases of social support. James Garbarino (1982) is one of many theorists who believe that large numbers of American children are likely to be mistreated because of political or economic decisions that have undermined the health and stability of low-risk family-oriented neighborhoods.

Some researchers have argued that child abuse is rampant in the United States because people in this society (1) have a permissive attitude about violence and (2) generally sanction the use of physical punishment as a means of controlling children's behavior. Indeed, there may be some truth to these assertions, for cross-cultural studies reveal that children are rarely abused in societies that discourage the use of physical punishment (see Belsky, 1980).

In sum, child abuse is a very complex phenomenon that has many causes and contributing factors. Figure 15-4 indicates that we have come a long way from those early theories that focused almost exclusively on the abusive parent (and his or her personality) as the primary contributor to the battered-child syndrome. But despite our better understanding of the causes of child abuse, we are still a long way from solving the problem. Rather than conclude on that depressing note, let's look at some of the methods that have been used to assist the abused child and his or her abusers.

"high risk" neighborhood: a residential area in which the incidence of child abuse is much higher than in other neighborhoods with the same demographic and socioeconomic characteristics.

How Can We Help Abusive Parents and Their Children?

A number of strategies have been devised in an attempt to prevent or control the problem of child abuse. For example, Kempe and Kempe (1978) report that a large percentage of abusive parents will stop physically mistreating their children if they can be persuaded to use certain services, such as 24-hour "hotlines" or crisis nurseries, that will enable them to discuss their hostile feelings with a volunteer or to get away from their children for a few hours when they are about to lose control. However, these are only stopgap measures that will probably not work for long unless the abuser also takes advantage of other services—such as **Parents Anonymous** or family therapy—that are designed to help the caregiver to understand his or her problem while providing the friendship and emotional support that an abusive parent so often lacks.[3]

Babies who are at risk for alienating their caregivers can be identified through neonatal assessment programs, and their parents can be taught how to make these infants respond more favorably to their caregiving. Indeed, we have already seen that Brazelton testing and training programs (see Box 5-2) are effective methods of preventing the "miscommunications" between infants and caregivers that could lead to child abuse. The Kempes (1978) also note that potential child abusers can often be identified in the delivery room by their reluctance to look at, touch, hold, or cuddle their infants. However, many of these reluctant caregivers will never abuse their child if they are visited regularly by a child-care professional who provides them with emotional support and encouragement and teaches them how to manage stress by relaxation techniques, by learning how to request help, and by building stronger social support networks (Kempe & Kempe, 1978; Schinke, Schilling, Barth, Gilchrist, & Maxwell, 1986).

Although its potential is largely untapped, television could become an effective ally in our efforts to prevent child abuse (Parke & Lewis, 1981). Thirty-second public service announcements might be an excellent method of publicizing formal support systems (for example, Parents Anonymous or crisis nurseries) that are locally available to abusive parents. Programming could be developed to teach parents effective, nonpunitive child-care techniques that would minimize social conflicts within the family and decrease the probability of child abuse (see McCall, Gregory, & Murray, 1984). Finally, television could be used to modify our attitudes about the rights of parents and their children. In the United States, the courts and welfare agencies are often hesitant to take children from their abusive parents, even when there is a history of repeated physical abuse (Rosenheim, 1973). One reason for their reluctant attitude is that, historically, children have been treated as their parents' possessions. Another is that abused children and their parents are often firmly attached to each other, so that neither the abusive adult nor the battered child wishes to be separated. However, it is essential that we carefully weigh the child's rights against the rights and wishes of parents, for some abusive adults will continue to seriously harm and occasionally even kill their children, regardless of the counseling they receive (Kempe & Kempe, 1978).

Although some people may disagree, most developmentalists have taken the position that no caregiver has the right to abuse a child. And in cases of severe abuse or neglect, developmentalists generally agree that our first priority must be to provide for the health and safety of mistreated children, even if that means terminating the abusers' legal rights of parenthood and placing their children in foster care or adoptive homes. The challenge that we now face is to become much more successful at preventing or controlling child abuse so that the difficult decision whether to separate children from their parents will need to be made less frequently than it is at present.

Summary

The family is the primary agent of socialization—the setting in which children begin to acquire the beliefs, attitudes, and values of their society. The most common arrangement in Western societies is the *nuclear family*, a social system that consists of three basic roles—wife/mother, husband/father, and child/sibling—although adaptive alternatives, such as the *extended family*, are quite common in many cultures and subcultures. Parents in all societies pursue three goals in raising their children: (1) ensuring the child's surviv-

---

[3]Fortunately these services are often free. Chapters of Parents Anonymous are now located in many cities and towns in the United States (for the location of a nearby chapter, one can consult a telephone directory or write to Parents Anonymous, 6733 South Sepulveda Blvd., Suite 270, Los Angeles, Calif. 90045). In addition, many cities and counties provide free family therapy to abusive parents. Often the therapists are lay volunteers who have been trained to serve in this capacity and who do so quite effectively.

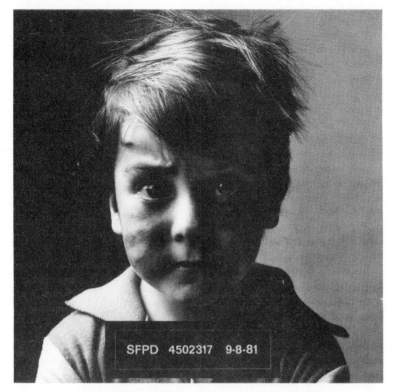

4 out of 5 convicts were abused children.

In the United States, an average of 80% of our prisoners were abused children. That is why we are working so hard to help these children today, before they develop into a threat to others tomorrow.

With your support, we can have a full staff of trained people available 24 hours a day. Abused children desperately need us. Please let us be there to help. Write for our free brochure, or send in your tax-deductible donation today.

San Francisco Child Abuse Council, Inc.
4093 24th Street, San Francisco, CA 94114

Photo 15-7. A number of programs and services have been created in an attempt to prevent or control the problem of child abuse.

al, (2) preparing the child for economic self-sufficiency, and (3) training the child to maximize other cultural values such as morality, religion, intellectual achievement, and personal satisfaction.

Traditionally, researchers have assumed that the flow of influence within a family was from parents, who did the shaping, to children, whose characters were molded by the child-rearing strategies of their elders. Today we recognize that families are complex social systems: parents influence each other and each of their children, who, in turn, may influence one another, each parent, and the parents' marital relationship. Families also live within a broader social context (for example,

---

Parents Anonymous: an organization of reformed child abusers (modeled after Alcoholics Anonymous) that functions as a support group and helps parents to understand and overcome their abusive tendencies.

a particular neighborhood, community, and society) that may affect family interactions and ultimately the development of the children within a family. To understand the influence of the family on developing children, one must treat the family as a social system rather than focusing exclusively on the ways parents may influence the child.

The birth of a child is a highly significant event that alters the behavior of both parents and may change the character of their marital relationship. The transition to parenthood tends to be less severe or disruptive when parents are older and have been married for some time before the child is conceived. Warm, responsive parenting during infancy contributes to the establishment of secure parent/child attachments and promotes the child's exploratory competence and intellectual growth. Although fathers interact less with their very young infants than mothers do, they soon become more involved with their children and begin to play a very special role in the child's life. The quality of the marital relationship is very important. Unhappily married couples often establish shaky emotional relations with their children, whereas parents who are happily married provide the mutual support and encouragement that usually enables them to establish good relations with their infants, even those who require special care or are temperamentally difficult.

Two important aspects of parenting are warmth/hostility and permissiveness/restrictiveness (parental control). These two parental dimensions are independent, so that we find parents who are warm and restrictive, warm and permissive, cool (rejecting) and restrictive, and cool and permissive. Generally speaking, warm and restrictive (that is, authoritative) parents who appeal to reason in order to enforce their demands are likely to raise cheerful, friendly children who are intellectually curious, self-confident, and well-behaved.

Parents from different social classes have different values, concerns, and outlooks on life that influence their child-rearing strategies. Lower- and working-class parents stress obedience, respect, neatness, cleanliness, and staying out of trouble—precisely the characteristics that their children will need to adapt to a position in the blue-collar economy. By contrast, middle-class parents are less restrictive and authoritarian and more likely than low-SES parents to stress independence, creativity, ambition, and self-control—the attributes that their children will need for success in business or the professions. Thus, parents from all socioeconomic strata tend to emphasize the character-

istics that contribute to success *as they know it*, and it is inappropriate to conclude that one particular style of parenting is somehow "better" or more competent than all others.

Interactions between siblings are generally more negative than those between children and their parents. But even though sibling rivalries are a normal aspect of family life, there is a positive side to having a sibling. Older sibs serve as attachment objects who may comfort their distressed brothers and sisters and provide a "secure base" for exploration. Moreover, the teacher/learner roles that siblings often assume at play are beneficial to all parties: older siblings learn by tutoring their younger brothers and sisters, while the younger tutees appear to profit from the instruction they receive. Although ordinal-position effects are not large, first-born children, who receive more attention and achievement training from their parents, tend to be more obedient, anxious, and achievement-oriented than later-borns. However, later-borns, who must acquire important social skills in order to negotiate with older, more powerful sibs, tend to establish better relations with peers than first-borns do.

Divorce represents a drastic change in family life that is stressful and unsettling for children and their parents. Children's initial reactions often include anger, fear, depression, and guilt—feelings that may last more than a year. The emotional upheaval that follows a divorce may influence the parent/child relationship. Children often become cranky, disobedient, or otherwise difficult, while the custodial parent may suddenly become more punitive and controlling. The stresses resulting from a divorce and this new coercive lifestyle often affect the child's peer relations and schoolwork. But after the first year, children of divorce are usually better adjusted than those who remain in conflict-ridden nuclear homes. Moreover, children of divorced parents may experience few if any long-term problems in adjustment when the parents are cordial and can agree on child-rearing strategies and when the noncustodial parent continues to provide adequate financial assistance.

Maternal employment does not seem to disrupt children's social and emotional development; in fact, children of working mothers are often found to be more independent and more sociable and to have less stereotyped views of men and women than children whose mothers are not employed. Although the data are scanty at this point, there is some evidence that children of working mothers score lower on tests of academic achievement than their classmates whose mothers have never worked. If this finding proves to be reliable, we will need to learn why maternal employment affects academic achievement so that working mothers can take the steps necessary to prevent these problems while continuing in the careers that they must (or very much hope to) pursue.

Child abuse is currently a very serious problem. Just about any child could become a target of abuse, although defiant children and those who are active, irritable, emotionally unresponsive, or ill are more vulnerable than happy, healthy children who are easy to care for. Child abusers come from all social strata, but many of them were themselves victims of abuse as children. Child abuse is more likely in families under social, financial, or environmental stress. Programs designed to assist abused children and their abusive parents have achieved some success. However, we are still a long way from solving the problem.

References

ABRAMOVITCH, R., Corter, C., & Pepler, D. J. (1980). Observations of mixed-sex sibling dyads. *Child Development, 51.* 1268–1271.

ABRAMOVITCH, R., Corter, C., Pepler, D. J., & Stanhope, L. (1986). Sibling and peer interaction: A final follow-up and a comparison. *Child Development, 57,* 217–229.

AINSWORTH, M. D. S. (1979). Attachment as related to mother-infant interaction. In J. S. Rosenblatt, R. A. Hinde, C. Beer, & M. Busnel (Eds.), *Advances in the study of behavior* (Vol. 9). Orlando, FL: Academic Press.

ALVAREZ, W. F. (1985). The meaning of maternal employment for mothers and their perceptions of three-year-old children. *Child Development, 56,* 350–360.

AMBERT, A. (1982). Differences in children's behavior toward custodial mothers and custodial fathers. *Journal of Marriage and the Family, 44,* 73–86.

ANDERSON, K. E., Lytton, H., & Romney, D. M. (1986). Mothers' interactions with normal and conduct-disordered boys: Who affects whom? *Developmental Psychology, 22,* 604–609.

BALDWIN, W., & Cain, V. (1980). The children of teenage parents. *Family Planning Perspectives, 12,* 34–43.

BARNETT, R. C., & Baruch, G. K. (1987). Determinants of father's participation in family work. *Journal of Marriage and the Family, 49,* 29–40.

BARRY, H., Child, I. L., & Bacon, M. K. (1959). The relation of child training to subsistence economy. *American Anthropologist, 61,* 51–63.

BASKETT, L. M. (1984). Ordinal position differences in children's family interactions. *Developmental Psychology, 20,* 1026–1031.

BASKETT, L. M. (1985). Sibling status effects: Adult expectations. *Developmental Psychology, 21,* 441–445.

BASKETT, L. M., & Johnson, S. M. (1982). The young child's interaction with parents versus siblings: A behavioral analysis. *Child Development, 53,* 643–650.

BAUMRIND, D. (1967). Child care practices anteceding three patterns of preschool behavior. *Genetic Psychology Monographs, 75,* 43–88.

BAUMRIND, D. (1971). Current patterns of parental authority. *Developmental Psychology Monographs, 4*(1, Pt. 2).

BAUMRIND, D. (1977, March). *Socialization determinants of personal agency.* Paper presented at the biennial meeting of the Society for Research in Child Development, New Orleans.

BECKER, W. C. (1964). Consequences of different kinds of parental discipline. In M. L. Hoffman & L. W. Hoffman (Eds.), *Review of child development research* (Vol. 1). New York: Russell Sage Foundation.

BELL, R. Q., & Chapman, M. (1986). Child effects in studies using experimental or brief longitudinal approaches to socialization. *Developmental Psychology, 22,* 595–603.

BELSKY, J. (1980). Child maltreatment: An ecological integration. *American Psychologist, 35,* 320–335.

BELSKY, J. (1981). Early human experience: A family perspective. *Developmental Psychology, 17,* 3–23.

BELSKY, J., Garduque, L., & Hrncir, E. (1984). Assessing performance, competence, and executive capacity in infant play: Relations to home environment and security of attachment. *Developmental Psychology, 20,* 406–417.

BELSKY, J., Gilstrap, B., & Rovine, M. (1984). The Pennsylvania infant and family development project: I. Stability and change in mother-infant and father-infant interaction in a family setting at one, three, and nine months. *Child Development, 55,* 692–705.

BELSKY, J., & Isabella, R. A. (1985). Marital and parent-child relationships in family of origin and marital change following the birth of a baby: A retrospective analysis. *Child Development, 56,* 342–349.

BELSKY, J., Lang, M. E., & Rovine, M. (1985). Stability and change in marriage across the transition to parenthood: A second study. *Journal of Marriage and the Family, 47,* 855–865.

BERNDT, T. J., & Bulleit, T. N. (1985). Effects of sibling relationships on preschoolers' behavior at home and at school. *Developmental Psychology, 21,* 761–767.

BERRY, J. W. (1967). Independence and conformity in subsistence-level societies. *Journal of Personality and Social Psychology, 7,* 415–418.

BLOCK, J. H., Block, J., & Gjerde, P. F. (1986). The personality of children prior to divorce: A prospective study. *Child Development, 57,* 827–840.

BRADLEY, R. H., Caldwell, B. M., & Elardo, R. (1979). Home environment and cognitive development in the first 2 years: A cross-lagged panel analysis. *Developmental Psychology, 15,* 246–250.

BRAZELTON, T. B. (1979). Behavioral competence of the newborn infant. *Seminars in Perinatology, 3,* 35–44.

BRODY, G. H., & Shaffer, D. R. (1982). Contributions of parents and peers to children's moral socialization. *Developmental Review, 2,* 31–75.

BRODY, G. H., Stoneman, Z., & MacKinnon, C. E. (1982). Role asymmetries in interactions among school-aged children, their younger siblings, and their friends. *Child Development, 53,* 1364–1370.

BRODY, G. H., Stoneman, Z., & Wheatley, P. (1984). Peer interaction in the presence and absence of observers. *Child Development, 55,* 1425–1428.

BRONFENBRENNER, U. (1986). Ecology of the family as a context for human development: Research perspectives. *Developmental Psychology, 22,* 723–742.

BUHRMESTER, D., & Furman, W. (1987). The development of companionship and intimacy. *Child Development, 58*, 1101–1113.

CAIN, L., Kelly, D., & Shannon, D. (1980). Parents' perceptions of the psychological and social impact of home monitoring. *Pediatrics, 66*, 37–40.

CASSIDY, J. (1986). The ability to negotiate the environment: An aspect of infant competence as related to quality of attachment. *Child Development, 57*, 331–337.

CHAPMAN, M. (1977). Father absence, stepfathers, and the cognitive performance of college students. *Child Development, 48*, 1155–1158.

CICIRELLI, V. G. (1982). Sibling influence throughout the lifespan. In M. E. Lamb & B. Sutton-Smith (Eds.), *Sibling relationships: Their nature and significance across the lifespan*. Hillsdale, NJ: Erlbaum.

CLARKE-STEWART, K. A. (1982). *Daycare*. Cambridge, MA: Harvard University Press.

CLINGEMPEEL, W. G., Ievoli, R., & Brand, E. (1984). Structural complexity and the quality of stepparent-stepchild relationships. *Family Processes, 23*, 547–560.

CLINGEMPEEL, W. G., & Segal, S. (1986). Stepparent-stepchild relationships and the psychological adjustment of children in stepmother and stepfather families. *Child Development, 57*, 474–484.

CONGER, R. D., Burgess, R., & Barrett, C. (1979). Child abuse related to life change and perceptions of illness: Some preliminary findings. *Family Coordinator, 28*, 73–78.

CONGER, R. D., McCarty, J. A., Yang, R. K., Lahey, B. B., & Kropp, J. (1984). Perception of child, child-rearing values, and emotional distress as mediating links between environmental stressors and observed maternal behavior. *Child Development, 55*, 2234–2247.

COOPERSMITH, S. (1967). *The antecedents of self-esteem*. New York: W. H. Freeman.

COVERMAN, S., & Sheley, J. F. (1986). Change in men's housework and childcare time, 1965–1975. *Journal of Marriage and the Family, 48*, 413–422.

COWAN, C. P., & Cowan, P. A. (1987). A preventive intervention for couples becoming parents. In C. F. Z. Boukydis (Ed.), *Research on support for parents and infants in the postnatal period*. New York: Ablex.

CRNIC, K. A., Greenberg, M. T., Ragozin, A. S., Robinson, N. M., & Basham, R. B. (1983). Effects of stress and social support on mothers and premature and full-term infants. *Child Development, 54*, 209–217.

CROCKENBERG, S. (1987). Predictors and correlates of anger toward and punitive control of toddlers by adolescent mothers. *Child Development, 58*, 964–975.

CROOK, T., Raskin, A., & Eliot, J. (1981). Parent-child relationships and adult depression. *Child Development, 52*, 950–957.

DESIMONE-LUIS, J., O'Mahoney, K., & Hunt, D. (1979). Children of separation and divorce: Factors influencing adjustment. *Journal of Divorce, 3*, 37–42.

DORNBUSCH, S. M., Carlsmith, J. M., Bushwall, S. J., Ritter, P. L., Leiderman, P. H., Hastorf, A. H., & Gross, R. T. (1985). Single parents, extended households, and the control of adolescents. *Child Development, 56*, 326–341.

DORNBUSCH, S. M., Ritter, P. L., Leiderman, P. H., Roberts, D. F., & Fraleigh, M. J. (1987). The relation of parenting style to adolescent school performance. *Child Development, 58*, 1244–1257.

DUBNOFF, S. J., Veroff, J., & Kulka, R. A. (1978, August). *Adjustment to work: 1957–1976*. Paper presented at the meeting of the American Psychological Association, Toronto.

DUNN, J. (1984). Sibling studies and the developmental impact of critical incidents. In P. B. Baltes & O. G. Brim, Jr. (Eds.), *Lifespan development and behavior* (Vol. 6). Orlando, FL: Academic Press.

DUNN, J., & Kendrick, C. (1981). Social behavior of young siblings in the family context: Differences between same-sex and different-sex dyads. *Child Development, 52*, 1265–1273.

DUNN, J., & Kendrick, C. (1982). *Siblings: Love, envy, and understanding*. Cambridge, MA: Harvard University Press.

DUNN, J., & Munn, P. (1985). Becoming a family member: Family conflict and the development of social understanding in the second year. *Child Development, 56*, 480–492.

EASTERBROOKS, M. A., & Goldberg, W. A. (1984). Toddler development in the family: Impact of father involvement and parenting characteristics. *Child Development, 55*, 740–752.

EGELAND, B. (1979). Preliminary results of a prospective study of the antecedents of child abuse. *International Journal of Child Abuse and Neglect, 3*, 269–278.

EGELAND, B., & Sroufe, L. A. (1981). Attachment and early maltreatment. *Child Development, 52*, 44–52.

EGELAND, B., Sroufe, L. A., & Erickson, M. (1983). The developmental consequences of different patterns of maltreatment. *International Journal of Child Abuse and Neglect, 7*, 459–469.

ERIKSON, E. H. (1963). *Childhood and society* (2nd ed.) New York: Norton.

ESTRADA, P., Arsenio, W. F., Hess, R. D., & Hol-loway, S. D. (1987). Affective quality of the mother-child relationship: Longitudinal consequences for children's school-relevant cognitive functioning. *Developmental Psychology, 23*, 210–215.

FALBO, T., & Polit, D. F. (1986). Quantitative review of the only child literature: Research evidence and theory development. *Psychological Bulletin, 100*, 176–189.

FELDMAN, R. S., Devin-Sheehan, L., & Allen, V. L. (1976). Children tutoring children: A critical review of research. In V. L. Allen (Ed.), *Children as teachers: Theory and research on tutoring*. Orlando, FL: Academic Press.

FELDMAN, S. S., & Aschenbrenner, B. (1983). Impact of parenthood on various aspects of masculinity and femininity: A short-term longitudinal study. *Developmental Psychology, 19*, 278–289.

FRODI, A. M., & Lamb, M. E. (1980). Child abusers' responses to infant smiles and cries. *Child Development, 51*, 238–241.

FURMAN, W., & Buhrmester, D. (1985a). Children's perceptions of the personal relationships in their social networks. *Developmental Psychology, 21*, 1016–1024.

FURMAN, W., & Buhrmester, D. (1985b). Children's perceptions of the qualities of sibling relationships. *Child Development, 56*, 448–461.

FURSTENBERG, F. F., & Seltzer, J. A. (1983, April). *Divorce and child development*. Paper presented at the meeting of the Orthopsychiatric Association, Boston.

GARBARINO, J. (1982). The human ecology of school crime. In B. Emrich (Ed.), *Theoretical perspectives on school crime*. Davis, CA: National Council on Crime and Delinquency.

GARBARINO, J., Sebes, J., & Schellenbach, C. (1984). Families at risk for destructive parent-child relations in adolescence. *Child Development, 55*, 174–183.

GARBARINO, J., & Sherman, D. (1980). High-risk neighborhoods and high-risk families: The human ecology of child maltreatment. *Child Development, 51*, 188–198.

GARCIA COLL, C. T., Hoffman, J., & Oh, W. (1987). The social ecology and early parenting of Caucasian adolescent mothers. *Child Development, 58*, 955–963.

GATH, A. (1978). *Down's syndrome and the family: The early years*. Orlando, FL: Academic Press.

GELLES, R. J. (1973). Child abuse as psychopathology: A sociological critique and reformulation. *American Journal of Orthopsychiatry, 43*, 611–621.

GJERDE, P. F. (1986). The interpersonal structure of family interaction settings: Parent-adolescent relations in dyads and triads. *Developmental Psychology, 22*, 297–304.

GLASS, D. C., Neulinger, J., & Brim, O. G. (1974). Birth order, verbal intelligence, and educational aspiration. *Child Development, 45*, 807–811.

GLICK, P. C. (1984). Marriage, divorce, and living arrangements: Prospective changes. *Journal of Family Issues, 5*, 7–26.

GOLD, D., & Andres, D. (1978a). Developmental comparisons between adolescent children with employed and nonemployed mothers. *Merrill-Palmer Quarterly, 24*, 243–254.

GOLD, D., & Andres, D. (1978b). Developmental comparisons between 10-year-old children with employed and non-employed mothers. *Child Development, 49*, 75–84.

GOLDBERG, S., Perrotta, M., Minde, K., & Corter, C. (1986). Maternal behavior and attachment in low-birth-weight twins and singletons. *Child Development, 57*, 34–46.

GOLDBERG, W. A., & Easterbrooks, M. A. (1984). Role of marital quality in toddler development. *Developmental Psychology, 20*, 504–514.

GROSSMAN, F. K., Eichler, L. S., Winickoff, S. A., & Associates. (1980). *Pregnancy, birth, and parenthood: Adaptations of mothers, fathers, and infants*. San Francisco: Jossey-Bass.

HARLOW, H. F., Harlow, M. K., Dodsworth, R. O., & Arling, G. L. (1966). Maternal behavior of rhesus monkeys deprived of mothering and peer associations as infants. *Proceedings of the American Philosophical Society, 110*, 88–98.

HENDERSON, R. W. (1981). Home environment and intellectual performance. In R. W. Henderson (Ed.), *Parent-child interaction: Theory, research, and prospects*. Orlando, FL: Academic Press.

HESS, R. D., (1970). Social class and ethnic influences upon socialization. In P. H. Mussen (Ed.), *Carmichael's manual of child psychology* (Vol. 2). New York: Wiley.

HESS, R. D., & Camara, K. A. (1979). Post divorce family relationships as mediating factors in the consequences of divorce for children. *Journal of Social Issues, 35*, 79–96.

HETHERINGTON, E. M. (1981). Children and divorce. In R. W. Henderson (Ed.), *Parent-child interaction: Theory, research, and prospects*. Orlando, FL: Academic Press.

HETHERINGTON, E. M., & Camara, K. A. (1984). Families in transition: The processes of dissolution and reconstitution. In R. D. Parke (Ed.), *Review of child development research*. Vol. 7: *The family*. Chicago: University of Chicago Press.

HETHERINGTON, E. M., Cox, M., & Cox, R. (1982). Effects of divorce on parents and children. In M. E. Lamb (Ed.), *Nontraditional families*. Hillsdale, NJ: Erlbaum.

HILTON, I. (1967). Differences in the behavior of mothers toward first and later born children. *Journal of Personality and Social Psychology, 7*, 282–290.

HOFFMAN, L. W. (1984). Work, family, and the socialization of the child. In R. D. Parke (Ed.), *Review of child development research*. Vol 7: *The family*. Chicago: University of Chicago Press.

HUDSON, M. F. (1986). Elder mistreatment: Current research. In K. A. Pillemer & R. S. Wolf (Eds.), *Elder abuse: Conflict in the family*. Dover, MA: Auburn House.

HWANG, C. P. (1986). Behavior of Swedish primary and secondary caretaking fathers in relation to mother's presence. *Developmental Psychology, 22*, 749–751.

JACOBS, B. S., & Moss, H. A. (1976). Birth order and sex of sibling as determinants of mother-infant interaction. *Child Development, 47*, 315–322.

KELLAGHAN, T., & MacNamara, J. (1972). Family correlates of verbal reasoning ability. *Developmental Psychology, 7*, 49–53.

KEMPE, R. S., & Kempe, C. H. (1978). *Child abuse*. Cambridge, MA: Harvard University Press.

KESSNER, D. M. (1973). *Infant death: An analysis by maternal risk and health care*. Washington, DC: National Academy of Sciences.

KINARD, E. M., & Reinherz, H. (1986). Effects of marital disruption on children's school aptitude and achievement. *Journal of Marriage and the Family, 48*, 285–293.

KLEIN, M., & Stern, L. (1971). Low birth weight and the battered child syndrome. *American Journal of Diseases of Childhood, 122*, 15–18.

KLINEBERG, S. L. (1984). Social change, world views, and cohort succession: The United States in the 1980s. In K. A. McCluskey & H. W. Reese (Eds.), *Life-span developmental psychology: Historical and generational effects*. Orlando, FL: Academic Press.

KOHN, M. L. (1979). The effects of social class on parental values and practices. In D. Reiss & H. A. Hoffman (Eds.), *The American family: Dying or developing?* New York: Plenum.

KURDEK, L. A., Blisk, D., & Siesky, A. E., Jr. (1981). Correlates of children's long-term adjustment to their parents' divorce. *Developmental Psychology, 17*, 565–579.

LAHEY, B. B., Hammer, D., Crumrine, P. L., & Forehand, R. L. (1980). Birth order × sex interactions in child behavior problems. *Developmental Psychology, 16*, 608–615.

LAMB, M. E. (1981). *The role of the father in child development*. New York: Wiley.

LAMB, M. E., & Elster, A. B. (1985). Adolescent mother-infant-father relationships. *Developmental Psychology, 21*, 768–773.

LAOSA, L. M. (1981). Maternal behavior: Sociocultural diversity in modes of family interaction. In R. W. Henderson (Ed.), *Parent-child interaction: Theory, research, and prospects*. Orlando, FL: Academic Press.

LASKO, J. K. (1954). Parent behavior towards first and second children. *Genetic Psychology Monographs, 49*, 96–137.

LEFKOWITZ, M. M., & Tesiny, E. P. (1984). Rejection and depression: Prospective and contemporaneous analyses. *Developmental Psychology, 20*, 776–785.

LERNER, J. V., & Galambos, N. L. (1985). Maternal role satisfaction, mother-child interaction, and child temperament: A process model. *Developmental Psychology, 21*, 1157–1164.

LeVINE, R. A. (1974). Parental goals: A cross-cultural view. *Teachers College Record, 76*, 226–239.

LEVITT, M. J., Weber, R. A., & Clark, M. C. (1986). Social network relationships as sources of maternal support and well-being. *Developmental Psychology, 22*, 310–316.

LIDDELL, C., Henzi, S. P., & Drew, M. (1987). Mothers, fathers, and children in an urban park playground: A comparison of dyads and triads. *Developmental Psychology, 23*, 262–266.

LIGHT, R. J. (1973). Abused and neglected children in America: A study of alternative policies. *Harvard Educational Review, 43*, 556–598.

MACCOBY, E. E. (1980). *Social development*. San Diego, CA: Harcourt Brace Jovanovich.

MAIN, M., & George, C. (1985). Responses of abused and disadvantaged toddlers to distress in agemates: A study in the day-care setting. *Developmental Psychology, 21*, 407–412.

MAIN, M., & Weston, D. R. (1981). The quality of the toddler's relationship to mother and to father: Related to conflict and the readiness to establish new relationships. *Child Development, 52*, 932–940.

MATEJCEK, Z., Dytrych, Z., & Schuller, V. (1979). The Prague study of children born from unwanted pregnancies. *International Journal of Mental Health, 7*, 63–74.

McCALL, R. B., Gregory, T. G., & Murray, J. P. (1984). Communicating developmental research results to the general public through television. *Developmental Psychology, 20*, 45–54.

MENAGHAN, E. G., & Lieberman, M. A. (1986). Changes in depression following divorce: A panel study. *Journal of Marriage and the Family, 48,* 319–328.

MENDES, H. A. (1976). Single fathers. *Family Coordinator, 25,* 439–440.

MILLER, N., & Maruyama, G. (1976). Ordinal position and peer popularity. *Journal of Personality and Social Psychology, 33,* 123–131.

MINNETT, A. M., Vandell, D. L., & Santrock, J. W. (1983). The effects of sibling status on sibling interaction: The influence of birth order, age spacing, sex of child and sex of sibling. *Child Development, 54,* 1064–1072.

MUSSEN, P. H., & Rutherford, E. (1963). Parent-child relations and parental personality in relation to young children's sex-role preferences. *Child Development, 34,* 589–607.

NATIONAL CENTER FOR HEALTH STATISTICS. (1980, January). *Provisional statistics* (Monthly Vital Statistics Report). Washington, DC: U.S. Department of Health, Education and Welfare.

NORMAN-JACKSON, J. (1982). Family interactions, language development, and primary reading achievement of Black children in families of low income. *Child Development, 53,* 349–358.

OGBU, J. U. (1981). Origins of human competence: A cultural-ethological perspective. *Child Development, 52,* 413–429.

PALKOWITZ, R. (1984). Parental attitudes and fathers' interactions with their 5-month-old infants. *Developmental Psychology, 20,* 1054–1060.

PARKE, R. D., & Lewis, N. G. (1981). The family in context: A multilevel interactional analysis of child abuse. In R. W. Henderson (Ed.), *Parent-child interaction: Theory, research, and prospects.* Orlando, FL: Academic Press.

PARKE, R. D., & Tinsley, B. R. (1984). Fatherhood: Historical and contemporary perspectives. In K. A. McCluskey & H. W. Reese (Eds.), *Life-span developmental psychology: Historical and generational effects.* Orlando, FL: Academic Press.

PATTERSON, G. R., & Stouthamer-Loeber, M. (1984). The correlation of family management practices and delinquency. *Child Development, 55,* 1299–1307.

PAULHUS, D., & Shaffer, D. R. (1981). Sex differences in the impact of number of older and number of younger siblings on scholastic aptitude. *Social Psychology Quarterly, 44,* 363–368.

PEDERSEN, F., Anderson, B., & Cain, R. (1977, March). *An approach to understanding linkages between parent-infant and spouse*

relationships. Paper presented at the biennial meeting of the Society for Research in Child Development, New Orleans.

PETERSON, J. L., & Zill, N. (1986). Marital disruption, parent-child relationships, and behavior problems in children. *Journal of Marriage and the Family, 48,* 295–307.

PHARES, E. J. (1976). *Locus of control in personality.* Morristown, NJ: General Learning Press.

PULKKINEN, L. (1982). Self-control and continuity from childhood to adolescence. In P. B. Baltes & O. G. Brim, Jr. (Eds.), *Life-span development and behavior* (Vol. 4). Orlando, FL: Academic Press.

RAGOZIN, A. S., Basham, R. B., Crnic, K. A., Greenberg, M. T., & Robinson, N. M. (1982). Effects of maternal age on parenting role. *Developmental Psychology, 18,* 627–634.

REBELSKY, F., & Hanks, C. (1971). Father verbal interaction with infants in the first three months of life. *Child Development, 42,* 63–68.

ROSEN, R. (1979). Some critical issues concerning children of divorce. *Journal of Divorce, 3,* 19–26.

ROSENHEIM, M. K. (1973). The child and the law. In B. M. Caldwell & H. N. Ricciuti (Eds.), *Review of child development research* (Vol. 3). Chicago: University of Chicago Press.

ROTHBART, M. K. (1971). Birth order and mother-child interaction in an achievement situation. *Journal of Personality and Social Psychology, 17,* 113–120.

SAMPSON, E. E., & Hancock, F. T. (1967). An examination of the relationship between ordinal position, personality, and conformity: An extension, replication, and partial verification. *Journal of Personality and Social Psychology, 5,* 398–407.

SAMUELS, H. R. (1977, March). *The sibling in the infant's social environment.* Paper presented at the biennial meeting of the Society for Research in Child Development, New Orleans.

SAMUELS, H. R. (1980). The effect of older sibling on infant locomotor exploration of a new environment. *Child Development, 51,* 607–609.

SANTROCK, J. W. (1972). The relations of type and onset of father absence to cognitive development. *Child Development, 43,* 455–469.

SANTROCK, J. W., & Minnett, A. M. (1981, April). *Sibling interaction: An observational study of sex of sibling, age spacing, and ordinal position.* Paper presented at the biennial meeting of the Society for Research in Child Development, Boston.

SANTROCK, J. W., & Warshak, R. A. (1979). Father custody and social development in

boys and girls. *Journal of Social Issues, 35,* 112–125.

SANTROCK, J. W., Warshak, R. A., Lindbergh, C., & Meadows, L. (1982). Children's and parents' observed social behavior in stepfather families. *Child Development, 53,* 472–480.

SCHACHTER, F. F. (1981). Toddlers with employed mothers. *Child Development, 52,* 958–964.

SCHACHTER, S. (1959). *The psychology of affiliation.* Stanford, CA: Stanford University Press.

SCHACHTER, S. (1963). Birth order, eminence, and higher education. *American Sociological Review, 28,* 757–767.

SCHAEFER, E. S., & Bayley, N. (1963). Maternal behavior, child behavior, and their intercorrelations from infancy through adolescence. *Monographs of the Society for Research in Child Development, 28*(3, Serial No. 87).

SCHINKE, S. P., Schilling, R. F., II, Barth, R. P., Gilchrist, L. D., & Maxwell, J. S. (1986). Stress-management intervention to prevent family violence. *Journal of Family Violence, 1,* 13–26.

SHERROD, K. B., O'Connor, S., Vietze, P. M., & Altemeier, W. A., III. (1984). Child health and maltreatment. *Child Development, 55,* 1174–1183.

SIRIGNANO, S. W., & Lachman, M. E. (1985). Personality change during the transition to parenthood: The role of perceived infant temperament. *Developmental Psychology, 21,* 558–567.

SNOW, M. E., Jacklin, C. N., & Maccoby, E. E. (1983). Sex-of-child differences in father-child interaction at one year of age. *Child Development, 54,* 227–232.

STARR, R. H., Jr. (1979). Child abuse. *American Psychologist, 34,* 872–878.

STEELE, B. F., & Pollack, C. B. (1974). A psychiatric study of parents who abuse infants and small children. In R. E. Helfer & C. H. Kempe (Eds.), *The battered child.* Chicago: University of Chicago Press.

STEINBERG, L. D. (1987). Single parents, stepparents, and the susceptibility of adolescents to antisocial peer pressure. *Child Development, 58,* 269–275.

STEINBERG, L. D., Catalano, R., & Dooley, D. (1981). Economic antecedents of child abuse and neglect. *Child Development, 52,* 975–985.

STEWART, R. B. (1983). Sibling attachment relationships: Child-infant interactions in the strange situation. *Developmental Psychology, 19,* 192–199.

STEWART, R. B., & Marvin, R. S. (1984). Sibling relations: The role of conceptual perspective-taking in the ontogeny of sibling caregiving. *Child Development, 55,* 1322–1332.

STEWART, R. B., Mobley, L. A., Van Tuyl, S. S., & Salvador, M. A. (1987). The firstborn's adjustment to the birth of a sibling: A longitudinal assessment. *Child Development, 58,* 341–355.

STUCKEY, M. F., McGhee, P. E., & Bell, N. J. (1982). Parent-child interaction: The influence of maternal employment. *Developmental Psychology, 18,* 635–644.

STUDY: Children with working mothers score lower on tests. (1983, June 26). *Atlanta Journal,* p. A4.

SUOMI, S. J. (1978). Maternal behavior by socially incompetent monkeys: Neglect and abuse of offspring. *Journal of Pediatric Psychology, 3,* 28–34.

SUTTON-SMITH, B., & Rosenberg, B. G. (1970). *The sibling.* New York: Holt, Rinehart and Winston.

U.S. BUREAU OF THE CENSUS. (1982). *Characteristics of American children and youth: 1980* (Current Population Reports. Series P-23, No. 114). Washington, DC: U.S. Government Printing Office.

U.S. DEPARTMENT OF COMMERCE. (1979). *Marital status and living arrangements: March 1978* (Current Population Reports, Series P-20, No. 338). Washington, DC: U.S. Government Printing Office.

WALLERSTEIN, J. S. (1984). Children of divorce: Preliminary report of a ten-year follow-up of young children. *American Journal of Orthopsychiatry, 54,* 444–458.

WALLERSTEIN, J. S., & Kelly, J. B. (1980a, January). California's children of divorce. *Psychology Today,* pp. 67–76.

WALLERSTEIN, J. S., & Kelly, J. B. (1980b). *Surviving the breakup: How children and parents cope with divorce.* New York: Basic Books.

WARREN, J. R. (1966). Birth order and social behavior. *Psychological Bulletin, 65,* 38–49.

WATERS, E., Wippman, J., & Sroufe, L. A. (1979). Attachment, positive affect, and competence in the peer group: Two studies in construct validation. *Child Development, 50,* 821–829.

WEAVER, K. F. (1985). Stones, bones, and early man: The search for our ancestors. *National Geographic, 168,* 561–623.

WEISNER, T. S., & Gallimore, R. (1977). My brother's keeper: Child and sibling caretaking. *Current Anthropology, 18,* 169–190.

WEISZ, J. R. (1980). Autonomy, control, and other reasons why "Mom is the greatest": A content analysis of children's Mother's Day letters. *Child Development, 51,* 801–807.

WILKIE, C. F., & Ames, E. W. (1986). The relationship of infant crying to parental stress in the transition to parenthood. *Journal of Marriage and the Family, 48,* 545–550.

WILSON, M. N. (1986). The black extended family: An analytical consideration. *Developmental Psychology, 22,* 246–258.

ZAJONC, R. B., Markus, H., & Markus, G. B. (1979). The birth order puzzle. *Journal of Personality and Social Psychology, 37,* 1325–1341.

ZEGOIB, L. E., Arnold, S., & Forehand, R. (1975). An examination of observer effects in parent-child interactions. *Child Development, 46,* 509–512.

ZUSSMAN, J. U. (1978). Relationship of demographic factors to parental disciplinary techniques. *Developmental Psychology, 14,* 685–686.

Beyond the Home Setting: Extrafamilial Influences

In Chapter 15 we focused on the family as an instrument of socialization, looking at the ways parents and siblings affect developing children. Although families have an enormous impact on their young throughout childhood and adolescence, it is only a matter of time before other societal institutions begin to exert their influence. For example, infants and toddlers are often exposed to alternative caregivers and a host of new playmates when their working parents place them in some kind of day care. Even those toddlers who remain at home will soon begin to learn about the outside world once they develop an interest in television. Between the ages of 2 and 5, many American children spend several hours of every weekday away from home as they attend nursery school. And by the age of 6 to 7, virtually all children in Western societies are going to elementary school, a setting that requires them to interact with other little people who are similar to themselves and to adjust to the rules and regulations of a brave new world—one that may be very dissimilar to the home environment from which they came.

So as they mature, children are becoming increasingly familiar with the outside world and will spend much less time under the watchful eyes of their parents. How do these experiences affect their lives? This is the issue to which we will now turn as we consider the impact of three **"extrafamilial"** agents of socialization: television, schools, and children's peer groups.

The Early Window: Effects of Television on Children and Youth[1]

It seems almost incomprehensible that only 40 years ago the average person in the United States could not have answered the question "What is a television?" When introduced in the late 1940s, television was an expensive luxury for the wealthy—one that made the children of well-to-do parents immensely popular with their peers. Today a television occupies a prominent location in virtually all American homes, and 70% of American families have more than one set. Robert Liebert and his associates (Liebert, Sprafkin, & Davidson, 1982) believe that television has changed our daily lives more than any other technological innovation of the 20th century. And they may be correct, for the average TV set in the United States runs for more than six hours a day, and it is not at all uncommon for people to alter their sleeping habits or plan their meals and leisure activities to accommodate television (Steinberg, 1980).

Does television undermine the quality of family life, as some critics have maintained? Are children who watch a lot of television likely to be socially withdrawn and less interested in schoolwork? How do children react to televised violence and to the social stereotyping of women and minorities that often appears in commercial programming? Can television be used to reduce social prejudices and to teach prosocial lessons such as cooperation and sharing? Does educational programming promote cognitive growth? In the pages that follow, we will discuss each of these issues as we consider what is known about the effects of television on children's social and intellectual development.

Children's Use of Television
In the United States, children between the ages of 3 and 11 watch an average of three to four hours of television a day. As we see in Figure 16-1, time spent in front of the television gradually increases until about age 12 and then declines somewhat during adolescence. A recent survey of television use in Australia, Canada, and several European countries reported virtually the same developmental trends in children's viewing habits (Murray, 1980). To place these findings in perspective, we need only note that by age 18 a child born today will

[1]The title of this section is taken from a book of the same name (Liebert, Sprafkin, & Davidson, 1982). I highly recommend this volume to those who are seeking a reasonably comprehensive and readable overview of the effects of television on developing children.

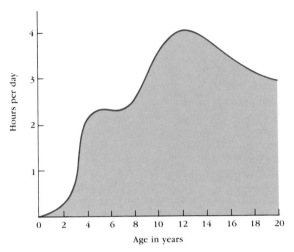

Figure 16-1. Average number of hours per day that American children and adolescents spend watching television. (*From Comstock, 1978.*)

have spent more time watching television than in any other single activity except sleeping (Liebert et al., 1982). Is it any wonder, then, that parents, educators, and those who study children are curious and often concerned about the possible effects of this incredible exposure to the electronic media?

Has television changed children's lifestyles and the character of family life? In some ways it has. One early survey found that a majority of families altered their sleeping patterns and mealtimes once they had purchased a television (Johnson, 1967). The presence of a TV at home also had the effect of decreasing the amount of time that parents spent with their youngsters in non-TV-related leisure activities such as games and family outings, and most parents at least occasionally used television as an "electronic babysitter." Although parents and children may spend many hours in close proximity as they watch TV together, some critics believe that this form of family interaction is not very meaningful for the younger set—particularly if they are told to sit still and keep their mouths shut until the commercials come on. Urie Bronfenbrenner (1970b) has argued:

> The primary danger of . . . television . . . lies not so much in the behavior it produces—although there is danger there—as in the behavior that it prevents: the talks, games, the family festivities and arguments through which much of the child's learning takes

place and through which his character is formed. Turning on the television set can turn off the process that transforms children into people.

Despite these warnings and protestations, there is little evidence that exposure to television deadens young minds or transforms children into social isolates who become less interested in playing games or making friends. Children who live in remote areas without television do spend significantly more time reading comics, going to movies, or listening to the radio than age mates who live in similar communities served by television (Huston & Wright, 1982; Schramm, Lyle, & Parker, 1961). But when television comes to an isolated area, children simply substitute TV viewing for these other roughly equivalent forms of entertainment. Apparently the availability of television does not affect the amount of time most children spend on homework—or leisure reading, for that matter, if we exclude comic books. Moreover, popular children who partake in many sports and extracurricular activities tend to read a lot and to watch a fair amount of TV (Lyle & Hoffman, 1972). So it is clearly inappropriate to argue that television viewing has replaced valuable pastimes such as reading or playing with one's peers.

The effects of television on cognitive growth and academic achievement are rather complex. It seems that the introduction of television into a remote area has little if any effect on children's basic cognitive abilities (Lonner, Thorndike, Forbes, & Ashworth, 1985), although at least one researcher found that the reading comprehension of elementary school students declined soon after television became available in their community (Williams, 1977, cited in Huston & Wright, 1982). And yet a recent study published by the U.S. Department of Education suggests that students in the lower grades may actually learn a great deal of useful information from watching television—particularly educational programming ("Study: Children with Working Mothers," 1983). It may be that the effects of television on academic performance depend largely on what the children are watching. An educational program such as *The Electric Company,* which is designed to teach reading concepts, may well reinforce the elementary school curriculum and have a positive effect on academic achievement, whereas popular programs such as *The Three Stooges*

---

extrafamilial influences: social agencies other than the family that influence a child's cognitive, social, and emotional development.

or *Magnum P.I.* have little educational value and could undermine academic achievement if they keep children from their lessons. Indeed, children and adolescents do perform better in school and score higher on standardized achievement tests when they spend more time on homework and watch less *commercial* television (Keith, Reimers, Fehrmann, Pottsbaum, & Aubey, 1986; "Study: Children with Working Mothers," 1983).

Some Potentially Undesirable Effects of Television

Aside from its potential for distracting children from schoolwork, there are several undesirable lessons that television could teach young viewers. In this section of the chapter, we will consider some possible concomitants of children's TV viewing that may annoy or even anger many adults.

Effects of televised violence

As early as 1954, complaints raised by parents, teachers, and students of human development prompted Senator Estes Kefauver, then chairman of the Senate Subcommittee on Juvenile Delinquency, to question the need for violence in television programming. As it turns out, American television is incredibly violent. Eighty percent of all prime-time television programs contain at least one incident of physical violence, with an average rate of 7.5 violent acts per hour (Gerbner, Gross, Morgan, & Signorielli, 1980). It is estimated that the average child of 16, who has already spent more time watching TV than in school, will have witnessed more than 13,000 killings on television (Liebert & Schwartzberg, 1977). And surprising as it may seem, the most violent programs on commercial television are some of those designed for children—especially Saturday morning cartoon shows, which contain nearly 25 violent incidents per hour (Gerbner et al., 1980).

Does TV violence instigate aggression?

In Chapter 7 we noted that children and adolescents who watch a lot of televised violence at home tend to be more aggressive than their classmates who watch little violence. Indeed, this positive relationship between the amount of violence one observes on TV and aggressive behavior in naturalistic settings has been documented over and over with preschool, grade school, high school, and adult subjects in the United States and with grade school girls and boys in Australia, Finland, Canada, Poland, and Great Britain (Parke & Slaby, 1983). In an early *longitudinal* survey, Leonard Eron and his

associates (Eron, Huesmann, Lefkowitz, & Walder, 1972) found that the best predictor of aggression among adolescent males was the boys' preference for violent TV programming as expressed 10 years earlier, when they were in the third grade. In other words, boys who favored violent programming at age 8 to 9 tended to be highly aggressive at age 19. Subsequent longitudinal studies of different populations indicate that (1) an earlier preference for televised violence predicts later aggression for both girls *and* boys and (2) children who are more aggressive are apt to watch more violence on television (Eron, 1980, 1982). The latter finding is important because it suggests that the link between televised violence and children's aggression is *circular*: viewing TV violence may instigate aggressive behavior, which stimulates interest in violent programming, which promotes further aggression, and so on down the line. Although the longitudinal surveys are correlational research and do *not* demonstrate causality, their results are at least consistent with the argument that early exposure to a heavy diet of televised violence may lead to the development of aggressive habits that persist over time.

One method of determining whether violent films really do instigate aggression is to expose children to either violent or nonviolent programming and then see whether the two experimental groups will differ when given an opportunity to commit aggressive responses. As early as 1972, 18 such experiments had been conducted, and 16 of them (89%) found that children became more aggressive after watching violent sequences on television (Liebert & Baron, 1972).

Several field experiments paint a similar picture. For example, Aletha Stein and Lynette Friedrich (1972) observed 97 preschool children over a three-week period to establish a "baseline" level of aggression for each child. The children were then randomly assigned to three experimental conditions. For a month, those who watched *violent programming* saw one *Batman* or one *Superman* cartoon a day in their nursery school classrooms. Children exposed to **prosocial television** watched daily episodes of *Mister Rogers' Neighborhood*, while those in the third group saw *neutral* (neither aggressive nor prosocial) films of circuses and farm scenes. After the month had passed, the children were observed at play for two additional weeks in order to measure the effects of the programming. Stein and Friedrich found that the children who had watched violent programming were subsequently more aggressive in nursery school than their classmates who had

Photo 16-1. Heavy exposure to media violence may blunt children's emotional reactions to real-life aggression and lead them to believe that the world is a violent place populated mainly by hostile and aggressive people.

watched either prosocial or neutral programming. Although the impact of the violent programming was greatest for children who had been above average in aggressiveness during the initial baseline period, these "initially aggressive" children were by no means extreme or deviant. They simply represented the more aggressive members of a typical nursery school peer group. So watching violent programming does indeed instigate aggression in many young children. Stein and Friedrich remind us that "these effects occurred in [a naturalistic setting] that was removed both in time and place from the viewing experience. They occurred with a small amount of exposure . . . and they endured the postviewing period" (1972, p. 247).

One reason that televised violence may instigate aggression is that children younger than 6 or 7 cannot easily distinguish appearances from reality (Flavell, 1986), and they are likely to believe that much of what they see on television is quite realistic. Thus, a young child who sees Wile E. Coyote spring back to form in good spirits after being disfigured by a blow to the head may assume that similar acts directed to playmates will produce no lasting harm. Moreover, a steady diet of violent programming may eventually convince the child that the outside world is a violent place inhabited by people who typically rely on aggressive strategies when faced with interpersonal conflicts. Indeed, Leonard Eron and his associates (Eron, Huesmann, Brice, Fischer, & Mermelstein, 1983) found that 7- to 9-year-old boys *and girls* who were judged highly aggressive by their peers

not only preferred violent television programs—they also believed that violent shows were an accurate portrayal of everyday life.

Desensitization to aggression. In addition to promoting aggressive behavior, a steady diet of televised violence may increase children's *tolerance* for aggression, even aggression that takes place around them in the real world. Ronald Drabman and Margaret Thomas (1974) tested this **desensitization hypothesis** with 8- to 10-year-olds. Half the children watched a violent Hopalong Cassidy film that contained several gun battles and fist fights. The remaining subjects were assigned to a control condition and did not see a film. Each child was then asked to watch a television monitor to ensure that two kindergarten children who were playing in another room didn't get into any trouble while the experimenter was away at the principal's office. The experimenter took great care to explain to the child that he or she was to come to the principal's office for help should *anything* go wrong. Each child then observed the same videotaped sequence, in which the two kindergartners got into an intense battle. The tape ended with a loud crash that occurred shortly after the camera had been knocked over and the video had gone dead.

The results of this study were straightforward: children who had watched the violent film reacted much more slowly to what they believed to be a real-life altercation than their classmates who had not seen a film. Drabman and Thomas suggested that exposure to media violence may blunt viewers' emotional reactions to later aggressive episodes and perhaps even make them feel that aggressive acts are a part of everyday life that do not necessarily warrant a response.

In a second experiment, Margaret Thomas and her colleagues (Thomas, Horton, Lippincott, & Drabman, 1977) exposed 8- to 10-year-olds to either a *violent* film from the popular police series *S.W.A.T.* or a *nonviolent* but exciting film of a championship volleyball match. The viewers were hooked up to a physiograph that re-

---

prosocial television: television programming that emphasizes socially desirable actions such as cooperation, helping, sharing, or comfort giving that benefit other people.

desensitization hypothesis: the notion that people who watch a lot of media violence will become less aroused by aggression and more tolerant of violent and aggressive acts.

corded their emotional reactions to the films (which were equally arousing). After the film, the experimenter switched channels and asked the child to monitor the activities of two younger children who were playing in an adjacent room. At this point the experimenter departed, leaving the subject hooked up to the physiograph. The child then observed the same videotaped altercation that Drabman and Thomas had used, and his or her emotional reactions to these events were recorded.

Once again, the results were clear: children who had watched the violent programming were less aroused by the *real-life* altercation than classmates who had seen the nonviolent film. Apparently an exposure to media violence does lessen a viewer's emotional sensitivity to later acts of aggression—a finding that may help to explain why children are more likely to *tolerate* aggression after witnessing violent acts on television.

Reducing the harmful effects of TV violence. Perhaps the most obvious method of reducing the potentially negative impact of violent programming is to carefully monitor what children are watching and to try to interest them in programs that contain little or no violence. Anyone who would like a list of programs that the experts consider too violent for young children can obtain one by writing to Action for Children's Television, 46 Austin Street, Boston, MA 02160.

Another step that concerned adults might take is to complain to the networks, to local network affiliates, and to sponsors of violent programs about the highly violent and aggressive programming directed at young children. Indeed, write-in campaigns organized by groups such as Action for Children's Television and the National Association for Better Broadcasting have been successful at persuading some advertisers to avoid sponsoring extremely violent television shows ("Cooling Off the Tube," 1976). And it is likely that these protests would be even more effective at reducing the level of violence on television if more concerned citizens became involved.

In the meantime, parents can help their children to critically evaluate media violence by pointing out subtleties that young viewers often miss—content such as the aggressor's motives, or intentions, and the unpleasant consequences that perpetrators suffer as a result of their aggressive acts (Collins, Sobol, & Westby, 1981). When adults highlight this information while strongly disapproving of a perpetrator's conduct, young children gain a much better understanding of media violence and are less affected by what they have seen—

particularly if the adult commentator also suggests how these perpetrators might have approached their problems in a more constructive way (Eron & Huesmann, 1984; Horton & Santogrossi, 1978).

Television as a source of social stereotypes

Television is often the young child's first exposure to the outside world and the people who live there. Indeed, many children have had little or no contact with police officers, teachers, people from different racial or ethnic groups, or the elderly (to name a few), and their "knowledge" of these groups is likely to consist of what they have seen on television. Unfortunately, these media portrayals are often inaccurate.

In Chapter 13 we noted that sex-role stereotyping is common on television and that children who watch a lot of commercial TV (and thus are often exposed to these stereotyped depictions) are likely to hold more conventional views of men and women than their classmates who watch little television. In fact, the youngsters who are affected most by sex-role stereotypes on television are girls of above-average intelligence from middle-class homes—precisely the group that is otherwise least likely to hold traditionally sexist attitudes (Morgan, 1982).

Stereotyping of minorities. Until the middle to late 1970s, ethnic minorities other than Blacks were practically ignored on television. Blacks tended to be given minor roles, and when foreigners or other non-Black minorities did appear, they were presented in an unfavorable light, often cast in the roles of swindlers or villains (Liebert et al., 1982). Today the representation of minorities on television has increased to approximate their proportions in the population. Yet, compared with Whites, a greater percentage of non-White characters are depicted as very poor people who work at service occupations, are prone to violence, or are involved in illegal activities (Liebert et al., 1982).

A study by Sheryl Graves (1975) suggests that these media stereotypes may affect children's racial attitudes. In Graves's experiment, both Black and White children watched a series of cartoons in which Black people were portrayed either positively (as competent, trustworthy, and hardworking) or negatively (as inept, lazy, and powerless). On a later test of racial attitudes, both Black and White children became more favorable toward Blacks if they had seen the positive portrayals.

But when the depictions of Blacks were negative, an interesting racial difference emerged: Black children once again became more favorable in their racial attitudes, while Whites became much *less* favorable. So the way Blacks are portrayed on television may have a striking effect on the racial attitudes of White viewers, whereas the mere presence of Black TV characters may be sufficient to produce more favorable attitudes toward Blacks among a young Black audience.

Countering stereotypes on television.

In recent years, attempts have been made to design programs for the younger set that counter inaccurate racial, sexual, and ethnic stereotypes while fostering goodwill among children from different social backgrounds. In 1969 *Sesame Street* led the way with positive portrayals of Blacks and Hispanics. And one early study (Gorn, Goldberg, & Kanungo, 1976) found that White preschool children soon became more willing to include non-Whites in their play activities after watching episodes of *Sesame Street* that depicted minority youngsters as cheerful companions. Among the other shows that have been effective at fostering international awareness and reducing children's ethnic stereotypes are *Big Blue Marble*, a program designed to teach children about people in other countries, and *Vegetable Soup*, a show that portrays many ethnic groups in a favorable light (Liebert et al., 1982).

In 1975 the National Institute of Education funded a program named *Freestyle*, designed to counter sex-role stereotypes. *Freestyle* is aimed at 9- to 12-year-olds, and its primary objective is to debunk the myths about females' lack of competence in traditionally masculine pastimes, educational pursuits, and occupations. The early results of this intervention are encouraging. After viewing 13 episodes of the program, grade school children showed the following changes (Johnston, Ettema, & Davidson, 1980):

1. Boys became more tolerant of girls who attempted sporting or mechanical activities, and girls became much more interested in these endeavors.
2. Both boys and girls became more accepting of boys who engage in "feminine" activities such as housework or caring for younger children.
3. Both boys and girls became more accepting of men and women who have nontraditional jobs.
4. Both boys and girls became less traditional and more egalitarian in their views about family roles such as who should cook, clean, or repair the house.

So we see that television can either reinforce or reduce inaccurate and potentially harmful social stereotypes, depending, of course, on the type of programming to which people are exposed. Unfortunately, the stereotyped depictions of gender, race, and ethnicity that often appear on commercial TV are presently far more numerous than the nonstereotyped portrayals, which are largely limited to selected programs that appear on public (educational) television.

Children's reactions to commercial messages

In the United States, the average child is exposed to nearly 20,000 television commercials each year—many of which extol the virtues of toys, fast foods, and sugary treats that adults may not wish to purchase. Nevertheless, young children continue to ask for products that they have seen advertised on television, and conflicts often ensue when parents refuse to honor their requests (Atkin, 1978). In one study, 4- and 5-year-olds saw a program that had either no commercials or two commercials for a particular toy. The children were later shown photographs of a father and son and were told that the father had refused to buy the advertised toy after his son had requested it. More than 60% of the youngsters who had seen the commercials felt that the boy would be resentful and would not want to play with his father, while the comparable figure among the no-commercial group was less than 40% (Goldberg & Gorn, 1977, cited in Liebert et al., 1982).

In addition to making children angry or resentful toward adults who refuse to buy advertised products, commercials may have an indirect effect on a child's peer relations. In the experiment by Goldberg and Gorn described above, children were asked whether they would rather play with the advertised toy or with friends in a sandbox. Those who had seen the commercials for the toy were much more likely to choose the toy over their friends than children who had not seen the commercials. When asked whether they would rather play with a "nice boy" without the toy or a "not-so-nice boy" with the toy, 65% of the commercial viewers chose the "not-so-nice boy" who possessed the advertised item, compared with only 30% of those in the no-commercial group. Is it any wonder, then, that parents are often concerned about the impact of commercials on their children? Not only do children's ads often push products that are unsafe or of poor nutritional value, they may also contribute to coercive family interactions and poor peer relations.

Television as an Educational Instrument

Thus far, we've cast a wary eye at television, talking mostly about its capacity to do harm. Yet, there is now reason to believe that this "early window" could become a most effective way of teaching a number of valuable lessons if only its content were altered to convey such information. Let's now examine some of the evidence to support this claim.

Educational television and children's prosocial behavior

A number of programs broadcast on the Public Broadcasting System (PBS) are designed to supplement the everyday learning experiences of preschool children. For example, *Sesame Street* was created to entertain preschoolers while fostering their intellectual and social development. A typical episode combines fast action and humorous incidents with a carefully designed educational curriculum designed to teach (among other things) letters of the alphabet, numbers, counting, vocabulary, and many social and emotional lessons. Another program, *Mister Rogers' Neighborhood*, is designed to facilitate the child's social and emotional development. To accomplish these objectives, Mister Rogers talks directly to his audience about things that may interest or puzzle children (for example, crises such as the death of a pet); he reassures them about common fears such as riding in airplanes; he encourages viewers to learn from and to cooperate with children of different races and social backgrounds; and he helps children to

Photo 16-2. Children learn many valuable lessons from educational TV programs such as *Sesame Street*.

see themselves in a favorable light by repeatedly emphasizing that "there is only one person in the whole wide world like you, and I like you just the way you are."

Both these programs have a positive influence on the social behavior of young viewers. When preschool children watch either program over a long period, they often become more affectionate, considerate, cooperative, and helpful toward their nursery school classmates (Coates, Pusser, & Goodman, 1976; Friedrich & Stein, 1973, 1975; Paulson, 1974). However, it is important to emphasize that merely parking nursery-schoolers in front of the tube to watch *Sesame Street* or *Mister Rogers* is not an effective training strategy, for this programming has few if any *lasting* benefits unless adults monitor the programs and encourage children to rehearse and enact the prosocial lessons they have learned (Friedrich & Stein, 1975; Friedrich-Cofer, Huston-Stein, Kipnis, Susman, & Clewett, 1979). Furthermore, children who are exposed to prosocial programming may well become more compassionate, helpful, or cooperative without becoming any less aggressive (Friedrich-Cofer et al., 1979). This puzzling finding may simply reflect the fact that children who watch prosocial programming typically become more outgoing and thus will have more opportunities to argue with their peers. Nevertheless, it seems that the positive effects of prosocial programming greatly outweigh the negatives, particularly if adults encourage children to pay close attention to episodes that emphasize constructive methods of resolving interpersonal conflicts.

Promoting good nutrition on television

Most food advertisements on children's television are for high-calorie or high-sodium foods and snacks that contain few beneficial nutrients (Stoneman & Brody, 1981). Since a diet containing too much of these foods has been established as a risk factor in a number of diseases (for example, high blood pressure) and dental problems, researchers have hoped to counter the influence of such advertising by producing pronutritional messages and commercials for nutritious snacks. Do these attempts to promote healthful eating practices affect children's dietary habits?

The evidence is somewhat mixed. Polly Peterson and her colleagues (Peterson, Jeffrey, Bridgwater, & Dawson, 1984) exposed 6-year-olds to pronutritional messages from shows such as *Mulligan Stew* (a PBS series) and *Captain Kangaroo* and found that children (1) *learned* the pronutritional information and (2) showed an increased *verbal preference* for more nutritious foods. But when given a choice between nutritious and nonnutritious snacks, these youngsters were no more likely to select nutritious foods than they had been before viewing the programs. However, Joan Galst (1980) found that 3- to 6-year-olds who had watched pronutritional programming did tend to choose nutritious rather than nonnutritious snacks if they had heard an adult comment on an ad for the nonnutritious foods by stressing these products' poor nutritional value and threats to one's dental health. So there is reason to believe that regular exposure to pronutritional television programming could be effective in teaching pronutritional concepts and perhaps even in altering children's dietary habits. Yet, the success of such programming may depend very critically on having an adult present to help children to interpret the implications of what they have seen and to translate those lessons into action.

Television as a contributor to cognitive development

In 1968 the U.S. government and a number of private foundations contributed the funding to create the **Children's Television Workshop (CTW),** an organization committed to producing TV programs that would hold children's interest and facilitate their intellectual development. CTW's first production, *Sesame Street,* became the world's most popular children's TV series—one that now reaches approximately 85% of the 3–5-year-olds in the United States and is broadcast to nearly 70 other countries around the world (Liebert et al., 1982; Wright & Huston, 1983).

The objectives of *Sesame Street*. As noted earlier, production artists, educators, and experts in child development worked together to design a program for preschool children that would foster important cognitive skills such as recognizing and discriminating numbers and letters, counting, ordering and classifying objects, and solving simple problems. It was hoped that children from disadvantaged backgrounds would be much better prepared for school after viewing this programming on a regular basis. In 1969 *Sesame Street* was unveiled and became an immediate hit. But was it accomplishing its objectives?

The evaluations. During the first season that *Sesame Street* was broadcast, its impact was assessed by the Educational Testing Service. About 950 children from five areas of the United States participated in the study. At the beginning of the project, children took a pretest that measured their cognitive skills and determined what they knew about letters, numbers, and geometric forms. At the end of the season, they took this test again to see what they had learned. Originally the sample had been divided into an experimental group that was encouraged to watch *Sesame Street* and a control group that received no such encouragement. However, the program proved so popular that the control children ended up watching nearly as often as the experimental group. As a result, the sample was divided into quartiles (a quartile equals 25% of the viewers) on the basis of the frequency of viewing. Children in Q_1 rarely watched *Sesame Street*; those in Q_2 watched two or three times a week; Q_3 watched about four or five times a week; and Q_4 watched more than five times a week.

When the data were analyzed, it was clear that *Sesame Street* was achieving its objectives. In Figure 16-2 we see that the children who watched *Sesame Street* the most (Q_3 and Q_4) were the ones who showed the biggest improvements in their total test scores (panel A), their scores on the alphabet test (panel B), and their ability to write their names (panel C). The 3-year-olds posted bigger gains than the 5-year-olds, probably because the younger children knew less to begin with.

During the second year a new sample of urban disadvantaged youngsters was selected from cities where *Sesame Street* had not been available during the first year. The investigators also followed up on 283 of the disadvantaged children from the original sample, many of whom were now in kindergarten or the first grade. The results of the second-year evaluation paralleled those of the original study—children who often watched *Sesame Street* posted larger cognitive gains than those who watched infrequently (Bogatz & Ball, 1972). In addition, the heavy viewers from the original sample were rated by their teachers as better prepared for school and more interested in school activities than their classmates who rarely watched the program.

The Electric Company. In 1970 CTW consulted with reading specialists to create *The Electric Company,* a TV series designed to teach reading skills

---

Children's Television Workshop (CTW): an organization committed to producing TV programs that hold children's interest and facilitate their social and intellectual development.

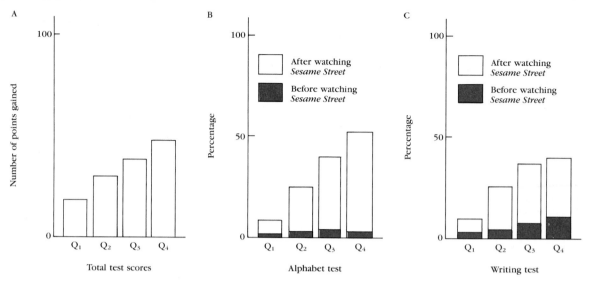

Figure 16-2. Relationship between amount of viewing of *Sesame Street* and children's abilities: A, improvement in total test scores for children grouped into different quartiles according to amount of viewing; B, percentage of children who recited the alphabet correctly, grouped according to quartiles of amount of viewing; C, percentage of children who wrote their first names correctly, grouped according to quartiles of amount of viewing. *(From Ball & Bogatz, 1970, as presented in Liebert, Sprafkin, & Davidson, 1982.)*

to young elementary school children. The programming was heavily animated, and to interest children in the content, well-known personalities such as Bill Cosby often appeared. The curriculum attempted to teach children the correspondence between letters (or letter combinations) and sounds—knowledge that should help them to decode words. Reading for meaning and syntax were also taught (Liebert et al., 1982).

The success of *Electric Company* was evaluated by administering a battery of reading tests to first-through fourth-grade children. Although home viewing had little or no effect on children's reading skills, those who watched *Electric Company* at school attained significantly higher scores on the reading battery than nonviewers (Ball & Bogatz, 1973). In other words, *Electric Company* was achieving many of its objectives when children watched the program with an adult, in this case the teacher, who could help them to apply what they had learned.

Other educational programs. In recent years, CTW and other noncommercial producers have created children's programs designed to teach subjects such as math (*Infinity Factory; Square One*), logical reasoning (*Think About*), science (*3-2-1 Contact*), and so-

cial studies (*Big Blue Marble*), to name a few. Most of these offerings have been quite popular in the areas where they are broadcast, although it remains to be seen how well they are achieving their stated objectives.

Criticisms of educational programming. One recurring criticism of educational television is that it is essentially a one-way medium in which the pupil is a passive recipient of information rather than an active constructor of knowledge. Indeed, we've seen that programs such as *The Electric Company* (as well as pro-nutritional messages and programs stressing prosocial behavior) are unlikely to achieve their objectives unless children watch *with an adult* who then encourages them to *apply* what they have learned. Perhaps John Wright and Aletha Huston (1983) are correct in arguing that television will soon be a much more powerful teaching device as it becomes *computer-integrated* and interactive, thereby allowing the viewer to be more actively involved in the learning process (see Box 16-1 for some early returns on the impact of computers on developing children).

Although *Sesame Street* was primarily targeted at disadvantaged preschoolers in an attempt to narrow the intellectual gap between these youngsters and their

Like television, the computer is a new technology that has the potential to affect children's development. But in what ways? If we take our cues from Hollywood, we might be led to believe that young computer "hackers" will grow up to be brainy but socially inept introverts, like those curiously lovable misfits from the movie *Revenge of the Nerds*. Indeed, many educators believe that the microcomputer is an effective supplement to classroom instruction—a tool that helps children to learn more and to have more fun doing so. And parents, many of whom may be "computer illiterates," are nevertheless rushing out to buy home computers, prompted, in part, by TV ads suggesting that they may be undermining their child's chances of success if they don't. Do computers really help children to learn? Is there a danger that young "hackers" will become so enamored of computer technology and so reclusive or socially unskilled that they risk being ostracized by their peers?

Only recently have researchers begun to explore the impact of computers on children's lives, and the early returns are interesting. For example, James Kulik and his associates (Kulik, Bangert, & Williams, 1983) find that children do learn more and seem to enjoy school more as well when they receive at least some *computer-assisted instruction*. One advantage of computer-assisted drills is that the machine can be programmed to diagnose learning problems (from the kinds of errors children make during the drill), to individualize questions for the student

to help him overcome deficiencies, and to provide instantaneous feedback, without criticism—the computer plays no favorites! This kind of instruction is similar in many respects to what a child might receive from an individual tutor. Other forms of computer-assisted instruction are more elaborate, allowing students to learn new academic material by playing highly motivating and thought-provoking games. After reviewing several recent studies, Kulik and his associates concluded that computer-assisted instruction can be more effective than traditional classroom instruction—particularly for disadvantaged students and other low achievers.

Douglas Clements (1986) believes that teaching students to *program* a computer has advantages beyond those associated with the performance of computer-assisted academic drills. In his own research, Clements gave first- and third-graders 22 weeks of training in Logo, a computer language that allows children to take drawings they've made and translate them into input statements so that they eventually succeed at reproducing their drawings on the computer monitor. Of what benefit is this kind of problem-solving activity? Although Clements's "Logo" children performed no better on achievement tests than age mates who participated in the more usual kinds of computer-assisted academic exercises, Logo users scored higher on tests of Piagetian concrete-operational abilities, metacognition (knowledge about thinking and thought processes), and creativity. These data are intriguing, for they suggest that computers are useful not only for teaching children academic lessons but for helping them to *think* in new ways as well.

Are young computer users likely to become reclusive misfits who are

shunned by their peers? Daniel Kee (1986) says no. Kee's observations led him to conclude that children often use the computer to attract playmates, almost as if it were any other desirable toy. And research in the classroom indicates that children who are learning Logo engage in *more* collaborative activities with classmates than students who are working on traditional assignments (Hawkins, Sheingold, Gearhart, & Berger, 1982). In sum, computers seem to promote, rather than inhibit, social interaction. Yet, it is possible that some children with poor social skills could become even more withdrawn should they find that their nonevaluative computer is more "user friendly" than most peers.

Obviously there is much more that we need to learn about the effects of computers on developing children. For example, there is some concern that economically disadvantaged students, who rarely have access to home computers, may fall even further behind in academic achievement. And since boys are much more likely than girls to take an active interest in computers and to sign up for computer camps, it is possible that the computer revolution may widen the gender gap that already exists in math and science achievement (Lepper, 1985). Judging from what we know about the effects of television, it is a good bet that computers will prove to influence children in many ways—some good, some bad. Outcomes may be less than desirable if a child's primary use of the machine is to hole up by himself in the bedroom, zapping Communist mutants from space. But the news may be rather positive indeed for children who use computers to learn, to think in new ways, and to collaborate with siblings and peers.

---

advantaged peers, it seems that children from advantaged backgrounds are the ones who are more likely to watch the program. As a result, *Sesame Street* may actually end up *widening* the intellectual and academic gaps between advantaged and disadvantaged youth (Cook et al., 1975). Yet, it seems fruitless to blame the program

itself, for disadvantaged youngsters who watch it regularly learn just as much as their more advantaged classmates (Bogatz & Ball, 1972). In other words, *Sesame Street* is *potentially* a valuable resource for all preschool children. The formidable task lies ahead—that being to convince parents that episodes of *Sesame Street* (and other educational programs) are indeed rewarding and valuable experiences, ones that they and their children should not be missing.

Should Television Be Used to Socialize Children?

Although television is often criticized as an instigator of violence or an "idiot box" that undermines the intellectual curiosity of our young, we have seen that the medium can have many positive effects on children's social, emotional, and intellectual development. Should we now work at harnessing television's potential—at using this "early window" as a means of socializing our children? Many developmentalists think so, although not everyone agrees, as we see in the following newspaper account of a conference on behavioral control through the media. To set the stage, the conference participants were reacting to the work of Dr. Robert M. Liebert, a psychologist who had produced some 30-second TV spots to teach children cooperative solutions to conflicts. Here is part of the account that appeared in the *New York Times*:

> The outburst that followed Liebert's presentation flashed around the conference table. Did he believe that he had a right to . . . deliberately impose values on children? Should children . . . be taught cooperation? Did ghetto kids perhaps need to be taught to slug it out in order to survive in this society? Was it not . . . immoral to create a TV advertisement . . . to influence kids' behavior? Liebert was accused of . . . manipulation and even brainwashing. One would have thought he had proposed setting up Hitler Youth Camps on Sesame Street. . . .
>
> However, I understand why the hackles had gone up around the . . . table. I am one of those people who [are] terrified of manipulation. A Skinnerian world filled with conditioned people scares the daylights out of me—even if those people do hate war and . . . love their fellow man. [Behavior control through technology may come] . . . at the cost of our freedom [Rivers, 1974, quoted in Liebert et al., 1982, pp. 210–211].

The concern of those conference participants is perhaps understandable, for television is often used as a means of political indoctrination in many countries. And is the use of television for socialization not a subtle form of brainwashing? Perhaps it is. However, one could argue that television in this country is already serving as a potent agent of socialization and that much of what children see in the media helps to create attitudes and to instigate actions that the majority of us may not con-

done. Perhaps the question we should be asking is "Can we somehow alter television to make it a more effective agent of socialization—one that teaches attitudes, values, and behaviors that more accurately reflect the mores of a free society?" Surely we can, although it remains to be seen whether we will.

The School as a Socialization Agent

Of all the formal institutions that children encounter in their lives away from home, few have as much of an opportunity to influence their behavior as the schools they attend. Starting at age 6, the typical child in the United States spends about five hours of each weekday at school. And children are staying there longer than ever before. In 1870 there were only 200 public high schools in the United States, and only half of all American children were attending during the three to five months that school was in session. Today the school term is about nine months long (180 school days); more than 75% of American youth are still attending high school at age 17; and nearly 50% of U.S. high school graduates enroll in some form of higher education. Yet these figures are somewhat unusual, even in the Western world. For example, only 29% of all Australians and 47% of Belgians complete the final year of high school (Copperman, 1978).

If asked to characterize the mission of the schools, we are likely to think of them as the place where children acquire basic knowledge and academic skills: reading, writing, arithmetic, and, later, computer skills, foreign languages, social studies, higher math, and science. But schools seem to have an **informal curriculum** as well. Children are expected to obey rules, to cooperate with their classmates, to respect authority, to learn about their society's way of life, and to become upstanding citizens. Today, we see the schools providing information and moral guidance in an attempt to combat social problems such as racism, teenage sex, and drug abuse. Although many social critics believe that educators should stick to academics and leave other forms of socialization to the church and the family, it is interesting to note that the push for compulsory education in the United States arose from the need to "Americanize" an immigrant population—to teach them the values and principles on which that country was founded so that they could be assimilated into the mainstream of American society and become productive citizens. Ironically, the need to produce a highly skilled work force was of only secondary importance, for most people earned a living from unskilled labor or farming—occupations that required little or no formal schooling (Rudolph, 1965).

So it is proper to think of the school as a socializing agent—one that is likely to affect children's social and emotional development as well as imparting knowledge and helping to prepare students for a job and economic self-sufficiency.

In this section of the chapter, we will focus on the ways in which schools influence children. First, we will consider whether formal classroom experiences are likely to promote children's intellectual development. Then we will see that schools clearly differ in "effectiveness"—that is, the ability to accomplish both curricular goals and noncurricular objectives that contribute to what educators often call "good citizenship." After reviewing the characteristics of effective and less effective schools, we will examine some of the ways in which teachers influence the social behavior and academic progress of their pupils. Finally, we will discuss a few of the problems that disadvantaged youth may encounter as they enter the middle-class environment of the schools.

Does Schooling Promote Cognitive Development?

If you have completed the first two years of college, you may already know far more biology, chemistry, and physics than many of the brightest college professors of only 100 years ago. Clearly, students acquire a vast amount of knowledge about their world from the schooling they receive. But when developmentalists ask "Do schools promote cognitive growth?," they want to know whether formal education hastens intellectual development or encourages modes of thinking and methods of problem solving that are less likely to develop in the absence of schooling.

To address these issues, investigators have typically studied the intellectual growth of children from developing countries where schooling is not yet available throughout the society. Studies of this type generally find that children who attend school are quicker to reach certain Piagetian milestones (for example, conservation) and will perform better on tests of memory and **metacognitive knowledge** than age mates from similar backgrounds who do not go to school (see Rogoff, 1981; Sharp, Cole, & Lave, 1979). And at least one study of very bright college students found a positive relationship between the amount of higher education

the students had completed and their proficiency at solving problems requiring formal-operational reasoning (Commons, Richards, & Kuhn, 1982). So schooling may indeed promote cognitive growth by teaching children general rules, principles, strategies, and problem-solving skills that they can apply to many different kinds of information. Yet, it is important to note that the differences between educated and uneducated subjects are likely to be small on any cognitive test (for example, recognition memory or nonverbal IQ) that does not depend on the use of strategies acquired at school (Sharp et al., 1979).

Determinants of Effective (and Ineffective) Schooling

One of the first questions that parents often ask when searching for a residence in a new town is "What are the schools like here?" or "Where should we live so that our children will get the best education?" These concerns reflect the common belief that some schools are "better" or "more effective" than others. But are they?

Michael Rutter (1983) is one theorist who thinks so. According to Rutter, **effective schools** are those that promote academic achievement, social skills, polite and attentive behavior, positive attitudes toward learning, low absenteeism, continuation of education beyond the age at which attendance is mandatory, and acquisition of skills that will enable students to find and hold a job. Rutter argues that some schools are more successful than others at accomplishing these objectives, regardless of the students' racial, ethnic, or socioeconomic backgrounds. Let's examine some of the evidence for this claim.

In one study, Rutter and his associates (Rutter, Maughan, Mortimore, Ouston, & Smith, 1979) conducted extensive interviews and observations in 12 secondary schools serving lower- to lower-middle-class pop-

---

informal curriculum: noncurricular objectives of schooling such as teaching children to cooperate, to respect authority, to obey rules, and to become good citizens.

metacognitive knowledge: one's knowledge about cognition and about the regulation of cognitive activities.

effective schools: schools that are generally successful at achieving curricular and noncurricular objectives, regardless of the racial, ethnic, or socioeconomic backgrounds of the student population.

ulations in London, England. As the children entered these schools, they were given a battery of achievement tests to measure their prior academic accomplishments. At the end of the secondary school experience, the pupils took another major exam to assess their academic progress. Other information such as attendance records and teacher ratings of classroom behavior was also available. When the data were analyzed, Rutter et al. found that the 12 schools clearly differed in "effectiveness": students from the "better" schools exhibited fewer problem behaviors, attended school more regularly, and made more academic progress than students from the less effective schools. We get some idea of the importance of these "schooling effects" from Figure 16-3. The "bands" on the graph refer to the pupils' academic accomplishments *at the time they entered* the secondary schools (band 3, low achievers; band 1, high achievers). In all three bands, students attending the "more effective" schools outperformed those in the "less effective" schools on the final assessment of academic achievement. Even more revealing is the finding that the initially poor students (band 3) who attended the "better" schools ended up scoring just as high on this final index of academic progress as the initially good (band 1) students who attended the least effective schools. Similar findings were also obtained in a large study of elementary schools in the United States. Even after controlling for important variables such as the racial composition and socioeconomic backgrounds of the student bodies and the type of communities served, some elementary schools were found to be much more "effective" than others (Brookover, Beady, Flood, Schweitzer, & Wisenbaker, 1979).

So the school that children attend can make a difference. And although the evidence is sketchy at this point, we are beginning to understand why some schools are able to accomplish many of their objectives while others are not. In the pages that follow, we will first consider some of the variables that are thought to contribute to an effective school environment and then try to determine how individual teachers might influence their students.

Some misconceptions about effective schooling

There are several factors that really contribute very little to a school's effectiveness, even though many people have stressed their importance. Let's briefly review some of the common misconceptions about effective schooling.

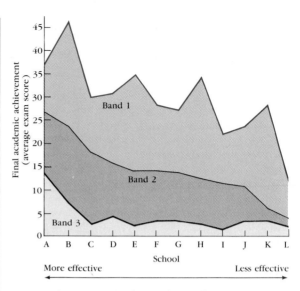

Figure 16-3. Average level of academic achievement in secondary school as a function of initial achievement at the time of entry (bands 1–3) and the school that pupils were attending (schools A–L). Note that pupils in all three bands performed at higher levels on this final academic assessment if they attended the more effective schools. Moreover, students in band 2 performed like band 1 students in the more effective schools but like band 3 students in the least effective schools. *(Adapted from Rutter et al., 1979.)*

Monetary support. Surprising as it may seem, factors such as the amount of money spent per pupil, the number of books in the school library, teachers' salaries, and teachers' academic credentials play only a minor role in determining student outcomes (Rutter, 1983). In two studies of secondary schools in England, the investigators found that neither the age nor the physical appearance of the school buildings predicted children's conduct or their academic accomplishments (Reynolds, Jones, St. Leger, & Murgatroyd, 1980; Rutter et al., 1979). Similar studies in the United States indicate that the level of "personnel support" (that is, teacher credentials and salaries) is positively related to student achievement only in the predominantly Black, inner-city schools where resources in some school districts are marginal at best (Brookover et al., 1979). The latter finding implies that there is some basic minimum level of support that is required for effective schooling. However, Rutter (1983) concludes :

Within the general range of resources usually available to schools, the precise level [of support] seems to be of limited importance with respect to pupil outcomes. We may conclude that an increase in resources is not likely to be an effective means of improving standards. Of course, the way resources are employed may well be important [p. 15].

School and class size. Another variable that contributes minimally, at best, to a school's effectiveness is average class size; in classes ranging from 20 to 40 students, class size has little or no effect on academic achievement. Consequently, it seems that across-the-board decreases in class size—say, from 36 to 24 students—are unlikely to improve student outcomes in any major way (Rutter, 1983). Yet, there are some exceptions to this very general rule. Michael Rutter and others (Educational Research Service, 1978) find that smaller classes are beneficial in the primary grades and for students who have special educational needs, as is often true of handicapped children or those from economically disadvantaged backgrounds. So if a school district were to have the money to hire additional instructors, the wisest course might be to devote these "personnel resources" to remedial instruction, special education, and the primary grades—precisely the settings in which smaller classes seem to promote academic achievement.

There is some evidence that the size of one's school affects student participation in structured extracurricular activities—settings in which aspects of the "informal curriculum" such as cooperation, fair play, and healthy attitudes toward competition are likely to be stressed. Roger Barker and Paul Gump (1964) surveyed the activities of high school students in schools ranging in size from fewer than 100 pupils to more than 2000. Although the larger schools offered more extracurricular activities to their students, it was the pupils in the smaller schools who were more heavily involved. Moreover, students in the smaller schools were more likely than those in larger schools to say that they enjoyed the challenge of working in and actually contributing to their extracurricular groups. Finally, there were few "isolates" in the small schools, where almost everyone was encouraged to join in one or more activities. By contrast, the marginal student in larger schools felt few pressures to participate and could easily get lost in the crowd. To the extent that a sense of belonging and the lessons stemming from extracurricular group activities are important aspects of schooling, these findings suggest that there may be some advantages to attending smaller schools.

Ability tracking. The merits of **ability tracking**—a procedure in which students are grouped by IQ or academic achievement and then taught in classes made up of students of comparable "ability"—have been debated for years. Some theorists believe that students learn more when surrounded by peers of equal ability. Others have argued that ability tracking will undermine the self-esteem of lower-ability students and contribute to their poor academic achievement and high dropout rate.

In his review of the literature, Rutter (1983) found that neither ability tracking nor mixed-ability teaching has decisive advantages: both procedures are common in highly effective and less effective schools. A closer inspection of the data suggested that mixed-ability instruction may be advantageous with younger children and that ability tracking makes more sense in secondary schools, where it is difficult to teach advanced subjects to students who vary considerably in their background knowledge. However, ability tracking is occasionally found to have negative effects on the self-esteem and academic achievement of low-ability students. After reviewing the tracking systems of effective and ineffective schools, Rutter (1983) concluded that *effective* ability tracking—

1. Categorizes students on the basis of their *tested abilities* in *particular subjects* rather than using an across-the-board assignment based on teachers' ratings or IQ scores.
2. Ensures that students in *all* ability groups have some exposure to the more experienced, popular, or "effective" teachers rather than simply assigning the best teachers to the high-ability groups.
3. Takes steps to integrate the bottom-track students into the nonacademic aspects of schooling, such as music, sports, and extracurricular activities. By taking part in these activities and occasionally being picked for positions of responsibility, bottom-track students are less likely to be stigmatized in a negative way or to suffer a loss of self-esteem.

Classroom structure. Although it may be difficult to remember your elementary school days,

---

ability tracking: the practice of placing students in categories on the basis of IQ or academic achievement and then educating them in classes with pupils of comparable academic or intellectual ability.

chances are you were educated in **traditional classrooms** where the seats were arranged in neat rows (or semicircles) facing the teacher, who lectured or gave demonstrations at a desk or a blackboard. In a traditional classroom, the curriculum is highly structured. Normally, everybody will be studying the same subject at a given moment, and students are expected to interact with the teacher rather than with one another. In recent years, however, many classrooms have become less formal or structured. "Open education" is a philosophy based on the premise that children are curious explorers who will achieve more by becoming *actively involved* in the learning process than by simply listening to a teacher recite facts, figures, and principles. In an **open classroom,** all the children are rarely doing the same thing at once. A more typical scenario is for students to distribute themselves around the room working individually or in small groups. For example,

> Two youngsters may be stretched out on a rug reading library books. The teacher is at the math table, showing four children how to use scales to learn about weights. Two children in the writing corner play a word game. Another takes notes about the nursing behavior of the class guinea pig. A sense of purpose pervades the room [Papalia & Olds, 1979, p. 401].

Is the open classroom more effective than the highly structured traditional setting? Proponents of open education certainly think so, although their claim is difficult to evaluate because students attending open nursery and elementary schools often come from different (usually more affluent) backgrounds than those who receive traditional instruction. It does seem that students generally prefer an "open" atmosphere and are more cooperative and create fewer disciplinary problems than students in traditional classrooms (Minuchin & Shapiro, 1983). Moreover, the open classroom may be effective at helping elementary school children to develop novel ideas and concepts (Rutter, 1983; Thomas & Berk, 1981), and one study found that children who had been randomly assigned to relatively unstructured nursery schools were later performing at higher levels in reading and math during the sixth, seventh, and eighth grades than age mates from comparable social backgrounds who had attended structured nursery schools (Miller & Bizzell, 1983). Yet, many investigators find no differences in the performance (or the conduct) of students in open and traditional classrooms, and others have concluded that students will actually learn more

Photo 16-3. Students at work in an open classroom.

in a *traditional* classroom whenever the subject matter requires teachers to illustrate very difficult concepts or transmit a lot of factual information (Good, 1979). So open education is hardly the panacea that its proponents claimed it to be. After reviewing the literature, Rutter (1983, p. 21) concluded that "debates on whether 'open classrooms' are better than traditional [ones] . . . or whether formal methods are preferable to 'informal' methods . . . are misplaced. Neither system has overall superiority, but both include elements of good practice."

Factors that do contribute to effective schooling

Composition of the student body. To some extent, the "effectiveness" of a school is a function of what it has to work with. On the average, academic achievement is lowest in schools with a preponderance of economically disadvantaged students (Brookover et al., 1979; Rutter et al., 1979), and it appears that *any* child is likely to make more academic progress if taught in a school with a higher concentration of intellectually capable peers. However, this does *not* mean that a school is only as good as the students it serves, for many schools that draw heavily from disadvantaged minority populations are highly effective at motivating students and preparing them for jobs or higher education (Rutter, 1983). The implication, then, is that there must be something about the "atmosphere" or "learning environment" that allows some schools to accomplish their objectives, regardless of the clientele they serve. Let's explore this idea further.

The scholastic atmosphere of successful schools. In his review of the literature, Rutter (1983) listed several values and practices that seem to characterize "effective" schools. For example:

1. *Academic emphasis.* Effective schools have a clear focus on academic goals. Children are regularly assigned homework, which is checked, corrected, and discussed with them. Teachers expect a lot of their students and devote a high proportion of their time to active teaching and planning lessons so that their expectations can be met. Instructors often plan their curriculum in groups and then monitor one another to ensure that they are doing what they can to achieve their objectives.

2. *Classroom management.* In effective schools, teachers spend little time setting up equipment, handing out papers, and dealing with disciplinary problems. Lessons begin and end on time. Pupils are told exactly what is expected of them and receive clear and unambiguous feedback about their academic performance. The classroom atmosphere is comfortable; all students are actively encouraged to work to the best of their abilities, and ample praise is given to acknowledge good work.

3. *Discipline.* In effective schools, the staff is firm in enforcing rules and does so on the spot rather than sending offenders off to the principal's office. Rarely do instructors resort to physical punishment. In fact, several studies suggest that corporal punishment and unofficial physical sanctions (slapping, cuffing) contribute to truancy, disobedient behavior, delinquency, and the establishment of a tense, negative atmosphere that is hardly conducive to effective learning.

4. *Staff organization and teacher morale.* Student conduct and academic achievement are better in schools where both the curriculum and approaches to discipline are agreed on by the staff working together as a team. Although it may be necessary for administrators to make decisions that individual instructors don't like, pupil outcomes are best in schools where all teachers feel that their points of view are taken seriously, even if they are not adopted.

In sum, we see that effective schools are those in which staff members work together to achieve well-defined, educational objectives based on what children want and need to know. Teachers are encouraged to offer helpful guidance and discouraged from commanding, ridiculing, or punishing their pupils. The emphasis in effective schools is on successes rather than failures, and ample praise and recognition are given to students for a job well done. In other words, the effective school environment is a comfortable but businesslike setting in which students are *motivated* to learn. After reviewing the literature, Michael Rutter (1983) concluded that the task of motivating students was of critical importance, for "in the long run, good pupil outcomes were [nearly always] dependent on pupils *wanting* to participate in the educational process" (p. 23).

And whose job is it to motivate students? Traditionally we have assigned this responsibility to the classroom instructor.

The Teacher's Influence

Once they reach school age, many children spend nearly as much time around their teachers as they do around their parents. Indeed, teachers are often the first adults outside the immediate family to play a major role in a child's life, and the functions that teachers serve will change rather dramatically as children progress through the educational system (Minuchin & Shapiro, 1983). Nursery school and kindergarten classes are in some ways similar to home life: teachers serve as companions or substitute caregivers who provide reassurance if needed while striving to help their pupils achieve the objectives of the preschool curriculum. Elementary school classrooms are more structured: teachers are focusing mainly on curricular goals, and grade school children are now more inclined to perceive their instructors as evaluators and authority figures rather than pals. During the adolescent years, teachers continue to serve as evaluators and authority figures. But since high school

---

traditional classroom: a classroom arrangement in which all pupils sit facing an instructor, who normally teaches one subject at a time by lecturing or giving demonstrations.

open classroom: a less structured classroom arrangement in which there is a separate area for each educational activity and children distribute themselves around the room, working individually or in small groups.

and college students change classes hourly and have many different teachers, it is less likely that any particular instructor will exert so much influence as was true during the grade school years.

Most of the research on teacher influences has focused on two very broad topics: (1) influences stemming from teachers' evaluation of students and (2) the effects of teaching styles on pupil outcomes.

Teacher expectancies and children's achievements: The Pygmalion effect

Teachers soon form distinct impressions of their students' scholastic potential, and these expectancies can have important effects on children's academic progress. In their landmark study of teacher expectancy effects, Robert Rosenthal and Lenore Jacobson (1968) gave first-through sixth-graders a nonverbal IQ test and then led their teachers to believe that this test predicted which students would show sudden bursts of intellectual growth during the academic year. Each teacher was given the names of five students who might very well prove to be "rapid bloomers." In fact, the so-called rapid bloomers had been randomly selected from the class rosters. The only way that they differed from the other children was that their teachers expected more of them. Yet, when the students were retested eight months later, Rosenthal and Jacobson found that, among the first- and second-graders, *the so-called rapid bloomers showed significantly greater gains in IQ and reading achievement than other students in the class.* In other words, the children who were expected to do well did, in fact, do better than other students of comparable ability.

Since the publication of this study, several other investigators have reported similar findings: students whom teachers expect to do well are apt to live up to these positive expectancies, whereas those expected to perform rather poorly often do earn lower grades and score lower on standardized tests than classmates of comparable ability for whom the teacher has no negative expectancies (see Harris & Rosenthal, 1985; Weinstein, Marshall, Sharp, & Botkin, 1987). Somehow teachers must be communicating their expectancies to students, thereby improving the self-concepts (and the will to achieve) of high-expectancy students while making the average- and low-expectancy students feel that they are not especially bright or expected to do well. The implication is that students are becoming the objects of their teachers' self-fulfilling prophecies in what Rosenthal and Jacobson called the **Pygmalion effect.**

Clearly, there is nothing mystical about the Pygmalion effect: it occurs because teachers treat high-expectancy students very differently from those who are expected to do poorly (Brophy, 1983; Harris & Rosenthal, 1985), and even first-graders are aware of this differential treatment (Weinstein et al., 1987). Basically, teachers expose high-expectancy students to more challenging materials, demand better performance from them, and are more likely to praise these youngsters for answering questions correctly (perhaps leading high-expectancy students to infer that they have *high ability*). And when high-expectancy students do not answer correctly, they often hear the question rephrased so that they can get it right (thus implying that failures can be overcome by *persisting* and *trying harder*). By contrast, low-expectancy students are not often challenged and are more likely to be criticized when they answer questions incorrectly (for example, "That's a stupid answer"), a practice that may convince them that their failures reflect a *lack of ability*. So teachers treat high-expectancy students in ways that promote a **mastery orientation** in the classroom, whereas low-expectancy students often receive the kinds of evaluative comments that could undermine achievement motivation or even contribute to **learned helplessness** (Dweck & Elliott, 1983).

But let's not be too critical of teachers for forming impressions of their students. All of us form impressions of the people in our lives, and these impressions often affect their behavior for better or worse. However, teachers should be made aware of the impact that their expectancies (and associated classroom behaviors) may have on their students. Indeed, the clever instructor might even use this knowledge to "get the most out of" nearly every child in the class by (1) setting educational objectives that the child can realistically achieve, (2) communicating these *positive* expectancies to the child, and then (3) praising the *ability* the child has shown whenever he or she reaches one of these academic milestones.

Teaching styles and instructional techniques

Earlier we saw that teachers in "effective" schools will typically set clear-cut standards for their students to achieve, emphasize successes more than failures, firmly enforce rules without derogating an offender or becoming overly punitive, and use praise rather than threats to encourage each child to work to the best of his or her ability. Perhaps you have noticed that these managerial characteristics are in some ways similar to the pattern of control that Diana Baumrind calls authoritative parenting. Indeed, Baumrind (1972) believes that the three major patterns of control that characterize parent/child interactions are also found in the classroom. Teachers who use an **authoritarian** style tend to dominate their pupils, relying on power-assertive methods to enforce their demands. The **authoritative** teacher is also controlling but will rely on reason to explain his or her demands, encourage verbal give-and-take, and value autonomy and creative expression as long as the child is willing to live within the rules that the teacher has established. Finally, the **laissez-faire** (or permissive) instructor makes few demands of students and provides little or no active guidance. Baumrind believes that teachers who use an authoritative style will contribute to children's intellectual curiosity, their academic achievement, and their social and emotional development.

A classic study by Kurt Lewin and his associates (Lewin, Lippitt, & White, 1939) is certainly relevant. Eleven-year-old boys who met after school to participate in hobby activities, such as making papier-mâché theater masks, were supervised by adults who functioned (1) as *authoritarian* leaders (by rigidly assigning jobs and work partners and by dictating policies without providing rationales for these edicts), (2) as authoritative, or *democratic*, leaders (by guiding the boys as they chose their own jobs and work partners and participated in policy making), or (3) as *laissez-faire* leaders (by providing little or no guidance and remaining noncommittal for the most part). How did the boys react to these supervisory styles? Authoritarian leadership produced tension, restlessness, aggressive outbursts, and a general dissatisfaction with the group experience. Productivity (as indexed by the number of theater masks constructed) was high under authoritarian leadership while the leader was present. But when the leader left the room, work patterns disintegrated. Democratic leadership was more effective; the boys were friendly toward one another and happier with the leader. Although productivity was not as high under democratic supervision, the boys continued working in the leader's absence, and the work they completed was of higher quality than that produced under authoritarian or laissez-faire leaders. Finally, the laissez-faire approach resulted in an apathetic group atmosphere and very low productivity. All

but 1 of the 20 boys in this experiment clearly favored democratic supervision.

These findings also seem to hold in the school setting. Students prefer a democratic atmosphere in the classroom (Rosenthal, Underwood, & Martin, 1969), and it appears that a flexible, nondictatorial instructional style is conducive to academic achievement (Minuchin & Shapiro, 1983). But a word of caution is in order, for the instructional techniques that a teacher uses will not affect all children in the same way. For example, Brophy (1979) notes that teachers get the most out of *high-ability* students by moving at a quick pace and demanding high standards of performance. By contrast, *low-ability* and *disadvantaged* children respond much more favorably to slow-paced instruction from a teacher who is warm and encouraging rather than intrusive and demanding.

In sum, authoritative instruction does seem to promote academic achievement. Yet, there are many ways that authoritative instructors might attempt to motivate their pupils, and the techniques that work best will depend, in part, on the type of student they are trying to reach.

Pygmalion effect: the tendency of students to perform better in the classroom when their teachers expect them to do well and to perform worse than they ordinarily would when the teacher expects them to do poorly (also called the teacher-expectancy effect).

mastery orientation: a tendency to persist at challenging tasks because of a belief that one has high ability and that earlier failures can be overcome by trying harder.

learned helplessness: a tendency to stop trying or to give up after failing because failures have been attributed to a lack of ability that one can do little about.

authoritarian instruction: a restrictive style of instruction in which the teacher makes absolute demands and uses threats or force (if necessary) to ensure that students comply.

authoritative instruction: a controlling style of instruction in which the teacher makes many demands but also allows some autonomy and individual expression as long as students are staying within the guidelines that the teacher has set.

laissez-faire instruction: a permissive style of instruction in which the teacher makes few demands of students and provides little or no active guidance.

The School as a Middle-Class Institution: Effects on Disadvantaged Youth

Public schools in the United States are middle-class institutions largely staffed by middle-class instructors who preach middle-class values. Some theorists have argued that this particular emphasis places children from lower-class or minority subcultures at an immediate disadvantage. After all, these youngsters must adjust to an environment that may seem altogether foreign and somewhat foreboding to them—a problem with which White middle-class students do not have to contend.

Scholastic outcomes

Many lower-income and minority students do have problems at school. They are more likely than middle-class youngsters to make poor marks, to be disciplined by the staff, to be "held back" in one or more grades, and to drop out before completing high school. Why is this? Let's consider three possibilities.

Parental expectancies and values. It seems that many lower-income and minority parents have rather modest academic expectancies for their children. Unlike middle-class parents, who stress "doing well" and "getting ahead," parents of disadvantaged youth are often satisfied if their children stay out of trouble and "get by" (Hess, 1970; Kohn, 1979). Moreover, parents from the lower socioeconomic strata are generally less knowledgeable about the school system and less involved in school activities, and this lack of participation may convince their children that school is not all that important. Yet, when lower-income or minority parents are interested and involved in school activities, their children do well in school (Brookover et al., 1979; Hess & Holloway, 1984). So it appears that parental encouragement and involvement can make a big difference.

"Relevance" of educational materials. The textbooks that children read are clearly centered on the lives and experiences of middle-class people, and it has been argued that lower-income and minority youth may simply be less inspired by these educational materials, which are often irrelevant to their own experiences. Indeed, there may be some truth to this assertion. Spencer Kagan and Lawrence Zahn (1975) found that third-generation Hispanic students who spoke only English were scoring far below their Anglo classmates in reading proficiency—an academic area in which textbooks adequately represent the middle-class Anglo culture but are largely irrelevant to Hispanics. However, these same minority students showed a much smaller achievement gap in mathematics, presumably because math texts contain less culturally irrelevant information. If Kagan and Zahn are correct in their interpretation, then perhaps we should be using more "culturally relevant" educational materials in school systems heavily populated by underachieving ethnic minorities.

Teachers' reactions to low-income and minority students. In his book *Dark Ghetto*, Kenneth Clark (1965) argues that the classroom represents a "clash of cultures" in which adults who have adopted middle-class values fail to appreciate the difficulties faced

Photo 16-4. Children are more likely to do well in school if their parents value education and are interested and involved in school activities.

by students from different subcultural and socioeconomic backgrounds. According to Clark, teachers in schools serving lower-income minority populations make nearly three times as many negative comments to their students as their colleagues in middle-income schools. Teachers often have lower expectancies for children from low-income families (Minuchin & Shapiro, 1983). Even before they have any academic information about their students, many instructors are already placing them into "ability groups" on the basis of their grooming, the quality of their clothing, and their use or misuse of standard English (Rist, 1970). In one study (Gottlieb, 1966), teachers were asked to select from a checklist those attributes that best described their lower-income and minority pupils. Middle-class respondents consistently checked adjectives such as *lazy, fun-loving,* and *rebellious.* Clearly, these instructors did not expect much of their disadvantaged students—an attitude that undoubtedly contributes to social-class and ethnic differences in achievement.

Ironically, lower-income and minority students may be convinced that they are doing well in school if their teachers evaluate them infrequently, assign them passing marks, and routinely promote them from grade to grade, regardless of their actual accomplishments (Mac Iver, 1987; Plummer, Hazzard-Lineberger, & Graziano, 1984). Indeed, Katherine Fulkerson and her associates (Fulkerson, Furr, & Brown, 1983) report that the academic expectancies of minority students increase and become more unrealistic from the third to the ninth grade. Is it a wise practice to give **"social promotions"** to children whose accomplishments are clearly substandard? Probably not. In fact, it could be argued that this practice actually perpetuates social inequalities by denying these underachievers the opportunity to repeat a grade and thereby acquire critical academic skills that they will need to do well in the future. But how do children feel about repeating a grade? Does it really help? As we see in Box 16-2, grade retention is a controversial practice that could have either positive or negative effects on retainees, depending on their age, the extent of their deficiencies, their self-esteem, and the amount of support they receive from parents, teachers, and peers.

Effects of school desegregation on minority youth

In its landmark decision in the 1954 case *Brown* v. *Board of Education,* the U.S. Supreme Court ruled that racially segregated schools were "inherently un-

equal" and declared that they be desegregated. The *Brown* decision was expected to have at least three positive effects on minority students (in this case, Blacks) and one favorable effect on Whites (Stephan, 1978):

1. For Whites, school desegregation was to lead to more positive attitudes toward Blacks.
2. For Blacks, desegregation was to lead to (a) more positive attitudes toward Whites, (b) increases in self-esteem, and (c) increases in academic achievement.

Since the *Brown* decision, several investigators have studied the impact of school desegregation on both Black and White students. Were the early predictions borne out? Let's take a look at the findings.

Has school desegregation improved race relations? The data on this issue are mixed. In one review of the literature, Black prejudice toward Whites was observed to decrease in about 50% of the studies, whereas White prejudice toward Blacks decreased in only 13% of the studies (Stephan, 1978). However, it is not at all uncommon for both Blacks and Whites in integrated schools to have more negative attitudes toward the other group than their counterparts in *segregated* schools. And this is often true even where integration was achieved voluntarily and without serious incidents (Green & Gerard, 1974; Stephan, 1977).

One reason that school desegregation has not been more successful at improving race relations is that members of various racial and ethnic groups tend to stick together without interacting much with their classmates from other groups. In fact, Neal Finkelstein and Ron Haskins (1983) found that kindergartners who were just entering an integrated school already preferred same-race peers and that these racial cleavages became even stronger over the course of the school year. Other investigators have noted that children's preferences for same-race friends become progressively stronger across grades in integrated schools (see Hartup, 1983). Yet, race relations often improve when students from different backgrounds are assigned to the same ability groups for instruction, are required to work together on important tasks, and/or have chosen to participate on multiethnic sports teams (Hallinan & Teixeira, 1987;

social promotion: the practice of promoting students to the next grade when their scholastic performance indicates that they should repeat their present grade.

Box 16-2
Repeating a Grade: Personal, Social, and Academic Consequences

If children do not attain the "minimal competencies" necessary for success in the next grade, they are often required to repeat the work that they have failed to master. Advocates of grade retention argue that repeating a grade is a beneficial experience—one that gives the underachieving child an opportunity to mature both socially and intellectually and to acquire academic skills that are absolutely essential to perform well in the higher grades (Kerzner, 1982). Yet, the critics have argued that retained children may often be stigmatized as "different" or even "stupid," an experience that could undermine their self-concepts, their academic expectancies, and their relations with teachers and peers.

For the most part, parents and teachers support grade retention because they believe that the positive aspects of this policy outweigh the negatives (Chase, 1968). Let's now consider the evidence to see whether there is any basis for this claim.

Grade retention and academic achievement. The primary purpose of retaining a child is to allow him or her to acquire important academic skills and thereby do better in school. Yet, an examination of the evidence available before 1970 suggests that the policy of holding children back in school was not meeting these objectives. The majority of nonpromoted children performed no better while repeating a grade than they had the first time around. Moreover, children of comparable ability who had been promoted generally outscored retainees on standardized achievement tests (see Plummer, Hazzard-Lineberger, & Graziano, 1984, for review). Even the most critical of these early reports, however, acknowledged that about 20% of the retainees were doing better academically after repeating a grade.

The recent literature on grade retention is more encouraging. Nonpromoted children are generally found to make better grades the second time around and to show definite improvements on standardized tests of academic achievement, particularly when they are retained in the lower grades (Ames, 1981; Kerzner, 1982). Retainees are more likely

to make good academic progress if (1) their parents support the decision to retain them, (2) they have a positive self-concept before being retained, (3) they have good social skills, and (4) *their academic deficiencies are not too extensive* (Plummer et al., 1984; Sandoval & Hughes, 1981). The last point is important, for it suggests that children who have received several "social promotions" and were not ready for the grade they failed may not profit by repeating it.

Grade retention and peer relations. Do peers stigmatize an older retainee as dumb, incompetent, or otherwise undesirable? Diane Plummer and William Graziano (1987) tried to answer this question by showing second- and fifth-graders photographs of retained and nonretained age mates (whom they did not know) and then asking them who would be liked better, who could give more help with schoolwork, and who would be a better playmate. The results were indeed interesting. On the liking item, a sizable minority of the children (38%) felt that the older, retained child would be liked better than a younger, *continued*

Minuchin & Shapiro, 1983). Clearly these latter findings support Finkelstein and Haskins's (1983) view that "school desegregation will not, by itself, . . . lead to a destruction of the color barriers that have plagued our society . . . if such barriers are to be reduced, schools will need to design, implement, and monitor programs aimed at facilitating social contacts between blacks and whites" (p. 508).

Has desegregation increased Black children's self-esteem? In his review of the literature, Walter Stephan (1978) found few differences in self-esteem between Black children in segregated and in integrated schools. In fact, none of the 20 studies found that desegregation had had a positive effect on Black self-esteem, while 5 studies (25%) reported that desegregation had had a negative effect. Unfortunately, this research has considered only the short-term effects of desegregation, and it remains to be seen whether the

self-concepts of minority children will improve after spending several years in integrated schools.

Has desegregation increased academic achievement? Do minority students achieve more in desegregated classrooms? In many cases they do, particularly if they begin to attend an integrated school early in their academic careers (Mahan & Mahan, 1970; Stephan, 1978; St. John, 1975). Although the academic gains that result from desegregation are often rather modest, it is worth noting that in only 1 of 34 studies have minority students in integrated classrooms performed at lower levels than their counterparts in segregated schools (Stephan, 1978).

Similar results have emerged from studies of handicapped children who are "integrated" into regular classrooms through a practice called **mainstreaming.** Although handicapped students who attend regular classes may perform a little better academically than

nonretained classmate. On the academic item, 86% of the second-graders and 66% of the fifth-graders felt that the older, retained child would be of more assistance with schoolwork. When asked why, they usually stated that the retainee had more experience with such assignments and would know more about them. Finally, more than half (52%) of the second-graders preferred the older, retained child as a playmate, and even 40% of the fifth-graders chose the retainee as a preferred companion. As a cautionary note, it is important to recall that the respondents were evaluating children whom they did not know. Nevertheless, their responses clearly question the notion that a child who has "failed" a grade will automatically be stigmatized as dull, incompetent, or otherwise undesirable.

Grade retention and self-esteem. How do children feel when they fail a grade? It is often assumed that they will be upset and depressed and may begin to lower their academic expectations or to question their self-worth. In fact, some theorists have argued that grade retention can produce a serious loss of self-esteem, which leads to further failure and

eventually to feelings of learned helplessness (Johnson, 1981). Do these reactions often occur when a child must repeat a grade?

Plummer and Graziano (1987) have recently studied some of the "personal" effects of grade retention in a rural school district in Georgia where a substantial percentage of Black and White students are retained at least once while in elementary school. Second- and fifth-grade retainees and nonretainees were asked to estimate the grades they would receive on their next report card (academic expectancy measure) and to indicate verbally how they viewed themselves on personal and social dimensions such as "lazy," "smart," "popular," "successful," and "honest" (self-esteem measure). The results would undoubtedly surprise many theorists. With one minor exception (second-grade retainees expected lower grades in reading than their nonretained classmates), retainees did not differ from nonretainees on the academic expectancy measure. Moreover, retainees in both the second and fifth grades actually had more favorable self-concepts than students who had not been retained. We must be cautious in

interpreting these results because nearly 40% of the children in this school had been held back at one time or another, so that being a retainee was in no way unusual. Nevertheless, there was little support for the idea that retainees view themselves as less capable of achieving or less "worthy" than nonretainees.

The policy of holding children back to facilitate their eventual academic progress remains highly controversial, and it is possible that alternative strategies such as promoting a child and providing special instruction in areas of deficiency will prove more effective than grade retention—if and when these techniques are tried on a large scale. Nevertheless, it appears that many children can benefit academically from repeating a grade without experiencing poor peer relations or a serious loss of self-esteem.

their handicapped age mates in special education classes (Madden & Slavin, 1983), they rarely show any increase in self-esteem. In fact, their perceived self-worth often declines because normal children tend to ridicule handicapped youngsters and will rarely choose them as playmates (Taylor, Asher, & Williams, 1987; Zigler & Muenchow, 1979). What can be done to make "integration" a more positive and fruitful experience for minority groups and the handicapped?

Robert Slavin (1986) and his colleagues have had some success using **cooperative learning methods** in which students of different races and ability levels are assigned to "math teams" and are reinforced for performing well *as a team*. Each team member is given problems to solve that are appropriate for his or her own ability level, but all children on a team are encouraged to monitor the activities of their teammates and to offer assistance when necessary. To encourage this teamwork, groups that complete the most "math

units" are rewarded in some way—for example, by earning special certificates designating the winning groups as "Superteams." Here, then, is a procedure ensuring that children of different races and ability levels will interact in a context where the efforts of even the least capable team members are important to the group's success.

Slavin finds that elementary school students in these cooperative learning groups come to like math

mainstreaming: an educational practice in which handicapped children are integrated into regular classrooms.

cooperative learning methods: an educational practice whereby children of different races or ability levels are assigned to teams; each team member works on problems geared to his or her ability level, and team members are reinforced for "pulling together" and performing well as a team.

better and will learn more about it than they do when they receive traditional math instruction. Moreover, team members gain self-esteem from their successes, and minority group and handicapped youngsters are more fully accepted by their peers. So it seems that racial integration and mainstreaming could have more positive academic and social consequences if educators were to deliberately design learning experiences that encourage students from different backgrounds to pull together, work hard, and pool their individual efforts for the accomplishment of group goals.

The Second World of Childhood: Peers as Socialization Agents

Although youngsters spend an enormous amount of time and energy playing with one another, only within the past 20 years have child developmentalists given much thought to how peer contacts affect developing children. Perhaps owing to early research on the behavior of adolescent gangs (see Hartup, 1983), peers have often been characterized as potentially subversive agents who may erode the influence of adults and lead the child into a life of delinquency and antisocial conduct. Popular novels and films such as *Lord of the Flies* and *A Clockwork Orange* reinforce this point of view.

However, this perspective on peer relations is distorted and unnecessarily negative. Although peers are occasionally "bad influences," they clearly have the potential to affect their playmates in positive ways. Try to imagine what your life would be like if other children had not been available as you were growing up. Would you have acquired the social skills to mix comfortably with others, to cooperate and to engage in socially acceptable forms of competition, or to make appropriate social (or sexual) responses to love objects other than your parents? No one can say for sure, but the following letter written by a farmer from the Midwestern United States provides a strong clue that interactions with other children may be an important aspect of the socialization process.[2]

[2]This letter appears by permission of its author and its recipient, Dr. Shirley G. Moore.

Dear Dr. Moore:

I read the report in the Oct. 30 issue of _____ about your study of only children. I am an only child, now 57 years old, and I want to tell you some things about my life. Not only was I an only child, but I grew up in the country where there were no nearby children to play with. My mother didn't want children around. She used to say "I don't want my kid to bother anybody and I don't want nobody's kids bothering me" . . .

From the first year of school, I was teased and made fun of. For example, in about third or fourth grade, I dreaded to get on the school bus and go to school because the other children on the bus called me "Mommy's baby." In about the second grade I heard the boys use a vulgar word. I asked what it meant and they made fun of me. So I learned a lesson—don't ask questions. This can lead to a lot of confusion to hear talk one doesn't understand and not be able to learn what it means.

I never went out with a girl while I was in school— in fact I hardly talked to them. In our school the boys and girls did not play together. Boys were sent to one part of the playground and girls to another. So I didn't learn anything about girls. When we got into high school and boys and girls started dating, I could only listen to their stories about their experiences.

I could tell you a lot more, but the important thing is I have never married or had any children. I have not been very successful in an occupation or vocation. I believe my troubles are not all due to being an only child . . . but I do believe you are right in recommending playmates for preschool children, and I will add playmates for . . . school agers and not have them strictly supervised by adults. . . . Parents of only children should make special efforts to provide playmates for them.

Sincerely yours,

_____

If we assume that peers are important agents of socialization, there are a number of questions that remain to be answered. For example, who qualifies as a peer? How do peers influence one another? What is it about peer influence that is unique? What are the consequences (if any) of poor peer relations? Do peers eventually become a more potent source of influence than parents or other adults? Are there cultural differences in the roles that peers play in a child's socialization? These are some of the issues that researchers are currently exploring as they turn in ever-increasing numbers to the study of children's peer groups.

Who or What Is a Peer?

Webster's New Collegiate Dictionary defines a **peer** as "one that is of equal standing with another." Developmentalists also think of peers as "social equals" or as individuals who, for the moment at least, are operating at similar levels of behavioral complexity (Lewis & Rosenblum, 1975).

We get some idea of why peer contacts are important by contrasting them to exchanges that occur within the family setting. A child's interactions with parents and older siblings are rarely equal-status contacts; typically children are placed in a subordinate position by an older member of the family who is trying to teach them something, issuing an order, or otherwise overseeing their activities. By contrast, peers are much less critical and directive, and children are freer to try out new roles, ideas, and behaviors when interacting with someone of similar status. And in so doing, they are likely to learn important lessons about themselves and others—lessons such as "She quits when I don't take turns," "He hits me when I push him," or "Nobody likes a cheater." Many theorists believe that peer contacts are important precisely because they are *equal-status* contacts—that is, they teach children to understand and appreciate the perspectives of people *just like themselves* and will thereby contribute to the development of social competencies that are difficult to acquire in the nonegalitarian atmosphere of the home.

Mixed-age interactions

According to Hartup (1983), interaction among children of *different* ages is also a critically important context for social and personality development. Although cross-age interactions tend to be somewhat *asymmetrical*, one child (typically the elder) possessing more power or status than the other, it is precisely these asymmetries that may help children to acquire certain social competencies. For example, the presence of younger peers may foster the development of sympathy and compassion, caregiving and prosocial inclinations, assertiveness, and leadership skills in older children (see, for example, French, Wass, Stright, & Baker, 1986). At the same time, younger children may benefit from mixed-age interactions by learning how to seek assistance and how to defer gracefully to the wishes and directives of older, more powerful peers. Moreover, younger children are potentially in a position to acquire many socially and intellectually adaptive patterns of behavior through direct instruction (tutoring) by elder playmates or by observing and imitating the competent behaviors of these "older and wiser" companions.

In their survey of children's social contacts in six cultures, Whiting and Whiting (1975) found that mixed-age interactions do differ in important ways from those among age mates. Nurturant and prosocial behaviors occurred more frequently in mixed-age groups, whereas casually sociable acts (such as conversation and interactive play) as well as antisocial ones (such as aggression) were more likely to occur among age mates. By the time children enter school, they already characterize older peers as more powerful and competent and younger peers as less powerful and competent than themselves (Graziano, Musser, & Brody, 1982). Given these observations, it should not be surprising to find, as Doran French (1984) recently has, that children's preferences for interacting with older, younger, or same-age peers depend on the purpose of that interaction. First- and third-graders clearly preferred age mates to either younger or older children when asked who might be more desirable as a friend. However, older children were preferred to age mates if the child felt the need for sympathy, help, or guidance, whereas younger children were the ones subjects chose if the situation called for them to display compassion or to teach another child what they already knew.

Frequency of peer contacts

As you might expect, the amount of contact that children have with their peers increases with age. Sharri Ellis and her colleagues (Ellis, Rogoff, & Cromer, 1981) observed the activities of 436 children aged 2 to 12 as they played in their homes and other locales around the neighborhood. The purpose of this research was to determine how often children interacted with adults, age mates, and other children who differed in age by more than a year. As we see in Figure 16-4, children's exposure to other children increases steadily from infancy through middle childhood, while their contacts with adult companions show a corresponding decrease.

---

peers: two or more persons who are operating at similar levels of behavioral complexity.

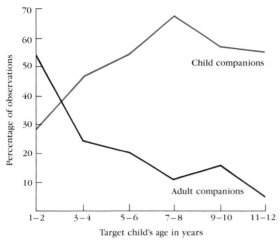

Figure 16-4. Developmental changes in children's companionship with adults and other children. *(From Ellis, Rogoff, & Cromer, 1981.)*

Same-age versus mixed-age interactions.
Since children attend age-graded schools, it seems reasonable to conclude that they would play most often with age mates. However, Ellis et al. (1981) found that they do not! As we see in Figure 16-5, youngsters of all ages spend much less time with age mates than with children who differ in age by more than a year. In another study of children's interactions in a neighborhood setting, Roger Barker and H. F. Wright (1955) found that 65% of peer contacts involved individuals who differed in age by more than 12 months.

Same-sex versus mixed-sex interactions.
In Chapter 13 we noted that preschool children already prefer playmates of their own sex. In their observational study, Ellis et al. found that even 1- to 2-year-olds were playing more often with same-sex companions and that this like-sex bias became increasingly apparent with age. The fact that infants are playing more often with children of their own sex probably reflects their parents' idea that boys should be playing with boys and girls with girls. And as children acquire gender stereotypes and sex-typed interests, it is hardly surprising that they would begin to choose same-sex playmates who enjoy the same kind of activities that they do.

What may be most surprising about the naturalistic studies of peer interaction is the sheer amount of contact that children have with one another before they go to school. Even 5–6-year-olds are spending as much

leisure time (or more) in the company of children as around adults (Barker & Wright, 1955; Ellis et al., 1981). And what is the "peer group" like? It consists primarily of same-sex children of *different* ages. Now we see why developmentalists define peers as "people who interact at similar levels of behavioral complexity," for only a small percentage of a child's associates are actually age mates.

Peers as Promoters of Social Competence and Personal Adjustment
To this point, we have speculated that interactions among children may promote the development of many social and personal competencies that are not easily acquired within the decidedly nonegalitarian parent/child relationship. Is there truly any basis for such a claim? And if so, just how important are those peer influences? Developmentalists became very interested in these questions after Harry Harlow showed that rhesus monkeys seem to require peer contacts in order to get along with other monkeys. Let's take a closer look.

Harlow's work with monkeys. Will youngsters who have little or no contact with peers turn out to be abnormal or maladjusted? To find out, Harry

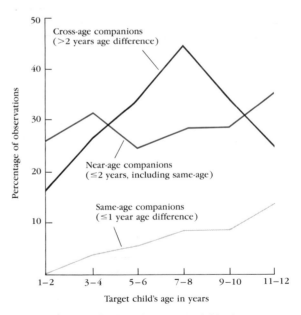

Figure 16-5. Developmental changes in children's companionship with children of different ages. *(From Ellis, Rogoff, & Cromer, 1981.)*

Photo 16-5. Monkeys raised only with peers form strong mutual attachments and will often attack other monkeys from outside their peer group.

Harlow and his associates (Alexander & Harlow, 1965; Suomi & Harlow, 1975, 1978) raised groups of rhesus monkeys with their mothers and denied them the opportunity to play with their peers. These **"mother only" monkeys** failed to develop normal patterns of social behavior. When finally exposed to age mates, the peer-deprived youngsters preferred to avoid them. On those occasions when they did approach a peer, these social misfits tended to be highly (and inappropriately) aggressive. Moreover, their antisocial tendencies often persisted into adulthood, particularly if they had been denied peer contacts for long periods.

Is peer contact the key to normal social development? Not entirely. In later experiments, Harlow and his colleagues separated rhesus monkeys from their mothers and raised them so that they had continuous exposure to their peers. These **"peer only" monkeys** were observed to cling tenaciously to one another and to form strong mutual attachments. Yet, their social development was somewhat atypical. Suomi and Harlow (1975) noted: "It is somewhat difficult for a baby monkey to explore its environment with another monkey hanging on for dear life and [when] even the most enthusiastic attempts at play are terminated by a big bearhug" (p. 167). The peer-only monkeys were often disturbed by minor stresses or frustrations, and as adults they became unusually aggressive toward monkeys from outside their peer groups.

And a human parallel. In 1951 Anna Freud and Sophie Dann reported a startling human parallel to Harlow's peer-only monkeys. During the summer of 1945, six 3-year-olds were found living by themselves in a German concentration camp. By the time these children were 12 months old, their parents had been put to death. Although they received minimal caregiving from a series of inmates who were periodically executed, these children had, in effect, reared themselves.

When rescued at the war's end, the six orphans were flown to a special treatment center in England, where attempts were made to "rehabilitate" them. How did these "peer only" children respond to this treatment? They began by breaking nearly all their toys and damaging their furniture. Moreover, they often reacted with cold indifference or open hostility toward the staff at the center. And like Harlow's monkeys, these children

> had no other wish than to be together and became upset when they were separated . . . even for short

---

"mother only" monkeys: monkeys who are raised with their mothers and denied any contacts with peers.

"peer only" monkeys: monkeys who are separated from their mothers (and other adults) soon after birth and raised with peers.

moments. No child would remain upstairs while the others were downstairs. . . . If anything of the kind happened, the single child would constantly ask for the other children, while the group would fret for the missing child. . . .

There was no occasion to urge the children to "take turns"; they did it spontaneously. They were extremely considerate of each other's feelings. . . . At mealtimes handing food to the neighbor was of greater importance than eating oneself [Freud & Dann, 1951, pp. 131–133].

Although these orphans were closely attached to one another and very suspicious of outsiders, they were certainly not psychotic. In fact, they eventually established positive relationships with their adult caregivers and acquired a new language during the first year at the center. The story even has a happy ending, for 35 years later, these orphans were leading effective, productive lives as middle-aged adults. According to Hartup (1983), "No more graphic account exists in the literature to demonstrate resilience in social development and to display that peer interaction can contribute importantly to the socialization of the individual child" (p. 158).

Taken together, Harlow's monkey research and Freud and Dann's observations of their war orphans suggest that parents and peers each contribute something different and perhaps unique to a monkey's (or a child's) social development. Under normal circumstances, parents may provide a sense of *security* that enables their young to explore the environment and discover that other people can be interesting companions. By contrast, contacts with peers seem to promote the development of competent and adaptive patterns of social behavior. Indeed, Harlow's "peer only" monkeys behaved in strange ways as adults only when exposed to strange companions; within their own peer groups, they generally displayed normal patterns of social and sexual behavior (Suomi & Harlow, 1978).

The importance of harmonious peer relations.   Just how important is it that human beings establish and maintain harmonious relations with their peers? Apparently it is very important. Merrill Roff (1974; Roff, Sells, & Golden, 1972) has collected longitudinal data on a large number of children who were clients at a child guidance center. After tracking these individuals for many years, Roff and his associates found that poor peer relations during childhood were a reliable predictor of severe emotional disturbances later in life. Children who had been actively shunned or rejected by their

classmates were more likely to be delinquent as adolescents, to receive bad-conduct discharges from the military service, and to display a large number of serious adjustment problems, including neuroses, psychoses, and sexual deviations. A second longitudinal study painted a similar picture: children who had been rejected by their peers in the third grade were more likely than those with good peer relations to be seeking treatment for emotional disturbances 11 years later as young adults (Cowen, Pederson, Babigan, Izzo, & Trost, 1973).

Researchers typically measure children's peer acceptance, or popularity, through *sociometric techniques*. In a sociometric survey, each child in a peer group might be asked to nominate several classmates whom she likes and several whom she dislikes; or alternatively, each child might be asked to rate all peer-group members in terms of their desirability as companions. Through the use of these procedures, it is usually possible to classify each group member into one of the following categories: (1) **sociometric stars** (children accepted by most peers and rejected by few), (2) **amiables,** or *"accepteds"* (those who receive fewer positive nominations than "stars" but who obtain a clear preponderance of positive nominations), (3) **isolates,** or **neglectees** (children who receive few positive or negative nominations and who seem almost invisible to peers), and (4) **rejectees** (those who are rejected by many peers and accepted by few).

Notice that there are two kinds of children—isolates and rejectees—who are low in peer acceptance. But interestingly enough, it is not nearly as bad to be ignored by one's peers as to be rejected by them. Isolated children whom peers often neglect do not feel as lonely as rejectees (Asher & Wheeler, 1985), and they are much more likely than rejected children to eventually be "accepted" or even achieve the status of sociometric star should they enter a new class or a new play group (Coie & Dodge, 1983; Coie & Kupersmidt, 1983). In addition, it is the rejected child, rather than the isolate, who faces the greater risk of suffering serious adjustment problems later in life (Cowen et al., 1973; Roff, 1974).

Why might poor peer relations in childhood be good prognostic indicators of later adjustment problems? Perhaps youngsters who are *rejected* by peers will face later difficulties because they have paid little attention to the values and teachings of the peer group and have simply failed to acquire many socially appropriate patterns of behavior. Indeed, Wyndol Furman and John Masters (1980) found that unpopular 5-year-olds were less likely than their popular classmates to follow rules endorsed by either peers or adults.

Of course, it is unlikely that poor peer relations are entirely responsible for the adjustment problems of a rejected child. Many unpopular children have shaky interpersonal relations with their parents or live in conflict-ridden homes—experiences that may create their own emotional difficulties while also hindering the child's attempts to establish adequate peer relations (Hetherington, 1981; Lewis, Feiring, McGuffog, & Jaskir, 1984). For example, we know that children who are abused by their parents often attain very low status in the peer group, perhaps owing to their tendency to be highly and inappropriately aggressive with peers (Hoffman-Plotkin & Twentyman, 1984; Main & George, 1985). Moreover, two recent studies have shown that preschoolers with a history of insecure attachments (particularly those who are "anxious and resistant" with their mothers) are likely to be picked on or ignored by peers and to be among the least popular members of a preschool play group (Jacobson & Wille, 1986; LaFreniere & Sroufe, 1985). So bad experiences at home may contribute in a *direct* way to later adjustment problems as well as coloring a child's relations with peers.

Surely, not all children whose home lives are shaky and insecure will be rejected by their peers; nor will all youngsters with amiable home lives be spared the pain of rejection (Skolnick, 1986). But since friendly and harmonious contacts with peers promote the development of adaptive social skills, it would seem that *any* child who fails to establish positive links to the peer group will run a far greater risk of displaying inappropriate and perhaps even pathological patterns of behavior as an adolescent or young adult.

How do children establish and maintain good relations with their peers? In Box 16-3 we will try to answer this question as we consider some of the determinants of one's social standing in the peer group.

Children and Their Friends

As young children become more outgoing and are exposed to a wider variety of peers, they typically form close ties to one or more of their playmates—bonds that we call *friendships*. According to Hartup (1983), true friendships are reciprocal relationships that in some ways resemble the attachments between children and their mothers. In this portion of the chapter, we will first consider how children define friendships and see what they expect from their "special" companions. We will then compare and contrast the social interactions of friends with those of acquaintances and discuss some of the roles that friends may play in a person's social and emotional development.

Children's conceptions of friendship

One way to determine what children think about the meaning of friendship is to ask them to tell you (1) what attributes friends should have and (2) what they should be able to expect from a friend. Bigelow (1977; Bigelow & LaGaipa, 1975) tried this approach with Canadian and Scottish first- through eighth-graders and found that children's expectations about friendship progress through three broad stages:

1. *Reward-cost stage.* In this stage, which emerges at about the second or third grade, a friend is a companion who lives nearby, has nice toys, likes to play with me, and plays the way I like to (that is, shares the child's expectations about play activities).
2. *Normative stage.* During grade four or five, shared values and rules become important. Friends are expected to stick up for and be loyal to each other. Friends are also supposed to share possessions, help each other, cooperate, and avoid fighting (Berndt, 1981; Furman & Bierman, 1983).
3. *Empathic stage.* Beginning at about the fifth to seventh grade, children begin to see friends as people who share similar interests, who make active attempts to understand each other, and who are willing to self-disclose intimate information or to listen and respond constructively to the child's own self-disclosures (Rotenberg & Mann, 1986).

Adolescents' expectations about the obligations of friendship represent an extension of this empathic stage, with a little less emphasis on shared interests and a much stronger focus on *reciprocal emotional relations.*

---

sociometric stars: children who are accepted by most members of their peer group and rejected by very few.

amiables: children who receive more positive nominations (acceptances) from their peers than negative ones (rejections).

isolates or neglectees: children who receive few nominations of any kind (acceptances or rejections) from members of their peer group.

rejectees: children who are rejected by many peers and accepted by very few.

At several points throughout the text, we have discussed factors that seem to contribute to children's popularity or social status. By way of review:

1. *Parenting styles.* Warm, sensitive, and authoritative caregivers tend to raise children who are securely attached and who establish good relations with both adults and peers (Putallaz, 1987; see Chapter 15). Unresponsive caregivers, particularly those who are also permissive, tend to raise children who are hostile and aggressive, while the children of more domineering or authoritarian caregivers are often rather anxious, reserved, and moody around their peers (see Chapters 12 and 15).

2. *Physical correlates.* Children with an athletic, or "mesomorphic," build tend to be more popular than those with linear (ectomorphic) or rounded (endomorphic) physiques. Rate of maturation may also matter: boys who reach puberty early tend to be more popular than boys who mature late (see Chapter 5).

3. *Ordinal-position effects.* Later-born children who must learn to negotiate with older and more powerful siblings tend to be more popular than first-borns (see Chapter 15).

4. *Cognitive skills.* Among groups of third- through eighth-graders, the most popular children are those who have well-developed role-taking skills (see Chapter 12). There is also a positive relationship between intelligence and peer acceptance: brighter children tend to be the more popular members of many peer groups (Hartup, 1983; Quay & Jarrett, 1984).

At least three additional characteristics may affect children's standing in the peer group: their names, their facial features, and their patterns of interpersonal behavior.

Names. Surprising as it may seem, John McDavid and Herbert Harari (1966) reported that children with attractive first names (for example, Steven or Susan) tend to be more popular than age mates with unusual or less attractive names (for example, Herman or Moon Muffin). And in a later study, Harari and McDavid (1973) found that teachers tend to have more positive achievement expectancies for children with attractive names.

These outcomes, like all correlational findings, must be interpreted with caution. Perhaps having a strange name does handicap children by making them the object of scorn or ridicule. However, we must consider the possibility that parents who give their children unusual names may also encourage unusual behaviors that contribute to the problems that the Myrtles and Mortimers may have with their peers.

Facial attractiveness. Despite the maxim that "beauty is only skin deep," many of us (children included) seem to think otherwise. Although it is difficult to specify exactly what combinations of features contribute to facial attractiveness, even 6- to 8-month-old infants can discriminate attractive faces from unattractive ones, and they show a clear preference for gazing at more attractive faces (Langlois et al., 1987). Attractive youngsters are often described in more favorable terms (for example, friendlier, more intelligent) than their less attractive playmates by both teachers and other children—even *preschool* children (Adams & Crane, 1980; Langlois, 1986). And when unattractive children do something wrong, they are often judged to be "meaner" or more chronically antisocial than an attractive child who commits the same act (Dion, 1972; Lerner & Lerner, 1977). So it seems that we are often swayed by a pretty face and will act as if whatever is beautiful must be good—or at least not too bad.

Attractive children are generally more popular than their less attrac-
continued

For 10- to 11-year-olds, the central obligation of friendship is "to be nice and help each other," whereas 16- to 17-year-olds say that, above all, friends are people whom they can count on for understanding and intimate emotional support (Smollar & Youniss, 1982; Tesch, 1983). So for older adolescents, close friendship seems to imply a unit relation or a "shared identity" in which "me and you" have become a "we" (Hartup, 1983).

Social interactions between friends and acquaintances

Although there is some question whether preschool children form solid, enduring friendships, they do have preferred playmates or "strong associates" (Hinde, Titmus, Easton, & Tamplin, 1985), and they tend to react differently to these youngsters than to mere acquaintances. For example, Masters and Furman (1981) found that nursery-schoolers both give and receive more positive reinforcers (approval, toys, and so forth) when interacting with preferred playmates than with acquaintances, whereas Hinde et al. (1985) noted that punitive or hostile exchanges are more frequent among acquaintances than among strong associates. Strong associates also respond more constructively to strange settings than pairs of unacquainted preschoolers do—suggesting that having a preferred companion may reduce a young child's anxiety about uncertain situations (Schwartz, 1972). Finally, 3- to 6-year-olds are generally willing to give up valuable play time to perform a dull task if their efforts will benefit a "friend"; yet, this kind

tive companions, and this link between facial attractiveness and peer acceptance begins to make some sense when we consider how attractive and unattractive children interact with their peers. Although attractive and unattractive 3-year-olds do not yet differ a great deal in the character of their social behaviors, by age 5, unattractive youngsters are more likely than attractive ones to be active and boisterous during play sessions and to respond aggressively toward their playmates (Langlois & Downs, 1979). So unattractive children do seem to develop patterns of social interaction that could alienate other children.

Why might this happen? Some theorists have argued that parents, teachers, and other children may contribute to a self-fulfilling prophecy by subtly (or not so subtly) communicating to attractive youngsters that they are smart and are expected to do well in school, behave pleasantly, and achieve good relationships with peers. Information of this sort undoubtedly has an effect on children. Attractive youngsters may become progressively more confident, friendly, and outgoing, whereas unattractive children who receive less favorable feedback may suffer a loss of self-esteem and become more resentful, defiant, and aggressive. This is precisely the way in which the "beautiful is good" stereotype could become a reality (Langlois & Downs, 1979).

Behavioral characteristics. Although physical characteristics associated with "attractiveness" contribute to peer acceptance, even highly attractive children may be very unpopular if playmates consider their conduct inappropriate or antisocial (Langlois & Styczynski, 1979). What behaviors seem to be important in determining a child's standing in the peer group? Several studies of preschool and grade school children report pretty much the same findings: popular children are observed to be reasonably calm, outgoing, cooperative, and supportive, whereas neglected children tend to be less talkative and more withdrawn, and extremely unpopular or rejected children can be described as highly active and disruptive braggarts who tend to be snobbish, short-tempered, and aggressive (Coie, Dodge, & Coppotelli, 1982; Coie & Kupersmidt, 1983; French & Wass, 1985; Ladd & Price, 1987).

Do popular children become popular because they are friendly, cooperative, and nonaggressive? Or is it that children become friendlier, more cooperative, and less aggressive after achieving their popularity? One way to test these competing hypotheses is to place children in play groups with *unfamiliar* peers and then see whether the patterns of behavior they display will predict their eventual status in the peer group. Several studies of this type have been conducted

(Coie & Kupersmidt, 1983; Dodge, 1983; Putallaz, 1983), and the results are reasonably consistent: the patterns of behavior that children display do predict the statuses they will achieve with their peers. Children who attain high status in the peer group tend to be warm and outgoing, and above all, *they know how to reward other children*. These popular youngsters are particularly skillful at initiating interactions, at giving attention or approval, and at complying with instructions or responding positively to others' bids for attention. Rather than bullying their way into a new group, children who ultimately attain high status will first attempt to understand the group's activities and then slowly make their entry, so as not to be perceived as pushy, disruptive, and self-serving. By contrast, children who will eventually be rejected by their peers are more likely to force themselves on the group and to insult, threaten, hit, or otherwise mistreat their new playmates (particularly if their intrusive social overtures are not well received), whereas passive youngsters who initiate few interactions and who shy away from others' bids for attention are likely to be ignored or neglected. Fortunately, both these groups of unpopular children can often be helped to achieve better peer relations through the kinds of social-skills training described in Box 12-2.

---

of self-sacrifice is almost never made for a mere acquaintance (Kanfer, Stifter, & Morris, 1981).

Children continue to respond more positively to friends than to nonfriends throughout the grade school years. When 6- to 8-year-olds play a tower-building game under cooperative or competitive guidelines, groups of friends do not necessarily build bigger towers than groups of acquaintances. However, friends are more talkative, pay closer attention to equity rules (for example, "If we take turns, we'll all make more points"), and usually direct their remarks to the group ("Let's do it this way") rather than to each other as individuals ("Put your block over there") (Newcomb, Brady, & Hartup, 1979). Friends don't always agree with each other. But as we noted in Chapter 12, disagreeing friends are more likely than

disagreeing acquaintances to fully explain the basis for their conflicting points of view and, thus, to provide each other with information that might foster the development of role-taking skills (Nelson & Aboud, 1985), as well as an ability to compromise.

We have seen that children's conceptions of friendship progress from a somewhat "egocentric" orientation in the early grade school years (that is, friends do what I like to do) to a more "empathic" orientation in later childhood and adolescence (that is, friends should recognize each other's needs and give help or emotional support whenever it is required). These changing views of the obligations of friendship are readily detectable in situations where children must pit their own personal interests against the needs of a friend. Thomas

Photo 16-6. Sometimes nothing is as reassuring as the affection and encouragement of a friend.

Berndt and his associates (Berndt, Hawkins, & Hoyle, 1986) recently had pairs of fourth-graders and pairs of eighth-graders work on a task in which they could choose to compete (and thereby maximize their own personal outcomes at the expense of the partner) or cooperate (thus enabling both of them to perform the task well). Fourth-graders were observed to compete more with friends than with acquaintances. They tended to view the task as a competitive one and seemed to be especially concerned about the prospect that a close friend would do better and thereby show them up. By contrast, eighth-graders chose to compete more with acquaintances than with friends and were more likely than fourth-graders to say that friends stress equality in their interactions. Clearly, these findings are consistent with the notion that friendships become more other-oriented and mutually supportive as children approach adolescence.

What roles might friends play in social development?

Do friends play a unique role in a child's social development? Do children who have established adequate peer relations but no close friendships turn out any different from those who have a number of these "special" companions? And might having a close friend or two help to protect a child against the problems associated with having a rejecting parent, being a rejectee in the eyes of most peers, or suffering other stresses such as parental divorce? Unfortunately, no one can answer these questions, for long-term studies of the effects of friendship have yet to be conducted. Nevertheless, the data we have reviewed might permit us to speculate a bit about the roles played by friends as socializing agents.

The fact that children respond more constructively to novel environments in the presence of friends suggests that friendships offer an emotional safety net— a kind of security that not only makes children a little bolder when faced with new challenges but may also make almost any other form of stress (for example, family dissolution, a rejecting parent) a little easier to bear. Indeed, we saw in Chapter 15 that children who respond most constructively to their parents' divorce are those who have the support of friends whose parents are also divorced.

Since friendships are usually described as pleasant or rewarding relationships that are worth preserving, children should be highly motivated to resolve any conflicts with these "special" companions. We've noted that disagreements among friends may foster the development of role-taking skills because friends try harder than acquaintances to fully explain the bases for their conflicting points of view. And given the possibility that one may lose something (or someone) valuable should conflicts remain unresolved, it is likely that squabbles among friends provide an impetus for compromise and cooperation that is simply not present to the same degree in interactions among acquaintances.

Although friendships of all ages are *reciprocal* relationships, we've seen that they are characterized by increasing intimacy and mutuality from middle childhood through adolescence. Could these relatively intense and intimate ties to what are overwhelmingly same-sex companions be necessary for the development of the deep interpersonal sensitivity and commitment so often observed in stable adult love relationships? Harry Stack Sullivan (1953) thought so. Sullivan reported that many of his mentally disturbed patients had failed to form close friendships when they were young, and he concluded that the close bonds that develop between same-sex friends (or "chums") during preadolescence provide the foundation of caring and compassion that a person needs to establish and maintain intimate love relationships (as well as close friendships) later in life.

So there are good reasons to suspect that close friends and friendships contribute in unique and important ways to social and personality development, and it will be interesting to see whether our speculations pan out in the years ahead as researchers begin to study the long-term implications of having (or not having) friends.

Mechanisms of Peer (and Peer-Group) Influence

To this point, we have seen that it is important for children to establish and maintain good peer relations because they will acquire many competent and adaptive patterns of social behavior through their interactions with peers. And exactly how do peers influence children? In many of the same ways that parents do—by reinforcing, modeling, discussing, and, in some cases, pressuring one another to comply with the values and behaviors they condone.

Peers as reinforcing agents

It is easy to see that parents, teachers, and other powerful authority figures are in a position to reward or punish the behavior of children. Yet, we might legitimately wonder whether a peer, who shares a similar status with the child, can become an effective agent of reinforcement. Wonder no longer—the evidence is clear: peers are rather potent sources of reinforcement.

Consider what Michael Lamb and his associates found while observing the reactions of 3- to 5-year-olds to their playmates' sex-appropriate or sex-inappropriate (cross-sex) activities. Children generally reinforced their companions for sex-appropriate play and were quick to criticize or disrupt a playmate's cross-sex activities. But were these playmates influenced by the treatment they received? Indeed they were. Children who were reinforced for sex-appropriate play tended to

keep playing, while those who were punished for sex-inappropriate play usually terminated this activity in less than a minute (Lamb, Easterbrooks, & Holden, 1980).

The reinforcers that children provide one another are often subtle or unintentional. For example, if Joey cries or withdraws when Rocky snatches a toy away from him, Joey may be unintentionally *reinforcing* his tormentor's aggressive behavior by allowing Rocky to obtain the toy at little or no cost. If so, Rocky should become more likely to attack Joey in the future. In an observational study of 3–5-year-olds, Gerald Patterson and his associates (Patterson, Littman, & Bricker, 1967) found that the most frequent victims of aggression were those children who often reinforced their attackers by crying, withdrawing, or giving in. And what happens if a victim suddenly begins to "punish" his tormentors by fighting back? Patterson et al. found that this strategy often persuaded the attackers to back off and seek new victims. Of course, victims who learn to repel their tormentors by counterattacking may conclude that aggression is a very rewarding activity and become more aggressive themselves. Indeed, few children remained chronic victims from session to session, and it was not at all unusual for one week's victim to become a later week's victimizer (Patterson et al., 1967).

So peers *are* important sources of social reinforcement. Although we have sampled but two studies from a voluminous literature, the evidence clearly indicates that children's social behaviors are often strengthened, maintained, or virtually eliminated by the favorable or unfavorable reactions they elicit from peers.

Peers as social models

Peers influence one another by serving not only as reinforcing and punishing agents but also as social models. For example, we have seen that children who are afraid of dogs will often overcome their phobic reactions after witnessing another child playing with these once-terrifying creatures (see Box 7-4). Among the other attributes and activities that are easily acquired by observing peer models are socially responsive behaviors (Cooke & Apolloni, 1976), achievement behaviors (see Sagotsky & Lepper, 1982), moral judgments (Dorr & Fey, 1974), an ability to delay gratification (Stumphauzer, 1972), and sex-typed attitudes and behaviors (Ruble, Balaban, & Cooper, 1981), to name a few. You may recall that several of these findings were discussed at length in earlier chapters.

Another function that peer models serve is to inform the child how he or she is supposed to behave in different situations. For example, a new child at school may not know whether it is acceptable to visit the water fountain during a study period without first asking the teacher—but she will quickly conclude that this behavior is allowed if she sees her classmates doing it.

The imitator's effect on the imitated.

Do children like to be imitated by their peers? Apparently so. In an interesting observational study, Joan Grusec and Rona Abramovitch (1982) found that when one preschool child imitated another, the model usually reacted very positively to his or her mimic by smiling, laughing, and even imitating the imitator, thereby prolonging a pleasant social interaction. This finding raises an interesting question: Do children learn to imitate their peers as a means of establishing friendly relations or influencing their companions? To find out, Mark Thelen and his associates (Thelen, Miller, Fehrenbach, Frautschi, & Fishbein, 1980) asked some fourth-, fifth-, and sixth-graders to do whatever they could to influence a younger peer to eat some horrible-tasting crackers (social-influence condition). Other children were not asked to influence the behavior of the peer (control condition). Before the crackers were to be eaten, each subject and his or her companion played a game, and the investigators noted how often subjects chose to imitate the strategies of their younger playmates. The results were clear: children who had been told to influence a younger child imitated that child's behavior to a much greater extent than those in the control group did. So it seems that children do like to be imitated and that their imitators know it.[3] And when do children begin to imitate as a means of establishing friendly relations or influencing their playmates? Perhaps as early as age 3, for Steve Dollinger and Melissa Gasser (1981) report that 3–5-year-olds who were instructed to influence a companion reliably chose to imitate the companion's behavior.

Peers as objects for social comparison.

Finally, children often reach conclusions about their competencies and other personality attributes by comparing their behaviors and accomplishments against those displayed by peers. If a 10-year-old consistently outperforms all her classmates on math tests, she is apt to conclude that she is "smart" or at least "good in math." A 6-year-old who loses every footrace that he has with peers will soon come to think of himself as a slow runner. Because peers are similar in age (and are presumed to be reasonably similar in many other respects), the peer group is the most logical choice for these kinds of *social comparisons* (see Festinger, 1954; France-Kaatrude & Smith, 1985). It matters little to our "smart" 10-year-old that she knows less math than her teenage sister. And our "snaillike" 6-year-old is not at all comforted by the fact that he can run faster than his 4-year-old brother. In matters of social comparison and self-definition, peers simply have no peer.

The normative function of "peer groups"

One of the most important ways that peers influence one another is by forming groups and setting norms that define how group members are supposed to look, think, and act. You may recall from your own childhood that pressures to conform to group norms are often intense and that those who ignore the dictates of their peers risk all sorts of penalties, ranging from simply being labeled a "nerd" to outright rejection. For many youngsters, it is quite an accomplishment to be accepted as "one of the gang" while somehow maintaining respectability in the eyes of parents, teachers, and other important adults.

Characteristics of true "peer groups."

It is difficult to specify the exact age at which group membership becomes important to a child. When social developmentalists talk about true **"peer groups,"** they are referring not merely to a collection of playmates but, rather, to a confederation that (1) interacts on a regular basis, (2) defines a sense of belonging, (3) shares implicit or explicit norms that specify how members are supposed to behave, and (4) develops a structure or hierarchical organization that enables the membership to work together toward the accomplishment of shared goals. Older nursery school children do share common interests, assume different roles while playing together, and conform to loosely defined norms or rules of conduct. But the membership of these preschool "play groups" may fluctuate from day to day, and the guidelines to which the children conform are often laid down by adults. The group activities of elementary school children, however, are very different. Members now share

---

[3]Of course, there are exceptions to this general rule. For example, a child who is mimicked in a derisive way or who has had a creative idea copied by her less competent peers is likely to be anything but flattered (Thelen & Kirkland, 1976).

norms that *they* have had a hand in creating, and they begin to assume stable roles or "statuses" within the peer society. Moreover, elementary school children clearly identify with their groups; to be a "Brownie," a "Blue Knight," or "one of Smitty's gang" is often a source of great personal pride. So it seems that middle childhood (ages 6–10) is the period when children are assuming membership in what we can call true peer groups.

Conformity to peer pressure. It is often assumed that children become increasingly responsive to peer pressure as they grow older and that adolescence is the period when the peer group has its greatest influence. Clearly there is an element of truth to these ideas. If peers are trying to convince an individual to partake in some kind of questionable or *antisocial* conduct, there is a curvilinear relationship between age and conformity: children become more and more inclined to go along with their peers between the ages of 6 and 15 but are then less and less likely to accede to deviant peer pressure from midadolescence onward (Berndt, 1979; Brown, Clasen, & Eicher, 1986; Steinberg & Silverberg, 1986). Yet, it is important to note that adolescents are not the "blind conformists" that our stereotypes would seem to suggest, for teenagers are much *less* likely than younger children to yield to peer influence when the norms or judgments of the peer group are nonsensical or lacking in credibility (Hamm, 1970; Hoving, Hamm, & Galvin, 1969). So even though the need for peer approval increases dramatically between childhood and early to middle adolescence, it seems that this approval motive may often be overridden by autonomy needs or by a desire to be correct (Hoving et al., 1969; Steinberg & Silverberg, 1986).

Peer versus Adult Influence: The Question of Cross-Pressures

Adolescence is often characterized as a stormy period when all children experience **cross-pressures**—severe conflicts between the practices advocated by parents and those favored by peers. How do they react to these conflicting demands? It is commonly assumed that parents and other adults make a stronger impression on the young child but that peers gradually become more influential than parents as children approach adolescence.

Ken Hoving and his associates tested this hypothesis by asking 8-, 10-, 12-, 14-, and 16-year-olds what a child should do in each of ten situations in which parents and peers gave conflicting advice. For example:

Susan likes music and is trying to decide whether to join the band or the choir. Her *mother and father think* that being in the band would be more fun because the band plays at all the basketball and football games. Susan's *friends think* that she would have more fun in the choir because the choir goes to many towns to sing. What do you think Susan will decide to do?

1. Do as her parents say and join the *band*.
2. Do as her friends say and join the *choir*.

Responsiveness to peers steadily increased with age. In other words, the older the subjects, the more likely they were to discount the advice of parents and favor the opinions of the peer group (Hamm & Hoving, 1971; Utech & Hoving, 1969). Berndt (1979) found a similar pattern of results, noting that peer influence increases most dramatically with age (at least through early adolescence) on matters of *antisocial* conduct. Similarly, Ed Bixenstine and his colleagues (Bixenstine, DeCorte, & Bixenstine, 1976) found an increase between the ages of 9 and 16 in children's readiness to participate in mischievous acts designed to annoy adults, such as soaping windows on Halloween.

Situational determinants of adolescents' reactions to cross-pressures

Although young adolescents are heavily influenced by their peers, there are situations in which they will typically react to cross-pressures by favoring the advice of their parents. *Peers* are likely to be more influential than parents in conflicts involving social activities, friendship choices, or questions of interpersonal and group identity; however, adolescents often prefer the advice of *parents* to that of peers whenever the issue involves scholastic goals or future-oriented decisions and aspirations (Brittain, 1963; Hunter, 1985; Sebald, 1986). Perhaps it is fair to say that peers are the primary reference group for questions of the form "Who am I?," whereas the advice of parents, teachers, and other significant adults will carry more weight when teenagers grapple with the question "Who am I to be?"

---

peer group: a confederation of peers who interact regularly, share norms, and work together toward the accomplishment of shared goals.

cross-pressures: conflicts between the practices advocated by parents and those favored by peers.

How important are these cross-pressures?

Even though 12- to 16-year-olds are so highly susceptible to peer influence, most parents need not worry about having protracted wars with their teenagers or about losing them to subversive peer groups (Hartup, 1983). It seems that adolescents who have established warm relations with parents who are neither too controlling nor too lax will rarely experience intense cross-pressures (Bixenstine et al., 1976; Brook, Whiteman, & Gordon, 1983). They have often internalized many of their parents' most basic values and, thus, may have little need to rebel or to desperately seek acceptance from peers when they are so warmly received at home. Fortunately, most adolescents do enjoy reasonably cordial relations with their parents and very much want their parents' approval (Youniss & Smollar, 1985). And even when teenagers are at odds with a parent over status issues, privileges, or academic matters, these disagreements do not necessarily make them any more susceptible to peer influence. In fact, Raymond Montemayor (1982) finds that adolescents who argue a lot with their mothers will often react to these conflicts by spending more time alone or with their fathers rather than becoming more involved with peers.

A second reason that the cross-pressures "problem" is not all that disruptive for most adolescents is that the values of the peer group are rarely as deviant as people have commonly assumed. Indeed, even though children perceive more peer pressure for deviant or antisocial conduct as they mature, it is important to emphasize that one's friends and associates are more likely to advise *against* or otherwise *discourage* antisocial behavior than to condone it (Brown et al., 1986). And on many issues for which parental and peer norms might seem to be in conflict, the child's behavior is actually a product of *both* parental and peer influences. Consider the following example. Denise Kandel (1973) studied a group of adolescents whose best friends either did or did not smoke marijuana and whose parents either did or did not use psychoactive drugs. Among those teenagers whose parents used drugs but whose friends did not, only 17% were marijuana users. When parents did not use drugs but best friends did, 56% of the adolescents were marijuana users. From these findings, we can conclude that the peer group is more influential than parents over marijuana use. However, the highest rate of marijuana smoking (67%) occurred among teenagers whose parents and peers *both* used psychoactive drugs,

and a similar pattern emerges when we look at parental and peer influences on use of alcohol and tobacco (Chassin, Presson, Sherman, Montello, & McGrew, 1986; Glynn, 1981; Krosnick & Judd, 1982). The implication is clear: rather than thinking about childhood or adolescent socialization as an issue of parents *versus* peers, we must now determine how parental and peer influences combine to affect developing children.

Some theorists have argued that peers eventually become the primary reference group on issues for which the opinions of an individual's parents and peers are generally *similar* but *varying in extremity* (for example, ideas about an acceptable curfew, appropriate conduct on a date, or access to the family car). Although this conclusion may well be correct, it may also underestimate the full impact of adult influence because the way peers feel about a particular behavior is often an expression of the *average level of parental support* for that behavior among the parents of *all* group members (Siman, 1977). For example, if a 17-year-old stays out with her friends until 11 P.M. when her parents want her in at 10, she may be returning home at a time that her friends' parents think is perfectly acceptable. She is rebellious by her parents' standards but not by those of other parents or the peer group. So parents have an effect on peer-group norms, and an adolescent's response to many issues may depend more on the group atmosphere (that is, the average parental opinion) than on the position of her own parents. The implication is that peer groups act as a filter for the attitudes and opinions of individual parents, serving to reinterpret these standards as reasonable or unreasonable and thereby exerting a powerful influence on an adolescent's attitudes, values, and behavior.

Cross-Cultural Variations in Peer Influence

We have seen that the peer group plays a very important role in the social and emotional development of American children. However, the United States is often characterized as a rather atypical, youth-oriented culture whose younger constituents (and, indeed, many of their elders) seem obsessed with the notions that "young is beautiful" and that "people over 30 are not to be trusted." This perspective is very different from that of many Oriental cultures, in which children soon learn to respect their elders and to treat the ideas of the aged as "words of wisdom" (Benedict, 1946). In many nonindustrialized societies, young boys and girls are routinely

Photo 16-7. Although teenagers are often characterized as wild or rebellious, typically their norms and values are a reflection of adult society.

assigned chores and responsibilities that restrict their opportunities for play (Leacock, 1971), and children in certain ethnic groups within Western societies may spend little time with peers because they are strongly encouraged to stay at home for family activities (Laosa, 1981). So there are reasons to believe that patterns of peer interaction and the nature of peer-group influences may vary considerably from culture to culture.

To date, the most extensive work on peer-group influences in other societies has been conducted by Urie Bronfenbrenner and his colleagues at Cornell University (Bronfenbrenner, 1967; Bronfenbrenner, Devereux, Suci, & Rodgers, 1965; Devereux, 1970). The subjects for these studies were 11–12-year-olds from England, Germany, the Soviet Union, and the United States. The children were asked to respond to a "dilemmas test" that consisted of 30 hypothetical situations, each of which pitted a norm endorsed by adults against peer pressure to deviate from that norm. Here is an example (Bronfenbrenner, 1967, p. 201):

You and your friends accidentally find a sheet of paper which the teacher must have lost. On this sheet are the questions and answers for a quiz that you are going to have tomorrow. Some of the kids suggest that you not say anything to the teacher about it, so that all of you can get better marks. What would you really do? Suppose your friends decide to go ahead. Would you go along with them or refuse?

Refuse to go along with my friends
Absolutely certain   Fairly certain   I guess so
or
Go along with my friends
Absolutely certain   Fairly certain   I guess so

Other dilemmas included situations such as neglecting homework to be with friends, wearing fashions approved by peers but not adults, and collaborating with friends to steal fruit from an orchard marked with "No Trespassing" signs.

Bronfenbrenner found that Russian children showed the greatest resistance to these deviant peer influences. U.S. and German children were more likely to go along with their peers than the Russians were, and English children showed the greatest willingness to take part in peer-sponsored misconduct. In all four cultures, boys showed more conformity to deviant peer influences than girls.

Further analyses revealed that the U.S., English, and German children who spent the most time with their peers were the ones who were more likely to say that they would participate in the deviant activities of the peer group. Yet, the amount of contact that a child had with peers was not the only factor that influenced his or her reactions to peer pressure. Both Soviet and American children have a great deal of contact with their peers during the first few years at school. However, these two groups react to examples of peer-sponsored misconduct in very different ways. Consider the following example.

Bronfenbrenner (1967) had Russian and American children take his "dilemmas test" under three conditions: (1) a *neutral* condition in which they were told that their answers would be confidential, (2) an *adult exposure* condition in which they believed that their answers would be seen by parents and teachers, and (3) a *peer exposure* condition in which they were told that their answers would be shown to their classmates. In both cultures, children assigned to the adult-exposure conditions were more likely than those in the neutral condition to conform to the socially desirable (adult) norms. However, the peer-exposure condition produced different reactions from the Soviet and the American samples. Soviet children responded as if their answers would be shown to adults—that is, their conformity to adult norms *increased* compared with their classmates in the neutral condition. By contrast, American children became much more willing to conform to the *deviant peer norms* when they were led to believe that classmates would see their answers.

So here are two groups of children, both of whom have a substantial amount of contact with their peers. Yet, members of one group (the Americans) often support peer-sponsored misconduct, while members of the second group (the Russians) do not. The reasons for this cultural difference become clearer if we look carefully at how Soviet children are socialized. Bronfenbrenner (1970a) points out that Russian educators use the peer group as an instrument for teaching and continually reinforcing the important sociopolitical values of Soviet society—values such as cooperation, teamwork, and group *esprit*. Children in a typical Russian classroom are divided into teams and encouraged to take part in cooperative, team-oriented activities. These teams frequently test their physical and academic skills against one another in regularly scheduled competitions, and group spirit is strengthened by administering rewards on the basis of team, rather than individual, accomplishments. Not surprisingly, Russian children learn to evaluate the individual in terms of his or her contributions to group goals, and indeed, they are instructed to keep tabs on their teammates, to assist them whenever possible, and to publicly censure those who are not inclined to "pull their weight." These lessons are apparently learned at an early age, as we see in the following conversations among third-graders:

> "Work more carefully" says Olga to her girlfriend. "See, on account of you our group got behind today. You come to me and we'll work together at home."
> Group leader to his classmates: "Today Valodya did the wrong problem. Marsha didn't write neatly and forgot to underline the right words in her lesson. Alyosha had a dirty shirt collar" [Bronfenbrenner, 1970a, p. 60].

In sum, the Soviet peer group is an extension of the adult sociopolitical system, whereas U.S. children are given a bit more leeway to evolve their own rules, norms, and customs—some of which will inevitably conflict with adult standards. Clearly, the peer group is an important socializing agent for both Russian and American children, and it would be inappropriate to conclude that Russians are less responsive than Americans to peer-group pressure. In fact, the Russian schoolchildren in Bronfenbrenner's (1967) study probably refused to endorse the misconduct of *hypothetical* peers because they expected little if any approval from their *real* classmates for doing so.

Summary

In this chapter we have focused on three extrafamilial agents of socialization: television, schools, and children's peer groups. When television became widely available, children soon began to watch it and spend less time in other leisure activities. Television programming is often violent, and there is evidence that a heavy diet of televised violence can instigate antisocial behavior and make children more tolerant of aggression. Television is also an important source of knowledge about people in the outside world. But, unfortunately, the information that children receive is often inaccurate and misleading—frequently consisting of stereotyped portrayals of men, women, and various racial and ethnic groups. Children are also influenced by television commercials, often becoming angry or resentful if a parent refuses to buy a product that they have requested.

Yet, the effects of television are not all bad. Children are likely to learn prosocial lessons and to put them into practice after watching acts of kindness on television. Parents can help by watching shows such as *Mister Rogers' Neighborhood* with their children and then encouraging them to verbalize or role-play the prosocial lessons they have observed. Educational programs such as *Sesame Street* and *The Electric Company* have been quite successful at fostering basic cognitive skills, particularly when children watch with an adult who discusses the material with them and helps them to apply what they have learned.

By age 6, children are spending several hours of each weekday at school. Schools seem to have two missions: to impart academic knowledge and to teach children how to become "good citizens." Schooling also appears to facilitate cognitive development by teaching children general rules, or intellectual strategies, that help them to solve problems.

Some schools are more "effective" than others at producing positive outcomes such as low absenteeism, an enthusiastic attitude about learning, academic achievement, occupational skills, and socially desirable patterns of behavior. Several factors, such as a school's resources, school and class size, and the ways classes and classrooms are organized, have been proposed as possible contributors to effective schooling. It turns out that "effective" schools are those in which the staff works together to achieve well-defined educational objectives. Teachers are helpful and supportive rather than commanding and punitive. The emphasis is on pupils' successes rather than failures, and students receive ample praise and recognition for good work. In short, the effective school environment is a comfortable but businesslike setting in which pupils are motivated to learn.

Traditionally, the task of motivating students has been assigned to classroom instructors. Teacher expectancies may create a self-fulfilling prophecy: students usually do well when teachers expect them to succeed, whereas they tend to fall short of their potential when teachers expect them to do poorly. Teaching style can also affect pupil outcomes. Generally speaking, it appears that an authoritative style is more likely than either authoritarian or permissive instruction to motivate stu-

dents to do their best. Yet, even the authoritative teacher may have to use different instructional techniques with different children in order to "get the most out of" each pupil.

The middle-class bias of most schools may hinder the academic progress of disadvantaged children or those from minority subcultures. Textbooks and other materials tend to portray middle-class values and experiences that may seem irrelevant and uninteresting to these students. Parents of lower-class children are often less knowledgeable about the school system, less involved in school activities, and less likely to encourage their children to excel in the classroom. Middle-class teachers are often more negative in their interactions with lower-income and minority students and do not expect them to do well. All these factors may contribute to the low levels of academic achievement often seen among disadvantaged and minority populations. It was hoped that school desegregation would help to cure some of these ills. Although minority students often do achieve more in integrated schools, there is little evidence that desegregation has accomplished other important goals such as reducing racial prejudice or raising minority students' self-esteem. However, newly developed cooperative learning programs hold some promise of making "integration" a more positive and fruitful experience for minority groups and the handicapped.

Peer contacts represent a second world for children—a world of equal-status interactions that is very different from the nonegalitarian environment of the home. Contacts with peers increase dramatically with age, and during the preschool or early elementary school years, children are spending at least as much of their leisure time with peers as with adults. The "peer group" consists mainly of *same sex* playmates of *different ages*. Indeed, developmentalists define peers as "those who interact at similar levels of behavioral complexity," because only a small percentage of the child's associates are actually age mates.

Research with monkeys and young children indicates that peer contacts are important for the development of competent and adaptive patterns of social behavior. Children who fail to establish and maintain adequate relations with their peers will run the risk of experiencing any number of severe emotional disturbances later in life. Among the factors that contribute to peer acceptance are secure emotional attachments to parents, physical attributes such as an attractive face, a mesomorphic physique, and early maturation, a popular name, good role-taking skills, and being a later-born child. Popular children are generally friendlier, more supportive, more cooperative, and less aggressive than unpopular children.

Children typically form close ties, or friendships, with one or more members of their play groups. Younger children view a friend as a harmonious playmate, whereas older children and adolescents think of friends as intimate companions who share similar interests and are willing to provide them with emotional support when it is needed. Although the roles that friends play in a child's social development have not been firmly established, it is likely that solid friendships (1) provide a sense of security that enables children to respond more constructively to stresses and challenges, (2) promote the development of role-taking skills and an ability to compromise, and (3) foster the growth of caring and compassionate feelings that are the foundation of intimate love relationships later in life.

Peers influence a child in many of the same ways that parents do—by modeling, reinforcing, and discussing the behaviors and values that they condone. During middle childhood, children form peer groups, evolve norms, and begin to pressure group members to conform to these normative codes of conduct. Susceptibility to peer influence peaks at early to middle adolescence, although even then, teenagers are hardly blind conformists. Children's reactions to cross-pressures depend on their age and the issue in question. In situations involving status norms, friendship choices, or questions of personal and group identity, children become increasingly responsive to peers as they mature. But even older children and adolescents prefer the advice of parents to that of peers in situations involving scholastic matters or future aspirations. Cross-pressures are not a major problem for most children, because the values of the peer group are often reasonably consistent with those of parents and other adults.

The influence of peer groups differs somewhat from culture to culture. For example, the Soviet peer group is a mechanism for teaching and maintaining the adult value system, and compliance with adult norms is rather uniform. By contrast, American children are allowed greater freedom to formulate their own rules, norms, and customs, some of which will inevitably conflict with adult standards.

References

ADAMS, G. R., & Crane, P. (1980). An assessment of parents' and teachers' expectations of preschool children's social preference for attractive or unattractive children and adults. *Child Development, 51,* 224–231.

ALEXANDER, B. K., & Harlow, H. F. (1965). Social behavior in juvenile rhesus monkeys subjected to different rearing conditions during the first 6 months of life. *Zoologische Jarbucher Physiologie, 60,* 167–174.

AMES, L. B. (1981, March). Retention in grade can be a step forward. *Education Digest,* pp. 36–37.

ASHER, S. R., & Wheeler, V. A. (1985). Children's loneliness: A comparison of rejected and neglected peer status. *Journal of Consulting and Clinical Psychology, 53,* 500–505.

ATKIN, C. (1978). Observation of parent-child interaction in supermarket decision-making. *Journal of Marketing, 42,* 41–45.

BALL, S., & Bogatz, C. (1970). *The first year of Sesame Street: An evaluation.* Princeton, NJ: Educational Testing Service.

BALL, S., & Bogatz, C. (1973). *Reading with television: An evaluation of The Electric Company.* Princeton, NJ: Educational Testing Service.

BARKER, R. G., & Gump, P. V. (1964). *Big school, small school.* Stanford, CA: Stanford University Press.

BARKER, R. G., & Wright, H. F. (1955). *Midwest and its children.* New York: Harper & Row.

BAUMRIND, D. (1972). From each according to her ability. *School Review, 80,* 161–197.

BENEDICT, R. (1946). *The chrysanthemum and the sword.* Boston: Houghton Mifflin.

BERNDT, T. J. (1979). Developmental changes in conformity to peers and parents. *Developmental Psychology, 15,* 608–616.

BERNDT, T. J. (1981). Age changes and changes over time in prosocial intentions and behavior between friends. *Developmental Psychology, 17,* 408–416.

BERNDT, T. J., Hawkins, J. A., & Hoyle, S. G. (1986). Changes in friendship during a school year: Effects on children's and adolescents' impressions of friendship and sharing with friends. *Child Development, 57,* 1284–1297.

BIGELOW, B. J. (1977). Children's friendship expectations: A cognitive-developmental study. *Child Development, 48,* 246–253.

BIGELOW, B. J., & LaGaipa, J. J. (1975). Children's written descriptions of friendship: A multidimensional analysis. *Developmental Psychology, 11,* 857–858.

BIXENSTINE, V. C., DeCorte, M. S., & Bixenstine, B. A. (1976). Conformity to peer-sponsored misconduct at four grade levels. *Developmental Psychology, 12,* 226–236.

BOGATZ, G. A., & Ball, S. (1972). *The second year of Sesame Street: A continuing evaluation.* Princeton, NJ: Educational Testing Service.

BRITTAIN, C. V. (1963). Adolescent choices and parent-peer cross pressures. *American Sociological Review, 28,* 358–391.

BRONFENBRENNER, U. (1967). Response to pressures from peers versus adults in Soviet and American school children. *International Journal of Psychology, 2,* 199–207.

BRONFENBRENNER, U. (1970a). *Two worlds of childhood.* New York: Russell Sage Foundation.

BRONFENBRENNER, U. (1970b). *Who cares for America's children?* Invited address presented at the conference of the National Association for the Education of Young Children, Washington, DC.

BRONFENBRENNER, U., Devereux, E. C., Suci,

G., & Rodgers, R. R. (1965). *Adults and peers as sources of conformity and autonomy*. Paper presented at the Conference for Socialization for Competence, San Juan, PR.

BROOK, J. S., Whiteman, M., & Gordon, A. S. (1983). Stages of drug use in adolescence: Personality, peer, and family correlates. *Developmental Psychology, 19,* 269–277.

BROOKOVER, W., Beady, C., Flood, P., Schweitzer, J., & Wisenbaker, J. (1979). *School social systems and student achievement: Schools can make a difference*. New York: Praeger.

BROPHY, J. E. (1979). Teacher behavior and its effects. *Journal of Educational Psychology, 71,* 733–750.

BROPHY, J. E. (1983). Research on the self-fulfilling prophecy and teacher expectations. *Journal of Educational Psychology, 75,* 631–661.

BROWN, B. B., Clasen D. R., & Eicher, S. A. (1986). Perceptions of peer pressure, peer conformity dispositions, and self-reported behavior among adolescents. *Developmental Psychology, 22,* 521–530.

CHASE, J. A. (1968). A study of the impact of grade retention on primary school children. *Journal of Psychology, 70,* 169–177.

CHASSIN, L., Presson, C. C., Sherman, S. J., Montello, D., & McGrew, J. (1986). Changes in peer and parent influence during adolescence: Longitudinal versus cross-sectional perspectives on smoking initiation. *Developmental Psychology, 22,* 327–334.

CLARK, K. B. (1965). *Dark ghetto*. New York: Harper & Row.

CLEMENTS, D. (1986). Effects of Logo and CAI environments on cognition and creativity. *Journal of Educational Psychology, 78,* 309–318.

COATES, B., Pusser, H. E., & Goodman, I. (1976). The influence of "Sesame Street" and "Mister Rogers' Neighborhood" on children's social behavior in the preschool. *Child Development, 47,* 138–144.

COIE, J. D., & Dodge, K. A. (1983). Continuities and changes in children's social status: A five-year longitudinal study. *Merrill-Palmer Quarterly, 19,* 261–282.

COIE, J. D., Dodge, K. A., & Coppotelli, H. (1982). Dimensions and types of social status: A cross-age perspective. *Developmental Psychology, 18,* 557–570.

COIE, J. D., & Kupersmidt, J. B. (1983). A behavioral analysis of emerging social status in boys' groups. *Child Development, 54,* 1400–1416.

COLLINS, W. A., Sobol, B. L., & Westby, S. (1981). Effects of adult commentary on children's comprehension and inferences about a televised aggressive portrayal. *Child Development, 52,* 158–163.

COMMONS, M. L., Richards, F. A., & Kuhn, D. (1982). Systematic and metasystematic reasoning: A case for levels of reasoning beyond Piaget's stage of formal operations. *Child Development, 53,* 1058–1069.

COMSTOCK, G. (1978). *Television and human behavior*. New York: Columbia University Press.

COOK, T. D., Appleton, H., Conner, R. F., Shaffer, A., Tabkin, G., & Weber, J. S. (1975). *Sesame Street revisited*. New York: Russell Sage Foundation.

COOKE, T., & Apolloni, T. (1976). Developing positive social-emotional behaviors: A study of training and generalization effects. *Journal of Applied Behavior Analysis, 9,* 65–78.

COOLING OFF THE TUBE. (1976, September 6). *Newsweek*, pp. 46–47.

COPPERMAN, P. (1978). *The literacy hoax*. New York: William Morrow.

COWEN, E. L., Pederson, A., Babigan, H., Izzo, L. D., & Trost, M. A. (1973). Long-term follow-up of early detected vulnerable children. *Journal of Consulting and Clinical Psychology, 41,* 438–446.

DEVEREUX, E. C. (1970). The role of peer group experience in moral development. In J. P. Hill (Ed.), *Minnesota Symposia on Child Psychology* (Vol. 4). Minneapolis: University of Minnesota Press.

DION, K. K. (1972). Physical attractiveness and evaluations of children's transgressions. *Journal of Personality and Social Psychology, 24,* 207–213.

DODGE, K. A. (1983). Behavioral antecedents of peer social status. *Child Development, 54,* 1386–1399.

DOLLINGER, S. J., & Gasser, M. (1981). Imitation as social influence. *Journal of Genetic Psychology, 138,* 149–150.

DORR, D., & Fey, S. (1974). Relative power of symbolic adult and peer models in the modification of children's moral choice behavior. *Journal of Personality and Social Psychology, 29,* 335–341.

DRABMAN, R. S., & Thomas, M. H. (1974). Does media violence increase children's toleration of real-life aggression? *Developmental Psychology, 10,* 418–421.

DWECK, C. S., & Elliott, E. S. (1983). Achievement motivation. In P. H. Mussen (Ed.), *Handbook of child psychology*. Vol. 4: *Socialization, personality, and social development*. New York: Wiley.

EDUCATIONAL RESEARCH SERVICE. (1978). *Class size: A summary of research*. Arlington, VA: Author.

ELLIS, S., Rogoff, B., & Cromer, C. C. (1981). Age segregation in children's social interactions. *Developmental Psychology, 17,* 399–407.

ERON, L. D. (1980). Prescription for the reduction of aggression. *American Psychologist, 35,* 244–252.

ERON, L. D. (1982). Parent-child interaction, television violence, and aggression of children. *American Psychologist, 37,* 197–211.

ERON, L. D., & Huesmann, L. R. (1984). The control of aggressive behavior by changes in attitudes, values, and the conditions of learning. In R. J. Blanchard & C. Blanchard (Eds.), *Advances in the study of aggression* (Vol. 2). Orlando, FL: Academic Press.

ERON, L. D., Huesmann, L. R., Brice, P., Fischer, P., & Mermelstein, R. (1983). Age trends in the development of aggression, sex-typing, and related television habits. *Developmental Psychology, 19,* 71–77.

ERON, L. D., Huesmann, L. R., Lefkowitz, M. M., & Walder, L. O. (1972). Does television violence cause aggression? *American Psychologist, 27,* 253–263.

FESTINGER, L. (1954). A theory of social comparison processes. *Human Relations, 7,* 117–140.

FINKELSTEIN, N. W., & Haskins, R. (1983). Kindergarten children prefer same-color peers. *Child Development, 54,* 502–508.

FLAVELL, J. H. (1986). The development of children's knowledge about the appearance-reality distinction. *American Psychologist, 41,* 418–425.

FRANCE-KAATRUDE, A., & Smith, W. P. (1985). Social comparison, task motivation, and the development of self-evaluative standards in children. *Developmental Psychology, 21,* 1080–1089.

FRENCH, D. C. (1984). Children's knowledge of the social functions of younger, older, and same-age peers. *Child Development, 55,* 1429–1433.

FRENCH, D. C., & Wass, G. A. (1985). Behavioral problems of peer-neglected and peer-rejected elementary-age children: Parent and teacher perspectives. *Child Development, 56,* 246–252.

FRENCH, D. C., Wass, G. A., Stright, A. L., & Baker, J. A. (1986). Leadership asymmetries in mixed-age children's groups. *Child Development, 57,* 1277–1283.

FREUD, A., & Dann, S. (1951). An experiment in group upbringing. In R. Eisler, A. Freud, H. Hartmann, & E. Kris (Eds.), *The psychoanalytic study of the child* (Vol. 6). New York: International Universities Press.

FRIEDRICH, L. K., & Stein, A. H. (1973). Aggressive and prosocial television programs and the natural behavior of preschool children. *Monographs of the Society for Research in Child Development, 38* (4, Serial No. 51).

FRIEDRICH, L. K., & Stein, A. H. (1975). Prosocial television and young children: The effects of verbal labeling and role-playing on learning and behavior. *Child Development, 46,* 27–38.

FRIEDRICH-COFER, L. K., Huston-Stein, A., Kipnis, D. M., Susman, E. J., & Clewett, A. S. (1979). Environmental enhancement of prosocial television content: Effects on interpersonal behavior. *Developmental Psychology, 15,* 637–646.

FULKERSON, K. F., Furr, S., & Brown, D. (1983). Expectations and achievement among third-, sixth-, and ninth-grade black and white males and females. *Developmental Psychology, 19,* 231–236.

FURMAN, W., & Bierman, K. L. (1983). Developmental changes in young children's conceptions of friendship. *Child Development, 54,* 549–556.

FURMAN, W., & Masters, J. C. (1980). Peer interactions, sociometric status, and resistance to deviation in young children. *Developmental Psychology, 16,* 229–236.

GALST, J. P. (1980). Television food commercials and pronutritional public service announcements as determinants of young children's snack choices. *Child Development, 51,* 935–938.

GERBNER, G., Gross, L., Morgan, M., & Signorielli, N. (1980). The "mainstreaming" of America: Violence profile no. 11. *Journal of Communication, 30,* 10–29.

GLYNN, T. J. (1981). From family to peer: A review of transitions of influence among drug-using youth. *Journal of Youth and Adolescence, 10,* 363–383.

GOOD, T. L. (1979). Teacher effectiveness in the elementary school: What do we know about it now? *Journal of Teacher Education, 30,* 52–64.

GORN, G. J., Goldberg, M. E., & Kanungo, R. N. (1976). The role of educational television in changing the intergroup attitudes of children. *Child Development, 47,* 277–280.

GOTTLIEB, D. (1966). Teaching and students: The views of Negro and white teachers. *Sociology of Education, 37,* 344–353.

GRAVES, S. B. (1975, April). *How to encourage positive racial attitudes.* Paper presented at the biennial meeting of the Society for Research in Child Development, Denver.

GRAZIANO, W. G., Musser, L. M., & Brody, G. H. (1982). *Children's cognitions and preferences regarding younger and older peers.*

Unpublished manuscript, University of Georgia.

GREEN, J. A., & Gerard, H. B. (1974). School desegregation and ethnic attitudes. In H. Franklin & J. Sherwood (Eds.), *Integrating the organization.* New York: Free Press.

GRUSEC, J. E., & Abramovitch, R. (1982). Imitation of peers and adults in a natural setting: A functional analysis. *Child Development, 53,* 636–642.

HALLINAN, M. T., & Teixeira, R. A. (1987). Opportunities and constraints: Black-white differences in the formation of interracial friendships. *Child Development, 58,* 1358–1371.

HAMM, N. H. (1970). A partial test of a social learning theory of children's conformity. *Journal of Experimental Child Psychology, 9,* 29–42.

HAMM, N. H., & Hoving, K. L. (1971). Conformity in children as a function of grade level, and real versus hypothetical adult and peer models. *Journal of Genetic Psychology, 118,* 253–263.

HARARI, H., & McDavid, J. W. (1973). Teachers' expectations and name stereotypes. *Journal of Educational Psychology, 65,* 222–225.

HARRIS, M. J., & Rosenthal, R. (1985). Mediation of interpersonal expectancy effects: 31 meta-analyses. *Psychological Bulletin, 97,* 363–386.

HARTUP, W. W. (1983). Peer relations. In P. H. Mussen (Ed.), *Handbook of child psychology.* Vol. 4: *Socialization, personality, and social development.* New York: Wiley.

HAWKINS, J., Sheingold, K., Gearhart, M., & Berger, C. (1982). Microcomputers in schools: Impact on the social life of elementary classrooms. *Journal of Applied Developmental Psychology, 3,* 361–373.

HESS, R. D. (1970). Social class and ethnic influences on socialization. In P. H. Mussen (Ed.), *Carmichael's manual of child psychology* (Vol. 2). New York: Wiley.

HESS, R. D., & Holloway, S. D. (1984). Family and school as educational institutions. In R. D. Parke (Ed.), *Review of child development research.* Vol. 7: *The family.* Chicago: University of Chicago Press.

HETHERINGTON, E. M. (1981). Children and divorce. In R. W. Henderson (Ed.), *Parent-child interaction: Theory, research and prospects.* Orlando, FL: Academic Press.

HINDE, R. A., Titmus, G., Easton, D., & Tamplin, A. (1985). Incidence of "friendship" and behavior toward strong associates versus nonassociates in preschoolers. *Child Development, 56,* 234–245.

HOFFMAN-PLOTKIN, D., & Twentyman, C. T. (1984). A multimodal assessment of behavioral and cognitive deficits in abused and neglected children. *Child Development, 55,* 794–802.

HORTON, R., & Santogrossi, O. (1978, August). *Mitigating the impact of televised violence through concurrent adult commentary.* Paper presented at the annual meeting of the American Psychological Association, Toronto.

HOVING, K. L., Hamm, N., & Galvin, P. (1969). Social influence as a function of stimulus ambiguity at three age levels. *Developmental Psychology, 6,* 631–636.

HUNTER, F. T. (1985). Adolescents' perception of discussions with parents and friends. *Developmental Psychology, 21,* 433–440.

HUSTON, A., & Wright, J. C. (1982). Effects of communications media on children. In C. B. Kopp & J. B. Krakow (Eds.), *The child: Development in a social context.* Reading, MA: Addison-Wesley.

JACOBSON, J. L., & Wille, D. N. (1986). The influence of attachment pattern on developmental changes in peer interaction from the toddler to the preschool period. *Child Development, 57,* 338–347.

JOHNSON, D. (1981). Naturally acquired learned helplessness: The relationship of school failure to achievement behavior, attributions, and self-concept. *Journal of Educational Psychology, 73,* 174–180.

JOHNSON, N. (1967). *How to talk back to your television.* Boston: Little, Brown.

JOHNSTON, J., Ettema, J., & Davidson, T. (1980). *An evaluation of "Freestyle": A television series designed to reduce sex-role stereotypes.* Ann Arbor, MI: Institute for Social Research.

KAGAN, S., & Zahn, G. L. (1975). Field dependence and the school achievement gap between Anglo-American and Mexican-American children. *Journal of Educational Psychology, 67,* 643–650.

KANDEL, D. (1973). Adolescent marijuana use: Role of parents and peers. *Science, 181,* 1067–1070.

KANFER, F. H., Stifter, E., & Morris, S. J. (1981). Self-control and altruism: Delay of gratification for another. *Child Development, 52,* 674–682.

KEE, D. W. (1986). Computer play. In A. W. Gottfried & C. C. Brown (Eds.), *Play interactions: The contribution of play materials and parental involvement to children's development.* Lexington, MA: Lexington Books.

KEITH, T. Z., Reimers, T. M., Fehrmann, P. G.,

Pottsbaum, S. M., & Aubey, L. W. (1986). Parental involvement, homework, and TV time: Direct and indirect effects on high school achievement. *Journal of Educational Psychology, 78,* 373–380.

KERZNER, R. L. (1982). *The effect of retention on achievement.* Unpublished master's thesis, Kean College.

KOHN, M. L. (1979). The effects of social class on parental values and practices. In D. Reiss & H. A. Hoffman (Eds.), *The American family: Dying or developing?* New York: Plenum.

KROSNICK, J. A., & Judd, C. M. (1982). Transitions in social influence at adolescence: Who induces cigarette smoking. *Developmental Psychology, 18,* 359–368.

KULIK, J. A., Bangert, R. L., & Williams, G. W. (1983). Effects of computer-based teaching on secondary school students. *Journal of Educational Psychology, 75,* 19–26.

LADD, G. W., & Price, J. M. (1987). Predicting children's social and school adjustment following the transition from preschool to kindergarten. *Child Development, 58,* 1168–1189.

LaFRENIERE, P. J., & Sroufe, L. A. (1985). Profiles of peer competence in the preschool: Interrelations between measures, influence of social ecology, and relation to attachment history. *Developmental Psychology, 21,* 56–69.

LAMB, M. E., Easterbrooks, M. A., & Holden, G. W. (1980). Reinforcement and punishment among preschoolers: Characteristics, effects, and correlates. *Child Development, 51,* 1230–1236.

LANGLOIS, J. H. (1986). From the eye of the beholder to behavioral reality: Development of social behaviors and social relations as a function of physical attractiveness. In C. P. Herman, M. P. Zanna, & E. T. Higgins (Eds.), *Physical appearance, stigma, and social behavior: The Ontario Symposium* (Vol. 3). Hillsdale, NJ: Erlbaum.

LANGLOIS, J. H., & Downs, A. C. (1979). Peer relations as a function of physical attractiveness: The eye of the beholder or behavioral reality. *Child Development, 50,* 409–418.

LANGLOIS, J. H., Roggman, L. A., Casey, R. J., Ritter, J. M., Rieser-Danner, L. A., & Jenkins, V. Y. (1987). Infant preferences for attractive faces: Rudiments of a stereotype. *Developmental Psychology, 23,* 363–369.

LANGLOIS, J. H., & Styczynski, L. (1979). The effects of physical attractiveness on the behavioral attributions and peer preferences in acquainted children. *International*

Journal of Behavioral Development, 2, 325–341.

LAOSA, L. M. (1981). Maternal behavior: Sociocultural diversity in modes of family interaction. In R. W. Henderson (Ed.), *Parent-child interaction: Theory, research, and prospects.* Orlando, FL: Academic Press.

LEACOCK, E. (1971, December). At play in African villages. *Natural History,* pp. 60–65.

LEPPER, M. R. (1985). Microcomputers in education: Motivation and social issues. *American Psychologist, 40,* 1–18.

LERNER, R. M., & Lerner, J. (1977). Effects of age, sex, and physical attractiveness in child-peer relations, academic performance, and elementary school adjustments. *Developmental Psychology, 13,* 585–590.

LEWIN, K., Lippitt, R., & White, R. K. (1939). Patterns of aggressive behavior in experimentally created "social climates." *Journal of Social Psychology, 10,* 271–299.

LEWIS, M., Feiring, C., McGuffog, C., & Jaskir, J. (1984). Predicting psychopathology in six-year-olds from early social relations. *Child Development, 55,* 123–136.

LEWIS, M., & Rosenblum, M. A. (1975). *Friendship and peer relations.* New York: Wiley.

LIEBERT, R. M., & Baron, R. A. (1972). Some immediate effects of televised violence on children's behavior. *Developmental Psychology, 6,* 469–475.

LIEBERT, R. M., & Schwartzberg, N. S. (1977). Effects of mass media. In M. R. Rosenzweig & L. W. Porter (Eds.), *Annual review of psychology* (Vol. 28). Palo Alto, CA: Annual Reviews.

LIEBERT, R. M., Sprafkin, J. N., & Davidson, E. S. (1982). *The early window: Effects of television on children and youth.* New York: Pergamon Press.

LONNER, W. J., Thorndike, R. M., Forbes, N. E., & Ashworth, C. (1985). The influence of television on measured cognitive abilities: A study with native Alaskan children. *Journal of Cross-Cultural Psychology, 16,* 355–380.

LYLE, J., & Hoffman, H. R. (1972). Children's use of television and other media. In E. H. Rubinstein, G. A. Comstock, & J. P. Murray (Eds.), *Television in day-to-day life: Patterns of use.* Washington, DC: U.S. Government Printing Office.

Mac IVER, D. (1987). Classroom factors and student characteristics predicting students' use of achievement standards during ability self-assessment. *Child Development, 58,* 1258–1271.

MADDEN, N. A., & Slavin, R. E. (1983). Mainstreaming students with mild handicaps:

Academic and social outcomes. *Review of Educational Research, 53,* 519–569.

MAHAN, A. M., & Mahan, T. W. (1970). Changes in cognitive style: An analysis of the impact of white suburban schools on inner city children. *Integrated Education, 8,* 58–61.

MAIN, M., & George, C. (1985). Responses of abused and disadvantaged toddlers to distress in agemates: A study in the day-care setting. *Developmental Psychology, 21,* 407–412.

MASTERS, J. C., & Furman, W. (1981). Popularity, individual friendship selection, and specific peer interaction among children. *Developmental Psychology, 17,* 344–350.

McDAVID, J. W., & Harari, H. (1966). Stereotyping of names and popularity in grade school children. *Child Development, 37,* 453–459.

MILLER, L. B., & Bizzell, R. P. (1983). Long-term effects of four preschool programs: Sixth, seventh, and eighth grades. *Child Development, 54,* 727–741.

MINUCHIN, P. P., & Shapiro, E. K. (1983). The school as a context for social development. In P. H. Mussen (Ed.), *Handbook of child psychology,* Vol. 4: *Socialization, personality, and social development.* New York: Wiley.

MONTEMAYOR, R. (1982). The relationship between parent-adolescent conflict and the amount of time adolescents spend alone and with parents and peers. *Child Development, 53,* 1512–1519.

MORGAN, M. (1982). Television and adolescents' sex-role stereotypes: A longitudinal study. *Journal of Personality and Social Psychology, 43,* 947–955.

MURRAY, J. P. (1980). *Television and youth: 25 years of research and controversy.* Boys Town, NB: Boys Town Center for the Study of Youth Development.

NELSON, J., & Aboud, F. E. (1985). The resolution of social conflict among friends. *Child Development, 56,* 1009–1017.

NEWCOMB, A. F., Brady, J. E., & Hartup, W. W. (1979). Friendship and incentive condition as determinants of children's task-oriented social behavior. *Child Development, 50,* 878–881.

PAPALIA, D. E., & Olds, S. W. (1979). *A child's world.* New York: McGraw-Hill.

PARKE, R. D., & Slaby, R. G. (1983). The development of aggression. In P. H. Mussen (Ed.), *Handbook of child psychology.* Vol. 4: *Socialization, personality, and social development.* New York: Wiley.

PATTERSON, G. R., Littman, R. A., & Bricker, W. (1967). Assertive behavior in children:

A step toward a theory of aggression. *Monographs of the Society for Research in Child Development, 32*(5, Serial No. 113).

PAULSON, F. L. (1974). Teaching cooperation on television: An evaluation of *Sesame Street's* social goals and programs. *AV Communication Review, 22*, 229–246.

PETERSON, P. E., Jeffrey, D. B., Bridgwater, C. A., & Dawson, B. (1984). How pronutritional television programming affects children's dietary habits. *Developmental Psychology, 20*, 55–63.

PLUMMER, D. L., & Graziano, W. G. (1987). The impact of grade retention on the social development of elementary school children. *Developmental Psychology, 23*, 267–275.

PLUMMER, D. L., Hazzard-Lineberger, M., & Graziano, W. G. (1984). The academic and social consequences of grade retention: A convergent analysis. In L. Katz (Ed.), *Current topics in early childhood education* (Vol. 6). New York: Ablex.

PUTALLAZ, M. (1983). Predicting children's sociometric status from their behavior. *Child Development, 54*, 1417–1426.

PUTALLAZ, M. (1987). Maternal behavior and children's sociometric status. *Child Development, 58*, 324–340.

QUAY, L. C., & Jarrett, O. S. (1984). Predictors of social acceptance in preschool children. *Developmental Psychology, 20*, 793–796.

REYNOLDS, D., Jones, D., St. Leger, S., & Murgatroyd, S. (1980). School factors and truancy. In L. Hersov & I. Berg (Eds.), *Out of school: Modern perspectives in truancy and school refusal*. Chichester: Wiley.

RIST, R. C. (1970). Student social class and teacher expectations: The self-fulfilling prophecy in ghetto education. *Harvard Educational Review, 40*, 411–451.

ROFF, M. F. (1974). Childhood antecedents of adult neurosis, severe bad conduct, and psychological health. In D. F. Ricks, A. Thomas, & M. Roff (Eds.), *Life history research in psychopathology* (Vol. 3). Minneapolis: University of Minnesota Press.

ROFF, M. F., Sells, S. B., & Golden, M. M. (1972). *Social adjustment and personality development in children*. Minneapolis: University of Minnesota Press.

ROGOFF, B. (1981). Schooling's influence on memory test performance. *Child Development, 52*, 260–267.

ROSENTHAL, R., & Jacobson, L. (1968). *Pygmalion in the classroom*. New York: Holt, Rinehart and Winston.

ROSENTHAL, T., Underwood, B., & Martin, M. (1969). Assessing classroom incentive

practices. *Journal of Educational Psychology, 60*, 370–376.

ROTENBERG, K. J., & Mann, L. (1986). The development of the norm of the reciprocity of self-disclosure and its function in children's attraction to peers. *Child Development, 57*, 1349–1357.

RUBLE, D. N., Balaban, T., & Cooper, J. (1981). Gender constancy and the effects of sex-typed televised toy commercials. *Child Development, 52*, 667–673.

RUDOLPH, F. (1965). *Essays on early education in the republic*. Cambridge, MA: Harvard University Press.

RUTTER, M. (1983). School effects on pupil progress: Research findings and policy implications. *Child Development, 54*, 1–29.

RUTTER, M., Maughan, B., Mortimore, P., Ouston, J., & Smith, A. (1979). *Fifteen thousand hours: Secondary schools and their effects on children*. Cambridge, MA: Harvard University Press.

SAGOTSKY, G., & Lepper, M. R. (1982). Generalization of changes in children's preferences for easy or difficult goals induced through peer modeling. *Child Development, 53*, 372–375.

St. JOHN, N. H. (1975). *School desegregation: Outcomes for children*. New York: Wiley.

SANDOVAL, J., & Hughes, G. P. (1981). Success in nonpromoted first grade children. *Resources in Education*, pp. 1–204. (ERIC Document Reproduction Service No. ED 212 371).

SCHRAMM, W., Lyle, J., & Parker, E. B. (1961). *Television in the lives of our children*. Stanford, CA: Stanford University Press.

SCHWARTZ, J. C. (1972). Effects of peer familiarity on the behavior of preschoolers in a novel situation. *Journal of Personality and Social Psychology, 24*, 276–284.

SEBALD, H. (1986). Adolescents' shifting orientation toward parents and peers: A curvilinear trend over recent decades. *Journal of Marriage and the Family, 48*, 5–13.

SHARP, D., Cole, M., & Lave, C. (1979). Education and cognitive development: The evidence from experimental research. *Monographs of the Society for Research in Child Development, 44*(1–2, Serial No. 178).

SIMAN, M. L. (1977). Application of a new model of peer group influence to naturally existing adolescent friendship groups. *Child Development, 48*, 270–274.

SKOLNICK, A. (1986). Early attachment and personal relationships across the life course. In P. B. Baltes, D. L. Featherman, & R. M. Lerner (Eds.), *Life-span development and behavior* (Vol. 7). Hillsdale, NJ: Erlbaum.

SLAVIN, R. E. (1986). Cooperative learning:

Engineering social psychology in the classroom. In R. S. Feldman (Ed.), *The social psychology of education: Current research and theory*. Cambridge: Cambridge University Press.

SMOLLAR, J., & Youniss, J. (1982). Social development through friendship. In K. H. Rubin & H. S. Ross (Eds.), *Peer relations and social skills in childhood*. New York: Springer-Verlag.

STEIN, A. H., & Friedrich, L. K. (1972). Television content and young children's behavior. In J. P. Murray, E. A. Rubinstein, & G. A. Comstock (Eds.), *Television and social behavior*. Vol. 2: *Television and social learning*. Washington, DC: U.S. Government Printing Office.

STEINBERG, C. S. (1980). *TV facts*. New York: Facts on File.

STEINBERG, L. & Silverberg, S. B. (1986). The vicissitudes of autonomy in early adolescence. *Child Development, 57*, 841–851.

STEPHAN, W. G. (1977). Cognitive differentiation and intergroup perception. *Sociometry, 40*, 50–58.

STEPHAN, W. G. (1978). School desegregation: An evaluation of the predictions made in *Brown* v. *Board of Education*. *Psychological Bulletin, 85*, 217–238.

STONEMAN, Z., & Brody, G. H. (1981). Peers as mediators of television food advertisements aimed at children. *Developmental Psychology, 17*, 853–858.

STUDY: Children with working mothers score lower on tests. (1983, June 26). *Atlanta Journal*, p. A4.

STUMPHAUZER, J. S. (1972). Increased delay of gratification in young inmates through imitation of high-delay peer models. *Journal of Personality and Social Psychology, 21*, 10–17.

SULLIVAN, H. S. (1953). *The interpersonal theory of psychiatry*. New York: Norton.

SUOMI, S. J., & Harlow, H. F. (1975). The role and reason of peer relationships in rhesus monkeys. In M. Lewis & L. A. Rosenblum (Eds.), *Friendship and peer relations*. New York: Wiley.

SUOMI, S. J., & Harlow, H. F. (1978). Early experience and social development in rhesus monkeys. In M. E. Lamb (Ed.), *Social and personality development*. New York: Holt, Rinehart and Winston.

TAYLOR, A. R., Asher, S. R., & Williams, G. A. (1987). The social adaptation of mainstreamed mildly retarded children. *Child Development, 58*, 1321–1334.

TESCH, S. A. (1983). Review of friendship development across the life span. *Human Development, 26*, 266–276.

THELEN, M. H., & Kirkland, K. D. (1976). On status and being imitated: Effects on reciprocal imitation and attraction. *Journal of Personality and Social Psychology, 33,* 691–697.

THELEN, M. H., Miller, D. J., Fehrenbach, P. A., Frautschi, N. M., & Fishbein, M. D. (1980). Imitation during play as a means of social influence. *Child Development, 51,* 918–920.

THOMAS, M. H., Horton, R. W., Lippincott, E. C., & Drabman, R. S. (1977). Desensitization to portrayals of real-life aggression as a function of exposure to television violence. *Journal of Personality and Social Psychology, 35,* 450–458.

THOMAS, N. G., & Berk, L. E. (1981). Effects of school environments on the development of young children's creativity. *Child Development, 52,* 1153–1162.

UTECH, D. A., & Hoving, K. L. (1969). Parents and peers as competing influences in the decisions of children of differing ages. *Journal of Social Psychology, 78,* 267–274.

WEINSTEIN, R. S., Marshall, H. H., Sharp, L., & Botkin, M. (1987). Pygmalion and the student: Age and classroom differences in children's awareness of teacher expectations. *Child Development, 58,* 1079–1093.

WHITING, B. B., & Whiting, J. W. M. (1975). *Children of six cultures.* Cambridge, MA: Harvard University Press.

WRIGHT, J. C., & Huston, A. C. (1983). A matter of form: Potentials of television for young viewers. *American Psychologist, 38,* 835–843.

YOUNISS, J., & Smollar, J. (1985). *Adolescent relations with mothers, fathers, and friends.* Chicago: University of Chicago Press.

ZIGLER, E., & Muenchow, S. (1979). Mainstreaming: The proof is in the implementation. *American Psychologist, 34,* 993–996.

Name Index

Huebner, R. R., 195, 395
Huesmann, L. R., 248, 254, 513, 604, 605, 606
Hughes, G. P., 622
Hughes, R., Jr., 526
Huie, K. S., 452
Hull, C., 53
Humphreys, A. P., 475
Humphreys, L. G., 361
Hunt, D., 584
Hunter, F. T., 635
Huntington, L., 155
Hurley, J. R., 403
Huston, A. C., 254, 480, 482, 483, 484, 489,
    492, 500, 502, 603, 609, 610
Huston, T. L., 419
Huston-Stein, A., 255, 608
Hutchings, B., 101
Hutchinson, C. A., 154
Hutt, C., 316, 475, 483, 484
Hutt, S. J., 153
Huttenlocher, P. R., 159, 160
Hwang, C. P., 416, 566
Hyde, J. S., 499, 513
Hymel, S., 455

Iannotti, R. J., 525, 527
Ievoli, R., 586
Ilg, F. L., 166
Ilgen, D. R., 477
Imperato-McGinley, J., 486
Ingram, D., 282
Inhelder, B., 316, 321, 323, 325, 342
Intons-Peterson, M. J., 472
Irwin, D. M., 532
Irwin, R. J., 194
Isabella, R. A., 568
Isseroff, A., 159
Ito, J., 87
Iwawaki, S., 441
Izard, C. E., 195, 200, 394, 395, 396, 414
Izzo, L. D., 628

Jacklin, C. N., 451, 475, 476, 477, 478, 481,
    485, 486, 491, 513, 569
Jackson, S., 325
Jacobs, B. S., 581
Jacobson, J. L., 130, 416, 629
Jacobson, L., 618
Jacobson, S. W., 130
Jagger, M., 334
Jakobson, R., 269
James, S. R., 85, 126
James, W., 148, 190, 205, 207, 209, 218
Janos, P. M., 367
Janowsky, J. S., 159
Jarrett, O. S., 630
Jarvik, F., 96
Jaskir, J., 417, 629
Jedlicka, D., 497
Jeffrey, D. B., 608
Jenkins, M. D., 378

Jennings, S., 442
Jensen, A. R., 39, 370, 376, 377, 378, 380, 383
Joffee, L. S., 120
Johnson, D., 623
Johnson, C. J., 279
Johnson, C. N., 437
Johnson, E. S., 475
Johnson, H., 285
Johnson, N., 603
Johnson, R. D., 474
Johnson, S. M., 578, 579
Johnson, W., 394
Johnston, J., 607
Jones, D., 614
Jones, K. L., 127
Jones, M. C., 172, 234
Jones, W. H., 500
Joos, S. K., 120
Judd, C. M., 636
Jusczyk, P. W., 193, 205
Justice, E. M., 340

Kaczala, C. M., 478, 479
Kagan, J., 41, 98, 212, 409, 410, 411, 415, 421,
    452, 453, 482, 513
Kagan, S., 523, 620
Kahan, L. D., 287
Kahle, L. R., 322
Kail, R., 336
Kallen, D. J., 499
Kandel, D., 636
Kanfer, F. H., 631
Kant, I., 190
Kanungo, R. N., 607
Kaplan, B., 38
Kaplan, B. J., 119
Kaplan, H., 180
Karabenick, J. D., 284
Katcher, A., 48, 480, 489
Katz, S., 91, 92
Kaufman, A. S., 361, 376
Kaufman, N. L., 361
Kaufmann, F., 198
Kaufmann-Hayoz, R., 198
Kavanaugh, R., 253, 450
Kay, N., 194
Kay, T., 87
Kaye, H., 235
Kaye, K., 252, 312
Kean, A. W. G., 10
Kearsley, R. B., 421
Keasey, B., 322
Keasey, C. B., 532, 539
Keating, D., 447
Keats, J. G., 475
Kee, D. W., 338, 611
Kefauver, E., 604
Keith, T. Z., 604
Kellaghan, T., 581
Keller, A., 436
Keller, H., 277, 395, 400

Kellman, P. J., 197, 199
Kellogg, L. A., 294
Kellogg, W. N., 294
Kelly, D., 568
Kelly, J. B., 583, 584, 585
Kempe, C. H., 588, 589, 590, 592
Kempe, R. S., 588, 589, 590, 592
Kendall, P. C., 455
Kendrick, C., 136, 578, 579
Keniston, A. H., 254
Kennedy, W. Z., 375
Kennell, J. H., 133, 397, 398, 399
Kenney, J., 364
Keough, J., 158, 166
Kerby, F. D., 454
Kerzner, R. L., 622
Kessen, W., 12, 13, 193, 424
Kessler, S., 101
Kessner, D. M., 117, 119, 577
Ketron, J. L., 356
Key, C. B., 370
Kiely, J. L., 138
Kiesler, S. B., 477
Kim, S. Y., 534
Kinard, E. M., 583
King, R. A., 520
King, S., 475
Kinsbourne, M., 162, 163
Kinsey, A. C., 496
Kipnis, D. M., 255, 608
Kirkland, K. D., 634
Kisilevsky, B. S., 195
Kister, M. C., 287
Klahr, D., 329
Klaus, M. H., 133, 398, 398, 399
Klaus, R. A., 380
Klee, L., 142
Klein, M., 589
Klein, R. E., 120, 406
Klein, R. P., 418
Klima, E. S., 278
Klineberg, O., 370
Klineberg, S. L., 567
Klinger, C. A., 443
Klinnert, M. D., 201, 396
Klusman, L., 133
Kohlberg, L., 61, 436, 449, 483, 491, 492,
    494, 495, 509, 530, 534, 535, 536, 537,
    538, 539, 540, 541, 542, 543, 551
Kohn, L. G., 518
Kohn, M. L., 563, 620
Kokenes, B., 440
Kolata, G. B., 137
Kolb, S., 180
Kolbe, R., 491
Konner, M. J., 326
Koperski, J. A., 154
Kopp, C. B., 137, 139
Korn, S., 99
Korner, A. F., 154, 155, 156, 402
Kotelchuck, M., 406

Kraemer, H. C., 154
Kram, K. M., 177
Kramer, D. A., 356
Kramer, S. J., 199
Krauss, R. M., 286, 287
Krebs, D. L., 523
Kreitzberg, V. S., 451
Kreutzer, M. A., 340
Kreye, M., 409, 410
Kriger, A., 400
Krile, D., 448
Kroll, J., 11
Kropp, J., 576
Krosnick, J. A., 636
Krowitz, A., 203
Kuchuk, A., 200, 396
Kuczaj, S. A., II, 281
Kuczynski, L., 248, 253, 402, 546, 548
Kuhn, D., 322, 326, 480, 492, 540, 613
Kulik, J. A., 611
Kulka, R. A., 588
Kunzinger, E. L., III, 336
Kupersmidt, J. B., 628, 631
Kurdek, L. A., 448, 583, 585
Kurtz, S. T., 320
Kuzmak, S. D., 320

La Barbera, J. D., 200, 396
Labouvie-Vief, G., 356
Lachmann, M. E., 568
Ladd, G. W., 455, 522, 631
LaGaipa, J. J., 629
LaFreniere, P. J., 451, 481, 629
Lahey, B. B., 576, 581
Lamaze, F., 134
Lamb, C., 139
Lamb, M. E., 86, 404, 415, 416, 418, 489, 569, 570, 583, 589, 633
Lamke, L. K., 500
Lando, B., 452
Lang, M. E., 568
Lange, G., 522
Langer, A., 203
Langer, J., 540
Langlois, J. H., 172, 400, 481, 490, 630, 631
Laosa, L. M., 577, 637
Larsen, R. J., 476
LaRue, A. A., 480
LaRussa, G. W., 474
Lasko, J. K., 582
Latchford, S. A., 119
Laupa, M., 534
Lave, C., 613
LaVoie, J. C., 491
Layzer, D., 377
Lazer, I., 380, 381
Leacock, E., 637
Leboyer, F., 135, 136
Lechelt, E. C., 221
Lechner, R. E., 284
Ledger, G. W., 338

Lee, E. S., 379
Leehy, S. C., 219
Leeuwenhoek, A., van, 74
Lefford, A., 209
Lefkowitz, M. M., 129, 140, 248, 254, 513, 575, 604
Leiderman, P. H., 573
Leinbach, M. D., 480
Lelwica, M., 201, 396
LeMare, L. J., 448
Lempers, J. D., 279
Lenard, H. G., 153
Lenneberg, E. H., 162, 266, 293, 294, 296
Lennon, E. M., 209
Lennon, R., 526
Leonard, C., 340
Leonard, L. B., 289
Lepper, M. R., 242, 611, 633
Lerner, J. V., 588, 630
Lerner, R. M., 441, 630
Lessen-Firestone, J. K., 130
Lester, B. M., 138, 139, 154, 401, 406
Leung, E. H. L., 277, 520
Levenstein, P., 381
Levenstein, S., 381
Leventhal, A. G., 216
Levin, H., 214, 244, 515
Levin, J. R., 338
LeVine, R. A., 561, 562, 563
Levitt, M. J., 244, 409, 415, 417, 521, 568, 570
Levy, N., 195
Levy, V. M., 340
Levy-Shiff, R., 424
Lewin, K., 38, 619
Lewin, R., 120, 176
Lewis, M., 201, 362, 402, 409, 410, 417, 436, 442, 451, 625, 629
Lewis, N. G., 589, 592
Lewontin, R. C., 377, 378
Liberty, C., 336, 337
Lickona, T., 532
Liddell, C., 566
Lieberman, M., 537
Lieberman, M. A., 584
Lieberman, P., 270
Liebert, R. M., 20, 254, 491, 602, 603, 604, 606, 607, 609, 610, 612
Liederman, J., 163
Liederman, P. H., 133
Light, R. J., 590
Lightbown, P., 289
Lindberg, M. A., 335, 339
Lindbergh, C., 567
Lindzey, G., 375
Linn, M. C., 475, 484
Lippincott, E. C., 605
Lippitt, R., 619
Lipsitt, L. P., 154, 178, 195, 235
Lipton, E. L., 155
Lipton, R. C., 423, 424
Littenberg, R., 412

Little, A. H., 235
Littman, R. A., 520, 633
Livesley, W. J., 444
Livson, F. B., 482
Livson, N., 172
Locke, J., 12, 190
Loehlin, J. C., 94, 103, 375, 377
Lollis, S. P., 270, 450
Londerville, S., 416, 451
London, P., 527
Longstreth, L., 372, 424
Lonky, E., 242
Lonner, W. J., 603
Lorch, E. P., 210, 254, 332
Lorenz, K. Z., 399, 407, 511
Loveland, K. K., 242
Low, H., 485
Lowe, C. R., 115
Lowell, E. L., 454, 458
Lower, J. E., 177
Lowery, C. R., 543
Lowery, G. H., 156, 166
Lubin, A. H., 177
Lucariello, J., 316
Lucas, T., 450
Lutkenhaus, P., 416, 450, 451
Lyle, J., 603
Lyons-Ruth, K., 414
Lytton, H., 516, 564

Maccoby, E. E., 211, 244, 437, 450, 451, 472, 475, 476, 477, 478, 481, 483, 485, 486, 491, 495, 513, 515, 521, 525, 526, 569, 573, 574, 576
MacDonald, A. P., 459
MacDonald, K., 452, 453
MacFarlane, A., 112, 136, 141, 195, 472
Macfarlane, J. W., 363
Mac Iver, D., 621
MacKain, K., 270
MacKay-Soroka, S., 278
MacKinnon, C. E., 490, 580
MacNamara, J., 581
MacPhee, D., 372
MacWhinney, B., 298
Madden, J., 381
Madden, N. A., 623
Madison, J. K., 231
Madison, L. S., 231
Madonna, 206
Maehr, M. L., 453
Magenis, R. E., 88
Mahan, A. M., 622
Mahan, T. W., 622
Mahler, M. S., 435, 442
Maier, H. W., 49
Main, D. S., 443
Main, M., 416, 417, 451, 569, 590, 629
Maio, M. L., 155
Maitland, K. A., 538
Major, B., 500, 501

Subject Index

Amniocentesis, 91, 92
Amnion, 114, 115
Analog experiments, 565
Anal stage, 45–46
Androgen:
    and aggression, 485–486
    and prenatal development, 485, 487
    and sexual development of adolescents, 175
Androgenized females, 485, 486, 487
Androgyny:
    advantages of, 500, 501, 502
    defined, 499
    development of, 500–501
Animism, 315, 319–320
Anorexia nervosa, 171
Anoxia:
    defined, 136, 137
    as a birth complication, 136
    obstetric medication and, 137
Anxious/avoidant attachment:
    defined, 414, 415
    development of, 414, 415
Anxious/resistant attachment:
    defined, 414, 415
    development of, 414, 415
    and peer relations, 416, 629
Anytime malformations, 122
Apgar test, 149, 150
Aphasia, defined, 293
Apnea monitor, 154
Arapesh society, 31, 486, 515
Assimilation:
    cognitive growth and, 60–61, 309–310, 328
    defined, 61, 309
Attachment:
    and achievement strivings, 456
    adaptive significance of, 63, 406–407
    caregiver-to-infant, 397–402
    day care and, 420–421
    defined, 397
    to fathers, 403, 406, 416–417, 419, 569
    individual differences in, 413–416
    infant-to-caregiver, 403–408
    long-term correlates, 416–418
    maternal employment and, 418–419
    and separation anxiety, 409
    and sociability, 451
    stability of, 417–419
    stages of, 403, 406
    and stranger anxiety, 408
    theories of, 398–399, 404–408
Attachment object:
    defined, 397
    fathers as, 404, 406, 416–417, 419, 569
    mothers as, 403–408, 413–416
    as a secure base, 411, 416
    siblings as, 580
Attention, development of, 210–212, 331–333

Attention span, 161, 210, 211
Audition, in neonates, 193–194
Auditory perception, development of, 205–206
Authoritarian instruction, 619
Authoritarian parenting, 571–573
Authoritative instruction, 619
Authoritative parenting, 571–573
Authority and social-order maintenance stage, of moral reasoning, 535, 536–537
Automatization, of information processing, 335–336, 341, 357
Autonomous morality, 531–532, 533
Autonomy, and self-concept, 437
Autostimulation theory, 154
Aversion therapy, 234

Babbling:
    as a contributor to attachments, 400, 407
    development of, 269
    relation to meaningful speech, 269–270
Babinski reflex, 152
Baby biography, 12–13
Balance-scale problems, 342–343
Basic gender identity:
    defined, 492, 493
    role in sex typing, 492–493, 494–495, 496
Basic trust vs. mistrust, defined, 49
Battered-child syndrome, 588, 598 (see also Child abuse)
Behavioral comparisons, phase of impression formation, 444
Behavioral inhibition, 98, 99
Behavioral schemata, 308, 309
Behavior genetics:
    defined, 39, 93
    research methods in, 93–96
Behaviorism, 52, 53 (see also Learning theory)
Biosocial theory, of sex typing, 487–488
Birthing room, 142
Birth order:
    and achievement, 581
    and achievement training, 373, 582
    and IQ, 373–374, 581
    and obedience, 581, 582
    and popularity, 581, 582, 630
    and sex typing, 581
    and sociability, 451–452, 581
Birth processes:
    in birthing rooms, 142
    by Caesarean section, 123, 136
    complications of, 136–137
    effects on baby, 134–136
    effects on older siblings, 136
    effects on parents, 132–134
    at home, 141–142
    stages of, 132, 133
Birth trauma, 134–135

Blastocyst, 113
Blastula, 113–114
Body build, and personality development, 170, 172, 630
Brain, development of, 158–163
Brain growth spurt, 159
Brazelton Neonatal Behavioral Assessment Scale, 149–151
Brazelton training, 151, 156, 402, 592
Breech birth, 136, 137
Bulimia, 171

Caesarean delivery, defined, 123, 140–141
Canalization, 102, 103
Caregiving hypothesis, of attachment, 415–416
Carpentered environment hypothesis, 218–219
Case study method, 18–19, 24
Castration anxiety, 46, 47, 488, 489, 529
Catch-up growth, 176, 177
Categorical self, 436, 437
Catharsis hypothesis, 517
Cathartic technique, 517–518
Causal attributions:
    defined, 461, 462
    in Dweck's learned-helplessness theory, 462–464
    in Weiner's achievement theory, 460–462
Centration, 319
Cephalocaudal development, 156–157, 158, 160, 164
Cerebral lateralization:
    defined, 162, 163
    developmental trends, 162–162
    and language development, 162, 293–294
Cerebral palsy, 136
Chewa society, 497
Child abuse:
    characteristics of abused children, 589, 591
    characteristics of child abusers, 589–590, 591
    environmental influences on, 590–591
    incidence of, 588
    treatment and prevention of, 592
Children's Television Workshop (CTW), 609, 610
Chorion, 114, 115
Chorionic villus sampling, 91–92
Chromosomal abnormalities, 85–93
Chromosome, defined, 76, 77
Cigarette smoking, and prenatal development, 128, 129
Classical conditioning:
    and attitude formation, 233
    compared to operant conditioning, 235
    defined, 52, 53, 232–233
    developmental trends in, 235

Empathy *(continued)*
and altruism, 65, 99, 521, 525–527
biological bases, 65
defined, 65, 521
Empiricist perspective *(see also* Nature/nurture controversy):
on language development, 267
on perceptual development, 190–191, 201, 202
Encoding, defined, 257
Endoderm, 114
Endomorphic physique:
defined, 170
and personality development, 170, 172, 178, 630
Engrossment, 133, 398
Enrichment theory of intersensory perception, 207–209
Enuresis, 234
Environmental determinism, 56, 57
Environmental hypothesis, of group differences in IQ, 378–380
Environmental influences *(see also* Cultural influences; Family influences; Parenting; Perinatal environment):
on caregiver-to-infant attachments, 402–403
on child abuse, 590–591
on intelligence, 97, 102, 105, 364, 367, 370–374, 378–380
on language development, 289–292, 298, 299
on moral reasoning, 538, 540
on neural development, 160, 161
on parenting, 576, 577
on perceptual development, 215–222
on personality and mental illness, 99, 100–102, 105
on physical development, 175–181
on prenatal development, 118–132
on sex typing, 474–475, 478–479, 486–487
on sexuality, 497
Epistemology, defined, 58
Equilibrium, and cognitive development, 58–60
Equipotentiality hypothesis, of cerebral lateralization, 162–163
Eros, defined, 43
Eskimo society, 218
Estrogen, and sexual development, 175
Ethnocentrism, defined, 577
Ethological theory:
of altruism, 65
of attachment, 406–407
compared to behavior genetics, 93
contributions and criticisms of, 64–66
philosophical assumptions of, 67
of separation anxiety, 411
of stranger anxiety, 411
Ethology, defined, 63

Evocative genotype/environment interactions, 104
Evoked potentials, 192, 193
Executive control processes, defined, 330, 331
Executive responses, 407
Expansions, 290–291, 292
Experimental control, defined, 20, 21
Experimental method, 19–22, 24
Expiatory punishment, 531
Expressive role, 473
Extended family, 561
Externalizers, defined, 459 *(see also* Locus of control)
Extinction, defined, 232, 233
Extrafamilial influences:
defined, 603
on developing children, 602–638
Extrinsic orientation, to achievement, 456, 457
Extrinsic reinforcement:
vs. intrinsic reinforcement, 242
and task performance, 242–243

Facial attractiveness:
and parent-to-infant attachment, 400
and popularity with peers, 630–631
Facial perception, 196, 200–201
Factor analysis, 353–355
Failure to thrive, 178–179
Fake cries, 268, 269
Falsifiability, 38, 39
Family(ies) *(see also* Family influences; Parenting; Siblings):
changing character of, 566–567
and childrearing patterns, 570–577
configuration of, and child development, 581–582
cross-cultural studies of, 562–563, 577
defined, 561
divorce and, 582–586
functions of, 561–563
methods of studying, 564–565
and parent/infant interactions, 562, 567–570
reconstituted, 567, 586–587
as social systems, 565–566, 570
television and, 603
Family influences *(see also* Parenting; Siblings):
on achievement, 456–457, 458, 460
on aggression, 515–517
on altruism, 520–521, 527
on intellectual performance, 364, 367, 371–374, 378–380
on moral development, 532, 546, 548–550
on obesity, 178
on perceptual development, 221
on sex typing, 478–479, 480–481, 487, 488–491, 494, 495, 500–501

Family influences *(continued)*
on sexuality, 498
on sociability, 451, 452–453
Family social system, 565–566, 570
Family studies:
defined, 94
of intelligence, 96–97, 369, 379–380
of mental illness, 101–102
of personality, 98–101
of physical development, 174
of sociability, 451
Fat Albert and the Cosby Kids, 255
Father/infant interactions, 404, 416–417, 569
Fathers *(see also* Family influences; Parenting):
as attachment objects, 416–417, 569
as custodial parents, 585
effects on birth outcomes, 133–134
effects on prenatal development, 130
as noncustodial parents, 584
reactions to neonates, 133, 398
and sex typing, 481, 488–489, 490, 569
stepchildren's reactions to, 586, 587
"Fear of separation" hypothesis, 409, 411
Feminine sex-typed individuals, 499, 500
Fetal alcohol syndrome (FAS), 127, 129
Fetus, period of the, 113, 116–118
Field dependence/independence, 221–222
Field experiment, 21–22
Fixation, 46
Fluid intelligence (g_f), 355–356
Fontanelles, defined, 157
"Forbidden toy" paradigm, 544, 545
Formal-operational stage:
defined, 61, 323
and higher stages, 326
and hypothetical-deductive reasoning, 323–324
and hypothetical propositions, 323, 324
incidence of, 325–326
and moral development, 539–540
schooling and, 613
and sex-role stereotyping, 494–495
Formats, defined, 270, 271
Form perception:
in childhood, 212–215
environmental influences on, 216, 218–219, 221–222
in infancy, 196–201
Four-beaker problem, 323–324
Fragile-X syndrome, 86, 90
Fraternal twins, *see* Dizygotic twins
Freestyle, 607
Friends:
children's conceptions of, 447, 629–630
as contributors to role-taking skills, 448–449, 631
as contributors to social/emotional development, 632–633
interactions between, 630–632

Impression formation *(continued)*
  role taking and, 445, 448–449
Imprinting, 407
Incompatible-response technique, 248, 249, 518–519
Incomplete dominance, 82–84
Independent assortment, principle of, 79
Independent variable, defined, 20, 21
Indifferent gonad, 115, 487
Indirect parental effects, 569–570
Indiscriminate attachment, stage of, 403
Induced labor, 140, 141
Inductive discipline:
  children's view of, 549–550
  defined, 548, 549
  and moral development, 548–549
Industry vs. inferiority:
  defined, 50, 440, 441
  and self-esteem, 440
Infantile amaurotic idiocy, *see* Tay-Sachs disease
Infant intelligence tests, *see* Developmental schedules
Infant mortality:
  birth weight and, 116–117, 137, 138
  chemicals and, 130–131
  disease and, 123–126, 131
  drugs and, 126–130, 131
  in home births, 141
  nutrition and, 120, 121, 131
  radiation and, 130, 131
Infant states, *see* States of consciousness
Informal curriculum, 612, 613
Information-processing theory:
  of cognitive development, 306, 329–345
  compared to Piaget's theory, 320, 336, 341–342, 344
  educational implications of, 345
  of punishment, 244–245, 246, 247, 545–546
  triarchic view of intelligence, 356–357
  view of learning phenomena, 255–257
Informed consent, 32, 33
"In-group/out-group" schema, 493
Inhibitory controls:
  defined, 545
  development of, 544–546, 547
Initiative, and self-concept, 437
Innate purity, 12, 13
Inner experimentation, 311–312
Insecure attachment (*see also* Anxious/ avoidant attachment; Anxious/resistant attachment):
  development of, 414–415
  long-term correlates of, 416–417, 629
  stability of, 417–419
  and stranger anxiety, 417
Instincts, 43 (*see also* Eros; Thanatos)
Institutionalized children, 419, 422–426
Instrumental aggression, 511, 512

Instrumental conditioning, *see* Operant conditioning
Instrumental role, 473
Integrative theory, of sex typing, 494–496
Intellectual Achievement Responsibility Questionnaire, 459
Intellectual content, 59 (*see also* Schema)
Intellectual development, *see* Cognitive development
Intellectual functions, 59–61, 309–310
Intellectual performance, 59, 364, 384 (*see also* IQ)
Intelligence (*see also* Cognitive development; IQ):
  components of, 58–61, 307–310, 353–357
  definitions of, 58, 307–308, 353
  environmental influences on, 364, 367, 370–374, 377–380
  information-processing view of, 329–345, 352–356
  and the nature/nurture controversy, 39–40, 353, 368–370, 377–380
  psychometric view of, 352–356
Intelligence quotient, *see* IQ
Intelligence testing (*see also* Intelligence; IQ):
  distribution of scores, 360–361
  group tests, 361
  of infants, 362–363
  information-processing perspectives, 356–357, 363
  methodological considerations, 365
  new approaches, 361–362
  origins of, 358–360
  stability of scores, 363–364
  uses and abuses of, 383–384
Interactional synchrony, 400–401
Interactionist theory:
  of language development, 298–299
  of perceptual development, 191, 201, 205, 215
Intermittent reinforcement, *see* Partial reinforcement
Internalization:
  defined, 44, 45
  and moral development, 46–47, 528, 529–530, 543, 545–546, 547
  and sex typing, 46–47, 488
Internalizers, defined, 459 (*see also* Locus of control)
Intersensory perception, 206–209
Interview method, 17–18, 564
Intrinsic orientation, to achievement, 456, 457
Intrinsic reinforcement:
  vs. extrinsic reinforcement, 242
  and task performance, 242–243
Introversion/extraversion, 99
Intuitive period, of intellectual development, 317–319

Invariant developmental sequence:
  of cognitive stages, 61, 310
  defined, 61, 310, 311, 531
  of gender identity stages, 492
  of moral stages, 530–532, 535–537, 539
IQ:
  compensatory education and, 380–383
  defined, 358, 359
  environmental influences on, 370–371, 378–380
  family influences on, 364, 367, 371–374, 379–380, 381–382
  and health, adjustment, and life satisfaction, 366–369
  hereditary influences on, 368–370, 377–378
  infant schedules and, 361–362
  and intellectual ability, 364, 384
  and intellectual performance, 364, 384
  and occupational status, 366
  and popularity, 630
  race differences in, 374–380
  and scholastic achievement, 364
  social class and, 374–380
  tests of, 358–364
  uses and abuses of, 383–384
Irregular sleep, 153 (*see also* REM sleep)
Isolate (neglectee), 628–629
Isolate monkeys, 420–422, 424, 425, 426
Isolette, 138

Kaluli culture, 292
Karotype, 80–81
Kaufman Assessment Battery for Children, 361
Kewpie-doll effect, 399–400
Kinesthetic sense, 209
Kinship, 92–93, 96, 97, 369
Klinefelter's syndrome, 87, 92
Knowledge base, and recall memory, 339
Kohlberg's theory:
  of moral development, 535–541
  of sex typing, 491–492
Kwashiorkor, 177
Kwoma society, 497

Labor:
  induced, 140–141
  stages of, 132, 133
Laissez-faire instruction, 619
Language:
  components of, 265–266
  defined, 265
  properties of, 264
Language acquisition device (LAD):
  defined, 267
  and language development, 268, 292–299
Language development:
  biological influences on, 267, 292–298

Monocular vision, and perceptual development, 216–217
Monozygotic (MZ) twins:
  defined, 80, 81
  as participants in family studies, 94–102, 105, 369, 451
Moral affect:
  defined, 528, 529
  and inductive discipline, 548
  relation to moral behavior, 541, 543
Moral behavior:
  cognitive rationales and, 545–546
  consistency of, 542–543
  defined, 528, 529
  discipline and, 546
  moral affect and, 548–549
  moral reasoning and, 540, 543
  observational learning of, 546
  punishment and, 544–546
  reinforcement and, 544
  self-concept training and, 547
  self-instructions and, 547
Moral development, 527–550 (see also Moral affect; Moral behavior; Moral reasoning)
Morality (see also Moral affect; Moral behavior; Moral reasoning):
  consistency of, 542–543
  defined, 528, 529
  development of, 528, 529–550
Morality of contract, individual rights, and democratically accepted law, stage of, 536, 537
Morality of individual principles of conscience, stage of, 536, 537
Moral realism, 531
Moral reasoning:
  cognitive development and, 532, 535, 539–540
  consistency of, 540–541
  cross-cultural studies of, 537, 538
  defined, 528, 529
  development of, 530–540
  discipline and, 548, 549
  invariance of stages, 530, 535, 538–539
  and moral behavior, 540, 543
  peer influences on, 532, 538–539, 633, 635, 637–638
  sex differences, 541, 542–543
  theories of, 529–546
Moral relativism, see Autonomous morality
Moral rules, defined, 534, 535
Moratorium status, of identity formation, 442–443
Moro reflex, 150, 152
Morphemes, defined, 265
Motherese, 290–291, 292
"Mother only" monkeys, 627
Motion hypothesis, of perceptual development, 218, 219

Motivational hypothesis, for group differences in IQ, 376–377
Motor development:
  in adolescence, 166–167
  in childhood, 165–166
  in infancy, 163–165
  practice and, 179–181
  secular trends, 179
  visual/motor coordination and, 164–165
Mullerian inhibiting substance (MIS), 487
Multiple attachments, stage of, 403
Multiple sclerosis, 161
Mundugumor society, 31, 486, 515
Muscular dystrophy, 84, 89, 90, 91
Mutations, 88–89
Myelinization, 160–161, 210, 211, 329

Naive hedonism stage, of moral reasoning, 535, 536
Names, as contributors to popularity, 630
Narcotics, and prenatal development, 128, 129–130
Nativist perspective:
  on intelligence, 353
  on language development, 267, 268, 292–298
  on perceptual development, 190, 202
Natural childbirth, 134, 135
Natural experiment, 22–24
Naturalistic observation, 16–17, 24, 63, 564–565
Natural selection, defined, 63
Nature/nurture controversy:
  defined, 39
  and intelligence, 39–40
  and language development, 266–268, 288–298
  and perceptual development, 190–191, 196–209
  and physical development, 173–181
Need for achievement (n Ach):
  components of, in Weiner's theory, 461, 462
  defined, 454, 455
  home environment and, 456–457
  quality of attachments and, 456
  parental influences, 458
Negative reinforcement:
  in coercive home environments, 516–517
  compared with punishment, 236–237
Neglectee (isolate), 628–629
Neo-Hullian theory, 53–54
Neonatal assessment, 149–150
Neonate:
  behavioral capabilities of, 150–152
  cognitive capabilities of, 59, 310
  defined, 119
  emotional capabilities of, 395
  learning capabilities of, 231, 235, 238

Neonate (continued)
  methods of soothing, 155–156
  perceptual capabilities of, 196–209
  sensory capabilities of, 193–196
  social capabilities of, 399–401, 407
  states of consciousness, 153–155
  temperamental differences, 98
Neurons:
  defined, 159
  destruction of, 159, 161
  experience, and development of, 160, 161
  trends in development of, 159
Neurotic disorders, defined, 101
Nonaggressive play environments, 519
Nonrepresentative sample, 27
Nonshared environmental influences, 100–101
Nonverbal communication:
  in animals, 264, 265, 294–295
  in deaf children, 278, 296
  in infants and toddlers, 274–275, 277, 279
Normal distribution, defined, 360, 361
Normative standards, in IQ testing, 365
Norm of social responsibility, 523
Nuclear family, defined, 561
Nutrition:
  adolescent dieting disorders, 171
  and intellectual development, 120–121
  and physical development, 175–178
  and prenatal development, 120–121, 131
  television and, 608–609

Obesity:
  defined, 179
  and physical development, 178
  and self-esteem, 441
Object concept:
  and attachment, 406
  defined, 312, 313
  development of, 312–314
  and self-recognition, 436
Object permanence, see Object concept
Oblique effect, 218, 219
Observational learning:
  of aggression, 354, 515, 604–606
  of altruism, 20, 255, 524, 608
  Bandura's theory of, 55–56, 249–255
  compared with trial-and-error learning, 249
  defined, 53, 249
  developmental trends, 252–253
  and the learning/performance distinction, 251
  and moral behavior, 546
  and moral reasoning, 538
  peers as models for, 256, 633–634
  of sex-typed attributes, 490–491

Observational learning *(continued)*
of social skills, 454–455
television and, 20, 253–255, 604–610
as a therapeutic technique, 256,
454–455
Observational method, *see* Naturalistic
observation
Observer bias, 16, 17
Observer reliability, 16, 17, 564
Obstetric medications, 136–137
Oedipal morality, 529–530
Oedipus complex:
defined, 47, 489
and moral development, 46, 529
and sex-role development, 46, 488–489
Only children, 582
Open classrooms, 616–617
Operant conditioning:
vs. classical conditioning, 235
defined, 52, 53, 235
developmental trends in, 238–239
and language development, 267,
288–289
principles of, 235–244
Operant learning theory, 54–55, 66,
235–244
Operational schemata, 308, 309 *(see also*
Cognitive operations)
Oral stage, 45
Ordinal position, defined, 581 *(see also*
Birth order)
"Ordinal position" hypothesis, of
sociability, 451–452
Organismic viewpoint, 58
Organization:
in information-processing theory, 337
in Piaget's theory, 59–61, 309–310
Original sin, 12, 13
Overextension, 272, 273
Overregularization, 281, 292
Ovists, 74
Ovulation, 76, 77
Own-sex schema, 493, 495, 496

Pain, neonates' sensitivity to, 195
Pain cry, 155
Parental control *(see also* Discipline; Parenting; Punishment):
and aggression, 516
children's view of, 574–575
effects on children, 572–573
patterns of, 571–572
social-class differences in, 576
Parenting *(see also* Family(ies); Family
influences):
children's impressions of, 574–575
children's influence on, 564–566, 568
effects on preschool children, 570–574
goals of, 561–563
and indirect parental effects, 569–570

Parenting *(continued)*
and infant development, 402, 414–417,
568–569
and peer relations, 452–453, 630
and perceptual development, 221
in reconstituted families, 586–587
in single-parent families, 583, 584, 585
social-class differences in, 575–577
stress and, 576, 577
among teenage mothers, 568
transition to parenthood and, 567–568
Parents Anonymous, 592
Parsimony, advantages of, 38, 39
Partial reinforcement:
vs. continuous reinforcement, 240
defined, 240–241
inconsistent punishment and, 246
"Partial reinforcement" effect, 241
Passive genotype/environment interactions,
103
Pattern perception, *see* Form perception
PCBs (polychlorinated biphenyls), and prenatal development, 130
Peer groups:
vs. adults as influence agents, 635–636
characteristics of, 634–635
cross-cultural studies of, 636–638
defined, 635
normative function of, 635
"Peer only" monkeys, 627
Peer relations, *see* Peers; Popularity,
determinants of
Peers:
contacts with, and role taking, 448–449
contacts with, and social competence,
626–629
defined, 625
frequency of contacts with, 625–626
impact on moral reasoning, 633,
637–638
popularity with, 628, 630–631
as reinforcing agents, 633
same-age vs. mixed-age interactions, 625,
626
and sex typing, 490, 633
and sexuality, 498
social comparison with, 634
as social models, 633–634
Penis envy, 489
Perception:
attention and, 210–212
defined, 190, 191
development of, during childhood,
209–215
development of, during infancy,
196–209
environmental influences on, 215–223
intersensory, 206–209
methods of studying, 192–193
of music, 206

Perception *(continued)*
of patterns and forms, 196–201,
212–215
and reading, 214
of spatial relations, 202–205
of speech and voices, 205–206
Perceptual learning, Gibson's theory of,
214–215
"Perceptual sets," and spatial perception,
220
Perinatal complications, 136–140
Perinatal environment, 132–142
defined, 132, 133
Permissiveness/restrictiveness, 571 *(see also*
Parental control)
Permissive parenting, 516–517, 549–550,
572–573
Permissive teacher, *see* Laissez-faire
instruction
Perspective cues, and spatial perception,
202–204
Perspective taking, *see* Role taking
Phallic stage, 46–47
Phenotype:
defined, 81
relation to genotype, 81–85, 102–106
Phenylketonuria (PKU), 89, 90, 92, 93
Phocomelia, 126, 127
Phonemes, defined, 265
Phonology:
defined, 265
development of, 268–270
Physical development:
in adolescence, 163–173
biological contributors to, 174–175
of the brain and central nervous system,
158–163
changes in body proportions, 156–157
changes in height and weight, 156
environmental influences on, 175–181
of motor skills, 163–167
of the muscles, 158
psychological consequences of, 169–173
secular trends, 169
sex differences, 158, 166–168
of the skeleton, 157–158
Piaget's theory of intellectual
development:
basic assumptions, 57, 58–61, 67,
307–310
definition of intelligence, 58, 307
educational implications of, 322–323
evaluation of, 61–63, 326–329
vs. information-processing theory, 320,
336, 341, 342, 344, 345
stages of, 61, 62, 310–326
Piaget's theory of moral development:
evaluation of, 532–534
stages of, 530–532
Pidgin language, 296

Radiation *(continued)*
  and prenatal development, 130, 131
Radical behaviorism, *see* Operant learning
    theory
Random assignment, 20–21
Range-of-reaction principle, 102–103
Rate of maturation:
  heritability of, 174
  and personality development, 172–173,
    630
Raven Progressive Matrices Test, 376
Reading:
  cognitive development and, 322, 341,
    345
  perceptual development and, 214
Reality principle, 44, 45
Recall memory:
  defined, 334, 335
  development of, 334–341
Recasts, 290–291
Receptive language, defined, 271
Recessive allele, 82–84
Reciprocal determinism, 56, 57, 564–565
Reciprocal punishment, 532, 533
Recognition memory:
  defined, 333
  development of, 334
Reconstituted families:
  children's adjustment to, 586
  defined, 567
  and delinquent behavior, 587
Referential communication:
  defined, 287
  development of, 286–288
Reflexes:
  adaptive significance of, 59, 150–151,
    152
  as contributors to attachment, 400, 407
  defined, 150, 151
  and intellectual development, 59, 310
  and neonatal status, 149–150
  and sudden infant death syndrome
    (SIDS), 154
Regression, 46
Rehearsal, 336–337
Reinforcement:
  and achievement motivation, 458
  of aggression, 516–517, 518, 633
  of altruism, 523–524
  and attachment, 404–406
  defined, 52, 53, 235
  information value of, 241, 243, 244
  and language development, 267,
    288–289
  and moral development, 544
  and observational learning, 249–251
  and peer popularity, 632
  among peers, 631, 633
  vs. punishment, 237–238, 248–249
  schedules of, 240–241
  and sex typing, 489–490

Reinforcement *(continued)*
  and shaping of complex responses,
    239–240
  use in social skills training, 454
  theories of, 241–244
  timing of, 240, 246, 545
  value of, 241
Reinforcer, defined, 52, 53
Rejectee:
  defined, 628, 629
  long-term implications, 628
Reliability, of IQ tests, 365 *(see also*
    Observer reliability)
REM sleep, 154, 155
Research ethics, 31–33
Research methods:
  in behavior genetics, 93–96
  in cognitive-development research, 307,
    335, 340, 342–343
  in developmental psychology, 15–31
  in early emotional development
    research, 394, 413, 420
  in family research, 564–565
  in moral development, 530, 534–535, 544
  in perceptual development, 191–193
  in self and social cognition research, 436,
    437, 439, 444, 445–446
Respiratory distress syndrome, *see* Hyaline
    membrane disease
Response-cost technique, 248, 249
Reticular formation, 161, 210, 211
Retrieval processes:
  development of, 338
  lack of, in infants, 238–239
Reversibility, 308–309, 319, 320, 321
Rh disease, 125, 131
Role taking:
  and aggression, 512–513
  and altruism, 448, 525
  cognitive development and, 447
  defined, 446
  friends as contributors to, 448–449, 631,
    632
  and friendship formation, 448
  and moral reasoning, 539–540
  and popularity, 448, 630
  and reactions to divorce, 585
  and social cognition, 445, 448
  social experience and, 448–449
  in social-skills training, 455
  stages of, 446
Rooting reflex, 150, 152, 153
Rouge test, 436
Rubella, 123, 125, 131
Rule assessment approach, to problem-
    solving research, 342–344

s, 355, 356
Samoan culture, 292
Schema:
  defined, 59, 308, 309

Schema *(continued)*
  development of, 59–61, 309–310
  varieties of, 59, 308–309
Schizophrenia, 101
Scholastic achievement *(see also* Schools;
    Teachers):
  ability tracking and, 615
  achievement expectancies and, 458–459,
    462
  class size and, 615
  compensatory education and, 380–383
  computers and, 611
  divorce and, 583
  in effective and ineffective schools,
    613–617
  grade retention and, 622–623
  home environment and, 456–457
  IQ and, 364
  locus of control and, 459
  monetary resources and, 614–615
  school desegregation and, 622
  teachers and, 462, 618–619, 620–621
  textbooks and, 620
Schools *(see also* Teachers):
  and cognitive development, 613
  desegregation of, 621–624
  education of handicapped children,
    622–623, 624
  effectiveness of, 613–617
  effects on moral reasoning, 523, 538
  functions of, 612–613
  as a middle-class institution, 620–621
Scientific method, 15
Secondary circular reactions:
  defined, 311
  and development of the self-concept,
    435
Secondary drive, defined, 54, 55
Secure attachment:
  defined, 413, 414
  development of, 414, 415
  long-term correlates of, 416–417
  stability of, 417–418, 419
  and stranger anxiety, 417
Secure-base phenomenon, 411, 416, 569
"Security of attachment" hypothesis, 451
Selective attention:
  defined, 211
  development of, 211–212, 332–333
  training of, 333
Selective breeding experiments, 93–94
Self *(see also* Self-concept; Self-esteem):
  defined, 434, 435
  development of, 435–441
Self-actualization goal, of parenting,
    562–563
Self-concept:
  in adolescence, 438–439
  cognitive development and, 436, 438,
    445
  defined, 435

Credits

CHAPTER 1. 23, Figure 1-1 adapted from "Age and Verbalization in Observational Learning," by B. Boates and W. W. Hartup, 1969, *Developmental Psychology, 1,* 556–562. Copyright 1969 by the American Psychological Association. Adapted by permission. **32,** Table 1-4 from *Ethical Principles in the Conduct of Research with Human Participants,* 1973. Copyright 1973 by the American Psychological Association. Reprinted by permission.

CHAPTER 2. 40, Figure 2-1 from *Perspectives on Social Psychology,* by D. R. Shaffer (Ed.). Copyright © 1977 by Lawrence Erlbaum Associates, Inc. Reprinted by permission of the publisher.

CHAPTER 3. 88, Table 3-2 adapted from "Genetic Counseling," by S. M. Pueschel and A. Goldstein. In J. L. Matson and J. A. Mulick (Eds.), *Handbook of Mental Retardation.* Copyright 1983 by Pergamon Press, Inc. Reprinted by permission. **94,** Figure 3-8 from *Behavioral Genetics: A Primer,* by R. Plomin, J. C. DeFries, and G. E. McClearn, 1980, W. H. Freeman. **96,** Table 3-4 from "Genetics and Intelligence: A Review," by L. Erlenmeyer-Kimling and F. Jarvik, *Science,* Vol. 142, *13,* 1477–1479, December 1963. Copyright 1963 by the AAAS. **103,** Figure 3-9 adapted from "Heritability of Personality: A Demonstration," by I. Gottesman, *Psychological Monographs,* 1963, *11* (Whole No. 572). Copyright 1963 by the American Psychological Association. Adapted by permission.

CHAPTER 4. 119, Figure 4-1 from *Infant Death: An Analysis by Maternal Risk and Health Care,* by D. Kessner, 1973, p. 100. Copyright 1973 by the National Academy of Sciences, Washington, D.C. **122,** Figure 4-2 adapted from a figure in *The Developing Human,* by K. L. Moore, 1977, W. B. Saunders. **139,** Figure 4-4 adapted from "Risk and Resilience in Early Mental Development," by R. S. Wilson, *Developmental Psychology,* 1985, *21,* 795–805. Copyright 1985 by the American Psychological Association. Adapted by permission.

CHAPTER 5. 164, Table 5-4 adapted from "The Denver Development Screening Test," by W. K. Frankenberg and J. B. Dodds, *Journal of Pediatrics,* 1967, *71,* 181–191. **166,** Figure 5-4 from "Motor Development," by A. Espenschlade. In W. R. Johnson (Ed.), *Science and Medicine of Exercise and Sports,* 1960, Harper & Row, Publishers, Inc. **169,** Figure 5-5 based on a figure from "Variations in the Pattern of Pubertal Changes in Boys," by W. A. Marshall and J. M. Tanner, *Archives of the Diseases of Childhood,* 1970, *45,* 13–23. **170,** Figure 5-6 from "Changes in the Stature and Body Weight of North American Boys during the Last 80 Years," by H. V. Meredith. In L. P. Spiker and C. C. Spiker (Eds.), *Advances in Child Development and Behavior* (Vol. 10). Copyright 1963 by Academic Press, Inc. Reprinted by permission. **176,** Figure 5-8 based on a figure from *Growth at Adolescence,* by J. M. Tanner, 1963, Blackwell Scientific Publications, Ltd., London.

CHAPTER 6. 196, Figure 6-1 from "The Origin of Form Perception," by R. L. Fantz, May 1961, *Scientific American, 204,* 66–72.

Copyright © 1961 by Scientific American, Inc. All rights reserved. **197,** Figure 6-2 adapted from "Infant Visual Perception," by M. S. Banks in collaboration with P. Salapatek. In M. M. Haith and J. J. Campos (Eds.), *Handbook of Child Psychology: Vol. 2, Infancy and Developmental Psychology.* Copyright 1983 by John Wiley & Sons. **198,** Box 6-1 adapted from "Pattern Perception in Infancy," by P. Salapatek. In L. B. Cohen and P. Salapatek (Eds.), *Infant Cognition: From Sensation to Perception,* 1975. Copyright 1975 by Academic Press, Inc. Adapted by permission. **199,** Figure 6-3 patterned after "Perception of Partly Occluded Objects in Infancy," by P. J. Kellman and E. S. Spelke, *Cognitive Psychology,* 1983, *15,* 483–524. Copyright 1983 by the American Psychological Association. **199,** Figure 6-4 adapted from "Development of Visual Organization: The Perception of Subjective Contours," by B. I. Bertenthal, J. J. Campos, and M. M. Haith, *Child Development,* 1980, *51,* 1077–1080. **200,** Figure 6-5 from "Infant Sensitivity to Figural Coherence in Biomechanical Motions," by B. I. Bertenthal, D. R. Proffitt, and J. E. Cutting, *Journal of Experimental Child Psychology,* 1984, *37,* 213–230. Copyright 1984 by Academic Press. Reprinted by permission. **204,** Figure 6-6 adapted from "Development of Sensitivity to Pictorial Depth," by A. Yonas, W. Cleaves, and L. Pettersen, *Science,* 1978, *200,* 77–79. Copyright 1978 by the AAAS. **211,** Figure 6-8 adapted from "Selective Auditory Attention in Children," by E. E. Maccoby. In L. P. Lipsitt and C. C. Spiker (Eds.), *Advances in Child Development and Behavior.* Copyright 1967 by Academic Press. Reprinted by permission. **213,** Figure 6-10 adapted from "Factors Affecting the Visual Recognition of Incomplete Objects: A Comparative Investigation of Children and Adults," by E. S. Gollin, *Perceptual and Motor Skills,* 1962, *15,* 583–590. **213,** Figure 6-11 from "Perception of Overlapping and Embedded Figures by Children of Different Ages," by L. Ghent, *American Journal of Psychology,* 1956, *69,* 575–587. University of Illinois Press. **214,** Figure 6-12 adapted from "A Developmental Study of the Discrimination of Letter-like Forms," by E. J. Gibson, A. D. Pick, and H. A. Osser, *Journal of Comparative and Physiological Psychology,* 1962, *55,* 897–906. Copyright 1962 by the American Psychological Association. Adapted by permission. **217,** Figure 6-13 adapted from "Movement Produced Stimulation in the Development of Visually-Guided Behavior," by R. Held and A. Hein, *Journal of Comparative and Physiological Psychology, 1963, 55,* 872–876. Copyright 1963 by the American Psychological Association. Adapted by permission. **220,** Box 6-2 adapted from "Perception of a Subjective Contour by Infants," by F. Treiber and S. Wilcox, *Child Development,* 1980, *51,* 915–917. © 1980 by The Society for Research in Child Development. Reprinted by permission.

CHAPTER 7. **250,** Figure 7-4 adapted from "Influence of Models' Reinforcement Contingencies on the Acquisition of Imitative Responses," by A. Bandura, *Journal of Personality and Social Psychology,* 1965, *1,* 589–595. Copyright 1965 by the American Psychological Association. Adapted by permission. **256,** Box 7-4 adapted from "Factors Determining Vicarious Extinction of Avoidance Behavior through Symbolic Modeling," by A. Bandura and F. L. Menlove, *Journal of Personality and Social Psychology,* 1968, *8,* 99–108. Copyright 1968 by the American Psychological Association. Adapted by permission.

CHAPTER 8. **272,** Table 8-1 adapted from "Structure and Strategy in Learning to Talk," by K. Nelson, *Monographs of the Society for Research in Child Development,* 1973, *38* (Whole No. 149). © 1973 by The Society for Research in Child Development. Adapted by permission. **274,** Figure 8-2 adapted from "The Influence of Functional Context on Children's Labeling Responses," by R. S. Prawat and S. Wildfong, *Child Development,* 1980, *51,* 1057–1060. © 1980 by The Society for Research in Child Development. Adapted by permission.

275, Table 8-2 adapted from *Psycholinguistics,* by D. I. Slobin. © 1979, Scott, Foresman & Co. **277,** Table 8-3 from *A First Language: The Early Stages,* by R. Brown. Copyright 1973 by Harvard University Press. **278,** Figure in Box 8-1 from *Talk to the Deaf,* by L. Riekehof. Copyright © 1963 by Gospel Publishing House. Adapted by permission. **279,** Table 8-4 adapted from *The Acquisition of Language: The Study of Developmental Psycholinguistics,* by D. McNeil, 1970, Harper & Row, Publishers, Inc. **280,** Table 8-5 from *Psychology and Language: An Introduction to Psycholinguistics,* by H. H. Clark and E. V. Clark, 1977, Harcourt Brace Jovanovich. **281,** Figure 8-3, a linguistic puzzle from "The Child's Learning of English Morphology," by J. Berko, *Word,* 1958, *14,* 150–177. **286,** Table 8-7 from "Social and Non-Social Speech," by R. M. Krauss and S. Glucksberg, *Scientific American,* February 1977, *236,* 100–105. Copyright © 1977 by Scientific American, Inc. All rights reserved. **287,** Figure 8-4 adapted from "The Development of Communication as a Function of Age," by R. M. Krause and S. Glucksberg, *Child Development,* 1969, *40,* 255–266. © 1969 by The Society for Research in Child Development. Adapted by permission.

CHAPTER 9. **330,** Figure 9-4 adapted from "Human Memory: A Proposed System and Its Control Processes," by R. C. Atkinson and R. M. Shiffrin. In K. W. Spence and J. T. Spence (Eds.), *The Psychology of Learning and Motivation* (Vol. 2). Copyright © 1968 by Academic Press. Adapted by permission. **339,** Figure in Box 9-3 from "From Knowledge Structures and Memory Development," by M. H. T. Chi. In R. S. Siegler (Ed.), *Children's Thinking: What Develops?* Copyright © 1978 by Lawrence Erlbaum Associates, Inc. Reprinted by permission. **343,** Table 9-2 adapted from "Developmental Sequences within and between Concepts," by R. S. Siegler, *Monographs of the Society for Research in Child Development,* 1981, *46* (Serial No. 189). © 1981 by The Society for Research in Child Development. Adapted by permission.

CHAPTER 10. **355,** Figure 10-1 adapted from a table in *The Nature of Human Intelligence,* by J. P. Guilford, 1967, McGraw-Hill Book Co. **359,** Table 10-2 adapted from the *Stanford-Binet Intelligence Scale—Manual for the Third Revision,* by L. M. Terman and M. A. Merrill, 1972, Houghton Mifflin Co. **363,** Table 10-4 adapted from "The Stability of Mental Test Performance between Two and Eighteen Years," by M. P. Honzik, J. W. MacFarlane, and L. Allen, *Journal of Experimental Education,* 1948, *17,* 309–324. **366,** Table 10-5 adapted from "Army General Classification Test Scores for Civilian Populations," by T. W. Harrell and M. S. Harrell, *Educational and Psychological Measurement,* 1945, *5,* 229–239. **369,** Table in Box 10-2 adapted from *Lives of the Mentally Retarded: A Forty-year Follow-up,* by R. T. Ross, M. J. Begab, E. H. Dondis, J. S. Giampiccolo, Jr., and C. E. Meyers. Copyright © 1985 by Stanford University Press. Adapted by permission. Table 10-6 adapted from the *Manual for Home Observation for Measurement of the Environment,* 1978, University of Arkansas, Little Rock. **374,** Figure 10-3 adapted from "Birth Order and Intellectual Development," by R. B. Zajonc and G. B. Marcus, *Psychological Review,* 1975, *82,* 74–88. Copyright 1975 by the American Psychological Association. Reprinted by permission. **375,** Figure 10-4 adapted from "A Normative Sample of Intelligence and Achievement of Negro Elementary School Children in the Southeastern United States," by W. Z. Kennedy, V. van de Reit, and J. C. White, *Monographs of the Society for Research in Child Development,* 1963, *28* (Serial No. 90). © 1963 by The Society for Research in Child Development. Adapted by permission. **376,** Table 10-7 adapted from "The Chitling Test," by A. Dove, *Newsweek,* July 15, 1968. **383,** Figure 10-6 adapted from "Preschool Compensatory Education and the Modifiability of Intelligence: A Critical Review," by C. T. Ramey, D. M. Bryant, and T. M. Suarez. In D. K. Detterman (Ed.), *Current Topics in Human Intelli-*

gence, Vol. 1: Research Methodology. Copyright 1985 by Ablex Publishing Corporation. Reprinted by permission.

CHAPTER 11. 401, Excerpts from *The First Relationship: Infant and Mother,* by D. Stern. Copyright © 1974 by Harvard University Press. Reprinted by permission. **404,** Figure 11-1 from "The Development of Social Attachments in Infancy," by H. R. Shaffer and R. E. Emerson, *Monographs of the Society for Research in Child Development,* 1964, *20,* p. 3. © 1964 by the Society for Research in Child Development. Reprinted by permission. **413,** Table 11-1 from *Patterns of Attachment,* by M. D. S. Ainsworth, M. Blehar, E. Waters, and W. Wall. Copyright © 1978 by Lawrence Erlbaum Associates, Inc. Reprinted by permission. **417,** Table in Box 11-2 adapted from "The Quality of the Toddler's Relationship to Mother and Father: Related to Conflict Behavior and the Readiness to Establish New Relationships," by A. Main and D. R. Weston, *Child Development,* 1981, *52,* 932–940. © 1981 by The Society for Research in Child Development, Inc. Adapted by permission. **426,** Figure 11-2 adapted from "Rehabilitation of Socially Withdrawn Preschool Children through Mixed-Age and Same-Age Socialization," by W. Furman, D. F. Rahe, and W. W. Hartup, *Child Development,* 1979, 915–922. © 1979 by The Society for Research in Child Development. Adapted by permission.

CHAPTER 12. 443, Figure in Box 12-1 adapted from "Cross-Sectional Age Changes in Ego Identity Status during Adolescence," by P. W. Meilman, *Developmental Psychology,* 1979, *15,* 230–231. Copyright 1979 by the American Psychological Association. Reprinted by permission. **444,** Figure 12-2 adapted from "The Development of Person Perception in Childhood and Adolescence: From Behavioral Comparisons," by C. Barenboim, *Child Development,* 1981, *52,* 129–144. © 1981 by The Society for Research in Child Development. Reprinted by permission. **446,** Table 12-1 adapted from "Social-Cognitive Understanding: A Guide to Educational and Clinical Experience," by R. L. Selman. In T. Lickona (Ed.), *Moral Development and Behavior: Theory, Research, and Social Issues,* 1976, Holt, Rinehart & Winston. **447,** Table 12-2 adapted from "Development of Physical and Social Reasoning in Adolescence," by K. P. Keating and L. V. Clark, *Developmental Psychology,* 1980, *16,* 23–30. Copyright 1980 by the American Psychological Association. Adapted by permission. **457,** Table 12-3 adapted from "The Relationship between Twelve-Month Home Stimulation and School Achievement," by W. J. van Doorninck, B. M. Caldwell, C. Wright, and W. K. Frankenberg, *Child Development,* 1981, *52,* 1080–1083. © 1981 by The Society for Research in Child Development. Adapted by permission.

CHAPTER 13. 474, Table 13-1 adapted from "Sex-Role Stereotypes: A Current Appraisal," by I. K. Broverman, S. R. Vogel, F. E. Clarkson, and P. S. Rosenkrantz, *Journal of Social Issues,* 1972, *28,* 59–78. Copyright 1972 by the Society for the Psychological Study of Social Issues. Used with permission. **475,** Table 13-2 adapted from "A Cross-Cultural Survey of Some Sex Differences in Socialization," by H. Barry III, M. K. Bacon, and I. L. Child, *Journal of Abnormal and Social Psychology,* 1957, *55,* 327–332. Copyright 1957 by the American Psychological Association. Adapted with permission. **477,** Table 13-3 adapted from *The Psychology of Sex Differences,* by Eleanor Emmons Maccoby and Carol Nagy Jacklin. Copyright © 1974 by Stanford University Press. Reprinted by permission of the Board of Trustees of the Leland Stanford Junior University. **481,** Figure 13-1 adapted from "Social Behavior at 33 Months in Same-Sex and Mixed-Sex Dyads," by C. N. Jacklin and E. E. Maccoby, *Child Development,* 1978, *49,* 557–569. © 1978 by The Society for Research in Child Development. Adapted with permission. **488,** Figure 13-2 adapted from *Man and Woman, Boy and Girl,* by J. Money and A. A. Ehrhardt, 1972. Johns Hopkins University Press. **499,** Table 13-6 adapted from

"Sexuality during Adolescence," by P. H. Dreyer. In B. B. Wolman (Ed.), *Handbook of Developmental Psychology,* 1982, John Wiley & Sons.

CHAPTER 14. 526, Table 14-3 from "Prosocial Development: A Longitudinal Study," by N. Eisenberg, R. Lennon, and K. Roth, *Developmental Psychology,* 1983, *19,* 846–855. Copyright 1983 by the American Psychological Association. Adapted by permission. **533,** Figure 14-1 and 14-2 adapted from "Factors Influencing Young Children's Use of Motives and Outcomes as Moral Criteria," by S. A. Nelson, *Child Development,* 1980, *51,* 823–829. © 1980 by The Society for Research in Child Development. Adapted by permission. **538,** Figure 14-3 from "A Longitudinal Study of Moral Judgment," by A. Colby, L. Kohlberg, J. Gibbs, and M. Lieberman, *Monographs of the Society for Research in Child Development,* 1983, *48.* © 1983 by The Society for Research in Child Development. Reprinted with permission. **548,** Quotes from "Moral Development," by M. L. Hoffman. In P. H. Mussen (Ed.), *Carmichael's Manual of Child Psychology,* Vol. 2. Copyright 1970 by John Wiley & Sons. Reprinted by permission. **549,** Table 14-5 adapted from "Contributions of Parents and Peers to Children's Moral Socialization," by G. H. Brody and D. R. Shaffer, *Developmental Review,* 1982, *2,* 31–75.

CHAPTER 15. 566, Figure 15-1 from "Early Human Experience: A Family Perspective," by J. Belsky, *Developmental Psychology,* 1981, *17,* 3–23. Copyright 1981 by the American Psychological Association. Reprinted by permission. **569,** Figure 15-2 adapted from "Effects of Maternal Age on Parenting Role," by A. S. Ragozin, R. B. Basham, K. A. Crnic, M. T. Greenberg, and N. M. Robinson, *Developmental Psychology,* 1982, *18,* 627–634. Copyright 1983 by the American Psychological Association. Adapted by permission. **572,** Table 15-1 based on data from *Socialization Determinants of Personal Agency.* Paper presented at biennial meeting of the Society for Research in Child Development, New Orleans, 1977. **590,** Figure 15-3 adapted from "Responses of Abused and Disadvantaged Toddlers to Distress in Agemates: A Study in the Day-Care Setting," by M. Main and C. George, *Developmental Psychology,* 1985, *21,* 407–412. Copyright 1985 by the American Psychological Association. Adapted by permission. **591,** Figure 15-4 adapted from "Child Abuse as Psychopathology: A Sociological Critique and Reformulation," by R. J. Gelles, *American Journal of Orthopsychiatry,* 1973, *43,* 611–621.

CHAPTER 16. 603, Figure 16-1 from *Television and Human Behavior,* by G. Comstock, 1978, Columbia University Press. **610,** Figure 16-2 from Ball and Bogatz, 1970, as presented in R. M. Lieberg, J. N. Sprafkin, and E. S. Davidson, *The Early Window: Effects of Television on Children and Youth,* 1982, Pergamon Press, Inc. **614,** Figure 16-3 adapted from *Fifteen Thousand Hours: Secondary Schools and Their Effects on Children,* by M. Rutter, B. Maughan, P. Mortimer, J. Ouston, and A. Smith, 1979, Harvard University Press. **626,** Figures 16-4 and 16-5 from "Age Segregation in Children's Social Interaction," by S. Ellis, B. Rogoff, and C. C. Cromer, *Developmental Psychology,* 1981, *17,* 399–407. Copyright 1981 by the American Psychological Association. Reprinted by permission.

Photo Credits

CHAPTER 1. 3, Eileen Copsey; **4,** Randolph Falk/Jeroboam; **11,** Philadelphia Museum of Art, W. P. Wilstach Collection; **16,** Nita Winter; **28,** (left) Historical Pictures Service, Chicago; **28,** (right) Kira Godbe; **30,** Richard Gordon/Wheeler Pictures; **33,** David M. Grossman/Photo Researchers.

CHAPTER 2. 36, Bill Bachman, Photo Researchers; **43,** Historical Pictures Service, Chicago; **45,** Frank Siteman/Jeroboam; **47,** James T. Coit/Jeroboam; **52,** Culver Pictures; **55,** (left) Christopher S. Johnson; **55,** (right) Chuck Painter/News and Publications Service, Stanford University; **57,** Yves de Braine/Black Star; **60,** Elizabeth Crews; **64,** Wayne Miller, Magnum Photos, Inc.

CHAPTER 3. 71, H. Mark Weidman; **72,** D. W. Fawcett/ Photo Researchers; **80,** Alice Kandell/Photo Researchers; **81,** (both) Dr. Uta Francke/Phototake-New York City; **83,** Nigel Calder/Photo Researchers; **88,** Bruce Roberts/Photo Researchers; **105,** Washington Post.

CHAPTER 4. 110, Cary Beth Cryor, from the "Rites of Passage" series; **113,** J. P. Revel, Caltech; **115–118,** Dr. Landrum B. Shettles; **126,** Heggemann/Black Star; **127,** James W. Hanson; **135,** E. Alan McGee/FPG International; **138,** James Holland/Stock, Boston.

CHAPTER 5. 146, Frank Siteman/Jeroboam; **148,** Ed Lettau/FPG International; **153,** (left) Ellis Herwig/Stock, Boston: (middle) Elizabeth Crews/Stock, Boston; (right) Elizabeth Crews; **165,** Elizabeth Crews; **168,** Elizabeth Crews/Stock, Boston; **177,** Chris Steele-Perkins/Magnum.

CHAPTER 6. 187, Ed Buryn/Jeroboam; **188,** Elizabeth Crews; **191,** David Linton from *Scientific American*; **194,** Micky Pfleter; **202,** William Vandivert from *Scientific American*; **208,** Ellis Herwig/Stock, Boston; **215,** Elizabeth Crews; **219,** UN Photo 150,094/ Milton Grant.

CHAPTER 7. 228, Kay Lawson/Jeroboam; **234,** Robert V. Eckert, Jr./EKM-Nepenthe; **239,** C. Rovee-Collier, Rutgers University; **247,** Barbara Alper/Stock, Boston; **248,** David Strickler/The PhotoFile; **250,** Burk Uzzle/Archive Pictures; **252,** Leonard Freed/ Magnum.

CHAPTER 8. 262, Tom Ballard/EKM-Nepenthe; **265,** R. Wrangham/Anthro-Photo; **273,** Elizabeth Crews/Stock, Boston; **277,** Elizabeth Crews; **284,** Christopher Morrow/Stock, Boston; **291,** Irene Kane/Jeroboam; **295,** Paul Fusco/Magnum.

CHAPTER 9. 304, Olof Kallstrom/Jeroboam; **311,** Grete Mannheim/DPI, Inc.; **313,** Peter Vandermark/Stock, Boston; **316,** Strang Photographics; **325,** Laimute Druskis/Jeroboam; **333,** Roger Malloch/ Magnum.

CHAPTER 10. 350, Elizabeth Crews; **358,** Bettmann Archive; **373,** (left) Karen Rosenthal/Stock, Boston; **373,** (right) Rebecca Chao/Archive Pictures; **382,** H. Mark Weidman; **385,** Elizabeth Crews.

CHAPTER 11. 391, Karen Stafford Rantzman; **392,** Jean-Claude Lejeune/Stock, Boston; **395,** (all) C. E. Izard, University of Delaware; **397,** Suzanne Arms/Jeroboam; **400,** Ken Gaghan/Jeroboam; **405,** Harry F. Harlow/University of Wisconsin Primate Laboratory; **408,** Steve Malone/Jeroboam; **410,** Suzanne Arms/Jeroboam; **416,** Robert V. Eckert, Jr./EKM-Nepenthe; **422,** Harry F. Harlow/University of Wisconsin Primate Laboratory; **423,** Suzanne Arms/Jeroboam.

CHAPTER 12. 432, Paul Damien, Click/Chicago; **437,** Peter Menzel/Stock, Boston; **441,** Roberta Hershenson/Photo Researchers; **449,** Dennis Hallinan/FPG International; **456,** David Shaffer; **458,** Michael Hayman/Stock, Boston; **461,** Mickey Pfleger.

CHAPTER 13. 470, Alice Kandell, Photo Researchers; **473,** J. Gleiter/H. Armstrong Roberts; **476,** Paul S. Conklin/Monkmeyer Press Photo Service; **483,** Gale Zucker/Stock, Boston; **484,** Rona Beame/Photo Researchers; **498,** Spencer Grant, Photo Researchers; **501,** H. Mark Weidman.

CHAPTER 14. 508, Nita Winter; **512,** Elizabeth Crews; **521,** Nita Winter; **524,** Ellis Herwig/Stock, Boston; **528,** Alice Kandell/ Photo Researchers; **531,** Ray Ellis/Photo Researchers; **544,** B. Kliewe/ Jeroboam.

CHAPTER 15. 557, Nita Winter; **558,** Mickey Pfleger; **562,** David Austen/Stock, Boston; **570,** Abigail Heyman/Archive Pictures; **574,** Erika Stone/Peter Arnold, Inc.; **579,** Robert Pacheco/EKM-Nepenthe; **584,** Randy Matusow/Monkmeyer Press Photo Service; **587,** Michael Kagan, Monkmeyer Press Photo Service; **593,** San Francisco Child Abuse Council, Inc.

CHAPTER 16. 600, Loren Santow, Click/Chicago; **605,** Arthur Tress/Magnum; **608,** © 1988 Children's Television Workshop. Used by permission; **616,** Elizabeth Crews/Stock, Boston; **620,** Michael Uffer/Photo Researchers; **627,** Harry F. Harlow/University of Wisconsin Primate Laboratory; **632,** Elizabeth Crews/Stock, Boston; **637,** Charles Gatewood/Stock, Boston.